Handbook of Research on Transitional Justice and Peace Building in Turbulent Regions

Fredy Cante
Universidad del Rosario, Colombia

Hartmut Quehl
Felsberg Institute, Germany

A volume in the Advances in Public Policy and Administration (APPA) Book Series

Information Science REFERENCE
An Imprint of IGI Global

Published in the United States of America by
Information Science Reference (an imprint of IGI Global)
701 E. Chocolate Avenue
Hershey PA, USA 17033
Tel: 717-533-8845
Fax: 717-533-8661
E-mail: cust@igi-global.com
Web site: http://www.igi-global.com

Library of Congress Cataloging-in-Publication Data

Names: Cante, Freddy, editor. | Quehl, Hartmut, editor.
Title: Handbook of research on transitional justice and peace building in turbulent regions / Fredy Cante and Hartmut Quehl, editors.
Description: Hershey : Information Science Reference, 2016. | Includes bibliographical references and index.
Identifiers: LCCN 2015037646| ISBN 9781466696754 (hardcover) | ISBN 9781466696761 (ebook)
Subjects: LCSH: Transitional justice--Case studies. | Peace-building--Case studies. | Conflict management--Case studies. | Poverty--Case studies. | Security, International--Case studies.
Classification: LCC JC571 .H34757 2016 | DDC 327.1/72--dc23 LC record available at http://lccn.loc.gov/2015037646

This book is published in the IGI Global book series Advances in Public Policy and Administration (APPA) (ISSN: Pending; eISSN: Pending)

British Cataloguing in Publication Data
A Cataloguing in Publication record for this book is available from the British Library.

For electronic access to this publication, please contact: eresources@igi-global.com.

Advances in Public Policy and Administration (APPA) Book Series

ISSN: Pending
EISSN: Pending

Mission

Proper management of the public sphere is necessary in order to maintain order in modern society. Research developments in the field of public policy and administration can assist in uncovering the latest tools, practices, and methodologies for governing societies around the world.

The **Advances in Public Policy and Administration (APPA) Book Series** aims to publish scholarly publications focused on topics pertaining to the governance of the public domain. APPA's focus on timely topics relating to government, public funding, politics, public safety, policy, and law enforcement is particularly relevant to academicians, government officials, and upper-level students seeking the most up-to-date research in their field.

Coverage

- Government
- Law enforcement
- Political Economy
- Politics
- Public Administration
- Public Funding
- Public Policy
- Resource allocation
- Urban Planning

The Advances in Public Policy and Administration (APPA) Book Series (ISSN Pending) is published by IGI Global, 701 E. Chocolate Avenue, Hershey, PA 17033-1240, USA, www.igi-global.com. This series is composed of titles available for purchase individually; each title is edited to be contextually exclusive from any other title within the series. For pricing and ordering information please visit http://www.igi-global.com/book-series/advances-public-policy-administration/97862. Postmaster: Send all address changes to above address.

Titles in this Series

For a list of additional titles in this series, please visit: www.igi-global.com

Management and Participation in the Public Sphere
Mika Markus Merviö (Kibi International University, Japan)
Information Science Reference • copyright 2015 • 400pp • H/C (ISBN: 9781466685536) • US $200.00 (our price)

Teaching Research Methods in Public Administration
Richard W. Schwester (City University of New York, USA)
Information Science Reference • copyright 2015 • 313pp • H/C (ISBN: 9781466681163) • US $185.00 (our price)

Emergency Management and Disaster Response Utilizing Public-Private Partnerships
Marvine Paula Hamner (LeaTech, LLC, USA) S. Shane Stovall (True North Emergency Management, USA) Doaa M. Taha (GMI, Ltd, USA) and Salah C. Brahimi (GMI, Ltd, USA)
Information Science Reference • copyright 2015 • 345pp • H/C (ISBN: 9781466681590) • US $200.00 (our price)

ICT Adoption and Application in the Malaysian Public Sector
Abdul Raufu Ambali (Universiti Teknologi MARA, Malaysia & Kwara State University Malete, Nigeria) and Ahmad Naqiyuddin Bakar (Universiti Teknologi MARA, Malaysia)
Information Science Reference • copyright 2015 • 316pp • H/C (ISBN: 9781466665798) • US $195.00 (our price)

Human Rights and the Impact of ICT in the Public Sphere Participation, Democracy, and Political Autonomy
Christina M. Akrivopoulou (Hellenic Open University, Greece) and N. Garipidis (Aristotle University of Thessaloniki, Greece)
Information Science Reference • copyright 2014 • 371pp • H/C (ISBN: 9781466662483) • US $185.00 (our price)

Chaos and Complexity Theory in World Politics
Şefika Şule Erçetin (Hacettepe University, Turkey) and Santo Banerjee (University Putra Malaysia, Malaysia)
Information Science Reference • copyright 2014 • 374pp • H/C (ISBN: 9781466660700) • US $210.00 (our price)

Transforming Politics and Policy in the Digital Age
Jonathan Bishop (Centre for Research into Online Communities and E-Learning Systems, Belgium)
Information Science Reference • copyright 2014 • 312pp • H/C (ISBN: 9781466660380) • US $200.00 (our price)

List of Contributors

Table of Contents

Section 4
The Turbulent Colombia

Detailed Table of Contents

A situation of turbulent peace is defined as an ambiguous transition from direct violence (which ends by means a fragile and incomplete peace agreement among enemies) to an indirect and subtle violence euphemistically denominated as progress. Indeed, a big rate of economic growth implies growing prosperity, incremented consumption, and increasing investment in the present but, sadly, the consequence of this material progress will be the suffering of future generations because the exhaustion and deterioration of nature in a world where the entropy is worsened by the rapacity of actual generations. The depletion and contamination of natural resources is the inherent cost of material progress and development of "productive" forces. The ideological, coercive and economic power of some organized minorities, and the acquiescence of a big majority of human beings constitutes the root of this problem. The antidote against this power is the critical examination of values by active citizens and the guide of ethics. In the long run this problem can be solved promoting a nonviolent economy.

This chapter understands reconciliation as an historical process, inseparably connected to communication processes, processes of remembrance, and the transformation processes of individual and collective memories. The author aims to link the issues of reconciliation and remembrance, and uses the historical example of the Germans coming to terms with their past ("Vergangenheitsbewältigung") after 1945 to categorize a specific reconciliation process into different contextual levels and thereby answer the question, whether or not the German reconciliation process has been successfully completed. This chapter also aims to seek possible fields of comparison with other reconciliation processes that have taken place in different time and spatial settings. Such a "comparison of differences and variables within the context of reconciliation processes" will be elaborated through an abstraction of structural components, using the example of Germany after the Second World War.

This chapter claims that non-violent action corresponds to a political dimension in which society has become a magnificent complex organism. Moreover, non-violent action corresponds to the phase of highest complexity in a social organization. Examples are provided ranging from ecology to population biology, from ethology to swarm intelligence. At the end, several conclusions are drawn that shed new lights on the social, cultural, and political understanding of our world and to the foreseeable future. The study of non-violent action provides sufficient arguments that allow the distinction between "politics" and "policy", i.e. "policies", so much so that politics is highlighted as a highest and most significant dimension of the human experience, and policies are then considered as secondary or lower. The human rights provide the ground for the understanding and comprehension of non-violent actions. In the core of the text a topology of non-violent actions is provided along with its explanation.

This analysis is a review of different negotiation theories by looking through the key documents of the United Nations on peace keeping and provides a review how negotiation theories could make an influence on them. Conflicts are an aspect of our daily life. They influence us not only in arguments with friends and family, but also in other dimensions of our discourse contributions. Therefore, it is significant to find practicable and conflict avoiding solutions for the parties involved. Negotiation is a form of discussion that helps find solutions for contradicting interests without using force. This violent free decision-making process is the most adequate form in a democratic culture. The growing denotation of political negotiations derives from an increasing interdependence, propagation of democracy, and a trend towards more peaceful dealings between governments. The main organization for peacekeeping and thus also peace negotiation documentation is the United Nations.

Violence against children and youth in war causes severe damage to individuals, communities and societies. This chapter aims to demonstrate the importance of reparations for children and youth as a peacebuilding mechanism in the context of transitional justice. On one hand, the chapter seeks to address reparations for children and youth understood as a political project, with a transformative and participatory potential for rebuilding societies and healing the wounds of those who have been affected by armed conflict. On the other hand, the paper attempts to overcome the conception of children and youth as passive victims, providing them with agency to become engaged political members in building peaceful societies. Thus, reparations should position them as subjects of rights, giving them voice as contributors in peacebuilding processes.

Section 2
Enduring Turbulences and Elusive Peace

This paper aims at analyzing the various forms of violence carried out by the different categories of people directly involved in the actual Syrian war: 'regular' soldiers, Alawite elite troops (plus the different security services), (mostly) Alawite militiamen, rebels from the (Sunni) mainstream armed opposition, and Islamist fighters, not to mention rogues who thrive on unruliness. This paper's hypothesis is that the demobilization of combatants is just partially connected to concrete issues – in the sense, for example, that any nationwide economic reconstruction will probably not be enough to promote reconciliation – since other factors impede any eventual transition from a violent civil war to a peaceful agreement, among them: a peculiar middle-eastern sense of masculinity plus the plague of sectarianism which builds organic barriers between people.

All the political systems of the Arab-Islamic zone are authoritarian, with the exception of Tunisia where fair elections recently took place and political alternation was accepted. Lebanon is another exception in the sense that state prerogatives – shared between antagonist religious communities – do not enjoy sufficient power to exert coercive policies. But apart from these two cases, this global authoritarian environment is of no avail vis-à-vis any initiative that would aim at forging some idea of citizenship – with its obligations and privileges – amongst the population, and particularly among the military. The present analysis will concentrate on the links existing between authoritarianism and citizenship, with an emphasis on Arab armed forces considered within their sociological contexts, since these entities are as much the emanation of the people(s) as the physical manifestation of the regimes' strength. The issue will be addressed through two perspectives: politics and philosophy.

Transnational migration has important implications on the respective country of departure and its political dynamics. This article addresses informal practices and processes of informalization during migration from dictatorially ruled Eritrea in North-East-Africa. On the base of dense ethnography among refugees and migrants in neighboring Ethiopia the article discusses migration's cultural and social effects and sheds a light on the potential role of migrants in Eritrea's expected political transition. It will be argued that refugees and migrants are unable to fully liberate themselves from Eritrea's authoritarian political culture while seeking prosperity, democracy and human rights elsewhere. Instead they blunder into informal practices such as deceit, exploitation and denial of solidarity, which inevitably backfire on social and political life.

This paper analyses South Sudan's long struggle for an inclusive reconciliatory process in the country from the Comprehensive Peace Agreement of 2005 to the peace negotiations in Addis Ababa in 2014/15 and highlights the difficulties that the country has faced in introducing a lasting initiative to bring about justice, achieve reconciliation and ensure accountability in the country. The author considers different judicial and non-judicial mechanisms as elements of a comprehensive transitional justice policy and suggests viable options for South Sudan to confront the historical grievances and to resolve the frictions and tensions that have persisted between the different warring groups and ethnic communities during the decades of war in South Sudan.

This paper looks at the role that the Extraordinary Chambers in the Courts of Cambodia play in the context of post-conflict justice in Cambodia. The first trial against one of the main perpetrators was completed in 2010; the first phase of the second case against two high-ranking leaders of the Khmer Rouge has been completed in 2014. This study includes an analysis of how the Tribunal has influenced the legal and political culture in Cambodia, and the ways in which the work of the Tribunal has changed the perception of common people concerning the Khmer Rouge period. The paper also looks at the proceedings before the Tribunal and discusses whether the Tribunal has, in the eyes of all relevant stakeholders, lived up to expectations. The interaction between the Cambodian government and the international community is crucial in this context. Finally, the Tribunal's lasting legacy is scrutinized in regard to its effect on the Cambodian legal system and in regard to the ECCC's outreach, education and documentation activities.

This article deals with the past activities of the gacaca courts in Rwanda. The first section of the article will review the reasons for reactivating the gacaca courts and consider its theoretical suitability as a means of resolving conflicts. The second part offers a survey of the actual implementation and results of the gacaca trials. In the final section, the concrete effects of these results on the inner-Rwandan processes of pacification and reconciliation are assessed.

Section 3
The Turbulent Iraq

This article brings together historical and political research in order to give an account of Iraq's recurring authoritarianism. Focusing on the agency of three distinct state elites, it will compare how these networks used cooptation and coercion to dominate their respective political arena. As a part of this, structural aspects like the allurement of the centralized state economic and the aspect of Western assistance in the (re)building of a central authority will join the analysis. However, the article will be primarily concerned with Iraqi politicians, their authorship of authoritarianism, their efforts to build a "modern" nation and their attempts to overrule dissent. The main interest of this inquiry is for the present and recent past: As Iraq has shaken off the oppression of 35 years of dictatorship, the new democratic system has shown to be extremely susceptible for a renewal of the authoritarian tradition.

This chapter argues that transition after critical junctures is heavily linked to the narratives which prevail the discourse of the respective country. Different political actors try to legitimize retroactively current claims to power. In such "zero hour" the extent of ability to organize, mobilize, set incentives, and protect followers is of the essence. This chapter uses the example of Iraq after 2003 where the split between Kurds, Shi'i Muslims, and Sunni Muslims, became the driving force behind political action and loyalty. An established counter-narrative deconstructs the claim that an eternal Shi'i – Sunni split determined all outcomes of Iraqi history, stating that religion was historically a rather subordinate identity. Then crucial contributions to the deepening of the sectarian cleavage by religious networks, the Iraqi constitution, and the policies of the Coalition Provisional Authority, (CPA) are shown and exemplified using the Iraqi trade union movement after 2003.

Since the parliamentary elections in 31st April 2014, the political process in Iraq described as a fragile, ethnic tension have mounted and security situation declined tremendously with the rises of Islamic State in Sunni Arab populated areas. Since 10th June 2014, over a million internally displaced people approached Iraqi Kurdistan Region in a two-week time period. More than 300,000 monitories, including Yazidi Kurds and Christians, have fled to Duhok city. Additionally, over 40,000 civilians Yazidis trapped for a week in the mountain of Snjar, running from Islamic State (IS). This text works out measures for accommodating conflicts and claims of Iraqi sectarian groups. In order to explore and assess application

This chapter aims to reflect upon the construction of historical memory in Colombia from an institutional framework and in the midst of an armed conflict that does not cease. The objective is to discuss the difficulties that emerge in this type of research when conducted under the political, conceptual and methodological parameters of a public entity. Therefore, three contexts that influenced the development of the research are analysed (institutional, social-political and scientific) and then the limits and difficulties that these implicate are exposed. Finally, a series of recommendations are presented as well as the learned lessons that should represent a contribution for future work related with the reconstruction of historical memory in contexts of violence and armed conflict.

Since the first implementation of a modern DDR program, implemented in Namibia in 1989, more than 60 programs became the initial stage of a stabilization process in countries, in which national governments and irregular forces have ended hostilities, reached a ceasefire or signed a peace agreement. This document aims to provide a comparative analysis between two of them: the reintegration policy led by Colombia and Indonesia, from a description of these DDR processes and the general experiences that have been accumulated through the DDR processes in both countries. This paper makes a brief analysis of the political contexts that were conductive to the implementation of the reintegration process in both cases, describes the challenges faced and currently being faced by these processes, pointing out the strategies to address them and the role of international cooperation. The analysis will be framed during the peace process and DDR program in Aceh, Indonesia, and the Republic of Colombia, since 2003 until nowadays.

Transitional justice and its range of mechanisms and goals appear to be an important debate about how to deal with past human rights abuses in transition societies or post conflicts. Because of the Peace and Justice Law 975 of 2005 and the actual Colombian scenario of a peace process between the Colombian state and FARC, the analysis of this kind of "justice" and the indigenous jurisdiction appear to be a

Different to previous attempts, negotiations currently under way in Havana between the Government and FARC, since 2012, were preceded by a decline in both parties' contentious tactics. This chapter seeks to analyze the relation between the conflict cycle and the start of a peace process, through the Colombian experience, and Dean Pruitt and Sun Lee Kim's perceived stalemate concept. It is argued that Havana dialogues are likely to be successful on the grounds that it seems that both parties share a mutual perception of stalemate. Finally, it is suggested that the context in which dialogues arose may also have an impact in an eventual DDR process.

Preface

In the classic tale "The Little Prince" appears the following remark about the only human inhabitant of a very small planet which is prone to a kind of instability or danger in form of gigantic trees:

... Indeed, as I learned, there were on the planet where the little prince lived--as on all planets--good plants and bad plants. In consequence, there were good seeds from good plants, and bad seeds from bad plants. But seeds are invisible. They sleep deep in the heart of the earth's darkness, until someone among them is seized with the desire to awaken. Then this little seed will stretch itself and begin--timidly at first--to push a charming little sprig inoffensively upward toward the sun. If it is only a sprout of radish or the sprig of a rose-bush, one would let it grow wherever it might wish. But when it is a bad plant, one must destroy it as soon as possible, the very first instant that one recognizes it ...Now there were some terrible seeds on the planet that was the home of the little prince; and these were the seeds of the baobab. The soil of that planet was infested with them. A baobab is something you will never, never be able to get rid of if you attend to it too late. It spreads over the entire planet. It bores clear through it with its roots. And if the planet is too small, and the baobabs are too many, they split it in pieces ... "It is a question of discipline," the little prince said to me later on. "When you've finished your own toilet in the morning, then it is time to attend to the toilet of your planet, just so, with the greatest care. You must see to it that you pull up regularly all the baobabs, at the very first moment when they can be distinguished from the rosebushes which they resemble so closely in their earliest youth. It is very tedious work," the little prince added, "but very easy" ... (De Saint-Exupéry, 2015)

The current world population is 7,361,062,100 and this huge number is increasing with dreadful velocity every second. Some experts in demography affirm that: "...At the dawn of agriculture, about 8000 B.C., the population of the world was approximately 5 million. Over the 8,000-year period up to 1 A.D. it grew to 200 million (some estimate 300 million or even 600, suggesting how imprecise population estimates of early historical periods can be), with a growth rate of under 0.05% per year...A tremendous change occurred with the industrial revolution: whereas it had taken all of human history until around 1800 for world population to reach one billion, the second billion was achieved in only 130 years (1930), the third billion in less than 30 years (1959), the fourth billion in 15 years (1974), and the fifth billion in only 13 years (1987)... Population in the world is currently (as of 2015-2016) growing at a rate of around 1.13% per year. The average population change is currently estimated at around 80 million per year..." (Worldometers, 2015).

Our problem is more complicated that the apparent simplicity of the little prince because a majority of human beings pursue an infinite diversity of caprices and ambitions inside a finite and fragile planet. Frequently each individual or collectivity keeps the accounts of their goods and services but ignores the damages and turbulences caused by their action.

Surely the readers of our Handbook of Research on Transitional Justice and Peace Building in Turbulent Regions may find that stormy societies are not always fixed anomalies lived in some isolated geographies: some countries can advance from turbulence towards calm and peace but sometimes disorder can be propagated regionally and globally. Indeed, in times of globalization a global propagation of dangers exists. Our main message in this short foreword is that we want to find global solutions in order to overcome the local, regional and global turbulences: a small turbulence is seed of a gigantic problem and, indeed, our finite planet is the small home to millions of human beings that create dozens of new problems but they can create cooperatively adequate solutions.

Utopian Global Welfare vs. Growing Planetary Turbulence

Some worldly philosophers known as utilitarian thinkers, specifically Bentham, Mill and Edgeworth suggested an idea of universal welfare (happiness). They defended the global well-being to the universe of sensitive beings (animals, plants and human beings).

In his wiser encyclical letter the Pope Francis quoted the words of Saint Francis of Assisi who proposed a more complete idea of a good and inclusive world:

... Francis helps us to see that an integral ecology calls for openness to categories which transcend the language of mathematics and biology, and take us to the heart of what it is to be human. Just as happens when we fall in love with someone, whenever he would gaze at the sun, the moon or the smallest of animals, he burst into song, drawing all other creatures into his praise. He communed with all creation, even preaching to the flowers, inviting them "to praise the Lord, just as if they were endowed with reason"... His response to the world around him was so much more than intellectual appreciation or economic calculus, for to him each and every creature was a sister united to him by bonds of affection. That is why he felt called to care for all that exists. His disciple Saint Bonaventure tells us that, "from a reflection on the primary source of all things, filled with even more abundant piety, he would call creatures, no matter how small, by the name of 'brother' or 'sister'"... Such a conviction cannot be written off as naive romanticism, for it affects the choices which determine our behaviour. If we approach nature and the environment without this openness to awe and wonder, if we no longer speak the language of fraternity and beauty in our relationship with the world, our attitude will be that of masters, consumers, ruthless exploiters, unable to set limits on their immediate needs. By contrast, if we feel intimately united with all that exists, then sobriety and care will well up spontaneously. The poverty and austerity of Saint Francis were no mere veneer of asceticism, but something much more radical: a refusal to turn reality into an object simply to be used and controlled. (Francis, 2015, p. 11)

The care of our common home is the main concern of the Pope Francis. He said that the entire world is suffering a permanent and growing destruction: seven decades after Hiroshima and Nagasaki the credible threat of a total destruction due to the possession of nuclear weapons by some powerful countries still persists; the global warming as a result of human activity is producing dramatic changes in the climate and the earth; pollution, climatic chaos, waste, contamination of water, loss of biodiversity, growing scarcity of clean water, breakdown of societies, increasing inequality, emergence of new wars, are the actual plagues propelled by the greed and indolence of human beings. Indeed, the mentioned problems are clear signals of a near destruction of the global commons. Approximately five decades ago the visionary biologist Garret Hardin proved the existence of an inexorable trend towards a tragedy of the commons due to the unrestrained growth of human population and the persistence of the most brutal greed (Hardin, 1968).

The modern history is a sequence of growing fragmentation of welfare from big universes (living beings, humanity) toward narrow and very exclusive collectivities (nations, social classes, communities, clubs, families and, finally, individuals). The consolidation of modern State Nations occurred in a context of severe competition: each nation has a chauvinist ambition in order to attain success despite the tragedy of its adversaries (Cuevas, 1998).

Sadly the world is not a public good without frontiers and rivalry. Indeed, the great economist Albert Hirschman reminded the remarks of Pascal about the Christian Divinity: God is the quintessential pure public good available to all the individuals and human collectivities at the same time, without exclusion (frontiers and barriers to entry), without rivalry (competition and jealously) and, perhaps, without subtraction (depletion of natural resources) (Hirschman, 1985, p. 7).

Exclusive groups (nations, social classes, communities, families, etc.) can be understood like very exclusive club goods. A club good, according to James Buchanan is a semi-public good that offers low levels of rivalry to its members but imposes high barriers to entry. The clubs are very exclusive because the utility that each individual receives from its consumption, use, access, "… depends upon the number of other persons with whom he must share its benefits." (Buchanan, 1965, p. 3)

The exclusive club of super riches comprises a minimal fraction of human kind. According to the most recent report by the NGO OXFAM: "Global wealth is increasingly being concentrated in the hands of small wealthy elite. These wealthy individuals have generated and sustained their vast riches through their interests and activities in a few important economic sectors, including finance and pharmaceuticals/healthcare … In 2014, the richest 1% of people in the world owned 48% of global wealth, leaving just 52% to be shared between the other 99% of adults on the planet. Almost all of that 52% is owned by those included in the richest 20%, leaving just 5.5% for the remaining 80% of people in the world. If this trend continues of an increasing wealth share to the richest, the top 1% will have more wealth than the remaining 99% of people in just two years … with the wealth share of the top 1% exceeding 50% by 2016 …" (Oxfam, 2015). Indeed, this means that the world is owned by an exclusive club (very powerful elite) that has the exclusive rights of property in order to take crucial decisions that, of course, affect the rest of the population.

A majority of human beings is condemned to live in turbulent regions, as victims of poverty and conflict. The economist Jeffrey Sachs, director of the Earth Institute at Colombia University, expressed the tragedies of millions of human beings in these terms:

Every morning our newspapers could report, "More than 20,000 people perished yesterday of extreme poverty." The stories would put the stark numbers in context—up to 8,000 children dead of malaria, 5,000 mothers and fathers dead of tuberculosis, 7,500 young adults dead of AIDS, and thousands more dead of diarrhea, respiratory infection, and other killer diseases that prey on bodies weakened by chronic hunger. The poor die in hospital wards that lack drugs, in villages that lack antimalarial bed nets, in houses that lack safe drinking water. They die namelessly, without public comment. Sadly, such stories rarely get written. Most people are unaware of the daily struggles for survival, and of the vast numbers *of impoverished people around the world who lose that struggle. Since September 11, 2001, the United States has launched a war on terror, but it has neglected the deeper causes of global instability. The $450 billion that the United States will spend this year on the military will never buy peace if it continues to spend around one thirtieth of that, just $15 billion, to address the plight of the world's poorest of the poor, whose societies are destabilized by extreme poverty and thereby become havens of unrest, violence, and even global terrorism. That $15 billion represents a tiny percentage of U.S. income, just 15 cents on every $100 of U.S. gross national product, or GNP. The share of U.S. GNP devoted to helping the poor has declined for decades, and is a tiny fraction of what the United States has repeatedly promised, and failed, to give. It is also much less than the United States should give, both to solve the crisis of extreme poverty and thereby to provide for U.S. national security. This book, then, is about making the right choices—choices that can lead to a much safer world based on a true reverence and respect for human life. (Sachs, 2005)*

The Existence of Turbulent Regions According To Two Different Views

The Institute for Economics and Peace produces annually an indicator of peace, named Global Peace Index. This index comprises three main domains, namely: ongoing domestic and international conflict (indicates the number and intensity of ongoing civil and international wars); societal safety and security (indicates the levels of safety and security within a country, such as the perception of criminality in society, the level of political instability and the rate of homicides and violent crimes) and, finally, militarization (indicates a nation's military capacity, both in terms of the economic resources committed to the military and support for multilateral operations). The Global Peace Index 2015 shows the next global photography where is highlighted the noisy turbulence in Middle-East, North Africa, Latin America and Russia, thus:

...The most substantial change in the index was recorded for the Middle East and North Africa (MENA) — where several countries suffered from an upsurge in violence related to sectarian strife and civil conflicts, as well as a rise in actions by Islamist extremist groups. It was followed by South America, where peacefulness was most affected in some countries by a rise in the perceptions of criminality and in popular protests. MENA now ranks as the most violent region, overtaking South Asia (which includes Afghanistan) from last year's GPI. Yet again, Europe maintained its position as the most peaceful region in the world, supported by a lack of domestic and external conflicts ... Although there were no new wars between countries, tense relationships between the two Koreas, concerns over China's growing military assertiveness in the Asia-Pacific region, the potential further expansion of the Middle East conflicts across borders, and the possibility that conflict between Russia and the Ukraine escalates into all out military confrontation suggest these may become hotspots for international conflict in the future. In the case of deaths from internal conflict, the scores for most regions deteriorated (the exceptions being South America and Central America and the Caribbean). The individual countries with the biggest score erosion for these indicators were Ukraine and Central African Republic, owing to ongoing and worsening civil wars. For the indicator of internal conflicts fought, internal conflict escalated most in the Middle East and North Africa. The situation improved in South America and South Asia... (Peace I. f., 2015, p. 8)

A more nuanced assessment is offered by the Fund for Peace with the Fragile States Index. This is "...an annual ranking of 178 nations based on their levels of stability and the pressures they face. The

Index is based on The Fund for Peace's proprietary Conflict Assessment Software Tool (CAST) analytical platform. Based on comprehensive social science methodology, data from three primary sources is triangulated and subjected to critical review to obtain final scores for the Fragile States Index. Millions of documents are analyzed every year, and by applying highly specialized search parameters, scores are apportioned for every country based on twelve key political, social and economic indicators and over 100 sub-indicators that are the result of years of painstaking expert social science research" (Peace F. F., 2015, p. 3).

This index comprises two big sets of indicators, namely: social indicators (demographic pressures, refugees and displaced people, group grievance, human flight and brain drain,); economic indicators (uneven economic development, and poverty and economic decline); and political and military indicators (state legitimacy, public services, human rights and rule of law, security apparatus, factionalized elites, and external intervention). According to this measurement, there are sustainable and stable "paradises" (Canada, Ireland, Iceland, Norway, Germany, Portugal, Australia and New Zealand); ambiguous "purgatories" (United States, United Kingdom, Poland, France, Spain, Costa Rica, Panama, Argentina, Chile, Uruguay, Romania, South Korea and Japan); turbulent hotter states (Mexico, Cuba, Brazil, Peru, Bolivia, Ecuador, Paraguay, Venezuela, Salvador, Nicaragua, Morocco, Algeria, Turkey, Ukraine, Belarus, Kazakhstan, Mongolia, China, India, Saudi Arabia, Malaysia, Indonesia, and South Africa); and, finally, burning turbulent hells (Guatemala, Haiti, Colombia, Sierra Leona, Liberia, Nigeria, Mauritania, Malik, Chad, Libya, Democratic Republic of Congo, Egypt, Kenia, Somalia, Ethiopia, Sudan, South Sudan, Yemen, Syria, Iraq, Afghanistan, Pakistan, Sri Lanka, Myanmar, Nepal, North Korea, and Russia).

The Dark Side of Peaceful and Prosperous Nations

The conventional economist assumes that the good health of a nation is equivalent to an incremented wealth (a growing gross domestic product, GDP). According to this odd assessment the healthiest nations are: United States, China, Japan, Germany, United Kingdom, France, Brazil, Italia, India and Russian Federation. According to the World Bank (Bank, 2015), some problematic regions like Latin America and Caribbean and Middle East and North Africa have lower economic income, and Sub Saharan Africa suffers a low income.

The less peaceful and more dangerous (militarized) countries are: Israel, North Korea, Russia, United States, Pakistan, France, India, Syria and Yemen (Peace I. f., 2015, pág. 36).

Nine potentially ultra-violent states exist that possess now a big arsenal of atomic weapons, namely: Russia, United States, France, China, United Kingdom, Israel, Pakistan, India and North Korea (Forbes, 2014).

The key message is that turbulence appears explicitly in some problematic regions (Latin America and Caribbean, Middle East and North Africa) but partially this is product of endogenous failures of each nation or particular region. Sadly the most prosperous and supposedly peaceful regions and countries can be actual and potential originators of waves of disorder and violence in the regions that today suffer turbulences.

The Essence of this Handbook

The reader of our collective work can find a complete theoretical discussion about conflict, violence, nonviolence, transitional justice, and peace building from different views and disciplines. Moreover, the specialized public can obtain exhaustive and nuanced explanation of some particular cases of transitional justice and peace building like Germany, Nicaragua, Sudan, Eritrea, Syria and Cambodia and, particularly, the situation of two very turbulent countries like Iraq and Colombia. This approach results from the cooperative work of researchers formed in different disciplines and with a direct knowledge on situations of violent conflicts and processes of restorative justice and peace building.

Freddy Cante
Universidad del Rosario, Colombia

Hartmut Quehl
Felsberg Institute, Germany

REFERENCES

Buchanan, J. (1965). An Economic Theory of Clubs. *Economica, 32*(125), 1–15. doi:10.2307/2552442

Cuevas, H. (1998). *Proceso Político y Bienestar Social*. Bogotá: Universidad Externado de Colombia.

De Saint-Exupéry, A. (2015). *genious.com*. Obtenido de The Little Prince, Chapter Five: http://genius.com/Antoine-de-saint-exupery-the-little-prince-chapter-5-annotated/

Forbes. (2014). *Forbes.com*. Obtenido de Nuclear Weapons States: http://www.forbes.com/sites/jamesconca/2014/09/25/the-nuclear-weapons-states-who-has-them-and-how-many/

Francis, P. (2015). *Vatican*. Obtenido de Francis Encyclicals: http://w2.vatican.va/content/francesco/en/encyclicals/documents/papa-francesco_20150524_enciclica-laudato-si.html

Hardin, G. (1968). The Tragedy of the Commons. *Science*, 1243–1248. PMID:5699198

Hirschman, A. (1985). *A Bias for Hope: Essays on Development and Latin America*. Boulder: Westview Press.

Oxfam. (2015). *Oxfam.org*. Obtenido de Oxfam International: https://www.oxfam.org/en/pressroom/pressreleases/2015-01-19/richest-1-will-own-more-all-rest-2016

Peace, F. F. (2015). *fundforpeace.org*. Obtenido de Fragile States Index: http://library.fundforpeace.org/fsi

Peace, I. f. (2015). *Visiionofhumanity*. Obtenido de Global Peace Index 2015: http://www.visionofhumanity.org/#/page/contact

Sachs, J. (2005). *The End of Poverty, Economic Possibilities for Our Time*. New York: Penguin Press.

World Bank. (2015). *databank.worldbank*. Obtenido de gross domestic product 2014: http://databank.worldbank.org/data/download/GDP.pdf

Worldometers. (19 de August de 2015). *worldometers.info*. Obtenido de worldometerspopulation: http://www.worldometers.info/world-population/

Acknowledgment

During the last week of May of 2014, inside the unforeseeable climate of Bogotá, Colombia (where you can frequently experience the four seasons in only one day and experience contradictory environments of peace and war), a remarkable academic discussion took place that also ended up in a fruitful process of consolidation of social ties.

The Rosario University was the host, and its Faculty of Political Science and Government held the workshop-conference on Realistic Peace and Turbulent Transitions. The successful organization of this seminal debate was the result of the joint efforts of the Rosario University and the Felsberg Institute for Education and Academic Research (FIBW) with additional support from the Colombian Organizations Icetex, Corpovisionarios and the Colombian Agency for Reintegration (ACR-Agencia Colombiana de Reintegración).

One of the most important attainments of this academic event was the encounter of numerous scholars, representing a wide variety of academic disciplines such as law, philosophy, economy, anthropology, history and sociology, among others, and carrying very singular experiences on social and political conflict from different parts of the world. Since the researchers know conflictive situations in determinate places and historical moments very well, the cases like Cambodia, Colombia, Eritrea, Germany, Iraq, Nicaragua, Rwanda, Syria, and Sudan were deeply discussed. Half of the participants are members of the *International Consortium for Research on Violence-ICRoV* (founded in Erbil, Iraq, in December 2013) and the other half were local professors and researchers who work in Colombian institutions.

The derived project of our mentioned event in Bogotá is the collective handbook of research on transitional justice and peace building in turbulent regions. The aggregated value of this academic product is the mixture of different points of view (different disciplines, varied analysis of conflict in dissimilar places and times) with a common denominator: how to promote processes of transitional justice and peace building in societies that suffer from endemic violence?

We are very grateful with the academic and managerial leaders and responsible persons that provided generous and opportune help. Of course, we are indebted with the academic participants of this collective effort (the authors and referees and my research assistant, Nathalie Mezza-Garcia), because of their responsibility and commitment to attain an optimal academic product. Finally we would like to express our sincere gratitude to the members of IGI GLOBAL disseminator of knowledge because their important contribution in the quality of this new handbook.

Section 1

Transitional Justice and Peace Building in Turbulent Regions

Chapter 1
Turbulent Peace, Power, and Ethics

Fredy Cante
Universidad del Rosario, Colombia

ABSTRACT

A situation of turbulent peace is defined as an ambiguous transition from direct violence (which ends by means a fragile and incomplete peace agreement among enemies) to an indirect and subtle violence euphemistically denominated as progress. Indeed, a big rate of economic growth implies growing prosperity, incremented consumption, and increasing investment in the present but, sadly, the consequence of this material progress will be the suffering of future generations because the exhaustion and deterioration of nature in a world where the entropy is worsened by the rapacity of actual generations. The depletion and contamination of natural resources is the inherent cost of material progress and development of "productive" forces. The ideological, coercive and economic power of some organized minorities, and the acquiescence of a big majority of human beings constitutes the root of this problem. The antidote against this power is the critical examination of values by active citizens and the guide of ethics. In the long run this problem can be solved promoting a nonviolent economy.

INTRODUCTION

A century ago a pessimistic visionary, the author of the Devil's Dictionary (Bierce, 2004), stated that peace is "… a period of cheating between two periods of fighting". This significance was referred to the arena of international affairs but also is valid in the context of internal conflict or civil war. Without doubts this accurate meaning is a variation by a minor composer on a theme composed by an original Master. The memorable Heraclitus of Ephesus stated wisely two famous sentences: "Everything flows and nothing stays" and "War is the father and king of all: some he has made gods, and some men; some slaves and some free."

The turbulence invades the different attempts to attain peace because destructive power and unethical deals are very frequent in the human relationships (and force, fraud and deception are the main strategies of powerful people). Exist at least three kinds of turbulences in the process of peace, namely: a) Peace agreements can be used like a Trojan horse by opportunistic rivals; b) Conflict

DOI: 10.4018/978-1-4666-9675-4.ch001

is an agonistic game among several adversaries and, consequently, peace agreements are partial consensus and, consequently, are source of new unconformity and renovated confrontations (all the sectors of a society want peace but each sector have different views of peace); and c) During and after a flourishing peacetime a reconciled society can promote material progress (unbound economic growth, incessant development of productive forces) which is in an inclement an violent process of creative destruction. Colombia and Iraq are paradigmatic and clear examples of turbulent peace because opportunistic rivals and biased peace agreements, nevertheless the rest of the supposedly peaceful and prosperous nations are carriers of others turbulences because they are promoting destructive progress.

In the recent history of Colombia (IEPRI, 2006) there are three process of turbulent peace, and each one has been cause of new kinds of war, and the next is the synthesis:

- **National Front (1958-1974):** Coalition between the leadership of two main traditional political parties (Liberal and Conservative), in order to finish the partisan violence, by means the rotation of power each four years between this two parties. Nevertheless this implied the abolition of a real political opposition, and the violent exclusion of leftist and populist political parties. The country experienced capitalist progress: urbanization, growth in the construction of cities and infrastructure and massive displacement of peasants to cities. Colombian governments followed the National Security Doctrine promoted by USA (in the context of Cold War). During these period was the birth of leftist guerrillas: Revolutionary Armed Forces of Colombia (originated in a repression of Colombian State against a peasant resistance), National Liberation Army, Popular Liberation Army, Quintin Lame (an armed resistance of indigenous people), and 19th of April Movement (created because the electoral fraud in 1974 against the populist National Popular Alliance).
- **Bittersweet Bargaining with Insurgent Guerrillas (1982-2002):** The quasi-annihilated 19th of April Movement attained a total demobilization and successful reintegration of combatants to the democratic competition (with a soft social-democratic proposal); after another peace agreement the Revolutionary Armed Forces of Colombia made a coalition with popular leaders, and a majority of its combatants were demobilized and they formed the Patriotic Union (UP) a party of left wing; indeed, the Patriotic Union was successful in local elections, but a majority of the militants of this party have been murdered by paramilitary groups of extreme-right and drug traffickers and, of course, this caused the radicalization of warriors in the ranks of the Revolutionary Armed Forces of Colombia ; posteriorly the neoliberal government of the President Cesar Gaviria and some sectors of the social-democratic political opposition construed a new Political Constitution at 1991 (which is a pact between soft social-democracy and neoliberalism); at the beginning of the century the government of Pastrana and Revolutionary Armed Forces of Colombia played a deceitful game of peace; and, simultaneously, some sectors of non-violent opposition founded the Democratic Pole which is a party of center left. During the same period evolved the drug-traffickers (from the market of marihuana to the most profitable business of cocaine), and they construed alliances with legal entrepreneurs and politicians, and even with guerrillas; a majority of the Colombian municipalities participated passively or actively in the organization and consolidation of the right-

wing violent counter-insurgence (cooperatives of agrarian self-defense, paramilitary groups and warlords) and near of 5 million of persons suffered forced displacement (about 10% of Colombian population).

- **Pacification and Deceitful Demobilization of Insurgent and Counterinsurgent Armies (2002-Today):** Partial demobilization of combatants from Paramilitary groups, and extradition of some important drug traffickers during the two administrations of the paradigmatic leader of the Colombian extreme-right Alvaro Uribe Velez (2002-2010); and today Colombia experiences a uncertain process of peace between the government of President Juan Manuel Santos (former minister of war of Alvaro Uribe Velez) and the weakened Revolutionary Armed Forces of Colombia (because the violent state repression known like Democratic Security of Uribe and Santos which is the dominant public policy). During the same period occur the next violent facts: democratic security and trust to foreign investors; repression against popular sectors; privatized security to foreign investors and opulent sectors, and economic incentives and privileges to foreign enterprises; neoliberal model of extractivism (legalized plunder of energy, water and alive organism by powerful transnational companies); and, notorious trend towards Kleptocracy (criminal alliances among corrupts politicians, private entrepreneurs, drug traffickers and others criminals).

The most violent and unstable Iraq lives a worse history. The state of tempestuous calm lived in Erbil (the prosperous Capital of Kurdistan) in the recent past (before the actual war between the Islamic State and its enemies) can be imagined like the most likely pattern of future development of Iraq (and other Arab countries) after this actual cycle of direct violence. The relative and stormy peace lived (during the past years) in the prosperous and small State of Kurdistan has been product of two very important factors, namely: First, the existence of high racial homogeneity (Kurdistan is called land of Kurdish because this ethnic group constituted the majority of the population of this region); Second, and most important, the government of this region offered trust and indulgences to foreign investors (mainly companies that works in the profitable business of oil extraction) like ten-year tax exemptions, total ownership of companies and repatriation of profits, reduced-price land allocation for investment project and, moreover, blind obedience to the precepts of neoliberalism (Fogoto, 2012).

A situation of turbulent peace is then defined as an ambiguous transition from direct violence (which ends by means a fragile and incomplete peace agreement among enemies) to an indirect, subtle but highly dangerous kind of violence euphemistically denominated as progress. Indeed, a big rate of economic growth implies growing prosperity, incremented consumption, and increasing investment in the present but, sadly, the consequence of this material progress will be the suffering of distant and people and future generations because the exhaustion and deterioration of nature in a world where the entropy is worsened by the rapacity of actual generations. The depletion and contamination of natural resources is the inherent cost of material progress and development of "productive" forces.

This document is organized in two big parts: in the first part (the background) is examined carefully the problem of turbulent peace; in the second part (conclusions and perspectives of future research) is explained the relationship among peace, power and ethics and, moreover, are insinuated some ways in order to find a prospect of solution. Key concepts (ethics, exosomatic and endosomatic instruments; moral, morality, power and turbulent peace) are synthetically explained at the end of the article.

BACKGROUND

Reality and Abstraction

According to Feyerabend "real" is what plays an important (functional) role in the kind of life one wants to live and today the people suffer the tyranny of experts (economist, agronomist, engineers, etc.) which exercise their power to construct realities by means science based principles . Indeed all cultures use abstractions in order to construct convenient and manageable realities:

The search for reality that accompanied the growth of Western civilization played an important role in the process of simplifying the world. It is usually presented as something positive, or an enterprise that leads to the discovery of new objects, features, relations. It is said that it widens our horizon and reveals the principles behind the most common phenomena. But this search has also a strong negative component. It does not accept the phenomena as they are, it changes them, and either in thought (abstraction) or by actively interfering with them experiment. Both types of changes involve simplifications. Abstractions remove the particulars that distinguish an object from another, together with some general properties such as color and smell. Experiments further remove or try to remove the links that tie every process to its surrounding —they create an artificial and somewhat impoverished environment and explore its peculiarities. In both cases, things are being taken away or "blocked off" from the totality that surrounds us. Interestingly enough, the remains are called "real", which means they are regarded as more important than the totality itself. Moreover, this totality is now described as consisting and of two parts: a hidden and partly distorted real world and a concealing and disturbing veil around it. The dichotomy occurs not only in Western philosophy and science, it also occurs in religious context it may be there combined with the dichotomy between Good and Evil ... (Feyerabend, 1999, p. 248)

Modern Power by Means of Abstractions

Nietzsche argued that the supreme aim of human beings is no the happiness or the welfare or at least the tranquility of contemplation (like has been assumed by economist from the times of Adam Smith). He said that even the most insignificant living being have an incorporate will to power and, consequently, this force impulse all human beings to growth, to exploit, to expand possessions and to become predominant ; and the will to power is the will to life and can be understood like a basic organic function. (Nietzsche, 2003)

According to Boulding there are three kinds of power: violent or military power which is exercised by means negative incentives (potential use of violence or coercion); economic power that is implemented across positive incentives (bribes) and the most powerful type of power: the charismatic and ideological influence of some influent leaders (like Jesus Christ, Gandhi, and different writers and intellectuals) that govern heart and minds of people. This power has two dimensions: Love and morality (capacity to construct communities, and social relationships through gifts, altruism, reciprocity and no interested contributions); and Ideology (ability to create feasible views of the world, and collective dreams), –for the purpose of this section I shall use only the first dimension. The power of the ruling class (political ideologist, military strategist, religious and moral authorities, intellectuals and writers, and journalist) is based in the construction of ideas which govern the decisions, actions, practices and behaviors of people that exercise more concrete and practical task (technical, economic and military powers and activities) and that belong to the ruled class (Boulding, 1989).

In all cultures and known societies human beings have exerted power, nevertheless there is a big and dramatic step from the power used by means stick and the power implemented through abstract concepts and models. The main characteristic of modern societies (including capitalism and socialism) is that rulers exert integrative power by means abstractions which govern the different modalities of technic, economic, and military actions of the modern subjects. A former scientific and posteriorly brilliant writer (Sábato, 1951) affirmed that money and reason endow modern man with secular power not despite abstraction but because of it. And today the power is multiplied because logarithms replace bludgeons and letters of exchange the gold ingots.

Following, complementing and amplifying the mentioned work of Sábato, the next are the main features of this kind of power exerted by means abstract ideas:

- **Profanation of the Sacred Nature:** Ancient people (and some contemporary aboriginal groups) have assumed wisely that the Sun is a God, and that the land is our mother. The pioneer of ecological economics (Georgescu-Roegen, 1971) wisely said that sun is the source of all of our available energy, in the form of direct flux of solar rays, and indirectly in the photosynthesis, and in the millenary formation of stocks of fossil fuels. Christianity, at least during fifteen centuries of Middle Ages, promoted indifference or contempt towards nature because–according to some interpretations of the Holly Bible–human beings are only ephemeral occupants (guest) of this earthly and impious material world, and this religion said that the most important human aim is the metaphysical paradise; the creators of modern ideology are a mixture of priest (lovers of abstractions and scholastic text) and materialist businessman (lovers of practical utility, and seekers of terrestrial paradises), consequently the creators of modern ideology have stated that nature is only a set of raw and functional materials and, consequently, this must be and object of exploitation, and must serve to new divinities in the form of human ideals of wants, desires, caprices and pleasures (Rifkin, 1981).
- **Deification of Abstract Ideals and Fetishism:** Modern people are governed by new divinities, the ancient God of the Holly Bible have been supplanted by new ideals: scientist (including atheist experts) are voluntarily ruled by abstract reason and platonic buildings of mathematics; policy makers and technocrats are followers of some magic idols and myths (invisible hand, unbound progress, eternal growth) and they preserve some sanctified entities or idealized aims (equilibrium, positive and growing rate of interest, positive and increasing rate of economic growth, and diminishing rate of discount over the future); designers of revolutions and some dreamers of social change are followers of abstracts ideals (some kinds of patriotism, and they express a suspicious love towards humanity); flocks of consumers are pursuing ideals of unbound success: they are seekers of pleasure and happiness without regard the negative consequences over another people, following the teaching of cruel and sadistic heroes – this means that Sade whit his libertine commandments of unbound success and unrestricted pleasure without take minimal care of victims (objects of pleasure) may be more influential than Smith. Hordes of consumers are addicts and loyal lovers of new fetish (cars, fashion, and ostensible consumption of expensive luxuries). Money is the new God for all the members of the market society because this is an abstract and pure exchange value (without utility, and material guaranty), it is an universal mean of pay and exchange which has magic attributes: unrestricted divisibility (which creates the illusion of measure to all the existing

things, values and merchandises); liquidity (the possessor of cash has economic freedom to attain indulgences and design business without cultural, ecologic and moral barriers … the unique frontier is his monetary budget); unbelievable accumulation and growth (deposits of money and diverse financial papers growth without limit by means the magical formula of compound interest) (Hardin, 1993). The new churches are the central banks (commanded by idiot technocrats obsessed to bless money, and dedicated to diminish the rate of inflation and to avoid falsification of money), and the financial institutions (houses of game, where well educated bandits construct buildings of imaginary numbers and play, by means speculative transactions, with the life and existence of natural environments and poor people that, indeed, they don't know). (Saul, 1993)

- **Mechanical Abstraction:** The biblical story of the creation, in six days, of all existent things, animals and human beings has been replaced by a new myth: modern thinkers have supposed that mankind constitute the center of the Universe, and that creators of abstract models can be architects of a man-made-universe and, consequently, this new race of autocratic intellectuals want to produce their own creatures: modern machines (exosomatic instruments moved mainly through petrochemical devices that consume nonrenewable deposits of fossil fuels). Illusory modern intellectuals assume that all the existent things and beings can be understood like machines, and consequently their abstractions are models of mechanism. The mechanic abstraction is the main model of thinking of modern people, and this is an interpretation of the world in which is assumed that big and complex universes (nature, society, individual, body, etc.) can be divided in small parts (pieces, components); and each part can be understood like an ideal unit, which belongs to a group of similar components (it has no singular features) and it is isolated of the rest. Abstract thinking permit the construction of ideal models (without complex process of interdependence and interaction, and without frictions), and the formulation of general laws, but it implies the erection of pure and ideal concepts (platonic entities without particular features and concrete realities), and the creation of unbelievable assumptions (in which the context and environment of each piece or component is assumed to be constant and inalterable).

This kind of power is imposed over people by means a combination of deception (indoctrination and instruction by means education) and coercion (against rebels and heretic persons). According to Sábato there is a trend towards homogeneity of this kind of thinking because the unification is abstracting: science led to a mathematical view of reality and capitalism led to an abstract society and ideal individuals (dispossessed of his freedom and personality), and this process occurs by means prizes and punishments in a process of repression and domestication across the education. Other liberal thinkers explained the danger of unrestricted experiments of social engineering that are the common denominator of two big social experiments – the totalitarianism of Nazis and the autocratic Socialism–, during part of the past century (Popper, 1945). This constitutes a deliberate and forced construction, by means violence and autocracy, of massive process of social change, according to a preliminary and utopian design (a platonic model or ideal) designed by influential theoreticians to be implemented by the best political leaders of a select human group, –respectively, a beauty and intelligent ethnic group, or a very productive and honest social class. The big scale of social experimentation leaded by dark politicians –Hitler, Lenin, Stalin, Mao and other minus famous– failed because the human limits of their commanders (characterized by serious bounds to know and to control, the diverse and uncertain behaviors of millions of human beings) and, of course, due the resistance of the lovers of freedom. Nevertheless today we live inside a renovated and systematic form of subtle totalitarianism, which is the market society that has the next main features: a set of seductive patterns (sleepless impulse of lucre or democratized greed, and massive and insatiable thirst of success), and a collection of autocratic organizations (families, schools, universities, enterprises, political parties, and different associations) which function like disciplined and obedient armies and, consequently, are managed by authoritarian bosses, watchman, and guides that govern a new race of vassals by means a set of selective incentives (prizes and punishments, breads and circus).

Unbound Power to Destroy and Transform Life

Warriors (armies, States, and terrorist) exercise destructive power by means credible threats (potential use of violence) because they have instruments of destruction (weapons). With the colossal advance in science and technology, the high qualified and prestigious armies of scientist and technics that work to States and enterprises have produced two powerful types of weapons: a) the atomic bomb which is the most advanced technic of destruction by means pyrotechnical knowledge, and leave behind the obsolete fashion of weapons with limited capacity to destroy; b) the intelligent weapons which are technological devices managed by remote control or endowed by powerful sensors, to destroy accurately military objectives (whit minimal intervention of fallible and scrupulous human soldiers). The main product of this dark knowledge is that now the war is an industry of massive destruction managed by cowards, and the groups of humans (old-fashioned guerrillas, discardable pawns of the military chess named euphemistically soldiers of the mother country, and unarmed citizens) can be hunt like insignificant flies or rats.

The maximum development of supposedly beneficial and constructive sciences and technics is danger and destruction in a planetary scale. The unrestricted advance of petrochemical technics has bad effects like exhaustion of fossil fuels (carbon and oil) and big increment in the global warming. The unbound growth and improvement in pyrotechnic weapons is represented in the ultra-destructive atomic bomb, and this kind of armament is a dissuasive force employed by all the powerful nations. Consequently, the total and fulminant destruction of the planet is a credible threat –even Schelling affirms that every new day is a miracle, and there are only some psychological barriers to the effective use of this demoniac device. The new field of biotechnology supposedly has been developed in order to overcome illness and to improve the quality of some plants and animals, nevertheless the uncontrolled expansion of this technology may produce a new hell in the nature and in the life. This technic is a fusion of informatics and genetic: computers are increasingly being used to decipher, manage and organize the immense genetic information that is considered like the raw resource of the global economy at the beginning of XXI century. Today there are two dangers caused by the impetuous advance in biotechnology, namely: transformation of animals, plants and human beings in patented products (private property of designers and big corporations) which can be "produced", transformed and adulterated like machines; creation of a new form of Eugenics, nor the more rudimentary eugenics implemented by Hitler but the more sophisticated and dangerous market-driven design of children, plants and animals, and the most brutal and capricious alteration of nature and life (Rifkin, El siglo de la biotecnología: el comercio genético y el nacimiento de un mundo feliz, 2009).

Economic Abstractions in Order to Plunder and Deceive

Businessman (entrepreneurs, dominant firms, managers of powerful commercial and financial empires), technocracy and policy makers exercise power of exchange and power to impose incentives over customers and employees by means deception, abstraction, bribes and war of prices.

The false accounts of economist: sadly a majority of economist (including the followers of Marx's theory, and mainly the dominant school of Neoclassical economic thinking) have omitted –with interested capacity to err– the productive role of nature. This fallacy has been destroyed by (Georgescu-Roegen, Energy and Economic Myths: Instituional and Economic Essays, 1976) in the next terms: a) nature produces all the energies, materials, and forms of life (which really are the irreplaceable input of all economy); b) human beings have big capacity of consumption, exhaustion and depletion of this resources (which are the unavoidable output of human works), c) natural resources are abstracted (leave out) by conventional economist and, consequently, this intellectuals have assumed that contribution of nature is equal to zero in the standard accounts; d) Suspiciously normal economist assume that the economic systems comprises only the exchange of services (different kinds of human labor) and payments (named rents) to owners of lands, mines, and positional goods (singular landscapes, extraordinary intelligence or beauty, and so on) and, consequently, they judge that nature is only a vulgar quarry (a deposit of indestructible energies and materials), a distant sewer (a place to put all the dangerous organic and inorganic waste, without bad consequences to humans), and raw material (a deformed clay, and a useless land) destined to be virtuously transformed by the glorified human work.; e) The inheritors of neoclassical and Marxist economist shamelessly disappear future generations (and distant people) by means the inter temporal rate of discount. All they agree that we can dilapidate the resources of the future (exploit today all the mineral and energetic reserves, destroy the soil, and contaminate the planet) because, "… long run is a misleading guide to current affairs. In the long run we are all dead" as the liberal gentleman Keynes said.

Reductionist economic thinking: following influential economist (Ricardo, 2004) and (Bastiat, 2004) the modern sheep have created the next kind of fantastic assumptions: ultra-abundant things like water and air (and all the nature) are free goods (without economic value), and only odd and scarce things like gold and diamonds have big economic value; despite the common sense observation brilliantly exposed by Shakespeare when he said that it is impossible to take a portion of flesh of a living body without remove blood (Shakespeare, 2004). Modern experts assume that it is possible to separate body and soul, soil and subsoil and so on. The defenders of conventional economic thinking have a simplistic view of humans and of nature. They take for granted that human beings are destined to be machines to maximize pleasures (if they are consumers), benefits (if they are entrepreneurs), and to wage an economic war (named "creative destruction"); this economic war produce winners (successful people) and losers (victims in form of unemployed, and human garbage). They believe –with lucrative blindness–, that nature is a passive object to be "productively" and "profitable" used, consequently, they abstract the qualitative features of a territory, namely: the complex set of physic, geologic, biologic, social, economic and cultural characteristics of the different socio-ecosystems inside a region.

Property rights to plunder and to deceit: from the denominated primitive accumulation of capital (Marx, 1993) until today, the creation of property rights has been a dirty enterprise of piracy, and arbitrary and constant enclosure. The logic of the all existent property rights has been built violently (Polanyi, 2001), following the next arbitrary ideas and actions: A) Nature is a passive object of appropriation, and can be fragmented in different segments (Countries, land, mines, waters, and air) by means the erection of fences, frontiers and barriers to exclude invasions (by poor persons, or foreign); B) The rent of land is the income of the landlord, who receives an usual payment (because he is owner of the supposedly non-destructible energies and materials of the soil), and an extraordinary profit due the increment in the demand of his land caused by the increment of population and the increase of the wealth (and the same logic applies to mines, and natural and artificial objects); C) A majority of Human beings have been victims of forced expulsion from the commons (collective properties of terrain by communities), and suffered forced displacement of people towards cities has been a key requisite in order to construct a market of labor; D) the salary is the income of workers (powerless people that have lost his sacred right to leisure, and that is paid for their mental or corporal work, and because their acquiescence); E) the interest paid to owners of money is due the arbitrary creation of a fictitious and fantastic merchandise (money), and the criminal appropriation of time by bankers. Polanyi emphasized that exist artificial and arbitrary merchandises which are product of fraud and plundering, namely: rent of land, market for labor, and monetary interest.

Revisiting Walter Benjamin's Thesis on History

In the aftermath of a war, a majority of people share a hopeful prospect of peace. They have a realistic view about some irreversible harms of violence (for example, they realize that it is impossible to recover corpses), and they believe in peace like a time of new opportunities to find a good life, and, consequently, they have a strong capacity to be resilient. Nevertheless, they innocently assume that history can be the outcome of a rational and binary choice –a bifurcation of ways (between a violent prospect and a violent future) where a people can reject a path towards violence and choice a peaceful road. Moreover they are prone to wishful thinking and have an ability to conceive optimist expectations about the uncertain future: individuals and societies, after a disaster, think that the future may be better than past.

The philosopher Walter Benjamin had a more complete and realistic picture in relationship with peace, he understood the impossibility of a complete restorative justice and exposed his doubts about the improvement of our civilization. An appropriate reading of his remark about the Angel of History help us to understand that history (Benjamin, 2009) is a continuous process (a non-divisible and turbulent flux between past and future) and, consequently, it is impossible to expect that the impure, violent and contaminate river of history finishes its course in a pure, peaceful and clean ocean. The destruction of nature and the physical and psychological violence against human beings are long run consequences of wars. In this famous text he stated that:

There is a painting by Klee called Angelus Novus. An angel is depicted there who looks as though he were about to distance himself from something which he is staring at. His eyes are opened wide, his mouth stands open and his wings are outstretched. The Angel of History must look just so. His face is turned towards the past. Where we see the appearance of a chain of events, he sees one single catastrophe, which unceasingly piles rubble on top of rubble and hurls it before his feet. He would like to pause for a moment so fair [verweilen: a reference to Goethe's Faust], to awaken the dead and to piece together what has been smashed. But a storm is blowing from Paradise, it has caught itself up in his wings and is so strong that the Angel can no longer close them. The storm drives him irresistibly into the future, to which his back is turned, while the rubble-heap before him grows sky-high. That which we call progress, is this storm.

Modern people blindly believe in progress, because they want to accept as true that this always means positive changes, net growth and constructive development. The common denominator of modern collectivities (from followers of liberal ideals of free markets to devotees of state intervention in order to attain social justice) is that all they do not conceive the negative and dangerous consequences of the storm named progress.

Seven decades after the World War Two the peace is even an illusory mirage, and the storm of progress has produced more dangers than benefits. Benjamin was correct and yet today his remarks are right because his reasonable suspects about progress, concretely in these words, in the mentioned text:

... Something unending (something corresponding to an endless perfectibility of humanity). ... something essentially unstoppable (as something self-activating, pursuing a straight or spiral path). Each of these predicates is controversial, and critique could be applied to each of them. This latter must, however, when push comes to shove, go behind all these predicates and direct itself at what they all have in common. The concept of the progress of the human race in history is not to be separated from the concept of its progression through a homogenous and empty time. The critique of the concept of this progress must ground the basis of its critique on the concept of progress itself.

From the point of view of realistic economist like (Schumpeter, 2008) time means radical historical changes, unexpected transformations, heterogeneous successions, and progress implies an inevitable process of creative destruction. Perhaps the divinities or the ideal genius of platonic and ideal worlds can create miracles without sacrifices (and profits without cost), but the human beings only can promote progress in some dimensions and retreat in another aspects. The socialism proposed by Marx and Engels (Marx, Manifiesto of the Communist Party, 1973) and their followers has only one virtue: the construction of a just society to all the workers (without the problems of exploitation of employees by corrupt and bad employers). Nevertheless there is a common denominator among capitalism, socialism and fascism, namely: a convenient economic trap which consists in the abstraction, suppression, and omission of nature which is the origin of all the energies, materials and forms of life that across human work and appropriation are used "productively" by societies and taken for free from nature. In the mentioned book about History Benjamin stated that:

The conformism which has dwelt within social democracy from the very beginning rests not merely on its political tactics, but also on its economic conceptions. It is a fundamental cause of the later collapse. There is nothing which has corrupted the German working-class so much as the opinion that they were swimming with the tide. Technical developments counted to them as the course of the stream, which they thought they were swimming in. From this, it was only a step to the illusion that the factory-labor set forth by the path of technological progress represented a political achievement. The old Protestant work ethic celebrated its resurrection among German workers in secularized form. The Gotha Program [dating from the 1875 Gotha Congress] already bore traces of this confusion. It defined labor as "the source of all wealth and all culture." Suspecting the worst, Marx responded that human being, who owned no other property aside from his labor-power, "must be the slave of other human beings, who... have made themselves into property-owners." Oblivious to this, the confusion only increased, and soon afterwards Josef Dietzgen announced: "Labor is the savior of modern times... In the... improvement... of labor... consists the wealth, which can now finally fulfill what no redeemer could hitherto achieve?" This vulgar-Marxist concept of what labor is, does not bother to ask the question of how its products affect workers, so long as these are no longer at their disposal. It wishes to perceive only the progression of the exploitation of nature, not the regression of society. It already bears the technocratic traces which would later be found in Fascism. Among these is a concept of nature which diverges in a worrisome manner from those in the socialist utopias of the Vormaerz period [pre-1848]. Labor, as it is henceforth conceived, is tantamount to the exploitation of nature, which is contrasted to the exploitation of the proletariat with naïve self-satisfaction. Compared to this positivistic conception, the fantasies which provided so much ammunition for the ridicule of Fourier exhibit a surprisingly healthy sensibility. According to Fourier, a beneficent division of social labor would have the following consequences: four moons would illuminate the night sky; ice would be removed from the polar cap; saltwater from the sea would no longer taste salty; and wild beasts would enter into the service of human beings. All this illustrates a labor which, far from exploiting nature, is instead capable of delivering creations whose possibility slumbers in her womb. To the corrupted concept of labor belongs, as its logical complement, that nature which, as Dietzgen put it, "is there gratis [for free].

Finally, Walter Benjamin's thesis on history can be complemented with the next remark about the triple suffering that the Angel of History could have about the human existence at the beginning of XXI century, thus: in the aftermath of each new war (direct violence) he establish that it is impossible to resuscitate corpses and to repair destroyed nature and injured human beings; and when he is pushed in the ephemeral present time towards the impetuous flow named progress he sadly corroborates that growth and economic development implies a new form of war (indirect violence) against nature and against distant persons in the geography and in the time (future generations). This occurs because to nature is assumed for free, and the value of life of future beings is fiercely discounted by the greedy present generations.

The Angel of History would like to stop the destructive machine of progress because he knows that modern human beings prefer to discount (depreciate) the future. He remembers the wise observations made by (Rae, 2010) two centuries ago, thus:

...The gratifications as may now be enjoyed generally awaken a passion strongly prompting to the partaking of them. The actual presence of the immediate object of desire in the mind by exciting the attention, seems to rouse all the faculties, as it were to fix their view on it, and leads to them to a very lively conception of the enjoyments which it offers to their instant possession. The prospects of future good, which future years may hold out to us, seem at such a moment dull and dubious, and are apt to be slighted, for objects on which the daylight is falling strongly, and showing us in all their freshness just within our grasp ... Everywhere we see, that to spend is easy, to spare hard.

A big part of nature is constituted of non-renewable natural resources and the rhythm of progress implies an intergenerational allocation of this kind of resources: a determined pace in the use of minerals and fossil fuels (including water and air) implies an inevitable and hard choice between distribution of scarce resources between actual human beings and future generations. This allocation of resources can be understood like a gift (positive or negative), a unilateral transaction, and an arbitrary choice made by a kind of dictator that, in the ephemeral present day decides the future of unborn people (without voice and vote).

If we assume an inter-temporal rate of discount equal to cero then the period of use of nonrenewable resources may be extended some centuries (and millions of future beings may be saved) but each generation may be condemned to a very frugal consumption of resources. Nevertheless, a big majority of human beings have a strong preference for consumption and joy in the present time (they are very impatient) because: the life of each human being is very short and his or her capacity to enjoy in perfection all its goods and experiences (mental and corporeal) is bounded by scarcity (nature and life are subject to entropy, decadence and deterioration); the majority of modern human beings are very eager and rapacious and, consequently, they prefer a pleasure (benefit) to be enjoyed sixty minutes hence and, of course, they prefer a pain (cost) to be endured a hundred years hence.

A Synthetic View of the Problem including some Empirical Evidence

The dozens of quantitative indicators made by orthodox economist about growth, investment, productivity, employment, profitability, rents, and rate of interest, etc. are a form of abstraction and a construction of illusions. Nevertheless when people observe directly or across qualitative reports the realities (deterioration of nature, physical discomfort, suffering and unhappiness of human beings), or when they know figures about environmental degradation and human misery, then they can doubt about the official reports.

According to Roegen the economic process can be represented in terms of the relation between low-entropy inputs (natural energies and minerals, plants and animals) and high-entropy outputs (instruments, machines, and goods of final and intermediate consumption, and waste produced by human beings). From the point of view of Kozo Mayumi the economic progress –understood like permanent growth and unrestricted development of productive forces– is assessed in terms of Economic Efficiency of Type 2 (EFT2), which refers to output per unit time. EFT2 constitutes and abstraction (omission) of the amount of natural inputs required in order to obtain the artificial outputs. The environmental destruction (deterioration of nature) –understood like extraction of minerals and energies, extinction of species of plants and animals, and growing production of waste and contamination – can be evaluated in terms of Ecological Efficiency of Type 1 (EFT1) that refers to the ratio of artificial output to natural input. EFT1 does not consider the sacred modern commandment of productivity (the time required to obtain the output). (Mayumi, 2012)

The figures of economic growth and productivity which are the modern symbols (flags and monuments) of progress are deceitful indicators because nature (and ecological efficiency) is not present in this fraudulent accountability. Indeed, the economic progress implies the production of ecological damages: extraction of billions tons of non-renewable fossil fuels and minerals; devastation of natural ecosystems and landscapes in order to obtain billions tons of wood and trillions tons of water; and production of billions tons of dangerous waste.

The vast research made by Angus Maddison and other academics offers an optimistic panoramic if we attend only the indicators of growth:

...Over the past millennium, world population rose 22–fold. Per capita income increased 13–fold, world GDP nearly 300–fold. This contrast sharply with the preceding millennium, when world population grew by only a sixth, and there was no advance in per capita income ... Per capita income growth is not the only indicator of welfare. Over the long run, there has been a dramatic increase in life expectation. In the year 1000, the average infant could expect to live about 24 years. A third would die in the first year of life, hunger and epidemic disease would ravage the survivors. There was an almost imperceptible rise up to 1820, mainly in Western Europe. Most of the improvement has occurred since then. Now the average infant can expect to survive 66 years ... The growth process was uneven in space as well as time. The rise in life expectation and income has been most rapid in Western Europe, North America, Australasia and Japan. By 1820, this group had forged ahead to an income level twice that in the rest of the world. By 1998, the gap

was 7:1. Between the United States and Africa the gap is now 20:1. This gap is still widening. Divergence is dominant but not inexorable. In the past half century, resurgent Asian countries have demonstrated that an important degree of catch–up is feasible. Nevertheless world economic growth has slowed substantially since 1973, and the Asian advance has been offset by stagnation or retrogression elsewhere ... (Maddison, The World Economy: A Millennial Perspective, 2001)

Situated on the edge of ecology, the academic Edward Goldsmith affirmed that three decades after the World War II the history registered its most disastrous facts: massive deforestation, soil erosion and desertification; floods and droughts, and growing poverty, millions of individuals live in vast shanty-towns, in which human life has attained a degree of sordidness probably unprecedented outside Hitler's concentration camps. (Goldsmith, 1985)

Seven decades ago finished the World War II, and now we suffer the consequences and risk of a progressive power of destruction: the storm named progress brings us new wars and big mountains of lots of fresh victims. In a recent journalistic report appears the next information about refugees:

...The number of people around the world forced by conflict to flee their homes, the United Nations High Commissioner for Refugees reported, has soared past 51 million, the highest number since World War II. That's more than six times the population of New York City, emptied into squalid camps. Half the refugees are children; a growing number of these are on their own, according to the report. More than half of the 6.3 million refugees under the refugee agency's care have been in exile for five years or more, testifying to conflicts that rage on and on. Most are what the United Nations refers to as "internally displaced" —people who have fled their homes but not their countries. (Schmemann, 2014)

The actual economic progress is like a machine of massive destruction more dangerous that the violent autocratic regimes of XX Century. People without sufficient acquisitive power (money) are invisible and non-existent in the market economy, and consequently they are outsiders of the economic reality. Hitler, Stalin and Mao were responsible of approximately 130 million of deaths, mainly by means economic weapons of massive destruction like famines and radical impoverishment (Jones, 2014). Today a part of human population suffer two kinds of hunger or acute starvation, namely: a) Immediate lack of food due war or natural disasters; and b) Daily undernourishment that is a less visible form of hunger -- but it affects many more people, from the shanty towns of Jakarta in Indonesia and the Cambodian capital Phnom Penh to the mountain villages of Bolivia and Nepal. In these places, hunger is much more than an empty stomach and can be the equivalent to a slow and painful way to death because for weeks, even months, its victims must live on significantly less than the recommended 2,100 kilocalories that the average person needs to lead a healthy life, and in that situation the body compensates for the lack of energy by slowing down its physical and mental activities. A hungry mind cannot concentrate, a hungry body does not take initiative, and a hungry child loses all desire to play and study and to live. Most of the world's hungry individuals live in developing countries. There are 805 million hungry people in the world and 98 percent of them are in developing countries. They are distributed as follows: 526 million (Asia and the Pacific); 227 million (Africa); 37 million (Latin American and Caribbean); 15 million (developed countries) The enormous paradox is that in the world there is enough food to feed everyone of this people (there is not a lack or scarcity of food in the sense assumed by Robert Malthus), and the available food is sufficient to provide everyone with at least 2.720 Kilocalories. (WFP, 2014) The main problem–following the remarks of Sen– is that very poor people is inexistent in the market economy because they do not have effective demand (they do not have sufficient or adequate land to grow, or income to purchase food). (Sen, 2009)

The poor people may be identified like forgotten and inexistent individuals (without the power and characteristics to be admitted like normal citizens). An influent international institution like the World Bank assumes (like the majority of States, and policy makers) that if a person lack of sufficient acquisitive monetary power then he or she may be considered as a poor individual. This institution informs that the people living in extreme poverty have below US$1.25 a day, and represent one billion of individuals; and approximately 2.2 billion of individuals live on less than US$2 dollars (according to recent statics). (World Bank, 2014)

According to a recent report by FAO exist 925 million in chronic hunger worldwide:

...the number of hungry people in the world remains unacceptably high despite expected recent gains that have pushed the figure below 1 billion. The new estimate of the number of people who will suffer chronic hunger this year is 925 million — 98 million down from 1.023 billion in 2009. ... (FAO, 2014)

During part of the past century a big share of the world was autocratically managed by dangerous leaders like Stalin, Hitler and Mao. Today, a minority of powerful and greedy super-magnates have unbound economic freedom in order to control the life and death of the rest of human beings. In a fresh report (OXFAM, 2014) appears a photography of the scale of rising wealth concentrations, capture of rents, unequal political representation which occurs because almost half of the world's wealth is now owned by just one percent of the population; the wealth of the one percent richest people in the world amounts to $110 trillion that is 65 times the total wealth of the bottom half of the world's population; and the bottom half of the world's population owns the same as the richest 85 people in the globe.

The economist T. Schelling, a polemic defender of the potential use of destructive force (dissuasion based on credible threats of terror, like the lesson of Hiroshima and Nagasaki), has offered the next arguments in relationship with the preservation of nuclear bombs:

...The most spectacular event of the past half century is one that did not occur ... We have enjoyed sixty years without nuclear weapons exploded in anger ... There has never been any doubt about the military effectiveness of nuclear weapons or their potential for terror ... How the inhibition arose, whether it was inevitable, whether it was the result of careful design, whether luck was involved, and whether we should assess it as robust or vulnerable in the coming decades, is worth examining. Preserving this tradition, and if possible helping to extend it to other countries that may yet acquire nuclear weapons, is as important as extending the Nuclear Non-Proliferation Treaty, now being renegotiated after its first twenty-five years ... (Schelling, Nobel Prize, 2005)

Perhaps the fragile illusion of the taboo may endure another seven decades more, but the material energies liberated by human beings don´t know about good manners and continence:

Globally around 30,000 nuclear weapons are held by various countries. More than one thousand five hundred of them are ready to launch at a moment's notice, 24 hours a day, seven days a week. On average, each of them has a destructive power thirty times that of the Hiroshima bomb. Through atmospheric effects, a few hundred could destroy a major part of the world... (Greenpeace, 2007)

Energy is an important ingredient in all phases of our opulent societies which are obsessed with growth, comfort and luxury. We live in a very interdependent world, and access to adequate and reliable energy resources is crucial for economic growth and for maintaining the material quality in the life of people. Nevertheless current levels of energy consumption (which are pushed by growth of population and greedy consumers and investors) production are not sustainable. About 40% of the world's energy comes from oil, and much of that goes to transportation uses. The U.S., with only 4.5% of the world's population, consumes 24% of the world's oil production per year; 66% of that oil is imported! About 85% of our energy comes from nonrenewable fossil fuels: oil, natural gas, coal. The likelihood of a link between global warming and fossil fuel use, with its production of carbon dioxide through combustion, is a signal of the dangerous consequences of this kind of energies (OpenStax, 2014)

Scientists have high confidence that global temperatures will continue to rise for decades to come, largely due to greenhouse gasses produced by human activities. The Intergovernmental Panel on Climate Change (IPCC), which includes more than 1,300 scientists from the United States and other countries, forecasts a temperature rise of 2.5 to 10 degrees Fahrenheit over the next century. The IPCC predicts that increases in global mean temperature of less than 1.8 to 5.4 degrees Fahrenheit (1 to 3 degrees Celsius) above 1990 levels will produce beneficial impacts in some regions and harmful ones in others. One of the most important conclusions is that net annual costs will increase over time as global temperatures increase. There is actualized information in: (Theguardian, 2013)

The constructors of realities also create images of demons, and of evil things. The market for addictive and psychoactive substances has a special feature: this is not result of voluntary and legal transactions inside an environment of economic freedoms. The extraordinary profitability of this market is product of the dangerous moral censure of some moral and political authorities (that argue that drugs are an anathema) and of the consequent legal prohibition of this merchandise. The consumption of this type of substances is normal in all the human societies because this is product of the different cultures. Due social and religious rituals or because the inherent dependence and pain of mortals, human beings normally consume diverse special substances which are denominated "sacred vegetables", "artificial paradises", and so on. Nevertheless some modern societies (especially in United States and Europa) have a false morality: their moral and religious authorities have the habit to forbid the consumption of some shunned substances like marihuana, cocaine, morphine, etc., because they argue that this products are dangerous and demoniac. However their arguments are impregnated of prejudice and lack of scientific rigor (for example the alcohol is accepted morally and legally but this substance may be more dangerous than some prohibited drugs). The designers of laws against drugs, concretely, the authors of the public policy named "War on Drugs" are –according to (Schelling, 1985)– creators of black markets which are protected and privileged commercial niches that are very profitable to organized crime and dangerous to consumers and growers of substances like marihuana, cocaine and opium. The named war on drugs produces losers: poor growers that suffer prosecution and aggression from members of their States and even from foreign powerful Nations; peasants that experiences destruction of nature because fumigations, and consumers that are exposed to bad quality substances and police repression; and, obviously, produces winners which are different forms of organized crime like Mafiosi, warlords, corrupt cooperators, and bankers.

The vicious and dangerous feedback of this market, and its contribution to civil war and corruption in countries like Colombia is product of an international public policy: from 1971 (during the polemic government of Nixon), the United States declared the War on Drugs and, as a result of this public policy, they created a black market (with high privileges and superb profitability due the illegal brand of this business). Indeed, without the abolition of this war and without the profitable business of prohibited drugs is impossible the attainment of peace in Colombia.

Transformation of Some Victims in Perpetrators and Markets of Victims

History is the product of war and competition, and this implies a dramatic change in all the things and human beings. It is impossible to catch an immutable or static reality, even situations like "peace" and "victims" can be transformed in its respective opposed states. Even victims of a violent conflict, sometimes, are transformed themselves in wrongdoers, and peace process are the germen of new clashes. Two millennium after the crucifixion of Jesus (and his generous sacrifice), some of the different religious organizations are rentable business; indeed, the Catholic Church is famous because the expensive indulgences of the hierarchs and the corruption of the named "Institute for the Works of Religion". In The Gospel according to Jesus Christ, the writer José Saramago (Saramago, 1992) wisely imagined that possibly God was acting strategically in order to create a paradigmatic Victim, and by means this kind of religious marketing he conquered the souls of millions of fervent followers. The moral message from this novel may be understood thus: some leaders know that being a victim sells, at least to the inheritors and political beneficiaries of the prey.

The political leaders and strategist of the Jewish people known very well the marketing of victims: every decade, from the end of World War Two until today, they and their sympathetic artist have produced dozens of books and films about the suffering of this people during the Holocaust. Besides the mentioned business, Jewish politicians are intellectual authors of a new apartheid: the territorial expansion of Israel and the consequent, exclusion, discrimination and violent actions of Jews against Palestinians (who not always are promoting pacifist resistance) constitutes a clear example of the dramatic historical changes: sometimes some victims and their representatives prefer to be perpetrators. The notorious expansionism of the State of Israel has been possible because the dramatic reduction of the Palestinian´s territory and the systematic extermination of Palestinians are legitimated by the words of political and intellectual leaders of Israel by means the modern power of abstraction (understood like the removal or extraction of undesirable and inconvenient realities). Golda Meir –a politician who was one of the founders of the State of Israel– has made abstraction of the Palestinians because in an interview she emitted the next message:

...There were no such things as Palestinians. When were there an independent Palestinian people with a Palestinian state? It was either southern Syria before the First World War, and then it was a Palestine including Jordan. It was not as though there were a Palestinian people in Palestine considering itself as a Palestinian people and we came and threw them out and took their country away from them. They did not exist. (Meir, 1969)

A prominent Jew intellectual leader specialized in games theory and who recently obtained the Nobel Prize of Economics, the Professor Aumann has made abstraction of Palestinian in the next terms:

Israel is the same as Palestine ...My wife has Palestinian documents. The Arabs say that Haifa and Tel Aviv are part of Palestine and they're right because this is indeed the land of Israel. We are both the Jews as well as the Palestinians. Referring to the Arabs as Palestinians is the root of our mistake. Therefore, it's important to say that we are the Palestinians and they are Arabs. (Benary, 2011)

Aumann has suggested the most hard and violent military strategies against Palestinians. He finished his Nobel Prize Lecture arguing in favor of war:

> *... We end with a passage from the prophet Isaiah (2, 2–4): "And it shall come to pass ... that ... many people shall go and say, let us go up to the mountain of the Lord, ... and He will teach us of His ways, and we will walk in His paths. ... And He shall judge among the nations, and shall rebuke many people; and they shall beat their swords into ploughshares, and their spears into pruning hooks; nation shall not lift up sword against nation, neither shall they learn war anymore." ...Isaiah is saying that the nations can beat their swords into ploughshares when there is a central government – a Lord, recognized by all. In the absence of that, one can perhaps have peace – no nation lifting up its sword against another. But the swords must continue to be there – they cannot be beaten into ploughshares – and the nations must continue to learn war, in order not to fight! (Aumann, 2005)*

Of course, the conflict between Jews and Palestinians is very complex, and without doubt the human beings of each state, the disarmed and pacific people, do not share the views of their violent and extremist representatives and, surely, in a near future, they can promote campaigns of resistance and disobedience against their violent and opportunist political and military leaders. For example the journalist Amy Kaufman is a voice of protest against the policy of mutual extermination. (Kaufman, 2015)

CONCLUSION

The Relationship among Peace, Power and Ethics

A virtuous collective action (voluntary social cooperation characterized by fraternity and solidarity) can be attained if a cooperative behavior (altruism and reciprocity) is realized by all or most individuals that have common goals (for example the rejection of war and the preservation of nature). The attainment of a genuine (no turbulent) peace can be understood like a successful virtuous collective action.

In our present world, the prevalent state of war (across direct violence and violent progress) occurs because a majority of individuals have selfish behavior, which means that each individual pursues mainly first-order benefits (pleasure, profit) in order to maximize his or her own consumption or investment. The selfish individual has an interested behavior, which may be narrow (the maximization of his or her own income or interest) or sophisticated (the maximum advantage, in terms of economic and political power to his or her collectivity: exclusive club or community, political party, enterprise, family, social class, country, etc.). Symptomatically the exponents of the dominant economic theory (neoclassic doctrine) assume that economic agents have only propensities, tastes, and cravings which are expressions of current economic preferences (first ordering volitions made by egoist agents) (Hirschman, Shifting Involvements: private interest and public action, 1982).

There is a relationship between egoism and the propensity to be obedient to powerful and dangerous leaders or groups. Five centuries ago a young irreverent writer named Etienne de la Boetié (Boetié, 2003), in his discourse on voluntary servitude, wisely suggested that the main problem of politics is the perverse behavior of blind and easy obedience (understood like the fatal propensity that a majority of human beings have to give up his freedom), and this thinker was the inspiration of nonviolent leaders like Thoreau, Tolstoy and Gandhi. Following the remarks of this author it is possible to affirm that if individuals have no moral values (meta-preferences, self-reflexive and critical choices) then they are prone to be blindly obedient. The main corollary of he is that wars, injustice and all the absurdities of power are possible because the voluntary acquiescence of vassals (wantons, and passive individuals which, voluntary, have renounced to be free persons). Of course some individuals obey because negative incentives (punishment) and others because positive incentives (gains, prizes and prestige).

The lack of a critical evaluation of moral values and economic preferences, and the propensity to obey are the main causes of modern injustice. Indeed, today the most dangerous and repugnant beings are the race of new vassals because they are docile employees and they blindly obey the most absurd orders from their bosses without doubts, questions, and critics –this modern disease has been judged by the German Philosopher Hannah Arendt (Arendt, 1999). She said that exist absurd finalities which are supposedly inevitable, imperative and absolutely necessary, and people acquiesce because, sadly, human beings avoid important questions about the ends, means and commandments; the obedient people (modern subjects) avoid questions about his or her culpability and they only care about the performance of his or her function. There is a collective guilt because blindly the society is obedient and is a collaborator of the evil and violence.

Indeed, the questions, doubts and remarks about social imperatives as economic growth and comfort of consumers are not an abstract exercise made by academic experts and, contrarily, all the people want to solve ethical questions even in the most minimal and apparently trivial choices, for example in the acquisition of a cell phone. In a recent article named "My search for a smartphone that is not soaked in blood" the active citizen George Monbiot expressed the next very interesting remarks:

...If you are too well connected, you stop thinking. The clamor, the immediacy, the tendency to absorb other people's thoughts, interrupts the deep abstraction required to find your own way. This is one of the reasons why I have not yet bought a smartphone. But the technology is becoming ever harder to resist. Perhaps this year I will have to succumb. So I have asked a simple question: can I buy an ethical smartphone? ... There are dozens of issues, such as starvation wages, bullying, abuse and 60-hour weeks in the sweatshops manufacturing them, the debt bondage into which some of the workers are pressed, the energy used, the hazardous waste produced. But I will concentrate on just one: are the components soaked in the blood of people from the eastern Democratic Republic of the Congo? For 17 years, rival armies and militias have been fighting over the region's minerals. Among them are metals critical to the manufacture of electronic gadgets, without which no smartphone would exist: tantalum, tungsten, tin and gold ... While these elements are by no means the only reason for conflict there, they help to fund it, supporting a fragmented war that – through direct killings, displacement, disease and malnutrition – has now killed several million people. Rival armies have forced local people to dig in extremely dangerous conditions, have extorted minerals and money from self-employed miners, have tortured, mutilated and murdered those who don't comply, and have spread terror and violence – including gang rape and child abduction – through the rest of the population. I do not want to participate... (Monbiot, 2013).

Then active citizens that have ethical choices and promote countervailing power against unjust orders from States, Markets and specific authorities can promote a non-turbulent peace.

Future Research Directions

At the end of this philosophical and historical remark are suggested and explained the next three perspectives of research, namely:

- **Revisiting Kant's Proposal about Perpetual Peace:** Kant emitted a very clear admonition at the beginning of his classic essay: "perpetual peace" is a very adequate message when this appears written at the entry of a cemetery (Kant, 1963). Without doubts, the world of the corpses is an environment of eternal peace and a perpetual steady state (without competence, conflicts and tensions). And his proposal to attain a state of perpetual peace among Nations requires a utopian state of equilibrated and symmetric relationships in the domestic arena (inside Countries) and in the international dimension. In the mentioned text Kant assumed a feasible perpetual peace as a result of the next set of rules of the game:

- No secret treaty of peace shall be held valid in which there is tacitly reserved matter for a future war.
- No independent states, large or small, shall come under the dominion of another state by inheritance, exchange, purchase, or donation.
- Standing armies shall in time be totally abolished.
- National debts shall not be contracted with a view to the external friction of states.
- No state shall by force interfere with the constitution or government of another state.
- No state shall, during war, permit such acts of hostility which would make mutual confidence in the subsequent peace impossible: such are the employment of assassins, breach of capitulation, and incitement to treason in the opposing state.

In order to transcend a mere cessation of hostilities, and build a durable peace, this influent philosopher proposed three additional rules, namely:

- The civil constitution of every state should be republican.
- The law of nations shall be founded on a federation of Free states.
- The law of world citizenship shall be limited to conditions of universal hospitality.

The world is moving in an opposed direction of Kant's proposal. At the beginning of XXI century exist convincing empirical evidence about the notable asymmetry in the arena of international affairs, and can be mentioned three cases: The prolonged blockage against the small and rebel island of Cube by the powerful United States; the pretense of the most riches countries of the named European Community in order to impose humiliating financial requirements over the impoverished Greece; and the structural condition of continents like Africa and Latin America as kinds of a backside (to put garbage) and a pantry to obtain cheaper energies and foods in benefit of powerful empires (China, United States and European Union).

From the point of view of spoilsport thinkers (or philosophers of material life), the war is inherent to human nature, is intrinsic to economic progress, is a relevant role of the ruling class, and moreover is an strategy in order to solve economic crises.

The economist Frank Knight affirmed that:

...Another important fact in the study of war is that man is a discontented animal, and particularly that he is likely to grow more discontented as he becomes better off. But this is mainly because he is prone to think someone else is getting the best of it or is putting something over on him. The conflict between different systems of conventionality or "culture", different customs, traditions, mores, on the one hand, and, on the other, increasing mass discontent as a direct consequence of an unprecedented increase in mass well-being in the last two centuries or so of our civilization re the two main cause of war which must be considered today in any thoughtful study of the problem of eliminating it.... (Knight, 1982, p. 361)

To Veblen the war is an occupation of the leisure class, and he reasoned thus in the first chapter of his Magnus opus (Veblen, The Theory of the Leisure Class: an Economic Study of Institutions, 1953):

Even if the institution of a leisure class had not come in with the first emergence of individual ownership, by force of the dishonor attaching to productive employment, it would in any case have come in as one of the early consequences of ownership. And it is to be remarked that while the leisure class existed in theory from the beginning of predatory culture, the institution takes on a new and fuller meaning with the transition from the predatory to the next succeeding pecuniary stage of culture ... the normal and characteristic occupations of the class in this mature phase of its life are in the form very much the same as in its earlier days. These occupations are government, war, sports, and devout observances ... government and war, at least in part, carried on for the pecuniary gain of those who engage in them; but it is gain obtained by the honorable method of seizure and conversion ... (p. 17)

At the end of his last book that justly was about the feasibility of peace the brilliant economist Thorstein Veblen said:

... Granting the premises, there should be no reasonable doubt as to this eventual cleavage between those who own and those who do not; and of the premises the only item that is not already an accomplished fact is the installation of peace at large. The rest of what goes into the argument is the well-known modern state of the industrial arts, and the equally well-known price-system; which, in combination, give its character to the modern state of business enterprise. It is only an unusually broad instance of an institutional arrangement which has in the course of time and changing conditions come to work at cross purposes with that underlying ground of institutional arrangements that takes form in the commonplace aphorism, Live and let live. With change setting in the direction familiar to all men today, it is only a question of limited time when the discrepancy will reach a critical pass, and the installation of peace may be counted on to hasten this course of things. That a decision will be sought by recourse to forcible measures, is also scarcely open to question; since the established law and order provides for a resort to coercion in the enforcement of these prescriptive rights, and since both parties in interest, in this as in other cases, are persuaded of the justice of their claims. A decision either way is an intolerable iniquity in the eyes of the losing side. History teaches that in such a quarrel the recourse has always been to force. History teaches also, but with an inflection of doubt, that the outworn institution in such a conjuncture faces disestablishment. At least, so men like to believe. What the experience of history does not leave in doubt is the grave damage, discomfort and shame incident to the displacement of such an institutional discrepancy by such recourse to force. What further appears to be clear in the premises, at least to the point of a strong presumption, is that in the present case the decision, or the choice, lies between two alternatives: either the price-system and its attendant business enterprise will yield and pass out; or the pacific nations will conserve their pecuniary scheme of law and order at the cost of returning to a war footing and letting their owners preserve the rights of ownership by force of arms. The reflection obviously suggests itself that this prospect of consequences to follow from the installation of peace at large might well be taken into account beforehand by those who are aiming to work out an enduring peace. It has appeared in the course of the argument that the preservation of the present pecuniary law and order, with all its incidents of ownership and investment, is incompatible with an unwarlike state of peace and security. This current scheme of investment, business, and sabotage, should have an appreciably better chance of survival in the long run if the present conditions of warlike preparation and national insecurity were maintained, or if the projected peace were left in a somewhat problematical state, sufficiently precarious to keep national animosities alert, and thereby to the neglect of domestic interests, particularly of such

interests as touch the popular well-being. On the other hand, it has also appeared that the cause of peace and its perpetuation might be materially advanced if precautions were taken beforehand to put out of the way as much as may be of those discrepancies of interest and sentiment between nations and between classes which make for dissension and eventual hostilities... (Veblen, An Inquiry into the Nature of Peace, 1964) (See the final paragraphs of the conclusions).

Keynes suggested that in order to solve the dangerous and recurrent economic crises the political leaders can promote the production of waste, extravagance and very absurd works by means the next task: luxurious castles and magnificent buildings; extraction of gold in order to construct goldbrick and then again bury this treasure to accumulate pure economic value of exchange; and, as ultimate resource, promote wars (Keynes, 2003). Indeed, the favorite disciple of Keynes, the professor Joan Robinson expressed that: "Hitler had already found how to cure unemployment before Keynes had finished explaining why it occurred" (Robinson, 1972).

It is crucial to have some utopians views about peace but without avoid the critical view of some economic and social thinkers.

- **New Remarks about the Concept of Ethics:** Following the wiser suggestion made by Hirschman about the combination between scientific knowledge and subjective moral sentiments, is pertinent to research about the next view in order to solve social problems:

... once we have become fully aware of our intellectual tradition with its deep split between head and heart and its not always beneficial consequences, the first step toward overcoming that tradition and toward dealing healing that split has already token. Down the road, it is then possible to visualize a kind of social science that would be very different form the one most of us have been practicing: a moral-social science where moral considerations are not repressed or kept apart, but are systematically commingled with analytical argument, without guilt feelings over an lack of integration; where the transition from preaching to proving and back again is performed frequently and with ease; and where moral considerations need no longer be smuggled in surreptitiously, but are displayed openly and disarmingly. Such would be, in part, my dream for a "social science for our grandchildren. (Hirschman, 2013, p.342)

An adequate mixture between the study of sciences and the critical reflection about moral values and morality can help us find responses to the next questions and other similar enquiries: how to be a citizen of the world and a member of the vast commonwealth of nature? It is possible to find some conciliation between private interest and the life of a great community that includes present and future generations and the preservation of other forms of life? How much de owe to the welfare of future generations? It is morally correct to promote a population size at which the average level of present welfare can be as high as possible? It is feasible and ethically desirably to promote the maximization of the total amount of welfare, assuming that is possible the mixture of different expectations of distinct persons about happiness?

- **An Exploration about the Feasibility of a Non-Turbulent Peace:** This may be understood like a form of progress characterized by de-growth, leisure and mediation. De-growth is a political, economic, and social movement based on ecological economics and anti-consumerist ideas. The thinkers and leaders that advocate in favor of De-growth are defenders of the downscaling of production and consumption (deliberate and sane contraction of economies), because overconsumption lies at the root of long term environmental issues and social inequalities. A pioneer of this trend is the French economist Serge Latouche (Latouche, 2010). In order to attain De-growth human beings can promote a peaceful and happy modality of life which implies the rescue of some very important actions like leisure (Russell, 1935) (Lafargue, 1989). Of course, the resource of meditation (Raghavan, 2014) can help us in order to attain a very tranquil and peaceful style of life. Finally the most important challenge is to construct a feasible solution based in an economy of nonviolence following the wise teachings of the heterodox economist Kenneth Boulding (Boulding, A Preface to Grants Economics: the Economy of Love and Fear, 1981).

REFERENCES

Arendt, H. (1999). *Eichmann en Jerusalén: un estudio sobre la banalidad del mal*. Barcelona: Lumen.

Aumann, R. (2005, December 8). Nobel Prize Organization. Retrieved from http://www.nobelprize.org/nobel_prizes/economic-sciences/laureates/2005/aumann-lecture.html

Bastiat, F. (2004). *Essays on Political Economy*. New York: G. P. Putnams and Sons.

Benary, E. (2011, September 22). We are the Palestinians and they are the Arabs. Retrieved from http://cjhsla.org/2011/09/22/we-are-the-palestinians-and-they-are-the-arabs/

Benjamin, W. (2009). *On the Concept of History*. New York: Classic Books America.

Bierce, A. (2004). *The Devil's Dictionary*. Washington: Bloomsbury.

Boetié, E. d. (2003). *El discurso de la servidumbre voluntaria, o el contra uno*. Bogotá: Universidad Nacional de Colombia.

Boulding, K. (1981). *A Preface to Grants Economics: the Economy of Love and Fear*. New York: Praeger.

Boulding, K. (1989). *Three Faces of Power: A General Theory*. London: Sage Publications.

FAO. (2014, November 21). FAO. Retrieved from http://www.fao.org/news/story/en/item/45210/icode/

Feyerabend, P. (1999). *The Conquest of Abundance: A Tale of Abstraction versus the Richnes of Being*. Chicago: Chicago University Press.

Fogoto, M. (2012, August 5). Is Erbil's Growth Spurt Hype or for Real? *Alpha Magazine*, 10-14.

Francis, P. (18 de June de 2015). *Papal Encyclicals on line*. Obtenido de papalencyclicas: http://www.papalencyclicals.net/

Georgescu-Roegen, N. (1971). *The Entropy Law and the Economic Process*. Boston: Harvard University Press. doi:10.4159/harvard.9780674281653

Georgescu-Roegen, N. (1976). *Energy and Economic Myths: Institutional and Economic Essays*. Toronto: Pergamon Press Inc.

Goldsmith, E. (1985). Is development the Solution or the Problem. *The Ecologist*, 210–219.

Greenpeace. (2007, February 9). Greenpeace Org. Abolish Nuclear Weapons: The Vital Statistics. Retrieved from http://www.greenpeace.org/international/en/campaigns/peace/abolish-nuclear-weapons/the-vital-statistics/

Hardin, G. (1993). *Living Within Limits: Ecology, Economics, and Population Taboos*. New York: Oxford University Press.

Hayek, F. (1991). *The Fatal Conceit: The Errors of Socialism*. Chicago: University of Chicago Press.

Hirsch, F. (1977). *Social Limits to Growth*. London: Routledge & Kegan Paul Ltd.

Hirschman, A. (1982). *Shifting Involvements: private interest and public action*. Princeton: Princeton University Press.

Hirschman, A. (2013). *The Essential Hirschman*. Princeton: Princeton University Press.

IEPRI. (2006). *Nuestra guerra sin nombre. Transformaciones del conflicto en Colombia*. Bogotá: Norma.

Jones, N. (2014, October 7). Mail Online. Retrieved from http://www.dailymail.co.uk/home/moslive/article-2091670/Hitler-Stalin-The-murderous-regimes-world.html

Kalecki, M. (1971). *Selected Essays on the Dynamic of Capitalist Economy 1933-1970*. Boston: Cambridge University Press.

Kant, I. (1963). *To perpetual peace: a philosophical sketch*. New York: Hackett Publishing.

Kaufman, A. (2015, June 19). Wake-up Call: Ami does his best Bibi impression [Video]. *972 Mag*. Retrieved from http://972mag.com/amik

Keynes, J. M. (2003). *The General Theory of Employment, Interest and Money*. London: Macmillan.

Knight, F. (1982). *Freedom and Reform: Essays in Economics and Social Philosophy*. Indianapolis: Liberty Fund.

Lafargue, P. (1989). *The Right to Be Lazy*. Chicago: Charles H. Kerr Publishing Company.

Latouche, S. (2010). *Farewell to Growth*. Cambridge: Polity Press.

Maddison, A. (2001, April 1). The World Economy: A Millennial Perspective. *The Unbroken window.com*. Retrieved from http://theunbrokenwindow.com/Development/MADDISON%20The%20World%20Economy--A%20Millennial.pdf

Maddison, A. (2014 November 1). World Economy. Retrieved from http://www.theworldeconomy.org/

Marx, K. (1973). *Manifiesto of the Communist Party*. New York: Inter Publisher.

Marx, K. (1993). *The Capital: A Critique of Political Economy* (Vol. 3). New York: Penguin Classics.

Mayumi, K. (2012). *The Origin of Ecological Economics: The Bioeconomics of Georgescu-Roegen*. New York: Routledge.

Meir, G. (1969, June 15). Interview. *Sunday Times*, 4.

Mishan, E. (1993). *The Cost of Economic Growth* (Revised Edition). London: Praeger Publishers.

Monbiot, G. (2013, March 11). My search for a smartphone that is not soaked in blood. *The Guardian*. Retrieved from http://www.theguardian.com/commentisfree/2013/mar/11/search-smartphone-soaked-blood

Nietzsche, F. (2003). *Beyond Good and Evil*. New York: Penguin Classics.

OpenStax. (2014 November 28). World Energy Use. Retrieved from http://cnx.org/contents/031da8d3-b525-429c-80cf-6c8e-d997733a@8.9:51/College_Physics

OXFAM International. (2014, January 20). *Working for the Few: Political Capture and Economic Inequality*. Retrieved from http://www.oxfam.org/sites/www.oxfam.org/files/file_attachments/bp-working-for-few-political-capture-economic-inequality-200114-en_3.pdf

Polanyi, K. (2001). *The Great Transformaton: The Poltical and Economic Origins of our Time*. Boston: Beacon Press.

Popper, K. (1945). The Open Society and its Enemies. London: Routledge.

Rae, J. (2010). *The sociological theory of capital, being a complete reprint of the new principles of political economy, 1834*. New York: Nabu Press.

Raghavan, L. (2014). *Mahatma Gandhi and Buddha's Path to Enlightenment*. Washington: Theosophy Trust Books.

Ricardo, D. (2004). *Principles of Political Economy and Taxation*. London: Dover Publications.

Rifkin, J. (1981). *Entropy: A New World View*. New York: Bantham.

Rifkin, J. (2009). *El siglo de la biotecnología: el comercio genético y el nacimiento de un mundo feliz*. Barcelona: Paidós.

Robinson, J. (1972). The second crises of economic theory. *The American Economic Review*, 62(1/2), 1-10.

Russell, B. (1935). *Praise of Idleness and other essays*. London: George Allen & Unwin.

Sábato, E. (1951). Hombres y engranajes. Buenos Aires: Emicé editores.

Saramago, J. (1992). *El evangelio según Jesucristo*. Barcelona: Seix Barral.

Saul, J. R. (1993). *Voltaire Bastard's: The Dictatorship of Reason in the West*. New York: Vintage.

Schelling, T. (1985). *Choice and Consequence: perspectives of an errant economist*. Boston: Harvard University Press.

Schelling, T. (2005, December 10). Nobel Prize. Retrieved from http://www.nobelprize.org/nobel_prizes/economic-sciences/laureates/2005/schelling-lecture.pdf

Schmemann, S. (2014, June 20). In Refugee Statistics, a Stark Tale of Global Strife. *The New York Times*. Retrieved from http://www.nytimes.com/2014/06/22/opinion/sunday/in-refugee-statistics-a-stark-tale-of-global-strife.html?_r=0

Schumpeter, J. (2008). *Capitalism, Socialism and Democracy*. New York: Harper Perennial Modern Classics.

Sen, A. (2009). *The Idea of Justice*. Boston: Harvard University Press.

Shakespeare, W. (2004). *The Merchant of Venice*. New York: Washington Square Press.

Smith, A. (2003). *Wealth of Nations*. New York: Oxford University Press.

Torres, L., Niland, L., & Allen, P. (2013, September 26). IPCC Climate Change Figures: then and now-interactive. *The Guardian*. Retrieved from http://www.theguardian.com/environment/interactive/2013/sep/26/ipcc-climate-change-figures-then-and-now-interactive

Veblen, T. (1953). *The Theory of the Leisure Class: an Economic Study of Institutions*. New York: The MacMillan Company.

Veblen, T. (1964). *An Inquiry into the Nature of Peace*. New York: Kelley.

Veblen, T. (2009). *The Theory of the Leisure Class*. New York: Oxford University Press.

WFP. (2014 October 1). Hunger Statistics. Retrieved from http://www.wfp.org/hunger/stats

World Bank. (2014, November 20). Poverty Overview. Retrieved from http://www.worldbank.org/en/topic/poverty/overview#1

ADDITIONAL READING

Arrow, K., Mnookin, R., Ross, L., Tversky, A., & Wilson, R. (Eds.). (1995). *Barriers to Conflict Resolution*. New York: W. W. Norton and Company.

Crocker, A. C., Hampson, F. O., & Aall, P. (Eds.), (2001). *Turbulent Peace, the Challenges of Managing International Conflict*. Washington: United States Institute of Peace.

Philpott, D. (2012). Just and Unjust Peace: An Ethic of Political Reconciliation (Studies in Strategic Peacebuilding. New York: Oxford University Press.

Ramsbotham, O., Woodhouse, T., & Miall, H. (2011). Contemporary Conflict Resolution. Cambridge: Polity Press.

Walzer, M. (2006). *Just and Unjust Wars: A Moral Argument with Historical Illustrations*. New York: Basic Books.

KEY TERMS AND DEFINITIONS

Endosomatic and Exosomatic Instruments: Human beings have a poor endowment of endosomatic instruments (compared with the natural skills and powerful tools of the rest of animals), but they have evolved by means the fabrication of artificial tools (means of production) which are inspired in organs and properties of humans and animals, and that potentiate their work (although consuming a lot of energy). The big increment in the production of this artificial instruments, and the notable sophistication and productivity (high capacity to work, and to produce faster a growing quantity of output), especially during the last five centuries of modern age, has caused dangerous and uncertain effects over nature and the life.

Ethics: Moral philosophy. The study of ethics constitutes a rescue of the very old academic tradition of economy which goes back at least to Aristotle that, justly affirmed that politics (including economics) legislates as to what we are to do and what we are to abstain from, and that the end of this science must include those of the others, so that this end must be good for man. In this order of ideas, the ethics has two central issues, namely: First, the question about human motivations and behaviors: "How should one live?" and; Second, the complex judgment of social achievement (the god for man, and the god for nature). The ethics, help us to overcome the next main difficulties of moral values and morality, namely: a) there is not a definitive and perfect set of moral values and an absolute and true guidance of morality; b) moral values and morality are circumscribed to cultural traditions and, moreover, they are dependent of the status quo (interest and power) of persons; c) there is not an universal agreement about the best moral values and about the better guidance of morality.

Moral: The meaning of moral has been developed by some thinkers like Hirschman, who has said that, sadly, a majority of human beings are wantons or immoral beings because they have only current economic preferences and, consequently, they lack of self-reflexive and critical view about the sense of his or her life, and in relationship with the collective aims of a desired social order. The big importance of moral choices, following the ideas of Sen, Frankfurt, Arendt and Hirschman, can be summarized in the next items: I) a person has the capacity of autonomous and self-reflexive thinking; II) the moral is part of high values: the legendary liberal J. S. Mill understood perfectly the importance of this behavior when he said: "is better to be Socrates dissatisfied than a pig satisfied"; III) a person has second order volitions (meta-preferences, moral values, ideologies), and, consequently, she or he is a moral agent that takes care about the problems of a society, and in relationship with a desirable social order; IV) a person is a lover of freedom and, consequently has moral dignity (the capacity to disobey absurd, incorrect and perverse orders) and, moreover, has the ability to exert countervailing power.

Morality: Morality is equivalent to voluntary cooperation, and can be understood like a behavior guided by the accomplishment of duties (which are selfless guidance and non-egoistic power that permit the social cohesion). Morality is the basis of this virtuous behavior and, consequently, the glue of societies. For example, a moral agent could be motivated by duty or by the desire to maximize average or perhaps minimum welfare. And, indeed, a moral agent could be animated by the desire to ensure the protection of certain rights (including the important wish to protect the environment).

Power: According to K. Boulding the power is exercised when men love, construct enterprise, create theories and scientific experiments, and expands markets, and, of course when they launch wars or compose poesy, in all their conceivable actions, human beings exercise power. The common denominator of these actions is, justly, that in order to attain our objectives we want to exercise influence and authority over our allies, and force and dissuasion over our enemies. To the influent T. Schelling –ideologist of cold war strategies and pioneer of the games theory– power is present in all human actions (love, sex, education, business, etc.) The individuals play games of strategy and, consequently, they exercise power: a player (an individual or a social group) has the capacity to get what he wants by exercising influence (or violent pressure) over his allies and enemies. Even a small baby has the capacity to get a toy because even the baby in arms –like the best actors and convincing girlfriends– uses their crocodile tears in order to exercise influence over his parents.

Turbulent Peace: A very ambiguous kind of peace which is characterized like a period of transition between a previous situation of war among people toward a new state of struggle by people against nature (and by opulent people against poor persons and future generations). A partial and incomplete peace can be attained among individuals that in the past were enemies, but that peace agreement open the doors to a process of unbound economic progress which generates indirect violence against marginal persons and future generations because the destruction of nature (depletion of natural resources and contamination that is condition to the development of "productive forces").

Chapter 2
Reconciliation as a Historical Process

Hartmut Quehl
Felsberg Institute, Germany

ABSTRACT

This chapter understands reconciliation as an historical process, inseparably connected to communication processes, processes of remembrance, and the transformation processes of individual and collective memories. The author aims to link the issues of reconciliation and remembrance, and uses the historical example of the Germans coming to terms with their past ("Vergangenheitsbewältigung") after 1945 to categorize a specific reconciliation process into different contextual levels and thereby answer the question, whether or not the German reconciliation process has been successfully completed. This chapter also aims to seek possible fields of comparison with other reconciliation processes that have taken place in different time and spatial settings. Such a "comparison of differences and variables within the context of reconciliation processes" will be elaborated through an abstraction of structural components, using the example of Germany after the Second World War.

Those who cannot remember their past are condemned to relive it. – G. Santayana in: Jan Assmann, Kultur und Gedächtnis

INTRODUCTION

When the German chancellor, Willy Brandt, kneeled down in front of the memorial for the exterminated Jews in Warsaw during a visit to Poland on 7th December 1970, the following photograph appeared in the press throughout Germany the next day[1] (Figure 1).

That same day, Brandt had signed the "Warsaw treaty" as part of a series of the so-called "Eastern treaties" with former war enemies Soviet Union, Poland, and Czechoslovakia, as well as with the Eastern German Democratic Republic (GDR), where the Federal Republic of Germany officially accepted the loss of its former Eastern territories for the first time and thus paved the way toward a new policy of détente in the middle of the Cold War. Brandt's genuflection manifested a demonstration of official German readiness for reconciliation and was highly contested within the German population. Only a few days later, the

DOI: 10.4018/978-1-4666-9675-4.ch002

Figure 1.

German weekly magazine "Der Spiegel" launched a public opinion poll into the deeply divided and polarized German public, which aimed at a representative investigation of West German public opinion. (Der Spiegel, 1970, p. 27) 84% of the interviewees stated, that they had already seen the photograph, of which 41% expressed their view that Brandt's genuflection was an appropriate action, whereas 48% viewed it as exaggerated. If we break this poll down into age groups, we find interesting results: within the age group of 30 to 59, a majority of 54% rated Brandt's action as exaggerated. This is precisely the generation of 1910 to 1940 that had made up the backbone of the war-supporting German population during the Nazi regime, or had been born during the peak of Nazi power.

What makes this photograph more interesting though, are the facts behind the image.

In this picture, we see a German radical socialist kneeling down in front of a Jewish memorial in a communist state, apparently begging for forgiveness for the atrocities of a regime that he himself had fought against as a member of the German clandestine resistance against the Nazi dictatorship. What is even more interesting is that his action is still subject to controversial dispute some 4 decades after the event, to such an extent that the consequences of a humanitarian catastrophe that had occurred roughly 40 years before Brandt's genuflection are still being debated. The discussion in 2005-2007 was mainly about whether Brandt acted spontaneously or whether his action was calculated, (Wolffsohn & Brechenmacher, 2005) and to what extent it is to be interpreted as a political symbol (Schneider, 2006).

But the most interesting are the following statements of members of the "fourth and fifth generation" when they were confronted with the photograph:

Oh, this is one of the former GDR guys, isn't he? (female, born in 1989)

This is the father of the famous German actor Matthias Brandt. (female, born in 1982)

This is Willy Brandt, he was a member of the Social Democrats, we had this in school. (male, born in 1998) (Quehl, 2014)

What can we learn from these episodes? First of all, we can see that reconciliation was a point of discussion for over 8 decades, i.e. more than a man's lifetime. And it shows that:

1. Reconciliation is a lengthy process, and
2. It is only the fourth and fifth generation that have obviously completed the process of historicization of an event, or a chain of events.

These are both important aspects of this chapter, which investigates the topic of reconciliation with a particular focus on the German reconciliation process after World War 2. In this chapter, reconciliation is understood as an historical process, inseparably connected to the processes of remembrance, and the transformation processes of individual and collective memories.

This article aims to link the issues of reconciliation and remembrance, and uses the historical example of the Germans coming to terms with their past ("Vergangenheitsbewältigung") after 1945 to categorize a specific reconciliation process into different contextual levels and thereby answer the question, whether or not the German reconciliation process has been successfully completed.

This chapter works with the following hypotheses:

- A reconciliation process has to be based on the principles of human security, transitional justice and participation, and has to offer a positive economic perspective.
- Stable reconciliation can only be achieved from the third generation onwards.
- Reconciliation processes need political breathing space, i.e. an absence of violence and a stable rule of law, although this does not automatically imply justice.
- Reconciliation has to be tied to multi-level democratic communication processes.

Based on these hypotheses, the following parameters may be deduced for an assessment of the reconciliation process after the Second World War:

1. Rule of law
2. Non-violence
3. Free and controversial discussion
4. Unrestricted political evolvement and participation
5. Positive economic perspective
6. Historicization of the past

The case of Germany has been thoroughly investigated and processed in German academic research. This chapter is based almost exclusively on German literature and research. It deliberately excludes the results of international research not merely to avoid exceeding the limitations of this evaluation, but rather to guarantee the required focus on specific aspects. This contribution does not claim to be complete. It works rather with certain reductions and somewhat arbitrarily selected case studies. This limitation is indicated and justified in each particular case.

This chapter also aims to seek possible fields of comparison with other reconciliation processes that have taken place in different time and spatial settings. Such a "comparison of differences and variables within the context of reconciliation processes" will be elaborated through an abstraction of structural components, using the example of Germany after the Second World War.

DEFINING THE SUBJECT

The handbook "Reconciliation after Violent Conflict" which was published by the International Institute for Democracy and Electoral Assistance (IDEA) in Stockholm defines reconciliation both idealistically and realistically:

Ideally reconciliation prevents, once and for all, the use of the past as the seed of renewed conflict. It consolidates peace, breaks the cycle of violence and strengthens newly established or reintroduced democratic institutions. As a backward-looking operation, reconciliation brings about the personal healing of survivors, the reparation of past injustices, the building or rebuilding of non-violent relationships between individuals and communities, and the acceptance by the former parties to a conflict of a common vision and understanding of the past. In its forward-looking dimension, reconciliation means enabling victims and perpetrators to get on with life and, at the level of society, the establishment of a civilized political dialogue and an adequate sharing of power ...

In practice such all-encompassing reconciliation is not easy to realize. The experience of a brutal past makes the search for peaceful coexistence a delicate and intricate operation. ... Each move demands changes in attitudes (e.g., tolerance instead of revenge), in conduct (e.g., joint commemoration of all the dead instead of separate, partisan memorials) and in the institutional environment (e.g., integrating the war veterans of both sides into one national army instead of keeping ex-combatants in quasi-private militias). ... (Bloomfield, 2003, Huyse, p.19)

These definitions do not suffice to explain the complexity of reconciliation processes. Reconciliation processes need a certain degree of segregation: under certain circumstances, partisans may need their separate memorials, and in some cases, war veterans will have to be excluded when it comes to establishing a new national army. The motives of vengeance and retaliation form an integral part of each reconciliation process and cannot be neglected by means of forced tolerance. Finally, reconciliation is not only an issue between victims and perpetrators, but also a task for the entire society and may at times include a vast majority of individuals who cannot be categorized into the one or the other side, but whose involvement is crucial for the initiation, realization and completion of a reconciliation process.

The German example in particular exposes that an investigation of the topic of reconciliation requires a very differentiated approach.

In an article "Verzeihen-Reconciliation-Versöhnung. Versuch einer Differenzierung verschiedener Konzepte" (Pardon – reconciliation - rapprochement: an attempt to differentiate the different concepts) which was published in 2012, the German psychoanalyst, André Karger, elaborates on the complexity of the subject of research. He rightly points out the different concepts that the English "reconciliation" and the German "Versöhnung" express:

Many authors use the terms appeasement, forgiveness, pardon or redress as similar in meaning to the English use of the term reconciliation. ... (Here)..., these terms shall be differentiated as follows: Rapprochement (the meaning of the German "Versöhnung") aims at defining the interpersonal relationship between victim and perpetrator (the terms restoration and recompense fall into this context). Forgiveness and pardon ("Verzeihen") signify the social act, with which the victim overcomes the negative emotions and attitudes that have evolved as a result of the damage both within himself as well as in relationship to the perpetrator .... "Reconciliation", on the other hand, means a social practice motivated primarily by society, as well as a goal-oriented peace agreement between victim and perpetrator which does not necessarily imply a complete compensation of guilt between victim and perpetrator or the individual entirely overcoming negative emotions and attitudes. "Reconciliation" can be achieved without forgiveness and pardon and signifies the political process. (Karger 2012, p. 15)

Karger defines the German "Versöhnung" as "rapprochement", and therefore as an intention to deal with the consequences of atrocities, especially the consequences of extreme violence resulting in trauma. In this sense, "Versöhnung" does not aim to restore relationships, but rather accepts the loss of the previous relationship and seeks for a new beginning. According to Karger, the following four aspects require special attention:

Firstly, the objective of reconciliation, secondly the (sometimes fundamentally) asymmetrical relation between victims and perpetrators, thirdly the problem of justice and the acknowledgment of guilt, and fourthly the question whether forgiveness or pardon is considered a conditional or an unconditional act. Within his differentiation between social and psychological dimensions, he states that pardon is an individual process which depends on individual contexts and which can be manifested in very different ways. The boundaries between the individual and society, and between individual pardoning and political reconciliation have to be differentiated. Whereas forgiveness stems from a religious-metaphorical context, pardon is related to an interpersonal, secular context. The English concept of reconciliation, in contrast, explicitly signifies a political-societal process.

He distinguishes four different dimensions of reconciliation (in the German meaning of "Versöhnung") as illustrated in Figure 2 and notes:

If "Versöhnung" is defined in the previously-mentioned sense of restoration of a relationship between enemies and/or victims and perpetrators, it makes sense to differentiate between four dimensions: an interpersonal dimension, which relates to the How, i.e. the process of building a relationship between victim and perpetrator; an intra-psychological dimension, which refers to the respective psychological process for victims and perpetrators; a social dimension which aims at the role of society within the process of "Versöhnung"; and a metaphysical dimension, which formulates the external frame for the conditions of "Versöhnung", as well as its possible phantasma. (Karger 2012, p. 14)

Figure 2. The four dimensions of reconciliation

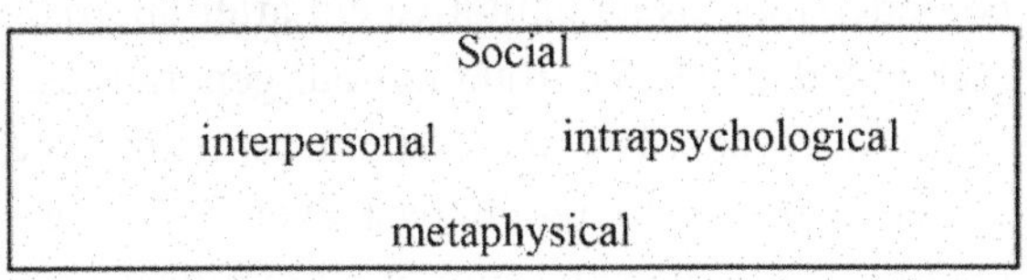

Within the context of his definition of "Versöhnung" as rapprochement, Karger also defines borderline cases such as vengeance as a motive for action: "Long before they can be overcome, the acceptance and experience of vengeance fantasies and impulses marks an important step towards the modification of a perpetrator's self-destructive introject." (Karger 2012a, p. 5) Furthermore, he sees certain qualitative cuts in the consideration of different contexts: comparing the rapprochement within a spousal relationship after a breach of confidence, and the rapprochement between victims and perpetrators after the Shoah, he points out the problem of the "unpardonable and unforgivable", and refers here to the limitations of comparison.

This highlights that reconciliation can never be accomplished as an isolated act. The act of reconciliation is based on the exchanges between many individuals about their past suffering. A reconciliation process is therefore always a communication process, in which the participants have to exercise their memory of the past as a basis for the exchange.

The German Egyptologist and cultural anthropologist, Jan Assmann, explicitly defines this interplay between communication and language as "communicative memory" and sees it as a product of the circular and reciprocal interconnection of the inside and the outside within an exchange with other people. Referring to the thoughts of Maurice Halbwachs, Assmann differentiates four sectors of external dimensions of memory: the mimetic memory (which refers to the act), the memory of things, the communicative memory (determined by language and communication), and the cultural memory as a transmission of sense and meaning. (Assmann, 2013, p. 20)

Assmann understands cultural memory as a collective term for all knowledge which gears action and experience within the specific frame of interaction in a society, and which is to be repeatedly introduced to and exercised from generation to generation.

He differentiates the collective term of "cultural memory from both "communicative memory" and from "science", a highly specialized form of memory building. "Communicative memory" is bound to the existence of living transmitters and communicators of experience and covers a range of approximately 80 years, i.e. 3 to 4 generations. The time zenith of a "communicative memory" moves on parallel to the progressing reference point of the present. The contents of such a memory can only be permanently fixed through a "cultural formation", i.e. through organized and ceremonialized communication about the past. (Assmann, Hölscher, 1988, p. 11)

Assmann defines cultural memory as "...the specific stock of texts, images and rites, that belong to every single society and epoch and which are at its respective disposal for repeated usage (...) The cultivation of this stock stabilizes and transmits its self-image, a collectively (but not exclusively) shared knowledge about the past on which a specific group fundamentally bases its consciousness of unity and uniqueness. This knowledge does not only differ from culture to culture, but also from epoch to epoch." (Assmann, 1988, p. 15)

Both Karger's subtly differentiated view on reconciliation, and Assmann's embedment of communication processes into the processes of memory transformation are essential for any historical analysis of reconciliation. They have been particularly valuable in informing this article where we have strived to construct a multidimensional, holistic analysis based on a concrete historic example and attempted an overall assessment of this particular societal example.

We therefore first need to formulate a working definition of reconciliation. Depending on the intention of the actor(s), reconciliation is

- An emotional desire and/or a mental necessity,
- A social action,
- A cultural convention and/or skill,
- A juridical term,
- An object of political regulation,
- An historical process, or
- The result of an historical process.

This chapter deals primarily with reconciliation as a process, so we clearly distinguish between "reconciliation" and "reconciliation processes" to avoid misunderstanding.

Referring to Karger's use of the term reconciliation as rapprochement, we will work with the most neutral definition possible. Here, reconciliation will be defined as a "shift among people towards a multilateral, positive and sustainable basic attitude of mutual trust, the willingness to stand by each other and/or jointly create a common future, people who had caused injury and damage to each other and had therefore formerly interacted with hostility or rejection." (Lexikon: Wortdeutung)

Referring to Assmann, the connection between remembrance, memory, communication and reconciliation will be outlined as follows:

Reconciliation is inseparably tied to the past, and inseparably embedded into the environment of those who are directly affected. Reconciliation is based on a willingness to overcome the past, and overcoming the past means the processing of past experiences. This process has to be closely linked to memory and the evolving of a cultural memory. In the course of a reconciliation process this can be understood as a qualitative cut after approximately 8 decades, i.e. roughly four generations.

In this regard, I understand remembrance as the capacity to retain past events in one's memory, as well as the sum of all reminiscences of an individual. Memory is understood as the capacity to store experiences and emotional impressions in order to recall them at a later stage. The importance of remembrance and memory becomes obvious, when we take into account that overcoming the past in the course of a reconciliation process means, first of all, dealing with the pain, injuries and suffering experienced. In this context, the experience of physical violence is an objective reality, whereas the experience of psychological violence, structural violence and cultural violence are subjective realities, strongly linked to perceptions.

Reconciliation cannot be forced, but rather has to be based on a voluntary decision, and reconciliation processes can only be planned to a very limited extent.

Out of the aforesaid, we can formulate the following working hypotheses:

- A reconciliation process has to be preceded by a traumatic experience.
- A reconciliation process can be regulated and steered only to a limited extent.
- A reconciliation process is directly connected to the collective memory of the affected societal groups.
- Reconciliation processes create new polarizations and cause social ruptures and marginalization.
- Successful reconciliation takes place only from the third generation onwards and is bound to the transformation of communicative memory into cultural memory.

These hypotheses are based on the conviction that reconciliation occurs on three different levels:

1. **Internal Relationships:** Coming to terms with the past, dealing with guilt and shame, creation of a collective memory
2. **External Relationships:** Communication with former enemies, regulation of relationships with neighbors
3. **Marginalized Groups:** Dealing with past and recent ruptures, with old and new groups and with old and new adversaries.

These hypotheses will be examined in the following using the example of Germany after the Second World War. We begin by defining the limits of research.

We have to take the specific characteristics of the conflict into account:

- Neither in the pre-war period (1933-1939), nor during the war period (1939-1945) or during the post-war period (after 1945), did Germany experience a civil war. Violent actions mostly took place during the time of the Weimar Republic after the end of the First World War (1918-1933). Violent actions between 1939 and 1945 were rare: no broad-based, armed partisan resistance structure or guerrilla force existed in Germany. In contrast, internal adversaries covered an extremely broad spectrum: at the one extreme, there was the tortured survivor of the concentration camp, and at the same time there was the other extreme, the opportunistic member of the Nazi party who had gone into "inner migration" caused by his hatred of the regime.
- The German population as a whole became victimized itself by allied bombings, forced expulsion etc. in the course of the war. This fact partly overshadowed the internal adversary structures.
- The main adversary lines existed on the national level, i.e. between nation states and politicized populations. One of the consequences of the war was the creation of forced territorial loyalties: on the one hand the allied states which did not tolerate any kind of internal dissent on war loyalty,

and on the other hand the occupied states and territories which experienced the creation of clandestine resistance and partisan groups, but at the same time created a stratum of collaborators.

- The collaboration phenomenon points out a second level of reconciliation which indirectly influenced the German internal process: even the allied war opponents had to deal with their internal adversary structures and overcome them.
- Finally, the division into two German states as a result of the war created a third line of reconciliation: after 1989, Germany once again had to face the challenge of an internal reconciliation process, this time between the victims of violent oppression and the perpetrators of a totalitarian regime. Again, we have to take into account that at no time did Germany experience any kind of civil war-like events, i.e. the extent of direct physical violence remained low.

Even with regard to the post conflict situation, the specific historical situation in post-war Germany after 1945 is unique in many respects. More than any other historical case of the 20th century, post-war Germany reflected the international and global political changes of the time. This is true with regard to international readiness for economic recovery, as well as to the German territorial division into two separate state entities, which basically connected the reconciliation process to the issue of re-unification and, at the same time, to the issue of European unification.

Last but not least, we have to mention the political and juridical development on the West German side, the Federal Republic of Germany: West Germany created a juridical system based on the principles of the rule of law, whose political system tried to process the negative experiences of the past within the frame of a specific democratic order.

The following chapters will inevitably have to generalize, so this chapter will therefore focus on the reconciliation process in the FRG without elaborating on the situation in the GDR. Moreover, we will exclusively elaborate general tendencies with regard to reconciliation constellations, without taking any specific subgroup into account. Finally, emphasis will be laid on the neighbor states of Poland and France regarding the external reconciliation processes, without taking other countries into consideration.

GENERATIONS

Even as we document the uniqueness of the German process, we can identify in parallel some important similarities that also apply to the enemies of Germany during the Second World War, and, in their abstraction, lay an important foundation for a general analysis of reconciliation processes.

One of these similarities is the classification of the various societal groups that had been affected by a reconciliation process by generation. Three categories may be distinguished:

1. Generations in terms of periods of life (two decades) within a family,
2. Generations in accordance with features of socialization, and
3. Generations in accordance with correlation of events, defined by decades in order to manifest the main discourses during shorter periods of time.

In this context we come across another peculiarity which applies not only to Germany but also to large parts of Europe: in terms of periods of life, the parents' and grandparents' generation - up to the so-called "bridge generation"[2] - were socialized and molded by the experiences of the First World War.

Today, it is considered an undisputed fact that the First World War and the Second World War are directly and inseparably interrelated with each other. When we take a closer look at the affected generations in terms of periods of life, this interrelationship becomes particularly obvious (Table 1).

The "bridge generation" of the First World War experienced violence and the economic and political crisis of the Weimar Republic during their personal formation phase. It was the first "fatherless" generation of a World War and later on formed the main contingents of the Nazi institutions (prior to the Second World War) and the German army, the "Wehrmacht" (during the Second World War). And, no less important: it produced the second "bridge generation".

The Göttingen sociologist, Gabriele Rosenthal, who has worked intensively on the Nazi period by conducting cross-generational biographical interviews, distinguishes the historical generations of the years 1933 to 1948 in terms of socialization in much more detail, elaborating on the particular year of birth and cultural youth impacts. By contrast, the Kassel based psychoanalyst Hartmut Radebold, who has intensively worked on the phenomenon of trans-generational dissemination of war memories and war traumata by investigating the subject of "war burdened childhood", classifies the entire age group born between 1933 and 1948 by event correlation, as "children of the war".

Table 2 exposes how differently the term "generation" can be used (Köttig, 2012).

In an article published in Radebold's volume on trans-generational dissemination of war-burdened childhood, the German researcher Bettina Völter points out in reference to Karl Mannheim and Gabriele Rosenthal, that we have to differentiate between a formal, familiar and historical definition of the label "generation". Alongside the purely chronological component, we need to ask how people with different biographical experiences in the same particular chronological time frame live, what they have in common, and how they shape their relationship to other generational contexts. As a consequence, biographical and cross-generational research has to be based rather on the phenomenon, i.e. the respective family, and not on an empirical pattern. (Völter, 2009) It is exactly this last phenomenon, the dimension of family, which reflects the complexity of generational interrelations.

My own family may exemplify this complexity. According to Rosenthal, the generation of my grandfathers and their brothers and sisters in both the patrilineal and the matrilineal prongs include the "Hitlerjugend" generation, the Weimar generation, the transitional generation, the Wilhelmine generation, as well as the pre-Wilhelmine generation (which is not included in Rosenthal's scheme)

Table 1. Generations in terms of periods of life

Prior to 1908:	Generation educated and raised according to Wilhelmine principles
1908-1918:	"bridge generation"
1918-1935:	Post-war children/ Weimer Republic (roughly 1.5 generations and two decades)
1935-1945:	Bridge generation

Table 2. Historical generations 1933 – 1948 according to Rosenthal and Radebold

Year of Birth	According to Rosenthal	According to Radebold
Ca. 1890-1900	Wilhelmine youth generation	
1906-1919	Weimer youth generation	
1919-1921	Transitional age groups	
1922-1929	Generation of "Hitlerjugend"	
1928/1929	Transitional age groups	
1930-1939	Children of the "Third Reich"	
1939-1945	Generation of "war children"	Generation of "war children"
II. 1948		

if we look at them in terms of socialization. The generation of my parents and their brothers and sisters included the generation of the Third Reich, the generation of "war children", as well as the generation after 1948, which Radebold defines all together as "war children".

The following brief insight into my own family history illustrates the intense interrelation of the three generational aspects of (1) phases of life, (2) features of socialization, and (3) correlation of events, and how these constellations have developed in terms of coming to terms with the past over a period of more than a century.

If we follow a distinction into "familial generations" we can identify five different generations: my grandparents as war participants, my parents as war children, my own generation as "baby boomers", my children as the post-unification generation, and grandchildren as the post-millennium generation.

My father's father was born in 1894 as a child of a middle class civil servant. He participated actively in the First World War, volunteering as a student, and attained the rank of officer. He joined the NSDAP as early as the late 1920s and reached the position of an "Obersturmbannführer SS" in Kassel. In the year 1934 he got married to my grandmother, who was born in 1908 as the youngest of four children in a civil servants' family from Kassel. This was already my grandfather's second marriage. He participated in the Second World War as member of the "Organisation Todt", holding the rank of Major. As an engineer, he was responsible for the construction of bridges and bunkers on all main European frontlines (Poland, France, and Russia). During the wartime bombardments after 1942, my grandmother was evacuated with her children to various places, partly seeking refuge with her family in Weimar, partly forcefully evacuated to different villages in Northern Hesse. After the end of the war, my grandfather was detained as a prisoner of war by the French army in Stuttgart for a short time, but since he had an excellent command of English, French and Russian, he was released shortly thereafter and worked as an interpreter for the allied forces. Directly after his release, he separated from his wife and family and married for a third time after his divorce from my grandmother. His third wife was half Jewish, and she knew about my grandfather's Nazi history. My grandfather can be considered as a staunch Nazi, although he never was politically active after the fall of the Third Reich. My grandmother, on the other hand, was basically a non-political person, although she became a convinced Nazi follower in the course of her marriage and upheld this conviction until her death in 1967. As family narrative relates, this firm Nazi conviction was mainly due to a certain nostalgic reminiscence of the "Golden Years" since she connected the "Third Reich" period with her personal epoch of wealth and social standing. She gave birth to three sons.

My mothers' parents both had their roots in the rural areas south of Kassel. My grandfather was born in 1903, my grandmother in 1916. As the family's narrative tells, both were nonpolitical, but grew up in a predominantly conservative, nationalist environment. They had four girls and one boy. In the year 1934, the family moved to the city of Kassel and purchased a small department store from a Jewish merchant in 1935. The family narrative goes on to relate that they were only allowed to purchase the shop on the condition that my grandfather became a member of the Nazi party. The family always preserved their rural roots and evacuated during the last years of the war back to their home village. My grandfather was drafted into the Wehrmacht in 1940, and was captured by the British as a regular rank–and-file soldier already in 1941. He stayed in British war captivity in various places like Libya, South Africa, Canada and the UK where he was assigned to forced labor. He finally returned home after 6 years in 1947. In contrast to my father's mother who had always been backed by her extended family, my mother's mother experienced the fate of the so-called "Trümmerfrauen" (literally "rubble women"): the generation of single mothers and women who all of a sudden found themselves being the head of the household and who had to shoulder the burden of reconstruction during the years of 1942 to 1947/48. During the long years of her husband's absence she had to care for children, family, household and income and having gained this position of authority never returned it to the male head of the household even after my grandfather's return from war captivity.

Neither family ever processed their Nazi history. The dominant pattern of behavior was the concealment of the political parts of the family history. The narration of everyday life in wartime and during the Third Reich was de-politicized and always contained a strong component telling of suffering from war atrocities: the bombardment of the Eder dam in 1943 and the flooding of the villages, the fire storm after the bombardment of Kassel, the "escape from the Russians" on foot with the baby stroller from Weimar to Kassel in 1945. Both families became literally "divided" in the year 1949: some brothers and sisters of both grandparents remained in the newly created German Democratic Republic, the former Soviet zone, whereas the greater part of both families lived in the West.

My parents were both born in the year 1936. They experienced the first bombardments and destruction of their homes at the age of 6-7 years and were 9 years old when the war ended. For my mother, the "fatherless" time of the war period lasted until 1947; for my father this condition became permanent after the separation of his parents in 1945. My parents married in 1960 at the age of 24. Both were and still are convinced pacifists, both became members of the Social Democratic Party, being part of its left wing, and both are firm opponents of any kind of rightist disposition. Both were politically active during the period of high tension between 1968 and 1972, but without becoming radical. Between them and the 1968-students' movement stood a gap of half a generation and the distance of an already completed higher education. There was seldom contact with family members in the GDR. My parents rarely went to visit and maintaining contact with them remained the task of my grandparents' generation. Processing their personal childhood experiences in wartime, and their parents' involvement in the Nazi regime had a lasting impact on my parents and made them become pacifist, socialistically oriented and cosmopolitan democrats. My parents tried to come to terms with the Nazi past of their parents and to understand their own childhood, with the intention to learn from the past and draw the necessary consequences. But defining their respective personal standpoints remained a highly individual process. It did not result in a generalizing demonization of the "fathers' generation", nor did it encourage them to enlighten and educate forthcoming generations.

This same distance from the "generation of 68" is also characteristic for my own generation. Born in 1961, half a generation separated me from the students' movement, I was too young for the wave of radicalization of the early 1970s. I was politically socialized by the peace movement and the No-Nuke movement of the late 1970s, at a time when the German RAF (Red Army Faction) had already reached the peak of its existence. In the political field, my generation oriented itself towards the squatter scene and the autonomous anarchist movements, but not with the RAF launched urban guerilla. For my generation, the GDR was a foreign country. I visited my matrilineal and patrilineal families in the East only once during my childhood, thereafter never again. I had friends in France and Spain, but not on the other side of the Iron Curtain.

But my generation was also the generation which started to process German Nazi history in a detailed manner. We formulated the relevant questions, and we worked in the History Workshops emerging all over Germany. My generation started to oppose each form of national pride and to reject all kinds of national symbols.

My eldest daughter was born during the situation of radical change in November and December 1989, immediately after the fall of the Berlin wall. The historical knowledge her generation has of the Nazi period relies on the family narratives of her grandparents, who themselves had experienced the Third Reich only during childhood. It is also based on the results of my generation's investigations, as well as on the official versions of school history books, which transmit a standardized knowledge about the Nazi period to the succeeding generations. For them, a visit to a concentration camp is a compulsory part of the school's curriculum, and a study of National Socialism is fixed in the syllabus according to age groups and school types. This generation experiences the time of the Nazi regime in a reprocessed and historicized version that my generation had compiled, prepared and shaped in didactics. Nevertheless, they still have access to primary sources: their grandparents, i.e. the "war children generation" which is still living and can continue to transmit the family narrative first hand.

The generation of my grandchildren will only be able to enjoy this opportunity of direct contact to contemporary witnesses to a limited extent. For them, the individual personality of Adolf Hitler is as far away as other historical figures such as Wallenstein, Bismarck, Wilhelm II, Charlemagne or "Herman the Cheruscan". The historicization of the Nazi past has been concluded. However, this generation has to deal with the issue of rightist radicalism, and it has to try to understand such ambivalent constellations as for instance the Israeli position within the conflict over Palestine. It remains a challenging question whether this generation will still classify these problems into a historicized Nazi continuity, or whether it will treat them as independent phenomena.

SYNCHRONISATION AND HISTORICIZATION

Reconciliation is a process that always involves at least two parties, whereas the processing of the past may be either an individual process or a group process. Depending on how many different groups can be identified during a reconciliation process, and how many commonalities the group members find in their shared history, the process of processing the past has to be viewed in different contexts: individual and collective memories have to be categorized, and these memories and categorizations need to become a subject of communication.

During a reconciliation process this happens by synchronization. An isolated memory can never be the basis for reconciliation and a variety of different isolated memories need at least a common historical background in order to communicate even about the possibility of reconciliation. The minimum feature of such commonality is the action of the perpetrator and the suffering of the victim. Synchronization is necessary in order to categorize remembrance as a precondition for reconciliation, and to provide a basis for interaction between the parties involved. This takes place on a variety of levels. In the following I would like to present three possible levels that are determinant for the process of remembering and communication about memories.

1. On the first level we find powerful external factors of influence, which have dominated the contemporary discourse. This level applies exclusively to internal reconciliation processes.
2. On the second level we find the conditions and circumstances, which accompany, determine, define and/or characterize the process of overcoming the past. This level applies to internal as well as external reconciliation processes.

3. On the third level we find the synchronization of the formative events of the former adversaries and recent reconciliation partners. This level applies exclusively to external reconciliation processes.

In the previous section I already indicated the importance of categorization into generations, and elaborated on a distinction between periods of life, features of socialization and correlation of events. In Table 3, I would like to work on the correlation of events and try to document the first level, i.e. the internal discourse, framed by decades. The attribution of the predominant discourse to respective time frames remains of necessity incomplete und subjective. Emphasis is put on those components that were important for collective processing of the Nazi past.

Table 4 points out some key factors for the elaboration of the second level. Again it needs

Table 3. Predominant discourses in Germany 1945 to present

Time Frame	Predominant Discourse
1945-1955	Reconstruction/ IDP's-Returnees-POW's/ Territorial Disintegration/ Constitution of two state entities FRG-GDR
1955-1965	Economic Rehabilitation ("Wirtschaftswunder")/ Hidden restoration vs. "Vergangenheitsbewältigung"
1965-1975	"Generation of 68"/ start of open debate on Nazi history/ societal division
1975-1985	Start of detailed processing of the past/ focus on overcoming Germany's Nazi history/ "History Workshops"/ Educational reform
1985-1995	Unification of GDR and FRG/ shift in focus of public discourse and academic research
After 1995	Processing of GDR history/investigation of unexplored fields of research of Nazi history

Table 4. Synchronization of events 1945 to present

Time Frame	Dominant Discourse	Institutions	Economy	International Politics	Domestic Politics
1945-1955	Reconstruction	East and West sectors in Germany	European Recovery Program (ERP) and "Trümmerfrauen"	Cold War	Partition of Germany
1955-1965	Economic Rehabilitation ("Wirtschaftswunder")/ Hidden restoration vs. "Vergangenheitsbewältigung"	European Coal and Steel Community (ECSC) between Germany and France	"Wirtschaftswunder"	De-Stalinization vs. McCarthy; first wave of decolonization	Rearmament
1965-1975	"Generation of 68"/ start of open debate on Nazi history/ societal division	EWG European Economic Community (EEC)	Energy Crisis	Hot Spot Middle East; second wave of decolonization	"68 movement." Red Army Faction (RAF), Eastern Treaties
1975-1985	Start of detailed processing of the past/ focus on overcoming Germany's Nazi history/"History Workshops"/Educational reform	EG European Community (EC)	Mass unemployment	Nuclear tests	Conservative shift
1985-1995	Unification of GDR and FRG/ shift in focus of public discourse and academic research	European Union (EU)	Reunification	Decay of the blocks	Reunification
After 1995	Processing of GDR history/ investigation of unexplored fields of research of Nazi history	EU-Enlargement	World economic crisis	Reconfiguration of international power structures	Consolidation of the unified Germany, new positioning in Europe and internationally

to be said that the selection of components is somewhat incomplete and arbitrary. It serves the purpose, however, of setting a possible framework in which memories can be classified and on which an exchange of experiences can be based, namely institutional development, economic aspects and international as well as national determinants. This may be seen as an extension of Table 1, correlated with additional components.

Looking at the last line of the table, some important features may be recognized:

- After 1995, the processing of GDR history takes priority over the processing of Nazi history
- Most of the "big issues" of Nazi history have already been dealt with and greater focus is placed on the study of details.
- Germany has become economically well positioned in an international context, resulting in new and more ambitious political aspirations.

While this latter point relating to the German economy is of central importance, it will not be investigated in this chapter. We address here instead the first two aspects which demonstrate an important component of reconciliation processes: the historicization of the past.

In this context, historicization means a reassessment, or a new assessment, of traumatic or traumatizing events, which require reconciliation, thus aiming at a mitigation of these events, and reducing their records to unemotional, historical fact.

The first of the aforementioned points describes the phenomenon of "overlapping layers": new historical events gain importance and push the primary traumatization to the background. The second point describes the "saturation" with processing of the past, coinciding with the ongoing fading of memories in the course of generational change. Both aspects, the strength of the "overlapping layers" and the "degree of saturation" of the succeeding generations, have a deep impact on the completion of historicization processes.

I would like to illustrate this by using the example of Brandt's genuflection in Warsaw described at the beginning of this chapter:

The public discussion in the year 1970 was about perceptions: the genuflection was subject to different interpretations, and a public debate on the moral eligibility and the consequences of the genuflection was sparked. Since 2005, however, this discussion has ceased to be held in public, but is rather discussed in a small circle of insiders and experts. It has become a debate about motives, i.e. an attempt at correcting the perceptions of 1970. But for the overwhelming majority of the German population, the 2005 debate doesn't play any role: the photograph of Brandt's genuflection had already become a positive symbol for the German reconciliation process. Any further debates on the issue are no longer of interest to the greater public.

In our context, where the structural components of an abstraction are our focus, we are confronted with the determining question of whether this process of historicization is accompanied by further experiences of violence. In the case of Germany, this may clearly be neglected.

Historicization can be seen as a result of de-emotionalization. This is a long-lasting process. An affected individual can de-emotionalize events only by working through them and through distance. The past can be processed through the continual recall of key events from memory, and their (new) interpretation on the basis of subsequent experiences. Distance can be achieved when memory-related emotions fade away, putting the event into perspective.

This refers once again to the phenomenon of "overlapping layers" whereby new memories overlap past events. This contributes to the eclipse of primary traumatization and may have a positive impact on a reconciliation process. Historicization is therefore closely connected to the way memorization proceeds. In relation to reconciliation, historicization is linked to the way individual violations are integrated into a generally accepted interpretation of facts, and thus pushed to the background.

One important precondition is the absence of violence. At the end of the day, the existence of violence and the extent of use of violence is determinant of how irreconcilability is transferred to succeeding generations.

When violent situations occur continuously, trauma is kept vivid and permanently fueled. The absence of violence prevents re-traumatization and "inheritance". This is true with regard to direct, i.e. physical and psychological violence, as well as structural and cultural violence. The first generation without experience of violence is the "generation of reconciliation". In the German example, this is the third generation.

Communication about the past also plays a prominent role in reconciliation. Ideally, it results in exhaustion and determines interest or disinterest on a certain topic. In cases where open communication is impossible, and where there is no chance to attain exhaustion, this absence of communication about the past results in a ticking time bomb.

Germany today can be considered an example of a completed historicization, as the example of Brandt's genuflection in Warsaw has demonstrated. A glance into the German daily press of 2014 confirms this statement. During the four week period between the 14 June and 15 July 2014 alone, not less than ten detailed articles, documentaries, essays and reviews were published in the daily newspaper "Frankfurter Allgemeine Zeitung", one of Germany's most renowned newspapers, which dealt at length with topics about Nazi history:

1. Report about new findings about Hitler's appointee for the German missile program, Hans Kammler, stating that Kammler was caught by American troops who presumably assisted him in going into hiding. (FAZamSo 2014)
2. Excerpts from the biography of Margarethe von Haase, wife of one of the Wehrmacht officers who participated in the attempt on Hitler's life on 20 July 1944, and were subsequently detained and killed, citing repressions against the family. (FAZ 2014a)
3. Article about a new exhibition on the German resistance in the Berlin "Bendlerblock", center of the German military resistance against Hitler under Stauffenberg in 1944. (FAZ 2014b)
4. Reviews of a book on the Hitler opponents Dietrich Bonnhoeffer and Hans von Dohnanyi. (FAZ 2014b)
5. Report on a book published by the German historian Sebastian Stopper, which was put on the index in Russia due to its research on the atrocities of Russian partisan contingents against the Russian civilian population during the Second World War. (FAZ 2014c)
6. Interview with Geoffrey Layton, successor of the owners of the German publishing house Ullstein, about the publishing house's history during and after the Nazi dictatorship. (FAZ 2014c)
7. Research findings of German scholars on their investigation in German and American military archives into the desertion of the German writer Alfred Andersch, who had claimed in his book "Die Kirschen der Freiheit" to have deserted his military unit in June 1944.(FAZ 2014d)
8. Article on the conversion of World War 2 bunkers into real estate. (FAZ 2014e)
9. Review of a book on children deported as forced laborers during the Third Reich. (FAZ 2014f)
10. Article on the vindication of Ilse Ströbe, former employee of the German Foreign Office who was executed in 1942 as an alleged communist spy. (FAZ 2014g)

Topics relating to Nazi history are regularly dealt with even in the local press, as illustrated by the report by one of the six survivors of the 1944 SS massacre in Oradour-sur-Glane in France. (HNA 2014)

Apart from the reports about Hans Kammler, Sebastian Stopper and the children forcefully deported during the Third Reich, these media articles clearly show that today's main topic of public and media discussion is no longer the examination of the past, but rather an elaboration of the process of its historicization.

We recognize here that the examination of the past takes places on multiple levels today. It has become culture. Memory has transferred from the various collective memories into a manifested cultural memory. Historicization has been concluded, a pre-condition – although not a guarantee – for a stable reconciliation process.

This has been a long road and the way has been marked by many milestones. I would like to present three of them in the following examples:

The first public discussion on the issue of the German "deserters" was initiated in Germany 35 years after the end of the war. That it was discussed at all, is owed to the results of the locally centered movement of a "history from below / grass root history" which spread all over Germany in the mid-1970s: local "history workshops" collected biographic material, conducted interviews with contemporary witnesses and thus initiated the collation of a local history of National Socialism in Germany. In the city of Kassel, the city council made the following decision on May 7 1979:

The magistrate as the municipal authority shall be entrusted to

1. *Contract eligible scholars for a local documentation of Kassel's history during the NS regime,*
2. *Publish the results of this documentation without delay in as widespread and publicly understandable manner as possible,*
3. *Contract eligible scholars for an historical investigation of the local self-administration and the political parties in Kassel from Carl Schomburg to the present date. (Kammler, Krause-Villmar, 1984, p. 6)*

Thereafter, a working group led by the historians, Dietfried Krause-Vilmar and Jörg Kammler, was established at the university of Kassel which in the following years not only published a local history of the Nazi regime in Kassel, but also initiated for the first time detailed research on local forms of resistance, and contributed to the vindication of deserters of the German armed forces. (Kammler, Krause-Villmar, 1984) At the same time, the working group succeeded in bringing one of the first concentration camps in Germany, the Breitenau detention center near Kassel, out of suppression and oblivion and back into the public eye, by creating an exemplary memorial.[3]

A second milestone was the so-called "Wehrmacht exposition". Accurately titled, "War of annihilation - Atrocities of the Wehrmacht from 1941 to 1944", this exhibition of the renowned Hamburg Institute for Social Research was inaugurated on 5 March 1995 in Hamburg. For the forthcoming four years it dominated much of the public debate on the Nazi period in Germany. In reaction to public criticism, the exhibition was revised, and the new catalogue of 2001 stated:

The exhibition's hypothesis that the Wehrmacht actively participated in the planning and realization of the war of annihilation against Jews, prisoners of war and civilian populations, was held as practically undisputed in historical scholarly research. In contrast, the response of the broader public exposes that an image of the "clean Wehrmacht" still prevails in parts of the German society even 50 years after the end of the war. (HIS, 2001)

The Wehrmacht exhibition was the subject of two parliamentary debates in the German Bundestag in 1997 (Thiele, 1997), and the controversy about the hypotheses finally led to a temporary interruption in 1999, initiated by the institute's director, Jan Philipp Reemtsma, who assigned an independent commission with the task of verifying photos and texts used in the exhibition in order to invalidate the accusation of manipulation and falsification. After one year's work, the commission recommended the exhibition's revision owing to some factual errors with regard to content, but relieved the creators of the exhibition from the accusations of manipulation and falsification.

The third milestone was set by the former German Minister of Foreign Affairs, Joschka Fischer, in the year 2005. He assigned an independent commission of historians with the task of investigating the involvement of the German Foreign Office during the Nazi period with the regime's crimes, with special regard to its involvement to the genocide of the European Jews. Five years later, the commission presented its findings to Fischer's successor, the then Minister of Foreign Affairs, Guido Westerwelle. The result of the investigation was distinct: from the very first day, the German Foreign Office actively took part in the annihilation policy of the Hitler regime, and was therefore actively involved in the deportation and annihilation of the Jewish population. (Conze, 2010) The findings of the commission became even more explosive, because they revealed the continuity of personnel of the German diplomatic corps from the Nazi period to the Federal Republic of Germany. The Foreign Office had already been charged by allied prosecution during the Nuremberg war crime trials, but at that time had managed to create a nimbus of clandestine resistance, a myth which the Foreign Office succeeded in keeping alive for about 60 years.

Each of these three milestone cases refers to a very specific stage of the German process of overcoming the past, showing it to be a protracted, and multi-level process: it took 35 years for resistance fighters and deserters to be rehabilitated and considered equivalent to "normal" members of the Wehrmacht; public acknowledgement of the atrocities committed by German soldiers during the war was delayed for about 50 years; and it took about 60 years to reveal the continuities of Nazi personnel in the Federal Republic of Germany by investigating the German Foreign Office, thus belying the myth of the Foreign Office as a bastion of resistance.

This latter research may already be divided into two areas: the first part elaborates on the crimes of the Nazi regime; the second documents the continuities into post war society. It was this transition that began the historicization of this complex field of research. The Foreign Office's involvement in the Nazi regime's crimes has now become part of German cultural memory, but the continuities to post war society are subject of new and current research.

The year 2015 marks the 70th anniversary of the end of the Second World War. This will be cause for a surge in new research, events, etc. But 2015 will definitely not create a wave of anti-Polish or anti-French campaigns or riots. It will not begin an anti-Jewish renaissance, even though the war waged by Israel in the Gaza strip in 2014 provoked the resurrection of old slogans in new forms. This bears no relevance to the stability of the reconciliation constellations of the Nazi regime. Historicization has been concluded through the transformation of collective memories into a cultural memory. Although, of course, this historicization can become the subject of new disputes at any time.

THE GERMAN "VERGANGENHEITSBEWÄLTIGUNG"

The term "Vergangenheitsbewältigung" is a well-established technical term in Germany that specifically describes the processing of Nazi history in the Federal Republic of Germany. Literally translated, it has the meaning of "overcoming the past". This term was defined by the first president of the newly founded FRG, Theodor Heuss, and developed out of the early debate about National Socialism and the issue of guilt, formulated by Eugen Kogon and Theodor Adorno. Following its early connotation as synonym for the German debate on guilt and shame, the term became a denomination of the failure of German society to clear its relationship to the past during the first few decades after 1945. The German Jewish author Ralph Giordano formulated in his book "Die zweite Schuld oder von der Last ein Deutscher zu sein" (The second guilt or the burden of being German – author's translation) (Giordano, 1987) the hypothesis that post-war Germany failed for decades to process its Nazi past and sabotaged the process by a "conspiracy of silence".

In contrast, the German historian, Eike Wolgast, refers in a 1997 essay to a peculiarity:

It remains an open field for research how the German population positioned itself to its very recent history, which had just ceased to be the present, under the immediate impression of the Nazi regime's collapse .... Generally speaking, it seems that in academic research there exists a tacit consensus that initially after 1945, a certain degree of normality had to be attained before an explicit discussion or examination of the Third Reich's past could have legitimately been expected. (Wolgast, 1997)

In fact, I consider these two aspects of "silence" and "attainment of normality" as the main characteristics of the German "Vergangenheitsbewältigung" in the first generation. In retrospect, we can state that more than a decade had to pass, before German society started to figure out its own position with regard to the Nazi regime, even though the long lines of freed former inmates of the concentration camps walking through a devastated Germany, and the forced visits of local populations to the concentration camp sites had made the regime's atrocities visible to a large part of the German population. This first post-war decade can be seen as the period in which internal German positions had to be clarified and the first new intra-societal polarizations came about. What contributed considerably to this extended period of silence was the fact, that it ultimately took four years to end the existing insecurity about the political and economic fate of post-war Germany by creating two German nation states. And even then this establishment remained provisional. What the end of the war certainly did initiate was a process of clarification of the internal relationships within the society of perpetrators.

This was of great importance to the reconciliation process. On the one hand, it illustrates that after 1945 in Germany, the boundaries between perpetrators and victims began to take shape, resulting in considerable "gray zones" which made a clear distinction difficult, especially with regard to the attitude of the masses. On the other hand, this was a necessary process to identify collective positions – whether national or international - on the reconciliation process with the "external" i.e. former war adversaries.

The encyclopedia "Lexikon der Vergangenheitsbewältigung", which was first published in 2007, tried to embrace in its entirety this internal process that we have tried to sketch for the immediate post-war period. (Fischer, Lorenz, 2009). In a total of 169 different articles, classified into a contextual and chronological order, the volume highlights those aspects which are considered of prime relevance. These aspects are distinguished according to the sub-categories of justice, discourse, culture and science, and are combined as reference points with the respective relevant events of each particular phase. What is important in this context, is the fact that revisionist and restorative features are also taken into account, as Table 5 illustrates.

Table 5 illustrates that the German "Vergangenheitsbewältigung" was a predominantly internal and purely German process after 1949 when the two German states were established. The clarification and definition of internal relationships within the perpetrators' society and the contention with

Table 5. Synchronization of events 1945 to present "Vergangenheitsbewältigung"

Time Frame	Dominant Discourse	Institutions	Economy	International Politics	Domestic Politics
1945-1955	Reconstruction	East and West sectors in Germany	European Recovery Program (ERP) and "Trümmerfrauen"	Cold War	Partition of Germany
1955-1965	Economic Rehabilitation („Wirtschaftswunder") / Hidden restoration vs. "Vergangenheitsbewältigung"	European Coal and Steel Community (ECSC) between Germany and France	"Wirtschaftswunder"	De-Stalinisation vs. McCarthy; first wave of decolonization	Rearmament
1965-1975	"Generation of 68" / start of open debate on Nazi history / societal division	EWG European Economic Community (EEC)	Energy crisis	Hot Spot Middle East; second wave of decolonization	"68 movement", Red Army Faction (RAF), Eastern Treaties
1975-1985	Start of detailed processing of the past / focus on overcoming Germany's Nazi history / "History Workshops" / Educational reform	EG European Community (EC)	Mass unemployment	Nuclear tests	Conservative shift
1985-1995	Unification of GDR and FRG / shift in focus of public discourse and academic research	European Union (EU)	Reunification	Decay of the blocks	Reunification
after 1995	Processing of GDR history / investigation of unexplored fields of research of Nazi history	EU-Enlargement	World economic crisis	Reconfiguration of international power structures	Consolidation of the unified Germany, new positioning in Europe and internationally

the victims' communities within Germany, were prominent characteristics of the second generation. "Vergangenheitsbewältigung" in relation to external parties had two major components, namely the debate about the Holocaust and the juridical investigation of the Nazi past. In these latter points, the two clarification processes of the internal and external relationships between perpetrators' and victims' communities were very much interconnected.

The table also highlights another important phenomenon that is characteristic for the German reconciliation process. When we look at the third column "Culture and Science" we recognize that the interaction of press and media, literature and academic research have pushed the German reconciliation process forward considerably. Sensitive issues were first processed in German literature. The media publicly exposed scandals and injustice. And academic research succeeded not only in documenting the overall history of the Third Reich, but also in controversially elaborating details which were connected to the larger picture of the Third Reich. Academic findings were presented to the public claiming optimal neutrality and maximum objectivity and these, together with the perceptions of people's various collective memories and the growing cultural memory, built up a documentation of the past. The result offered only limited toeholds for polemics, propaganda, populism and falsification of history.

In his book "Das umstrittene Gedächtnis" (The contested memory), the German historian, Arnd Braukämper, investigated and analyzed in depth how world war history was handled in various European countries. (Braukämper, 2012)

He states that the victim-perpetrator-relationship determines the level of reconciliation and that the first step required is a clarification of the interior relationships within the victims' society as well as within the perpetrators' society.

Braukämper also understands this process as a process of change, during which "communicative memory" (which can be instrumentalized by state or group interests) is transformed into a differentiated "cultural memory" that evolves from within a society.

He basically differentiates between individual memory, family memory, communicative memory and cultural memory. He sees reconciliation as an interaction between victim and perpetrator, although this interaction is based on an unequal relationship.

In this context, he finds an important correlation: perpetrators undergo a process of auto-victimization, i.e. an auto-protection mechanism in order to relativize their own deeds and thus survive physically and mentally. Perpetrators are in this way also victims, but the converse is not automatic: victims are not perpetrators, except in cases of retaliation. A victims' society can however host perpetrators' communities.

The process of auto-victimization can be traced easily in Germany. Refugees and returning POW's conveyed the image of victimization from expulsion, war captivity, forced labor and mass rapes. The German civil population identified its own suffering with the destructive air raids, and German society as a whole saw itself as a victim of political seduction.

By contrast, when we consider German victims' communities, it is indeed difficult to identify groups of perpetrators, although there is evidence of acts of violent retaliation. To date this remains an unexplored field of research.

As shown in the previous chapter, a long time had to pass before this simplified, collective auto-victimization could be corrected and the sensitive issue of perpetrators within victims' communities could be discussed.

The clarification of internal as well as external relationships thus requires a process of differentiation that lasts at least two to three generations. The initiation of a debate on all the facets of the relationship between victims and perpetrators alone needs a minimum of two generations. In the case of our core theme, i.e. the German reconciliation process, this is not a peculiarity on the part of the Germans, but applies similarly to all sides.

I would like to illustrate this in Table 5 by using the example of the two German nation states, FRG and GRD, and their respective Eastern and Western neighbors, Poland and France. Table 6 describes the above-mentioned third level of synchronization, the "external reconciliation process" described in the previous chapter.

In both France and Poland, the "National guiding principle" can be clearly connected to a heroization of the past, whereas in the case of the two German national states we see that both regimes tried to extract themselves from direct responsibilities: the FRG positioned itself as the "legal successor of the Third Reich" but without acknowledging any moral confession of collective guilt, and the GDR presented itself as the collective homeland of German anti-fascism. The second and third rows of the table show that the tasks of reprocessing and coming to terms with the relationships between victims and perpetrators were sensitive and painful for all four countries alike. The "succeeding main discourse" refers to some events that began to have an important influence on the reprocessing of world war history. Here, we can recognize that the differentiation process that had begun, found its parallel in new and growing memory experiences which themselves influenced the process of coming to terms with the past, resulting in the gradual construction of overlapping layers (see Table 7).

We can deduce some basic similarities and differences with regard to the initiation of a differentiation process from this very simplified table.

France is the only country that was involved in de-colonization processes and was thus actively

Table 6. Synchronization of events 1945 to present: reconciliation processes

State/Category	France	FRG	GDR	Poland
National guiding principles after 1945/49	Resistance	"Vergangenheitsbewältigung" legal succession of the Third Reich	Anti-fascism	Communist resistance
Topics of reprocessing	Collaboration Period of the Vichy regime	Denazification	In cases of apology: collective "whitewash certificate"	Collaboration
Own offenses vs. auto-victimization	Own offenses: deportation of Jews Participation in the war Bi-national relationships/ marriages	Victims of political seduction, war captivity and forced labor, mass rape, expulsion, air raids	Victims of Nazi clique in alliance with great land owners and big capitalists	Own offenses: massacre of Jewish population Non-communist resistance
Succeeding main discourse	De-colonization in: Indochina and Algeria	German emigrants Returnees from war captivity	Revolt of 17 June 1953	De-Stalinization Solidarmosc Pope John Paul II

Table 7. Synchronization of events 1945 to 1995: Germany and its neighbors

	1945-1955	1955-1965	1965-1975	1975-1985	1985-1995
France	Indochina	Algeria	Paris May riots	Change from socialists to conservatives	Dissolution of the blocs
FRG		Berlin wall	Movement of 1968	Change from social democrats to conservatives	Re-unification
GDR	Revolt of 17 June 1953		Prague spring	Rise of civilian opposition	Re-unification
Poland		Posen revolt of June 1956	Prague spring	Solidarmosc + Wyotila	Dissolution of the blocs

involved in new wars in Indochina and Algeria. In Poland, we repeatedly see forms of national, non-communist resistance, which manifest in various revolts and riots, and at a later stage in the foundation of the independent union movement of Solidarnosc. Poland possesses another particularity: in the midst of the Cold War, Karol Woytila, a citizen from a regime which had dedicated itself to atheism, was elected pope.

It is also an interesting feature that at the end of the 1960s all four countries were influenced by the effects of worldwide rebellion and the drive for revolution, reforms, and change. In all cases, the following decade was characterized by political and societal restructuring. The dissolution of the blocs in the last decade (1985-1995) constituted a further binding element.

In all cases, it was the grandchildren's generation that contested the various versions of communicative memories, and began to unveil both national heroism and auto-victimization.

But the German reconciliation process was not a product of the efforts of the third generation: the third generation was simply the generation which pushed the process of differentiation forwards and, as a result of this differentiation process, completed the transformation from collective to cultural memory.

It was the first generation that attempted to clarify reconciliation partners. In the case of Germany and its neighbors, these included:

- Combatants/soldiers with combatants/ soldiers
- Civilians with civilians
- Civilians with combatants/soldiers (anonymously, or with the perpetrators exposing their identities)
- Neighbors and neighbors (here, it is still unexplored to what extent this is applicable in Germany for the years 1945-1949).

Based on these constellations, a variety of institutions were founded in the succeeding years, which worked on the national as well as transnational levels as agents of reconciliation, some of them are still active to date. These were, among others:

- Town twinning
- Veterans' associations/ POW associations
- War graves commissions
- Youth exchange - school contacts - student exchange
- Franco-German Youth Office and German-Polish Youth Office
- "Aktion Sühnezeichen-Friedensdienste" (Action Reconciliation Service for Peace)

At the other end of the spectrum, Germany also experienced the rise of revisionist and restorative organizations: displaced associations, war veterans' comradeship associations etc. that tried to gather all those societal forces which were reluctant to embrace reconciliation or rejected it outright.

During the first two generations, certain societal constellations thus came into existence that had both polarizing and marginalizing effects on the respective societies.[4] The proportion of political hardliners and how great the chances for restoration were, were determined by political stability and societal embedding of the will to reconcile. This is neither a German nor a European phenomenon, but rather a global phenomenon.

As already stated above, the relationship between victims and perpetrators is basically an unequal relationship. It is also a fact that perpetrators activate a certain protection mechanism by claiming auto-victimization. Depending on the severity of their offenses and guilt, and depending on the resulting degree of the perpetrator's traumatization, this protection mechanism guarantees physical and mental survival. The same is true for the victims: victimization needs a certain protection mechanism, and the severity of traumatization determines the individual degree of encapsulation.

PARAMETERS OF ASSESSMENT AND EVALUATION

Has the German reconciliation process been concluded? If so, has it been successfully concluded? These questions can be answered differently, depending on the parameters set for assessment.

If the success of the reconciliation process were measured by the extent to which the atrocities of the Nazi regime have been fully investigated and sentenced, the answer will be no. If we continue to ask whether justice has been achieved and whether the victims have been fully compensated, the answer will again be no. If such an assessment depended on the question whether racism and anti-Semitism still exist in Germany today, the answer cannot clearly been formulated, and becomes a question of belief.

At the outset we defined the following parameters for an assessment of the reconciliation process after the Second World War:

1. Rule of law
2. Non-violence
3. Free and controversial discussion
4. Unrestricted political evolvement and participation
5. Positive economic perspective
6. Historicization of the past

With regard to Germany, we have to differentiate in our assessment between the two German nation states, the GDR and the FRG. The two states were based on fundamentally different political and economic systems and each addressed and handled the issue of reconciliation in totally different ways, as we will see in the following. In the chart below, emphasis has been laid exclusively on the FRG. Table 8 illustrates that while the parameters used, marked here as "structures", can

Table 8. Parameters of assessment and evaluation

Structure	Success	Exceptions
Open and unrestricted communication processes (freedom of opinion)	Open discussion and freedom of opinion are guaranteed. Each individual has the opportunity to express his standpoint in public.	Incitement of the people and Holocaust denial are elements of an offense Murder is not time-barred (§ 211 STGB), but there is a period of limitation for the commencement of prosecution of a crime Nazi symbols are prohibited "Mein Kampf" is not permitted to be published in its original version
Absence from violent conflict resolution	The post-war processes ran/run mostly without violent action. After the Second World War, the FRG did not experience any serious violent confrontations - the principle of non-violent coexistence successfully prevailed.	RAF Right wing terrorism and NSU
Economic prosperity / safeguard of living standards	Germany became a global political power, ERP program (Marshall-Plan), economic reconstruction and „Wirtschaftswunder", European unity	Oil crisis Mass unemployment Economic injustice / increasing social and economic disparities
Historicization of the process	A general change in consciousness and perspectives among the German population has come about, the Nazi and World War 2 past has become part of cultural memory, distance has been gained from the fourth generation onwards	Percentage of neo-nazi dispositions (4,1 – 9,7 %), anti-Semitic dispositions (9,3 %) and racist (5,3 %) dispositions
Monopoly of use of force by a recognized institution, checks and balances through the separation of powers	The use of force is monopolized by the state (executive power), the constitutional state guarantees the right to life and physical integrity (abolition of death sentence, prohibition of torture) and the right to freedom of expression	Even the state itself continually tends to curtail and abrogate these principles: anti-terrorist measures during the „Deutscher Herbst", state of emergency laws, restrictions on the right to hold demonstrations, decree on occupational ban for members of "radical parties" (Radikalenerlaß)
Participation	Participation is secured to a large extent, each individual has the right to formulate his political opinion and establish himself politically, even revisionist institutions are allowed	Exclusion from public service jobs if evidence is found for unconstitutional activities Crime Political participation in parliament is restricted: a minimum of 5% of votes required High obstacles for plebiscites
Rule of law, "Checks and Balance"	The state controls compliance to the rule of law, and is at the same time controlled by the constitutional principles of separation of powers, as well as by the independence of the judiciary and the constitutional ban on the prosecution of dissention	The rule of law does not guarantee justice.

certainly be assessed as successfully achieved, a number of exceptions can also be identified.

By applying the parameters defined above, we can state that the German reconciliation process, as seen by the state of affairs in 2015, has been successfully concluded. The transformation of collective memories into a cultural memory can be considered to be complete. The course of time has positioned the fourth and fifth generation at a certain distance, and the process of historicization has also widely been concluded. However, the multitude of exceptions shows that this process is multi-leveled and it has in no way succeeded in creating a society that has a homogenous understanding of the past. Nevertheless, the important conclusion is that societal priorities have shifted.

However, we have to accept that at least one part of the dark history of Germany seems to have survived these processes: the phenomenon of neo-Nazism. But can we really interpret the rise of neo-Nazism as a manifestation of continuity, or is it rather a novel phenomenon?

The statistical data of the year 2014 provide a largely differentiated picture: only 21,700 individuals in Germany are known to be part of the right wing extremist spectrum (by comparison in 2009: 30,000). (Netz gegen Nazis 2009) A recent study at Leipzig University presents results shown in Table 9 regarding current German world views (Brähler, Decker, Kiess 2014).

Table 9. Current German world views (Leipzig study 2014)

Coherent right wing extremist world view	5.6%	2002: 9.7%
Xenophobia	18.1%	2002: 26.9%
Chauvinism	13.6%	2002:18.3%
Anti-Semitism	5.1%	2002: 9.3%
Advocacy of authoritarian regime	3.6%	2002: 7.7%
Social Darwinism	2.9%	2002: 5.3%
Trivialization of National Socialism	2.2%	2002: 4.1%

In the year 2010, the overall membership figures of all associations which are organized under the umbrella of the Union of the Displaced (Bund der Vertriebenen BdV), were estimated at approximately 550,000. The BdV, which was one of the most influential political pressure groups on the revanchist spectrum, has ceased to play any important role today. (RP-Online 2010)

When we consider the example of "anti-Semitism", we see that not only the focus, but also the connotations of propaganda have changed. A clear enemy image of the "Jew" as projected during the Nazi regime is now virtually non-existent. Instead, anti-Semitism today is either diffusely mixed with racism and chauvinism and characterized by the slogan "Ausländer raus!" (i.e. demanding the expulsion of foreigners from Germany), or it takes the shape of a specific form of Anti-Zionist or Anti-Israeli. An enemy concept of Israel currently exists which paradoxically mingles right-wing propaganda ("World Zionism and Israel suck Germany dry") and left-wing propaganda ("Israel annihilates the Palestinian people").

It is important to state that owing to the chronological distance from the primary generation of perpetrators (over 80 years) and the majority of the victims (70 years), the historicization process of the Nazi past and the transformation of collective memories into a cultural memory have to be considered to be completed. Recent German neo-Nazism and anti-Semitism call this historicization into question and raise a new dispute about cultural memory while rejecting current social, economic and political constellations. But this is part of the present, a new epoch.

The assessment of the German reconciliation process cannot, however, be limited to the question of success or failure. A second factor of assessment has to deal with the internal contradictions of the process. These internal contradictions are disclosed in the discrepancy between the two columns "Success" and "Exceptions" in the table presented above. A closer look reveals some core areas that may put the image of a successfully completed reconciliation process into perspective. In the following, I want to elaborate on two of these core sectors in more detail:

- The issue of injustice and
- The issue of continuity.

The juridical prosecution and due punishment of Nazi crimes illustrates the ambivalence of the reconciliation process best. The 5-year period of transitional justice between 1945 and 1950 was characterized by a partition of jurisdiction with regard to crime prosecution between the allied juridical bodies and German judiciary, which was being reconstructed at that time. The Law No. 4 from 30 October 1945, and No. 10 from 20 December 1945, issued by the Allied Control Council, placed responsibility for civil cases and crime prosecution into the hands of the German courts, with the exception of criminal activities committed by Nazis and/or individuals targeting the Allied forces, in addition to war crimes and crimes against humanity. After 1950 and 1955, respectively, all responsibility for the prosecution of Nazi crimes was handed over to the German judiciary. (Rücker, 1979)

Theoretically, the political and judicial order that was established in the FRG offered and still offers the opportunity to inflict penalty for every single Nazi crime. In practice, however, the prosecution of crimes was confronted with various rather trivial obstacles. The main problem hindering prosecution was not the period of limitation for capital crimes, e.g. for murder, which according to German law never falls under statute of limitation. The problem lay in the period of limitation for the initialization of prosecution for murder, which can be assumed to be applicable for the vast majority of homicides committed during the Nazi regime. This period amounts in accordance with § 211 STGB (German criminal law) to thirty years. This signified in practical application, that even perpetrators whose crimes had been revealed and who had been found guilty could no longer be prosecuted when the period of limitation had passed. The extreme difficulty in taking evidence and the prolonged process and longtime delay in arraignment meant that not all perpetrators could be brought to justice.

The second problem was that prosecution, trials and judgments could only be duly executed in a relatively small number of cases. In many cases, the perpetrators had died in the war or had passed away subsequently. Some had committed suicide or could not be brought to court due to their age. Let us consider for example, the fates of former concentration camp commanders (Rücker, 1979, 130pp) shown in Table 10.

The third problem was that victims' denouncements and the initiation of prosecution often happened on very limited evidence, so that the public prosecutors were forced to open blanket investigations which targeted at times entire military units. At the end of the day only a fraction of the suspects were actually brought to court. Rücker's statistics on legally binding sentences and regularly concluded court cases that did not result in sentencing of the defendant or continued prosecution of a suspect, show interesting figures for the years 1965 to 1977. In the year 1971 alone, 13 judgments with life sentences were rendered, 26 judgments with sentences for fixed-term imprisonment, but a total of 3859 cases were terminated without sentence. (Rücker, 1979, p. 126) Similar proportions could be seen in all other years of that period.

Table 10. Fate of former concentration camp commanders

Overall Figure	Died in the War	Executed with/ without Trial	Suicide	Sentenced	Died in Detention	Without Trial	Fate Unknown
45	5	14	5	10	4	6	1

During the period of transitional justice, it proved problematic that the allied war crimes trials, exclusively enacted by the United States after 1946, were based on military jurisdiction outside of national or international legislation, Of course, this extraordinary situation might have arisen since the genocide of the Jews and the war crimes committed, especially on the Eastern front, had reached a dimension of extermination which had never been known before. But the situation of a virtually extra-territorial jurisdiction also included the problematic tendency that in the course of time, the sentences rendered by the American judges became more and more influenced by the political developments of the approaching Cold War era. The trials against the German industrial magnates, tycoons and trusts (Case 5: Friedrich Flick et. al.; Case 6: IG Farben, Case 10: Krupp) ended with comparatively mild punishments, acquittals, or amnesty and untimely discharge. (Ueberschär, 2008) The global polarization at the start of the Cold War needed continuity in economy as well as in politics, so the last allied sentences were rendered in a pragmatic spirit.

The famous "Wilhelmstraßen trial" or "Ministries trial" against leading figures in the former Foreign Office leads to the second problematic complex of continuity. Two aspects require special attention. The fact, that denazification in the FRG was implemented on the basis of self -disclosure in the form of a questionnaire, had the consequence that only those Nazis who had been denounced by others were excluded from public service and denied political activity. But this was only a small number of individuals. Secondly, there was a severe lack of qualified personnel in nearly every sector of public administration after 1945, so that the responsible leaders resorted to the re-recruitment of nearly all personnel who were not officially accused of having committed war crimes. The case of the German Foreign Office illustrates the dilemma of continuity very well. When the FRG re-established the Ministry of Foreign Affairs in 1951, the diplomatic corps consisted in large part of staff who had served under von Ribbentrop in Wilhelmsstraße.

At this point, the phenomenon of continuity starts to become sensitive. The so-called "Wilhelmsstraßen trial" (named after the street in Berlin where the Nazi Foreign office was located) was the longest of the Nuremberg follow-up trials and lasted from 4 November 1947 until 4 April 1949. The complicity and active involvement of the Foreign Office in the planning and implementation of Hitler's policy of extermination was proved beyond doubt, thus proving the guilt of the so-called "desk-murderers". Although sentences were rendered, the first all-encompassing amnesties and discharges took place as early as 1950. Only one year later, the new Foreign Office of the FRG was founded, including many of the former Nazi "desk-murderers".

Once again, two important factors must be taken into consideration, although we will not be able to elaborate on them in great detail. Firstly, the continuity in employment of the "desk-murderers" did not automatically imply a continuation of their criminal activities. The newly founded FRG did not allow for this. There has been, however, insufficient investigation and research done on the issue of whether the "desk-murderers" transferred any of the spirit of the Third Reich into the Federal Republic of Germany. The above-mentioned work of the Historical Commission of 2005 – 2010 was a first serious attempt to trace such continuity, and this indicates a second important factor. Exactly 60 years had to pass until the time was ripe for such an all-encompassing investigation of the Foreign Office's past. Still, it is characteristic of the political and societal change in the FRG after 1945 that such wholehearted clarification of its crimes could be possible. (Conze, 2010)

The third and last component of assessment has to deal with the issue of comparison and the benefit an analysis of the German reconciliation process has for cases in other countries. In the introduction, I formulated the intention to elaborate on the possibility of "comparison of differences and variables within the context of reconciliation processes" by means of an abstraction of structural components, using the example of Germany after the Second World War. This needs to be related to recent conflict settings and discussed against the backdrop of the permanently changing faces of violent conflict resolution in recent times.

In retrospect, the German example can be categorized as follows:

- The conflict was both an inter-state and an internal conflict:
    - The reconciliation process was at first predominantly directed towards the exterior = transnational.
    - The internal reconciliation process took place on a reduced level.
- The conflict has been terminated.
- There were / are no more violent activities.

Whereas the dividing lines between victims and perpetrators with regard to external relationships are relatively clear from a German viewpoint (Axis powers vs. Allies, Germany vs. neighboring countries), the internal dividing lines are far more difficult to distinguish.

Even a basic perpetrator-victim constellation of Nazi to non-Nazi does not fit. There were too many overlaps and blurring of contours. Not all industrial magnates were Nazis, though they had a common interest with the NSDAP. (Neebe, 1981) In the early years, a socialist-oriented opposition even existed inside the NSDAP, which could have developed into a real threat to Adolf Hitler's position in the early 1930s. (Bracher, 1955) Lastly, the example of the two major Christian denominations in Germany, the protestant and the catholic churches, shows that the entire spectrum of resistance from "inner emigration" and opportunism to unconditional support for the Nazi regime could be found within one single organization.

It is relatively easy to define which potential victim groups evolved during the Nazi regime: Jews, homosexuals, Sinti and Roma, national resistance, political parties and organizations in opposition to the regime, victims of the Gestapo, concentration camp inmates and many more.

These victim groups were the basis for the formation of reconciliation constellations after the end of the Second World War. Within Germany, this spectrum can roughly be described as follows:

- Genocide victims (Jews)
- Persecuted minorities (homosexuals, Sinti and Roma)
- Political dissenters
- Victims of arbitrariness and misuse of power
- Emigrants
- "Inner emigration"

External reconciliation constellations referred primarily to the following groups:

- Civilians in attacked countries
- Civilians in annexed and occupied countries
- Enemy soldiers
- Forced laborers and deportees
- POW's

The fact that the victim groups of the Nazi period were not identical with the reconciliation constellations after the end of the war points out once again the uniqueness of the German case. The genocide of the Jewish population, the mass murder in the concentration camps and the far-reaching exodus of the German opposition had the effect that the internal reconciliation process slid into the background, since the overwhelming majority of victims had either been annihilated or were living abroad.[5] In addition to that, the division of Germany into two state entities produced the extraordinary situation that both states applied totally different reconciliation concepts, so that, after the reunification in 1990, the unified Federal Republic of Germany had to deal with a new, delayed and double-pronged task of reconciliation, i.e. the processing of the GDR regime's omission to overcome its Nazi past as well as the introduction of a new (now internal) reconciliation process between the victims and perpetrators of the authoritarian GDR regime.

Is such a complex setting really appropriate for gaining an understanding of recent and ongoing reconciliation processes?

Our response must be ambivalent. On the one hand the parameters which were used in this investigation for assessing the success of a reconciliation process, can indeed be acknowledged as universal.

On the other hand, we have to continually adjust and modify these parameters against the backdrop of the constantly changing face of violent conflict resolution. The ongoing wars of the 21st century appear very different to the Second World War. Victim-perpetrator constellations, as elaborated in the German example, exist in different compositions and under different conditions today. In some cases, reconciliation processes are enacted during the course of an ongoing conflict. This might indicate that the parameters for assessment are permanently overridden and have to be re-determined. Violent conflict resolutions are prolonged today. They do not have clear lines of distinction and it becomes more and more difficult to evaluate success or failure, because they barely enter into resting phases and rarely reach a third generation which is not affected by continuous violence.

By contrast, a certain universal consistency can be traced in some parameters. According to the results of this investigation, it is doubtful whether a reconciliation which had been ordered "from above" could ever have any sustainable effect in the absence of the parameters of "democratic structures" and "free expression".

This adds a whole new challenge to the examination of reconciliation processes.

FUTURE RESEARCH DIRECTIONS

The preceding discussion has handled reconciliation as an historical process. I would like, therefore, to identify potential future research directions and tie them to the German example discussed here and its relevance for the comparative analysis of reconciliation processes after the dissolution of the blocs after 1989-1990.

As already presented, the processes of 'Vergangenheitsbewältigung' and reconciliation in Germany after the Second World War have been comprehensively documented and researched. These investigations rest on the abundant materials available today for the examination and analysis of the time before, during and after the 'thousand year Reich' of the Nazis and the Second World War. This chapter has attempted to identify some gaps in this research. It has at the same time, however, made very clear that the list of possible research topics may be extended indefinitely. Just consideration of the topics of 'Neo-Nazism' and 'anti-Semitism' opens up a multitude of possibilities for academic research. If one agrees with the thesis put forward in this chapter, in their current forms these are not necessarily to be seen as a follow-on of the Nazi period, but rather as independent phenomena that may have arisen from specific constellations of social interactions within the changing dimensions of time and space in the post-Cold War era. Investigations of this kind primarily address the analysis of the process of historicization.

In the context of this chapter, the question of future research possibilities is much simpler to handle. The first main question is: where can gaps in research be found that are relevant to the topic of 'Reconciliation as an historical process'? The second main question is: what can be learned from the German example and what practical applications could the analysis of the German process of coming to terms with the past offer?

Out of the foregoing, the following areas for future research may be put forward:

Transition Research: "Zero Hour"

Revenge and retribution can be understood as compensatory acts in which victims act on their own initiative in reaction to their inflicted suffering. Such compensatory activities imply the transformation of victims to perpetrators and communities of perpetrators arise within victims' communities. Compensatory acts may take place systematically, but they primarily occur in situations of radical change and in a vacuum. Such a vacuum arises, for example, at the end of a war. There is a great deficiency in German historical research in the analysis of the so-called 'zero hour' which is characterized by such a situation of radical change.

The German economist, Werner Abelshauser, vehemently denied the existence of a time of radical change called 'zero hour' in his book 'Deutsche Wirtschaftsgeschichte nach 1945' (A history of German economics post 1945) and presented evidence that certain economic transition developments may be traced to either well before or long after the official end of the Second World War on May 8, 1945. (Abelshauser, 2004) This dissention has limited relevance for historians and those in the humanities or other social disciplines. We understand the term 'zero hour' not as a date on which political and economic upheavals can be pinned, but as a synonym for a vacuum: the old order had fallen, a new order had not yet been constituted. This situation can only be fixed in time to a limited degree. Many dates and stations in German history can be named between 1944 and 1946. Stefan Heym described this vacuum in his novel 'Schwarzenberg' by means of an example: a small, fictitious district on the border between Hesse and Thuringia gets forgotten during the Allied occupation of Germany and division into occupied zones in 1945. Located between the Red Army and the American troops, the district is forced to organize itself in a political vacuum with an uncertain future (Heym, 1984). Other non-literary sources sum up the idea of a vacuum more directly. Holocaust survivors in the publication 'Nirgendwo und überall zu Haus' (At home nowhere and everywhere) tell of confrontations between victims and perpetrators in the legal vacuum of 'zero hour' and of the drive for vigilante justice. It is precisely this that is a core theme of reconciliation research: revenge and retribution (Doerry, 2006). In the same publication it is made clear that the eschewal of revenge and retribution can be a long and very individual process and one that constantly needs to be readdressed. If we want to analyze these decision processes, we need a combined approach from both an historical and a psychological perspective.

'Zero hour' had other aspects too. My paternal grandfather admitted to my father that he had been given the order of blowing up the Stuttgart electricity works in 1945 should the war end and the city be occupied by allied troops. He did not carry this out, however, but rather gave himself up as a prisoner of war. This event describes a further core theme of reconciliation research: the turning point in the actions of individuals and societal groups. If we abstract these two constellations, the following research questions may be formulated: what happens when victims become perpetrators in an act of revenge and what consequence does this have on reconciliation processes? Furthermore, what happens when perpetrators cease their actions and what influence does this have on reconciliation processes?

We know too little about such courses of events and decision processes. This is a task for biographical research that combines historical and psychological approaches and which may have to work reconstructively when there is no longer access to contemporary witnesses.

Academic Frontiers: Reconstructive, Interdisciplinary, Biographical Research on Trauma, Continuity and Transgenerational Transfer

Two further fields of research in which historical and psychological research must combine are the topics of trauma and transgenerational transfer. Are traumatic experiences transferred from affected individuals to their children and grandchildren? If so, how do such transmission processes function? If not, can the traumatic experiences of the affected party be the reason for secondary or tertiary traumatization of the generations thereafter? Can we identify inheritance mechanisms in which hatred and violent dispositions are kept alive over generations to come?

The topic of transgenerational transfer has gained importance in German educational and sociological research in recent years, although some analyses seem more speculative than factually-based. One reason for this is the discipline-specific, focused handling of orally transferred sources. Certainly, familial continuities can be traced over generations from biographical interviews, but from the point of view of the historian, an appropriate contextual and environmental analysis is paramount. On the flip side, a purely historical documentation and factual analysis is not expedient if the personality profile of the affected party has not been adequately investigated. This is where research frontiers need to be crossed. In an analysis of reconciliation as an historical process, these are primarily the boundaries between psychology, social psychology and historical studies.

In the foregoing chapter, the continuity of Foreign Office staff from the Nazi period into the Federal Republic of Germany, was referred to by the example of the Wilhelmstraße trial. Harry Waibel lists *ca.* 2000 short biographies of former National Socialist functionaries in his examination of staff continuities among the decision-makers of the Nazi regime in the GDR, who took over official positions in civil service, administration, political parties and the military in the Soviet occupied zone or rather, the GDR, after the end of the war (Waibel, 2006). Both cases indicate that the reconstruction of Germany, in the GDR as well as in the FRG was supported by the incorporation of former perpetrators, who would support the state in both 'real socialistic ant-fascism' and in the western, capitalistic democratic model. In order to establish an appropriate empirical basis for analysis which is not solely focused on totalitarianism research, we must attempt to track down continuities in the mental attitudes of individual protagonists both in the GDR and the FRG and to prove that also they acted in the respective new orders according to such a restorative mind-set. This is a difficult undertaking. Such fundamental, interdisciplinary and comparative research would certainly bring important results in the fields of 'continuities and discontinuities' and 'transgenerational transfer' which are an essential part of reconciliation research.

The phenomena described above bear another very interesting component. Continuity of staff had a system-stabilizing effect in both cases, although the two systems involved were economically, politically and ideologically completely different.

Why?

Theodor Adorno's 1959 analysis of the totalitarian system of National Socialism and Stalinism, also referred to by Waibel, provides an only partially suitable explanation:

However, the same character types are susceptible to both forms of totalitarianism. Authoritar-

ian personalities are altogether misunderstood when they are construed from the vantage point of a particular political-economic ideology; the well-known oscillations of millions of voters before 1933 between the National Socialist and Communist parties is no accident from the social-psychological perspective either. (...) Authoritarian personalities identify themselves with real-existing power per se, prior to any particular contents. Basically, they possess weak egos and therefore require the compensation of identifying themselves with, and finding security in, great collectives. (Adorno, 1981, p. 17)

So, what 'character types' maintained continuity in the GDR? If the disposition of the individual character is not the only factor determining how bound he was by authority, then what other factors play a role and to what extent? And how do dispositions change in the course of time under changing conditions and a changing 'Zeitgeist'?

Finally, which continuities can still be recognized during the process of the reunification of the two German states after 1989-1990? In contrast to the first German reconciliation process, the second German reconciliation process, after the fall of the GDR, has not even begun to be adequately researched.

Cross-Time and Cross-Culture Comparison

This leads us to the limitations of comparison. We can take for granted that each reconciliation process is unique. A comparison is simply an attempt to use practical experience as well as theoretical reflection. The three dimensions of time, space and the specific constellations of event correlation, demonstrate the limits of comparison.

When we consider the dimension of time, the German example quickly shows up the limitations of comparison. The German example has a second distinctive feature: the processing of GDR injustices is a second reconciliation process that has been unfolding in German society since 1989. The reunification of the two German states represents the overlapping of two fundamentally different forms of authoritarian rule. The innumerable dead left by the Nazi regime lies in stark contrast to the comparatively few politically motivated deaths in the GDR. The exact number of people murdered in prison, while attempting to escape or by execution is unknown, but may be estimated as between 2,500 and 5,000 between 1949 and 1989. (Borbe, 2010) There is still no reliable record of the number of GDR prisoners held between 1949 and 1989. The estimates vary from 150,000 to 350,000. In processing the history of the GDR, there is neither a clear perpetrator-victim distinction nor a clear separation between victim and injustice.

In the light of this shocking lack of clarity in the processing of recent German history, public opinion of the history of the GDR appears almost cynical. A poll issued in 2014 by the federal foundation for the reappraisal of the Communist dictatorship in East Germany, revealed that every second person in Germany had "had enough of the GDR story". 54% of West Germans and 51% of East Germans do not want to know any more about the GDR past (HNA 2014b).

We can see in the German example as we consider the factor of time, that different forms of violence determine the nature and extent of public discourse and thereby also influence the nature of the reconciliation process. We can also see that resistance to the essential step of historical reappraisal in a reconciliation process can spread through an entire cross-section of society and affect not only the perpetrators and victims. The relevance of globally interconnected events can be recognized in an historical examination. The nature and practice of authoritarian politics in the GDR were closely linked to the framework of the Cold War. German society finds itself still wrapped up in a silent, hidden reconciliation process today. The concrete form of this process has been suppressed in public. Its extent and relevance are hard to measure and its consequences are impossible to predict.

When we consider the dimension of space by referring to international examples, while we can unequivocally apply the assessment parameters noted earlier, each different conflict constellation over the past 50 years shows unique characteristics.

The conflict in Israel and Palestine can be regarded as a long-lasting, ongoing, extreme concentration of direct, structural and cultural violence. This has a very specific impact on the phenomenon of trans-generational transfer. It results in a spiral of violence that continually reproduces itself with a kind of "inheritance mechanism" in which the principle of irreconcilability is passed from generation to generation.

A conflict that lasted just as long, with a similar concentration of direct, structural and cultural violence, was that of South Africa under the apartheid regime. Here though, a reconciliation process was begun when apartheid ended. Now, just under 25 years later, we can see that serious changes have been brought about in government, economics and society. It is also clear that the South Africans have set themselves the challenge of undergoing a long and difficult historical process. Since the third generation has not yet been reached, any evaluation of the process thus far must remain provisional.

Another African conflict that ended two and a half decades ago had completely different consequences again. When the Eritrean war of independence ended in 1991, the victorious liberation front that made up the new government, simply denied the need for either inter-statal or intra-societal reconciliation. Eritrea is now in a kind of permanent state of emergency with constant military mobilization. When we add to this the specific Eritrean characteristic of being a "Diaspora society" (approximately one third of the total population lives outside of the country), it is clear that if a reconciliation process should one day be initiated in Eritrea, that the government and its people will be faced with new and unique challenges in its implementation.

Governmental dominance in handling the problem of reconciliation is also seen in Rwanda. The reconciliation process of coming to terms with the genocide can be characterized as a state-imposed process, which raises substantial doubt over its sustainability.

The reconciliation process in Colombia is once again completely different. Here we find the unique situation that elements of reconciliation processes and transitional justice were initiated during ongoing conflict situations. Both of which have been exploited to a high degree by the contending parties. Here too, the interconnection of regional and international events make it clear that at the present moment it is nearly impossible to make a prognosis of how it will proceed, especially as the faces of the conflict are changing dynamically and it is in many cases hard to distinguish clearly between perpetrator and victim.

Colombia is the only example given here that does not coincide with a change in system. This makes it particularly interesting in view of reconciliation, since the guerilla war and the anti-guerillas actually represent a system conflict, which in its refusal to compromise bears the greatest responsibility for the fact that the conflict has now raged for over 60 years.

It is still very difficult to judge what effect the changes in recent violent conflicts will have on the initiation, realization and form of future reconciliation processes. This can best be illustrated by the current example of the conflicts in Syria and Iraq. It is hard to imagine a process of rapprochement in a post-conflict scenario when the face of these wars is constantly changing and it has become nearly impossible to keep tabs on all the protagonists and their particular goals.

We will definitely have to face these new challenges when it comes to reconciliation processes.

CONCLUSION

This chapter has shown reconciliation to be a lengthy and complex process. It has made clear that reconciliation cannot be equated with securing justice. And, it has demonstrated that even under ideal conditions, a reconciliation process can only be successfully concluded by the third generation at the earliest.

It has also been shown that reconciliation processes require a period of peace and stability in order to succeed and that success is integrally linked to the absence of violence. When we attempt an abstraction of these processes from a structural point of view, we see that reconciliation is closely connected to the following generations' experiences of violence. Communication about these experiences has a decisive influence on the chance of success of reconciliation processes.

Reconciliation does not mean the end of a conflict constellation. When we understand it as "rapprochement", it simply means the readiness to risk a new beginning within a certain conflict constellation and to approach possible solutions. A reconciliation process does not necessarily imply the parallel transformation of potential conflict sources. Nor does it automatically imply peace, although a reconciliation process is a major part of a peace process.

The example of Germany post-World War 2 has shown that a successful reconciliation process has to be tied to democratic institutions and a system governed by rule of law. Whether the system is poor or unjust is not relevant. It still secures fundamental rights. The system itself may violate those basic rights, but it still guarantees the individual his right to claim physical and mental integrity.

We applied the parameters given at the outset for measuring the success of a reconciliation process to the German example and have established that the reconciliation process after the second World War may be regarded as having been successfully concluded.

These parameters are universal and may be applied to other cases.

Herein lies an opportunity for comparison. The absence of violence, principles of rule of law and participation are prerequisites for all reconciliation processes and every reconciliation process has to face the problems of continuity, injustice and the losing side. The strength of comparison lies in being able to make use of the experiences gained in earlier examples. What sub-processes may be identified? Which institutionalizations and inspirations were successful and which failed? The art of comparison lies in applying such findings to the specific parameters of a process.

REFERENCES

Abelshauser, W. (2004). Deutsche Wirtschaftsgeschichte nach 1945, München: becksche Reihe.

Assmann, J. (1988). Kollektives Gedächtnis und kulturelle Identität. In J. Assmann, & T. Hölscher (Ed.), Kultur und Gedächtnis. Frankfurt: Suhrkamp.

Assmann, J. (2013). Das kulturelle Gedächtnis. Schrift, Erinnerung und politische Identität in frühen Hochkulturen (7th ed.). München: C.H. Beck.

Bloomfield, D., Barnes, T., & Huyse, L. (Eds.), (2003). *Reconciliation after Violent Conflict. A Handbook*. Stockholm: International Institute for Democracy and Electoral Assistance.

Borbet, A. (2010). *Die Zahl der Opfer des DDR-Regimes*. Erfurt: Landeszentrale für politische Bildung Thüringen.

Bracher, K. D. (1955). Die Auflösung der Weimarer Republik. Eine Studie zum Problem des Machtverfalls in der Demokratie. Villingen: Ring-Verlag.

Brähler, E., Decker, O., & Kiess, J. (2014). *Die stabilisierte Mitte. Rechtsextreme Einstellungen in Deutschland 2014*. Amadeo Antonio Stiftung.

Braukämper, A. (2012). *Das umstrittene Gedächtnis. Die Erinnerung an Nationalsozialismus, Faschismus und Krieg in Europa seit 1945 (The disputed memory. Remembering National Socialism, Fascism and War in Europe after 1945)*. Paderborn: Schoenings.

Conze, E., Frei, N., Hayes, P., & Zimmermann, M. (Eds.), (2010). *Das Amt und die Vergangenheit. Deutsche Diplomaten im Dritten Reich und in der Bundesrepublik*. München: Karl Blessing Verlag.

Netz-gegen-Nazis.de. (n. d.). Data from the Website. Retrieved from http://www.netz-gegen-nazis.de/artikel/rechtsextremismus-zahlen-755

Doerry, M. (2006). "Nirgendwo und überall zu Haus": Gespräche mit Überlebenden des Holocaust. München. In Ders. Erziehung zur Mündigkeit (7th ed.). Frankfurt/Main. Retrieved from http://signale.cornell.edu/text/meaning-working-through-past

Fischer, T., & Lorenz, M. N. (Eds.). (2009). *Lexikon der Vergangenheitsbewältigung in Deutschland. Debatten- und Diskursgeschichte des Nationalsozialismus nach 1945* (2nd ed.). Bielefeld: Transkript.

Frankfurter Allgemeine Zeitung (FAZ). (2014a). In Sippenhaft. *FAZ*, 137.

Frankfurter Allgemeine Zeitung (FAZ). (2014b). Lasst euch euren freien Willen nicht nehmen. *FAZ*, 149.

Frankfurter Allgemeine Zeitung (FAZ). (2014c). Klarheit im Urteil. *FAZ*, 149.

Frankfurter Allgemeine Zeitung (FAZ). (2014d). Extremistisches Material? *FAZ*, 150.

Frankfurter Allgemeine Zeitung (FAZ). (2014e). Wie meine Familie von den Nazis enteignet wurde. *FAZ*, 150.

Frankfurter Allgemeine Zeitung (FAZ). (2014f). Der berühmteste Deserteur der Wehrmacht. FAZ, 151.

Frankfurter Allgemeine Zeitung (FAZ). (2014g). Geknechtet und überfordert. *FAZ*, 155.

Frankfurter Allgemeine Zeitung (FAZ). (2014h). Steinmeiers Widerstandskämpferin. FAZ, 157.

Frankfurter Allgemeine Zeitung am Sonntag (FAZamSO). (2014a). Was wurde aus Hans Kammler? *FAZamSo*, 24.

Frankfurter Allgemeine Zeitung am Sonntag (FAZamSo). (2014b). Bunker als Wohnhaus. FAZamSo, 27.

Giordano, R. (1987). *Die zweite Schuld oder Von der Last Deutscher zu sein*. Hamburg: Rasch und Röhring Verlag.

Hamburger Institut für Sozialforschung (Ed.). (2001). *Verbrechen der Wehrmacht. Dimensionen des Vernichtungskrieges 1941 – 1944. Begleitbroschüre zur Ausstellung*. Hamburg: Hamburger Edition.

Hessisch-Niedersächsische Allgemeine (HNA). (2014). Ruinen des Grauens.

Hessisch-Niedersächsische Allgemeine (HNA). (2014b). Jeder zweite hat genug von DDR-Geschichte.

Heym, S. (1984). Schwarzenberg, München: btb Verlag.

Kammler, J. (1985). Ich habe die Metzelei satt und laufe über … Kasseler Soldaten zwischen Verweigerung und Widerstand (1939 – 1945); Kasseler Quellen und Studien, Schriftenreihe des Magistrats der Stadt Kassel 6, Fuldabrück: Hesse GmbH.

Sitzungsbericht über die 26. Stadtverordneten-versammlungs in: Kammler, J., Krause-Villmar, D. (1984). Volksgemeinschaft und Volksfeinde. Kassel 1933 -1945. Eine Dokumentation. Kassel in der Zeit des Nationalsozialismus I, Fuldabrück: Hesse GmbH.

Karger, A. (2012). Verzeihen – Reconciliation – Versöhnung. Versuch einer Differenzierung verschiedener Konzepte. In A. Karger (Ed.), *Vergessen, vergelten, vergeben, versöhnen? Weiterleben mit dem Trauma, Psychoanalytische Blätter 30*. Göttingen: Vandenhoeck & Ruprecht Verlag.

Köttig, M. (2009). Die Bedeutung der intergenerationalen Weitergabe in Familien- und Lebensgeschichten rechtsextrem orientierter junger Frauen. In H. Radebold, W. Bohlleber, & J. Zinnecker (Eds.), *Transgenerationale Weitergabe kriegsbelasteter Kindheiten. Interdisziplinäre Studien zur Nachhaltigkeit historischer Erfahrungen über vier Generationen 2* (pp. 201–214). Weinheim, München: Beltz Juventa.

Neebe, R. (1981). Großindustrie, Staat und NSDAP 1930-1933. Göttingen: Vandenhoeck + Ruprecht GmbH.

Online, R. P. (2010). BdV hat nur noch rund 550.000 Mitglieder. Retrieved from http://www.rp-online.de/politik/deutschland/bdv-hat-nur-noch-rund-550000-mitglieder-aid-1.478970

Picture 1 - http://www.move-magazin.eu/wp-content/uploads/2011/07/Kniefall-von-Warschau-Copyright-Deutscher-Bundestag.jpg, 20.09.2014

Quehl, H. (2014). Interviews - All interviews were conducted by the author in May 2014.

Rückerl, A. (1979). *Die Strafverfolgung von NS-Verbrechen 1945 – 1978. Eine Dokumentation*. Karlsruhe: C.F. Müller Juristischer Verlag.

Schneider, C. (2006). *Der Warschauer Kniefall. Ritual, Ereignis und Erzählung (Historische Kulturwissenschaften 9)*. Konstanz: UVK.

Der Spiegel. (1970) Kniefall angemessen oder übertrieben? *Der Spiegel*, 1970(51).

Thiele, H.-G. (Ed.). (1997). Die Wehrmachtsausstellung. Dokumentation einer Kontroverse. Dokumentation der Fachtagung in Bremen am 26. Februar 1997 und der Bundestagsdebatten am 13. März und 24. April 1997, Bremen: Bundeszentrale für politische Bildung.

Trobisch-Lütge, S. (2010). *Das späte Gift. Folgen politischer Traumatisierung in der DDR und ihre Behandlung, 2*. Gießen: Psychosozial-Verlag.

Ueberschär, G. R. (Ed.), (2008). Der Nationalsozialismus vor Gericht. Die alliierten Prozesse gegen Kriegsverbrecher und Soldaten 1943-1952 (3rd ed.). Frankfurt/Main: Fischer Taschenbuch Verlag. Retrieved from http://www.wortbedeutung.info/Versöhnung/

Völter, B. (2009). Generationenforschung und transgenerationale Weitergabe aus biografietheoretischer Perspektive. In H. Radebold, W. Bohlleber, & J. Zinnecker (Eds.), *Transgenerationale Weitergabe kriegsbelasteter Kindheiten. Interdisziplinäre Studien zur Nachhaltigkeit historischer Erfahrungen über vier Generationen Weinheim* (pp. 95–106). München: Beltz Juventa.

Waibel, H. (2011). *Diener vieler Herren. Ehemalige NS-Funktionäre in der SBZ/DDR*. Frankfurt: Peter Lang Verlag.

Wolffsohn, M., & Brechenmacher, T. (2005). *Denkmalsturz? Brandts Kniefall*. München: Olzog.

Wolgast, E. (1997). Vergangenheitsbewältigung in der unmittelbaren Nachkriegszeit. In R. Carola (Ed.), Forschungsmagazin der Universität Heidelberg. Retrieved from http://www.uni-heidelberg.de/uni/presse/RuCa3_97/wolgast.htm

ENDNOTES

1 http://www.move-magazin.eu/wp-content/uploads/2011/07/Kniefall-von-Warschau-Copyright-Deutscher-Bundestag.jpgtag.jpg

2 The "Brückengeneration" or "bridge generation" refers to the group of people whose earliest childhood experiences were during wartime, but were still too young at the end of the war to have been involved in any way in wartime activities and too young to have developed any ideological consciousness such as their fathers' and grandfathers' generations had.

3 http://www.gedenkstaette-breitenau.de/

4 In this context I would like to highlight another very important side aspect of the German reconciliation process, which cannot be further elaborated in this chapter. From the 1960s onwards, the German internal controversy about the various displaced associations in the FRG led to a heated debate, charged with emotions to such an extent that an irreconcilable confrontation between the two adversary camps evolved: on the one side were the displaced associations under the umbrella of the Union of the Displaced (BdV) who insisted on their right to return to their respective homes in the segregated Eastern territories even after the ratification of the Eastern Treaties. On the other side were various leftist groups and factions who declared this position as "revisionist", thus insinuating that the displaced association were not only proposing to restore the territorial boundaries of Germany from 1937, but also aiming to restore the former regime. The debate became such a polemic that from a certain point onwards every public discussion about the victimization of the German refugees after 1945 – which had without any doubt taken place – became discredited as "fueling revisionism". It was only during the first decade of the 21st century that an atmosphere evolved in Germany that allowed for a new assessment of the events and an acknowledgement of the sufferings of the displaced. In the year 2008, a Federal Foundation for Flight, Displacement and Reconciliation ("Bundessstiftung Flucht, Vertreibung, Versöhnung") was created with the objective of documenting the sufferings of the German displaced, though just as one main issue within the broader context of refuge seeking and displacement in the 20th century. The opening of a permanent exhibition in the newly built documentation center is envisaged only for 2016 (see http://www.sfvv.de).

5 In the year 1925, statistics gave the number of Jews in Germany to be 563.733 (cf. http://www.bundesarchiv.de/gedenkbuch/einfuehrung.html.de?page=2). The first post-war Jewish communities were established as early as 1945 in Berlin, Frankfurt and Munich. From all the of Jewish communities which became members of the Central Jewish Council established in Germany in 1950, an estimate of 17,000 people can be made. (cf. http://www.zeit.de/2000/02/200002.beitext.lau_.xml).

Chapter 3
The Complexity of Non-Violence Action

Carlos Eduardo Maldonado
Universidad del Rosario, Colombia

ABSTRACT

This chapter claims that non-violent action corresponds to a political dimension in which society has become a magnificent complex organism. Moreover, non-violent action corresponds to the phase of highest complexity in a social organization. Examples are provided ranging from ecology to population biology, from ethology to swarm intelligence. At the end, several conclusions are drawn that shed new lights on the social, cultural, and political understanding of our world and to the foreseeable future. The study of non-violent action provides sufficient arguments that allow the distinction between "politics" and "policy", i.e. "policies", so much so that politics is highlighted as a highest and most significant dimension of the human experience, and policies are then considered as secondary or lower. The human rights provide the ground for the understanding and comprehension of non-violent actions. In the core of the text a topology of non-violent actions is provided along with its explanation.

To the memory of my friend Kamel Shiyaa Abdullah.

INTRODUCTION

Non-violent action is – and has been throughout history, a non-evident social and political move of societies. For, the rule has been violence in its manifold forms, layers and expressions. Violence has been served in history as sort of gratis principle. Henceforth, it has had a scandalous value. This paper argues that non-violent action is worthy in a variety of modes precisely because of its complexity. Arguments about such a complexity are provided that, at the same time, shed light on the linearity of violence. This paper claims that non-violent action corresponds to a political dimension in which society has become a magnificent complex organism. Moreover, non-violent action corresponds to the phase of highest complexity in a social organization. Examples are provided ranging from ecology to population biology, from ethology to swarm intelligence. At the end, several conclusions are drawn that shed new lights on the social, cultural, and political understanding of our world and to the foreseeable future.

DOI: 10.4018/978-1-4666-9675-4.ch003

A PRIMARY DISTINCTION: VIOLENCE AND AGGRESSION

It will never be too much working, once and again, on a basic distinction, namely between violence and aggression. Behind such a differentiation lies in fact the difference between nature and society or also between nature and culture – an epistemological issue that entails, however, far serious consequences.

The Marxist tradition believes that violence is the midwife of history, an idea that really sends us back to the archaic Greece. It was, indeed, Heraclitus who used to say that it is pollemos what begets nearly almost everything:

One should be aware that pollemos pervades, with discord, and that things are naturally born by discord (frag. 80), and

Pollemos our genesis, governing us all to bring forth some gods, some mortal beings with some unfettered yet others kept bound (frag. 53).

However, as we know, violence does not exist in nature, at all. Nature is not violent and does not know about violence. When people speak of the violence of an earthquake or a tornado, a typhoon or a hurricane, for example, they just mean how struck they are, period. They speak their own suffering and passiveness, rather than about mother nature as being violent. Not vis-à-vis physical forces, but neither in the relationship between pray and predator, for instance, does violence take place.

Instead, violence is particularly a human feature - hence, precisely its scandalous character. Whether we speak of physical or emotional, open or psychological, military or subtle forms of violence – whichever its character or nature, violence is to be blame because it bears, so to speak, its own justification. I shall come back later on this point.

I would like to stress that violence is opprobrious because it is free and it adds no evolutionary advantage on the wellbeing of humans. Violence, as it happens, has been used in many ways and justified in a variety of ways that range from religion to politics, from philosophy to metaphysics, for instance (Walzer, 2006). Yet, nearly all those justifications rely on cultural arguments – in the largest and deepest sense of the word, even if some times (as it was the case with nazism[1]) some of the arguments are drawn from science or philosophy, as it happens.

Indeed, properly speaking in the sphere of human culture, we can rather speak of aggression as having a valuable worth for survival, learning and adaptation. A single example can illustrate this:

Suppose there is gentleman crossing the street with his pregnant wife, a couple of little kids that hold their parents hands, and with his own mother who is already aged enough. As he crosses the street, say, through the zebra-pad, suddenly a car driven at a high speed comes by and almost hit the family. Luckily the driver could deviate the car and stop some meters ahead.

Well, the man with the family loses control and goes screaming, yelling and showing his hands closed as fist to the driver, while he complains about the mad way of driving the car.

Well, the father and husband's reaction cannot be judged as violent. Instead it is an *aggressive* reaction against the driver by which ultimately what comes at stake is the biological survival of the family group. The reaction of the man is fully justified from the point of view of both culture and evolution. That act of aggression is biologically justified, for it aims at enhancing life and survival. As for the reaction of the driver, it is something that can be left here aside out of focus.

Nature is not driven, in any sense by violence – a notoriously cultural concept. Even in the pray-predator relationship it has been shown that, on the one hand, the predator does never mean to eliminate a population, or a group of possible prays. She just wants to satisfy her immediate needs in due time. Correspondingly, the pray is not afraid of disappearing as group or species, for she knows that the predator will only catch one single pray and that will be enough. That, of course, does not mean the absence of fear and a sort of panic. It is the natural duty of a pray to run as fast as possible and try to escape from the predator. However, it is the nature of a predator not to eliminate a whole group in a niche, but only one of its members in order to satisfy its biological needs.

This brings us farther to an additional point, namely the fact that violence has always been free against an individual, but also a systemic or systematic "policy" against large groups – of enemies. Thus, the concept of violence goes hand in hand with the undervaluing of others as distinct, inferior or foreigners throughout the western history.

Probably the most dramatic moments in the history of mankind have been generated or accompanied by violent regimes, governments, policies or whimsically decisions. However, one is to be cautious enough not to claim that the most important moments in the history of mankind have been triggered by violence, for that would not be true.

As for aggression, it can be said to enhance the adaptability to new and even perilous situations by human beings. If so, then aggressive situations entail a process of learning and adaptation that is characterized by sudden and unexpected circumstances.

THE NATURE OF VIOLENCE

The concept and practice of violence is closely intertwined with the idea of hierarchical systems, control, and manipulation. Indeed, there are to conditions for violence to exist, namely a hierarchy, so that a stance orders and the other executes, and a strong control system. It is usually the commander the one who justifies any violent action, although it has also been the case that that they command just following orders from higher hierarchies, and the justifications lies somewhere else – even probably in a non-entirely public sphere.

I do not want to enter here into a typology of the various kinds of violence that exist in the world, such as psychological, physical, military, symbolic, and others. I prefer instead to dig into what can be labeled as the nature of violence. In other words, this is about trying to find a rationale for a behavior that, as I shall mention, does not have any rationality whatsoever.

Can anything be truly justified? What is the proper nature of a *good* justification? When discussing what science is, Socrates concludes in the *Theatetus* that science is a justified belief. This means that any one is entitled to have his or her beliefs – no matter the content or the intention of the belief. There is no problem in here. On the contrary, the entire trouble – the one that most notably differentiates the philosopher (Socrates) from the sophist (such as Thrasymachus, Protagoras, and others) – lies in the justification provided to any given belief.

Thus, overlapping the issue about science on to the more general of human action, we can then safely say that any people is entirely entitled to act or do whatever he or she considers as necessary or convenient, for instance. The real trouble, the highest sensitive issue pertains the justification – ex ante or ex post of the action considered.

These are, indeed the two basic modes of justification, ex ante and ex post. Important as they are, they do not suffice though to clarify the concern about the feasibility of justifying any kind of human action. The justification can either be moral or intellectual, logical or religious, to name but a few types of possible justifications.

In real world life, most justifications usually come ex post. Trying to identify whether there was a kind of ex ante justification is a central concern of legal considerations, moral, or religious concerns, and that is called as the *intention* of the action, i.e. the intention that both drives and originates any action. As it is well known from the spheres just mentioned, when the intention can be safely identified, the judgment upon the action or person is more severe and heavier than if the situation happens otherwise.

Violence is a justified action that is accompanied or triggered by evil intentions, concerns or feelings. In other words, violence is a harmful action that can be justified with or as malicious sentiments or beliefs. The nature and origins of such sentiments and beliefs is varied, rich and deep, and is not the central topic here. The perversity of violence roots in the maleficent beliefs and sentiments that either trigger or accompany the action under consideration.

VIOLENCE AND WAR

To be sure, war is of al the neatest and best achieved product wherein violence exists and can be appreciated and valued. War is a specific human behavior. War, in its various ways and expressions, scales and times, is the best product of violence. There are and there have been religiously as well as economic, political or defensive wars, as it happens.

The time of wars is the time when past, present and future become compacted by the gravity of the present. The past remains as a long nostalgia, and the future is shaped as a horizon to be – who knows truly when. Wilderness and savage, brutality and crime live together in an atmosphere made up with solidarity and fellowship, love, tenderness and caring – fortuitous though strong and robust.

In any case, the atrocities of wars allow for the following distinction:

A. On the one hand, wars convert people – in fact, normal regular people -, into evil human beings, senseless and efficient and efficacious machines;
B. On the other hand, wars need of inhumane, insensitive and mad people in order to either obey unconditionally any order from upper or outer control stances.

H. Arendt (2006) has studied as anyone else the case of such a regular human being as R. Eichmann, and has pointed out to the banality of evil. Indeed, violence can be easily identified to evil – a category that surpasses any singular field or domain. Evil people do not appear as demoniac or monstrous, as possessed or anything of the sort people, but as regular nearly anonymous ones.

The banality of evil consists in following the rules, the standards, the norms and accepted prescriptions of the majority, or of the ruling power in each case. Thus, they do not act against the normal impositions upon everyone else. On the contrary, they are obedient, efficient, efficacious, and keen. Their costumes and language, their proxemics and relations are according to the correct standards from any point of view. The perversity of evil consists either in using such people or also in being embodied in such personnel.

Violence has become a most serious hurdle in history due to two basic developments: it has become a systemic phenomenon and also a systematic problem. To be sure, we have come to live in a non-zero sum world in which, as a consequence, all possible forms of violence have come to be integrated, reinforced, and closely linked among each other form of violence. The phenomenology of violence is an obscure chapter in the history of mankind where psychologists and psychiatrists, lawyers and philosophers, historians and sociologists, anthropologists and economists have come to work together and make joint discoveries about the forms, expressions, and justifications of violence.

Thus, the many-faces of violence or violent behavior throughout which basically self-interests, self-image, self-prestige and the like are the triggering factors for violent violence, whether systematic or not have come to the fore and become a public concern. If there might have been a time in the past when violence was originated in the darkness and under the shadows, it has increasingly become clear that violence has operated also under the brightest light and in the open air. In other words, violence is not to be associated with unclearness or shadows, as complot or sabotages, for instance.

The truth is that in most of cases in the past people have mainly appreciated the consequences or effects of violence and not always, and not necessarily, their causes or reasons. It is the advancement of knowledge and research that has permitted a different understanding of the phenomenon. Such an understanding has precisely brought to the fore the many-faces of violence, the sinuous justifications by all prevailing powers in the past and present, and the culturally exclusive nature of such a behavior.

Let us say it frankly: violence is an *exclusively* human behavior that is not be seen anywhere in the entire realm of nature. If so, then the issue becomes the un-natural character of violence, whence its scandalous fact – regardless of the philosophical, religious or scientific conception of nature. That unnatural nature of violence is to be simply called as evil. Evil, then, is a non-natural behavior among human beings, a telluric force and appearance of violence.

This is not to claim – à la Rousseau – that human beings are naturally born as good but society perverts and distorts them[2].

One salient feature should be mentioned here, though. It is the fact that the entire history of technology has since ever been the history of technology with military purposes. Only very recently –specifically in the last five to eight years can the history of technology be devoiced to some extent from military interests and goals. Some examples about this is the development of the convergent technologies, namely the NBIC+S: nanotechnology, biotechnology, the technologies of information, the technologies of cognition, and the social dimension of technology (such as the social networks).

ALTERNATIVE POLITICAL AND MILITARY ACTIONS

Politically speaking, collective action, as well as political actions, are indeed possible using some military implements and yet being non-violent. To be sure, alternative politics has historically been a right – very much as a moral or fundamental human right. Already present in Hobbes and Locke as the *natural right to subversion*, it was aimed as the right to revolt against tyranny and despotism. The times were ripe when the bourgeoisie had not yet reached power, particularly before 1789. In the course of the years, after 1789 such a natural and moral right was to be left in the oblivion, in the backstage of political philosophy – not to mention social philosophy and social movements.

There is key remark, though. Such an acknowledgement about the moral and natural right to subversion is previous to the differentiation between *politics* and *policy* (*policies*). Such a distinction was introduced some time during the 1950s by an anonymous clerk from the U.S. State Department, when, in the middle of the cold war, he/she sent a memo to the Federal offices and bureaus asking them questions such as: what do you do, what do you need, what are your assets, what are your goals, how do you intend to reach those goals, and the like. Thus, the policy, i.e. policies were born, which were to be later on systematized in the form they have come to be known; that is, as formulation, control, regulation, evaluation, and the like of goals and actions.

With such a turn, politics, in its most pregnant sense suffered a distinction. On the one hand, there was the policy, i.e. state and governmental policies with all their technologies, strata, layers, and procedures. On the other hand, there is politics, which was to remain to-date as a non-institutional, corporative or establishment-like goal and action. With due time, policy, i.e. policies was to be

Table 1. Kinds of non-violent actions

• Civil disobedience – articulated as: strikes, boycotts, general strike • Resistance • Subversion – consists of: civil and military subversion, leaking, sabotage, hacking, occupation, neutralization of a real or potential enemy • Insubordination • Rebellion • Resistance and collective actions • Absence of collaboration • Non-violent intervention • Non-violent armed revolt • Insurrection

Source: Taken from (Maldonado, 2002)

understand, as it is indeed the case nowadays, as strictly intertwined with institutionalism, legality, national symbols, and the like. Policy, i.e. policies has come to be, doubtless, a concept that both belongs to, and characterizes, mainstream science.

Here, I would like to lead our regard towards the other concept: politics. In my view it is a wider and deeper one, even though it might also accept some fuzziness and permeability. However, the current concept of politics resumes the ancient distinction among the Greeks between *politeia* and *politiké*, which was to be taken in history as the legacy of politics, period. Thus, the reflections by authors like Montaigne, Machiavelli, Hobbes, Locke or Marx, for example, among many others, refers to the concept I want to highlight here.

Politics, I claim, not only supports but also is made out possible thanks/via non-violent actions. Table 1 presents the kinds of non-violent actions.

The philosophical and political rationale of non-violent actions are the human rights. Thus, a human rights-based politics can be conceived as non-violent politics, so much so that the very ground of human rights consists in making life possible and every time as possible as it can be imagined.

Now, the politics of non-violence allows for the differentiation between policy, i.e. policies and politics. Politics has been displaced by policy, whereby it has been reduced or assimilated to institutionalism, legality, legitimacy, and law-like behaviors and stances. In other words politics has been deviated, i.e. routed as voting, electing the people's representatives and caring for the accountability of governance. More radically, the ancient role of opposition has been contrived to the law of vote-and-elect, period. Democracy has thus become republican, something that is quite clear from Habermas' social, philosophical and political works (cfr. particularly his *Facts and Norms*).

According to Table 1, civil disobedience is essentially an individual action, whereas subversion and resistance are collective actions. However, a god understanding of the concepts, social, cultural and historical frames, individual action cannot be displaced nor reduced to collective action, or vice versa. Both entail a dynamic unity that encompasses the engagement of the individual with his/her own time and circumstances. And the other way round, the importance of collective action cannot be explained any longer in terms of the addition of individual actions. Such, indeed is the case of the traditional comprehension of game theory very much as the theory of rational choice and the theory of collective action – three closely intertwined levels of one and the same assumption, namely the individual is rational and therefrom on grounds the rationality of society as a whole, too.

Let us say it with other words: the complexity of non-violent action lies in opening up the gates of policy on to a broader, larger and deeper space. Such is the politics of civil society. A politics of civil society is not to be taken as indifferent to the policies of the state, and yet it can and must be regarded as independent of those policies. Some examples of politics of the civil society are: the right to one's own body, the right to a sound environment, all the common goods – that go far beyond the classical distinction between private and public goods -, and a politics of knowledge, namely knowledge and information. Herein one can include the right to free wifi – which leads further on to the importance of wimax -, and the care for future in all its manners, ways, modes and comprehensions.

Indeed, according to Wallerstein, policies are essentially about the present. Thus, the time density of policies is short sighted. This is exactly what all the various national programs of development or also the governmental policies are all about. Policies must be nurtured with a deeper or denser time scale. It is my contention that a twofold argument can be provided.

On the one hand, opening policies to nature and the environment gives them a greater time density thanks to which they are to be named then as politics, precisely. On the other hand, at the same time, understanding that the very core of any policy are people, in other words, the civil population, civil society, and the individuals as such. The link must be established then between nature and the environment, on the one hand, and civil society as a whole, on the other. After all, for the individuals the very first experience of nature are their own bodies, in each case. If so, then a politics of non-violent action roots in the corporeity of society and the individuals – and this sends us back to the unity between the environment and the living body: an organic unity, indeed.

To be sure, a politics of civil society is not reduced to policies, but broadens up the window of self-organization, spontaneity and trust among people. Some of the actions of non-violent politics include the outraged and incensed – a morally totally justified movement in times of financial and political crises. Non-violent actions are justified on the level of the dignity of life together with the striving for a life with quality. This means, a moral issue and an economical one. The large scope of non-violent action, i.e. politics is anything but a reductionist understanding of history, culture and society. On the contrary, it aims at providing enough open forms of action and organization. The preference of the opportunity of one of those actions over others is a matter of convenience and chance, of intelligence and cleverness. The wisdom of people knows what and when to choose one, when the moment comes – under the proviso that the policies do permit and sponsor non-violent politics – which, to say the truth, rarely happens in history.

In the name of nature and life revolt and subversion are justified if necessary. In the name of dignity and outrage, very much as in the name of quality of life is insubordination and resistance right actions to defend one's honesty, truthfulness and right to live, period.

Civil disobedience, resistance and subversion, strike, boycotts, general strike, insubordination, rebellion, absence of collaboration, non-violent intervention, very much as civil and military subversion, are carried out via leaking, sabotage, spying, hacking, occupation, neutralization of a real or potential enemy, and non-violent armed revolt or insurrection. As it can be easily seen, such forms of non-violent action, i.e. politics are not just a matter of military versus civilians, but a jointure of chance and planning, where various forms of organization, expertise and skills joint together to enhance the chances and possibilities of life.

In any case, however, it should be stressed that non-violent actions do not exclude normal political participation.

ON ECOLOGY AND BIOLOGY

The question I would like to raise here is, how does nature avoid violence? The equations Lotka-Volterra set up early in 1925-26 open up the gate to a sound answer. The framework is, as it is known, the prey-predator relationship. For a long while such equations were just taken between a single predator and a single pray. However, more recent studies on the equations allow for a broader view in which sets of predators are considered along with sets of prays. A dynamic understanding of the balance in nature has been so reached. Table 2 provides an example of the most basic ecological, i.e. political relations following the Lotka-Volterra equations.

Table 2. Basic ecological relations after the Lotka-Volterra equations

Mutualism	Depredation
Parasitism	Commensalism

Source: own

To be sure, the interplay of the various scenarios shown in table 2 allows conclude that the rule in nature is not so much competition and struggle, but cooperation and commensalism. Population biology along with landscape biology and together with mathematics and ecology serve here as conspicuous milestones for getting a cooperative view of nature. Now, originally the Lotka-Volterra equations dealt with linear equations. More recent studies include non-linear equations in the Lotka-Volterra equations (Temkin, 2012).

Put in one word, nature does not know of violence as the concept has been grasped traditionally from mainstream science. At its best – or worst – nature just knows about aggression.

Mutualism refers to mutual benefits for different parts, sets or elements that allow them a better well-being. The most important discovery made up on the basis of mutualism is *symbiosis*. Symbiosis is the real rule that explains the weave of live (Margulis & Saga, 2003) – from biology to economics. Moreover, widening the Darwinian conception about the origins of life, symbiosis explains life as an everlasting process of mutual dependence, mutual help and mutual benefit. Depredation, on the contrary is the concept that stands for egotism, selfishness and individualization, in all concerns and levels of nature and society. Depredation entails fighting and suspicion, distancing and caution over against the environment, no matter what. As for parasitism, it is the complement of depredation in that no mutual benefit exists at all, and one species exists at the expense of other. In game theory this is explained as the free-rider. Finally, commensalism is that relationship in nature or society in which one species benefits from the other, but the other one does not derive benefit or harm.

Of course, in nature all four expressions (co-) exist – very much as in society. However, by and large it is mutualism that prevails and pervades the interplay of all sorts of species on Earth. In contrast, when looking at history, it is parasitism and depredation what rules in nearly all stances of the human organizations – from military to economic, from political to cultural space.

As it can be easily seen, a rigorous study of violence – which usually comprises just social sciences at large - is not possible without taking into account, at the same time, the comparison or contrast with what happens in nature. If so, then, the study of social sciences entails also the inclusion of sciences such as synthetic biology, landscape biology, evolutionary biology, population biology, ecology and the life sciences. Well, the result of such a dialogue is the acknowledgement of policies and the need to broaden up the very concept of politics. It is my contention that such a broadening brings us face to face with the complexity of non-violent actions. After all, politics is the realm of action – in society, for the others. Policy, by contrast, identifies "politics" with governance and government.

From an evolutionary standpoint, violence is a concept that pretends to make some people just *culturally* better; thus, for instance, economically better, or geographically, if not politically, for instance. However, violence does not make anyone *biologically*, i.e. *evolutionary* better. In other words, it does not fulfill any positive role in enhancing our chances for survival and adaptation. In the contrary, violence is one of the names for death.

Indeed, violence is a culturally nurtured concept that lacks any support in the living world, only in human history and culture; for example in the realm of beliefs, in the sphere of ego's; in the level of self-images, and interests, whether conscious or subconscious. We become less representatives of the living weave, and: yes, more humans: alas!

Now, one reason why violence does not exist in nature is because nature is grounded on abundant information, i.e. continuous processes of exchange, interplay, collaboration and mutualism. One species profits from others but at the same time benefits from other species in a long and unending chain of mutual benefit and co-evolution - from bacteria on to plants to animals of all kinds along the geography and regardless of geographical particularities – such as whether, humidity, dryness, etc.

One of the conditions – condition sine qua non – for violence to be is a limitation or scarcity of information. This is why strategy and tactics, surprise and massive force, and the like have traditionally accompanied violence. The story of the four generations of warfare – till to-date is clear enough about this[3]. In a world where most information is shared and common to all, violence is unviable, for the damage to one species would certainly harm the species that exerts violence first.

Well, information abounds in nature, and according to a number of authors form various disciplines, life as such is information and knowledge (Maturana and Varela, S. Kauffman, B. Jacob, and many others – ranging from disciplines as diverse as complexity theory, biology, microbial biology). All in all, the weave of life is sustained via a continuous information processing that occurs in a manifold of manners, thus: distributive, parallel, fuzzy, massively parallel, quantum – in sum: non-algorithmically. Consistent research in this sense is being carried out currently – comprising emergent and distributed systems, unconventional computing, non-classical computation, and hypercomputation[4].

THE TURN TO SWARM INTELLIGENCE AND COOPERATION

To be sure, cooperation is the rule in nature, whereas competition – technically called as "natural selection", is just an exception. After all, as it has been said above, nature abounds in information.

In other words, nature can be grasped, as it has indeed been the case, in terms of collective intelligence, technically called as swarm intelligence. A recent discovery, swarm intelligence shows that school of fish, herds, bird flocks, and collective insects – as the best and most common cases studied to-date, are collective behaviors based on simple rules that allow identifying those swarm as an individual. However, some examples regarding human systems have also been collected in the literature and studied, such as traffic jam, crowd during escape behavior, crowd walking in a big city, etc.

The rules that explain swarm intelligence have been thoroughly studied, but the reason why such a behavior emerges in nature is not clear as yet. Probably it is a defensive behavior, but also a game, or a way to mean something, probably. In any case, it is a behavior that looks harmonious if not aesthetical and by all means non- violent.

Besides, from a thermodynamic point of view, cooperating implies much less effort and a lower cost, that defeating and fighting. Fighting is a highly entropic behavior for any species, at any scale of nature or society. In contrast, cooperation is make up possible at a much smoother cost and almost effortlessly, regardless of whether we consider normal circumstances or critical ones, such as wars, famines, epidemics, and others. Violence is a highly entropic behavior: history offers uncountable examples and political science is full of case studies – when looked carefully.

Every single human being is a collection of cells and, moreover, a set of bacteria. Our individuality is the outcome of highly cooperative cells that make up possible tissues, organs, and systems. One single cell that does not want to cooperate – most conspicuously, it appears, a cell with "junk DNA", is enough for a cancer to arise. Cancer, thus, is a wonderful example of the outcome of one single cell that is selfish and un-cooperative. All in all, health is but the result of cooperation, for example between the immune system and the rest of our body, between the brain and our environment, and so forth. If so, then normality – in the broadest philosophical sense – can be taken as the result of cooperation and collaboration. A disease, in contrast, looks aggressive and violent just because it is the outcome of a lack of harmonious collaboration between cells, or tissues, organs or systems.

That said, nature does not know about hierarchies of any kind, neither in plants nor in animals. The habit to see and read nature in terms of hierarchies – queens, soldiers, laborers, and the like (as in the case of bees, for instance), is just a cultural deformation of a strongly anthropomorphized and anthropological tradition. At its best we can speak of levels of organization but definitely not as pyramidal-like structures or dynamics.

Nature, that in the deepest sense of ancient wisdom also means wisdom, can be properly seen as a wide weave of cooperation and collaboration. Competition does exist, but as the Lotka-Volterra equations show, predatory behaviors are sustainable only in short time and at an individual scale. No predator will ever devour every single prey, for a dynamic balance would be broken. The chain of life, so to speak would thus become impossible.

Violence is a sick behavior in society, very much as in nature. To be sure, violent behavior makes up human beings a plague – a rough but sincere conclusion when the entire landscape is seen from above, so to speak. In one word, violence makes human life impossible and brings the chain of life at stake.

WHERE LIES THE COMPLEXITY OF NON-VIOLENT ACTION, REVISITED

Very much as, mathematically speaking, complexity science should not be confused with a huge amount of equations, analogously, a great number of variables does not mean that we are facing a complex system or behavior. Moreover, even though closely intertwined complexity and nonlinearity should not be automatically identified and, at the end of the day, one must distinguish them. To be sure, complexity does entail non-determinism and a rejection to any kind of reductionism. As it happens, a complex system has never been defined so far, but it is understood and explained by the features, properties or characteristics a complex system exhibits or has.

Complexity theory, I would to highlight, is not just a framework, for example a theoretical or conceptual framework. Instead, when a system exhibits characteristics or else when a behavior becomes so that it can be safely called as "complex" (for instance, because there is a power law distribution, or it is highly unpredictable, and so on), then complexity theory becomes valuable. My argument here is that one should focus on whether a system is complex or not, or if a behavior is complex; if so, then complexity theory can be helpful to explain it and understand it.

More precisely, let us rephrase the problem here. What does the complexity of non-violent consist of? Various features help providing together a solid argument.

First and most important, the aim of pointing at the complexity of non-violent action consists in showing a *plurality* of actions possible or necessary, according to time and space. Whereas the management of policies is rather reductionist vis-à-vis politics, it is important to bring into evidence that politics is and should be a realm of open adaptive collective and individual actions. The standard conception of policies as it is identifies with governance and institutionalism does not allow, an on the contrary, it rather impedes seeing, accepting, and possibly fostering other ways for acting.

Accordingly, the rationale for non-violent action are the human rights, wherein the absolute right to life should by all means be brought to the focus, right upon the table under the day-light. Thus, whereas policies are mostly and most generally concerned with government and the state, the human rights clearly point out to the fact that the care for life – namely the dignity of life and a life with quality, is the only rational, moral and natural ground that universally affirms the importance and necessity of each living being, i.e. person.

It is history and culture, in other words, the combination of necessity and chance, which calls for one or some of the various forms of non-violent action. This means, non-violent actions should not, by any means, be taken as a normative or canonical enterprise. As long as normal political action is possible, all the means should be put on to enhancing and broadening those possibilities. However, when a political regime, a government or a state hinder normal political action, non-violent actions become feasible and necessary. It all depends on the people and their capacity to interpret the moment and reality. Something that, besides, is easily said, but very hard to do.

Let us put it straightforwardly, thus: the very conception of policy or policies is both the outcome and the enhancement of the most crucial political achievement of the modern age, namely the nation state. A public policy is one and the same issue as the concern for and about the nation state. Nonetheless, the importance of political life – hence *politeia* – cannot be simply identified with the state, i.e. the national government. As it happens, alas, in many times the main reason for the violation of the human rights is the state or government itself. Let's not forget in the backstage the significance of *state terrorism*. In sound and safe terms, one thing is the use of language from officials and clerks and political leaders, and quite another thing is a critical, reflexive use of language. (Between brackets, the mass media should be warned hereon).

Non-violent actions are, therefore, not to be grasped in a binary and probably Manichean sense, such as facing a potential external enemy, but it can also be considered in situations between different countries, different nations, and different national frontiers, or else within one and the same state or government. The complexity of the very political life and historical circumstances defines the entire need for non-violent actions. In times of globalized and networked systems and crises, it is not so much the legitimacy of this or that state what is truly at stake. Rather, it is the very viability and sustainability of life what is at stake – life as we know it, and life-as-it-could-be-possible; life on earth or else life possible in another place within the solar system.

Ecology and the environmental challenges and problems allow or even impose us to think in terms other than history and geography. To be sure, thinking far beyond the boundaries of national history and political geography brings us face to face with natural, life-like phenomena that largely surpass the traditional frames for thinking about violence as such; that is, culture and the social sciences, even the human sciences and the humanities.

At the end of the day, the complexity of non-violent actions shows us that the various forms of such actions do coincide or nurture from other species, or from biology ad evolution theory, for instance. In its soundest sense, politics, i.e. policies is or should be nothings else that allowing and providing possibilities for life – as many possibilities as can be imagined and achieved. Rather than just constraining and limiting, instead of normalizing and retrieving, the very sound task of the state and government should be to dignify life, to enhance it and making it possible, well, to care about as such quality for it to be graceful and joyful.

This, of course, pertains human life, but human life is just one single moment of much larger and broader landscape that includes all known and knowable forms of life. After all, in contrast with culture, we have come to reckon that there is no essential or fundamental species on life, and that there is no one key species so that without it life on earth would not exist at all.

Thinking about life in general means linking, networking, matching, and thinking in terms of set theory, for instance. Non-violent actions aim at digging into the phase space of the possible when life is at stake. Violence as such is undesirable and unnecessary – in the economics of the universe: hence, the sense and meaning of non-violent actions – here and always.

CONCLUSION

Passivity and acceptance may be morally or religiously sound arguments. However, in the framework of political studies or political philosophy they are untenable. As said, politics is the field of action – hence decisions and organization (de Waal, 2007). I have argued here than when it comes to the defense of life any argument is acceptable under the proviso that violent be suppressed or superseded. The call for non-violent action grounds on both the acknowledgement of the absolute necessity of life very much as the rejection of violence in any form: whether physical or symbolical, open or subtle, for instance.

The most basic of all forms against any kind of violence is, to be sure, resistance. However, once we open up the doors for resistance, so to say, then the array of other non-violent actions follows. Nietzsche used to say that life wants us all as warriors – never giving up, surrendering or faltering. Life, as we know, is after al a long-term game.

There are no higher values or principles above the absolute necessity and right to live. Any other idea, principle or value that is placed above the right to life is sheer ideology and hides violence (to-come). The human rights serve then as the rationale for non-violent action in any form and under any circumstance. We are to be able to defeat violence, but violence cannot be defeated by some other (better or finer or stringer) violence. A vicious circle is then produced: the rest is history.

Astonishingly, non-violent actions have not been the rule along the history of western civilization. On the contrary, as Marx rightly pointed out, violence has been the midwife of history. Such a history must be ended. Yet, it is not by violence that it can be overturned.

We, I have the hunch, are at the dawn of a new civilization. That however should by no means be taken as an automatic claim. The common least expression of the new civilization is sketched out as the end of violence. Philosophical and moral, even economic and social arguments and experiences can be shown in the direction of the aurora of a new civilization. That, however, is not my goal here. Politically, some basic elements of the new daybreak are non-violent actions. In any case, the whole point brings us to a sudden horizon, namely the complexification of the human experience. Only one proviso is brought up here: complexity does not have anything to do with complicate, hard, tough or difficult – systems, times, or behaviors. The complexity of life just brings to the fore the dignity, the quality, the enhancement and possibility of a better life. Living-well is after all, a matter of wisdom. And yet, we strive for it.

REFERENCES

Arendt, H. (2006). *Eichmann in Jerusalem: A Report on the Banality of Evil*. London: Penguin Classics.

De Waals, F. (2007). *Chimpanzee Politics: Power and Sex among Apes*. Baltimore: Johns Hopkins University Press.

Maldonado, C. E. (2002). *Filosofía de la sociedad civil*. Bogotá: Siglo del Hombre Editores.

Maldonado, C. E., & Gómez-Cruz, N. (2012). The Complexification of Engineering. *Complexity*, *17*(4), 8–15. doi:10.1002/cplx.20395

Maldonado, C. E., & Gómez-Cruz, N. (2015). Biological Hypercomputation: A New Research Problem in Complexity Theory. Complexity, 20(4), 8-18.

Maldonado, C. E., & Gómez-Cruz, N. A. (2014). Synchronicity Among Biological and Computational Levels of an Organism: Quantum Biology and Complexity. *Procedia Computer Science*, *36*, 177–184. doi:10.1016/j.procs.2014.09.076

Margulis, L., & Sagan, D. (2003). *Acquiring Genomes: A Theory of the Origin of Species*. New York: Basic Books.

Temkin, A. Y. (2012). Equations for the Quantum Mind Evolution in the Struggle for Life. NeuroQuantology, June(2), 305-310. doi:10.14704/nq.2012.10.2.535

Walzer, M. (2006). *Just and Unjust Wars: A Moral Argument with Historical Illustrations*. New York: Basic Books.

ADDITIONAL READING

Grover, J. (2001). *Humanity: a Moral History of the Twentieth Century*. London: Yale Nota Bene.

Nowak, M. A. (2011). *SuperCooperators. Altruism, Evolution, and Why We Need Each Other to Succeed*. New York: Free Press. With R. Highfield.

Pinker, S. (2012). *The Better Angels of our Nature: Why Violence Has Declined*. London: Penguin Books.

Seeley, T. D. (2010). *Honeybee Democracy*. Princeton, NJ: Princeton University Press.

ENDNOTES

1 Cfr. G. Lukacs, *The Destruction of Reason*, Merlin, Pr., 1980.

2 See, in contrast O. Stone's fantastic movie *Natural Born Killers*, from 1994.

3 I prefer to leave aside here the story about the four generations of war, namely: i) massive unity of body; ii) massive fire force; iii) *blitzkrieg*; iv) fourth generation warfare. The discussion is going about a fifth generation of warfare, namely the war-net.

4 Some work on these and close subjects have been carried out and can be seen in: (Maldonado, Gómez, 2015; Maldonado, Gómez, 2014; Maldonado, Gómez, 2012).

Chapter 4
Negotiation for Sustainable Peace:
Negotiation Theories vs. Peacekeeping in the UN Documents

Mirjam Wolfstein
Felsberg Institute, Germany

ABSTRACT

This analysis is a review of different negotiation theories by looking through the key documents of the United Nations on peace keeping and provides a review how negotiation theories could make an influence on them. Conflicts are an aspect of our daily life. They influence us not only in arguments with friends and family, but also in other dimensions of our discourse contributions. Therefore, it is significant to find practicable and conflict avoiding solutions for the parties involved. Negotiation is a form of discussion that helps find solutions for contradicting interests without using force. This violent free decision-making process is the most adequate form in a democratic culture. The growing denotation of political negotiations derives from an increasing interdependence, propagation of democracy, and a trend towards more peaceful dealings between governments. The main organization for peacekeeping and thus also peace negotiation documentation is the United Nations.

INTRODUCTION

"The natural state of men is not peaceful coexistence but war - not always open hostilities, but at least an unceasing threat of war" (Kant 1795). As Immanuel Kant states that human kind has cultivated conflict situations since its beginnings, normally to survive the various situations which it has been facing, but also to rule others. The conflicts are different types, varying from macro conflicts - between international organization or states - to micro conflicts - between people. It is imaginable that there are different solutions for the different types of conflicts. The most widely applied solution is to force one's own solution upon the opponent, however.

Conflicts are characterized not only by the variance of their outcome but also by their intensity, by mediators, the conflict parties, and the parties' willingness to solve conflicts. Since the uprising

DOI: 10.4018/978-1-4666-9675-4.ch004

of humanism, it has been tried to solve conflicts without violence or even war as it has be been widely accepted that to solve a conflict with violence is the huge defeat. Therefore, diplomacy and the negotiations which go along became a central to conflict solution. Especially armed conflicts are meant to be solved by negotiation so as they can reach sustainable peace building measures.

Since the United Nations founding in 1945 after the Second World War, peace building, peace keeping, and sustainable peace consolidation have been a primary objective. In this line of thought, the UN passed various resolutions during the Cold War era to keep at least the "cold peace" between the Blocks preserved. However, it can be assumed that the implicit threat of nuclear devastation was more frightening, and thus contributing to peace, than any of the UN resolution passed.

Above all, after the end of the conflict between the East and the West, the main problems of the United Nations became noteworthy as "the political new beginning of 1990 found no unified world, but pre-industrial clan rule, industrial nation states and post-industrial society world" (Czempiel, 1994, p 15). The end of the block confrontation did not bring the desired or expected world peace with it. Instead, since the 1990s wars are more and more regional but not fewer in number. At the same time small weapons and other war objects are more widely spread. The consequences of which can be observed in the conflicts in the Middle East and Africa which appear to be aggravating. "Peace has also two sides: absence of personal violence, and absence of structural violence. We shall refer to them as negative peace and positive peace respectively" (Galtung, 1969). Thus, to keep a sustainable peace in all aspects from daily small conflicts such direct human interaction to macro conflicts such as international disputes, the conflict parties have to discuss the problems with each other. Therefore, negotiations as a means are more essential to international relations than ever before. This analysis tries to clarify how negotiation theories affect modern diplomacy strategies and its role in the UN peace building agendas since the end of the cold war. The United Nations reports have been created to provide detailed documentation, also for cases in which negotiations were not successful. Consequentially, they not only include valuable information on what negotiations accomplished, but also on what they were not able to resolve.

This paper gives a small overview about negotiations and the theories on which they are based. Essentially, three different negotiation theories for conflict situations are applied: the first two are the International Multilateral Negotiation and the Ripeness theory both by William I. Zartman. The third theory is the Transcend-Method according to Johan Galtung. After a theoretical introduction, key UN documents on the subjects of peace keeping, peace building, and peace concerning are analyzed in light of the afore mentioned theories. The conclusion will then elaborate on how theoretical negotiation concepts can be (more) valuable means in the UN decision and implementation process concerning peace keeping and building operations.

BACKGROUND

The solutions of conflicts in our era are evidently has to made through the diplomatic way. In fact, the United Nation was founded to monitor and solve the international conflicts which could turn into armed conflicts.

As already stated - since the world is full of conflicts, their study and solution have been a key element in the subjects of not only the executive political organs but also of any social sciences. To begin with, the key documents of the UN were subjects of many articles and books over the last six decades, since it's foundation. As an overview on the international law a book of Norman Paech and Gerhard Stuby is essential: Völkerrecht und Machtpoltik in den internationalen Beziehungen" (International Law and Power Politics in the International Relations) (2001), as well as the book of the German political scientist Ernst-Otto Czempiel on the reform the United Nations: "Die Reform der UNO" (The reform of the UN) published in 1994.

Negotiations were theorized also by numerous scientists since the beginning of the 19th century. French, English and US-American political scientists have published over the last centuries, lot of different theories and approaches along negotiation and modern diplomacy. In the modern era is William I. Zartman one of the leading scientist on negotiation theories. He have published over 30 books and articles on this subject. Zartmans focus on the mutually enciting opportunities and mutual hurting stalemate are well explained in his works "Mutually Enciting Opportunities and Durable Settlements" (2004) and in "The timing of peace initiatives: Hurting stalemates and ripe moments" (2001).

Besides, Johan Galtung published since the 1970th many books and articles on the subject of peace and conflict solutions. His article "Violence, Peace, and Peace Research" was published in 1975 and it was a grassroot for many upcoming publications on the subject of peace research since then. In the book "Transcend and Transform: An Introduction to Conflict Work (Peace By Peaceful Means)" took Galtung peace research to the next level by combining diplomatical elements with the basics of peace research.

Though, this article is focusing on the theoretical approaches of William I. Zartman and Johan Galtung, their publications over the decades made clear that a change in the diplomacy is necessary for peaceful solution of conflicts. As already mentioned the amount of publications is so huge that it cannot take place here and list every essential article.

MAIN FOCUS OF THE CHAPTER

Negotiation Theories

General Negotiation Theory

"Negotiation is a form of finding solutions without the use of force for contradicting interests. This non-violent process free of power is the form adequate the democratic culture of the quarrel discussion" (Pfetsch, 2006, p. 1). The growing importance of political negotiations is marked by an increasing interdependence of a globalizing world, the propagation of democracy and a trend towards more peaceful dealings between governments. Therefore, negotiations manifest not only a central component in the national policy-making processes, but also in international policy efforts. "Negotiations are a vehicle of communication and stakeholder management. As such, they can play a vital role in assisting policy-makers to obtain a better grasp of the complex issue, factors and human dynamics behind important policy issues" (Alfredson, Cungu', 2008).

Frank Pfetsch defines negotiation, while he refers to Guy O. Faure, in the following manner: "Negotiation is a social process, in which two or several parties for a certain time interoperate with the search for a satisfactory position for their differences regarding one matter of dispute" (Pfetsch, 2006, p. 20). This definition contains all points which define negotiations, as it describes the process character, the contradictory interests concerning the matter of dispute, the actors who are involved in the conflict and, as a result, a solution that is acceptable for both sides. In fact, it even requires the intention of both parties to find a solution which Pfetch originally refers to as *Lösungsfindung*.

From the afore mentioned negotiation definition, it can be inferred that negotiations can manifest themselves in different manners, direct or indirect:

1. Direct negotiation means that the conflict parties communicate directly with each other, either alone or with or more mediators together.
2. Indirect negotiation, in contrast, can also be conducted secretly by one or more mediators.

There are different preconditions necessary for the conflict parties in order to agree to negotiate. The first precondition is the involved parties' willingness to settle a conflict. "The willingness to settle a conflict today versus continuing to fight until victory is a function of expectation of future victory an current and anticipated costs (Regan, 2000, p. 11). This cost-benefit calculation has been transcribed in an analytic formula by Patrick Regan shown in Box 1.

The formula shows the optimum balance necessary to settle a conflict peacefully between the poles, victory and defeat, for each conflict party (Regan, 2000, p. 11).

Conflict parties have different assuming during a negotiation process the general characteristics have been summarized by John S. Murray in his article "Understanding competing theories of negotiation". In this article, he depicts two kinds of negotiators - competitive and problem-solving negotiators: According to Murray, these negotiator characteristics are presented in Table 1.

The patterns Murray lists are easy to recognize and stereotypical. Furthermore Murray explains that this classification of the patterns of negotiators also contribute to principal assumptions that can be made concerning negotiators as depicted in Table 2.

Table 1. Recognized patterns of negotiators

Competitive	Problem-solving
The negotiator:	The negotiator:
Tries to maximize tangible resource gain for own client within limits of current dispute/problem.	Tries to maximize returns for own client including any joint gains available.
Makes high opening demands and is slow to concede.	Focuses on common interests of parties.
Uses threats, confrontation argumentation	Tries to understand the merits as objectively as possible
Manipulates people and process	Uses non-confrontational debating techniques
Is not open to persuasion on substance	Is open to persuasion on substance
Is oriented to quantitative and competitive goals	Is oriented to qualitative goals, a fair/wise/durable agreement, effectively negotiated

Table 2. Basic assumptions

Competitive	Problem-solving
Negotiating world is controlled by egocentric self-interest.	Negotiating world is controlled by enlightened self-interest.
Underlying motivation is competitive/antagonistic.	Common interest valued.
Limited resources.	Interdependence recognized.
Independent choices: tomorrow's decision unaffected materially by today's	Limited resources with unlimited variation in personal preferences.
Resource distribution system is disruptive in nature (either-or).	Resource distribution system in integrative in nature (joint).
Goal: win as much as you can – and especially more than the other side	Goal: mutually agreeable solution that is fair to all parties and efficient for community.

Box 1.

$$\sum_{t=0}^{n} \mathrm{EU}_{\mathrm{t}}^{\mathrm{settle}} = \sum_{t}^{n} \left[\left(C_t^{settle} + B_t^{settle} \right) - p\left(C_{tn}^{victory} + B_{tn}^{victory} \right) + \left(1 - p \right) \left(C_{tn}^{defeat} + B_{th}^{defeat} \right) \right]$$

More than just the conflict parties and their negotiators involved in a conflict solution, often a mediator is needed to mediate. The role of the mediator has historic roots. Mediators of have been active in clans and tribal societies to mediate not only internal conflict but also intertribal or inter-clan conflict. As the list of skills required by the mediator is quite extensive, the mediator has to have special characteristics to be able to operate, and not to act as a new different party in a dispute. As Patrick Regan states in his analysis: "Presumably then outside parties intervene in an internal conflict at the core of their motivation is some form of conflict management. Interveners may prefer their ally to prevail, but one would think that prevailing at an acceptable cost and in a reasonable time frame would be critical to an effective outcome" (Regan, 2000, p. 3).

A mediator has to be equipped with five main characteristics: credibility, objectivity and self-control adaptability, perseverance, and finally appearance and demeanor. These skills guide him through any mediation or negotiation. Based on these characteristics, a mediator should bring to the negotiation table, he or she will have to follow four guiding principles (Friedmann, Himmelstein, 2013, p.43):

1. **Voluntariness:** From all parties included the mediator can every time determinate the negotiation.
2. **Discretion:** A mediator never comments on the subject beyond the negotiation.
3. **Openness to Any Result:** All parties have to participate the negotiation with willingness. This also includes the negotiation as the ability of completion.
4. **Multipartiality:** The mediator is on the side of all parties - this means more than a simple neutrality and, thus, defines the mediator's as beyond that of balancing positions.

To achieve their objectives an intervener must manipulate the cost of continued fighting, the benefits from settlement, and do so in a way that convinces both sides that settling now is preferable to the same outcome at some future time, so might think of this as using an intervention to create a 'ripe' moment (e.g. Haass, 1990). (Regan, 2000, p. 8)

After this generalization of the preconditions, as well the patterns as the assumptions of negotiators and the mediators, the following stages of this chapter discuss the theorization of negotiation as a process.

"There is yet no satisfactory theory of negotiation", framed by William I. Zartman in 1975 in his article "Negotiations: Theory and Reality," for the journal of *International Affairs* (P. 69). Negotiation theories are concerned with and based in several complex theoretical approaches which have their origins in different other theories. The approaches that contribute to the theoretical framework are: decision theory, game theory, the organization theory, small group theory, coalition theory and leadership theory.

Negotiation theories were taken no account in Germany up to now like in Anglo-Saxon countries. They have been used, applied, and studied in England and the United States for decades, however. Essentially they are based on the basic principles of diplomacy. Although negotiation techniques have been applied for as long as human kind exists in everyday life, the economic and the political sphere, there is still no coherent uniform negotiation theory in political science.

In political science, work on a negotiation theory began in the 1950s and 1960s on grounds of the nuclear threat which forced both super powers to solve their conflicts in a diplomatic way instead of leading a warlike contention.

In the centre of the negotiation theories that were developed is, on the one hand, the negotiation process, possible motives as well as interests of the actors and the explanation of the results and, on the other hand, the conditions required for successful or unsuccessful negotiations (Pfetsch, 2006, p. 19).

According to Frank Pfetsch, the negotiation process is based on and conducted in three phases: the pre-, main-, and post-phase. The pre-phase is directed to questions concerning the opposing parties' characteristics regarding organizational-technical problems and negotiation objectives.

The main phase is characterized by tools such as bilateral or multilateral diplomacy, assignment of means of information, choice of economic and military means, operations of secret services, informal contacts, as well as alliance and alliance questions and/or effort of domestic means. (cf. Pfetsch, 2006, pp. 20). Finally, follows the post phase or so-called implementing phase; it deals above all with the implementation of the achieved arrangements and concerns the permanence of the result (Pfetsch, 2006, p. 23).

Tanya Alfredson and Azeta Cungru' characterize the negotiation phases in their article "Negotiation Theory and Practice" likewise: "Realistically, one could conceptualize a model that recognizes the importance of negotiation theory and skills across the core phases - agenda setting, policy analysis, formulation, implementation and evaluation - of the policy cycle" (Alfredson, Cungru', 2008, p. 4). In this characterization, agenda setting is the phase in which the choice of items and frameworks are defined, the analysis phase describes the navigation through a complex issue of areas and topics in which the parties can compromise with each other. During the phase of formulation, policy makers may "organize their policy options into coherent selection base from which to negotiate." The implementation phase is characterized by the assertion of the outcomes of the negotiation. Finally the stage of evaluation is the monitoring of the implemented outcomes which is represented by the factors awareness of accountability to constituencies and the structure (Alfredson, Cungru', 2008).

"Moreover, the timing if an intervention should significantly influence the duration of a conflict through its effect on expectations. At the early stages of a conflict opposition movements will generally be small, lightly armed, and lacking the crucial support of the general public.

The different theoretical approaches have also different characteristics concerning their potential outcome, assumption, and limitation. The main negotiation theories can be categorized as (Alfredson, Cungru', 2008, p. 17):

1. **Structural Negotiation Theory:** Focuses on means, position. The primary focus is on the so called "Win-lose". This also contributes to its limitations which, on the one hand, lock this approach on a premise that might lead to lost opportunity for mutually beneficial agreement, and, on the other hand, its focus on an over-emphasis of power.
2. **Strategic Negotiation Theories:** (e.g. game theory) Characterized by the focus on the result, rationality, and positions as its basic features. Such as the structural negotiation theory, this also focuses on a "win-lose" outcome with the supplement of existence of optimal solutions and rationality of players, however. The limitation of these approaches is rooted in their exclusion of powers and players undifferentiated apart from differences in the quality of options open to each other.
3. **Behavioral Negotiation Theory:** (e.g. diplomatic treatises, personality types) Focuses on basic features such as personality traits and analyzes in light of a "win-lose" assumption rooted in the role of perceptions and expectations. The limitation of this theory is its emphasis on position.
4. **Concession Exchange Negotiation Theory:** (processual) Focuses on the concession making behavior as well as on positions, with the expected assumption of "win-lose" based in the "moves as learned" (reactive) response.

Its limitations are on the one side emphasis on positions and the lack of predictiveness on the other side.

5. **Integrative Negotiation Theories:** (e.g. phase theories, process models principled negotiations) Focus on problem solution, on creating values, communicating and "win-win" solutions. The assumption of this approach is creating more "win-win" potentials. The parties should still recognize and be prepared for encounters with non-integrative bargainers and the time consuming aspects of this approach are valuable limits.

In order to reach an acceptable solution for the negotiating parties it is important to all theoretical approaches that the parties compromise with each other in their aims. As we see, negotiation is the part of the daily policy making. In the international decision making process negotiations are especially vital as they can prevent an armed conflict or a war.

Negotiation Theory According to William Zartman

Beyond the theories just introduced, William Zartman's analysis of various negotiation theories is particularly helpful. He developed several theory attempts to the negotiation process that point to the fact that no theory offers a generally applicable solution, but is a joint decision making process. He is the author and publisher of several books and essays on the topic of negotiations, for example, "The negotiation process, the dynamics of escalation and negotiation in the omnibus Escalation" and "Negotiation in International Conflicts, Preventive Diplomacy, Peacemaking in International Conflict: Methods" and "Techniques, Negotiating from Asymmetry: The North-South Stalemate".

This analysis looks on two of his theories which were considered in more detail with regard to negotiation: first Zartman's article about multilateral negotiations: "Introduction: Two's Company and More's Crowd: The complexities of multilateral negotiation" and secondly his ripe theory, in his article "Negotiations the ace a Mechanism for resolution in the Arab Israelis conflict" which he wrote for the Leonard Davis institute. The "ripe theory" applied in this notebook described from William Zartman in detail in his book "Ripe for resolution: Conflict and intervention in Africa works on".

Both attempts are briefly introduced in the following. The multilateral negotiation theory was discussed in the International Multilateral Negotiation by Zartman. This theory includes also other theories, for example, the decision theory, the game theory, the organization theory, and others.

The multilateral negotiation theory characterizes six signs of multilateral negotiations which differ from bilateral negotiations. First several parties are involved in the negotiations, these are meant that in comparison to bilateral negotiations not only two parties are integrated. Secondly, there is not only a contentious issue between the opponents, but several. "...the multi-issue nature of multilateral negotiations. This attribute is based in reality, but is not inherent; ..." (Zartman, 1997, p. 4.).

Thirdly, the multirole of the negotiations, "Precisely ace texture is present on the issue dimension, adding role differential to numbers and interest groups" (Zartman, 1997, p. 5). The fourth characteristic feature is the formation of coalitions; this allows the opposing parties to establish alliances with different contentious issues.

The fifth and the sixth aspects of the multilateral negotiations concern the result, "consensus decision-making: Multilateral negotiations by their nature do not lend themselves to either unanimous decision or majority-rule decisions". Thus the sixth attribute is the so-called "Rule-making as the main outcome" (Hoadley, 1996, p. 10).

The first problem of this theory is the role of the third parties, which often operate not only as mediators but as a conflict party. In this case the third party has its own interest to seek, this is why

Figure 1. Mutually hurting stalemate (Brahms, 2003)

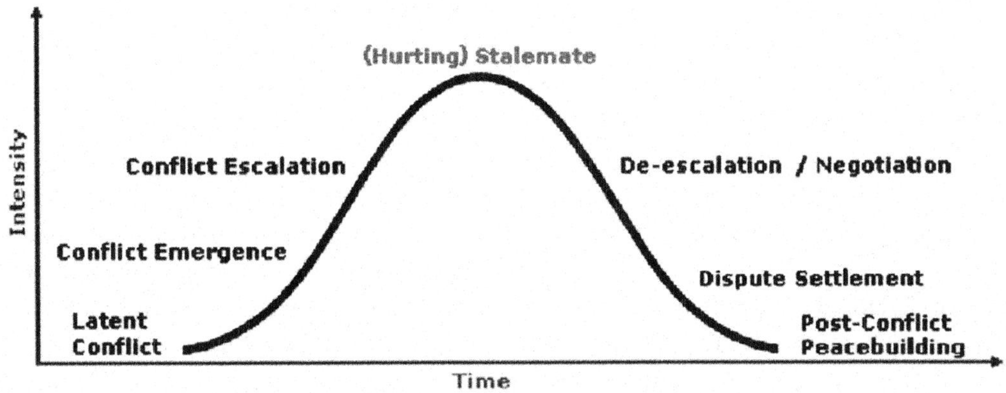

it is not able to follow the rules of mediation. In a multilateral negotiation are already more than two parties involved, therefore the way out of the conflict is more difficult. The second problem of this theory is that it assumes the common intention of the opposing parties for the solution. For that reason the negotiations serve only for condition purification.

The second theory in view of negotiations which was developed by William Zartman is the ripe theory. For this attempt it is unimportant how many parties are involved in the conflict, because he refers to the beginnings or conditions of negotiations. Zartman defines the ripe theory as follows: "Ripeness theory is intended to explain why, and therefore when, parties to a conflict are susceptible to their own or other efforts to turn the conflict toward resolution through negotiation" (Zartman, 1999, p. 2.). The ripe moment is entirely connected with diplomacy - John Campbell describes in the following words: "Ripeness of time is if the absolute essences of diplomacy." (Campbell, 1976, p. 73)

For successful negotiations, which have a lasting effect on a conflict ripeness, justice and their penetration are required. "The ripe moment is necessarily a perpetual event [,…], it can be created if outside parties can cultivate the perception of painful present vs. preferable alternative, and therefore can be resisted so long as the party in question refuses or is otherwise able to block out that perception" (Zartman, 1999, p. 3).

Three central elements are integrated in the ripeness theory:

1. Mutually Hurting Stalemate
2. Way Out
3. Valid Spokesman

In the centre of the ripe theory stands the Mutually Hurting Stalemate (MHS), "the idea behind the concept is that the parties find themselves locked in a conflict from which they cannot escalate their way out and this deadlock is painful to both of them" (Zartman, 1999, p. 3), or in other words: MHS gives the impulse for the search for the way out from a conflict. The MHS is defeated by a cost-benefit analysis which the opposing parties themselves gauge. In addition, it is fully consistent with public choice notions of rationality (Zartman, 2001, p. 1).

The element MHS (Figure 1) has been added with the component of Mutually Enticing Opportunity (MEO). The concept of a MEO is a conceptual advancement after which lasting conflict resolutions should be found. MEO is a "prospect for a more attractive future to pull them [conflict parties] out of their conflict, once a MHS pushed them into negotiations."(Zartman, 2001, p. 14) MEO has been created just like MHS as a prospect, it is a subjective awareness of objective elements and it must be produced by the parties. (Zartman, 2004) "When a MEO is not developed in the negotiation, they remain truncated and unstable, even if they reach a conflict management agreement to suspend violence..." (Zartman, 2001, p. 14)

Beside the MHS, the ripe theory contains another important component: the perception of the Way Out. Because ripeness is actually one necessary condition, however it is not sufficient for the initiation of negotiations. For that reason, Way Out is a necessary component of ripeness and offers also the possible expedient of conflicts, even if the parties not able to identify special solutions. This element could be accompanied by mediators.

As the third element of ripeness Valid Spokesman have been pointed out by Zartman; it has a second level importance, because a presence of strong leaders on both sides are necessary to deliver compliance to the agreements (Zartman, 2001, p. 10).

After conducting extensive research, Zartman himself points to the deficiencies in his approach that still exist. He thus emphasizes the ripe moment as a potential key element in negotiation and conflict solution theory which requires further research. To find the ripe moment in conflict situations there a still research necessary all aspects of the conflicts, like objective and subjective elements (pain, impass, inability to bear the cost of further escalation, related and objective evidence of stalemate etc.)

Transcend Method According to Johan Galtung

Now the third attempt of the negotiations theories – the Transcend method – is shown. Although Johan Galtung, the developer of the method, reluctantly counts it as part of negotiation theories, it is applied here. The reason for Galtung's reluctant position towards the transcend method of negotiation theories lies in the differentiation between hard and soft negotiating: Hard negotiations would result only in "a decayed compromise" (Galtung, 2007, p. 236), in soft negotiations the result is satisfactory to both parties, namely in such a way that it would have a sustainable effect.

The transcend method appeals to the dialogue between opposing parties, and negotiations are also a form of the dialogue. In this context, the word 'transcend' can be understood as overstepping the borders of experience. The conflicts are worked on "by transcendency and transformation," "so that the parties can live with it." (Galtung, 1998) This approach was published by Johan Galtung in 1998 in an essay on conflict transformation with peaceful means in the journal *Science and Peace*. He deals with conflicts at different levels. Micro (conflicts within and between people), meso-(social conflicts), macro (conflicts between states or nations) and mega conflicts (which will concern regions or cultures) are described categorized and with the Transcend method, a potential solution is offered.

In this paper the attempt is considered by Galtung for so-called macro-conflicts. To be able to understand the conflict resolution method, Galtung believes, the life cycle of conflicts must be understood. "You appear, reach an emotional, even violent climax, then become weaker, disappear – and often come again." This refers to the fact that the opposing parties have not achieved her aims. Galtung writes about states: „States were created, around war and not to bring peace in the world." (Galtung, 2007, p. 106). In the state structures statesmen and diplomats have the monopoly to lead peace negotiations. They do this, while they protect their national interests, "also if their interests lie beyond their state borders, affect in their "sphere of influence", even if these influence the interests of the human basic needs or prevent even their fulfillment. Instead of people rebelling against this nonsense, there are really some people that state that the "harmony of the interests" is the

Table 3.

Nr.	Position	Outcome	Process	Sum	Work
[1]	1,0 Either – or	Win	Conflict	1	1
[2]	0,1 Either – or	Win	Conflict	1	1
[3]	0,0 Neither – nor	Retreat	Respite	0	2
[4]	½, ½ Half-Half	Compromise	Negotiation	1	1
[5]	1,1 "As also"	Transcend	Dialog	2	0

only realistic way to the peace." (Galtung, 2007, p. 106) The research limits itself to diagnosis or analyzes, it is based on data, therefore the past is put in the foreground, ergo the research leaves the "therapy proposals" to the statesmen and diplomats, as predictions contain uncertainties. In consequence is why the Transcend method is aimed at diluting this monopoly.

Conflicts can dissolve themselves on the basis of their past, or they can be solved in such a way that conflicts which stretch over a longer time period and "with those where for a long time violence is carried out, the knowledge of the past is not enough." (Galtung, 2007, p. 107). In order to solve this conflict, the antagonists need not only knowledge of the past but also an image of the future since concrete suggestions for a better future are contributions to a peace culture.

During those conflicts which take place on macro-levels, the fear of violence plays a great role, argues Galtung. Therefore, he describes five possible aspects of fear of violence in interstate conflicts between nations. The first aspect is violence as a political means in which the culprit puts through its interests. The second aspect is that violence also meets the uninvolved and innocent. Thirdly the panic linking up by force, humiliation and fright are demonstrated. The fourth aspect concerns the unpredictability of violence, because one can give no prediction about when, where, and whom violence will hit. As the fifth basic idea he applies the attempt of the culprit of protecting itself from possible repayment. (Galtung, 2007, pp. 110)

Galtung ascertains in a conflict, all the same of which way, five possible solutions. First only one of the parties achieves its will and secondly only the other party asserts itself, both lead to a fight. Thirdly neither one nor the other can assert itself, here deferment will be the next step. In fourth place both parties accept compromises which are negotiated. The fifth possibility is the ideal type after Galtung to solve a conflict, he calls this way "As also". This solution approach leads to the fact that the opposing parties enter a dialogue with each other. All these alternatives describe a process which stands at the end of an attempt. From it he derives Table 3 (Galtung, 2007, p. 34).

The Transcend method aims to master a conflict in such a way that it leads as a result to a solution which is satisfactory to both opposing parties and fulfils the interests of both so a "Win-Win" situation originates. If these possibilities showed a process, the result lies already in the process itself, and "… the elective process depends on the desired result of a conflict." (Galtung, 1998)

To be able to work on a conflict with the Transcend method, three steps are necessary: First the marking of the extreme positions of the parties. Secondly the introduction of these positions in a base diagram, and finally the search for interpretations in the schema, becomes renowned particularly on "neither" - and on him "as an also" attempt. Since these both attempts cause the so-called "ah-effect" with the opposing parties. (Galtung, 2007, p. 108)

The three manifestations to which the Transcend method appeals are empathy, creativity and dialogue. These must be used to solve conflicts. "If creativity is the key to the conflict what is then the key to peace?" – Galtung asks in his book "Konflikte und Konfliktlösungen", and he provides as answer that equality is the key to peace. (Galtung, 2007, 145)

The deficit of the Transcend method as well as with other attempts of the negotiations theory is the condition of the will of the opposing parties to solve the conflict. "The great question is whether the participants are ready for negotiations on a high level and if they are, they should also be able to carry out something similar." (Galtung, 2007, p. 237)

Frameworks for Peace from the United Nation

United Nation Peace Building and Peace Keeping Agendas

Agenda for Peace

45 years after the creation of the United Nations, the political situation of the world has changed, the end of the East-West conflict rang in a new era in international policy, therefore a reorganization is necessary also within UN.

"An Agenda for Peace" originated in 1992 by Boutros-Ghali, the secretary general at that time of UN. In his report Boutros-Ghali referred to in the segment about the peace building on chapter 6 of the charter. (United Nations, General Assembly, 1992)

The Agenda for Peace placed special emphasis on conflict prevention and reacted with thus above all to them – by the end of the cold war – modified situation of the international politics. The rash of existing conflicts should be avoided by measures like humanitarian aid and preventive diplomacy. Based on the agenda is due the foundation of "Department of Political Affairs" which has to observe the duty political developments all over the world to be able to warn early about menacing conflicts.

In the Agenda for Peace three outlines are treated: Preventive diplomacy, peace building and peace keeping. These three aspects contribute to peace consolidation. To be able to carry out preventive diplomacy, confidence-building measures are arranged. This means that the fact inquiry as well as preventive operations and demilitarized zones can relapse.

Peace building is one of the most important aspects of this agenda. It is divided into further measures: Strengthening and recognition of the International Court of Justice and defusing of the conflicts by assistance for displaced persons. In addition, the UN Security Council should accept the economic problems which come up along with sanctions (according to art. 41. UN-Charter).

If all peaceful resources fail, it must be fallen back - based on article 42. of the UN-Charter - on military measures. Such armed forces should be available not only in isolated cases, but permanently to the UN. In order to allow those permanent troops, these should be created for the enforcement of peace. The troops should be heavier armed than the present peacekeeping forces, and they may be used only if an aggression has already begun (United Nations, General Assembly, 1992, art.44).

Member states of UN would make available these troops available voluntarily. Such troops for the peace enforcement would be justified as a temporary measure according to article 40 of the charter. However, peace keeping troops should not be mistaken for the armed forces according art. 43. of the charter which can be put up to given time „to deal with acts of aggression or with the military personnel which Governments may agree to keep on stand-by for possible contribution to peace-keeping operations" (United Nations, General Assembly, 1992, art. 44.).

Peace building is the first step for peace keeping. Therefore, the basic conditions for its success are rooted peace protection which manifest itself in: a clear and practicable order, the cooperation of the parties by the implementation of this order to make available the continuous support on the part of the security council, the readiness of the member states, the required military staff, police staff and civil staff including experts; an effective guidance of the United Nations in the official jurisdiction and on site, as well as an adequate financial and logistic support.

"As the international climate has changed and peace-keeping operations are increasingly fielded to help implement settlements that have been negotiated by peacemakers, a new array of demands and problems has emerged regarding logistics, equipment, personnel and finance, all of which could be corrected if Member States so wished and were ready to make the necessary resources available" (United Nations, General Assembly, 1992, art. 50.).

Peace consolidation in conflict future will be applied as a counterpart to the preventive diplomacy. To be successful here, peace-construction and peace keeping missions must also contain comprehensive efforts to the determination and support of structures which are likely to consolidate peace and promote confidence and well-being of the people.

Some elements that contribute to the support of a lasting peace are:

- To speed up cooperation projects around economic and social development
- Dismantling of enemy stereotypes by student and teacher exchange
- De-mining is the most important aim, because without this the development cannot be sped up, and the landmines are a threat for peace because thereby the conflict can trigger once more.

The issue of landmines is picked up as a central theme in all the reports of Boutros-Ghali and are looked as one of the most important issue during the peace building.

In addition, the support of new democratic structures by UN and the better cooperation based on regional agreements and organizations is mentioned. "Under the Charter, the Security Council has and will continue to have primary responsibility for maintaining international peace and security, but regional action as a matter of decentralization, delegation and cooperation with United Nations efforts could not only lighten the burden of the Council but also contribute to a deeper sense of participation, consensus and democratization in international affairs" (United Nations, General Assembly, 1992, art. 64.).

To be able to finance peace building measures, the peace keeping and the peace consolidation in future conflict three proposals were made: (United Nations, General Assembly 1992, Art. 69.-74.)

- **Proposal One:** Acceptance of a package of measures for mastering the liquidity problems which are caused by the extremely high amount unpaid contributions by the member states, as well as the problem of insufficient company means: a) charge of interest on the not-on-time-paid contribution; b) suspension definite article of the finance order of the United Nations to allow the deduction of budgetary profits; c) increase of the company means fund to 250 million US dollars and approval of the principle after which the circumference of the fund should amount to about 25 percent of the inclined contributions of one year to the well-arranged household; d) establishment of a limited-period reserve fund endowed with 50 million dollars for the peace keeping from which the launching costs are covered by peace operations up to the entrance of the compulsory contributions to take out loans; e) authorization of the secretary general, at the market if other cash springs should not be sufficient.
- **Proposal Two:** Creation of a fund for humanitarian purposes of about 50 million

US dollars for the use in humanitarian emergency situations. This proposal has been transformed, in the meantime

- **Proposal Three:** Creation of an endowment fund of the United Nations for peace duties by an aimed amount of 1 billion US dollars first. The fund would be fed from a combination by compulsory and voluntary contributions from governments the private sector. As soon as the aimed financing is achieved, the profit from the arrangement of the capital would be used for the financing the costs of approved peace operations, other measures of the conflict resolution and related operations.

In 1995, the Agenda for Peace was reworked and was supplemented – 86 to 105 were added. This improved version of the Agenda for Peace manifested a reflection of the prior 3 years (1992-1995) and, above all, the catastrophe in Rwanda. The new Agenda for Peace enumerates some changes in comparison to 1989 and the new imminent scenarios as for example disintegrating states in Africa (Somalia) or the wide armament of chemical, biological or atomic weapons. A great origin for change was also the growing number of the armed conflicts since the end of the Cold War.

Agenda for Development

After the acceptance of the Agenda for Peace, Boutros-Ghali got a mandate to draft an Agenda for Development, because development problems were not sufficiently regarded in the Agenda for Peace. Since development is a safe basis for peace, and peace is valid as a basis for development, but many must speed up their development with the background of the past, in existence or imminent conflicts.

"Development cannot proceed easily in societies where military concerns are at or near the centre of life. Societies whose economic effort is given in substantial part to military production inevitably diminish the prospects of their people for development. The absence of peace often leads societies to devote a higher percentage of their budget to the military than to development needs in health, education and housing. Preparation for war absorbs inordinate resources and impedes the development of social institutions" (United Nations, General Assembly, 1994, Art. 17).

Boutros-Ghali contributes the lack of development into international tensions and into a chasing for military power. For the societies which are in such a circulation, it is difficult not to be involved in conflicts or a war. (United Nations, General Assembly, 1994, art. 18).

Another point in Boutros-Ghali's Agenda for Development is that conflict situations require other developing strategies than during peacetime. Therefore, development work should be already begun before ending of the conflict to be able to achieve a better result in peacetime.

The measures to peace consolidation which this development allow are the following: Determination and support of the structures which strengthen the peace and strengthen to prevent a relapse in conflict situation.

That's why peace consolidation is the task of all countries on all stages of development. Above all, for the countries which have just left behind a conflict, peace consolidation offers the opportunity to construct new social, political, and judicial institutions. Developing countries are able to remodel their economic system on grounds of the peace consolidation to guarantee a sustainable development. (United Nations, General Assembly, 1994, art. 23.).

Therefore, the most urgent duty of peace consolidation consists in reducing the war's effects on the population (e.g.: Food aid, support of the health and hygiene sector, de-mining as well as the logistic support of important organizations).

In future conflicts, de-mining will be particularly important, because the removal of landmines and the determination of fighting action is a necessary pre-condition for all other measures of peace consolidation. Capacities must be created to carry out de-mining, supervise, and evaluate and the state norms in harmony with the international directives.

Along with de-mining, the reintegration of the combatants is another important aspect of peace consolidation. This is a difficult endeavor with speaks to the stability concerning the conflict future. The reintegration of the combatants is vital for the course of the conflict future and, moreover, it is an essential condition for the supply of peace. (United Nations, General Assembly, 1994, art. 27.) So the revitalization of the occupation growth will show a strong incentive for young people to give a refusal to the war trade.

Not only the population suffers from conflict, but conflict also affects the government and administrative apparatus. Therefore, the efforts made in the future of conflict must be directed particularly towards rebuilding them. Thus key institutions of the civil society, as for example the justice system, need to be strengthened or, in some cases, be recreated.

Boutros-Ghali believes that one must expose the conditions that created a conflict. Hence, it is valid that different conflicts may require different approaches. Peace consolidation tells to promote a culture of the peace. For example: A land reform, regulations to the common use of water occurrence, to common economic support zones, to common tourism projects and cultural exchange can induce positive developments.

To avoid wars and armed conflicts, the reduction of military expenses is an important link in the chain of measures which support socio-cultural development as well as peace.

"Demilitarization has also produced painful strains among the industrialized market economies, though less severe than those in countries in transition. Particular localities and firms have been severely affected, but the market mechanism has made it easier for resources to be absorbed in other sectors of the economy. Alternative employment has often been difficult to find for many workers however, and retraining remains sporadic." (United Nations, General Assembly, 1994, Art. 36.). Thus, demilitarization offers not only chances but also challenges to come as various kind of tensions resulting from economic decline, for example.

According to this agenda peace, security, and development belong together firmly. Therefore, a sustainable development is indispensable for peace and security. Boutros-Ghali places special value on the consolidation of peace in the future of conflicts. In this consolidation process, removing the causes of the conflicts, the reintegration of former combatants, and de-mining are all important aspects of sustainable peace.

Peace Keeping in the Reform Documents of the UN

A More Secure World

In 2004 the secretary general gave an order to the High-Level Panel to work out a renewal and reform of the United Nations. Though since Boutros-Ghali's Agenda for Development the organization did not stop in area of reshaping, however, there was little progress concerning peace keeping. One of the proposals since 1994 was the millennium explanation of Kofi Annan which proposed the new challenges as well as the role of the United Nations in the 21st century.

In the revision, central challenges of globalization and the problems of the developing countries and transitional countries were integrated. In the last decade, 5 million people died during wars and civil wars. Therefore, decisions were made for the protection of peace. Among them are:: Removal of the danger of the weapons of mass destruction, strengthening international and national law, - member states should act in harmony with the charter of the UN and the International Court of Justice.

To make the United Nations more effective in maintaining peace and security by giving it the resources and tools it needs for conflict prevention, peaceful resolution of disputes, peacekeeping, post-conflict peace-building and reconstruction. In this context, we take note of the report of the Panel on United Nations Peace Operations and request the General Assembly to consider its recommendations expeditiously. (United Nations, General Assembly, 2000, Art. 9.)

On this occasion, the point of the obligation of the signatories is for the observance of the arms control and disarmament, international law, as well as human rights especially important.

Further measures for the peace keeping were determined, measures against international terrorism, fight against drug trafficking, fight against organized international criminal activity, wide disarmament of the weapons of mass destruction, compared with measures unauthorized small arms trade and light arms trade.

Furthermore all states were asked to take into consideration the entry to the agreement on ban of the usage, the storage, the production and the passing on of anti-personnel mines and about destruction as well as to the mine protocol to the arrangement about conventional weapons in its changed version.

The next step in the direction of changes was the Brahimi report of 2000 which examined the changed international situation concerning peace keeping missions and gave its proposals in addition. The report of the High-Level Panel is based on the Brahimi report of threats, challenges and changes – A more secure world: Our shared responsibility. Chapters X and XI of the report are devoted to peace keeping missions.

A statement of the High-Level Panel is the difference between peace keeping missions which allow the acceptance that the use of force will not be necessary. With peace-enforcement missions the use of force would be from the outset a component of the mission and both operations kinds of the approval of the Security Council require, unless it concerns self-defense cases (United Nations, High-level Panel on Threats, Challenges and Change 2004, Art. 212-213.)

For the installation of peace-enforcement troops the developed states bear the responsibility "to transform their existing force capacities into suitable contingents for peace operations" (United Nations, High-level Panel on Threats, Challenges and Change 2004, art. 216.)

The member states should provide not only the troops, but also support the work of the expert groups for the peace missions of UN. This group is subordinate to the secretariat of the United Nations. The peace missions should be stronger integrated into the regional cooperations.

The role of the peace keeping forces is many-sided, from the support of the development of a peace agreement up to police operations. The most important duty is the sustained peace consolidation, however. Moreover, the installation of the peacekeeping forces is not suitable as a longer term solution. Therefore, special representatives should take over this work partly. For the peace consolidation, a constant *fonds* should be arranged. From that "the recurrent expenditures of a nascent Government, as well as critical agency programmes in the areas of rehabilitation and reintegration." (United Nations, High-level Panel on Threats, Challenges and Change 2004, article. 228.)

In the report of the High-Level Panel the proposal was made to found a commission for peace consolidation which was not planned in the charter. This had to go after art. 29. of the UN charter in consultation with the security council and the Economic and Social Council are arranged. Their duty should be to strengthen the new role of the United Nations concerning domestic conflicts. The composition of the commission should be held relatively small, should meet in different composition and stand at least for a year under the chairmanship of a member approved by the security council. (United Nations, High-level Panel on Threats, Challenges and Change 2004, art. 261-265.).

To support this commission, an office should be established in the secretary. This should lead a number of national and international expert. (United Nations, High-level Panel on Threats, Challenges and Change 2004, Art. 266-269.) With this report, renewals were suggested concerning peace keeping, one of the most important ones is the institution of the commission for peace consolidation which should support the work of UN and the peace protection forces.

"In Larger Freedom" and the 60th Summit Document 2005

After the recommendations of the High-level Panel on Threats, Challenges and Change Kofi Annan proposed the report of the general assembly with the title In larger Freedom in March, 2005: towards development, security and human rights for all. This report is based on the millennium declaration, on the Brahimi report, the agenda for further changes, and on the recommendations of the high-level panel. Nevertheless, it can be said that in the preceding reports the problems of peace enforcement, peace keeping, and peace consolidation had higher rank than in the report of Annan. In chapter III (Freedom from Fear) peace keeping and peace consolidation are discussed in one chapter.

For the peace keeping Kofi Annan spotted concerning the report of the expert's group for peace missions (Brahimi report) that the number the peace keeping operations since 2000 has been increased, above all in Africa – because here "developed countries are increasingly reluctant to contribute troops. As a result, our capacity is severely stretched." (United Nations, General Assembly, 2005, art. 111.)

Annan requested the member states to assist the United Nations to form its peace keeping capacity more efficiently. The goal was to achieve a quicker deploy ability of the troops and better cooperation with regional organizations.

The disregard of the international law and the law on the peace keeping forces should be pursued criminal, because these has undermined the reputation of the United Nations and the international law.

Concerning peace consolidation Annan takes over the proposal of the High-Level Panel for threats challenge and change about the foundation of a commission for peace consolidation and also within the UN secretary an establishment of the office to the support peace consolidation.

The duties of the commission for peace consolidation would be supported by the UN after a war to guarantee the financing of the reconstruction and to check the progress of the realization of the medium-term reconstruction aims. Therefore, the commission would have no early warning or supervision function, however, it could stand to advice.

The 60th summit of the United Nations took place on September 15, 2005. Many hoped for appropriate reforms and renewals within UN. However, these expectations were disappointed early on by new reform suggestions from the US ambassador to the UN - John Bolton. Bolton submitted an amendment of approx. 400 points shortly before the summit. Thus, one could be sure that constructive changes could not be expected from the summit.

Concerning peace keeping, like in other areas of UN, few innovations were achieved. The support of the peace keeping operations was confirmed and the creation of a constant police capacity was demanded. In addition, a stronger cooperation with regional organizations like the African union was found necessary. On this occasion, it was pointed out to the chapter VIII of the UN charter and this should be strengthened. Beside the cooperation with regional organizations, a concrete case about anti-personnel mines was particularly found.

Also the jurisdiction of the peace keeping forces was emphasized on grounds of the incidents of the sexual exploitation and the sexual abuse during the operations. Concerning peace consolidation, the installation of a commission was decided on. The commission would also be in charge of peace consolidation and its purpose and duties were determined.

"The main purpose of the Peace building Commission is to bring together all relevant actors to marshal resources and to advise on and propose integrated strategies for post-conflict peace building and recovery. The Commission should focus attention on the reconstruction and institution-building efforts necessary for recovery from conflict and support the development of integrated strategies in order to lay the foundation for sustainable development. In addition, it should provide recommendations and information to improve the coordination of all relevant actors within and outside the United Nations, develop best practices, help to ensure predictable financing for early recovery activities and extend the period of attention by the international community to post-conflict recovery. The Commission should act in all matters on the basis of consensus of its members." (United Nations, General Assembly 2005, art. 98.)

The composition of the commission was determined. The commission should dispose of an organization committee whose arrangement was also described. To guarantee the financing, should be invited to the sessions of the World Bank, the International Monetary Fund, and other donors. In addition, the establishment of a peace consolidation fund was suggested. Indeed, there voluntary contributions were announced.

From both documents, it is evident that the intention of strengthening peace keeping operations was actually followed through and the commission for peace manifest another milestone. Nevertheless, there are deficits above all by armed operations and the legitimacy of the "humanitarian operations." Since the strict ban of violence which determines the UN charter is contradicted.

CONCLUSION

Negotiations are embedded in history, and they have been a part of diplomacy since ancient times. Still, in modern history, they have been a decisive part of the international policy making of the UN, whose role it is to keep and monitor peace all over the world. More precisely, also to contribute towards avoiding armed conflicts and solve existing conflicts sustainably.

The general development of the political situation around the world in the last two decades supports the need of reform of the United Nations structurally as well as its engagement in peace keeping and peace consolidation efforts. After the East-West conflict, the expected pacification of the world became no reality. Instead, the world's conflicts became more regionalized and did not concern the whole world. At the same time, grew in number and intensity to a level that the UN could no longer successfully engage with. The conflicts in the Middle East, particularly the Iraq war 1991, undermined the reputation of UN. Also the civil wars in Africa (Somalia and Rwanda) where the UN sent peace keeping manifested setbacks for the peace keeping operations.

Boutros-Ghalis' attempt failed to renew the UN, not only because the USA had positioned themselves against it. In the Agenda for Peace, Boutros-Ghali indicated many needs in the area of peace keeping and peace consolidation, however, only a few were put into action.

Only with the Brahimi report were essential changes realized. Being based on the High-Level Panel delivered in 2004 the report's proposals for peace keeping and peace consolidation, were adapted in the reform paper by Kofi Annan.

A thorough analysis of the development of peace keeping in the UN documents shows that the concentration of the peace protection on armed operations is a backward step in comparison to the original idea which was formulated in the charter. According to article 33 the member states shall peacefully quarrel. For this reason - in my opinion - the UN should have concentrate on preventive measures instead of peace creation.

Unfortunately, the relation was lost to chapter VI of the charter which still existed in the Agenda for Peace and the result document referred primarily to chapter VIII of the charter which regulates regional agreements. Czempiel wrote the following about chapter VI of the charter: "This chapter is underdeveloped and is hardly used" (Czempiel, 1994, p. 186.).

In existence conflicts should be resorted on military measures according to the charter only after failure of all peaceful means. (United Nations, Security Council, 1945: Art. 42.) This article was still exactly considered with Boutros-Ghali. It loses essence in the newer papers, however.

The summit in September 2005 did not produce the desired result as the new emphasize was put on the disarmament and the fight against the spread of weapons of mass destruction. A positive point was resolved, namely the foundation of the commission for peace consolidation which should take over the coordination of peace consolidation missions.

An important point which stretches through all papers is the possible legitimacy of the preventive war strategy. This would mean for UN that its principles (organ of the peace preservation and the collective security) would have to surrender (Horn, 2005). This direction would also contradict the demanded proposals in the areas of peace protection and peace consolidation.

The conversion of the proposals in the resulting document concerning peace keeping and peace consolidation is thin and tailored towards US politics. This is essentially do to the fact that the legitimacy of the military operations after the beginning of peacekeeping operations throws no good light on the United Nations. The goal of the United Nations should be to avoid armed hostilities and promote peaceful solutions. "Nevertheless just if UN should play a bigger role with the international military operations (which make sense excluding the proven form of the blue helmet missions [UN peace keeping or peace building operations]), the compatibility of such deployment with the valid international law and the UN charter would have to be able to be checked by an independent judicial authority. Nevertheless, such reforms are not planned up to now" (Strutynski, 2005).

If we take a look back on the different described negotiation theories and on the various agendas and papers of the United Nations, we can point out different role of the UN:

1. The role of a mediator
2. The role as a conflict party
3. The role as a peace builder to defuse conflict situations

As defined in the UN charter, the UN should hold the position of a strong and neutral mediator, to lead the conflict parties out of dangerous situations. In this assessment the basic approaches of all three theory, specified above, can be found. Especially the MHS and MEO, as the main elements of the ripeness theory could become more handling in the management of peace building and peace keeping because through this attempt the UN could lead the conflict parties to negotiation and therewith to peaceful solution.

The theory of multilateral negotiations is mainly a basic theoretical attempt for the UN. Although it may has shortcomings in the management of negotiations with many parties, it manifests the natural negotiating process for an international organization like the United Nations, and even if the UN have been blocked often in multilateral negotiations by its members, and also by its own system.

A cost-benefit analysis of conflicts should be carried out prior to deciding on conflict resolutions by the UN as well because a frequent accomplishment of sanctions as they may be imposed on in resolutions could lead to economic problems and radicalization of the stakeholders (e.g.: Israel-Palestine conflict).

The main regards of the transcend method is understanding the conflict history and promoting empathy for others, despite the awareness that interest conflicts at the centre of policy. For these reasons is the UN forced - as explained in the agendas and in the reform papers - to reconsider its present peace building and peace keeping approaches.

Also, the UN has not always the financial means to carry out sustainable peace building or peace keeping operations, but only emergency missions. For sustainable peace keeping, the ripeness theory as well as the transcend method connect the possible solutions for a conflict with a positive future - like MEO by Zartman and imagination of future by Galtung. Therefore the United Nations should focus in their peace building operations more on this elements (aspects of a positive future) than on military peace brought by armed troops.

A stronger leadership role of the United Nations is essential to its position in international policy making. In other words, it take on the challenges that come with its self-understanding as a principal agent in international policy making. This holds true even if the five permanent members are more capable independently from the international community. Joint efforts of the international community remain a desirable goal.

"The gap between necessity and sufficiency is in the hands of the negotiator himself to seize the ripe moment or ripen the moment yet unripe, to create a formula of justice that attracts both parties to an agreement, and to conduct a follow-trough strategy that will carry the agreement into acceptance and implementation. Concepts in negotiation only codify good practice, opening the way for skilled, committed negotiators who seek the end the conflict." (Zartman, 1998, 16.) In this short statement, Zartman points to the deficiencies of all theoretical negotiation approaches. As long the negotiator are not truly seeking for a peaceful solutions, as long all the conflict players are incapable of action, sustainable conflict resolution remains but a mere goal.

FUTURE RESEARCH DIRECTIONS

Negotiation vs. economic development: Even if these two terms are depending on each other's, it is conspicuous that the modern economic system relying on capitalism and on profit orientation are often obstacle peaceful conflict solution and even negotiations. Therefore, it is important to look the development of the capitalistic system and ask how it influences conflict development either in to peace or to armed hostilities.

Future questions should be on the economic, political and interests of the conflict parties, no matter in internal or international conflicts. Another focus should be on the adaptation of social system in developing and emerging countries so the risk of armed conflict could be reduced.

A research direction could spotlight the global movements in diplomacy, economic and politics and their dependency on each other. A crucial point hereby is the focus on cost-benefit analysis of the interdisciplinary fields and the influence of the so called industrialized countries on international conflict cases.

The role of the United Nations in conflict resolutions should be also a research field in the future, and how the position of the UN could become stronger in the diplomatic fields instead of member states of the UN play the role of a mediator. So, the UN could be a strong global player, after losing trust in most parts of the world through internal corruption and lack of transparency. Therefore, the discussion on a reform of the UN is necessary, because there cannot be a prevention of violence until the member states are using their legitimate use of force in their foreign policy.

REFERENCES

Alfredson, T., & Cungu', A. (2008). *Negotiation Theory and Practice: A review of literature*. Retrieved from http://www.fao.org/docs/up/easypol/550/4-5_negotiation_background_paper_179en.pdf

Brahm, E. (2003). *Hurting Stalemate Stage*. Retrieved from http://www.beyondintractability.org/essay/stalemate/

Campbell, J. (1976). *Successful Negotiation: Trieste*. Princeton: Princeton University Press.

Czempiel, E.-O. (1994). *Die Reform der UNO. Möglichkeiten und Missverständnisse*. München: Beck.

Friedman, G., & Himmelstein, J. (2013). *Konflikte fordern uns heraus. Mediation als Brücke zur Verständigung*. Frankfurt am Main: Wolfgang Metzner Verlag.

Galtung, J. (1969). Violence, peace and peace research. *Journal of Peace Research*, *6*(3), 167–191, Retrieved fromhttp://www.jstor.org/discover/10.2307/422690?uid=3737864&uid=2129&uid=2&uid=70&uid=4&sid=21105242745363. doi:10.1177/002234336900600301

Galtung, J. (1998). Konflikttransformation mit friedlichen Mitteln. *Die Methode der Transzendenz*. Retrieved from http://www.transcend.at/methode.html

Galtung, J. (2007). *Konflikte und Konfliktlösungen. Die Transcend-Methode und ihre Anwendung*. Berlin: Kai Homilius Verlag.

Hoadley, S. (1996). *The 1995 NPT Conference: An Application of Zartman's multilateral negotiation theory* (The Australian National University, Research School of Pacific Studies, Peace Research Centre: Working Paper 164) Canberra: National Library of Australia.

Horn, H. v. (2005). *Die Vereinten Nationen nach 60 Jahren: Ein Sanierungsfall? Mit Kriegseinsätzen zur neuen Welt-UN-Ordnung*. Retrieved from http://www.ag-friedensforschung.de/themen/UN-Reform/horn.html

Kant, I. (1795). *Perpetual Peace: A Philosophical Sketch*. Retrieved from https://www.mtholyoke.edu/acad/intrel/kant/kant1.htm

Murray, J. (1986). Understanding Competing theories of negotiation. Negotiation Journal, 1986(April). Retrieved from http://repository.law.ttu.edu/bitstream/handle/10601/1634/Negotiations.pdf?sequence=1

Pfetsch, F. R. (2006). *Verhandeln in Konflikten. Grundlage – Theorie – Praxis*. Wiesbaden: VS Verlag für Sozialwissenschaften.

Regan, P. (2000). *Third party interventions and the duration of interstate conflicts*. Retrieved from http://web.worldbank.org/archive/website01241/WEB/IMAGES/THIRDPAR.PDF

Strutynski, P. (2005). *UN-Reform – ein Schritt zurück*. Retrieved from http://www.ag-friedens-forschung.de/themen/UNO/reform5.html

UN-General Assembly. (2000). *Resolution 55/2: United Nations Millennium Declaration* Retrieved November 18, 2014, from http://www.un.org/millennium/declaration/ares552e.pdf

UN-General Assembly. (2005). *Resolution adopted by the General Assembly: 60/1. 2005 World Summit Outcome* – (A/60/L.1) Retrieved from http://www.un.org/womenwatch/ods/A-RES-60-1-E.pdf

UN-High-Level Panel on Threats. Challenges and Change (2004). *A more secure World: Our shared responsibility* (A/59/565). Retrieved from http://www.un.org/en/peacebuilding/pdf/historical/hlp_more_secure_world.pdf

UN-Secretary General - Annan. K., (2005). *In larger Freedom: Towards development, security and human rights for all* (A/59/2005) Retrieved from http://www.un.org/en/ga/search/view_doc.asp?symbol=A/59/2005

UN-Secretary General - Boutros-Ghali. (1992). *Report of the Secretary-General. An Agenda for Peace. Preventive diplomacy, peacemaking and peace keeping* (A/47/277-S/24111). Retrieved from http://www.unrol.org/files/a_47_277.pdf

UN-Secretary General - Boutros-Ghali. (1994). *Report of the Secretary-General. Agenda für Entwicklung* (A/48/935). Retrieved from https://www.globalpolicy.org/component/content/article/226-initiatives/32314-an-agenda-for-development-report-of-the-secretary-general.html

UN-Security Council. (2000). *Report of the Panel on United Nations Peace Operations. The Brahimi Report* A/55/305-S/2000/809. Retrieved from http://www.unrol.org/files/brahimi%20report%20peacekeeping.pdf

United Nations. (1945). *Charter of the United Nations: We the people of the United Nations... United for a better World*, Retrieved from http://www.unrol.org/files/UNcharter.pdf

Zartman, I. W. (1975). Negotiation: Theory and Reality. *Journal of International Affairs*, *29*(1), 69–77.

Zartman, I. W. (1997). Introduction: Toward the Resolution of International Conflicts. In I. W. Zartman, & J.L. Rasmussen. (Ed.), Peacemaking in international Conflict. Methods and Techniques. Washington, D.C.: United States Institute of Peace Press.

Zartman, I. W. (1999). *Negotiations as a Mechanism for Resolution in the Arab-Israeli conflict* (Davis Occasional Papers 72). Jerusalem: The Leonard Davis Institute for International Relations.

Zartman, I. W. (2001). The timing of peace initiatives: Hurting stalemates and ripe moments. *The Global Review of Ethnopolitics*, *1*(1), 8–18. doi:10.1080/14718800108405087

Zartman, I. W. (2004, September 2). *Mutually Exciting Opportunities and Durable Settlements.* Paper presented at the annual meeting of the American Political Science Association, Hilton Chicago and the Palmer House, Chicago, IL. Retrieved from http://www.allacademic.com/meta/p60174_index.html

Chapter 5
Reparations for Children and Youth:
A Peacebuilding Mechanism

Sinthya Rubio Escolar
Universidad Carlos III de Madrid, Spain

ABSTRACT

Violence against children and youth in war causes severe damage to individuals, communities and societies. This chapter aims to demonstrate the importance of reparations for children and youth as a peacebuilding mechanism in the context of transitional justice. On one hand, the chapter seeks to address reparations for children and youth understood as a political project, with a transformative and participatory potential for rebuilding societies and healing the wounds of those who have been affected by armed conflict. On the other hand, the paper attempts to overcome the conception of children and youth as passive victims, providing them with agency to become engaged political members in building peaceful societies. Thus, reparations should position them as subjects of rights, giving them voice as contributors in peacebuilding processes.

INTRODUCTION

Children and youth are amongst the most affected groups by armed conflicts. The brutalities committed against these groups pose enormous challenges to local and international communities aiming at ending tolerance for war and calling for accountability for human rights atrocities. Violence against children and youth in war causes severe damage to individuals, communities and societies. Transitional justice has been positioning itself in the international political and legal scene, as well as in the academic and professional sphere for already the past two decades. In this context, reparations programs are conceived as a political project based on rights and refer to the attempts to provide recognition and benefits directly to the victims of systematic abuses of human rights and international humanitarian law.

Nevertheless, the field of transitional, both in theory and practice, has frequently ignored children's and youths' views and interests and has paid extremely limited attention to their possible role in it. Aptel and Ladisch (2011) argue that this

DOI: 10.4018/978-1-4666-9675-4.ch005

failure is due to the disempowerment of children in a general, and of child and youth victims in particular, as a result of their lack of representation in and by political entities and civil society organizations. Indeed, it is important to recognize children and youth as rights holders. Failure to acknowledge crimes committed against them may reflect misperceptions regarding children and youth as political actors and agents (Mazurana & Carlson, 2009). Besides this, at least in theory, effective participation results in policies and public agendas that respond to the real needs and priorities of stakeholders, taking into account opinions and proposals of local communities (Laplante & Rivera, 2006).

The international human rights movement has been focusing on the instrumental value of a participatory approach to design, implementation and monitoring policies and programs. Transitional justice is not the exception, and here my interest does not lie simply in pointing out the importance of reparations, but also in how participatory reparations could contribute to the positioning of children and youth as peacemakers.

To overlook children and youth as part of sustainable peacebuilding mechanisms is self-defeating (Helsing, 2006). It is necessary to include young people in the political process so that they can move from a position of being disenfranchised to a position of sharing power (Cairns, McLernon, Moore & Hakvoort, 2006). Reparations for children and youth have a participatory and transformative potential - to heal the wounds (to the extent that they can) and to contribute to rebuilding societies.

My aim in this chapter, therefore, is to demonstrate the importance of reparations for children and youth as a peacebuilding mechanism in the context of transitional justice. On one hand, the chapter seeks to address reparations for children and youth understood as a political project which seeks recognition by means of participatory processes. On the other hand, the paper attempts to overcome the conception of children and youth as passive victims. To achieve this, this paper proposes to focus on the instrumental value of participation, based on the recognition of the right of the children to participate in the processes that affect them, providing them agency to become engaged political members in building peaceful societies. Accordingly, the proposed thesis is that reparations should be sensitive to address the realities of children and youth affected by war, positioning them as subjects of rights, giving them a voice and taking into account their role as contributors in peacebuilding processes.

BACKGROUND

Who Are Considered as Children and Youth?

Our world is not seen as an easy place for children (Farson, 1974). Nevertheless, there is no consensus about a proper definition of who are consider as children and youth; many authors agree that these categories are socially constructed, historically variable, and highly contestable (Dallaire, 2010; Farson, 1974; McEvoy-Levy, 2006; Singer, 2006; Wessels, 2007; Woodhead & Montgomery, 2003). In most cases, the label "adult" tends to mean competent, reliable, wise; whilst the labels "child" and "youth" mean incompetent, unreliable, and ignorant. Furthermore, the concept of childhood is inevitably linked to that of adulthood, and it is defined as "that which lacks the capacities, skills and powers of adulthood" (Archard, 1993, p.30). As Garbarino and Kostelny (1996) argue, there is a human relationship that unites children and adults, but there are important cognitive, linguistic, emotional, and physical differences that separate us.

In legal terms, according to the Convention on the Rights of the Child (CRC) a child means every human being below the age of eighteen years unless under the law applicable to the child, majority is attained earlier (1981, art.1). But children are more than a chronological category for analysis, intervention, protection, and care; they must be recognized as rights holders. The Convention calls for recognition and inclusion. Children's rights are important because they recognize the respect children are entitled to, as well as their dignity (Freeman, 2007). Likewise, inclusion refers to basic assumptions based on children's differences from adults and the discriminatory practices that can result from it (White, 2002).

If the distinction between child and adult is difficult, the definition of who is a youth is disputable.

According to the United Nations, youth is defined as those persons between the ages of 15 and 24 (United Nations, 1981). In western cultures, the term 'youth' refers to people in transition between childhood and adulthood. However, in some cultures a person may be considered an adult at the age of twelve or fourteen if they are married or have completed certain "rites of passage", such as in the case of some indigenous communities in Colombia, where the concept of the term 'adolescent' does not exist. Besides this, Wessells and Jonah (2006) argue that many African societies have an expansive conception of youth; in South Africa and Sierra Leone this term can include people up to their mid-thirties and forties.

The term 'youth' can encompass a lot in terms of age and experience (Borer, Darby & McEvoy-Levy, 2006). Most often, this label is synonymous with 'adolescents' or 'teenagers'. Experience says that identifying youth as a category for analysis and policy is complicated, due to the fact that youths are not a homogeneous entity either locally or globally (McEvoy-Levy, 2006). Despite the fact that children and youth are overlapping categories, this circumstance does not dispute their recognition as subjects of rights. Accordingly, the terms children and youth in this paper refer to those individuals between twelve and twenty five years old.

Children and Youth Affected by Armed Conflicts

A lot has been written about children and armed conflict but, above all, after Machel's 1996 report "Impact of armed conflict on children", which drew universal attention to the devastating effects war produces on children. Conflicts not only affect the children and youth physically, but also mentally and emotionally. If they are exposed either directly or indirectly to violence, their lives are interrupted, their social protection mechanisms are weakened and their vulnerability as well as the probabilities of a re-victimization in the future increases (Apfel & Simon, 1996; Barber, 2009; Cairns, 1996; Thomas & Wall, 2011; United Nations, 2006).

For instance, according to the Report from the Working Group on Children and Armed Conflict regarding the situation of children in the Syrian Arab Republic presented to the Security Council (2014); over 10.000 children have been killed; 5.500.000 children have been affected since March 2011 and up to 1 million children live under siege (UNICEF, 2014). The widespread violations of human rights and international humanitarian law by the Syrian authorities and armed groups committed against children include: recruitment and use of children; arbitrary arrest and detention; ill-treatment and torture; maiming; and sexual and gender-based violence.

On the other hand, the Colombian case is similar in victimization of children and youth but differs from the Syrian conflict in statistics and duration of the conflict. The country is in the midst of a half-century long conflict between the government, guerrillas and paramilitaries groups. Colombia's official register of armed conflict victims from 1985 onwards lists 7.392.679 victims, including 2.210.615 children and 1.241.655 young people (between 18 and 26 years old) for a total of 3.452.270 children and youth (Unidad para la

Atención y Reparación Integral a las Víctimas, 2015). Major victimizations suffered by children and youth are displacement, homicide, forced disappearance, recruitment and use of children, threats and sexual violence.

Fortunately, recent studies have not only focused on the victimization of children and youth but have also focused on their resilience. According to Kostelny (2006), children's level of resilience in war-torn countries depends on the balance of risk (stressful and traumatic events, vulnerability factors) and protective factors (family or community support). Therefore, the coping abilities demonstrated by children and youth in dealing with the impact of armed conflict on them are influenced by their social environment, such as families, peers, and communities. A general conclusion is that children and youth may be at once traumatized and resilient, victimized and agentive, vulnerable and empowered, individuals and members of communities (Thomas & Wall, 2011).

Moreover, as Siobhán McEvoy-Levy (2006) notes, "the experiences of young people in warfare around the world are highly variable and their pathways into violence different" (p.282). In the same way, victimization is different. Children and youth can be victims of direct violations such as torture, forced recruitment, abduction, sexual violence, maiming; or they may experience the violence committed against their caretakers, the tearing apart of their families and communities; as well as suffer the violation of their civil, political, social, economic and cultural rights (Ladisch & Ramírez-Barat, 2014). In this paper, I will not address the reparations for a specific type of victimization but for all children and youth affected by an armed conflict, this of course, in spite of acknowledging the need for an in-depth study per type of victimization.

Transitional Justice and Peacebuilding

For already two decades, transitional justice has been positioning itself in the international political and legal scene, as well as in the academic and professional sphere. Transitional justice makes reference to a set of measures designed to face the legacy of systematic violations of human rights and international humanitarian law, that has the aim of the administration of justice in a comprehensive manner and to promote reconciliation. Moreover, as Pablo de Greiff (2012) observes, is it indispensable that transitional justice measures (such as truth-seeking, criminal justice, reparations and institutional reforms) accomplish to recognize that "the other is the bearer of rights and therefore to engage in modes of redress that can not only assuage suffering but also to restore the rights that were so brutally violated and affirm victims' standing as full citizens" (p.43).

On the other hand, reparations attempt to promote justice, empower victims and preserve their dignity (Freedson, 2011). In the context of transitional justice, reparations are understood as a political project based on rights, and as an expression of a dignified message that is manifested in concrete terms, both material and symbolic, individual and collective. Similarly, reparations refer to the attempts to provide benefits directly to the victims, that is, sets of reparative measures with massive coverage (De Greiff, 2006). Reparations are about more than responding to the basic needs of victims (i.e. development programs), but to respond to the real impact of violations in victims' lives, and to acknowledge what happened to them (Correa, Guillerot & Magarrell, 2009) in the process of achieving justice (here I refer to a substantive conception of justice).

What do we understand by peace? Generally, peace is conceived as the absence of armed conflict or the antonym of war. Galtung (1996) finds two compatible definitions of peace: the absence or reduction of violence of all kinds, and non-violent and creative conflict transformation. Moreover, the concept of peace is understood in a large sense. As Jon Elster (2012) points out, it includes the notion of civic peace, which consists of a low level of criminal violence, some form of psychological healing, and the cooperation by public officials towards the post-transitional regime.

Given the consensus in the field, the task will not be to offer a novel definition of peacekeeping, peacemaking and peacebuilding. This tripartite conflict resolution strategy first emerged when Galtung (1976) in his work "Three Approaches to Peace: Peacekeeping, Peacemaking, and Peacebuilding", called for building infrastructure to promote sustainable peace by addressing the 'root causes' of violent conflict and supporting indigenous capacities for peace management and conflict resolution. However, it was after 1992 with Boutros-Ghali's landmark report "An Agenda for Peace" that these concepts entered into the mainstream.

On the one hand, peacemaking generally refers to the processes of diplomacy, negotiation, mediation or other forms of settlement to put an end to violent dispute and address the issues that led to it. On the other hand, peacekeeping is considered by United Nations (2008) as a technique designed to preserve the peace and to assist implementing agreements achieved by the peacemakers. The concept of a peacekeeping mission limited to strictly military tasks has evolved to a multidimensional model (military, police and civilian elements) to contribute to lay the foundations for sustainable peace.

Meanwhile, peacebuilding is understood as the reestablishment of the bonds that have been broken. Lederach (2007) defines it as "an array of processes, approaches, and stages needed to transform conflict towards more sustainable, peaceful relationships" (p.20). In this way, the measures to be implemented have as goals the establishing of peace, the prevention of the re-emerging of violence, strengthening the capacity for conflict management, and sustaining peace over the long-term by addressing the root causes and the consequences of conflict. In addition, peacebuilding requires a long-term commitment to addressing the underlying causes of conflict through both structural and relational transformation (Lederach, 2007). This can include building institutions, socioeconomic development, social reconstruction, community development, empowerment, reconciliation, mechanisms to address the past and developing effective governance (Hamber & Kelly, 2005).

Finally, there is a clear relationship between reparations and peacebuilding. Firchow and Ginty (2013) develop some interesting questions about whether reparations can produce a more sustainable and better quality peace. On the other hand, Brett and Malagon (2013) argue that emancipatory peacebuilding and reparation processes should seek to transform those structural conditions that represent the embedded root causes of conflict. Meanwhile, Lambourne (2009) proposes a model of transformative justice that supports sustainable peacebuilding. Hence, the fact that reparations form part of an effective transition to sustainable peace after an armed conflict is uncontested (Firchow & Ginty, 2013).

Reparations have a forward-looking aim in the sense that they can address past violations and contribute to prevent their recurrence, whilst also laying the foundations for a durable peace (Ladisch & Ramírez-Barat, 2014). Lambourne (2009) notes that analyzing and evaluating transitional justice (and its measures) with respect to its contribution to peacebuilding, enables a more holistic perspective that takes into account the expectations of conflict participants. Consequently, articulating reparations and peacebuilding efforts in a post-conflict context is fundamental for a comprehensive response to deal with gross human rights violations.

MAIN FOCUS OF THE CHAPTER

Reparations for Children and Youth

In terms of rights, the Convention on the Rights of the Child calls on States parties to "take all appropriate measures to promote physical and psychological recovery and social reintegration of a child victim of: any form of neglect, exploitation, or abuse; torture or any other form of cruel, inhuman or degrading treatment or punishment; or armed conflicts. Such recovery and reintegration shall take place in an environment which fosters the health, self-respect and dignity of the child" (United Nations, 1989, art.39).

In the same vein, the Guidelines on Justice in Matters Involving Child Victims (2005) recall the recognition of the rights of children and that "child victims should, wherever possible, receive reparation in order to achieve full redress, reintegration and recovery. Procedures for obtaining and enforcing reparation should be readily accessible and child-sensitive".

On the other hand, reparations programs (unlike reparation in international law that respond to judicial mechanisms that assess violations on a case-by-case basis that compensate victims in proportion to the harm suffered and can take the forms of restitution, compensation, rehabilitation, satisfaction and guarantees of nonrecurrence), are focused on victims' rights and well-being. These are state administrative programs with concrete measures aimed at dignifying victims as rights holders and designed for a massive coverage.

Reparations programs have as goals to provide structural and restorative elements to contribute to the process of reconciliation and the consolidation of peace (Firchow & Ginty, 2013). In the context of large scale political violence context, reparations are better understood as a political project based on rights, with the purpose of giving victims due recognition and to build up civic trust between citizens, and between citizens and state institutions (Rubio-Marín & De Greiff, 2007).

Reparations shall be effective, adequate and prompt. Furthermore, reparations for children and youth shall be transformative, participative and inclusive. I take the concept of transformative reparations from the authors Uprimny and Guzmán-Rodríguez (2010), who argues that in transitional scenarios, reparations should be understood not only as a mechanism to deal with past injustice, but as an opportunity to strive for a better future.

Having said this, there are further aspects of reparations for children and youth that should be considered. Notwithstanding the high level of victimization that children and youth experience in armed conflicts, they often do not see themselves as citizens whose rights have been violated. Reparations, like other transitional justice measures, send a message to those who were victimized as children in order for them to understand that what they suffered was a violation of rights instead of a normal incident or some form of punishment (Ladisch & Ramírez-Barat, 2014) and that their future role in society is based on rights, not violence (Aptel & Ladisch, 2011).

Therefore, the public message sent by the State to children and society through reparations is fundamental, since it demonstrates that the past occurrence cannot be tolerated any longer, that the state is offering the possibility of a future free from violence, and that there are the conditions for citizens to exercise their rights (Instituto Colombiano de Bienestar Familiar, 2013). Additionally, reparations for children and youth shall facilitate the possibility that their voices are heard and that they will be able to enrich history and provide a wider view of the impact that violations of rights have on society (Ladisch & Ramírez-Barat, 2014).

Here I will take De Greiff's normative conception of transitional justice (2012), to reaffirm how reparations for children and youth contribute to the promotion of justice, which provide recognition, and promote civic trust, reconciliation and democratization. As this author states, transitional justice measures, and in this case I make an emphasis on reparations programs, seek to provide recognition to victims; and this recognition means to seeing children and youth as rights-holders and citizens. For this reason, reparations for children and youth demonstrate that the "government has made a sufficiently serious commitment to justice that it is willing to invest resources and, in well-crafted programs, by giving beneficiaries the sense that the state has taken their interest to heart" (De Greiff, 2012, p.43). Regarding civic trust, as an aim reparations seek to attain, it refers to the trust between citizens (children and youth), as well as between the citizens and the State's institutions. Thus, reparations programs can foster civic trust in children and youth when they receive a concrete response derived from the responsibility of the state for the denial of their human rights.

To promote reconciliation and democratization are the final[1] goals of transitional justice (De Greiff, 2012). Reconciliation understood as the position in which citizens can trust to one another and have the possibility to think of a common future; meanwhile, the strengthening of democracy must be understood in the measure that it reinforce the rule of law through norm affirmation. Hence, reparations for children and youth can contribute to reconciliation as reconciliation is based on recognition and trust. To the same extent, reparations for children and youth must affirm their rights and positioning them as rights-bearers; representing a commitment to the rule of as reparations programs try to redress the violation of rights.

In a similar vein, as Mazurana and Carlson (2010) note, reparations at the national level can play an important role in strengthening societies' abilities to preserve the rights of children. In the same vein, grassroots reparations processes (which, of course, should be supported by the State), could more successfully heal the wounds of children, youth, families and communities, as well as contribute to rebuild the social fabric that was destroyed.

There are some obstacles towards establishing accountability for violations of children's rights in the context of armed conflicts as well as in the implementation of child-specific reparations. They involve the lack of political will, scarcity of resources, low technical capacity and low priority attention for children (Freedson, 2011). Fortunately, in recent years some publications focusing on transitional justice and children have been published,[2] and some actions have been taken, i.e. In Sierra Leone, UNICEF published a child-friendly version of the Truth and Reconciliation Commission Report. In Colombia, there is a child-friendly version of the Victims and Land Restitution Law "Déjala Volar" in an effort to explain the main features of the law. As Miano (2013) pointed out: "this may help build momentum for a reparative process focused on the long-term wellbeing of children after conflict" (p.41).

Children may be eligible for reparations both as individuals and as part of a group. Nevertheless, providing reparations to children is a relatively new development and involves a number of challenges (Freedson, 2011). It is important that reparations acknowledge children as rights bearers and citizens who suffered specific violations in light of their vulnerability (Aptel & Ladisch, 2011). It is also very important to consider the age of the victim at the time of the victimization, in order to understand its impact and possible reparative measures to take.

The needs, perspectives, realities and rights of children and youth should become a lens through which transitional justice and, more specific reparations define their objectives, modalities and results (Aptel & Ladisch, 2011). Therefore, access to education, employment, skills training, and options for positive roles in community life are some of the most urgent needs of youth moving out of war (Borer, Darby & McEvoy-Levy, 2006). The work with children and youth should be designed to give them hope, for them to move beyond the past and to look towards the future with a hopeful attitude (Helsing, 2006). Thus, children and youth need to be aware of the past in order to be able to play a constructive role in building the future (Aptel & Ladisch, 2011).

Finally, establishing a protective environment that includes networks of support is an important reparative mechanism for children and youth. Nosworthy (2009) argues that the most effective way to guide any interventions for children and youth is to encourage and assist families and communities to take responsibility for providing the necessary support and protection.

A Participatory and Continuous Process

The instrumental value of participation is indeed recognized in numerous areas of human rights law. This "participatory approach" is especially taken into account for the design, implementation and monitoring of human rights practices, policies and programs (Abregú, 2008). Similarly, Melish (2010) has analyzed the importance of participation with relation to the "new governance" and "new accountability" movements, which recognize participation as a fundamental part to effective public policy making.

Regarding children and youth, it is noteworthy that the three overarching principles in the CRC (non-discrimination, participation and best interest) must offer a normative framework and guideline for the implementation of reparations for children and youth. It is therefore necessary to bring the best interest of the child and non-discrimination principles to the forefront of action for a comprehensive approach of the participatory process. Thus, these principles are not simply instruments, but rather determine how to implement reparations. By doing so, children's rights it are put into perspective and are articulated with a transitional justice approach.

In socio-political scenarios, the exclusion of large parts of the population is an obstacle for democratization and reconciliation (Kemper, 2005). Generally, for ideological or pragmatic reasons, children and youth are excluded from social and political processes and institutions. In fact, as Borer pointed out children and youth are more likely than their elders to lack access to resources and essential services (Borer, Darby & McEvoy-Levy, 2006). Therefore, it is necessary to include them in these processes so that their position as marginal subjects changes to a position where they are empowered subjects that exercise, and learn how to exercise, their citizenship.

Here, I take the concept of participation used by Crisitán Correa and his colleagues (2009), which highlights three main components: effective participation (that recognizes complexity and builds capacity); information and knowledge that flow in two reciprocal directions; and meaningful and transparent impact. "Participation that is respectful, knowledgeable, and transparent, and that is achieved through effective forms of representation, allows victims to feel that they are valued and recognized as rights-holders under the law and as relevant actors in their society" (p.389).

Hence, participation is effective as a framework for the involvement of young people in activities that develop their potential. For young people, participation is a holistic mechanism to support their development and protection in the process of community engagement as well as to lay the foundations for a democratic society (UNICEF, 2004). Ladisch and Ramírez-Barat (2014) reaffirm that first-hand experience is essential for the promotion of engagement. They note that participation can contribute to build a sense of ownership and can help to develop the capacity of civic engagement of those allowed to participate.

Participation can help to foster resilience in children and youth, and make changes in their lives (O'Kane, 2009). Nevertheless, children and youth participation requires a long-term commitment to develop their capacities and achieve realistic goals. Meaningful participation and space to come together with their peers, to share their experiences and express their views can give them strength and increase their life skills, and self-confidence as well as reinforce their capacity for critical thinking and self-awareness as citizens (Ladisch & Ramírez-Barat, 2014).

Participation in their home, school and community is the most effective way to develop the potential of children and youth and increase their protection, especially during times of conflict (or post-conflict). Involving adolescents gives them the opportunity to express themselves and contribute their voice, opinions and ideas to the social dialogue, and understand that they are not part of the problem, but part of the solution (UNICEF, 2004).

Furthermore, the continuity of the process constitutes a major challenge for reparations. The efficacy of the reparations programs will depend, to a large extent, on the perception children and youth have regarding the attempts the state has made to redress the facts and its serious commitment with the process. Hence, for children and youth to trust institutions, and reparations programs implemented by them, they need to know and comprehend the process, and trust people involved in it. Therefore, reparations for children and youth cannot be merely isolated and fragmented actions; a continuous process with results is needed.

Reparations for Children and Youth as a Peacebuilding Mechanism

In this context, reparations are understood in a programmatic sense, involving children and youth as active participants in the design, implementation, monitoring and evaluation of reparations process. According to Nosworthy, restoring normality to young lives requires that actions aimed at addressing the legacies of conflict involve young people directly, including their active participation, allowing a better understanding of how they have been affected and how to design as well as and implement appropriate programs to assist them in dealing with the consequences of conflict (Nosworthy, 2009), in this case, reparations programs.

As reparations are best conceptualized as a political project based on rights (in this case, those that arise from the recognition of children and youth as subjects with rights) it is paramount when referring to reparations that they exercise their right to participation, listed in Article 12 of the Convention on the Rights of the Child, where it determines that children have the right to express their opinion freely in those matters that affect them, considering their age and maturity. It is essential to focus on the best interest of the child during participation processes and to take into account evolving capacities of children (Suchkova, 2011). Additionally, special efforts should be made to avoid re-traumatization of children and youth in the course of participation processes. The involvement of children in any participatory process should have the principle of the best interest of the child and should take into account international law in relation to children, including their right to be treated with dignity and compassion, the right to be protected from the hardships of the justice process and the right to privacy.

The challenges inherent in promoting and guaranteeing processes of participation are great and need to be carefully considered in implementing a participatory-focus to reparations (Laplante, 2012). For example, managing the expectations of victims, balancing interests of diverse groups of victims, establishing effective communication strategies, ensuring the safety of victims, ensuring that all relevant stakeholders are consulted, early outreach and sensitization on the reparations process and reaching the victims (Suchkova, 2011). Although the participation of victims in reparations is a complex undertaking (it can be staged, manipulated for political ends, and frustrated by unrealistic mechanisms), it has the potential to help reparations play an important role in the broader agenda of achieving justice and creating respect for human rights and democracy (Correa, Guillerot & Magarrell, 2009).

A participatory process creates a sense of local ownership of a reparations programs (Suchkova, 2011). Through this approach, participation becomes a concrete manifestation in the process but, at the same time, it can be a symbolic message with a reparative effect. As Laplante (2010) argues, the participatory approach constitutes an inherent reparative effect because it recognizes and treats the formerly marginalized as equal citizens under the law, a process that can restore dignity and empower the formerly voiceless.

Therefore, participation can itself become a guarantee of non-repetition, especially for children and youth, and play a role in institutional changes that allow societies learning from what happened and secure respect for human rights in the future (Correa, Guillerot & Magarrell, 2009). Also, participation of children and youth in defining and implementing reparations contributes to rebuilding social links within communities and protective environments which might have been destroyed as a result of the conflict (Suchkova, 2011). In addition, the more space for children and youth to take part in their design, the more participatory the activity will be. While direct experience and longer term involvement in the work of reparations is an excellent way to ensure an understanding of the process and its goals, the simple act of participating is in itself an important learning experience (Ladisch & Ramírez-Barat, 2014).

The intervention of children and youth may also contribute to linking their experiences with the rest of society, including government. Dialogue, consultation and exchange of information make it easier (Correa, Guillerot & Magarrell, 2009), in this case, for children and youth to feel recognized as full rights holders with the capacity to make proposals and contribute. Therefore, enabling participation concerning reparations gives children and youth citizen status and ultimately constitutes a form of political restitution (Laplante, 2012). I definitely agree with Laplante (2012) when she highlights that "the success of any transitional justice project rests greatly on it being perceived as legitimate by the public" (p.230). Consequently, reparations for children and youth will be more effective if they make sense to them and if the priorities respond to the real impacts in their lives and honour their realistic expectations (Correa, Guillerot & Magarrell, 2009).

Cairns and his colleagues mention to the impact of the peace process in Northern Ireland on children and youth, and emphasis that they may take part in telling these stories themselves and articulating their own experiences of conflict as a part of healing and envisioning a better future (Cairns, McLernon, Moore & Hakvoort, 2006). The participation of children and youth aims to empower them as citizens, to construct an effective "peace architecture" and enact visions of state, society and government that respond directly to their self-defined and specific needs, priorities and cultural values (Brett & Malagón, 2013). Additionally, here I reaffirm what Lambourne (2009) notes about the importance of involving local citizens in the development of transitional justice mechanisms that are consistent with needs, culture and local customs.

Thus, I propose reparations for children and youth as a peacebuidling mechanism. The argument is that reparations for children and youth can be used as a catalytic mechanism to reduce the factors that may violate their rights and, at the same time, to reaffirm their rights. I would like to emphasise how through participative reparations processes the historic discrimination and power imbalance faced by children and youth turns into participation, empowerment, recognition, decision-making opportunities and a platform for action. Accordingly, through reparations, children and youth can reinforce transformative capacities, reconciliation, guarantees of non-recurrence, conflict resolution initiatives, and therefore, strengthen democracy and become agents of peace. Consequently, reparations and peacebuilding entail long-term processes and the strengthening of democracy, thus reparations connect with peacebuilding.

In the same vein, Brett and Malagón did interesting research in *Overcoming the original sin of the "original condition:" How reparations may contribute to emancipatory peacebuilding,* arguing for a greater integration of reparations in peacebuilding and for a more transformative approach on the part of Transitional Justice agendas, with the purpose of transforming relationships, infrastructures and structural conditions which caused the conflict (Brett & Malagón, 2013). According to the authors, what they call "emancipatory peacebuilding" should be a set of long-term interrelated and deeply transformative processes oriented towards changing the relations of power and reducing structural exclusion, shaped and strengthened by local initiatives. Hence, transitional justice and peacebuilding become transformative when they focus on the principles of local participation and empowerment (Lambourne, 2009).

There are significant ways in which reparations can contribute to reconciliation through symbolic and transformative mechanisms for healing and reconstruction (Firchow & Ginty, 2013). As Ramírez-Barat (2012) emphasizes, working with younger generations on transitional justice measures is essential to building democratic societies. At a crucial moment in the political history of a country, the direct involvement of children and youth in transitional justice and reparations processes can contribute to building children and youth's understanding of human rights as well as their capacity for active citizenship.

Children and Youth as Peacebuilders

Agency

Although children and youth represent a considerable proportion of the population in any country, they have little or no participation in social and political processes. Even when they are rights bearers, they are not considered as civil society actors. When they feel that their views and perspectives are taken into account, when their needs and concerns are addressed, and when they have the opportunity to exercise their rights, they will position themselves as political agents in society.

I would like to emphasise that agency gives meaning to reparations. Only through participation will children and youth can feel that they are in a process that means something and that it is valuable for them. In such cases, the agency (understood as the capacity to carry out actions with an intention) must also be understood as the possibility to give voice to the children and youth and transform, in a way, the identity of victims to one of active agents and members of the political community that assume a role as contributors in the processes of peacebuilding.

As mentioned before, children and youth are fundamental actors in contributing to the guarantees of non-recurrence. They need to hear the message "never again", they need to observe that there is an acknowledgement of the harm they suffered, perceive that certain institutions are accountable for what happened, to envision a different future, a vision of peace and to nurture their capacity for agency (Ladisch & Ramírez-Barat, 2014). Political engagement will provide them with practice in power sharing, developing skills and values essential to a sustainable peace (McEvoy-Levy, 2006). Consequently, they may move from a position of being disenfranchised to sharing power (Cairns, McLernon, Moore & Hakvoort, 2006).

One clear idea is that there cannot be peace if children and young people are excluded. They can be peacemakers in many ways, through conflict resolution mechanisms, sensitization of children's rights, development of technical skills, community based processes of reconciliation, and the recovery of traditional values that allow them to transform their realities and relationships. Therefore, excluding children and youth not only runs the risk of jeopardizing peace but also deprives societies of "a potential driving force for peace and development" (Ladisch & Ramírez-Barat, 2014, p.182).

A youth perspective helps to perceive a more complete picture of the dynamics of conflict reproduction and transformation, as well as the challenge of reconciliation (McEvoy-Levy, 2006). Along the same lines, it is essential to understand the link between opportunity (economic, education) and children and youth believing in a better future as well as in a sustainable peace and their motivation to invest in them (Helsing, 2006). Otherwise, it will not make sense for them to support peace and they could try to change the status quo by violent means. Unfortunately, very often children and young people are marginalized by their leaders, their societies and by the peace processes (Helsing, 2006) and here reparations with a participatory approach may play a crucial role.

During armed conflicts, the political awareness of adolescents is likely to be very high. Due to the violence and injustice they face, young people may feel forced to take action (UNICEF, 2004). Therefore, young people should be "supported as peace constituencies because they can both promote peace but also endanger it" (Kemper, 2005, p.38). In other words, youth symbolize a dual identity, they may be potential threats to peace and important peacebuilding resources.

Identity

In the book *In the Name of Identity: Violence and the Need to Belong* by Amin Maalouf (2004), the author notes that identity is not a one-time subject, but something that continues building and transforming throughout our lives. Therefore, young people - whether victims, perpetrators, bystanders, street fighters, war orphans, rioters, refugees, homeless persons, family heads, rights activists, students, ex-combatants, or peacemakers, are all survivors (McEvoy-Levy, 2006).

The tendency is to depict children as victims and youth as perpetrators. But young people are more than that. We need to move beyond the concept of these groups are vulnerable or spoilers, receivers of protection and care, but we need to start seeing them as contributors and active citizens with diverse realities, and especially, as subjects with rights. The state, society and communities have to visualize youth in their roles related to peace rather than restrict them to their roles during war (Kemper, 2005). Thus, the agency turns into the possibility of transforming "militarized" identities, with which most of the youth are labeled in most of today's armed conflicts, to that of social actors with capacities for peacebuilding. In this way, reparations with a participatory approach could send a powerful message which challenges the victim perpetrator dichotomy by giving young people the chance of overcoming violence and hate on their own initiative (Kemper, 2005).

As a final point, children and youth are passive agents of conflict transformation when they are the *raison d'etre* of peace efforts, but they can become active peacemakers. They are citizens who have their own point of view that they need spaces and mechanisms to help articulate their voices (Ladisch & Ramírez-Barat, 2014). Viewing young people only as victims minimizes their capacities; in their process of reparations, to overlook the other roles they can play such as being resilient persons, social actors in post-conflict reconstruction and potential agents for change, could jeopardize the chance to achieve a durable peace.

SOLUTIONS AND RECOMMENDATIONS

At this point, I would like to highlight my argument regarding the role children and youth may play in participatory reparations and how this process may function as a peacebuilding mechanism. It is important to reaffirm that adult support to young people's contributions to peacebuilding is a must. Additionally, failure to take into account experiences of children and youth wastes the capacity and potential of young people to be a catalyst for change, for reconciliation and for peacebuilding in their communities (Aptel & Ladisch, 2011).

Reparations as a peacebuilding mechanism can take advantage from youths' considerable independence from traditional structures and help them find their role in communities. Moreover, young people may have less of an interest in maintaining the status quo than their adult counterparts, having more incentives for change. As Galtung (2006) argues, a "very strong point for youth would be creativity coming from their less closed, more open mind" (p.274). Therefore, reparations should take advantage of youth's typical characteristics such as their entrepreneurial spirit, their creativity, and their search for meaning (Kemper, 2005). Their energy, enthusiasm, resilience and strong desire for justice and peace can be valuable in peacebuilding efforts (UNICEF, 2004).

Finally, I mention Lederach's *Moral Imagination* (2005) to emphasise the potential of children and youth to become peacemakers. Moral imagination is all about innovation, and it implies the ability to imagine a collective world, a world that includes "us" but also includes "them"; it is the capacity to see what does not yet exist. As the author argues, the challenge is how "to invoke, set free, and sustain innovative responses to the roots of violence while rising above it" (p.172). Therefore, it is necessary to find ways to nurture a questioning capacity that explores and interacts constructively with the complex relationships and realities that face communities (p.173).

Consequently, who better than young people should assume this challenging role? As pointed out by Drummond-Mundal and Cave (2006): "social and political inclusion of children, in particular youth, in conflict transformation and peacebuilding makes pragmatic and constructive sense. These young people may have experience and capacities that can either work for or against new social and political constructions. For peace to be sustainable, the adults of tomorrow need to feel a sense of ownership and responsibility for the creation and maintenance of a climate of peace". Finally, as Galtung (2006) notes, to be young is to have less past and more future, less trauma suffered and more hope. Youth may well be our best protection against further deterioration towards total war.

FUTURE RESEARCH DIRECTIONS

There is a need to pay more attention to the reparations processes for children and youth. This field is practically underexplored. Despite the growing field of transitional justice, very little research has addressed reparations for these groups. Children and youth as victims, and as vulnerable groups, are not always given sufficient attention during and after conflict.

More work is clearly needed in this area, giving the lack of knowledge on how reparations programs and measures could impact the lives of children and youth, provide real benefits to them, and what are the institutional and material challenges for its effective implementation. Consistent and rigorous evaluations of reparations programs impact will be at the heart of efforts to provide an accurate answer for war-affected children and youth. Transitional justice researchers, practitioners, and policy professionals face the challenge of moving towards a better understanding of children and youth as subjects of rights and as social actors. In this way, there is an urgent need to design and implement particular strategies and mechanisms for children and youth to address their reparation.

Furthermore, the role of children and youth in reparations processes has been non-existent. It is needed to go deeper into certain concepts such as participation, agency, transformative potential, identity, empowerment and citizenship, all of which contribute to reparations and connect it to peacebuilding. In this respect, this subject requires a more expansive understanding of the participatory role that children and youth can play in reparations and its effects on peacebuilding.

Additionally, more research about the role that reparations may play in peacebuilding is needed. Despite the growing debate, Firchow and Ginty

(Firchow & Ginty, 2013) note that literature on transitional justice and peacebuilding is relatively compartmentalized and that there is little crossover between the two; these authors also raise the question about whether reparations can produce a more sustainable and better quality peace. Thus, the complex nature of the impact of armed conflict on children and youth calls for comprehensive approaches to post-conflict interventions and to pay more attention to each other's perspective.

CONCLUSION

In 2004, the United Nations Secretary-General issued the first report on The Rule of Law and Transitional Justice in Conflict and Post-Conflict Societies (United Nations, 2004); in this document the rebuilding of the rule of law and transitional justice mechanisms were articulated and connected to post-conflict peacebuilding. Reparations, participation, self-agency, empowerment, respect for human rights and democratic values are at the core of this proposal.

Young people can be dynamic and active agents in their process of reparations, as well as in the other transitional justice mechanisms. Furthermore, children and youth can contribute in a myriad of ways to peacebuilding through rebuilding social relationships, supporting a culture of peace through conflict resolution mechanism, being a source of resilience for their communities and engaging in local based initiatives of reconciliation.

Unfortunately, for ideological or pragmatic reasons, children and youth are excluded from social and political processes and institutions. Reparations for children and youth must be understood as a political project based on the rights that arise from the recognition of children and youth as subjects with rights. Therefore, it is necessary to include them in these processes so that their position as marginal subjects changes to empowered subjects who are able to exercise, and learn how to exercise, their citizenship. Thus, reparations for children and youth have a participatory and transformative potential, to heal wounds as much as possible, and to contribute to the rebuilding societies.

Unless young people who are affected by armed conflicts are provided with positive alternatives, they will be more likely to perpetuate violence. The value of participation, either instrumental or intrinsic, creates a space for children and youth to reaffirm their condition as rights holders and citizens. For children and youth a participatory reparations program will provide a sense of ownership; the agency will give meaning to the process, and the participatory approach will constitute a reparative effect itself. In this way, a participatory reparations program will make sense to children and youth, will create understanding of the process and its goals, and fulfill their expectations.

For this reason, participatory reparations for children and youth become a mechanism to provide agency and the opportunity to transform their identities, above all, to one of peacemakers. In conclusion, thinking of children and youth as peacemakers pose the challenge of sharing power, which means adults to willingly give power up, in order for children and youth to assume leading roles in reparations and in the peacebuilding process.

REFERENCES

Abregú, M. (2008). Human Rights for All: From the Struggle against Authoritarianism to the Construction of an All-Inclusive Democracy - A View from the Southern Cone and Andean Region. *Sur International Journal of Human Rights*, *5*(8), 7–41.

Afpel, R., & Simon, B. (Eds.). (1996). *Minefields in their hearts. The mental health of children in war and communal violence*. New Haven: Yale University Press.

Aptel, C., & Ladisch, V. (2011). *Through a new lens: a child-sensitive approach to transitional justice*. New York: International Center for Transitional Justice.

Archard, D. (1993). *Children. Rights and childhood*. New York: Routledge.

Barber, B. (Ed.). (2009). *Adolescents and war. How youth deal with political violence*. New York: Oxford University Press. doi:10.1093/acprof:oso/9780195343359.001.0001

Borer, T. A., Darby, J., McEvoy-Levy, S., & RIREC Project on Post-Accord Peace Building. (2006). *Peacebuilding after peace accords: The challenges of violence, truth, and youth*. Notre Dame, Ind: University of Notre Dame Press.

Brett, R., & Malagón, L. (2013). Overcoming the original sin of the "original condition:" How reparations may contribute to emancipatory peacebuilding. *Human Rights Review (Piscataway, N.J.), 14*(3), 257–271. doi:10.1007/s12142-013-0271-5

Cairns, E. (1996). *Children and political violence*. Cambridge: Blackwell Publishers.

Cairns, E., McLernon, F., Moore, W., & Hakvoort, I. (2006). The impact of the peace process in Northern Ireland on children's and adolescents' ideas about war and peace. In S. McEvoy-Levy (Ed.), *Troublemakers or Peacemakers? Youth and post-accord peace building* (pp. 117–138). Notre Dame, IN: University of Notre Dame Press.

Correa, C., Guillerot, J., & Magarrell, L. (2009). Reparations and victim participation: a look at the Truth Commission Experience. In C. Ferstman (Ed.), *M. Goetz., & A. Stephens. Reparations for victims of genocide, war crimes and crimes against humanity. Systems in place and Systems in the Making* (pp. 383–414). The Netherlands: Martinus Nijhoff Publishers. doi:10.1163/ej.9789004174498.i-576.103

Dallaire, R. (2010). *They fight like soldiers they die like children. The global quest to eradicate the use of child soldiers*. New York: Walker & Company.

De Greiff, P. (2006). Justice and Reparations. In P. De Greiff (Ed.), *The Handbook of Reparations* (pp. 451–477). New York: Oxford University Press. doi:10.1093/0199291926.003.0013

De Greiff, P. (2012). Theorizing Transitional Justice. In M. Williams, R. Nagy, & J. Elster (Eds.), Transitional Justice (pp.31-77). New York: New York University Press.

Drummond-Mundal, L., & Cave, D. (2006). Children as the seeds of peace: Exploring children's potential contribution to conflict transformation and peacebuilding. Draft submitted to *The Journal of Peacebuilding and Development*. (Unpublished manuscript).

Elster, J. (2012). Justice, Truth, Peace. In M. Williams, R. Nagy, & J. Elster (Eds.), Transitional Justice (pp.78-97). New York: New York University Press.

Farson, R. (1974). *Birthrights*. New York: Macmillan Publishing Co., Inc.

Firchow, P., Ginty, R., & M., (2013). Reparations and Peacebuilding: Issues and Controversies. *Human Rights Review (Piscataway, N.J.), 14*(3), 231–239. doi:10.1007/s12142-013-0275-1

Freedson, J. (2011). *Bridging the accountability gap: new approaches to addressing violations against children in armed conflict*. Cambridge: Conflict Dynamics International.

Freeman, M. (2007). Why it remains important to take children's rights seriously. *International Journal of Children's Rights, 15*(1), 5–23. doi:10.1163/092755607X181711

Galtung, J. (1976). Three realistic approaches to peace: Peacekeeping, peacemaking and peacebuilding. *Impact of Science on Society*, *26*, 103–115.

Galtung, J. (1996). *Peace by Peaceful Means: Peace and Conflict, Development and Civilization*. London: SAGE Publications Ltd.

Galtung, J. (2006). Theoretical challenges of peace building with and for youth. In S. McEvoy-Levy (Ed.), *Troublemakers or Peacemakers? Youth and post-accord peace building* (pp. 259–279). Notre Dame, IN: University of Notre Dame Press.

Garbarino, J., & Kostelny, K. (1996). What do we need to know to understand children in war and community violence? In R. Afpel, & B. Simon (Eds.), Minefields in their hearts. The mental health of children in war and communal violence. New Haven: Yale University Press.

Hamber, B., & Kelly, G. (2005). A place for reconciliation? Conflict and locality in Northern Ireland. *Democratic Dialogue*, Report 18.

Helsing, J. (2006). Young people's activism and the transition to peace. Bosnia, Northern Ireland and Israel. In S. McEvoy-Levy (Ed.), *Troublemakers or Peacemakers? Youth and post-accord peace building* (pp. 195–216). Notre Dame, IN: University of Notre Dame Press.

Instituto Colombiano de Bienestar Familiar. (2013). *Reparación con sentido. Guía pedagógica*. Bogotá: Author.

Kemper, Y. (2005). *Youth in war to peace transitions. Approaches of International Organizations*. Berlin: Berghof Research Center for Constructive Conflict Management.

Kostelny, K. (2006). A culture-based, integrative approach. Helping war-affected children. In N. Boothby, A. Strang, & M. Wessells (Eds.), *A world turned upside down. Social ecological approaches to children in war zones* (pp. 19–38). United States of America: Kumarian Press, Inc.

Ladisch, V., & Ramirez-Barat, C. (2014). Between Protection and Participation: Involving Children and Youth in Transitional Justice Processes. In C. Ramirez-Barat (Ed.), *Transitional Justice, culture and society. Beyond outreach* (pp. 173–210). New York: Social Science Research Council.

Lambourne, W. (2009). Transitional Justice and Peacebuilding after mass violence. *The International Journal of Transitional Justice*, *3*(1), 28–48. doi:10.1093/ijtj/ijn037

Laplante, L. (2010). Evaluating Truth Commissions and Reparations through the Eyes of Victims. *L'observateur des Nations Unies*, *28*(1), 167–176.

Laplante, L. (2012). Negotiating reparations rights: The participatory and symbolic quotients. *Buffalo Human Rights Law Review*, *19*, 217–250.

Lederach, J. (1997). *Building Peace: Sustainable Reconciliation in Divided Societies*. Washington, DC: United States Institute of Peace.

Lederach, J. (2005). *Moral Imagination: the art and soul of building peace*. New York: Oxford University Press. doi:10.1093/0195174542.001.0001

Maalouf, A. (2004). *Identidades asesinas* (F. Villaverde, Trans.). Madrid: Alianza Editorial.

Mazurana, D., & Carlson, K. (2009). Reparations as a Means for Recognizing and Addressing Crimes and Grave Rights Violations against Girls and Boys during Situations of Armed Conflict and under Authoritarian and Dictatorial Regimes. In R. Rubio-Marín (Ed.), *The Gender of Reparations: Unsettling Sexual Hierarchies While Redressing Human Rights Violations* (pp. 162–214). Cambridge: Cambridge University Press. doi:10.1017/CBO9780511596711.007

Mazurana, D., & Carlson, K. (2010). *Children and reparation: past lessons and new directions*. Innocenti Working Paper, UNICEF, Florence.

McEvoy-Levy, S. (2006). Introduction: youth and the post-accord environment. In S. McEvoy-Levy (Ed.), *Troublemakers or Peacemakers? Youth and post-accord peace building* (pp. 1–26). Notre Dame, IN: University of Notre Dame Press.

McEvoy-Levy, S. (2006). Conclusion. Youth and post-accord peace building. In S. McEvoy-Levy (Ed.), *Troublemakers or Peacemakers? Youth and post-accord peace building* (pp. 281–305). Notre Dame, IN: University of Notre Dame Press.

Melish, T. (2010). Maximum Feasible Participation of the Poor: New Governance, New Accountability, and a 21st Century War on the Sources of Poverty. *Yale Human Rights and Development Law Journal, 13*(1), 1–134.

Miano, M. (2013). Toward a Child-Oriented Approach to Reparations: Reflecting on the Rights and Needs of Child Victims of Armed Conflict. *PRAXIS The Fletcher Journal of Human Security, 28*, 28–45.

Nosworthy, D. (Ed.). (2009). *Seen, but not Heard: Placing Children and Youth on the Security Governance Agenda*. Zurich: LIT Verlag.

O'Kane, C., Feinstein, C., & Giertsen, A. (2009). In D. Nosworthy (Ed.), *Seen, but not Heard: Placing Children and Youth on the Security Governance Agenda* (pp. 259–286). Zurich: LIT Verlag.

Ramírez-Barat, C. (2012). *Engaging children and youth in transitional justice processes: guidance for outreach programs*. New York: International Center for transitional Justice.

Rubio-Marín, R., & De Greiff, P. (2007). Women and reparations. *The International Journal of Transitional Justice, 1*(3), 318–337. doi:10.1093/ijtj/ijm035

Singer, P. W. (2006). *Children at war*. Berkeley: University of California Press.

Suchkova, M. (2011). *The importance of a participatory reparations process and its relationships to the principles of reparation (Reparations Unit, Briefing Paper No.5)*. Colchester: University of Essex.

Thomas, D., & Wall, J. (Eds.). (2011). *Children and armed conflict. Cross-disciplinary investigations*. Great Britain: Palgrave Macmillan.

UNICEF. (2004). *Adolescent programming experiences during conflict and post-conflict. Case studies*. New York: Author.

UNICEF. (2014). *Under Siege. The devastating impact on children of three years of conflict in Syria*. New York: Author.

Unidad para la Atención y Reparación Integral a las Víctimas. (2015). *Registro Único de Víctimas*. Retrieved from http://www.unidadvictimas.gov.co/index.php/en/

United Nations. (1981). *Secretary-General's Report to the General Assembly, (A/36/215)*. New York: Author.

United Nations. (1989). *Convention on the Rights of the Child, (Adopted by General Assembly Resolution 44/25)*. New York: Author.

United Nations. (1996). Impact of armed conflict on children (Report from the expert of the Secretary-General Graça Machel, (General Assembly resolution A/51/306). New York: Author.

United Nations. (2004). *The rule of law and transitional justice in conflict and post-conflict societies: Report of the Secretary-General to the Security Council, (S/2004/616)*. New York: Author.

United Nations. (2005). *Guidelines on justice in matters involving child victims and witnesses of crime, (Ecosoc Resolution 2005/20)*. New York: Author.

United Nations. (2008). *United Nations Peace-keeping Operations. Principles and Guidelines*. New York: Author.

United Nations. (2014). *Working Group on Children and Armed Conflict. Conclusions on children and armed conflict in the Syrian Arab Republic, (S/AC.51/2014/4)*. New York: Author.

Uprimny, R., & Guzmán-Rodríguez, D. (2010). En búsqueda de un concepto transformador y participativo para las reparaciones en contextos transicionales. *International Law: Revista Colombiana de Derecho Internacional, 17*, 231–286.

Wessells, M. (2007). *Child soldiers: From violence to prevention*. Boston: Harvard University Press.

Wessells, M., & Jonah, D. (2006). Recruitment and reintegration of former youth soldiers in Sierra Leone. Challenges of reconciliation and post-accord peace building. In S. McEvoy-Levy (Ed.), *Troublemakers or Peacemakers? Youth and post-accord peace building* (pp. 27–47). Notre Dame, IN: University of Notre Dame Press.

White, S. (2002). Being, becoming and relationship: Conceptual challenges of a child rights approach in development. *Journal of International Development, 14*(8), 1095–1104. doi:10.1002/jid.950

Woodhead, M., & Montgomery, H. (Eds.), (2003) Understanding childhood: an interdisciplinary approach. United Kingdom: John & Sons Ltd.

ADDITIONAL READINGS

Barash, D. P. (2000). *Approaches to peace. A reader in peace studies*. New York: Oxford University Press.

Barber, B., & Doty, S. B. (2013). How can a majority be resilient? Critiquing the utility of the construct of resilience through a focus on youth in contexts of political conflict. In C. Fernando, & M. Ferrari (Eds.), Handbook of resilience in children of war (pp. 233-252). Toronto: Springer. doi:10.1007/978-1-4614-6375-7_17

Birchall, E., Francq, E., & Pijnenburg, A. (2011). C. Sandoval (Ed.), The International Criminal Court and Reparations for Child Victims of Armed Conflict. Colchester: University of Essex.

Ciurlizza, J. (2012). And the children learned not to cry: stories about children and transitional justice in Latin America. In I. Derluyn, C. Mels, S. Parmentier, & W. Vandenhole (Eds.), Re-Member. Rehabilitation, reintegration and reconciliation of war-affected children (pp.105-126). Cambridge: Intersentia.

Cole, E., & Murphy, K. (2011). History Education Reform, Transitional Justice, and Transformation of Identities. In P. Arthur (Ed.), *Identities in Transition*. New York: Cambridge University Press.

Del Felice, C., & Wisler, A. (2007). The Unexplored Power and Potential of Youth as Peacebuilders. *Journal of Peace Conflict & Development, 11*, 1–29.

Fisher, K. (2013). *Transitional Justice for Child Soldiers. Accountability and Social Reconstruction in Post-Conflict Contexts. Rethinking Peace and Conflict Studies Series*. London: Palgrave Macmillan.

Hancock, L. (2013). Zones of peace. In R. M. Ginty (Ed.), *Routledge handbook of peacebuilding* (pp. 237–248). Oxon: Routledge.

Kostelny, K., & Wessells, M. (2013). Child friendly spaces: promoting children's resiliency amidst war. In C. Fernando, & M. Ferrari (Eds.), Handbook of resilience in children of war (pp. 119-130). Toronto: Springer. doi:10.1007/978-1-4614-6375-7_9

Ladisch, V. (2013). Children and youth participation in transitional justice processes. *Journal of the History of Childhood and Youth*, *6*(3), 505–513. doi:10.1353/hcy.2013.0040

Magid, B., & Boothby, N. (2013). Promoting resilience in children of war. In C. Fernando, & M. Ferrari (Eds.), Handbook of resilience in children of war (pp.39-50). Toronto: Springer. doi:10.1007/978-1-4614-6375-7_4

Mani, R. (2002). The three dimensions of justice in post-conflict peacebuilding. In R. Mani (Ed.), *Beyond retribution. Seeking justice in the shadows of war* (pp. 3–22). Cambridge: Polity Press.

McEvoy-Levy, S. (2013). Youth. In R. M. Ginty (Ed.), *Routledge handbook of peacebuilding* (pp. 296–308). Oxon: Routledge.

McKay, S., Veale, A., Worthen, M., & Wessells, M. (2011). Building meaningful participation in reintegration among war-affected young mothers in Liberia, Sierra Leone and northern Uganda. *Intervention (Amstelveen, Netherlands)*, *9*(2), 108–124. doi:10.1097/WTF.0b013e328348dfe7

Olson, K. (2004). Children in the Grey Spaces Between War and Peace: the Uncertain Truth of Memory Acts. In J. Boyden & J. De Berry (Eds.), *Children and Youth on the Front Line: Ethnography, Armed Conflict and Displacement*. Oxford: Berghahn Books.

Parmar, S., Roseman, M., Siegrist, S., & Sowa, T. (2010). *Children and Transitional Justice. Truth-Telling, Accountability and Reconciliation. Human Rights Program Series*. Cambridge: Harvard University Press.

Paulson, J. (2011). *Education and Reconciliation. Exploring Conflict and Post-Conflict Situations. Education as a Humanitarian Response*. London: Continuum International Publishing Group.

Pells, K. (2012). "We have life without living": addressing the legacies of genocide for Rwanda's children and youth. In I. Derluyn, C. Mels, S. Parmentier, & W. Vandenhole (Eds.), Re-Member. Rehabilitation, reintegration and reconciliation of war-affected children (pp. 153-184). Cambridge: Intersentia.

Pruitt, L. (2008). They Drop Beats, Not Bombs: Music and Dance in Youth Peace-Building. *Australian Journal of Peace Studies*, *3*, 14–32.

Quénivet, N. (2014). Transitional and Generational Justice: Children Involved in Armed Conflicts. In N. Szablewska & S. Bachmann (Eds.), *Current Issues in Transitional Justice: Towards a More Holistic Approach (Springer Series in Transitional Justice)* (pp. 55–81). London: Springer.

Sarkin, J. (2012). Integrating Transitional Justice and Disarmament, Demobilisation and Reintegration: The need to achieve rehabilitation, reintegration and reconciliation for child soldiers and child victims of enforced disappearances. In I. Derluyn, C. Mels, S. Parmentier, & W. Vandenhole (Eds.), Re-Member. Rehabilitation, reintegration and reconciliation of war-affected children (pp. 77-101). Cambridge: Intersentia.

UNICEF. (2010). *Children and Truth Commissions*. Innocenti Research Center, International Center for Transitional Justice, Florence.

United Nations. (2011). *Children and Justice during and in the aftermath of armed conflict* (Working Paper No.3). Office of the Special Representative of the Secretary General for Children and Armed Conflict, New York.

United Nations Development Programs. (2006). *Youth and violent conflict. Society and development in crisis?* New York: Author.

Weyns, Y. (2012). On children's rights and wrongs: the challenges for a rights-based approach to reintegration. In I. Derluyn, C. Mels, S. Parmentier, & W. Vandenhole (Eds.), Re-Member. Rehabilitation, reintegration and reconciliation of war-affected children (pp.533-556). Cambridge: Intersentia.

KEY TERMS AND DEFINITIONS

Agency: The capacity to carry out actions with an intention. The capacity children and youth have to make their own free choices. In the context of this chapter must also be understood as the possibility to give voice to the children and youth in political and social processes.

Children: In legal terms, according to the Convention on the Rights of the Child, a child means every human being below the age of eighteen years unless under the law applicable to the child, majority is attained earlier. But children are more than a chronological category for analysis, intervention, protection, and care; they must be recognized as rights holders.

Participation: A process in which children and youth get involve in social and political processes and institutions. Through participation is recognized the capacity and value that children and youth have to contribute to society, as well as is develop their potential.

Peacebuilding: Is understood as the reestablishment of the human and systemic bonds that have been broken. The measures to be implemented for peacebuilding have as goals establish peace, prevent violence re-emerging, strengthening capacity for conflict management and sustain peace over the long-term.

Reparations: In the context of transitional justice, are understood as a political project based on rights, and as an expression of a dignified message that is manifested in concrete terms. In this context, refers to massive programs that distribute different benefits. These may include material and symbolic reparations and can be distributed individually or collectively.

Transitional Justice: A set of judicial and non-judicial measures designed to face the legacy of systematic abuse of human rights and international humanitarian law, that has the aim of the administration of justice in a comprehensive manner and promote reconciliation. These measures include criminal prosecutions, truth seeking mechanisms, reparations programs, and different kinds of institutional reforms.

Youth: This term can include a lot in terms of age and experience. Most often, this category is synonymous with 'adolescents' or 'teenagers'. Identifying youth as a category for analysis and policy is complicated, due to the fact that youths are not a homogeneous group. Accordingly, in the context of this paper, I use the terms children and youth to refer to those individuals between twelve and twenty five years old.

ENDNOTES

1 Here the term final refers to distance (not in time) but in causal chains. When De Greiff makes reference to "final goals" indicates that its realization depends upon the contribution of a larger number of factors. The author classifies the aims in two axes: (1) the number of intervening factors, and (2) their relative importance in bringing about the desired results. See De Greiff, P. (2012). Theorizing Transitional Justice. In M. Williams., R. Nagy., & J. Elster (Eds.). *Transitional Justice*. (pp.31-77). New York: New York University Press.

2 See UNICEF. (2010). *Children and Truth Commissions* (Innocenti Research Center, International Center for Transitional Justice). Florence: Author; Aptel, C., & Ladisch, V. (2011). *Through a new lens: a child-sensitive approach to transitional justice*. New York: International Center for Transitional Justice; Derluyn, I., Mels, C., Parmentier, S., & Vandenhole, W. (2012). *Re-Member. Rehabilitation, reintegration and reconciliation of war-affected children*. Cambridge: Intersentia; Parmar, S., Roseman, M., Siegrist, S., & Sowa, T. (2010). *Children and Transitional Justice. Truth-Telling, Accountability and Reconciliation*. Human Rights Program Series. Cambridge: Harvard University Press.

Section 2
Enduring Turbulences and Elusive Peace

Chapter 6
Violence and Masculinity in the Syrian Conflict

Stéphane Valter
University of Le Havre, France

ABSTRACT

This paper aims at analyzing the various forms of violence carried out by the different categories of people directly involved in the actual Syrian war: 'regular' soldiers, Alawite elite troops (plus the different security services), (mostly) Alawite militiamen, rebels from the (Sunni) mainstream armed opposition, and Islamist fighters, not to mention rogues who thrive on unruliness. This paper's hypothesis is that the demobilization of combatants is just partially connected to concrete issues – in the sense, for example, that any nationwide economic reconstruction will probably not be enough to promote reconciliation – since other factors impede any eventual transition from a violent civil war to a peaceful agreement, among them: a peculiar middle-eastern sense of masculinity plus the plague of sectarianism which builds organic barriers between people.

INTRODUCTION

This paper aims at analyzing the various forms of violence carried out by the different categories of people directly involved in the actual Syrian war: 'regular' soldiers, Alawite elite troops (plus the different security services), (mostly) Alawite militiamen, rebels from the (Sunni) mainstream armed opposition, and Islamist fighters, not to mention rogues who thrive on unruliness. This paper's hypothesis is that the still very distant demobilization of combatants is just partially connected to concrete issues. For instance, any nationwide economic reconstruction project – probably the most tangible of incentives – will certainly not be enough for the time being to promote reconciliation between warring factions. When, some weeks after the first demonstrations, the regime started to fear the consequences of the upheaval and realized that it was finally not that strong, its supporters (from the Alawite-dominated security services and special combat units) wrote on the walls: 'Either Asad, or we will burn the country.' And that is exactly what they have been doing. The Islamic State, a newcomer on the war scene, has adopted the same strategy. The other armed groups' attitude may be described as in-between. In such a furious outburst of mutual destruction, envisaging mutually profitable economic projects seems a bit odd.

DOI: 10.4018/978-1-4666-9675-4.ch006

Indeed, other dominant factors seriously impede any eventual transition from a violent civil war to a peaceful agreement. Among these multiple domineering factors, a peculiar middle-eastern sense of masculinity can be identified plus, above all, the plague of sectarianism which has built organic barriers between people. Not to mention the 'natural' desire of harmed and offended people to take revenge, sometimes irrationally, particularly when there is no justice at all. The mechanism of violence, after the conflict turned bloody (a few months after March 2011), seems therefore to be only partially linked to concrete and practical questions, which renders any solution very remote, in the sense that the struggle is first of all perceived by many as being existential, and thus non-negotiable. Syria's distressing situation, after more than four years of conflict, does not allow the author to envisage any reasonable solution for the near future, since all indicators point to the fact that the country is very far from accepting the simple idea of implementing any form of transitional justice, in the wide framework of a peace building process. Syria is now *de facto* divided, geographically and mentally, to the point that any attempt at fostering citizenship, trust, and recognition is doomed to failure. Thus, if many people long for a ceasefire (reconciliation still being too far-off), this may not be on the same premises. In any case, no faction is actually able to articulate an encompassing, coherent, and inclusive political agenda. To this gloomy picture must be added the material interests of armed groups for continuing a fighting that sounds for them much more preferable than making reasonable concessions.

From an academic point of view, it could assuredly be interesting to discuss methodically what lays at the intersection between categories like gender, ethnicity, and religion in a war context. It would appear that Kurdish ladies and women play a paramount military role, especially when they are recruited into PKK-monitored units. Alawite ladies and women now also do take part in the regime military effort, especially in police and control missions, because of the huge male bleeding within the community. From a Sunni Arab point of view, women have generally remained in the military background. Whatever these remarks, it remains difficult to see what could be the implications of these three categories (gender, ethnicity, and religion), with their respective stances towards violence, on any still inconceivable peaceful solution. War is usually a man's business, while women have to comply with males' decisions and errors, especially in the patriarchal Middle East, which signifies that the sole gender category is probably not the most adequate paradigm to use for analyzing the Syrian war (with the exception of the Kurds, who are by the way rather peripheral actors). So, in such a context where (transitional) justice is totally absent and where peace building is too frequently understood as the destruction of enemies, the dynamics of primordial identities (religion and ethnicity), together with personal interests, shapes the course of the conflict. Finally, the author admits that he perceives the exclusive gender perspective, albeit interesting, as too narrow since the Syrian war is infuriated and global.

The role of social media in contemporary wars is something that has no previous antecedent. Syria is in this sense an interesting case study. Although no thorough analysis of this issue will be carried out here, this issue has to be kept in mind. First because social media have played a paramount role in disclosing the regime's crimes, and then jihadist groups' abuses. Secondly because social media have become an easy way of promoting violence, either for personal virile bragging or for scaring foes. There is therefore a close link between social media and the containment / promotion of violence. Moreover, the role of the cellular phone, slowly introduced in the early 2000s, may deserve some reflection: the regime was then torn between its economic interests (taking people's money through its providing a useful service monopolized by a few individuals connected to power) and security concerns (controlling society), probably mixed with a small technological development scheme for the country. The seemingly sluggish introduction of the internet, around the same period (Bashar's access to power in 2000), was related to the same paradox: enrichment *versus* control. Albeit very controlled, these new communication devices have prepared the ground for the Spring 2011 mobilization and then upheaval.

The methodological perspective that has been followed is based on constant interrogation and doubt. Whereas data and facts have been gathered through regular field research (before and during the war), the analysis – or, more modestly, the attempt at giving some coherence to a very confused situation – has relied mostly on gender discrimination, sectarian divisions, ethnic specificities, and political considerations, taken from a wider moral and philosophical viewpoint when this has seemed useful. In any case, the prolegomena are that violence is part of the banality of (Syrian) life, although it can take different forms and can be regulated by various causes. The focus will moreover not be so much on providing multiple concrete examples of violence (which would amount to a distressing accountancy) than on supplying analysis tools. The structure of this paper is divided into three main sections: the first one aims at presenting the various forms of violence in the Syrian war; the second at investigating the links between masculinity and violence; the third at pondering on the contradictions between an eventual political reconciliation and the prevailing sectarian resilience.

BACKGROUND

The 'regular' army,[1] based on conscription, includes recruits from all communities but for the fact that many elements have defected and that Sunni brigades are scarcely engaged for fear of desertion. The total would make about 300,000 soldiers, or a little less. But the core of the 'regular' armed forces is essentially constituted by professional Alawite soldiers:[2] around 70,000 men at the beginning of the insurrection and probably less than 50,000 now (from the 3rd and 4th divisions as well as from the Republican Guard). The security services are almost exclusively made of Alawites (some tens of thousands of people) whereas the pro-government militias (or *shabbiha*) include many Alawites (but not only) and consist of some 100,000 persons.[3] To this pro-regime body must be added Shiite foreign fighters, some of them mercenaries, others volunteers, who are around 40,000 and who come from Iran, Iraq, and Lebanon. And finally, some Russian advisers and soldiers who struggle for the regime's survival (and for their own interests).

The mainstream armed opposition is mostly Sunni – which clearly indicates the religious rift between both camps – and includes the Free Syrian Army. The FSA – which has adopted a nationalist stance more or less secular although stamped with obvious religious references (in variable proportions according to the places) – regrouped the bulk of the fighters (about 60% at its highest, out of some 150,000 rebels) until the attractiveness of other more equipped Islamist groups progressively depleted its ranks. Thus, the creation of the Islamic Front in late 2013 stroke a decisive blow to its predominance. Finally, a number of (sometimes) smaller but well equipped and influential power-wielding fighting groups are clearly Islamist, when not openly jihadist (Lund, 2012).[4] Foreign fighters (not that numerous yet probably more than 5% of the rebels some two years after the start of the uprising) have seen a regular increase in numbers with an overrepresentation of jihadists, and as far as (Syrian and non-native) elements performing *jihad* are concerned, they rapidly constituted more than 10% of all fighters (Valter, 2012),[5] and much more now with the radicalization of the conflict and the attractivity of very violent groups (like the Islamic State).

The *modus operandi* for expressing violence and asserting masculinity varies in form and motivation from one of the above-mentioned categories to another, although self-perception and assessment of masculinity may in the end be quite similar in most cases. We assume that the Oriental general pattern of patriarchy, with male domination and gender segregation, has mold the collective psychology and imposed determined behaviours on social actors, in spite of the more or less socialist and secular ideology of the Baath party, in power since 1963, which has tried to build a new society, theoretically regardless of genders and creeds, although there has been no direct and bold attempt to refashion radically the societal relations of power. In particular, the Baath party has globally eschewed any straight confrontation with Sunni Islam (some 70% of the population) on societal issues (like marriage, divorce, inheritance, and all that is connected to male dominance), and when clashes have occurred, it has been mainly about power stakes.

In this case, males are supposed to stand for the honour of the group: family, clan, tribe, neighbourhood, confessional community, and eventually the whole nation (although this latter concept has lost must of its substance – despite decades of Arab nationalism – since the civil war's sparking off). Male individuals are thus required – as in most human societies – to take up arms when the group is perceived to be threatened or when sacred values are subjected to (real or imagined) humiliations. It can be presumed that among the most important Oriental values are respect towards religion and kinship security (with an emphasis on women's chastity). The Syrian civil war fits into this model since the religious dimension has antagonized Sunnis against Alawites (a despised medieval split from Imami – that is, mainstream – Shiism) together with other minorities (Islamic ones: Druses and Ismailis, plus the Christians), although political divergences have also blurred confessional allegiances. Secondly, the abuse of women, through rape as a source of proud – viewed as a manly feat against the foes' honour –, has also been a widespread feature of the conflict, especially on the part of the regime's soldiers and militiamen.[6]

One can wonder whether it is useful to consider this bloody conflict – in fact any war – through the lenses of literature. Thus, is Stephen Crane's *The Red Badge of Courage*, about the American civil war (1861-1865), helpful to apprehend the violence exerted against fellow citizens, in Syria as well as in other cases? 'It was revealed to him that he had been a barbarian, a beast. He had fought like a pagan who defends his religion' (chapter 17). Moreover, contradictory perceptions of the same war are obviously possible depending on the vision, for instance whether it is close or distant: the regime leadership, secluded in highly protected places, cannot but see the course of the military operations very differently from the men engaged on the battlefield. Elaborating on vision, it seems as well that the distinction between civilian and military perceptions is sometimes indistinct, particularly when the suffering concerns everybody directly, which is especially the case in civil wars, to the point where it becomes almost irrelevant to speak of civilians and soldier. Other general issues will have to be addressed as well, like the frequency and length of civil wars, and the impact of the former on the intensity of the latter. The longer a civil war, the more chance there is that elements of lower social classes will participate and thus modify the expressions of violence in a way corresponding to their deficient education and behavioural patterns (which may probably be connected to brutal codes of interaction), and human personality may regress to negative forms of animality.

Conflicts based on community mobilization seem to rely on an exclusive sense of identity, when the state has collapsed and rules of coexistence are no more relevant: national disintegration therefore leads to the creation of antagonistic territories that resemble ghettos, which is strange in a way since the state's authority is supposed to be based on reason and common interests, but for the fact that ghettos are based on culture, nature, and self-assertion, and not on politics, contracts, and the acceptance of others. A question to be addressed (generally and in the Syrian case) is the extent to which certain forms of violence are, or are not, connected to historical processes of modernity, with a determining post-colonial heritage and subsequent social, political, industrial, etc., transformations (Keane, 1996). Another way to ponder on violence is to look at it as a process made up of narratives related to experiencing and imagining violence, as did the Australian anthropologist Michael Taussig (Taussig, 1987). We have moreover to admit that violence is to be found everywhere, in every society (before, during, and after war), and that it should be analyzed from a semiological point of view, through structures of significations. For example, what are the deep aims of violence when not rationally oriented towards a military victory? The tribal nature of violence and masculinity just need here be mentioned,[7] since tribes are not numerically very important; yet, some forms of tribal (in the sense of extended kinship) behaviour can definitely be found in urban contexts.

THE VARIOUS FORMS OF VIOLENCE

With regards Syria, although it seems a bit anachronistic to speak of civil war in the absence of a unified territory (the Syrian state's boundaries date from only the end of the first world war), many feuds occurred between Sunnis and Alawites since 1305, that is after the promulgation of a *fatwa* (a generally constraining juridical opinion) by a Sunni theologian of Hanbali rite, Ibn Taymiyya, who considered the Alawite 'religion' as outrageous doctrinal deviancies deserving the capital punishment. He thus anathematized this community and called for its extermination on the ground of both conspiracy with the Christians (the Crusaders) and apostasy (Friedman, 2010, p. 188-197).[8] An Alawite revolt in 1317 led to a repression commanded by the (Egyptian) Mamluk sultan which left some 20,000 dead. In 1516, another repression led by the Ottoman sultan resulted in some 10,000 dead. And bloody internecine fights happened between Alawite and Ismaili peasants in the 19th century, with the frequent interference of Sunni (Egyptian or Ottoman) forces. The theoretical end of these massacres came after the promulgation of the 1909 Ottoman law on religious freedom, which calmed down the old climate of mutual aggressions. But it was the French mandate (1920-1946) which decisively contributed to ease the community tensions, through the military promotion of Alawite, Druse, and Ismaili officers within what was to become the new national armed forces. After the independence (1946), the conservative political forces (aided by military rulers) did not create a situation where the Sunni animosities against the minorities could be exacerbated, in the sense that the traditional order was maintained: dominance of the Sunni landowners and bourgeoisie. But after the Baathist takeover in February 1963, the minorities (among them the Alawites) started to break off their ancestral marginalization since the new regime included many officers from the edged out communities, and these ones began their ascension within the state's apparatus, which was to generate Sunni dissatisfaction. And this growing frustration created a fierce political crisis which culminated in February 1982 when an Islamist insurrection flared in Hama (with the killing of Alawites, Baathist members, and Christians) before being crushed by the regime's forces: a part of the city was totally destroyed and an unknown number of people were decimated (maybe up to 20,000 in about two weeks).

This is the sad legacy of the actual conflict, although Montesquieu (1689-1755) suggested that the major political virtue is the courage to forget the past. Yet, for others, amnesia may contribute to the reproduction of violence in the sense that the best way to avert it is to keep alive memory. Whatever it may be, violence and masculinity can be analyzed – in the actual war context – through the following items: intimidation, sexuality (rape, forced marriage, etc.), torture, (military and extrajudicial) killing, plundering, graft, all of these abuses and crimes being largely documented. The necessary taxonomy must take into account the following oppositions: men (as actors and victims) / women (always as victims in this patriarchal and predominantly Sunni Muslim society where they are not supposed to battle); locals (with shared culturally inherited behaviours) / foreigners (characterized by other traditions for expressing violence); Alawis / Sunnis (although any cultural distinction may not be huge in spite of two clearly distinct historical experiences: secular oppression *versus* domination – until the mid-1960's); Arabs / Kurds (particularly in the areas where the latest are numerous, with irredentist claims denied by all brands of Arab chauvinism). The general climate is one of global insurrection where military targets are rarely distinguished from civilian areas, from all sides involved in the conflict, and with governmental forces carrying out brutal and indiscriminate counter-insurgency operations.[9]

If all kinds of torture are not an invention of the Syrian conflict, and originate from humanity's barbarism, a few of these brutal expressions of violence have yet been prominent and even publicized, due to the savagery of the fighting (which indiscriminately targets civilians) and the extensive use of social media (unknown in previous wars) – mostly through amateur pictures and videos – for justification or propaganda. Whereas acts of mutilation have generally been displayed to stress the other camp's cruelty, some manifestations of viciousness and insanity have also been exhibited for purposes of self-pride and intimidation, like probable cases of cannibalism (May 2013) when a governmental helicopter pilot's head was shown cooking on a grill[10] or when a rebel commander proudly exposed himself tearing out the heart (or the liver) of a regime dead soldier and eating it.[11] But probably the fiercest expression of violence was the bombing of the Damascene oasis (Ghuta) in August 2013 with chemical weapons, which left hundreds of supposed rebel civilians dead or agonizing.

In all these outbursts of ferocity, one may ponder on the nature of the arms used – primitive (knives), 'conventional' (guns), or advanced (missiles and chemicals) – and wonder about the collective perceptions concerning the use of such and such. For violence is differently perceived in accordance with specific cultural codes: a certain type of weapon may be deemed 'clean' in a particular context, and gruesome in another, depending on the circumstances and the actors, national and foreign. In this sense, the awareness about violence differs evidently with time and place.[12] The nature and the intensity of violence are related to different items, among them silence or noise, whenever evidence is revealed to the public (for different purposes: inspiring commiseration or terror). Notwithstanding the suffering endured by the victims, the expression of violence may differ between a silent photography and a video with recorded sound, all of them being plentiful on social media which propose different forms of visual staging. In this respect, the widespread registering of violence through the abundant use of cellular phones, from all sides, in the secret services' gaols as well as through summary executions carried out by Islamist rebels, assuredly leads to an appalling sense of banality.

War may be described by visibility or absence: perceptible sufferings (via voices and proximity) or lack of human presence (when torment and death are just alluded to), both ways of presentation having been used by the conflicting sides to justify their cause and frighten foes. In this sense, could the end of war and of violence be likened to the contemplation of silence, after saturation? If noise (through bombing, shelling, shooting) resembles too well an intolerable acoustic aggression, silence may on the contrary express some kind of liberation, unless it conveys a frustrating and maddening impossibility to express oneself. Moreover, the visual representations of corpses, via all sorts of media, daily expose bodies which are identified or not, sometimes mutilated and even torn to pieces, when not totally pulverized, to the point that this recurrent show of violence is gnawing at people's physical and psychological integrity, like a collective cancer which spares no one. Images – in which people are actors, victims, and spectators – may thus suggest, through the last traces of perpetuity, cruelty and (often) degraded death rather than calmness and dignity.

The French philosopher Maurice Merleau-Ponty (1908-1961) tried to conceptualize the images expressing both the visible (what is perceived) and the invisible (what is imagined) through the concepts of wild being and the experience of flesh (Merleau-Ponty, 1979). Starting from the paradoxes which perception raises, he assumes that the latter instils both an absolute proximity of the world and an irremediable distance, to the extent that the 'natural posture' is supposed to be pure passivity (a body which endures) or pure activity (a vision which is connected to things). Vision is thus distance and ubiquity, a sort of detachment from (others' and one's) sufferings, as well as a capacity to distinguish and experience misery in different parts of the same national space, if we attempt to formulate this theory in the context of the Syrian civil war. This ambivalent yet complementary perception is reinforced by the fact that the available images are either modified or raw, all this genuine or fake visibility aiming at boasting one's feats and condemning others' crimes, which makes of violence the exacerbated result of a war of representation, in addition to its very real tragedy.

It can be surely assumed that violence is geographically widespread as much as it is symbolically extensive. Almost no place of the defunct 'national' territory is now safe from military operations and individual acts of vengeance and prevarication, while all aspects of public and private life have been affected by misery, torment, and distress. Apart from the torture and killing, people have been displaced, inside and outside the country (some 9 million people displaced out of a population of some 22 million, with some 2.5 million refugees in neighbouring countries), and the infrastructure has been destroyed: houses, factories, hospitals, schools, mosques, roads, agriculture, etc. Violence is thus both humane and material to the point of no return: all that gave a sense of common belonging – the possibility of moving within a familiar landscape where fellow citizens could be met and cultural monuments admired – has been wiped out. And suffering extends to everyday life even without any battling, when the scarcity of essential commodities renders life a fight against nature and one's basic needs. Voluntarily cutting the electricity grid or disrupting the distribution of water (not to mention food and medicine) must in this sense be considered as weapons designed at killing by inches.

On the symbolic level, the damage may be even worse. The state's structures (with the army as the nation's guardian) have been more than largely discredited since they are widely perceived to be biased and functioning for the sole benefit of a single group: the Alawite community (to which the president and the power nucleus belong) and its stooges (the other minorities plus some Sunni 'parasites'[13]). The previously shared (yet fragile) sense of being part of the same monotheistic family has exploded in the face of narrow community allegiances: the notion of collective sacred has hence collapsed. And although there are a lot of variations in the Syrian dialect, even language, as a binding identity element, has been affected in the sense that violence is expressed towards people who speak roughly the same idiom (with the exception of the Kurds): violence and its consubstantial linguistic expression are accordingly exerted against others as much as towards oneself, war being thus internal and wielded against one's own identity. This has been dramatically expressed on the social media by a governmental officer who stopped fighting, dropped his arm and went to the astonished rebels, addressing them in these terms: 'I love my country. I love all nationals. I even love the stones.' But in spite of his noble desire for reconciliation, he was shot some time later, which may mean that the most wanted 'national' body is disintegrating to the point of putridity.

HOW MAY MASCULINITY BE CONNECTED TO VIOLENCE?

Although many civilians did not fear at the beginning of the crisis (March 2011) to demonstrate with bare chests, in order to show that they carried no weapons and were ready to assume the final sacrifice for freedom's sake, when a lot of them began to fall victims to purpose or random shooting, peaceful and courageous expressions of discontent (considering the regime's tradition of brutality and lawlessness) rapidly turned more violent. In this way, the kind of mass mobilization initiated in a different context by Gandhi through hunger strikes was not experimented, certainly because it seemed to be of no efficacy in face of systemic brutality and also, perhaps, because the Levantine assertion of masculinity was not accustomed to such mortification.[14] From the regime's point of view, acceding to wide and popular demands (although they were not clearly articulated at first) was not acceptable for fear of seeing the whole system fall down, and undoubtedly because entering into negotiation under pressure was perceived as an unendurable sign of manly weakness. 'Asad for eternity or we burn out the country', the frightful and premonitory slogan written on public walls, was therefore considered a nihilist option preferable to any kind of power sharing.

Masculinity undoubtedly shares common features whatever the cultural environment, and many manifestations of virility are connected to the group to which individuals belong, such as the warlike songs and dances performed by all the male members of the western Sunni tribes opposed to the Shiite-dominated central government in Iraq. The Syrian opposition has its famous singers whose role has been to galvanize protesters, like Ibrahim Qashush, from the conservative Sunni city of Hama, whose throat was cut and vocal cords pulled out in July 2011 by pro-regime ruffians. His celebrated song carried the following stimulating words: 'You lost your legitimacy and the price for the martyrs' blood will be high. Bashar, go to hell with your speeches, for liberty is by our doors.' Expressing a defiant fervour to the sound of this revolutionary anthem has been an efficient – yet very dangerous – way of indulging in collective protest based on proximity (neighbourhood and community) bonds. The regime also has its musical spokespersons, such as the renowned Alawite singer Ali Dik,[15] whose works praise the country and extol the president with straight expressions of masculine enthusiasm. All this kind of cultural drumming up shares sociological characteristics the purpose of which is to strengthen group and community ties while publicly stressing men's preparedness to resist and combat.

The rape of women (and even of men, although homosexuality is theoretically forbidden in Islam) may be the most publicized way to emphasize one's manliness. Videos have been showed on social media of regime soldiers and militiamen captured by rebels who found undisputed filmed evidence that these (para) military had abused women and even recorded their baleful misdeeds on their own cellular phones in order to brag in front of their criminal comrades. Given the extent of this phenomenon and the Islamic taboo on illegal sexuality, one has to wonder whether this type of sinister affirmation of virility is connected to collective sexual frustration. Although no precise data are available, it seems well that the global hindrances to gender mixing, the frequency of arranged weddings, plus the difficulties of making a decent living (like having separate rooms), which sometimes delay marriage and ineluctably impede its harmonious course, have created a global atmosphere of intense sexual dissatisfaction. Although the desire for sexual domination of women is a general trend of human animality, which is all the more brutal and vicious when directed at enemies' women in times of chaos, the intensity of such a tragedy reflects definitely the baseness and depravity of the civil war, and presages ominously of any future reconciliation. Islamist and jihadist fighters, for their part, have expressed masculinity in their unwavering willingness to fight the regime, until the ultimate sacrifice, so as to avenge Sunni women's honour.[16]

If there is a link between masculinity and sexuality, is there a relation between the latter and morbidity? The ritual of rape, with the unilateral staging of sexual pleasure and enjoyment, displays not only violence and obscenity, but also sadism, which can be expressed through primitive or 'refined' techniques, like the above-mentioned video recording. Freud (1856-1939) analyzed the death wish that pushes someone to kill others, physically or symbolically (through the profanation of their honour), after having taken pleasure in their torment, as far as this can be a convincing explanation to understand violence. The morbid expression of violence lies for a large part in the observing process, that is: on the other (as victim or torturer) as well as on oneself, which explains the extensive use of social media to show very cruel forms of violence, not only for edification purposes but also for evil self-satisfaction.

In this respect, we can suggest that the point of saturation has not been reached yet. As Freud wrote, the intensity and duration of violence, when it shows no sign of dwindling, can be explained as a way to scare fellow-soldiers so as to avert individuals from thinking to their own interests (out of self-preservation) and consequently to prevent the group's cohesion from fading away (which could cause at first a general panic because of the loss of references). Warding off saturation therefore means buttressing the system and avoiding military demobilization. Nietzsche's (1844-1900) thought may also be useful to distinguish between power of self-assertion (the positive strength of hefty people) and repressive force (the perverted force of weak people). Perverted might has thus been employed by the regime's security apparatus solely to frighten and impose domestication, as if people were not citizens but only bondsmen – slaves – toiling in feudal lands. Probably to a lesser quantitative degree, Islamist rebels (and especially the most extremist ones, close to al-Qaeda) have indulged in ghastly public executions where their victims are humiliated before being slaughtered. Thus, is this kind of depraved violence the privilege of valiant men, of heroes?

Conversely, an extreme sense of masculine self-righteousness has pushed many rebels, the majority of them being Islamist combatants (from radical armed groups, like Jabhat al-Nusra, or the Front of Victory), to commit damaging suicide attacks against governmental positions. Whatever one may think of the ideological motivations of these candidates to martyrdom, it must be admitted that such acts assuredly represent the peak of bravery, though sometimes in desperate forms. It should be noted that no pro-regime military (as far as we know) has ever carried out such a lethal attack on enemy targets. Finally, and not to mention random shelling of civilian zones by the regime's air force, some rebel groups have not shunned from firing rockets at Alawite districts or from letting bombs explode in populated areas close to security bases. If masculinity is certainly the main prod behind such dangerous and mortal attacks, it cannot be ignored that its manifestations take different and contradictory forms which are rather difficult to evaluate and classify.

Masculinity also stems from observation and imitation. In the rebel ranks, if there is no attested use of children soldiers, many youngsters have taken up arms, either for surveillance or for military engagement, which is quite 'natural' since a whole generation has been materially destroyed and psychologically ruined because of the destruction of the educational infrastructure and the regular exposition of young people to the worst forms of violence. The codes of masculinity are therefore transmitted in a way essentially based on mostly irrational reactions to violence, which will negatively determine the sociological context of what will eventually emerge from the war. Indeed, videos have been displayed of rebel teenagers publicly decapitating governmental captured soldiers in what appeared to be the sordid implementation of judicial farces.

The words used to describe the violence directed towards adversaries may sometimes carry obscene and degrading meanings so as better to stress some sense of (dubious) masculinity. The term 'dogs' widely employed by rebels to scoff at president Asad's soldiers and militiamen suggests that these (para)military are only servile creatures, aggressive when in pack but fearful as soon as they get into thorny situations.[17] The obscenity aimed at enemies, the purpose of which is to deny them any pretension to humanity, is therefore to be found in images as well as in words, which often reach an offensive and injurious degree that hampers any kind of further truce. The power of language to describe scorn and hatred, spirit and bravery, violence and death, can be analyzed through Michel Foucault (1926-1984)'s theory (Foucault, 1966): a 'bad' behaviour may in the end signify that one is telling some kind of fundamental truth, which means that the realm of what is possible and acceptable remains delimited by certain cultural conditions of truth. Here, that exacerbated violence has become the normal – or at least the main – way of expression, which is partly corroborated by the rare available Syrian writings about the civil war, in which humanity and hope are permanently threatened by blind violence (Leverrier, 2014). We may add that there is a necessary need for precedents before engaging in description.

An exacerbated sense of masculine superiority, combined with perversity, may in the end lead to the banality of evil, as Hanna Arendt (1906-1975) showed in different circumstances (Arendt, 2006; Revault d'Allonnes, 1995, p. 21-72). Since it is not exaggerated to speak about mass murder in the Syrian civil war, as far as the regime is concerned – as best exemplified by the August 2013 chemical attack on some Damascene suburbs – and also to some lesser extent as indicated by collective reprisals on Alawites on the part of some extreme Islamist factions, we may suggest that the Syrian context resembles to a certain degree Nazi violence. If we follow Arendt, we have thus to admit that most of those who have organized and carried out the killings are sociologically 'normal', that is: they come from all segments of society (before entering the security apparatus) and have no particular predisposition to violence (before being subjected to mass – mainly based on community – mobilization). For Arendt, vicious and denatured soldierly virility (like the one which created the Nazi criminal industry) originates from an incapacity to communicate (to exchange ideas and emotions) and even to think, and especially to think from others' point of view. And this incapacity derives from a general lie and a shortfall of judgment. Finally, extremely aggressive masculinity, spurred by a perverse ideology and an unrelenting terror, bans plurality, erases the realm of (normal) politics, and deprives human beings from their humanity (Arendt, 1958a and 1958b).

POLITICAL RECONCILIATION OR SECTARIAN RESILIENCE

Kant (1724-1804) takes a different view since he speaks of radical evil, in the sense that it is fundamentally antagonistic to moral law. Here, the banality of evil comes from the fact that it is radical. And evil is perversion because the respect due to moral law finally depends on narrow self-interests, that is, concerning the Syrian war, each side disregards wider (national) interests.[18] Thus, the supreme evil consists for Kant in lie and falsification, or the abuse of reality on ideology's part, since understanding (the others) means in a way justifying (their claims). For Aristotle, the process of identification with others' suffering arises from the principle of analogy: I may suffer as much as the person who is hurt in front of me. Moreover, his conception of *philia* sustains that amity can only express itself through verbal exchanges (*logos*) within the political framework of the city. So amity, viewed as a dialog with others that aims at conciliating multiple private interests, stands for the core of politics, which here means having the capacity to understand the world from others' point of view. But this broad-mindedness towards others' verity unquestionably lacks in civil wars.

But, as alluded to *supra*, the warring protagonists' mental and sectarian backgrounds differ widely, in the sense that a huge amount of Alawis perceive themselves as a threatened minority which could be slaughtered again by Sunni extremists, whereas Sunnis view themselves as an oppressed majority. And both claims are partly true. In this perspective, the actors' legitimizing discourses – *i.e.* competing claims to power monopoly and quasi-exclusive conceptions of order (or of disorder) – have to be deconstructed essentially through the prism of community animosities and political divergences. The aggressive Islamist posture of some FSA-affiliated brigades (not to talk about jihadists sympathizing or associated with al-Qaeda) occasionally – and sometimes frequently – conveys a very hostile attitude towards Alawites *per se*. This daunting martial speech is combined with an intimidating behaviour on the part of some FSA groups, to the point that one may speak of 'Free Syrian secret services'[19] which behave in some circumstances as arbitrarily and unlawfully as the regime's gloomily notorious intelligence agencies, though on a smaller scale. This has helped the 'official' authorities to portray their adversaries as intolerant and fanatical so-called Muslims who want to slay coreligionists, as well as domineering and tyrannical fighters who reject law and order.

Albeit precise statistics are scarcely available, the following religion-based figures can be advanced with some caution: Sunnis form some 70 (and even 75%) of the population (Arabs and Kurds included), Christians are about 10% (maybe a bit more, or probably less due to emigration because of the war), Alawites are around 12% (or a bit more), Murshidites[20] stand for some 1.5% (or a bit less), each of the Druse and Ismaili communities represents around 3% plus, finally, very few Imami Shiites. According to ethnic criteria, Kurds are between 10 and 15%, Armenians under 3% (probably less because of emigration), as much as the Turkomans and the Tcherkesses united. Lastly, between 60 and 65% are Sunni Arabs (that is, in the regime's eyes, the potential or real foes). One can easily see from these approximate demographic data based on religion and ethnicity that the Syrian crisis holds a clearly pronounced religious character, in spite of genuine political differences: a not negligible amount of Alawite officers have deserted (which indicates deep cleavages within the community) as well as many Sunni high ranking officers (rather close from the power centre) who made defection, plus politicians and diplomats (who benefited from the system). Whereas Christians (or at least the Christian ecclesiastic authorities) have remained quiet, a certain 'Saint-George Brigade' in central Syria has fought with the rebels. Druses as well, traditionally supportive of the regime because of a shared sense of religious marginality within Islam, have been crossed by internal splits.

If the battlefield can be considered as a theatre stage on which war is dramatized under certain rules, like the art of dissimulating corpses or, on the contrary, that of bringing them to the fore to stress male hysteria, why not supposing that civilians constitute a kind of audience? This public may even form an imaginary tribunal, aided by (partly) professional and (mostly) amateur journalism (via social media), away from cynical political maneuvering and misleading ideological intransigence, devoted to re-establish truth and institute the reign of virtue. The testimony of witnesses, if allowed, could bring about a collective sense of guilt and stop the spilling of blood. But after all the material damage, the physical pain, and the psychological sorrow, even the liberty of speech has been fettered when not brutally suppressed. Journalists in particular have seen their work impeded when they were not noxiously targeted by all the conflicting sides,[21] as if the power of speech was in a way stronger that arms' might. The question yet is how to move from a crowd to a public, as Shaftesbury (1671-1713), an English philosopher and politician, asked (Caillé, Senellart & Lazerri, 2007, p. 23-31). The public means here a collective space of discussion and of converging social practices where one's individuality accepts others', within a moral framework based on reflection and (self-)criticism, or the perpetual questioning of one's own representations.

To counter the Syrian conflict's ideological – and even mythological – impassioned background, it has to be publicly stated and accepted that the ancient wars are over: between Arabs (here, Syrian rebels) and Persians (*i.e.* the *pasdaran* fighters sent by Teheran to help the regime), between the Crusaders (today, the Orthodox Russian military advisers and troops) and Sunni Muslims (the majority of the population whom rebels pretend to represent), between Arabs (the whole Syrian people which the regime claims it is standing for) and Turks (the descendants of the Ottoman empire which colonized the Middle East for centuries, now accused of plotting to annex Damascus again with the help of mercenaries: the rebels), or between Sunnis (the main current of Islam, symbolically captured by the rebellion) and Shiites (the Iranian brand of Islam, plus the national minorities accused of being the heirs of medieval heterodox and extremist sects: Alawites, Druses, and Ismailis). In this sense, history, when just considered as a long experience fraught with hatred and massacres, assuredly remains an insuperable obstacle to overcome. And it is probably only through free dialogue – through a re-invention of an inclusive national identity – that all kinds of narrow antagonizing mythologies, be they religious or nationalist, can be neutralized to the benefit of a more comprehensive vision of coreligionists and adversaries.

Violence in the Syrian civil war is definitely connected to the preservation of material interests, as far as the (mostly Alawite) governmental side is concerned: monopoly and prevarication for the top, petty trafficking and quiet survival for the mass. Many (Alawite) security men have also thrived on the detention of arrested persons, who can be freed only after the payment of a ransom, not to mention administrative corruption which compensates for losses due to the crumbling – civil – economy. With regards rebels, this is also partly true since some fight out of economic necessity, to garner money (to be well-off in a devastated economic environment) and accumulate prestige (to obtain the needed weapons to wield power and prove their masculinity). Some brigades do not even hesitate to shift loyalty as soon as better equipment and more abundant financing are proposed by foreign donors, while others indulge in criminal business – unscrupulous kidnapping[22] and lucrative traffics – to finance their military activities, the economy of war being sometimes very appealing.

Thus, the idea that some kind of economic recovery could attenuate tension and lead to the reconstruction of the country, with some kind of reconciliation, is tantalizing, although nobody knows from where the enormous sums of needed money would come. The Iraqi example moreover shows that wealth is not enough to bring rival factions and communities together unless an unattainable consensual sense of equity is achieved. The logic of economic exchange, which relies on reasonable passions to promote a general rationality susceptible of satisfying everybody's needs (from a liberal and mercantile point of view), seems absent. It can be therefore assumed, for the majority of the population's misfortune, that the self-destroying violence in Syria has not still reached the point where actors prefer to negotiate and share power instead of killing each other. And insurmountable barriers still stand in the way of rapprochement between challenging sides which seem to consider the conflict more as a mortal fight between religious communities – perceived as organic groups – rather than as a struggle which can be solved politically through mutual concessions with some economic incentive.

A common sense of law may reduce the gap between the regime and the rebels, as well as between the latter ones themselves who are greatly divided (Islamo-nationalists *versus* Islamists, Arabs *versus* Kurds), if accountability was accepted and implemented, as what happened, sometimes arduously, in other places. 'Weapons gave you independence, laws will give you freedom', proclaimed Francisco de Paula Santander (1792-1840). Walter Benjamin (1892-1940) put it in a more conceptualized form when he stated that law must monopolize violence so as to protect itself (Benjamin, 2012). As Aristotle pointed out in *Politics*, man may be the best of creatures when improved by institutions (law and justice) whereas he can also be the worst when separated from them. But the regime's security apparatus has totally ignored human beings' basic rights, even under the rules of war, whereas some rebel armed groups have implemented an expeditious, arbitrary, and cruel medieval justice allegedly based on Islamic law, that is on a very regressive and pitiless interpretation of sharia (Valter, 2014). Moreover, is it possible to forgive unpardonable and indefensible crimes? If the prime award of justice is the feeling that we are putting it into practice, as Rousseau (1712-1778) used to say (in *Émile*), serious doubts may be cast on an eventual solution to the war in Syria, given the prevalent intransigence.

The deliquescence of education, which was already very dogmatic under the Baath's rule before almost all the infrastructure was destroyed, will impede human beings (and especially men) from bringing welfare and happiness to themselves, their families, and to the whole nation, since they will have no chance of being positively moulded by instruction, as the German-French philosopher d'Holbach (1723-1789) remarked in his *Universal Moral*. And this education, which is essentially political, depends on politicians in general and jurists in particular to steer men toward the common good, as the Dutch philosopher Mandeville (1670-1732) said (Caillé, Senellart & Lazerri, 2007, p. 17-23).

FUTURE RESEARCH DIRECTIONS

Although violence may be explained from different perspectives, it remains in the end difficult to comprehend. It looks quite obvious that any regulation of physical violence partly depends on an intense social conditioning which pushes individuals to rigorously control their (emotional) acts, in a long historical and cultural process, which has been a long process in the West as demonstrated by Norbert Elias (1897-1990) (Elias, 1969/1982). If we assume that violence can also be symbolic, as Pierre Bourdieu (1930-2002) showed (Bourdieu, 1979), and that inequality can be presented as natural whereas it reflects in reality the dominating class's capacity to impose its own references, the possibility of breaking the vicious circle of violence seems thin. And this is especially true when depreciative processes against others, with particular modes for justifying violence, are under way. Another obstacle is the cultural and psychological weight of tradition, when one tries to emancipate himself from particular forms of violence he endured (in childhood) through some kind of wicked mimicry, or when one has been trained in an environment prone to violence, like in the army or the security services, and above all in situations of arbitrariness and lawlessness (when violence is encouraged and recognized as paying).

Favouring strength to violence may stabilize situations of war, in the sense that strength (a phenomenon which can be politically legitimated) aims at imposing some kind of social order whereas violence (a phenomenon which can easily become illegitimate) plans to destroy it, as the

French sociologist and philosopher Georges Sorel (1847-1922) pointed out (Sorel, 1972). Or, in the impossibility to put an end to violence, looking positively at it may in a way resolve the problem. Carl Schmitt (1892-1985) thus stated that the notion of political dignity must be attached to violence and war since the fundamental purpose of any political system is to distinguish between friends and enemies. But if any given conflict is supposed to create a distinction between the warring sides, in the sense that they must – even reluctantly – mutually recognize each other, what about the conflicts in which the other's identity is totally denied? The Syrian regime only mentions 'terrorists', thus ignoring legitimate demands for political reforms, whereas most of the rebels refuse to engage in any serious negotiation before the resignation of the whole political and military leadership, these two rigid positions boding of course very badly for any future solution. We are here rather close to the two extreme cases envisaged by Georg Simmel (1858-1918), the German sociologist, when he wrote that peace cannot succeed fighting as long as people wage war either for crapulous motives or out of pleasure (Simmel, 1995).

Another aspect to consider is the very nature of the troubles: is the conflict (here in Syria) animated by clearly defined revolutionary purposes? Is there a genuine revolutionary process, with clear political aims, or is it just a situation of turmoil, madness, and chaos? Revolutionary violence may abate when some goals have been attained, whereas mayhem seems to know no limits. This is all the more true when no recognized institution is able to remind basic norms to belligerents and render some kind of justice. In Syria, as in many other tragic situations, norm and justice are only defined within and by both sides' political and military leaderships: the un-negotiable legitimacy of a president chosen by plebiscite (with no other candidate) *versus* the absolute truth supposedly revealed by God (for the extreme Islamist fighters). Betwixt and between, there is a small space for rebels who fight on a political basis, that is, with identified, eventually acceptable, and in due course inclusive objectives (in one of the best scenarii).

Although this paper has alluded here and there to the role of the diverse social media in unveiling, condemning, or boasting cruelty, according to circumstances and actors, a deeper study may certainly be needed on this subject (Gonzalez-Quijano, 2012). An assessment of the social media's huge contribution to the disclosure of serious and reliable information about the Syrian war has to be carried out. Similarly, examining the dynamics of social mobilization through the use of social media, in opposition to the atomization of society encouraged by the authoritarian Syrian regime as well as by the various brutal armed groups, would certainly bring about interesting results. For the structuring of civil society – the Syrian one for instance – definitely owes a lot to these new ways of communication and exchange. In parallel, the morbid use of social media to terrorize people (like the Islamic State has done) also deserves some interest in future researches.

CONCLUSION

The following lines are the result of a last field research conducted in the Bekaa valley (Lebanon) and in Damascus (Syria) in September 2014, and are supposed to complete the previous ones, written a few months before. On a general level, it can be assumed that the regional situation has deteriorated, with the rise of the monstrous creature called the Islamic State, this criminal organization having raided and/or occupied many Iraqi cities. One of the most gruesome manifestations of IS's cruelty was its fighters' morbid determination to torture, kill, and eradicate members of the Kurdish Yazidi community, erroneously dubbed Satan's worshippers. Thus entire families and whole villages were forced to escape in the arid, barren, and scorched Sinjar Mountain, preferring to die out of thirst and starvation instead of falling captives to the jihadist warriors who would have executed them for supposed apostasy, heresy, heterodoxy, etc. It indeed appeared from documents released on the web by IS that the jihadist and terrorist fighters were pleased at imagining these fleeing civilians being burnt by the sun's summer hotness, as if they were roasting in hell because of their deviant creed and subsequent sins. IS's trademark is thus brutality, mercilessness, and even some kind of sadism (with ghastly ritual and theatrical executions) towards whomever may be perceived as a foe to Sunni Islam… and to the organization.

Such a criminal gang, with its preposterous yet terrifying religious stamp, has succeeded in mobilizing many frustrated, unemployed, and marginalized Muslims, locally and around the world, who only assert their virility through parading among scared civilians, shooting prisoners, decapitating hostages, capturing and raping women, etc. Their hatred of whatever is different and considered as hostile is such that there seems to be for them no possible assertion of the personality if it is not expressed through the unleashing of an extreme form of barbaric masculinity. Yet some reports mention that IS's almost nihilist violence – since its actions deal with destruction and not development – is tempered by the fact that the deserving fighters sometimes indulge themselves in sentimental titbits with – voluntarily or reluctantly – consenting ladies, in arranged marriages which presumably take the form of the legal Islamic matrimonial unions.[23] It has also been reported that the praiseworthy combatants, after being married (whatever the length of the hymen), are now and then allowed to undertake tourist trips between Syria and Iraq in air-conditioned buses charted by the organization and guarded by fellow fighters, in the company of their integrally veiled sweethearts. But when confronted to Kurdish female *peshmergas* waging war like Amazons, as around the city of Kobane (north of Syria) since September 2014, and even committing suicide operations,[24] the jihadist fighters' masculinity seems no longer to be so high and mighty. Yet IS has also its – mainly foreign – female fighters, but whose military prowess is not much documented.[25] From the regime's side (and with the exception of women officers), it has now been some time that (mostly Alawite but also Christian) women have enlisted in what may be called the civil defense: controlling check-points for instance, one of the traditional male prerogatives. In the dreary context of a war which will probably last for many years, unless the balance of external aid radically changes and clearly leans towards one side, women are obviously supposed to suffer more, as indirect casualties, deliberate targets, direct victims, or even committed combatants. Therefore, one may question the validity of the masculinity paradigm, as a structuring process, to understand the (real or symbolic) violence of a war in which some women have begun to take an active role.

If virility is to be connected to morality, IS's fighters score very poor marks. One report heard from a Hizbollah militiaman in Lebanon clearly indicates – if it were still needed – that primitive and barbaric cruelty largely prevails over what could be called bravery or intrepidity, the paramount virtue of the heroes. After being caught in a skirmish in the eastern Bekaa valley, not far from the border between Lebanon and Syria, actually a den of terrorists, one IS jihadist was roughly interrogated by Hizbollah members. But although being brusquely punched, the captured jihadist was laughing to such an extent that his questioners asked him the reason: he knew that he would neither be tortured nor killed but handed over to the Lebanese army, adding that Hizbollah militiamen were notorious for their discipline and morality, whereas 'we have no ethics', as he concluded. The level and nature of violence can thus be paralleled to the ethical commitment of the fighters involved.

In a different context, Lebanese police officers – supervised by (Shiite) Hizbollah secret services which work hand in hand with their (Alawite) Syrian counterparts – controlling the border with Syria (at al-Masna' crossing-point, halfway between Beirut and Damascus) were unevenly treating all the Syrians who desired to go back to their country: very few officers for a lot of travelers, an interminable queue, no place to rest, no toilets, etc., frequent rebukes, regular insults, ill-treatment and sometimes blows. For the ordinary Syrians wishing to enter Lebanon, it was (mid-September 2014) impossible since the border was closed, except for those traveling for an official purpose, or connected to the Syrian regime. These humiliation and violence against probably innocent civilians can be understood as a collective punishment against people who prefer (or have preferred) to quit their country instead of fighting with the regime, and are thus considered as potential traitors (from an official Syrian point of view), or who come (or have come) to Lebanon to increase the refugees' burden on the state and destabilize the country (from a xenophobic and anti-Sunni Lebanese stance). In such a sense, this rude behaviour represents a double and blind vengeance towards an unidentified and anonymous group of persons, despised by (mostly Shiite) Lebanese military and police because of their supposed poor social status and (Sunni) religious allegiance, and abandoned by their national authorities which view them as cowards or defectors. To put the finishing touches to this picture, one must remind that the Syrian military were feared in Lebanon during the occupation years (1976-2005) whereas they are now looked down on and scorned, when not exploited, beaten, and even killed.

When collective revenge is linked to disrespect for civilians, far from any consideration of superior martial pluckiness, violence appears in a despicable – and lasting – form. Moreover, when the settling of scores constitutes a process with no limits of time, deeply rooted in community memory, and when domination takes the form of a brutal and indiscriminate behaviour, one can hardly see any possible end to violence. Another aggravating element is the fact that the already complex Syrian civil war has become a battlefield for regional and international frustrated and irascible fighters, who seem if not to wage war against chimeras at least to desperately look for foes to vent their accumulated anger (under the pretext of punishing God's enemies). Finally it appears that many people, considered primarily as members of the different (religious) communities – the primordial social groups –, view the conflict first of all as an existential war – and not a political clash – in which males (and now females, to a lesser yet increasing degree) have to stand for the collectivity's honour and security.

REFERENCES

Al-Khatib, M. K. (n. d.). *Mi'at 'Am min al-'Adhab [One Hundred Years of Suffering]*. Beirut: Manshurat.

Angelova, I. (2014). *Rebel-Held Suburbs of Damascus: Resilience Mechanisms in the Face of Chemical Attacks. Policy Alternatives.* Arab Reform Initiative.

Arendt, H. (1958a). *The Human Condition*. Chicago: University of Chicago Press.

Arendt, H. (1958b). *The Origins of Totalitarianism*. Cleveland: The World Publishing Company.

Arendt, H. (2006). *Eichmann in Jerusalem: A Report on the Banality of Evil*. New York: Penguin Books. (Original work published 1963)

Benjamin, W. (2012). *Critique de la Violence* (Original work published 1921). Paris: Petite Bibliothèque Payot.

Bocco, R. (1995). *'Asabiyât* Tribales et États au Moyen-Orient. Confrontations et Connivences. *Monde Arabe Maghreb-Machrek*, *147*, 3–12.

Bourdieu, P. (1979). *La Distinction. Critique Sociale du Jugement*. Paris: Les Éditions de Minuit.

Bozarslan, H. (2008). *Une Histoire de la Violence au Moyen-Orient, de la Fin de l'Empire Ottoman à Al-Qaida*. Paris: La Découverte.

Bucaille, L. (Dir.). (2013). Femmes combattantes (dossier). *Critique Internationale, 60*, 7–88.

Caillé, A., Senellart, M., & Lazerri, C. (Eds.), (2007). Histoire Raisonnée de la Philosophie Morale et Politiquees. Paris: Flammarion.

Chouet, A. (1995). L'Espace Tribal Alaouite à l'Épreuve du Pouvoir. La Désintégration par le Politique. *Monde Arabe Maghreb-Machrek, 147*, 93–119.

Elias, N. (1969/1982). *The Civilizing Process: Sociogenetic and Psychogenetic Investigations*. Oxford: Blackwell.

Foucault, M. (1966). *Les Mots et les Choses (Une Archéologie des Sciences Humaines)*. Paris: Gallimard.

Friedman, Y. (2010). *The Nusayri-Alawis: An Introduction to the Religion, History, and Identity of the Leading Minority in Syria*. Leiden: Brill.

Ghassûb, M., & Sinclair-Webb, E. (2000). *Imagined Masculinities: Male Identity and Culture in the Modern Middle East*. Londres: Saqi Books.

Gonzalez-Quijano, Y. (2012). *Arabités Numériques. Le Printemps du Web Arabe*. Arles: Actes Sud/Sindbad.

Hannoyer, J. (Coord.) (1999). Guerres Civiles. Économies de la Violence, Dimensions de la Civilité. Paris: Karthala / Beirut: CERMOC.

Hassan, H. (2012, July 16). A Bamascus loyalist defects as violence affects the tribes. *The National*. Retrieved from http://www.thenational.ae/thenationalconversation/comment/a-damascus-loyalist-defects-as-violence-affects-the-tribes

Keane, J. (1996). *Reflections on Violence*. London: Verso.

Le Gac, D. (1991). *La Syrie du Général Assad*. Bruxelles: Éditions Complexe.

Leverrier, I. (2014). *Joumana Maarouf's Letters from Syria*. Retrieved from http://syrie.blog.lemonde.fr/2014/04/08/les-lettres-de-syrie-de-joumana-maarouf-en-librairie/

Lund, A. (2012). *Syrian Jihadism. UIbrief, 13*. Stockholm: Swedish Institute of International Affairs.

Merleau-Ponty, M. (1979). *Le Visible et l'Invisible, followed by Notes de Travail*. Paris: Gallimard. (Original work published 1964)

Michaud, G. (pseudonym for Seurat, M.). (1983). L'État de Barbarie: Syrie 1979-1982. *Esprit (Paris, France)*, (November): 16–30.

No Author. (2011). Syrian Tribes Start Creating Unrest. Sheikhs are Using Force to Oppress the Youth. *Al-Sharq al-Awsat*. Retrieved from http://www.aawsat.com/details.asp?section=4&article=647031&issueno=12021

Revault d'Allonnes, M. (1995). *Ce que l'Homme Fait à l'Homme. Essai sur le Mal Politique*. Paris: Flammarion.

Simmel, G. (1995). *Le Conflit* (Original work published 1908). Strasbourg: Circé.

Sorel, G. (1972). *Réflexions sur la Violence* (Original work published 1908). Paris: Marcel Rivière.

Taussig, M. T. (1987). *Shamanism, Colonialism, and the Wild Man: A Study in Terror and Healing*. Chicago: University of Chicago Press. doi:10.7208/chicago/9780226790114.001.0001

Valter, S. (2012). Rivalités et Complémentarités au Sein des Forces Armées: le Facteur Confessionnel en Syrie. *Les Champs de Mars*, 23, 79-96.

Valter, S. (2014). La Justice Chariatique en Syrie 'Libérée'. *Confluences Méditerranée, 90*(3), 155–173. doi:10.3917/come.090.0155

Van Dam, N. (1996). *The Struggle for Power in Syria. Politics and Society under Asad and the Ba'th Party*. Londres: I.B. Tauris.

ADDITIONAL READING

Abbud, S. (2002). *Thaqafat al-'Unf fi al-'Iraq, (The Culture of Violence in Iraq)*. Köln, Beirut: Dar al-Jamal.

Accad, E. (1992). *Sexuality and War. Literary Masks of the Middle East*. New York, London: New York University Press.

Al-Rachid, L., & Méténier, É. (2008). À Propos de la Violence 'Irakienne'. Quelques Éléments de Réflexion sur un Lieu Commun. *A Contrario*, 1/5, 114-133.

Arthur, P. (Ed.). (2014). *Identities in Transition. Challenges for Transitional Justice in Divided Societies*. Cambridge, NY: Cambridge University Press.

Böttcher, A. (1998). Syrische Religionspolitik unter Asad. Freiburg im Breisgau: Arnold-Bergstraesser-Institut (Freiburger Beiträge zu Entwicklung und Politik, 25).

Bozarslan, H. (2009). *Conflit Kurde. Le Brasier Oublié du Moyen-Orient*. Paris: Autrement.

Chatty, D. (2010). The Bedouin in Contemporary Syria: The Persistence of Tribal Authority and Control. *The Middle East Journal*, *64*(1), 29–49. doi:10.3751/64.1.12

Clastres, P. (2013). *Archéologie de la Violence. La Guerre dans les Sociétés Primitives* (first edition in 1977). La Tour d'Aigues: Éditions de l'Aube.

Colas, D. (1992). *Le Glaive et le Fléau. Généalogie du Fanatisme et de la Société Civile*. Paris: Grasset.

Corbin, A., Courtine, J.-J., & Vigarello, G. (Dir.) (2011). Histoire de la Virilité (de l'Antiquité au XXIe siècle), 3 volumes. Paris: Le Seuil.

Foucault, M. (1994/1997). *Histoire de la Sexualité*. Paris: Gallimard. (Original work published 1976)

Girard, R. (2011). La Violence et le Sacré (first edition in 1972). Paris: Fayard (Pluriel).

Jabar, F., & Dawod, H. (Eds.), (2003). Tribes and Power: Nationalism and Ethnicity in the Middle East. London: Saqi Books.

Lazreg, M. (2008). *Torture and the Twilight of Empire: From Algiers to Baghdad*. Princeton, NJ: Princeton University Press.

Moser, C. N. O., & Clark, F. (Eds.). (2001). *Victims, Perpetrators or Actors? Gender, Armed Conflict and Political Violence*. London, New York: Zed Books.

Richani, N. (2002). *Systems of Violence: the Political Economy of War and Peace in Colombia*. Albany: State University of New York Press.

Richani, N. (2010). Fragmentation of Sovereignty and Violent non-State Actors in Colombia. In K. Mulaj (Ed.), Violent non-State Actors in World Politics (pp. 27-44). London: Hurst.

Safford, F., & Palacios, M. (2002). *Colombia: Fragmented Land, Divided Society*. New York: Oxford University Press.

Taussig, M. T. (2005). *Law in a Lawless Land: Diary of a Limpieza in Colombia*. Chicago: University of Chicago Press.

Winter, S. (2015). The 'Alawis in the Ottoman Period. In M. Kerr & C. Larkin (Eds.), *The Alawis of Syria: War, Faith and Politics in the Levant. London*. Hurst.

Winter, S. (in press). A Secular History of the 'Alawis: From Medieval Syria to the Turkish Republic, 947-1939. Princeton, NJ: Princeton University Press.

KEY TERMS AND DEFINITIONS

Alawites: Medieval split from Shiism. Many of the security apparatus members hail from this religious community.

Baathism: A pan-Arabist ideology founded in Syria in the 1940s, rather secular and socialist, yet authoritarian.

Druses: A scission from Ismaili Islam after the death of the Ismaili (Fatimid) Egyptian caliph al-Hakim. They represent about 3% of the Syrian people.

Free Syrian Army: Probably the first armed group opposed to the regime, and constituted of deserters. Now, this rather moderate group has lost a lot of influence in front of more extremist groups.

Hanbalism: One of the four (remaining) schools of Islamic jurisprudence, founded in the mid-IXth century. It actually constitutes the official doctrine of Saudi Arabia.

Hizbollah: A Lebanese Shiite party-cum-militia created in the 1980s. It represents a large part of the Imami (or mainstream) Shiite community. It is supported by Iran and Syria, and is devoted to the fight against Zionist expansionism.

Ismailis: A division within Shiism, from 765 (death of the imam Jaafar al-Sadiq) onwards. Probably around 3% of the Syrian population.

Jihadists: Those who (want to) perform *jihad*, in the sense of a merciless fight against Western values and interests, against Zionism, moderate Arab regimes, Jews and Christians, and even Muslim people considered as renegades.

Kurds: An ethno-linguistic group leaving in four countries (Turkey, Iraq, Iran, and Syria), deprived of statehood at the end of the First World War. In Syria, the Kurdish factions are numerous, but the most influential are the People's Protection Units (or YPG), an emanation of the Turkish Marxist-Leninist highly militarized Kurdistan Workers' Party (or PKK).

Murshidis: Members of a religious community which is a split from the Alawite tribes. Although dogmatically different and with no particular connection to the regime, they are frequently assimilated to Alawites.

Shiites: A minority trend of Islam (around 10%, with a few subdivisions) found in Iran, southern Iraq, Syria, Lebanon, etc.

Sunnis: Followers of mainstream Islam, in the world and also in Syria (some 70% of the population). Most of the armed rebellion is made up of Sunnis.

Yazidis: A Kurdish religious group living in northwest Iraq. Their esoteric religion is syncretic and borrows from Islam, Judaism, Christianity, and local pagan cults. They are mistakenly called the devil's worshippers.

ENDNOTES

1 Insofar as this expression has any meaning in an insurrectionary context.

2 Some 70% of 'regular' soldiers and a huge amount of senior officers out of more than a thousand.

3 Rough figures indicate that some 135,000 soldiers, intelligence officers, and militiamen have been killed since March 2011, about half of them being Alawite. http://www.adnkronos.com/AKI/Arabic/Security/?id=3.2.1098461728. An important amount of absconding has occurred among Alawite soldiers and officers, which indicates that the conflict between the regime and the non-Islamist rebel groups can sometimes be more political than religious. http://all4syria.info/Archive/73461, http://all4syria.info/Archive/72951.

4 On the Islamist Ansar al-Sham battalions (March 2014), http://carnegieendowment.org/syriaincrisis/?fa=55066. On the al-Qaeda franchise in Syria, the Islamic State in Iraq and the Levant (ISIL, December 2013), http://carnegieendowment.org/syriaincrisis/?fa=54017.

5 See also http://mideastafrica.foreignpolicy.com/posts/2013/08/09/external_support_and_the_syrian_insurgency. And http://www.saudigazette.com.sa/index.cfm?method=home.regcon&contentid=20140125193596.

6 Outraging women's honour (mother, wife, sister, or daughter), or *'ird* in Arabic, constitutes the supreme wound – physical or symbolic – inflicted upon enemies, in the sense that men's virility must fundamentally manifest itself in the defense of this honour.

7 See the works of Haian Dukhan, a Phd candidate at the School of International Relations, University of St-Andrews (Scotland).

8 This *fatwa* was partially translated by Edward Salisbury, *Journal of the American Oriental Society*, tome II, 1851. A more complete translation was written in French by Stanislas Guyard, 'Le Fetwa d'Ibn Taimiyyah sur les Nosairis', *Journal Asiatique*, sixth series, tome XVIII, August-September 1871, p. 158-198.

9 See Usahma Darrah, http://alhayat.com/OpinionsDetails/543499.

10 http://www.frontpagemag.com/2013/theodore-shoebat/syria-cannibalism-and-videotape/.

11 http://www.independent.co.uk/news/world/middle-east/syrian-civil-war-the-day-i-met-the-organ-eating-cannibal-rebel-abu-sakkars-fearsome-followers-8617828.html. And http://www.youtube.com/watch?v=JF6dqvLxKTQ.

12 In Albania for instance, at least until the communist rule, the traditional code of honour obliged any man to face his future victim and tell him overtly why he was going to shoot him, the only excusable reason for the slaying being to exert the right of revenge for familial or tribal reputation's sake (like avenging a member of the group previously murdered).

13 To the point that they are hostages of the regime more than they may profit from it.

14 The ancient mystic (sufi) figures of the classical Islamic period are but a bygone experience and an outdated model.

15 For example, http://www.elnashrafan.com/news/show/1006882.

16 Yet, their abuse of Alawite, Christian, etc., women, although not much documented and thus subjected to speculations, seems nevertheless to have occurred at least in some instances. So the fighting cannot be said to be between viciousness and decency, which would be too simplistic.

17 In this respect, the militiaman must be distinguished from the traditional Oriental 'tough guy', the former one wielding an unbridled violence that resembles a general social challenge, whereas defiance towards the latter one is more individualistic and respectful of some degree of social conformity.

18 And this is particularly true of the regime and of extreme Islamists.

19 See for instance the creation of an extended security branch within the resistance around the capital, http://www.youtube.com/watch?v=dbkvB_8OylY.

20 An almost centenary scission from the Alawites with whom they are often erroneously amalgamated, because of different tribal allegiances and dissimilar doctrinal creeds.

21 Foreign journalists, when not killed, have been taken hostages by Islamist rebel groups for ransom.

22 Some 15,000 since March 2011, plus the huge amount of arrested persons.

23 The Kuran stipulates that the woman's (even implicit) consent is obligatory: II, 238/237.

24 On October, 5th, a female Kurdish fighter seems to have carried out the first suicide mission against IS in Kobane.

25 Some 150 French women and tens of European women have travelled to areas occupied by IS (west of Iraq and northeast of Syria). According to activists, for example, a Tunisian woman is leading a brigade in Raqqa (north of Syria), which includes 60 women (who need to be single and between 18 and 25 to join in) known for carrying heavy weapons.

Chapter 7
Military vs. Citizens in the Arab Zone:
An Assessment from Political Philosophy

Stéphane Valter
University of Le Havre, France

ABSTRACT

All the political systems of the Arab-Islamic zone are authoritarian, with the exception of Tunisia where fair elections recently took place and political alternation was accepted. Lebanon is another exception in the sense that state prerogatives – shared between antagonist religious communities – do not enjoy sufficient power to exert coercive policies. But apart from these two cases, this global authoritarian environment is of no avail vis-à-vis any initiative that would aim at forging some idea of citizenship – with its obligations and privileges – amongst the population, and particularly among the military. The present analysis will concentrate on the links existing between authoritarianism and citizenship, with an emphasis on Arab armed forces considered within their sociological contexts, since these entities are as much the emanation of the people(s) as the physical manifestation of the regimes' strength. The issue will be addressed through two perspectives: politics and philosophy.

INTRODUCTION

All the political systems of the Arab-Islamic zone are authoritarian, with the exception of Tunisia where fair elections recently took place and political alternation was accepted. Lebanon is another exception in the sense that state prerogatives – shared between antagonist religious communities – do not enjoy sufficient power to exert coercive policies. But apart from these two cases, this global authoritarian environment is of no avail *vis-à-vis* any initiative that would aim at forging some idea of citizenship – with its obligations and privileges – amongst the population, and particularly among the military. The present analysis will concentrate on the links existing between authoritarianism and citizenship, with an emphasis on Arab armed forces considered within their sociological contexts, since these entities are as much the emanation of the people(s) as the physical manifestation of the regimes' strength. The issue will be addressed through two perspec-

DOI: 10.4018/978-1-4666-9675-4.ch007

tives: politics and philosophy. It will be as much a general reflection as a precise study of some cases taken from the Arab world's present history. As indicated, the idea is to consider the role played by Arab military in actual political transitions. Are they factors of repression or of evolution? And in which way can they contribute to implement the notion of citizenship within peoples long deprived of fundamental political rights? Finally, which considerations may urge them to push towards peaceful and negotiated solutions, or on the contrary, prevent them from doing so? It must be noted that the requests articulated by the recent popular uprisings, since the end of 2010, were formulated in terms of liberty, democracy, elections, participation, development, etc., all of these being but universal demands (even if the concerned sociological contexts were specific).

BACKGROUND

It has to be admitted that the Arab political systems do not globally suit the criteria of the accomplished State in the sense that the different civil services do not function according to competence, that is, with a full participation of all citizens. On the contrary, through nepotism and corruption, when it is not terror, the general reinforcement of the administration (including the armed forces) aims mostly at increasing the repressive ability and resources monopolization, for the sole benefit of a small group. This model fits all the Arab world, except the two aforementioned cases. Doubtlessly, the re-examination of some philosophers who pondered over what links warrior's condition to citizenship will help us comprehend, within the framework of (Arab) authoritarian and despotic systems, the reasons behind: the refusal to govern men through the acquiescence of their free will; the systematic use of violence against the people; the enrolling of soldiers separated from society; the absence of any ethical finality among the political elite; and the instilling of distrust between citizens to prevent any coordinated action. It seems impossible, within the limited scope of this chapter, to go through all the philosophical literature that has been written on the subject. If exhaustivity remains impossible, it is also certainly useless since few good and relevant references suffice, as the stoic Seneca (Nero's tutor) used to say.[1] Secondly, the classical philosophers do not appear to have been surpassed on fundamental issues by neither modern nor contemporary ones, who have finally just reformulated in their own terms their predecessors' analysis. Thirdly, it would seem curious if a given political philosopher arrived at totally different conclusions than another one, especially if we take for granted that reason aims at apprehending the truth, which can only be one (even if it can be perceived and expressed differently according to diverse cultural contexts). In this sense, since we are dealing with human experience, we have relied on authors whose ideas seem particularly appropriate for our purpose.

As far as we know, classical Arab philosophers were scarce and largely influenced by the prism of religion, according to which God' will must remain the supreme reference (whereas, in theory, pure reasoning should only be based on a rational approach).[2] Reflecting on citizenship was therefore not really relevant since one could only speak of obedient and submissive subjects towards the religious and political leader: the caliph (that is to say God's deputy on earth). For reasons probably specific to Arab and Islamic culture, medieval philosophy was completely supplanted – in terms of legitimacy – over the centuries by jurisprudence (*fiqh*), the essential principle of which is to base legal reasoning on Islamic law's prescriptions, with a slight amount of intellectual independence (Tibi, 2005, p. 64). In the end, this tendency was reinforced by what may be called the Islamic revival (*nahda*, from the end of the XIXth century onwards) that took the form – yet with some notable exceptions – of religious, historical, cultural, ethnic, linguistic, etc., self-apologia, to the detriment of methodical investigation and systematic criticism. This self-justification combined to harsh denigration of the West later took two main shapes: self-centred politico-religious movements (emanating from the Egyptian Muslim Brotherhood) and chauvinist Arab nationalism (Nasserism in Egypt, Baathism in Syria and Iraq). None of which has been known for cultivating any inclination for conflicting voices: for example, the sectarian policy of Muslim Brother first freely elected Egyptian president Muhammad Morsi has not been a paragon of political virtue (and the same can be said of general-turned-president Sisi, Nasser's heir).

Last but not least, the poor level of public education systems in Arab countries has aggravated this tendency, with imperfect methods for teaching foreign languages (not even to mention ancient Greek and Latin, the foremost vectors of classical philosophy), inadequate endeavours for translating useful books into Arabic, and restricted places devoted to philosophy within curricula. To summarize, the general environment of oppression, exerted by colonial powers, then by newly independent authoritarian states, and most of all by traditional cultural contexts impervious to free thought and individual emancipation, has not been a favourable leaf-mould for Arab political philosophy, which therefore does not represent a huge contribution to universal thought. Since we can assume that reason should institute mutual relations of justice and utility between humankind, it is most certainly through educating the people to politics that the Arab armed forces will be able to carry out their missions while benefiting from the nation's respect. In this regard, according to Aristotle, politics is assuredly the prime of sciences because of its direct connection with (personal and collective) perfection that life is supposed to attain. As we said, the aim of this paper is to ponder over the possibility of Arab military to become full citizens.

ARAB AUTHORITARIANISM AND ARMIES

Significant cases will be considered, among them Syria and Iraq, for their numerous similarities: ethnic divisions between Arab and Kurds; fierce antagonisms between Sunni and Shiite Islam; presence of Christian minorities and Islamic sects; authoritarian baathist regimes (now a bygone legacy in Iraq and a system on the wane in Syria); over-equipped armies (warplanes, missiles, etc., even chemical weapons as in Syria); presence of transnational terrorist Islamist organizations. All these analogous elements cannot but lead to the same analysis. Moreover, if we admit that the collapse of the Iraqi state (2003) took place a bit more than ten years before the Syrian one is scheduled to crumble (which seems inevitable), we may see in the terrible Iraqi experience[3] a guideline for what should be done or avoided in Syria after the regime will have changed. Inversely, the actual woes that beleaguer and overtake Syria may be an acute reminder of what must be eschewed if Iraq wishes once and for all not to fall back into the throes of civil war. The common threat constituted by the Islamic State (EI), the Sunni terrorist and jihadist group that controls swathes of both countries, renders the comparison more pertinent. We mean that the present violence and destruction that befall the Syrian people,[4] with no solution in sight, cannot be considered as a definitely remote danger towards Iraq, even after the election of a more consensual government (August 2014) led by a Shiite prime minister who is at great pains healing the wounds of past sectarian marginalization and ethnic tensions. Thus, both cases (as well as others) are mutually enriching since interconnected, and may give some insights about the possibility for Arab military to become full citizens, both respected and respectful. Respected as individuals enjoying full political rights (in the limit allowed by their particular status), and respectful of civilians and fellow countrymen under the paramount supervision of the law.

Before asking oneself whether Arab military can make some pretensions to the citizen status, it seems important to tackle the armed forces (be they official or not) in a larger context that consists mainly of particular political systems, social structures, and religious references.[5] For the armed forces are indeed, through conscription and professionalization, the emanation of the people inasmuch as they are – mostly – the physical manifestation of the regimes' might. One should also take into account the fact that the security situation in the Middle East as is very tense, with profound complex causes and ancient inextricable conflicts, without any serious kind of regional security arrangements. On the contrary, the existing security alliances only involve a few states and are offensively directed against others: Iran and Syria (plus Shiite Iraq and Lebanese Hezbollah, the party-cum-militia) *versus* the Syrian armed groups; Egypt, Saudi Arabia, and the United Arab Emirates with regard to the Libyan chaos and the internal Yemeni conflict; Qatar and Turkey (which support the Syrian armed opposition and reject the *coup d'État* against Egyptian president Morsi in July 2013) *versus* other Sunni states; etc. Lebanon remains too fragile to prevent proxy conflicts from taking place on its territory. Jordan tries for its part to remain stable in the midst of all the regional conflicts. Palestine, although a sacred Arab cause, seems to have ceased to interest anybody in spite of symbolic gesticulation, whereas Israel deals discretely with some Arab regimes and maintains a low-profile military cooperation with the Kurdistan Regional Government (KRG) of Iraq. Finally, one could say that the only uniting factor is the rapid and EI scaring expansion of the Islamic State, the radical Sunni terrorist organization that threatens the whole Arab region and menaces Kurdish territorial claims (in Syria and northwest Iraq), with the notable exception of Turkey that looks rather satisfied – for the time being – to have let thousands of international jihadists cross its borders to pour in droves into Syria.

Three main theoretical frameworks may be useful to understand middle-eastern societies and, subsequently, their armed forces. The first is based on viewing political systems as networks of relations existing within basic communities and then transposed to the national level. Political stakes (which involve the armed forces) must thus be analysed as alliances determined by kinship, ethnicity, religious communities, patronage, and clientship (Gellner, 1981; Eisenstadt, 1973). The second, the production framework, perceives societies as economic structures characterized by a certain level of economic development that generates specific socio-economic relationships plus, most importantly, a particular political process and a special ideological legitimization. In this respect, it appears, in the Middle East in particular, that class mobilization remains much weaker than primordial community solidarities whenever the matter deals with the quest for material advantages; and the armed forces are no exception. Thirdly, what can be dubbed the paradigm of centre-periphery links aims at studying the system's heart as possessing an innate tendency to dominating thrown off sectors. The political community may thus be viewed (according to M. Weber) as a moral order of authority, with the state (the centre) possessing (or pretending to do so) the legitimate monopoly of authority.[6] If one wanted to ponder over the eventual existence of a separation between social structures and political functions, he would certainly reckon that the Arab world (and the Middle East more particularly) does not really suit what may be named the accomplished and model state (which necessarily includes the armed forces).[7] Similarly, he would grasp that the functioning of the civil service does not globally correspond to any criteria solely based on competence.

Some structural elements seem to favour the use of force (with the exception of the Lebanese case). These are the building process of the 'oriental' state, that can be paralleled with the administration's constant strengthening in order to increase the repressive capacities and the cornering of resources (Tilly, 1985, pp. 169-187).[8] And also the fact that this kind of state functions less with depersonalized bureaucratic procedures than with interdependencies between groups (Geertz, 1977, pp. 255-310). Can we therefore talk about some sort of authoritarian exception in the Arab world (with the neighbouring zones included: mostly Turkey and Iran)? Indeed, two other cultural elements keen to encourage coercion, within the state and the security apparatus, may be spotted: patriarchate and the master-disciple relation (Camau, 2006, p. 66-70). In Tunisia and Egypt, it can be supposed that the army (considered as the disciple *vis-à-vis* the political leadership) has moved (late 2010 and early 2011) towards some kind of autonomy from the central power (the master in the above model). The Tunisian army, contrary to the interior ministry's forces, did not intervene to crash the popular upheaval, which led to President Ben Ali's flight. In Egypt, the army remained on the sidelines before finally deciding to drop ex-general Hosni Mubarak, when the military hierarchy realised that the preservation of its interests compelled it not to oppose the uprising. In both cases, but out of different motives (sense of patriotic duty in Tunisia, narrow calculations in Egypt), the military institution refused to support the dictator any more.

But this has not been at all the case in Syria where political power and military might were, and still are, two sides of the same reality (Cook, 2007). Before the March 2011 rebellion, the civil government was just a folding screen behind which the multiple security agencies were pulling the strings. After the popular demonstrations were very violently crashed, the regime's repressive and military character appeared in broad daylight (if it were needed), since every political decision has been subjected to what can be called counter-insurgency tactics (in spite of some cosmetic measures). A huge amount of Sunni officers and soldiers have deserted to join the armed rebellion, while an important number of Alawite military staff and personnel have also run away (sometimes to openly mutiny). Yet the core of the regime's armed forces has remained faithful to president Asad, because many soldiers and security personnel hail from the same (Alawite) religious community, which creates – really or just out of propaganda – a shared destiny. Already militarized, the Syrian regime shows, in the actual tragic circumstances, an exemplary manifestation of symbiosis between political leadership's policy and top brass's strategy.

In Algeria, the Arab spring has not blossomed, certainly because of the frightful remembrances of the bloody civil war (in the 1990s): some 150,000 killed persons, about one million displaced people, etc. So the repercussions of neighbouring Tunisia's agitation could not but be cautious. Notwithstanding the fact that the military are omnipresent in the political arena since independence in 1962, and that coordination between security services and army intelligence remains high (Bourrat, 2012, p. 21-37). Some minor concessions were made to the people in order to prevent any contagion from Tunisia and beyond, and the system thus spared the cost of a major repression. The only potential point of disagreement between politicians (who act under the supervision of the dominant National Liberation Front) and military is about the successor of the aged and ailing president, since the nominee will have to maintain the *status quo* of organized prevarication. In Morocco, the king has made some negligible concessions so as to defer, as long as possible, more radical reforms for the benefit of his subjects. Whether Arab authoritarianism is analyzed through the lenses of patriarchate and master-disciple relation, or through another model, it remains true that democracy has not taken root within the Arab world, where the whole security apparatus is used to stamp out any claim for citizenship.

Moreover, whereas the armed forces' field of action is traditionally and theoretically defined according to the notion of border – the limits of the national territory (real or claimed) –, the security services' mission is rather devoted to exert control and repression within the national boundaries (Bocco & Meier, 2005). The German philosopher and sociologist Georg Simmel used to say, in reference to this topic, that 'the border is not so much a spatial fact with sociological effects as it is a sociological fact which takes on a spatial form' (Simmel, 1999, p. 607). And, obviously, this type of definition classifies individuals and groups through aggregating them to the political body or separating them from it, according to their allegiances. In the case of Syria, whole contesting districts and rebellious areas are collectively repressed and bombed while others, sometimes within the same city, are spared and protected, according to a non-appealable and clear-cut logic of either loyalty or exclusion, which the military are forced to implement whatever the cost in terms of nation building. For comparison's sake, one should remind that Lenin thought that the people could not rise and conduct a revolution against the army, which he conceived of as the entire group's emanation. On the contrary, in most Arab countries, and also partially in Turkey and Iran, the armed forces generally constitute a reactionary element associated to despised regimes.

To a certain extent, even in the cases where the army did not fire on the protesters, like in Tunisia and Egypt, one may wonder whether the fraternizing was more motivated by the feeling of a common revolutionary action or rather by conservatism and corporatism (both due to a dubious moral and civic stance) (Lindemann, 2008, p. 55-56). But in some instances, certain armies (which have to be differentiated from the brutal and ruthless security services) have been progressively accustomed to some kind of normalization. By normalization, we mean the acceptance of 'modern' moral and cultural norms. And this qualitative process can be considered as an important cause behind some armies' adoption of pragmatic positions that sometimes led to acceptable endings to crisis (Geisser & Krefa, 2011, p. 93-95). Moreover, when counter-insurgency carries more weight than the defence of borders (like in Syria and Iraq where both regimes' foes are internal), it remains highly doubtful that the armies' appertaining missions may bestow on them any lacking legitimacy (Caylus, 2012).

Samuel Huntington,[9] followed by Juan J. Linz (Linz, 2000), argued that the professionalization of the armies should normally direct their interest towards interior security and development rather than repression, although this thesis is not incompatible with a certain amount of political authoritarianism (Gresle, 2005). It could also be that some armies' involvement in peace-keeping international missions (under the United Nations' or the African Unity's auspices) may have provided them with a pragmatic spirit appropriate to defend democratic institutions. Whereas in the recent uprisings and conflicts, most Arab regimes have cherished the delusion that the system was protecting the people while being threatened by external plots. Conversely, the different oppositions have insisted on the deplorable implication of the armed forces in graft and cruelty, and have subsequently called for their patriotic awakening. It is finally obvious that any approach purely based on security concerns – which implies repression, killing, and destruction – can only forbid a finally less costly imposition of order that, it is true, implies compromises. Needless to say, in all the mentioned cases, the political consciousness of the military determines their attitude towards the orders given to them.

WARRIORS AND MIGHT THROUGH PHILOSOPHY

Ancient thinkers and political philosophers can assuredly give interesting clues as to the possible links between warlike status and access to citizenship. The following examples and quotes, obviously not exhaustive, are yet probably sufficient to delineate a useful scope of philosophical and political thought that should allow for a better understanding of the Arab region (the specificity of which must be questioned). Xenophon (430/425-355/352), a disciple of Socrates and a rival of Plato, in his *Hiero or the Treatise on Tyranny*, argues that 'tyrants [...] are reluctant either to inspire bravery into the citizens or to arm them properly, since it is more pleasing to them to turn foreigners into more fearful persons than the citizens themselves, so they resort to them as body guards.' (Strauss, 1997, p. 21). The contemporary version of this sound (and deplorable) analysis consists in the fact that Arab regimes make a systematic use of violence against their own peoples, and that they even tend to enrol soldiers sociologically separated from the whole social body (especially when power is wielded from minorities, like in Syria where the elite units are very largely sectarian). These regimes may also resort to mercenaries, again as in Syria where Iranian Pasdaran soldiers and Lebanese Shiite Hezbollah fighters, along with Iraqi Shiite militiamen and Afghan Shiite Hazara tribesmen, wage war with the government army; or in the Gulf states which usually contract foreign soldiers and vigilantes (from Pakistan, Colombia, etc.).

In Plato's (424/423-348/347) *Gorgias*, the Socratic thesis (which denounces rhetoric as the art of lying) is opposed to the Sophist stance (which admits the resort to violence). And through the occurring dialogue between the two sides, Plato endeavours to show that philosophy naturally rejects violence since the human being is supposed to argue with freedom and reason in order to convince without compelling. In *The Republic*, Plato makes a clear distinction between tyranny and politics: whereas the first means governing men through might, the second implies that they be ruled through the acquiescence of their free will. Under the theoretical hierarchy that is supposed to organize the ideal city, Plato defines the universal principle of order as existing both within the city and the individual. So whenever conflict can be transformed into unity – that is when all categories belonging to the ideal political organization (from which the military are a part) fulfil scrupulously their natural functions –, Plato's city (we would say the nation today) can live in harmony and bliss. Actually, in modern societies, the only political system close to this ideal model must most probably be based on consensus and stable institutions in order for everybody to play a useful and gratifying role in public life.

But the state may also be terrorist when it wants to prevent the emergence of plain citizenship, particularly among the armed forces that could then threaten the entire system. The pillars of this terrorizing policy were described by Aristotle (384-322), in his *Politics*, as the following: the debasement of the citizens, the establishment of mistrust between them, and the impossibility of conducting any coordinated action. The expression 'political animal' reflects in this sense all the ambiguity of the various situations as well as the conflict between the existing potentialities. Thus, the human being can get close to, or away from, citizenship depending on the nature of the political system. In this respect, Aristotle insisted on the fact that man could only have a fulfilling existence and become an accomplished citizen (within the framework of the ideal city) through reason. And reason has to be expressed by language, via dialogue and criticism, which sets up in the end mutual links of justice and equity. In the *Nicomachean Ethics*, Aristotle identified politics as the prime science since it is, according to him, in direct connection with perfection: the aim of life, that is the desired outcome of collective behaviour and personal conduct. Therefore, politics would even surpass morals since the quest for the common good constitutes the human condition's honour. It can be added that Aristotle only viewed positively the goods acquired and utilized for a domestic use, in a perspective of temperance and moderation. He thus disapproved of any economic activity aiming not only at resources capturing or speculation but also at the simple fact of trading (which he names *chrematistics*, or the art of enrichment).

Needless to say, the immixture of many Arab militaries in dubious economic affairs, not to mention open corruption and aggressive prevarication, constitutes a crippling impediment to the principles defended by Aristotle, we mean: when the virtuous man desires to become a respectable citizen. In the context of state terror mentioned by Aristotle, which ignores all legal constraints and pushes to the manifestation of 'legitimate' violence but outside the rule of law (that normally implies continuity, regularity, and publicity), the military rapidly loose their souls. This is especially true if they intervene in brutal counter-insurgency, while freeing themselves from all legal and moral norms that may curb violence. Finally, fear, suspicion, the restriction of public life, and even the total splitting up of the social scope all wipe out whatever attempt there may be at building some kind of citizenship – while the requirements of citizenship may (re)integrate the military at the end of conflicts – because of a generalized depoliticizing process.

Saint Augustine (354-430), while reflecting on strength and law, distinguished, in a similar way but from a theological angle, between self-love and love of God, the first corresponding to the terrestrial city (conducted by the passion of domination) and the second referring to the celestial one (with 'citizens united in charity').[10] Joining the armed forces may thus be discrepant with the Augustinian conception of purity, in the sense that justice remains absolutely anterior and superior to power. In this manner, justice is immutable and sovereign, and any attempt at subordinating justice to power constitutes a very serious moral mistake. Machiavelli (1469-1527) was more pragmatic: in order to impose domination, the regime must resort to all the rules of politics (and even to violence) in order to avert what could turn out unforeseeable and fatal (like a popular uprising). With this rather cynical vision, the moral considerations are supposed to slip away in front of the requirements needed for maintaining political stability, and this whatever the sacrifice demanded towards public liberties as well as the constraints imposed on citizens. Machiavelli's ideas, expressed in *The Prince*, do not seem to be obsolete since all the Arab leaders apply his precepts, to a greater or lesser degree. Thus the implication of the Arab armed forces in security and repressive measures resembles too well the case of the Italian statelets from Machiavelli's epoch during which power remained precarious.

According to the English philosopher Hobbes (1588-1679), when the relations between authority (the monarch) and the people deteriorate to the point that violence predominates, it can be assumed that society is close to a primitive (and negatively perceived) state of nature. And this disastrous situation is characterized by unpredictability, insecurity, and chaos.[11] When it becomes almost impossible to identify military who remain respectful of laws and institutions, or even mere ordinary citizens behaving with a high sense of responsibility, the situation may be described as primitively natural. Although the Scottish philosopher Hume (1711-1776) had pointed to the fact that men always need rules, even to kill themselves,[12] this ritualized frame can nevertheless explode in certain situations. The armed forces are thus allowed to perpetrate all possible excesses, thus forgoing the moral commitment that appertains to a reasoned citizenship. This is the case today in Syria where the civil strife is no more codified (killing of civilians, rape, etc.) and where war prisoners are scarce, from both sides (with sometimes the exception of the Free Syrian Army), as if no reconciliation process was ever envisaged. In the Iraqi conflict, between the central government and the EI, pro-regime revengeful Shiite militias do not hesitate to commit atrocities against Sunni compatriots whom they suspect of being accomplices of the jihadists and traitors to the country.[13]

For his part, Locke (1632-1704)[14] aimed at the containment of authority by limiting it through both people's consent and natural law, in order to forestall any danger of arbitrariness, since he believed that all men were fundamentally equal and independent, and that reason could teach them how to respect each other. Human feeling was thus supposed to naturally protect the innocent and punish any abuse. He viewed civil society as a body of people united and controlled by a magistrature applying a common and general law, and thus he did not consider it as liberticide since even the authorities had to submit to the rules. Civil society was indeed seen as a protecting body against destruction, bondage, and plundering in the sense that natural law remains the ultimate bulwark for the defence of liberty. But when power becomes too authoritarian and even too savage, Locke recognizes to the people the right of resisting. One may assume that what has been known in Syria as civil coordinating committees (also present in other Arab countries where uprisings have taken place) are in a way concrete examples of successful civil resilience in the face of brutal and indiscriminate state warfare. These committees have documented (with improvised technical devices) the misdeeds of the regime's armed forces when they crushed what was at the beginning rather peaceful demonstrations. And they continue to offer a rather precise coverage of the state's indiscriminate violence. They have also tried in some places to organize the distribution of whatever relief could be given to suffering people. These civil committees, made up of activists and volunteers, now document, at their own peril, EI's atrocities.

While reflecting on the importance of juridical relationships, Montesquieu (1689-1755) was on the opinion, in *De l'Esprit des Lois* (*The Spirit of Laws*), that all the citizen's acts (as far as he is a political being) are regulated by laws, whereas man's actions (as a social being) are rather controlled by manners and morals. Yet, in the Arab world, the various situations of oppression and violence do not allow for a sufficiently strong juridical supervision, able to efficiently control the armed forces' prerogatives and instructions that may – and indeed do – act in almost total impunity. They act so in such a morally degrading way (first of all towards themselves) that they quickly end up, according to Montesquieu, irrevocably deprived of the citizenship status. The coarse and even inhumane behaviour of many members of the Syrian regime's armed forces, and sometimes also of rebel fighters, denies them all access to mankind since the basic rules of sociability have been ignored. The question is then, after such an accumulation of hatred and distrust: how to reintegrate the belligerents in an encompassing social body once civil strife is over? How to judge and pardon whom has committed humiliation, torture, cold killing, rape, mass murder? Most of the security services and of the elite army units in Syria, like many Islamist fighting groups,[15] can surely be put into the category of animality (and not civility), in so far as the quintessence of man's condition is liberty and the marrow of social condition is justice, as Montesquieu pointed out.

Rousseau (1712-1778) represents a turning point in political philosophy since he does not regard so much the practice of power as aiming at the achievement of man's liberty. Rather, he declares that power must belong in the first place to the people who thus become sovereign in an inalienable way. The republican regime remains in this way the best system of government, and the old feudal-like relationships between mankind, based on exploitation and subjection (and sometimes fright), have to be replaced by interdependencies between citizens defined by law. Concerning war, he adds that it cannot be defined as 'a relation between men but rather between states, in which individuals have incidentally become foes, not as human beings but as soldiers'. He moreover defines what the rules of war should be, in such a way that moderation and mercy may be applied with not too much reticence, and even naturally: 'Even in the midst of war, a just prince who grabs in enemy territory all that belongs to the public realm must respect individual persons and properties [...].' Finally, with regard to the treatment of prisoners: 'Since the aim of war is the destruction of the hostile state, it is thus permissible to kill its defenders as long as they carry weapons; but as soon as they lay them down and surrender [...], they become ordinary men and nobody has any right on their lives.' But such a humanist theory barely applies in many conflicts where prisoners are just abused, tortured, and killed, whereas 'the right of servitude is null [...] since the words *servitude* and *right* are contradictory and mutually exclusive'.[16]

In total contradiction to these noble ideas, the violence perpetrated by EI fighters derives from general patterns of human barbarism, from cruel examples belonging to the Prophet's tradition, and from pure and sadistic criminality. Their violence also derives, without the slightest doubt, of the ignominies committed by the regime. Violence and counter-violence. Among the worst cases of viciousness, and those which received a wide media coverage (intentionally on the EI's part as a form of terrifying propaganda), are the slaughtering of some 1,500 (mostly Shiite) cadets at Camp Speicher near Tikrit, in Iraq (June 2014), after they were exhibited like sacrificial sheep; and the massacre committed at Tabqa, in a military air base located in northern Syria, when some 220 captured government soldiers were gruesomely killed in a filmed mass execution (August 2014). On the other side, industrial kinds of violence have been carried out by the Syrian regime, with sarin gas and chlorine against civilians.

VIOLENCE: OPPRESSION OR EMANCIPATION

When one tries to imagine an ethical frame by which military discipline and conduct should abide, the gap between this ideal reference and the real functioning of the armed forces may certainly reflect a saddening degree of moral deliquescence, first within the soldiers themselves and then within their society as a whole. This reflection may serve as a useful perspective to imagine future political transitions, in which Arab military could play a stabilizing role. The marquess of Vauvenargues (1715-1747), an impecunious aristocrat, a valetudinarian officer, and a moralist, wrote an *Introduction à la Connaissance de l'Esprit Humain* (*Introduction to the Knowledge of Human Mind*) the sapiential teaching of which endeavoured to promote a martial ideal exalting duty, honour, and virtue. But it is clear that the Arab military remain a long way from this model, even in Egypt where, as we said, the army finally decided not to side with the deposed president (H. Mubarak) in order to install (yet not without some reluctance) a more democratic system. But the military took one year later an active part in ousting the first elected president (M. Morsi) who was accused (along with his party) of bringing the country to the edge of collapse. This sequence of events ended when the Muslim Brotherhood was declared a terrorist organization, thus putting a final end to any idea of free political participation.

Although the issue is general and universal, it seems difficult to end this reflection based on the Arab zone without mentioning an Arab and Muslim thinker: the reformist sheikh from Aleppo Abd al-Rahman al-Kawakibi (1849-1902) who wrote the famous *Taba'i' al-istibdad* (or *The Characteristics of Despotism*). In his book, he uttered the idea that the fear experienced by a despot towards an eventual vengeance of his subjects remains much stronger than their apprehension about his brutal force. He thus means that the despot's fear emanates from the fact that he knows too well what to expect from his subjects, whose fright is only caused by ignorance, which may obviously change. Thus, if the despot's fear results from an organic incapability that is impossible to modify without shattering (to his own disadvantage) the political order, the subjects' dread solely arises from a (largely imagined) lack of collective cohesion, which is amendable via social interactions and political coordination. And when his fear originates from the idea that he may lose everything (power and life), the subjects are generally only afraid of just having to give up scanty means of subsistence as well as to relinquish a miserable life (Tapiéro, 1956). We can incidentally notice that the issue of the relationship between ruler and subjects – which we view today in terms of access to full citizenship – was already reflected upon in the Levant, even before the emergence of modern authoritarian and military Arab regimes.

Another penniless nobleman, disillusioned officer, and French writer, Alfred-Victor de Vigny (1797-1863), took his inspiration from the idea that the progress of philosophy should normally diminish the resort to war. In *Servitude et Grandeur Militaires* (*Military Servitude and Greatness*), he appears both disappointed and admiring towards the army. He brands the backwardness and the barbarianism of his epoch's armies where 'the warrior is separated from the citizen and where man remains miserable and ferocious.' Similarly, he laments the difficulties to live in a time 'when the armies will identify with the Nation,' that is when the soldier will no more be a tool of repression against civil troubles under a temporary chief's orders. This idea of a missing link between military and society desperately applies to the Arab world (as well as to other cultural zones where development, liberty, and justice are impeded). Vigny moreover compared, in civil war contexts, the soldier to the gladiator: 'How can we live under laws that we find reasonable to deliver death to whomever would refuse [...] blind submission?,' and this because of 'absolute orders given to the Armies by the sovereign Power, so frequently fallen into undeserving hands' (Vigny, 1949, p. 13, 14, 21, 43, 44).

German thought in particular has mused upon the question of violence. Hegel (1770-1831) thus constructed the theory of (asymmetric) dialectic relationships between lord and slave, in an unremitting and unavoidable fight between antagonistic consciences, each aiming at asserting itself at the prejudice of others. From this conflict between individuals about recognition and submission, social life finally evolved towards the first manifestations of the state. In this matter, Hegel considered that the ideal modern state – were it to exist – was necessarily characterized by a full harmony combining unity and difference.[17] His vision of the deterministic struggle between master and thrall may help to explain, to a certain point, recent evolutions in the Arab world, especially when some military – as actors of repression as well as victims of the general authoritarianism – have defected to express their disapproval of iniquitous systems. This has been the case in Syria where the 500,000 odd army has been largely reduced because of desertions, for liberty's sake. Inversely, one could also argue that some violence-prone elements have just switched formal camps and only joined the armed rebellion so as to give full vent to their long contained desire of revenge. In doing so, they have disregarded any strong moral commitment to fight the regime alone, and not the Alawi community *per se*, which constitutes *nolens volens* its core power basis. In other words, is the Syrian crisis a patriotic surge to eradicate oppression or just the last manifestation of boisterous Sunni vengeance against a brutal sectarian (minority) regime? The noteworthy exception of Tunisia must be reminded since the army, at the beginning of the protests, protected the people from a tentacular and repressive police apparatus and then, after Ben Ali's forced departure, played the role of the Constitution's guarantor.[18]

If the second example (probably a little more than the first one) may reflect Hegel's conception of harmony (unity and difference), other different cases seem to fit more or less in the same frame. Many Arab military, previously used to engage in fierce repression in order to impose non-consensual systems, have thus been affected by internal insubordination, both in their quest to cast out from power unbearable yokes (detrimental in the end to their own interests) and to restore a minimum amount of essential public liberties (out of moral conviction). In Libya, the army, based on tribal and geographical allegiances, disintegrated when some units raised to sweep away Ghadaffi's dictatorial grip (February – October 2011). What remains now of the state's security apparatus painfully endeavours to control and include the various militias into the state building process, which is highly contested by warlords and their tribesmen (sometimes purporting to follow the right religious tradition, or *salaf*, and sometimes brandishing the flag of *jihad* to cover criminal activities). In Egypt, the military were the backbone of the old system until the hierarchy decided to drop the president (February 2011) and then, dubiously, pretended to restore democracy by overthrowing the second one (July 2013). And in Yemen, the army, split on tribal, religious, and political basis, still remains far from representing either state or society, particularly after the Shiite Huthi northern tribesmen – manipulated by former president Saleh and supported by Iran – launched a large-scale attack (end of 2014) towards the centre and the south of the country. The last three cases seem far from Hegel's model, when global social life is supposed to evolve towards the consolidation of an ideal modern state, united yet accepting political, religious, and cultural differences.

Nietzsche's (1844-1900) thesis distinguishes between power of self-assertion (the positive strength of hefty people) and repressive force (the perverted force of weak ones).[19] If we follow him, the might employed by many Arab military should without ambiguity be put into the second category. (Overt or disguised) violence has generally been exerted solely to impose domestication, as if people were not citizens, with equal rights and obligations according to the state's laws, but only bondsmen toiling in feudal lands. In his *Critique of Violence*, the German philosopher Walter B. S. Benjamin (1892-1940) considered that the unleashing of violence could be paralleled with a manifestation of God's wrath, in the sense that the biblical divinity's impetuous ire could express, by amplification, man's extreme anger. The complexity of this analysis may not conveniently explain either the intensity of many political, economic, and sociological conflicts or the military's stances towards them. Yet Benjamin's point may be kept in mind in the sense that many crisis have taken place in a climate of extreme violence loaded with narrow community references which, once stirred up, usually set up insuperable fences between people (who thus become organically governed by their own non-negotiable and exclusive innermost identities).[20] Benjamin's idea that violence can sometimes be freely destructive and irrational may be useful to the analysis. But can spontaneous violence be pure?

Hannah Arendt appears to accept this hypothesis even if she admits that this eventual purity can easily be rendered instrumental by institutional corrupting processes (Arendt, 1996). If we follow Arendt on the idea that the outburst of violence goes along with a high unpredictability (an increasing concatenation of furious misdemeanours), we may therefore suggest *a contrario* that the less respectful of law (by essence predictable) military's acts are, the less chance they have of being able to pretend to the status of responsible state servants, and thus of citizens. The case of the Tunisian army, which rejected violence and instability in the first place, has already been mentioned as a body mindful of the citizens' security and of the state's durability. Whereas in Syria, violence has totally gone out of control, from all sides, with apparently few military coordination even within the state's security services and army units. With such complete leeway and uncontrolled full powers, the numerous atrocities will certainly be impossible to forget during any (still very distant) reconciliation process. It is certainly true that pure and total violence may sometimes allow oppressed people to regain a part of their dignity, even with some amount of irrationality and savagery during revolts, as suggested by the French psychiatrist and essayist Frantz Fanon (1925-1961).[21] Yet one cannot defend the idea that the whole Syrian security apparatus, which relies on extremely violent means (sometimes similar to the rebels' but for the fact that they are carried out on an industrial scale), may pretend to the same qualification – fighters for humanity – since their only purpose is to keep up the exploitation system. Fanon thus could have said that the Syrian rebellion acts with full legitimacy as long as it strives to get rid of a more than forty-year old cruel oppression.[22] Or at least, he could have said that concerning a part of the rebellion: those who fight for liberty, and not just to spill Alawite and 'unfaithful' blood in order to impose some medieval Islamist ideology, not to mention the roving criminal gangs.

Systems of domination, in which warriors give orders to producers, can be analyzed from an anthropological point of view. That is how Ernest Gellner usefully contributed to this field of research. So when this kind of systems vanished a long time ago in the West, they gave way to more refined commercial and bureaucratic links between people, as more or less happened quite recently in the socialist block after the collapse of the communist and repressive regimes.[23] Concerning the Arab zone, these interactions based on intimidation and exploitation are doubtlessly the norm, in the sense that the warriors' (the military) role consists usually to closely keep watch on the people through coercion and brutality, so as to extract from them the maximum of resources. In so doing, they are subordinated to the sole interests of a greedy and imperious political leadership (whatever its outward characteristics). Obviously, the preceding ethical theories on violence cannot be dissociated from non-egalitarian and competitive societies where interactions between groups and individuals are essentially based on confrontation. From this angle, the military could hardly escape from these morally restricting particulars, intrinsically connected to their function, even if they attempted to redefine their socio-political role in a more rational way (that is in a legal and democratic framework) (Michaud, 2012, p. 115; Farago, 1998).

FUTURE RESEARCH DIRECTIONS

The rare but significant case of the German armed forces must be pointed out since they are submitted to important limits concerning the use of force, even when they act as the state's legitimate protectors. Thus in Germany, Bundeswehr soldiers and officers are compelled by the Constitution to disobey any order which might seem to them contrary to the accomplishment of their mission in a democratic spirit.[24] These legal and moral bounds imposed on the military (because of the weight of a painful national past) certainly inculcate in them respect towards the political institutions. Moreover, due to these democratic limitations, they can be viewed with consideration by the civil society that is enticed to perceive them as normal citizens in their own rights. Definitely, the German example is outstanding and probably an exception rarely to be seen elsewhere, for historical reasons. Yet, after taking this example as an ideal norm, a comparative analysis will have to be carried out, for instance between the Arab world and south-east Asia to understand why the military's role has led to rather calm institutional transitions in some places (Burma, the Philippines, Thailand, etc.) whereas the multiple security agencies have played a subverting and repressing game in many Arab countries. We mean that instead of contributing to the achievement of some kind of consensus, they have generally engaged in preserving old, obsolete, and corrupted regimes to the detriment of progress, welfare, and durable stability.

Even if all the mentioned theories on the nature of authoritarianism, monopoly of power, and violence have been articulated (for some of them) in bygone times, they remain nevertheless totally relevant to understand the political systems of the Arab area today. Indeed, almost all these systems are based on coercion – in spite of some recent positive evolutions, like the free legislative and presidential elections in Tunisia (end of 2014) – and thus they rely heavily on the various armed forces to implement control, surveillance, and exploitation. The widespread lack of interest, on the part of these authoritarian and corrupt systems, in promoting democracy and rooting citizenship may probably ensure their survival for some time, but assuredly sows the seeds of public discontent. The governmental armed forces' stance, whether in accompanying democratic transitions or, on the contrary, in curbing legitimate popular demands, can only determine on which side of History they will remain. One may wonder whether the lessons of the Iraqi baathist state's collapse and of the ensuing chaos that resembles a civil war (fuelled by international jihadist organizations, the most terrifying of them being the Islamic State) between the different denominations and ethnic groups and that has been plaguing the country for years, have been memorized by the concerned actors in Syria.

CONCLUSION

Since it appears, in Syria, Iraq, Libya, Yemen, and elsewhere, that more emphasis is given to plunder, torture, destruction, and slaughter than to the possible ways of finding negotiated solutions. The armed forces, from the governmental side or from the various rebel factions' one (which sometimes fight furiously against each other), prefer to carry on obstinately their respective military campaigns instead of following clear political objectives that could be useful guidelines to reconstruct the country. Instead of defining inclusive plans for the after-war period, the displayed efforts rather give way to political bickering among decision-makers as well as pitiless battling between the regime military and the rebel militias (and even among themselves). Protecting properties, defending civilians, behaving humanely towards prisoners, abstaining from ill-treatment, abiding by the law, and showing consideration for ethics, are definitely the supreme standards by which soldiers and officers will be considered by whatever national community there may be once war is over; and all these parameters will determine the nature of the political transition, for better or worse. If the history of the Iraqi disintegration, chaos, marginalization, and now slow and harrowing reconstruction process cannot be rewritten, some lessons may nevertheless be learnt from Syria's calamities. These are that military must always stand for the people rather than protect nonconsensual and brutal regimes. Thus, they can gain the admiration and the respect of the whole population in order for stability to be perennial and democracy to be unwavering, whatever the religious, linguistic, and ethnic problems of the national social fabric, too often marred by class antagonism, sectarian animosity, and territorial irredentism. This long-term goal can clearly only be achieved through civic education.

REFERENCES

Arendt, H. (1996). *Essai sur la Violence* (trans. plus foreword by M.-I. B. de Launay). *La Nature du Totalitarisme*. Paris: Bibliothèque philosophique Payot.

Bocco, R., & Meier, D. (2005). Penser la Notion de Frontière au Moyen-Orient. *A Contrario*, 2/3, 3-10.

Bourrat, F. (dir.) (2012). La Place et le Rôle des Armées dans le Monde Arabe Contemporain. In Les Champs de Mars, 23. Paris: La Documentation Française (Institut de Recherche Stratégique de l'École militaire).

Camau, M. (2006). Globalisation Démocratique et Exception Autoritaire Arabe. *Critique Internationale*, *30*(1), 59–81. doi:10.3917/crii.030.0059

Caylus, H. (2012). Le Choix d'une Démilitarisation Brutale: le Cas de l'Armée Irakienne. In F. Bourrat (Ed.), La Place et le Rôle des Armées dans le Monde Arabe Contemporain (pp. 97-117). In Les Champs de Mars, 23. Paris: La Documentation Française (Institut de Recherche Stratégique de l'École militaire).

Cook, S. A. (2007). *Ruling but not Governing: the Military and Political Development in Egypt, Algeria and Turkey*. Baltimore: John Hopkins University Press.

de Vigny, A.-V. (1949). B. Grillet (Ed.), *Servitude et Grandeur Militaires*. Paris: Librairie Larousse (collection Classiques Larousse).

Eisenstadt, S. N. (1973). *Traditional Patrimonialism and Modern Neopatrimonialism*. Thousand Oaks, London: SAGE Publications.

Farago, F. (1998). *Les Grands Courants de la Pensée Politique*. Paris: Armand Colin.

Geertz, C. (1977). The Integrative Revolution: Primordial Sentiments and Civil Politics in the New States. In C. Geertz (Ed.), *The Interpretation of Cultures* (pp. 255–310). New York: Basic Books.

Geisser, V., & Krefa, A. (2011). L'Uniforme ne Fait plus le Régime, les Militaires Arabes face aux 'Révolutions'. *La Revue Internationale et Stratégique*, *83*(3), 93–102. doi:10.3917/ris.083.0093

Gellner, E. (1981). *Muslim Society*. Cambridge: Cambridge University Press.

Gresle, F. (dir.) (2005). *Sociologie du Milieu Militaire. Les Conséquences de la Professionnalisation sur les Armées et l'Identité Militaire*. Paris: L'Harmattan.

Lindemann, T. (2008). Faucons et Colombes. Le Choix Stratégique des Forces Armées entre Intérêt Corporatiste et Identités Militaires. *Revue Internationale de Politique Comparée*, *1/15*(1), 55–76. doi:10.3917/ripc.151.0055

Linz, J. J. (2000). *Totalitarian and Authoritarian Regimes*. Boulder, London: Lynne Rienner Publishers.

Michaud, Y. (2012). *La Violence* (7th ed.). Paris: PUF.

Simmel, G. (1999). *Sociologie. Études sur les Formes de Socialisation* (Original work published 1908). Paris: PUF.

Strauss, L. (1997). De la Tyrannie, followed by Correspondance avec Alexandre Kojève (1932-1965). Paris: Éditions Gallimard (NRF, Bibliothèque de philosophie).

Tapiéro, N. (1956). *Les Idées Réformistes d'al-Kawâkibî, 1265-1320 – 1849-1902. Contribution à l'Étude de l'Islam Moderne*. Paris: Les Éditions arabes.

Tibi, B. (2005). *Islam between Culture and Politics* (2nd ed.). Basingstoke (Hampshire) / New York: Palgrave Macmillan. doi:10.1057/9780230204157

Tilly, C. (1985). War Making and State Making as Organized Crime. In *P. B. Evans, D. Rueschemeyer, & T. Skocpol (dir.), Bringing the State back* (pp. 169–187). Cambridge: Cambridge University Press. doi:10.1017/CBO9780511628283.008

ADDITIONAL READING

Aristotle. *Nicomachean Ethics* and *Politics*.

Benraad, M. (2015). *Irak, la revanche de l'histoire. De l'occupation étrangère à l'État islamique*. Paris: Vendémiaire.

Bozarslan, H. (2008). *Une Histoire de la Violence au Moyen-Orient*. Paris: La Découverte.

Burgat, F., & Paoli, B. (Eds.), (2013). *Pas de Printemps pour la Syrie. Les Clés pour Comprendre les Acteurs et les Défis de la Crise (2011-2013)*. Paris: La Découverte.

Daguzan, J.-F., & Valter, S. (Eds.), (2014). *Les Forces Armées Arabes et Moyen-Orientales (après les Printemps Arabes)*. Paris: ESKA – Fondation pour la recherche stratégique.

Kutschera, C. (Ed.), (2005). *Le livre noir de Saddam Hussein*. Paris: Oh ! Éditions.

Machiavelli. (n. d.). *The Prince*.

Plato. (n. d.). *The Republic*.

Seneca. (n. d.). *Epistulæ morales ad Lucilium*.

Vauvenargues, (L. de Clapiers, marquess of) (1956). *Noblesse de Vauvenargues*. Paris: Les Libraires Associés.

KEY TERMS AND DEFINITIONS

Alawites: The Alawite 'religion' can be considered as a medieval split from Imami (mainstream) Shiism. Their specificities are considered as grave anomalies by conservative Sunnism which brands them as evident proofs of irreligiousness.

Baathism: An Arab nationalist, secular, and more or less socialist ideology, created in Syria in the 1940s by people hailing from all religious communities (Alawites, Christians, Sunnis, etc.).

Huthis: A Shiite (from the Zaydi subdivision) group operating in Yemen which carried out a *coup d'État* in 2014.

Jihad: Koranic word meaning 'effort' (personal, piety-related, defensive, or offensive effort, according to the context).

Kurds: An ethnic and (Indo-European) linguistic group leaving in the Middle East, deprived of statehood by the 1923 Lausanne treaty. Some 40 million people today.

Muslim Brotherhood: A confessional and (non-overtly) political organization created in Egypt in 1927, with social, educative, religious, etc., aims. Always in conflict with the political power (first during the monarchy, and then from 1952 onwards).

Nasserism: Ideology (vaguely) articulated by Nasser and based on Egyptian patriotism, Arab nationalism, African commitment, and non-aligned sympathies, with a non-negligible amount of (late) socialism.

Shiism: A split in Islam dating back to the time of the Prophet's succession, more precisely after the assassination of the third caliph in 656. The Arabic word means 'party' (that is, of 'Ali, Muhammad's cousin and son-in-law).

Sunnism: The main trend in Islam (some 90% of all Muslims). The Arabic word signifies 'those who follow Muhammad's tradition (words and deeds)' and do not think that 'Ali (and his descendants later on) had any particular right to the succession.

ENDNOTES

1 In his *Epistulæ morales ad Lucilium*.

2 Farabi (872-950), who commented Plato's works, is an outstanding exception, within as well as outside Islam.

3 From 1991 (the first Gulf war) to 2003, more than 1,5 million victims (because of the American-led attacks and embargo); and probably more than 1 million (direct and indirect) victims from 2003 (the second Gulf war) up to now, according to UN and independent sources. http://www.voltairenet.org/article187295.html.

4 According to some sources, since March 2011, there are about 230,000 (direct) victims, but it can be assumed that this number can be doubled if we add disappeared people (that is, killed in jails and buried in mass graves) and indirect victims (because of disease, malnutrition, etc.). Plus some 2 million refugees and some 6 million internally displaced people.

5 Any sound analysis should consider with care and scepticism (which does not mean necessarily rejection) all the theories according to which Islam and democracy are organically

incompatible. The American orientalist Bernard Lewis seems to support the theory of incompatibility whereas the Franco-Tunisian academic Mohamed-Chérif Ferjani opines that Islam is not fundamentally opposed to democracy (contrary to the political use of Islam which does not often get along well with human rights).

6 Especially in his *Politics as a Vocation*, first published in 1919.

7 If we continue to follow Gellner who perceives patronage as a consequence of an incompletely centralized state (from a capitalist point of view), with an ineffective and corrupted bureaucracy as well as with narrow group-based dynamics.

8 State building and use of the army are here intertwined.

9 Particularly in his *Soldier and the State: The Theory and Politics of Civil-Military Relations*, first published in 1957.

10 *The City of God*, book XIV, chapter 23.

11 For Hobbes, as articulated in his *Leviathan*, these relations are not yet conceived on the basis of reciprocity (that is, they are deprived of any synallagmatic character).

12 See his *Treatise of Human Nature*, first publication in 1739. The rules of war were enacted from 1864 onwards in Geneva.

13 Many Shiite militiamen have even recently declared that some Sunni members of Parliament were only representing the despised Islamic State, whereas many segments of the Sunni population (tribes, local groups, individuals) also suffer from this terrorist organization.

14 Especially in his *Two Treatises of Government*.

15 Some of them are made up of a rather huge percentage of foreigners coming to perform *jihad* against the Alawi sect.

16 See his *Du Contrat Social, ou Principes du Droit Politique*, (*On the Social Contract, or the Principles of Political Law*), book first, chapter IV ('On Slavery').

17 See both *Phenomenology of Spirit* (for the slave – master relationship) and *Philosophy of Right* (about state and freedom).

18 The army only consisted of some 35,000 men (with some 23,000 conscripts among them) whereas the police forces were made up of more than 100,000 persons, which proves in a way that the army had been marginalized and was therefore not ready to support heartily the regime.

19 In *Beyond Good and Evil*.

20 Among the examples of this kind of conflicting situations are the fierce cleavages between Sunnism and Shiism, and even within Sunnism itself, with fiery words of anathematization towards whoever is perceived as schismatic and heterodox.

21 Who sided with the Algerian independence fight. See his famous *Les Damnés de la Terre*, first published in 1961.

22 As Ignace Leverrier (see his blog on Syria) pointed out during a private correspondence with the author: 'Evil and ferocity are everywhere. In Syria, there are not two sides but much more, and all those whom the regime brands in an unequivocal manner as 'rebels' or 'terrorists' cannot be ranked together. Criminals, jihadists, terrorists, are not interested in (pacific or not) political change since, from a certain point of view, they are the offshoots of a situation which gets less and less under control and on which they thrive. In doing so, and probably in spite of their will, they serve the regime's interests (which tries to find his salvation in anarchy) and not the revolutionaries' who want to install peace and order. Manipulation and abuse *versus* outbreaks and excesses'.

23 See in particular his *Nations and Nationalism*, 1983.

24 Article 10 of the military justice code thus defines officers' duties: orders 'cannot be given for another purpose than service needs', and they must be 'in conformity with the rules of international law, legal acts, and military rules.' Article 11 stipulates that any soldier can refuse to obey an order the execution of which may constitute an offence. According to article 25 of the Constitution, the general rules of international law (that is chapter VII and article 51 of the United Nations Charter: 'a State that, for whatever reason, [...] disregards the prohibition to resort to force, as has been enacted in the United Nations Charter, and uses the force of weapons violates international law and commits an armed aggression') are part of German law. Therefore, the members of the German armed forces themselves must submit to them. Moreover, any measure which might disrupt peaceful coexistence between peoples (like the preparations for a war of aggression, etc.) contravenes article 26 of the Constitution; and this article has been reinforced by article 80 of the penal code which specifies that these aggression-oriented measures may be punished by harsh sentences (up to life imprisonment). Finally, the foundation in 1994 of the Zentrum Innere Führung (or Centre for the moral and civic training of the German armed forces), located in Koblenz, is a genuine German specificity.

Chapter 8
Informality and Informalization among Eritrean Refugees:
Why Migration Does Not Provide a Lesson in Democracy

Magnus Treiber
Felsberg Institute, Germany

ABSTRACT

Transnational migration has important implications on the respective country of departure and its political dynamics. This article addresses informal practices and processes of informalization during migration from dictatorially ruled Eritrea in North-East-Africa. On the base of dense ethnography among refugees and migrants in neighboring Ethiopia the article discusses migration's cultural and social effects and sheds a light on the potential role of migrants in Eritrea's expected political transition. It will be argued that refugees and migrants are unable to fully liberate themselves from Eritrea's authoritarian political culture while seeking prosperity, democracy and human rights elsewhere. Instead they blunder into informal practices such as deceit, exploitation and denial of solidarity, which inevitably backfire on social and political life.

INTRODUCTION

This article is based on findings and conclusions that result from anthropological research on informality and informalization in migration from Eritrea in North-East Africa. Respective research aimed at studying, conceptualizing and evaluating informal practices among Eritrean refugees in various stations and stages of their transnational migration. It attempts to grasp refugees' informal praxis in detail, then to conceptualize informality and survival practices within the broader context of migration from Eritrea and finally to elucidate social, political and cultural implications the emergence of informality in migration will have on Eritrea's imminent transition. Theoretical reflections combine the viewpoint of existentialist anthropology with an anthropological concept of informality and are based on extensive ethnographic fieldwork in the migratory milieu. This article focuses on Shimelba Refugee Camp in Northern Ethiopia and on the Ethiopian capital

DOI: 10.4018/978-1-4666-9675-4.ch008

Addis Ababa. On the basis of ethnographic examples and stories it will be discussed if Eritrea's refugee generation should be regarded as a critical mass to bring democracy and a new political culture and society.

BACKGROUND

Migration from Eritrea

Eritrea, a small African country at the shores of the Red Sea, reached formal independence only in 1993, after the *Eritrean People's Liberation Front* (EPLF) had finally won a war of 30 years against neighboring Ethiopia. Eritrea has a total population of roughly six million people, plus a global Diaspora abroad that may make up another million people at best. This Diaspora originates from emigration during the 1980s and again after 2002. In the 1990s, however, Eritrea was widely considered a promising example for Africa's progress towards development, peace and democracy. Such hopes did not come true. During the last decade the country has become internationally known for its harsh and brutal dictatorship.

Since its fall-back into undisguised dictatorship in September 2001, Eritrea has experienced enduring political and economic crises. The historic struggle for national unity – considered to be still and always under threat – has become a political cult of Eritrea's guerilla-government under President Isaias Afewerki and justified to mute and persecute all critique and opposition. In this sense literally everything in Eritrea has become political – including the country's coercive and practically open-ended national-service in administration or the military. This national service does not allow following individual life projects, but subjects its members for long years (women up to their mid-twenties, men up to their forties) to inadequate symbolic pay and the arbitrariness of mistrustful superiors. Certainly, Eritrea's record of human rights violations is extraordinary – even measured by the rather low standard of comparable Third World countries. Refugees are indeed Eritrea's main export good. Desertions from national service as well as emigration have become mass phenomena, despite draconic punishment and a shoot-to-kill-policy at the country's borders (Hirt, & Mohammad 2013, Kibreab 2009, Hepner 2009, Treiber 2007, Treiber 2005). The *United Nations High Commissioner for Refugees* (UNHCR) currently lists almost 306.000 people in its statistical category "total population of concern" and tens of thousands of refugees in both of Eritrea's neighboring countries, Ethiopia and Sudan.[1] From here refugees seek formal and informal ways into a better world that guarantees the rule of law and human rights as well as the opportunity to build up a more promising existence. Northern America and Europe are imagined to be the most attractive goals Eritrean refugees aspire to reach. Continuous catastrophes near Lampedusa Island in the Mediterranean Sea, where many Eritreans have perished, show again and again which risks refugees take to make these dreams come true (Treiber 2013a).[2]

In order to develop an anthropological understanding of these risks and hopes, the subsequently emerging culture of migration and its potential consequences for a political future of the country, theoretical concepts such as informality and existence will be discussed.

Informality and Existential Anthropology

The notion of informality originates from economic and political anthropology (Lindell 2010; AlSayyad 2004, Tickamyer & Bohon 2000). In African studies the term first illustrated the urban economic sphere (Hart 1973); it was later also used to describe African politics in general and the African state in particular (Chabal 2009, Mbembe 2001, Chabal & Daloz 1999, Bayart, Ellis & Hibou 1993). In this sense, Africa is perceived as the 'informal continent', with regard both to the economic and the political domains. Informality, however, cannot be easily claimed for the state in Eritrea and Ethiopia (see Chabal & Daloz 1999: xxi). Both countries have a long tradition of formal state administration and tight control of their subjects (Bozzini 2011, Aalen & Tronvoll 2009, Quehl 2005; cf. Zewde 2001, Marcus 1994).

The perception of Africa as the 'informal continent' does not mean that Africans are experts in informal practices; informality cannot be simply deduced as an African essence. This paper argues that informal practices, so typical in the field of migration, have to be learned during migration itself. Providing false information in formal interviews or attempts to bribe staff and circumvent regulations seemingly has become as common among Eritrean refugees as paid-for sham marriages with members of the Diaspora. Some Eritrean refugees completely enter the 'informal world': they leave Addis Ababa and move on to Khartoum, giving up any claim for resettlement and relying exclusively on informal ways of onwards-migration.

Informal practices are means to become active, where decreed passivity and helplessness prevail. Informality has the potential to transgress actual situations of deficiency; informal action hints at a better future elsewhere. For Eritrean refugees neither returning back home, nor 'local integration' in Addis Ababa or Khartoum would be attractive options; to advance by all means has become existential (Schielke 2012). In this sense, informality may refer to the existential gap between now and here and then and there, which is characteristic for migration. This dimension of unprivileged migration cannot exclusively be explained with conventional concepts such as 'coping strategies', 'agency' or by simply attributing to migrants 'tactic' (e.g. Essed et al. 2004) or 'creative' agency (Piot 2010, Knörr 2005). Migrants do not always act in a rational way as these concepts suggest; they also make rather irrational and overhasty decisions – at least from the anthropologist's more distant point of view. To describe their acting as mere anti-state resistance (Scott 1990, Skalnik 1989) is therefore likewise inadequate. Whereas informal practices in migration have been described elsewhere (van Liempt 2009, Horst 2006, Schuster 2005, Kibreab 2004), migration's inherent entanglement of informality and existentialism – the migrants' need to advance[3] – has not yet been sufficiently studied.

While the existentialist dimension inherent in migration has already been stressed by Jackson (2006) and Graw and Schielke (2012), considerations from existential anthropology have not yet been linked up to the concept of informality. The combination of both concepts, however, promises to generate an innovative theoretical approach in migration studies.

According to Keith Hart informality emerges from an "informal/formal dialectic" (2010: 379). Indeed, Eritrean refugees in Addis Ababa find themselves stuck between formal procedures and requirements and a precarious life-world that demands informal praxis. Their struggle to survive and to advance in difficult interaction with national and international refugee administration proved an essential site for research on informality in migration. Furthermore, the ethnographic example of Eritrean refugees contributes to a broader understanding of migration from Africa in general (e.g. Abdalla, Dias Barros & Berthet 2014, Triulzi & McKenzie 2013, Westin & Hassanen 2014, Graw & Schielke 2012) and migration's informal/formal dialectic in particular. Respective practices of circumvention, evasion or deceit in the interface with immigration authorities or social workers after arrival in a new host country may result from the migration process itself.

Political Implications

Certainly emigration has important implications on the country of departure. Eritrea's political situation is complex. Its inherent secretiveness, dating back to the liberation war, makes it impossible to fully understand internal dynamics, processes and power struggles from the outside. In any case, Eritrea's former guerrilla leaders are in their 60s now. Some of the most powerful supporters of President Isaias Afewerki have already passed away and a next generation of political leaders from within the country's single political party, *People's Front for Democracy and Justice* (PFDJ), or its military apparatus is not in sight.

National political debate is now mainly led abroad; exiled opposition parties are in the Diaspora and numerous new political alliances are formed (cf. Radtke 2006, Bernal 2006). Besides their common lip service to democracy and human rights Eritrean opposition parties, movements and alliances remain, however, highly fragmented and essentially based on regional, religious and kinship affiliations. While the (present-day) *Eritrean Liberation Front* (ELF) and the *Eritrean People's Democratic Party* (EPDP) try to link up to the now historic liberation fronts ELF and EPLF, the *Eritrean Solidarity Movement for National Salvation* (ESMNS) and the *Eritrean National Council for Democratic Change* (ENCDC) claim to represent the younger generations, who lost trust in the political authority of Eritrea's freedom fighters from both, EPLF and ELF. Others such as the *Red Sea Afar Democratic Organization* (RSADO) and the *Eritrean Afar State in Exile* (EASE) or the (Saho-based) *Eritrean National Salvation Front* (ENSF) and the *Democratic Movement of Eritrean Saho (DMES)* are rivaling on the legitimate representation of ethnic groups. Some of these groups pursue peaceful means, others believe in militancy and violence. One indeed active guerilla is the *Democratic Movement for the Liberation of Eritrean Kunama* (DMLEK). According to its Diaspora, its religious program, funding and support these political groups are based in Ethiopia, in the Sudan, the Arab Peninsula as well as in Europe, Australia and the United States.

An open political transition (cf. Holtmann & Wiesenthal 2009) towards a post-Isaias-era is commonly expected in the nearer future with respective scenarios ranging from democratization (with or without PFDJ) to civil war (cf. Gebreluel & Tronvoll 2013; ICG 2013). Eritrea's young generation, however, does not only lack any experience with political participation and democracy, it also adopted a specific authoritarian habitus (cf. Quehl 2013, 2003) that is carried on and reproduced during migration and in the Diaspora. This becomes especially apparent in the opposition parties' recruitment and indoctrination of young refugees in Addis Ababa and the Eritrean refugee camps in Ethiopia.

On the other hand, Eritrean refugees learn and adopt informal practices during migration. It can be assumed that typical practices among Eritrean migrants are both at the same time: authoritarian and informal. Apparently, migration does not promote solidarity and democracy, even though refuge from dictatorship and desire for democracy and human rights are constantly referred to. The Eritrean opposition abroad, blaming solely the country's president for the decay of the country, seems unaware of or even unwilling to acknowledge these problems. Having Eritrea's future in mind, this issue certainly is of urgent importance (Treiber 2013b).

Ethnographic fieldwork on the topic has mainly been done in in Khartoum/Sudan and Addis Ababa/Ethiopia (2009-2012) within the research project 'Dynamic Worlds of Imagination – Learning Processes, Knowledge, and Communication among Young Urban Migrants from Eritrea and Ethiopia' (together with Kurt Beck and Délia Nicoué, Bayreuth University, Bavarian Research Network 'Migration and Knowledge' ForMig, 2009-2013), following earlier research in Asmara (2001-2005), Shimelba Refugee Camp (2007), Washington DC and Minneapolis, Cairo and Jerusalem (2007-2009).

REFUGEES AND MIGRATION BETWEEN THE FORMAL AND THE INFORMAL

Eritreans are formally acknowledged as international refugees on the broad basis of UNHCR's 'Eligibility Guidelines for Assessing the International Protection Need of Asylum Seekers from Eritrea' (2011a). Practically everybody who did not violate article 1F of 1951s Geneva Refugee Convention, but committed "a crime against peace, a war crime, or a crime against humanity" can claim political repression or – in case of Evangelical Christians – religious persecution. Formally excluded are those, who belonged to the core of the country's dictatorial system, and/or filled leading military positions during the last war with Ethiopia, 1998-2000. From a formal point of view, represented by the United Nations and their humanitarian refugee agency, the status of an international refugee (and his or her degree of exposure) is provided on the basis of 1951s Geneva Refugee Convention and successive administrative regulations and guidelines. Respective categories are clear-cut and lawful. However they do not always fit.

Besides youths who left the country before they could be drafted, the majority of Eritrea's refugees abroad inevitably had to compromise. Within the framework of Eritrea's national service recruits fulfill crucial administrative tasks that – after all – put the state into practical existence. Recruits are involved into repression and persecution as policeman, soldiers, prison guards or spies. Some had hoped for a well-respected career in a ministry or in the military and complied until this dream turned sour. And many fearfully looked the other way, when they noticed injustice and crime. Under dictatorial rule few people can claim to be free from moral guilt; leaving does not necessarily negate structural involvement and everyday complicity. While a refugee's past may therefore be rather ambiguous, it is the formal acknowledgment as an international refugee under protection of the United Nations that attests – ex post – unlawful persecution and moral justification of one's escape.

Thus, one should not be surprised that officials from within Eritrea's dictatorial system have apparently been resettled to the United States with the help of UNHCR. This also applies to various members of Ethiopian-backed guerrilla groups, who simply denied any political engagement in formal interviews.

Of course there are other – informal – ways to move on, too. Thousands try their luck and board dangerous transports crossing the Sahara desert and the Mediterranean Sea. Many hundreds have died or have been killed during their journey, while others made it to Europe or Israel. Today most member states of the European Union accept asylum seekers from Eritrea or at least provide provisional protection, years after the UNHCR – usually a cautious political actor – prominently appealed to suspend deportations already back in 2004. Still in 2008, however, two Eritrean asylum seekers were deported from Frankfurt/ Germany and subsequently imprisoned in Eritrea.[4] Switzerland recently tightened its asylum law, not least because of the influx of Eritrean refugees, and Israel's government discussed the possible deportation of Eritrean and Ethiopian migrants, labeled 'infiltrators', to Uganda. Europe, self-proclaimed custodian of human rights in the World, has obviously closed its doors. Only those might be allowed in, who have already reached its shores – by whatever means. Therefore informal migration has spread sideward. Nowadays Eritrean migrant communities can be found from Ecuador to Hong Kong or Indonesia. These informal ways and routes are more expensive, more risky, but available, if needed. Formal resettlement on the contrary offers a unique chance and privilege, though it may currently mainly apply to Eritrean refugees in Ethiopia. Since few years resettlement processes have indeed started. People who stayed for years in isolated and malaria-infested camps in the country's north have now reached the United States or Australia. Still the formal process may take long years and finally lacks any guarantee. Informal migration will therefore go on. Motivation to leave Eritrea and seek a secure and more promising life elsewhere is huge, especially among urban youths. They have given up on the state and do not want to wait for the expected transition yet to come. In contrast to the Arab world there is no critical mass left that could instigate demonstrations and eventually topple the government. At present a coup d'état by discontent military brass is far more likely.

From the 1990s onwards the new paradigm of transnationalism allowed to perceive complex mutual ties between established Diaspora and home countries. In this context Nina Glick-Schiller coined the concept of 'long-distance nationalism', exposing the Diaspora's potential involvement abroad into processes of political transition (Glick-Schiller & Fouron 2001). Proponents of democratization abroad could then also be considered a gain for the respective home country. And indeed Eritrean and international human rights activists, concerned NGO's (*Human Rights Watch, Amnesty International, Reporters Without Borders* or *Human Rights Concern – Eritrea* to name only the most prominent), and political parties in exile try to lobby, provide insights – where otherwise little is known – and exert pressure on the Eritrean dictator and his ruling clique. This is well-understandable and certainly justified.

It is, however, intriguing to shed a light on processes underneath: Even if many migrants from Eritrea into the world have an urban background very few migrate under favorable conditions. Despite their formal acknowledgement as international refugees, people feel marginalized, even forgotten by the world. In global media their plight appears only when the number of dead is particularly high. The UNHCR is considered overburdened and helpless at best. Especially young people who experienced life in Eritrea as a frustrating standstill without prospects and development, do not want to wait again, they want to become active, make use of their life time, their dreams and motivation. They risked their lives to leave a brutal regime. Now they want to participate in a world that promised civilization, the rule of law and opportunities to make a living. In various stages and stations beyond the Eritrean borders – in refugee camps and urban centers in Ethiopia and the Sudan – people feel excluded again. They indeed face constant exclusion and subjection. Political, legal and social marginalization result in a typical perception and interpretation of self and world from below. Here human rights generate their own discursive power. The call for respect and justice expressed by political youth sections, local refugee associations or individuals in their approach to refugee agencies and authorities explicitly refers to human rights and self-confidently uses common NGO-newspeak. Human rights are identified as the moral base of the Western world – and human rights talk as its political language. To claim human rights then also becomes an attempt to establish contact to the Western world and bridge the global gap between here and there. Frustration arises when the call is ignored – or assigned to the local UNHCR office and its usual go-slow administration. Two aspects of this phenomenon are especially remarkable.

First of all, very few migrants have concrete knowledge about origins, history and content of 1946s 'Universal Declaration of Human Rights' (cf. Harmon-Gross 2009: 100-105). From a perspective from below human rights become important as an imagined opposite to social, personal and also bodily experiences of exclusion in the past and in the present. The original declaration's wording is considered to be of minor importance, while necessary keywords can easily be picked up from NGOs' and activists' daily work. This actually turns human rights into "Rumours of Rights", as Julia Eckert has put it (2012).

Second, human rights and the formal acknowledgement as an international refugee offer a moral identification and express an unfulfilled existential need – but they are unable to lead through daily life in a migrants' world.

Unprivileged migration demands individual learning processes and transforms social worlds. If you feel in need to exaggerate your personal reasons to flee the country in the UNHCR-interview – because everybody does so and you do not want to be crossed over – if you feel forced to bribe national or even international staff, if you are frustrated and leave illegally from the refugee camp to town, if you are in need of a sleeping-berth, a job and a smuggler to move on, the claim for human rights will not help: You will have to find informal ways to get along and to advance or otherwise to acquiesce to ordered passivity, heteronomy and year-long waiting.

'I see no future for myself sitting here, and waiting does not make change... so I gotta do something…' Aron (30) wrote me from Khartoum, preparing his onward journey through the Sahara. In his typical understanding, the need to advance in migration is existential. Waiting without hope means to give up, to finally surrender after all the risks taken and sacrifices made. If you see an opportunity to take action, you rather will try to grab it. So you will find yourself lying, breaking various laws and taking dangerous risks. To some such practices bring serious moral problems along; others sniff a chance to do business with migrants' inevitable needs.

Doubtlessly informality is a key phenomenon of migration to the Global North and its wider informal economy. Not least it evolves from contact with formal authorities, rules and processes and further ripens in the migrants' local and at the same time transnational milieu.

Those who manage to cross Eritrea's highly militarized southern border to Ethiopia have to pass through a security screening; they are then allocated in one of the large refugee camps in Northern Ethiopia (Mai Ayni, Shimelba, Hitsats or Adi Harish). While Eritreans are officially acknowledged as international refugees and placed under the formal protection of the UNHCR, life in camp is restricted to survival from day to day, to boredom and frustration (Treiber & Tesfaye 2008, see also Lüdeke 2012, Tesfaye 2011, Kirk 2010, Harmon-Gross 2009).

Eventually – usually after several years – the administrative process accelerates and leads to transfer to Addis Ababa, Ethiopia's capital, and from there hopefully to resettlement in the US, Australia or elsewhere. Ethiopia formally refuses "local integration" of Eritrean refugees, as suggested in the UNHCR handbook for resettlement (2011b). This forces the UNHCR to seek for third host countries, willing to permanently receive these refugees. The legal status as refugee, however, does not include the right to work within Ethiopia, which renders thousands of people, among them many educated and well trained, dependent from aid money. Still, life in the city is much more attractive than life in the camp. The city is believed to offer more (informal) chances than the camp and to allow for own initiatives as compared to the decreed passivity to which refugees are condemned in the camp (see also Kibreab 2004, Sendker 1990).

As Ethiopia's administrative control is tight and resettlement regulations ask for legal status in the country, refugees need to obtain a formal permit if they want to live outside the camp; most of these legalized migrants – then labeled 'urban refugees' – choose the capital Addis Ababa as residence. Being allowed to live in the city does not necessarily mean that departure is on the eve. Most urban refugees still have to stay and survive in the country for several years, during which time they struggle hard with different national and international agencies and authorities in order to be resettled or at least to get clearance. In the meantime they depend on family members in the Diaspora or have to seek informal work in town.

While Eritreans outside Ethiopia are clearly visible and discernible as strangers, the complex social, historical and cultural ties existing between Eritreans and Ethiopians as well as phenotypic similarities allow Eritrean refugees to hide within

Addis Ababa's urban fabric. At the same time, most of them live in peripheral areas outside the city centre; social life is pre-dominantly restricted to the Eritrean milieu.

It is a frustrating experience to be forced waiting for the resettlement process to accelerate and yield fruit while lacking concrete opportunities as well as reliable prospects for the future. Hence, people become active, circumvent formal restrictions and find informal ways in those situations, where formal status and formal procedures are thought to be unpromising or even obstructive. Refugees thus blunder into arbitrary situations and (informal) forms of action they originally intended to flee.

An exemplary look into Shimelba Refugee Camp and Addis Ababa will allow a more detailed perspective.

Shimelba Refugee Camp

Shimelba Refugee Camp (cf. Treiber & Tesfaye 2008) is located in Ethiopia's Northern Province, Tigray. In May 2000 Ethiopian troops withdrew from occupied areas within Eritrea after two years of war over the precise line of the border. Under protection of the Ethiopian military several thousand lowland agro pastoralists and few highland peasants left Eritrea for fear of reprisals by returning Eritrean security forces. The first camp – Wala Nihibi – was established in immediate proximity of the contested border, still on former battleground. The area was littered with unexploded ammunition and rotting body parts, and infiltration or even attacks from the Eritrean side had to be feared. Thus people were relocated to Shimelba in 2004, some 10 kilometers from Sheraro, a small market town in Northern Ethiopia. Since then there is continuous influx, now, predominantly from urban youth. In 2012, 800 to 1000 Eritrean refugees per months arrived in Ethiopia at the risk of their life.[5] At times far more than 10,000 people lived in Shimelba, so three other camps, exclusively for Eritrean refugees, have been established more recently further South. Shimelba Refugee Camp is strategically situated in a remote valley at the foot of a hill on which the camp administration has its fenced and guarded compounds. From here the whole camp can be overlooked. It is apparently divided into two larger living areas:

The greener and calmer, even village-like neighbourhood with its grass-roofed round huts, typical for Eritrea's Gash-Barka-province, is inhabited by ethnic Kunama families. The other half of the camp has densely build rectangular houses, covered by plastic sheets or corrugated iron. It also offers a boulevard, numerous shops, bars and cafés. Here loud music and electric light extend the day into the night, while the rest of the camp turns silent at nightfall. To some extent Shimelba is a youth planet.

The area's urban character cannot surprise. Inhabitants of this side of the camp are predominantly urban youths, comprising far more men than women. Most of them are Tigrinya-speakers and have relatives in Eritrea's global Diaspora, established during the struggle for independence; these are now actively approached and addressed through electronic communication. Already small sums allow improving quality in life, some two or three hundred dollars allow opening up one's own small business.

The refugee's dwellings have been built from mud bricks by the camps' first generation and are since then handed on to newcomers. As most of the Kunama lowland agro-pastoralists have been granted a 'group case' as persecuted ethnic minority and subsequently leave, more and more of their houses are taken over by urban youths.

The camp as a whole is not fenced. However the only way out – a dirt road towards the small town Sheraro – starts from the camp administration's hill and passes a check-point, where travel documents are controlled. In the opposite direction a mountain stream, deeply carved into the rocks, limits the camp territory. The rest is enclosed by agricultural land that belongs to local peasants.

This is where history comes in: 30 years ago the area belonged to the heartland of Tigray's major guerilla movement, the TPLF (*Tigray People's Liberation Front*) which forms the core of today's national government. Shimelba valley was then used to hide and maintain the guerrilla's motor pool. Therefore the local population counted for staunch and loyal political support and effectively guarded the camps borders. Especially in the first years inmates were considered enemies and suffered from open contempt; violent clashes between youths and rape cases were reported. Since then Eritrean political opposition groups tried to ease tensions with support of the Ethiopian government and its responsible national authority ARRA (*Administration for Refugee and Returnees Affairs*) that administers the camp. Tensions however have just shifted.

While an assigned US-based NGO bravely educates on 'gbv' (gender-based violence) and 'std' (sexually transmitted diseases), trying to render the mass of refugees into morally valuable, peaceful, clean and certainly not too political individuals, the Ethiopian backed Eritrean political groups and movements put considerable pressure on individual refugees to join them. Back in 2007 all the formally elected Kunama representatives were said to be guerrilla-members of DMLEK (*Democratic Movement for the Liberation of Eritrean Kunama*). Alexander, a young Kunama and UNHCR translator, did not comply with DMLEKs agenda and thus had to fear abduction and assassination during night time. He used to sleep with a club within reach. Young Tigrinya- and Saho-speakers at least feared to be blacklisted by officials and their supported political groups and risk malicious gossip.

The stay in Shimelba Refugee Camp is everything else than an attractive option to pursue a better life in a better world. Many inmates ran away to Khartoum, from where they hoped to move further by informal means. Some reached Israel, then far more promising than today. Many tried to reach Malta or Italy, but many also lost their health or even their lives in the Sahara, in Libyan prisons or in the Mediterranean Sea.

Ruta's husband was reported dead after one of the numerous boat accidents in the Mediterranean Sea. He had left his wife and his two little children in his brothers' care and did not inform them about his plans in order to make goodbye easier. Things got even worse, when her husband's brother tried to rape her, blaming her for his brothers' death. She tried to present her problems to different institutions of the camp administration, but failed to be relocated to another house. Though she got assistance from helpful friends, she lacked sufficient command of English and also self-confidence to fight for protection and support. She survived from laundry services and injera-backing (injera is the traditional Abyssinian flat bread), hard work that resulted in a miscarriage and continuous health problems. Isayas was a more public figure. He, a man in his thirties, had already managed to reach Malta. In 2002 Malta deported a whole group of Eritreans back to their home country. Their fate is well known, as some managed to run away from Adi Abeito prison, while others were shot.[6] Isayas was part of the Malta group and somehow he had managed to get to Shimelba, however he lost his mental health. When we met him, he was hardly responsive, socially avoided and isolated, a madman. After medical treatment in hospital did not bring change he was sent back to Shimelba to eke out his miserable existence. Everyone in the camp knew people like Ruta or Isayas and everyone took their example as a warning.

Since about 2010 there has been some noticeable change. Resettlement processes to third host countries – usually USA or Australia – have gained speed. People awaiting their flight out of the country are transferred to Addis Ababa, where the *International Organization for Migration* (IOM) – an international service agency processing legal migration – takes care of them. They are transitorily hosted in a guarded residence hall near

Bole Airport and sent through final interviews, a medical check-up and so-called 'cultural orientation'. Thousands have already reached their new homes and sent back information about their whereabouts and wellbeing. However there is no guarantee and waiting without certainty – Alcinda Honwana speaks of "waithood" (2012) – invites and even provokes informal self-help at the expense of more honest and more vulnerable others. Yohannes' example may serve as an illustration.

I knew Yohannes still from Asmara and found him here in Shimelba, he had just arrived few weeks before. He was one of the numerous single urban youths in the camp, who still hoped to get along and advance. Yohannes took the opportunity of my presence and wrote a letter to the UNHCR, naming me as an international reference. And here is what he wrote:

My name is Yohannes K., I was born, raised and completed my Elementary, Junior and High school Education in Addis Ababa Ethiopia. In September 1998, I along with my whole family was deported from Addis Ababa to Eritrea [as so-called ethnic Eritreans and enemy people, MT]. We were not welcomed by the society we at first considered ours. Shortly after my arrival, I was registered and continued my higher education in Asmara University.

After 3 years of my study, I and many other students were arrested in places called Wia and Gelalo. We were imprisoned [be]cause we strongly criticized the government's corrupted administration and were detained for about 40 days.

After the so called mercy from the government most of the students were released, but I was actually not lucky to be released. I was listed as a protest organizer and kept along with 19 other students in an isolated underground cell. After being isolated for another 30 days, we were forced to sign a paper, officially approving to be guilty. [...]

Between 2003 and 2005 I was working in some private owned companies and later on I started working on my own. But in March 2005, about 5 a.m. in the morning security forces came to me while I was sleeping and took me to prison in Asmara and later a place called Mai Serwa. I was detained there until a person who paid 5000 Nakfa claimed responsibility.

I went to Addis and stayed there, leading my life for about a year, [but then] was arrested by Ethiopian security forces. I was caught and imprisoned in a place called Qera. I was arrested and questioned several times by different security members, after cross-examining me. I answered that I didn't have any political interest; I told them that I came in order to lead a peaceful and settled life. After that I was deported to Shimelba Refugee Camp. Shortly after my arrival to Shimelba I gave my fingerprints to the ARRA office here in Shimelba and was sent to Endabaguna for further investigation. [...] I was again investigated by immigration and security officers. They then sent me back to Shimelba by informing that they would call me whenever they want to hold talks. Ever since I had talks with the security I had been stressed and faced traumas from the day I set my foot here in Shimelba.

When I was back in Eritrea I had the chance of meeting several foreigners who came by many purposes and due to unofficial personal meetings with them, the officials started to suspect me and were warning me each time. One among my friends is currently in the camp to perform a research. When he first met me, he was shocked and showed me his sympathy. He was upset about the way my life turned up-side-down. So dear Madam, dear Sir I would like to forward my application and seek a solution for my problems.

While Yohannes indeed grew up in Addis Ababa and was deported to Eritrea after the border war erupted in 1998, he has never been a student at Asmara University. Therefore he was not arrested and sent to Wia or Gelalo and he certainly was no ringleader of the protesting students in 2001. Yohannes was not arrested in 2005 either, he never spent time in an Eritrean prison and so, he was never bailed out. The private business he refers to was a friend's bar, where he worked as a waiter. There he came into contact with some foreigners and members of the Diaspora, but political debate was carefully avoided. He was a draft dodger, illegally staying in Asmara, and always at risk to be controlled by military police, but he was not targeted by Eritrean security. However he was indeed caught in Addis Ababa and sent to Shimelba; it seems he was denounced to Ethiopian police. Certainly he dreamed of a "peaceful and settled life" and understandably arrest and interviews caused unease and stress, but to speak of a trauma sounds exaggerated to me.

Why did he fabricate such a story? First of all he could not foresee that mere conscientious objection would be sufficient to be put under international refugee protection. Then he saw what life in a refugee camp means at best: boredom, deprivation and frustration, if not complete marginalization and surrender. Waiting drives you crazy, people say in Shimelba. Thus attempts to upgrade one's "case" (and indeed, 'case' is the locally used word in the refugees' newspeak adopted from administration and NGOs) are only a matter of consequence. So, Yohannes tried to manipulate his formal refugee determination process with his means at hand: He resorted to own, but self-evident bodily experiences to constitute a heightened medical risk and to contemporary public knowledge to create a history of political persecution. In order to increase credibility he referred to my person, using our acquaintance as a competitive advantage. Remarkably he completely omits his adventurous escape from Eritrea; he had managed to bribe an African soldier of the United Nations' then peacekeeping mission and crossed the numerous checkpoints of the Eritrean and the Ethiopian side hidden in the boot of a light tank.

Beteseb, a man in his early forties, remembers that he was not fully aware of the words' meaning, when he was told: "You are now a refugee!" I met him first in Shimelba in August 2007 and since then during several stays in Addis Ababa. He has now been a refugee for almost a decade and had enough time to think about it. For him being a refugee means first of all being denied to act and to decide on your own. All responsibility is transferred to an opaque and restrictive administrative body. Refugees are simply ordered to sit and wait. At the same time waiting bears no guarantees. Refugee administration consists of heterogeneous, even contradictory institutions, who all claim expertise and promise to do their best, but may not be trusted. Not even reliable protection is provided. Refugees feel subjected to various forces, to national and international administration, regional politics, and violence, to deprivation and reeducation programs. Possible ways to influence one's fate consist in certain informal practices adopted within the camp context:

Theoretically a formal administrative process is based on clear-cut categories, decision-making follows an inherent logic, is legitimate and just. Therefore this process has to be protected from external corrupting and contaminating influences, including the applicant him/herself. In contrast to Ruta, Yohannes managed to open up at least a potential room for manipulation. He built on previous contacts to the outside world, education and communicative skills and he tried to anticipate what counted in his favor. Being a relative newcomer to the camp he failed, however, and was not promoted out-of-band.

Yohannes' example shows that not only ARRA and UNHCR attempted to overlook and to control the refugee population from the top of their hill, the refugees tried to do likewise from below. ARRAs and UNHCRs staff members were constantly under observation; their statements and decisions were interpreted and anticipations were made where possible. Various education programs on gender, hygiene and human rights provided a useful vocabulary to approach international staff in particular and thus further widened the gap between the educated and the illiterate instead of spreading knowledge in a democratic way. Personal ties to decision-makers – or at least to their friends and colleagues on the hill – were considered most important, to learn about the outside world, one longs to see, but of course also to gain trust and ex post witnesses of one's story. To dramatize reports of one's own escape was seen as a competitive measure, indispensable to leave this unpromising place as soon as possible, also to the detriment of more needy, less able people. Deceit appeared to be intrinsic to the camp as a whole, everyone did it and rumors ranged from embezzled food rations to the sale of ID-numbers (for which official staff was held responsible). The silent rule demanded: Seek to promote your process, protect and conceal your story and status, consider others as competitors and mistrust them!

Migrations' informal practices are obviously born in the encounter with formal refugee administration and are perpetuated within the refugees' own social world. This may sound rather dystopic, and to some extent it certainly is. On the other hand it is exactly in this unpleasant social environment that friendship and solidarity prove of value. Here in isolation and seclusion the promised world beyond has come one step closer, can already be sensed and further imagined. And even here, in the refugee camp, the liberating effect of migration becomes obvious – future takes shape due to one's own action, venture and ability. Informality becomes a policy of active influence.

Addis Ababa

Addis Ababa again is the real world, a metropolis even, and it is expected to offer multiple opportunities or at least a few – usually opportunities remain few. Nonetheless refugees in Addis Ababa prefer the city to the camp. From being exposed in a hidden camp, life changes towards hiding in a public place, however.

In the surroundings of Shimelba or Mai Ayni refugees – at least those with an urban background – can easily be spotted. They dress in neat T-shirt and Jeans, their shape and skin color is different from local peasantry, who are exposed to heat and rain on the field, and finally urban Eritrean Tigrinya sounds clearly different from rural Tigrinya in Western Tigray. In Addis Ababa urban Eritreans can be taken for Ethiopians. While there is no discrimination on first sight (as in Khartoum or Jerusalem, where Eritreans and Ethiopians are usually perceived as one ethnic other), Addis Ababa does not offer a large informal, ethnically segmented labor market in which Eritreans could easily fit in as waitresses and waiters, cleaners, guards, construction workers or rickshaw-drivers. Jobs are very rare in Addis Ababa, and this applies to blue-collar as well as to white-collar work. After all, high unemployment is a main reason for Ethiopian citizens to migrate in masses to the Sudan, the Middle East, South Africa and the so-called Western world.

As refugees are not allowed to work, their return to self-dependence and their hoped-for participation in city life is hampered from the beginning. Dating back to imperial times Ethiopia has a longstanding and authoritarian tradition of national administration; documents and stamps are of vital importance. Besides their refugee card – in banks or post-offices sometimes mistaken for a diplomatic UN-ID – Eritreans do not possess and usually do not get necessary papers, including even a driving license. Additionally employers may ask to prove membership in the ruling party, which of course is out of reach for Eritreans.

Being effectively disadvantaged by law entails further social marginalization. The Amharic language is a problem, at least for newcomers. Dwelling is sought in Addis Ababa's peripheral neighborhoods, in Haya Arat, in Gerji or in Qera. Wherever they will settle, however, the Kebele, the local neighborhood committee, will be informed of their presence. The Kebele representatives secure the state on a micro level. In Addis Ababa you may feel freed from the camps' immediate and unavoidable paternalism, but you will know, you are under supervision. Many urban refugees, who do not want to be drawn into political games – an option which Ethiopia seems to reward with administrative privileges, such as travel permits and educational programs – try to keep a low profile. Actually the Ethiopian state and its institutions look quite familiar to Eritreans, still one is not far enough from home. Waiting, however, continues.

Even those urban refugees who are already listed for resettlement face unforeseeable problems. Ermias had successfully passed all necessary interviews by the UNHCR and the US *Department of Homeland Security*, but the date for his medical checkup was delayed. Successively his security clearance expired. In order to renew it, he had to wait for the American staff to fly over from Kenya again. Another year was lost. Despite his frustration he insisted that he was not a victim. He managed to leave Mai Ayni after three months only and pushed his resettlement process into an overall reliable state. And certainly he was not in financial need; he found a job as computer expert and translated on behalf of UNHCR, IOM and various host countries' immigration authorities. As a translator he was considered to have expert knowledge on resettlement procedures. And while he was usually approached by intimidated, even scared applicants before or after a decisive interview, he also quoted a lady who wanted to extend her stay in Addis for another year. Why? She managed to set up a booming business and sought to profit as much as possible before leaving.

Nonetheless the majority of Eritrean refugees live from irregular financial support from outside; women may also bake injera and brew beer to get along. Some will fail again and again in getting their migration done. Promising informal options may be sham marriage or bribe, but these are expensive. Lying is considered everyman's chance to success, even a necessity to pass. Ermias tells me that interviewees finally failed because their stories were inconsistent, but also because applicants claimed membership in the armed opposition – which is not at all an advantageous asset, but necessarily results in the loss of the refugee status.

Moges is a former air force pilot, who spent a year and a half in prison without charges. After his eventual release he found a smuggler, who brought him to the border and then crossed Gash River, a dangerous undertaking. Initially Moges was considered of military use by the Ethiopians and to be at risk by the UNHCR. After that he felt forgotten for more than four years – until September 2013, when the US *Department of Homeland Security* considered him 'eligible' after his interview. In summer 2014 he reached the United States.

In 2004 Beteseb stole an army jeep, took an Indian UN officer hostage and broke through the border fortification while being haunted under fire. The US authority categorized his case as 'pending' for six long years. After intervention at UNHCR head quarter in Geneva his case was taken up again and referred to Australia. Refugees, who had their interview together with him or even afterwards, again left since long. In May 2015 IOM finally called him in for medical examination – a check-up that usually precedes an already scheduled resettlement.

Both men, Moges and Beteseb, were active, even heroic subjects in their escape from Eritrea. Since then they have been reduced to passive objects in administrative processes that did not always promise progress. Both felt more and more fragile under the plight of an uncertain future. So, Beteseb was unable to sleep and to eat properly for at least one week before his official appointments. I had the chance to accompany both of them to the UNHCR office for a couple of times, to witness their fearful anticipation and to be part of the secretive discussions in the cage-like waiting room. Once, due to my unannounced presence that violated the institution's rules and regulations we were referred to the division manager, an Ethiopian lady who, then, never seemed to be at her desk. When we tried to analyze and discuss afterwards what had happened, we both felt reminded of civil servants in Eritrea who behave likewise – in order to avoid responsibility. The seemingly separated spheres of international and national politics – represented by ARRA and UNHCR – collapsed into one opaque bureaucratic machine with whatever hidden agenda. Susan Whyte reminds us that uncertainty is less a state of reality, but a "process of minding" (2009: 13). Explaining the world from below through interpretation of experience and acquired knowledge thus becomes likewise informal: it becomes gnostic. After Moges left Beteseb found it increasingly hard to keep up moral discipline, to divide between right and wrong and to consider himself and others still human. This quote from a conversation (in English language, recorded in May 2012) may illustrate his existential fragility as well as the long process of individual and social transformation that accompanied his migration from Eritrea via Shimelba to Addis Ababa:

Yes, things, [...] all things [are] messed up like you see, and I don't have any person who could deal with my case. Just I am trying to live in my inside beauty, just I am doing my work and something. [He's a talented singer and guitar player. MT] Just I am trying to forget help from ARRA and UNHCR, so I am doing good – what will be the result, I don't know. But security wise always there is (...), you feel every second about your security this time. You can't entertain yourself even in Bulgaria [neighborhood in AA].

Here an incident comes to his mind, which in his line of thought seems to fit in well, he reports from a recent attack by two Ethiopian citizens who had been deported from Eritrea:

They [...] want to quarrel, but I'm fit. So I should [...] leave and most probably both of them, they are [physically weaker than me], [...] one of them is trying to hit me and I hold his hand and he can't do nothing. So I am peaceful. (...) 'Your question is with Isaias [Afewerki, the Eritrean president]. Leave it for him! I am an Eritrean citizen; I came here because of Isaias, so both of us should [...] insist [on him]. It's not the matter of us, this is politics, you are civil, I am civil [sic! I think he means "civilised"], so we don't have to do such kind of stuff.

In his narration he refrains from violence, which he denounces as animalistic, though it might have been a natural, understandable reaction even. Instead he offers something as obvious as surprising: solidarity in shared misery – however not at any price. After all he has gone through he stands with his back to the wall:

So from now on you are my friend. Don't think about that, if you think about that, maybe I can harm you, I can harm you. You are weak, I'm not tolerant. So first I [...] have to be [a] real human being, second if you [wish], I will be wild. So take care.'

Eritrea's Refugees: A New Generation towards a Democratic Future?

Eritrea's political transition is open, but imminent. The country's nationalist ideology has become hollow as promised peace, development and prosperity did not materialize, whereas older conflict lines such as religious, ethnic or regional differences have gained importance again. The president's argument that no democracy is needed, as long as the national leader embodies the will and identity of his people, exposes nothing but his uncompromising will to stick to power with the help of a paranoid security apparatus and corrupted military generals. Particularly military middle ranks apparently feel more and more unsatisfied. Ethiopian incursions in spring 2012 proved the military's disastrous state, an attempted coup (the so-called Forto-incident) had to be tackled in January 2013 and in the following October troops searching the capital Asmara for draft-dodgers refused to shoot when people in the streets rebelled.

Eritrea's ruling clique grows old; a second generation of political leaders from within the former guerrilla movement has not been bred successfully – most potential 'candidates' went into exile or were silenced. Also the important economic and political support of loyalists in the Diaspora becomes weaker; prominent officials have subsequently defected and initial emigration after the border war with Ethiopia has become a large-scale mass migration – and a rewarding business for corrupt militaries, cooperating with bandits in the Sudan and Egypt's Sinai (cf. Mekonnen & Estefanos 2011, Tesfagiorgis 2013 & Gebreluel, Tronvoll 2013).

Eritrean politics is infested with crime, hubris and sectarianism. Working on Eritrea since more than a decade I doubt that many of these predominantly young refugees are still very much interested in politics, when they put their life on the line and leave their home country. They hope for a better life elsewhere, which their country is unable and their government unwilling to provide. Most Eritrean refugees worry about family, not about politics which people learned to avoid and finally tried to flee.

Other than in the Arab spring migration has become much more attractive than social revolution in order to access the world's promises of human rights, democracy and prosperity. Reaching the other side of the border, however, draws people into a complex and unforeseen political constellation that does not allow an easy exit.

Migrants from the Global South heading for the Global North try to cross into privileged, but tightly controlled territory, as mass migration from the Global South is largely unwanted. This certainly is migration's most general political dimension. To claim political asylum provides one of the few legal entry options into the 'better world'. Being an acknowledged international refugee or asylum-seeker may therefore legitimize your individual migration project and convince otherwise skeptical refugees to present themselves as political activists.

Certainly refugee camps intend to seclude migrants from the rest of society and create a temporarily distinct territory. Its administration, usually made up of national authorities and international agencies, most prominently the UNHCR, as well as different national and international NGOs, aims at both, accommodation and shelter for the camp's inmates and protection of the outside society from potential dangers, such as criminality, disease and political unrest. After all, UNHCR's camp policy dates back to military disaster management during and after World War II. Contrary to this prudent seclusion refugee camps attract political mobilization, as the camps' inhabitants are kept available. It has been shown repeatedly since Liisa Malkki's study on Hutu refugees in Tanzania (1995) that refugees are in fact a political resource, in our case in favor of Ethiopia. Ethiopia is interested in both, initiating political transition in neighboring Eritrea and keeping eventual change under control. Ethiopia's government shares an uneasy history of cooperation and rivalry with its Eritrean counterpart (both have been guerilla fronts before 1991). After the regime-change the Ethiopian government imposed an administrative 'Ethnic Federalism' – that also allows to divide and rule – and now tries to shape the Eritrean opposition accordingly. Whoever is ready to become active in one of the Ethiopia-backed ethnic opposition groups, such as the Kunama-Guerilla DMLEK, the Saho movements (DMES and ENSF) or the young Tigrinya patriots within the *Solidarity Movement for National Salvation* may – unofficially – profit from certain privileges such as travel permission or enrolment into formal education programs out of camp. And while these emerging political groups all postulate human rights and democracy they bully other refugees and instigate conflict inside the refugee camp and within the larger refugee milieu. Besides – and this should not be forgotten – such political engagement promises important social contacts abroad and integration into globally organized political networks, a resource that other refugees and applicants for resettlement lack.

Traditionally, the field of Eritrean opposition groups is extremely confusing and volatile. Alliances are formed and broken. From an anthropological perspective it is therefore more interesting to explore how refugees themselves deal with this widely unexpected, but complex political constellation they find themselves in: Cheru is a young man of about 30 years; when we met in 2010 he acted on behalf of the ethnic Saho radicals and eagerly informed me on political activities in the refugee camp. In his clear-cut view refugees were victims of the regime, their wish to reach a safe haven was understandable, but more importantly resistance against the government had to be organized. Remarkably these political seminars and demonstrations that serve to disseminate political doctrine lack free and open discussion. These forms of political education are apparently imported from Eritrea's political guerrilla-culture. Also political programs look alike: "Lives have to be lost", Cheru told me pathetically, lowering his voice and cautiously observing the people around us.

During my stay in Shimelba in 2007, Tesfai, a young Tigrinya patriot had already suggested to set off bombs in strategic places inside Eritrea and kidnap the children of military officers and government officials. While talking he got all enthusiastic and his eyes started glowing – and I imagine, that Eritrea's current dictator in his younger, still revolutionary days might have looked alike.

This kind of talk may have dangerous consequences, but there is reason to doubt, that young radicals like Cheru or Tesfai will risk their own life in armed struggle. Still they were refugees in a difficult situation and their political activism has to be seen in this context. They enjoyed moving freely throughout Ethiopia, being courted by its leaders and assigned a mission – while their countrymen, confined to the camp and its depressing daily life, struggled to keep up their mental health. Cheru and Tesfai did certainly not give up their own individual plea for resettlement, but tried to build bridges into a world they had not yet entered – and everyone guessed exactly that. Such prominent political activists are cautiously observed by others; they are mistrusted by most and envied at the same time. However no one seems able to fully evade the political field – as Yohannes' example has shown.

FUTURE RESEARCH DIRECTIONS

To further explore on and accompany Eritrea's political transition towards a post-Isaias-era is certainly of high importance and will provide lessons to peace & conflict studies far beyond Eritrea's case. Despite its small size and international marginality Eritrea's transition into an open political future provides a unique chance for joint intensive research from different interdisciplinary perspectives. Until today history and political situation are well documented considering both Eritrea and its international Diaspora (cf. Quehl 2005, O'Kane & Hepner 2009). While few attempts have been made to question the political role of refugees for the country's future, mass migration from Eritrea has indeed become a topic in various academic fields as well as in international media. Most interestingly more and more young African researchers have started to work on the matter; most of them are themselves of Eritrean or Ethiopian origin. Although they went through very different ways, the historian Mussie Tesfagiorgis (University of Winnepeg/Canada), the lawyer Daniel R. Mekonnen (International Law and Policy Institute, Oslo/Norway) and the geographer Sadia Hassanen (Stockholm University) – a now established second generation of Eritrean scholars – have themselves been migrants.

Several Ph.D. projects that address migration from Eritrea (and Ethiopia) from an anthropologist viewpoint have recently been started at the universities of Bayreuth (Délia Nicoué), Stockholm (Tekalign Ayalew), Khartoum (Netsereab G. Andom) or Addis Ababa (Mulu Getachew). These highlight learning processes during migration and after arrival in Europe, the relationship between migrants and Diaspora, migration's informality and obstacles in Khartoum or the linkage of biographical and political histories in Mai Ayni refugee camp. Mirjam Wolfstein's doctoral project on the integration of unaccompanied minors into the German and European educational systems (Felsberg Institute) refers to a large extent on experiences with young refugees from Eritrea. Thus academic research on migration from Eritrea is developing and diversifying. Additionally the refugee experience is increasingly covered by autobiographical publications and refugee journalists addressing the Diaspora abroad as well as the interested public in refugee-receiving countries.

It will be central to ongoing and future research to deal with Eritrea's political trajectory and to provide knowledge and voices for a peaceful change towards the better. Furthermore research has to address changes, that migration itself induced: More and more rural youths – often unaccompanied – arrive in Europe. These lack school education and have lived for years without parents or older relatives; instead youths have been involved into an increasingly informal culture of migration that will create problems and challenges for generations inside and outside of Eritrea.

CONCLUSION

Eritrean refugees may arrive somehow naïve in the refugee camp, but they quickly learn that they cannot flee the meshwork of political questions and demands; inevitably they get trapped in its local and global dimensions. Longing for a peaceful life, sustained by human rights, democracy and a chance for prosperity and personal development, refugees face a tedious struggle with international refugee administration and exclusive migration policy. Political persecution provides one of the few arguments to be granted access to the Global North. Eritreans thus become active to defend and promote their migration processes, literally putting their existence at stake. While trying to exit Eritrea's political (and economic) dead end street and participate in the world beyond, they remain rooted in Eritrea's authoritarian guerrilla-culture at the same time, perpetuating secrecy, rivalry, blackmailing and violence.

In refugees' complex political constellation Eritreans are no privileged actors, they are applicants without strong influence and playthings in confusing political games, but they are certainly not only victims. They are decisive political subjects of a new Eritrea yet to come, a new Eritrea that will neither be free from its authoritarian past nor from the embodied refugee experience and its resulting culture of migration.

Experiences of continuous postponement and opacity in the administrative decision-making process and resulting helplessness and impotence have an enduring and frustrating effect. The perception of being marginalized and forgotten by the Global North sediments down into their own interpretation of the world and becomes a basis for further action – that is informal praxis.

Blundering into informality mirrors an existential yearning to stay active and to influence one's own fate and progress. Refugees and migrants from Eritrea find themselves in a remarkable dilemma. Their broad recognition as international refugees morally justifies escape and migration – while daily life demands informal and also illegal practices. This discrepancy backfires on the migrant's milieu: Far beyond isolated Eritrea and its dictatorial rule, in the encounter with the world beyond – that promised prosperity, democracy, human rights and the rule of law – Eritrean migrants broadly reproduce mutual mistrust, rude competition, deceit and exploitation of co-migrants instead of social solidarity. Not everyone becomes a criminal, of course, but no one is fully exempt either. While calling for democratic participation, trust in formal rules and the respect of human rights social decay is instigated and perpetuated. The way towards a better life in a better world turns out to be much more challenging, than one could have predicted. What Eritrean migrants wanted to overcome by leaving, sticks to them and comes along. Thus it would certainly be too easy to proclaim Eritrea's refugees the new democratic generation and hope of tomorrow. Social decay, conflict and authoritarian political culture are likely to persist.

In a more general sense, migration may indeed offer a way out of violence, where local changes for the better seem impossible, but it may not create a moral base for democracy and sustainable peace.

REFERENCES

Aalen, L., & Tronvoll, K. (2009). The End of Democracy? Curtailing Political and Civil Rights in Ethiopia. *Review of African Political Economy*, *36*(120), 193–207. doi:10.1080/03056240903065067

Abdalla, M., Dias Barros, D., & Berthet Ribeiro, M. (Eds.), (2014). *Spaces in Movement: New Perspectives on Migration in African Settings*. Köln: Köppe.

AlSayyad, N. (2004). Urban Informality as a ,New' Way of Life. In A. Roy & N. AlSayyad (Eds.), *Urban Informality. Transnational Perspectives from the Middle East, Latin America and South Asia* (pp. 7–30). Lanham, MD: Lexington Books.

Bayart, J.-F., Ellis, S., & Hibou, B. (1999). *The Criminalization of the State in Africa*. Oxford: James Currey.

Bernal, V. (2013). Civil Society and Cyberspace: Reflections on Dehai, Asmarino, and Awate. *Africa Today*, *60*(2), 21–36. doi:10.2979/africatoday.60.2.21

Bozzini, D. (2011). Low-tech Surveillance and the Despotic State in Eritrea. *Surveillance & Society*, *9*, 93–113.

Chabal, P. (2009). *Africa: the politics of suffering and smiling*. London: Zed Books.

Chabal, P., & Daloz, J.-P. (1999). *Afrika Works. Disorder as political instrument*. Oxford: James Currey.

Eckert, J. (2012). Rumours of Rights. In J. Eckert, B. Donahoe, Ch. Strümpell, & Z. Ö. Biner (Eds.), *Law against the State. Ethnographic Forays into Law's Transformations* (pp. 147–170). Cambridge: Cambridge University Press. doi:10.1017/CBO9781139043786.007

Essed, Ph., Frerks, G., & Schrijvers, J. (2004). Introduction. Refugees, Agency and Social Transformation. In P. Essed, G. Frerks, & J. Schrijvers (Eds.), Refugees and the Transformation of Societies. Agency, Policies, Ethics and Politics. New York, Oxford: Berghahn.

Gebreluel, G., & Tronvoll, K. (2013, October 15). Is the Horn of Africa facing another collapsing state? Eritrea's refugee crisis threatens to undermine the stability of the secretive country. *Al Jazeera*. Retrieved from http://www.aljazeera.com/indepth/opinion/2013/10/horn-africa-facing-another-collapsing-state-201310611177564655.html

Glick-Schiller, N., & Fouron, G. (2001). *Georges Woke Up Laughing: Long-Distance Nationalism and the Search for Home*. Durham, NC: Duke University Press. doi:10.1215/9780822383239

Graw, K., & Schielke, S. (Eds.). (2012). *The Global Horizon. Expectations of Migration in Africa and the Middle East*. Leuven: Leuven University Press.

Harmon-Gross, E. (2009). *Seeking Resettlement and Navigating Transnational Politics. The Intersection of Policies, Human Rights and Individuals in Shimelba Refugee Camp* [MA Thesis]. University of Tennessee. Retrieved from http://trace.tennessee.edu/utk_gradthes/84

Hart, K. (1973). Informal Income Opportunities and Urban Employment in Ghana. *The Journal of Modern African Studies*, *11*(1), 61–89. doi:10.1017/S0022278X00008089

Hart, K. (2010). Africa's urban revolution and the informal economy. In V. Padayachee (Ed.), *The Political Economy of Africa* (pp. 371–388). London, New York: Routledge.

Hepner, T. R. (2009). Seeking Asylum in a Transnational Social Field. New Refugees and Struggles for Autonomy and Rights. In D. O'Kane & T. R. Hepner (Eds.), *Biopolitics, Militarism and Development. Eritrea in the Twenty-First Century* (pp. 115–133). New York: Berghahn.

Hirt, N., & Mohammad, A. S. (2013). 'Dreams Don't Come True in Eritrea'. Anomie and Family Disintegration due to the Structural Militarization of Society. *The Journal of Modern African Studies*, *51*(1), 139–168. doi:10.1017/S0022278X12000572

Holtmann, E., & Wiesenthal, H. (2009): *Transition. Transformation. Posttransformation.* Jena: SFB 580 Mitteilungen, 31.

Honwana, A. (2012). *The Time of Youth. Work, Social Change, and Politics in Africa.* Sterling, VA: Kumarian Press.

Horst, C. (2006). *Transnational Nomads. How Somalis Cope with Refugee Life in the Dadaab Camps of Kenya.* New York, Oxford: Berghahn.

International Crisis Group. (2013). *International Crisis Group: Eritrea. Scenarios for Future Transition.* Africa Report No. 200.

Jackson, M. (2006). *The Politics of Storytelling. Violence, Transgression and Intersubjectivity.* Copenhagen: Museum Tusculanum Press.

Kibreab, G. (2004). Pulling the Wool over the Eyes of the Strangers. Refugee Deceit and Trickery in Institutionalized Settings. *Journal of Refugee Studies*, *17*(1), 1–26. doi:10.1093/jrs/17.1.1

Kibreab, G. (2009). Forced Labour in Eritrea. *The Journal of Modern African Studies*, *47*(1), 41–72. doi:10.1017/S0022278X08003650

Kirk, J. (2010). Gender, forced migration and education. Identities and experiences of refugee women teachers. *Gender and Education*, *22*(2), 161–176. doi:10.1080/09540251003606925

Knörr, J. (2005). Introduction. In J. Knörr (Ed.), Childhood and Migration (pp. 9-21). Bielefeld: transcript.

Liempt, I. v. (2007). *Navigating Borders. Inside Perspectives on the Process of Human Smuggling into the Netherlands.* Amsterdam: Amsterdam University Press. doi:10.5117/9789053569306

Lindell, I. (2010). Introduction. The changing politics of informality – collective organizing, alliances and scales of engagement. In I. Lindell (Ed.), *Africa's informal workers. Collective agency, alliances and transnational organizing in urban Africa* (pp. 1–32). London, New York: Zed Books.

Lüdeke, F. (2012). *'Der weibliche Flüchtling' zwischen Bild und Aushandlung: Eine Feldforschung in Shimelba/Äthiopien* [MA Thesis]. Bayreuth University, Germany

Malkki, L. (1995). *Purity and exile. Violence, memory, and national cosmology among Hutu refugees in Tanzania.* Chicago: University of Chicago Press.

Marcus, H. (1994). *A History of Ethiopia.* Berkeley: University of California Press.

Mbembe, A. (2001). *On the Postcolony.* Berkeley: University of California Press.

Meconnen, D. R., & Estefanos, M. (2011). *From Sawa to the Sinai Desert. The Eritrean Tragedy of Human Trafficking.* Discussion Paper. Retrieved from http://ssrn.com/abstract=2055303

Piot, Ch. (2010). Border Practices. In A.-M. Makhulu, B. Buggenhagen, & S. Jackson (Eds.), Hard Work, Hard Times. Global Volatility and African Subjectivities (pp. 150-164). Berkeley, & Los Angeles: University of California Press.

Quehl, H. (2003). Oral History on War. Tagadelti in and after Eritrea's War of Independence. In E.-M. Bruchhaus (Ed.), *Hot Spot Horn of Africa. Between Integration and Disintegration* (pp. 136–147). Münster: LIT.

Quehl, H. (2005). *Kämpferinnen und Kämpfer im eritreischen Unabhängigkeitskrieg 1961-1991. Faktoren der Diversität und der Koherenz. Eine historische Untersuchung zur Alltagsgeschichte des Krieges*. Felsberg: Edition Eins.

Quehl, H. (2013). Zum Umbau von Kriegsgesellschaften. Eritrea, Kurdistan und Nicaragua zwischen Pragmatismus, Isolation und Assimilation. In B. Greiner, T. Müller, & K. Voß (Eds.), *Erbe des Kalten Krieges. Studien zum Kalten Krieg* (Vol. 6, pp. 480–498). Hamburg: Hamburger Edition.

Radtke, K. (2006). Die Finanzierung von Bürgerkriegen aus der Diaspora. Eritreer in Frankfurt und Tamilen in Toronto. In K. Inhetveen (Ed.), *Flucht als Politik. Berichte von fünf Kontinenten* (pp. 163–182). Köln: Köppe.

Sartre, J.-P. (1968). *Search for a method*. New York: Random House.

Schielke, S. (2012). Engaging the world on the Alexandria waterfront. In K. Graw & S. Schielke (Eds.), *The Global Horizon. Expectations of Migration in Africa and the Middle East* (pp. 175–193). Leuven: Leuven University Press.

Schuster, L. (2005). The Continuing Mobility of Migrants in Italy. Shifting between Places and Statuses. *Journal of Ethnic and Migration Studies, 31*(4), 757–774. doi:10.1080/13691830500109993

Scott, J. (1990). *Domination and the Arts of Resistance: Hidden Transcripts*. New Haven: Yale University Press.

Sendker, L. (1990). *Eritreische Flüchtlinge im Sudan. Zwischen Assimilation und Segregation* (Vol. 70). Hamburg: Institut für Afrika-Kunde.

Skalník, P. (1989). Outwitting the State. An Introduction. In P. Skalník (Ed.), *Outwitting the State* (pp. 1–22). New Brunswick: Transaction Publ.

Tesfagiorgis, M. (2013). From Troubled Homes to Human Organ Harvesters. The Odysee of African Refugees in North Africa. In D. R. Mekonnen, & M. Tesfagiorgis (Eds.), The Horn of Africa at the Brink of the 21st Century. Coping with Fragmentation, Isolation and Marginalization in a Globalizing Environment (pp. 61-98). Felsberg: Edition Eins.

Tesfaye, L. (2011). *Stationen mobiler Fluchtgeschichten: Migration als Verhandlungsfeld zwischen Kontrollregimen, Handlungsräumen und der Verwirklichung persönlicher Lebensvorstellungen am Beispiel eritreischer Flüchtlinge in Äthiopien* [MA Thesis]. Munich University.

Tickamyer, A., & Bohon, S. (2000). The Informal Economy. In E. F. Borgatta, & Rh. Montgomery (Eds), Encyclopedia of Sociology (2nd ed., Vol. 2, pp. 1337-1344). New York: Macmillan.

Treiber, M. (2005). *Der Traum vom guten Leben. Die eritreische warsay-Generation im Asmara der zweiten Nachkriegszeit*. Münster: LIT.

Treiber, M. (2007). Dreaming of a good life. Young urban refugees from the Horn of Africa between refusal of politics and political asylum seeking. In H. P. Hahn & G. Klute (Eds.), *Cultures of Migration. African perspectives* (pp. 239–260). Berlin: LIT.

Treiber, M. (2009). Trapped in Adolescence. The Post-War Urban Generation. In D. O'Kane & T. R. Hepner (Eds.), *Biopolitics, Militarism, and the Developmental State: Eritrea in the 21st Century* (pp. 92–114). New York: Berghahn.

Treiber, M. (2010). The Choice between Clean and Dirty. Discourses of Aesthetics, Morality and Progress in Post-revolutionary Asmara, Eritrea. In E. Dürr & R. Jaffe (Eds.), *Urban Pollution. Cultural Meanings, Social Practices* (pp. 123–143). Oxford: Berghahn.

Treiber, M. (2013a). Lessons for Life. Two migratory portraits from Eritrea. In A. Triulzi & R. McKenzie (Eds.), *Long Journeys. African Migrants on the Road* (pp. 187–212). Leiden: Brill. doi:10.1163/9789004250390_011

Treiber, M. (2013b, September 11-13). Flucht aus Eritrea und die Zersetzung des Sozialen. *Rundbrief KDV im Krieg*. Connection e.V. Internationale Arbeit für Kriegsdienstverweigerer und Deserteure,

Treiber, M. (2013c). Leaving Eritrea, Entering the World – Migrants in the Making. In M. Tesfagiorgis, & D. R. Mekonnen (Eds), *The Horn of Africa at the Brink of the 21st Century. Coping with Fragmentation, Isolation and Marginalization in a Globalizing Environment* (pp. 127-138). Felsberg: Edition Eins.

Treiber, M. (2013d). Grasping Kiflu's Fear – Informality and Existentialism in Migration from North-East Africa. *Modern Africa. Politics. Historia y Sociedad (Rio Piedras, San Juan, P.R.)*, *1*(2), 111–139.

Treiber, M. (2014). Becoming by Moving. Khartoum and Addis Ababa as migratory stages between Eritrea and 'something. In M. Abdalla, D. Dias Barros Denise, & M. Berthet Ribeiro (Eds.), *Spaces in Movement: New Perspectives on Migration in African Settings* (pp. 189–205). Köln: Köppe.

Treiber, M., & Tesfaye, L. (2008). Step by Step. Migration from Eritrea. In E.-M. Bruchhaus & M. Sommer (Eds.), *Hot Spot Horn of Africa revisited. Approaches to make sense of conflict* (pp. 280–295). Berlin: LIT.

Triulzi, A., & McKenzie, R. L. (Eds.). (2013). *Long Journeys. African Migrants on the Road*. Leiden: Brill. doi:10.1163/9789004250390

UN High Commissioner for Refugees. (2007). *Refugee Protection and Mixed Migration. A 10-Point Plan of Action*. Retrieved from http://www.unhcr.org/4742a30b4.html

UN High Commissioner for Refugees. (2011a). *Eligibility Guidelines for Assessing the International Protection Need of Asylum Seekers from Eritrea*. Retrieved from www.refworld.org

UN High Commissioner for Refugees. (2011b). *UNHCR Resettlement Handbook*. Retrieved from http://www.refworld.org/docid/4ecb973c2.html

Westin, Ch., & Hassanen, S. (Eds.), (2014). *People on the Move. Experiences of forced migration, with examples from various parts of the world*. Trenton, NJ: Red Sea Press.

Whyte, S. R. (2009). Epilogue. In L. Haram & C. Bawa Yamba (Eds.), *Dealing with Uncertainty in Contemporary African Lives* (pp. 213–216). Uppsala: Nordic Africa Institute.

Zewde, B. (2001). *A History of Modern Ethiopia 1855-1991*. Oxford: James Currey.

ADDITIONAL READING

Abdalla, M., Dias Barros, D., & Berthet Ribeiro, M. (Eds.). (2014). *Spaces in Movement: New Perspectives on Migration in African Settings*. Köln: Köppe.

Agier, M. (2008). *On the Margins of the World. The Refugee Experiences Today*. Cambridge, UK: Polity Press.

Agier, M. (2011). *Managing the Undesirables. Refugee Camps and Humanitarian Government*. Cambridge, UK: Polity Press.

Bozzini, D. (2011) *En état de siège: ethnographie de la mobilisation nationale et de la surveillance en Erythrée*. Thèse de doctorat, Université de Neuchâtel, Switzerland.

Friedman, J., & Randeria, S. (Eds.). (2004). *Worlds on the Move. Globalization, Migration and Cultural Security*. London: I.B. Tauris.

Graw, K., & Schielke, S. (Eds.). (2012). *The Global Horizon. Expectations of Migration in Africa and the Middle East*. Leuven: Leuven University Press.

Hirt, N., & Mohammad, A. S. (2013). "Dreams Don't Come True in Eritrea". Anomie and Family Disintegration due to the Structural Militarization of Society. *The Journal of Modern African Studies, 51*(1), 139–168. doi:10.1017/S0022278X12000572

Honwana, A. (2012). *The Time of Youth. Work, Social Change, and Politics in Africa*. Sterling, VA: Kumarian Press.

Horst, C. (2006). *Transnational Nomads. How Somalis Cope with Refugee Life in the Dadaab Camps of Kenya*. New York, Oxford: Berghahn.

Iosifides, Th., & Sporton, D. (2009). Biographical methods in migration research. *Migration Letters, 6*(2), 101–108.

Jackson, M. (2006). *The Politics of Storytelling. Violence, Transgression and Intersubjectivity*. Copenhagen: Museum Tusculanum Press.

Mekonnen, D. R., & Tesfagiorgis, M. (Eds.). (2013). The Horn of Africa at the Brink of the 21st Century. Coping with Fragmentation, Isolation and Marginalization in a Globalizing Environment. Felsberg: edition eins.

O'Kane, D., & Hepner, T. R. (Eds.). (2009). *Biopolitics, Militarism and Development. Eritrea in the Twenty-First Century*. New York: Berghahn.

Portes, A., & DeWind, J. (Eds.). (2007). *Rethinking Migration. New Theoretical and Empirical Perspectives*. New York: Berghahn.

Sayad, A. (2004). *The Suffering of the Immigrant*. Cambridge: Polity Press.

Schutz, A. (1944). The Stranger. An Essay in Social Psychology. *American Journal of Sociology, 49*(6), 499–507. doi:10.1086/219472

Stoller, P. (2001). *Money has no Smell. The Africanization of New York City*. Chicago: Chicago University Press.

Thomas, W., & Znaniecki, F. (1918–20). *The Polish Peasant in Europe and America* (2 vols). Boston: Richard G. Badger.

Triulzi, A., & McKenzie, R. L. (Eds.). (2013). *Long Journeys. African Migrants on the Road*. Leiden: Brill. doi:10.1163/9789004250390

Tsianos, V., Hess, S., & Karakayali, S. (2009). *Transnational migration. Theory and method of an ethnographic analysis of border regimes*. Working Paper 55. Brighton: University of Sussex, Sussex Centre for Migration Research.

Westin, Ch., & Hassanen, S. (Eds.). (2014). *People on the Move. Experiences of forced migration, with examples from various parts of the world*. Trenton, NJ: Red Sea Press.

KEY TERMS AND DEFINITIONS

Existentialism: Inspired by Albert Camus and Jean-Paul Sartre the anthropologist Michael Jackson tried to make key concepts of philosophical existentialism useful for anthropological research and theory. These focus on subjectivity and subjective experience of the outside world, on life's processual character and its therefore inevitable gap between now and then.

Informality: According to Keith Hart's informal/formal dialectic, informality emerges in the encounter with formality. In unprivileged migration informal practices encompass bribe and corruption, false and forged documents, illegal immigration and the like. Besides these criminal offences less clear-cut practices, such as circumvention of formal rules, evasion, manipulation and mistrust, have become characteristic for the transnational migratory milieu of Eritreans. Informality and the process of informalization therefore also describe an ambivalent culture of migration.

Refugee: The category 'refugee' is first of all a legal label, referring to respective national law as well as to the international Geneva Convention of 1951, which forms the UNHCR's working base. Refugees formally underlie international protection and care. From a refugee's perspective, however, this rather ambivalent status also implies decreed passivity, indefinite waiting, administrative categorization and paternalistic control – as it has been shown by Liisa Malkki, Barbara Harrell-Bond or Michel Agier. In the case of Eritreans the international refugee status may lead to resettlement to a third country, but informal alternatives may occasionally seem more promising. On the other hand it is the formal refugee status (on the base of nationality) that morally legitimizes even informal onward-journeys and asylum-claims.

Transnational Milieu: Transnationalism – as developed by Nina Glick-Schiller, Peggy Levitt and others – is not limited to the complex mutual ties between diasporas and their places of origins. The concept is also useful to describe processual migrations through different stages and stations of a specific migration and its temporal as well as spatial dimensions and interconnections. A respective milieu – that proves similar life situations, shared experiences and internal communication – consists of a local level, where people meet temporarily in cities or refugee camps and an eventually global level which connects migrants in different stations and stages on the base of electronic communication.

Unprivileged Migration: Migration seeks to bridge both a temporal and spatial gap, seeking for future establishment elsewhere. If migration is not privileged by lawful procedures, economic promises, comfort and social respect, but faces political and social exclusion and criminal exploitation, its underlying life project becomes an existential risk. Unprivileged migration here is a dangerous travel for one's own sake to a better, but not a welcoming world.

ENDNOTES

1. UNHCR Statistical Yearbook 2012, Annex, Tables 2 and 5.
2. See BBC News, 7 Oct 2013: Lampedusa boat disaster – Death Toll rises to 232; BBC News, 30 Jun 2014: Italy finds 30 bodies in migrant boat (news.bbc.co.uk).
3. In his existential philosophy Sartre describes "need" as "a lack seeking to be denied" and "hence a surpassing-toward (a rudimentary pro-ject)" (1968: 171, FN 3).
4. Both men had to be granted formal asylum in Germany in 2010, after their second escape from Eritrea. Despite immediate protests and broadly available country-of-origin information they had been extradited to torture and prison. Their case has been documented in detail by concerned human rights groups (Connection e.V.; Pro Asyl; Eritreische Antimilitaristische Initiative: Eritrea - Desertion, Flucht & Asyl. 09/2010; http://www.connection-ev.de/article-1286).
5. UNHCR: 2013 UNHCR country operations profile – Ethiopia. Retrieved November 7, 2013 from http://www.unhcr.org/pages/49e483986.html
6. See Human Rights Concern – Eritrea: Voices of Torture. Documentary. 2006 (hrc-eritrea.org).

Chapter 9
Of Justice, Accountability, and Reconciliation:
Preliminary Stocktaking on Transitional Justice Efforts in South Sudan

Kathrin Maria Scherr
Max Planck Foundation for International Peace and the Rule of Law, Germany

ABSTRACT

This paper analyses South Sudan's long struggle for an inclusive reconciliatory process in the country from the Comprehensive Peace Agreement of 2005 to the peace negotiations in Addis Ababa in 2014/15 and highlights the difficulties that the country has faced in introducing a lasting initiative to bring about justice, achieve reconciliation and ensure accountability in the country. The author considers different judicial and non-judicial mechanisms as elements of a comprehensive transitional justice policy and suggests viable options for South Sudan to confront the historical grievances and to resolve the frictions and tensions that have persisted between the different warring groups and ethnic communities during the decades of war in South Sudan.

In any country ravaged by a legacy of conflict, mass violence, and human rights abuses, there are many challenges to rebuilding a society and effectively addressing the past. In conflict and post-conflict societies transitional justice embodies an attempt to build a sustainable peace through a process that involves complementary measures such as prosecuting perpetrators, revealing the truth about past crimes, providing victims with reparations, promoting reconciliation and reforming abusive government structures (Seibert-Fohr, 2012, pp. 1042). The UN's approach to transitional justice was set out in detail in two consecutive reports of the UN Secretary-General to the UN Security Council in 2004 and 2011 (United Nations, S/2004/616 (2004); United Nations, S/2011/634 (2011)). According to the definition contained in the latter report transitional justice "consists of both judicial and non-judicial processes and mechanisms, including prosecution initiatives, facilitating initiatives in the right to truth, delivering reparations, institutional reform and national consultations" (UN, S/2011/634 (2011), p. 2). Transitional justice is guided by the multidimen-

DOI: 10.4018/978-1-4666-9675-4.ch009

sional notion of *reconciliation* and while it is difficult to find a holistic definition of the concept as such, in the particular context of post-conflict peacebuilding reconciliation usually encompasses two core principles: Seeking the truth about the crimes committed and rendering justice through elements of criminal and/or restorative justice (Hazan, 2009, p. 261).

When war ends the inevitable question arises concerning how to deal with crimes and human rights abuses committed during times of conflict. Thereby, the key considerations evolve around elements of retributive and restorative justice. Whereas the notion of retributive justice encompasses issues such as how to punish the perpetrators having committed grave offences, deliver justice to the victims and repair the damages caused to them, elements of restorative justice focus on victim-offender mediation with a view to rehabilitating the offenders through reconciliation with the victims and the community at large (Clamp & Doak, 2012, pp. 342). In the context of transitional justice the more community-centric approach of restorative justice frequently co-exists with the victims' desire for punishment of the offenders. This often creates a natural tension between the elements of restorative and retributive justice and raises the question whether peace and justice can be achieved at the same time (UN, S/2004/616 (2004), p. 8; African Union Panel of the Wise, 2013, pp. 10). In many instances transitional justice strategies are shaped in situations where peace is fragile or perpetrators retain power. Thus, any attempt to secure a durable peace and deliver justice at the same time must carefully balance the demands of justice with the political realities on the ground. There is an inherent tension between the pursuit of justice on the one hand and the process of reconciliation on the other. In cases where perpetrators continue to hold power or are part of a post-conflict power-sharing agreement, mechanisms of retributive justice might be obstructed by those in power since they may very well be the targets of that justice (Van Zyl, 2005, p. 209). Effective transitional justice policies therefore require a balancing act between the quest for societal peace and the pursuit of justice and largely depend on the prevailing political, legal, social and economic realities of the country coming out of conflict. Every country's transitional justice experience is unique and there is no "one-size-fits-all formula" (UN, S/2004/616 (2004), p. 1) providing a blueprint and guarantee for a successful process of reconciliation and healing. Accordingly, in order to develop a legitimate strategy that helps to bring about stability and peace in a post-conflict setting, it is important to take into account both the victims' desire for justice as well as the local populations' needs, perceptions and expectations towards reconciliation and social reconstruction (Hazan, 2009, pp. 263).

South Sudan is the world's youngest nation, a state that emerged on 9 July 2011 after decades of civil war and whose coming into existence was preceded by a long and gruesome fight for independence. Peace between the warring parties was eventually achieved with the Comprehensive Peace Agreement in 2005 and South Sudan's claim for statehood was finally sealed by a positive referendum on self-determination in January 2011. After decades of intermittent civil war South Sudanese society is deeply fractured and scarred. When speaking about South Sudan's violent history, the focus is usually on the North-South conflict in (the then still united) Sudan and the decades of civil war that preceded South Sudan's independence. What is often overlooked is the fact that the "South" has been marred by a history of tribal tensions, sectarian fights and interethnic violence over scarce resources such as water and land necessary for cattle grazing. During the decades of civil war the ethicized, South-on-South, military violence was further instigated by the North, which in an effort to weaken the Southern enemy, recruited some of the ethnic groups from the South and deployed them against others (Copnall, 2014, p. 167; Johnson, 2011, p. 131). Furthermore, leadership struggles within the main southern opposition movement – the Sudan People's Liberation Army (SPLA) – quickly degenerated into an ethnic confrontation between the fighters loyal to John Garang, an ethnic Dinka, and the Nuer fighters, led by Riek Machar (Elhag, 2008, pp. 164; Johnson, 2011, pp. 127). While South Sudan's quest for nationhood was marked by a gruesome war against the North, interethnic violence in the country also accounted for numerous victims and grave offences against human rights. In November 1991, for instance, forces led by the SPLA's breakaway faction of Riek Machar deliberately killed an estimated 2000 civilians of the Bor community, mostly ethnic Dinka, and wounded several thousand more over the course of a few weeks. Only in August 2011, twenty years after the bloodshed, which became known as the 'Bor Massacre', Riek Machar publicly apologized for his role in the massacre. Despite the large-scale violence and human rights abuses during the years of civil war, to this day a comprehensive process of justice and reconciliation has not been conducted in South Sudan and the few initiatives attempting to set in motion transitional justice efforts so far have produced scant results. Even before the most recent outbreak of violence between forces loyal to President Salva Kiir and anti-government forces known as the Sudan People's Liberation Movement in Opposition (SPLM/A in Opposition, SPLM/A-IO) in December 2013, the conversation about transitional justice in the country remained severely obstructed by inter-communal clashes, continued armed militia activities, incomplete disarmament processes and severe infrastructure and governance challenges. In the most recent past a constructive dialogue on transitional justice issues has been silenced by the return to a renewed and devastating armed conflict in the country.

The recent history of South Sudan shows a pattern of the country's leading officials looking to the future by putting the painful legacies of the past behind them. Consequently, such policy approach neglected to legitimately deal with previous conflicts. While a constructive engagement with its violent history has not been possible so far, the omission to deal with these issues beforehand has forced the country to face much greater grievances later on. This paper seeks to shed light on South Sudan's flawed attempts since the signing of the CPA in 2005 to develop a comprehensive strategy of justice, peace and reconciliation in the country. Furthermore, it links the roots of the present conflict, and the difficulties and challenges that the parties are facing in the course of the current peace process, directly to the neglectful attitude the nation has taken with respect to a thorough confrontation with past injustices and crimes committed during the years of conflict.

A FLAWED HISTORY OF JUSTICE AND RECONCILIATION IN SOUTH SUDAN

Justice and Reconciliation under the Comprehensive Peace Agreement

South Sudan fought two civil wars against the Government of Sudan (1955-1972 and 1983-2005), which in total claimed an estimated 2.5 million lives and displaced around four million people (Esposito & Crocker, 2004, p. 1). After decades of a devastating war in Sudan between the North and the South, and tedious peace negotiations starting with the Machakos Protocol in 2002, which at the time provided the basis for a ceasefire and peace talks, war officially ended with the signing of the Comprehensive Peace Agreement (CPA) between the Government of Sudan and the Sudan People's Liberation Movement/Army (SPLM/A) in the Nyayo Stadium in Nairobi, Kenya on 9 January 2005. The CPA of 2005 was comprised of six protocols, which were concluded between 2002 and 2005 and in which the warring parties in Sudan committed to embark on a negotiated roadmap for peace.

The CPA sought to create sustainable peace in the country through a number of power-sharing arrangements that triggered the necessary legislative and institutional changes, as well as a new constitutional framework for Sudan, all of which were necessary to secure a balanced compromise between the demands of the North and the South at the time. In line with the arrangements agreed upon in the CPA, a Government of National Unity (GNU) was established in Sudan, while the South set up a largely autonomous government at the same time, the Government of Southern Sudan (GoSS). In addition to the principles on power sharing, the CPA contained extensive wealth-sharing arrangements including provisions to share the country's oil revenues between the North and South (CPA, Agreement on Wealth Sharing, Chapter III; International Crisis Group, 2007, pp. 2). With reference to the security arrangements under the CPA, the South was able to retain its army while joint security units were created to patrol the border between the North and the South (CPA, Agreement on Security Arrangements, Chapter VI). Most importantly, the Peace Agreement foresaw a six-year interim period that was to be followed by a referendum on self-determination in the South (Articles 2.4-2.6 CPA, The Machakos Protocol, Chapter I). While both the SPLM and the National Congress Party (NCP), the ruling party in the North, had committed themselves in the CPA to promote national unity during the interim period, the South could choose to become an independent nation in a referendum in 2011. Despite the fact that the CPA's implementation suffered considerable delays, national elections were held in Sudan in 2010, followed by the referendum on self-determination of the South at the beginning of 2011.

From the start of the negotiations the international community was heavily involved in the peace process leading up to the signing of the Comprehensive Peace Agreement. Already in the early talks the Intergovernmental Authority on Development (IGAD) and in particular Kenya, took a lead in the negotiations. The breadth of international involvement in the peace negotiations was mirrored in the number of signed witnesses to the CPA: Kenya, the United States, the United Kingdom, Italy, Norway, the Netherlands, Uganda, Egypt, the IGAD Partners Forum, the Arab League, the United Nations, the European Union, and the African Union (AU). Considering the extensive international attention and heavy involvement in the consultations leading up to the CPA, it is all the more surprising that despite the extensive power- and wealth-sharing arrangements outlined in the final document, the Peace Agreement only contained a brief reference to the need for reconciliation in the country and entirely excluded the question of accountability for the crimes, atrocities and human rights abuses that had been committed in the country during the decades of civil war. Generally speaking, the parties at the negotiating table adopted a rather narrow, forward-looking approach in the consultations by focusing the terms of the final Peace Agreement on a future framework for political transition and wealth sharing rather than contemplating a mechanism within the terms of the final agreement to confront the country's militant past and to remedy the legacies of violence and injustice that had occurred during the years of civil war in Sudan (Oette, 2011, pp. 25). Of even further interest, during the negotiations the parties openly considered inserting general amnesties in the wording of the final peace agreement. On this point, however, the international advisors present at the negotiation table made their voices heard to not include such provisions in the CPA (Crawford-Browne, Basha & Alexander, 2006, pp. 141).

In the end the final wording of the Comprehensive Peace Agreement gave very limited consideration to examining Sudan's painful past and merely included a general commitment to a national reconciliation and healing process to be conducted by the then National Government of Unity based in Khartoum during the six-year interim period. The promise to initiate a National

Reconciliation and Healing Process (NRHP) was spelled out in Article 1.7 of the CPA's Power-Sharing Agreement (Chapter II, Part I (Reconciliation)) signed in Naivasha, Kenya on 26 May 2004, wherein both parties agreed

[…] to initiate a comprehensive process of national reconciliation and healing throughout the country as part of the peace building process. Its mechanisms and forms shall be worked out by the Government of National Unity.

Apart from the general clause referring to the need for reconciliation and healing, the CPA did not provide any parameters regarding the implementation of such a policy, nor did it contain a requirement to hold the instigators of past violence culpable or remedy the atrocities and injustices that had been committed by both sides during the decades of war between the North and the South. This approach was replicated in the post-CPA constitutional framework, the Interim National Constitution (INC) and the Interim Constitution of Southern Sudan (ICSS) of 2005, which both only included vague references to a national process of reconciliation and healing. In fact, while Article 21 INC stated that "[t]he State shall initiate a comprehensive process of national reconciliation and healing that shall promote national harmony and peaceful co-existence among all Sudanese", Article 82 (d) INC merely declared as one of the duties of the Government of National Unity the "implementation of an information campaign throughout the Sudan in all national languages to popularize the Comprehensive Peace Agreement, foster national unity, reconciliation and mutual understanding." The Interim Constitution of Southern Sudan of 2005 (ICSS) contained similar references in Articles 39 (2), 126 (5)(d) and 173 (6)(g) ICSS. In terms of justice and accountability, there was reluctance on the side of both parties to commit to a thorough investigation and prosecution of serious crimes that had been committed in the course of the decades of conflict – a practice that was perpetuated in the years after the signing of the CPA.

Post-CPA Developments and Failed Attempts to Live Up to the Pledge of Reconciliation

As part of the CPA, the Agreement on Security Arrangements called for armed groups outside the SPLA and SAF (Sudan Armed Forces) structures to incorporate into the organized forces (army, police, prisons and wildlife forces) of either polity or being reintegrated into the civil service or civil-society institutions (Article 7 (b) CPA, Chapter VI; Article 11 Permanent Ceasefire and Security Arrangements Implementation Modalities). South Sudan's practice of military integration, i.e. the process of incorporating armed militia groups into the national army and the police, thereby stands in stark contrast to a regular policy of disarmament, demobilization and reintegration (DDR), which was also part of the CPA and constitutes the practice of reintegrating ex-combatants into civil society. Moreover, in the years following the signing of the Peace Agreement a growing habit of granting blanket amnesties to reintegrate rebels and militia leaders was the South's answer to confronting its militant past. In fact, a culture of impunity, especially with respect to the armed forces, has reigned in the country in the ten years since the signing of the CPA (Warner, 2013, p. 40).

The so-called 'Juba Declaration on Unity and Integration', which was issued by Salva Kiir in January 2006, attests to the recurrent phenomenon in the South of military integration and amnesty for armed-group leaders in the post-CPA era. After the signing of the Comprehensive Peace Agreement the South increasingly faced the threat of so-called "Other Armed Groups (OAGs)" (Article 7 CPA, Chapter VI), armed militia groups, which had not been party to the CPA and thereby threatened to derail the fragile peace. In 2005 in the South a total of 18 armed groups had to be integrated into the Sudan People's Liberation Army (SPLA) (Munive, 2013, p. 12). One of these armed groups were the South Sudan Defense Forces (SSDF), a loose alliance of forces largely affiliated with the North and led by Paulino Matiep (Young, 2006, p. 14). While previous attempts to neutralize the group had failed, Salva Kiir pursued a vigorous policy of integration and unity by fully absorbing the SSDF into the structures of the SPLA. This process was laid out in the Juba Declaration, signed on 8 January 2006 between the Sudan People's Liberation Army and the South Sudan Defense Forces (International Crisis Group, 2014, p. 14). In addition to the amalgamation of SPLA and SSDF to form one unified, non-partisan army, the document also included "a declaration of general amnesty to cover any criminal acts committed in previous times of hostilities between the two forces" (Juba Declaration, 2006). This implied an outright exemption from prosecution for all members of the SSDF for past crimes.

Previous attempts to neutralize rebel groups in Jonglei, Unity and Upper Nile states have repeatedly been accompanied by offers of blanket amnesties for militia leaders. Similarly, a presidential decree of 25 April 2013 granted general amnesties to the rebel commanders of six militia groups in South Sudan, namely Major General David Yau Yau, Major General Munto Abdahala Munto, Major General Johnson Olwin, Major General Bapiny Monytuil Wicjang, Major General Oyuog Ogot and Major General Gordon Kong, and to all the forces serving under them, which resulted in the surrender and reintegration of thousands of militias into the SPLA (Doki, 2013). In fact, the practice of amnesty and integration has been one of the government's strategies in dealing with OAGs ever since the Comprehensive Peace Agreement. So far no member of the SPLA or of any armed group in South Sudan has been held accountable in front of a court for wrongdoings and abuses committed during the years of war or after. Until the most recent peace negotiations under the auspices of IGAD in Addis Ababa, truth and justice for alleged atrocities committed by members of the armed forces in South Sudan have not been seriously contemplated.

Amid the growing culture of impunity, in the aftermath of the signing of the Peace Agreement in 2005 both parties did not live up to their commitment of implementing an effective Process of National Reconciliation and Healing (NRHP) as mandated under Article 1.7 of the CPA (Chapter II, Part I (Reconciliation)). While there was a general acknowledgement of the need to conduct a comprehensive reconciliation process in the aftermath of the civil war, only half-hearted attempts were made on both sides to turn Article 1.7 CPA into more than a loosely formulated, general pledge for reconciliation. During the six-year interim period between the signing of the CPA and the referendum on self-determination in the South, the GNU failed in pursuing a committed and inclusive process of healing and reconciliation in the country. Despite the GoSS's attempts to establish an institutional structure to address the quest for reconciliation, also these initiatives did not yield any tangible and lasting results.

On 27 June 2006, in a string of presidential orders Salva Kiir established a number of Commissions whose formation was partly mandated under Articles 149, 150, 152 and 153 ICSS. In three consecutive decrees (Presidential Decrees No. 46/2006; No. 48/2006; No. 44/2006) President Kiir appointed the members of the Southern Sudan Peace Commission (SSPC), which changed its name to South Sudan Peace Commission (SSPC) after the country's independence, the Southern Sudan Human Rights Commission (SSHRC) and the Southern Sudan Relief and Rehabilitation Commission (SSRRC). All commissions played a more or less significant role in the task of assisting with the implementation of the CPA and ICSS clauses on reconciliation. While the SSPC's mandate included the reconciliation of all armed and political groups through dialogue and consensus building, the Commission was also tasked with the integration of armed and political forces into the SPLM/A. Thereby, the SSPC embraced the Government's policy of amnesty and integration for OAGs. The SSPC's work was guided by a Strategic Plan for Peace and Reconciliation (Southern Sudan Peace Commission Strategic Plan 2007–2011, Southern Sudan Peace Commission 2007; Revised Strategic Plan 2010-2011, Ministry of Peace and CPA Implementation, 2010). Based on Articles 149 and 150 ICSS, the SSHRC was directed "to uphold, protect and promote human rights in Southern Sudan and monitor the application and enforcement of the rights and freedoms enshrined in the Interim Constitution of Southern Sudan, 2005 [...]," (Presidential Decree No. 48/2006; Human Rights Commission Act, 2009). Furthermore, the SSRRC was formed to support repatriation, relief, resettlement, rehabilitation, reintegration of internally displaced persons and to facilitate the reconstruction of the conflict affected areas in Southern Sudan (Presidential Decree No. 44/2006). While all three commissions made some progress in monitoring and reporting on past and ongoing abuses and human rights violations, truth-telling and accountability efforts remained weak.

Overall, during the interim period government-led efforts for justice and reconciliation in Southern Sudan did not succeed in fostering a national dialogue. While there was general recognition of the need for a process of peacebuilding and reconciliation in the country, the Government struggled to find a clear vision on what type of reconciliation was needed and how to implement and coordinate such an initiative. Even though civil society initiated several reconciliation programs in the South, the government agencies did not take on a leading role in coordinating the multiplicity of initiatives and programs that were all working on the same issues. Grassroots reconciliation approaches by civil society included, for example, the South Sudan Centre for Conflict Resolution (SSCCR), an organization which started in 2008 as an initiative to engage young people with ideas of peace and human rights in South Sudan. Furthermore, the former Bishop of Torit, Paride Taban, set up the Holy Trinity Peace Village in Kuron, Eastern Equatoria, a village where different ethnic communities live together peacefully. For this project Paride Taban was awarded the UN Sergio de Vieira Prize 2013 (Sergio Vieira de Mello Foundation, 2013).

Though the country was aware of its need for a comprehensive national dialogue, it lacked a holistic and coordinated approach to implement such an initiative. The result was a highly fragmented, costly and uncoordinated set of reconciliation initiatives, which failed to create a lasting impact and steered away entirely from holding perpetrators accountable for serious crimes and atrocities committed during the civil war. By cultivating a growing tradition of impunity to appease rogue militia forces, the GoSS also squandered the chance to initiate a true dialogue on peace and national reconciliation among the communities of Southern Sudan.

Justice and Reconciliation in the Newborn Nation

After the referendum on self-determination in January 2011, in which an overwhelming majority of South Sudanese voted for secession, Sudan split in two. South Sudan declared its independence on 9 July 2011 and became the world's youngest nation. After decades of war, the challenges were many for the young nation, whereby the task of state building in South Sudan's multiethnic society proved to be the most difficult. South Sudan's 11 million people include more than 60 indigenous ethnic groups and 80 linguistic groups (UNMISS, 2014b, p. 14). In its first few years of independence the country struggled with its weak institutional framework, ethnic clashes, sectarian violence and waves of inter-communal fighting. Especially South Sudan's largest and most populous state Jonglei, which is inhabited by several ethnic groups such as the Murle, the

Lou Nuer, the Anyuak and the Gawaar Nuer, was the scene of many ethnic clashes (Copnall, 2014, pp. 169). The armed skirmishes of cattle herders mostly evolve around scarce resources such as water and grazing areas. Those who killed and raided during these clashes have not been brought to justice. Inter-ethnic slaughter and the lack of a thorough South-South dialogue, i.e. an open dialogue between the different ethnicities and tribes in South Sudan, exacerbated the challenge of building a nation out of the mosaic of ethnic and regional communities that were once united by a common enemy during the years of civil war.

With a view to building upon existing peace and reconciliation initiatives, the South Sudan Peace and Reconciliation Commission (SSPRC) was established in 2011 by Presidential Decrees No. 62/2011 and No. 63/2011. The Commission was supposed to follow in the footsteps of the previous SSPC, which had carried the same mandate under the lead of the former Ministry of Peace and CPA Implementation during the six-year interim period. The duties and powers of the newly created Commission were laid out in the Peace and Reconciliation Commission Act of 2012 and concerned the coordination of all peace-related activities in South Sudan. In 2012 a nationwide campaign was launched by the Office of the President and the SSPRC entitled "A Journey of Healing for National Reconciliation", which was headed by the erstwhile Vice President Riek Machar Teny. The campaign was a renewed attempt by the Government of South Sudan to drive the process of national reconciliation under the guidance of the Vice President. As outlined in the Commission's Strategic Plan 2013-2015, the reconciliation initiative's stated aims were to promote reconciliation and build trust among and between South Sudanese communities (SSPRC Strategic Plan, 2013, p. 4). It thereby mirrored the objectives that had already been proclaimed in the preamble of the Transitional Constitution of South Sudan (TCSS) of 2011 calling for "a genuine national healing process and the building of trust and confidence in our society through dialogue" and referring specifically to reconciliation, committing all levels of government to "initiate a comprehensive process of national reconciliation and healing that shall promote national harmony, unity and peaceful co-existence among the people of South Sudan." (Article 36 (b) TCSS, 2011). While the need for a nationwide dialogue between communities and tribes in South Sudan remained undisputed, skepticism emerged as to the government's motives for initiating such a campaign and criticism arose with respect to its planned implementation. Not only was the involvement of the (then) Vice President, Riek Machar, questioned, but the government generated the process as a top-down initiative which emerged without previous consultation of the public at large on their expectations regarding such a campaign. Moreover, the initiative was to be conducted without involvement of the numerous reconciliation programs and grassroots initiatives that had evolved in South Sudan under the guidance of church and civil society organizations over the years (The Sudd Institute, 2013, p. 13).

In the framework of its action plan, which included a renewed attempt to foster dialogue between the fractured communities in South Sudan, a comprehensive peace and national reconciliation conference, the first of its kind, was planned and scheduled to take place in Juba in April 2013 in the presence of community leaders from the ten states of South Sudan. However, after President Kiir initially postponed the conference to June 2013, he issued a presidential order on 15 April 2013 withdrawing all delegated executive powers from the Vice President and relieving Riek Machar of his leading role in the reconciliation initiative. As stipulated in the presidential order the powers of the Vice President were restricted to those listed in Article 105 (a)-(c) TCSS, 2011 (Presidential Decree No. 03/2013). Moreover, in a separate order the President dissolved the National Reconciliation Committee and cancelled the entire process until he formed his own committee to organize the announced conference (Presidential Decree No. 04/2013). While critics had accused Riek Machar early on of misusing the forum of the reconciliation process to bring forward his own political aspirations, the bold move by Salva Kiir could retrospectively be seen as a precursor to the dismissal of Riek Machar as Vice President only a few months later. Once again government-led peace and reconciliation efforts in South Sudan were influenced by political power games and eventually fell victim to political rivalries.

Following the dissolution of the National Reconciliation Committee spearheaded by Riek Machar, the President ordered the formation of a church-led process under the chairmanship of Archbishop Daniel Deng Bul. The Committee for National Healing, Peace and Reconciliation (CNHPR; <reconciliationsouthsudan.org>) was set up in April 2013 and charged with conducting a nation-wide consultation process on how best to pursue a sustainable and effective national reconciliation process in South Sudan.

The Current Conflict: Political Power Struggles and Unresolved Historical Grievances

Only a few months after the suspension of the reconciliation initiative, on 23 July 2013 as part of a major cabinet reshuffle President Salva Kiir dismissed his Vice President Riek Machar as well as a large part of his Cabinet (Presidential Decrees No. 49/2013 & No. 50/2013). In the weeks following his dismissal, Riek Machar announced that he would challenge Kiir in the 2015 presidential elections. Moreover, in the middle of November 2013 Salva Kiir, President and Chairman of the Sudan People's Liberation Movement (SPLM), issued an order to dissolve all party structures and concurrently dismissed several high-ranking SPLM leaders (Sudan Tribune, 2013a). Political tensions were rising and during the meeting of the SPLM National Liberation Council, the party's second highest organ, on 14 and 15 December 2013, fighting broke out at the SPLA Headquarters in Juba between the Nuer and the Dinka fractions of the Presidential Guard, which is the 8th Division of the South Sudan People's Liberation Army (SPLA), also called the Republican Guard or the Tiger Division. The armed conflict between supporters of President Kiir and those loyal to former Vice President Riek Machar quickly escalated and spread to Jonglei, Unity, and Upper Nile State. With reference to the events of 15-16 December the Government of South Sudan accused Riek Machar and his supporters of staging a failed *coup d'état*, a charge that was adamantly denied by Riek Machar (Copnall, 2014, pp. 254; Manrique Gil, 2014, pp. 4; Human Rights Watch, 2014, pp. 22). While the perceptions of the precise unfolding of events differ, the intensity and promptness of the outbreak of violence in December 2013 surprised many and attested to the fragility of the young nation. Political disputes between the country's leadership and open rifts within the ruling party quickly escalated into a full-blown armed conflict in parts of South Sudan, which was further goaded by an instrumentalization of the ethnic identities of both parties to the conflict. While ethnic tensions were not the initial trigger for the outbreak of violence, in the political power struggle between Salva Kiir, an ethnic Dinka, and Riek Machar, from the Nuer community, both relied on ethnicity to propel their agenda and to mobilize for support.

In the course of the most recent conflict forces on both sides have committed egregious crimes, often along ethnic lines between soldiers and militias from the country's two largest ethnic communities – the Dinka and the Nuer. These have included targeted attacks against civilians and civilian objects, beatings, rape and sexual violence, acts of torture, arbitrary arrests, massive looting and widespread destruction of civilian property as well as ethnically motivated extrajudicial and targeted killings. Several major towns have been destroyed and numerous villages have been razed. The impact on the population has been profound: since the conflict erupted on 15 December 2013, thousands of people have been killed, about 1.6 million people have been internally displaced and almost 600,000 have been forced to flee to neighboring countries (UN, S/2014/537 (2014), p. 6). The United Nations Mission in South Sudan (UNMISS) is hosting more than 135,000 internally displaced people who have been fleeing violence and ethnic reprisals (UNMISS, 2015).

UNMISS was established on 9 July 2011 by a Resolution of the United Nations Security Council (Resolution 1996(2011)), which tasked the mission in Point 3 (b)(iii) of the Resolution, inter alia, with

[...] monitoring, investigating, verifying, and reporting regularly on human rights and potential threats against the civilian population as well as actual and potential violations of international humanitarian and human rights law, working as appropriate with the Office of the High Commissioner for Human Rights, bringing these to the attention of the authorities as necessary, and immediately reporting gross violations of human rights to the UN Security Council.

Based on an assessment of the current crisis, the Human Rights Division of UNMISS presented its findings in two consecutive reports on the human rights situation in South Sudan. On 21 February 2014 UNMISS released an "Interim Report on Human Rights" (UNMISS, 2014a), which preceded a second Report of 8 May 2014 entitled "Conflict in South Sudan: A Human Rights Report" (UNMISS, 2014b). The latter report, which is based on 900 interviews with victims and witnesses of the events since 15 December 2013, determines that there are reasonable grounds to conclude that from the very outset of the violence "violations of international human rights and humanitarian law have been committed by both parties to the conflict" (UNMISS, 2014b, p. 3). Focusing on the conflict hot spots in the northeast of the country an additional report entitled "Flash Human Rights Report on the Escalation of Fighting in Greater Upper Nile" (UNMISS, 2015) was issued by UNMISS on 29 June 2015. The report reiterated allegations of killings, rape, abduction, looting, torture, displacement and other atrocities amounting to serious human rights abuses and grave violations of international humanitarian law committed by both government and opposition forces. After decades of civil war the current conflict has once again taken a heavy toll on the civilian population and a few years after independence the vision of peace and stability in the young nation lies in tatters.

How to Move Forward by Looking Back: The Need for Justice, Accountability and Open Dialogue

Despite the efforts to broker a peace deal between the belligerent forces, South Sudan currently remains in a state of armed conflict. What initially started as a political crisis has quickly developed into a civil war accompanied by a mounting humanitarian disaster due to, inter alia, growing food insecurity in the country (UN, S/2014/537 (2014), p. 6). In February 2014 the UN designated South Sudan a Level 3 humanitarian emergency, which is the UN classification for the most severe, large-scale humanitarian crises. As a result of the mediation efforts in Addis Ababa facilitated by the International Authority on Development (IGAD) to end the intractable conflict, several agreements were signed between the warring parties since the outbreak of violence in December 2013. An "Agreement on Cessation of Hostilities" (CoH) was concluded on 23 January 2014, followed by a "Recommitment on Humanitarian Matters in the CoH Agreement" on 5 May 2014, an "Agreement to Resolve the Crisis in South Sudan" on 9 May 2014 and the Agreement of 25 August 2014 entitled "Re-Dedication of and Implementation Modalities for the Cessation of Hostilities Agreement". All of these negotiated settlements were violated within days of being signed and bear testimony to the fragility and complexity of the situation. As a result of the failure to secure a peace deal, in March 2015 IGAD announced a revised, expanded mediation team – 'IGAD-Plus', which included the African Union (AU), the United Nations, China, the U.S., the UK, the European Union, Norway and the IGAD Partners Forum (International Crisis Group, 2015, p. 3). While in July 2015 the IGAD-Plus representatives proposed a "Compromise Agreement on the Resolution of the Conflict in South Sudan" for consideration to the warring parties, the UN Security Council has in the meantime imposed sanctions on six South Sudanese commanders, i.e. three individuals from the SPLA (Major General Marial Chanuong Yol Mangok, Lieutenant General Gabriel Jok Riak and Major General Santino Deng Wol) and three individuals from the SPLA in Opposition forces (Major General Simon Gatwech Dual, Major General James Koang Chuol and Major General Peter Gadet).

While justice for serious crimes should be an essential part of any peace agreement, the drafters of the Comprehensive Peace Agreement of 2005 deliberately excluded questions of accountability for past abuses and violations. After the Comprehensive Peace Agreement set the tone on this issue, the post-CPA period was marked by an absence of lasting initiatives to bring about justice, reconciliation and restitution to resolve the frictions and tensions that had evolved between the different warring groups and ethnic communities during the decades of war in South Sudan. In the years since the signing of the CPA, no lasting attempts have been undertaken to confront the historical grievances and to introduce an inclusive reconciliatory process in South Sudan.

Whereas the need for a comprehensive transitional justice strategy in South Sudan seems evident, the elements comprised in such a process are not. The multiple building blocks of South Sudan's future transitional justice framework are yet to be chosen. While the instruments used to bring about justice and accountability in post-conflict settings are many, the best transitional justice strategies have historically been those which simultaneously looked backwards to mend the past and forwards to build a peaceful future (Waldorf, 2006, pp. 86-87). As (then) UN Secretary-General Kofi Annan declared in front of the UN Security Council in 2004: "Where transitional justice is concerned, the better approach is usually not an either/or choice between prosecutions and truth commissions. Instead, a nationally determined combination of mechanisms will generally work best [...]" (UN Press Release, 2004).

Apart from the prosecution of perpetrators, past peace processes have successfully used complementary measures such as reparations, vetting, truth commissions and other judicial and non-judicial means in order to serve justice and achieve accountability. In addition to that, many societies have resorted to customary traditions of dispute settlement and reconciliation, a practice which was also highlighted by the UN Secretary-General in the 2004 UN Report on Transitional Justice (S/2004/616 (2004), p. 12):

> *Due regard must be given to indigenous and informal traditions for administering justice or settling disputes, to help them to continue their often vital role and to do so in conformity with both international standards and local tradition.*

Out of the plethora of tools that are available to shape an enduring transitional justice strategy, what are the most promising options for South Sudan?

The case of South Sudan confirms the assertion that peace without justice can foster renewed cycles of violence. In order to break the vicious cycle of interethnic clashes and to initiate a process of nation building in the country, ending the culture of impunity and forging justice and accountability are imperative. A South Sudanese reconciliatory process presents an opportunity to address the contentious policy of granting impunity to militia forces, which still is a recurrent practice in the young nation. In line with international law, UN

Security Council Resolution 2132 (2013) demanded explicitly that those responsible for violations of international humanitarian and human rights law in South Sudan must be held accountable. Furthermore, international treaties including the 1949 Geneva Conventions, which South Sudan has ratified, require parties to a conflict to ensure that people responsible for serious offences are prosecuted. The ongoing IGAD-led peace talks in Addis Ababa have to recognize the importance of justice to long-term peace and security in South Sudan. In a similar vein (former) Special Representative of the United Nations Secretary-General in South Sudan, Hilde F. Johnson, stated at the presentation of the UNMISS Human Rights Report in early May 2014 that "[a]ccountability is critical to end the legacy of impunity in South Sudan and prevent similar atrocities in the future" (UNMISS, 2014b). In his Christmas speech on 24 December 2013, President Salva Kiir acknowledged for the first time that targeted killings had been committed in Juba in December 2013 and announced that those responsible would be punished (Sudan Tribune, 2013b).

Fair and credible prosecutions of perpetrators having committed gross offences and flagrant human rights violations against unarmed civilians in the course of the conflict not only serve to punish the instigators of such crimes, but can also function as a deterrence mechanism for future crimes. Apart from providing recourse to victims of serious crimes, criminal prosecutions also help to build respect for the rule of law in a war-torn country and rebuild trust in government institutions. Moreover, it forces the perpetrators and the society at large to confront the country's violent past (AU Panel of the Wise, 2013, pp. 16). Criminal prosecutions in post-conflict societies can occur on three different levels, i.e. on the national level, in front of hybrid or mixed special courts and at the level of specialized international tribunals. While in this case all three options may be considered, some will be more suited to the particular context of South Sudan than others.

In order to adequately address the crimes that have been committed in front of national courts in South Sudan, the country must first ensure that its legal framework provides for the substantial and procedural requirements needed to prosecute international crimes, such as war crimes and crimes against humanity. In case the South Sudanese penal law does not conform to the standards prescribed by international law, amendments to the country's criminal justice system would be required prior to an indictment of the alleged perpetrators (Oette, 2011, p. 157). In addition to that, due to the lack of capacity of the local justice system to investigate and prosecute such complex international crimes, the South Sudanese judiciary would require specialized training and capacity-building. So far the idea of holding domestic trials has received little support outside South Sudan.

On the other hand, the proposal to set up a hybrid or mixed special court in South Sudan in order to remedy the human rights violations that were committed in the course of the current conflict has been voiced by UN Secretary-General Ban Ki-moon, who recommended the creation of a mixed tribunal for South Sudan to the UN Security Council (UN, 2014a). Furthermore, the idea to establish a hybrid court was advocated by UNMISS in its Human Rights Report of 8 May 2014. The seven recommendations listed in the Report's conclusion include, among others, an urgent appeal to set up "a credible accountability mechanism, consistent with international standards, [...] to hold the perpetrators of violations individually accountable" (UNMISS, 2014b, pp. 60-61). Not only does the Report encourage the judiciary to "establish serious investigations into allegations of violations of international human rights and humanitarian law", but goes as far as recommending the establishment of "a special or hybrid tribunal with international involvement", should the "government prove unwilling or unable to pursue genuine accountability" (pp. 60-61). It is suggested that the composition of a mixed special court for South Sudan consists of a combination of national and international lawyers and judges. Thereby, a hybrid court would "avoid the drawbacks of purely domestic trials and proceedings by purely international courts" (Nouwen, 2006, p. 190). A similar proposal was put forward in July 2015 in Chapter V of the IGAD-Plus "Compromise Agreement on the Resolution of the Conflict in South Sudan." The Agreement foresees the establishment of a 'Hybrid Court for South Sudan (HCSS)' "to investigate and prosecute individuals bearing the responsibility for violations of international law and/or applicable South Sudanese law" (Chapter V, Section 3.1.1; p. 43). Furthermore, the Agreement states in Chapter V, Section 3.3.2 that the HCSS shall be composed of "a majority of judges [...] from African states other than the Republic of South Sudan" (p. 44).

While the involvement of national judges and jurists enhances domestic ownership of the trials, the international involvement is supposed to secure the credibility of the process. Trials in front of a hybrid court can, however, only capture those perpetrators who bear the primary responsibility for planning, ordering and carrying out the most heinous crimes. Moreover, a hybrid court can only be established in full cooperation with and under the terms agreed to by the Government of South Sudan (UN, S/2004/616, pp. 13). In the past hybrid courts have been set up in post-conflict countries such as Sierra Leone, Kosovo, East Timor, Senegal and Cambodia (Nouwen, 2006, pp. 194).

The International Criminal Court is designed to secure accountability "for the most serious crimes of concern to the international community as a whole" (Article 5 ICC Rome Statute, 1998). However, as South Sudan is not a signatory to the Rome Statute of the International Criminal Court (ICC), the Court does not have jurisdiction to investigate or prosecute alleged crimes committed in the current conflict in South Sudan. The only ways in which investigations could be authorized and proceedings could be instigated in front of the ICC would either be by the Government of South Sudan's voluntary declaration to accept the ICC's jurisdiction in line with Article 12 (3) of the Rome Statute or according to Article 13 (b) of the ICC's Rome Statute on the basis of an official authorization for investigations by the UN Security Council under Chapter VII. A Chapter VII Resolution of the UN Security Council (UN Doc. S/RES/1593 (2005)) provided, for example, the basis of the ICC's jurisdiction over certain crimes allegedly committed in the course of the Darfur conflict.

A third option is provided by Article 15 (1) of the Rome Statute according to which under specific conditions the Office of the Prosecutor has the possibility to initiate investigations *proprio motu*. With respect to the option of opening investigations *proprio motu*, a previous authorization for an investigation has to be granted by the Pre-Trial Chamber according to Article 15 (3) of the Rome Statute. In addition to that, according to Article 17 of the Rome Statute the ICC is bound by the principle of complementarity, which only permits the referral of cases to the Court as far as a state is unwilling or unable to investigate and prosecute international crimes. A prior investigation as to the capability and willingness of South Sudan's criminal justice system to prosecute serious human rights offences would therefore be required (AU Panel of the Wise, 2013, p. 18).

The choice of retributive justice is a necessary element for a successful and lasting peace and reconciliation effort in the country. Nevertheless, criminal prosecution can only ever be a partial response to dealing with the conflict in South Sudan. While the perpetrators of the most serious offenses should be subject to full criminal responsibility, it is equally important for governments, citizens and perpetrators to openly acknowledge the wrongfulness of human rights abuses and to come to terms with the country's violent past in a nationwide dialogue. In an effort to heal the wounds of victims and establish a collective narrative about the atrocities, crimes and grave human rights violations that were committed in the country's recent past, a truth commission could be set up in South Sudan to complement criminal prosecutions (Deng, 2014, p. 9; AU Commission of Inquiry, 2014, pp. 13). The 2004 Report on Transitional Justice by the UN Secretary-General refers to truth commissions as "official, temporary, non-judicial fact-finding bodies that investigate a pattern of abuses of human rights or humanitarian law committed over a number of years" (UN, S/2004/616, p. 17; La Rosa, 2009, pp. 371). In fact, truth commissions have proven to be an effective mechanism to initiate a process of victim-perpetrator confrontation and to help rebut official lies and myths regarding past human rights abuses through a thorough investigation and a comprehensive documentation of past offences. Truth commissions have regularly been set up in post-conflict environments and successfully contributed to the process of reconciliation and healing (Seibert-Fohr, 2012, pp. 1042). In fact, from 1991 to 2013 a total of about 25 truth commissions were established in various post-conflict countries (AU Panel of the Wise, 2013, pp. 21). Apart from the prominent example of South Africa's Truth and Reconciliation Commission, similar commissions have, amongst others, been set up in Sierra Leone, Panama, Peru, East Timor, Uganda, Ghana, Argentina, Guatemala and Liberia (Deng, 2014, pp. 2; Tomuschat, 1999, p. 49). The establishment of a truth commission in South Sudan would constitute an additional path to accountability and reconciliation in the country by providing a public forum for victims to address their grievances and for perpetrators to confess their crimes. Moreover, such a mechanism would help to extend truth, justice and reconciliation efforts to the grassroots level. The establishment of a 'Commission for Truth, Reconciliation and Healing (CTRH)' has also been included in Chapter V, Section 2 of the proposed "Compromise Agreement on the Resolution of the Conflict in South Sudan", which was issued by the IGAD-Plus mediation team in July 2015.

Proposals have also been made with respect to the involvement of South Sudan's customary legal traditions and practices in the country's overall reconciliation efforts. After all, it is a regular practice for chiefs and traditional authorities in customary court proceedings in South Sudan to encourage disputing parties to discuss their differences in order to come to a solution that is acceptable to both sides. While according to Section 98 (2) of South Sudan's Local Government Act of 2009 customary courts in South Sudan do not have jurisdiction when it comes to criminal matters, such traditional reconciliatory mechanisms and mediatory practices could also serve to negotiate compensations and other civil remedies for the victims. After all, the state also has an obligation to provide reparation to victims of gross human rights violations, which can take various forms including material assistance, such as compensation payments, as well as symbolic measures like monuments, memorials and national days of remembrance (Barsalou, 2007, p. 10).

An inclusive constitutional drafting process will be another important step to foster dialogue and reconciliation among the people of South Sudan. The involvement of civil society, traditional leaders and other actors could initiate a comprehensive nationwide discourse on the country's permanent constitutional framework and at the same time instigate a collective dialogue on identity and nation-building in South Sudan. In view of the aim to set up an expansive and lasting transitional justice process in the country, South Sudan must adopt an integrated response that incorporates formal prosecutions complemented by elements of truth-telling, memorialization, compensation, restitution, rehabilitation and meaningful reconciliation.

The international community reacted with great concern to the renewed outbreak of violence in South Sudan and expressed dismay at the reports of targeted killings and atrocities committed by the conflicting parties. Immediately after the outbreak of violence in December 2013, the African Union as well as UNMISS set up separate mechanisms to provide for a thorough investigation and documentation of alleged human rights offences committed in the course of the conflict in South Sudan. While UNMISS published several meticulous and detailed reports on the human rights situation in South Sudan (UNMISS, 2014a, 2014b & 2015), the African Union reacted with the formation of the 'African Union Commission of Inquiry on South Sudan'. The Commission was established at the 411th Meeting of the Peace and Security Council of the African Union (AUPSC) at the level of Heads of State and Government held in Banjul, The Gambia on 30 December 2013 and is the first of its kind. Headed by former Nigerian President Olusegun Obasanjo, the Commission is tasked with investigating "the human rights violations and other abuses committed during the armed conflict in South Sudan, and make recommendations on the best way and means to ensure accountability, reconciliation and healing among all South Sudanese communities." (AUPSC, 2013, para. 8).

The Government of South Sudan has meanwhile acknowledged that human rights violations were committed in the course of the current conflict and has reacted to international pressure by establishing various accountability measures, among them an SPLA-led investigation committee to explore and report on abuses committed by state security personnel in Juba and an 'Investigation Committee on Human Rights Abuses' headed by former Chief Justice John Wuol Makec that carried a similar mandate (Presidential Decree No. 06/2014). However, no public information has been available since on any of the ongoing investigations (Human Rights Watch, pp. 96). In addition to various accountability mechanisms, the Government started an initiative to confront South Sudan's history of conflict through the establishment of a 'National Platform for Peace and Reconciliation (NPPR)'. The platform, which was set up in April 2014, is comprised of three national bodies, i.e. the 'Independent Committee for National Healing, Peace and Reconciliation' headed by Archbishop Daniel Deng Bul, the 'South Sudan Peace and Reconciliation Commission (SSPRC)' headed by Hon. Chuol Rambang, and the 'Specialized Parliamentary Committee for Peace and Reconciliation' headed by Hon. Lt. Gen. David Okwier. The platform, which is proclaiming to be the "voice of the grassroots", is aiming to "construct a national dialogue for peace and reconciliation" by organizing workshops at the local, state and national level with a view to focusing on a bottom-up approach in developing an agenda for peace and reconciliation in South Sudan (NPPR Website). It will, however, be of crucial importance that the ongoing efforts of this new initiative do not shy away from raising the question of accountability in the current conflict.

CONCLUSION

Peace talks are underway in Addis Ababa to resolve the ongoing conflict that has ravaged the country since the outbreak of violence on 15-16 December 2013, between troops loyal to the country's President Salva Kiir and rebel forces loyal to his former deputy Riek Machar. While there are currently still two serious obstacles to any kind of transitional justice process in South Sudan, i.e. the absence of real peace and the lack of commitment from all warring parties to seek reconciliation, lessons can already be drawn from past mistakes in order to prepare for an effective process of reconciliation and healing to be initiated in the country when the time is ripe. The 2005 Comprehensive Peace Agreement, which brought an end to the 22-year civil war in Sudan, included only a vague reference to national reconciliation and neglected to provide a framework to bring the perpetrators of human rights violations committed during the years of civil war to justice. Moreover, the aftermath of the signing of the Peace Agreement in 2005 was marked by half-hearted reconciliatory efforts and most of all by the absence of a genuine and inclusive "South-South Dialogue", i.e. a proper reconciliatory discourse between the fighting ethnic communities in the South.

The current conflict is in part a result of unresolved issues carried over from the CPA throughout the interim period to the new nation of South Sudan. The memory of the abuses perpetrated during the civil war and the lack of accountability mechanisms in the CPA for serious crimes committed in the long history of South Sudan's violent struggle have had direct implications for the current conflict. The omissions of the CPA and post-CPA period as well as the persistent culture of impunity have sown the seeds for continued abuses by the country's armed fighters. South Sudan should draw its lessons from the past by avoiding the shortfalls of previous peace attempts. In order to avoid repeating past mistakes, an integrated process of truth-telling, justice and reconciliation has to be a crucial component of the final peace agreement between the country's warring factions. A superficial political agreement sealed with handshakes and smiles under the watchful eye of the international community will not be enough to resolve the crisis and to secure lasting peace and stability in South Sudan. In fact, "[t]he credibility of a political solution for the future depends partly on accountability for what happened in the past" (Zoellick, 2005).

Both sides should therefore be obliged to submit themselves and their supporters to a transparent and independent investigation consistent with international legal standards to bring justice to the perpetrators of grave offences and human rights violations. If South Sudan is to come to terms with its troubled past, it is crucial that the issue of accountability is openly addressed and that those who are found to be responsible are tried and punished through fair and impartial justice mechanisms. The question of accountability had been entirely omitted from the terms of the Comprehensive Peace Agreement of 2005. Hence, the only way to bring about the long-awaited peace in South Sudan is not to let history repeat itself.

REFERENCES

African Union Commission of Inquiry on South Sudan (CISS). (2014 June 26-27). Interim Report, African Union, Assembly of the Union, Twenty-Third Ordinary Session, Assembly/AU/19(XXIII).

African Union Panel of the Wise. (2013, February). Peace, Justice, and Reconciliation in Africa: Opportunities and Challenges in the Fight Against Impunity. The African Union Series. International Peace Institute.

African Union Peace and Security Council (AUPSC). (2013, December 30). Communiqué. 411th Meeting of the Peace and Security Council at the Level of Heads of State and Government on the Situation in South Sudan. PSC/AHG/COMM.1 (CDXI).

Agreement on a Cessation of Hostilities between the Government of the Republic of South Sudan and the South Sudan Democratic Movement/Defense Army Cobra Faction. (2014, January 23). Retrieved from http://www.gurtong.net/LinkClick.aspx?fileticket=mvVHdl-Wsd4=&tabid=124.

Agreement on Permanent Ceasefire and Security Arrangements Implementation Modalities between the Government of the Sudan (GoS) and the Sudan People's Liberation Movement/Sudan People's Liberation Army (SPLM/SPLA) during the Pre-Interim and Interim Periods, signed in Naivasha, Kenya on 31 December 2004.

Agreement to Resolve the Crisis in South Sudan. (2014, May 9). Retrieved from http://www.southsudan.igad.int/attachments/article/249/Agreement%20to%20Resolve%20the%20crisis%20in%20S.%20Sudan,%209%20May'14.pdf.

Barsalou, J. & Baxter, V. (2007, January). *The Urge To Remember, The Role of Memorials in Social Reconstruction and Traditional Justice.* United States Institute of Peace, Stabilization and Reconstruction Series No. 5.

Clamp, K. L., & Doak, J. (2012). More than words: Restorative Justice Concepts in Transitional Justice Settings. *International Criminal Law Review*, *12*(3), 339–360. doi:10.1163/157181212X648824

Copnall, J. (2014). *A Poisonous Thorn in Our Hearts: Sudan and South Sudan's Bitter and Incomplete Divorce*. London: Hurst Publishers.

Crawford-Browne, S., Basha, S., & Alexander, K. (2005). Obstacles to Transitional Justice in Sudan. In B. Raftopoulos & K. Alexander (Eds.), *Peace in the Balance: The Crisis in Sudan* (pp. 139–157). Cape Town, South Africa: Institute for Justice and Reconciliation.

Deng, D. K. (2014, July). *Memory, Healing and Transformation in South Sudan*. Transitional Justice Working Paper. South Sudan Law Society.

Doki, C. (2013, May 2). Scant hope for South Sudan's latest amnesty offer to rebels. *The Niles*. Retrieved from http://www.hrw.org/sites/default/files/reports/southsudan0814_ForUpload.pdf.

Elhag, N. (2008). A Tale of Two Wars: The Militarization of Dinka and Nuer Identities in South Sudan. In J. Abbink & A. van Dokkum (Eds.), *Dilemmas of Development: Conflicts of Interest and their Resolutions in Modernizing Africa* (pp. 164–186). Leiden: African Studies Centre.

Esposito, D. & Crocker, B. (2004, January). *To Guarantee the Peace: An Action Strategy for a Post-Conflict Sudan*. Centre for Strategic and International Studies.

Government of Southern Sudan Presidential Decree No. 44/2006. (2006 June). Retrieved from http://www.unmis.unmissions.org/Portals/UNMIS/CPA%20Monitor/Annexes/Annex%20 4427%20-%20GoSS%20Commissioners.pdf.

Government of Southern Sudan Presidential Decree No. 46/2006. (2006, June 27). Retrieved from http://www.unmis.unmissions.org/Portals/UNMIS/CPA%20Monitor/Annexes/Annex%20 44%20-%20GoSS%20Commissioners.pdf.

Government of Southern Sudan Presidential Decree No. 48/2006. (2006, June 27). Retrieved from http://www.unmis.unmissions.org/Portals/UNMIS/CPA%20Monitor/Annexes/Annex%20 44%20-%20GoSS%20Commissioners.pdf.

Hazan, P. (2009). Reconciliation. In V. Chetail (Ed.), *Post-Conflict Peacebuilding: A Lexicon* (pp. 256–266). Oxford: Oxford University Press.

Human Rights Watch. (2014, August). *South Sudan's New War: Abuses by Government and Opposition Forces*. Report. Retrieved from http://www.hrw.org/sites/default/files/reports/southsudan0814_ForUpload.pdf.>

International Crisis Group. (2007, July 26). *A Strategy for Comprehensive Peace in Sudan*. Africa Report N°130.

International Crisis Group. (2014, April 10). *South Sudan: A Civil War by Any Other Name*. Africa Report N°217.

International Crisis Group. (2015 July 27). *South Sudan: keeping Faith with the IGAD Peace Process*. Africa Report N°228.

Johnson, D. H. (2011). Twentieth Century Civil Wars. In J. Ryle, J. Willis, & S. Baldo (Eds.), The Sudan Handbook (pp. 207-222). London: Rift Valley Institute.

Juba Declaration on Unity and Integration between the Sudan People's Liberation Army (SPLA) and the South Sudan Defence Forces (SSDF). (2006, January 8). Retrieved from http://www.peacemaker.un.org/sudan-juba-declaration2006.

La Rosa, A.-M., & Philippe, X. (2009). Transitional Justice. In V. Chetail (Ed.), *Post-Conflict Peacebuilding: A Lexicon* (pp. 1–28). Oxford: Oxford University Press.

Manrique Gil, M. (2014, March). South Sudan: The Roots and Prospects of a Multifaceted Crisis. European Parliament, Directorate-General for External Policies DG EXPO/B/PolDep/Note/2014_55.

Munive, J. (2013). Disarmament, Demobilisation and Reintegration in South Sudan: The Limits of Conventional Peace and Security Templates. Danish Institute for International Studies, 2013:07.

National Platform for Peace and Reconciliation (NPPR). (2014, April). Retrieved from http://www.reconciliationsouthsudan.org/index.php?option=com_content&view=featured&Itemid=101.

Natsios, A. S. (2012). *Sudan, South Sudan & Darfur: What Everyone Needs to Know*. New York: Oxford University Press.

Nouwen, S. (2006). Hybrid courts: The Hybrid Category of a New Type of International Crimes Courts. *Utrecht Law Review*, *2*(2), 190–214. doi:10.18352/ulr.32

Oette, L. (2011). Law Reform in Times of Peace Processes and Transitional Justice: The Sudanese Dimension. In L. Oette (Ed.), *Criminal Law Reform and Transitional Justice, Human Rights Perspectives for Sudan* (pp. 11–31). Surrey, UK: Ashgate.

Peace and Reconciliation Commission Act of 2012. (2012 May 4). Retrieved from http://www.peacecommission.org/wp-content/uploads/2014/03/Peace-and-Reconciliation-Commission-Act-2012.pdf.

Presidential Decree No. 03/2013. (2013, April 15). RSS/RO/J/03/2013. Retrieved from http://www.sudantribune.com/IMG/pdf/presidential_decree_reducing_powers_of_the_vp.pdf.

Presidential Decree No. 04/2013. (2013, April 15). RSS/RO/J/04/2013. Retrieved from http://www.sudantribune.com/IMG/pdf/presidential_decree_reducing_powers_of_the_vp.pdf.

Presidential Decree No. 49/2013. (2013, July 23). RSS/RD/J/49/2013. Retrieved from http://www.gurtong.net/LinkClick.aspx?fileticket=ZOejD0cc1w%3d&tabid=124.

Presidential Decree No. 50/2013. (2013, July 23). RSS/RD/J/50/2013. Retrieved from http://www.gurtong.net/LinkClick.aspx?fileticket=7cD-9Y4z904%3d&tabid=124.

Proposed Compromise Agreement on the Resolution of the Conflict in the Republic of South Sudan. Retrieved from http://southsudan.igad.int.

Re-Dedication of and Implementation Modalities (2014). The Cessation of Hostilities Agreement signed on 23rd January 2014 between the Government of the Republic of South Sudan and the Sudan People's Liberation Movement/Army (In Opposition), signed on 25 August 2014 in Addis Ababa.

Seibert-Fohr, A. (2012). Transitional Justice in Post-Conflict Situations. In R. Wolfrum (Ed.), *The Max Planck Encyclopedia of Public International Law* (Vol. IX, pp. 1042–1049). Oxford: Oxford University Press.

South Sudan Peace and Reconciliation Commission. (2013, January). Strategic Plan 2013-2015. Retrieved from http://www.cmi.fi/images/stories/publications/reports/2013/SSPRC_SP%202013-2015_FINAL.pdf.

Southern Sudan Human Rights Commission Act of 2009. (2009). Retrieved from http://www.icnl.org/research/library/files/South%20Sudan/SSHumanRights%20CommissionAct2009.pdf.

Sudan Tribune. (2013, November 15). Audio Recording. Retrieved from <http://www.sudantribune.com/spip.php?article48818.>

Sudan Tribune. (2013, December 25). *Kiir denounces Killing of Civilians on Tribal Basis, says "Criminals" to be punished*. Retrieved from <http://www.sudantribune.com/IMG/pdf/president_salva_kiir_christmas_message.pdf.>

The Comprehensive Peace Agreement of 2005. (2005). Retrieved from http://www.unmis.unmissions.org/Portals/UNMIS/Documents/General/cpa-en.pdf consisting of, *inter alia,*

- The Agreement on Security Arrangements (Chapter VI), signed in Naivasha, Kenya on 25 September 2003.

- The Agreement on Wealth Sharing (Chapter III), signed in Naivasha, Kenya on 7 January 2004.

- The Machakos Protocol (Chapter I), signed in Machakos, Kenya on 20 July 2002.

- The Protocol on Power Sharing (Chapter II), signed in Naivasha, Kenya on 26 May 2004.

The Local Government Act of 2009. (2009). Retrieved from http://mlgi.org.za/resources/local-government-database/by-country/sudan/sub-national-legislation/The%20Local%20Government%20Act%202009.pdf/view

The Sudd Institute. (2013, June 7). *Peace and Reconciliation in South Sudan: A Conversation for Justice and Stability*. Retrieved from http://www.suddinstitute.org/assets/Publications/National-Reconciliation-formattedSudd-Institute.pdf.

Tomuschat, C., De Coti, O. L., & Tojo, A. B. (1999, February 25). *Guatemala, Memory of Silence*. Report of the Commission for Historical Clarification. Conclusions and Recommendations. Retrieved from www.aaas.org/sites/default/files/migrate/uploads/mos_en.pdf.

UN General Assembly. (1998, July 17). Rome Statute of the International Criminal Court. Retrieved from http://legal.un.org/icc/statute/99_corr/cstatute.htm.

UN Security Council Resolution 1593 (2005, March 31). UN Doc. S/RES/1593. Retrieved from http://www.un.org/en/ga/search/view_doc.asp?symbol=S/RES/1593(2005).

UN Security Council Resolution 1996 (2011, July 8). UN Doc. S/RES/1996 (2011). Retrieved from http://www.un.org/en/ga/search/view_doc.asp?symbol=S/RES/1996(2011).

UN Security Council Resolution 2132 (2013, December 24). UN Doc. S/RES/2132. Retrieved from http://www.un.org/en/ga/search/view_doc.asp?symbol=S/RES/2132(2013).

United Nations. (2004). *The Rule of Law and Transitional Justice in Conflict and Post-Conflict Societies.* Report of the Secretary General to the Security Council (S/2004/616 (2004)).

United Nations. (2004, October 6). Press Release of the Secretary-General. Department of Public Information (SG/SM/9519, SC/8210). Retrieved from http://www.un.org/News/Press/docs/2004/sgsm9519.doc.htm

United Nations. (2011). *The Rule of Law and Transitional Justice in Conflict and Post-Conflict Societies.* Report of the Secretary General to the Security Council (S/2011/634 (2011).

United Nations. (2014, May 12). Secretary-General's Briefing to the Security Council on South Sudan. Statement. Retrieved from <http://www.un.org/sg/statements/index.asp?nid=7666.

United Nations. (2014, July 25). Report of the Secretary-General on South Sudan (S/2014/537).

United Nations. (2015, July 1). Press Release. Department of Public Information (SC/11958). Retrieved 30 June 2015 from http://www.un.org/press/en/2015/sc11958.doc.htm.

United Nations Mission In South Sudan. (2014, February 21). *Interim Report on Human Rights: Crisis in South Sudan, Report Coverage 15 December 2013–31 January 2014*. Human Rights Division. Retrieved from http://unmiss.unmissions.org/Default.aspx?tabid=5805&language=en-US.

United Nations Mission In South Sudan. (2014, May 8). *Conflict in South Sudan: A Human Rights Report*. Human Rights Division. Retrieved from http://unmiss.unmissions.org/Default.aspx?tabid=5805&language=en-US.

United Nations Mission In South Sudan. (2015, June 29). *Flash Human Rights Report on the Escalation of Fighting in Greater Upper Nile. April/May 2015*. Retrieved from http://unmiss.unmissions.org/Default.aspx?tabid=5805&language=en-US.

Van Zyl, P. (2005). Promoting Transitional Justice in Post-Conflict Societies. In A. Bryden, & H. Hanggi (Eds.), *Security Governance in Post-Conflict Peacebuilding* (pp. 209–231). Geneva: Geneva Centre for the Democratic Control of Armed Forces.

Waldorf, L. (2006). Mass Justice for Mass Atrocity: Rethinking Local Justice as Transitional Justice. *Temple Law Review*, *79*(1), 1–87.

Warner, L. A. (2013). Armed Group Amnesty and Military Integration in South Sudan. *The Rusi Journal*, *158*(6), 40–47.

Young, J. (2006). *The South Sudan Defense Forces in the Wake of the Juba Declaration. Small Arms Survey*. Graduate Institute of International Studies.

Zoellick, R. B. (2005). *The Hard Work Of Peace. Prepared For Delivery University Of Khartoum, Sudan On 9 November 2005*. Sudan. Retrieved from .http://2001-2009.State.Gov/S/D/Former/Zoellick/Rem/56654.Htm

Chapter 10
Post-Conflict Justice in Cambodia:
The Legacy of the Khmer Rouge Tribunal

Daniel Heilmann
Independent Researcher, Germany

ABSTRACT

This paper looks at the role that the Extraordinary Chambers in the Courts of Cambodia play in the context of post-conflict justice in Cambodia. The first trial against one of the main perpetrators was completed in 2010; the first phase of the second case against two high-ranking leaders of the Khmer Rouge has been completed in 2014. This study includes an analysis of how the Tribunal has influenced the legal and political culture in Cambodia, and the ways in which the work of the Tribunal has changed the perception of common people concerning the Khmer Rouge period. The paper also looks at the proceedings before the Tribunal and discusses whether the Tribunal has, in the eyes of all relevant stakeholders, lived up to expectations. The interaction between the Cambodian government and the international community is crucial in this context. Finally, the Tribunal's lasting legacy is scrutinized in regard to its effect on the Cambodian legal system and in regard to the ECCC's outreach, education and documentation activities.

INTRODUCTION

The traumatic experiences of the 1960s and 1970s, especially the Vietnam War and the authoritarian regime of the Khmer Rouge, have deeply influenced Cambodian society. The Cambodian experience is in many ways unique and different from other countries' experiences, because of the multidimensionality of the conflict. It is particularly remarkable that while the Khmer Rouge have been removed from power over thirty-five years ago, only over the last decade modest progress has been made in Cambodia towards sustainable social and economic development.

This paper looks at the role that the Extraordinary Chambers in the Courts of Cambodia play in the context of post-conflict justice in Cambodia. The Extraordinary Chambers in the Courts of Cambodia (also known as the Khmer Rouge Tribunal; hereinafter ECCC or Tribunal) were established in 2006 – more than 25 years after the crimes were committed. Their establishment marks an important step in Cambodia's attempt to come to terms with its past.

DOI: 10.4018/978-1-4666-9675-4.ch010

The first trial (Case 001) against one of the main perpetrators was completed in 2010; the first part of the second trial against some of the high-ranking leaders of the Khmer Rouge was completed in 2014. It is unclear whether and how the Tribunal will proceed after the appeal judgment and the completion of the second phase of that trial (Case 02/002). Additional cases are under investigation. However, the Cambodian government is reluctant to support the work of the Tribunal for much longer.

This paper tackles important questions, including an analysis of the extent to which the Tribunal has influenced the legal and political culture in Cambodia, and in which ways the work of the Tribunal may have changed the perception of the Khmer Rouge regime in society. First, a brief historic overview including the process of establishing the ECCC will be given. The paper will then look at the proceedings before the Tribunal and discuss whether the Tribunal has, in the eyes of the stakeholders, lived up to the expectations. Especially important in this context is the interaction between the Cambodian government and the international community. Finally, some thoughts will be shared on the Tribunal's lasting legacy in regard to improvement of the Cambodian legal system and post-conflict justice in general.

BACKGROUND

Cambodia had been a French protectorate since 1863 and King Norodom Sihanouk declared Cambodian independence in 1945 during Japanese occupation (at the request of the Japanese occupiers). However, the French were able to reimpose their colonial administration in October 1945. Cambodia finally became independent in 1953/54 in the context of the first Indochina War. Independence was followed by a period of Cambodian political non-alignment and neutrality in the 1950s and 1960s (for a detailed account of the Cambodian history after independence see Kamm, 2002). King Norodom Sihanouk, who had abdicated in 1955 in favor of his father, became Head of State again in 1960. His policy successfully maneuvered Cambodia through the Cold War, when the superpowers fiercely fought over influence in the region. But ultimately Cambodia could not avoid being dragged into the Vietnam War. Genuine neutrality became impossible under pressure from various stakeholders, and, in 1965, Sihanouk made a pact with North Vietnam and allowed Chinese military supplies to reach North Vietnam via Cambodian territory. Increasingly, Cambodia's eastern provinces were serving as bases for the Viet Cong. Hence, the United States began a bombing campaign to weaken Vietnamese logistical lines running through Cambodia in 1969. Sihanouk feared that the Vietnamese conflict would spill over into Cambodia and therefore opposed the U.S. bombing campaign. At the same time, domestic opposition to Sihanouk grew (already since 1964 the government faced an underground insurgent movement - the Khmer Rouge).

In 1970, while he was on a state visit in China, Sihanouk was ousted in a military coup by Prime Minister Lon Nol. The Lon Nol government issued an ultimatum for North Vietnamese troops to leave Cambodian soil. Although the role of the United States during that time remains unclear, the Lon Nol government was ultimately supported by the United States in the civil war that raged from 1970 to 1975. Despite support from the United States, the Lon Nol government remained weak and lost rapidly territory to the advancing Khmer Rouge guerilla forces. The intense U.S. bombing campaign further helped the advancing Khmer Rouge forces, because it brought them support and sympathy of the common people. In addition, the Khmer Rouge insurgency could count on military support from North Vietnam. Eventually, American support for the Lon Nol government ceased in the context of broader geo-strategic considerations. The Cambodian government was unable to sustain itself any longer and broke down when in April 1975 the Khmer Rouge marched triumphantly into Phnom Penh.

At first, the Khmer Rouge troops were hailed as liberators by the Cambodian people, who had suffered a great lot during the years of civil war and the Vietnam War (for a detailed account of the Khmer Rouge regime see Kiernan, 2005). But it became clear to everyone within a matter of days that the Khmer Rouge had a radical Maoist ideology and intended to act on it without compromise. The country was renamed "Democratic Kampuchea" and it was subjected to a radical experiment of social re-engineering: the Khmer Rouge planned to establish a self-sufficient rural society. To that end they evacuated all major cities within days after coming to power. Following the takeover, the Khmer Rouge mercilessly moved the population out of Phnom Penh. Many thousands died during death marches to the countryside. Once people arrived in the rural areas they were coerced to agricultural work and other forms of hard physical labor. All social, economic and legal institutions were abolished over the course of the following years. Such radical policies led to food shortages, lack of sanitation, medical care and medication (Schrey & Meisenberg, 2013, p. 77). Those who had lived in the cities had lost the basic skills to survive in the harsh environment of the rural areas and the jungle.

No authoritative figures exist, but it is estimated that approx. 1.7 million people died through killings, torture, starvation and disease during the roughly four years of the Khmer Rouge regime from April 1975 to January 1979 (Scheffer, 2008). Anyone who stood in the way of the radical ideology of the Khmer Rouge was tortured and eliminated. In the infamous Tuol Sleng prison alone 12.000 political prisoners were killed and tortured to death. Many more died on the "killing fields". Alone at the Choeung Ek killing field, just outside Phnom Penh, more than 9.000 common people were executed with barbaric means.

Finally, at the beginning of 1979, and after a campaign of cross-border raids into Vietnam, the Khmer Rouge were driven out of Phnom Penh and all other large cities by Vietnamese troops. Khmer Rouge forces were simply overpowered by the Vietnamese army and they retreated to a remote area close to the Thai border where they planned to regroup. The ensuing civil war between the Vietnam installed government and the Khmer Rouge lasted for another ten years, but the Khmer Rouge were never again in a position to seriously threaten to take power. Ultimately, in 1987, under international diplomatic pressure, peace talks began. As a result, in September 1989 Vietnam withdrew its troops from Cambodian territory. Fighting between the warring Cambodian groups continued for a while, but two years later, in October 1991, a United Nations brokered peace agreement was signed - the Paris Agreement (Agreement on a Comprehensive Political Settlement of the Cambodia Conflict, 23 October 1991). Under the Paris Agreement, the United Nations were given broad powers to monitor the implementation of all components of the peace agreement, to enforce the ceasefire and to deal with questions of demobilization and the return of refugees and internally displaced persons. To that end the United Nations Transitional Authority in Cambodia (UNTAC) was established in 1992. Besides overseeing the implementation of the Paris Agreement, UNTAC was also tasked with organizing free and democratic elections. The Khmer Rouge boycotted the elections and resumed their insurgency (on a low scale and only in the regions on the Thai border). But the 1993 elections were a success and resulted in the appointment of two Co-Prime Ministers, Norodom Ranariddh and Hun Sen. They entered into an uneasy coalition government that was stable for a few years only. Both opponents accused each other of staging a coup and Hun Sen finally took sole power when Norodom Ranariddh was forced to leave the country in summer of 1997.

This is still the situation today: Hun Sen's Cambodian Peoples' Party (CCP) runs the country. The CPP has won every major election since 1997 - although in the last general elections in 2013 the opposition Cambodian National Rescue Party won 44.5% of the votes and took 55 out of 123 seats in the National Assembly.

The Khmer Rouge continued their fight in certain areas along the Thai border until 1998, when they finally collapsed after internal power struggles. Pol Pot, the former leader of the Khmer Rouge was denounced by his comrades in a show trial in 1997 and died soon thereafter in 1998, which marked the factual end of the Khmer Rouge.

Given the magnitude of human suffering and atrocities that were committed during the four years of the Khmer Rouge reign, it is quite surprising that it took almost three decades to address these atrocities through a judicial process. However, it must be borne in mind, that international criminal justice is a rather new legal discipline, which was after the Nuremburg and Tokyo trials in the wake of World War II dormant for the coming 50 years (Schrey & Meisenberg, 2013, p. 78).

Mock prosecutions and trials against a handful of Khmer Rouge cadres took place after the Vietnamese invasion in 1979. Pol Pot was sentenced to death in absentia by the Vietnam-backed government. However, these judgments were of a symbolic nature. The Khmer Rouge were still fighting a guerilla war in the jungles close to the Thai border during the 1980s. Therefore they were out of reach for the Phnom Penh government.

Problematic was also the fact that, due to geo-strategic interests of the super powers, the Khmer Rouge were still recognized as the official government of Cambodia by the United Nations until 1993. This explains why for a long time no initiatives were taken in regard to post-conflict justice, although the atrocities were already well-known and documented by that time.

Finally, in 1997, things changed when the two co-prime ministers and the United Nations Commission on Human Rights called for the investigation of crimes against humanity and genocide during the Khmer Rouge regime. During the Cold War period, mass atrocities and grave human rights violations had largely been considered a matter of internal affairs and they remained mostly unpunished (Schrey & Meisenberg, 2013, p. 79). This changed in the new global landscape after the fall of the iron curtain, when in 1993 and 1994 the ad-hoc criminal tribunals for the former Yugoslavia and for Rwanda were established through resolutions by the United Nations Security Council. Given these dynamics, and also the move in the international community towards establishing an international criminal court, the call for post-conflict justice in Cambodia gained attention and new momentum.

However, it took another decade until the Khmer Rouge Tribunal was finally established. One of the reasons was that the establishment of the Tribunal had, for political reasons and reasons of international law, to be different from the procedure of establishing the ICTY and ICTR. China argued that there did no longer exist a thread to international peace and security. A threat to international peace and security is, however, a prerequisite to action of the Security Council under Chapter VII of the UN Charter. The option to create an ad-hoc tribunal similar to the ICTY and ICR was therefore off the table. Another reason was that there were simply no local experts who could handle the complex process of gathering evidence and prosecuting high-level criminals. Lawyers, judges and other members of the judicial professions had been among those targeted and eliminated by the Khmer Rouge. In the 1990s a huge capacity void existed in Cambodia. Obviously, the Khmer Rouge had had a devastating impact on the Cambodian judiciary and legal profession. They successfully exterminated the country's intellectual elite and, when the Khmer Rouge were ousted in 1979, there were only ten qualified lawyers left in the country (Amnesty International, 2002). The justice system had been completely deconstructed and has, for various reasons, been slow to recover ever since. Partly due to the civil strife prolonging into the late 1990s, the country's legal institutions have not recovered until today. Obviously, prosecutions for genocide and crimes against humanity must be – not least because they are international crimes - subject to highest international standards. Cambodian institutions lacked the capacity and knowledge for undertaking such a complex endeavor without sufficient help and support from the international community.

Due to conflicting interests, the negotiations between the Cambodian government and the United Nations to establish the Tribunal turned out to be complicated. The Cambodian government insisted that the Tribunal would remain under Cambodian control and that the United Nations should play purely an advisory role. This was difficult, if not impossible, to accept for the UN who insisted on an impartial and independent tribunal that adhered to international standards. The negotiations extended over several years, more than once reaching a deadlock (Scheffer, 2008, provides a detailed inside view of the negotiations between the UN and the Cambodian government). Finally, the Cambodian government and the United Nations signed an agreement on 6 June 2003. The ECCC was taking shape in 2006, when the national as well as the international judges were sworn in.

THE SET-UP OF THE TRIBUNAL

Before evaluating the work of the Tribunal, one must note that multiple crucial legal experiments have been undertaken in the context of the ECCC - as a result of the above-mentioned difficult negotiations between the UN and the Cambodian government. For example, in contrast to most other United Nations backed hybrid courts, the ECCC was established within the national judiciary. The ECCC is the first hybrid court that mandates a majority of national judges and divides key legal and administrative offices and funding mechanisms into distinct national and international sides. Ergo, the judicial officers, prosecutors and judges appointed by the UN cannot determine issues unilaterally (and vice versa).

The temporal jurisdiction of the ECCC extends from 17 April 1975, the day the Khmer Rouge took power, to 6 January 1979. With this limited temporal jurisdiction a fully-fledged inquiry into the Cambodia conflict - i.e. the crimes that were committed during the civil war before the Khmer Rouge came to power, as well as the time beyond the Khmer Rouge period - is not possible. Furthermore, the jurisdiction ratione personae of the Tribunal is limited to the senior leaders of Democratic Kampuchea and those most responsible for the crimes committed at that time.

The limited scope of jurisdiction of the Tribunal has been at the center of the negotiations between the Cambodian government and the United Nations in the years leading up to the establishment of the Tribunal. The eventual outcome of these negotiations is an unorthodox set of sui generis hybrid chambers within the existing Cambodian court system - as is signified by the name "Extraordinary Chambers in the Courts of Cambodia". Some of the unique features have proven to be problematic, for example the ECCC's inclusion of two pairs of investigators modelled after the French criminal law system. This led to inevitable redundancy and gridlock. Both, the existence of investigating judges, and the fact that both the Office of the Co-Prosecutors and the Office of the Co-Investigating Judges are two-headed (national and international) have contributed to the inefficiency of the Tribunal (Ciorciari & Heindel, p. 6).

Hybrid courts were created at the end of the 1990s, because the international community was not fully satisfied with the expensive and slow work of the international ad-hoc tribunals that had been established in the cases of Yugoslavia (ICTY) and Rwanda (ICTR). The hope was that hybrid courts would better accommodate sovereignty concerns of the affected states, promote local ownership and legitimacy, connect trials to local survivor populations, build host government capacity, and deliver credible justice at a lower cost than fully international proceedings (Ciorciari & Heindel, p. 2). Yet, over time it has become clear that hybrid courts can also suffer from serious deficiencies. For example, they are frequently exposed to power struggles and they are vulnerable to domestic political interference. Furthermore, they are susceptible to confusion and inefficiency as they merge multiple legal systems and personnel with different approaches to justice. As will be shown, these issues prove troublesome in the case of the ECCC.

THE CASES

Only one case has so far been fully adjudicated by the ECCC. Case 001 saw Kaing Guek Eav (also called "Duch") stand trial. He served as director of S-21, a security center tasked with interrogating and executing persons perceived as enemies of Democratic Kampuchea and the Khmer Rouge ideology. The S-21 prison was operational between 1975 and 1979. In addition to mass executions many detainees died as a result of torture and their conditions of detention.

The Tribunal found that a minimum of 12,272 individuals were detained and executed at S-21 (this number is based on prisoner's lists, the Tribunal however stated that the actual number of detainees is likely to have been considerably greater). The Tribunal found that Duch possessed and exercised significant authority at S-21 and that he voluntarily ensured that S-21 ran as efficiently as possible and did so out of loyalty to his superiors and the Communist Party of Kampuchea. Ultimately, the trial chamber convicted Duch of crimes against humanity, as well as numerous grave breaches of the Geneva Conventions, for which it imposed a sentence of 35 years of imprisonment (ECCC, 2010, para. 679). The judgment did not hold up on appeal and the appeals chamber sentenced Duch to life imprisonment, the maximum sentence available under the law (ECCC, 2012). The appeals chamber held that the trial chamber had insufficiently weighted the gravity of the crimes committed by Duch and that he had held a central leadership role at the S-21 prison (ECCC, 2012, para. 377). The appeals chamber pointed out that the high number of victims along with the extended period of time over which the crimes were committed (more than three years), place the case among the gravest that have ever been adjudicated before international criminal tribunals (ECCC, 2012, para. 376).

Only one other case has been before the Tribunal: Case 002. For various reasons, mainly the high age of the defendants, Case 002 has been split up in mini-trials. A judgment in the first mini-trial (Case 002/01) was rendered in August 2014. Case 02/002 is currently in the initial phase. In Case 002 four senior leaders of the Khmer Rouge regime were indicted for their leadership involvement in the Khmer Rouge atrocities. The accused were charged with crimes against humanity, grave breaches of the Geneva Conventions, and genocide against the Muslim Cham (a religious minority which makes up approx. 2% of the Cambodian population) and the Vietnamese minority. The trial in Case 002 began in June 2011. However, over the course of the trial the proceedings had to be terminated with regard to two of the accused in 2012 and 2013 respectively: Ieng Sary (the Minister of Foreign Affairs under the Khmer Rouge) died on 14 March 2013, and Ieng Thirith (Minister of Social Affairs under the Khmer Rouge) was found unfit to stand trial due to her progressing dementia. Of the original four accused in Case 002 only two of the accused, Nuon Chea (the Chairman of the Democratic Kampuchea National Assembly and Deputy Secretary of the Communist Party of Kampuchea) and Khieu Samphan (the Head of State of Democratic Kampuchea), lived to see the end of the first part of the trial in the court room.

Case 002 was severed into separate trials, each addressing a different section of the indictment. The first mini-trial (Case 002/01) focused on alleged crimes against humanity related to the forced movement of the population from Phnom Penh (and later from other regions) and the execution of soldiers immediately after the Khmer Rouge takeover in 1975. Over the course of the trial 92 individuals gave testimony (including three experts, 53 fact witnesses, five character witnesses and 31

Civil Parties); more than 5800 evidentiary documents were subjected to examination (totalling over 222,000 pages); and the Chamber admitted 1,124 written statements and transcripts of witnesses and Civil Parties. The closing statements concluded on 31 October 2013 and the judgment was rendered on 7 August 2014.

In Case 001/02, the two remaining defendants were sentenced to imprisonment for life for committing crimes against humanity (ECCC, 2014, para. 1105). In particular the trial chamber found that at least two million people were forcibly transferred from Phnom Penh by Khmer Rouge soldiers under false pretexts and threats and that immediately after 17 April 1975, at least 250 Lon Nol officials were executed. The Trial Chamber did not find credible the defense claims that Phnom Penh was evacuated to protect the inhabitants from American bombing and food shortage (ECCC, 2014, para. 525 et seqq). The Chamber found that a widespread and systematic attack against the civilian population of Cambodia was purposefully carried out in furtherance of party policies and plans to build socialism. In its judgment that Trial Chamber awarded civil party reparations on a collective level and endorsed eleven projects (ECCC, 2014, para. 1109 et seqq). Amongst the endorsed projects are the institution of a National Remembrance Day; the construction of a memorial in Phnom Penh to honor victims of forced evacuations; a permanent exhibition as well as a mobile exhibition; the inclusion of a chapter on forced population movement within the Cambodian school curriculum; and the construction of a peace learning centre. In this context, in March 2015, a memorial to Victims of the Democratic Kampuchea Regime, and especially to the victims who were killed at S-21, was inaugurated at the Tuol Sleng museum (The Court Reporter, April 2015, p.8).

The second trial against Khieu Samphan and Nuon Chea (Case 002/02) is underway and the trial chamber decided that charges related to genocide, forced marriage and rape, treatment of Buddhists, internal purges and the targeting of former Khmer Republic officials, form the basis of the trial (ECCC, 24 December 2013).

Two more cases, Cases 003 and 004, are under investigation. On 3 March 2015, two suspects in Case 003 and Case 004 were charged in absentia by the international co-investigating Judge (The Court Report, March 2015, p.1). In Case 003, Meas Muth, who is believed to be a former navy commander under the Khmer Rouge regime, was charged with allegations of crimes against humanity and grave breaches of the Geneva Conventions. In Case 004, Im Chaem, who is believed to be a former district secretary, was charged with allegations of homicide and multiple categories of crimes against humanity. However, due to the tensions between national and international judges, it remains unclear whether the Tribunal will be in a position to push through with trials in these cases. As will be discussed in the following section, there is significant disagreement between the Cambodian judges and investigators and their international counterparts on the direction and future of the Tribunal.

CO-OPERATION BETWEEN CAMBODIA AND THE INTERNATIONAL COMMUNITY

Judicial Independence

Cambodia has an intricate relationship with the ECCC and the official position regarding the proceedings before the ECCC is ambivalent. In 2010, Prime Minister Hun Sen informed United Nations Secretary-General Ban Ki-Moon that "Case 003 will not be allowed. [t]he court will try the four senior leaders successfully and then finish with Case 002" (Crowther, 2010, p. 4). Arguably, the main reason behind the government's denial to support the prosecution of more than the Khmer Rouge leaders which have already been indicted, is to protect members of the government who were also in the Khmer Rouge. Further trials could potentially bring attention to acts of (prominent and high-ranking) persons which so far have gone unnoticed.

The repercussions of the government's opposition to the investigation of further crimes are immense. In the struggles surrounding investigations of alleged crimes two international investigating judges have resigned, reportedly because of perceived interference in their work. In 2011, a considerable number of international staff members in the Office of the Co-Investigating Judges walked out to protest the failure of the co-investigating judges to investigate the crimes that form the basis of Case 003. The international co-investigating judge ultimately bowed to pressure and stepped down. However, his successor – while having a different approach - did also not hold this position for long and stepped down (for a summary of these events see Coughlan, Ghouse & Smith, 2012, pp. 31-32). An order delivered prior to his departure invited the co-prosecutors to file a supplementary submission in the Case 003 investigation. This action was considered highly controversial because the international co-investigating judge recommended that four high-ranking officials in the sitting Cambodian government be interviewed concerning allegations of Khmer Rouge war crimes. The order is a confidential document, but its contents were widely reported in the media (see for example Di Certo). The opposing interests of the United Nations on the one side, and the Cambodian government on the other side, complicate the work of the ECCC.

Additionally, the independence of Cambodian judges and prosecutors from the government is doubtful. Political influence on the Cambodian judiciary is, for example, evidenced by politically-motivated prosecutions coupled with a failure to prosecute suspects who are well-connected (Coughlan, Ghouse & Smith, 2012, p.19). The relevant laws are in place, enforcement is the problem. Judicial independence and the separation of powers are enshrined in the Cambodian Constitution in Articles 128 and 51 respectively. These articles provide checks and balances against interference by other branches of government. In practice, however, the judiciary, including the ECCC, seems susceptible to political interference (Coughlan, Ghouse & Smith, 2012, p. 18). For example, pressure has been exerted when the Cambodian government rejected that sitting officials are summoned as witnesses and when it opposed the investigation of additional suspects in Cases 003 and 004. Concerning the issue of high-ranking officials being summoned, the international judges of the pre-trial chamber have (in a separate opinion to a decision) stated that they find it reasonable to believe that one or more members of the government may have knowingly and willfully interfered with or threatened and intimidated witnesses who may give evidence before the co-investigating judges (ECCC, 9 September 2010, para. 6).

Concerning the contentious issue of investigation of additional cases and suspects in Cases 003 and 004, the international co-prosecutor (unable to reach an agreement with his national counterpart) filed a notice of disagreement and asked the pre-trial chamber to resolve it. An affirmative vote by the pre-trial judges could not be reached because the three Cambodian judges voted against additional investigations and the two international judges voted in favor (ECCC, 18 August 2009). This is a symptomatic decision amongst many which are all divided on national/international lines.

However, it must be pointed out that the Cambodian government's position is predicated on the law. The government argues that the Law on the Establishment of the Extraordinary Chambers must be interpreted restrictive. Art. 2 of the Law on the Establishment of the ECCC states that the Tribunal shall "bring to trial senior leaders of Democratic Kampuchea and those who were most responsible for the crimes and serious violations of Cambodian laws related to crimes". The law speaks of those "most" responsible. The government's position is that the major culprits have been tried and that justice has been done after the conclusion of Case 002. This is a valid interpretation of the law, but it is strongly opposed by advocacy groups and the international community.

Both sides, national and international, have interests which seem irreconcilable. That the government's position is replicated by the Cambodian judges at the Tribunal is no surprise. There is a thin line between voluntarily aligning with the government view and bowing to pressure. Definitely the situation of the national judges at the ECCC is difficult. Clashes and struggles between the Cambodian stakeholders and their international counterparts are inevitable in an environment of mistrust. Ultimately, the opposing objectives of the Cambodian stakeholders and the international community may overshadow the legacy of the Tribunal.

Funding and Budget

Other issues are also problematic, prominently the budget of the Tribunal. The ECCC is funded solely through voluntary contributions. Each side, national and international, receives independent streams of funding from donor states. So far, more than 30 states have contributed funds and the donor community is led by Japan, several European states, the United States, and Australia (The Court Report, April 2014, p. 2). While the Cambodian government oversees the finances of the national side, the United Nations side is overseen by a mix of offices in the UN Secretariat. Until the end of 2015 the ECCC will have spent USD 265 million in total (The Court Report, April 2014, p. 2). It currently operates with an annual budget of roughly USD 30 million, which comes mostly from the United Nations side, while the Cambodian side also (through international donors) substantially contributes. In 2014, the United Nations side provides 25.2 million to the budget, while the Cambodian side provides USD 6.4 million· By the end of 2015, when two trials will likely have been completed, the total cost runs up to approx. USD 265 million.

From the very beginning, critics of the ECCC's split structure feared that without clear international leadership, the Court would be vulnerable to the same bureaucratic dysfunction that plagues Cambodia's domestic judicial system. Such issues have indeed surfaced. Allegations of kickbacks from Cambodian staff to politicians in exchange for their positions arose in 2007 (Coughlan, Ghouse & Smith, 2012, p. 29). An audit carried out by the UN Development Programme in 2007 on human resources management and hiring procedures found that of 29 staff investigated, 18 individuals did not meet the minimum requirements specified in the vacancy announcements and that 28 positions were filled by government appointment without following a competitive selection process (UNDP, 2007, pp- 3-5). Substantial mismanagement of human resources and financial means seems to have occurred at the Tribunal.

Given this mismanagement of resources, it is not surprising that the donor community is asking for speeding up the procedure. The ECCC predicts that its timeline will run beyond 2018 (The Court Report, p.2), but the international community seems to be unwilling to provide additional financial resources. Donor fatigue is a serious issue. The UN and other donors have indicated a commitment to provide funds for the current Case 002 through to completion. But the situation is not so clear concerning Cases 003 and 004 – if they should finally go ahead. When one takes into account that over the course of almost ten years more than USD 230 million have been spent on what basically amounts to two trials, it is understandable that the United Nations and other donors make no clear commitment regarding future cases.

Without a turnaround in the approach of international donors, Cases 003 and 004 may ultimately be prevented from reaching the trial phase. It has been argued by NGOs that in this event the ECCC's historical record would be tainted because the ECCC would then provide only a limited account of the Khmer Rouge atrocities. Obviously, the international community is caught between a rock and a hard place when it comes to deciding on the future of the ECCC, especially so because support from the Cambodian government is not to be expected.

THE PERCEPTION OF THE TRIBUNAL IN CAMBODIAN SOCIETY

An important factor that will determine the legacy of the Khmer Rouge Tribunal is how the Tribunal's work is perceived by ordinary Cambodians. Although it is too early to draw definitive conclusions about the ECCC's impact on Cambodian society, it is clear that over the last years the knowledge on the Khmer Rouge regime and the understanding of the scale of crimes that have been committed during that time has increased among Cambodians, and especially the young population. While in 2008 39% of participants in a public opinion survey said that they had no knowledge of the ECCC, this number decreased to only 25% in 2010 (Pham, Vinck, Balthazard & Hen, 2011, p. 21). An impressive number of people know by now that the Tribunal exists and what it stands for. This in itself is an impressive success. However, there is little evidence that ordinary Cambodians understand the background and legal process in much depth. Therefore, people may have unrealistic expectations about what the ECCC can achieve. For example, it is not uncommon that people hope, because of the deep international involvement in the process, that the Court will bring complete understanding and truth about what happened. A high percentage (more than 80%) of Cambodians believes that the ECCC will not only bring justice to the victims, but also help the reconciliation effort (Pham, Vinck, Balthazard & Hen, 2011, p. 39). Ultimately, many also hope that the work of the ECCC will result in generous reparations and compensation (Ciorciari & Heindel, p. 55).

Overall, it seems that Cambodian society is divided over the Tribunal's existence and how trials are handled. Naturally, Cambodians are more concerned about how the trials will affect the future of their country. Cambodians have, for a long time, been very positive concerning the progress and the direction of development of the country. This has, according to a public opinion survey changed drastically after the general elections of 2013. It seems that Cambodians are increasingly impatient and discontent with the direction of the country, and, more importantly, do not trust the state and its institutions any longer. In the survey of November 2013, 43% of participants stated that they believe Cambodia is headed in the wrong direction, in January 2013 only 21% of respondents had stated this (International Republican Institute, 2013, p. 4). Making the judicial system more fair and independent has been highlighted as the area of reform that is most important to make Cambodia a democratic state (International Republican Institute, 2013, p. 7). The ECCC and its work must be assessed against this sentiment of discontent with the state and its judicial institutions.

Different groups in society view the ECCC from different perspectives. One of the most important groups with a view to the Tribunal is the survivors of the Khmer Rouge regime. While the average age in Cambodia is roughly 23 years, this group is comprised of elderly people in their sixties and seventies. The elderly are not homogenous in their assessment of the Tribunal. A first group of the survivors support the work of the Tribunal unconditionally. They are victims and almost all of them have lost family during the Khmer Rouge regime. They are motivated by the belief that the Tribunal will not only bring justice, but hopefully also reparations for victims. However, in other societal groups there is an increasing distrust of the international community. The opinion is widespread that the UN is at least partly at fault for the country's culture of impunity and corruption. Many Cambodians still seem to be somewhat supportive of the government and therefore argue that the focus and efforts should be concentrated on national problems like poverty and corruption. To many Cambodians these are more important problems that need to be tackled than the truth about past atrocities. A considerably large group of people have in one way or the other collaborated with the Khmer Rouge or were Khmer Rouges themselves. They are afraid that their former lives might be revealed if the Tribunal was to get a mandate to investigate crimes on a broad base. Naturally they are opposed to the Tribunal's work. Overall, elderly Cambodians and survivors of the Khmer Rouge seems to be heterogeneous and rather apolitical.

For demographic reasons the youth are becoming rapidly a more and more important group in Cambodian society. The youth have been born after the collapse of the Khmer Rouge regime in 1979, and while they are not very politicized, they are an increasingly vocal part of society. Their beliefs and expectations must therefore be taken into account. It seems that the youth is more cohesive and homogenous than the elderly. In general, they are not well informed about the Khmer Rouge and they find it difficult to believe that Cambodians could have killed each other on such a large scale. Schools only slowly start to give an objective account of the Khmer Rouge regime. Some youth are curious to learn what happened and support justice and truth processes to the benefit of the victims. Most, however, remain largely ignorant and uninterested when it comes to the atrocities committed by the Khmer Rouge. For many young people their own economic perspectives and the immediate future is much more important that the history of the country. Another influential group, which is also divided, are Cambodian expatriates. Some support the tribunal, because many Cambodians from the diaspora have returned to Cambodia and are engaged in tribunal issues while working for international non-governmental organizations. Others oppose the Tribunal for various reasons. A common argument is that the money dedicated to the trials could be better spent on alleviating poverty and improving infrastructure in the country.

Overall, it seems that Cambodian society is split over the existence of the Tribunal as a truth and justice mechanism. Most Cambodians, just in line with their government, seem to prefer to move on and to concentrate on the tasks and challenges that lie ahead for the country. A common sentiment is that Cambodians should focus on improving the future of their country instead of scrutinizing the past.

LEGACY OF THE TRIBUNAL

Given the disputes surrounding the Tribunal, what can its legacy ultimately be and what does legacy mean in the context of a hybrid court? The Office of the United Nations High Commissioner for Human Rights (OHCHR) defines legacy as "a hybrid court's lasting impact on bolstering the rule of law in a particular society, by conducting effective trials to contribute to ending impunity, while also strengthening domestic judicial capacity. The aim is for this impact to continue even after the work of the hybrid court is complete" (Office of the United Nations High Commissioner for Human Rights, 2008, pp. 4-5). OHCHR describes several categories of potential legacy initiatives. Among them are (1) professional development projects, such as mentoring and training, which are designed to facilitate capacity-building within the host country; (2) physical infrastructure projects, which include archiving court records; (3) catalyzing domestic legal reform, and having an impact on domestic and international jurisprudence; and (4) a rule of law legacy including the promotion of fair trial rights, judicial independence, impartiality and due process by showcasing these values at the hybrid court (Office of the United Nations High Commissioner for Human Rights, 2008). Taking the OHCHR categories as a benchmark, how does the ECCC fare when it comes to creating a lasting legacy?

Impact on Rule of Law and the Domestic Judicial System

Many projects beyond the actual trials are being implemented in the vicinity of the Tribunal. This includes projects to institutionalize education about the Khmer Rouge, memoralize the victims, foster reconciliation and built capacity in the legal sector.

In theory, the ECCC appears well-positioned to impact the national judicial system because it is part of the national legal system and its internal rules are based on the Cambodian Code of Criminal Procedure. As a tribunal established under Cambodian law, the ECCC should embody the values of judicial independence and due process. These principles are enshrined in the Cambodian Constitution, for example in Articles 128 and 38. The idea for hybrid courts in general, and for the ECCC in particular, includes an important demonstration effect in that they foster a cultural shift in how the domestic courts are perceived by society. Ideally, hybrid courts aspire to the highest standards of independence, impartiality, due process and human rights norms and demonstrate the supremacy of law and the ability of a court to operate free from political interference. Clearly a hybrid court must aspire to the highest standards of independence, impartiality, and application of norms of due process and international human rights, because it is regarded as a model.

As has been outlined above, independence and impartiality are some of the problematic issues surrounding the Tribunal. When judges fail to act in a transparent manner, the message sent to the domestic judicial system is that of a lack of professionality at the Tribunal. The United Nations have been criticized by non-governmental organizations and advocacy groups for ignoring, or at least failing to adequately respond to the allegations of political interference at the Tribunal. The question must indeed be asked, to what extent the ECCC can have a positive impact on the national legal system and the rule of law in Cambodia, when it is perceived as being a politically influenced institution. However, a thorough understanding of the Cambodian context is needed before arriving at a conclusion. A rather large part of Cambodian society seems to support the government policies concerning the Tribunal. While it is true that the independence and professionalism of the Tribunal will shape its legacy, it is also important to take into account the perception of Cambodians themselves. Cambodians want judicial and legal reform and a trustworthy, independent judiciary. However, they do not seem to believe that the ECCC is instrumental in achieving these goals. A lingering sentiment seems to be that the money spent on the Tribunal could probably be spent better elsewhere. Maybe it would be worthwhile to consider an approach that supports Cambodian institutions such as courts and prosecutors directly, instead of overfunding the inefficient and expensive ECCC for years to come. So far the impact of the ECCC on the domestic judicial system has been minuscule at best.

Capacity-Building and Professional Development

Former UN Secretary-General Kofi Annan is on record stating that the ECCC should have "considerable legacy value, inasmuch as it will result in the transfer of skills and know-how to Cambodian court personnel" (United Nations, para. 27). Ideally, the ECCC will have a lasting impact and influence on the domestic judiciary's understanding of international standards and it will provide the domestic judiciary with experience in conducting trials according to international best practices in areas such as fair trial rights and court administration. This is particularly important with a view to Cambodia's past as a country where the legal profession was dramatically decimated under the Khmer Rouge and where there still is a serious lack of qualified and experienced legal personnel.

The ECCC provides much needed legal training. For example, the Defense Support Section organizes training for defense lawyers in cooperation with the Bar Association. The training for lawyers includes courses on legal skills and international law and they are provided to both national staff and lawyers outside of the ECCC. The Tribunal's in-country location, hybrid composition, and inclusion of Khmer language make it possible for its Cambodian personnel to learn about international standards and best practices (Ciorciari & Heindel, p. 70).

Notwithstanding these efforts, the ECCC has been criticized for not taking a sufficiently active role concerning the outreach to the regular Cambodian courts. Clearly the daily trial work has the highest priority, and all personnel development initiatives are viewed as ancillary to this objective. However, some capacity-building and skills transfer occurs organically without the need for extra activities. In order to ensure the most effective skill transfer, it is of course preferable that such activities are additionally to the regular court work undertaken (Coughlan, Ghouse & Smith, 2012, p. 27).

In order for capacity-building projects to influence domestic practice, it is essential that national staff are able to find relevant employment in the national judiciary after leaving the ECCC. It is unlikely that the ECCC will have a major impact on legal reform in Cambodia, but nevertheless, its impact on the Cambodian staff at the Tribunal may have positive effects once the Tribunal winds down and the staff works in the regular Cambodian judiciary again. However, it is not guaranteed that national staff will choose to return to the national judicial system when they finish working at the ECCC. A report on the Special Court for Sierra Leone noted that many Sierra Leoneans who had worked at the SCSL would leave the country once the court finishes, minimizing the benefits to the national system (Kerr & Lincoln, 2007, p. 17). The same could happen in Cambodia. The main reason of such a negative outlook is that the salary in the Cambodian judiciary is simply not attractive enough, for the rather highly paid (by local standards) national ECCC staffers to return to the national judiciary. Qualified national staff may choose to work at other international tribunals instead of returning to domestic practice.

Change in the Cambodian legal culture is a long-term project and the near-term payoffs of the ECCC are likely to be not too many. The ECCC helps to develop local legal skills, but sustainable and lasting change in Cambodia's legal culture will only occur when there is a fundamental commitment to the rule of law (Ciorciari & Heindel, p. 70). While there are only limited resources for capacity-building and training activities available, the ECCC's most important capacity-building activity is undoubtedly to hold trials that set a positive example of due process and judicial integrity and impartiality. As has been scrutinized above, this is unfortunately a cumbersome and not very successful endeavor.

Documentation and Public Outreach

In addition to carrying out criminal trials, the ECCC performs non-judicial functions. Importantly, it was designed to help connect survivors to the criminal process, but also to educate the Cambodian youth about the Khmer Rouge. It is an advantage that the ECCC are located within Cambodia. However, in situ proceedings and national participation do not guarantee a strong outreach component per se. As with international courts, hybrid courts' perceived institutional priorities, usually favor core judicial functions. The ECCC is no exception, and the advantages that its location and composition afford have been tempered by shortcomings in its institutional design, endowment, and political will (Ciorciari & Heindel, p. 53). Public outreach and information activities are part of its objective. However, neither of the ECCC's foundational documents (the Framework Agreement between the UN and the Cambodian Government and the Cambodian law establishing the ECCC) mention outreach programmes. But the Tribunal's Internal Rules mention outreach and legacy projects indirectly. The Internal Rules divide outreach functions and assign responsibilities to two separate offices: the Public Affairs Section and the Victim Support Section (Internal Rules, Rule 12bis 1 (h)). Neither the Public Affairs Section nor the Victim Support Section are outreach offices per se. Their mandates overlap. The Public Affairs Section has concentrated on focusing on public information and a broad audience of donors, organizations and the general population, while the Victim Support Unit has concentrated on facilitating participation by civil parties. Twice a week, the Public Affairs Section of the ECCC organizes Khmer Rouge Tribunal study tours (The Court Report, March 2015, p.11). Each time groups of approx. 200 to 300 villagers from across Cambodia visit the ECCC, the Tuol Sleng Genocide Museum and the Choeung Ek killing fields and receive a guided tour and briefings. Furthermroe, during trial recesses, the Public Affairs Section conducts school visits and hosts community video screenings across the country. In this context, a good number of outreach materials has been created by the Public Affairs Section. An even bigger number has been published by NGOs. Additionally, the ECCC maintains an informative website on which all court documents are available online. These efforts have made information about the Tribunal easy to find for Cambodians and foreigners alike. The Tribunal even had its own radio program, which was suspended after one year due to a lack of funds (The Court Report, January 2013, p. 6). Many other outreach events related to the ECCC have been led by civil society organizations and not by the Tribunal itself.

Atrocities and crimes are not only documented by the Tribunal itself, but notably also by non-governmental organizations such as, for example, the Documentation Centre of Cambodia (DC-Cam). DC-Cam was originally established as part of Yale University's Cambodia Genocide Programme and became an independent NGO in 1997. By now, DC-Cam owns the largest archive on the Khmer Rouge period, including over 155,000 pages of documents. Besides that, DC-Cam just like many other Cambodian NGOs, is active in research, outreach, and educational projects concerning the Khmer Rouge period.

As the OHCHR toolbox rightfully states, "legacy may also come in the form of physical infrastructure, such as facilities, as well as the physical domain of evidence and archives of court records. Physical legacy is an important factor since issues such as the choice of court premises may have significant symbolic meaning" (Office of the United Nations High Commissioner for Human Rights, 2008, p. 35). In this regard, i.e. infrastructure, outreach and documentation, it seems that the ECCC could ultimately be successful and leave a lasting legacy.

CONCLUSION

Concerning the legal discipline of international criminal law, the Khmer Rouge Tribunal has not brought about many developments. It is also unfortunate that the ECCC did not have much of an impact on the domestic judiciary. Corruption and incompetence in the Cambodian judiciary are still problematic.

While, from a legal viewpoint, one can make the argument that so far the Tribunal has not been overly efficient, this may not hold true if one looks at the larger picture. Although the prosecutions have come late, maybe too late, and the trials have been complicated by political interests, something important has been gained: the facts about atrocious crimes have been discovered, investigated and are now well documented. The truth has been established. In that sense, the legacy of the Khmer Rouge Tribunal is more than bringing justice to the victims or improving the rule of law in Cambodia.

The Tribunal is as much about truth, reconciliation and remembrance as it is about justice in the legal sense. From the beginning it was clear that the prosecution of perpetrators, almost forty years after the Khmer Rouge atrocities have been committed, is rather symbolic. Especially so, since most perpetrators and victims are not alive anymore. Therefore, the legacy of the Khmer Rouge Tribunal cannot only be seen in the judgments rendered by the Tribunal. The lasting value of the Tribunal's work is to be found elsewhere. It is the investigations, the archiving of evidence and the outreach that took (and still takes) place at the Tribunal and in its vicinity.

FUTURE RESEARCH DIRECTIONS

The focus of this paper was to scrutinize the Khmer Rouge Tribunal and to assess the perception of the Tribunal's work. The key question, what the Tribunal's legacy ultimately can and will be must remain without a definite answer. The jury is still out, as, at this moment, the fate of Cases 003 and 004 has not been decided. The adjudication (or not) of these cases, as well as the appeals judgment in Case 002, will play a pivotal role for the overall legacy of the Khmer Rouge Tribunal. All analysis of the Tribunal's work and effectiveness can, at this point in time, only be a preliminary stocktaking. Future research will have to focus on a thorough analysis of the upcoming judgments and decisions of the ECCC. Such research should also include observations on the perception of the Tribunal's jurisprudence in academia and by other international courts, such as the International Criminal Court, in order to provide a more in-depth understanding of how, if at all, the ECCC has shaped international criminal law.

REFERENCES

Amnesty International. (2002). *Kingdom of Cambodia: Urgent need for Judicial Reform*. Retrieved from http://www.unhcr.org/refworld/pdfid/3deb63334.pdf

Ciorciari, J. D., & Heindel, A. (in press). Experiments in International Criminal Justice: Lessons from the Khmer Rouge Tribunal. *Michigan Journal of International Law*.

Coughlan, J., Ghouse, S., & Smith, R. (2012). The Legacy of the Khmer Rouge Tribunal: Maintaining the Status Quo of Cambodia's Judicial and Legal System. *Amsterdam Law Forum, (4)*, 17-35.

Crowther, S. (2013). *The Election and the ECCC*. Cambodia Tribunal Monitor.

Di Certo, B. (2012, June 4). Top officials eyed in KRT probe: report. *Phnom Penh Post*, 1, 6.

Extraordinary Chambers in the Courts of Cambodia. (2009, August 18). *Considerations of the Pre-Trial Chamber Regarding the Disagreement Between the Co-Prosecutors Pursuant to Internal Rule 71* (Doc. 001/18-11-2008-ECCC/PTC).

Extraordinary Chambers in the Courts of Cambodia. (2010). *Judgment in Case 001* (Doc. 001/18-07/ECCC/TC).

Extraordinary Chambers in the Courts of Cambodia. (2010, September 9). *Second Decision on Nuon Chea's and Ieng Sary's Appeal Against OCIJ Order on Request to Summon Witnesses, Opinion of Judges Downing and Marchi-Uhel* (Doc. 002/19-09-2007-EEEC-OPIJ (PTC 50)).

Extraordinary Chambers in the Courts of Cambodia. (2012). *Appeal Judgment in Case 0001* (Doc. 001/18-07-2007-ECCC/SC).

Extraordinary Chambers in the Courts of Cambodia. (2013, December 24). *Case 0002/02 Trial Chamber Workplan* (Doc. E301/5).

Extraordinary Chambers in the Courts of Cambodia (2014, August 7). *Case 002/01 Judgment* (Doc 002/19-09-2007/ECCC/TC).

International Republican Institute. (2014). *Survey of Cambodian Public Opinion*. Retrieved from http://www.iri.org/sites/default/files/Cambodian%20Poll%209%20Final%20PUBLIC.pdf

Kamm, H. (2002). *Cambodia. Reports from a Stricken Land*. New York, NY: Arcade Publisher.

Kerr, R. & Lincoln, J. (2007). *The Special Court for Sierra Leone: Outreach, Legacy, and Impact, Draft Interim Report*. War Crimes Research Group Department of War Studies, King's College London.

Kiernan, B. (2005). *The Pol Pot Regime: Race, Power and Genocide in Cambodia under the Khmer Rouge 1975-1979*. New Haven: Yale University Press.

Office of the United Nations High Commissioner for Human Rights. (2008). *Rule of Law Tools for Post-conflict States: Maximizing the Legacy of Hybrid Courts*. Doc. E.08.XIV.12.

Open Society Justice Initiative. (2010). *Salvaging Judicial Independence: the Need for a Principled Completion Plan for the Extraordinary Chambers in the Courts of Cambodia*. Retrieved from http://www.opensocietyfoundations.org/reports/salvaging-judicial-independence-need-principled-completion-plan-extraordinary-chambers-courts

Open Society Justice Initiative. (2012). *The Future of Cases 003/004 at the Extraordinary Chambers in the Courts of Cambodia*. Retrieved from http://www.opensocietyfoundations.org/sites/default/files/eccc-report-cases3and4-100112_0.pdf

Pham, P., Vinck, P., & Hen, S. (2011). *After the first trial: a Population based Survey on Knowledge and Perceptions of Justice and the ECCC*. Berkley University Human Rights Centre.

Scheffer, D. (2008). The Extraordinary Chambers in the Courts of Cambodia. In C. Bassiouni (Ed.), International Criminal Law (Vol. III, pp. 219-256). Martinus Nijhoff, Netherlands.

Schrey, D. & Meisenberg, S. (2013). The Contribution of the Khmer Rouge Tribunal to Reconciliation, Remembrance and Memoralisation in Cambodia. *KAS International Reports*, 2013(4), 75-94.

The Court Report. Issue 71. (2014, April).

The Court Report. Issue 83. (2015, March).

The Court Report. Issue 84. (2015, April).

United Nations. (2004). *Report of Secretary-General on Khmer Rouge Trials* (Doc. A/59/432). Retrieved from http://www.unakrt-online.org/documents/report-secretary-general-khmer-rouge-trials-1

United Nations Development Programme. (2007). *Special Audit: Audit of Human Resources Management at the ECCC* (Report No. RCM0172). Retrieved on 05 October 2014, from http://www.unakrt-online.org/Docs/Other/2007-06-04%20UNDP%20Special%20Audit%20of%20ECCC%20HR.pdf

ADDITIONAL READING

Becker, E. (1998). *When the War was over: Cambodia and the Khmer Rouge Revolution*. New York, NY: Public Affairs.

Chandler, D. (1999). *Brother Number One: A Political Biography of Pol Pot*. Westview Press.

Chandler, D. (2008). *A history of Cambodia* (4th ed.). Westview Press.

Short, P. (2013). *Pol Pot: The History of a Nightmare*. Hodder & Stoughton.

Strangio, S. (2014). *Hun Sen's Cambodia*. Yale University Press.

KEY TERMS AND DEFINITIONS

Crimes Against Humanity: Crimes against humanity are certain acts when committed as part of a widespread or systematic attack directed against any civilian population. Unlike war crimes, crimes against humanity can be committed during peace or war. They are not isolated or sporadic events, but are part either of a government policy (although the perpetrators need not identify themselves with this policy) or of a wide practice of atrocities tolerated or condoned by a government or a de facto authority.

Genocide: Genocide means any of the following acts committed with intent to destroy, in whole or in part, a national, ethnical, racial or religious group, as such (a) Killing members of the group; (b) Causing serious bodily or mental harm to members of the group; (c) Deliberately inflicting on the group conditions of life calculated to bring about its physical destruction in whole or in part; (d) Imposing measures intended to prevent births within the group; (e) Forcibly transferring children of the group to another group.

Hybrid Court: Hybrid Courts usually apply a mix of national and international law (both procedural and substantial and feature a blend of international and national elements, in particular international and national judges and staff.

Khmer Rouge: A Cambodian Communist movement that was active as a guerrilla force from the 1960s to the 1990s and held power under the leadership of Pol Pot from 1975 to 1979.

Transitional Justice: Transitional justice refers to the set of judicial and non-judicial measures which are implemented in order to redress the legacy of massive human rights abuses. These measures include criminal prosecutions, truth commissions, reparations programs, and various kinds of institutional reforms.

Chapter 11
Gacaca Courts in Rwanda:
Experience and Perspectives

Gerd Hankel
Hamburg Institute for Social Research, Germany

ABSTRACT

This article deals with the past activities of the gacaca courts in Rwanda. The first section of the article will review the reasons for reactivating the gacaca courts and consider its theoretical suitability as a means of resolving conflicts. The second part offers a survey of the actual implementation and results of the gacaca trials. In the final section, the concrete effects of these results on the inner-Rwandan processes of pacification and reconciliation are assessed.

GACACA COURTS IN RWANDA: EXPERIENCE AND PERSPECTIVES

The topic that is the focus of this contribution is controversial. That is by no means surprising, since the occurrences—the genocide in Rwanda—which lead to its emerging as an issue are themselves highly controversial. What is contested is not the genocide itself. That it occurred is recognized by all but a few extremists. The debate centers instead around the question of which side one tends to support in interpreting the genocide and reaching the appropriate conclusions. On the one side, there is the official version of the current Rwandan government. Its representatives can rightly point to the fact that they ended the mass killings in an atmosphere of global indifference towards what was happening and therefore consider themselves morally justified in deciding alone in what forms and with what content the genocide, its perpetrators, and the memories of the crimes should be dealt with. On the other side, which includes many Rwandans in exile abroad, there are those who charge that the official Rwandan position and its supporters instrumentalize the genocide; they call for a historical narrative that can incorporate the experience of all Rwandans.

For reasons that will be presented below, the author of this text is also skeptical regarding the official Rwandan claim to the exclusive right to decide how to deal with the country's recent past. Despite some positive initiatives, the sum of the various measures and especially the ideology behind them reveal that Rwanda is in the midst of a problematic and potentially dangerous development.

DOI: 10.4018/978-1-4666-9675-4.ch011

At this point one might assert—and this is clearly the position taken by official German development aid policy[1]—that it is up to Rwandan policy makers alone to define and implement the path they choose to take to achieve a peaceful future for their country. One must agree with this in so far as, by definition, a government that meets the minimal requirements of a liberal-democratic order must fulfill the task of responsible and engaged efforts to meet the needs of its citizens. But what makes Rwanda, independent of these minimal requirements, a special case, is its history as the site of a crime against humanity that affects the international community as a whole.[2] This is the case despite the fact that the United Nations failed to attempt to prevent or at least curb the genocide, for the dimensions of the crime alone renders it a severe violation of the basic moral values of humankind. As a result, conversely, the manner in which these crimes are dealt with, including the judicial consequences and the means of achieving social peace in the country, are also significant beyond the borders of Rwanda. The international tribunal in Arusha, which prosecutes the planers and organizers of the genocide, was thus established by the United Nations (UN). The UN appointed non-Rwandan judges to try the cases. The reactivation of the traditional Gacaca justice system within Rwanda has been propagated by the Rwandan government itself as a model for resolving conflicts in the region (Ngoga, 2008, pp. 326-327) and indeed Rwanda takes great pains to present itself as a champion of peace and human rights, whose efforts are legitimated by its own experience of violence.[3] In view of these activities that go beyond the domestic sphere, criticism from outside Rwanda thus seems appropriate, especially since it focuses on aspects that are related not only to the modalities of these activities but indeed also to the understanding of Rwandan society in an ongoing process of modernization that underlies them.

Before the critique of Rwandan policy is explicated here, the first section of this text will review the reasons for reactivating the gacaca courts and consider its theoretical suitability as a means of resolving conflicts. The second part offers a survey of the actual implementation and results of the gacaca trials. In the final section, the concrete effects of these results on the inner-Rwandan processes of pacification and reconciliation are assessed. This assessment will examine whether and, if so, how Rwanda's ambivalent development can be considered compatible with the concept of transitional justice and the work of non-governmental organizations (NGOs) in Rwanda who support the concept and its implementation.

1. Reactivating the Gacaca Courts

During the Rwandan genocide, which occurred between April and July 1994, approximately eight hundred thousand people were murdered. The majority of the victims were Tutsi, a minority group within Rwanda's population, or Hutu who either supported the political opposition and were therefore suspected of siding with the Tutsi, had attracted envy and malevolence due to their social position, or had simply refused to participate in killing other Rwandans.[4]

Soon after the genocide ended on 4 July 1994, it was clear to both the international community and to those who had assumed political control in Rwanda that the perpetrators of the crimes committed during the genocide had to be prosecuted. The number of victims was much too high and the dimensions of terror too great to allow for a form of dealing with the crimes outside the realm of criminal justice. In November 1994, the UN Security Council, no doubt spurred by hopes that this step would mean that its failure to prevent or end the genocide might be forgotten more quickly, established the International Criminal Tribunal for

Rwanda, which was to prosecute those Rwandans who had used their high positions in politics, the military, or the police to prepare and carry out the genocide.[5] Arusha, a small town in Rwanda's neighboring country of Tanzania about one hour by plane from the Rwandan capital of Kigali was chosen as the court's seat. The distance of the court from the site of the crimes generated objections in Rwanda, which were further fueled by the decisions not to appoint a Rwandan judge and to exclude the death sentence as a possible punishment for those convicted[6] and, most especially, by the agreement that the court's jurisdiction would, according to its statute, not only extend to crimes of genocide but also to crimes against humanity and war crimes. Theoretically, at least, this meant that investigations could also be initiated against those who were in power in Rwanda after the genocide ended.[7]

Since its first judgment in September 1998, the court in Arusha has to date (July 2014) handed down fifty-two decisions; eleven are still pending. Twelve of these were acquittals; the rest of the defendants received long prison sentences, some life imprisonment. So far, the new ruling class in Rwanda has not had to face serious investigation and, as the chief prosecutor has stated, this is not at all likely to change.[8] Nonetheless, criticism of the court has continued to be voiced in Rwanda. However, these critiques address primarily what are seen, for example by Rwandan political figures, as modest and disappointing results on the backdrop of the court's million-dollar budget and the fact that it has been in existence for twenty years.[9]

It is thus unsurprising that Rwanda soon began prosecuting those accused of having been involved in the genocide itself. In August 1996, as a wave of Hutu who had fled to Zaire towards the end of the war—many of whom were suspected of being perpetrators of genocidal crimes—returned to Rwanda,[10] the new transitional parliament passed a law that was supposed to make it possible to prosecute genocidal crimes.[11] To speed the process of dealing with these cases, special courts were established in the criminal and military judicial bodies, which were to deal solely with genocidal crimes and other crimes committed during the period of the mass murder.

In the following years these courts processed some eight thousand cases.[12] This was obviously too few to cope with the constantly rising numbers of accused who were awaiting trial in Rwandan prisons. In 1996 already about one hundred thousand such prisoners were incarcerated, and by the end of the decade their number had risen to around one hundred thirty thousand. With about one thousand five hundred cases being decided per year, the special courts would have taken decades to try these accused, not even counting all the additional suspects who were identified during the course of other proceedings, because, for example, they were accomplices of others standing trial. Moreover, this would have meant that the accused were to be imprisoned under conditions that only euphemistically could be termed "difficult". The government prisons and municipal *cachots*, which had been built during the colonial period, were equipped to house only a fraction of the numbers of prisoners now held there. Disease and death were daily occurrences, one could only speculate about the long-term psychological effects, and it went without saying that the incarceration of so many Rwandans for an indefinite period was bound to exacerbate the already daunting preconditions for establishing social peace in this conflict-ridden country.

In this situation, a solution seemed to lie in making use of an adjudicative tradition that could be institutionalized on the scale required without excessive cost and effort and also offered the advantage of moving the proceedings from the limited space of the existing courts and opening them up for a larger public, to serve educational goals. Gacaca [13] was this traditional Rwandan adjudicative form, which, as the name suggests—*gacaca* means grass or meadow—was aimed at involving as many people as possible in the proceedings. Under the leadership of people respected by the local community, the *Inyangamugayo* (meaning roughly "those who abhor dishonor"), the inhabitants of a village gather outdoors for the gacaca to resolve disputes. In this assembly, the focus was not on assigning blame to a specific individual or to her or his family or clan. Rather, it was important that the accused or a member of his or her family admit that specific behavior was unacceptable and, if necessary, undertake some form of reparation or contrition. The chief goal of a gacaca proceeding was thus to restore social peace; to this end, a ritual act was performed at the end of the public assembly.[14]

Gacaca justice was originally applicable for all disputes and perceived violations of the legal order but was limited to disputes within the realm of civil law by the colonial government in 1924. (Rwanda became a Belgian mandate territory after World War I). This state did not change after the country gained independence in 1962, but throughout these decades, the importance of the gacaca system generally declined, as this traditional adjudicative form was increasingly supplanted by the government court system.[15]

Reactivation of traditional gacaca justice to deal with criminal offenses resulted in two problems. First, this form of justice had to be extended to again apply to criminal acts while continuing to adhere to the prohibition of collective punishment that was also one of the basis legal principles in Rwandan jurisprudence. Guilt therefore had to be individualized and a specific perpetrator identified without a doubt for a specific crime.[16] Second, rules had to be drawn up for the proceedings and for the courts' composition, their jurisdiction, and their capacity to pass sentences, as well as for opportunities to appeal decisions. Both of these preconditions were met with five further laws passed by the Rwandan parliament beginning in 2001, with the last law passed in 2008.[17] These changes in the laws had become necessary because earlier regulations had proven impractical, lacking in clarity, or simply counterproductive. For example, the number of lay judges elected by the local population[18] as Inyangamugayo was reduced from nearly twenty per gacaca court to seven. Negotiations within the gacaca courts had been too time consuming, but, more importantly, numerous judges had had to be replaced because it was discovered that they have been involved in the genocide in one way or another. Furthermore, the categories that had been developed for classifying suspects were changed. The original four categories, which paralleled the provisions of the 1996 law establishing the special genocide courts, were later reduced to three. At the same time, opportunities to differentiate within the category, especially with respect to individual participation in a crime and the severity of the sentence, were improved. Perpetrators in category 1 were again defined as those who had used their high-ranking positions in politics or as a member of the military or police to plan, organize, or implement the genocide and those suspected of committing sexual torture or rape.[19] Category 2 was now extended considerably and encompassed those accused of crimes that effected or threatened other persons' life and health, thus ranging from murder (including multiple murders) to manslaughter and assault and battery.[20] Category 3 included those suspected of property offenses such as theft or looting.[21] Finally, in another change in the relevant laws, attendance at the gacaca trials was made mandatory for the local adult population. In the introductory phase of gacaca in 2002, there had been no such provision, since the authorities had expected a high level of interest in the proceedings. However, participation by the local inhabitants had soon declined considerably, so there were fears that the expected broad educational effect would not be forthcoming. The provisions on mandatory attendance and participation went into effect in June 2004,[22] and sanctions in the form of fines and short prison sentences were effective, as experience showed, in enforcing this law.

Following a pilot phase that began at selected sites in 2002 and ended in 2004, gacaca courts were established in all of the almost ten thousand cells and about one thousand five hundred sectors of Rwanda.[23] Gacaca courts on the cell level were charged with collecting information on the occurrences within that cell in the period from 1 October 1990 (beginning of the civil war) to 31 December 1994 (final suppression of uprisings by extremist Hutu in Rwanda). On the basis of this information, they were then to assign the accused to one of the three categories and to preside over the cases of suspects from category 3. Gacaca courts on the sector level were to deal with crimes in category 2 and were also the appeals courts for decisions reached on the cell level. A third type of gacaca courts were the appeals courts for decisions of the sectoral-level gacaca courts pertaining to category 2-crimes.[24] Crimes of the first category fell exclusively into the jurisdiction of the regular courts or the military courts until spring 2008. The assumption behind this was that the type of crime to be dealt with (sexual torture, rape) precluded public proceedings, and the complexity of the cases and the educational status of the accused organization of the genocide by national and local elites might be too great a challenge for the gacaca judges. Since May 2008, however, rape and sexual torture crimes as well as crimes perpetrated by planers and organizers of the genocide who had previously worked in the country's administration, the police, army, or the churches up to the level of municipalities and sub-prefectures (*commune*, *sous-préfecture*) could also be tried before sector-level gacaca courts.[25] This extension of the sphere of jurisdiction of the gacaca courts had become necessary because, due to the investigations and trials conducted up to 2008, the number of accused in category 1 had risen to a level that made it impossible for the regular criminal and military courts to deal with these cases in an acceptable period of time.

Gacaca courts were authorized to hand down sentences that ranged from imprisonment for one to thirty years for category-2 crimes and between twenty years and life imprisonment for category-1 crimes. Those convicted of property offenses (category 3) were subject only to compensation of damages. Minors who were between the ages of 14 and 18 at the time of the crime could be sentenced to imprisonment for six months to twenty years in category 2 and between six and one half months and twenty-five years for category 1.[26] The remarkably wide range of possible sentences for crimes form category 1 and 2 is a result of the intention of the relevant laws to reflect the traditional gacaca purpose of reestablishing social peace. Those who confessed to their crimes and asked publically for the forgiveness of the local population in credible form could receive a milder sentence.[27] The earlier the defendant confessed and expressed remorse, the milder the sentence would be. In the best possible case, that is, if the confession and declaration of remorse was forthcoming before the gacaca court had begun dealing with the concrete charges, those accused of category-1 crimes could receive prison sentence of "only" twenty years (for minors six and one half years). The sentence of a category-2 defendant might be reduced in the case of murder, including even multiple murders, to only eight years (two and one half years for minors). Moreover, accused who had confessed to category-2 crimes (for category-1 crimes only minors) were eligible for generous opportunities for probation and substitute sentenced. Even in murder cases, the law provided that decisions could be reached that meant that the perpetrators would only serve one-sixth of the complete prison term. One-third of the sentence would be changed to probation and for the remaining one-half of the original prison sentence, the convicted individual would be obliged to do public-service work (*travaux d'intérêt général*) such as building houses for survivors of the genocide, repairing streets, or building irrigation systems and clearing new fields.

Public-service work as an expression of active remorse, reduced sentences and sentences commuted to probation, large public groups as witnesses of the trials that can also testify to the credibility of the process of investigating occurrences and identifying the guilty, based on experience—all of these are elements that would seem to make the gacaca courts an ideal means of resolving conflicts. Few arguments to the contrary are in sight and these are easily refuted. The potential alternative of a reconciliation commission was not feasible in a situation in which for many weeks similar numbers of people were killed daily as died throughout the final decades of the South African apartheid regime. And to rigorously insist on passing sentences that, at face value, would have been in keeping with the dimensions of the genocide was ultimately not a viable alternative, since long prison sentences for a large number of perpetrators would have divided the country for many more years to come. Gacaca justice and its combination of punishment and reconciliatory elements thus was, so a tentative conclusion, the most appropriate form of adjudicative system for ensuring that after the genocide Rwanda would not only experience pacification in the short term but also achieve sustainable peace, thanks to rapprochement within society and the perspective of reconciliation.

2. Implementation and Results of the Gacaca Trials

Whoever traveled in Rwanda in the summer of 2002 saw large roadside billboards depicting scenes of violence and people weighted down by great pain and suffering. These images reminding people of the horrors of the genocide and its aftermath bore the headline "Gacaca Justice" and below these words, in somewhat smaller type, "The truth heals. When we say, what we have seen, when we confess, what we have done, our wounds will be closed." This sensitization campaign, as it was called in Rwanda, was accompanied by various measures in preparation for beginning the gacaca trials. More than ten thousand judges—including, for the first time in the history of the gacaca system, female judges—were prepared for their work in courses lasting several weeks; they learned about the make-up and function of the gacaca courts and how the trials were to be conducted (How can one determine whether a confession is complete and sincere? What are the rights of victims and witnesses during the proceedings? How are charges to be assessed in legal terms, and how is a decision formulated?).[28] Special attention was paid to presenting the three steps that made up the core elements of the gacaca trial, since these are the litmus test for the significance of the trials as a motor of national reconciliation. The first of these procedural steps is to determine what occurred during the genocide on the territory of a specific cell. To this end, the inhabitants of a hill assemble, and each is called on to report on everything she or he observed. The intention is that the truth will be determined, the suffering of the victims is recounted, and the perpetrators' crimes are identified. In the second step, occurrences are attributed to individual accused persons; in other words, the community of inhabitants of the cell determines in a process of public debate to what extent a specific person committed criminal acts or not. If there is substantial reason to suspect an individual was involved in crimes, the accused are classified into one of the three categories of crimes. The third step is finally the trial itself, in which the court decides in a public assembly[29] whether the defendant did in fact perpetrate the crimes. The decisions reached must be documented in written form (Cour Suprême, 2001, pp. 18 ff). At no point during the trial are the accused provided with legal counsel. But the defendants also do not have to face a prosecutor who attempts to implement the state's intention to impose punishment. In the gacaca tradition, the local community alone is supposed to take sides for or against the accused and thus determine the decision of the "wise men and women".

When the gacaca trials began on 19 June 2002 (at first in twelve sectors, then, from November 2002 on, in another 106 sectors) (Inkiko, 2014), expectations were high on all sides. The victims, or rather survivors of the genocide sought, finally justice. They wanted those responsible for the death of their relatives and their own injuries to be punished, wanted to know where and how the murders occurred, and where the bodies were buried. Those in prison, in turn, hoped that they would get no more than a short sentence or the confirmation that they were innocent. The Rwandan state hoped that its rhetoric of reconciliation would soon be made concrete and confirmed, and the international community, represented locally by numerous NGOs, was highly interested in observing whether the gacaca courts would fulfill expectations and perhaps even serve as a model for dealing with other conflicts in the region.

The beginnings were encouraging. Participation in many places was high. Sitting in a semicircle in front of the judges, the inhabitants of the villages spoke about what had happened, voiced accusations, called on prisoners who were brought before the assembly to make confessions, offered detailed testimony, or vehemently defended the accused. They were willing to accept the fact that this meant, once a week for several hours, they would be unable to cultivate their fields or do other work. What emerged was something like a collective feeling that a historical moment had opened up, which could not be allowed to pass without being put to use, since it might be an opportunity to secure peace for their country. Unfortunately, the feeling soon disappeared. People's interest in gacaca dwindled, due at first to the fact that the trials dragged on for months without tangible results. After having to report on their suffering again and again, having to wait longer and longer for the court decisions and for reparations, finally many people simply stayed home. The survivors had had very different notions of how justice would be administered, especially since thousands of prisoners had been set free following a communiqué issued by transitional president Paul Kagame on 1 January 2003.[30] Although this was not a final decision that the released would remain in freedom, because these former prisoners still had to stand trial before gacaca courts, the victims nonetheless now might face meeting the perpetrators of crimes against themselves or their families in their neighborhood. Indeed, as reports show, such encounters in fact often did occur and, in the eyes of many victims, soon became a symbol of the authorities' disregard for their plight.

That the perpetrators and the Hutu more generally were increasingly dissatisfied was due to what they perceived as a disappointing development of the proceedings. The reconstruction of occurrences proved to be an intensive, time-consuming process, and decisions, including acquittals, were a long time in coming. As already noted above, the numbers of the accused increased significantly as a result of witness testimony. This last aspect in particular—by no means an unusual phenomenon when mass crimes are dealt with by the judiciary—was perceived as proof of a desire for revenge. Although this impression was grounded only in references to isolated cases, for the vast majority of the Hutu population it was convincingly confirmed by the fact that the gacaca courts only investigated crimes perpetrated against the Tutsi. Hutu were focused on as the victims of crimes only if these crimes occurred within the context of the genocide—in other words, when the Hutu had died in connection with acts of violence that had targeted Tutsi. As a result, the murders of Hutu by Tutsi soldiers during the civil war—it was estimated that several ten thousand such murders had been committed (Des Forges, 1999)—were not considered, although they should have been investigated according to the letter of the various laws that had been passed to reactivate the gacaca courts.[31]

This problematic constellation did not change after 2005, when gacaca trials began in all sectors of the country. Although in the interim and concomitant with the trials the Rwandan state had implemented intensified measures to improve the genocide victims' situation (free medical care in some cases, exemption from school fee, help in building housing), many victims remain highly skeptical in view of the generous reductions of sentences for perpetrators who have confessed and the provisional release of prisoners. And among Hutu, discontent over the victor's justice, which is how they refer to the gacaca courts off the record, has even increased.

Those who arrived at Kigali airport in summer 2012 could see a poster hanging behind the counter where visas were issued that announced in German "Gacaca: the foundation for sustainable justice and reconciliation". The poster could also be seen elsewhere in Rwanda and was intended to be an unequivocal and compelling summary of gacaca justice, which was ended with an official ceremony in Rwanda's parliament on 18 June 2012, ten years to the day after it began. At that event, President Paul Kagame had a similar message to convey. "We all know the value and the role of Gacaca." And he added, "What these courts achieved went beyond anyone's expectations. They administered justice and united Rwandans at the same time. These courts were evidence of our ability to find solutions for the challenges that seemed insurmountable."[32]

Indeed, what the gacaca courts have achieved in the past ten years is impressive. Some thirteen thousand courts reached decisions on nearly two million criminal charges; about one million people were prosecuted, the vast majority of them (90 percent) male. By far the largest group of trials (67 percent) involved category-3 crimes such as theft and property damage; these were followed by category 2 with murder, manslaughter, or aggravated assault and battery (29 percent), and by crimes from category 1, the planning and organizing of genocide or perpetrating sexual violence, for example in the form of rape (4 percent). Exactly how many defendants were acquitted is not known. According to estimates, on an average 15 percent were acquitted, with the numbers varying from one category to the next.

The process of dealing with the history of the genocide on the judicial level is thus now completed for the most part. Rwanda will conduct a few more trials of individuals accused of crimes in association with the genocide in the next few years, but these are proceedings that have been referred to the Rwandan courts by the International Criminal Tribunal for Rwanda in Arusha. The mandate of that court ends in 2014. These proceedings will take place under international supervision, as it were, and, because they involve representatives or henchman of the genocidal regime, they have little or nothing to do with the events on a local level, which were dealt with by the gacaca courts. It was there, in particular, that the foundation was to be created for a new, socially united, and peaceful Rwanda.

3. Assessment of Results

It would be no doubt exaggerated to expect that any form of dealing with the history of mass crimes of dimensions like those of Rwandan genocide could produce solutions that satisfy all those involved. This is especially the case because the Rwandan genocide has several specific features that distinguish it from others, such as the Shoa or the genocide perpetrated against the Armenians. First, it occurred in only one country, and there were no special units that terrorized specific groups of the population who lived outside its borders. Second, a large majority of the country's inhabitants participated in the crimes, and no one could convincingly claim that they had no knowledge of the massacres. Third, survivors had no opportunities to emigrate permanently. They were forced to live with the perpetrators and their supporters in one country, in Rwanda.

From this perspective, it is almost surprising that criticism of the gacaca justice has not been more vehement. But as foreign observers can ascertain after a relatively short time, Rwandan society is locked into a reconciliation postulate that absorbs all criticism. Not a single day goes by without the media disseminating this postulate, politicians evoking it, or representatives of civil society calling for its implementation. The aim is to reconstruct Rwanda, making it a country that, as the preamble of the constitution states, has learned its lessons from its disastrous past and now turns, in a state of national unity, to a peaceful future.[33]

This determination, together with a commitment to human and civil rights that is also part of the constitution,[34] has made Rwanda the focus of attention for international NGOs for many years and has rendered it a popular object of academic research focusing on so-called transitional justice. Not all of those who have followed events in Rwanda are convinced that the country is following the right path. Nonetheless, the voices of those whose assessment is positive, whether with or without qualifications, are considerably more numerous. Anglo-American literature, in particular, has followed the Rwandan process of dealing with the country's history from a decidedly affirmative perspective (Longman, 2008, pp. 206-228; Clark, 2009, pp. 297-319). But approval is also clearly the dominant reaction in the offices of organizations from continental Europe who are active in the country. Both in Rwanda and elsewhere, this approval stems from the impression that seems to be confirmed by the determination described above. Rwanda is in motion, its leadership is addressing the country's problems with pragmatic energy; the economic upswing is apparent, and the government's plan for the future, called Vision 2020, offers a clearly defined perspective.[35] According to these positive opinions, if we compare Rwanda with its neighbors, then it becomes obvious that Rwanda has taken an impressive leap in its development. Although it is also impossible to ignore the fact that the state authorities and their control are very much in evidence in nearly all areas of life, the need of many Rwandans, especially the genocide survivors,[36] for reassurances with respect to security should not be underestimated.

All these are no doubt substantial reasons for confirming an overall positive assessment. But what is problematic, and may perhaps have dangerous consequences, is the fact that these reasons are based on a foundation, the stability of which is far from being secure. This fundament consists of a historiographical narrative that can be heard and read throughout the country in the media, in the schools, and on every level of governmental administration. It can be summarized as follows—without oversimplifying: The poison of racism was introduced into Rwanda by the colonial powers, first the Germans and then the Belgians. A society that had lived in harmony up to that point developed two antagonistic groups within the population, one of which, the Hutu as the majority, claimed exclusive power for itself when the country became independent (1 July 1962). It was supported in this aim by Belgium as the former colonial power and by the Catholic Church, since both feared a loss of their own influence. As a result of the new state ideology, referred to as Hutuism, hundreds of thousands of Tutsi were driven out of the country. Attempts to return were suppressed with military force and lead to massacres against the Tutsi who had remained in Rwanda, massacres that became pogroms. The sustained climate of suppression and violence spawned an ideology of annihilation, which intensified from 1990 on, when the extremist Hutu regime of Juvénal Habyarimana saw its power threatened, and lead to concrete plans to perpetrate a genocide. According to this narrative, the crash of Habyarimana's plane on the evening of 6 April 1994[37] was a welcome trigger but not the actual reason for the genocide (Sebasoni, 2007, pp. 9.29, 160.178)[38].

This narrative has little in common with the historical realities that are substantiated by numerous documents and can be corroborated by examining the evidence. That the genocide took place is incontestable. Also incontestable is the way in which the militant opposition of the *Front patriotique rwandais* (FPR)/*Rwandan Patriotic Front* (RPF), which was the predecessor of Paul Kagame's rebel army, significantly contributed with its aggressive-apodictical policies to fueling hatred and an annihilatory mindset. The FPR/RPF were responsible for beginning the civil war on 1 October 1990. As a result of the conflict, large numbers of refugees, most of whom were Hutu, were forced to live under inhuman conditions in huge camps (Dallaire, R. & Beardsley, B. 2003). While it is unclear whether the FPR/RPF actually shot down the presidential airplane, it is responsible for murdering Hutu during the war, during the genocide, and in the ensuing phase in which the power relations in the country were being consolidated; by legal definition, these are crimes against humanity. There were more than one hundred thousand such murders. It is likely that the number actually exceeds two hundred thousand (Hintjens, 2009, pp. 82-85; Prunier, 2009, pp. 147-8), and although not all of these murders fall under the jurisdiction *ratione temporis* of the gacaca courts, in the collective memory of Rwanda's Hutu population, they form a single unit that warrants assigning the Hutu the status not only of perpetrators but also of victims. But this perspective was absolutely taboo in the gacaca trials: those who merely allude to such an idea were the targets of intense threats and attempts at intimidation coming from members of the military or the police who present at the trials. Tutsi are not perpetrators—that is, very briefly, the subtext of gacaca justice. And by disseminating this message, the gacaca system—which has even been established in Rwanda's constitution—[39] has been assigned a significant, if not the most significant function in cementing a historical narrative that serves to maintain power relations and their justification. The gacaca message is complemented and intensified through *ingando*, an institution that is also rooted in Rwandan traditions (originally conceptualized as an obligatory reintegration program lasting as long as three months for those formerly imprisoned for genocidal crimes, in which as many as one thousand participants, including school and university students and civil servants, were instructed in the official Rwandan version of the country's history and in civics),[40] and *itorero* (obligatory training programs lasting several weeks, especially for educators and others whose work involves dissemination and outreach functions)[41] as well as a variety of measures implemented by the legislature, all of which aim, with increasingly rigid methods,[42] to install the historical narrative presented by the state as the uncontested truth. It is as if an increasingly tight net is being spread over Rwandan society and stifling every expression of a view that is critical, or perceived as such. It is thus unsurprising that recognized NGOs that are engaged in maintaining and promoting human rights consider Rwanda to be a restrictive state with a highly problematic track record in this area (N.A., 2008).

Nonetheless, should we not consider the perceived need of a country and many of its citizens for security more important than a flawless or at least acceptable record in maintaining human rights? Is it not imperative that peace be established, if necessary with heavy-handed methods, before, after a period of general consolidation, a more comprehensive perspective on the past can be adopted? To answer these questions in the affirmative would mean one condones the way journalists are threatened and attacked; condones the status of freedom of the press, which in Rwanda is on a level similar to that in Iran or Somalia; condones the way the secret police creates a climate of fear and mistrust; condones abuse of prisoners and the disappearance of undesirable persons.[43] If we consider that the fundamental understanding of transitional justice defines as obligatory goals, whether in the short-term or the long-term, recognition of victims and the promotion of peace, reconciliation, and democracy,[44] and presents these as goals that cannot be pursued in name only or as a camouflage, then Rwanda's gacaca courts can hardly be referred to as a form of transitional justice. There is no reason to expect that numerous and massive violations of (human) rights will at some point give way to just practices, just as it is unlikely that mere empty catchwords about democracy and freedom will contribute to the emergence of truly democratic and peaceful conditions. To rely on civil society where there is no such entity, where the state—from the highest echelons of power down to the smallest administrative unit of the *nyumbakumi* (who heads ten households)—determines the course of political and social life is a mistake, which becomes no less serious if human rights standards are verbosely evoked in developmental cooperation.[45] In this situation, it may indeed be more honest to leave it up to the Rwandans to decide how to deal with their past. But in this case one should also be prepared to accept the possible consequence, i.e., that this undertaking might go very wrong. Should that occur, then one would at least have the reassurance of not having contributed to this outcome due to a *déformation professionnelle* that spawns unwarranted optimism, a lack of knowledge, or a naïve outlook.

REFERENCES

Aftrol Staff Writer. (2008). Rwanda's Commonwealth accession questioned. *Afrol News*. Retrieved from http://www.afrol.com/articles/33812

Centre de Gestions des Conflits. (2001). *Les juridictions Gacaca et le processus de réconciliation nationale*. Kigali.

Clark, P. (2009). The Rules (and Politics) of Engagement: The Gacaca Courts and Post-Genocide Justice, Healing and Reconciliation in Rwanda. In P. Clark, & Z. Kaufman (Eds.), After Genocide (pp. 297-319).

Cour Suprême. (2001). *Manuel explicatif sur la loi organique portant création des juridictions Gacaca.*

Dallaire, R. & Beardsley, B. (2003). Shake hands with the devil: the failure of humanity in Rwanda.

Des Forges, A. (1999). *Leave None to Tell the Story: Genocide in Rwanda*. New York: Human Rights Watch.

Digneffe, F., & Fierens, J. (2003). *Justice et gacaca. L'expérience rwandaise et le genocide*. Namur: Presses Universitaires de Namur.

Hassan, B. J. (2009, June 22). Rwanda: Letter from Hassan B. Jallow to Kenneth Roth. Retrieved from http://reliefweb.int/report/rwanda/rwanda-letter-hassan-b-jallow-kenneth-roth-22-jun-2009

Hintjens, H. (2009). Reconstructing political identities in Rwanda. In P Clark, & Z.D. Kaufman (Eds.), After Genocide (pp. 82-85).

Kagame, G. (2008). UN Security Council extends ICTR mandate. *New Times*, 1–2.

Lichterbeck, P. (2009). *Der Aufbruch von Kigali* (p. 5). Der Tagesspiegel.

Longman, T. (2008). Justice at the grassroots? Gacaca trials in Rwanda. In N. Roht-Arriaza & J. Mariezcurrena (Eds.), *Transitional justice in the twenty-first century. Beyond truth versus justice* (pp. 206–228). Cambridge.

Muesi, F. (2008, September 6). Rwanda's input to solve part of UNAMID's problems – Karake. *New Times*, 3.

Mutara, E. (2009, March 7). 156 genocide survivors and witnesses killed. The New Times.

Ngoga, M. (2008). The institutionalisation of impunity: A judicial perspective on the Rwandan Genocide. In P. Clark & Z. D. Kaufman (Eds.), *After genocide: Transitional justice, post-conflict reconstruction and reconciliation in Rwanda and beyond, London* (pp. 326–327). Hurst.

Prunier, G. (2009). *From genocide to continental war. The 'Congolese' conflict and the crisis of contemporary Africa*. London: Hurst & Co.

Prunier G. (2008). *The Rwanda crisis: History of a genocide* (6th ed., p. 312). London: Colombia University Press.

Sebasoni, S. (2001, December 18-31). Gacaca: Une justice que le peuple rwandais comprend. *Grands Lacs Hebdo* (pp. 25f).

Servilien, M. S. (2007). Le Rwanda. Reconstruire une nation (pp. 9-29, 160-178).

Wibabara, C. (2014). *Gacaca Courts versus the International Criminal Tribunal for Rwanda and the National Courts* (pp. 107–159). Baden-Baden.

World Health Organization. (2014). VISION 2020. Retrieved from http://www.theeye.co.rw/vision_2020.php

ENDNOTES

1 Eva Gmelin, director of the Rwandan office of the Deutscher Entwicklungsdienst (German Development Service), declared in a conversation with the author in May 2009 that it was to be "taken for granted" that it was up to the Rwandans to decide how to deal with their past.

2 The preamble to the Rome Statute for the International Criminal Court affirms "that the most serious crimes of concern to the international community as a whole must not go unpunished…." (http://www.un.org/law/icc/, accessed September 6, 2014). Among the most serious crimes listed in article 5 of the Statute are, in this order, a) genocide, b) crimes against humanity, c) war crimes, d) the crime of aggression.

3 This is, for example, the case through the Rwanda's involvement in the UN mission in Darfur, UNAMID. See (Muesi, 2008). Rwanda's input to solve part of UNAMID's problems – Karake. *The New Times*, p. 3.

4 In 1994, about ten percent of Rwanda's population of 7.5 million were Tutsi, 85 percent were Hutu, and only about one percent belonged to the group called Twa, who were hardly involved in the genocide; see (Des Forges, 1999, pp. 37).

5 See Resolution 955 (1994) from November 8, 1994, http://www1.umn.edu/humanrts/peace/docs/scres955.html, accessed September 6, 2014.

6 According to Article 23, paragraph 1 of the resolution, in determining the terms of imprisonment, the courts "shall have recourse to the general practice regarding prison sentences in the courts of Rwanda." The death sentence was in effect in Rwanda until summer 2007.

7 The genocide was the extreme occurrence in a war that began with an attack of the *Armée patriotique rwandaise* (APR), the military organization of the *Front patriotique rwandaise* (FPR) or Rwandan Patriotic Front (RPF), on the northern border of Rwanda on 1 October 1990. Commander-in-chief of the APR was Paul Kagame, who is the current president of Rwanda and also the head of the FPR.

8 See the letter of Hassan B. Jallow, prosecutor of the ICTR, at http://reliefweb.int/report/rwanda/rwanda-letter-hassan-b-jallow-kenneth-roth-22-jun-2009 (Jallow, 2008).

9 The most recent such statement: (Kagame, 2008).

10 As a result of the APR's successful advance, beginning in late Ende April 1994, some two million Hutu fled to Rwanda's neighboring countries, with the largest group, about 1.3 million people seeking refuge in Zaire. See (Prunier, 2008, pp. 312).

11 Loi organique n° 8/96 du 30/8/1996 sur l'organisation des poursuites des infractions constitutives du crime du génocide ou des crimes contre l'humanité, commises à partir du 1er octobre 1990. In *Journal Officiel* no. 17, September 1, 1996.

12 On the trials see (Charity Wibabara, 2014, pp. 107-159).

13 The letter c in the word gacaca is pronounced like the ch in the English word "church".

14 This could involve drinking a mug of beer together. Serious crimes such as murder might lead to a marriage being arranged between the feuding parties. See (Digneffe, f. & fierens, J. 2003, pp. 12).

15 Université nationale du Ruanda (Centre de Gestions des Conflits, 2001; Servilien M. Sebasoni, 2001, pp. 25f).

16 This is stipulated in article 14 of the International Covenant on Civil and Political Rights of 1966, which Rwanda ratified in 1975.

17 Loi organique n° 40/2000 du 26/01/2001 portant création des "juridictions Gacaca" et organisation des poursuites des infractions constitutives du crime du génocide ou de crimes contre l'humanité, commises entre le 1er octobre 1990 et le 31 décembre 1994. The last law past is Loi organique n° 13/2008 du 19/05/2008 modifiant et complétant la Loi Organique no. 16/2004 du 19/6/2004 portant organisation, compétence et fonctionnement des Juridictions Gacaca chargées des poursuites et du jugement des infractions constitutives du crime de génocide et d'autres crimes contre l'humanité commis entre le 1er octobre 1990 et le 31 décembre 1994 telle que modifiée et complétée à ce jour.

18 Every Rwandan above the age of eighteen is eligible to vote.

19 See article 11 of the Loi Organique n° 10/2007 of 1 March 2007.

20 Ibid.

21 Ibid.

22 See article 29 of the Loi Organique n° 16/2004 of 9 June 2004.

23 Rwanda has four administrative levels; beginning on the lowest level there are cells, sectors, districts, and finally the four provinces (the Northern, Southern, Eastern, and Western Provinces) and the capital, Kigali.

24 See article 41, 42, 43, and 53 of the law of June 2004 and article 7, 8, and 9 of the law of March 2007.

25 See article 7 and 9 of the law of May 2008.

26 See article 14 of the law of June 2007 and article 17 and 20 of the law of 2008.

27 This was already the case for trials before the special courts but was revised for the gacaca courts.

28 For more information see (Cour Suprême, 2001, pp. 32ff., 117f., 133ff) -*Manuel explicatif sur la loi organique portant création des juridictions Gacaca*, n.p.,.

29 Closed session trials were obligatory in rape cases, see article 6 of the law of May 2008.

30 Further communiqués followed; they all were related to old (seventy years and above) or young (less than eighteen) prisoners or those who were ill who had been accused of less serious crimes or who had made complete confessions.

31 The jurisdiction of the Gacaca courts, which had been set out by law, was from 1 October 1990, the beginning of the civil war, to 31 December 1994, the official end of the fighting. The courts' jurisdiction applies to crimes of genocide and other crimes against humanity. The latter includes crimes against civilians, if they were perpetrated systematically on a larger scale.

32 Quoted from President's speech, at the 18th Commemoration of the 1994 Genocide against the Tutsi. In: *Rwanda Dispatch*, April-May 2012, p. 8.

33 See Nr. 1, 4, 5 in der preamble to the constitution of 4 June 2003.

34 Paragraph 9 of the preamble, article 10-44 (Chapter one: Fundamental Human Rights).

35 On Vision 2020 see the document retrieved from http://www.theeye.co.rw/vision_2020.php, accessed September 6, 2014; on economic development see http://allafrica.com/stories/200909110208.html, accessed September 6, 2014.

36 Between 1995 and 2008, 156 genocide survivors and witnesses who had testified in trials against those suspected of genocide crimes were reportedly killed. (Mutara, 2009, p.2).

37 On board the plane were, besides President Habyarimana, the president of Burundi, also a Hutu, and a number of high-ranking officers of the Rwandan army. The plane was shot down by a missile.

38 See Servilien M. Sebasoni: *Le Rwanda. Reconstruire une nation*. Kigali 2007, pp. 9-29, 160-178.

39 See articles 143 and 152 of the constitution from 4 June 2003.

40 See http://www.nurc.gov.rw/index.php?option=com_content&view=article&id=50&Itemid=12, accessed September 6, 2014.

41 See the document retrieved from http://allafrica.com/stories/200805190212.html.

42 The last law to go into effect, on 23 July 2008, was the Law Relating to the Punishment of the Crime of Genocide Ideology, which, despite the lack of clarity regarding what constituted genocidal ideology (see article 2), imposed heavy sentences for disseminating such ideologies, such as arrest in a home for delinquent minors foras much as twelve months; for youths between fourteen and sixteen prison between five and twelve and one-half years and for their parents prison sentences between fifteen and twenty-five years (see article 9 and 11).

43 An Italian priest told the author in September 2009 that in his parish in northern Rwanda people who had "problems" with the authorities regularly disappeared.

44 See the definition on http://ictj.org/en/tj/#, accessed September 6, 2014.

45 On the status of human rights in development cooperation see, for example, the brochure published by the Deutsche Gesellschaft für Technische Zusammenarbeit (GTZ), one of the predecessors of the Gesellschaft für internationale Zusammenarbeit (GIZ, German Federal Enterprise for International Cooperation), which was founded on 1 January 2011: *Das ABC der Menschenrechte in der Entwicklungszusammenarbeit*, Eschborn, February 2009.

Section 3

The Turbulent Iraq

Chapter 12
Enforcing Central Authority:
Nuri al-Maliki and the Tradition of Iraq's Authoritarian State

Hauke Feickert
Center for Near- and Middle Eastern Studies (CNMS), Germany

ABSTRACT

This article brings together historical and political research in order to give an account of Iraq's recurring authoritarianism. Focusing on the agency of three distinct state elites, it will compare how these networks used cooptation and coercion to dominate their respective political arena. As a part of this, structural aspects like the allurement of the centralized state economic and the aspect of Western assistance in the (re)building of a central authority will join the analysis. However, the article will be primarily concerned with Iraqi politicians, their authorship of authoritarianism, their efforts to build a "modern" nation and their attempts to overrule dissent. The main interest of this inquiry is for the present and recent past: As Iraq has shaken off the oppression of 35 years of dictatorship, the new democratic system has shown to be extremely susceptible for a renewal of the authoritarian tradition.

INTRODUCTION

In April 2014 Nuri al-Maliki campaigned as Iraq's strongman and led his "State of Law" alliance to victory in the national elections. While many had called him a tyrant, incapable of uniting a divided country, Iraq's prime minister obviously had not lost his appeal: Gathering 24% of the vote, his party became the strongest force in parliament. Especially in the Shia-Arab community of the south many had subscribed to his call for a new majority government, stronger, more efficient, and free from quarrels with the other parties of the outgoing national unity coalition. Right after the results were published Maliki called on various smaller entities to rally behind him, threatening thereby to divide his opponents and to exclude prominent politicians from the Sunni-Arab and Sunni-Kurdish constituencies. After eight years in power Maliki's party now seemed close to gain absolute control over the state. Indeed, many scholars had predicted this new Iraqi authoritarian-

DOI: 10.4018/978-1-4666-9675-4.ch012

ism, as Maliki had sidelined the constitution and outmaneuvered parliamentary opposition for years (Dodge 2013; Rayburn 2014; Visser 2010). Building a considerable network of support, Maliki had increasingly answered demands for power-sharing, protests against corruption and calls for provincial autonomy with force. However, all of Maliki's efforts were crushed in June of 2014, when the government lost control over the city of Mosul to the jihadist group "Islamic State". Public opinion turned sharply against the prime minister, who had to step down within weeks. Nevertheless, many observers have been arguing that a mere change in personal would not be enough to protect Iraqis from a transgressive state (Russel & Sambanis 2014). For as much as the recent rise in authoritarianism has been caused by the now dismissed prime minister, its roots can be traced back to a particular perseverance of elite politics. Joining this debate, the present article seeks to analyze and compare how various political elites in the history of the country envisioned Iraq's central state as the essential tool for social unification and economic modernization.

BACKGROUND

The article will use the classical definition of authoritarianism by Juan Linz to review the rule of the three elitist social groups who shaped Iraq in the 20th century (Linz 2000). Drawing on Linz, the article will discuss their claims for legitimacy and analyze their amount of popular support. It will then view the disconnect of the regimes with society and their efforts to control the population. In this part, the weakening of legal and institutional power as well as the recourse to violence will be examined. In the final conclusion, the recurrence of elitist rule and of claims for modernization as well as the persistent significance of cooptation and coercion will be juxtaposed to explain authoritarian instability in Iraq.

MAIN FOCUS OF THE CHAPTER

The first period to be discussed will be the Hashemite Monarchy and the rule of the Sharifian Officers (1922-1958). Drawing on the works of Hanna Batatu, Toby Dodge, Peter Sluglett and Charles Tripp the article will focus on how Iraq's Sunni-Arab elite was using the distribution of agricultural wealth as well as British colonial power to realize their vision of a unified central state. This concept quickly became dependent on open violence in order to silence large segments of resistance, in particular among Iraq's Shi'a-Arabs and the Kurds. The article will then move on to the period of the Iraqi Republic under the rule of the Tikriti Ba'ath and the personal dictatorship of Saddam Hussein (1968-2003). It will especially use the works of Eric Davis, Fanar Haddad and Joseph Sassoon to show how the state's new leadership used the recently acquired oil wealth to fulfill past promises of state modernization, but ended up weakening and discrediting the central state by intensifying intercommunal conflicts with Iraq's Shiites and Kurds. In a third part the article will cover contemporary politics, analyzing the new Iraqi Republic's development under Nuri al-Maliki and the rise of the Da'awa Malikiyoon (2006-2014). In particular the works by Toby Dodge, Joel Rayburn and Raidar Visser will be assembled here to give an account of how the new power elite abandoned the idea of a coalition government, representing all communities of society, to revive a strong central state in an effort to enforce unity under Shia-Arab leadership.

THE RISE OF IRAQ'S AUTHORITARIAN STATE

Claims for Legitimacy

In 1921 the British government allowed the Hashemite Prince Faisal Ibn Husain to become king of the new state of Iraq. The new ruler, a son of the revered Sharif of Mecca, had no prior links to the country and was chosen by the British colonial administrators because of his family background and his leadership role in the Arab National Movement. Faisal was accompanied to Baghdad by Sunni-Arab officers who had fought alongside him against the forces of the Ottoman Empire. These so called "Hashemite" or "Sharifian" officers were eager to develop Iraq into a prosperous urban country after years of what they perceived as having been Turkish oppression and misrule (Batatu 1978, p. 319). Many of them had been born in Iraq and had been groomed for leadership in the Ottoman military, like Nuri al-Sa'id, Ja'far al-'Askari, or Taha and Yasin al-Hashimi. Indeed, even Faisal himself had been educated in Istanbul and had been active in the capitol as an MP. Thus, although the new ruling elite advocated a break with the Ottoman past, it shared much of the Turkish outlook on modernization. The late Ottoman Empire had been a split multiethnic society trying to keep its unity by propagating a common national identity, centralizing control, investing in means of communication and ensuring comprehensive military service. The Sharifian Officers made these ideals their own, continuing in fact a policy which had shaped the administration of Ottoman Iraq since the 1860ies (Çetinsaya 2006, p. 28). Since the rule of Midhat Pasha, the Ottoman state had tried to bring the country under direct control, using new jobs in the bureaucracy and new titles for landholders as incentives for the local elites to cooperate. Its ultimate aim was to include the larger tribal part of the population into its system of taxation and conscription, a goal which by the advent of the First World War had not been achieved.

Popular Support

Where the Empire had failed, the Sharifian Officers hoped to succeed. For them, the protection and support of Great Britain were to ensure, that the locals would comply with their ideals. Faisal already stated on his journey to Baghdad, that he might require the help of British forces to rule Iraq. His view was, that his new subjects were "unimaginable masses of human beings, devoid of any national consciousness or sense of unity, imbued with religious traditions and absurdities, receptive to evil, prone to anarchy, and always willing to rise against the government" (Walker 2003, p. 33). As undifferentiated as this view seems, it would soon become evident that Faisal and his followers regarded some Iraqis to be more civilized than others. Thus, the king quickly established a relationship with urban notables like 'Abd al-Rahman al-Kailani, who had been warning against the implementation of democratic principles since the fall of Ottoman rule (Wilson 1931, Appendix III). For Sunni-Arab nobles like al-Kailani, the prospect of majoritarianism raised fears that the poor farmers, rural tribes and Shi'a-Arabs would decide the country's future. But the Hashemite monarchy opened up the possibility for them to align with an Arab National Movement that was heavily influenced by elitist notions and led mostly by urban Sunnis. In 1922 al-Kailani became the crown's first prime minister. Later that year he was succeeded by another prominent Sunni, 'Abd al-Muhsin al-Sa'dun, who was the paramount Sheik of the Muntafiq confederation in southern Iraq. His rise to high office was indicative of the other fundamental alliance which the palace concluded: Like the urban elite, the countries tribal chiefs were mostly affirmed in their pre-war status (Dodge 2003, p. 106). This included their ownership of the tribal demesne, the formerly communal land that had become the exclusive property of the Sheiks during Ottoman times. Indeed, as the Sheiks were entrusted by the state with judiciary rights over their tribes, their power was even advanced. Additionally, many Sheiks received tax exemptions and gained parliamentary seats in exchange for their support. With their compliance assured, the government would take the risk to exclude and affront those parts of the citizenry that did not fit into its vision for the new state.

Disconnect with Society

Opposition against the Hashemite monarchy was to be found in areas where there had been tensions before. The region of the middle-Euphrates, with the holy cities of Shi'a Islam and the surrounding tribal areas, had long been able to keep a distance from any government residing in nearby Baghdad. Attempts to enforce taxation and to conscript the population had in fact resulted in repeated uprisings, which strengthened the cooperation between the local Sheiks and the scholars, or marja'iyya, of the "Houza 'Ilmyya", the religious schools and faculties in Najaf and Karbala (Çetinsaya 2006, p. 125). Instability at the mid-Euphrates was especially sensitive, as troubles could spread quickly to other rural parts of the country. Here, Shi'a and Sunni tenants could profit from the government's weakness by attacking their landlords whose power rested greatly on state support (Dodge 2003, p. 87). Particularly prone to unrest was the region of the Muntafiq just to the north of the harbor city of Basra. In this area, strong local liegemen of the paramount Sheik, the so called Sarkals, were quick to rise in rebellion against their overlord, if the central authority backing him seemed to falter. Yet another region that would be in need of a special approach from any central government was the mountainous northeast with its Kurdish population. Repeated tribal revolts, appeals for autonomy and even the declaration of independence by Shaik Mahmud Barzinji in 1919 had shown great opposition to interference from outside. However, as the "only possible markets [for Kurdish trade] were Mosul and Baghdad" and as "the only communication ran through Mesopotamia" the Kurdish region was included in the new Iraqi state by the British authorities. (Wilson 1932, p. 133).

Control of the Population

The Sharifian administration soon proved to be rather insensitive towards these local particularities. The first confrontation occurred in 1922/1923, when representatives for the constitutional assembly were to be elected. Shi'a marja'iyya under the leadership of Mahdi al-Khalisi demanded a boycott as the elections would "injure the future prosperity of Iraq" (Sluglett 2007, p. 56). This was chiefly because the clerics were against setting up any institutions that could legitimize a new order based on British protection. However, hostility was also caused by the new election law which granted voting rights only to subjects of "original" Iraqi descend (Haddad 2011, p. 42). As many Iraqi Shi'a had Iranian origins, especially in the clerical establishment, this would cut them out of the political process. Furthermore, the boycott was a reaction towards a state building process that so far had left out any Shi'a contribution. To level the Sunni hold on power, al-Khalisi demanded that half of all the state's employees should be from the Shi'a sect (Sluglett 2007, p. 224). Great support for the Houza's protest came from the tribal areas. Here, the prospect of permanent taxation and subjection to Baghdad raised the possibility of rebellion. Indeed, the Bani Huchaim tribe did in fact rise against the state in the winter of 1923. The Iraqi government under Muhsin al-Sa'dun reacted to this situation by on the one hand bribing Sheiks to quit the boycott and allowing the British air force to bomb the unresponsive. On the other hand, Mahdi al-Khalisi was expelled from the country, a measure which triggered the voluntary exile of many more Shi'a clerics to Iran. This procedure eventually secured the elections and the establishment of a parliament in which Shiites had little to say.

Yet, excluding representatives from the country's majority group did not dissolve local resistance to the new state institutions. Instead, uncooperative Iraqis were subject to a continuous use of force from 1922 onwards. As Faisal had foreseen, British military support had become vital for suppressing discontent. However, as the Sharifian administration was demanding independence from its colonial protector, the need for an indigenous force for suppression became increasingly urgent. Thus, three years after establishing a biased legislature, the new Prime Minister Ja'far al-'Askari tried to raise the state's power of coercion. Having formed the nucleus of a new military from Sunni ex-officers in 1921, the Hashemite administration asked parliament in 1927 to introduce conscription. In the years between, discussions of the matter had shown that the government wanted this in order to build a large army, which would be able to repress great internal revolts and would act as an educational institution for the nation: Every Iraqi was to experience the national community via his service in the armed forces (Dodge 2003, p. 140). But as conscription was so unpopular that its introduction risked mass violence, the British informed King Faisal that they would not help him to impose it. Thus forced to gain allies in the population, the government approached Shi'a tribesmen and politicians of the newly formed Nahda party, offering them posts in exchange for their support (Sluglett 2007, p. 94). An agreement could not be reached, however, and for the time being conscription remained unattainable, resulting in the perception of Shi'a opposition to the army and in doubts about their loyalty to the Arab Nationalist cause. These feelings were indeed openly expressed in the summer of 1927 by a Sunni government employee whose anti-Shiite writings sparked street protests and a fatal clash between demonstrators and the army. This script of events was again repeated in early 1933 leading to minor tribal rebellions at the Euphrates.

Although conscription would not be achieved until 1934, the repressive power of the state continued to be established even without it. Numbering only 3000 soldiers in 1921, the military had expanded to 12,000 men in 1932. By this time, the government's leading men, Nuri al-Sa'id and Ja'far al-'Askari, seemed prepared to use it in order to demonstrate Iraq's independence from British power. The first objective for this goal would be the Kurdish independence movement under its leader, Sheik Mahmud Barzinji. In 1926 the Iraqi government had agreed to support the free expression of the Kurdish language and culture and to establish an autonomous local administration. But by 1930 the ministry of education still blocked the establishment of cultural institutions and the promised Kurdish administration was all but inexistent. The situation deteriorated as Baghdad seemed to purposefully delay the promised reforms (Sluglett 2007, p. 124). The Sharifian government, set on its doctrine of a strong unifying central state and fearing other calls for provincial self-rule, dismissed Kurdish demands as attempts to weaken the nation. Thus, in 1930 large parts of the Kurdish territories fell out of central control as local tribes rallied under the leadership of Sheik Mahmud. Reacting to the insurrection, the government sent two thirds of the Iraqi army into Kurdistan to subject the rebels. However, these forces proved to be unable to reestablish public order so that the government had to plead for British support. This outcome was highly unsatisfying for the Iraqi government, as it underlined rather than dissolved public perception of its dependence on Great Britain. A year later the government's inability to enforce its authority by using indigenous forces could again be observed in the guerilla campaign of the Kurdish Sheik Ahmed Barzani (Sluglett 2007, p. 152) and during the great general strike which triggered tribal rebellions along the Euphrates (Tripp 2007, p. 69).

Relieve for the humiliated proponents of a strong central state came in 1933, when the new army could eventually "triumph" by violently subjecting the Assyrian minority, who had been identified as servants of colonialism and a "threat" to national independence. This demonstration of the state's growing ability to suppress was additionally affirmed by events right before the military coup d'état in 1936: After parliament had passed the conscription bill in early 1934 and had voted for an increase in military spending, a protest movement formed among discontented Shi'a politicians, the marja'iyya and the tribal population. Petitions raised the issue of Shi'a underrepresentation, the framing of elections, the increased taxation, and specific grievances of certain Sheiks (Tripp 2007,

p. 80). After a change of cabinet and the granting of state benefits to some protest leaders had calmed and split the opposition, the new Prime Minister Yasin al-Hashimi used the army and the new Iraqi air force to suppress the remaining rebels. Similarly, smaller uprisings in 1935 and 1936 of Kurdish and Shiite tribesmen were now crushed by superior Iraqi forces.

Collapse of the Regime

Eventually however, the series of repressive campaigns against the population proved to be the governments undoing. Unable to envision a solution to the countries chronic instability, the governing elites of the monarchy lost much legitimacy. Thus, as social criticism against the power of the landowners grew and as Sharifian disregard for "uneducated" Shi'a-Arabs appeared too uncompromising, the military itself orchestrated a violent change. By the end of the coup of October 1936, two of the most prominent Sharifian Officers had lost power: Yasin al-Hashimi was forced into exile and Ja'far al-'Askari was even killed. The incoming administration, supported by the military, included social reformers and encompassed more Shi'a ministers than ever before. These developments proved to be a foreshadowing of things to come. For although the conspirators soon abandoned their reform agenda and three years later the Sharifians were back in power under Nuri al-Sa'id, the Sharifian vision for Iraq had been exposed as a failure: After 1936 it was clear that power in Iraq had to be shared with other groups, if stability ever was to be won. The near exclusive hold on power, which the Sharifian Sunni-Arabs had enjoyed since 1921 could not be maintained. Their failure to correct this dangerous imbalance by significantly opening up the political system and enact social reforms would eventually result in the revolution of 1958 that destroyed the monarchy for good.

However, by the time the monarchy was overthrown, elitist institutions and patterns of autocratic behavior had long been established in Iraq. As was already noted at the time, only an elite of prominent politicians loyal to the crown could gain high office. The socio-economic leaders of the country, who were competing among themselves for government patronage and protection, soon became dependent clients of the incumbent chief executive. This prompted Prime Minister Nuri al-Sa'id to claim, that it was unlikely for any person "[to] become a member of parliament unless the government nominates him" (Bengio 2003, p. 19). The dependence of agrarian elites on state protection and distribution increased the central authority from the start. In addition to this, Sunni-Arab communal solidarity and the exclusion of popular representation further heightened elite control, as access to power was not only a matter of class but was even unequal for the different ethno-sectarian groups. Thus, the number of Shiite MP's was never above 35% although their constituency consisted of roughly 55% of the population (Bengio 2003, p. 20). This government structure was quite unstable, as the disenfranchised rebelled periodically and even the fighting among the elite continued. Right away, the use of military force was necessary to uphold the system. During the 1950ies Nuri al-Sa'id had hoped, that the development of the oil industry would gradually increase the ability of the government to buy off the dissenters and to pacify society (Tripp 2007, p. 106). Indeed, oil revenues would become an important asset to appease the population and to raise acceptance for authoritarian rule (Haj 1997, p. 137). But it would be the rule of the Ba'ath party of Saddam Hussein, which would profit from this new instrument of power, not the discredited monarchy.

THE PEAK AND CRISIS OF IRAQ'S AUTHORITARIAN STATE

Claims for Legitimacy

The Ba'ath party took power in a bloodless coup in July 1968, ending the authoritarian government of 'Abd al-Rahman 'Arif, with whom it had been allied only a few years before. Indeed, like 'Arif the new president of Iraq, Hasan al-Bakr, had been a member of the "Free Officers Movement" that overthrew the monarchy and later disintegrated into competing factions. His native base of support lay in the Sunni tribal areas of northwestern Iraq as well as in the Sunni-Arab officer corps, which had become his professional home. Additionally, much like during the 'Arif presidency, al-Bakr came to employ relatives, using strong family ties to gain loyal supporters. His deputy and kinsman Saddam Hussein would later intensify this method, drawing heavily on the citizenry of his native town of Tikrit and his home tribe of the al-Bu Nasir. Thus, the rule under Bakr and Saddam became known as the rule of the "Tikriti Ba'ath" (Batatu 1978, p. 1088). Like the monarchy and the Sunni regimes which had preceded them, the Tikritis subscribed to the idea of modernizing the state. Quite unlike them, however, Hasan al-Bakr and Saddam Hussein were in fact able to finance a massive expansion of the central bureaucracy due to the vastly increased oil revenues: Since the nationalization of the British based "Iraqi Petroleum Company" in 1972, profits had risen from 218.6 million Pounds to 29 billion Pounds in just a decade (Haj 1997, p. 137). This income terminated any socio-economic restrictions the state previously had. The mutual dependence between landowners and the state, which had marked the monarchy, was dissolved. With state building accomplished and society finally completely subservient, the government would now seek to unify the population by encouraging nationalism. This nationalism would be based on the government's own definition of true Iraqi ethnicity, customs and history (Davis 2005, p. 153-57). Using the new oil wealth for mass-patronage and the state apparatus for coercion, the regime had powerful means and the will to enforce its own cultural views: As an associate of Saddam Hussein reported, the Iraqi leader was prepared to "turn this country into a Stalinist dictatorship" to achieve his aims (Sassoon 2012, p. 194). However, by the time of Iraq's defeat in the war of 1991, major parts of the population had still not been assimilated to the unifying vision of an essentially Sunni-Arab government.

Popular Support

Coming to power, the Tikritis proved to be able to build wide-ranging alliances and were seeking to establish a popular image. As the Iraqi branch of the Arab Ba'ath party had been founded by Shiites, the party was at first even considerably open for inter-communal cooperation. It's vision of popular Arab solidarity was appealing to many, especially to the lower and rising middle classes. In the early years of the regime, when the party entertained socialist convictions, it even pledged to rid Iraq from the oppression of great landowners, "backward" tribal chiefs and "pre-modern" clerics. This rhetoric was useful to gain support from left-leaning citizens and secular nationalists alike. Eventually even the Soviet Union was courted by the regime and the Iraqi Communist Party under Aziz Muhammad was drawn into an unstable alliance between 1973 and 1979. However, the longer the regime lasted, the more did it fell back upon an alliance with the property owners whom it had originally promised to weaken. So, starting in the 1980ies, tribalism was culturally revived. Saddam Hussein praised it for its ability to bridge social and ethnic cleavages, as many tribes held Shiite and Sunni members. The popular outreach in the 1970ies and the outreach to the tribes in the 1980ies attracted Sunnis, Shiites, and Kurds alike. Indeed, the party could soon point out prominent Shi'a prime ministers like Sa'dun Hammadi and Naim Haddad or Kurdish allies like 'Ubayd Allah al-Barzani or Taha al-Jizrawi. But despite this, a "multiethnic" government was never really implemented. For underneath the party's proclaimed nationalism, encompassing all Iraqis regardless of their identity, lay the informal "shadow state", a network of clientism and nepotism at the centre of which remained the Sunni-Arab elite and the ruling Tikritis (Tripp 2007, p. 259). During the 35 years of their reign they would use the substantially increased resources of the central state to enforce their understanding of Iraqi national identity.

Disconnect with Society

From the start, the new government's effort in modernizing Iraq by central control was open to violence. As Saddam Hussein put it, the regime had to be ready "[to] chop heads off to serve fifteen million [Iraqis]" (Sassoon 2012, p. 196). This attitude was applied primarily against fellow countrymen by the party's numerous internal security services, which held changing definitions of the enemy of the nation. The communist party was at times courted and persecuted simultaneously. Arab Nationalists and supporters of unification with Egypt and Syria were offered a platform only to be targeted along with Ba'ath officials who criticized the leadership from a leftist position. Potential competitors were constantly searched for and harassed. However, aside from the popular communists, this kind of opposition largely consisted of scattered urbanized groups who could be easily suppressed or co-opted. Much more insecure was the government's control in areas where the central state traditionally had been viewed critically. Thus, as scholars in the Shi'a holy cities of Najaf and Karbala began to criticize the government's secularism and its empty promises of a land reform, the Houza 'Ilmyya became once again a focal point of resistance. Drawing on support from the conservative Shiite peasantry, the marja'iyya could instigate mass protests throughout the south and even in urban settlements to which many impoverished fellahs had been forced to migrate in the decades before (Tripp 2007, p. 195). Particularly suitable for undermining the state's authority were the teachings of Ayatollah Mohammad Baqir al-Sadr, who's popular Islamism reached out to both Sunni and Shi'a Muslims. Sadr's ideas on democratic government in harmony with the Koran inspired the formation of the Islamic Da'awa party, a movement which would soon organize guerilla attacks against the Ba'ath regime. Another area of conflict remained Iraqi Kurdistan, in which the Tikritis inherited a military conflict from their predecessors. Here, the Kurdish Democratic Party (KDP) under Mullah Mustafa al-Barzani had repeatedly organized tribal rebellions against previous military governments, largely supported by more urbanized Kurds who flocked around Jalal Talabani. However, the autocratic leadership of Mullah Mustafa would weaken the Kurdish resistance several times, eventually resulting in the secession of Mullah Mustafa's son 'Ubayd Allah, who joined the Ba'athist national unity government in 1974, as well as the separation of the Talabani faction which formed the Patriotic Union of Kurdistan (PUK) in 1975.

Control of the Population

Conflict between the Tikriti Ba'ath and the Shiite and Kurdish communities began almost immediately. In June 1969 thousands of followers of Grand Ayatollah al-Hakim, took the streets of Najaf and Baghdad to present well known grievances. The paramount representative of the Houza, Muhsin al-Hakim called for a fair representation of the Shi'a and respect for their rights, a complaint which repeated the content of an earlier petition. In this text, the government was specifically urged to "cultivat[e] justice and equality among the people of this nation and refrain [...] from any discrimination to achieve the unity of the nation" (Kadhem 2012, p. 229). This also included the end of the political discrimination against Iraqis who had been considered Persian citizens since

Ottoman times. The demands were widely supported in Shiite settlements, were a large protest movement had formed among students, peasants, and middle class Shiites who all had suffered from economic nationalization. The government reacted violently to suppress the demonstrations. In addition, the regime publicly accused Shi'a leaders of plotting with Israel. With the public divided and insecurity spreading, many marja'iyya left the country or fell back on silent dissent.

The crackdown on the protest movement in 69' was a starting point for further clashes between religious Shiites and the regime. After smaller uprisings in 1974 and 1976 the pinnacle was reached in 1977: A march on the event of the 'Ashura festivities grew into a mass demonstration with about 30.000 people, who were rioting against Ba'athist policies. The underground Da'awa party and sympathetic clerics were said to have instigated the rising, which resulted in a massive effort of the regime to uproot the dissenters. The government now clearly felt endangered by the gathering Islamic opposition, an insecurity that was further deepened by the revolution in neighboring Iran and the rise of Ayatollah Khomeini. It reacted by drastically intensifying measures which the state had already been employing for some years: The banning of religious rites like the 'Ashura celebration, the closing of faculties and of funding for the Houza, the expelling of Iranian students as well as of tens of thousands of Iraqis with "Persian" ancestry. However, as the coming war with revolutionary Iran would depend on the mass conscription of Shiites, the authorities simultaneously tried to extort compliance from the marja'iyya (Kadhem 2012, p. 325). This was largely successful, as the remaining clerics accepted government supervision of its sermons and its donations, thus becoming paid government officials supporting the war against Khomeini's Iran (Tripp 2007, p. 225). After that, internal resistance became tragically symbolic, like the opposition of the prominent Ayatollahs Mohammed Bakir al-Sadr and Mohammed Sadiq al-Sadr, who were murdered by the regime in 1980 and 1999 respectively. Still, Islamism continued to trouble the regime considerably from the outside, as exiled Iraqis working with the Da'awa party or the Supreme Council for the Islamic Revolution in Iraq (SCIRI) carried out assassination attempts and guerilla attacks throughout the 1980ies and 1990ies.

Although the regime's use of state power had already been gross up to the beginning of the Gulf War, the worst was yet to come. An unprecedented policy of mass murder would now be used against whole communities. Its first victim would be the rural Kurdish population, which became the specific target of the 'Anfal campaign. Carried out in 1987 and 1988, the campaign aimed at reestablishing the authority of the central government in Kurdistan. Here, fighters of the KDP and PUK, supported by Iran, had taken up arms after Ba'athist promises of an autonomous region had proven to be a sham. The Iraqi army started by rounding up Kurdish villagers for mass-resettlement. Later on, villages associated with the Kurdish resistance were completely annihilated and all of their inhabitants murdered. During the campaign the military extensively used poison gas against Kurdish guerillas and civilians alike. The government was successful in regaining complete control over the Kurdish region at the price of destroying about 80% of Kurdistan's rural settlements and killing more than 100,000 people (Tripp 2007, p. 236). To the Arab public the fighting against the Kurds was presented as an effort to save the nation from traitors in league with Iran. This rhetoric was given some credibility by Kurds who joined the national unity government in Baghdad in 1974 and who strengthened the impression that the central state was impartial and cared for all of Iraq's communities alike.

This chimera would eventually be dissolved by the so called Iraqi Intifada of 1991, which as a nation-wide event was much more apt to expose the narrow backing of the regime. As government control over the country broke down in the aftermath of Iraq's military defeat in Kuwait, a series of spontaneous uprisings took place. Starting with expressions of anger against Saddam Hussein personally, locals in southern towns and cities rose in arms and began to expel state officials. Joined by mutinous army units, tribes, and underground resistance fighters, the Intifada swiftly expanded to the Kurdish northeast. With 14 out of 18 governorates in rebellion, the regime's survival eventually depended on the loyalty of the Sunni heartland and the Sunni-Arab army reserve. By then, the Intifada seemed to divide the country along ethno-sectarian lines as many southern rebels offered their loyalty to the Houza and as officials from the Kurdish region defected to advancing KDP and PUK guerillas. The impression of intercommunal hostility was in fact promoted by the staggering Tikriti regime, which tried to rally Sunnis to their cause by depicting the rebels as a danger to their position in the state. Thus, in a series of seven articles in the party newspaper "al-Thawra", Saddam Hussein himself described his rebellious countrymen as being "foreigners to Iraq in mind, conscience and feeling" (Haddad 2011, p. 120). Defying the legitimacy of cultural particularities, he indicated that it were the non-authentic Iraqis, who had endangered the survival of the nation in various phases of the country's history (Davis 2005, p. 248). This reading of events was clearly adopted by some of the regime's forces, who moved against the rebels with the slogan "No Shi'a after today". In the end, loyalist troops succeeded in crushing the Intifada in the south, resulting in the death of tens of thousands and the displacement of nearly two million people. But under economic sanctions of the UN and protective no-flight-zones, the government's victory was hardly complete. The Kurdish north gained virtual independence and even in the Shi'a south the state was no longer powerful enough to reclaim local control, as neighborhoods established their own defences and social services. In the aftermath, the Shi'a clergy was harassed and allegedly rebellious populations in the south were collectively resettled, culminating in the destructive draining of the Mesopotamian marshes. While the mass of the people suffered from insufficient access to shrinking government resources, the regime tried to placate its Sunni power base by expanding its networks of personal patronage.

Collapse of the Regime

Although the Tikriti elite maintained control, the credibility of its claims to unify and modernize the nation was shattered by the events of 1991. The regime had been exposed as elitist and sectarian, lacking enthusiastic support even in much of Iraq's Sunni community. Nationalism was as popular as ever, but the Tikritis were no longer able to impose their definition of the term from the top down and to use it as a justification for their rule. Instead, the weakening of the state's power as well as the remembrance of Ba'athist atrocities strengthened the call for a government truly representative of its Shiite majority and its Kurdish community. This was clearly expressed by the Iraqi opposition in exile. Formed in 1992 by the Kurdish parties and several Arab entities, the Iraqi National Congress (INC) brought together a wide range of political actors. In it, Socialists, Communists, Nationalists, former Ba'athists, and Islamists endorsed the country's multiethnic composition, agreed upon future democratic elections and accepted full autonomy for the Kurdish region (U.S. DoS 2002). In such a system, the traditional Iraqi state, which had tried to enforce a Sunni vision for the country since the monarchy, seemed at last unusable. However, when the regime of Saddam Hussein was forced from power by the U.S. military intervention in 2003, authoritarianism proved to be much harder to eliminate.

The country the Tikritis left behind was impoverished by over 20 years of war and economic sanctions. With private enterprise crippled, the population depended on state distributions of food and consumer goods. Access to these resources was linked to compliance with the regime. Additional provisions would depend on the degree of association with Saddam Hussein himself, who used the power of patronage more than ever to co-opt the country's social and economic elites (Tripp 2007, p. 259). By the turn of the millennium this system of clientage had largely replaced bureaucratic government (Sassoon 2012, p. 206). The means for this system largely originated from the sale of oil, which even under the international restrictions placed on Iraq's trade after the Second Gulf War amounted to six billion Dollars in 1999 (U.S. DoS 1999). The centralized control over the marketing of Iraq's oil would continue even after the regime's fall. This would prove to be a major asset for the later resurgence of an authoritarian central state: As provincial budgets remained dependent on oil revenues distributed by the central government, the building of self-sufficient federal powerbases was impossible. Also, the influence of charismatic leaders in several opposition parties, like the KDP, PUK, and SCIRI, did not bode well for democratic decision-making after the demise of the Tikriti regime. The importance of personalized politics, with its temptations for nepotism and corruption, observable since the monarchy, was there to stay. More trouble lay in the distortion of the countries heterogeneous identity after 80 years of Sunni predominance. Soon, many Sunnis would fight against their loss of influence and even reject independent statistics exposing their minority status: Since 2003 various politicians with a Sunni-Arab background have falsely emphasized that their community makes up 42% of the population, or have even claimed that "the number of Sunni Arabs [are] the same as that of Shi'a Arabs" (Haddad 2011, p. 155). Thus, the new government found itself almost immediately at odds with a large part of its citizens. From then on, attempts to give Sunni representatives a share in government were in contest with instincts to impose the interest of the new majority.

THE REVIVAL OF IRAQ'S CENTRAL STATE

Claims for Legitimacy

In April 2006 Nuri al-Maliki, a member of parliament for the Islamist Da'awa party, was elected prime minister of Iraq. His accession was preceded by a loss of confidence in the leadership of Ibrahim al-Ja'afari, a fellow party member, who seemed to be unwilling to contain the rising spread of sectarian violence in Baghdad. Especially the occupying Americans had become wary of Ja'afari's leniency towards vigilantism and became the driving force in building support for change. After months of consultation Maliki emerged as a compromise candidate. As a former operator of the Da'awa exile resistance against Saddam Hussein, Maliki was viewed as a resourceful and capable organizer. At the same time, being only a second-rank politician from the smallest of the Shiite parties, he was expected to be controllable and to serve as a mediator for the governing coalition. However, this hope was misplaced as the new prime minister quickly established his independence. In this Maliki was supported by close relatives, foremost Maliki's son Ahmad and his brother-in-law Ali al-Musawi. They were joined by friends and former Da'awa operatives like Tareq Najim, Ali al-'Allaq and Gata Njaiman al-Rikabi. As a collective group these followers were referred to as the "Malikiyoon" (Rayburn 2014, p. 50). Like the prime minister himself, most of them originated from lower middle class families from the rural south. Having been persecuted and exiled, the first concern of this new governing elite was to secure the recently won power and preeminence for the Shi'a Islamist movement. Inspired by the discussions in the seminars of Najaf in the 1970ies and the teachings of democratic Islamism by Bakir al-Sadr, their party's agenda envisioned a modern bureaucratic central state, efficiently governed by a popular elected executive, but also under Islamic law and traditions. For guidance in this effort, Da'awa bowed to the authority of the religious scholars of the Houza in Najaf and Karbala. However, this system was not similar to Khomeini's doctrine of direct political rule by religious jurists (wilayat al-faqih), as the marja'iyya were only to give advice to the democratic government (wilayat al-ummah). Although this distinction was important in preventing an Iranian-style government, it demonstrated how far the Da'awa party was integrated in Shi'a Islamist discourse. This explicit Shi'a identity would be a novelty. Yet, for Iraqi politics the implicit communalism and elitism of the Malikiyoon was far from unique.

Popular Support

From the beginning, the Malikiyoon displayed a deep insecurity about their support in Iraq. Having joined the "United Iraqi Alliance" in 2005, Da'awa had integrated itself into an all-Shi'a political movement, consisting of the prominent "Supreme Council for the Islamic Revolution in Iraq" (SCIRI) and the mass-movement of Muqtada al-Sadr, a son of the "martyred" Sadiq al-Sadr. As Iraqi patriots, the Malikiyoon were however deeply suspicious of the Iranian ties of SCIRI and its armed wing, the "Badr-Organization". As middle-class politicians, they were further repelled by the social revolutionary posture of their Sadrist allies, who were very popular among the Shi'a poor. The new elite was even more suspicious of the new Sunni parties and their continuing sympathies for the fallen regime. In their opinion, the Sunni heartland of Iraq should be punished for its complicity in the crimes of the Tikriti regime. Former Ba'athists down to the mid-party level should be liable to prosecution and exclusion from state positions. As a member of the established de-Ba'athification committee, Maliki himself had acted accordingly by advocating a harsh vetting of government employees: "I told myself, those people should feel shy after what they did to us. [...] We have the right to seek revenge [...]" (Parker & Salman 2013, p.71). A thorough exchange of civil servants seemed especially urgent, as remaining regime loyalists could undermine the new state so that "whatever had been built could be gone, and the Ba'ath could be back" (Filkins 2014, p. 10). This fear was not diluted by the continuing U.S. military presence, which protected the newly established government in Baghdad against a growing resistance movement led by former regime operatives and foreign jihadists. Becoming prime minister, Maliki therefore began an intensive purge, particularly of the security services. Having established his personal oversight, Maliki then began to broaden his support base by luring supporters away from his Shi'a rivals and by even reemploying Ba'athist who would be loyal only to himself. Patronizing former army officers like Farouq al-'Arraji and 'Amar al-Basri, Maliki connected his rule with parts of the clientage of the former regime. Especially useful became his leverage over the senior judge of Iraq's Supreme Court, Medhat al-Mahmoud, who provided rulings favoring the power of the executive in order to avoid his own prosecution for his Ba'athist past (Sullivan 2013, p. 19). In addition, Maliki also succeeded in connecting his regime with rural tribes through newly formed "Tribal Support Councils" in the provinces. These councils acted in fact as a platform to mobilize street support for the new prime minister. However, redirecting state funds and distributing jobs and contracts to his clients quickly drew the attention of rival parties. Thus by 2008, Maliki had come under growing pressure from within his own coalition, adding their resistance to the continuing Sunni insurgency.

Disconnect with Society

As fighting for political power, social strife, and sectarian conflict had openly engulfed the country in 2006, opposition towards the Da'awa government became wide-spread. The rejection was most intense in the northwest, were the Sunni population refused the democratic process and Shiite majoritarianism. Here, the sacking of Ba'athist army officers and party members resulted in a growing sympathy for rebel forces. Random attacks by Shi'a militiamen on alleged Ba'athists, the seizure of Sunni mosques by Shi'a organizations, the escalating mass expulsion of Sunnis from Baghdad and the takeover of their homes by pauperized Shiites escalated the conflict further (Rayburn 2014, 84). Discontent also reached the Sunni tribes in the provinces of Anbar Salah al-Din and Nineveh, who had been especially patronized by Saddam Hussein, but now were lacking access to state resources. Particularly capricious was the situation in the town of Fallujah at the middle-Euphrates and the city of Mosul on the Nineveh plains, where open fighting had already broken out in 2004. A much more amicable opposition came from the prosperous Kurdish region, for which Masoud Barzani's KDP and Jalal Talabani's PUK had secured constitutional autonomy. Although the Kurds supported the Shi'a-led government in Baghdad and agreed with a harsh de-Ba'athification process, which would exclude even former school-teachers from state employment, tensions remained. This was especially because of Kurdish claims on "unredeemed" territories outside of the new autonomous region. Additionally, the Kurds demanded a new oil law allowing them to export their natural resources on their own to secure independent revenues. Both issues resulted in several rounds of increasingly bitter negotiations. However, conflict was not limited to northern Iraq, as the different Shiite Islamists competed for primacy in the south. Especially in Baghdad's Shi'a neighborhoods as well as in Basra, the movement of Muqtada al-Sadr gathered great support by providing social services for the poor and staffing a popular militia which defied the U.S. occupation. Building on its personal contacts with the Houza al-'Ilmyya, the SCIRI also vied for influence in the Shia constituency. Much more elitist in appearance, SCIRI distinguished itself especially by its enthusiastic embrace of federalism, demonstrated by its call for a Shia autonomous "Region of the Center and the South" that was to encompass Iraq's main oilfields.

Control of the Population

On each of the ongoing grievances the new government would prove to be unwilling to give in. The main dispute would be with the Sunni-Arab community, whose leaders had protested since 2003 against the ascendance of parties with a distinctly Shi'a identity. This had reached a climax in 2005, when the Islamic Party, led by Mohsen Abdul Hamid, and the Association of Muslim Scholars under Harith al-Dhari called for a boycott of the political process. For them, any vote taken under foreign occupation would legitimize the American presence and likely be prone to "fraud" (Morrow 2005, p. 6). More immediate, they objected to a new constitution which offered representation based on ethnicity and religion, weakened Arabism as the core identity of the state, and prohibited political participation for many ex-Ba'ath members. By appealing to their constituency they sought to outvote the constitution's adherents in a country-wide referendum in October 2005 and thus reclaim national leadership. However, the Sunnis suffered defeat at the polls, losing not only the plebiscite but also the parliamentary election in December. Helpless to stop the Ja'afari and Maliki government's sack of Sunni bureaucrats, the ousted elite compared its situation to the Safavid or Persian occupation in the 17th century (Tripp 2007, p. 297). Political frustration increased Sunni support for the insurgency, as remaining officials and even prominent politicians like Mahmoud Mashhadani from the Islamic Party or Adnan al-Dulaimi and Tariq al-Hashimi from the Tawafuq bloc turned secretly against the state (Rayburn 2014, p. 113). The government reacted by accelerating the takeover of jobs by loyal Shi'a party members and by directing U.S. forces against the violent uprising.

However, the socio-political transformation that occurred in 2006 and 2007 did not achieve new stability. Instead, as control over the central government was passed to the different Shi'a parties, their internal rivalry for the greatest share of revenues paralyzed the administration and escalated into street fighting. Thus in August 2007, members of the Badr Organization and the Sadrist movement engaged in a shootout over the control of the shrine of Imam Hussein in Karbala, killing 50 people in the process. This gang warfare eventually ended, when Iraqi troops, backed by U.S. forces cleared the city (Rayburn 2014, p. 28). The incident demonstrated that even among the Shi'a stability was lacking and U.S. assistance was vital to assert state authority. In order to change this, Prime Minister Maliki committed himself to build a security force, unaffected by the splits within the Shi'a coalition and loyal to him as commander in chief. To do this, Maliki would empower personal associates like Shirwan al-Waeli and Abboud Qanbar to unconstitutionally direct security affairs from offices linked directly to the prime minister's secretariat (Dodge 2013, p. 249). This parallel governing structure sidelined the authority of the defense and interior ministries and increasingly cut out the Malikiyoon's Shi'a allies. In addition, the prime minister took advantage of the new "Accountability and Justice Law", passed in January 2008, to bring former Ba'athist officers back into service under his own patronage (Sullivan 2013, p. 32). Finally, with the new security forces having expanded from 227.000 in 2006 to 425.000 in 2008, Maliki felt secure to use the state's new power to enforce central authority upon his own Shi'a partners (U.S. DoD 2006, p. 34/ U.S. DoD 2008, p.31). His attacks against warring militias in Basra in March 2008 and against the Sadrist militia in Baghdad two months later succeeded in reestablishing government control, although the necessity to request American military assistance still showed the government's limits.

Falling short to impress militarily, the submission of the militias nevertheless did establish Maliki as a credible leader for Iraq's Shi'a middle class, which feared an outbreak of anarchy and mob rule. In addition, the targeting of Shiites was publicized by the Malikiyoon to proof to the Sunnis the impartiality of the government. They increased this image by retreating from the all-Shi'a "United Iraqi Alliance" to campaign independently with the "State of Law Alliance" in the elections of 2010. The Malikiyoon's inclusion of Sunni candidates, the cooptation of Sheiks from the Sunni "Awakening Movement" and coalition talks with ex-Ba'athist politicians like Saleh al-Mutlaq did indeed increase their national standing. As an important part of this Sunni outreach, the confrontation of Kurdish demands became a useful government strategy. Indeed, the Malikiyoon could generate support among Sunni-Arabs who were living along the border of the "Kurdish Autonomous Region" (KAR). Fearing their eventual expulsion, the locals resisted Kurdish ambitions for territorial annexations. Most of the population instinctively looked towards Baghdad for protection and held sympathies for the reestablishment of a strong, Arab-led central-government. This notion in itself conflicted with the Kurds, who had long fought against an over-powerful state and who insisted on the establishment of a federal government system. These conflicting visions for the state's administrative structure became even more pressing, when the governorates of Anbar, Salah ad-Din and Diyalah began demanding federal rights for themselves, based on the model of the KAR (Sullivan 2013, p. 32). Blocking legal procedures and even overturning Diyalah's provincial government by force, Maliki thwarted these attempts. Criticizing federalism as a system which would make the central state "extremely weak, no more than a mere instrument for delivering funds and distributing them", Maliki advocated a "strong state, capable of controlling the situation" (Visser 2008). With centrifugal forces unfolding in the provinces, the prime minister was eager to demonstrate central control. Thus, in 2012 Maliki ordered the Iraqi army to occupy the disputed territories along the Kurdish border. This move triggered gun battles between the military and paramilitary units of the KAR. However, a greater escalation was avoided by a quick American diplomatic intervention in favor of the Kurds. As a result, instead of demonstrating the government's strength, the failed attack signified that violence would no longer work to subdue a near-independent and well-supported KAR.

The central government could achieve much greater success against the Sunni community, who were lacking U.S. protection. Indeed, right after Washington had handed security matters back to Iraq, the new military authorities were much inclined to use raw military force in provinces like Anbar and Nineveh. In an approach reminiscent of the failed U.S. Search + Destroy strategy of 2003/2004, Iraqi forces conducted arbitrary raids to gain information on rebel networks and to discourage the population from making common cause with the ongoing insurgency. Thus, in an event like the murder of the mayor of Fallujah in 2013 about 400 people were imprisoned for two weeks. These mass-arrests of civilians were accompanied by maltreatment and torture, which only served to increase Sunni alienation from the Shi'a government. Since 2011 this expressed itself in growing street demonstrations, where people additionally objected to the overall corruption of the government and the lack of jobs and services (Amnesty International 2011). These protests gained support even in the Shiite south, were violent clashes made the unpopularity of the government very clear. The government partially succeeded to quell the uproar by harassing the demonstrators and defying their assemblies as gathering points for Sunni radicals. Further arrests against social leaders were justified with claims that these individuals were trying to overthrow the republic with the help of outside powers like Turkey, Saudi-Arabia, or Qatar.

The growing opposition was further embittered by the failure of the newly formed "Iraqiyya Alliance" to increase the Sunni's political influence. Instead, the government succeeded to outmaneuver Iraqiyya during the government formation talks of 2010, ignored its repeated boycotts of parliament by reviving Shi'a-Kurdish cooperation, and thwarted its efforts to depose the prime minister (Sullivan 2013, p. 28). The weakness of the opposition was made plainly obvious in September 2012, when a compliant judiciary convicted Vice-President Tariq al-Hashimi, Iraq's highest-ranking Sunni official, for having supported resistance groups in 2006/2007. This was followed-up by investigations against Iraq's Minister of Finance, Rafi al-Issawi, who was also charged with corruption and terrorism (Dodge 2013, p. 241). However, the persecution of Issawi intensified the protest movement in the Sunni northwest, which set up permanent camps and started to call for the resignation of Maliki's administration. Tribal leaders, who had worked with the government against jihadist groups like al-Qaida in Iraq, also joined the protests, accusing the government of insufficient respect and support. The increasingly violent demonstrations were again denigrated as a hotbed for jihadist- and Ba'athist-fighters, who were indeed infiltrating the movement. Thus, in late December 2013 the Iraqi army cleared major protest camps in an effort to quell the resistance in the Sunni provinces.

Collapse of the Regime

The initial success of the military operation was quickly overturned however, as gunmen linked to the jihadist group "Islamic State in Iraq" began an attack of their own, taking over several protest strongholds and occupying the city of Fallujah. Yet as dramatic as the outbreak of open warfare was, in itself it did not constitute a danger to the government's power-base in the Shi'a community. Indeed, as the Malikiyoon had constantly been warning against the danger of Sunni revanchism, the eruption of violence now seemed to vindicate the government's hard line. Because of this, Maliki could campaign in the national elections in April 2014 as a guardian of the new republic. It was not until the Iraqi army collapsed under attacks from the Islamic State and ceded the northern metropolis of Mosul to the jihadists that the Malikiyoon lost support. With all political parties having been aggrieved during Maliki's reign and refusing now to work with him, Ali al-Sistani, the Houza's leading ayatollah, urged the Da'awa party to "speed up the selection of a new prime minister who has wide national acceptance" (Morris 2014). The party agreed to nominate Haider al-Abadi, one of their own leaders who had kept his distance form the Malikiyoon, to succeed Maliki as prime minister. Abadi immediately called for the restoration of the national unity government, guaranteeing all parties a fair representation and shared power. Thereby the repressive approach of the Da'awa Malikiyoon had been rejected. However, as of now, the Malikiyoon remain a powerful network inside the government with many followers embedded in the public service and even Nuri al-Maliki himself resurfacing as Iraqi vice-president.

More importantly, the setback for the Malikiyoon did not in itself terminate the renewal of authoritarianism in the new Iraqi Republic. None of the Shi'a Islamist parties has revoked the notion that leadership of the country should be reserved for them, since they represent Iraq's predominant community. The political exclusion of Sunni-Arabs will continue, as Da'awa, the Supreme Council and the Sadr Movement all agree on harsh de-Ba'athification and are equally fearful of secret support for the insurgency. Also, conflict with the Kurds might restart, as a strong Arab-led central government remains widely popular. With this in mind, further campaigns for more provincial autonomy and provincial control of oil-exports have a great possibility to produce violent response from the state. Thus, aside from the intercommunal strife, elitism and the centralized oil-economy also continue to undermine democratic change. The prevailing patron-client-system and personalized access to state revenues have concentrated influence in the hands of a few prominent party leaders. As clientism is so important for gaining and rewarding political loyalty in Iraq, the interest in preserving independent checks and balances is extremely low. This is why the state's politization of the anti-corruption Integrity Commission, the Human Rights Commission, the independent Media Commission, the judiciary and the banking sector did produce little protest or debate: Every party hoped to profit from a lack of oversight (Sullivan 2013, p. 21). As the party elites try to bind local leaders to their cause by distributing money gained from oil-exports, large parts of the population are unable to profit and participate. As long as infighting among the elite and conflict with Iraq's excluded Sunnis continues, authoritarian rule will keep its attraction by promising false hopes of order and unity.

FUTURE RESEARCH DIRECTIONS

Whatever the course of future events, the past has demonstrated that Iraqi authoritarianism has in the end always failed in its attempts to dominate and assimilate. However, it seems to resurface because of the continuance of segregated elites, who disagree on the idea of what the Iraqi national identity should be. As politics in modern Iraq has been dominated by elites, further research on these networks could be more helpful to understand the shortcomings of democratization in the country. Furthermore, to avoid any repetition of autocratic rule, possibilities for federalization, the disbanding of centralism and the strengthening of non-sectarian movements should be examined.

CONCLUSION

In comparing the rule of the three elites, the "Sharifian Officers", the "Tikriti Ba'ath", and the "Da'awa Malikiyoon", similarities can be deduced to explain the persistency of authoritarianism in Iraq. Thus, in every period the rulers aimed at modernizing the country through political, economic and social initiatives of the state. Establishing centralized control over all of Iraq's population was deemed to be essential to increase the state's authority and to unify the heterogeneous country.

However, this effort was led by communal elites, who promoted their own group identity at the expense of larger parts of the population. Thus, Arab nationalism, although presented as a secular ideology, was rooted in Sunni-Arab culture and patronized by the predominantly Sunni-Arab networks of the Sharifians and the Ba'ath. More overt, Shi'a-Islamism was linked to networks in the Shi'a-Arab community and legitimized as majoritarian rule for Iraq's largest community. Yet, while all of the elites claimed to embody the Iraqi nation, their popular support was rather limited. Indeed, their inability to integrate local interest groups and their disrespect for desires of self-government and autonomy repeatedly demonstrated a lack of connection with the multiethnic society which is Iraq. The confrontation with perceived "internal enemies", who held rather different views for the government of their country, resulted in feelings of mutual alienation. Thus, Kurdish citizens, various tribal groups, the peasantry, the marja'iyya, or contemporary Sunnis experienced the state as a foreign oppressor. In turn, they themselves were repeatedly cast as outsiders by the government. These feelings were intensified by violent oppression.

Thus, because the state's power was concentrated in elite networks originating from only one community, centralization, justified to overcome centrifugal forces, in fact invigorated the country's differences. The means to make this centralization possible rested on the state's monopoly on the distribution of key economic resources: Land-titles and oil-exports. Other means of cooptation and coercion were occasionally derived from foreign occupiers, although this was not as forthcoming as desired by Iraqi rulers. To establish full control over these resources, all regimes resorted to patronage and established personalized networks, which in turn weakened independent state institutions and the rule of law. In the case of the Tikriti Ba'ath this structure proved to be so successful, that the regime could not be overthrown from within. Both the control of the Sharifian and the Da'awa Malikiyoon were much more contested. In these cases, the prevailing instability led to attempts to change the government in order to integrate dissent and to establish a more legitimate, broad-based government. As could be seen in the case of the Hashemit monarchy, these efforts to increase government appeal fell short, resulting in a violent revolution and the ousting of the Sharifian elite. In the case of the new Iraqi Republic the outcome is still open, but with the current difficulties of reform and the amount of popular dissatisfaction a similar end might await the Da'awa Islamists.

REFERENCES

Al-Khafaji, I. (2004). *In Search of Legitimacy: The Post-Rentier Iraqi State.* Retrieved from http://conconflicts.ssrc.org/archives/iraq/khafaji/

Al-Marashi, I. (2003). An Insight into the Mindset of Iraq's Security Apparatus. *Intelligence and National Security*, *18*(3), 1–23. doi:10.1080/02684520412331306900

Amnesty International. (2011). *Days of rage: Protests and Repression in Iraq.* Retrieved from http://www.amnesty.ca/sites/default/files/mde140132011en.pdf

Batatu, H. (1978). *The Old Social Classes and the Revolutionary Movements of Iraq*. Princeton, NJ: Princeton University Press.

Bellin, E. (2004). The Robustness of Authoritarianism in the Middle East: Exceptionalism in Comparative Perspective. *Comparative Politics*, *36*(2), 139–157. doi:10.2307/4150140

Bengio, O. (2003). Pitfalls of Instant Democracy. In M. Eisenstadt & E. Mathewson (Eds.), *U.S. Policy in Post-Saddam Iraq: Lessons from the British Experience* (pp. 15–26). Washington, DC: Washington Institute for Near East Policy.

Çetinsaya, G. (2005). *Ottoman Administration of Iraq, 1890–1908*. London, New York: Routledge.

Davis, E. (2005). *Memories of state, politics, history and collective identity in modern Iraq*. Berkeley, CA: University of California Press.

Dodge, T. (2003). *Inventing Iraq. The Failure of Nation-Building and a History Denied*. New York: Columbia University Press.

Dodge, T. (2013). State and society in Iraq ten years after regime change: The rise of a new authoritarianism. *International Affairs*, *89*(2), 241–257. doi:10.1111/1468-2346.12016

Filkins, D. (2014, April 28). Letter from Iraq. What We Left Behind. *The New*.

Haddad, F. (2011). *Sectarianism in Iraq. Antagonistic Views of Unity*. London: Hurst & Co.

Haj, S. (1997). *The Making of Iraq. 1900 – 1963. Capital, Power, and Ideology*. Albany, NY: State University of New York Press.

Kadhem, F. J. (2012). *The Sacred and the Secular: The 'ulama of Najaf in Iraqi politics between 1950 and 1980* [Unpublished doctoral dissertation]. University of Exeter.

Linz, J. (2000). *Totalitarian and Authoritarian Regimes*. New York: McGraw-Hill.

Morris, L. (2014). A letter from Sistani turned the tide against Iraq's leader. *Washington Post*. Retrieved from http://www.washingtonpost.com/world/middle_east/a-letter-from-sistani-turned-the-tide-against-iraqs-leader/2014/08/13/3b3426cf-60ee-4856-ad26-d01a9c6cc9c3_story.html

Morrow, J. (2005). *Iraq's Constitutional Process II. A Lost Opportunity. Special Report 155*. Washington, DC: United States Institute of Peace.

Parker, N., & Salman, R. (2013). Notes from the Underground: The Rise of Nouri al-Maliki and the New Islamists. *World Policy Journal*, *30*(1), 63–76. doi:10.1177/0740277513482618

Rayburn, J. (2014). *Iraq after America: Strongmen, Sectarians, Resistance*. Washington, DC: Hoover Institution Press.

Russell, K., & Sambanis, N. (2014). Maliki Isn't the Problem. The Roots of Sectarianism in Iraq. In: *Foreign Affairs*. Retrieved from http://www.foreignaffairs.com/articles/141599/kevin-russell-and-nicholas-sambanis/maliki-isnt-the-problem

Sassoon, J. (2012). *Saddam Hussein's Ba'ath Party. Inside an Authoritarian Regime*. New York, Cambridge: Cambridge University Press.

Sluglett, P. (2007). *Britain in Iraq*. New York: Columbia University Press.

Sullivan, M. (2013). *Maliki's Authoritarian Regime. Middle East Security Report No. 10*. Washington, DC: Institute for the Study of War.

Tripp, C. (2007). *A History of Iraq*. New York, Cambridge: Cambridge University Press. doi:10.1017/CBO9780511804304

U.S. Department of Defense. (2006). *Measuring Stability and Security in Iraq. Report to Congress*. Retrieved from http://www.defense.gov/home/features/Iraq_Reports/

U.S. Department of Defense. (2008). *Measuring Stability and Security in Iraq. Report to Congress*. Retrieved from http://www.defense.gov/home/features/Iraq_Reports/

U.S. Department of State. (1999). *Saddam Hussein's Iraq*. Retrieved from http://www2.gwu.edu/~nsarchiv/NSAEBB/NSAEBB167/13.pdf

U.S. Department of State. (2002). *Future of Iraq Project*. Retrieved from http://www2.gwu.edu/~nsarchiv/NSAEBB/NSAEBB198/

Visser, R. (2008). Iraqi Shiite Factionalism and Iran's Role in the Basra Fighting. Terrorism Focus, 5(14).

Visser, R. (2010). *Once More, Washington Puts the Cart before the Horse in Iraq*. Retrieved from https://gulfanalysis.wordpress.com/2010/12/15/once-more-washington-puts-the-cart-before-the-horse-in-iraq/

Walker, M. (2003). The Making of Modern Iraq. *The Wilson Quarterly*, *27*, 29–40.

Wilson, A. T. (1931). *A Clash of Loyalties. Mesopotamia 1914-1917. A Personal and Historical Record*. London: Humphrey & Milford.

Wilson, A. T. (1932). *A Clash of Loyalties. Mesopotamia 1917-1920. A Personal and Historical Record*. London: Humphrey & Milford.

ADDITIONAL READING

Al-Qarawee, H. (2012). *Imagining the Nation: Nationalism, Sectarianism, and Socio-Political Conflict in Iraq*. Lancashire: Rossendale.

Al-Qarawee, H. (2013, April 5). The Rise of Sunni Identity in Iraq. The National Interest.

Lijphart, A. (1995). Multiethnic democracy. The Encyclopedia of Democracy, 3, 853-865.

Visser, R. (2010). The territorial aspect of sectarianism in Iraq. *International Journal of Contemporary Iraqi Studies*, *4*(3), 295–304. doi:10.1386/ijcis.4.3.295_1

Watts, R. (1998). Federalism, Federal Political Systems, and Federations. *Annual Review of Political Science*, *1*(1), 117–137. doi:10.1146/annurev.polisci.1.1.117

Zubaida, S. (2002). The Fragments Imagine the Nation. *International Journal of Middle East Studies*, *34*(2), 202–215.

KEY TERMS AND DEFINITIONS

Authoritarianism: Juan Linz defined authoritarian power as a system in which political pluralism is constrained, a state of emergency is evoked to gain legitimacy, political participation is controlled, and the government's rights are ill defined.

Centralism: This describes a state structure which defers most of the decision-making to the central government and forces cities and provinces to send most of their revenues to the capital, where (political and economic) means are redistributed.

Da'awa Malikiyoon: The Da'awa party (i.e. the party of Islamic Calling) was founded in the 1960ies as an Islamic movement to challenge the rise of communism and secularism in Iraq. Like many middle class Shi'ites from the countryside, Nuri al-Maliki, Iraq's future prime minister, was attracted to its conservative message. Radicalized by state repression, Maliki helped to organize the party's militant resistance, thus gaining a network of followers. These associates, who mostly originated from a similar social background, became to be known as the Malikiyoon.

Democratization: This is understood as a process in which authority is gradually handed over from an authoritarian regime to representatives of the whole population. Political pluralism is granted and the government's power is reduced by law. Eventually the people gain the right to elect a government and to engage in peaceful opposition.

Hashemite Monarchy: This family still rules in contemporary Jordan and once ruled Syria, Iraq, and the Hejaz province (Mekka and Medina). Its ancestry includes the great-grandfather of the prophet Muhammad. This lineage is valued by Sunni and Shi'a Muslims alike.

Power Elite: The term is closely linked to C Wright Mills, who used it for describing the personal bonds and combined social influence of political and economic leaders.

State-Structure: This term refers to the organizational form of the state, i.e. the distribution of power among agencies, the working of these agencies, and the underlying self-perception influencing the exchange between these agencies as well as between the government and society at large.

Tikriti Ba'ath: The inhabitants of the Iraqi city of Tikrit are referred to as Tikriti. As Iraq's dictator, Saddam Hussein, originated from this area and used his influence to bring relatives or plain residents of his home-town into positions of authority, either within the ruling party (Ba'ath, i.e. the party of Arabic Renaissance) or the state bureaucracy, his regime came to be known by this term.

Chapter 13
The Trade Union Movement of Iraq after 2003:
Exploring the Role of Narratives in Turbulent Regions

Thomas Erich Jakob
Philipps University of Marburg, Germany

ABSTRACT

This chapter argues that transition after critical junctures is heavily linked to the narratives which prevail the discourse of the respective country. Different political actors try to legitimize retroactively current claims to power. In such "zero hour" the extent of ability to organize, mobilize, set incentives, and protect followers is of the essence. This chapter uses the example of Iraq after 2003 where the split between Kurds, Shi'i Muslims, and Sunni Muslims, became the driving force behind political action and loyalty. An established counter-narrative deconstructs the claim that an eternal Shi'i – Sunni split determined all outcomes of Iraqi history, stating that religion was historically a rather subordinate identity. Then crucial contributions to the deepening of the sectarian cleavage by religious networks, the Iraqi constitution, and the policies of the Coalition Provisional Authority, (CPA) are shown and exemplified using the Iraqi trade union movement after 2003.

INTRODUCTION

We all know the allegory of an elephant standing in a dark room while several people enter the room from several sides, touch, feel, smell, and hear what they face and afterwards discuss what that silly thing in that room might have been. Of course, everyone has an own version, an own view, own experiences, and thus an own focus.

Such games are played more than often in scientific and political discourses. They can be applied to the history of countries and peoples, constructing path dependencies and thus legitimizing current policies, forming current identities, and societal fractions. These versions of events, opinions and views are called narratives. They constitute bonds, nations, or ethnicities and may affect directly or indirectly the distribution of power.

DOI: 10.4018/978-1-4666-9675-4.ch013

A recent illustration of the distribution of power against the background of narratives can be witnessed in Iraq. The narrative of the eternal and always underlying Sunna – Shi'a-dichotomy prevailed and led the country into an ethnosectarian division to an extent never witnessed before in its history. The reasons, of course, are complex and the case of Iraq will preoccupy scientists for at least some decades.

However, the notion that tensions in Iraq derive from an ethnosectarian division anchored in the history of Iraq because of a steady suppression of the Shi'a majority by a Sunni minority is consensus in the media, think tanks and even some scientific papers nowadays. This chapter argues that this perception is too narrow, even dangerous, and perpetuates itself. Hence, the chapter describes a vicious circle that started with the occupation in 2003 and ended with the almost complete destruction of secular civil society institutions and growing sectarian violence in Iraq.

This chapter is divided into three sections which descend from the described vicious circle, summed up in figure 1 (see appendix). The three main questions are: Is the ethnosectarian reading of Iraq's history unavoidable? Second, how did this reading become the dominant one after 2003? And third, how did it contribute to the destruction of secular civil society institutions?

The first part deals with the modern history of Iraq showing three things: First, it is much more likely that discrimination of certain groups started before the wave of mass conversion to Shi'ism in southern Iraq and that this discrimination had no genuine religious background. Second, Iraq witnessed a time of flourishing civil society with little importance of religious affiliations. Third, the religious question entered the political landscape in 1991 – and only to a marginal extent before – strongly influencing the US perception of Iraq.

Because of the above mentioned atmosphere of consensus about the leading role of religion in the tensions of Iraq and its history, it is difficult to make a contradictory point about the importance of the ethnosectarian division. Therefore, the first section is the most important pillar of the entire chapter. If this part fails to convince the reader, all other parts become more or less worthless. This is why it is the longest and probably the most elaborated section. However, those readers who are familiar with the modern history of Iraq can have only a short look or even skip this section.

In the second part, it will be shown how the occupational forces perpetuated the deepening of the sectarian cleavage by the state building strategy. This strategy consisted of a consociationalist system according to the perception of a religious divided country on the one hand and of a quick reactivation of the oil industry on the other. Additionally, clerical networks grew in importance in the shadow of the crushed political system, providing infrastructure and money for organization of interests.

So, the distribution of rents and resources and thereby questions of security after 2003 were tied to religious affiliation and other, mostly secular currents rapidly lost influence. This was particularly problematic, as consociationalism needs plurality to function effectively. To exemplify this loss of influence, the third section will, underlining the thesis proposed in part one and part two, show how the trade union movement, being one of the most secular movements after 2003 in Iraq, declined from 2003 – 2012. Again, coming back to figure 1, the perception of a religiously divided country was nourished, and the vicious circle started all over again.

Today, even the idea of splitting the country into three states, which tended to be considered as the least likely of all possibilities of constitutional engineering and their long term outcomes ten years ago (Anderson & Stansfield, 2005, pp. 213-215), became accepted in public discourse, sometimes promoted as an inevitable result of the democratic transition in Iraq and whole Middle East (Ashdown, 2014).

BACKGROUND

The sudden attention that gained Iraq in 2003 posed a dilemma to policymakers and scientists. Before, Iraq was rather unknown to western people and politicians, isolated, and of less interest as it was not providing opportunities for business or a possible ally in international organizations. Saddam Hussein's grip on Iraq was strong and, although not cherished, widely accepted in the international community.

In 2003 things changed. After the quick defeat of the Iraqi Army, the US Administration needed a quick and understandable version of Iraq's history and societal tensions as well as a plan to show that the situation in Iraq was under control. This is where a simplified, ethnosectarian reading of Iraq's history became prevalent. The result was among other things, a complex system of consociationalism with fixed representation of Kurds, Sunnis, and Shi'is, although disliked by most Iraqi exile opposition groups. While leading and young academic experts on Iraq threw their hands up in horror attesting a failure of nation building and a history denied (Dodge 2003) or criticizing the way of (mis)use of historical memory (Davis, 2005), the promoters of such a split, anchored in the Iraqi constitution, succeeded at least in convincing the persons in charge for State Building inside the Bush Administration and the Coalition Provisional Authority (CPA).

For those interested in theoretic classifications, the social constructive basic tenor of the chapter is obvious. The chapter invokes constructivist rhetoric and views itself standing in an (old) interpretative tradition. Indeed, the awareness of narratives as constructing social realities and influencing decisions is about more than four decades old. The notion that meaning-making leads to real outcomes can be found in Blumer's first premise of interactionism, stating that "people act based on what things mean to them" (Blumer, 1969), as well as in the famous monography "The social construction of reality" of Berger and Luckman from 1966, encouraging the analysis of the dialectical relationship of what we do and what we think.

Such studies of self-perception ground on the assumption that the answer to the question "who we are" is a permanently negotiated and socially created (Gabrium & Goldstein 2001). A particular understanding of past and present is not the only understanding possible, and what is taken as the "truth" depends on people's agendas, orientations, horizons, basic needs and environmental influences. The chapter tries to consider all these, explaining the decline of secular civil society institutions in Iraq after 2003. Now, and first, it has to be shown that a different reading of Iraq's modern history is possible.

IRAQ'S MODERN HISTORY: ALL ABOUT SHI'A AND SUNNA?

The Root of Shi'ism: Suspicion towards the Center

One of the most misleading side effects of the emphasis on the split of the Iraqi population into Sunnis and Shi'is is the impression that past and current conflicts or uprisings derive from religious issues. This may even include the perception that people truly want to fight for their specific kind of faith and that clashes are about rituals, dogmas, the right sources of jurisdiction, and so forth. This is, at least for Iraq, not the case. But religion has a special status in discourses within the international community, as it is often regarded as holy cow, as untouchable feature which nobody dares to challenge or put into question. This particular unique attitude renders religion an attractive label for any kind of elites struggling for the corridors of power in a country. So, if religion can be merely a tool for organization and mobilization, we should focus more on the concrete issues and maybe other underlying patterns of problems in the country.

One of these patterns is a long-lasting conflict between the different centers and peripheries in the history of Iraq.

To start this reasoning, one should ask why parts of the population converted apparently very late in history after the sectarian division to Shi'ism. A simple look at the geographical and topographical map of Iraq gives more information. For many years Iraq and especially its southern provinces formed a frontier between the Ottoman and Persian Empire both claiming to be the sovereigns of Islam (Nakash, 1996, p.14). Both empires invoked rhetorics stressing the Shi'a and Sunna differences from the 16th century on, mostly meant to weld together the population against the regional enemy. But, the waves of mass conversion in the southern provinces of Iraq can be regarded as relatively independent, as they took place in the 18th and 19th century (Luizard, 2002, pp.17-18). To understand this dynamics the role of the tribes and local leaders, especially in the barely accessible marshlands and desert regions, has to be taken into account. The tribes were used to have a semi-autonomous status since the breakdown of the Abasside Empire in 1258. The remoteness and difficult terrain of the region made it almost uncontrollable for the urban elites. Additionally, similar to the Kurdish tribes in the north, the tribes in the southern provinces took advantage of being schmoozed by both empires. Without relinquishing their independence, the tribes managed to adopt the best offers proposed by both parties depending on the current needs. This attitude towards the ruling elites had a crucial side effect: As the risk of side change of a tribe was continuously present the efforts considering investment in infrastructure, innovation concerning administration, agriculture, and education in that region were very low. This approach lead to a disparity in infrastructural progress between the centers of power and the peripheral borderland. Additionally, the high reliance on animal breeding and nomadic traditions stood in contrast to the agricultural dominated northern provinces of Iraq, which were easier to control from Constantinople because of their relative closeness to the heartland of the Ottoman Empire. The result was an educational and infrastructural shortfall of vast regions in the southern provinces.

After 1831, when the Ottomans drove off the Mamluks and reestablished their formal control over the provinces of Basra and east of Tigris, they implemented land and administrative reforms. The implementation of the Land Law of 1858 had widespread consequences. Collective landownership was abolished and the registration of the title deeds could only be done in the name of an individual. These individuals were often sheikhs or even civil servants, abusing their connection to the capital, and so most simple tribal cultivators did not register (Tripp, 2000, p.17). This can be explained by illiteracy, blind trust in the sheikhs, and connected, suspicion against politics amounting to a downright apolitical culture. Not for nothing, there was a widespread saying among Iraqi people stating that: "Politics is not *shughli* (my work). I need *shughl* that feeds me" (Dawisha, 2009, p.42).

The transfer of land ownership to the sheikhs meant a shift in the meaning of tribal identity. The sheikhs legitimized their power more and more by their state-granted land ownership which led to several uprisings, especially of the underprivileged social strata which suddenly became tenant farmers.

At this point, religion comes into play. There is no reason to pretend that the high degree of conversions to Shi'ism in the southern provinces in these days posed a mere coincidence. It can be argued that the glorification of the fight against oppression celebrated in Shi'ism attracted many disappointed tribesmen, and the conversion posed an act of civil disobedience towards the ruling elites: The Sunni Ottoman centre, on the one hand, and the Sheikhs on the other (Luizard, 2002, p.17). Surely, it would be too much to reduce Shi'ism to a "schematic theory of Shi'ism as a religion of perpetual protest" or consider it as "Islamic version of the myth of Sisyphus—condemned to roll the fiction of its own reality up the hill, against the grain of history, then watch it hopelessly roll down to ground zero of its cyclical desperation for salvation" (Dabasha, 2011, p.309). Nevertheless, after a closer look at the historical and socio-economic circumstances, the motif of protest and victimization can be considered as a driving force for the conversion in Iraq.

This development was reinforced by the Vilayet Law of 1864 which intended to include via councils all hitherto untouched entities into the state administration. Meanwhile the Ottoman policies forced many nomadic tribes to settle down and engage in agriculture. The new ways of life, disputes about water and soil distribution, and administration of land grew beyond the control and competence of the tribal Sheikhs. Thus, religious arbitrators and brokers, so called sayyads (Arabic: master or mister) especially form the holy cities of Kerbala and Nadjaf, claiming to be descendants of the prophet, became important players (Nakash, 1996, p.36). The new referees were skilled in verbal reasoning and moral argumentation. This, and the growing economic prosperity of the region around Kerbala due to the building of the Hamidiyya channel, led to a spread of Shi'ism in the south of Iraq. Nevertheless, as the conversion did not require special rituals, it was, if anything, subtle. Additionally, the amalgamation of tribal traditions and religious rituals eased the entry into the new confession. However, a common Shi'i consciousness was rather absent, especially as tribes, the village, and family bounds were still the most important communities and were often mixed in terms of sectarian affiliation. Indeed, till 1958 it can be said that at

...the level of the poor and illiterate masses, who constituted the vast majority of the population, matters of identity were an esoteric subject, of which they had no real cognizance, and to which they accorded little importance, let alone much loyalty. (Dawisha, 2009, p.140)

In a short summary we can assume, that broad parts of the community avowing themselves to Shi'ism or at least following its rituals were often geographically marginalized, used to a high degree of self-determination stemming from economically underdeveloped, structurally weak areas, and were relatively under-educated in terms of modern sciences compared to the dwellers of the northern regions more close to the center. At least, they suffered from subjective discrimination by the center or local landlords, and/or lacked civic capital to manage the new agricultural life after being forced to settle down.

It shall not be denied that ideological convictions, personal opinions, and so forth might have played a role in the waves of conversion in the 19th century. But first, facing the historical and societal evidences, these reasons seem rather subordinate. Secondly, the awareness of the fact, that the Shi'is were not simply discriminated because of their religion, but that those who felt discriminated and disadvantaged tended to turn to Shi'ism, helps to have a more differentiated look at the tensions in the modern state of Iraq which more than often derive from the socio-economic pattern and structural disparities found by the British after the first world war. To put it in the words of Hanna Batatu (1978):

"In the light of the existing factual evidence, it is not possible to affirm or deny that here class differences were fundamental and religious differences derivative. [...] At the same time, it should be pointed out, that Shi'ism, as an ideology and in its practical form, had a natural appeal to underdogs that stemmed from its preoccupation with suffering and from the centrality of its passion motif in its Islam."

The Monarchy: A Modern State Needs Modern Bureaucrats

Despite the promise of full independence after the Arab revolution against the Ottoman Empire, Britain aimed to keep its influence in Iraq. The

British Acting Civil Commissioner in Iraq, Captain Arnold T. Wilson, was in favor of a strict colonial and British dominated system, mainly for three reasons. First, he emphasized the abundance of knowledge about state structures and modern administration among the Iraqi population. Second, he regarded those agitating for self-rule in Iraq, which were mainly located in a thin nationalist and urban settled social strata, as self-interested mal-content clique trying to enrich themselves on the expense of the population. Third, he stressed the strategical importance of Iraq for the British Empire, concerning its geographical position and its oil wealth. With King Faysal then, an extern was implemented as monarch, who was to a certain degree dependent on the security forces of the former colonial power and an apparatus was installed, consisting of bureaucrats and technocrats. Against the background of the aforementioned composition of the vast majority of the Shi'a population, it seems less surprising that the key positions in the new state were held predominantly by individuals from the northern provinces and thus of Sunni confession. Moreover, it legitimizes the question, if the absence of the conversion waves of the 19th century in the southern provinces and hence an entirely Sunni Iraq would not have rendered at least similar cabinets with similar players in charge in the first twenty years of the infant state. No doubt, imported King Faysal relied on his loyal officers who already supported him against the Ottomans and which were mainly Sunni. But the administration of a modern state, which the heavily influential British governments had in mind, required human capital that could barely be found among the locals in the southern provinces. Besides, the interest of participation of the southern tribes was more than questionable, as the suspicion against the center did not decrease after the disappointment regarding the refusal of an own, fully independent nation by the British. Regulations about the requirements for entering a leading position in a public office hampered additionally the integration of the southern population. The constitution of 1924 stated that only those who had the Iraqi citizenship were allowed to run for public office and occupy a leading position. All those who once had the Ottoman citizenship, or whose parents or grandparents held it, qualified for Iraqi citizenship. All others had to make official demands, no matter for how long their families had been living in the territory of Iraq (Luizard, 2002, p.52). Of course, this was viewed as another humiliation and many refused to get involved, as the way into public office seemed unattainable. We do not know how much time such a demand would have taken, and which kind of harassment dwellers of the southern provinces would have had to suffer. But we can acknowledge that the big run on authorities to gain the citizenship failed to materialize.

Regardless of strategies and origins at that time, revolutionary movements that had emerged wanted to bypass the established alliance of Sunni politicians and rural landlords, redistributing power and privileges and developing a broader-based constituency among the middle and lower classes (Marr, 2004, p.47). This was true for the tribal uprisings, especially between 1935 and 1937, but also for the emerging political movements of communism in the mid-1920s and Ba'athism in the late 1940s, which should play a major role in the era to come.

The Era of Revolutions and Civil Society (1958 - 1968)

Policies already started under the monarchy and fostering the unity of Iraq built the basis for the "era of revolutions". One of the central pillars was education. Well aware of the hazards deriving from a socio-economical divided Iraq, King Faysal appointed a fervent nationalist to reform the educational system: Sati' al-Husri who would manage to increase the number of Shi'i students in schools and universities and to fight illiteracy (Dawisha, 2009, p.180). Indeed, it "was clearly the intention of the new rulers to alleviate what had been the monarchy's Achilles heel: the pitifully wide gap between the obscenely rich and the abject poor" (Dawisha, 2009, p.181). Slums in the bigger cities, where peasants lived who escaped exploitation by Sheikhs, were replaced by social housing including brick houses with running water and a school system. Accordingly, construction reduced unemployment and improved the socio-economic situation of the working class mainly consisting of Shi'i workers. The higher level of education was a cornerstone for a deepening national consciousness and led to at least two major developments:

First of all, the economic chances of Shi'ites, just as the number of Shi'ites in leading positions – at least outside the army – improved. The differences between Shi'ites and Sunnis dwarfed facing the ideas of pan-Arabism and nationalism. Under the rule of Abd Al-Karim Qasim 1958-1963, high politicians even remarked that they more than often were not aware of the religious background of their colleagues. Nonetheless, the higher ranks of the army, i.e. the officers and commanders in chief remained Sunnis. The only difference after 1958 was that the background of the officers shifted to more provincial towns in a triangle between Mosul, Tikrit and Al-Qa'im. This was due to the network character of Arab social interaction, widespread known as *wasta* and the hermetic character of military officer corps without control mechanisms. We can, however, assume the Sunni dominance in the officer corps as oddment of the infant days of the country.

The second development refers to a phenomenon often witnessed in developing countries but also in the history of Europe. The growing middle class was more and more amenable to revolutionary ideas. Thus, communist and Marxist ideology grew in importance. The socio-economically and politically still backward south, especially, turned to be a fertile soil for those ideas.

Unsurprisingly, the clandestine communist party, founded in the 1920s, had, besides some quarters in its nucleus Baghdad, Basrah and Nasiriya, its strongholds in the southern cities of Nadjaf, Kufa and Hilla (Dawisha, 2009, p.115). In 1959 the ICP was at its peak, mobilizing almost two million people on May first – while the entire population of Iraq was about 14 million. In 1955 the party's members were mainly Shi'i Arabs, equally to the composition of the other, pan-Arab socialist movement, the Ba'ath party, simply reflecting the ethnosectarian composition of the country (Batatu, 1978, p.700: p.748).

At the same time, the Da'wa party was founded, presenting itself as religious alternative. But, unlike its successor today providing the prime minister of Iraq, the party did not have sectarian inclinations, but rather pan-Islamic features (Dai, 2008, p.245). It formed cells in a Leninist manner and called itself rather revolutionary than evolutionary or reformist, as reforms would only modify the superstructure above the real basis. The basis was the Shari'a and the utopia promoted was not a communist society but an Islamic state (Jabar, 2003; p.79). At the beginning, the main supporters were influential Shi'i merchants and only some reformist Iraqi Shi'a clerics. The bulk of the clergy opposed the idea of a religious party in Iraq for many reasons: The fear of losing power and potential of mass mobilization, the fight about scarce resources and above all, it was claimed that the foundation of an Islamic state was impossible before the return of the Hidden Imam (Jabar, 2003; p.81). The Da'wa party was a reactionary religious answer to spreading secularism and aimed among other things to win back the hearts of the lower classes.

After all, the Da'wa, communist, and Ba'ath party were a symptom of a generally growing civil society. The Iraqi nationalist movement developed a broad political coalition encompassing members of all Iraq's ethnic groups, including Sunni and Shiite Arabs, Kurds, Jews, Christians, Armenians, and other minority groups. Iraqi civil society began to flourish with the formation of numerous student and professional associations, including a highly respected legal profession, a vibrant press, artist ateliers, writers' associations, labor unions, and an extensive coffeehouse culture (Davis, 2005, p.232). Hence, it can be said that in everyday life, the sectarian gap did not play a notable role. Only the officer corps seemed a relic of the days of the monarchy, when most of Shi'ites were simply not willing, competent, or educated enough to meet the British requirements for an Iraqi state.

The Ba'ath and Saddam: Using Disparities to Consolidate Power

When Saddam Hussein entered the political landscape in the early 1960ies, several groups fought for the corridors of power in Iraq. Tribes had their own parallel legal system till 1958 and local Sheikhs constituted roughly up to 35% of the national assembly. Although weakened by nationalists´ policies, drawing on family bounds and blood they still posed an influential player, especially in the lower rural classes. The tribes faced a more urban pan-Arabist and nationalist movement. Because of the successes of the charismatic Gamal Abd Al-Nasr in Egypt, his often stressed and celebrated toughness against the western powers, and his rhetorics about a third, Arab way, pan-Arabism emerged as the predominant Ideology of that time.

However, the Iraqi society was split into many fractions. There was, for instance, the "Unity Now" fraction, which promoted unification with other Arab countries as soon as possible or the "Iraq First" fraction claiming that domestic problems in Iraq should be solved first. The communist movement and the vast majority of tribal sheikhs could be counted to the latter fraction; sectarian affiliation, again, did not play a major role. Also, the Ba'ath party was split up into a fraction favoring a major role of civilians in government and a fraction favoring army influence and the officer corps was split into a fraction from the big cities Baghdad and Mosul and a fraction from more provincial areas and towns, still in the triangle between Mosul, Tikrit and Al-Abid. The latter favored the "Iraq first" agenda, while the former stuck – at least in their rhetorics more to the idea of a quick unification with other Arab countries. This bulk of political players were challenged on another level: Due to their proposed mix of secularism and socialism from clerics and mujtahids, but also from urban merchants often of Shi'i background such as the al-Khalibi clan, and eventually from the growing political Islamism of which the Da'wa party was a descendant. Hence, it was a confusing constellation of political currents and most Iraqis had at least two movements corresponding to their identity and self-perception. Then the, in 1963 and again in 1968 established, Ba'ath regime grew more and more authoritarian.

In 1979 Saddam Hussein succeeded al-Bakr, who had been from the same tribe. His success in lingering in power for over three decades can be traced back to two main pillars of his regime. The first was extraordinary violence. As an admirer of Stalin he was convinced that political persecution, censorship, and punitive strikes against the own population were legal means to secure the stability of a country. Additionally, he was influenced by the ideology and thoughts of Michel Aflaq, a key figure of the early pan-Arab movement. Aflaq, himself not averse to violence, wrote: "When we are cruel to others, we know that our cruelty is meant to bring them back to their true selves, of which they are ignorant" (Dawisha, 2009, p.215). The results were bombings, gas attacks, persecution and torture of real or imagined enemies of his rule or person.

The second pillar of Hussein's long lasting power maintenance was the ability to counter, involve, use, and misuse several political streams for the cult of his own person. When he seized power in 1979, he had already been the most influential man in the background of the country for about 10 years. In the following decades he would succeed in eliminating the communist movement, seriously weaken the political Islamism, and silence his critics inside the army.

The tactics considering the communist movement was to dispute their socio-economic basis and alienate voters. While forming a "Progressive Patriotic and National Front" with the communist and some Kurdish parties in 1973, the Ba'ath had implemented a broad welfare program financed by the recent oil boom. The Ba'ath then claimed these policies to be part of their own agenda, trying to make the communist superfluous in the eyes of the lower income classes. Waves of repression since 1963, and even before under Qasim, had led additionally to the structural infirmity of the ICP. In 1979, Hussein launched a final campaign against the party and removed violently the residues of the mass movement in government, army, and civil society.

Concerning political Islam, things turned to be more complex. Two characteristics of the Da'wa party disturbed the new Ba'ath regime. First, the religious attitude and the connected de facto power of mobilization of mass protests in religious, mostly rural areas, challenging the rule of the secular, mostly urban supported regime. Second, the clearly anti-authoritarian tendency, criticizing the national elites in the aftermath of the Arab-national catastrophes of the defeat of June 1967, the shift to market economy and the secession of Bangladesh (Jabar, 2003, p.51). In the case of Iraq, a drought in the southern provinces in the late 1970 increased political and economic frustrations among the dwellers in the southern provinces. The Da'wa Party managed successfully to mobilized those frustrated masses (Dai, 2008, p.259). It is nothing but consequent that the Da'wa party turned more and more to Shi'i rhetorics, as it was an ideal connecting platform for the disenchanted masses of the south. At the same time the religious establishment and the Da'wa party became more and more involved with each other. Revolutionary tendencies, enforced by the successful Iranian revolution of 1979 in the neighboring Persia led to an intensification of persecution and discrimination of the party members and eventually drove the party into exile in Iran.

But Hussein´s brutality was not only directed against Shi'ites and communists. He managed to silence and oust his competitors within the army and the party by conspiratorial, intriguing, and partly cunning methods. Without further scientific foundation, here a little legend told in Iraq about the craftiness of Saddam Hussein:

The city of Mosul was always a city of education, science, culture, civic and human capital. Many of the key figures of modern Iraq, and even before, were from Mosul or had consultants stemming from the city. Once, Saddam Hussein had in one of his attacks of paranoia the fear of being betrayed and driven off by Mosul's elite which still constituted some of the cleverest heads of Iraq. So, Hussein equipped pickups with sacks filled with money and sent them to the countryside around Mosul and its outskirts. The money was distributed without consideration in return and soon incredibly rich but uneducated and administratively incompetent simple peasants, workers, and tribesmen entered the city and bought weapons, buildings, shops, influence and governmental positions. From that day on, Mosul for several years would not pose a threat to Saddam Hussein's autocratic regime.[1]

Hussein cultivated differences between several groups, deepening their enmity, steering the power balance in the country by oil revenues and changed sides if one of his allies grew a possible challenge to his regime. This policy of domestic counterbalancing included the support of certain Shi'i and Kurdish tribes, whenever it seemed suitable for him. Then, after the disaster of the first and second gulf war, Hussein tried to consolidate his power basis even by changing classical Ba'ath attitudes. He turned from secularism to a more religious view, adding the words "God is great" to the Iraqi flag and fawned over the tribes. He admitted again, a since 1958 abolished parallel tribal judicial system, involving tribal penalties like the amputation of extremities or honor killings (Dawisha, 2009, p.235). His main source of power became personal networks and relatives, especially from his hometown and tribe, the al-Bu Nasir, and their allies al-Dulaim. The secret service, the National Guard and his personal bodyguards were mainly or exclusively recruited from the al-Bu Nasir (Dodge, 2003, p.161).

Because of this paternalistic pattern, and despite the fact that in the Iran- Iraq war most Iraqi Shi'ites fought for the regime in Baghdad which eventually led Teheran to the conclusion that the supported Iraqi movements, especially the Da'wa and Islamic Supreme Council of Iraq (ISCI) failed in their attempt to "export Islamic revolution" (Dai, 2008, p.254), it can be clearly stated for Saddam's era:

One of the most persistent misconceptions about Iraqi politics [...] is the belief there is a fundamental 'from-time-immemorial' division between 'Sunnis' and 'Shi'is', and that a principal objective of 'the Shi'is' is the creation of an Islamic state in some sort of close relationship to Iran. A far more meaningful division is the one between the Takriti power-holders and the majority of the disenchanted and disenfranchised population, both Sunni and Shi'i.

(Farouk-Suglett & Suglett, 2001, p. 299).

NARRATIVES, STATE BUILDING, AND CONSOCIONALISM

Consolidating the Narrative: Politics and Science after 2003

After having developed an alternative reading of Iraq's modern history, it is time to encounter the *State Building Process* after 2003. The coalition forces had the difficult task of building an entire nation with history, schoolbooks, heroes and legends. The task was not only to build up an administrative system. The difficult part was to choose a narrative for Iraq and consolidate this narrative with institutions. This was a crucial point, as it would set the course for the country's development and self- perception. In John Knights´ words:

Cognition affects rational decision making, rational decision making affects the development of institutions, institutions affect rational decision making, institutions affect cognition, institutions affect social outcomes. (Knight, 2000, p.11)

In 1991, after the second gulf war, displaced Iraqi soldiers driven out of Kuwait, dwellers mostly from the southern marches of Iraq at the Iranian border, Kurds and parts of the population of major southern cites rose against the regime in Baghdad. The uprising was put down brutally and was viewed and made history as 'Shi'a uprising' in western media, although the sect was rather a platform for organization and the underlying reasons complex. However, the dichotomy of Sunna and Shi'a finally entered the political discourse of modern Iraq (Davis, 2005, p.243, Dai, 2008, p.253), and shaped the perception held by the policy makers in the state building process after 2003.

A dichotomy, or taking the Kurds into account, a threefold divided Iraq is a constellation very easy to grasp and is something that can be easily explained to the public and to policymakers not familiar with the Middle East. A huge problem arose when the United States entered Iraq without real reconstructing plans. A quick and understandable solution had to be found after 2003. Thus, the Coalition Provisional Authority (CPA) adopted the narrative of the ethnosectarian divided country which came up after 1991 aiming to implement a proportional representation election system.

Even more problematic turned the fact that Iraq lacks a tradition of scientific history writing. As the scientific discourse was undermined by the authoritarian regimes, a discussion about different interpretations of the past did not take place. Even simple information about tribal history, the monarchy, or the era of Revolutions is missing. The CPA cleaned the schoolbooks from Ba'ath ideology.

But a complete renewal of the views of the Ba'ath regime on Iraq's past did not happen. For instance, the developments of the era of revolutions concerning civil society are widely unknown among the youth, while many elder Iraqis, especially from the urban regions, still refer to Adb al-Karim Qasim as the leader (as-sa'im) and tell in which clubs and associations they were members. At the same time it must be stressed that the fear injected under the Ba'th regime prevents many from talking freely about that era.

A very interesting development is the growing literature about Shi'ism in Iraq. From 1991 on and again in 2003, sectarianism was more and more promoted as the "always underlying split". Dawisha, for instance, writes in 2003 about the nationalist era after World War II, arguing that the Shi'i identity was simply "concealed" (Dawisha, 2009, p.240), unfortunately not providing any sources. In 2006, Vali Nasr announces on 254 pages "The Shia Revival", explaining with little scientific evidence and quotations "how conflicts within Islam will shape the future", claiming that "the Shia-Sunni conflict [...] has been far more important in shaping the Middle East than many realize and acknowledge" (Nasr, 2006, p.22).

Jabar writes about disturbances of the national integration after the revolution of 1958, citing Hanna Batatu. Then he continues: "This point is brought home when we remember that the officer corps was historically Sunni Arab-dominated" (Jabar, 2003, p.58). But, taking a look at the quoted passage in Batatus´ work, he merely mentions that "the revolution has disturbed the delicate balance between the various ethnic and sectarian communities of Iraq, [...] mainly owing to the unevenness in the social development of these communities" (Batatu, 1978, p.807). He does not refer to the leadership, but to the socio-economic *enhancement* of the Shi'a community. So this quotation is, if not deliberately wrong, at least a very free interpretation. Another inconsistency appears, when Jabar refers to Phebe Marr. He writes:

The composition of state elites in this period, as Marr has suggested, revealed three major tendencies: an increase in the role of the career officers, a decline in Shi'ite and Kurdish representation and, lastly, a shift from upper to lower middle-class provincial elites (Jabar, 2003, p.58).

The centrality of the discrimination of Shi'ites is stressed, as it is put alongside two other main developments. But as Marr refers to more than these three developments, namely education, agricultural and industrial backgrounds, the centrality seems highly constructed. Taking a look at the cited passage in the Middle East Journal, she merely writes:

The figures below show that Arab Sunnis (about 25 per cent of the population) still predominate among the leaders, while the Shi'ah (about 50 to 55 per cent of the population) and the Kurds (about 17 to 20 per cent) are underrepresented. While the new regime has not created this situation, it has done little to relieve it, and in the case of the Kurds (up to the time of the present regime), it has done much to exacerbate it. (Marr, 1970, p. 288)

The mentioned figures then show a decline of Shi'a representation from 32 to 30%. The centrality suggested by Jabar seems therefore rather misleading.

For sure, there could be found more examples, constructing on a rather contested basis an eternal sectarian conflict. Especially after 2003 this kind of literature exploded. Such theses often derive from the will of an author to force history into a straightjacket to clarify his point. Basically, this way of dealing with history is not problematic, as no scientific work will ever be able to reflect all narratives, and therefore there will always, no matter how long the research had taken, remain a narrative among others. It becomes problematic, however, when the authors claim their view to be the only, underlying, and everlasting view, while other views just conceal its truth. The second problem arises when religion enters the play or when claims contending the discrimination of a certain religious community, are not contested. Often it remains forgotten that individual identities may change, and a religion will never cover the entire spectrum of a population and can therefore never be its only attribute. This is to be considered especially in the very sensitive field of State Building. For Iraqi individuals, self-unfolding was almost impossible in the era of Saddam Hussain. After 2003, they had to orient themselves in the new environment and evaluate chances, dangers, and utility of joining a certain political group. Therefore, I suggest a "zero hour research agenda", decoupled from sectarian rethorics, simply examining how the sectarian aspect could grow so important in Iraq nowadays and what happened to other political currents.

2003: Zero Hour

When George W. Bush visited Iraq on May 1, 2003, he declared the end of all major combat operations. While in his back a banner stated "mission accomplished", he acknowledged that "We have difficult work to do in Iraq." He was blatantly right.

The gap left by the Ba'ath regime turned to be a more serious problem than estimated by the coalition forces. Like the opening of Pandora´s box, the removal of the old authorities caused havoc and a crisis of identity. Looting and violence broke out and could not be brought under control for several weeks. Many observers define this mismanagement of security governance as the biggest fault of the entire operation. This is genuinely true, however, to a broader extent than estimated.

After about a quarter of a decade without the right to define itself the people of Iraq were in a sudden and deep identity crisis. As history showed there are many identities for an Iraqi to build upon. But, the lesson bitterly learned by the communists in Iran after 1979 was that in a "hour zero" situation peoples true desires and characters are not of importance. It is rather of importance, which group is to a higher extent able to organize, to mobilize, to set incentives, and to protect its followers. In Iraq, many groups entered the political landscape after the fall of Saddam. In the environment of violence and uncertainty the tribes became a major player in the rural areas. Citizens who had cut their ties to their kinship many years or decades ago assumed their tribes' names again, searching shelter in the areas protected by the tribes' militias. Elected inter-tribal and inter-ethnical city councils emerged without any interference from outside, like in Fallujah or Mosul.[2] Although for the latter it could be anticipated that a bloodbath would happen due to its ethnic diversity. However, the group that was equipped and networked the best, were the religious leaders from the south relying on their sectarian identity. Mosques had traditionally not only been places for religious worship, but also a gathering place to discuss recent political developments within the Muslim community (*Umma*). This is already anchored in the language, the Arab word for mosque (jami'a) derives from the root ja-ma-'a, meaning "to collect" or "to gather". Due to the places for gathering, a feasible organizational structure, connections to clandestine networks and to Iran, and financial means, clerics became powerful political players in Iraq's 2003 *Zero Hour*. This went so far that the Mahdi Army, which prevented especially the slums in Baghdad from looting, was so much en vouge that it was able to oppose coalition forces in 2006 and seize vast parts of Baghdad and the city of Basra. It is controlled by Muqdar Al-Sadr, a descendant of a well-respected family of Sayyds, and son in law of Mohammad Sadeq al-Sadr, who was ideological leader of the Da'wa party in the 1980s and executed by the Ba'ath regime. The clerics attached great importance to their sect, legitimizing their leadership; and Sunnis soon would follow this identity game (Feldman, 2004, pp.78-80).

The extraordinary bad security situation in Iraq after the invasion was due to the lack of an elaborated plan for Iraq after *Zero Hour*. When the CPA started its work its information was biased due to three reasons:

First, the knowledge about Iraq was poor and what had entered especially the U.S. collective memory was the second Gulf War of 1991 and the aforementioned emphasis on Shi'i and Sunni identities in the media. Second, the above described ongoing developments in Iraq after 2003 seemed to prove this dichotomy to be true. Third, the CPA worked closely together with the secular opposition, but especially with the INC which was the only party that viewed proportionality as a central point, underestimating the power of the clerics and tribe leaders (Feldman, 2004, p.79).

Table 1 (see appendix) shows that most opposition groups did not favour a proportional system. This was partly due to the hope to obtain a bigger part of the cake in a non-proportional system, and partly due to the real will to unify the nation. As a matter of fact, the Iraqi Governing Council implemented by the CPA was the first ethnosectarian committee in Iraq's history. It set up a constitution, anchoring the ethnosectarian division by a proportional representation election system. The widening of the sectarian gap which had already caused small scratches in Iraqi society became the basis of the new Iraq.

Proportionality and Consociationalism: The Political Dimension of State Building

The idea of proportionality in politics is widely discussed and is found in the archetypal form in Switzerland and the Netherlands. It derives from the concept of *consociationalism*, where the main pillars constitute an oversized coalition, a mutual veto system, and a high degree of autonomy for each segment to run its own internal affairs (Lijphart, 1977, p.27). But the core fact about consociational democracies is the plurality of political relevant groups. A closer look at Switzerland, which can be termed as the most stable form, reveals that indeed the key positions in government are distributed along ethnic lines, mostly coined by the language. But more is considered, namely confession, religiosity or secularism, urban or rural respectively centre or periphery origins, and eventually class (Lipset & Rokkan, 1967, p.554). Government formation therefore is a very long and sensible process. The Kantons have ample rights through the federal system. Furthermore an independent central bank, professional associations, trade unions, and NGOs shape the decision making process.

In Iraq, proportionality was indirectly introduced by articles 55, 61, and 139 stating that the post of the Parliaments' Speaker, the President, and the Prime Minister consist of councils of three members. In practice, these councils are designed for a Shi'i, a Sunni, and a Kurd. Additionally it became custom to divide the posts of the cabinet, and hence the Ministries, along these lines. In a very short time, this system called "muhassasa" became part of the discourse in many strata of life and lead to less stress on competence and more on the ethnosectarian group in hiring processes. Outcomes were sometimes quite strange, like the occupation of the post of the Minister for Higher Education and Research (2005 – 2010) with someone who was not able to speak English at all.

But the real crux of Iraqi was its rentier state pattern. 90% of the state budget derives from oil rents or taxes related to the petrol industries. Considering the fact that these Industries only employ 300.000 workers, it becomes obvious that a vast majority is – concerning GDP – bluntly speaking superfluous. Over 90% of the workforce are employed in the public sector, as this is, due to the difficulties of starting an own business in the private sector, the easiest and safest way to earn money. Every public sector worker is supervised in the end by a ministry. Now, it has to be taken into account that the ministries, similar to the key positions in government, were distributed along the three major groups – Shi'is, Sunnis and Kurds. The system of muhassasa encouraged simple administrative staff as well as political decision makers to turn to their sect, as the chances to have a career were better within that community than outside. Moreover, an unforeseen side effect was the increased influence of the clergy, which lead to the pervert outcome, that not only the post in the country were distributed along sectarian lines despite of competence, but ethnosectarian groups often did not chose the most competent candidate but the most religious. Religiosity became a way to have a career, and so religion entered the strata of the citizens´ lives where it had not been important before. The result was a "sectarization" of the public sector. Dawisha reports of a young Shiite, who had lined up in front of the Ministry of the Interior to join the police force but had expressed a preference for soldiering. When he was asked why he was not applying to the Ministry of Defense, his immediate answer was: "it does not belong to us" (Dawesha, 2012, p.10).

Before the regional elections in 2009 and the governmental elections 2010 a remarkable development took place. As religiosity doesn't make a candidate a good politician, and politics involve skills in administration and deal mostly with profane issues like electricity, water supply, and reconstruction projects, the elected representatives of the religious parties were overstrained. Disappointed of the religious parties due to corruption, lack of civil services, and administrative incompetence, public opinion turned away from sectarianism. Even the most influential Shi'i cleric, Ayatollah as-Sistani withdraw from politics, prohibiting the use of his picture at any political occasion. The top candidate of the secular front, Iyad Allawi and the ruling Prime Minister from Da'wa topped each other in nationalist rhetoric, emphasizing the unity of the country, the fight against corruption, and showing their infrastructural efforts. Allawi's front won the election, but in the aftermath, technically speaking, the secularists broke down because of al-Maliki hanging on to power backed by the Kurds. The Kurds were promised a hydrocarbon law, so they could run their oil industries more efficiently. The law has been disputed until today between oil rich and oil poor regions and shows that the underlying struggles of Iraq today remain non-religious.

In any case, the Allawi`s front did not obtain the post of the Prime Minister, lost credibility, had to decide whether to support Maliki forming a national government and, against their own believes distribute posts according to muhassasa. The sectarian gap had overruled all other perceptions of parties and its members, and Iraq was on a slippery slope towards sectarian violence.

But how could it happen, that elites did not or only hardly cooperate, while consociationalism's aim is actually to foster cooperation?

The Flaws of Iraqi's Consociationalist System

An answer can be found in the missing factors welding elites together. The main feature of consociationalism is an opposition potent enough to oppose the elites and to form overreaching loyalties (Guelke, 2013; pp.176-178, Lijphard, 197, p.66). This may be from the outside an exterior enemy or from the inside a pluralist federalism, threatening with secession, or a strong civil society or, such as in the case of Switzerland, all at once.

An exterior enemy is in the constellation of the international system rather unlikely to appear. However, US troops were at least in the elections of 2005 an important issue. In 2010 the occupation played only a marginal role. More complex is the problem of federalism: The governorates could have become the nucleus of a subsidiary identity. However, federalism was rejected by many parts of society, as nationalism persists as a very strong feeling. Moreover, people were simply used to the central power in Baghdad, thus all the networks were aligned and targeted towards the capital. In a country without rule of law, networks are of utmost importance (Schlumberger, 2008, p.633-635). In return, the central power had eminent rights to intervene within the provinces. This phenomenon was already addressed in Germany under the term *Politikverflechtungsfalle* (*Joint Decision Trap*) (Scharpf, 1988, p.242). Actors concur with a pending constitutional amendment as potential veto players who benefit from the implementation. In German federalism, these are the provincial governments. In - in Iraq these are local networks, tribes and clans. The *Joint Decision Trap* is thus not the blockade by veto players in the daily decision-making, but the inability of the political system to bring about institutional changes to resolve these blockages. The uncertainty of a decentralized local government in Iraq generated fears among its population, superposing its possible advantages. This is particularly true, as especially under Saddam the local groups were often instrumentalized and played off against each other, so rivalries grew stronger. Therefore, and as only the Kurds insisted on an own federal state, a system of asymmetrical federalism was introduced, where at least tree governorates could join to form a Region which had extraordinary rights and relations to the central government. All other governorates would initially remain under the control of Baghdad, until a "Federation Council" was established, representing the governorates. So, Iraq was built as a two chamber system, but the concrete competencies were not fixed. Article 62 states:

A legislative council shall be established named the "Federation Council" to include representatives from the regions and the governorates that are not organized in a region. A law, enacted by a two-third majority of the members of the Council of representatives, shall regulate the Federation Councilformation, its membership conditions and its specialization's and all that is connected with it.

This has never happened until today, so the governorates which could be a strong player in the political system, remain marginalized.

Concerning civil society, just under 1 Billion dollar had to be spent by the United States to expand civil society institutions such as civic education, independent media, and women issues (Dawisha, 2009, p.267). Compared with the overall costs of the Iraq war these efforts seem rather neglectful. Against the background of a lack of an overall reconstruction plan, this is rather unsurprising, but in the end disastrous, as civil society organizations, in which people can gather and organize alongside their particular interests are a key pillar of consociotonalism. Besides, local networks provide a better access to the people and help to identify their needs. Admitted lessons learned were clearly: "Working through indigenous networks seems to increase community acceptance and provide a higher and more lasting degree of local security than military or private-security protection alone could achieve" (Bowen, 2009, p.4). The biggest problem is that these networks often work beyond the control and surveillance of the coalition forces, or work against their priorities. One of the most concrete examples is the treatment of the trade union movement after 2003.

THE DECLINE OF A SECULAR CIVIL SOCIETY PLAYER: TRADE UNIOS AFTER 2003

Trade Unions in Iraq - A History of Anti-Authoritarian Secularism

Trade unions in Iraq were founded in the late 1920s and had their heyday in the Qasim era. They had been a mouthpiece and tool for mobilization of the communist party. So, the trade unions struggled, besides microlevel negotiations and collective bargain issues, for similar points like the ICP:

Withdrawal of foreign troops, better working and living conditions for the lower income classes, and secularism. The communist party was in its beginning influenced by the British labor movement and less by Soviet socialism, although the party capitalized financial and structural aid from the USSR. This led to some tensions, as parts of the party, like in other Communist movements in Europe of the same time (e.g. KPD in Germany), accepted Stalin in the 1950s as leading figure and lost popularity among the local people. Despite, trade unions had grown quite strong and the Ba'ath party started to court its leaders and members. Connections to union leaders resembled a certain power of agenda setting in the ongoing discourses of civil society. This was particularly of strategic interest, as citizens could not find the main venue for political articulation and aggregation in political parties, and that space was to be occupied by professional associations and trade unions. Anywise, unions had become the domains for the wider political and ideological contestation that was being fought out nationally (Dawisha, 2009, p.191).

The Ba'ath party, and especially Saddam Hussein started from the second seize of power in 1968 on to fight the communist party and trade unions heavily, exchanged the entire leadership ranks, and prohibited or crashed strikes and collective bargaining. Nevertheless, in unions were still strong enough to enforce the 8 hours day and wider recognition in Law No. 151 of 1970. But slowly trade unions were turned into state controlled "yellow" unions. Discrimination and intimidation of independent union members and leaders increased, involving dismissal, expulsion, interrogation under torture, and executions in front of factory gates. All unions were forced to join the General Federation of Trade Unions (GFTU) which was founded 1959 and became 1986 the only recognized trade union association by law.

This campaign was systematic and seemed to be a priority of Saddam Hussein. As he did not tolerate powerful actors beside him, in 1979, right after his seize of power, he arrested and partly executed vast parts of the union's leadership. Among those executed were the General Secretary of GFTU being himself a minister and a member of the "Revolution Command Council" which ruled the country by decrees, the Chairman of GFTU, and other officials, despite they were all Ba'athist appointees (LabourNet UK, 2004). With Labor Law No.71 and the Law about the Organization of Trade Unions No. 52 amending the new Labor Code of 1987, Hussein finally domesticated unions completely. Strikes were nearly forbidden, just like collective bargaining, and public sector unions banned. As the public sector had grown to the sector with the far most employees, this move happened to consolidate the regimes power over the employees, and was promoted as abolishment of the unnecessary: Hussein himself stated a in speech: From now on, the title "Worker" is abolished and all workers shall become official employees by the State [...] As everybody is now a government employee, there is no more need for trade unions." (LabourNet UK, 2004).

This move cut the historical ties between the union movement in Iraq and the British Trade Union Confederation (TUC). First the "sovjetization" of the movement and then the control of government made it unbearable for the TUC to view the GTFU as independent partner. The TUC turned to and supported an underground trade union organization which was formed in Iraq in 1980 named the Workers' Democratic Trade Union Movement (WDTUM, 2005). The movement managed to stay active till 2003, organizing under huge dangers labor action, mostly in the Kurdish regions.

After the invasion, trade unionists in exile and within the country were aware of the possibilities and chances in zero hour. Only one week after the official collapse of the Ba'ath regime on May 9, 2003, partly with help from the WDTUM, partly from other organizations, a meeting in Baghdad attended by over 400 unionists elected several committees, preparing and structuring country wide campaigns. Moreover, a new association was founded: The Iraqi Federation of Trade Unions (IFTU). In August 2003, according to the figures of the WDTUM, trade unions existed in the oil and gas industry, in the railway industry, in the transport and communications industry, and in teaching, operating in 10 cities (Muhsin, 2003).

Actually, most claimed aims of the Federation would make every democracy promoting secular westerner's heart miss a beat. They included an end to the occupation, building democracy, a halt to privatization, establishment of social welfare, women's equality, scrapping anti-union laws, implementation of basic workers' rights, and banning forced and child labor. The movement supported from the beginning democratization in Iraq and searched to overcome the sectarian gap at the same time. Indeed, the elected committees worked on a secular basis. Furthermore, the trade union movement was the very first independent civil society organization in Iraq endorsing U.N. Resolution 1546, which sets the time table for Iraq's transition into a democracy. Moreover, unions managed to oppose influence from sectarian parties as well as from ex-Ba'athists.

A dispute arose after 2003 about the assets of the old state steered GFTU. As the GFTU still formally existed, the union movement was de facto split, and both Federations were courted by religious parties. After the invasion and elopement of many former GFTU leaders, a meeting was held between the GFTU and the Shi'i sectarian SCIRI, at which formalities for a cooperation should be negotiated (Tudor, 2004). It failed, thus preventing a form of "union capture" widely witnessed in developing countries. This was mostly due to the composition of the GTFU, still containing many ex-Ba'athists at that time. The composition posed as well a serious hurdle for a cooperation with the WDTUM. Remarkably, two years after the breakdown of the old regime, the GFTU managed to clean itself from ex-Ba'athist influences, and the movement in general managed to keep its independence despite the dominance of the sectarian cleavages. So, the WDTUM agreed to amalgamate both federations to the General Federation of Iraqi Workers (GFTW) in 2005.

Trade Unions, the Coalition Forces, and the CPA

The CPA was not very eager to support the trade union movement in Iraq after 2003. While implementing laws concerning child labor (CPA Order 89, 2003) the law No. 150 of 1987 stayed in force. But it would be overhasty to assume intentional harassment. The enormity of the tasks to accomplish overwhelmed the small staff anyways, which led to prioritisations (Ward, 2011, p.10). The neglect of the trade union movement derives from three sources.

First, in the U.S., unions still bear a certain aura of illegitimacy, market distortion, and a connection with communist thought. The Labor Management Relations Act of 1947 (29 U.S.C. § 401-531), better known as Taft–Hartley Act, banned unions from the political landscape by prohibiting political strikes and monetary donations by unions to federal political campaigns. Moreover, important tools of collective labor action were penalized. It was part of the policies developed in the so called McCarthy era and is still in force today.

Additionally, the question whether unions benefit or harm society is scientifically contested. Among economists, the discussions are mostly grounding on a book from 1984, confronting the monopoly model, in which unions act as monopolist of labor and hence lead to gross weight losses, with a collective voice model, emphasizing reduction of labor turnover, enhancement of worker morale and cooperation, resolution of grievances, and the pressuring of management into stricter efficiency. The authors, Freemann and Medoff (1984) state in this book (p.247):

In most settings the positive elements of the voice/ respose face of union offset or dominate the nega-

tive elements of the monopoly face. [...] (T)here is a place for unions to improve the well-being not only of their members but of the entire society.

One of the main critics of Freemann and Medoff and of trade unions in general, Morgan O. Reynolds, stating that "to many economists and businesspeople, I suspect, these claims appear fantastic and absurd on their face" (Reynold, 1985, p.269), would become chief economist for the United States Department of Labor under the first Bush administration in 2001 – 2002. Bush himself had invoked in 2002 the 1947 Taft-Hartley Act, unused since the 1970s, in a labor dispute with dockworkers at the west coast. All in all, the atmosphere at the administration was less labor union friendly and the CPA was created and founded as a division of the United States Department of Defense, reporting to the Secretary of Defense.

Second, the union movement had opposed the invasion and opposed the occupation and the new introduced political system since its first day. The movement organized and participated in protests against the coalition, demanded a quick withdrawal, and denied cooperation. It followed thereby an old tradition, deriving from the time of British occupation, considering itself as anti-colonialist. Additionally, as finances and wages of the state sector were controlled by the CPA, again protest emerged against the CPA. The wage ($60 a month) was the same as the Hussein regime. But, in times of the old regime, it included frequent bonuses, profit sharing, medical coverage, and food subsidies. There was no overtime pay, benefits, or medical coverage under the CPA.

Third, trade unions opposed the policies of quick privatization and *Reconstructing Iraq* strategy of the World Bank (World Bank, 2004). When Paul Bremer issued Order 39, paving the road for international privatization of the whole economy except natural resources, massive protests organized by Iraqi labor unions ensued (Harwood, 2005). On December 6, 2003, coalition forces stormed and destroyed the IFTU headquarter in Baghdad. It was at the time, when U.S. forces started heavy and heavily criticized counterinsurgency measures due to the worsening security situation (Hersh, 2003). However, unions had some successes. The first huge labor dispute after the occupation was between the Oil Workers Union and Bechtel and Halliburton. The latter company was known for formerly being headed by Vice President Dick Cheney, and is suspicious of having won projects in Iraq due to their good relations to the Bush administration. In early 2004, Oil workers protested against hiring of foreign workers, which were considered as much cheaper and a lesser security risk to the companies. Although the Iraqi labor code forbids such hiring when there is an equally qualified Iraq, it was legal, as the CPA ordered that foreign companies did not stand under Iraqi jurisdiction. However, after tribe leaders joined the strike, the companies agreed in a new hiring system and even increased the wage to $125 per month. Such actions are particularly annoying for the CPA and the Bush administration, as the reconstruction of Iraq should be paid by oil revenues. Hence, after all, it would not have been logically for the planning board nor the U.S. Administration to support a movement agitating against and discrediting the Provisional Authority's authority and reconstruction plans.

Trade Unions in the Iraqi Political Power Structure

The trade union movement had till 2005 another frontline to fight at besides the struggles with the CPA. The struggle between the 2003 still Ba'ath driven GFTU and IFTU, involving former Ba'athists now acting as insurgencies claimed a prominent victim. Saleh Hadi, International Secretary of the IFTU and well-respected figurehead of the entire movement was tortured and murdered in his own home on January 04, 2005. The manner how he was brought to death bore the handwriting of the secret service of the Ba'ath regime. Despite the loss of an important intellectual leader, this assault had a much broader and destructive message. In the atmosphere of growing violence it aimed to show, that the secular movement around the trade unions were not able to protect even its most prominent figure. Indeed, more and more supporters turned to sectarian groups to gain protection and financial outcome.

It was only two month later, the Iraqi Freedom Conference (IFC) was founded by labor groups, women's groups, students, and neighborhood groups agitating among other things against the occupation troops as well as against sectarian militias (IFC, 2006). Armed safety guards would patrol in the ethnically divided districts of Baghdad; 40% of the IFC's members belonged to the trade union movement. Its motto was "No Shi'ism, no Sunnism, our identity is humanity! And the occupation is the humanity's enemy", revealing the strategy: to mobilize against the occupation and against sectarianism by that way offering a third path. This strategy seemed to have failed, the IFC's trail went cold after the last raid of coalition troops on January 12, 2008; its former official website is cracked down.[3] On July 04, 2007, the leader of the Security Guards, Abdel-Hussein Saddam, was executed at night in his home. The IFC blames coalition forces. All in all, although many of the protected districts remained mixed for a long time, the IFC militias seem annihilated facing the coalition forces and sectarian militias.

Besides these two adversaries, trade union politics opened up another frontier: The new Iraqi administration and government. According to United States Labor Against the War (USLAW), freezing union bank accounts and assets, banning union leaders from traveling outside Iraq without prior government approval, transferring union leaders to remote locations far from their homes, families and union members, issuing criminal charges against Oil Union Federation officers alleging they are undermining the Iraqi economy by protesting privatization of oil resources and companies are regularly undertaken measures of the authorities to discipline union members and leaders (Lyderson, 2010).

This was, first, due to the rejection of the system of muhassassa and hence the indirect denial of legitimacy concerning many politicians in charge. Second, due to the anti - privatization and anti-corruption agenda of the unions. The Oil Workers Union IFOU, a member of the GFIW, had become the most powerful union in the country. Hussein Shahrastani, Iraq's oil minister, had issued a directive in 2007 banning unions from participating in any official discussions or negotiations about the new hydrocarbon law, since unions have no legal status to work within the state sector. However, unions claimed the right to participate in labor issues on behalf of Iraq's workforce. The union opposed the first draws, as they gave vast rights to international companies and aimed to open the path for privatization. But Iraqi unions believed that the Iraqi government is weak in comparison to savvy and powerfully connected international oil companies, which would be in the end more responsive and loyal to their shareholders than to the government and the needs of the Iraqi people, although Article 111 of Iraq's constitution states that natural resources belong to the people of Iraq (Bader-Blau, 2007, p.19).

The dispute about the oil law goes on in Iraq till today. The Iraqi government eventually drafted "no bid contracts" with some, mainly US oil companies. These no bid contracts are contracts only negotiated with one company respectively without public tendering procedure. Some negotiations were canceled, due to critics from within Iraq, but maybe mostly because some U.S. Senators feared that the contracts could undermine the efforts of Kurds, Sunnis and Shiites to reach agreement on a hydrocarbon law and a revenue-sharing agreement (Cramer & Robertson, 2008), however, some no bid contractors still work in Iraq till today.

Relations between the Iraqi administration and government and trade unions worsened as well due to disputes in the electricity sector. Unions conducted demonstrations against the worsening supply of electricity in Baghdad, at the same time asking where $13 billion went which were assigned for electrical infrastructure. The response was a complete crackdown of union offices in the electricity sector across Iraq. As these measures were not justified with Labor Law 150 but with a Ministerial Order under the Terrorism act of 2005, the consequences were much harsher than the years before (ITUC, 2011). Additionally, religious issues were more and more used to harass the mostly secular unions. Security forces stormed the head office of the Writers Union in December 2010 under the pretext that the union's social club sold alcohol, which was perceived by the head of Baghdad's council as 'un-Islamic' (ITUC, 2012). In 2011, the Iraqi Cabinet issued two decrees withdrawing its recognition of the General Federation of Iraqi Workers (GFIW) and its member trade unions, and instead appointed an unelected and unrepresentative "Ministerial Preparatory Committee (MPC)" to take over all union structures and assets and oversee the upcoming trade union elections. This attempt to turn the movement again into a "yellow union" was a reaction to mass protests among oil workers belonging to the IFOU against low wages and poor working conditions in the public sector compared to foreign enterprises before (Isakhan, 2014, pp.124-126).

Although trade unions had played a virtual role in mobilizing people across the country in the small Arab spring in January 2011, widely ignored by the western media, its power is restricted by harassment by the state and hostilities by religious groups. Since, unions focused on the struggle about a new labor code recognizing union rights in the public sector. Although several drafts were made, the last in 2014, none did suffice by a mile Iraq's ratified ILO conventions. Despite solidarity campaigns especially from the U.S., the UK and Japan, the issues did not find their way into the mainstream media. The movement is widely marginalized and gains mostly attention by infrequent statements. With hindsight, it seems, that the sectarian cleavage has prevailed all other noteworthy developments in Iraq, and from that point of view, western media and scientists run the risk of not simply explaining the sectarian gap in their reports, but to deepen it.

FUTURE RESEARCH DIRECTIONS

One thing is for sure: Iraq, facing IS a demoralized army and sectarian discrimination on all sides, should remain a memorial as warning for future generations. The State Building process failed to achieve peace and prosperity. Maybe other reasons can be found for that failure, besides the ones showed in this chapter.

In general terms, research about the roles of narratives, perceptions and views about history remains an important task to understand the dynamics of transition. Which groups or players invoked which view of history at which time and for what purpose? Or was it just a chain of coincidences that led to a certain self-perception of individuals or groups? What role do economic necessities, struggle for security, and the infrastructure of networks play? These questions could not only be asked in the Islamic world. However, especially as the sectarian gap grows in importance in the perceptions of all important Middle Eastern players, the region is a fruitful research field. Bahrain and the Gulf States could be the next objects of research, especially in the context of the Arab Spring, but also concerning future developments. Do people clinch to the nation-state, to their sect, to their employers or maybe to other categories of identity? When did which identity become en vogue? And even maybe: How long will sect play a role in the region? Is there another possible spit appearing at the horizon? Or will we find out only when the borders of Middle East are redrawn according to a sectarian reading, just to realize that the tensions in the region do not stop? The answers are still to be found.

Concerning trade unions as civil society institutions, research has to be done not only about their role in Arab Spring but in general about the relationship to authoritarian regimes. Valenzuela (1991) made a quite comprehensive attempt to close that gap drawing on European and South American unions. Middle East is still uncharted waters concerning such research agenda. But not only trade unions could be objects, other civil society groups and their influence regarding regime change and transition could be of interest, especially in the context of the Arab Spring. Civic associations, sport clubs, local parties, environmental groups etc. played and play their role as well.

CONCLUSION

In this essay questioned the prevailing assumption that the ongoing violence in Iraq would stem from an insuperable antagonism between Shi'ites and Sunnis. It was shown, that conflicts in the past did often derive from structural disparities, gaps in education, disputes among elites, rural and urban conflicts, and eventually authoritarianism. Consequently, religious issues were rather seldom at stage but rather issues of redistribution and self governance. However, the perception of a religiously split state coined the state building process and perpetuated the deepening of the sectarian cleavage in the country.

The trade union movement bore all requirements for enhancing a secular, democratic state. But the negative attitudes towards occupation and privatization made the CPA neglecting the movement, despite its potentials. In the aftermath of the invasion, the trade union movement was annihilated caught three fronts: the occupation forces due to the anti-colonial heritage and the delay of oil revenues, the Iraqi authorities due to protests against corruption, the proportional system as well as the demand for workers' rights, and the sectarian militias due to the movement's secular attitude. As the form of consociationalism introduced in Iraq fostered the gap and made sectarian groups the most important in the country, the secular movement was pushed into oblivion. It seems, as if the word was watching the sectarian cleavage grow and split the country, while a suitable partner for development was struggling unseen in the blind angle of the cameras.

REFERENCES

Anceschi, L., Gervasio, G., & Teti, A. (2014). *Informal Power in the Greater Middle East. Hidden Geographies*. London: Routledge.

Anderson, L., & Stansfield, G. (Eds.), (2005). *The Future of Iraq. Dictatorship, Democracy, or Division?* Macmillan.

Ashdow, P. (2014). Western Intervention over Isis won't prevent the Break-up of Iraq. Retrieved from http://www.theguardian.com/commentisfree/2014/aug/14/western-intervention-isis-iraq-muslim

Bader-Blau, S. (2007). Iraqi Unions vs. Big *Oil. Middle East Report (New York, N.Y.)*, *37*, 16–21.

Batatu, H. (1978). *The Old Social Classes and the Revolutionary Movements of Iraq. A Study of Iraq's Old Landed and Commercial Classes and of its Communists, Ba'athists, and Free Officers*. Princeton: Princeton University Press.

Berger, P. L., & Luckmann, T. (1966). *The Social Construction of Reality. A Treatise in the Sociology of Knowledge*. New York: Anchor Books.

Blumer, H. (1969). *Symbolic Interactionism: Perspective and Method*. New Jersey: Prentice Hall.

Dabasha, H. (2011). *Shi'ism. A Religion of Protest. Harvard*. Harvard University Press.

Dai, Y. (2008). Transformation of the Islamic Da'wa Party in Iraq: From the Revolutionary Period to the Diaspora Era. *Asian and African Area Studies*, *7*(2), 238–267.

Davis, E. (2005). History Matters: Past as Prologue in Building Democracy in Iraq. *Orbis*, *49*(2), 229–244. doi:10.1016/j.orbis.2005.01.004

Dawisha, A. (2009). *Iraq. A Political History from Independence to Occupation*. Princeton: Princeton University Press.

Dawisha, A. (2012). Post Occupation Iraq. The Brittleness of political Institutions. *The Woodrow Wilson International Center for Scholars: Occasional Paper Series,* Spring, 1-15.

Dodge, T. (2003). *Inventing Iraq: The Failure of Nation-Building and a History Denied*. New York: Columbia University Press.

Farouk-Souglett, M., & Suglett, P. (2001). *Iraq since 1958. From Revolution to Dictatorship*. New York: I. B. Tauris.

Feldman, N. (2004). *What We Owe Iraq: War and the Ethics of Nation Building*. Princeton: Princeton University Press.

Freemann, R. B., & Medoff, J. (1984). *What Do Unions Do?* New York: Basic Books.

Gubrium, J. F., & Goldstein, J. A. (2001). *Handbook of interview research*. London: Sage. doi:10.4135/9781412973588

Harwood, M. (2005, April). Pinkertons at the CPA. *Washington Monthly*. Retrieved from http://www.washingtonmonthly.com/features/2005/0504.harwood.html

Hersh, S. M. (2003, December 15). Moving Targets. Will the counter-insurgency plan in Iraq repeat the mistakes of Vietnam? *The New Yorker.*

IFC. (2006). Founding declaration of the Congress of Freedom in Iraq (in French). Retrieved from http://solidariteirak.org/spip.php?article301

ITUC. (2011). International Trade Union Confederation, *2011 Annual Survey of violations of trade union rights - Iraq*. Retrieved from http://www.refworld.org/docid/4ea66205c.html

ITUC. (2012). International Trade Union Confederation, *2012 Annual Survey of Violations of Trade Union Rights – Iraq*. Retrieved from http://www.refworld.org/docid/4fd88946c.html

Jabar, F. A. (2003). *The Shi'ite Movement in Iraq*. London: Saqi Books.

Jakob, T. E. (2014). The Islamic State in Iraq. The Key Lies in Baghdad (in German). Retrieved from http://www.fokus-nahost.de/?p=161360

Kramer, A. E., & Robertson, C. (2008, September 10). Iraq Cancels Six No-Bid Oil Contracts. *New York Times.*

LabourNet UK. (2004). The 'Yellow' Unions in Saddam's Iraq. Workers Democratic Trade Union Movement (WDTUM) in Iraq. Retrieved from http://www.labournet.net/world/0408/ukiraq03.html

Lijphart, A. (1977). *Democracy in Plural Societies. A Comarative Exploration*. London: Yale University Press.

Lipset, S. M., & Rokkan, S. (1967). *Party Systems and Voter Alignments. Cross-National Perspectives*. New York: Free Press.

Luizard, P.-J. (2002). *La question irakienne*. Paris: Fayard.

Lyderson, K. (2010). Iraqi Electricity Union Offices Raided Under Minister's Draconian Decree. Retrieved from https://www.globalpolicy.org/political-issues-in-iraq/oil-in-iraq/49337-iraqi-electricity-union-offices-raided-under-ministers-draconian-decree.html

Marr, P. (1970). Iraq's Leadership Dilemma: A Study in Leadership Trends. *The Middle East Journal*, *24*(3), 283–301.

Marr, P. (2004). *The Modern History of Iraq*. Boulder: Westview Press.

Muhsin, A. (2003). Address of the UK Representative of the Workers' Democratic Trade Unions of Iraq before the TUC in Sheffield on 23.09.2003 [Speech]. Retrieved from http://www.labournet.net/ukunion/0310/shefftuc1.html

Nakash, Y. (1996). *The Shi'is of Iraq*. Princeton: Princeton University Press.

Nasr, V. (2006). *The Shia Revival. How Conflicts within Islam will shape the Future*. New York: W. W. Norton & Company.

CPA Order 89. (2003). Amendments to the Labor Code Law No. 71, 1987.

People's World. (2006). Gripping narrative of an Iraqi trade unionist. Retrieved from http://www.peoplesworld.org/gripping-narrative-of-an-iraqi-trade-unionist/

Reynolds, M. O. (1988). A Critique of What Do Unions Do? *The Review of Austrian Economics*, *2*(1), 259–271. doi:10.1007/BF01539312

Scharpf, F. W. (1988). The Joint-Decision Trap: Lessons from German Federalism and European Integration. *Public Administration*, *66*(3), 239–278. doi:10.1111/j.1467-9299.1988.tb00694.x

Schlumberger, O. (2008). Structural Reform, Economic Order, and Development: Patrimonial Capitalism. *Review of International Political Economy*, *15*(4), 622–649. doi:10.1080/09692290802260670

Streit, M. E., Mummert, U., & Kiwit, D. (2000). *Cognition, Rationality and Institutions. Berlin et al.* Springer. doi:10.1007/978-3-642-59783-1

Tripp, C. (2000). *A History of Iraq*. Cambridge: Cambridge University Press.

Tudor, O. (2004). TUC report of an ICFTU fact-finding visit. Retrieved from http://www.tuc.org.uk/international-issues/iraq-appeal/iraq-unions-and-law

Wallach, J. (1995). *The Desert Queen. The Extraordinary Life of Gertrude Bell*. New York: Anchor Books.

Ward, C. J. (2011). *The Coalition Provisional Authority's Experience with Governance in Iraq: Lessons Identified*. United States Institute for Peace Special Report No.139. Washington D.C., United States Institute of Peace.

Webb, S. (2003). U.S. military attacks Iraqi trade unions. Retrieved from http://www.peoplesworld.org/u-s-military-attacks-iraqi-trade-unions/

Williams, M. H. (2013). *The Multicultural Dilemma. Migration, ethnic politics, and state intermediation*. New York: Routledge.

World Bank. (2004, July 26). State Owned Enterprises Reform In Iraq (Working Paper No. 2). *The World Bank*.

ADDITIONAL READING

Davis, E. (2005). *Memories of State: Politics, History, and Collective Identity in Modern Iraq*. Berkeley: University of California Press.

Dodge, T. (2003). *Inventing Iraq: The Failure of Nation-Building and a History Denied*. New York: Columbia University Press.

Johnson, A., & Muhsin, A. (2006). *Hadi Never died: Hadi Saleh and the Iraqi trade unions*. London: TUC Publications.

Tripp, C. (2000). *A History of Iraq*. Cambridge: Cambridge University Press.

KEY TERMS AND DEFINITIONS

Consociationalism: Form of political power sharing between elites in an along several cleavages divided state aiming on stability

CPA: (*Coalition Provisional Authority*) Transitional government established by the United States and their allies with legislative, executive, and judicial power in 2003 – 2004.

Kurds: Populace in northern Iraq and neighboring states with strong linguistic and traditional ties to the Persian cultural area struggling for recognition as nation

Narrative: A particular view of the past, neglecting or dumping some information down and focusing on other to get a coherent version and explanation of past and present events

Shi'ism: Current of Islam deriving from a dispute about the successor of prophet Muhammed with slightly different traditions and religious jurisdiction

State Building: Planned construction of a functioning state in post war countries focused on the power enforcement of state in society

Trade Union: Body of organized labor providing mutual aid benefits and representing workers' rights in civil society and politics

Zero Hour: The point of time where an old system has collapsed and society has to define its identity, ways of cohabitation, and political rules of the game again

ENDNOTES

1 I owe this little story to Prof. Dr. Raid Ramzi S. Al-Omari, stemming from Mosul and working at Al-Nahrain University, College of Engeneering, Baghdad, Iraq.

2 In Mosul some claim, that the council was implemented by David Petreus, the commander of the 101st Airborne. See: Celeste; p.4. But all Iraqis I had conversions with about this issue state that it was only *backed* by the coalition forces.

3 The information about the IFC is indeed very weak. Despite some conversations I had with Iraqi scholars visiting the Center of Iraq Studies (CIS) in Erlangen between 2012 and 2014 and some Internet articles on the movement, the only sources are Arabic and the French Wikipedia articles. Unfortunately, most of their links lead to the shutdown site www.ifcongress.com.

APPENDIX

Figure 1. The Circle of perception and action in Iraq after 2003 (© Thomas E. Jakob, 2015)

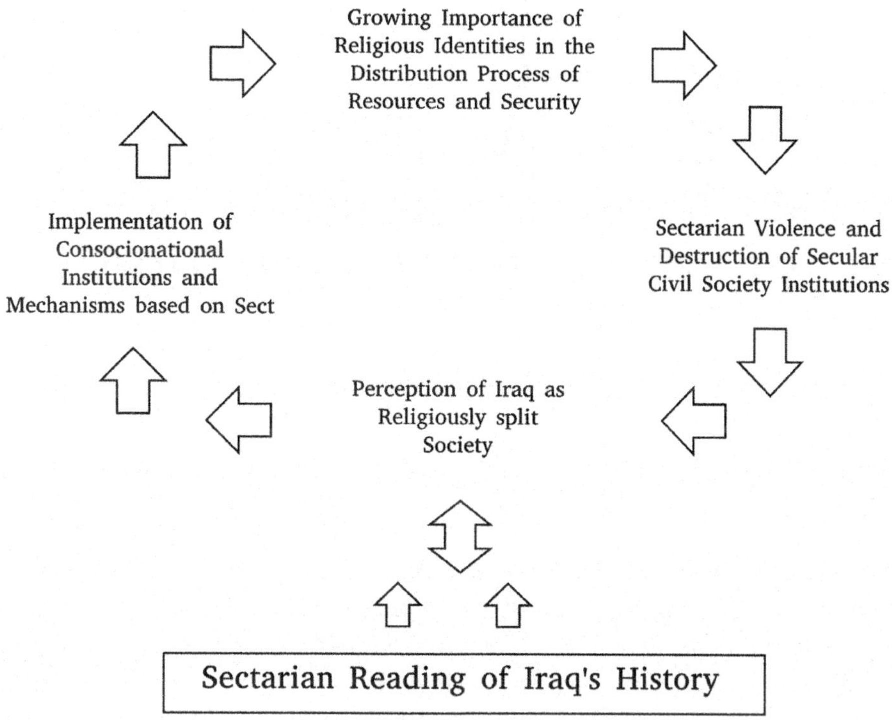

Table 1. Attitudes towards an ethnosectarian political system of the exile opposition groups in 2003

Exile Group	Attitudes towards an ethnosectarian political system
Da'wa	• Abolition of divide policy based on ethnicities, religions, sects. • Guarantee of the right to vote for all ethnicities, sects. • (Denial of division of posts based on ethnicities, sects).
Other Islamic Parties	• Islamic state comprehends all people regardless of ethnicities and sects (I). • Abolition of divide policy based on ethnicities, sects (I). • Negative attitude to sectarianism (S/M). • Abolition of racism (I). • Approval of racial, sectarian, and linguistic diversity (K/I).
INC and Secularist Parties	(Division of posts based on ethnicities, sects; INC).
Democrat Organizations	Abolition of divide policy based on ethnicities, religions, sects (B).

Abbreviations: (B) Iraqi Democratic Movement in Britain (IDMB); (I): al-Kutla al-Islamiya fil-Iraq (Sunni-Islamic); (K) Haraka al-Kawadir (Split of Da'wa); (S) Supreme Council for Islamic Revolution in Iraq (SCIRI) (Iran connected); (M) Munnazama al-'amal al-Islamy (islamic workers party). Full table see: Yamao, 2008, p.257.

Chapter 14
Reconciliation of Identity Groups in Iraq:
Conflict Analysis and Political Means of Ethnic Accommodation

Nazar Jamil Abdulazeez
Felsberg Institute, Germany

ABSTRACT

Since the parliamentary elections in 31st April 2014, the political process in Iraq described as a fragile, ethnic tension have mounted and security situation declined tremendously with the rises of Islamic State in Sunni Arab populated areas. Since 10th June 2014, over a million internally displaced people approached Iraqi Kurdistan Region in a two-week time period. More than 300,000 monitories, including Yazidi Kurds and Christians, have fled to Duhok city. Additionally, over 40,000 civilians Yazidis trapped for a week in the mountain of Snjar, running from Islamic State (IS). This text works out measures for accommodating conflicts and claims of Iraqi sectarian groups. In order to explore and assess application of those means in conflict accommodation in Iraq, first, this text analyses the conflict through identifying actors, outlines the structure of the conflict and change in the dynamic of the conflict over the time. Second section of this text, illustrates the means for reconciliation of different identities in the world of politics based on the conflict analysis.

INTRODUCTION

Violence against children and youth in war causes severe damage to individuals, communities and societies. This chapter aims to demonstrate the importance of reparations to children and youth as a peace building mechanism in the context of transitional justice. On one hand, the chapter seeks to address reparations for children and youth understood as a political project, with a transformative and participatory potential for rebuilding societies and healing the wounds of those who have been affected by armed conflict. On the other hand, the paper attempts to overcome the conception of children and youth as passive victims, providing them with agency to become engaged political members in building peaceful societies. Thus, reparations should position them as subjects of rights, giving them voice as contributors in peace building processes.

DOI: 10.4018/978-1-4666-9675-4.ch014

BACKGROUND

Since the parliamentary elections on 31st April 2014, the political process in Iraq described as a fragile. Ethnic tensions have mounted and security situation declined tremendously. Meanwhile, Islamic State in Iraq and Levant (ISIL) occupied most of the Sunni Arab populated areas. By 10th June 2014, over a million internally displaced people moved to the Iraqi Kurdistan Region (IKR). More than 300,000 monitories, including Yazidi Kurds and Christians, have fled to Duhok city. Additionally, over 40,000 civilians Yazidis trapped for a week in the mountain of Snjar, running from Islamic State (IS), without food and water (see UNHCR, UNOCHA and UNPO 2014). Furthermore, UN has declared a "level 3 Emergency" in Iraq due to the humanitarian crisis and gross violations of human rights especially against minority groups (ABC news, 2014).

The current crisis in Iraq was foreseen. This is because of tracking conflicts over the last two decades and comparison process among intra-state and inter-state conflicts; illustrate the fact that intra-state conflicts represent the majority (see Wallensteen 2007; Sisk and Varennes 2003). Additionally, Sisk (2003, p.139) points out that according to the evidences, most of the present-day wars are fought in the name of religion or ethnicity, which applies to the current circumstance in Iraq.

However, what this text works out are measures in the world of politics for accommodating conflicts among Iraqi identity groups. The first section of this text analyses the conflict in Iraq through identifying direct and indirect actors. Also, it outlines the structure of the conflict and change in the dynamic of the conflict over time. Second section of this text, illustrates the means for reconciliation of different identities in the world of politics and applies them to the crisis in Iraq. Initially, this paper stress the fact that eradication of discrimination and human rights violation are essential procedures before coming up with a resolution that meets the needs of various identities. In world of politics, power-sharing solution is an answer for a reform in the political system after deadly conflict or for a process of forming new government such as in Iraq after 2003, taking into account that there is no territorial claim by one of the conflict parties. Additionally, autonomy is an option that could either bring secessionist towards integration or a step on the ladder towards separation as a last resort (Ghai 2003, p.186). However, there is no comprehensive cure that would be suitable in all cases and situations. Therefore, this paper utilizes the conflict in Iraq as an example of accommodating ethnic conflict.

CONFLICT ANALYSIS

According to the definitions pointed out by UPPSALA Conflict Data Program (UCDP), the current conflict in Iraq is regarded as an armed conflict[1]. However, in order to provide sufficient analysis, this section stresses the social conflict among Iraqi identities. Since, the social conflict occurs when two or more actors work hard simultaneously to obtain an available set of inadequate resources (Wallensteen 2007, p.15).

Concentration of this analysis is on area that has been suffering for more than 50 years and regarded as infamous religious conflict around the world, which is the Middle East (Nye 2007, p.185). More precisely is Iraq, which is located at the heart of this area. Iraq was violently administrated by Saddam Hussein and Baath party for three decades. "Forced disappearance, torturing, arbitrary custodies and executions" were used widely. Consequently these practices resulted in eviction of 500,000 Shi'a Arabs from Iraq to Iran. Also, the Iraqi government carried out the well-known notorious genocide campaign "Anfal" against Kurds that led to arresting and group executions of at least 100,000 Kurds in 1988 (ICTJ 2012). In March 2003, Iraq was invaded by US-led collation forces that continued until 2011. During this period tension and conflict among

Iraqi identities have increased. The tension among Iraqi identities mounted in period between 2005 to 2008 civil war (see Dodge 2012; Percy 2009; Barak 2007; Simon 2007). Civil war in Iraq cost 112,000 lives of civilians, including children, men, women, young people and elderly people (IBC 2014).

The focus of this paper is analysis of the conflict after withdrawal of the US-led forces from Iraq in 2011. This is because of three reasons. First, the USA role in Iraq has changed from direct actor to being as in-direct. Second, Iranian influence in the political process in Iraq have increased, which was a long lasting aim for Iran. As an evidence, tracking the history, one of the reasons for Saddam Hussein to fight Iran and one of reasons for Reagan administration to support Iraq was to prevent the wide spread of "Ayatollah Khomeini's revolution to southern and central of Iraq, eastern Saudi Arabia and Bahrain", area in which Shi'a and oil are located (O'leary 2009, p.270). Third, new actor named ISIL gained more power and was able to control wide geographical areas in Iraq. In recent days (June, 10th 2014) Sunni insurgents have seized the cities of Mosul and Tikrit, and were moving closer to Baghdad (BBC news 2014). Growths of Islamic State (IS), previously named ISIL, in Iraq resulted in one and half million internally displaced people who have approached Iraqi Kurdistan Region in a two-week time period. Minorities such us Yazidi Kurds and Christians have been victimized by IS armed groups. Consequently, over 300,000 minorities have left their homes and escaped to the IKR. Additionally, over 40,000 civilians Yazidis trapped for a week in the mountain of Snjar, running from IS groups, without food and water (see UNHCR, UNOCHA and UNPO 2014). In several meetings of the writer of this text with survivals in Duhok province, three cases of unaccompanied children was recorded and kidnapping of seventy-three Yezidi girls and women by IS armed groups was documented. Also, cases of dead children and elderly people at the mountains of Snjar were reported by survivals to the text author.

The analysis of the conflict in this paper focuses on the three elements; actors, structures and dynamics of the conflict analysis, which have been used by agencies such as World Bank, Department of Intentional Development (DFID) and Swedish International Development Cooperation (SIDA).

Actors of the Conflict

One of the three main elements of conflict analysis is identifying actors that have been affected or able to influence the direction of the conflict, on domestic, regional and global level (SIDA 2006, p.10). According to the constitution, Iraq is a country of "multiple nationalities, religions, and sects" (ICR P.6). Moreover, although the Iraqi constitution identifies both Kurds and Arabs, who portrayed by Sunni and Shiite, represents the majority of population, there are minorities such as Turkmen, Christians, Yazidis, and Assyrians living in Iraq too. Political entities in Iraq are representing their sectarian groups, which reinforced through creation of alliances and parliamentary blocs in four processes of parliamentary elections. One of the reasons is the anarchy and security vacuums in Iraq after the US-led invasion in 2003. In such circumstance, ethnicity was important for individuals and victimized people, as their lives were under threat due to their identity (Abdulazeez, 2013, p.37). In this regard, individuals understand their ethnic group as a source of protection (Blagojevic 2009, p.11).

Accordingly, the direct actors of the conflict in Iraq are Shi'a Arabs, Sunni Arabs and Kurds. They are estimated to constitute 55%, 18.5% and 21% of the population in Iraq, respectively (Abdulazeez 2013, p.31). Shi'a Arabs are represented by the Iraqi National Coalition (INC) (Aljazeera 2010). The INC is constituted of Shi'a Arab political parties, including Islamic Dawa party, Iraqi nationalist "Sadr movement" and Islamic Supreme Council of Iraq. They are mainly living in the south and centre of Iraq. Before 2003, only Islamic Dawa party and Islamic Supreme Council of Iraq were existed and they were in an armed conflict with Iraqi regime. After 2003, Shi'a Arab came to the power in Iraq as the size of Shi'a Arab population enabled them gain more than 50% of votes.

The second actor in Iraq is Kurds who have been represented in the Iraqi parliament by the Kurdistan alliance since 2003. Kurdistan alliance is constituted of Kurdistan Democratic Party (KDP), Patriotic Union of Kurdistan (PUK), Gorran movement and Islamic parties. They are mainly living in the north and north-east of Iraq. After the first Gulf-War in 1991, Kurds have formed their own government, voted for their own parliament and reinforced "Peshmarga" forces in the Iraqi Kurdistan region. Peshmarga forces are recognized by the Iraqi constitution as part of defending forces in Iraq (O'leary 2009, p.10). After 2003, they have participated actively in Iraqi parliamentary elections and in forming the cabinets of Iraq governments.

The third direct actor in Iraq is Sunni Arabs who ruled Iraq for more than 84 years (Dodge 2005, p.44). After 2003, Sunni Arabs were fought the US-led occupation forces via insurgency, as well as, they boycotted the first parliamentarian election in 2005. Sunni Arabs "suffered from demographic delusion of grandeur", whereas, high participation rate was recorded for both Shi'a Arabs and Kurds (O'leary 2009, pp.17-18). Political entities that represent Sunni Arabs have created a new bloc named National Coalition Forces (NCF). The NCF constitute of several political parties including United for Reform and Iraqi Islamic Party. Sunni Arabs are mainly living in the centre and north-west of Iraq. However, some of the provinces in Iraq such Kirkuk and Baghdad are accommodating various Iraqi sectarian groups.

Additionally, since 2003, only AL Iraqiya List, led by former Prime Minister Ayad Allawi, had attempted to maintain their ideology through representing nationalist from different identities in Iraq, rather than representing a specific ethnic group. Based on the election results, it was clear that Iraqi people are mobilized by the political parties based on their identity. Therefore, AL Iraqiya list was able to gain only 22 seats in the Iraqi parliamentary elections 2014. Even though, Al – Iraqiya list is predominantly Sunni and still important party in the current political crisis (Hiltermann 2012).

There is another type of actors who do not participate directly in the conflict. However, they support a direct actor either publicly or secretly. Consequently, they are indirect actors in the conflict and have played a vital role in Iraq conflict after 2003 (Nye 2007, p.49). After 2003, neighbouring states have been working on advancing their interest in Iraq through influencing the political process, developing economic relations and even providing military support (Dodge 2005, p.8).

The role of the United States of America was always changing. In 2003, the US invaded Iraq and ruled the country through CPA. In 2004, they handed over the sovereignty of Iraq to the transitional government and the US government withdrew forces from Iraq in 2011. There are various arguments that debate US goal for invading Iraq, one of which is "removal of Saddam would be the key to unlock the Middle East" (Dodge 2005, p.58). Again by June 2014, the president Obama decided to take part in the new conflict in Iraq. The USA involvement portrayed by; carrying out limited operation of the US air forces in Iraq in order to target IS, provision of military support, sending military advisors to train Iraqi forces including Peshmarga forces[2] and providing humanitarian assistant to trapped civilians in Snjar Mountains (the guardian 2014).

Since 2003, terrorist groups and militia have devastated the life of Iraq people and cost over 100,000 lives of civilians (IBC 2014). At the beginning of the US-led invasion of Iraq, many Sunni Arabs and some Shi'a Arabs created their insurgency groups, claiming that they were fighting the U.S. led forces. Sunni insurgency groups "have been supported by terrorist organizations like Abu Musaab Al Zarqawee" (Nye Jr. 2007, p.196). Another infamous terrorist group named ISIL have already gained human and military resources through occupying majority of Sunni populated areas. Islamic State, previously named ISIL, is an extension to the Islamic State in Iraq, which is a terrorist organization established in 2006 by AL Qaida organization in Iraq (Mapping Militant Organizations 2012).

Structure of the Conflict

Regardless the conflict actors, states or parties, Galtung (2000, p.52) in his text classified conflict formation in any part of the world into five categories; economic, military, political, cultural and geographical conflict. Additionally, the purpose of structure analysis is to identify the main reasons of the conflict (SIDA 2006, p.9). Accordingly, the paragraphs in this section explain the structure of the conflict among Iraqi sectarian group. In Iraq, the issues in the structure of the conflict are varies according to identity of the group. In another words, the issues of the conflict between Kurds and the central Government of Iraq, which ruled by Shi'a Arabs, are different form conflict issues between Sunni Arabs and the Iraqi central government.

Initially, structure of the conflict between Kurds and Shi'a Arabs that rule the government are; nationality, oil production, oil revenue and control over the contested areas.

Nye (2007, p.186) described a nation by a group of people who share common characteristics such us "ethnicity, linguistic, religion". One of the long standing conflicts in Iraq is between Kurds and the Iraqi former governments. Galtung (2000, pp.109-110) in TRANSCEND program, he identified five armed conflicts between the Kurds as a nation with the state of Iraq during 1952 until 1999.

The urgency of recognizing Kurdish nationality in Iraq as a step in the ladder towards independency was essential for Kurdish parties in the Iraqi Kurdistan region, which led to unification of their political message after fall of Iraqi regime in 2003 (Dodge 2005, p.53). As strategy, Kurds have worked on economic development through legislation of their own laws for investments and enhancing practises for attraction of foreign firms to their region. Since the new Iraqi constitution shared this power with federal regions (Iraqi constitution article 112 second). Kurds were successful in this regard and remaining IKR as a safe region in Iraq after 2003 assists them to achieve this strategy.

Additionally, the second pillar of this economic development in the Iraqi Kurdistan Region is oil production. Since 2008, IKR have started attacking firms to their region. Consequently, by 2013 IKR singed contracts for oil production with world known firms such as DNO, Exxonmobile and chevron[3].

In contrast, the desire of Kurds in Kurdistan region for independency and gaining more power was opposed by the Iraqi state. Until 2015, the Iraqi central government refused to recognize IKR contracts for oil production. Also, Iraqi central government made more pressure on IKR through blocking IKR budget share in the Iraqi general budget for 2014. Additionally, the Iraqi government paused spending on human and military resources for Peshmarga. Although, Peshmarga forces are formally recognized in the Iraqi constitution as part of Iraqi defence system, Peshmarga forces deprived form all Iraqi military supports and resources. Another, challenge between Iraqi central government and Iraqi Kurdistan region is article 140 of the new Iraqi constitution, which provided a road map to resolve contested areas. Kirkuk is one of those areas which claimed by Kurds as a part of their region and been separated from their region by Saddam Hussein (Hiltermann 2010).

The above paragraphs illustrated the structure of the conflict between Kurds and Iraqi central government. The coming paragraphs point out conflict structure between Sunni Arabs and Shi'a Arabs, portrayed by the Iraqi central government.

Power control has remained one of the main structures of the conflict among Sunni Arabs and Shi'a Arabs and it has been obvious in the political scene after 2003. This is because one of the on-going old conflicts in politics is the control of the power (Nye, Jr. 2007, p.68). Since March 2003 until now, the number of Iraqi parliament seats that belong to Shi'a Arabs enabled them to rule Iraqi government.

Sunni Arabs did not represent the majority in Iraq. However, they have ruled Iraq for over 30 years through Ba'ath party. Invasion of Iraq and defeating Ba'athist regime was a clear vision for Americans. However, political mission was more complicated and unexpected (Dodge 2005, p.58). This is because Iraqi sectarian groups, precisely religious, looked at gaining power and authority in new Iraq (Wallensteen 2007, p.61). Shi'a Arabs established and organized their own militia. On the other hand, Sunni Arabs aimed at retaking the power in Iraq through the insurgency (O'leary 2009, pp.8-10). Additionally, lack of stability and lack of enforcing law and order in Iraq by occupation forces led to grow of militia. Militia groups claimed that they were fighting occupation forces and the Iraqi government figures. However, "car –jacking, house –breaking and kidnapping the middle class community" were widely practiced by militia groups (see Dodge 2005, p.15-19). As evidence, analysts counted at least 56 organizations and small fictions that claimed to be involved in organized insurgency, self-defences, or "Jihad" in new Iraq (O'leary 2009, p.6). Beside militia and insurgency groups, the new government in Iraq deprived Sunni Arabs form participation in the political process through justices and accountability law[4].

Another conflict structure is economic discrimination of Sunni Arabs in Iraq. Iraq is coming second in the top list of countries that reserve the largest amount of oil (Dodge 2005, p.8). However, Iraqi debt in 2003 ranged between 130-140 Billion US Dollars, where most of them cancelled according to Paris club agreement (BBC Arabic 2012)[5]. In order to recover from war, it was imperative for Iraqi state to work on developing its economy, precisely oil production. However, discrimination in distribution of oil revenue and lack of investment due to bad security situation led to "displacement of more than one and a half million families during 2006-2010" (IOM cited in BBC 2011).

As a result, Sunni Arabs deprived from economic development and participation in the political process. Consequently, insurgency was the approach for many skilled Iraqi officers who remained without job and pensions. During negotiations process carried out among Iraqi political elites, Shi'a Arabs, and Sunni Arabs in February 2006, Sunni Arabs negotiators had 8 demands, two of which were reconstruction of new Iraqi army and security forces that guarantee inclusion of all ethnic groups without discrimination. Additionally, Sunni Arabs requested termination of both articles 7 and 135 in the Iraqi constitution, which deal with De-Baathification, because they are inconsistent with equality in front of the law (USIP 2007, p.9).

In this section, conflict structures among Iraqi identity groups were explained. The latter two paragraphs stressed on-going political competition among Shi'a Arabs and Sunni Arabs and economic discrimination of Sunni Arabs. The next section outlines dynamic of the conflict through explaining role of conflict actors in specific episodes that have great impact on the life of Iraqis.

Dynamic of the Conflict

Attitude and behaviour of the actors, Sunni Arab, Shi'a Arab and Kurds, are changing over time in order to gain more power and economic prosperity of their identity groups. In the following paragraph, this text concentrates on; the political development and participation of Kurds, Sunni Arabs and Shi'a in the political process in Iraq after 2010. Later on, it explores the economic situation and security development in Iraq.

A result of the Iraqi parliamentary elections in 2010 was a turning point in the political process especially for Sunni Arabs. This is because Sunni Arabs, who boycotted the elections process in 2005, actively participated in order to ensure their representation in the political process. However, the De-Baathification law was still in practice. Consequently, many Sunni Arabs including the leader of Al Arabia political entity deprived from running to the public office as a candidate for Sunni Arabs. Later on, as a part of responding to the claims of Sunni Arab, the leader of Al Arabia list was appointed as the deputy of Prime minister. Additionally, former Iraqi officers were deprived from running to the public office or hold senior positions at the new Iraqi Government.

Since 2003, Kurds in Iraq have participated in the process of elections and referendum in order to enhance political position of Kurds in Iraq and to advance economic prosperity in the IKR. Iraqi government was representing Shi'a group that was led by Nuri Al Maliki, the leader of the State of Law – political entity. The new established government in 2010 did not respond to the claims of both Kurds and Sunni Arabs as it has been explained in previous section. Additionally, Al Maliki concentrated on the notion of powerful central government. Due to political struggle among politicians form Shi'a Arabs, Sunni Arabs and Kurds, The prime minister utilized his position to expand his own power through appointment of his son as a leader of special troop and himself as acting minster for four ministries including ministry of interior. Moreover, in 2013 the Vice president of Iraq "Tariq Al Hashimi", who is another Sunni Arab leader in Iraq, escaped to Turkey. Iraqi court claimed that his accusation was because of his terrorism conduct.

Economically, Iraqi people were suffering from bad economic situation. However, unemployment rate in Iraq was over 30% in 2004 and dropped to 11% by the end of 2012 (Iraq Media NET 2012). Additionally, in comparison with the civil war period, 2005 and 2008, security situation in Iraq improved tremendously. For example, number of Iraqi victims dropped to 4000 after 2009, number of casualties among Iraqi civilian dropped by 87% in 2010 (IBC 2014).

The above two paragraphs illustrated willingness of Iraqi identity groups to participate in the political process. At the same time, it explained the fact that Iraqi central government was not able to fulfilling demands of Sunni Arabs and Kurds in Iraq after 2010. The coming paragraphs stress declines in the political development in Iraq and economic discrimination by Iraqi central government.

In theory, Abdulazeez (2013, p.6) worked out that applying 'the framework analysis[6]' model in the case of ethnic conflict in Iraq, political exclusion motivated Ethnic Mobilization due to grievance caused by discrimination, strong group-identity among all Iraqi sectarian groups and also the groups' cohesiveness. Continuous pressure and use of violence by government upon mobilized ethnic groups increased the sense of threat and stimulated violent political actions (Abdulazeez 2013, p.6).

March 2012, "Sunni Muslims stage mass rallies across the country over several months, protesting against what they see as marginalisation by the Shia-led government" (BBC news 2014). Iraqi provinces have seen mass demonstration especially in AL Anbar province and in town of Hawija, which is located at the south of Kirkuk. After few months of continues demonstrations, Iraqi government decided to use violence in Al Anbar and Hawija in order to separate protestors. As a result of the military action, at least 50 civilians were killed in Hawija (BBC news 2014). In the meanwhile, Sunni Arabs were not successful in establishing federal system in their provinces such us in Tikrit as the notion was opposed strongly by Iraqi central government and Shi'a Arabs7 (AL SHARQ AL AWSAT 2011). Later, Sunni Arabs in Al Anabar and Nenawa provinces were deprived from participating in Iraqi parliamentary elections 2014 due to security reasons, which is one of the political rights granted by universal declaration of human rights and Iraqi constitution.

On the other hand, Kurds were struggling with the Iraqi central government. Politically, Kurds have realized that the prime-minister is not welling to implement article 140 and release the allocated budget share for Peshmarga. Consequently, Kurds, Sunni Arabs jointly with Sadri movement, which is one of the Shi'a groups, have worked on replacing the Prime minister 2012 but their attempt was not successful.

Economic tension mounted between the Iraqi central Government and Kurdistan regional Government regarding oil production. For Kurd having direct contract with firm for oil production is a step on the ladder towards independency. Hiltermann (ICG 2012) pointed out that the latter is characterized to be open and developed society, they signed contracts with the famous and the biggest oil companies in the world such "ExxonMobil, Chevron, Total and Gazprom", which is strongly condemned by the Iraqi state.

Human rights and rights of minority groups remained one of the challenging and threatening new Iraq government. HRW (2010) pointed out that "human rights conditions across Iraq remain extremely poor for vulnerable groups, particularly women, minorities, and men suspected of homosexual conduct". This is in addition to 20 Iraqi media worker killed in a two- year time, torture and bad treatment, overcrowd and abuse by police and military were reported in Iraqi prisons.

Minorities have been targeted by explosions, threatening life, kidnapping and forced deportation. As a result, many families moved from central and south of Iraq towards Kurdistan region. IOM (2012) illustrated that after terrorist attack on Saidat al-Najat church in Baghdad in 2012 the number of Christian were moved to Kurdistan region reached to 1350 families. One of the distinguished achievements of Iraqi constitution is recognition of identity, cultural, educational and religion rights of minorities. However, they have been a victim for terrorist and militia groups. Christians do not worry about Islam rather than "the interpretation of jihad as unconditional war against infields" (Galtung 2000, p.59).

In such political and economic discrimination, IS have utilized grievances of Sunni Arabs to mobilize people. Additionally, they have attacked prisons in Baghdad and Nenawa, where many of Sunni Arabs arrested including terrorists. As a result, "at least 500 prisoners, mainly senior al-Qaeda members, escaped from Taji and Abu Ghraib jails in a mass breakout". IS was able to maintain and strengthen their position in Al Anbar province. By 9th of June, IS started expanding their operations into areas beyond Al Anbar. In the few days they were able to control over 40% of Iraqi state including Slahadeen, Diala and Nenawa provinces. IS had clear strategy in terms of expanding their operation in Iraq especially in Sunni populated areas. Local factors that enabled IS are; first is common identity among people in Nenawa, Salahadeen, Diala and Alanbar, which is Sunni Arabs. Second, International Crisis Group pointed out that "accumulated grievances of Sunnis in the area meant that IS pushed against a house of cards" (ICR 2014). Third, high unemployed rate pushed people to join armed groups as a source of income. Fourth, IS mobilized former Ba'ath party members and former Iraqi officers in their armed groups. By 10th June, IS appointed former Ba'ath party member and former senior Iraqi officer as new governor and mayor of Slahdeen and Nenawa. Finally, Iraqi army forces in those areas did not fight IS group.

At this stage Kurds reacted immediately and send Peshmarga to areas such as Kirkuk in order to protect it from IS occupation. However, it was the golden opportunity for Kurds to control contested areas after 14 years of negotiations. Senior Official form Iraqi Kurdistan Region claimed that, Peshmarga went to Kirkuk in order to protect it from IS occupation based on the request of Iraqi prime minister. Similarly to Kurds, Shi'a Arabs established a militia and send it to Samara, which is located in the South of Salahadeen, in order to protect "Imam Al Askari" shrine from IS occupation.

The above two paragraphs pointed out new conflict actors, which is IS. Also, it explained response of both Kurds and Shi'a Arabs to the IS expansion. The following paragraphs illustrate new roles of in-direct actors with change in the dynamic of the conflict.

Occupation of large areas in Iraq by IS armed groups stimulated involvement of in–direct actors in the conflict in Iraq. First of all, Iran has seen IS operations in Iraq as a threat upon Shi'a in Iraq and Iran. One of the important issues for Iran is "Shi'a crescent" which has not only an implication upon Iraq, also affects other countries such as Syria, Jordan, Lebanon and other countries in the Persian Gulf (Parasiliti 2012, p.130 and Norell 2007, p.3). In Iraq, it is clear is that Iran has supported one of the main Shi'a political parties, the Sader Movement and created the Islamic Supreme Council of Iraq (ISCI), for the purpose of influencing the decision of furthering the interests of Iran in Iraq (O'Leary 2009, p.9 and Dodge 2005, p.20). Iran have directly involved in the conflict through sending military troops, airplanes and military support for both Iraqi central Government and Iraqi Kurdistan region. As evidence, by 7th July 2014, Iranian government announced that one of the Iranian pilots killed in Iraq during fighting IS armed groups (Al Arabia 2014). Additionally, on the 26th August 2014, in a press conference with the president of Iraqi Kurdistan Region, Iranian foreign minister stated that they have supported Iraqi army and Peshmarga in their fighting with IS armed groups by sending military equipment (Rudaw 2014).

Another involvement of in-direct actor in the Iraqi conflict is the USA. IS operations stimulated threats upon US interests in Iraq especially in the Iraqi Kurdistan Region. Additionally, direct involvement of Iran in the conflict increases Iranian position in Iraq, which is against the interest of the USA. Consequently, the USA involvement constituted of carrying out limited operation by the US air forces in Iraq against IS armed group, sending military advisors, providing humanitarian assistant to trapped civilians in Snjar Mountains and finally military support of Iraqi forces including Peshmarga (the guardian 2014).

The above paragraphs illustrated the dynamic of the conflict and roles of the actors, which is the last part of the conflict analysis section. In the coming section, this text explores the ethnic accommodation/ reconciliation means in the world of politics. Meanwhile, it utilizes the conflict in Iraq.

POLITICAL MEANS FOR ETHNIC ACCOMMODATION IN WORLD OF POLITICS

Iraq is a multiple nationality, cultures and religions from its inception. Rival and tension among Iraqi sectarian groups is in a continual manner. Therefore the beginning and the end of the conflict life are not recognized by causes and effects. Rather than, specific episodes in the conflict life have influential impact on escalating or taming the conflict among Iraqi identities.

If the causes of conflict such as discrimination and violation of human rights have been resolved then it means we have accommodated ethnic identities. Without doubts no, Wallensteen (2007, p.171-3) pointed out that it is hard to eliminate the demand for territory once it has been raised and dealing with human rights issues remain either preventive measures of conflict or means reconciliation after the stalemate of the conflict such as Bosnia-Herzegovina case 'agreement Dayton' in 1995. He continued, nevertheless, it is possible to step back claims to autonomy as an interim or final solution for the conflict, such as Kurds in Turkey whom scaled back their demand from independence to autonomy. However, Varennes (2003, p.153) concluded that the accord beyond fighting stalemate and negotiation process involves at least one of the three options, which are independency, power-sharing or autonomy and human rights guarantee.

This paper demonstrates political means for accommodation or reconciliation of various identity groups in five options. Firstly, measures to be taken in order to eradicate discrimination and human rights violation as essential procedures, which are essential in both negative and positive peace8situations. Secondly, decentralization is an option to guarantee response to one group will not affect the rights of others. Thirdly, power-sharing is suitable in the cases of reform in the political process after armed conflict, taking into account that there is no territorial claim. Additionally, power-sharing solution is applicable in the process of forming new government. Fourthly, autonomy is as an option that could either bring secessionist towards integration or a step in the ladder towards separation (Ghai 2003, p.186). Fifthly, the final option is independency, which is the final resort.

Eradication of Discrimination and Human Rights Violation

Initially, one of the crucial means for prevention of ethnic conflict is human right protection and non-discrimination policies. Both (Wallensteen 2007, p.166) and (Varennes 2003, p.153- 5) have stressed that discrimination against minorities may enhance violence activities. Discrimination itself takes various forms such as lack of economic development, restriction on religious practice and use of language in addition to other forms of discrimination such as legal and administration. Moreover the latter focused on employment opportunity or holding governmental positions, landownership, transmigration programs which could change the demography of specific areas and citizenship denial. While, the former added lack of political representation, oppression by security forces and difficulty for crossing borders and he concluded that all above are rights declared in "the universal declaration of human rights 1949 and the convention of human rights 1966". It is commonly known that all above discriminations were widely practiced during ruling Iraq by Saddam Hussein (see Iraqi Constitution; ITCJ 2012 and HRW 2006). However, after 2003 security situation declined, people organized according to their ethnicity and religion significantly. Steele (2008, p.5) argued that when the security situation reached to the level of survival, religion, ethnicity, tribe or any other classifications of identity will be drawn more narrowly.

In order to prevent violence activities and/ or escalating the conflict into armed conflict, it is imperative, not only recognize human rights principles constitutionally as it is regarded as a guarantee for protection of the rights of minorities (Varennes 2003, p.159), but also put those rights into practice and fulfil them. Also, legal recognition of human right principles is essential in a peace making and peace building processes such as in Iraq 2003.

In peace accord in Angola and Dayton General Frame work agreement for peace in Bosnia and Herzegovina, Varennes (2003, p.152) pointed out that the common features in many peace agreements are inclusion of human rights principles and more precisely protection of minorities, and indigenous rights and non-discrimination. Application of human right principles enables civil society institutions to monitor fulfilling rights of entities and to work on reversing the ethnic cleansing (Bell 2003, p.169). Moreover, new established governments after intra-state armed conflict may seek democratic accreditation, which facilitate support of the international community in a post war era efforts (Reilly 2003, p.174). In the case of Iraq, Security Council delegated a mission to Iraq[9] in order to monitor human rights situation and to provide political assistance in forming new democratic government. Additionally, although the constitution affirmed establishment of Human rights commission since early 2005, article 102, the first commission has not been established until April 2012 (Aswat Al Iraq 2012). Furthermore, many civil society organizations have been established to monitor and work on human rights education.

In sum the list of rights that acquires to meet is firstly, elimination of the various forms of discriminations that we have already mentioned previously such as equal access to natural resource, freedom of population movements and protection of indigenous settlement, international transparency and secular state that is separated from religious (Wallensteen 2007, p.167). Secondly, Bell (2003, p.166) pointed out that in addition to the bill of rights, what is required as an ideal framework for human rights provision are; reform in policing, fair and transparent criminal justices and judiciary system, setting up human right commission, prisoner release and amnesties.

Human rights principles well illustrated in the articles of new Iraqi constitution. This is in addition to articles 9, 45 and 84 that focus on the protection of human rights during activities of intelligence, and other security forces and prohibiting some traditional activities that contradict with human rights principles (Iraqi constitution). In comparison with period before 2003, there are progress made in distribution of oil revenue, amnesty, delegation of authority to the provincial level and constitutional reform. However, there are issues needs to be address. For example, good governance, development of economic sector, enhancing security, reinforcing rule of the law and provision of infrastructure services (Steele 2008, p.3).

Decentralization

Second, decentralization of authority and power delegation at the lower level is another option. Theoretically, connection between peace building and human rights is clear and it is recognized in human rights instruments but practically the nature of this connection is challenging and controversial (Bell 2003, p.161). This is because responding to the rights of one group may affect the other ones'. Therefore, is it imperative at the end to find solution that serves the interests of all groups and to have a chance for a revision after a specific period of time (Wallensteen 2007, p.167). Sunni Arabs and partly Shi'a Arabs have opposed the decentralization option in Iraq, which was demonstrated during voting on new constitution. In contrast, Kurds and many Shi'a Arabs favoured weak central government. This is because the latter group claimed that genocide and annihilation had been practiced against them when Iraq was centralized and ruled by Sunni Arabs. However, Sunni Arabs claimed that they may be punished collectively because of sins of the Ba'athists (McGarry and O'Leary 2008, p.354-5).

Wallensteen (2007, p.168-70) argued that a sever discrimination lead to conflict, one of which is armed conflict. In contrast, nationalism is regarded as a root cause for violent ethnic conflict since "absences of good governance and democratic tradition, or lack of economic development, do not breed ethnic conflict" (Varennes 2003, pp.155-8). It is commonly known that Kurds have continued claiming for independency since the inception of Iraqi state. Thus, decentralization is integrated into Iraqi constitution, by which the preamble recognize that reserving Iraqi free union and sovereignty is reserved by implementing Iraqi constitution only. In another words Kurds have the rights to announce their state when Iraqi central government do not adhere the constitution articles (Iraqi constitution Preamble).

Power-Sharing Solution

Third, in the worlds of politics power-sharing solution is another option after civil war or when independency is a demand of an identity group. Within the border of a state when the conflict enhanced into armed conflict, precisely into civil war, peacemaking, peace building and peacekeeping will be a difficult process. Generally, there are two reasons for that, civil war is more destructive than inter-state war both socially and psychologically, and conflict parties are ingrained within the same state (Wallensteen 2007, pp.122-3). The common feature of nowadays conflict is upon either territorial organization or partition of the states (Ghai 2003, p.184). However, preferences and use of power by the states are seen as the root causes for the majority of conflict that resulted in demand for autonomy and power sharing solutions (Varennes 2003, p.157). Three groups in Iraq, Sunni Arabs, Shi'a Arabs and Kurds have different concerns and arguments. Kurds were cautious about their independency and self-administration that they have enjoyed since 1991. Shi'a Arabs had concerned about not lose their political weight in new Iraq due to attacks of Sunni insurgents. Finally Sunni Arabs afraid from Iranian influence upon Shi'a political parties, whom running government (Steele 2008, p.3). In the coming paragraphs, this text explores two options for power-sharing approaches in handling a conflict, in which they are integrative and consociational power-sharing approach. Then it will explore autonomy as political form of self-administration.

The first option is power sharing–integrative approach, which is; unified state, non-ethnic based classification, centralized, inclusive, has federal structure and take on the majority electoral system. However, the consociational power-sharing approach considers ethnic based -territorial autonomy, establishes confederal structure, develop quota system to guarantee minimum level of representation, has high proportional electoral system and recognizes cooperation rights. It deals with ethnic groups as a "building blocks" (Sisk 2003, p.146-8). Moreover, the first approach needs more attention because it urges all groups to work within the same unified structure. In contrast, the second approach is decentralized and not inclusive in a way that the overall framework remains same with treating a group positively (Wallensteen 2007, p.168). People, who adhere integrative approach in Iraq, claim that it is appropriate solution as it could protect state unitary, defeat crime, enhance civic national identity and can stand against threats from neighbours. While, Joseph Biden, Leslie Gelb, Peter Galbraith who claimed that consociational approach meets new Iraq situation and concentrates on Iraqi identities by forming decentralized government along three lines Kurds, Sunni Arabs and Shi'a Arabs (Mc Garry and O'Leary 2008, p.345).

Tracking successful peace accord in specific areas that has no territorial demand or dispread minorities, adopting proportional representation such as sharing legislative and administrative positions may be regarded as the best solution (Varennes 2003, p.157). Moreover, the purpose of power-sharing solution in multiethnic societies is designed to develop conflict management requirements with the principles of democracy (Sisk 2003, p.139). In this political system human rights protection, election campaign with fair election process supervised by independent election committee and the results of elections shape the new government are supposed to be the main features of this option "integrative approach" (Wallensteen 2007, p.130). However, democratic legitimacy during the transition period, after peace agreement, is crucial step towards legitimate democracy (Reilly 2003, p.175). Meanwhile, what the consociational power sharing approach adds to integrative approach is means to protect a specific group (Bell 2003, p.167).

In contrast, power sharing solution is not always successful because in divided societies it is preferred as an exit from war rather than a long–term solution (Sisk 2003, p.140). Moreover, the duration of peace agreement process is another factor, which affects the whole process. Wallensteen (2007, p.124) pointed out that "spoilers" interference increases when the duration of peace process is longer and may result in to revert into war. Furthermore, in a fragile situation, "as quickly as possible" transition into democratic process is unable to consider long-term and sustainable democracy (Reilly 2003, p.176). One of the intriguing issues is dealing with violated rights or crimes committed before agreement of power sharing. This is because human rights issues supposed to look at both past and future circumstances (Bell 2003, p.172). Finally, central government[10] is often blamed for failure peace process because they are the actor who loses in terms of power and authority. Therefore, central government may decline its agreement (Varennes 2003, p.157). Reconciliation in Iraq should not only focus on the primary factors of identity which are religion, ethnicity, and tribe, but also on secondary actors of identity which are internal displaced people, class and professions (Steele 2008, p.1). Steele continues that it is essential "to start with people at where they are not where we wish to be", in another words dealing with people that have experienced victimization before and during the conflict. Therefore, institutions such as ministry of reconciliation, high Iraqi tribunal, Martyrs foundation, political prisoner foundation and ministry of immigrants and migration have been established in Iraq to deal past and recent victimization.

Additionally, successful peace process considers four main elements for power–sharing solution that are; inclusion of all main conflict actors through involvement in making and taking decisions, investigate common ground and continued negation within peace agreement rules (Sisk 2003, p.143). Moreover, participation of indigenous people, territorial autonomy, recognition and empowering tradition and cultures are the main features of successful negation elements among conflict parties (Varennes 2003, p.157). Furthermore, election processes during transitional period is only a step in the ladder for long-term democracy.

All above analysis of power-sharing solution does not mean that it works as final remedy in any conflict. This is because based on experiences after the Cold-War, there is no comprehensive and final solution (Wallensteen 2007, p.124). Another reason is power sharing solution may not meet the goals of central state and secessionists because the former concerns about integration of its territory and the latter may seek independency (Sisk 2003, p.144). Finally, lack of trusts, control of benefits, resources and political representation could be fairly achieved by either autonomy or independency which is the main functioning believes of ethnic minorities (Varennes 2003, p.155)

Autonomy

Fourth, autonomy is regarded as a political form of sharing power, precisely consociationalism that has been gaining popularity and continuous support regionally and internationally. The reason behind that is despite of wider agenda of the conflicts parties, it has ability to bring conflict parties into negotiation process (Ghai 2003, pp.187-8). Moreover, focus on autonomy has been a feature trend of governments that works on handling the root causes of the conflict or at least respond to claims (Varennes 2003, p.152). Furthermore, Wallensteen (2007, p.176) described autonomy as a "tailor –made answer to a particular problems". This is because he claimed that it responds to the needs of both conflicting parties, people claim self-determination and central government aim at keeping the territorial integrity. In another words, it is middle ground that bridge between one or more groups with the central government in order to keep state unitary. However, one of the global examples that went beyond state to regional level is the European Union (Ghai 2003, pp.187-8). In our case the constitution of Iraq, not only recognized federal regional government of Kurdistan region, that consist of three governorates/ provinces, but also it paved the road for all other governorates to organize in federal regions (Mc Garry & O'Leary 2008, p.348). However, there is an exception for both Baghdad and Kirkuk city because they are characterized by being multinational, and multi ethnic cities, Baghdad is the capital of Iraq and during Saddam Hussein ruling of Iraq, ethnic cleansing and transmigration program implemented in Kirkuk (Iraq constitution article 140).

However, there is sceptical view towards autonomy by both central authority and ethnic groups. Three reasons to explain that are; it is argued that the autonomy region may be ruled by criminal groups, war has created lack of trust especially central authority may give the priority of right of return to other identity groups and due to security dilemma during transitional period, a period of demilitarization, sharing power and negotiation etc. (Wallensteen 2007, pp.123-176).

The unsuccessful example of autonomy has already exercised in Iraq. In 1971 Kurds for the first time in their history were able to gain their self-administration region as an outcome of peace agreement with central authority "11th Adar Agreement". However, the central authority reoccupied Kurdistan region by the end of 1975 and put to end this experience. Therefore, even autonomy when it is agreed and granted it may not succeed. Ghai (2003, p.180) explained two causes for unsuccessful autonomy practises, which are: first, on-going legitimacy inquire and problems with its management by state. Second, the claim of specific group may be independency, therefore, autonomy either it did not meets the original goal or it may be a temporary solution for further negotiation. Additionally, regardless serious or sophisticated design, it may not able to solve problems that are inherited and came to the surface after post war (Sisk 2003, p.149). Furthermore, autonomy may fail due to partial implementation of accords (Varennes 2003, p.156). Finally, the most important point is that "most of the functioning autonomies have not seen ethnic cleansing in their territories or considerable refugee flows", this is apart from Dayton agreement of 1995 between Bosnia and Herzegovina (Wallensteen 2007, p.173-7).

Independency

Fifth: independency, Annihilation of identity group and discrimination are main motivations to claim independency (Bell 2003, p.166). In such conflict over territory between the state and opponents groups, loses of a state clearly means born of new states (Wallensteen 2007, p.179). However, the contemporary civil wars unusually end up with partition and creation of new states (Sisk 2003, p.141). Nevertheless, there are cases were the state accepts independencies of identity groups, which are; when border with the new state remain open for movements of people and materials, if creating new state will not "damage its self-understanding" and if there is possibility of future integration. However, one of the reasons that the central government refuse the partition option is the new border do not solve current problems rather it may create new problems (Wallensteen 2007, pp.180-3).

Although partitioning Iraq into three states for Kurds, Shi'a Arabs and Sunni Arabs was initiated by the US senior positions, they have stepped back into creating three federal regions (Mc Garry and O'Leary 2008, p.345). Additionally, after 2003 Kurds are the only actor that claims independency. Until IS occupation of Sunni Arab populated provinces in June 2014, Kurds were not in a position to announce the born of new state named "Kurdistan" for several reasons; the US administration were not encounter for independency of Kurdistan, Turkey regards such option as threat upon its national security, infrastructure in Kurdistan region still in development process and areas named disputes such as Kirkuk city, which is claimed by Kurds as part of their region, and known for its multiethnic and oil-rich city, remained unsolved..

However, after 10th June 2014, Kurds have clearly stated that they going to announce their independency (BBC 2014). For Kurds it is regarded as golden opportunity because they have already controlled contested areas including Kirkuk city after 10th June 2014. They have built economic infrastructure through making contracts with world known firms of oil production. Kurds established economic cooperation with Turkey that enabled them to export their oil. They started selling their oil production separately from Iraqi central Government as the latter stopped paying IKRG budget share in the Iraqi budget. Finally, neither Turkey nor the USA opposed the IKR statements for independency. Additionally, other countries such Israel and Hungary publically announced their support to the Kurdish claim for independency (Deutsche Welle 2014).

FUTURE RESEARCH DIRECTIONS

Conflicts among ethnic groups have been seen in the political arena. These are often continuous and old-type conflicts in politics (Nye, Jr. 2007, p.68). According to the scholarly research that has been stated above, there is no single cause of the conflict in Iraq. Instead, there are multiple factors. Political exclusion, indeed, is one of those factors.

However, there are questions which have not been answered yet, such as, what is the relation between the political process in Iraq and rise of radical elites? How communal groups were mobilized based on identity? And why is mobilization based on ethnic identity rather than any other classification? What factors have increased the threat on group identity? Is there a link between discrimination and the rise of militia? What is the aim of militia? is it "defence of offensive"?

CONCLUSION

Nowadays, fulfilling Human rights principles by the ruling states is essential approaches towards prevention of conflict from escalating into armed one. Moreover, it is imperative to sustain it through constitutional legislation and put them into practice. Conflict in Iraq devastated various identity groups. The outcomes of 30 years of Sunni Arab ruling were fighting neighbouring countries, gross human rights violations, genocide against Kurds and displacement of Shi'a Arabs. Whereas, the outcomes of 10 years of Shi'a Arab ruling were displacement of millions of people, gross human rights violations, rise of militia and terrorist organizations activities, crimes against humanity in Snjar area. The affected people are mainly minorities, part of Sunni Arabs, Kurds and Shi'a Turkmen. Similarly to the period during Saddam Hussein, new Iraqi government after 2003, represented by the State Of Law, have carried out economic and political discrimination against other Identity groups. Federalism and decentralized governing have been adopted in the Iraqi constitution, but both Sunni Arabs and Shi'a Arabs opposed practising it, except in the Iraqi Kurdistan region. Kurds have worked on economic and political development in their region, which resulted in having democratic accreditation, safety and economic prosperity.

The new Iraq is lacking common identity, rather than, there are three or more identities named Shi'a Arab, Sunni Arab and Kurds. The period after 2003, proved that Kurds, Shi'a Arabs and Sunni Arabs failed to live in a unified country named Iraq.

New state for Kurds named State of Kurdistan is a difficult born, however, it is a matter of time and the current circumstance is the regarded as the golden opportunity. This is because change in approaches of neighbouring country and the USA towards independent Kurdistan. Kurds have established their own economic infrastructure including oil production. Additionally, they are the second biggest nation without state around the world. The five past decades proved that it is impossible to impose an identity upon Kurds, not only in Iraq but also in other countries. Finally, recent availability of international support for Peshmarge in fighting IS groups reinforce Kurdish position for independency.

Sunni Arabs and Shi'a Arabs were not successful in peace-making, rather than, they were practicing political and economic discrimination against each other, which resulted in armed conflict and civil war. Nationalists from both Sunni Arabs and Shi'a Arabs are seeking unified Iraq. In such case, Iraq government joining two federal states is the possible means for accommodating demands of both identities. In such case, independent state of Kurdistan is inevitable. This is because Kurds have experienced both Sunni Arab and Shi'a Arab ruling of Iraq and the outcomes were adverse for Kurds.

Colonialism drew the borders of states, joining various identity groups in countries did not exist before. Colonialism borders are neither bibles nor Holly Quran that cannot be touched. Three new states based on Identity is a solution. However, it requires mutually hurting stalemate position in order to reach a point where independent states become identity requirement.

REFERENCES

ABC news. (2014). *Iraqi Army, Militants Clash West of Baghdad*. Retrieved from http://abcnews.go.com/International/wireStory/iraq-humanitarian-crisis-highest-level-24967762

Abdulazeez, N. (2013). *Ethnic conflict in the Middle East, Causes, Reconciliation and Negotiation*. Kent: Parker.

Al Arabiya. (2014, July 5). Iranian pilot killed fighting in Iraq, state media report. Retrieved from https://english.alarabiya.net/en/News/middle-east/2014/07/05/Iranian-pilot-killed-fighting-in-Iraq-state-media-reports.html

Al Jazeera. (2010). *Iraq's most powerful coalitions*. Retrieved from http://www.aljazeera.com/focus/iraqelection2010/2010/03/20103493048404203.html

Al Sharq Al Awsat. (2011). *The national alliances discuss "Sunni Insurgency" and "Al Sader" calls Tikrit to retreat federalism*.http://www.aawsat.com/details.asp?section=4&issueno=12023&article=647358&feature=

Arabic, B. B. C. (2012). Iraq asks states whom participated in Baghdad meeting to drop his debts. Retrieved from http://www.bbc.co.uk/arabic/middleeast/2012/03/120327_iraq_arabs_summit.shtml

Aswat Al Iraq. (2012). *First independent human rights organization, historical accomplishment-UNAMI*. Retrieved from http://en.aswataliraq.info/(S(ucrz3s55x5512p3hnjk0pj55))/Default1.aspx?page=article_page&id=147956

BBC. (2011). *Iraq crisis: Where will ISIS attack next?* Retrieved from http://www.bbc.com/news/world-middle-east-27846706

BBC. (2011). *Iraq war in figures*. Retrieved from http://www.bbc.co.uk/news/world-middle-east-11107739

BBC. (2014). Iraq Kurdistan independence referendum planned. Retrieved from http://www.bbc.com/news/world-middle-east-28103124

BBC. (2014). Iraq Profile. Retrieved from http://www.bbc.com/news/world-middle-east-14546763

Christine, B. (2003). Human rights and minority protection. In J. Darby & R. MacGinty (Eds.), *Contemporary Peacemaking Conflict, violence and Peace Processes*. New York: Palgrave Macmillan.

Deutsche Welle. (2014). Kurdistan, public referendum towards independency. Retrieved from http://www.dw.de/كردستان-استفتاء-شعبي-باتجاه-الاستقلال/a-17757172

Dodge, T. (2005). *IRAQ'S FUTURE The aftermath of regime change*. London: Routledge.

Galtung, J. (1967). Theories of peace: a synthetic approach to peace thinking. TRANSCEND International. Retrieved from http://www.transcend.org/files/Galtung_Book_unpub_Theories_of_Peace_-_A_Synthetic_Approach_to_Peace_Thinking_1967.pdf

Galtung, J. (2000). Leaving the Twentieth Century, Entering the twenty-first: Some Basic conflict Formations. In *J. Galtung and C. Jacobsen, searching for Peace the Road to TRANSCEND*. London: Pluto Press.

Ghai, Y. (2003). Territorial options. In J. Darby & R. MacGinty (Eds.), *Contemporary Peacemaking Conflict, violence and Peace Processes*. New York: Palgrave Macmillan.

Hiltermann, J. (2010). *Kurds no closer to taking Kirkuk after Iraqi elections*. Foreign Policy. International crisis group. Retrieved from http://www.crisisgroup.org/en/regions/middle-east-north-africa/iraq-iran-gulf/iraq/kurds-no-closer-to-taking-kirkuk-after-iraqi-elections.aspx

Hiltermann, J. (2012). *A Kurdish Wedge between Iraq and Turkey*. International Crisis Group. Retrieved from http://www.crisisgroup.org/en/regions/middle-east-north-africa/iraq-iran-gulf/iraq/op-eds/hiltermann-a-kurdish-wedge-between-iraq-turkey.aspx

Hiltermann, J. (2012). *Ruling Baghdad*. The National Interest. Retrieved from http://nationalinterest.org/commentary/ruling-baghdad-3604

Human Right Watch. (2006). *Iraq: Saddam Hussein Put to Death*. Retrieved from http://www.hrw.org/news/2006/12/29/iraq-saddam-hussein-put-death

Human Rights Watch. (2010). *Iraq's 2010 National Election, A human rights Platform for Candidates*. Retrieved from http://www.hrw.org/news/2010/02/25/iraq-s-2010-national-elections

International Center for Transitional Justices. Middle East and North Africa, Iraq (2012). *Background: A Repressive Recent History*. Retrieved from http://ictj.org/our-work/regions-and-countries/iraq

International Crisis Group. Middle East Report N°12. (2012). *Iraq's Secular Opposition: The Rise and Decline of Al-Iraqiya*. Brussels/Baghdad. Retrieved from http://www.crisisgroup.org/en/regions/middle-east-north-africa/iraq-iran-gulf/iraq/127-iraqs-secular-opposition-the-rise-and-decline-of-al-iraqiya.aspx

International Crisis Group. (2104) *The Iraq's Jihadi Jack-in-the-Box*. Retrieved from http://www.crisisgroup.org/en/regions/middle-east-north-africa/iraq-iran-gulf/iraq/b038-iraq-s-jihadi-jack-in-the-box.aspx

International Organization for Migration. (2012). *Internal Displacement of Christian Families in Northern Iraq Subsides, Emigration rises*: IOM Report. Retrieved from http://www.iom.int/cms/en/sites/iom/home/news-and-views/press-briefing-notes/pbn-2012/pbn-listing/internal-displacement-of-christian-famil.html

Iraq Body Count. (2012). *Documented civilian deaths from violence*. Retrieved from http://www.iraqbodycount.org/database/

Iraq Media, N. E. T. (2012). *Ministry of Planning announces unemployment rate reduced to 11%.* Retrieved from http://imn.iq/news/view.16192/

Iraqi Council of representative (2012). *Constitution.* Retrieved from http://parliament.iq/english/index.php?newlang=english

Mapping Militant Organizations Project. (2012). *Iraq.* Retrieved from http://www.stanford.edu/group/mappingmilitants/cgi-bin/maps/view/iraq

McGarry, J., & O'Leary, B. (2008). Iraq's constitution of 2005: Liberal Consociation as political prescription. In S. Choudhry (Ed.), *Constitutional design for divided societies: integration of accommodation?* Oxford: Oxford University press.

Nye, J. (2007). *Understanding international conflicts an Introduction to Theory and History* (6th ed.). New York, London: PEARSON/LONGMAN.

O'leary, B. (2009). How to Get Out of Iraq with Integrity. Pennsylvania: University of Pennsylvania Press.

Reilly, B. (2003). Democratic validation. In J. Darby & R. MacGinty (Eds.), *Contemporary Peacemaking Conflict, violence and Peace Processes.* New York: Palgrave Macmillan.

Rudaw. (2014). Barzani's meeting with the minister of foreign affairs of Iran. Retrieved from http://rudaw.net/sorani/kurdistan/270820142

Sisk, D. T. (2003). Power–sharing after civil wars: matching Problem to Solutions. In J. Darby & R. MacGinty (Eds.), *Contemporary Peacemaking Conflict, violence and Peace Processes.* New York: Palgrave Macmillan.

Steele, A. D. (2008). *Special report reconciliation strategies in Iraq.* United States Institute of Peace. Retrieved from http://www.usip.org/publications/reconciliation-strategies-iraq

Swedish International Development Cooperation Agency. (2006). *Manual for Conflict Analysis.* Retrieved from http://www2.sida.se/sida/jsp/sida.jsp?d=118&a=3351&language=en_US&searchWords=manual%20for%20conflict%20analysis%2020th%20October%202012

The guardian (2014). Obama hails 'promising step forward' as Iraq names new prime minister http://www.theguardian.com/world/live/2014/aug/11/iraq-crisis-us-air-strikes-help-kurds-retake-territory-live-updates

UNHCR. (2014). *UNHCR country operations profile - Iraq.* Retrieved from http://www.unhcr.org/pages/49e486426.html

United Nations Assistant Mission for Iraq. (2012). *Iraqi Constitution.* Retrieved from http://www.uniraq.org/documents/iraqi_constitution.pdf

UNOCHA. (2014). *Iraq.* Retrieved from http://www.unocha.org/iraq

UNPO. (2014). *Urgent Action For Iraq's Vulnerable Components Needed.* Retrieved from http://www.unpo.org/article/17220

Uppsala University, Department of Peace and Conflict Research. (2012). Definitions. Available from http://www.pcr.uu.se/research/ucdp/definitions/#Ceasefire_agreements

USIP. (2006). *Weak Viability The Iraqi Federal State and the Constitutional Amendment Process.* Retrieved from http://www.usip.org/files/resources/Morrow_SR168.pdf

Varennes, D. F. (2003). Peace Accords and Ethnic Conflicts: a comparative Analysis of content and approaches. In J. Darby & R. MacGinty (Eds.), *Contemporary Peacemaking Conflict, violence and Peace Processes*. New York: Palgrave Macmillan.

Wallensteen, P. (2007). Understanding Conflict Resolution (2nd ed.). London: SAGE publication.

ADDITIONAL READING

Choudhry, S. (Ed.). (2005). *Constitutional design for divided societies: integration of accommodation?* Oxford University Press.

Darby, J., & Mac Ginty, R. (2002). Contemporary Peace-making Conflict, violence and Peace Processes. McMillian publication.

Dodge, T. (2005). Iraq's Future: The aftermath of regime change. Routledge publication.

Nye, J. (2007). Understanding international conflicts: an Introduction to Theory and History. PEARSON/ LONGMAN publication

Wallensteen, P. (2002). *Understanding Conflict Resolution*. SAGE publications.

KEY TERMS AND DEFINITIONS

CPA: Coalition Provisional Authority.

HRW: Human Rights Watch.

ICTJ: International Centre of Transitional Justices.

ICR: International Conflict Centre.

IKR: Iraqi Kurdistan Region.

IS: Islamic State.

ISIL: Islamic State in Iraq and Levant.

KDP: Kurdistan Democratic Party.

NCF: National Coalition Forces.

IOM: International Office for Migrations.

PUK: Patriotic Union of Kurdistan.

SIDA: Swedish International Development Cooperation Agency.

UCDP: UPPSALA Conflict Data Program.

UNAMI: United Nation Assistant Mission for Iraq.

ENDNOTES

1 "it is a contested incompatibility that concerns government and/or territory where the use of armed force between two parties, in which at least one is the government of a state, results in at least 25 battle –related death in one calendar year" (UCDP 2014)

2 Peshmarga is Kurdish forces that belong to Iraqi Kurdistan Regional Government.

3 DNO https://www.dno.no/about-dno/
Exxonmobile http://corporate.exxonmobil.com/en/company/worldwide-operations/locations/iraq/about/overview
Chevron http://www.chevron.com/chevron/speeches/article/12052012_threepillarsof-partnership.news

4 Previously known as De-Baathification law, which is aimed at preventing Ba'ath party members and former Iraqi officers from participation in the political process.

5 This has been translated from Arabic to English by the author of this essay.

6 The framework analysis' model consists of seven interlinked concepts that motivate ethnic mobilization and conflict formation. Those concepts are: 'discrimination, ethnic group identity, ethno-political leadership and group cohesion, political environment, use of violence by governments, external support and international economic status' (Gurr and Harff 1994, p.78).

7 This has been translated from Arabic to English by the author of this text.

8 Johan Galtung described the negative peace by a situation where organized group violence is absence, while the positive peace is a situation where exercised physical violence.

9 "UNAMI" United Nation Assistant Mission for Iraq http://unami.unmissions.org/

10 It refers to the actor who holds the authority at the central government before the peace process with opponents.

Chapter 15
The Neo-Colonial State of Exception in Occupied Iraq

David Whyte
University of Liverpool, UK

ABSTRACT

This paper explores the immediate post-conflict period following the 2003 Coalition invasion of Iraq, analysing the political strategy of economic exceptionalism violently and illegally imposed by the Coalition partners. The government of occupation, Coalition Provisional Authority, (CPA) ensured the disbursal of revenue and the accumulation of profits at an accelerated rate with few administrative controls or mechanisms of accountability. In the case of the post-invasion transformation of Iraq, routine corporate criminality, facilitated by the government of occupation, is revealed as an important means of producing and reproducing (neo) colonial power relations. The systematic corruption of the reconstruction economy unfolded in a liminal space opened up by the suspension of law. This neo-colonial 'state of exception' became the mode of domination that sough political and social transformation as part of the 'reconstruction' process in post-Saddam Iraq.

INTRODUCTION

This paper explores the immediate post-conflict period following the 2003 Coalition invasion of Iraq. It describes a post-conflict period that can be characterised as a strategy of economic exceptionalism that was violently and illegally imposed by the Coalition partners. Elsewhere, I have argued that the routine law breaking and corruption that dominated the Iraqi reconstruction economy quickly became normalised as part and parcel of the occupation (Whyte, 2007 and 2008). This research showed how systematic fraud and bribery served a useful purpose for the Anglo-American occupation as part of a wider system of economic domination designed to provide structural advantages to Western firms entering the Iraqi economy. The government of occupation, Coalition Provisional Authority, (CPA) ensured the disbursal of revenue and the accumulation of profits at an accelerated rate with few administrative controls or mechanisms of accountability. In the case of the post-invasion transformation of Iraq, routine corporate criminality, facilitated by the government of occupation, was revealed as an important means of producing and reproducing (neo) colonial power relations.

DOI: 10.4018/978-1-4666-9675-4.ch015

The systematic corruption of the reconstruction economy unfolded in a liminal space opened up by the suspension of law. As this paper will show, this 'state of exception' was most visible in the suspension of Iraqi sovereign law and the establishment of impunity for all US nationals (and some categories of the nationals of all Coalition states). The paper therefore explores a specific moment of state/law/power in which the normal rule of law was suspended under emergency conditions. In this case, the extreme form of neo-colonialism imposed on Iraq was made possible by a military invasion which, in so far as it constituted a violent and illegal crime of aggression, suspended the international legal order. The neo-colonial project was subsequently secured by the imposition of a wholesale suspension of the country's constitutional order.

In this paper, I argue, following Nader (2007), that a principle of 'lack' or 'deficit' was the core justification for the plunder and 'reconstruction' of Iraqi society. This was justified on the basis that the system of rules that governed the Iraqi economy and society were primitive and therefore lacked the necessary values that enabled proper integration into the global economy. It was the primitiveness of the Iraqi economy and 'lack' of conformity with the so-called Washington Consensus that provided the chief rationale for tearing-up the Iraqi constitution and re-writing the country's laws.

BACKGROUND

Giorgio Agamben (2005) is perhaps the best known writer to analyse the form of contemporary states of exception. In his book *State of Exception*, he points out that the tendency of governments to resort to non-lawful means under the pretext of a 'war on terror' is nothing new. In a historical analysis that includes Napoleon's state of siege in 1811, Lincoln's suspension of *habeus corpus* in 1861, the Italian states of siege in Palermo, Naples and Milan in the latter half of the 19th century, Roosevelt's assumption of extraordinary powers in 1933 and the Third Reich's suspension of the Weimar Constitution, Agamben maps out the resort to 'state of exception' as a regular feature of modern states.

In so far as the state of exception depends upon the suspension of law to impose a new force of law, it's relationship to the rule of law cannot be defined easily; it exists neither as a lawful state nor as a state of complete lawlessness. Rather a state of exception is a state of limbo that exists in an indeterminate space, oscillating between law (in so far as a sovereign authority issues a degree or order that is, by virtue of the fact it has been made by the sovereign, claims a legal source) and non-law (in so far as the normal rule of law, or the normal rules of legal procedure have been suspended or erased).

For Agamben, the state of exception represents something fundamental to state power. It is not merely a result of bad government, or a pathological condition, but, is, following Schmitt's famous statement that the sovereign is "he who decides on the state of exception" (Schmitt, 1950/2003) the very foundation of state sovereignty. Starting from this point Agamben shows how the state of exception has become an almost permanent condition in the most powerful and advanced states. The US detention centres of Abu Ghraib and Guantanamo represent the highest stage of development of the state of exception, and rather than being understood as aberrations or the extremes at the margins of state power, they represent the latest manifestations of an ever-present core of state/law/power. The state of exception that is so clearly discernible at Abu Ghraib and Guantanamo therefore acts as a kind of hidden matrix that we can use to chart the course of contemporary politics.

A key aspect of sovereign power that his analysis reveals is the relation between the sovereign and its ability to reproduce the space between law and non-law in which a "secret solidarity between law and anomie" is revealed. The state of exception normally occurs under conditions of national emergency involving a security crisis or challenge to state sovereignty (whether real or imagined), when the state invokes the right to suspend the normal rule of law as a matter of *necessity*. Agamben argues that the concept of necessity that is derived directly from Carl Schmitt is the figure that enables the state of exception to appear "as an 'illegal' but perfectly 'juridical and constitutional' measure that is realised in the production of new norms (or of a new juridical order)" (Agamben, 2008: 28). As Hannah Arendt noted in the context of the Third Reich, suspension of the law is generally justified using a principle of *raison d'etat* (literally, 'reason of state' which is normally equated to the 'national interest') – an over-riding concern that requires the state to use extreme means to defend its integrity (Arendt, 1965/1977). So, in the case of in the 2003 invasion and occupation of Iraq, Saddam's fictitious weapons of mass destruction acted as the *raison d'etat*. It is not difficult to deconstruct this narrative to show how it was almost entirely fictional but this is not the point. The point is that the state always needs to locate its resort to exception - by definition, a resort to extreme measures - in the context of a legitimating narrative.

Such legitimations of state power can be read from this perspective as having a claim about of a legal lacunae - or lack of law – at their heart. Harvard Professor of Torture Alan Dershowitz's assertion that torture is necessary to save lives provides a stark example of how a fictional necessity is designed to fill a vacuum of law - a lawlessness or lack of legal order. Dershowitz merely provides a means of bridging the gap between the law and its need to address the situation for which it is required. In this sense, Dershowitz might be likened to a modern day Schmitt – an apologist for the state of exception. Similarly, the extra-legal intervention by the Coalition in Iraq was necessary in order to bridge the gap between international law and its need to address the situation for which it is required (the removal of Saddam and the protection of the international order).

It is this legal lacunae, always at the heart of the defence of the 'state of exception', that Walter Benjamin famously contested. For Schmitt, the Third Reich's legal theorist, necessity was a grounding principle in law – a principle that enabled states to normatively address what is *missing* in law. For Schmitt the state of exception thus arises from the separation of norm from its practical implementation and seeks merely to fit the norm to the situation for which it is required. For his critics however, the principle of necessity is not one that seeks to address a lacuna – because the lacuna is always fictitious in any case.

In her work on legal plunder, Nader (2007) identifies an enduring theory of lack at the heart of Western colonialism and argues that the idea that there is a legal space to be filled is a primary dynamic in the transplant of law from the so-called 'developed' to the 'developing' world. 'Lack' the identification of a 'gap' in law has been a primary justification for the spread of legal systems that support colonisation and 'globalisation' and aid the economic plunder of the Global South. This "theory of lack" positions western cultural values as the norm where western "rule of law" is a key ingredient for the betterment of societies that lack a developed rule of law. Yet, for Nader, it is crucial to always note that the idea of a 'lack' is never based upon a knowledge of the legal traditions in the target societies. For the colonised societies are societies that always had developed sets of norms and values that are shared and upheld as 'law'. Often, as we shall see, this boils down to a violent and vicious "storm of progress", to paraphrase the opening comments in Cante's's chapter in this volume.

A STATE OF EXCEPTION?

In many ways, the transformation of the Iraqi economy can be understood as a *prima facie* example of a "state of exception". But what has been described here is more complex and nuanced than

Agamben's account of the structure of state/law/power. Agamben's "state of exception" needs to be more fully developed in the context of this case.

In the state of exception imposed on Iraq, we find an entirely different structure than that of Guantanamo or Belmarsh – or indeed, more generally in anti-terror legislation that introduces special powers or suspends *habeas corpus*. In those cases the state imposes a state of exception on the status of the individual to enable the eradication of the legal status of the individual. The individual is captured in a legal limbo, with no rights as a human being or as a citizen; a state of "bare life". Where the status of an entire territory or nation state is the target of the state of exception, then a very different set of dynamics come into play.[1] In occupied Iraq the general aim was socio-economic re-ordering. In Guantanamo and Belmarsh prisons, where the focus is upon the re-categorisation and absolute control over particular individuals, this is not so immediately clear, though of course, we cannot imagine the existence of such places were Britain and the US not involved in a global struggle for socio-economic dominance. But in the sense that focus is not the individual - in terms of the eradication of individually created rights or the arbitrary condemnation of individuals to the status of *homo sacer* - this is a state of exception that seeks the control of a territory and its socio-economic structure.

One consequence of this focus on the individual object of power is that state power is conceptualised in negative, or controlling terms. This is a feature of the concept of state of exception that Lemke has drawn our attention to: "Agamben pursues a concept of power that is grounded in the categories of repression, reproduction and reduction, without taking into account the relational, decentralised and productive aspects of power" (Lemke, 2005: 9).. In reflecting upon this point, it is significant that the form taken by the suspension of law in occupied Iraq was imposed using both positive and negative functions of law. That is to say, it sought the creation of particular social conditions, at the same time as it imposed coercive or controlling measures. In this sense, the state of exception that we find in the transformation of the Iraqi economy cannot simply be understood in terms of the "state as policeman" (Coleman et. al., 2009) or embodied in the "figure of the police." (Agamben, 2000).

Of course, the imposition of a new legal order in occupied Iraq was at partly based upon a 'negative' dynamic of law. Indeed, it might be said that the overbearing dynamic in the context of the transformation of the Iraqi economy was not a formal (or even informal) suspension of law, but obliteration of the law. And this might be described in entirely negative terms. But it is crucial to recognise that the (negative) obliteration of the law was coupled to a creative or positive reconstruction of the legal basis for economic activity. On the face of things, the law created new possibilities for economic activity - especially for economic activity by foreign multi-nationals. Now those positive or creative capacities created by CPA law also had devastating consequences for Iraqi industry in so far as the removal of commercial protectionism forced many Iraqi producers out of business. This dynamic, best described as the *creative destruction* of the Iraqi economy, is a contradictory one, and one that cannot be simply understood in the negative terms invoked by categories of "suspension" or "eradication" of law.

In this sense, the year zero approach to the Iraqi economy which swept aside international and national law in order to establish the foundations of a neo-liberal economic infrastructure cannot simply be understood as part of the continuum of historical cases that Agamben draws our attention to, but more closely approximates to what Benjamin (1978) called "law-making violence", whereby the previous rule of law is obliterated and a new law created as a result of the ability of a social group to violently enforce its will. Revolutionary transformation – the eradication of particular sets of social relations and their replacement with new sets of social relations – is, for Benjamin, always premised upon law-making violence. Thus, the eradication of political and military elites, their replacement with new elites and the social and economic transformation that followed can be understood as a supreme act of law-making violence.

Moreover, this obliteration of law was given legitimacy by a particular form of humanitarian discourse that does not fit closely to Agamben's typical necessity justifications. Whilst the framing of Executive Order 13303 draws upon a *raison d'etat* of protecting US national interests, more general claims as to the necessity of reconstructing the economy are based upon the premise of promoting economic success and survival for the Iraqis, as opposed to some kind of defence against an external or internal threat. Discourses of economic liberation were important in both Coalition and Iraqi government sources supporting reform. Here, the basic claim was that the reforms would free the Iraqi people from the "tyranny of the planned economy"; Saddam's economic policies were in such discourses represented as a key mechanism of political and social repression (Whyte, 2008). The Coalition, then, invoked an economic, as well as a political, humanitarianism. In this context, the concept of 'necessity' is framed rather differently, whereby the rationale used to support economic transformation is made with reference to *economic* necessity. The reasoning behind the suspension of law, then, is rather more circumspect and connected more closely to what we might call a 'civilising mission'.

We will develop this brief discussion of the shortcomings of Agamben's formulation of the state of exception in the conclusion to this chapter. For the time being, the discussion turns to explore the historical context and current ideological turn that allows us to better understand the relationship between law-making violence and Imperialist 'civilising missions'.

THE RIGHT TYPE OF VALUE

For Santiago, the legitimate authority for the expansion of the US Empire in its earliest moments was provided by the demarcation of a notional line between the inside/civilised notion of self and the outside/savage notion of self (Santiago, 2006). As long as the Native American was on the other side of the divide, theft of land, brutalisation and genocide would remain legitimate. Boiled down to its most simple logic, otherness or being outside of our civilisation justified - in law and in practice - the most extreme measures of violence and expropriation.

The notion of civilisation has, certainly since the colonisation of the Americas, always projected a "civilised" social order based upon a very specific set of economic relationships. Ellen Meiksins Wood (1998 and 2003) has shown how early ideological justifications for the colonisation of the Americas rested on the idea that land and property could be legitimately taken by colonisers if it was not 'productive'. This justification for the violent expropriation of Native American populations was later transformed by English liberal philosopher John Locke into the efficient production of *value* whereby land could be seized if it did not produce value (or, more accurately, the type of value that counted in the European money system). Thus:

New conceptions of property were also being theorized more systematically, most famously in John Locke's Second Treatise of Government. Chapter 5 of that work is the classic statement of a theory of property based on the principles of improvement. Here, property as a "natural" right is based on what Locke regards as the divine injunction to make the earth productive and profitable, to improve it. (Meiksins Wood, 1998).

The Marshall trilogy that developed the lasting jurisprudential justifications for the colonisation of territories that the Native American inhabited contained implicit references to the "savages" whose lack of civilisation "would leave the country a wilderness", or in Lockean terms would not produce the right type of value.[2]

As Nader argues, commenting upon the relationship between colonisation and a *legal* civilising mission, legal imperialism often exhibits itself with an internal cultural logic that views all other legal cultures as basically empty (Nader, 2005). Legal systems that do not conform to our standard of civilisation can therefore be treated as blank canvasses that lack law and lack the means to develop. The Anglo-American strategy in Iraq did precisely this and mobilised a civilising mission that provided the rationale to treat the country's economic and legal system as a blank canvass. Just as the US Patriot Acts and the cages of Guantanamo, not to mention the UK Anti-Terrorism Acts and the cells of Belmarsh, have effectively erased any legal status of the individual, so the Anglo-American invasion and occupation of Iraq instantly erased the nation's legal status and replaced it with a new system of law in the name of civilisation and progress.

To concept of the state of exception, then, we must incorporate a broader understanding of necessity than that captured by *raison d'etat*. On one hand this is the notion of a lack or a deficit in the ability of the indigenous peoples to fully exploit their environment (ibid.). And in the context of the contemporary global economy, they cannot afford to hold themselves back. The civilising mission - always one dripping with rhetorical benevolence - is now a drowning in a very different rhetoric of economic survival. And it is only by full incorporation into the global economy that survival can be made possible. On the other hand, law is becoming more responsive to the infrastructural needs of global economic restructuring whereby the national interest is explicitly aligned with a universalising, civilising rationale that subjugates us, to paraphrase Thomas Frank (2000) to the obedience of "one market under god". And "one market under god" could well have been the motto of the CPA, for it describes precisely the occupation's enterprise. The first priority for the government of occupation in its first year was not the protection of public assets or the protection of the rights or living conditions of the Iraqi people, but the imposition of a neoliberal economy on Iraq.

THE OCCUPATION AND THE TRANSFORMATION OF PROPERTY RELATIONS

In many ways it was a claim to a legal 'lack' that characterised the occupation of Iraq following the 2003 invasion. The form of legal deficit or 'lack' that characterised this conflict was not one that conforms precisely to the John Lock notion of lack, but it has very close similarities, since the aim is a transformation of property relations. In the brief analysis that follows, it will become clearer as to how this transformation of property relations was sought.

Iraq was portrayed as a nation that was, due to its mode of property relations, was fundamentally corrupt. According to George W. Bush in his address to the Iraqi people immediately following the April 2003 invasion: "You will be free to build a better life, instead of building more palaces for Saddam and his sons…You deserve better than tyranny and corruption…." (*The Guardian*, April 10th, 2003).

Elsewhere, I have noted how a succession of key conferences on the reconstruction of Iraq after the invasion made clear the true aim of the occupation (Whyte, 2007 and 2008). At the *Rebuild Iraq* conference, held in Amman, Jordan in April 2005 US Under-Secretary of State for Commerce William Lash used his keynote address as an opportunity to castigate Saddam for the "economic sins" of his regime (Whyte,

2008). A speaker representing the US Embassy in Baghdad reinforced this position by highlighting to the assembled audience - largely comprising Iraqi and Western business representatives - that Saddam's corruption and "hatred for economic freedom" prevented the prosperous development of the country: "Iraq could have been an Asian tiger with the democratic free will of the people" (ibid.). Another speaker representing the US State Department Baghdad condemned the "tyranny of Saddam's planned economy", which bred "lawlessness", "economic corruption", an "insecure business environment", and "decades of subsidies for Iraqi industry" (ibid.). Thus, he continued: "[t]he transition from a command economy to a modern economy doesn't just mean sorting out the mess, it requires social and cultural change..." by "...imparting an efficient system of commercial law".

Paul Bremer's position as the bureaucratic head of the CPA carried with it the authority to both make and administer the law, to set the budget for reconstruction and to spend revenue, to allocate funds to government ministries, to write the new constitution and to design the new political system. In the bureaucratic structure of the CPA we find the collapse of political and legal authority into the figure of the bureaucratic official; in other words, the negation of the separation of powers that is supposed to characterise modern liberal democracies.

The CPA's dual aim was both to kick-start the reconstruction by injecting funds into the private interests that swarmed around the Authority like the proverbial flies and to simultaneously establish a neo-liberal capitalist economy in Iraq. The administrative tools used in fulfilling the latter aim consisted of 100 orders issued during the first 14 months of the occupation. The general force of the CPA legal regime - officially approved by the UN Security Council in May 2003 - was the imposition of a model of monopoly capitalism dominated by powerful overseas firms and the minimum of protections for local producers and industrial workers, spearheaded by the wholesale privatisation of state assets to foreign multinationals. The substance of those orders gets us closer to the real agenda in the war on terrorism in Iraq, for together they constitute a programme of enforced privatisation; the extraction from host states of natural resources; and the establishment of low wage economies ostensibly designed to bring 'freedom' to the Iraqi people. Just as the military invasion calls itself Operation Iraqi Freedom, the CPA administrative orders are carefully couched in the language of market freedom. Order 12 on Trade Liberalization Policy is a case in point. The Order notes:

Reaffirming the provisions of General Franks' Freedom Message to the Iraqi people of April 16, 2003, Recognizing the central role of international trade in Iraq's recovery and its development of a free market economy, Acting on behalf, and for the benefit, of the Iraqi people, I hereby promulgate the following:... (Coalition Provisional Authority, 2003a)

The order, introduced about a month after Bush declared major hostilities over, suspended all customs and duty charges on goods entering the country. It had an immediate effect. The Iraqi economy was suddenly became a target for the economic 'dumping' of manufactured products, food and raw materials. For example, within a few days of the order being passed, chicken legs that had been mass-produced in the US were being shipped in by American company Tyson, forcing the market price of chicken down to $1.25 a kilo (Colliers, 2003). Before the corporate invasion, chicken produced in Iraq cost $1.30 a kilo, and the state controlled the price to protect producers and butchers. Now it is no longer economical to produce Iraqi chicken and many have been forced out of business by this classic example of commodity dumping.

The legally binding administrative orders issued by the CPA thus created a trade regime that eradicated 'protections' for local industry and opened the way for product dumping on Iraq. The orders also demanded privatisation and encouraged full foreign ownership of a wide range of state-owned Iraqi assets industries and banks and generally created a WTO compliant regime that protected foreign capital at the expense of local business. Neo-liberal reforms imposed by the CPA radically transformed industrial policy, import and export rules and the structure of taxation. Together those reforms represented a formidable crowbar that had the single purpose of prising open the Iraq economy for global (but mainly US) capital. *The Economist* described the CPA's policies as a "wish-list of foreign investors" (*The Economist,* 27th September 2003). The final Order made by Bremer was the decree that those reforms would have a lasting and binding authority on future Iraqi governments.

Order 39 issued by CPA on September 19th 2003 permitted full foreign ownership of a wide range of state-owned Iraqi assets, opening the economy up for the next wave of invasion by occupying powers' corporations.

Those orders also sought to bring Iraq into line with the World Trade Organisation regime. Added to the creation of a general patent regime which will protect foreign countries at the expense of local business, also included are some very specific measures to ensure that agricultural production will in the future depend upon foreign agri-biotech firms. Order 81 on "Patent, Industrial Design, Undisclosed Information, Integrated Circuits and Plant Variety" for example, effectively outlawed the informal sharing of farm seed supply system that has survived in Iraqi farming for years to force farmers to use the protected varieties that are sold to them by trans-national corporations in the name of agricultural reconstruction. The following extract from Order 81 captures accurately the tone and general tenure of the CPA's regime:

Acknowledging the Governing Council's desire to bring about significant change to the Iraqi intellectual property system as necessary to improve the economic condition of the people of Iraq, Determined to improve the conditions of life, technical skills, and opportunities for all Iraqis and to fight unemployment with its associated deleterious effect on public security, Recognizing that companies, lenders and entrepreneurs require a fair, efficient, and predictable environment for protection of their intellectual property....the need for the development of Iraq and its transition from a non-transparent centrally planned economy to a market economy characterized by sustainable economic growth through the establishment of a dynamic private sector... (Coalition Provisional Authority, 2003b).

So this was the aim: transition from a centrally planned economy to a market economy. And both the method and purpose of this transition required reforms that opened new market spaces for foreign capital and indeed provided significant structural advantages to large corporations. Those reforms, in establishing the conditions of structural advantage sought nothing less than a transformation of the relationship between public and private sectors and between local and international capital in Iraq.

THE OCCUPATION AND INTERNATIONAL LAW

In March 2003, anticipating the Anglo-American occupation of Iraq, the British Attorney General Lord Goldsmith had issued a legal opinion on the economic governance of Iraq that was unequivocal about the occupiers' obligations under international law. Goldsmith reminded the UK government that "[a]rticle 43 of the Hague Regulations imposes an obligation to respect the laws in force in the occupied territory 'unless absolutely prevented'", and issued a clear warning that, "...the imposition of major structural economic reforms would not be authorised by international law."[3] The occupiers, then, were well aware of their legal obligations under international law. They chose not to observe them (see also Kramer and Michalowski, 2005).

The Iraqi constitution at the time of the occupation enshrined the principles of central planning by national authorities and asserted that private enterprise must be compatible with those principles. Thus, the transformation of the Iraqi economy should not merely be regarded as a matter of policy, but should be considered a constitutional matter which effectively destroyed Iraq's distinctive political and social identity and obliterated the existing (constitutional) legal order. Certainly this effect of the CPA rule of law makes it unambiguously illegal under international law. And given the amount of work that went on in the CPA debating and writing a new constitution for Iraq, there can be little doubt that key CPA personnel were well aware that they were involved in a process that breached the Geneva and Hague rules.

If CPA officials were wilfully ignoring their obligations under international law, as seems most likely, they did so in the knowledge that their government was fully committed to ensuring the legal impunity of its officials. At the beginning of the occupation, the United States government made a remarkable decision to ensure that its own personnel would remain outside the reach of normal legal procedures. On the same day that the CPA was created by United Nations Security Council Resolution 1483, George W Bush signed and issued Executive Order 13303. The Order, which passed almost entirely without comment in the US media, never mind in public debate, declared a state of emergency in order to suspend all personal legal liabilities of the occupiers. The text of the Order read as follows:

I, GEORGE W. BUSH, President of the United States of America, find that the threat of attachment or other judicial process against the Development Fund for Iraq, Iraqi petroleum and petroleum products, and interests therein, and proceeds, obligations, or any financial instruments of any nature whatsoever arising from or related to the sale or marketing thereof, and interests therein, obstructs the orderly reconstruction of Iraq, the restoration and maintenance of peace and security in the country, and the development of political, administrative, and economic institutions in Iraq. This situation constitutes an unusual and extraordinary threat to the national security and foreign policy of the United States and I hereby declare a national emergency to deal with that threat.

As a result of this "unusual and extraordinary threat" (although it is hardly clear from the text of the order whether the threat is from the risk of judicial process or the business of occupation itself), US citizens were exempted from any "attachment, judgement, decree, lien, execution, garnishment, or other judicial process" with respect to the proceeds from the sale of petroleum, or any interests in Iraqi petroleum held by the United States government or any national of the United States.[4] The Order quite clearly sought to exempt US citizens from judicial process in the US and in Iraq.

From text it is clear that the Order also intended exemption from international law. In what looks like a nod to article 64 of the 1949 Geneva Convention, Executive Order 13303 notes that judicial interference or financial instruments are likely to obstruct "the orderly reconstruction of Iraq." Article 64 had broadened the remit of the "public order and safety" clause in the Hague rules to permit occupiers to maintain "the orderly government of the territory." Bush's Order, then, rather clumsily attempts to connect the immunity of US personnel to orderly reconstruction. But this can be considered as neither in the spirit or the letter of Geneva or Hague. The legality of Executive Order 13303 has subsequently been challenged by academic lawyers (for example, Kelly, 2004), but this challenge has failed to provoke public debate.

The terms of the exemption first of all provides immunity from the theft or embezzlement of oil revenue, and second, from any safety, human rights or environmental violation, or indeed any criminal offence that might be committed in the course of producing Iraqi oil. Now unless you were a close observer of the CPA's regime, the significance of providing immunity from the first category - the theft or embezzlement of oil revenue - might not be immediately obvious. But its significance, particularly in the first 14 months or so of the occupation is that it covered upwards of $30b worth of Iraqi oil revenue held in the Development Fund for Iraq (DFI) and spent by the CPA. Executive Order 13303 quite deliberately provided a cover of immunity for the use and abuse of DFI funds made available to the CPA by United Nations Security Council Resolution 1483. This is significant, since it was those funds that were used to fund the entry of Western corporations into the reconstruction economy.

Any doubts as to the application of Bush's Order in Iraqi law were eradicated on 23rd June 2003 by Paul Bremer. CPA Order 17 declared that all CPA personnel and personnel who were members of Coalition forces, along with their property, funds and assets "shall be immune from Iraqi Legal Process". The Order also declared that "all Coalition contractors and their sub-contractors as well as their employees not normally resident in Iraq, shall not be subject to Iraqi laws or regulations in matters relating to the terms and conditions of their contracts in relation to the Coalition Forces or the CPA." Once again, there is a nod to the provisions of the Hague and Geneva rules. Thus, the Order notes that states are contributing personnel, equipment and other resources to the Coalition in order to contribute to the *security and stability* that will enable the relief, recovery and development of Iraq"[5]

Order 17 was extended again in June 2004 as one of the final acts of the CPA. Taken together Executive Order 13303 and CPA Order 17 provided a *carte blanche* provision of immunity from prosecution for white-collar and corporate crimes in Iraq. Executive Order 13303/CPA Order 17 represent very simply and clearly an act of suspension of the law. The effect was a state of limbo between law and lawlessness that produced fertile conditions for US capital to exploit newly opened up markets in 'reconstruction', security and the production and sale of Iraqi oil; a liminal space in which a particular form of a 'state of exception' provides those companies and their employees with legal immunity.

Those specific provisions of immunity, granted by government Order, were supported during the CPA's term of office between 2003 and 2004 by the deliberate circumnavigation and obstruction of external auditing procedures. The establishment of the International Advisory and Monitoring Board (IMAB), the body required under the terms of United Nations Security Council Resolution 1483, was deliberately delayed by the US authorities and prevented from receiving its mandate until a full 5 months into the CPA's term of office (Iraq Revenue Watch, 2003). In addition, investigative and enforcement powers were denied IMAB after successful lobbying by US government representatives (Lawson and Halford, 2004). Subsequently, the CPA took 11 months to appoint its internal auditor, the Special Inspector General for Iraq Reconstruction (SIGIR; Iraq Revenue Watch, 2003). Those delays were crucial in hindering the ongoing audit of CPA activities. The CPA and the US government continued to block audits and investigations throughout the Authority's term of office (*Washington Post* 16th July 2004; *Financial Times* June 22nd, 2004; KPMG Bahrain, 2004).

In another explicit breach of UNSCR 1483, the CPA failed to meter oil production and export and did not keep an adequate record of oil export income. In addition, the CPA kept no list of companies it issued contracts to. One report by IMAB (2005) found evidence of incomplete DFI accounting records; untimely recording, reporting, reconciliation and follow-up of spending by Iraqi ministries; incomplete records maintained by US agencies, including disbursements that were not recorded in the Iraqi budget.

The systematic obstruction of auditing procedures preserved the zone of liminality in which few records were kept and few mechanisms of accountability existed. This disruption to the operation of audit procedures constituted clear breaches of both the specific requirements of UNSCR 1483 and of the norms of international accounting. It was estimated that in the first year of occupation, between $8.8 billion and $12 billion of DFI revenue remained accounted for.[6]

LEX MERCATORIA AND THE WASHINGTON CONSENSUS

Audi has argued that the rationale for the overnight transformation of the Iraqi economy can be found in a new 'standard of civilisation'. In so far as this standard of civilisation seeks the adoption of the neo-liberal terms and condition of entry into the global economy, it boils down to little more than the Washington Consensus. Thus, "the implementation of liberal, market oriented reforms becomes the prerequisite for a country's integration into international society" (Audi, 2004-05).

If there is a general principle of international law that has always existed, it is one that is based upon the promotion of values of 'civilisation'. If we can put aside the oxymoronic qualities and hypocrisies of the Western concept of civilisation for a moment, it is important to recognise the enduring centrality of an idea of a universal 'civilisation' in international law. Thus Article 38 of the International Court of Justice statute asserts a jurisprudential benchmark of "general principles of law recognised by civilised nations." Now, of course there is some controversy about what "civilised" constitutes here, but if there is one common theme that runs through bodies of rules and norms that have been described as a 'standard of civilisation', they are rules for the functioning of a global economic system (Panezi, 2007). The standard of civilisation is most clearly expressed in the mysterious, imprecise, legal concept of *lex mercatoria* that supports liberalised markets and 'free' trade and in contractual, trade and property relationships that has its origins in the 11th century legal system used by European merchants. Infrastructurally, the rules and norms described as *lex mercantoria* have expanded rapidly as international transactions have intensified (de Souza Santos, 1995). The neo-liberal institutions, the World Bank, IMF, alongside the World Bank, have been key sites of the new *lex mercatoria*, as have the institutional structures of trading blocs such as the European Union and NAFTA. To this we can add the pre-dominance of US initiated and organised *fora* for dispute resolution at an international level that are established and guided by the norms of American informal law (amongst them, for example, the International Chamber of Commerce; Heydebrand, 2001).

In articulating a position that reeks of the end of history thesis, David Fidler argues that the new 'standard of civilisation' is given force by a "liberal victory" that is clearly discernible in international law and international relations: "In international law, liberal dominance appears in the prominence given to free trade, democratic governance, human rights, the rule of law, and good governance" (Fidler, 2001: 147). Accordingly international lawyers must get over their embarrassment with 18th and 19th century colonialist association with the term 'standard of civilisation' since the world is now moving gradually, but assuredly, towards a new "civilisational pluralism" (ibid.: 154). In this account, the progress towards this neo-liberal standard of civilisation appears as consensual, guaranteed by the evolution of mutually agreed upon processes and procedures. Now Fidler wrote this piece a matter of months before the September 2001 attacks on the World Trade Centre and the Pentagon. And perhaps, without those events, his analysis might have had more persuasive power as a portent of a smoothly running legal order, organised around a relatively consensual agenda. But, given the long history of how the US has dealt with those that stand outside the 'standard of civilisation', it is the long march of US Imperialism rather than the sudden events of September 2001 that reveals the naivety of Fidler's analysis. After all, if Iraq was hardly the first time a military invasion or coup, initiated or backed by the US, produced a wholesale transformation of an economy resistant to US capital into an economy open for business. The key shock therapy experiments of Chile and Indonesia stand as key examples. But to those we might add the low level military operations in the 1980s in Nicaragua and Guatemala, the war to defeat the left as part of Plan Colombia, the invasions of Panama, Grenada and Haiti and the ongoing military blockade of Cuba. All of those military operations aim to consolidate a US political and economic and legal hegemony, and specifically establish US-friendly economic policies as a 'standard of civilisation'.

If Fidler and his colleagues'[7] narrative about a steady, consensual, transition to a universal law of the market tells us something important about how the US law scholarship provides intellectual support to US global hegemony. Just as academics such as Alan Dershowitz, Harvard's own 'Professor of Torture' have obediently concocted a new line in novel, if entirely spurious, legal justifications for torture and for the existence of Guantanamo Bay[8], so a handful of US lawyers have emerged to justify the illegal economic transformation of Iraq. The new *lex mercatorialists* – find in the complex of common practice norms, rules, and transnational institutions a normative structure that is apparently strong enough to brush aside the Hague and Geneva agreements and to brush aside the terms of the US Security Council agreement that applied to the occupying forces.

FUTURE RESEARCH DIRECTIONS: CHALLENGING LEX MERCATORIA

There is, however, good reason to doubt the legal status, or even the existence of *lex mercatoria*. Without devaluing the hegemonic significance of this legal architecture, what we are describing here is by no means a linear or logically integrated process of law making. Those norms have developed over at least 5 centuries and in its contemporary context *lex mercatoria* can be said to have multiple sources of varying political and juridical status (international treaties, established custom in TNCs and other transnational organisations, the decisions of international courts, the United Nations and its various sub-committees and affiliated organisations, NGOs and so on). And each of those sources incorporate their own conflicts, debates, unresolved battles whose protagonistis may or may not have popular support and may indeed be challenged by counter-hegemonic groups. It is therefore important to understand this 'standard of civilisation' not as a closely coupled system that has developed smoothly or rationally, but as something that is fought over and involves hegemonic struggles in an almost unfathomable range of sites, with outcomes that invariably contradict and conflict with other outcomes. In this sense, *lex mercantoria* cannot seriously be considered consensual. Neither does *lex mercantoria* have a hierarchy of rule or decision making processes that can be located in time or space. It may be a customary form of law, but this again raises all kind of questions about the relationship between custom, norm and law, particularly if those customs have been arbitrarily imposed 'from above'.

Boaventura de Souza Santos (1995) argues that we can challenge *lex mercatoria* on two main grounds. First, its validity has been the subject of some debate between civil law scholars and common law scholars, the latter disputing its legal status, largely because a major source of *lex mercatoria* has not been the courts or law-making authorities, but in private bodies such as corporate in-house lawyers and American corporate law firms. Second, in the absence of a developed institutional architecture capable of guaranteeing, at a global level, the regulation and reproduction of a new global regime of (capitalist) accumulation, the American law firm has adopted a central role (see also Gessner, 1998). This indicates that *lex mercatoria*, rather than being based on a universal set of norms, is emerging as a highly parochial US-centric normative structure. This has also been the criticism of other key institutions that may be capable of developing such an architecture, namely the WTO and the IFIs.

It is therefore not credible to claim that *lex mercatoria* constitutes a truly global legal normative framework. The growing significance of the Chinese economy on the world stage provides evidence of an entirely separate set of normative standards and values, exemplified by the *guanxi* system of exchange. Moreover the current US-led assault upon Hawali and Hundi systems of exchange provide evidence of the ongoing struggles between competing norms. *Lex mercatoria* might be better described as part of a set of "faked rules and institutions" that aim to enlarge the structural power of capital by relinquishing the law's role in constraining market actors, based in turn upon a faked consensus (Mattei, 2003).

Yet the lack of a convincing claim to embody a standard of international law has not prevented the *new lex mercatorialists* proclaiming it as a deep structure of law. For Audi, Iraq remains a lawless space until it complies with the new 'standard of civilisation' Audi, 2004-05). For as long as it exists on the wrong side of the boundary between civilised and uncivilised economy, it cannot claim the protection of international law more generally. This is a circular argument that Kafka would have been proud of: Iraq can be subject to a suspension of law and forced to swallow the prescriptions of the neo-liberal order, precisely because it remains outside the protection of international law. And it remains outside the protection of international law because it has not become fully integrated into the neo-liberal order. Most simply boiled down this 'standard of civilisation' reads: "if you don't agree to what we say, then you must agree to what we say." Just as the inmates of Guantanamo find themselves in legal limbo, in a state of bare life, under the command of a law that eradicates their legal status and yet at the same time determines precisely their conditions of existence, so it goes for the Iraqi nation state.

In the case that this paper explored earlier, we find a set of legitimating narratives that are too complex to be described as *raison d'etat*, for they are based upon the premise of a civilising mission as well as upon the granting of political freedoms, and they are openly connected to the creative destruction and reconstruction of an economic and political system, rather than simply being based upon the survival or integrity of the sovereign. But *Lex mercantoria* is a law that is not really law, for it is an ephemeral, arbitrary and highly contentious body of rules that can make no credible claim to universal application. It is a fake law. Yet, it is this law, the arbitrary law of the occupier that sweeps aside the international laws of war and the sovereign law of the Iraqi constitution. Those laws, which once appeared as concrete law, are turned instantly to dust by an act of military force.

CONCLUSION

This chapter has sought to expand Agamben's formulation of the state of exception to more fully understand the particularities of neo-colonial rule in the case of occupied Iraq. In so far as Agamben limits himself to understanding the consequences of the relationship between sovereign power and anomie for the individual, he does not contemplate the connection of law – and indeed the liminal spaces created in the state of exception - to the deeper structures of social relations that the law supports. As Santiago has noted, "Agamben's argument privileges a liberal interpretation of the law that situates the emergence of the state of exception in the relationship between the state and the individual" (Santiago, 2006: 21). In this sense, Agamben's formulation remains asocial. But as this case shows us, states of exception are always connected to a project of power that constitutes social relations in general terms as well as constituting legal relations between the individual and the state, and indeed property relations.

What happened to the Iraqi society in the immediate aftermath of the invasion was an attempt to establish a new set of commercial practices that would restructure the economy by transforming property relationships. In so far as frequent reference was made to the reforms as part of an effort to bring Iraq closer to the conditions required for membership of the WTO, those practices were introduced with reference to international institutions and the normative standards that they promulgate, but not with reference to *international law*. In the conceptual universe occupied by the US governing elite, it was Saddam's planned economy that constituted the exception; an economically uncivilised and barren space that had hitherto remained, to use the British colonial term 'beyond the pale'. The aim of the occupation was not to merely impose a law of exception, but to establish the global neo-colonial norm – the new *lex mercatoria*.

In advanced capitalist states, the state of exception has a range of simultaneous functions: as ideological or propaganda supports, as a means of expanding or enhancing state security apparatuses, to legitimise colonial reach externally and so on. In so far as it is able to reveal the core of a brutal relationship between the state and the law, the concept of the state of exception is made more powerful when we understand the 'lack' or the 'deficit' that it seeks to address. In other cases in which exceptional rule has been applied, this lack is positioned as a lack of law or a lack of public order. In this case, the deficit was positioned as resulting from particular economic and political structures.

Just as in the case of John Locke's theory of property based on the principles of improvement, in Iraq, social transformation was predicated upon the injunction to make the economy productive and profitable. The rationale for the violent expropriation of the Iraqi people was simply a modern day theory of deficit/lack: that the constitution was not equipped for a fully functioning capitalist society. If this theory of deficit/lack is the doctrine, and the new 'standard of civilisation' seeks to address this deficit, then the state of exception measures described here are merely the technical means to achieve neo-colonial rule.

REFERENCES

Agamben, G. (2000) Sovereign Police. In V. Binetti, & C. Casarino, (trans.), Means Without End: notes on politics. Minneapolis: University of Minnesota Press.

Agamben, G. (2005). *State of Exception* (K. Attel, Trans.). Chicago: University of Chicago Press. doi:10.1215/9780822386735-013

Arendt, H. (1965/1977). *Eichman in Jerusalem: a report on the banality of evil*. London: Penguin.

Audi, A. (2004-05). Iraq's New Investment laws and the Standard of Civilisation: A case study on the limits of international law. *The Georgetown Law Journal*, *93*, 335–364.

Bahrain, K. P. M. G. (2004). *Development Fund for Iraq: Report of Factual Findings in connection with Disbursements For the period from 1 January 2004 to 28 June 2004*. Baghdad: International Advisory and Monitoring Board of the Development Fund for Iraq and the Project and Contracting Office.

Benjamin, W. (1978). Critique of Violence. In P. Demetz (Ed.), *Reflections: Essays, Aphorisms*. Autobiographical Writings, New York: Schoken Books.

Coalition Provisional Authority (2003a). Order Number 12, Trade Liberalisation Policy, CPA/ORD/7 June 2003/12: 1, emphasis in the original.

Coalition Provisional Authority (2003b). Order Number 81, Patent, Industrial Design, Undisclosed Information, Integrated Circuits and Plant Variety, CPA/ORD/26 April 04/81: 1, emphasis in the original.

Coleman, R., Sim, J., Tombs, S., & Whyte, D. (2009). Introduction. In R. Coleman, J. Sim, S. Tombs, & D. Whyte (Eds.), *State, Power, Crime*. London: Sage. doi:10.4135/9781446269527.n1

Colliers, R. (2003) Imports Inundate Iraq under new U.S. Policy, San Francisco Chronicle, 10th July.

de Souza Santos, B. (1995). *Towards a New Common Sense: law, science and politics in the paradigmatic transition*. London: Routledge.

Dershowitz, A. (2002, January 22). Want to torture? Get a warrant. *San Francisco Chronicle*.

Fidler, D. (2001). The Return of the Standard of Civilisation. *Chicago Journal of International Law*, *2*(1), 147.

Fidler, D. (2001). The Return of the Standard of Civilisation. *Chicago Journal of International Law*, *2*(1), 154.

Frank, T. (2000). *One Market Under God: Extreme Capitalism, Market Populism, and the End of Economic Democracy*. New York: Doubleday.

Gessner, V. (1998). Globalisation and Legal Certainty. In V. Gessner & A. Budak (Eds.), *Emerging Legal Certainty: empirical studies on the globalisation of law, Aldershot*. Dartmouth.

Heydebrand, W. (2001). From Globalisation of Law to Law Under Globalisation. In D. Nelken, & J. Feest (Eds.), Adapting Legal Cultures (p. 119). Oxford: Hart.

IMAB. (2005). Statement by the International Advisory and Monitoring Board on the Development Fund for Iraq, 4th November.

IMAB. (2005). Statement by the International Advisory and Monitoring Board on the Development Fund for Iraq, 23rd May.

Iraq Revenue Watch. (2003). *Iraq Keeping Secrets: America and Iraq's public finances. Iraq Revenue Watch, report no. 3*. New York: Open Society Institute.

Kampfner, J (2003, May26). Blair Was Told it Would be Illegal to Occupy Iraq. New Statesman.

Kelly, C. (2004). The War on Jurisdiction: Troubling questions about Executive Order 13303. *Arizona Law Review*, *46*(483).

Kramer, R., & Michalowski, R. (2005). War, Aggression and State Crime. *The British Journal of Criminology*, *45*(4), 446–469. doi:10.1093/bjc/azi032

Lawson, A., & Halford, S. (2004). Fuelling Suspicion: the Coalition and Iraq's oil billions. London: Christian Aid.

Lemke, T. (2005). A Zone of Indistinction – A Critique of Giorgio Agamben's Concept of Biopolitics, Outlines. *Critical Social Studies*, *7*(1), 9.

Mattei, U. (2003). A Theory of Imperial Law: A study on U.S. hegemony and the Latin resistance. *Global Jurist Frontiers*, *3*(2), 4. doi:10.2202/1535-1653.1088

Meiksins-Wood, E. (1998). The Agrarian Origins of Capitalism. *Monthly Review (New York, N.Y.)*, *50*(3), 14. doi:10.14452/MR-050-03-1998-07_2

Meiksins-Wood, E. (2003). *Empire of Capital* (pp. 97–99). London: Verso.

Mustill, L.J. (1988). The New Lex Mercatoria: The first twenty five years. *Arbitration International*, *4*(2), 86–119. doi:10.1093/arbitration/4.2.86

Nader, L. (2005). The Americanisation of International Law. In F. von Benda-Beckman, K. von Benda-Beckman, & A. Griffiths (Eds.), Mobile People, Mobile Law: expanding legal relations in a contracting world (pp. 200-201). Aldershot: Ashgate.

Nader, L. (2007). Promise or Plunder? A Past and Future Look at Law and Development. Global Jurist, 7(1).

Panezi, M. (2007). Source of Law in Transition: re-visiting general principles of international law. *Ancilla Iuris*, 66-79.

Santiago, C (2006). From Insular Cases to Camp X-Ray: Agamben's state of exception and United States territorial law. *Studies in Law, Politics and Society*, 39, 15-55.

Schmitt, C. (2003). *The Nomos of the Earth: in the international law of the jus publicum Europaeum* (Original work published 1950). New York: Telos.

Teubner, G. (2002). Breaking Frames: Economic globalisation and the emergence of lex mercatoria. *European Journal of Social Theory*, *5*(2), 199–217. doi:10.1177/1368431022225414

Whyte, D. (2007). The Crimes of Neo-liberal Rule in Occupied Iraq. *The British Journal of Criminology*, *47*(2), 177–195. doi:10.1093/bjc/azl065

Whyte, D. (2008). Hire an American! Tyranny and Corruption in Occupied Iraq. *Social Justice (San Francisco, Calif.)*, *35*(3).

ENDNOTES

1 I am grateful to Jose Atiles for pointing this out to me in conversation.

2 This argument and direct quotes can be found in Johnson v. M'Intosh, 21 U.S. 543, 590 (1823).

3 Memorandum from Lord Goldsmith, Attorney General to the Prime Minister March 26th 2003, reproduced in Kampfner, 2003.

4 The full text of this Executive Order 13303 can be found in Office of the Press Secretary, White House Press Release, 22nd May, 2003, published online at: http://www.whitehouse.gov/news/releases/2003/05/20030522-15.html.

5 My emphasis.

6 The lower and upper limits of those figures are derived from SIGIR audits analyses by investigative journalist. See Reuters report 'Audit Shows $8.8billion in Iraqi funds missing', 19th August 2004, available at: http://www.msnbc.msn.com/id/5763483/print/1/displaymode/1098 and Harriman, 2006.

7 For the classic statement of the new *lex mercatoria*, see Mustill, 1988; for a complex sociological legitimisation of *lex mercatoria*, see Teubner, 2002.

8 In an infamous article in the *San Francisco Chronical* in January 2002, Dershowitz followed in the footsteps of his intellectual forbearer Carl Schmitt by proclaiming his own support for a state of exception. In an article supporting judicial torture warrants, he observed, "Every democracy, including our own, has employed torture outside of the law."

Section 4
The Turbulent Colombia

Chapter 16
Retaliation in Transitional Justice Scenarios:
The Experiences of Argentina and Colombia

Gustavo Rojas Paez
Universidad Libre, Colombia

ABSTRACT

This chapter discusses the role of retaliation in the Transitional Justice Scenarios of Argentina and Colombia, drawing attention to the continuation of state violence and human rights violations in these two South American countries following the implementation of legal and non- legal mechanisms of TJ. Subsequently, it attempts to demonstrate how the implementation of TJ mechanisms may fall short in preventing cycles of violence that allow powerful actors, linked to the interests of the state, to continue performing the retaliatory practices that historically caused major 'social harm' in the transitional societies . The rationale of this article consists of two central questions: How can transitional societies deal with both the legacy and reconfiguration of state violence? Moreover, to what extent do orthodox understandings of law and TJ serve as a means for the recreation of the retaliatory practices that shaped the conflicts that TJ measures are supposed to address?

INTRODUCTION

Transitional justice (hereafter TJ) has become a buzzword in the jargon of both policy makers and scholars. Broadly understood as the type of justice mechanisms implemented after periods of harsh political confrontation, mass atrocity and gross human rights violations, the configuration of the idea of TJ has been significantly influenced by the political experiences of Latin American societies (Teitel 2000). Reference to the transitional scenarios of the Southern Cone, and most recently to the implementation of TJ mechanisms in the ongoing-armed conflict of Colombia, constitutes a common component of the ample but diffuse literature on the subject (Bell 2009; Uprimny & Saffon 2007).

This chapter discusses the role of retaliation in the TJ scenarios[1] of Argentina and Colombia, drawing attention to the continuation of state

DOI: 10.4018/978-1-4666-9675-4.ch016

violence and human rights violations in these two South American countries following the implementation of legal and non-legal mechanisms of TJ. Subsequently, it attempts to demonstrate how the implementation of TJ mechanisms may fall short in preventing cycles of violence that allow power groups, linked to the interests of the state, to continue performing the retaliatory practices that historically caused major 'social harm' in the so called transitional societies[2].

The rationale of the chapter consists of two central questions: How can transitional societies deal with both the legacy and reconfiguration of state violence? Moreover, to what extent the understandings of law that inform TJ processes facilitate the continuation retaliatory practices that serve the interests of major power groups, who benefited from the violence of both the conflict and the transitional period?

In order to address these two questions, this chapter uses elements of critical criminology such as Cohen's concept of 'states of denial' (2004) and draws attention to the performance of TJ. In particular, the chapter examines the role of the state as both a regulator and generator of crime before and after TJ processes (Chamblis 2010). In so doing, the chapter uses insights of anthropological accounts (Gugliemucci 2007; Castillejo 2007) on TJ and highlights the importance of thinking about transitional justice from a critical perspective. The article argues that retaliation can also be present in TJS and shows that the discourse on rights surrounding the notion of TJ is imbued with multiple meanings, shaped by political, legal and social actors[3]. In this vein, concepts from the work of P. Bourdieu, such as social capital and legal field, also inform the theoretical framework of the chapter.

The chapter is structured in three sections. Firstly, I provide an overview of the transitional scenario of Argentina, outlining the historical assemblage of state terror in Argentina and two commemorations on March 24th - the National day of Memory in Argentina. Secondly, I trace a depiction of the TJ scenario of Colombia, based on an analysis of the legal framework of the transition and its political configuration. Finally, in the third section, I draw some conclusions by reflecting on the role and intensity of retaliation in the two cases.[4].Throughout the article, the relationship between law and state violence is evinced. In highlighting this relationship, my intention is to underscore that that law can be instrumentalized in TJ processes and leave aside the idea of "justice" from an ethical perspective.

Despite there being no single definition of TJ, for the purpose of this article I will take Joanna's Quinn definition of the notion as an analytical tool. For Quinn, 'TJ is the process by which societies move either from war to peace or from a repressive regime to democracy while dealing with resulting questions of justice and what to do with social, political, and economic institutions' (Quinn 2009). Quinn's definition is illustrative of the models of TJ mechanisms implemented in Colombia and Argentina.

Notwithstanding state violence having constituted the most harmful form of retaliation in Latin American societies, the phenomenon of persistent state criminality and its surrounding social, political and economic forces remain largely unaddressed in TJ research. This contribution aims to draw attention to this phenomenon and the role of the state as a retaliatory actor in contexts where the historically asymmetric relationships of power remain – largely intact, even after the implementation of TJ mechanisms.

ARGENTINA: AN ARCHIVE OF STATE CRIME

Authoritarianism and state violence have been characteristic features of Argentinean history (Aguila 2010), with violence having played a fundamental role in the foundation of the state, as reported by historical accounts on the genocide of indigenous peoples and the perpetration of extreme violence against black Argentineans in the nineteenth century (Seri 2010). This foundational violence persisted at the beginning of the twentieth century, when the military and their trained paramilitary forces *Liga Patriotica*, assassinated hundreds of strikers (Seri 2010). Both groups targeted workers, students, university professors and school teachers whose political beliefs represented a threat to the nationalistic interests of Argentina's Catholic-Nationalist elites (Robben 2005)[5].

State violence intensified prior to the 1976 coup, with many paramilitary groups having formed during 1970-75. The *Argentine Anti-Communist Alliance,* or *Triple A,* integrated by civilians, the military and police, was the most voracious among them (Malamud 1995), estimated to have murdered 2,500 civilians (Seri 2011). Against such a backdrop, it can be argued that state terror in Argentina should not be understood as a by-product of the 1976 dictatorship, but rather as the result of a complex historical process in which state violence was normalised and supported by influential groups of society such as the elites and Catholic Church (Robben 2005; Lesa 2011). The police benefited from a permissive legal framework in which a misdemeanor was not treated within the judicial system, but regulated by edict police (Taylor 1999).

Despite state involvement in the formation of paramilitary groups being evident before the transition, lawyers and other institutional actors turned a blind eye to this phenomenon, falling within what S. Cohen terms the 'state of official denial,' through which 'the state makes it impossible or dangerous to acknowledge the existence of past and present realities' (Cohen 2004). The state is thus provided with a moral context for the denial of its servants' deviant behaviour, and is consequently able to impose their narrative of history and ignore a present created by atrocity (Whyte 2009).

El Proceso 1976 to 1983

The military dictatorship ruling Argentina from 1976 to 1983 emerged as a result of the *coup de etat* led by Lieutenant Jorge Rafael Videla, who overthrew the debilitated government of Maria Stella Dominguez de Peron (Aguila 2010). With the purpose of reforming the economic, social and political organization, which had resulted from popular mobilization of the early 1970s, the military besieged power starting what is known in Argentinean history as *El Proceso* or the *Process of National Reorganization* (Kratz 2011). To achieve their political and economic aims, the military declared war against any opposition or 'supposed opposition' including guerrilla forces or any other societal sector (Taylor 1999; Robben 2005). From the military regime's perspective, reorganising Argentina meant replacing a 'chaotic but participatory democratic system with a hierarchical one centred on reactionary Catholicism and non-redistributive capitalism' (Katz 2011).

According to CONADEP (National Commission on the disappeared-Spanish Acronym), between 10,000 and 30,000 people 'forcibly disappeared' during the dictatorship, many of whom were political dissidents tortured by state agents in clandestine detention centers. Having been tortured and questioned, victims were taken on airplanes over the Atlantic Ocean and the "Rio de la Plata", into which they were thrown alive (Verdeja 2010-Inter-American Human Rights Court-*Scilingo case)*[6]. The ongoing Cold War meant that the US sponsored dictatorship spread terror among the Argentinean population, by implementing practices such as Enforced Disappearances (hereafter ED), torture and arbitrary detentions, committed in 500 clandestine centres located throughout the entire country (CONADEP). The military considered themselves as guardians of the nation and were inspired by the US Doctrine of National Security (Lesa 2011), which promoted the idea that 'the world faced an ultimate war between communist and non-communist forces and that this battle would be waged through nonconventional warfare with each nation (Taylor 1999). The dictatorship came to an end in 1983, as a result of the humiliating military defeat of Argentinean forces in the *Malvinas War* (Crenzel 2008).

The Argentine society has since struggled to elaborate what Derrida referred to as the *Archive*. In a transitional society, as Derridian-inspired accounts on memory suggest, an archive is the place where social order, law and authority are determined (Derrida 1995; Castillejo 2007; Van Marle 2007). Judicial and non-judicial frameworks of TJ work as archives aiming to assist societies in coming to terms with a violent past and to eventually achieve reconciliation or peace. The ways in which the violence of the dictatorship has been confronted both institutionally and socially within the Argentinean transitional scenario are described below, based on two recent commemorations of the day for Memory, Truth and Justice[7].

March 24th: A Day for Memory, Truth and Justice

According to Law 26.085-2006, March 24th is the day for Argentineans' remembrance of the horrors of the dictatorial regime. The law resulted from multiple mobilisations that intensified after the end of the dictatorship. To this day, a significant number of victims' organisations contest the way that state terror has been dealt with by democratic governments. A close observation of this day's commemorations allows us to explore the narratives and discourses of victimhood that have moulded the transition to democracy in Argentina. These narratives and discourses are presented in a ritualistic manner, through which the different organisations expose their social capital in an event capturing an entire country's attention[8].

March 24th 2002

Argentina was seriously struck by bankruptcy at the outset of this century, culminating in five different presidents in less than a month. This situation brought about nationwide mobilisations, which the governments responded to with extreme police repression, with twenty-seven people dying due to police brutality.

Against this backdrop, a massive mobilisation took place in the midst of extreme social and political turmoil in Plaza de Mayo on March 24th 2002, with thousands of people and victims organizations gathering to demand justice. Their motto was *"Justice! For yesterday and today"* (Gugliemucci 2007). In her analysis of the commemoration of this event, Argentine anthropologist Ana Gugliuemucci draws attention to the wide participation of social organisations that joined the massive mobilisations in 2002 (Gugliemucci 2007). Gugliemucci stresses that in addition to the well-known number of victims' organisations, a new organisation took part in the mobilisation in 2002- *Mothers of Pain*. This organisation unites the mothers of the assassinated youngsters, killed by *Gatillo Facil (Easy Trigger)*, a selective form of extrajudicial killing perpetrated by police forces during the democratic regime. These new victims of state violence are young, poor men living in marginal areas of Argentina's biggest cities. The participation of Mothers of Pain added a further element of motherhood to the mobilisation, following the presence of two other well-known organisations of the mothers of victims of state violence - Mothers of Plaza de Mayo and Grandmothers of Plaza de Mayo. Thus, the mothers of victims of state violence of both the democratic period and the dictatorship gathered together at this particular moment in time.

Plaza de Mayo is a place where retaliatory feelings towards state violence from the past and present have convened since the end of the dictatorship. On March 24th 2002, the motto *Justice for today and yesterday* highlighted the experiences of injustice emerging from the state violence of both the dictatorial regime and democratic period. The cry for justice has also represented the 'symbolic power' of the victims' organisations and the 'liminality' of the Argentine transition[910]. When reflecting on the victims of state crime's predicament and mobilisation, two questions come to mind: What path has the Argentine society taken during the past 27 years? To what extent have the retaliatory practices of the state shifted?

Similar to the "enforcedly disappeared" of the dictatorial regime, the victims' bodies of *Easy Trigger* represent the existence of those individuals whose life is not worthy of value and therefore become killable, and what Foucault called the 'let die' (Foucault 1988)[11]. In contrast to the "enforcedly disappeared" of the dictatorship, the victims of *Easy Trigger* are not killed due to political beliefs. However, they are the recipients of the state's retaliatory power, deployed through '*mano dura*' policies(*hereupon hardline)* in which poor youngsters from marginalised lower classes are portrayed as the "dangerous others". Consequently, the poor are branded as suspected criminals who deserve to be morally and socially excluded (Chiller and Varela 2009). As Lessa has put it: 'Those 'morally excluded' from society can be subjected to anything-the perception is that human rights do not apply to them' (Lessa 2011).

Hard-line policies are reinforced by state institutions, such as the judiciary. Cases of *Easy Trigger* are not afforded the necessary attention, as exemplified in the case of Walter Bulicio. In 1991, Walter was detained along with 72 other youngsters for attempting to sneak into a rock concert without paying. He was taken to 35th Police Station, where he was severely beaten. The youngsters were later freed without the reasons for their detention being explained, however Walter was taken to hospital and died following a brain haemorrhage, aged 17 (IAHRC-Inter American Human Rights Court). The case remained in the Argentine courts for almost 10 years without a ruling, with Walter's parents subsequently taking the case to the IAHRC, which ordered the Argentine government to hold those responsible for Walter's death. However, twenty years after the incident, no culprit has been found. The impunity of Easy Trigger replicates Cohen's "state of denial", which was characteristic of the dictatorship, whereby during military rule the judicial system did little to prevent enforced disappearance (Skaar 2003). Today, preventing the killings of victims of Easy Trigger remains unimportant within the Argentinean legal system. According to CELS (CELS-Centre for Social and Legal studies-Spanish acronym 2010), around 2753 people have died due to state violence over the past decade (CELS 2007-2010). The impunity of these heinous crimes has given rise to cycles of retaliation that contribute to the idea of the state as a retaliatory agent, consolidating its power through violence and impunity (Lessa 2011).

March 24th 2004.

The election of Nestor Kichner as president held great significance for the Argentine human rights movement (Druliolle 2011), with President Kichner being responsive to the demand for *Memory, Truth and Justice*, which human rights organisations had upheld for almost thirty years after the dictatorship. During his term, Kichner instigated congress to overturn laws prohibiting the prosecutions of the members of the military juntas. (Crenzel 2011). The so-called Full Stop (1986) and Due Obedience (1987) laws had been perceived as a harsh blow to the victims movement, whose members celebrated the declaration of the unconstitutionality of such laws and the reopening of proceedings against the former military (Crenzel 2008).

In addition to these important changes in the contested legal framework of the transition, the Kirchner government also promoted programmes for the preservation of memory. Since the mid-1990s, victims had struggled for the remembrance of the "forcibly disappeared," contesting the politics of oblivion promoted by the legal framework of the transition (Druliolle 2011).

One of the Kirchner governments' most important memory projects is the transformation of ESMA, the Navy School Mechanics, into a space of memory and the promotion and defence of human rights (Glueccini 2007; Druliolle 2011), with the official inauguration of this transformation taking place on March 24th 2004. Significantly, ESMA was one of the biggest clandestine centres in which the military had kept political dissidents under clandestine detention. The massive military facility had also been a maternity ward, and given that many of the detained mothers who gave birth in these clandestine detention centres were tortured, assassinated and forcibly disappeared, the children born in secret were abducted and given up for adoption by the military. It is estimated that around 200 children were born clandestinely, with their bodies representing a war trophy for the military[12].

Many of the sinister events that took place in ESMA influenced the repertoire of the victims' organisations that have resisted state terror since the dictatorship. Many of these organisations were invited by the Kirchner administration to the inauguration of the 'Museum of Memory' that will be built as a result of the government's decision to pay tribute to the victims of state terror. Through this invitation, the government set a milestone in the politics of memory in Argentina by acknowledging the 'social capital' of those most affected by state terror: the relatives and parents of enforcedly disappeared persons during the dictatorship.

Against this backdrop, I will briefly refer to the retaliatory responses on state terror of three victims' organisations: Mothers of Plaza de Mayo, Grand Mothers of Plaza de Mayo and HIJOS. The narratives of these organisations are emblematic of the resistance to state crime and oblivion influencing the transitional interplay in Argentina. As will be exposed, this resistance is imbued by retaliatory responses and interpretations of state violence deployed on the commemoration of March 24th.

Motherhood, Sons and Scratches in a Museum of Memory

The participation of Mothers of Plaza de Mayo in the inauguration of the Museum of Memory was particularly symbolic. Despite military repression and the killings of two of their founding members, this group of mothers of forcibly disappeared children started their fight against state terror back in 1977, since managing to both influence and sensitise the Argentine transitional scenario. Although they had always been reluctant to participate in memory projects promoted by state organisations, in 2004 they informed the government of their interest to take part in the inauguration ceremony of the Museum of Memory, on the condition that some members of the local government were not present, particularly the governor of the province of Buenos Aires (Guegleccini 2007). The government was responsive to the demand of the mothers, banning the participation of some of its members from the event.

In a ritualistic ceremony in front of a heterogeneous audience, President Kichner addressed the mothers and other victims' organisations present (Sosa 2011). In his speech, Kichner highlighted the courage of three organisations: Mothers of Plaza de Mayo, the Grandmothers of Plaza de Mayo and the HIJOS (*Sons and Daughters for Identity and Justice, against Forgetting and Silence*), highlighting their archetypal struggle for the Argentine nation. His recognition of their fight to keep these memories alive marked a new beginning in the politics of remembering its temporalities and places in Argentina.

Prior to Kitchener's speech, different victims' organisations were given an opportunity to speak out on stage. The narratives of the organisations had a cathartic character, influenced by retaliatory feelings towards what happened in ESMA. Not only was what happened at issue, but also how to remember the victims of heinous crimes committed in ESMA. In their speech, HIJOS cried out their countrywide-known motto: *no forgetfulness, no pardon, we do not reconcile!* HIJOS is an organisation integrated by abducted children who never met their disappeared parents, struggling for their identification and remembrance. In their speech, they demanded the punishment not only of the perpetrators but also those public servants who signed the decree that legally recognised the beginning of the dictatorship, reading out a list with the names of many public servants who continued to work for the government during the democratic period. These demands replicated that of *scratching*, which has become characteristic of this organisation, whereby the youths decided to graffiti the houses inhabited by the perpetrators as a retaliatory reaction to the non-prosecution of former members of the dictatorship . The so-called *scrachers* would paint the houses of former military with messages such as: *Assassin you should be in jail!*. Following the demand for justice, one of the children who had recently found the identity of his parents thanked Grandmothers of Plaza Mayo for their struggle that had led to the recuperation of 95 children abducted during the dictatorial regime (CELS 2010). One common element of these three organizations' narratives is their insistence for the punishment of the perpetrators. Accordingly, the lawyers of the Grandmothers made a plea requesting a 50 years prison sentence for the former dictator Rafael Videla (Grandmothers' website 2012). The other two organisations support this plea, emphasising that only the harsh punishment of perpetrators will guarantee that the horrors of the dictatorship will *Never Again* occur. Thus, the motto Never Again also somewhat started to influence the interpretive paradigms of the judiciary.

The Judicial Reading of the Past

Following the commemorations, a series of judicial rulings against former members of the military and its supporters took place, establishing that what occurred during the dictatorships was genocide (Feirstein 2010). This innovative form of framing the events of the dictatorship evokes two questions: On the one hand, to what extent will individual accountability help Argentineans to come to terms with a past of state crime and gross human rights violations? On the other hand, can individual responsibility at the local level shed light on our understanding of state violence and the structural forces that led to it? As previously mentioned, the judiciary did little to combat the culture of denial promoted by the military and its supporters within the dictatorship and at the beginning of the democratic era. On the contrary, by developing a model of "judicial reasoning" known as the *two demons theory*, the judiciary treated the violence exercised by both the military and the Argentine guerrilla groups as equal criminal behaviour, and in so doing, the motivational component of political violence was put aside. This legalistic approach of producing truth via legal adjudication distorted the political character of violence and somewhat legitimated state violence. The Argentine Archive is still being completed and is composed of multifarious layers of meaning, which are permanently moving back and forth. After all, as Feirstein reminds us: "Unlike war, genocide does not end with the deaths it causes-it begins with them" (Feirstein 2010).

COLOMBIA: CONSTELLATIONS OF VIOLENCE IN TRANSITION

The Colombian armed conflict has been one of the longest ongoing conflicts in the world (Meertens and Zambrano 2010), involving a complex array of actors in which the interests of guerrilla groups, paramilitary forces, mafia barons and state agents intertwine (Uprimny & Saffon 2007). The modern origins of the conflict date back to the 1950s, when the conservative and liberal parties started to fight for political control of the country (Pecaut 1978). This period, known as "La violencia," left a death toll of nearly 200,000 people (Laplante & Theidon 2007).

Violence persists as a central element of the Colombian reality, with retaliation manifesting itself at different contexts in the confrontation. The events of November 2011, when four captive members of the security forces were shot dead by FARC, are representative of this dynamic. The guerrilla force killed their hostages in response to the rescuing attempt of the Colombian troops approaching one of FARC's camps, in which the hostages had been kept for 12 years (BBC 2011)[13]. It is intriguing that these images of war take place in a country whose government claims to be experiencing a political transition from war to peace (Mahler and Thomson 2011). In contrast to Argentina where TJ mechanisms have been implemented to come to terms with a violent past, Colombia's are being implemented within an ongoing armed conflict (Urpimny & Saffon 2007). Rather than a thorough analysis of the Colombian conflict, this section of the article addresses the Colombian transitional scenario and its retaliatory dynamics. This scenario emerged from the peace negotiations between the Colombian government and the United Self Defense of Colombia in 2003, with the paramilitaries agreeing to demobilise and announcing a unilateral ceasefire on the condition that none of their members would face prison sentences or extradition to the US (Laplante & Theidon 2007).

The configuration of paramilitary groups is marked by the historical uneasy link between the Colombian state and the paramilitary. In what follows, I will highlight the difficulties of negotiating with pro-state forces in a transitional scenario. Whose interests prevail in a negotiation among supporters? To what extent can the state condemn those whose power has emerged from its legal and political authority? In addressing such questions, I contend that bypassing the retaliatory potential of the state and its proxy forces, the legal framework of the Colombian "transition" has allowed for the continuation of serious human rights violations such as Forced Displacement (hereafter FD), ED and extrajudicial killings such as the so-called false positives (Gomez Santamaria 2010, HRW 2015).

Causing major social harm within society, these crimes also represent the normalisation of forms of retaliation involving the state and powerful groups of interests. The civilian population has been severely affected due to the retaliatory dynamics of the confrontation and the diverse interests maintaining it, with contemporary Colombia currently experiencing a humanitarian crisis in which around 50,000 FD have been reported and approximately 3.5 million persons are estimated to have been forcibly displaced (Uprimny, Diaz & Sanchez 2010; Codhes 2011). [14]

The Formation of the Paramilitary: Law and State Violence

The formation of paramilitary groups in Colombia dates back to the cold war. Similar to the Argentinean dictatorship, the Colombian government embarked on the war against insurgency with the support of the US (Stokes 2006). However, the use of law as a means to legitimize state violence has been more apparent in Colombia than in the Southern cone, exemplified by the passing of Decree 3398 / 1965 and Statute of Security/ 1978, both of which have subsequently led to the formation of pro-systemic groups such as paramilitary forces, in purporting to defend democracy against communism. This legal framework also granted the military the right to "exterminate social workers, trade unionists, men and women who did not support the establishment" (Giraldo 1996). According to Human Rights Watch, paramilitary groups have been responsible for most human rights violations throughout both the conflict and transitional period (Human Rights Watch 2010).

State Crime and the Inter-American Court's Ruling on UP Extermination

Union Patriotica (UP) was a political party that emerged out of the peace negotiations between the Colombian government, FARC and other guerrilla movements such as ELN and M19 in 1984 (Laplante & Theidon 2007). Despite a declared countrywide cease-fire, around 4,000 UP activists were assassinated during the 1980s and 1990s by paramilitary groups supported by a complex network comprising members of the Colombian military, traditional elites, multinational corporations, and drug traffickers (Raphael 2010; Gomez -Suarez 2007).

The destruction of a complete political group was also legitimized through the almost non-existent prosecutions against perpetrators of the systematic killings of members of UP, with 93% of crimes in Colombia remaining unpunished during the 1990s (Gomez -Suarez 2007). Moreover, only 11.1% of the 3,000 cases of the murders of the UP members faced prosecutions. This level of impunity prompted victims' organisations to bring the case to the Inter-American Commission of Human Rights, which reached the conclusion that the extermination of the UP was a collective murder (ICHR 1997). In this decision, the Commission highlighted that the extermination of UP was close to the defining elements of genocide, but however fell short within the international criminal law definition due to the way the events developed (Gomez-Suarez 2007).

PEACE AND JUSTICE LAW: FRAMEWORK OF TRANSITION

Following four turbulent and failing years of negotiations with FARC, the government of Alvaro Uribe commenced dialogue with the Colombian paramilitary- the United Self-Defence Forces of Colombia in 2003 (AUC -Spanish acronym) (Diaz 2009).These conversations resulted in the *Santa Fe de Ralito* agreement, which gave rise to the so-called *Peace and Justice* law (hereupon PJL), enacted in 2005. The paramilitaries agreed to demobilise, announcing a unilateral ceasefire on the condition that none of its members would face prison sentences or extradition to the US (Laplante & Theidon 2007). It is against this backdrop that the contested Colombian transitional justice framework came into being.

A Contested "Transitional" Setting

Prior to the enactment of law 975 PJL, the Colombian government presented a preliminary draft of the statute, entitled Alternative Penal Draft Legislation (Diaz 2009). From then on, the legal framework of the TJ scenario of Colombia has raised contestation, mainly from the victims of both paramilitary and state violence. This first attempt to produce a legal framework for the demobilisation of the paramilitary featured two problematic elements that triggered social mobilisation at both local and international levels. First, the draft did not establish any penal punishment for the demobilised paramilitary, and second, it did not provide an adequate program of reparations for the victims of paramilitary violence (Uprimny, Sanchez & Guzman 2010). Social protests from indigenous movements, African-Colombian organisations, peasant communities and local and international NGOs raised concerns from the international community and the UN High Commissioner for Human Rights (Diaz 2009). As a consequence of the social mobilisation and influence of the international community, two main changes were incorporated into the resulting PJL of 2005: a maximum sentence of 8 years for the demobilised paramilitary members, and a reparation program implemented by the National Commission of Reparations (CNR- Spanish acronym) (Laplante & Theidon 2007).

Outcomes of Implementation

After almost 10 years of implementation, the views of advocates of the PJL differ visibly from those of the victims' movement and human rights organisations, with the former arguing that the law should be regarded as a successful TJ mechanism implemented in an ongoing armed conflict. By contrast, the latter contends that the law and its highly controversial implementation have clearly failed to fulfil the aims of TJ, drawing attention to three problematic and interrelated aspects of Colombia's transitional scenario. Firstly, the judicial procedure established by PJL and the way in which the truth has been delivered through it. Secondly, the failure to consolidate the guarantees of non-repetition amongst the parties after the peace negotiations, and, thirdly, in connection to the previous aspects, the "re-emergence" of paramilitary violence that has given rise to the ensuing persistence of violence towards vulnerable groups of society. This mounting violence can also be attributed to the political-economic setting in which the interests of neoliberal globalisation and the Colombian government are favoured (Maher & Thompson 2011)[15].

A Limited Judicial Truth

The judicial process of PJL encompasses three interrelated and potentially problematic phases: massive demobilization, the voluntary confession (or - free version) of crimes committed, and the eventual prosecution of crimes committed by ex-combatants. As already stated, the procedure's worst outcome for the perpetrators would be a maximum prison sentence of 8 years, even if the ex-combatant in question has been involved in gross human rights violations such as massacres, extrajudicial killings or the recruitment of child soldiers. Since the free versions are not compulsory, the truth about the crimes is yet to be wholly unveiled, and many victims of paramilitary violence therefore remain doubtful about the whereabouts of their disappeared relatives. This has had a detrimental effect on to the victims' right to truth, illustrated by the fact that of an estimated 48,000 demobilised paramilitaries, only 3,284 have decided to cooperate with the truth-telling proceedings of PJL (Uribe 2011). The transparency of the demobilisations has recently been questioned by Maher and Thomson, describing them as farcical demobilisations within their critique of the negotiations with the Colombian paramilitary (Maher and Thompson 2011). Based on data from the American States Mission to support the peace process in Colombia MAPP/OEA, Maher and Thompson highlight that 7,000 demobilised members of AUC 'pulled out of the demobilisation process' (Maher and Thompson 2011). By the same token, MAPP/OEAA has shown that there has not been true disarmament and that the paramilitary continues to operate in various regions of the country (MAPP/ OEAA 2009 cited by Maher and Thompson 2011). A further incident violating victims' right to truth was the 2008 extradition of 13 paramilitary leaders to the US, without being heard at the free versions hearings (Uprimny, Sanchez & Guzman 2010). They will be prosecuted for drug trafficking, and it therefore seems unlikely that they will confess further human rights crimes committed in Colombia. Ultimately, the judicial procedure established by PJL has been inefficient given that only 11 definite sentences have been produced in almost 10 years (Verdad Abierta 2015)

Lack of Guarantees of Non-Repetition

The lack of guarantees of non-repetition is a fundamental flaw of the TJ scenario of Colombia, giving rise to cyclical violence influenced by retaliatory practices and responses. According to the Colombian Commission of Jurists (CCJ), there were 4,720 human rights violations perpetrated by paramilitary groups during 2002-2008 (CCJ 2010), with their report also highlighting that 880 paramilitary massacres were carried out in the post-demobilization period. The lack of guarantees of non-repetition has deeply affected the "transitional process" and its legitimacy as a means of achieving peace. Furthermore, it is claimed that around 2,000 demobilised ex-combatants have been assassinated since demobilization (CCJ 2010).

The paramilitaries are the main perpetrators of FD in the country, as indicated by the National Register of Displaced Population (RUPD-Spanish acronym 2008), which asserts their responsibility for 32% of FD in Colombia, followed by the guerrillas accounting for 26%. In effect, FD through terror tactics has been used by all armed groups in the Colombian conflict (Maher and Thomson 2011) Nevertheless, FD caused by paramilitary violence is linked to economic motives and has a strong relationship with the accumulation of land by multinational companies (RUPD 2008). Thus, the "reorganised" paramilitaries operate in regions where valuable natural resources are located, such as the case of the palm oil industry (Leech 2009). As Fidel Mignorance reports, paramilitary groups have forcibly displaced persons from their territories and have been instrumental in serving the interests and expansion of multinationals significantly benefitting from free trade agreements and neoliberal globalisation (Mignorance 2006)

State Crime and Its Impunity

The engagement of the Colombian victims' movement with the cosmopolitan discourse on human rights has prompted them to bring their case to the Inter-American Court of Human Rights Court (IACHR). Following the adoption of this legal strategy and the IACH's positive response to the claims of the victims, the Colombian state has been condemned four times in the jurisprudence of the IACHR (CCJ 2010). The rulings of the IACHR have not only confirmed the responsibility of the Colombian state in the creation of paramilitary groups, but have also evinced how the legal framework produced by the Colombian state has enabled and fostered the organization of such groups (IACHR 2004, 2005, 2006 and 2007). Alas, the significance of these rulings has been at issue during the implementation of PJL, due to the continuation of both state violence and paramilitary violence in Colombia since 2005.

The former is exemplified by the extrajudicial executions perpetrated by members of the Colombian state forces, the so-called *false positives* (Gomez Santamaria 2010, HRW 2015). 'A false positive occurs when the army kills innocent civilians and passes them off as enemy guerrilla combatants in order to falsely inflate their kill counts' (Impunity Watch 2011). According to CINEP, extrajudicial killings increased during the "transitional" period, as indicated by the 3,000 cases reported from 2002 to 2010 (CINEP 2010)[16], many of which remain unpunished to this day. Similar to the case of Easy Trigger in Argentina, victims of extrajudicial executions belong to marginal sectors of the Colombian society. Regrettably, the situation in Colombia is worsened by PJL, which does not include victims of state violence in its definition of victims (Uprimny, Sanchez & Guzman 2010).

The "re-emergence" of paramilitary groups has been denied by the Colombian government (CCJ 2010). Thus, the Colombian government uses the term "New Emergent Criminal Bands" (BACRIM-Spanish Acronym) when referring to them. This form of institutionalised denial will be highly detrimental for the victims and may leave a wide array of Human Rights violations unaddressed, including forced displacement, ED, and the recruitment of child soldiers committed by reorganised paramilitaries during the "transitional period". The re-organised paramilitaries have been responsible for 47% of the homicides reported in 2010 (Arcanos 2011)

Various peasants have been assassinated by BACRIM, within the implementation of the land restitution program that emerged in 2011. The March 2012 deaths of African Colombian leader

Miguel Ruiz and his son Samir Ruiz exemplify the retaliatory dynamics of Colombia's TJ scenario, as Miguel had been actively involved in the land restitution process in Chocó, one of the regions seriously affected by Colombia's war, forced displacement and land dispossession. They were killed by reorganised paramilitaries who may be providing security services to businessmen in the region, days before the government began to receive the testimonies of peasants concerning the location of their dispossessed territories (Civico 2012, Semana 2012). Since 2010, over 20 land claimers have been assassinated in regions where the land restitution program has been implemented (Civico 2012). In November 2012, 10 peasants were massacred by one of the criminal bands in which the paramilitary have reincarnated, imbuing terror in the peasantry of Santa Rosa de Osos, a municipality of Antioquia (El Colombiano 2012). This practise of terrorising vulnerable population does not greatly differ from the violence exercised by the "demobilized" paramilitary in 2003.

CONCLUSION

Within this chapter, I set out to explore both the role of retaliation and state crime in the TJ scenarios of Argentina and Colombia. The two TJ scenarios have brought about legal fields giving way to narratives of history and institutional arrangements that show that TJ cannot simply be understood as a set of practices that will lead societies through the path of progress and reconciliation. On the contrary, this chapter suggests that the historical configuration of conflicts and the narratives of survival and resistance should be part of the discussion on TJ. This may shed light on our understanding of the social and epistemic structures that perpetuate social harm.

Despite the implementation of TJ mechanisms, both countries and their legal systems remain highly authoritarian and exclusionary (Iturralde 2010), as exemplified by institutional forms of retaliation such the extreme use of criminal punishment for petty crimes (Iturralde 2010, Gargarella 2008). Criminal law is extremely punitive in both countries, and those subjected to imprisonment are mostly poor marginal citizens (Gargarella 2008). On the other hand, the high impunity rates of state crime represent a particularly harmful form of retaliation to victims of state violence from both past and present. The latter not only replicates S. Cohen's states of denial addressed at the outset of this chapter, but also appears to perpetuate the retaliatory practices of punitive states and the groups of interests that support them, as in the Colombian case.

In the two cases, the non-prosecution of powerful structures has become a normalised practice that takes place within the legal field, whose rationality can be understood through the lens of S Cohen notion of 'implicatory denial', namely the vocabularies, justifications, rationalizations, and evasions used to deal with 'our awareness of so many images of unmitigated suffering' (Cohen 2004). In this vein, it can be argued that the legal narratives that emerge out of transitional processes embody a relationship between violence and historical injustice that leads to the denial of the political configuration of the transitional scenarios, which recalls W. Benjamin's remark on law–making violence (Benjamin 1978)." Violence is inherent to law. There is darkness at the heart of the law, an injustice for which the institution will be paying its restitution in the fullness of time" (Benjamim 1978). This should warn us to be more creative and historically sensitive when using the emerging global paradigms of legal and non-legal knowledge for transitional periods.

REFERENCES

Aguila, G. (2010). State violence and repression in Rosario during the Argentine dictatorship, 1976-83. In M. Esparza, H.R. Huttenbach, & D. Feierstein (Eds.), *State Violence and Genocide in Latin America* (pp. 137-151). Oxfordshire, UK: Routledge.

Arcanos 2011. (n. d.). Retrieved from http://www.arcoiris.com.co/2012/05/arcanos-17/

Bell, C. (2009). The "New" law of Transitional Justice. In K. Ambos, J. Large, & M. Wierda (Eds.), Building a future on Peace and Justice (pp. 105-126). Springer.

Benjamin, W. (1978). Critique of violence. In P Demetz (Ed.), *Reflections*. New York: Shoken Books.

Bourdieu, P. (1987). The Force of Law: Toward a Sociology of the Juridical Field. Hastings Law Journal, 38.

Castillejo, A.C. (2007). La Globalización del Testimonio:Silencio endémico y los usos de la palabra. *Revista Antípoda*, 4.

Chamblis, W., & Michalowsky, R. (2010). *State Crime in the Global Age*. Collumpton.

Civico, A. (2012, Spring) This has been a cruel war: paramilitary violence and democracy in Colombia. Paper presented in the panel What is Political about Violence in Post- Conflict Latin America? American Ethnological Society.

Cohen, S. (2004). *States of Denial*. Oxford University Press.

El Colombiano. (2012, November 8). ONU condenó masacre de 10 campesinos en Santa Rosa de Osos. Retrieved from http://www.elcolombiano.com/BancoConocimiento/S/santa_rosa_de_osos_masacre_de_campesinos_fue_condenada_por_la_onu/santa_rosa_de_osos_masacre_de_campesinos_fue_condenada_por_la_onu.asp

Crenzel, E. (2008). Present Pasts: Memory (ies) of State Terrorism in the Southern Cone of Latin America. In F. Lessa (Ed.), *The Memory of State Terrorism in the Southern Cone*.

Derrida, J. (1995). *Archive Fever: A Freudian Impression*. Chicago: Chicago University Press.

Diaz, C. (2009) Colombia's bid for justice and peace. In K. Ambos, J. Large, M. Wierda (Eds.), Building a future on Peace and Justice (pp. 469-501). Springer. Berlin

Druliolle, V. (2011). Remembering and its Places in Post-dictatorship Argentina. In F. Lessa (Ed.), *The Memory of State Terrorism in the Southern Cone*.

Giraldo, J. (1996). Colombia: The Genocidal Democracy. Common Courage Press.

Gomez Santamaria, S.M. (2010) Constructions of the Violent State: The Case of Extrajudicial Executions of Civilians by State Military Forces in Antioquia, Colombia. Oñati Socio-Legal Series, 1(1).

Gomez Suarez, A. (2007). Perpetrator Blocs, genocidal mentalities and geographies: the destruction of Union Patriotica in Colombia and its lessons for genocide studies. *Journal of Genocide Research, 9(4)*. London: Routledge. doi:10.1080/14623520701644440

Gugliemucci, A. (2007). *La Objetivación de las Memorias Públicas sobre la última dictadura militar. Revista Antípoda. Número 4*. Uniandes Bogotá.

Human Rights Watch. (2015). Rol de los altos mandos en Falsos positivos: evidencias de responsabilidad de generales y coroneles del Ejército Colombiano por ejecuciones de civiles. Human Rights Watch. Retrieved from http://www.eltiempo.com/contenido/politica/justicia/ARCHIVO/ARCHIVO-15997016-0.pdf

Iturralde, M. (2010). Democracies without Citizenship: Crime and Punishment in Latin America. *New Criminal Law Review: An International and Interdisciplinary Journal, 13(2)*. University of California Press. doi:10.1525/nclr.2010.13.2.309

Katz, P. (2011). A new "normal" Political complicity: exclusionary violence and the delegation of Argentine Jewish associations during the Argentine dirty war. International Journal of Transitional Justice, 5(3).

Laplante, L., & Theidon, K. (2006). *Transitional Justice in times of conflict: Colombia's Ley de Justicia y Paz. Michigan Journal of International Law*, 49.

Laplante, L. J. (2011). Reviewed Work: Reconciliation(s): Transitional Justice in Postconflict Societies by Joanna R. Quinn. *Law & Society Review*, *45*(1), 230–232. doi:10.1111/j.1540-5893.2011.00433_5.x

Lesa, F. (2011). *Beyond Transitional Justice: Exploring continuities in Human Rights Abuses in Argentina between 1976 and 2010. Journal of Human Rights Practice, 3(1), 25-48*. Oxford University Press.

Maher, D., & Thomson, A. (2011). The terror that underpins the ′peace:′ the political economy of Colombia's paramilitary demobilization process. In E. Herring, & D. Stokes (Eds.), Critical studies on terrorism, 4(1), 95-113.

Malamud-Goti, J. (1995). Punishing Human Rights Abuses in fledgling democracies: The case of Argentina. In N. Roht-Arriaza (Ed.), Impunity and Human Rights in International Law and Practice (pp. 160-170). Oxford University Press.

Marle, V. (2007) Constitution as Archive. In S. Veitch (Ed.), Law and the Politics of Reconciliation. Hampshire, England: Ashgate.

Marteen, D., & Zambrano, M. (2010). Citizenship Deferred: The politics of Victimhood, Land Restitution and Gender Justice in the Colombian (Post?) Conflict. International Journal of Transitional Justice, 4(2), 189-206.

Mignorance, F. (2006). The flow of palm oil Colombia / Belgium/ Europe. A study from human Rights perspective. Human Rights Everywhere. Retrieved from http://www.cbc.collectifs.net/doc/informe_en_v3-1.pdf

Peacaut, D. (1978). Orden y Violencia en Colombia 1930-1954. Bogotá. CEREC. Siglo XXI.

Raphael, S. (2010). Paramilitarism and state terrorism in Colombia. In R. Jackson, E. Murphy, & S. Poynting (Eds.), *Contemporary state terrorism: theory and practice*. London: Routledge.

Robben, A. (2005). *Political Violence and Trauma in Argentina*. University of Pennsylvania Press. doi:10.9783/9780812203318

Semana. (2012, March 28). Asesinatos de Manuel Ruiz y su hijo, otro golpe a la restitución de tierras. Retrieved from http://www.semana.com/nacion/articulo/asesinatos-manuel-ruiz-su-hijo-otro-golpe-restitucion-tierras/255592-3

Seri, G. (2010). Vicious Legacies? State violence in Argentina. In M. Esparza, H. R. Huttenbach, & D. Feierstein (Eds.), *State Violence and Genocide in Latin America* (pp. 182–195). Oxfordshire, UK: Routledge.

Skaar, E. (2001). *Judicial Independence and Human Rights Policies in Argentina and Chile*. Bergen, Norway: Chr Michelsen Institute.

Sosa, C. (2011). Queering Acts of Mourning in the Aftermath of Argentina's Dictatorship: The Mothers of Plaza de Mayo. In F. Lessa (Ed.), *The Memory of State Terrorism in the Southern Cone*.

Stokes, D. (2006). Iron Fists in Iron Gloves: The Political Economy of US Terrocracy Promotion in Colombia. *British Journal of Politics and International Relations*, *8*(3), 368–387. doi:10.1111/j.1467-856X.2006.00219.x

Taylor, (1999) A Juridical Frankenstein, or death in the hands of the state. In A. Sarat (Ed.), *The Killing State: Capital Punishment, Law, Politics and Culture* (pp. 60-80). New York: Oxford University Press.

Teitel, R.G. (2000). *Transitional Justice*. Oxford University Press

El Tiempo. (2015, June). ONU condenó masacre de 10 campesinos en Santa Rosa de Osos Retrieved from http://www.eltiempo.com/contenido/politica/justicia/ARCHIVO/ARCHIVO-15997016-0.pdf

Uprimny, R., & Saffon, M. (2007). *Uses and abuses of Transitional Justice discourse in Colombia*. PRIO Policy Brief 6, Oslo International Peace Research Institute.

Uprimny, R., Sanchez, C., & Guzman, D. (2010). Informe sobre Colombia. En Las victimas y la Justicia Transicional. Fundación para el debido proceso legal. Washington D.C.

Uribe, C. (2011). *Amnistias y responsabilidad de la corte penal internacional. Lecciones del proceso de Paz con la AUC. In G. Gallego, & M. González (Eds.), Conflicto armado interno derechos humanos e impunidad.*

VerdadAbierta.com. (2015, January). Los retos de la Ley de Justicia y Paz en su noveno año. Retrieved from http://www.verdadabierta.com/justicia-y-paz/legislacion/5563-los-retos-de-la-ley-de-justicia-y-paz-en-su-noveno-ano

Verdeja, E. (2010). Political Violence, justice and reconciliation in Latin America. In M. Esparza, H. R. Huttenbach, & D. Feierstein (Eds.), *State Violence and Genocide in Latin America* (pp. 169–181). Oxfordshire, UK: Routledge.

Wang, Y. (Ed.), (2012, November 9). Colombian paramilitary gang kills 10 peasant. Xinhuanet.com. Retrieved from http://news.xinhuanet.com/english/world/2012-11/09/c_131961167.htm

Impunity Watch. (2012, November 12). Paramilitary Drug Gang Slaughters 10 Farmworkers. Retrieved from http://impunitywatch.com/paramilitary-drug-gang-slaughters-10-farmworkers/

Whyte, D. (2009). Crimes of the Powerful: a reader (Readings in Criminology and Criminal Justice). Open University Press.

ENDNOTES

1. For the notion of Transitional Justice Scenarios see A. Castillejo (2007).
2. At the core of both criminology and criminal law lies a fundamental problem- the undertheorisation of state crime. This theoretical void is reflected in the TJ experiences addressed here. In both countries, crimes committed by the state such as political repression and enforced disappearances served the political project of the state and its supporters. As research focuses mainly on a type of criminology and criminal law, whose research agenda is mostly informed by state definitions of crime, a detrimental normalization of state violence has taken place in both societies. The situation draws attention to Chamblis, Michalowsky and

Kramer's call for a shift of paradigm in Criminology, whereby criminology should change its focus from the state definitions of crime to a broader definition of crime based on the notion of social harm. For a timely explanation see Chamblis, Michalowsky and Kremmer 2010.

3 I frame the notion of retaliation in a broad sense, in which asymmetric power relations are not really changed through TJ arrangements. Contrariwise, it seems to be the case that asymmetric power relations are reinforced and recreated by the criminal laws that emerge form the transitional political periods.

4 In spite of having significant sociological differences, the Argentine and Colombian transitional scenarios have been marked by the continuation of state violence and the emergence of repressive crime control fields over the past decades. The common elements of criminalization of the poor and prison overcrowding in both countries prompt us to reflect on the role of criminal law in contexts of social inequality. For an analysis of Latin American crime control fields see Iturralde 2010. For a timely critique on the role of punishment in contexts of social inequality see Gargarella 2008.

5 Robben has described el Proceso as a form of 'cultural war'.

6 For more on this heinous practice see Verbisky, H (1996) The flight: Confessions of an Argentine Dirty warrior. New York: New Press.

7 My analysis draws mainly on Ana Glugliemucci's insightful work. Based on her ethnography, I provide an account of the role of retaliation in the TJ scenario of Argentina.

8 For the purpose of my analysis, TJ scenarios should be observed through the lens of P Bourdieu's notion of the Legal Field, an arena where struggle takes place among different agents. See Madsen and Dezaley (2005).

9 According to Bourdeau symbolic power is the power to transform the world, by transforming the words for naming it. See Madsen and Dezaley(2005)

10 Liminality is a useful concept to counter the linear understanding of transition promoted by mainstream narratives of TJ. Similar to the ritual subject, the trajectory taken by transitional societies is neither homogeneous nor progressive, but much more complex. The term was first used by T. Adorno in his critique of Enlightenment. Anthropologist V Turner also used it in his study of rituals.

11 The notion of 'the let die' proves useful to understand the dynamics of state violence and its contemporary political configuration. The concept was put forth by Foucault in his analysis of bio power, which helped explain how power is exercised over life and death. Violence is exercised on behalf of everyone's existence not only on behalf of the sovereign who was to be defended in the past. As a result, there is a dividing line between those whose life is worthy of respect and those whose life is thought of as not worth living-necropolitics. See Foucault 1978. Also Membe 2003.

12 See http://www.abuelas.org.ar/institucional.php?institucional=historia.htm&der1=der1_hist.php&der2=der2_inst.php

13 See http://www.bbc.co.uk/news/world-latin-america-15905488

14 i Data on displacement varies and it is highly likely that the number of displaced population exceeds the 3.5 million estimated by the sources cited here.

15 Neoliberal Globalisation is a process that started at the end of the cold war under the motto TNA- There is no alternative to Neoliberalism. The process has been driven by the principles of the Washington consensus, which promote the worldwide expansion

of market oriented democracy. For a very important analysis of this phenomenon see Santos 2002. For the Colombian case and its relationship with the TJ process see Maher and Thompson 2011.

16 According to UN special Rapporteur on extrajudicial killings, the False Positives are a systematic practice throughout the country and intensified from 2004 to 2008. In 2010 The United Nations office of the High Commissioner for Human Rights reported 3000 extrajudicial killings perpetrated principally by the Colombian army. For an important overview of False Positives see: http://www.fidh.org/IMG/pdf/colombie589e.pdf

Chapter 17
From the Studies of Violences to Memories:
The Construction of Victims and its Articulations with the State

Yomaira García Acuña
Universidad Simón Bolivar, Colombia

ABSTRACT

This paper presents some of the effects of Colombia´s armed conflict in people who were displaced from their territories, and the institutional mechanisms proposed to address this problem. The author studies the cases of El Salado (Bolívar Department) and Nueva Venecia (Department of Magdalena) in a research conducted in these populations after the massacres of the years 2000 by paramilitary groups, and articulates the notions of violence and memories in order to question the current interventions on them in terms of transitional justice.

INTRODUCTION

Violence has always been part of Colombia´s history and violence studies have occupied a central role in the country. However, only in the last years the subject of memory has gained increasing relevance in public sceneries. The reason why the latter social construct was not a focus of interest until recently is due mainly to a lack of language appropriation of the term.

In order to address the evolution of the interest mentioned above, the author resorts to her PhD project on Memories in the case study of Nueva Venecia and to some of the results of the project entitled "Familias y Construcción de Memorias" [1] (Families and Memory Building), which focuses on the massacres of El Salado and Nueva Venecia, where more than forty people were murdered in February and November of 2000.

The first part of this chapter tackles the subject of violence. The second part focuses on memories and provides a summary of the theoretical aspects of the work and literature review-mainly Colombian and South American authors. The third part presents some of the results of workshops conducted with victims of the massacres that migrated to the municipalities Barranquilla and Soledad in the department Atlántico in the north

DOI: 10.4018/978-1-4666-9675-4.ch017

coast of Colombia, with victims that years later returned to their populations of origin. Lastly, some final reflections and conclusions are drawn.

BACKGROUND: VIOLENCE STUDIES IN COLOMBIA

Refering to cases of violence in Colombia seems to be an imperative for human and social sciences in Latin-America. Questions regarding the violent or not-violent nature of Colombians and the place that the country occupies in international violence rankings have been object of interest of the general population and especially of researchers working on the subject. In fact, there is a lot of literature written, since Colombia´s armed conflict[2] has been approached by many disciplines in numerous studies. This chapter presents the summary[3] and context of the country´s situation, in order to address more accurately the concept of memories.

Usually studies of Colombia´s armed conflict tend to allude to long-term studies, starting from Colombia´s independence wars, the battles of governors aiming to appropriate power in the country in the XIXth Century and the subsequent conflicts between members of the most important political parties, Liberals and Conservators, in the middle of the XXth Century. The assassination of the political leader Jorge Eliecer Gaitán, on the 9th of April of 1948, is considered as the event that triggered what is known as the First Period of Violence, which ended in 1953 with the arrival of the Army General Gustavo Rojas Pinilla to the presidency. This event generated a considerable amount of written works. Not only in the academia but also in the literature and media. This event tends to overshadow other important events[4] and it is considered as the foundational incident of contemporary violence in Colombia. At least in the collective imaginary because violence was already present before Gaitán´s assassination.

After Rojas Pinilla came to power, the Second Period of Violence initiated in the country, which ended with the fall of the General. This episode led to the creation of the Frente Nacional, which was an agreement between Liberals and Conservators to take turns in the presidency for sixteen years. That is, from 1958 to 1974.

The Third Period of Violence started with the fight against armed groups, which had already been conformed in the sixties in the form of rural guerrillas, and that still exists under the name of FARC (an acronym that translates as Revolutionary Armed Forces of Colombia). After the formation of the FARC, other guerrillas such as the ELN (National Liberation Army) and the M-19 were created.

The appearance of drug trafficking as an actor in violence gives rise to the Fourth Period of Violence. Since the seventies, the departments of the North Coast of Colombia experienced an economic boom with massive production of marihuana. At the end of this decade the traffic of cocaine in the departments of the center of the country and the formation of drug cartels for the production and distribution of this drug generated a war between, towards and against the latter, as well as a unification of some other sectors of the guerrillas.

At the same time, paramilitary forces, the AUC, were being created with the aim of defending the dominant classes from the guerrillas. Since the nineties, paramilitary forces have had an important incidence in politics in the country. Although at first it was mainly in rural areas, by 2002 33% of the Congress was proven to either have active links with paramilitaries or had arrived to that political position with their support.

Generalized Violence is the term coined by Daniel Pécaut to refer to this situation, in which there is an articulation of weapons and politics. In rural areas, this control is wielded through fear, murders, appropriation of land, forced displacement, rapes, control over aspects of quotidian life, such as dressing or hair styles, choice over partners, etc. The control also extends to modes of production derived from the cultivation of the land, as farmers have to pay money to paramilitaries or guerrillas (sometimes both), similarly to a tax that has an extorsive nature.

One of the pioneer studies in the subject of violence in Colombia was the work by Umañan Luna, Guzmán and Fals Borda[5] entitled Violence in Colombia: a Study of a Social Process (1962)[6]. This book was object of critiques coming from the government and other sectors of societies, especially regarding its explanations for the causes of violence. In this study some structural aspects of violence are analyzed, like the subject of land and land ownership. The incorporation of testimonies made it stand out.

In 1987, the government of the president Belisario Betancourt created a Commission on Violence Studies as a way to look for ways to avoid violence in Colombia. The final product is a document entitled *Colombia: Violencia y Democracia* (Colombia: Violence and democracy). This report proposed a general perspective on violence and divided it into different types (urban, against ethnical minorities, related to media, etc.). The document included recommendations as well as policies related to criminality, peace-building, among others[7]. The raising interest in conducting research on violence generated a great volume of academic production, to the point where the expression *violentólogos* "violentists" was coined to allude to those interested on the subject.

The academic production of that time also reflects the characteristics and increasing importance of violence. This can be seen in texts like those of Gonzalo Sanchez and Donny Meertens (1987), Bandits, Squires and Peasants (Bandoleros, *gamonales y campesinos. El caso de la violencia en Colombia).* The case of violence in Colombia, as well as in the book by Maria Victoria Uribe (1990) Killing, Spiking and Over-Killing, the massacres of violence in Tolima, 1948-1964 (*Matar, Rematar y Contramatar, las masacres de la violencia en Tolima, 1948-1964*). One of the first texts that showed this problem and gave voice to those who did not have it through telling their stories is the book by Edilma Flor Perez (1993). In it, adults, boys and girls coming mostly from the eastern plains region tell their story, in the crossroads between the armed outlaw groups, the military, persecution by being branded Communists. At that time victims of violence had little relevance in governmental programs, despite how syndicalist and agrarian leaders, as well as women and students, reclaimed their visibilisation. The Political Constitution of 1991 is seen as the responsible for their acknowledgment and of other ways of facing relations with the State, at least in perspective.

The exacerbation of other forms of violence became evident thanks to the massive displacement of inhabitants from rural areas of Colombia, although this has been present since the Second Period of Violence. It is these series of massive displacements the responsible for Colombia occupying the second position in the world, after Sudan, as the country with most internal displacement. In the traffic lights of the biggest cities of Colombia, for example, it is commonplace to see numerous families who have been forcedly displaced from their territories asking for money and help. This situation also extends to the main roads connecting different parts of the country.

Until 1997, people who had been displaced by Colombia´s armed conflict were encapsulated into the term "historical poors". In that year the government issued the Law 387 in *order to adopt specific measures to prevent, address, protect, stabilize and consolidate socioeconomic conditions of displaced people from Colombia*[8]. Currently this legal framework still prevails.

Failed attempts to achieve peace in the country through conversations with the FARC and the ELN after various presidential periods culminated in the government of Andrés Pastrana in 2002, when conversations in San Vicente del Caguán stopped.

After Álvaro Uribe became president, paramilitaries, who by then had around 30.000 members, made public their intention of demobilizing[9]. The government proposed a law entitled *Ley de Alternatividad penal* (Law of Penal Alternative), which generated many controversies. Mainly because paramilitaries who demobilized and who were covered by it were not prosecuted for the crimes they committed and because it did not allude to victims at all. Some years later, the law was re-examined and the Law 975 or *Ley de Justicia y Paz* (Law of Justice and Peace) was created.

The attempts for consolidating peace have been accompanied by symbols, which have varied through time. For instance, the white pigeon, the green ribbon, the pink ribbon, mass mobilizations, among others, the most notable taking place in February and March of 2008. Explanations to the existence of violence made evident the complexity of the phenomenon: conflicts between political parties, the emergence of the guerrillas, the abandon from the State, the unfinished process of building a nation, the role of drug trafficking, the consolidation of paramilitarism, as well as the articulation guerrillas-paramilitaries-drug-trafficking and the cultural argument that Colombian citizens are violent by nature coming together in one place.

When in the nineties forced displacement became a national problem, governmental institutions and the academy addressed the subject. Thus, methodological responses to categorize the population were created. This included relevant information related to ethnic groups, age, gender, places of expulsion and maps of the conflict, to mention a few.

Nowadays, the work by scholars that examines the conflict is also plentiful. This can be seen in the works of Marta Nubia Bello, particularly Forced displacement, Dynamics of war, exclusion and rootlessness (2004)[10], a book she compiled. In the book the authors make an analysis of the issue of displacement, the consequences of it, attempts to rebuild their lives of displaced, indigenous and afro populations. The subjects of gender and displacement are also discussed. The book also includes institutional responses to the problem, the role of the media and mechanisms to address what has been described as a psychosocial.

The intensification of the conflict in the 90 places at the centre the concern for the effect on women, though the term was not yet coined until the early years of the 2000: violence based on gender (VSB)[11]. The aggressions suffered by women show differences in treatment towards them and particularities that exist in the armed conflict. The Bureau of Women and Armed Conflict (La mesa de la Mujer y el Conflicto Armado) has been issuing an annual report to account for this, as shown in its publications posted on the website. Also important are the analyses by the Historical Memory Group of the National Commission for Reparation and Reconciliation[12], CNRR, particularly worth noting the Women and War Report: Victims and resistant in the Colombian Caribbean, which was coordinated by María Emma Wills. In the General Report of the Historical Memory Group, Enough already! Colombia: War Memoirs and dignity (2013) there is a comprehensive analysis of the violence in Colombia.

All these are advances in terms of quantifying the problem. However, the quote of Nicolás Rodríguez Idárraga (2008:31) still prevails: "Despite the great advances in terms of reconstructing the period of violence, none of the previous cases ask for the meaning that the actors involved give to their own experiences"[13].

The sense given by the actors, the victims to the events is what shapes memory studies. The inclusion of the issue of subjectivity in studies sets a concern in the social sciences in Colombia. Gonzalo Sanchez's book, War, memory and history (2003), raises significant debates about the non-recording of events but rather the attribution of meaning given to them. However, the recovery of the lived experience is what is mostly transmitted or the centre of field studies[14].

STUDIES ON MEMORIES

The term *memory* in singular alludes to the act of registering, recalling and evoking. In this way, the subject is usually studied by cognitive psychology and neurosciences. In social sciences, human sciences, literature and arts, memory is an important resource for accounting for the past, as well as an instrument of denunciation and search for justice.

Memory is not a faithful register of experiences, but a reconstruction of what we do. The past is organized, or better, it reorganizes. It is the *meaning* attributed to what we remember what reconfigures memory. Memory, in this way, is an essential source for accessing the past. At the same time, it is the basis for future planning. Here, the individual and the social intercept, but also the present, the past and the future. This has remained similarly throughout the history of humanity by means of rituals and commemorations, among others. Although in the XXth Century it acquired other dimensions.

The proliferation of studies of memory start with the text by Maurice Halbwachs of 2004, *Memoria Colectiva (Collective Memory).* His work opened the sociological research on the subject. Halbwach´s emphasized on the importance of space as meaningful for creating social ties, where sudden changes on it had notable effects on individuals, as well as on objects and images that played a role in the collective memory. Places receive the footmark of those who inhabit them, and individuals also receive the impact of the places where they inhabit. This chapter also relates to the work of Zambrano (2006), who points out that memory is a reflexive construction of referents for collective action, instead of the signature for remembering and forgetting in a society.

Two important concepts when studying memories are experience and transmission, which lead to affirming that there does not exist a single version of a past event; not even a recent one. The subject of experience is studied by LaCapra (2005) and Scott (2002). Considering lived experiences within historical studies goes hand by hand with recovering the voices of the oppressed, minorities and victims who have been forgotten in the official history. This is one of the main causes for the recent interest in oral history and for the increasing value of the latter when talking about experiences, which has historically been set aside by the "hard" part of the studies due to its apparent subjective nature. Nonetheless, contemporary authors of human sciences, such as philosophers, literary theorists and psychoanalysts have made it their focus of study.

Most of the contributions related to memory transmission have been made by Agamben (2000), Todorov, (2000), Jelin (2002), Kaufman (2006) ane Tisseron (2007), among others. The research presented here finds difficulties in processes of transmitting memories intergenerationally. For instance, people who have been forcedly displaced tend to remain in silence, as well as people who have been victims of kidnapping and wars. Not only silence towards institutions but also to their families. They remain in silence due to the fear of being involved with one or another band but also due to fear and trauma. Lechner & Guell (1999) claim that memories are composed by silences, which is different to forgetting. Especially because stories are known, but silenced. Kaufman (2000) adds that families can remain in silence, as well as sharing narratives or make them invisible. Sometimes taking care or protecting someone means to remain in silence, other times it means sharing. Sometimes, as the author above mentions, silence it is the only possibility for survival. In sum, the term transmission is always present as collective memory or as an absent one.

There are three elements of Pollak´s work (1992) that are crucial for organizing memories: events, people or characters, and places. These three aspects are not necessary experienced by one individual, but rather they can be transmitted from one person to another one. This means that deformations and idealizations of the facts are present. Events and characters play the central role in memory studies. Until recent years memory was of those who won. Leading to an unequal distribution of it.

Wars, indeed, have always been the quintessential example of subjects that led to memory building processes. This is why there are many reports that deal with the First and Second World War. Particularly, findings such as those of Freud´s on trauma and his daughter´s in children´s trauma. The most remarkable ones are related to the Holocaust.

According to Enzo Traverso (2007), the wars of recent years have also been wars of memory; they have been justified by the ritual evocation of the duty of memory. Traverso mentions numerous examples in many countries where revindications make allusion to revenges after the events of the Second World War. Thus, the Holocaust becomes a symbol of memory, and it is usually taken as the best model to look at the past. This is why it has been used by the cinematographic industry and television to spread memories, contributing beyond the realm of academic disciplines.

Many authors refer to "the duty of memory" as in imperative. Todorov invites to reflect on this subject through his publication *Los Abusos de la Memoria* (2000) (The Abuses of Memory). His theory alerts us about the problem of processes of memory recovery that promote themselves without considering the use that they will have. This is included in the distinction made between literal and exemplary memory. The abuses of the memory are also discussed by Ricoeur (2000:96) in three levels: the pathological, the hindered memory; the practical, the manipulated memory; and the ethical-political level, the forced memory. In this respect, Ricoeur´s work has similarities with Todorov´s, particularly on the issue of justice within the exemplary memory. Although he extends it further by including working with memory, grief and justice linked to alterity, which also includes the concept of *debt*.

Memory studies in Latin America come mostly from Argentina, Chile and Uruguay and are linked to the dictatorships that those countries experienced in the eighties and nineties. Usually these studies are urban and are conducted by middle socioeconomic strata. The situation in Colombia is more akin to what occurred in Peru, Salvador and Guatemala. However, in all these countries the distance to the past is greater than in the case of Colombia.

Despite that in Colombia there has not been a solution to the armed conflict, memory is highly important, as it can be seen in different areas such as academics, the media and the collective claiming of social rights. In this paper, the issue of memory is linked to sociopolitical violence. When referring to violence, it is seen chronologically. Hence collective actions that report, dilate and demand rights also have a long history. This also applies to other forms of dilation such as film, literature[15] and painting, even if they do not use the term *memory*.

Unlike other countries, in which the term *memory* has been used broadly in mass media and in the academic production, the situation only appears recently to the Colombian case. Other authors have also noticed the absence of the subject in academia, particularly in the social sciences. Sánchez (2003: 98) wonders why only recently the subject started to be thematized and why it remains an "*interdit*" or a non-purged guilt that has been difficult to transpose into national historical memory. His explanation to this question relies on the uncertainty over the nation's future and on the omnipresence, real or imaginary, of the role of war on it, which has made Colombians live a perpetual present where little or nothing seems to change. The author continues to ask himself: how to accumulate memory, to remember, in a stationary story that takes place in an ongoing war. A second explanation is that war makes living this way so overwhelming that it seems as if all time concentrated together at the same moment in which we live. The third explanation is that the Periods of Violence mentioned above crossed every institution and the lives of every Colombian citizen, making it difficult to define the historical responsibility, more than in any other Latin American country. Lastly, he considers that what we see today has ceased to be outstanding; the nature of this envelope and the loss of the sense of succession seem to be hallmarks of our political representations.

Alberto Verón Ospina (2011) refers to this interest of academia for Memory (capitalized according to the author), distinguishing it from the type of memory scholars referred to a few years ago. The main reason for it was the use of the latter as a mantra whose invocation was thought to unveil all of the old problems besetting the world. The term *vindicating* past injustices is politically dangerous due to its challenging nature.

According to the literature, it is plausible to say that the past can be used as a political weapon, an instrumentation and sacralisation of memory. As stated by Sergio Grez Toso (2007), in a naive way it is believed, as history did with written sources, that through memory you could access the "true story"; that of the majority, the forgotten, the neglected or any other group despised by the official story. Nowadays, the vignettes of victim´s NGOs and movements are full of expressions of great expectations related to the topic of memory, assuming that memory equals truth, reparation or justice.

It is also important to highlight the importance of the latter questions, especially in the face of the Law 441 of 2011, *Ley de Víctimas y Restitución de Tierras* (Law of Victims and Restitution of the Land), which was created as a framework for victims seeking restitution. Also in this sense, the approaches made by Georges Bensoussan in his text *¿Auschwitz en Heritage?* (2010) are important. Benssoussan mentions the characteristics of memory, of forgetting and of duty. Especially his work A New Vision of the Defeated? which indicates that memory is not synonymous with a "vaccine that would preserve us from the horror." This also allows us to query the slogan used by groups of relatives of victims and human rights organizations: "Remember not to repeat." He argues that the operation of our daily lives and the media try to forget more than to spread the knowledge. The following section presents some of the outcomes of the project Families and Memory Building (Familias y Construcción de Memorias), related to the massacres of New Venice and El Salado.

THE MASSACRES OF EL SALADO AND NUEVA VENECIA

El Salado is a township located 18 km away from Carmen de Bolivar, connected to it by a path and 2 hours away from the touristic city Cartagena. It once had around 5000 inhabitants mainly engaged in agriculture and the cultivation of products for daily consumption. However since the nineties, guerrillas began to increase their influence on the area by forcing landowners to give them their farms. The slaughter of El Salado began on February 17th of 2000 when 450 paramilitary of the North Block entered several townships surrounding this population, committing all sorts of atrocities such as burning vehicles, damaging properties and murdering people. This was in order to spread fear among the population to control El Salado. The massacre lasted for 5 days, which gave some people time to escape. The paramilitaries came to El Salado on February 18th at 9 am. They kicked the doors of houses and took people to the main square, which was in front of the church. They divided women and men, but both were tortured, strangled and beheaded, leaving more than 60 people dead. First they started with men and then they proceeded with murdering women. They sexually abused some of them by inserting barbed wires, blades and weapons into their genitals. One woman, after being accused of being the partner of a member of the guerrillas, was dragged by her hair through the main square. Other women were forced to cook for them during the two days they were in the village. According to what survivors narrate, from the House of Culture they took bagpipes and drums and played them each time they killed someone. Men were also stripped naked to see if they had scars from fighting or if their legs lacked hair due to the use of boots by guerrilla members.

On the other side, New Venice, is a township that belongs to the municipality of Sitio Nuevo, located 50 minutes by boat from the town of Ciénaga. It is part of the department Magdalena, whose capital is the touristic city Santa Marta, in the north coast of Colombia. Most of the inhabitants are fishermen, due to the palafitic conditions of the village (Image 1). In the study by Alfredo Correa de Andreis (1999:3)[16] on palafitic populations he referred to the poverty of the region, the abandonment of the State, the low credibility of its inhabitants by the public and private sectors, and how both had influenced the development of a perverse social capital, supported by a culture of fear in a tenebrous environment. As an example, the replacement of the state in regulating production activities such as fishing with actors from outside of the towns (P.14).

The slaughter of Nueva Venecia, occurred on November 22d of the year 2000. According to a report by the Commission on Human Rights conformed by 3 NGOs, a paramilitary group of 70 people wearing uniforms of military forces and caring ranged weapons rented 6 speedboats in a neighbouring town. As they went through the pipe that leads to Nueva Venecia, they killed three fishermen. Once in town, they called a group of fishermen they had on a list and who were being accused of collaborating with the guerrilla group ELN. They gathered them, together with another group of suspected criminals in the area. As they could not find every one on the list, they made one of the hostages lead them through the town. Later on they went back to the church where they had gathered about 15 fishermen at 5:30 am, asked them to lie on the floor facing down, proceeded to shoot them indiscriminately by shooting them to their head and disfiguring their faces. This made it difficult to identify the bodies. According to

Figure 1. Housing in Nueva Venecia, Magdalena-Colombia (the author)

the Commission of Human Rights, the latter has the aim of generating terror among the population. The report also highlights the attempts of family members to contact the nearest military battalion, Battalion Vergara Vergara, which were not taken into account. The Army arrived in the afternoon of the next day, landed on the football field and stayed for only five minutes, according to citizen´s testimonies. Most of the inhabitants migrated after the massacre, leaving the town deserted. Although reports from Social Action and the Ombudsman indicate that most of the population returned weeks later.

RESEARCH PROBLEM, OBJECTIVES, METHODOLOGY, AND RESULTS

The research of the project addressed the question of how are the memories in families of El Salado and Nueva Venecia that were expelled from their lands in 2000? Some additional questions were how have the various actors involved re-signified the events in different public political and historical spaces? Which rituals have been developed, on what dates, in which places? How is forgetting built? How do groups rebuild their memories? What do they talk about? Who are the entrepreneurs of memory and which meanings of the past they promote? Lastly, from a gender perspective, which specific features can give account of the memories of families that have been victims of violence? The main goal of the research was to analyse the processes of construction and transmission of memories in families that were displaced from El Salado and Nueva Venecia in 2000. The specific objectives were recognizing the transformations of family ties after the events of 2000 in El Salado and Nueva Venecia; studying the processes of memory transmission in the reports related to the events of El Salado and Nueva Venecia and the meaning given to them; understanding how the processes of memory building and forgetting the events have been built from a gender perspective; and analysing the organizational processes of the victims of the massacres in El Salado and Nueva Venecia.

The identification of families in Barranquilla and Soledad who were forcedly displaced from El Salado and Nueva Venecia was the first step of the investigation. Various sectors, such as the National Commission for Reparation and Reconciliation, NCRR, have studied it. The massacre of El Salado has been more studied than the one that took place in Nueva Venecia. The study of the first one by the NCRR produced the document "Esa guerra no era nuestra" (This War is not ours), which is available on the Web. The fact that the media widely informed about the events that took place in El Salado facilitated contacting more than 100 of a the displaced in two neighbourhoods of Barranquilla. However, since the massacre of Nueva Venecia and the adjacent palafitic town Buenavista is not widely known, it took over a year to access a group of 60 people.

In both populations, a survey was initially performed, which allowed us to obtain socio-demographic information including data relationship, age, eating habits, aspects of housing, access to health resources, education subsidies, but also data about their relationship with care entities such as Acción Social. This initial contact was obtained through institutional approaches and 2 leaders of an organisation that represents them. In addition to the aforementioned survey, the team conducted 20 semi-structured interviews with members of both populations and 6 in-depth interviews. Since the interviews took place in the homes of the interviewees, some participants were the father and mother, other mother and sons or daughters, etc. allowing also to consider other aspects of family dynamics, such as roles, leadership, communication, agreements and disagreements. 4 Workshops focus groups were made to construct stories of neighbourhoods, one exclusively for women displaced from Buenavista and Nueva Venecia and another with population under 12 years, children and grandchildren from New Venice and El Salado. All interviews were recorded, some filmed, transcribed and then the information was returned to the people who were interviewed for them to check the notes that were taken, adding or removing information.

Another strategy used was the one of the neighbourhoods, by means of which information from the four neighbourhoods, La Chinita, La Luz, Santo Domingo and La Candelaria I and II, where most of the study population resides, was obtained. This allowed accessing other content and reaffirmed the one found in the previous step by other means.

For the project, media analysis was very important; particularly the press. The proposal of Eliseo Verón's in his text *Construcción de Memoria* (2002) was very relevant. In Memory studies the media is an important source. Considering memory as a process subject to reinterpretation, re-significations and in this sense being something unfinished-, the media easily can show this aspect. It can be considered that the media, to certain extent, gives voice to victims and witnesses. Especially in situations such as those discussed in this research, allowing an extension of the institutional panorama and, in that sense, it can also bring not only better knowledge of the truth, but also help seeking justice –in some cases.

It was also explored how from other fields such as the Arts have referred to the events of El Salado and New Venice. In this respect the work of the painter Nitho Cecilio on Nueva Venecia, with more than 10 paintings representing this slaughter, has to be mentioned.

RESULTS

The displacement should not be considered as an event that occurs in a given time. It is a process in which one can identify several stages. Our interviewees, for instance, expressed the failure of the authorities whose mission was to protect the lives of people during and after the two massacres. Faced with threats in the case of El Salado, after having suffered similar situations in 1997, the inhabitants lived in a permanent anxiety. But like many of them said "everyone thought they were not going to return".

After the displacement, the narrations regarding the initial coexistence in the new territory, Barranquilla and Soledad, show the stigmatization by people of the city, as it can be seen in the following testimonies, although this is not completely generalizable:

With the neighbours we have made good friends because we are known already, you ask around for us and then they say where we live and we are called "the Salaos[17]. (Interview displaced from El Salado).

With regard to changes in family relationships, it is important to note that while families in general are constantly changing, we were interested in finding the transformations to families after to the massacres occurred in their populations. It is necessary to start with the most obvious facts, the lives lost in the slaughter itself, which are recalled in the following testimony quotes[18]:

They killed my nephew Orlando, who was about 20 years.

They killed my nephew Jair who was 17.

They killed my cousin Joaquin.

Yes, it was horrible, they killed the family. The husband of a member of my family wasn't killed because a paramilitary said he looked like his father, but he has been sick of his heart ever since.

My husband was not killed because he hid in the water but he also became very ill from grief, sadness, and had no health and died.

Deaths, murders of their loved ones are part of the losses mentioned, but another also immediate effect of displacement is the breaking of family ties, which beyond the biological link, it is also a break with their culture. Some have been unable to return due to the pain that causes them to see their town and people in the deteriorating conditions in which they are. Some women and men died of related causes, according to interviewees, after the death of a family member during the events.

Before displacement, although nuclear households were common, it was characteristic of the families of El Salado to have extended family forms, unrelated to the size of the house. Interviewees of El Salado mentioned that the houses resembled small ranches or farms, as can be seen in the following comment "... in the town we lived together in the same house, it was a neighbourhood of houses, many large houses, some *ranchones,* you can say". In the case of Nueva Venecia and Buenavista, houses were smaller and precarious, but an essential aspect stressed by families of these populations was the closeness to relatives.

Another aspect of families that was explored was couple relationships. These are described generally as good before the events. Some couples have remained together after the slaughter; others saw their relationship deteriorate, or broke up because of reasons associated with the displacement itself because they took different paths in search of opportunity and security. A resident of Buenavista commented: "It was here, when he came to Barranquilla and he fell in love, because before in the town there was not an atmosphere for that. The only fun was going to the canteen and every once in a while when a young woman said "let´s do a house party".

But there is evidence of domestic violence, and neglectfulness of men even before displacement:

He was bad with me, bad, bad, but as one respects and one was from a small village, inexperienced ... my mom had come here before, and lived on the ferrocaril, and I was suffering far away, until I said no, I just grabbed a bag like those of rice, and put my clothes and then a Johnson brought me here, and I said I'm going to my mom´s, and I came. Then he came back and I said, I'll just leave it there, and I suffered a lot. (Woman interviewed from New Venice).

Changes in gender roles are evident especially in the transformation of traditional productive activities. We found that it was easier for women to adapt to the city because doing housework and working in family houses was similar to activities practiced before displacement. Most men, however, felt deep nostalgia and sadness as a consequence of the inability brought by not being able to work the land in the case of Salado and fishing in the case Nueva Venecia.

After the displacement men have presented more tendency to be sick, according to the testimonies gathered. However, this might due to diseases being more visible in men due to the new role of supplier of the vast majority of women in these populations and the permanence of the traditional role of caregiver, preventing women to freely and openly express their sorrows and pains.

... Now I have my husband sick, he has to have dialysis done, sometimes he helps me work and sometimes not, because the disease does not allow him... (New Venice)

Resilience is a theoretical category has been used to describe the processes of recovery of people in situations of adversity. It has been linked to the analysis of the effects of the armed conflict in Colombia, as shown by several studies in the country.

With regard to the transmission of memory, the following expression is used: "We talked about what happened to our children and grandchildren, but the grandchildren do not want to go there. For fear, I would say, I'm not going to El Morro. During the day maybe, but at night one is afraid" (Interviewed New Venice). Assuming that the phenomenon of transmission as a mental functioning of human beings, this paper assumes that it is always present, expressed either in nostalgia from parents evoking the territories from which they were expelled or by means of the silence about the events that led to the displacement and the believe that children should not know the truths.

The transmission from one generation to another, from brutal isolated events to wars, has been part of the work of social and human sciences. Within these, psychoanalysis is known for its contributions to the field of subjectivity, providing the basis to articulate the individual, the family and social studies of memory of this research. Transmission is defined by Jelin (2002) as the process by which a shared cultural knowledge linked to a vision of the past is constructed. That is, the sense that people involved give to events. Who, what and how it is transmitted is part of what is presented. Within the first question it is necessary to mention the differences in the experiences of the massacres according to the age of the person when the events occurred, the sex, education level, whether or not they witnessed the events, the distance from them, etc.

According to Susana Kaufman in her paper *Lo legado y lo propio, Lazos familiares y transmisión* (2006), transmission is the central founder of subjectivity, senses and affiliation. Her work incorporates the contributions made by Freud on trauma, war neurosis and other aspects that were studied by psychoanalysts who succeeded him. Clearly, violence and fear work by destroying and breaking transmissions via intersubjective ties. Kaës (1996) reminds us that "the horror is transmitted when no processing or representation of the violence is registered as a nameless excess in the psyche of the parents in the body and in subsequent generations". The contributions of psychoanalysis to the interpretation of trauma have transcended disciplinary boundaries to history, anthropology and sociology, among others. All have taken aspects of Freud's initial proposals. This is the case of Lacapra Dominick (2005) (2006), who articulates history, psychoanalysis and literature and has made significant analysis not only to understand the concept of trauma, but also the victim-perpetrator relationship, the role of witness and a crucial aspect, not only from the theoretical but also methodological point of view, the "management" of the interviews.

The difficulty to narrate the unspeakable, to talk about a pain that escapes language and imprisons them individually, leads to Gampel (2002) referring to the term "radioactive influences", a term evidently borrowed from physics to show the inability to escape from the destructive effects that sociopolitical violence brings: "no one is safe from the destructive effects caused by humans to other humans," he says. And adds: "We can all be passive transmitters or receivers of that radioactivity at random, just because we belong to a nation or territory, we live in society and in the world. The radioactive identification circulates unpredictably, it has to do with a particular person operating remotely modifying the relationships between individuals and between States and its effects are not limited to a fixed time". This can be evident in the following story:

Oh, no, I tell you, that when I'm talking, I feel bad because ... that's terrible, one thing is having lived it and another one is to tell. (Interviewed New Venice).

We are dealing with a voluntary process of silence from the part of families. The expression said by one of our interviewed "they can´t know" has dramatic consequences. Viñar (1991) studied them and found that society is divided between those who know and those who do not know. Those who lived become "the extreme experience" and those who did not lived lack some knowledge, a division that brings profound implications for psychic life and for building a society.

There is an intention to protect with the belief "they should not know". It can safely be said that the transmission of reports in most cases is done unintentionally, where children and grandchildren are brought to the village, and are present in the celebrations and in groups of people involved in the situation and they listen when people talk about the violent events.

Every day someone brings out with that or me, but anyone does it because one still has family there.

Currently no one has been commissioned to speak of what happened to the children, although they are interested in knowing. People from the village are always coming and discussing their experiences, which arouses curiosity in children and they request to be taken back there to know the place.

No, I do not tell them what happened, I do not tell them that. Sure, I tell them that we lived in union, that one went fishing with one´s woman, and that the town was water, that we fished with atarraya, that we sat on the terrace to catch the cool breeze, and that I liked to drink, for a whole week, back then when this was possible; not now, because we had friends there, but here your friend is your enemy.

We say we lived in the village, the village was water, but the other part was not discussed with them.

They ask me and they ask mom too. Mom, how it happened and why it happened ... and they tell you, oh, no, mommy, then in there people cannot live. But, look, that town was nice, spacious, there was nothing to worry about, no worrying for the young people smoking dope, but I now have so many things that I have fear of.

However, in other families the communication is different:

When adults talk about what happened and children are present, they ask you what that site was, and what happened, and we explain.

The affectation to generations is obvious and even more when those affected did not receive the psychological help needed. Here we must mention that "the absence of social compensation policies makes these situations encapsulated in the 'private' space of it and one of the effects of this is the depoliticisation of the victims and of life, a phenomenon which can also be explained by other factors.

With respect to age at the time the events occurred, we also found differences in interpretation and in recalling experiences, as it was observed in an interview with a young leader of the repair process of El Salado and an adult, leader of the Association of displaced Bolivar ASODESBOL.

The generational aspect is also important to consider, in the face of the Law 975 of 2005 of Justice and Peace, as well as in the Law of Victims and Land Restitution. The confessions and denials of perpetrators of the events give rise to many questions about memory transmission, but also about the dynamics that have occurred in the families open other questions regarding the Law of victims. Parents, especially mothers, have used in some cases different procedures so that their children do not find out about the slaughters. For example, hiding the newspapers that talk about it, to turning off the TV when a victimizer is going to give the report or declaration. This hinders the possibility to discuss the facts with children following a sense of protection and to avoid revenge. It is important to ask, however, how could they be able to request to the authorities the access to their rights if they lack crucial information?

The management of pain and the problem of Truth, which arises particularly in the Framework of Transitional Justice, could be seen under the framework of the work of Alejandro Castillejo in his studies in South Africa, such as those described in the text *Archivos del Dolor* (2009). We face collective forms of memory (installed institutionally many times) and in individual forms. As an example, this can be seen in the

Figure 2. Abandoned house in El Salado (the author)

case of acts of remembrance and commemoration of people and events, part of processes that integrate a group either a family or a community around them. A tour of El Salado shows several houses collapsed as a result of the armed conflict. These ones, however, hold no inscription. There are others that show the economic boom that there was once due to the tabaco industry. The Images 2 and 3 show this situation. Many of the houses are painted in very live colours as a result of government policy. We lack, however, a sound proposal that answers why the use of such bright colors to paint the houses there.

Figure 3. Abandoned wealthy house in El Salado (the author)

In relation to gender, in the case of the armed conflict in Colombia, there are several investigations that have linked gender and conflict, gender and political movement and gender and reparation. The impact of the armed conflict on women in Colombia has been reported by various women's organizations and the academia since the eighties with the intensification of the conflict and increased displacement of populations.

For our work, the use of the gender category is useful for its potential critical use according to the work of Joan Scott (1996), which also helps to show the differences between men and women product of cultural construction, relations of inequality between and with regard to armed conflicts, and differential involvement plus or simultaneously with the institutional articulation. Here the focus is acknowledging that violence, the armed conflict and forced displacement have differential effects depending on gender, age and ethnicity.

With regard to the content of their narratives, the results of our investigation agree with those reported by Elizabeth Jelin (2002), who mentions some differences between men and women linked largely to the daily life of both. Women being more likely to show care for others, especially family, and generally expressing more feelings while men tend to be synthetic.

It is clear that women play various activities outside the home, but these changes do not indicate changes in the way of conceiving the traditional roles assigned to men and women and this is reflected strongly in activities such as food preparation. The research confirms this through the stories of women and social mapping of work activities. This is so because the culture has imposed a division of labour based on gender. The testimonies clearly tell us about traditional roles played by both genders:

... There were people that went fishing around three o'clock in the morning, and returned in the evening. Those who went to fish early and returned to the town during the evening, and those who went fishing with a net, who came back the next day.

Becoming the emotional support of families, as has been noted by the author (García Acuña, 2008), is also part of the gender tasks assigned to women. Hence talking of events is a topic mostly of them, narrating the events and the impact on their lives, and even more on the suffering and the effects on their loved ones, but not on themselves"

The gender balance of Donny Meertens (2004) on the issue of displacement showed differential involvement of genders. The findings coincide with the results we present here. The first milestone is that among the displaced population, adult women slightly outnumber men. This is consistent with data from other entities. Increased female heads of household (due to murder of husbands or partners) and family breakdown associated with anonymity, or dynamics proper of big cities, are some of the main causes.

Arriving at the places where they settle, men and women both live the stigma of being displaced and with the distrust that the war generates. Men are stigmatized in labour-related aspects, while women feel in their neighbourhoods. But more significantly, the stigmatization of state institutions due to the lack of identity documents, which in many cases were lost during the displacement, or even lacking the *military card,* since it was not required to be a fisherman or a farmer, the main previous work activity of men. Likewise many children were not admitted to school immediately because they did not have their identity documents.

That one was ... was in better conditions than here, that our rights were violated and still are by state entities that violate it ... So at least ... if you're going to claim your rights and you go badly dressed, if you do not go stinky, they said you are not a displaced person ... who said a displaced always has to look poor?

The expression that summarizes this stigmatization and its use by official personnel (mostly women) in charge of responding to your requirements, was discussed by María, one of our interviewees:

You do not seem displaced, you're not dressed as a displaced.

Although even in these situations, women tend to prefer urban integration over returning. According to Meertens, mentioned earlier, these different positions reflect the difficulties of adaptation of both genders and should be considered in differential policies by government agencies. Another aspect that the author mentions is related to the impact of the events. At the time of the violence and recent displacements, losses and changes tend to be stronger for rural women that come from a world characterized by the neighbourhood, domesticity, with a narrowed geographical mobility and less participation in public aspects than men. But when the process of settlement and reconstruction of everyday life in the place of arrival starts, the balance sheet shows a reverse trend; unemployment affects men harder than women.

The research reports show that women have more opportunities to find work, which is usually located within informality. It can be seen that for many women their pain is overcame, especially if it is supported by entities. In addition to exercising a role as guarantors, women also play a formative function, which enables not only the modification of traditional roles but also foments leadership in the public space and the promotion their rights. This, in addition to having an educational role and to the acquisition of skills for speaking in public and having a greater capacity for critical self-evaluation and improving themselves, which ultimately leads to an increase in esteem. As said by one of our female interviewees: "Now I'm not afraid to talk and no one can stop me".

However, as it has been documented in other spaces (García, Acuña 2008), changes on gender aspects take place within the home and in the relationships between family members, as it can be seen in the expression of Neivis (name not changed), one of the women leaders of El Salado:

But this process was not easy. Initially we had conflicts with our husbands. But we ... We reported the problems of education and health of El Salado. We sued asking for better health conditions.

Previous experience of participation in organizational activities before displacement is one factor that helps explaining why some women show higher strengths when being forcedly displacement. The ability to create networks through "community kitchens" and other collective activities are some of these.

Violence during the massacre also show gender differences.

Doris was the first one to die in the slaughter of 1997. (Interviewed by El Salado).

Nayibis Osorio was dragged by the hair from her home, accused of being partner of a guerrilla Member (Interviewed by El Salado).

The above expressions reveal how war makes women have their rights violated, particularly sexual and reproductive rights. It is commonplace that domestic violence and sexual violence are used as a weapon of war -sexual assault by armed actors, which can take place in the form of forced prostitution, sexual harassment, and other forms of violence that women still do not identify as violence, like forced domestic services, control over their behaviour, their way of dressing and, particularly, their emotional lives. That is, their choices on their partners.

The text *Mujeres y Guerra: Víctimas y Resistencia en el Caribe Colombiano* (Women and War: Victims and Resistance in the Colombian Caribbean), published by the Historical Memory Group of the CNRR (National Commission of Reparation and Reconciliation) (2011), under the coordination of Maria Emma Wills, works extensively with violence based on gender in an analysis that includes women not only as victims but also as victimizers. Likewise, it describes cases of rapes mostly by groups of the paramilitaries AUC. It also discloses the dense tissue of women's organizations in the Colombian Caribbean that through various expressions has been acting to address this violence.

The obligation to make women work as cooks of paramilitaries or guerrilla groups is part of the forms of violence against women that are rarely recognized or noted by the ones who suffer it. This is understandable if one considers the history of service to others that has accompanied the lives of women, especially in the countryside, in poverty and inside their homes.

All these forms of violence towards populations and particularly in the case of women have been denounced by many scholars, but especially by the broad spectrum of organizations and women's networks since the nineties. However, at the institutional level the prevailing trend is silence and while there are small steps in terms of recognizing the problem, this is not accompanied by the opportunity of justice. It is important to ensure the rights of the displaced population and overcome the unconstitutional state of affairs (ECI). The Judicial Sentence 025 of 2004 generated a number of Autos, one of which is the 092 of 2008 for the protection of fundamental rights of women victims of forced displacement due to armed conflict. However, the institutional approach is in its infancy still.

Regarding organizational processes, the following quote explains the perspective that displaced people the vision they have of it:

And as you may notice they tried to weaken the organizational structure of El Salado, the strongest ones, people who most excelled in culture, citizen rights, who were nice to everyone, who were very charismatic, very kind people, community mothers, teachers, the best leaders, the one who was a councilman... finally they weakened the organizational structure of Salado and terror did its evil. The entire community was a victim.

Product of displacement, a fragmentation of the social network takes place, and of the relationship with others. Hence, the possibility for forming groups and strong organizational processes is reduced or hindered. At the governmental level, many Sentences, Laws and Autos of high courts have been signed to improve the situation, but much remains to be done. The organization and participation of displaced populations has been the subject of laws, judgments and orders as discussed below. With the Law 387 of 1997, the Service System proposed to design a care plan for prevention and humanitarian emergency care that helped guaranty socio-economic stabilization of displaced people. The Law states that this population should be included in the design of the programs, as well as in the plans established for their attention.

Faced with the failure of the State and based on 1150 sues to the state by displaced populations across the country, the Constitutional Court issued the judgment T-025 of 2004, which was considered an important step not only to reiterate and enforce commitments to these populations but also because it analysed the role of institutions of displaced population, stating that they could act as informal agents through their legal representatives. In the Auto 027, 109 indicators are adopted to measure the state of unconstitutional things for displaced populations and also 233 indicators of 2007 were revised again. As a consequence, the Court reiterated these commitments and critically analysed the issue of participation and indicators that the government had established to measure -the scenarios and issues, conditions, guarantees and appropriate responses. This led to concreting a list of indicators for measuring the performance of the relevant national and regional authorities working with displaced people in the Auto 116 of 2008, which incorporated suggestions of the organizations PLAN and SIGMA.

In the Auto 116 of 2008, the Constitutional Court urged the government to adopt a protocol of participation that enabled to show progress, setbacks or stagnation in the implementation of the indicators that the Court ordered. In this protocol it is considered that the effective participation "is a right belonging to the Mesas de Fortalecimiento para la Población Desplazada (MFOPD) -Bureau for Support of the Displaced Population- that support organizations of displaced people. They were the consultants regarding the definition, implementation, monitoring and evaluation of the public policy for the caring and prevention of forced displacement".

It can be seen how these bureaus that were created by the Decree 250 of 2004 had the function that was latter better specified with the approval of the Law 1448 of 2011, *Ley de Víctimas y de Restitución de Tierras* (Law of Victims and Land Restitution), which allowed a new process to begin. The Decree 790 of the 20th of April 2012 replaced the institutions that worked with the attention and participation of the displaced population with Tables, creating the Tables of Victims and adopting new protocols. At the time of the interviews the law was being regulated, so there were many voids in terms of a proper understanding of the processes. As one of the displaced said "we´ve now gone from being displaced to victims". This expression was used not only by the displaced population, but also by officials.

Faced with all these processes related to legislation and that tried to improve what repeatedly has been considered as an Unconstitutional State of Things IST (Estado de Cosas Institucional ECI), it is also necessary to review the organizations ISTs. The characteristics of these have been analysed by various researches, such as the Donny Meertens (2004), in his work on the differential gender analysis in relation to armed conflict. He mentions some of the characteristics of the organizations of the displaced population, some of which we have been mentioned in the previous section. According to Meertens, male leadership characterizes ISTs of organizations that have emerged. The participation of displaced women as managers has been little and their activities are mostly been focused on income generation through projects of low sustainability. He mentions that the cohesion of IST organizations headed by men in big cities like Bogotá, the capital of Colombia, has been characterized by transience, naturally linked to specific sues, while organizations of displaced women have developed more strongly in cities like Medellin, Cartagena, Barrancabermeja and smaller cities.

In the analysis of organisational processes, we also consider how they relate to institutions, but also how they are seen by the displaced population. Regarding the first aspect mentioned above, in interviews about the appreciation for the institutions some of them said:

I had a good concept of the government before it happened; Now, not so much.

We have only received a "cooking kit" by Pastoral Social and a starter subsidy. An official of the Department of Government made us sign some papers promising us aid and never returned anymore.

Regarding the second point, we heard from officials (Mostly women):

We have given them everything.

It is important to question what this scarcity of help means for government entities, what is considered as the "right to have rights"? On the other hand, it is clear that there are differences in the organizational processes and the involvement of the populations of El Salado and Nueva Venecia. Both populations were associated at first for reasons related to the need of commencing legal procedures, that in case of El Salado resulted in an association of displaced of El Salado, Bolivar, ASODESBOL, Atlantic Chapter, unlike the Population of New Venice where they have not

Figure 4. Church of El Salado. (The author)

achieved yet building an organization that allows them to demand their rights as victims of forced displacement, collectively.

In the absence of recognition and gaps in justice in Colombia, coupled with the fact that there has not been an end to the armed conflict in the country, victims' organizations often find themselves trapped and in a paradoxical situation that puts them in a situation of disability and vulnerability but where, at the same time, they are expected to have an enormous capacity to make the arrangements that allow them to put the legislation and procedures into practice. Which is why they unite and organize but with big fractures that do not allow them to achieve their demands.

We also found that organizations lack motivation, both financially and emotionally, which generates the failure of local authorities, so that an overall fragmentation and weak processes are the result due to constant and fruitless struggles with the State in terms of fighting for the guarantees of participating effectively in its processes.

FINAL REFLECTIONS AND FUTURE WORK

As stated above, memory as a process is subject to reinterpretation, re-significations and in this sense is always unfinished. Hence, when analysing *fights for memory* it is important to consider the possibility of denunciation and impact of its actions and how can the organizations of families transcend mostly from the scope of private to public and political stage. One that values and recognizes their experiences, allowing them to achieve their demands. It is in this sense that the analysis by Castillejo (2009) in his studies in South Africa are very enlightening for our case, particularly what he mentions in the epilogue of his book *Los Archivos del Dolor* (The Archives of pain). Castillejo´s studies serve as foundations for scholars to interrogate about the articulation between the academy and the governmental aspects of each case. For example, the Laws of Justice and Peace (justicia y Paz) and the Law of Victims and Land Restitution (Víctimas y Restitución de Tierras), -both proposals that point towards Transitional Justice-, involve the participation of university researches, groups of victims and victims individually. In respect to these issues we make the following concluding remarks:

Firstly, the recognition not only of poverty but of exclusion that has historically been experienced by victims of massacres. Access to health care, education and basic services has been limited. In both populations notable deficiencies persist in terms of public services: water, electricity, sewerage. It is important not to fall within what Pierre Bourdieu and Loic Quant (2000) referred to when they mentioned moralism as one of the vices of multiculturalism, where the social and economic were left aside due to the focus and attention on the recognition of identities, while outside there were many (as in the case of the victims of the massacres of el Salado and Nueva Venecia) school children and people without access to health. For Bourdieu, these choices are related to the functional, where it is expected for institutions to serve on their names, but not factual aspects. Many NGOs of humanitarian character retake this.

Secondly, the impact in terms of gender and generations and the view on the conflict and its resolution varies. In the case of the elderly, the years of life lost due to displacement and violence in general are incalculable. But there is also a big population of children and adolescents with serious historical effects that have not yet been addressed.

Lastly, it is important to recognize the difference between the official memory and the technocracy that is installed regarding victims. Clearly there is a policy for the victims and it is a window for the State to analyse suffering. Policies are defined and the affected respond within their framework. Thus, leaders are defined; it is established who are the holders of the words and decisions, who are also carriers of truth, who represents whom. But this performance is passive; it is a dynamic process marked by controversies, disputes and protests. The provision of this technicality is organized so that people are compiled to talk about their suffering. The silence makes them invisible. And from other perspectives, also suspects. From another logic, as posed by Kaufman (2006) and Oberti (2006), it is assumed that silence is not therapeutic. The state, in that respect, builds other subjectivities. Institutional regulations define what is expected of the population of officials (mostly female staff), responsible of implementing the programs. In this way, new languages and new ways of naming the pain take place, generating a process of depoliticisation due to for fear or shame. But this framework makes the same structural conditions associated with the armed conflict to maintain. And the academy? Well, it usually only makes echo to the State.

REFERENCES

Agamben, G. (2004). (A. Hidalgo, Ed.), *Infancia e historia.* Buenos Aires.

Bello, M. N. (Ed.), (2004). Desplazamiento forzado, Dinámicas de guerra, exclusión y desarraigo. Bogotá: Universidad Nacional de Colombia, sede Bogotá.

Bensssousan, G. (2010). *Auschwitz por herencia? Sobre un buen uso de la memoria.* Barcelona: Anthropos.

Blair, E. (2012). *Un itinerario de investigación sobre la violencia. Contribución a una sociología de la ciencia.* Medellín: Editorial Universidad de Antioquia.

Braun, H. (2008). *Mataron a Gaitán. Vida pública y Violencia urbana en Colombia.* Madrid: Editora Aguilar.

Caracol Radio. (2005) Oral Interview with Orlando Fals Borda Orlando due to the book Violence in Colombia. *El Heraldo.* Ediciones 21, 22 y 23 de Febrero de 2000. Retrieved from www.caracol.com.co/oir.aspx? Id=168502

Castillejo, A. (2009). Los archivos el dolor. Ensayos sobre la violencia y el recuerdo en la Sudáfrica contemporánea. Bogotá: Universidad de los Andes.

Centro Nacional de Memoria Histórica. (2012). ¡Basta Ya!. Colombia: Memorias de guerra y dignidad. Informe general Grupo Memoria Histórica. DPS.

Comisión Nacional de Rearación y Reconciliación, CNRR, (2010), May.

COMISIÓN NACIONAL DE REPARACIÓN Y RECONCILIACIÓN, CNRR. . (2011). Mujeres y Guerra. Victimas y resistentes en el Caribe Colombiano. Informe del Grupo de Memoria Histórica coordinado por María Emma Wills. Taurus, Fundación Semana.

Constitución Política de Colombia, 1991

Correa De Andreis, A. (2001). *La mirada que mira la mirada. Un caso de alianza en la Ciénaga Grande de Santa Marta*. Barranquilla: Universidad del Norte.

Das Veena. (2008). Trauma y Testimonio. In A. Ortega Francisco (Ed.), Veena Das: Sujetos del dolor, agentes de dignidad. Bogotá: Universidad Javeriana, Instituto pensar, Universidad Nacional de Colombia, Colección CES.

Del Pino, P., & Jelin, E. (2003). *Luchas locales, comunidades e identidades*. Madrid: Siglo XXI Editores.

Eribon, D. (1982). Entrevista a Pierre Bourdieu. Retrieved from http://pierre-bourdieu.blogspot.com/2008/01/entrevista-pierre-bourdieu-qu-significa.html

Fals Borda, O., Guzmá, G., & Umaña, E. (1962). *La violencia en Colombia*. Bogotá: Universidad Nacional.

Galeano, E. (1995). *Ser como ellos y otros artículos*. Bogotá: Tercer Mundo Editores.

Gampel, Y. (2002). El dolor de lo social. Psicoanálisis APdeBA. Vol. XXIV - N° 1/2.

García, Y. (2012). *Rutas por la memoria. Voces de Nueva Venecia y El Salado*. Barranquilla: Universidad Simón Bolívar -Colciencias.

García Acuña, Y. (2008). *Familias en Colombia. Transiciones hacia el siglo XXI*. Barranquilla: Ediciones Universidad Simón Bolívar.

García Márquez, G. (2007). Cien años de soledad, Edición conmemorativa. Bogotá: Real Academia Española, Asociación de Academias de la Lengua española

Gres Toso S. (2007). Historiografía, memoria y política. Observaciones para un debate. *Cyber Humanitatis,* 41.

Halbwachs, M. (2004). La memoria colectiva, Zaragoza: Prensa Universitarias de Zaragoza. Retrieved from http://es.scribd.com/doc/36199740/Halbwachs-Maurice-La-Memoria-Colectiva

Informe de la Comisión de Organismos de Derechos Humanos sobre la Masacre en la Ciénaga Grande de Santa Marta. (2000, December 22). Retrieved from http://www.derechos.org/nizkor/colombia/doc/cienaga.html

Jelin, E. (2002). *Trabajos de la memoria*. Madrid: Siglo XXI Editores.

Jelin, E. (2007). Familiares, víctimas y ciudadan@s: Las luchas por la legitimidad de a palabra. *Cadernos Pagu*, *29*, 37–60.

Jimenez Becerra, A., & Guerra García, F. (2009). Las luchas por la memoria. Bogotá: Instituto por la Pedagogía, la Paz y el Conflicto Urbano, IPAZUD, Universidad Distrital francisco José de Caldas.

Kaës, R. (1996). *El sujeto y la herencia. Transmisión de la vida psíquica entre generaciones*. Buenos Aires: Amorrortu Editores.

Kaufman, S. (2006). *Lo legado y lo propio. Lazos familiares y transmisión de memorias. En Jelin, E. & Kaufman, S. (Comps). Subjetividad y figuras de la memoria*. Buenos Aires: Siglo XXI Editora Iberoamericana, Siglo XXI de España Editores.

Lacapra, D. (2006). Historia en transito. Experiencia, identidad, teoría crítica. permanente Buenos Aires: Fondo de Cultura Económica de la Argentina.

Law 1448 de 2011. Ley de Víctimas y Restitución de Tierras. Decree 250 de 2004. Decree 2244 del 20 de junio de 2011. Decree 790, 20 Abril de 2012. Sentence T-025 de 2004.

Law 387 de julio of 1997. Por la cual se dictan medidas para la prevención de desplazamiento forzado; la atención, protección y estabilización socioeconómica de los desplazados internos por la violencia en Colombia.

Law 975 de 2005. (2005). Ley de Justicia y Paz

Lechner, N., & Güell, P. (2006). Construcción social de las memorias en la transición chilena. In Jelin, E. & Kaufman, S. (Comps). Subjetividad y figuras de la memoria. Ciudad Autónoma de Buenos Aires: Siglo XXI Editora Iberoamericana.

Meertens, D. (2004). Género, Desplazamiento, Derechos. In M. N. Bello (Ed.), *Desplazamiento forzado. Dinámicas de guerra, exclusión y desarraigo*. Bogotá: Universidad Nacional de Colombia.

Mesa Mujer y Conflicto armado. Informe sobre la violencia sociopolitical contra mujeres, jóvenes y niñas en Colombia (2005, November). Retrieved from http://www.coljuristas.org/documentos/libros_e_informes/v_informe_mesa_mujer_y_conflicto.pdf

Oberti, A. (2006). La memoria y sus sombras. In E. Jelin & S. Kaufman (Eds.), *Comps). Subjetividad y figuras de la memoria*. Buenos Aires: Siglo XXI Editora Iberoamericana, Siglo XXI de España Editores.

Pecaut, D. (1997). *Pasado, presente y futuro de la violencia. Análisis Político. No 30*. Enero-Abril.

Pollak, M. (1992). Memoria e identidad social. In memoria, olvido, silencio. La producción social de identidades frente a situaciones límites. Introducción Ludmila da Silva Catela (2006). La Plata: Buenos Aires: Ediciones Al Margen.

Ricoeur, P. (2000). *La memoria, la historia, el olvido*. Buenos Aires: Fondo de Cultura Económica.

Sánchez, G. (2003). *Guerras, Memoria e Historia*. Medellín: La Carreta Histórica.

Sánchez, G., & Meertens, D. (1983). *Bandoleros, gamonales y campesinos. El caso de la Violencia en Colombia*. Bogotá: El Áncora Editores.

Scott, J. W. (2015). Experiência. *Revista de Estudios de Gênero. La Ventana, 2*(13), 42–74.

Todorov, J. (2000). *Los abusos de la memoria*. Buenos Aires: Paidós.

Traverso, E. (2007). *El pasado, instrucciones de uso. Historia, memoria, política*. Madrid: Marcial Pons. Ediciones Jurídicas y Sociales.

Uribe, M. V. (1990). *Matar, rematar y contramatar: las masacres de la violencia en el Tolima, 1948-1964*. Bogotá: CINEP, Controversia.

Verón, E. (2002). *Construir el acontecimiento. Los medios de comunicación masiva y el accidente en la central nuclear de Three Mile Island*. Barcelona: Gedisa.

Viñar, M. (2006). *Violencia social y realidad en psicoanálisis. En Puget Janine y Käes René, (Compils)*. Buenos Aires: Editorial Lumen SRL.

Zambrano Carlos Vladimir (2006). *Memoria colectiva y Comunidad Política, Propedéutica Etnográfica-Constructivista,* Bogotá: Universidad Nacional, sede Bogotá, Instituto Unidad de Investigaciones Jurídico-Sociales Gerardo Molina, UNIJUS

ENDNOTES

1 This project was financed by the Instituto Colombiano para la Ciencia, Tecnología e Innovación, COLCIENCIAS, and was developed from 2010 to 2012 by an interdisciplinary team coordinated by the author. The results of the research are detailed in the book *Rutas por la Memoria. Voces de Nueva Venecia y El Salado* (2012) by the author.

2 It is important to mention that until the year 2011, when the government of President Juan Manuel Santos officially informed it, every president of Colombia had denied the existence of an internal armed conflict in the country.

3 In the text of Elsa Blair (2012) An itinerary of research on violence. Contribution to a sociology of science, an extensively discussion on the matter can be found.

4 Like the case of the persecutions to syndicalist leaders previous to the assassination of Gaitán and that are described in Daniel Pécaut´s book (1987).

5 The book was conceived as a text of complaint with the intention of making visible a phenomenon and later inducing change, but the increase in violence showed that this was not possible. Monsignor Guzman, one of the coauthors was forced into exile in Mexico; the son of Eduardo Umaña was murdered years later and Fals Borda was tortured by government forces and was exiled a while. During a radio interview with Caracol Radio on the occasion of the reissue of the book 40 years later, April 25 of 2005, Fals Borda spoke about his frustration over the increasing violence.

6 La Violencia en Colombia: Estudio de un Proceso Social.

7 The Committee of violence consisted of academics from different disciplines and it is important to highlight two aspects; first, that in its conformation there was no woman, although in order to prepare the chapter on violence in families, the committee requested the help of Mary Himelda Ramirez. The second aspect is related to institutional arrangements, where two of the Commissioners became coordinators of the entity called the National Commission for Reparation and Reconciliation, CNRR, -entity created in 2005 to which I shall refer later; one as director of the NCRR and the other one as coordinator of the Memory Aerea of it.

8 According to the Law 387 of 1997: Someone displaced is that person who has been forced to migrate inside the national territory, abandoning its residency and usual economic activities because his or her life, physical integrity, security or personal freedom have been venerated or are threatened due to any of the following reasons: internal armed conflict, riots and internal tensions, generalized violence, massive violations of Human Rights, infractions against International Humanitarian Rights and other circumstances that arise from the latter situation that have or can alter public order". (Es desplazado toda persona que se ha visto forzada a migrar dentro del territorio nacional abandonando su localidad de residencia o actividades económicas habituales, porque su vida, su integridad física, su seguridad o libertad personales han sido vulneradas o se encuentran directamente amenazadas, con ocasión de cualquiera de las siguientes situaciones: Conflicto armado interno, disturbios y tensiones interiores, violencia generalizada, violaciones masivas de los Derechos Humanos, infracciones al Derecho Internacional Humanitario u otras circunstancias emanadas de las situaciones anteriores que puedan alterar o alteren drásticamente el orden público").

9 At the end of the presidential period of Álvaro Uribe demobilizations conducted by the National Fiscal Agency (Fiscalía Gen-

eral de la Nación) started to be questioned. Especially due to the proliferation of "false demobilized"; subsequently, the number of demobilized paramilitaries is not précised.

10 *Desplazamiento forzado. Dinámicas de guerra, exclusión y desarraigo*

11 Due to space reasons I will not extend in this analysis, which I develop better in the book Routes through Memory: Voices of Nueva Venecia and El Salado (Rutas por la Memoria, Voces de nueva Venecia y El Salado) (García, 2012), which was one of the objectives of the project and construction Families memory.

12 Grupo de Memoria Histórica de la Comisión Nacional de Reparación y Reconciliación.

13 "A pesar de los inmensos avances logrados en el plano de la reconstrucción del período de la Violencia, ninguno de los casos anteriores se pregunta por el sentido que le dan los actores involucrados a sus vivencias particulares".

14 The publication of the text of Elizabeth Jelin (2002), The Works of Memory (*Los Trabajos de la Memoria*) and the texts that follow priduct of a research program on the subject of memories about the dictatorships in the Southern Cone, developed at the Institute of Social development, IDES, Buenos Aires, in the period of 1998-2004, is a reference that has to be mentioned.

15 The Slaughter of the Zona Bananera occurred in 1929 and retaken by Gabriel García Márquez in One Hundred Years of Solitude, the book that awarded him the Nobel Award in Literature in 1982, is perhaps the best known story that narrates it.

16 Sociologist killed in 2004 by order of Jorge 40, paramilitary of the Caribbean Region and who also directed the slaughter of Nueva Venecia. This was established in the Free Versions that have provided by demobilized members who have demobilised under the guarantees of the Justice and Peace Law. Jorge 40 was extradited along with 12 other paramilitary leaders to the United States by decision of President Alvaro Uribe Vélez during his period of government.

17 A colloquial expression of the North Coast for someone who has bad luck.

18 More testimonies can be found in the Book by García (2012).

Chapter 18
Reconstruction of Historical Memory In The Midst Of the Armed Conflict in Colombia:
Questions, Reflections, Difficulties and Learnings

María Angélica Garzón
Universidad Pedagógica y Tecnológica de Colombia UPTC, Colombia

Paula A. Timcke Rey
Felsberg Institute, Germany

ABSTRACT

This chapter aims to reflect upon the construction of historical memory in Colombia from an institutional framework and in the midst of an armed conflict that does not cease. The objective is to discuss the difficulties that emerge in this type of research when conducted under the political, conceptual and methodological parameters of a public entity. Therefore, three contexts that influenced the development of the research are analysed (institutional, social-political and scientific) and then the limits and difficulties that these implicate are exposed. Finally, a series of recommendations are presented as well as the learned lessons that should represent a contribution for future work related with the reconstruction of historical memory in contexts of violence and armed conflict.

INTRODUCTION

Colombia has experienced one of the longest and most violent armed conflicts in the world. For more than 50 years a large proportion of its population has been affected by this conflict that has resulted in the loss of family and friends, life projects, territories and cultural expressions. In practice, the armed conflict expresses itself in murder, kidnapping, forced displacement and other forms of human rights violations. In this country, war has become a structural element of everyday life, with violence as a determining aspect of how people live in a large part of rural and urban areas.

DOI: 10.4018/978-1-4666-9675-4.ch018

Over the years the conflict has become more complex in regard to the participation of diverse protagonists coming from the drug-trafficking business, corruption and other mechanisms of criminality. In addition to this, leftist guerrillas, paramilitary groups and the Government have transformed the conflict into an internal conflict with no ideological reference other than the unjust enrichment of such groups. The consequence of all this has been the configuration of a diffuse context in which there is no clarity in terms of motives and actors. This scenario, in combination with an intensification of violent acts and therefore a significant number of victims, has overwhelmed the Government ´s response.

Indeed, the levels of violence reached at the present time are unprecedented as they are characterized by extreme cruelty, dehumanisation and the denigration of the human being. These experiences have marked not only the lives of the victims but have also determined the lives of Colombians and the way the country works. The Colombian Government has tried throughout its history – without any success until now – to achieve peace and consolidate a democratic society.

For example, in recent times Álvaro Uribe Vélez (2002-2010) undertook the demobilisation of paramilitary groups during his Presidency through the Law of Justice and Peace (*Ley de Justicia y Paz –Ley 975- Congreso de la República de Colombia, 2005*). This involved groups confessing to their crimes in return for reduced sentences being handed down and ex-combatants being given the chance to reintegrate into society. This law was laid out through transitional justice with the aim of achieving peace in post-conflict Colombia. At the present time, President Juan Manuel Santos´s administration (2010-present) has been conducting conversations with the group known as the *Fuerzas Armadas Revolucionarias de Colombia* (Revolutionary Armed Forces of Colombia), the *FARC. The aim of these peace talks includes the* creation of accords that will lead to the laying down of arms. Additionally, the Colombian Government has claimed it has initiated conversations with the second largest guerrilla group known as the ELN (National Liberation Army, *Ejército de Liberación Nacional* in Spanish), to join the attempt of reaching a peace agreement.

These initiatives have contributed to the mobilisation of a discourse that supports the transition of Colombia towards the end of the conflict, seeking to place the victims at the centre while the armed conflict has not been solved. However, in Colombia victims have acquired prominence in diverse processes that seek to repair the harm caused by violence, as well as to guarantee rights to truth, justice and reparation and reconstruct the historical memory. The intention is to know what happened, why it happened, who the perpetrators and the victims were, and what actions can be taken to prevent this violence from happening again.

The Colombian Government has deployed a series of efforts to meet the demands of the transition from the armed conflict into the consolidation of a democratic society or, to put it another way, the requirements that imply moving from war to peace. Thus, institutions have been created with the objective of assisting victims in dimensions such as psychosocial, economic, material, symbolic and access to justice. Efforts have also been made to create reliable databases that give a real account of the actual number of victims, the violent acts and the perpetrators. Work and action is ongoing to restitute land to people who have been victimised by forced displacement, to promote the return to the land and generate the conditions to end forced displacement. Finally, the need to rebuild the historical memory of the conflict has been emphasised in order to document the violence, dignify victims (by giving them names and faces) and conduct a symbolic reparation process.

Nonetheless, what is exceptional about this case is that these efforts have been carried out while the conflict is still ongoing. This stands in contrast to previous experiences where this process is carried out in the post-conflict phase when distance from the violent past can be taken and advances towards the consolidation of an inclusive democracy guaranteeing the right of non-repetition, justice and truth can take place. One of these important initiatives has been reconstructing the historical memory of the country´s armed conflict that involves diverse actors, interests and manifestations becoming a complex web of violence and human rights violations. In this sense, the reconstruction of historical memory, being in the midst of a conflict, becomes a challenge that both generates questions and allows extensive discussions and explorations about its possibilities.

Thus, the goal of this article is to reflect upon the work of rebuilding historical memory when carried out by a public institution in order to create an account of the past that is still present and to put into discussion questions such as the pertinence of the reconstructing memory in the middle of the war, the role of the victims in this work, the definition of an "object" of study and its social impact. The reflection emerges from the authors' experience as researchers who build historical memory from a mandate and some institutional logics in highly conflictive areas of Colombia, which has forced them to question their work, the way they develop it, its limits and also its potential. At the same time, they allowed the authors to critically reflect and propose a series of recommendations that arise from the lessons learnt and possible ways to overcome the difficulties that have come upon in their work.

In the next section, a brief review of the imperative of rebuilding memory is presented in order to give an account of *violent pasts* – defined as *the duty of memory* – and to show how this has been translated into an institutionalism for this purpose in Colombia's case. Subsequently, three different contexts in which the research has been developed are exposed with the aim of showing the limits and the scope they provided to this work.

The first context is the institutional, which contains a theoretical and conceptual framework as well as some specific guidelines for the conception, development and presentations of the research. The second context is the socio-political, which determines a framework of action in terms of gathering information, validating it and presenting it as research results as it is characterised by the dynamics of the armed conflict, the violence and state response. Finally, the scientific context dictates a series of premises and rules that validate the research work and define it as successful, robust and with quality standards. In the last section some reflections are presented such as questions, challenges and lessons learned from the conducted work in relation to the contexts announced and conclude with a series of recommendations that the authors, as researchers in this field, want to share with others interested in or dedicated to the reconstruction of historical memory.

BACKGROUND

The Duty of Memory: Reconstruction of Historical Memory as an Institutional Mandate

The duty of memory appeared in Europe towards the second half of the 20th century when it became necessary to revise recent pasts in order to understand *why* is it possible to have such devastating violence as the one endured during the Holocaust, which was mainly responsible for the breakdown of the modern Enlightenment project. Scenarios such as those in Rwanda, Bosnia and Kosovo during the 1990s, in which the image of desecrated towns and thousands of people crossing national frontiers revived the policy of European guilt and mobilised questions concerning lessons learnt after Auschwitz (Huyssen, 2000). Thus, in Europe it became necessary to turn back to the past, reflect upon its effects in the present and propose memory policies that set aside the old method of endpoint and forgetfulness.

In this way, *to remember* does not appear as an option but as a *duty*; as an imperative that translates under the motto: "you will remember" or, for authors such as Ricoeur (2008), the duty of memory emerges with the aim of exorcising a history marked to trauma. In Reyes Mate´s words (2011), the duty of memory makes reference by recognising that the unthinkable has occurred and thus to become aware of knowledge´s limits. The duty of memory, in the 20th century, offers *what* to think (Reyes Mate, 2011).

For Latin America, the duty of memory emerges from the post-dictatorial experiences of 1990s when countries such as Argentina, Chile, Brazil, Paraguay and Uruguay abandoned their dictatorial pasts and turned towards democracy. In this context a new collective model was endorsed where anyone can account for information about the past from the mobilisation of the concept of *Never Again (Nunca más),* that is, the revision of the past with the intention of guaranteeing the non-repetition of violent acts associated with dictatorship and armed conflicts. Through this, the duty of memory in Latin America became the central axis that articulates complaints about the past with projects for the future by proposing a political practice that demands truth and justice for victims (Jelin, 2001).

The need to revise the past or revisit it as a collective in Latin America, as much as in Europe, responds to the situation where the current redefinition of limits and boundaries of the Nation-State and the concern to determine its validity has led to the creation of historical review of struggles, protagonists and silent and excluded voices (Jelin, 2001). Thus, the duty of memory not only proposes a review of the past in terms of lessons learned but rather pretends to achieve a redefinition of the identity of historically excluded groups and the reconstruction of a social fabric deteriorated by violence. Following this, the duty of memory translates into a demand to reconstruct the memories of excluded, silent, victimised or vanquished groups.

In Colombia, such a duty becomes relevant in a national context in which initiatives are presented that seek for a political solution to the armed conflict and where victims are essential because guaranteeing their rights becomes an important part of pacification processes (Reátegui in: ICTJ, 2009). For example, in the case of Uribe's Law of Justice and Peace (Law 975 of 2005) in which the process of paramilitary demobilisation was carried out, it was demanded that the Colombian Government fulfil its duty of preserving the historical memory of the conflict. This involved exposing violations of human rights, their motives and effects, to strive for the non-repetition of these victimising actions and the restoration of victims´ dignity (Law 975 of 2005).

With this intention, the Law contemplated the creation of a group of specialists dedicated to the documentation of the conflict and the reconstruction of historical memory: the Historical Memory Group ascribed to the National Commission of Reparation and Reconciliation (*Comisión Nacional de Reparación y Reconciliación, CNRR* in Spanish). During its tenure this Group, composed of academics and researchers, was able to document prominent cases of forced displacement, massacres, dispossession of land, kidnapping and victimisation of indigenous groups, women, public officials, syndicate or union leaders in specific places or regions. By the end of its mandate, the Group published a final report[1] of more than 50 years of armed conflict, the causes that originated it, its dynamics, logic, effects and the way in which civilians have resisted throughout different artistic, political and organisational initiatives.

The documentation of particular cases and the final report performed by this Group were disseminated through free circulation publications, photographic exhibitions, commemorations and diverse public acts. The aim of this was to attempt to divulge such memories, to create awareness among the population, to generate political platforms to defend rights and to carry out a reflection regarding a *desired* present and future. However, with the completion of the Historical Memory Group´s tenure the process of the duty of memory was not finished in Colombia. On the contrary, it was strengthened by the creation of the National Centre of Historical Memory[2] (*Centro Nacional de Memoria Histórica, CNMH* in Spanish), which aims to recover documents as well as oral and journalistic material that can give an account of human rights and international humanitarian law violations that occurred during the Colombian armed conflict. Therefore, the goal and purpose of this Centre is the integral reparation of victims through the Government's fulfilment of the duty of memory.

In order to do this, the Centre is structured into different working areas, including those dedicated to the documentation of cases, the creation of official archives, the dissemination and support of local initiatives and the setup of a museum of memory. This Centre aims to elaborate the conflict´s historical memory in Colombia from an institutional perspective. This does not exclude the fact that memory initiatives originated by communities and non-governmental organisations are also present in the country constituting what Jelin (2001) denominates the struggles for memory or the struggles to impose an official version of the past.

Undoubtedly, manifestations and expressions of memory in Colombia that have been constituted outside the Government and empowered victims and collectiveness are diverse. Various experiences have become part of victims' daily lives, such as community museums, literature, photographic exhibitions, marches, festivals, dance, music, documents and a broad number of other type of expressions that seek to expose the past, document it, revise its meaning and raise the population´s awareness towards the violence endured. The duty of memory is also part of these initiatives.

Moreover, the rebuilding of historical memory done from institutions and design for such purposes and the one done by the community can be different in terms of content, evidences and narrations; as in matter of methods, resources and times. Hence, it is interesting to reflect on these differences and, for this work, to think about rebuilding historical memory from a spatial perspective; that is, from the place where it is reconstructed.

MAIN FOCUS OF THE CHAPTER

Contexts That Configure the Work of Reconstruction of Historical Memory and Its Limiting Factors

The Institutional Context

The institutional context makes reference to the framework from which the parameters for research and the reconstruction of historical memory are defined. In our case, from the Colombian State´s duty of memory and the preservation of the armed conflict´s memory. This context is important because it is the one that proposes, in a first instance, political, conceptual and methodological definitions in order to carry on this work.

Therefore, in this context memory is understood as a tool that allows victims´ visibility including their stories, with the objective to reconstruct a sense of the past. This is accompanied by the possibility of rebuilding the mentioned *past* from the present and with this identify and express political demands for truth, justice, reparation and guarantees of non-repetition. In this way, memory works as a bridge that connects past, present and future (Riaño, 2006).

Memory also works as a tool that allows the victim population to review the meaning of its experience of violence to understand it as the result of a complex social, cultural, political and economical framework that is determined by the logic and interests of the armed conflict. Thus, it is expected that with the reconstruction of these memories victims go through symbolic reparation or social recognition of what happened to them. Finally, memory is understood as a methodological tool whereby it is possible to reconstruct the near past prioritising the voices of individuals who have suffered violence and linking their narratives with others giving account of how the Colombian armed conflict has been configured at regional, political, economic and cultural levels (CNRR, 2009).

In this context memory is understood as an *object*, *source* and *method* of conflicting character, that is to say, where it is fought for the inclusion of voices and versions of the past. By this means, memory is defined as a diverse and polyphonic political platform (CNRR, 2009). According to the previous definition, the work of historical memory reconstruction should aim to:

1. Give relevance to victims´ voices without excluding those of interest, such as the voices of perpetrators, justice and public officials, for the reconstruction of an historical narrative.
2. Be concerned less about the veracity of stated facts and more about narrative forms, the moments in which these are made, silences, pauses and meanings. Be concerned more, as stated by Jelin (2001), about the process through which the past is given a meaning, in Castillejo words, by trying to understand what these narratives are telling us (Castillejo, 2009).
3. Understand memory reconstruction as an activity, a process that involves remembrance, memory, forgotten facts and emotions. Understand that a process of reconstruction is neither uniform nor harmonic; tensions, disagreements, exclusions and silence are present (Passerini, 2006).
4. Understand the experience of violence in other ways by living the present according to the meaning given to the past and proposing a different future that diverges from the one that the armed conflict dictates. As a personal, social, cultural and political process, the reconstruction of memory emerges from experience and modifies it (Riaño, 2006).

The previous assumptions guide the work of historical memory reconstruction that is done from an institutional logic and represents research guidelines in which the victims´ participation in the process is central. It also demands the joint stipulation regarding the way that the work should be conducted, the persons that should participate, the audience that it should be addressed to and pointing out the aspects that should be prioritised and become known to the public. Overall, the conception of rebuilding historical memory as reparation requires research that integrates *research-action* and *do no harm* paradigms.

The previous paradigms propose, on one hand, the relation not with an object of research but with individuals that actively participate, who also produce knowledge from their own lives´ conditions with the purpose of modifying them. On the other hand, it has to be guaranteed that no harm occurs given that working with conflict victims involves reviving experiences of violence and suffering. This is why the monitoring of intervention processes and the do no harm approach are central and aim to avoid detrimental impact of research actions related to or promoted by institutional frameworks (Rodríguez, 2008). Consequently, the work of rebuilding historical memory implies a relation based on dialogue, this means, understanding that the relation of research is constructed from individual to individual and that victims have the capacity to reflect and build knowledge from their own experience and modify it.

However, research work developed from an institutional framework does not necessarily meet all the previously enunciated premises due to lack of correspondence between the research and the administrative and bureaucratic logics. Time frames, for example, emerged as a factor that determined the research´s development as schedules, activities and work stages had to be constantly modified. This hindered the creation of reliable relationships with key members of the community and possible participants, affecting the trust needed to conduct this kind of testimonial and experiential work. What is more, bonds of trust and confidentiality between the participant and the researcher had to be constructed and reinforced through constant visits and field activities that were undermined by constant disruption to the schedule and due to bureaucratic requirements.

The temporal instability complicated the strengthening of relationships with victims. Scheduled meetings were often postponed or cancelled, activities and sessions were carried out in short periods of time that did not correspond to a given methodology, deadline, and furthermore a debriefing to the participants was not completed. This undermined the trust of participants in the process, who questioned the work of the research team that had to cope with a constant failure to comply with the agreed schedule.

Another consequence of the disparity between research and institutional time frames was the postponement of agreements made by researchers and victims. This turned out to be a significant problem because when working with violence victims in the reconstruction of their experiences, compromises and agreements become very important. It is precisely because of these types of agreements that it is possible to make a participative research in which the experiences of victims become the main axis. Therefore, to proceed with these types of research it is necessary to have temporal and spatial flexibility that adheres to the dynamics that this activity entails. These can vary depending on the specific reconstruction case, composition of the group, context where it happens, security situation at the time, etc.

Furthermore, in the construction of historical memory the figure of the researcher as an individual is important, as well as his or her previous experience and training. To proceed with this type of work it is recommended to create interdisciplinary teams that combine capacities and skills that allow a complex reading of violence and its consequences. In this specific case, the research team was mostly made up of lawyers and economists with professionals of human sciences such as anthropologists, sociologists and social communicators being a minority. The team´s structure seemed enriching at first but did not fulfil expectations because instead of generating interdisciplinary dialogues it proposed disciplinary disputes in which quantitative paradigms were imposed over qualitative perspectives. The latter are more accurate for memory reconstruction.

This made the team's work a difficult process as it was not orientated towards a collective construction of ideas but rather to a defence of methodologies and concepts of each discipline according to the researchers preferences. Furthermore, an important part of the research was dedicated to endless discussions, and given that validating research decisions according to principles of all disciplines became incredibly difficult. Instead of being an opportunity to create knowledge from different perspectives, it became an obstacle and a constant struggle, especially in regard to the analysis and presentation of the results.

In addition, the team´s arrangement, the project´s structure and above all the connection between its elements resulted in the lack of coherence and internal cohesion of the research. Discussing results, giving feedback, collective analysis and exchange of knowledge and experiences among the research are essential for moving forward collectively and not individually. In our case, the repercussions were important since the different disciplinary groups had their own rhythm, progress and results that made the research project uneven and the development of the particular purposes inconsistent. The discrepancies negatively affected the internal coherence of the project as a whole.

Finally, institutional support at the moment of gathering information in areas of the country where armed conflict continues with great intensity represents a risk both to the victims who participate in the research and to the team of researchers. Security protocols, key contacts and safeguards were necessary to carry out this work with a reduced risk. However, in many cases research groups lacked these security protocols, making researchers feel threatened, and resulting in them taking significant risks and requiring the use of personal resources to minimise them. Moreover, in other research cases, this type of support has not guaranteed a real security on the field and has even turned out to be counterproductive. In both cases, a security strategy should be agreed upon to avoid the lack of institutional support for the researcher.

In the following section a short outline of the Colombian armed conflict is presented with the purpose of showing the current and complex political and social context in which this fieldwork has been conducted and also in which the human rights violations have taken and are still taking place.

The Socio-Political Context

As noted above, the work of memory reconstruction in Colombia has become a challenge of interest because such reconstruction is done in the midst of, paraphrasing Jelin, "a past that doesn´t want to pass" (2001, p.35). Certainly, the armed conflict that has been present in Colombia for decades keeps itself alive even though its dynamics have changed throughout time. This makes the process of taking a step back from the past in order to reconstruct it and re-signify it a complex task. Thus, historical memory´s reconstruction is performed in a scenario in which perpetrators continue to act, violence becomes recurrent and victimisation is constant.

The fact that the research is carried out from an institutional framework implies a series of criteria and a specific logic that make it particular and give it numerous limitations. In addition to that, the place, its history and its conditions at the moment of performing the research also present a series of restrictions or characteristics that provide a determined framework of action. The national, regional and local logics of the armed conflict plus the government´s response must be taken into account at the moment of designing the methodology plan of the research. However, it is necessary for this design to include a margin for unforeseen events as well as for improvisation because security situations do not always allow the development of activities according to a plan.

In general terms and according to what existing figures show[3], the Colombian armed conflict has left 220,000 fatal victims (between 1958 and 2012) and 40,787 dead combatants. Of those killed, 81.5% have been civilians and 18.5% combatants (Centro Nacional de Memoria Histórica; 2013, p. 32). In terms of other types of victims, there have been (until March, 2013) 25,007 disappearances, 1,754 victims of sexual violence and the recruitment of 6,421 children and teenagers in the RUV reported (Ibid p.33). Regarding forced displacement the situation is even more worrying:

The Americas region hosted the second largest number of IDPs in 2012 with a total of 5.8 million, an increase of 3 per cent. Colombia remains the country with the highest number of IDPs in the world, with a total of between 4.9 and 5.5 million, according to the IDMC. The country's internal armed conflict forced an estimated 230,000 people to flee their homes during the year. (Internally Displaced People in Figures UNHCR http://www.unhcr.org/pages/49c3646c23.html; 19th November 2014)

As mentioned previously, the existing records and the way they are constructed lead to the existence of different figures about this phenomenon. According to official statistics of the RUV, until March 2013 there were a total of 4,744,046 displaced persons in Colombia. Armed actors in the conflict have been mainly guerrillas, paramilitaries and the State itself. More recently, after the demobilisation of paramilitary groups between 2003 and 2006, new criminal groups began to emerge known as "BACRIM" (bandas criminales – "criminal bands"). These groups gather recidivist paramilitaries (who did not really demobilise) and criminal actors linked to drug trafficking, contract killing and other types of violence. Some of them have not been conceptually and theoretically understood as part of the Colombian armed conflict4 but have become important illegal actors that perpetuate violence, in the places where our research was conducted, although this time with a different name.

These features of the Colombian armed conflict represent a threat to field-research because as figures indicate, it is mostly civilians and not combatants who suffer consequences. Therefore, working in areas where violence is still perpetuated by these actors who are also monitoring the research process represents an imminent risk for both researchers and victims. Given that confrontations do not necessarily occur in remote rural areas but also in cities and their urban surroundings, it is very easy to become exposed to interventions, interactions and even threats from these actors.

The repertoire of violence includes massacres, tortures, threats, brutality, forced displacement (individual and massive), murders, extortion, sexual violence, invasion of private space, abductions and kidnappings, public and private property attacks, illicit recruitment, bomb explosions, attacks directed to specific groups of people in strategic and meaningful places with demonstrative effects, landmines, forced recruitment of children and teenagers and the disappearance especially of community leaders or opponents to dominant force of a given actor. Finally, in many cases State actors have acted in alliance with illegal actors leaving the community with no institutional support and breaking the trust towards the State and citizens. Informants also referred in Colombia as "sapos" (i.e. "snitchers" or "rats"), make an important part of this work. Thus, despite efforts made by the State, there has not been an adequate rights or protection guarantee made to victims.

The physical and psychological consequences of excessive and constant use of violence affect the social fabric, trust among members of the same community and even of the same family. This is why the work of historical memory becomes complicated, as it requires a minimum level of trust among participants that is not always possible. Building this trust and creating a peaceful environment to proceed with exercises is not an easy task and a lot of times it requires a physical and geographical distance from the place of residence in order to participate. This implies transfers, meetings, routine changes in the life of participants, which can call the attention of armed illegal actors who are present at the areas of research. As researchers mainly coming from the capital city who don´t belonging to that context, their presence is questioned and revised constantly. This is why the idea that the researcher is being watched, spied, and followed by one or more (armed) actors must be accepted and assumed from the beginning.

The logics of violence aim to an appropriation of territory in order to dominate strategic routes and thus maintain position, smuggle drugs, weapons or other type contraband. This is why civilians are attacked, taken out of their houses, their lands, stripped from their properties and their social-fabric is destroyed in a great measure with the intention of breaking solidarity bonds and assuring no resistance at all. Fortunately this does not always happen and there are different forms of resistance. It is precisely these mechanisms, which researchers want to rescue, get to know, point out and share. This implies entering places of fear and horror where uncertainty and insecurity are part of an everyday violence. Given that armed actors do not respect civilians, the researcher can easily become just another victim.

In such a context, methodological design and research objectives must be adjusted permanently according to the situation and security, even though the tools used do not comply with classical research standards, having in mind that part of the work is also living the experience in order to know the situation narrated by the victim. Consequently, all data and every sentence and number gathered – mostly from non-official sources – have an immense value and must be understood and treated as such. It is not a systematic, library type recollection but rather a flexible one, in some cases improvised, with the main aim of getting to know the experience of an individual that has lived this violence. In many cases an old picture, a newspaper clipping, a personal object, a map or a smell becomes an input for reconstructing what happened, without losing value just because of the fact that it is not hard data collected in the most objective way possible.

On several occasions, the gathered information is small and the fieldwork very limited due to conditions already discussed. Although there is a generally determined research objective, it is necessary to work upon material gathered during visits to communities, even if it is fragmented or incomplete. This is why, it is not always possible to contrast or compare hypothesis and ideas, make additional recollections or ask again about certain topics. However, this is not the main purpose of the methodology of reconstruction of historical memory from the perspective that was proposed. As such it is more important what victims say – or don't say– than corroborating a hypothesis that has been previously developed in a deductive process, disconnected from the particular context. At this point, the limits of the socio-political and the scientific context are reached, since the first determines a specific action framework, and the second one demands the fulfilling of a set of parameters and conditions that can't always be considered.

The Scientific Context

The reconstruction of historical memory can be subscribed to the field of knowledge, denominated as field of human rights, repressed memories and political violence (Jelin, 2003). This field was configured during the 1960s (20th century) and was consolidated during the 1990s. For Castillejo (2009) this field is characterised by its interdisciplinary nature and its connection to intellectual traditions that raise questions regarding the way in which representations from the past are produced and used.

As a field of knowledge, the field of human rights, repressed memories and political violence postulates conceptual and methodological statements that characterise researchers inscribed to it. First, its main question explores the past. Second, it understands memory as a process, as a construction, as an arena of conflict in which there is a struggle for an imposition of a version of the past. Third, qualitative approaches are privileged and represented in the use of testimonies, narratives, photographs, artistic practices and other mechanisms used for presenting memories publically. Fourth, it aims to make victims visible, dignifying them and creating social consciousness regarding the violence they had to endure.

From this field the following questions emerge as important: localisation (from where is this work done), enunciation (from whose voices is it being spoken and who is listening) and narration (what is mentioned, omitted, how it is narrated and under what logic or institutional mandate). It also implies a work of reflexivity[5] (Bourdieu & Wacquant, 2005) in which the researcher asks about political, ethical and personal commitments that motivate his choice of working topics related with armed conflict, victims and memory. Hence, the subjectivity of who investigates becomes evident and his or her feelings, experiences and expectations are exposed. Therefore, questions regarding the work of reconstruction of historical memory not only have to make reference to *how, who* and *what for,* but also have to include: *who does it* and *from where.*

Methodologically, as stated before, the field privileges qualitative approach and the use of narratives. By this way it is intended to recreate memories, evidence the forgotten ones and rebuild stories that can tell something about the past. In doing this, techniques that allow the collective to remember as a group are carried out. Workshops, timelines, group interviews, social cartographies, etc., are used in a special way. In general, techniques that allow a reactivation of memory are used. In the framework of this research, the use of these techniques was a clear parameter for gathering information. However, the team was constantly pressured to involve quantitative paradigms from the use of figures and statistical data. It is important to point out that reconstruction of historical memory does not exclude the use of figures. On the contrary, the exercise of a dialogue between narratives and statistics can be extremely productive as long as it is proposed by the needs of the research and does not end up being an imposition of ideas or disciplinary premises.

This research adopted an inductive approach that followed the line of thought of methodological premises of construction of historical memory mentioned in this article, giving priority to the way participating victims define prominent events perpetrators, causes and effects of violence. By doing so, the voice of those affected by the conflict took a central place in the research. However, the approximation became distorted by a more deductive approach, which included previous hypothesis, the construction of timelines from secondary material such as newspapers, relevant literature and official reports, putting in second place key milestones or information that emerged from the victims´ testimonies or was gathered from non-official sources.

The attempt to achieve a balance between types of data (primary-secondary, qualitative-quantitative), the way of recollection and its validity failed in the sense that there was no serious discussion about the meaning, use and role that each type of data was going to have in the research. The relation between primary and secondary information should be complementary, without diminishing importance to the first one because the second one has weaknesses already mentioned and officially recognised. In this study case, for example, there were no numbers or figures regarding some phenomena, which obliged the researchers to give an even more central use to the testimonial material as it was the first time these phenomena were mentioned.

This way of constructing information (as timelines) from some testimonies given by victims is not based on deductive principles or statistical analyses that ensure representativeness, objectivity in data collection and a positivist position towards the research. The authors have been very conscious of this and therefore have chosen to give the qualitative data gathered a specific value, this means, as life stories, testimonies, lives and opinions. The authors have never intended to present them as homogeneous information regarding victims´ ways of thinking, acting, living and reacting.

The authors consider that testimonies are never used in excess if they aim to show the experiences of violence and suffering from the victims´ voices and understanding. In fact, one of the main premises of the work of historical memory is placing these voices at the forefront. In this case, the testimony lost relevance because space had to be given to statistical analysis of official sources and legal material about the development of laws related to the armed conflict in Colombia. The latter should have been part of a legal framework for the whole research and not another research question for victims. What is worse, this perspective became the starting point from where the interpretation and analysis of the testimonies should be done rather one result that could turn into policy recommendations.

A further difficulty has been the different objectives of the project, a project with a functionality that obeys different interests beyond the scientific one and therefore also includes some research questions that had to be answered in several ways, thus making more complex its methodological design and development. Concentrating on specific aspects for further analysis was extremely difficult because of the variety of aspects that had to be considered. Besides from each team´s research features, there were overarching ones such as gender, age, age groups, ethnicity as well as territorial, legal and public policy approaches. These demanded taking into account many elements at the same time without necessarily focusing on the ones that became relevant during fieldwork. This hindered the analysis of some aspects of which proper information was not found and diminished the time that could have been used for deepening the analysis of other key aspects that appeared or emerged as relevant.

This simultaneous multiplicity of objectives also hindered the development of workshops and memory reconstruction exercises because despite the resulting dynamic, they had to be included, creating an approach that was not only oriented to remembering violent acts experienced by victims and their re-signification of these, but to other topics that had to be included such as reparation policies and institutional responses. This demand, added to the short period of time planned for data recollection, resulted in exhausting work sessions for both, victims and research teams. These sessions always followed a procedure of question-answer and had no psychosocial support, which is an essential and necessary element in these types of inquiries.

Regarding the presentation of results and the writing of the final research report, several requirements had to be fulfilled as they should give account of the different objectives proposed initially and additionally, they must be directed at a heterogeneous audience. In many cases and erroneously, it is considered that the victims of the armed conflict lack the reading and intellectual capacity owned by individuals dedicated to the academic field. Therefore research reports are orientated towards expert audiences and other ways of presenting the research results in a way that is "easy" to understand are proposed for the victims. In that sense, the same rigour of research in social sciences is being expected of a report about reconstruction of historical memory without necessarily having the same purpose or function.

Even though the authors share the idea of demanding rigorousness, they do not agree with the fact that the use of official sources and statistic data will guarantee it in this case. They also disagree with the statement that in one single report different publics have to be addressed. There has to be a prioritisation regarding *who* is being addressed and with *what* purposes in order to determine a type of, a structure, a language and a specific content for the final report.

Finally, on the construction of knowledge inside the project, as mentioned in the institutional framework, the teams´ arrangement was interdisciplinary and the influence of different disciplines was asymmetric, generating an imbalance favouring legal, economic and public policies analysis perspectives over anthropological, sociological and cultural perspectives, that tend to analyse social expressions, in this case the expression of violence and memory rebuilding. Thus, this field was also characterised by the negotiation between approaches, perspectives adding another motive to the project´s discussion, differences and ineffectiveness. With this the authors do not want to reject the idea of interdisciplinary work. On the contrary, they want to highlight the need of proceeding throughout agreements, tasks division, deepening in areas and methodologies in order to build knowledge collectively and coherently.

The need of formulating public policy recommendations of attention to victims, the access to rights guaranteeing and to repairing dimensions by the end of the final report comes from a more consultative work rather than a research one. While it is possible to make general recommendations from the results found or give guidelines for eventual development of a specific policy, the objective of the work is not to resolve shortcomings or policy problems or to demand a particular institutional response. Rather, it is to identify them, make them visible and raise awareness about them. How to solve them is the responsibility of an additional analysis or a consultative work, if possible done by experts in translating social problems into effective regulations, as it is about recommendations that do not necessarily emerge from the completion of a couple of exercises of memory reactivation with a specific community victim of the conflict.

Challenges, Questions, and Lessons

The question about historical memory reconstruction in the midst of the armed conflict is political, methodological and ethical. Therefore, reflecting about this type of work has to become something vital and necessary for researchers that work in this field from institutional mandates or from communitarian experiences. This is the first major challenge and learning demanded by the work. The reflection exercise implies making the researcher interests, motivations and expectations explicit but also asking himself about the work itself. Demands and requirements are even bigger from a do no harm paradigm, which implies a constant surveillance of the work done in order to avoid damaging effects on the participants.

However, the development of a reflexive perspective when done from an institution is not simple to address because, as mentioned before, there are multiple factors and bureaucratic logics that turn the research exercise into a race seeking to delivering products, achieving goals, performing negotiations and responding to conceptual and methodological orientations that are not necessarily done including the research´s interests. This means responding to scientific criteria but responding to institutional interests and political criteria.

The research then becomes a scenario of constant negotiation, re-elaboration and adjustments seeking to fulfil victims´ and institutional expectations at the same time dealing with the stakes and risks implied in the research work. This generates the following questions, challenges and lessons:

Questions

A series of reflexive questions arose during the research because of the limits and demands of each context, as discussed previously. These questions appear when doing this type of work in the midst of the armed conflict and are presented with the intention of generating discussion.

The first and perhaps the most important question is: How convenient is it to perform the reconstruction of a past that has yet not passed? This means, interrogating the pertinence of reconstructing historical memory in the midst of the armed conflict. It is also necessary to generate a question regarding the aim of this reconstruction, to whom is it useful? What for? One must also think in terms of questions of the participants, which voices should be privileged, through what means, what could be the implications or consequences for those who decide to participate, how could the re-victimisation be avoided with these type of exercises?

What part of the population is willing to talk about victimising experiences when these narrations can generate more victimising actions or suffering? How can these narrations be proposed and memories triggered when pain and victimisation are present? How could the interference of violent ones be avoided in these types of processes? How can security be guaranteed to population that participates in these processes and to the research teams involved? What audience is the research outcomes expected to reach? How can memory be diffused to broader public? How can reparation be guaranteed from the reconstruction of historical memory?

Challenges

As discussed throughout this article, the challenges presented when reconstructing historical memory while the armed conflict is still going on are varied. In this case they were divided into those related to the institutional framework in which the research is carried out; to the socio-political context, that implies the armed conflict itself; and finally to the scientific parameters, which poses criteria and ways of proceeding and thinking which cannot always be implemented in a violent and politicised context.

A part of these challenges has to do with work done with victims and how to truly develop a do no harm approach. This, considering that the research proposal is to reconstruct memory of violent experiences, can place the population of victims in a risky situation and that many times institutional logic ends up obstructing the research. This raises challenges at a methodological level as it becomes necessary to innovate in this area with the intention of performing works that allow a greater closeness and participation of the victims.

Other challenges that arise here are the conceptual ones that demand that researchers involved in these types of works consider notions of memory, history, conflict, victims that are coherent and in accordance with the Colombian context. The utilised concept of duty of memory includes a series of statements and premises, partly from an European provenance and partly with a South American, in particular of the Southern Cone, which reflect realities that possibly do not necessarily relate to the current situation of Colombia. In this sense, constructing conceptual elaborations regarding memory is another big challenge that has to be assumed in a dialogue in which multidisciplinarity exists in order to complement and strengthen, and not in order to divide or fragment.

Lessons

From the research experience and the reflection of such experience the authors return to the basic questions made when reconstructing historical memory and validate them as a necessary part of the research activities. In this sense, the first lesson is always asking: in what field of knowledge are we? What does the research in this field demand? How do we define our research object? What are the adequate methodological strategies for the research´s development? How can the subject-researcher and subject-researched relations be built? What kink of outcome should be reached? How can the research´s results be "given back" and presented to a broader audience? For whom is it written?

Doing research from an institutional context requires, as well as from an academic one, an understanding of the topic and the research question, acknowledging what its purposes are, what it should reach and under what criteria. The exercise of placing oneself in a field of knowledge, laying out or defining an object of research, constructing questions and hypothesis and proposing methodological approaches is valid in the duty of reconstructing memories and historical memory. A research of this style developed in an armed conflict´s framework demands a constant revision and adjustment of the design of the research in order to create an account of the reality that is faced in the collection of information. In this sense, the reconstruction of memory demands not only an adequate methodological approach but also a flexible one that allows a response to the different expectations of those who narrate their stories of violence and pain and the institutional demands of reconstructing certain past and the violence situation of a country that is still immersed in an armed conflict.

Indeed, facing the mandate of reconstructing historical memory, of pointing out the voices of conflict victims and with daily events such as terrorist attacks, kidnappings, murders, etc., is not performed by remembering the past from the present in order to find a meaning to what happened, but rather by remembering the past from the present and still keep on living it. In that sense the task is not only to re-signify but to denounce the life conditions that allow the perpetration of such past, so that immediate actions that seek to guarantee human rights can be taken and hopefully be more optimistic about future expectations.

Here, the victims´ voices become completely relevant because from these voices the narrative of memory is thread and also because they allow to understand why the past does not cease and how violence is lived at present time. These voices, that seem to be strong sources of information, move towards the constitution of political subjects and citizens that demand a rigorous fulfilment of their rights. Thus, it is important to ask, if the researcher willing to understand that he is not dealing with an object of investigation – i.e. memories – but rather, that he has established a subject based relation that visits the past and raises demands and claims in the moment in which hearing these voices becomes urgent.

The previous question is not easy to solve, especially when the work of memory reconstruction gets constantly confused with the work of gathering the truth of what happened and also when institutional bureaucracy usually obstructs the managing of resources and time that the current political context and violence demands. There is also the institutional mandate that implies a series of limits for the work of memories reconstruction in a context of violence. Limits referred to contractual objects, working equipment, economic resources, research times, products to deliver and even epistemological demands where the use of testimonies or figures becomes mandatory.

In this regard, it is necessary to mention that there is not one single epistemological, conceptual or methodological approach in order to reconstruct historical memory. However, an interesting option is the approach through a qualitative, narrative and experiential procedure since historical memory reconstruction demands putting the voices of its protagonists – the victims of violence – at the forefront. This does not exclude the incorporation of other sources of information such as the one gathered through press releases, academic studies, film and literary sources, official figures, etc.

Here, statistical perspective is not necessarily excluded. On the contrary, it allows us to measure the phenomenon of violence in broader scales, as well as to find trends and correlations between variables. In terms of research it can be used as a backdrop, a second referent, as an element in order to create dialogue between the context and the experience (victims´ voices) or simply to show a different perspective upon the studied episode of violence.

In personal terms, researching in the midst of the Colombian armed conflict and performing workshops and exercises in areas where there is a presence of armed actors, dangers and risks, demands a special disposition of the researcher and an essential social and human commitment. Otherwise, it is not possible to explain how an academic, an expert or a scientist, decides consciously to get involved in these types of complicated contexts, giving up of certain comforts and going to the places where victims have something to say. Returning to everyday working and personal life becomes difficult for the researcher once the fieldwork is over. The links and bonds created with these people during the research and fieldwork and their human suffering usually becomes more than just a researcher-subject relation and narrations tend to leave a strong mark on the researchers. The contribution for understanding what is really happening in Colombia is invaluable and by leaving his desk, figures, reports and other secondary sources, the researcher experiences a change in his practice which challenges him to question about his work, roll, objectives, professional goals and contributions to a better understanding of what has happened and is still happening in the country.

RECOMMENDATIONS FOR THE WORK OF RECONSTRUCTION OF HISTORICAL MEMORY IN CONTEXTS OF CONFLICT

In this sense and from the authors' own experience the following recommendations are presented:

1. Placing victims´ narratives in the forefront, their voices, feelings, expressions, etc. This way the use of testimonies becomes fundamental and never excessive, on the contrary, its use allows illustrating a situation from experience and thus raises awareness regarding violence and suffering. In addition, through testimonies, new aspects, facts and strategies become known that could not be found or identified by other means.
2. Prioritising the use of testimony does not mean discarding other information sources or types; on the contrary, it is possible to thread complex realities from testimonies, secondary documents, press releases, statistical analysis, etc. Historical memory implies reconstructing complex contexts and in order to achieve this it is required to appeal to and validate diverse sources of information. What needs to be cleared is the role that each information source is going to play in the research as well as its value.
3. Historical memory´s reconstruction, that is, a reconstruction that depends on established intersubjective relations, context conditions, the narrator´s interests and expectations of an institution. Under this measure, the research questions must be orientated towards how this is process done, how specific memories are re-signified through construction of memory, what confrontations are faced by imposing an official version, generally, questions should ask about how sense is given to the past -rather than asking about the past itself- (Jelin, 2001; Castillejo, 2009).
4. This enables responding to the questions proposed by Riaño regarding the pertinence of this type of research: What is the research´s contribution to the research subjects? (Riaño, Memorias Metodológicas, 2007). For us, the answer is in turning the research exercise into a platform in order to politically empower, and through this begin to reclaim the guaranteeing of truth, justice and reparation rights. For this it is necessary to understand that historical memory reconstrcuction is a long and demanding process, especially when done from harmless action research perspectives. Therefore, research dedicated to this topic should contemplate wise and prudent implementation time without limits of time stipulated from institutionality or funding sources. In particular this regards institutional research that have the goal of achieveing and fulfillng the duty of memory.
5. Reconstruction of historical memory should involve the questioning of ethnographic authority (Riaño, Memorias Metodológicas, 2007, p. 10) this is, questioning the role played by researchers, their methods and truths. Horizontal knowledge relationships should be established with the subject, in this case the victims, recognising their voices, epistemological places and powers within the relation. In general, making of the process of historical memory reconstruction a shared and committed project.
6. Finally, space and time should be granted in order to think about and validate the process of forgetting. Even though historical memory emphasises going back to the past through memories, silence, forgetting and leaving the past behind must also be alternatives for victims. The authors are referring here to the happiness of something that has been forgotten which is mentioned by Ricoeur (2008) when the action of not remembering becomes an option and not an imposition. Working historical memory therefore involves a deep respect towards victims´ options and the legitimacy of both the right of forgetting and the right of remembering.

With these series of recommendations the authors aim to contribute to the discussion about reconstruction of historical memory, not from theory but from practice. Secondly, they hope to understand this contribution as part of a process of reflection researchers working on the reconstruction of memory need to do. It is useful and beneficial to express the difficulties, challenges, and lessons that emerged from this experience. Sharing these thoughts and reflections with other researchers of this field is a compromise between historical memory and the ethics and political implications it generates. It also contributes to a more human understanding of this approach and the work carried out by researchers committed to it. Therefore this type of research point to a constant reflection of what has to be done, how it has to be done, with whom and for whom, in order to continue questioning the work of historical memory reconstruction in a context where the justification for the existence of this approach, the armed conflict, is still going on.

REFERENCES

Bourdieu, P., & Wacquant, L. (2005). Una invitación a la sociología reflexiva. Buenos Aires, Argentina: Siglo XXI Editores.

Castillejo, A. (2009). *Los archivos del dolor. Ensayos sobre la violencia y el recuerdo en la Sudáfrica contemporánea.* Bogotá: Universidad de los Andes CESU.

Centro Nacional de Memoria Histórica. (2013). Basta Ya. Colombia: memorias de guerra y dignidad. Bogotá: Imprenta Nacional.

Comisión Nacional de Reparación y Reconciliación. (2009). Recordar y narrar el conflicto. Herramientas para reconstruir memoria histórica. Bogotá: Fotoletras S.A.

de la República de Colombia, C. (2005). *Ley 975 de 2005 por la cual se dictan disposiciones para la reincorporación de miembros de grupos armados organizados al margen de la ley que contribuyan de manera efectiva a la consecusión de la paz nacional y se dictan otras disposiciones para acuerdos humanitarios.* Colombia.

Huyssen, A. (2000). En busca del tiempo futuro. *Revista Puentes, 1*(2). Argentina.

Jelin, E. (2001). Los trabajos de la memoria. Madrid: Siglo XXI Editores.

Passerini, L. (2006). *Memoria y utopía. La primacía de la intersubjetividad* (1st ed.). España: Publicacions de la Universitat de València.

Reátegui. (2009). En: International Center for Transitional Justice Colombia (2009). *Recordar en conflicto: iniciativas no oficiales de memoria en Colombia.* Bogotá: Unión Europea.

Reyes Mate, M. (2011). *Auschwitz, justicia y deber de memoria.* Fronterad. Retrieved from http://fronterad.com/?q=auschwitz-justicia-y-deber-de-la-memoria&page=0,0

Riaño, P. (2006). *Jóvenes, memoria y violencia en Medellín. Una antropología del recuerdo y el olvido.* Medellín: Editorial Universidad de Antioquia, ICAHN.

Riaño, P. (2007). Memorias Metodológicas. Revista de Estudios Sociales.

Ricoeur, P. (2008). La memoria, la historia, el olvido. Buenos Aires: Fondo de Cultura Económica.

KEY TERMS AND DEFINITIONS

Bandas Criminales (BACRIM): "Criminal groups" term that refers to new emerging groups of organized crime and drug trafficking in Colombia adopted after the demobilization process of paramilitaries in 2003 and 2006.

Centro Nacional de Memoria Histórica (CNMH): National Centre for Historical Memory. Public institution that succeeded the GMH, officially created by the Law of Victims and Land Restitution (Law 1448/2011) and with a broader mandate that the GMH. Official website: www.centrodememoriahistorica.gov.co.

Comisión Nacional de Reparación y Reconciliación (CNRR): National Commission for Reparation and Reconciliation. Created in Colombia by the Justice and Peace Law (Law 975/2005, article 50) as part of the transitional justice program and for a period of 8 years. One of the components of this commission was the creation of a special unit to investigate and narrate the reasons and the evolution of the armed conflict giving a central role to the victims. This unit was called *Grupo de Memoria Histórica-GMH* (Historical Memory Group) and was in charge of distinguished scholars, experts on Colombian political history, sociology, anthropology and social work.

Ejército de Liberación Nacional (ELN): National Liberation Army, is also a leftist guerrilla organization, smaller than the FARC-EP, but also considered as a terrorist group by some states (Colombia, USA, among others) since it actively participate in the armed conflict through military operations in different parts of the country.

Fuerzas Armadas Revolucionarias de Colombia - Ejército del Pueblo (FARC-EP): Revolutionary armed forces of Colombia – People's Army, are a leftist guerrilla organization that actively participates in the armed conflict for over 50 years. Some states classify it as a terrorist group (Colombia, USA among others) and it is well known for kidnaping, extortion, bombing oil pipelines and electrical power towers, illegal mining as well as drug production and trafficking.

ENDNOTES

1 Centro Nacional de Memoria Histórica (2013). *¡Basta ya!: Colombia: memorias de guerra y dignidad*. Bogotá: Centro Nacional de Memoria Histórica: DPS. Departamento para la Prosperidad Social.

2 The official website is: www.centrodememoriahistorica.gov.co. It contains all the material (books, reports, videos, etc.) produced by the Group and the Center for free consultation.

3 These figures are subject to discussion because they have not been done systematically and judiciously hence underreporting of the armed conflict. The Government has made an important effort in order to gather all the information in the *RUV –Registro Único de Víctimas-* (Official Record of Victims). However, this record only includes victims from 1985 onwards leaving an important number of historical victims ignored. This situation, regarding the gathering of information, has been and still is a significant discussion in the country.

4 This is also a very important (political and legal) discussion in the country: How should these actors be classified? What consequences does this type of classification imply?

5 Reflexivity is understood here from the proposal of Pierre Bourdieu (Bourdieu & Wacquant, 2005) in which reflection about the research work becomes an epistemological imperative for whom performs the investigation. With this not only the subject of knowledge but also the political and moral compromises are stated.

Chapter 19
Different Paths to Peace Building:
A Comparative Analysis of DDR Programs in Colombia and the Province of Aceh, Indonesia

Javier Cardenas
Universidad de los Andes, Colombia

Nadia Stefania Pérez
Universidad del Rosario, Colombia

Sergio Triana
University of Cambridge, UK

ABSTRACT

Since the first implementation of a modern DDR program, implemented in Namibia in 1989, more than 60 programs became the initial stage of a stabilization process in countries, in which national governments and irregular forces have ended hostilities, reached a ceasefire or signed a peace agreement. This document aims to provide a comparative analysis between two of them: the reintegration policy led by Colombia and Indonesia, from a description of these DDR processes and the general experiences that have been accumulated through the DDR processes in both countries. This paper makes a brief analysis of the political contexts that were conductive to the implementation of the reintegration process in both cases, describes the challenges faced and currently being faced by these processes, pointing out the strategies to address them and the role of international cooperation. The analysis will be framed during the peace process and DDR program in Aceh, Indonesia, and the Republic of Colombia, since 2003 until nowadays.

DOI: 10.4018/978-1-4666-9675-4.ch019

INTRODUCTION

The process of disarmament, demobilization and reintegration (DDR) is considered by many practitioners and theorists as a key phase in a peace process. Modern DDR processes arose in the late eighties with the aim of becoming a tool to build stability after settling a formal peace agreement or adoption of a ceasefire in context of post war torn situations. These processes had a set of activities, which include interventions and operations, like controlled discharge of combatants from armed groups, the collection and documentation of heavy weapons, ammunition, small arms, as well as short-term transitional assistance designed to cover the basic needs of ex combatants and their families. As their first implementations, DDR mechanisms included safety allowances, such as food, medical services, clothes, training and occasionally also employment.

Once the fall of the Berlin wall and the end of Cold War occurred, employment of several stabilization and peace building missions, undertaken by international organizations like the United Nations, became frequent, in order to deal with a growing number of internal conflicts in regions such as Africa and Asia. Since the first implementation of a modern DDR program, which was implemented in Namibia in 1989 (Meek, & Mallan, 2004), more than 60 programs became the initial stage of a stabilization process in countries, in which national governments and irregular forces have ended hostilities, reached a ceasefire or signed a peace agreement (other typical cases reported are Burundi, Côte d'Ivoire, Democratic Republic of the Congo, Haiti, Liberia, Sudan, Indonesia, Rwanda, among others).

The degree of success of these programs greatly varies, especially since there are no unified indicators to measure it. Still, the international community agrees on recognizing cases of successful reintegration, such as Colombia, Indonesia and Rwanda (Edmonds, Mills & McNamee, 2009). These cases are recognized by its best practices, the sustainability of improvement, their contribution to greater development processes and the achieved peace. This document aims to provide a comparative analysis between reintegration policy led by Colombia and Indonesia, from a description of these DDR processes and the general experiences that have been accumulated through the DDR processes in both countries. Under the idea of highlighting the efforts that have been developed in Colombia and Indonesia on reinsertion, reincorporation and reintegration over time, this paper makes a brief analysis of the political contexts that were conductive to the implementation of the reintegration process in both cases, describes the challenges faced and currently being faced by these processes, pointing out the strategies to address them and the role of international cooperation. The analysis will be framed during the peace process and DDR program in Aceh, Indonesia, and the Republic of Colombia, since 2003 until nowadays.

BACKGROUND

Over the years, DDR programs have been considered as a fundamental component for an effective transition from conflict to peace. Ultimately DDR processes have been considered as largely standardized techniques and procedures that include lessons learned from other crisis situations. Most of them were carried out without a previous design or theorization, and thus their evolution was mainly determined by trial and error. Later on, literature based on the experiences started to emerge. The Stockholm Initiative on Disarmament, Demobilization and Reintegration (SIDDR) in 2005, the Integrated DDR Standards of the United Nations (IDDRS) in 2006, the Cartagena Contribution to DDR (CIDDR) of 2009, and the First Global DDR Summit (2013), in which experiences on peace, rural development, technical cooperation and DDR in different parts of the world were discussed, are some of the examples.

Traditional DDR literature focused on short-term goals and emphasized the topic of security and stabilization in post conflict situations. It also gave priority to determine which mechanisms and technical components would ensure DDR success. This first generation was mainly explored by political or other social scientists (Stankovic and Torjesen, 2010). Later on the focus of the DDR research was expanded and started to include new factors. Now also medium and long-term goals of DDR were included and its importance to peace building and the development of the country were highlighted. Rather than only focusing on standardized procedures, literature started to pay attention to contexts, and relationships between DDR and its environment. This second generation tries to understand the dynamics of DDR with other essential topics, such as transitional justice, institutional capacities and reparation of victims. Other disciplines, such as anthropology, econometrics, psychology, geography and public health are now exploring DDR research.

Nevertheless, comparative analyses on DDR are still scarce and limited. This paper aims at helping to overcome the shortage of academic literature on the topic and contributes to a better understanding of the situation.

DDR IN PERSPECTIVE: COLOMBIA AND ACEH, INDONESIA

Colombia

Up to now, Colombia faces the longest internal armed conflict in the Western Hemisphere (Laplante and Theidon, 2007). Although the conflict started at the end of the 40's, as a violent confrontation between the two main political parties (Liberal and Conservative Party) it has been growing away from its original ideological purpose. Many factors contributed to trigger and fuel the conflict, including political exclusion of left parties during the National Front period (1958-1974); strong centralization of the State resulting in its weak presence in different regions and peripheral zones; inadequate distribution of land, extreme poverty, among other social inequalities.

During the 70´s and 80´s the emergence of new actors such as drugs-trafficking organizations, right-wing paramilitary groups, and self-defense forces, transformed the ideological feature of the conflict, enhancing the focus towards economic factors. Confrontation spread throughout the whole territory, and violence, –confined to rural and periphery areas until then -, reached urban and strategic areas (Pizarro Leongomez, 2004). Financial autonomy of illegal groups, as a result of their participation in illicit activities, reduced their need of popular support to survive and changed their interests and objectives (Echandia, 2000). The evolution of the conflict has allowed the growth of criminal dynamics that made the conflict even more complex. Hence, finding exclusively a political solution to the conflict is insufficient, and structural change is needed in order to achieve peace.

Throughout the years, most of the public support of illegal groups has faded. Constant attacks on civil population, forced displacement, and massive violation of human rights including children recruitment, perpetuated by illegal groups, has undermined the legitimacy of all actors involved. Therefore, reintegrating ex-combatants into communities represents a huge challenge.

Up to 2012, the conflict has claimed over 218.000 deaths, up to 5 million of displaced people, and more than 27.000 kidnappings (Centro de Memoria Historica, 2013), besides significant economic costs to Colombia in terms of lack of development and opportunities. The conflict continues after over six decades. Accordingly, the Colombian case displayed a lack of State capacity to provide security and maintain the monopoly of power, which has been changing in the last decade. Hence, the Colombian internal conflict may share more similarities with other conflicts in Asia or Africa than with other type conflicts and violence in the Americas.

Indonesia

The intrastate conflict between the province of Aceh and the central government of Indonesia started in 1976 when first incompatibilities were addressed. The conflict is a result of combined factors such as territorial disputes, religious and economical grievance, and criminal organizations. The province of Aceh is located at the northern-west tip of the Indonesian island of Sumatra. It has known a long period of insurgencies, fighting the Dutch and the British since 1873. In 1976 a descendent of the Sultan`s dynasty, Hasan de Tiro, formed the Free Aceh Movement (*Gerakan Aceh Merdeka* GMA) and declared the independence of Aceh. The Indonesian government initiated military response to the insurgencies. In 1989 the Aceh province was declared a military zone and the ensuing war led to massive human rights violations committed by both sides, killings, disappearances, tortures, forced displacement and countless deaths (Froedin, 2008).

This region is known for being rich in natural resources such as oil and natural gas, but suffered from an uneven repartition of wealth. These grievances were a key trigger for the conflict. In 1970 only 5% of the revenue from oil exploitation went to the local government (Uppsala Database, 24/02/2015). All revenues went to Jakarta and the province of Aceh could slightly benefit from its own resources. In addition, the land appropriation and trans-migration inflicted a negative impact on the region's development. Resentment at perceived inequalities in the flow of rents gave a significant popular support to the GAM's cause. Peasants and rebels fought for the same objectives, and the ones who did not take the arms, largely supported the ones in the front. There was a strong link between the armed rebels and its base support, opposing to the Colombian case.

Aceh would have been the door of entry of Islam into Indonesia, but it distinguishes itself from the rest of Indonesia for its more conservative form of Islam. Leaders felt distant from Jakarta, which promoted a unified Indonesian culture and cared little for the local needs and customs of the province. But religion would not have been the main reason for the conflict, as GMA never intended to create a fundamentalist Islam State. It would nevertheless have been a unifying factor in the Acehnese nationalism (Beck, 2007)

Between 2002 and 2004, GMA lost 50% of its members, including its commander due to martial law. This put the GAM members in a difficult position to continue their cause. On the other hand, the new president and vice-president elected in 2004 favored a political rather than a military approach to ending the Aceh civil war. At the beginning of 2004, conditions to negotiate the end of the conflict were slowly beginning to emerge. But it was not until the end of the year that they were accelerated. On December 2004, a tsunami affected the whole area. The aftermath of the tsunami led to a ceasefire and cessation of hostilities in the disputed area. The Indonesian government temporarily removed restriction to north Sumatra to allow humanitarian help. In 2005 the GMA and the Indonesian government signed the Memorandum of Understanding (MoU) in Helsinki. GMA agreed to disarm and the government agreed to withdraw all military forces by the end of 2005. Hasan di Tiro, founder of the rebel movement was allowed to return to Indonesia on the 11th of October 2008 after 30 years of exile (*Aljazeera*, October 2008). Conflict has officially terminated following the peace agreement signed in 2005 in Helsinki.

The Aceh conflict claimed an estimated 30,000 lives, displaced 400,000 people, and approximately 39 percent of the population consider themselves to be victims of conflict. The conflict damage and losses have been estimated at USD 10.7 billion (Multi-Stakeholder Review of Post-Conflict Programming, MSR, 2010).

As shown by the brief context, there are significant similarities between these two case studies. They both have faced a long internal conflict, which has configured their social, economic and political dynamics. Geography played a key part of the conflict, as the central State presence was weak in the conflicted areas, and gave comparative advantages to the illegal groups. Thus, a stronger non-military State presence is one of the biggest challenges in post conflict contexts. Moreover, during both conflicts, there have been more than two parties involved. The different and often opposing interests of the various stakeholders resulted in a more complicated peace process while prolonging the development of an integral solution. Furthermore, economic resources are not the main cause of the conflict, but along the years became an essential variable that needs to be address in order to put an end to the conflict.

However, some differences can also be found. Islamic practices in the Province of Aceh have influenced social practices and contributed to unify Aceh inhabitants. In this aspect, Indonesia has certain advantage over the Colombian case; the religion of Islam has a strong influence on all parts of society and therefore acts as a unifying factor, which facilitated the finding of an approach of dealing with the situation that is understandable for all parts of the society and with which the majority can identify themselves. In Colombia the case is different. Although the majority of the population is catholic, it does not have such a deep influence on the society and culture as it has in the case of Islam. Therefore the common ground of understanding that is given through common religious values does not exist, making it harder to find a solution that includes all believes of the society. Additionally, a major natural catastrophe in the Province of Aceh forced parties to reach an agreement, while in Colombia conflict has continued regardless of minor natural tragedies.

The particularities of each case have transformed and conditioned the ways the government and other stakeholders react to the challenges they faced. Thus, although significant similarities can be found between the Province of Aceh and Colombia, their approach to DDR program has been widely different and addressing diverse needs. The next sections will describe and explain how each DDR was designed, develop and carried out.

THE LONG PATH TO PEACE: EVOLUTION OF PEACE BUILDING AND DDR

Colombia

Colombia has made many attempts to negotiate peace with different armed groups and put an end to the internal conflict. In the last twenty years, diverse approaches have failed to deal with radical demands from the Revolutionary Armed Forces of Colombia (FARC) and the inflexibility of other sectors influencing the country's economic and politics.

The Belisario Betancur administration (1982-1986) was the first one to initiate a negotiated solution in 1982, declaring amnesty. Meanwhile, the FARC focused on their political party Patriotic Union (UP), and Betancur believed their political participation would lead FARC on the path of legality. But both actors failed to assume their responsibilities, leading to a relapse of the conflict (Posso, 2004).

At the same time, the government also had negotiations with the guerrilla movement M-19 that ended in the Agreement of Corinto where a ceasefire was agreed as well as the demobilization of the guerrillas. The National Rehabilitation Plan was set up to contribute to reinsertion of former combatants. The M-19 gave up weapons and became the political party *Alianza Democrática M-19,* renouncing to armed struggle and willing to implement changes in the country by legal means. They achieved favorable electoral results at a local level and participated in forging the 1991 Constitution, as a part of the Constituent Assembly. Their M19 influence has been declining with their integration into the democratic system.

The 1991 Constitution was an attempt to bring together all sectors of society, so they could determine a political democratic system that would include them all, and put an end to the armed conflict. It addressed some issues such as social exclusion, inequalities and minorities' rights, which also contributed to mitigate some insurgent groups. However, the ideological feature of the main guerrillas had changed and the Constitution was not enough to put an end to the conflict.

In the early 1990s, the FARC, the National Liberation Army (ELN), and the Popular Liberation Army (EPL) worked together on developing a common position for negotiations through the Simon Bolívar Guerrilla Coordination Body (CGSB). The government agreed to initiate new negotiations for the first time outside the country, in Venezuela where four rounds of talks were held in Caracas in 1991. Time was spent on negotiating the conditions of a ceasefire, and meanwhile the FARC took the opportunity to increase their military positions. The government refused to make a consensus and both parties failed to find a common ground. Negotiations were suspended with the rapid escalation of violent events, leading to the declaration of "integral war" and a political crisis. The only negotiations that took place in 1997 were on humanitarian matters and prisoners exchanges (Fernandez, Garcia-Duran, & Sarmiento, 2004).

From 1998 to 2002, the Pastrana administration and its policy of new state initiated a new round of negotiations. At the same period Colombia witnessed a change in military relations, with multiplications of paramilitary presence in agriculture, coca, oil area and drugs and arms trafficking. Government security forces also increased with the support of the United States' "war on drugs" through Plan Colombia, being also used against insurgencies. The Demilitarized Zone (DMZ) was a main condition to peace talks. The DMZ was a zone free of all military activities. The rebels could use it as a haven but instead used it to reinforce their military capacities and engage into drug-trafficking (CNN, 12/08/2012). International backing was at the lowest point, with the FARC being labeled by the USA as "the most dangerous terrorist group" (Washington Times, 19/03/2002), leading to a massive loss of popular support. A decisive turnover was in 2002 with the end of the demilitarized zone which led to the end of negotiations.

In 2002 the United Self-Defense Forces (AUC) decided upon a ceasefire and entered formal negotiations with the Colombian government. After the signed of the Ralito II Accord, AUC announced they would demobilize by the end of 2005. A legislation *Ley de Justicia y Paz*[1] (Justice and Peace Law) was put in forward to establish a transitional justice framework and guarantee "contribution to achieving national peace, collaboration with the justice system, reparation for the victims, and adequate re-socialization" (ICTJ, 2012). The AUC would have demobilized completely by 2006. Some leaders also have been extradited in 2008 to the US after refusing to comply with the Peace and Justice Law. If rebels could comply with the government and benefit from a special treatment, victims did not have a special right to reparation or apologies. This gap triggered social conflicts and slowed down the reintegration of former combatants. More than 6.5 million people have registered as victims of the armed conflict in Colombia, and now peace negotiations in La Havana are looking at addressing their rights and allowing them to be spokesmen for their condition.

After the death of the FARC top leader Alfonso Cano in 2011, President Manuel Santos initiated in 2012 the current peace negotiations with the FARC, first in Norway and then in Cuba's capital. They address the end of the armed conflict, the land reform, guarantees for the exercise of political opposition and citizen participation, drug trafficking and the rights of the victims of the conflict. The government still battles to find a better balance between central government control and local autonomy, to implement an effective state presence in remote areas and provide the guerrillas from replacing the state`s prerogatives. Public opinion still has to be convinced; forgiveness should be anticipated by truth commission in order to move population towards a common peace.

If the negotiations were to succeed, between 8000 and 10000 combatants would demobilize. Most importantly, they would need to be reintegrated into society. This presents a challenge since Colombian social fabric is affected after 60 years of conflict. Important questions remain unresolved, such as, how they are all going to be reintegrated? Will they enter politics? What will be done with their weapons? (Nussio and Howe, 2010). These questions should be addressed in further research and continue to be a central issue in the public debate.

Indonesia

In the case of Aceh, before the Helsinki peace talks, which led to the final Peace Agreement, several negotiations failed due to the incompatibilities between the parties. However, in 2004 the situation changed after a tsunami devastated Indonesia, and raised international community's attention on Indonesia, and specially the Aceh Province. The catastrophe made GAM start to take steps towards a peaceful cooperation, by declaring a unilateral ceasefire in order to facilitate the work of the emergency assistance. Meanwhile, Central government temporarily removed restrictions to north Sumatra to allow humanitarian help deployment. Moreover, external pressure was added, as the existence of a peace process was a condition of the international community in order to start paying out funds for the reconstruction process. The opportune intervention of the Finland Government and its Crisis Management Initiative (CMI), who had the support of both the Indonesian Central Government and the GAM, help to build trust and credibility to carry out the peace process (Aspinall, 2005).

After a difficult start of negotiations, involved actors managed to solve crucial problems such as the territorial status of Aceh, the number of remaining troops in this territory, as well as the formation of formal parties. While the foregoing ceasefire agreements did not treat the main grievances of the problem, the "Memorandum of Understanding" (MoU), signed on August of 2005, included all main topics of the conflict. The Memorandun of Understanding addressed 6 general points:

- **Governing of Aceh:** Indonesian Government granted self-governance to Aceh, which received autonomy in most of public issues[2]. The region of Aceh would now be consulted with respect to international agreements and had the right to have its own flag and hymn. The government also facilitated the creation of Aceh political parties.

In addition, the MOU allowed Aceh to raise funds and set its own interest rates beyond those set by the Central Bank. It earned jurisdiction on its natural resources and its territorial sea, and could retain 70% of its revenues from these natural resources.

- **Human Rights:** A Truth and Reconciliation Commission was to be created, and military personnel responsible of crimes would be trialed in front of a Human Rights Court. A legal code for Aceh would be drafted on the universal principles of human rights.
- **Amnesty and Reintegration in Society:** General Amnesty was granted to all GAM members and prisoners who were involved in the insurgency, except to those who committed crimes, and granting them all rights, including the right to political participation. Around 500 GAM members in exile

also received amnesty, including Hasan di Tiro, founder of the rebel movement, who was allowed to return to Indonesia after 30 years of exile. The amnesties were implemented rapidly to gain trust from GAM, and so already two days after the signing of the MoU ex-combatants were released. Nevertheless, disputes arose about the ex-combatants having committed crimes or not. After the amnesty, the decommissioning should take place in 4 phases.

The Disarmament, Demobilization and Reintegration (DDR) process was designed focusing on three main groups: GAM ex-combatants and supporters, amnestied political prisoners and civilians (Froedin, 2008). After decades of war, almost every sector of Indonesia was affected somehow by the conflict. The peace agreement was facing the challenge of reintegrating 25.000 ex-GAM combatants, active supporters and associated dependents into society.

- **Security Arrangements:** Hostilities would end with the signing of MOU. GMA agreed to disarm and the government agreed to withdraw all military forces by the end of 2005. GAM was required to demobilize 3000 troops and hand in 840 weapons. In exchange Indonesia had to withdraw all non-organic military and police, and effectives had to be reduced to 14700 military and 9100 police officers.
- **Establishment of the Aceh Monitoring Mission:** The Aceh Monitoring Mission had to established, including European Union and ASEAN countries, in order to monitor the demobilization of the GAM, the decommissioning of the weapons, the redeployment of non-organic military and police, the human rights situation, the legislative change and the application of the amnesty.
- **Dispute Settlement:** If disputes were to be raised regarding the implementation of the MoU, they were to be solved by the Head of Monitoring Mission, in dialogue with the parties, and with all parties providing required information.

There were several reasons that finally lead to the signing of the peace agreement. As a starting point, the humanitarian crisis caused by the Tsunami, facilitated cooperation for both sides. Through this inevitable cooperation, trust in the process was developed by all the parties involved. It furthermore allowed the international community to exercise more pressure in pushing the peace process forward, by granting humanitarian and strong financial assistance and allowing international monitoring of the process. Also the international training in Helsinki in accordance to the reintegration of the ex-combatants contributed to peace in Indonesia.

Finally, it facilitated the process that the agreements in the MoU were kept quite general and simple. Nevertheless, there are various points of the MoU that have not been implemented yet, for example a judicial process for human rights violations and historic memory. Although the MoU can be regarded as successful, further challenges for a stable peace in Indonesia are the sustainability of the agreement, the economic development of the Aceh region and high crime rates.

One of the core issues of peace negotiations is the trust in the process. As shown by both cases, international participation and support help to build this confidence, but is not enough. National public support turns out to be decisive to the sustainability of the process and to facilitate the implementation of the agreements. In this sense, Aceh demonstrates that a strong popular support for the GAM's cause increased the trust in the process and promoted the participation of civil society. On the other hand, the lack of support and acceptance of the illegal groups' discourse by civil society has obstructed the confidence in the process, in the Colombian case. Since building trust is a process that grows along with negotiations, peace processes should be open to the public, as the case of Aceh, and involved parties should be interested in providing enough information so the civil society can better understand and take part into it. Although a peace agreement could be reach without social support, its implementation cannot be done without it.

Moreover, Aceh's experience shows that negotiating general issues during the peace process can contribute to reach agreements in shorter time. This can be positive to end a long-term conflict and start implementing actions for peace-building. As shown in the Colombian case, a detailed and specify agenda to negotiate upon, could prolong the time to reach agreements, or even worst to make it impossible. However, agreements that tend to be too general could also be problematic as some core issues could be left unattended if there is not enough political will. Neither approach (general or specific agenda) can guarantee a successful peace process, unless there is genuine political will and interests by stakeholders to carry on with their responsibilities. In this sense, mechanisms for accountability should be set from the beginning.

Although both Colombia and Indonesia have negotiated with the main armed group in the conflict, they both have failed to carry out a comprehensive peace process, leaving unattended sectors that can become potential spoilers of the peace-building process. One of the main lessons from the two cases is that the peace processes need to take into account all stakeholders involved. In most cases, explicitly include all actors in a peace agreement is simply not possible. However, the implementation of the agreements should bear in mind all sectors, and find different mechanisms and common ground to collectively build peace.

Finally, different experiences around the world, and specially these two cases illustrate the importance of including during the peace process programs dealing with ex combatants in the aftermath of the conflict. There has been plenty of debate around the issue of whether former combatants should receive favorable treatment in comparison with ordinary civilians or other affected groups. However, failing to attend their needs would most likely evolved into a relapse of the conflict and certainly will fuel to instability in the transition phase. Thus, DDR policy needs to be plan while negotiating peace. Now it will be explain how these two countries faced the challenge of designing a DDR program.

TAILOR MADE DDR PROGRAMS AND LOCAL OWNERSHIP

Colombia

In Colombia, the current public policy dealing with ex-combatants' reincorporation into civil life started in 2003 with the Reincorporation into Civil Life Program (PRVC for its initials in Spanish), which was carried out until 2006 by the Ministry of Interior and Justice. Its main goal was to provide humanitarian aid to former combatants, right after a peace agreement was reached between the Government of Colombia and the united self-defense Forces of Colombia AUC (Alta Consejeria para la Reintegración, 2010).

Since the beginning there have been two ways of entering the program: individual demobilization and collective demobilization. The first refers to those who individually and voluntarily decide to drop out of an armed group, either by leaving or escaping from it in order to return to legality. Individuals in this situation can go before any civil or military authority, including local government offices, police and military staff, or even public schools and local churches, and express their intention to demobilize. They are redirected to the Ministry of Defense, where they are received through the Program of Humanitarian Attention to Demobilized (people) (PAHD). They start a process of disarmament, demobilization and stabilization that last between 60 and 90 days. During this period a verification protocol is followed, to ensure their belonging to an illegal armed group, as well as their will to reintegrate into civil life. Ex-combatants are held in a *Hogar de Paz* ("Peace home") where psychological help and basic services are provided. At the end of it, the Operative Committee for Laying down Weapons (CODA) issues a certificate, which allows them to start their reintegration process (Ministerio de Defensa Nacional, 2006).

On the other hand, collective demobilization refers to ex-combatants giving up weapons as a result of a negotiation process with the government. In this scenario, they are received through the Office of the High Commission for Peace (OACP), ascribed to the Presidency Office. They equally receive basic services and go through a process of verification, in order to obtain a certificate to start their reintegration process. Most AUC members entered the program through this mechanism. This also implies that some of the former combatants might not be as committed to process as desired, since they give up their weapons following an order, and not necessarily as a result of a personal decision.

In both cases, if ex-combatants are underage (18 or younger) at the moment of demobilization, they are considered victims of child recruitment and go to the Colombian Institute of Family Welfare (ICBF). If they are 18 or older they can directly access to reintegration benefits (Agencia Colombiana para la Reintegración, 2014).

Initially in 2003, this policy focused on a reinsertion process. Assistance given to demobilized people consisted mainly in offering them subsides and humanitarian-aid kits, which allowed ex-combatants to survive for a limited period of time. The PRVC had different mechanisms to attend ex-combatants according to how they had entered the program. For example, attention to a person individually demobilized could last around 24 months; meanwhile attention to an ex-combatant who had been collectively demobilized would only last around 18 months. These differences were equally reflected on financial subsides. An individually demobilized person could receive approximately 895,000 Colombian pesos (around 450 US dollars) a month, plus 179.000 Colombian pesos (around 100 US dollars) for each person of his/her family. On the other hand, a collectively demobilized ex-combatant would receive in average 380.000 Colombian pesos (around 200 US dollars) a month, not-conditioned to his or her commitment with the program. Additionally, the program had a reduced number of professionals working to provide attention to each demobilized, a ratio of 1 professional for 1000 ex-combatants. These professionals promoted access to health services, education and financial assistance to the ex-combatants in massive sessions. As a result, an individual could be attended by different workers at collective meetings (Cardenas & ACR, 2015).

Services to demobilized groups were mostly given at shelters and *fincas* (farms) near big cities –mainly Bogota-, or at Centers for Reference and Opportunities (CRO) of the PRVC. The lack of a clear regulation for these places led to tensions, coexistence´s conflicts and disagreements with host communities. Moreover, if the reinsertion policy managed from Bogota guaranteed efficiency, it also generated strong centralization and it did not take into account local social needs and regional institutions.

In 2006, the Colombian Office of the High Presidential Counselor for Reintegration (ACR) was established. The creation of the ACR meant a higher level of administrative autonomy, the implementation of a new strategy focused on Social and Economic Reintegration Policy (PRSE), as well as a radical change in attention given to demobilized people (Gomez, 2013). This new policy transformed the vision of adopting short-term reactive actions and organized multidisciplinary groups to overcome the notion of immediacy and replaced it with a distinctive long-term approach towards all participants. Personal services given to ex-combatants and their families were integrated, and they were the same for both individually and collectively demobilized people.

In 2010, a significant change was introduced with the creation of a “Reintegration Route”, focused on the development of skills and abilities of the Participants in the Reintegration Process (PRP). This route addresses 8 dimensions: personal, family, education, productive, housing, health, citizenship and security. These 8 dimensions are intended to offer PRP opportunities in all the main aspects of their lives. The Route allows having clear standards to measure the progress of participants during the reintegration process, by monitoring their advancement through the System of Information for Reintegration (SIR). This system provides data on all dimensions of each PRP. To January of 2014, 2489 participants had completed their Reintegration Route (ACR, 2014).

The Reintegration Route is inspired by a multidimensional perspective to guarantee integrated services to the PRP. The Route ensures access to the Social Security Subsidized System for participants and their close family, as well as psychosocial services for at least two and a half years, and access to the national educative system. Once a PRP has at least reached fifth grade, the Route provides access to job training and different levels of technical courses. The Route encourages economic insertion through two methods. First, it supports business initiatives through an initial capital. On the other hand, it provides access to new or used housing through an incentive to employability. In the same way, PRPs can use these economic resources to pay half of university’s tuition, in case they want to continue their education. Moreover, the Route does an important effort strengthening skills and abilities of PRP and their families in order to face risky situations and/or recidivism situations. The Route also encourages PRP to build-up their legal status as citizens, and thus recognizes their rights and duties. Accordingly, the Route increases social service and community service initiatives made by participants, allowing them to interact with host communities and victims. According to the ACR reports, there have been over 2.200 of these social service activities to June of 2014.

The Reintegration Route´s approach is overcoming vulnerability and accordingly it intends to promote autonomy, exercise of rights and duties, and PRPs’ attachment to law. Participants and ACR professionals work together to determine a particular route for each individual, taking into account his or her personal needs, age, gender, ethnic group and educational level, among other factors. This process has allowed the ACR to identify needs of the attended population based on their psychological, social and cultural features, which are vital to develop an effective reintegration practice. The plan of action agreed between each participant and the ACR looks for redefining and reorienting the participant´s vocation, life’s aspirations and projects, considering his or her immediate social context as well as his or her abilities. Therefore, the work done by the ACR is realistic and objective since it is based on specific expectations of each individual, and existing means provided by the State and other actors to achieve them.

It is important to clarify that all of these benefits are available as long as the PRP stays in legality and does not commit any illicit activity again. As soon as a judicial process is open to a PRP, they will be investigated and expelled from the program.

As a cross-cutting aspect, the ACR has implemented a model of communitarian reintegration (Holguin, 2010). Since 2007, there has been a model of intervention targeting host communities and promoting coexistence and reconciliation. These interventions intend to promote awareness and democratic education between the host communities and former combatants. Each project is developed in a specific zone of a municipality, and last 12 months. Initially, it includes formation and workshops with the community and the PRPs. Then, the community participates in the designing, fundraising and implementation of a communitarian project that has been agreed on. Simultaneously, the community decides on a symbolic action that makes emphasis on reconciliation. In the same way, the ACR has enhanced its scope to promote prevention campaigns on children and adolescents' recruitment with the program *Mambru no va a la Guerra, este es otro cuento* (Mambru does not go to war, that is a different story). There have been around 130 interventions in over 100 municipalities with this strategy. Although communitarian interventions aim to create spaces of mutual recognition and reconciliation between demobilized people and the community, it does not always reach its objective. Participation for demobilized people is optional, and it doesn't register big attendance numbers. Also, even if they participate, most of them prefer to keep their status conceal, getting in the way of genuine reconciliation. Finally, the time period (a year) doesn't guarantee sustainability and sometimes these spaces disappear after the ACR finished its intervention.

The reintegration program has had a significant impact on Colombia. Since 2003, around 47,124 out of a total of 56.514 demobilized people have gone through the reintegration process; 12, 06% were woman and 6, 67% between 18 and 25 years old. Over 10.000 people have gained a high-school degree, and over 21.000 have completed elementary education. Around 700 participants have entered college education, half of them going into law studies. Up to November 2013, over 20.000 people had a formal job and about the same amount had accessed job training programs. Likewise, around 31.000 participants are now part of the financial system. Despite different shortfalls and challenges, the ACR has delivered relevant results contributing to the peace consolidation of Colombia (ACR, 2014).

Indonesia

The DDR process in Indonesia emerges as a result of the Memorandum of Understanding of 2005. The 3000 people who entered the program and the amount of weapons handed-in were a number agreed as a result of political interests and calculations of both parties. It implies that the total number of GAM members was not included in the DDR process and most of them just came back to society without help from the State.

Amnesty was granted to around 500 GAM members in exile and 1400 members who had been put in jail were released. The disarmament and demobilization process of the GAM was progressive along the withdrawing of the official Armed Forces. Around 14.000 soldiers of the Central Government stayed in the province to ensure transition and stability, and more than 30.000 left the region. Up to December 31st of 2005, the GAM handed in a total of 840 weapons at 12 centers, which were destroyed with the presence of 300 observers from ASEAN and EU representatives (Small Arms Survey, 2006). It has been calculated that 15% of combatants were women, mostly underage and who joined the GAM voluntarily. In 2005 leaders of the GMA announced that they had disbanded their military wing. The period of disarmament and demobilization lasted until 2006. An Aceh Monitoring Mission was set up by the EU and ASEAN to monitor the process of DDR.

To facilitate the return to normal life for ex-combatants, pardoned political prisoners and affected civilians, a reintegration fund was set up to cover the economical reintegration. All groups would receive either a suitable piece of farming land, employment or social security if they had a disability to work. The Government of Indonesia would allocate funds for the rehabilitation of destroyed property and GAM was allowed to keep 70% of the profits, what further stabilized their economic situation. However, keeping these commitments related to land property, was not possible for the central government.

In February 2006, the Indonesian government set up the Aceh Reintegration Agency (BRA) of the GAM, in order to assist the implementation of the process. The BRA established a socio-cultural and an economic component, to indicate that the program wanted to go further than cash grants. But due to a lack of time and capacities to build and design a need-based reintegration program which would include land reforms, recovery of livelihoods and creation of opportunity, the BRA resigned to economical allocation for all beneficiaries. As Froedin (2008) pointed out, "in doing so the BRA opted for the immediate gratification of vulnerable stakeholders, rather than the sustainable economic development of its target community.

It was estimated that reinsertion would last only 6 months and reintegration around 18 months. In both cases, the process would be framed in a communitarian perspective. 4 phases were implemented: 1) Assisting population, prisoners who had found amnesty and ex-combatants. 2) Community finances and short term programs, which included reconstruction of health points, schools, bridges, with remuneration for the community 3) Development from below and above, with compensation for all victims of the armed conflict. 4) Transition to long term development and construction of peace, as well as reinforcement of institutional basis (Agencia Catalana de Cooperació al Desenvolupament, 2008).

Initially, ex-combatants that were part of the program would receive a check every two months. According to the Transitional Safety Net Allowance indicators, members could also receive land or material resources for fishing or agriculture. Demobilized people also had the chance to become part of the Armed Forces or Policy. However, after the first payment was done, problems arise. Those who did not enter the program felt they should be included, and former commanders, using their command chain, tried to redistribute the money, with virtually no success.

Being overwhelmed by the huge amount of people turning to BRA for help, the organization soon was seeking support from the Kecamatan Development Program (KDP) from the Indonesian government and supported by the World Bank. As a response, the National Program for Community Reintegration (PNPM) was established by the Indonesian Government in 2007 and also aimed at reducing poverty, strengthening local governments and service delivery, but also in other areas, such as environmental protection (UNSDN, 2013). It is still working in more than 80.000 villages of Indonesia today. The program aimed at helping victims of the war by implementing a community-based approach, meaning that villages get a grant which they can divide and use by themselves for either finance public infrastructure or economically beneficial private goods. Both the BRA-KDP and the PNPM programs were implementing community-based approaches to reintegration, which empower villages to decide on their own what to do with the granted funds and thereby improve their economic position and strengthen society relations.

The amount of the grant was calculated by the population size of the village and the conflict intensity and was between 6.000 and 17.000 USUSD (Morel, Watanabe, & Wrobel, 2009). In total, the fund held 21.7 USD million, and helped 1724 villages. In village meetings the habitants decided who should be declared as a victim, and how the grants should be divided. In Aceh, 90% of the grant was spent on infrastructure.

Due to the popular support of GAM, ex-combatants were easily received by their communities. Around 90% of demobilized people feel accepted among their villages. In Aceh, the relation with the community has never been a problem, as social ties stayed strong and the line between the rebel in the jungle and the supporting peasant was blurry. The combatants were able to return to their homes and families and were often welcomed and celebrated. They were even more employed and more active in the community life, as they enjoyed greater responsibilities and respect from their former positions (Small Arm Survey, 2006). This process, along with traditional ceremonies of reconciliation, has facilitated implementing the communitarian-based approach. The Colombian case is completely opposite, as paramilitaries and guerrillas groups are seen as responsible for massive violations of human rights and communities are not initially willing to receive them. Rejection, stigmatization and discrimination are some of the problems most former combatants face when they return to communities. Thus, a significant part of them prefer to keep their past hidden and anonymously live in big cities and away from their hometowns.

In the Province of Aceh, reconciliation within communities has been an important process with the returnees and has been mostly based on religious traditions. Ceremonies called *peusijuek* were attended by Aceh Monitoring Mission Peacekeepers, police officers, military, victims and often the whole village. *Peusijuek* usually involved pouring sacred water, yellow rice or powder on those blessed after reconciliation of a dispute. It symbolizes that the parties are at peace, by 'cooling them down'. Such rituals come from pre-Islamic tradition with a Buddhist influence from earlier Aceh. 77% of surveyed GMA's members said they attended a welcoming ceremony in their villages (World Bank, 2006). Ex-combatants also experienced reconciliations ceremonies and sermons from imams in the mosque or in their villages. Sometimes people who had been in conflict would be asked to shake hands in presence of a traditional leader, and recite selected prayers and verses from the Koran. Another ritual inherited from Muslim tradition was the *halal bi halal*, were Christians would go to Muslims home to beg for pardon, being part of Indonesia's specific tradition of mutual forgiveness (Llewellyn and Philpott, 2014).

Islam would have also been a contributing factor to the successful reintegration of ex-combatants, for example with one of the programs being based upon the legal concept of *diyat*. It refers to payments made to the victim`s families in the case of intentional murder or unintentional murder in the classic Islamic jurisprudence. This specific procedure would later be taken up by the Aceh Reintegration Agency, and in the same sense Islamic Law influenced transitional justice in the region of Aceh (Stewart, 2014)

Moreover, a central issue in Aceh was the political participation. An important part of the reintegration of former combatants was the right for them to run for political offices and the self-governance of the Aceh territory. Since the MoU, the governor is directly elected. The 23 districts and cities of the province's directly elected leaders have wide fiscal and political power. (Aguswandi, 2006). The former armed group GAM converted into a political movement and was legalized together with 11 local parties as a formal political party in 2008. Already in December 2006, the first elections took place and Irwandi Yusuf was elected as Aceh`s governor and GAM came to power on provincial and district offices. The reason for voting GAM into office, might be justified by the population seeing GAM as a drive for change, since it has became a part of rural life while the conflict and was known for its good organization skills. Furthermore, supporting the GAM through their vote was seen as a contribution to the peace process (Aspinall, 2008). Nevertheless, there have been severe challenges for the GAM to run the office due to a lack of administration skills, and support from other political parties, as well as the splitting of GAM into different groups. The missing modernizations of the Acehnese administration, as well as weak capacities of local government were further challenges for a working parliament in Aceh.

Furthermore, improvements in security led to increased mobility of labor and reduced transaction costs and risk for investment. Unemployment was very low among former combatants, but did not result from the reintegration program as ex-combatants who would have been reintegrated outside the program were equally employed. Instead, the 2004 tsunami devastated the region and great labor force was needed for the reconstruction process. This conjuncture allowed most of former combatants to easily reintegrate into the economic market. A significant number of them went from combatants to constructors and contractors without mayor obstacles (Aspinall, 2009). However, quality of such jobs is often poor and many are still living at or below the poverty line. Economic growth rates in Aceh for the first half of 2008 were less than half of those across Indonesia as a whole, with Aceh's economy actually contracting by 5.8 per cent over the first six months of 2008 (World Bank, 2008). As Rolston (2007) claims, it does not make sense merely to reintegrate ex-combatants into poverty; such a move can lead to fresh conflict or a rise in violent crime.

One of the main features of the Indonesian case is that reintegration process in Aceh was part of a wider strategy of peace keeping and sustainable development in the area. The European Union implemented the Peace Process Support Package APPS to support police and justice reforms in Aceh, support organizations of local elections and support for local governance reforms and applications of the New Law on Governing Aceh. All these measure were intended to fast forward democratization in the region. The project was also part of the UNDP-GOI Strengthening Sustainable Peace and Development Program in Aceh SSPDA, to support the GoI in the implementation of the MoU and contribute to wider reconstruction, recovery and development of Aceh. It addressed supporting mid-term and long-term livelihood and increase of opportunities for both victims and former combatants, as well as emphasizing social reintegration and reducing tensions and violence (Conflict Recovery, 2007).

However, the DDR process in Aceh was confronted with many obstacles. One of them is the specific geography of the islands, which results in an uneven influence of the central government over the territory. Also local customs still enter in conflict with the national government. On top of it, rebels who were not part of GMA have been excluded from the DDR process and a variety of armed actors, such as women, separatists, radical Islamists, paramilitaries and criminal organized groups, still act as spoilers of the negotiated peace, following different objectives (Barron, 2009).

One of the main failures of the reintegration was due to lack of technical methods to implement an effective monitoring of who would benefit from the programs. No ID was delivered, criteria of selection remained unclear and verification mechanisms were flawed. Many victims of the conflict still remain in a position of disadvantage compared to others. The money was given without technical assistance or advices on how to spend it and provided beneficent from using it effectively. Funds have been spread widely in unproductive consumption. Former combatants too, asked why they were only being given *uang rokok* (money for cigarettes) when they deserved more and when the MoU mandated that assistance should economically empower them (World Bank, 2006). This brought disillusion to former combatants and increased mistrust in the government of Indonesia. Building a state legitimacy was put in second plan as skepticism grew stronger. Unequal access to benefits, lack of transparency in delivery mechanisms, and perceptions of corruption undermined the influence of the government. However, DDR has been successful in the sense that Aceh habitants are now committed to resolve these differences through political means, and the return to armed conflict is highly unlikely.

In Aceh, human rights' violations and accountability for crimes committed during the conflict still have not been address. The Truth and Reconciliation Commission has not been set up yet. This issue is algid since both parties don't want to be judged by their acts. Similarly, in Colombia the reparation of victims has been a long process with tremendous efforts but minor results. In both cases, accountability of the State and illegal groups for their actions during the conflict remains uncertain.

To conclude, community is a vital stakeholder of the process, since reintegration actually occurs in a daily basis in local contexts. Although an individual approach to reintegration programs can be necessary when the conflict is still ongoing, to ensure the protection of participants, as the case of Colombia, community still needs to be taken into account. Empowering communities and providing them with enough resources not only help to reintegrate ex combatants into the economic market, but also contribute to reconciliation and the reconstruction of social fabric. When host communities and other vulnerable groups perceive they are also being benefit from the DDR program, they would be more willing and open to embrace and participate on it, as the Aceh case proves. Accordingly, the articulation with local institutions and authorities is vital to implement the program. When public and social local institutions take part into the program, it generates trust among communities. Moreover, organized registration and monitoring mechanisms allow to easily follow the process of the policy and identify problems, shortcomings and strengths of the program in in real-time. It is also useful to measure the impact of the program as the Colombian case shows.

Finally, as both cases demonstrated it is necessary to ensure mechanisms allowing ex combatants to participate into decision-making processes and have a successful political reintegration. An active political life would also reduce the chances of recidivism, as people would agree to resolve their differences through formal means, instead of returning to the weapons.

WHO IS BUILDING PEACE?

Colombia

The Colombian case on DDR is quite different from the global process. In Colombia, the DDR program started as a national initiative rather than as a product of international interventions. Over the years, there has been an institutional evolution, since Colombia has not only designed the reintegration public policy, but it has also guaranteed its continuity by including it in national and regional development plans. Reintegration is a government policy, intending to become a State policy (Cárdenas & ACR, 2015).

DDR program started in 2003 as a joint action between the Ministry of Defense, managing the disarmament and demobilization processes, and the Ministry of Interior, in charge of the reintegration part. However, the increasing number of people demobilizing and the new challenges that came along with it, called for stronger institutions.

In 2006, a governmental decision created the Colombian Office of the High Presidential Counselor for Reintegration (ACR) and made it possible to unify a more ambitious policy. The Ministry of Defense stayed in charge of the Disarmament and Demobilization (DD) processes, and the ACR became the safe keeper of the Reintegration process of the DDR policy. At this point, the ACR decentralized its functions, by establishing over 32 regional offices throughout 26 departments of Colombia. Hence, attention given to people at the 10 Centers of Reference and Opportunities (CRO) improved. Likewise, it brought the public policy and the process of the Participants in the Reintegration Process (PRP) closer to local contexts (ACR, 2014). It was not about subsidies anymore, but rather psychosocial attention, access to education, job training, legal advice, and opportunities to promote productive initiatives. These aspects had proven to be relevant to determine whether participants were going to success or not at reintegrating in society (Cárdenas & ACR, 2015).

The 2010 change of government was the appropriate occasion to redesign the institutional program in order to face the challenges of a latent post-conflict scenario. At this point, the Colombian Office of the High Counselor for Reintegration became the current Colombian Agency for Reintegration (ACR), with higher levels of administrative and financial autonomy, since it is not ascribed to the Administrative Department of Presidency (DAPRE) anymore, but rather has its own resources (Cárdenas & ACR, 2015). The reintegration policy is mostly funded (around 95%) by the Colombian State. Moreover, International Cooperation provides both financial and technical assistance. The financial cooperation is usually operated by donors, and external actors.

The personalized reintegration model has required a significant change of administrative schemes and program management. Indeed, the program went from having only 1 professional worker for 1.200 ex-combatants in 2003, to 1 worker for 80 in 2010, and a proportion of 1 professional for 40 PRPs in 2014 (Cárdenas & ACR, 2015). Thus, it is guaranteed a personalized, effective and on-time attention to participants, even for those who live in remote rural areas.

Reintegration policy has become not only compatible, but also complementary to the State Security policy, the National Development policy and other initiatives related with peace and social, economic and political development. In this sense, it needs a well-articulated management of the process, involving other public entities (both at national and local levels) such as the Ministry of Health, the Ministry of Education, and the National Learning Service (SENA), among others. It also includes a shared-responsibility strategy to connect this process with the civil society, the private sectors and the international community. For the ACR it is essential that other actors, public and private, contribute actively to the Reintegration Policy and assume their responsibility with it.

Over the last decade, the Colombian State has built-up an institutional articulation, which allows perceiving the DDR process as a mean of peace-building instead of a goal. The consolidation of this process has been made possible as a result of progressive articulation of different state entities such as the Ministry of Defense, the National Prosecution Office (Fiscalía), the Colombian Institute of Family Welfare (ICBF) and the Office of the High Commissioned for Peace (OACP) (Cárdenas & ACR, 2015).

Indonesia

After the peace negotiation, the government of Indonesia was financially tied to assisting the humanitarian crisis resulting from the tsunami. But it still made it clear that efforts should be put into reintegration. In 2006 the National Reintegration Agency was created (Badan Reintegrasi Aceh BRA) by governor's decree to oversee the reintegration process. Forbes Bersama was integrated to the BRA, consisting of four advising groups. The BRA quickly evolved into a government-led agency, receiving financial aid from the government covering 80% of the entire reintegration assistance. The Agency was responsible in front of the Governor of Aceh and the government of Indonesia was scheduled to work on reintegration until 2009, when it would delegate to local governments. Since 2009, reintegration has taken a new turn by being mostly concentrated on political reintegration through political participation. GAM has changed itself into Komisi Peralihan Aceh (KPA). During the national elections, which were free and fair as observed by independent institutions such as UE and UNDP, GMA won first place with 48% of votes at local legislature seats, before the other national parties such as Partai Demokrat or Golkar. They also won 16 out of 23 regions were the conflict was most intense. Elections show that the Acehnese population still sees GMA candidates as potential leaders (Aguswandi, 2008).

The government of Indonesia has provided in total almost 77 million USD for reintegration (Froedin, 2008). As for the GAM, its National Council created in 2005 the Aceh Transition Committee to oversee the demobilization and reintegration of its ex combatants. Through this, the Governor of Aceh provided rounds of payment for each ex combatants, which rounded up to a total of around one million USD.

International Community played an important role during the whole process. At first, the international communities and NGOs emphasized their help towards the tsunami, neglecting the post conflict reconstruction. The Agency for Reconstruction and Rehabilitation enjoyed more resources and funding, as well as better technical assistance from worldwide experts than the BRA. For example in 2007, if 8000 USD would be allocated to reconstruction of houses destroyed by the tsunami, only 4000 USD would be allocated to houses destructed by the conflict (Froedin, 2008). EU and ASEN, with Switzerland and Norway, brought their assistance through the Aceh Monitoring Mission. The cost of the mission was of 10.524.810 USD (EU Council Secretariat, 2006).

The European Commission is said to have provided 4.526.800 USD to support the peace implementation and the DDR process of GAM fighters, in order to assist immediately the "2000 detainees and 3000 GAM fighters in the field at the point of release/demobilization. This will take the form of medical screening, a subsistence package and in the case of prisoner's release, the cost of transportation". Furthermore, they provide an allowance benefiting to approximately 25000 beneficiaries and their families for up to 6 months, evaluated with the level of assistance provided to victims of the tsunami and finance the mediation and communication of information on the reintegration process "to encourage reconciliation and acceptance in the communities" (European Security Review, 2005). This assistance was implemented by the OIM.

The World Bank was in charge of conducting a GAM Needs Assessment between October 2005 and March 2006 to provide a framework for the reintegration. This GAM Needs Assessments had three aims: respect the timeframe for reintegration, assess the socio economic needs and aspirations of former combatants, GAM noncombatants and political prisoners, and help development of programs to aid the reintegration (World Bank, 2006). Such an assessment was used as an example for further programs, such as the German Technical Cooperation (GTZ). Also, Japan has supported the programs since March 2006 with funds of USD8.74 million.

On the other hand, civil society did a significant contribution to the process. The province of Aceh benefited from a specific social structure which made the reintegration easier. The relationships remained strong between GAM fighters and civilians throughout the conflict and combatants often returned to their villages without problems. The border between combatants and noncombatants remained blurry and the reintegration was well accepted, even celebrated, after the peace negotiation. Less than 1% of former combatants reported integration problems, and surveys show "a high level of community trust and combatants playing a large role in their village associational life"(Small Arms Survey, 2006) A World Bank report states that the needs of returning combatants were very similar to the ones of conflict affected populations in general. In fact a special attention given only to ex combatants would create tension, and the process had to be analyze as a whole, for the community and from the community.

Some lessons are learned from this. As Colombia exemplifies, national leadership and state participation, despite international aid and support, is efficient. When the program is led and funded by the State, sustainability can be guaranteed as it is not coordinated to international pressure. Furthermore, join efforts with local and regional institutions, as well as promote the reintegration as part of a bigger development agenda contribute to the success of peace-building.

CONCLUSION

This brief comparative analysis highlighted important issues that contribute to the success of DDR programs. A common idea among DDR practitioners and academics is that programs that start before the end of the conflict have less chance of being successful. However, the Colombian case adds evidence to the idea that despite huge challenges DDR programs can start before the end of the conflict and still be fruitful.

Stronger no-military presence of central state in conflicted areas is one of the first challenges that needs to be addressed. DDR programs could be used as that tool of intervention to undermine structural flaws and contribute to economic and social development. Accordingly, DDR programs will always be more effective if they are part of a wider development strategy and it gets articulated with other peace building initiatives.

Another important factor for success is fostering national support and trust towards the process. Although international participation is necessary and gives credibility to the process, the implementation of the program will need a big involvement of national actors, and civil society to be connected to local contexts and communities. Consequently, national ownership and leadership will increase the reliability and would likely ensure sustainability of the process. Accountability mechanisms should also be set up to this goal.

A fundamental issue in peace building is the need to include, or at least bear in mind, not only ex combatants but all actors involved. Host communities, as well as other groups affected by the conflict must be included as an essential part of any reintegration program, and should be equally benefit from it. Consequently, potential spoilers would be neutralized and committed to peace.

Although significant similarities can be found between the Province of Aceh and Colombia, their approach to DDR program has been widely different and addressing different needs, depending on the following factors: type of DDR implemented focus (withdrawal vs. demobilization and reinsertion vs. reintegration); involvement of international actors; local ownership of the process; international pressure; transitional justice system (trust, reparation and forgiveness). This paper analyzes how two different DDR processes, under the umbrella of peace building, can be tailor made designed and implemented depending on the different contexts of each country (endogenous and exogenous). The aim of this analysis is not only to show what are the "good practices on DDR" based on these two case studies, but to illustrate the effect that local ownership of the process, local technical knowledge and consensus-trust between parties is key in order to have a sustainable DDR process towards strengthening peace building scenarios

FUTURE RESEARCH DIRECTIONS

Since DDR programs highly depend on the context, most academic research is based on in-depth case-studies. As this paper tries to show, comparative analysis of cases can further help to give evidence about the impact implemented measures in different contexts can cause. It also helps to find common grounds and facilitates identifying key factors that can contribute to the success of a DDR program. Bearing in mind that context is determinant at the time of implementing DDR programs, best practices and learned lessons from international cases can show the effect of policies. Research can also explore and compare the impact of DDR programs after they are finished. Therefore focus on comparative analysis can be support for improving DDR literature.

Further research should also take into account the after-DDR situations of the countries. Specifically, it would be useful to develop deeper research on the impact of the DDR program on the Aceh province. Similar to studies done in Liberia and Sierra Leona, control groups of former combatants who did not enter the program can highlight the strengths and shortcomings of the DDR process. The Colombian case would present more difficulties about this kind of research as the conflict continues, and the reintegration progress is far from being over. Rather, in the case of the Colombia, it will be important to further investigate the situation of DDR if the current peace negotiations are successful.

As a final note, this paper shortly mentions the role of Islam practices and their impact on the reintegration process. However, further research on how religious values and practices influence these programs, not only on their designing and implementations, but also on their long-term impact could be useful, especially for peace-building contexts with strong religious traditions.

REFERENCES

Agencia Catalana de Cooperació al Desenvolupament. (2008). *Indonesia (Aceh). Aguswandi. (2008). The Political Process in Aceh: A New Beginning? Conciliation Resources Accord, 20.* London: Conciliation Resources.

Agencia Colombiana para la Reintegración. (2014). *Memorias III Congreso de Responsabilidad Social. Justicia Transicional y Escenarios de Reconciliación,* Universidad Externado De Colombia, Colombia.

Agencia Colombiana para la Reintegración. (2014). *Estrategia de Reintegración.* Bogotá, Colombia: Presentación Power Point.

Agencia Colombiana para la Reintegración. (2014). Por la paz soy capaz. Informe de gestión ACR, enero – diciembre 2013. Bogotá, Colombia.

Agencia Colombiana para la Reintegración. (2014). Evolución del Proceso de Reintegración. Bogotá: ACR. Retrieved from: www.reintegracion.gov.co

Agencia Colombiana para la Reintegración. (2015). *First Global Disarmament, Demovilization and Reintegration (DDR).* Colombia: Summit. Agencia Colombiana para la Reintegración.

Aljazeera. (2008, October 11). Exiled Aceh Leader Returns. Retrieved from http://www.aljazeera.com/news/asia-pacific/2008/10/2008101144652814370.html

Alta Consejería para la Reintegración. (2010). Desarme, Desmovilización y Reintegración en Colombia. Lecciones aprendidas y resultados del proceso 2002-2010. Bogotá, Colombia.

Aspinall, E. (2008 April). Peace without Justice? The Aceh Peace Process in Indonesia. Centre for Humanitarian Dialogue, Helsinki.

Aspinall, E. (2009). Combatants to contractors: The political economy of peace in Aceh. *Indonesia.*

Barron, P. (2009). The limits of DDR: Reintegration lessons from Aceh. *Small Arms Survey Yearbook,* 249–283.

BBC News Latin America. (2015, January 15). Q&A: Colombia Peace Talks. Retrieved from http://www.bbc.com/news/world-latin-america-19875363

Beck, C. (2007). Re-paving the road to peace: Analysis of the implementation of DD&R in Aceh Province, Indonesia. Bonn: Bonn International Center for Conversion. Retrieved from https://www.bicc.de/uploads/tx_bicctools/brief35.pdf

Cárdenas, J & ACR (2015). Evolución del proceso de reintegración. Fortaleza institucional basada en la experiencia y lecciones aprendidas. Bogotá: ACR.

Carillo, M. (2012, August 29). Time is right, but past failures haunt Colombia's peace talks. *CNN.* Retrieved from http://edition.cnn.com/2012/08/28/world/americas/colombia-farc-peace-talks/

Castillo, M. (2012, August 29). Time is right, but past failures haunt Colombia Peace Talks. *CNN Latin America.* Retrieved from http://edition.cnn.com/2012/08/28/world/americas/colombia-farc-peace-talks/

Centro de Memoria Histórica. (2013). *Basta ya! Colombia: memorias de guerra y dignidad (General Report)*. Bogotá, Colombia: Grupo de Memoria Histórica.

Conflictrecovery.org. (2007). Support to Aceh Reintegration and Peace Agency. Retrieved from http://www.conflictrecovery.org/bin/Annexe_I-a.pdf

Echandía Castilla, C. (2000). El conflicto armado colombiano en los años noventa: cambios en las estrategias y efectos económicos. *Revista Colombia Internacional*, 49 – 50, 117 – 134

Edmonds, M., Mills, G., & McNamee, T. (2009). Disarmament, Demobilization, and Reintegration and Local Ownership in the Great Lakes: The Experience of Rwanda, Burundi, and the Democratic Republic of Congo. *African Security*, *2*(1), 29–58. doi:10.1080/19362200902766383

EU Council Secretariat. (2006). EU Monitoring Mission in Aceh. Retrieved from http://www.eeas.europa.eu/csdp/missions-and-operations/aceh-amm/pdf/15122006_factsheet_aceh-amm_en.pdf

European Security Review. (2005). Aceh Monitoring Mission: a New Challenge for ESDP. Retrieved from eeas.europa.eu/us/docs/infopack_06_en.pdf

Fernández, C., García-Durán, M., & Sarmiento, F. (2004). Peace mobilisation in Colombia: 1978 – 2002. Retrieved from http://www.c-r.org/accord-article/peace-mobilisation-colombia-1978-2002

Froedin, L. (2008). The Challenges of Reintegration in Aceh. Retrieved from http://www.c-r.org/es/node/1125

Gomez, C. (2014, October 6) Victims of Colombia conflict fight to be recognized as such. Quartz. Retrieved from http://qz.com/274647/victims-of-colombias-conflict-fight-to-be-recognized-as-such/

Gómez, S. G. (2013). Contextualización teórica e histórica de la reintegración social y económica de desmovilizados en Colombia. *Poliantea*, *6*(11).

Holguin, J. (2010). Communitarian Reintegration in DDR Programs: An Analysis of the Communitarian Component of the Reintegration Program in Colombia, 2002-2008 [Doctoral dissertation]. University of Notre Dame.

International Center for Transitional Justice. (2012). Feature Series: Colombia's Justice and Peace Process. Retrieved from https://www.ictj.org/news/feature-series-colombia%E2%80%99s-justice-and-peace-process

Llewellyn, J., & Philpott, D. (2014). *Restorative Justice, Reconciliation and Peacebuilding*. New York: Oxford University Press. doi:10.1093/acprof:oso/9780199364862.001.0001

Meek, S., & Malan, M. (2004). Identifying lessons from DDR experiences in Africa: workshop report. *Institute for Security Studies* (Monograph 106).

Memorandum of Understanding between the Government of the Republic of Indonesia and the Free Aceh Movement. (2005). Retrieved from http://news.bbc.co.uk/2/shared/bsp/hi/pdfs/15_08_05_aceh.pdf

Ministerio de Defensa Nacional. Republica de Colombia (2006). Programa de Atención Humanitaria para el desmovilizado. Retrieved from https://www.mindefensa.gov.co

Morel, A., Wratanabe, M., & Wrobe, R. (2009). Delivering assistance to conflict-affected communities: the BRA-KDP program in Aceh. *World Bank*. Retrieved from http://documentos.bancomundial.org/curated/es/2009/12/12022794/delivering-assistance-conflict-affected-communities-bra-kdp-program-aceh

Multi-Stakeholder Review. (2009). *Multi-Stakeholder Review of Post-Conflicting in Aceh – Identifying the Foundations for Sustainable Peace and Development in Aceh* (Vol. 2). Washington, DC: World Bank.

Nussio, E., & Howe, K. (2010). What if the FARC Demobilizes? *International Journal Stability of Security and Development, 1*(1), 58–67. doi:10.5334/sta.aj

Posso, C. M. (2004). Alternatives to War: Colombia's Peace Process. Conciliation Resources. Retrieved from http://www.c-r.org/accord-article/negotiations-farc-1982-2002

Pugel, J. (2009). Measuring Reintegration in Liberia: Assessing the Gap between Outputs and Outcome. In R. Muggah (Ed.), *Security and Post-Conflict Reconstruction: Dealing with Fighters in the Aftermath of War* (p. 90). Abingdon, Great Britain: Routledge.

Quartz. (2014). Victims of Colombia's Conflict Fight to be Recognized as such. Retrieved from http://qz.com/274647/victims-of-colombias-conflict-fight-to-be-recognized-as-such/

Rolston, B. (2007). Demobilization and reintegration of ex-combatants: The Irish case in international perspective. *Social & Legal Studies, 16*(2), 259–280. doi:10.1177/0964663907076534

Small Arms Survey 2006: Unfinished Business. (2006). Small Arms Survey. Geneva: Graduate Institute of International and Development Studies. Retrieved from http://www.smallarmssurvey.org/

Stankovic, T., & Torjesen, S. (2010). *Fresh Insights on Disarmament, Demobilization and Reintegration: A Survey for Practitioners. Norwegian Institute of International Affairs*. Oslo: NUPI.

Stewart, R. (2014). *Incorporating Cultural and Religious Practices into Transitional Justice: Lessons Related to Islam in Tunisia and Aceh, Indonesia*. McGill University. Retrieved from http://www.mei.edu/content/map/incorporating-cultural-and-religious-practices-transitional-justice-lessons-related-islam-tunisia

Sujatmiko, I. G. (2012). Conflict Transformation and Social Reconciliation: The Case of Aceh, Indonesia. *Asian Social Science, 8*(2). doi:10.5539/ass.v8n2p104

The Washington Times. (2002, March 19) FARC leaders indicted in US. Retrieved from http://www.washingtontimes.com/news/2002/mar/19/20020319-041134-7938r/

UNSDN. (2013). Indonesian National Program for Community Empowerment. Retrieved from http://unsdn.org/indonesian-national-program-for-community-empowerment/

Uppsala Conflict Data Program. (2015, February 25). UCDP Conflict Encyclopedia. Retrieved from www.ucdp.uu.se/database

Uppsala University World Bank. (2006). *GAM Reintegration Needs Assessment: Enhancing Peace through Community-Level Development Programming*. Jakarta: The World Bank.

World Bank Indicators. (2015, February 2) Retrieved from http://data.worldbank.org/indicator/NY.GDP.MKTP.KD.ZG

KEY TERMS AND DEFINITIONS

Demobilization: The formal and controlled discharge of active combatants from armed forces and groups, including a phase of "reinsertion" which provides short-term assistance to ex-combatants.

Disarmament: The collection, documentation, control and disposal of small arms, ammunition, explosives and light and heavy weapons from combatants and often from the civilian population.

Interim Stabilization Measures: A set of actions aiming to create holding patterns and control imminent threats, in order to provide some time and space for political dialogue during an ongoing conflict.

Peacebuilding: A long-term process involving a wide range of actions designed to prevent relapsing into conflict as well as to provide conditions for sustainable peace. Peacebuilding is a complex process and implies strengthening institutional capacities at different areas, so as to create the bases of development and peace.

Psycho-Social Support: Counseling and support services that focus on helping ex-combatants and victims of violence improve psychological well-being, and manage trauma and mental illness stemming from conflict.

Reconciliation: The re-knitting of social fabric through long-term processes of healing and forgiveness. Reconciliation is a deeply individual process, but is linked to the broader reconstruction of civic trust and communal association.

Reinsertion: The assistance offered to ex-combatants during demobilization but prior to the longer-term process of reintegration. Reinsertion is a form of transitional assistance to help cover the basic needs of ex-combatants and their families and can include transitional safety allowances, food, clothes, shelter, medical services, short-term education, training, employment and tools.

Reintegration: The process by which ex-combatants acquire civilian status and gain sustainable employment and income. It is a political, social and economic process with an open time-frame, primarily taking place in communities at the local level.

ENDNOTES

1 For additional reading on the subject see Laplante and Theidon, 2007.

2 The central government of Indonesia only retains sovereignty on Aceh about issues related with foreign affairs, external defense, national security, monetary and fiscal matters, justice and freedom of religion.

Chapter 20
Transitional Justice and Indigenous Jurisdictions Processes in Colombia:
Four Case-Studies and Multi-Sited Ethnography

Angela Santamaria
Universidad del Rosario, Colombia

Monica Acosta
Universidad del Rosario, Colombia

Mauricio Alejandro Fernandez
Universidad del Rosario, Colombia

ABSTRACT

Transitional justice and its range of mechanisms and goals appear to be an important debate about how to deal with past human rights abuses in transition societies or post conflicts. Because of the Peace and Justice Law 975 of 2005 and the actual Colombian scenario of a peace process between the Colombian state and FARC, the analysis of this kind of "justice" and the indigenous jurisdiction appear to be a complex subject in Colombia. The authors would like to discuss, the different uses of international and national laws concerning Indigenous peoples in Colombia, as a social process of complex interactions involving different types of agents (State actors, NGOs, international organizations, indigenous organizations, lawyers, etc.). In addition, it will be important to discuss how the transitional justice framework in Colombia brings up some incongruence to coordinate and apply concepts accordingly to the indigenous jurisdiction, drawing on four case studies and ethnographical work dealing with the international production of customary law.

DOI: 10.4018/978-1-4666-9675-4.ch020

INTRODUCTION

Colombia is one of the two countries in Latin America where Indigenous governments benefit from formal political autonomy. They are in Colombia 102 Indigenous nations and 1.378.000 persons (3.4% of the national population). This "consociation" model, instituted in the Constitution of 1991, granted local Indigenous authorities *(cabildos)* the right to exercise jurisdiction in their *resguardos* according to their own norms and procedures (Special Jurisdiction, article 246 of the Constitution of Colombia). The indigenous councils were granted the right to design and implement development plans, to promote public investments, to receive and administer public funds, to preserve natural resources, to cooperate in the maintenance of public order and to represent their own territories (Art. 330 Colombian Constitution).

Nevertheless, after twenty-four years, this model had partial regulations established in the 1953 act of 2014 that settle several provisions in order to administer the *resguardos* as an autonomic indigenous territory. This political autonomy is the base for the functioning of autonomous systems and procedures in Education, health, justice and life plans (strategies that organize and structure the community based on its future prospects). However, most of the times, these autonomous systems enter in conflict with the Colombian central state policies and governments political will. It is important to remark, that each indigenous group have their own system within their *resguardo* according to their costumes and culture.

This situation in relation to the juridical autonomous system is considered as an entanglement for the coordination between ordinary justice and indigenous justice, especially on issues such as the application of punishment. Recently, a mediated case that involved an armed conflict actor (Revolutionary Armed Forces of Colombia –FARC- guerrilla), put on discussion the legitimacy, effectiveness and guarantees of both jurisdiction due to the sentence of sixty years of prison to a rebel accused of killing two indigenous from the Nasa community at Toribio, Cauca in 2014. The supporters of the ordinary jurisdiction have questioned the guarantees and protection of human rights in a seven hour judgment. Nevertheless, other examinations praise the effectiveness and pragmatism of the indigenous jurisdiction contrasting with the inefficiency of the ordinary justice.

By itself, the study and analysis of the indigenous jurisdiction is a complex subject. However, this complexity becomes more difficult because the Peace and Justice Law 975 of 2005 and the actual Colombian scenario of a peace process between the Colombian state and FARC, that will bring several changes in all levels based on the "field" of transitional justice1. This kind of justice with a "conception of justice in periods of political transition" (Teitel, 2003: 1) has four purposes: firstly, to establish the truth of what happened and collect data of human rights violation cases. Secondly, the application of justice is not necessary trough the penal system. Thirdly, the realization of a democratic reform is needed. Finally, to ensure a peaceful post conflict processes (Benavides, 2013: 11).

This peace process has put into work many juridical frameworks in order to adequate the institutions for a social scenario in peace. Therefore, in order to attend all the indigenous rights violations, the transitional justice is based on the law 1448 of 2011 (land restitutions and victims law) with its differential application for the indigenous groups (4633 of 2011). This juridical framework aims not only at repairing indigenous individuals but also at considering indigenous groups as subjects of collective reparation (Art. 3 Act 4633). This transitional justice framework in Colombia brings up some incongruences when it comes to coordinate and apply the concepts accordingly to the indigenous jurisdiction that as we mentioned, is diverse depending on each indigenous group.

It is important to remark that the critic situation suffered by the indigenous groups in terms of a systematic violation of human rights due to the armed conflict, demands the application of methods (dialogue between society' and indigenous' knowledge) that will articulate the ordinary justice and the ancestral law of the indigenous groups. Within this context of application of justice are based the individual and collective rights that have place in a political and juridical system on transition.

This paper will expose a brief description of transitional justice, right to the truth and memory according to the worldviews and major law practices from the Nasa, Wayuu and Arhuaco indigenous groups. These groups are important because historically their juridical practices based on the Major Law or the Law of Origin has opened the discussion of the way to articulate international and national jurisdictions with indigenous justice.

Moreover, indigenous peoples all over the world have emerged as legitimate subjects of international law with rights to exist as distinct peoples. In this context, we would like to analyze the different uses of international and national laws concerning Indigenous peoples in Colombia. Within the scenario where the government has included a range of mechanism of transitional justice, such as criminal prosecutions, truth telling that publicly recognizes the abuse, often in a form of an official truth commission, massive reparations programs and different kinds of institutional reforms (Orentlicher, 1991, 2005, 2007; Arthur, 2009; De Greiff, 2011). This paper also will show that the recognition of international Indigenous governments and the production of law by indigenous peoples constitute a social process of complex interactions involving different types of agents (State actors, NGOs, international organizations, indigenous organizations, lawyers, etc.).

In addition, it will presented the recognition of international Indigenous governments and the production of law by indigenous peoples constitute a social process of complex interactions involving different types of agents (State actors, NGOs, international organizations, indigenous organizations, lawyers, etc.).

Finally, the importance of this paper lies on addressing the question of how the globalization of law, which includes the processes of importation and exportation of legal transitional justice technologies, resources, and juridical hierarchies like a "legal transplant" upon indigenous jurisdiction, affects the position and importance of traditional authorities in law production (Dezalay and Garth, 2002; Merry, 2007, 2010; Bonilla, 2009; Twinning, 2000, 2005 y 2006 in Bonilla, 2009). The research explores this. The research explores this general question at different levels (local, national and international), drawing on four case studies and ethnographical work dealing with the international production of customary law.

ORGANIZATION OF THE PAPER

This paper contains three sections. The first part consist in a local ethnographic study of juridical practices in the Indigenous Law School of Tierradentro (Cauca), which included the local production of customary law following the new Constitution. The second part emphasizes the international process of the Indigenous peoples´ Rights Draft Declaration at the U.N, focusing on the participation of Arhuaco and Wayuu indigenous organizations and the articulation between national and international level. Finally, we will explore this cases-studies that challenge the Transitional Justice framework in Colombia at national level.

Case-Study No 1: Tierradentro Indigenous School of Justice (Cauca, Colombia)

The case of a local school of justice in Tierradentro shows the processes of law production at a local level in a context of armed conflict, involving a variety of actors with competing agendas (indigenous leaders, non-indigenous anthropologists and lawyers, academics and European experts). On important actor was the European Union, which funded the project, and wanted to homogenize and rationalize the customary law (in order to put it in conformity with international standards of human rights). In addition, this international organization used the term of "transitional justice" as a label under it could work to strengthen the protection of "individual" human rights. On the other hand, the local indigenous actors aiming to reinforce its local practices of law and local political institutions.

The question of justice administration occupied a central place in the programs of indigenous development in Colombia during the end of the 1990's. This fact is particularly explicit within the framework of the "Community development" program in the Tierradentro project: the Indigenous Law School (2000-2005).

Colombia and in particular the state of Cauca have been since the year of 1990 an area for experimentation and production of the articulation between indigenous and national jurisdiction. During this process, there was an increase in the struggle for the control of the Indigenous Law School. The interest of social agents on indigenous justice is related to the recognition of the indigenous territories in the new Constitution and the economic exploitation of natural and energetic resources. The principal objective behind the funding of indigenous justice programs is the transformation from the customary law into positive law and the homogenization of legal practices. The international agencies paying for the justice programs (like BID, European Union and American agencies) wants to control or at least influence the legal and political strategies (collective rights, cultural diversity and legal pluralism) of the regional indigenous organizations. In this sense, we want to show some of the characteristics observed in the Indigenous Law School of Tierradentro.

This case study helps to understand the "transplantation" of legal expertise. For the traditional authorities the School is a training space for the indigenous political leaders who defend the right of the *Cabildos* to control and organize the social and political life of indigenous *Resguardos,* and the right to resist the external juridical policies. The Indigenous School was the *pilot project* of the 'Indigenous Research Center' in the European Union program. Its three axis of work were:

1. The *customary law* reflection.
2. The construction of "intercultural spaces."
3. The articulation of *national law* in the context of intercultural dialogue.

The School was an academic and political project to build a space for the formation and consolidation of indigenous justice and indigenous leaders (Consejo de Autoridad y Territorio, 2003: 4). In this way, the school intended to contribute to the development of what the indigenous authorities call the "life plan" *(Plan de vida)* of Tierradentro. The school was itinerant and covered 24 *Resguardos* of the area. The seminars, which lasted from one to three days, took place each month. In four academic years, nearly 300 students (governors, ex-governors, elders, members of the councils of justice, etc.) participated in these seminars. A mixed group (indigenous and non-indigenous) of coordinators was responsible of the working sessions of the School: it included a non-indigenous anthropologist who had worked with the CRIC (Indigenous Regional Council of Cauca), the governor of the Calderas *Resguardo*, an indigenous ex-governor, a non-indigenous lawyer and the coordinator of the young indigenous group. The Indigenous School following the recommendation of the European Union wanted to propose, with this project, a space for discussion among the indigenous authorities about the production of minimum standards in the application of indigenous justice. It is wised to contribute to the homogenization process of legal practices.

According to the Delegation of the European Commission, the topic of indigenous justice was conceived as a component of the development model in the framework of human rights and the fight against impunity. In July 2005, at the conclusion of the Tierradentro program, there was a debate about the type of penalties applied by the indigenous special jurisdiction in Cauca. Specifically considered were the cases of the application of *cepo* (punishment where the prisoner is suspended by the feet for 10 to 20 minutes), of the *fuete* (punishment of 40 to 50 blows of whiplashes) and the prison sentences of more than sixty years (the maximum punishment in Colombia is 40 years) (Suescun, 1998).

These practices of indigenous justice were embarrassing the international institutions, in particular the European Union, who funded formation spaces for the reinforcement of these jurisdictions. For the Delegation of the European Union in Colombia, the Indigenous Law School was part of a judicial reform project within the framework of the "good governance" model, "peace-building from below", the Human Rights Program and the reduction of impunity, as Christine Bell says, "transitional justice[2] became a label under which nongovernmental organizations (NGOs) and international organizations worked (Bell, 2009).

In this part, the paper advise that the production of customary law is a complex process involving many interactions between the various agents: EU officials, local experts (anthropologists and lawyers) and indigenous authorities. In the book "Redes transnacionales y emergencia de la diplomacia indígena. Un estudio a partir del caso colombiano" (2008), there are some details about the interactions and power struggles between some of those agents. In this paper, the authors do not have the space to enter into more details.

Two Indigenous School Projects in Competition

In order to implant a legal formation model, the local indigenous organizations set up explicit strategies, in order to have access to the European Union and BID's funding, which had invested important sums on the issue of indigenous justice in the years 2000-2005. In the meantime, the indigenous association *Juan Tama*, which was not part of the Indigenous Law School of Tierradentro, settled its own parallel project of School of Justice and the "traditional authorities" of Calderas *Resguardo* supported it.

The leaders of the Calderas school presented their project as a self-managed local initiative in contrast with the school funded by European Union. The local leader, brother of an Indigenous senator started the project. His family was very important in political decisions at a regional and national level. This young indigenous man aimed to start a political career just as his brother had done. Through this school, he hoped to gain a privileged position at the local government and to achieve academic legitimacy. This project could make this possible due to his family's prominent position in the national debate about intercultural education and the application of the indigenous special jurisdiction. His sister, who had studied political science, was a community CEO for the production of Coca products *-NASA Esh-*.

The Calderas School project represented a political strategy of the indigenous *elite* of the Calderas *Resguardo.* Interestingly, the Calderas governor (the uncle of the young man) was also the coordinator of the first school and he occupied a privileged position in local government. The two competitive projects coexisted for one year in a movement of exacerbation and competition. The new school of justice held formation workshops in particular by mobilizing law students. Then it managed to sign a convention with the National

University for academic and financial support. When the approval of more funding to the Law School of Tierradentro by the European Union was confirmed, the defenders of the alternative project playing with their political power undertook a radical action, by putting the local indigenous authorities against the mixed group.

A "traditional" trial took place in August 2004. The experts were blamed for using the product of the workshops to publish books and articles. The decision made in the traditional trial resulted in the obligation of the project's non-indigenous members to leave the territory. This example shows how the production of customary law depends also of local power struggles within the local indigenous groups themselves. In the next part, we want to analyze the international dimension of customary law production.

Case-Study No 2: The International Process of Draft Declaration of Indigenous Peoples' Rights at the UN: The Colombian Case

The authors are introducing during the second part of this paper some ethnographic materials produced during the research carried out at the United Nations (UN) specialized groups (Geneva, 2004-2005; 2013-2015). This part will focus on two particular events: the WG meeting in July 2004 and the discussion session on Item 15a) at the Human Rights Commission in April 2005. There were four indigenous leaders from Colombia attending the specialized groups. Three of them were leaders of the Colombian Indigenous National Organizations (ONIC): Luis Evelis, Aparicio Rios and Leonor Zalabata. By last, a young woman Luz Mila working for a local Wayuu organization. This case it is interesting because the analysis of the participation of the Colombian indigenous leaders, their speeches, their strategies of insertion in this social space and the uses of international law and indigenous peoples' rights.

The Working Group on Indigenous Populations, Geneva, July 2004

At the Working Group in Geneva were those Colombian indigenous leaders who represented an improvised diplomatic indigenous delegation due to budgetary constraints and who gave their speeches in front of the plenary WG. Leonor Zalabata is an important arhuaco indigenous leader at a national level and has taken part in the international groups for the last few years. She participated in discussions on "protection of biodiversity and human rights". She also denounced the Colombian State on cases of indigenous forced displacements due to violence and the consequences of illegal drug plantation fumigations trough the Colombian Plan. She also proposed the establishment of economic projects as well as an alternative indigenous program in the fight against the illegal plantations[3].

The second representative is a young woman from Guajira: Luz Mila of the Wayuu people. She made a presentation of the indigenous groups' right of free, prior and informed consent (Convention 169. ILO) in relation to private and state-owned projects, that affects their lands and natural resources. She explained that there were 25 economic megaprojects set up by multinational companies in the Guajira region in 2000.

Wayuu Organizations of Colombia announced that in spite of the obligatory ratification of the 169th ILO Convention, many economic projects were established in the indigenous territories without considering their opinion. There is a pressing need for the Colombian State to set up indigenous territorial entities established by the national Constitution. The Indigenous entities make it possible for the indigenous communities to have an administrative and political autonomy. (Intervention, Luz Mila, "Alternative resolution mechanisms for conflicts, July 2004)

The last representative is Aparicio Rios, a Nasa of the Indigenous Regional Council of Cauca (CRIC). He intervened on the case of the Naya massacre (2001) in the discussion on "Globalization, neo-liberalism and Indigenous people's Rights". He denounced the imposition of the neo-liberal economic model in Colombia and the distinction between the economic dominating model and the alternative economic model for the indigenous peoples. He introduced two categories for the alternative development model: the "ethno-development" and the "Life Plans". He also presented the experience of the Naya School of Justice that is a similar experience to the one presented in the first part of the paper. This school of justice was established after the forced displacement of approximately 6.000 people due to violence. Important to remark the interventions and concepts that registered those leaders: The conservation of biodiversity and cultural diversity. Also the demands of the defense of Human Rights in a context of armed conflict and finally the promotion of alternative economic, political and juridical models.

Specialized Agents and the Point 15A at the Human Rights Commission (HRC) in UN (April 2005)

The materials that will appear in this part of the paper are the product obtained through the ethnographic observations during the working session of the Human Rights Commission (HRC) about point 15a, which dealt with indigenous rights within the Human Rights agenda at the UN. The HRC met during one month every year and the talks about point 15a lasted only a few hours but involved weeks of preparation and lobbying by NGOs and indigenous organizations. The session started with the presentation of the activities of the special Rapporteur on the situation of the human rights and fundamental freedoms of Indigenous peoples (Rodolfo Stavenhagen, Mexico) and of the activities of the president of the Working Draft Declaration Group (Chávez, Perú).

The presentation made by the Special Rapporteur presented in loco the missions in specific countries (Canada, Colombia, Mexico and Philippines) and the conclusions of the meeting of the justice experts group (this group is made up of legal scholars from universities in Spain, Canada and Latin America and of indigenous lawyers). It centered on the documentation of human rights violations by different states.

As well as the president of the working Draft Declaration Group, he was mainly concerned with an abstract discussion on international law. These two presentations evidence the articulation of various levels of law application and the characteristics of legal rationality. There was indeed a social division of juridical work between the two UN experts on the indigenous questions. The president of the working group is in charge of the privileged function of "law creation" which is at the base of the universalization effect introduced by Pierre Bourdieu.

The ethnographic work enables to recognize at the HRC some participants of the Draft Declaration Working Group: Armand Mackenzie (Canada), Adelard Blackman (Canada) and Sylvain Duez (CSIA, France). In an interview given by A. Mackenzie during the morning session.

Lobbying in the U.N is very important. In two weeks, we have succeeded in making modifications and introducing new concepts in the report by the Special Rapporteur in the Canadian mission. We can use the new judicial concepts at the national and local level for our social struggle. It is a question of having clear strategies and of negotiating with the States. The negotiation of block per block and at the end of a few years resulted in the collapse of the whole judicial wall. (April 2005, Geneva, Grand Palais)

In this General Assembly, in contrast to the specialized indigenous working groups, the representatives of the indigenous organizations intervened by using only one microphone and only one seat[4]. The indigenous organizations within the General Assembly of States do not have a recognized place. In this sense, alliances between indigenous organizations and Human rights NGOs are the one of the most effective ways to discuss the "indigenous question" within the General Assembly.

The participation within the Human Rights Commission implies a change of mental space for the treatment of the "indigenous question". The legal field is imposed on those who agree to participate in the making of indigenous peoples' law and this becomes a professional legal monopoly. Within the framework of this meeting, there are local and international representatives of human rights NGOs, who manage the lobbying of indigenous organizations. However, for these NGOs the "indigenous question" appears as a victimization of indigenous organizations in the Colombian conflict. A parallel meeting under the coordination of the Colombian Federation of NGOs was created to permit the monopoly of the multi-level lobbying.

In the UN Accreditations office Luis Evelis Andrade[5], the president of the Indigenous National Organization of Colombia (ONIC), had arrived with two indigenous representatives who took part at the session: Leonor Zalabata[6] and Abadio Green[7]. Abadio Green is well known among the representatives of the indigenous organization members of the Latin American Caucus. Interventions made by the leaders were very short and precise. Throughout the morning, the three representatives of the Colombian organizations made separated interventions on the same subject in the same spaces. In this context, each document presented and the intervention of the three indigenous organizations reveals the tensions and alliances between them.

Related to this, Luis Evelis Andrade, the president of the ONIC at that time[8] said:

It is the first time that I come here. It is a pity because we do not know how the UN system work and because of that, we cannot profit from it at all. We prepared three principal points to present at the General meeting. The situation of violation of the indigenous peoples rights within the framework of the Colombian conflict. The precise case of the Kankuamo people of the Sierra Nevada de Santa Marta, and finally, our need to discuss with the Special Rapporteur about the State recommendations of the Colombian report. (Luis Evelis Andrade, April 2005, Geneva)

Luis Evelis Andrade said that they were to remain the rest of the week in order to meet with human rights NGO's in Geneva. The work of multi-level lobbying of the Colombian indigenous organizations are controlled by the human rights NGO's federation.

Abadio Green had confiscated several publications by the security control. This entrance is recognized as a privileged space for the circulation of specialized information. This is a privileged occasion for the personal and formal exchange of books and reports with U.N. experts, representatives of the States and indigenous leaders (Table 1).

The 3 indigenous leaders use 3 principal concepts to build his discursive strategies: human right's violation, displacements forced due to violence and economic violence. His speeches show implicitly the central question of impunity. This subject is the heart of national debate in the context of negotiations with the paramilitaries groups. Despite the different uses of international and national laws and the juridical strategies concerning Indigenous peoples in Colombia, the term "transitional justice" entered to the political and legal debate in 2005, based on the Justice and Peace Law of Colombia or Law 975 of 2005 (Table 2). Since then, some agents, local experts and

Table 1. Different uses of juridical fields in UN Indigenous Colombian Delegation Geneva

OIA: Abadio Green (president) **Strategies:** 1. Denunciation action of indigenous people's rights violations 2. Denunciation of Indigenous displacements forced due to violence 3. Denunciation of economic project implantation in Colombia 4. Denunciation of Drugs Policies and Colombian Plan	**Wayuu people: Luz Mila (indigenous lawyer)** **Strategies:** 1. Alternative projects presentation 2. Denunciation of control policies of illegal plantations 3. Appropiation process of international law and uses of prior, free and informed and consultation (169th Convention)
CRIC: Aparicio Ríos (Human Rights program) 1. Denunciation of global economic model and the human rights violations for the transnational economics agents. 2. Presentation of indigenous and alternative economic development models. 3. Presentation of autonomy and ethno-development project 4. Plan of life	

NGO have focused their attention and struggles in terms of "transitional justice". As Christine Bell writes, as the focus of transitional justice expanded from human rights accountability in democratic transitions to a broader conception of transition, nowadays the transitional justice involving a range of legal regimes and mechanisms, as well as a complex set of goals beyond those of 'accountability' and 'democratization' (Bell, 2009: 9).

In the next part, we want to analyze the discourses of leaders in a parallel meeting with the Special Rapporteur.

A Parallel Meeting between the Indigenous Caucus and the Special Rapporteur Immediately After Talks about Point 15A (Geneva, April 2005)

The first part of the aforementioned meeting focused on the subject of intercultural indigenous education. The Rapporteur introduced the conclusions of the Canadian and Colombian missions and the abysm between the laws and the applications in different countries. The Colombian indigenous representatives made interventions about specific violations cases of indigenous people's rights. The Colombian indigenous organizations introduced the "indigenous question" in the speech of "international humanitarian law" in a restrictive manner. Until now, only members of the indigenous organizations spoke and not the dominant social agents (NGOs of Human Rights who enabled the Colombian indigenous leaders to attend the HRC) produced "the social image" of the "indigenous question" through the uses of homogenizing symbols and stereotypes in the frame of victimization process.

Table 2. Legal technologies for the Penal justice of transitional Model (Law 975/2005, "Justice and Peace")

Object of the model: The model aims to make the peace process possible, through the individual and collective reincorporation to the civil life of the armed groups' members and to guarantee the respect of victims' rights. Legal technologies: - Alternative punishment: five to eight years of prison within the framework of the war crimes commission (article 3), victims' rights to justice, reparation and truth (article 4) - Collective Reparation Programs of the displacements due to African palm plantations; communitarian projects between victims and aggressors The Constitution of National Restitution and Reparation Commission (CNRR)

Leonor Zalabata: The policy of militarization of the Colombian government and the negotiations with the paramilitary groups, introduced one of the most serious problems in Colombia, the return of the displaced indigenous peoples due to violence and the problem of the rights of abandoned territories. I would like to know what we can do, and what the mechanisms are in order to control and apply UN recommendations. During meetings with U.N agencies, many of them did not know that you had made a mission in Colombia! (Intervention represents Indigenous Confederation Tayrona (CIT), meeting with the Special Rapporteur, Grand Palais, April 2005)

This intervention shows characteristics of the Colombian indigenous organization's struggles: the problem of the "indigenous displacement population due to violence", the question of "territorial rights violations" and the problem of legitimizing "legal expropriation of indigenous territories". In spite of the existence of multiple frameworks in the formulation of indigenous struggles, the Colombian indigenous organizations could not formulate the "indigenous Colombian question" in other registers different from that of human rights. In this sense, this framework is becoming dominant in the international arenas.

Abadio Green: In the Colombian case there are 31 million hectares of tropical forest occupied by armed actors. We work in Colombia for the installation of the International Court of Indigenous People's rights. We want to set up International Commissions of Observation and Verification for which we do not need a government invitation. We work for the installation of Alternative Human rights Observatories to criticize state policies. An Ethnocide, genocide and ecocide exist in Colombia! (Intervention, meeting with the special reporter, Grand Palais, April 2005)

This intervention shows a dynamic appropriation of international law, both penal and humanitarian, as well as categories and practices by the indigenous organizations. In this sense, international organizations appropriated the model of international courts in the framework of alternative uses for the indigenous Special Jurisdiction in Colombia. The "indigenous authorities" created a hybridization of justice between "customary law", "Special Indigenous jurisdiction" and international and humanitarian justice. This intervention privileges the register of self-determination, cultural resistance and the production of "alternative Human Rights policies".

The last intervention of the ONIC president centered on the dynamic victimization of indigenous peoples by the "Democratic Security" state policy, the agro-industrial economic policy and the territorial policy.

In 2000, twenty indigenous leaders were assassinated in the context of the installation of economic projects in indigenous territories. The obligation to make preliminary consultations with the indigenous communities was violated and there are many cases of indigenous forced displacements due to violence. Eighteen indigenous groups are in danger of disappearing. We need an International verification and Humanitarian Commission for the Colombian case and we need international cooperation, solidarity and support. (Luis Evelis Intervention, meeting with the special reporter, Large Palate, April 2005)

In contrast with the HRC, were the States have the monopoly of international law production, the indigenous representatives enjoyed a much larger freedom of speech at the parallel meeting. In particular, they could propose forms of appropriation of international law.

Years later, at the Permanent Forum on Indigenous Issues (UNPFII), Indigenous organizations including the Tayrona Indigenous Conference (CIT) insist on issues related to the prior consultation, the protection of the traditional knowledge and the access to genetic resources:

Even though the declining situation in terms of human rights suffered by the indigenous groups in Colombia between 2005-2010, with very few cases of transitional justice that have advanced, leaving most unpunished, the authors observed that international agencies specialized as the UNPFII not considered as a central theme the human right situation. Meanwhile Colombia in 2005 was discussing a law for political transition to paramilitary groups, internationally the discussions of the transitional justice for indigenous groups was marginal. However, indigenous organizations continued to strengthen the construction of strategies in these scenarios.

Ten years later (2014-2015) another ethnographic work is essential in these places to observe the dynamics, discussions and key players related to the discussion of the Colombian indigenous cause in the United Nations. Nowadays, the discussion about the indigenous women has a central position at the agenda under the peace process. Various indigenous women around the world have expressed in the Permanent Forum on Indigenous Issues (UNPFII) and other UN agencies a variety of violent practices based on gender, ethnicity and race. Since 2004 the UNPFII gives recommendations on the issue of indigenous women in the context of militarization of indigenous territories, social dislocation due to political conflicts, migration and the violation based on sex that causes a worsening of their situation of poverty and marginalization due to cultural differences and their minority status.

Although there is a growing participation of the international cooperation in the empowerment of the indigenous women and their various violence, internationally only 0.08% of the resources are assigned to support processes of political participation and analysis of violence in general (observation notes UNPFII, 2014 and 2015). The forms of violence expressed in many reports of the UN agencies (1999, 2005) and in the report of the UN Rapporteur on violence against women (2001) are critic. Also, in the Inter-American Commission on Human Rights Commission (IACHR, 2006 cited in Mesa de Trabajo Mujer y Conflicto Armado, 2006) and in the Constitutional Court Act 092 and its monitoring reports (2008-2010), concluded that there is an imposition to assume other roles in familiar, economic and social spaces. This situation, leads the indigenous woman to overcome "material and psychological burdens of extreme and abrupt nature" because they are exposed to particular risks by their gender-specific vulnerabilities in the armed conflict (Auto 092/2008).

In some cases, women can be direct targets but mostly the violent situations occur because of their relationships as "daughters, mothers, wives, partners or sisters". Their honor is related to men and therefore, It is a form of "damaging the honor of the enemy", a form of revenge (Mesa de Trabajo Mujer y Conflicto Armado, 2006: 33). The case of the Arhuaco people is interesting. In 2010, the CIT began to develop an international strategy through Geremías Torres. Nationally, the Constitutional Court established the order 092 of 2004 calling on all entities of the national government to create 13 programs for the protection of women's rights. This Auto functioned as a launch pad for the process of empowerment of indigenous women. During this participation, new items come into the Arhuaco people agenda. The rights of Mother Earth and the defense of the four elements (water, earth, fire and air) and various forms of violence against women (sexual, economic, spiritual, cultural). Also at the session of the UNPFII (2014, 2015), was observed how the arrival of the representative of Latin America to the Forum, the Aymara indigenous Maria Eugenia Choque will put the issue of indigenous women in a more visible way.

Despite the different uses of international and national laws and the juridical strategies concerning Indigenous peoples in Colombia, the term "transitional justice" entered to the political and legal debate in 2005, based on the Justice and Peace Law of Colombia or Law 975 of 2005. Since then, some agents, local experts and NGO have focused their attention and struggles in terms of "transitional justice". As Christine Bell writes, as the focus of transitional justice expanded from human rights accountability in democratic transitions to a broader conception of transition, nowadays the transitional justice involving a range of legal regimes and mechanisms, as well as a complex set of goals beyond those of 'accountability' and 'democratization' (Bell, 2009: 9). In the next part, We will revisit the national level and analyze the arhuaco and wayuu cases.

EMBLEMATIC CASES THAT CHALLENGES TRANSITIONAL JUSTICE AT NATIONAL LEVEL: INDIGENOUS PEOPLES ARHUACO AND WAYUU

Transitional justice as normative conception refers to "the set of actions that can be implemented to deal with the legacy of massive human rights abuses, where 'to deal with the legacy' of such abuses means, firstly, to demonstrate the validity of human rights norms that were systematically violated. A non-exhaustive list of such measures includes trial before the penal system, truth seeking, reparations and institutional reform. Far from being components of a list, these measures are part of transitional justice because they share two goals. One is to provide recognition to victims and promote civic trust. Finally, to contribute to strength the democratic rule of law" (De Greiff, 2011: 28).

Regularly, the South African case is treated as an iconic case in terms of transitional process, reparation and justice and truth clarification. This has meant that "the affinities of the transition policies are then developed based on similar schemes, but with the accommodations pointing to learn from the lessons of other countries in particular" (Presentation Castillejos, Gatti and Visacovsky, 2013). Thus, the apparent overcoming of a violent past in Latin America (mainly dictatorships and armed conflicts) has led from these specific locations and contexts, to explore policies that reflect the relationship between violence and past to build and clarify the truth:

> *The historical and factual nature of that past (through, for example, truth commissions or Historical Clarification); 2) And how that past is updated in the present through agendas embedded in pain communities or support groups, survivors or victims, and its contradictions within such upgrade raises. (Presentation Castillejos, Gatti and Visacovsky, 2013)*

However, the development of this has meant, that these practices entered into the order of "guiding concepts", a sort of "globalized gospel" that functions as a roadmap at different processes, called "transitional justice (international justice), liberal peace building and policies of memory and repair" (Presentation Castillejos, Gatti and Visacovsky, 2013). The use of these concepts according to the consensus of justice and international politics, it fails in the visibility and the reparation of the violent practices that Latin American societies have lived. Indeed, those politics maintain dynamics of exclusion, marginalization and silence that are meant to be repair. In Pablo de Greiff's words, the variety of proposed policies cannot be abstracted from the political and economic reality. This is because they include varying degrees of support and opposition locally, different degrees of legislation and development capacity, different legislative and administrative instruments which do not necessarily coincide regarding to the different measures (De Greiff, 2011: 22-23).

The above-mentioned shows that there is a need to "think properly the enunciation contexts where "the past", "the victims", "the suffering", "the forgiveness" and especially "the future" constitute political artifacts that articulate the possibilities of a more prompt justice (Presentation Castillejos, Gatti and Visacovsky, 2013). In the same way, Rodriguez - Garavito and Lam said that the logic of transitional justice is problematic regarding the resolution of rights violations to indigenous communities, mainly because:

The concept that indigenous peoples have about the conflict that led to the deprivation of their rights may differ significantly from the concept of traditional and dominant sectors of society. For instance, for indigenous peoples the conflict have origin in the past, with the era of colonization and therefore, they not agree with the temporary focus and more restricted transitional justice policies, which tend to focus on a specific period of armed conflict or a totalitarian regime. (Rodriguez - Garavito and Lam, 2013: 21)

Beyond than a mere matter of time definition, the difference points to complex situations, as in many cases the transitional justice emphasizes in the responsibility of some actors (mainly illegal) while the responsibility of the state or private companies in the systematic violation of rights remains without any trial. The standardization or the concealment of the violent practices of these actors falls directly in the process of uncovering the truth. The impossibility of access to certain information (the relationship between public officials and members of the security forces and illegal armed groups, for example) undermines any intention of overcoming violence. This situation shows a need to re-define the meaning of "the violent", overcoming the idea of power abuse, that takes asides the "others at social contexts immersed in, structural and standardized violence, with permanent crisis and profound divisions and fractures that have defined, paradoxically, the world order (Presentation Castillejos, Gatti and Visacovsky, 2013).

Case-Study No 3: Wayuu People

The Wayuu Indigenous People is located in the Guajira Peninsula in northern Colombia, and in the state of Zulia in northwestern Venezuela. The Wayuu indigenous inhabit the municipalities of Barrancas, Diversion, Fonseca, Maicao, Uribia, Manaure and Riohacha. Divided in the *Resguardos* of Upper and Middle Guajira. Other *Resguardos* are located in the southern part of the peninsula and in the Carraipia reserve. There are about 270,000 people, according to DANE Census 2005 composed by 18,211 families, representing 20.5% of the national indigenous population (DANE, 2010). These statistics represents for the Guajira department 48% of the population and 8% of the population of the state of Zulia. The Portete Bay is located in the municipality of Uribia (municipality with the highest concentration of indigenous people), ancestral territory of the clans Uriana and Epinayú. This territory is considered a place of great strategic location, found between Cabo de la Vela and Punta Gallinas where the tourist routes moves to the upper Guajira. Another important location found in Bahia Portete is Puerto Bolivar, port of shipment of coal from the Cerrejon mine (CNRR- Group of Historical Memory, 2010: 37).

Wayuu Mayor Law and Transitional Justice

The Wayuu people has its own conception of criminal justice. There are three important principles. First, there is *Putchi* (the entity that generates material damage to a victim). For the Wayuu justice there is an equivalent concept for a victim: *Asiruu*. *Putchi* arises from the right to a *maunaa* (compensation). From the perspective of the ordinary jurisdiction and in the context of transitional justice, it would be the compensation or reparation. The *Maunnaa* is the base for a law of compensation. The role of traditional authority is central because through their participation, society is able to avoid immediate vengeance (Colmenares, 1993). According to the Wayuu law, physical violence causing injury or death of a person, moral offenses that undermine the prestige of an individual or a family group must be compensated materially. Indeed, also the actions and expressions that cause sorrow in the spirit (Guerra, 2002: 171).

The offenses for the Wayuu cause two types of loss of social status: 1) by the offender, because violates a rule or social norm. 2) By the victim because of the offense made against himself. Therefore, in the process of negotiating for the compensation, it is important to maintain or increase the lost status (Guerra, 2002: 93). When an offense (murder, theft of animals, etc.) occurs, the affected family group carried out a thorough investigation of the incident to identify the people involved and establish the family groups that will be required financial compensation. It is within the family group that is decided to continue with the solution of the dispute, not only traditional chiefs Wayuu take the decision, but also the brothers are consulted, uterine nephews and women. Once the decision is taken, the affected family group determinate to send a *Palabrero* or *Pütchipü'üi* (kind of a lawyer) to request compensation according to the status of the affected group (Guerra, 2002).

The women take an important role within the development of disputes. The women are whom "usually gives advice to their male relatives, help to mobilize support in the problems, contribute with their properties to pay compensation and some of them talk strongly in the negotiations" (Saler quoted by Guerra, 2002: 121).

Transitional Justice Elements and Perspectives for the Wayuu people

The Wayuu are organized socially in a family uterine system, that is, by matrilineality. In the Wayuu society women acquires a central role of representation, mediation and connection between the outside worlds. Similarly, the ancestral territory is an indispensable element of the Wayuu culture, to its rituals and spirituality. The territory is the space in which the cultural views of life and death take place.

Contrasting the Victims Decree with the concepts of victims for the Wayuu people, while for the Decree 4633 of 2011 "for indigenous peoples the territory is victim, given their worldview and special and collective bond that unites with Mother Earth", for the *Pütchipü'üi* this view does not appear in the Wayuu cosmovision. Only the familiar clans are subject to be considered as victims.

In relation about the reparation, the Ipuana clan says that only we can know how much we demand for each victim. It has to be take into account how the murder was realized. You can calculate the damage in 200 bulls. For example not only pays who committed the crime but also who saw it. In the case of massacres is so complicated, where the bodies fall apart... that has not been seen in the culture historical violent events. However, that has value. For example if were 40 spectators, all are guilty. Let's say 200 bulls, necklaces, 600 goats, two mules, two pumas are requested. (Interview Orangel, September 2013)

However, according to the *Pütchipü'üi*, for such cases it should be considered a collective reparation through social projects (cemeteries construction, farms, goats, road construction, etc.) that will benefit many clans. Instead, individual compensation will divide the clans. The decree insists on a reparation that is contradictory from the vision of justice, conflict resolution and reparation of the Wayuu People, while payment in Wayuu justice means a symbolic and relational process where the material and moral damages caused by a person or a group to the family group of the victim (maternal side as parental). That is that the payment is not limited materially to another individual. It has a clear clan sense, product of a consensual agreement, and expresses what both parts have in common in terms of justice (CNRR, 2010).

The repair process has been problematic due to the lack of coordination between the special jurisdiction of the Wayuu cultural regulatory system and the ordinary law. For instance, in the Wayuu culture social events are meant to be resolved on based of the application of a principle of compensation where every damage deserves a reparation (Perrin, 1965: 65; Guerra, 2002: 135; Prieto y Molina, 2010:). Any criminological action that causes a material or moral damage to a person or victim brings up the right to a material compensation. The resolution of the conflict and its verdict its settle by a *Palabrero* (in Wayuu language *pütchipü'üi*) which acts as a kind of lawyer for both parts in conflict to avoid future revenge (Colmenares, 2006; Guerra, 2002).

In addition, another characteristic of this regulatory system of the Wayuu people is the collective reparation to the entire family collectively. This material compensation may vary depending on the case but is done most of the time in a payment in kind with beasts, necklaces and other item stablished by the *pütchipü'üi*. Beyond this important point, the treatment of the case of Bahia Portete initially pretended to be assume by the indigenous jurisdiction. However, the complexity of the transcended the own cultural particularity and was assumed by the ordinary jurisdiction. The ordinary justice of the Colombian state despite having the case of Bahia Portete must not overlook the cultural codes and costumes of the Wayuu people of Portete in order to a successful reparation of the victims, cause of transitional justice has emerged to develop new norms at the international level, based on "first generation" human rights (Arthur, 2010). Thus, this kind of legal strategies concern to civil and political human rights violations non-collective human rights abuses.

Aiming for the articulation of the rehabilitation and satisfaction procedures, it can be said according to the previous point, that the State will establish permanent mechanisms for each specific case of physical and psychological rehabilitation and social and legal support in order to restore individual and collective autonomy of the victims. However, this does not meet the necessary cultural differentiation for the Wayuu People, that in word of the Pütchipü'üi Andronico, compensation is measure by the value of the blood in various stages:

The reparation of tears is done to the relatives of the father, in case the absence of the father the brothers are responsible of the clan. After this is set the value of the blood, requested by the maternal uncle, when it was committed in front of someone. Following is set the value of the flesh of the victim that corresponds to the maternal family. Depending on the possibilities of the family the payment, it is made in two or three parts. Also there is a small symbolic reparation where the family of the victim meets the victimizer, in a short ceremony where they drink three shots and animals and necklaces are gifted, symbolizing the harmonization of the two families (Interview Andronico Urbay, Autonomous Board of Pütchipü'üi, Maicao, September 2013).

It is important to evoke that the Wayuu People, like many other indigenous groups in Colombia develops special bonds with the territory from its worldview. For this reason, in the social and cultural rehabilitation presented in the Article 118 of the 4633 decree, the State shall take measures and support with intercultural spaces of collective and individual ceremonies and rites, and recovery of traditions and cultural practices. This is not complete unless the access to the physical spaces where the rites and ceremonies are practiced are not guaranteed. Similarly, the limited access to ancestral territory difficult to achieve the satisfaction for the victims, due to the importance that represents for the Wayuu people their territory and its importance in restoring its cultural, social and economic conditions.

Case-Study 4: The Arhuaco People

The Arhuaco people inhabit the southern part of the Sierra Nevada de Santa Marta Mountain, located at the north of Colombia that rises from the Caribbean Sea to the 5,800 meters above sea level. The Sierra Nevada is the ancestral territory of four indigenous groups descendants of the Tayrona group (Arhuaco, Kogi, Wiwa, Kankuamo). According to the statistics of the Tayrona Indigenous Confederation there are an estimated of 45.000

Arhuaco indigenous who live in the Resguardo of the Sierra Nevada at the bottom of the southern part of the Sierra called expansion zone.

Justice as Equilibrium: Arhuaco Law of Origins and Worldview of the Arhuaco People

The concept of Justice of the Arhuaco People is intimately related to the commitment of the Law of Origin and the balance of all what exist in the universe, and not with the application of codes or laws of human origin (Table 3). In the same way, all "beings" that exist in the physical and spiritual world are subjects of justice. To contextualize the Arhuaco Justice a brief reference will be made from a philosophical field, to understand the actions of material justice. The idea is to conceive a role of Justice Arhuaca from an "own" approach.

The Arhuaco People and the Transitional Justice: Definitions

This chapter will approach what the Arhuaco People perceived as truth, justice, reparation and guarantees of non-repetition. These concepts are important to establish a dialogue between transitional justice and the concept of balance of Indigenous Peoples. In this way, an approximation is made for the concept of indigenous peoples as "victims" for Transitional Justice and coordination of technology with legal cultures.

The damage should be understood as the disturbance of balance and the material manifestation of Zaku-Kaku Jinn due to the non-fulfillment of the Law of Origin. This is the reason of why any action to be repaired, should be focused in rebalancing the harmony. It is imperative to heal and repair, however, is essential to have the necessary material elements, the most important of them is the ancestral territory, where are the Zaku-Kaku Jinn or "institutions" of justice. Therefore, as the authors shall see in the case of damages to the Arhuaco people, the demand of returning the ancestral lands is a constant. Significantly, according to the Arhuaco philosophy, in the territory are found the "institutions" and "officials" of justice capable to restore the balance of all kinds of negative actions and spirits. What it means that there are material elements necessary to clean up the damage caused by external factors to the Arhuaco people, because everything is linked to the spirit from creation and is reflected in the Law of Origin.

To the Arhuaco people, justice is not a matter between humans but embraces everything what exist in the universe. For this reason, when it is

Table 3. Major law and Arhuaco people

The exercise of the Arhuaco Major Law
The Arhuaco people have the mission to accomplish and enforce their own laws, in a spiritual and the material sense referred to the Law of Origin. When there is a non-fulfillment of the traditional exercise, internal dynamics and governance is interrupted. Then, comes the problems that are manifested in the involvement of individuals, society and nature. Thus, the individual must be in harmony with nature, with life and with other people. Of all this will depend the conduct and behavior in society of the people. In this sense the Arhuaco people, must practice permanently the mandates issued by the Law of Origin, expressed on the traditional knowledge that is what it gives the meaning and recognition of the experience of being indigenous. The exercise and implementation of the justice system are key elements that give a meaning to the self-government of the Arhuaco people. However, the authorities should ensure and enforce traditional commitments to be in harmony with Mother Nature and among the people in order to predict and prevent problems and diseases at the territory. In addition, the exercise and implementation of the Mayor Law enables and empower the political autonomy. This due to the faculty to judge and punish the violation of internal rules issued by the Law of Origin that is the source of our law. Two phases are identified in the application of justice: the first one determines the material damage and its reparation by the authorities. This is a public process. The second phase is the spiritual and traditional reorganization under the guidance of Mamo (spiritual authority). Traditional justice is different from the ordinary because of the principle of the spiritual balance that committing a crime or failure affects the whole family, the community and the environment. Therefore, part of the sentence obeys a spiritual remedy for the person committing the offense, in turn must repair the damage already caused to the affected community (Pueblo Arhuaco, 2012).

Source: Own elaboration

treated the Arhuaco people as "victims", it must be taken into account the context of the Law of Origin, where the *Zaku-Kaku Jinas* are "victims" and also the territory and its vital cycle. For this motive, all the reparation actions should be oriented towards the healing of all kind of "victims" and rebalancing the territory.

When a human being is affected the damage should be measured integrally. In other words, beside the material affection as an impossibility to fulfil the mission of the Arhuaco people, it must seek the conservation of the balance of the territory. This is why every verdict contemplate two ways: in one hand, the reparation actions must be conducted to repair the spiritual damge and in the other hand to repair, the material damage caused to the *Zaku-Kaku Jinas*. For instance, when a person is murdered, the affectation is because the impossibility of the "victim" to complete his duty in life, rather than the physical disappearance.

At last, it is important to expose an idea of "truth" and guarrantee of non-repetition. The truth is associated to a spiritual consult from the *Mamo* to the spiritual institutions of justice, complemented by the sensorial experience of the human being. Thus, the Mamos and the authorities (Cabildo and Comisario) apply the justice. The guarantee of non-repetition are the guarantees to fulfill the mission and the destiny imposed by the Law of Origin, its practices over the autonomy of the ancestral territory and the respect of all the cultural practices.

The Arhuaco People: Informal and Formal Justice

The universal conceptions of justice, truth, reparation and guarantees of non-repetition is not compatible with the healing and balancing practices of the indigenous groups. Because of this, the main difficulties that challenges the Transitional Justice in Colombia, is to put into dialogue "the approximation of the conception of justice from the State with the approximation of the conception of justice from the victims", what Uprimmy and Guzman as "Transitional Justice from below" (2010: 20) consider. In this particular case, the indigenous peoples as an indivisible cultural body and the consideration of the territory as a victim, puts an especial challenge to the successful transitional justice process.

A first element that difficult the implementation of the 4633 decree is that this legal instrument does not respond to the culture of the Arhuaco People. The rules created to regulate the human affairs are based on a particular way of understand life. It is understood that the understanding of the law and justice of the decree are based on the conception of life and justice of the majority of the society and the institutions of the State. The Arhuaco people do not think that the decree correspond to their philosophy, thoughts and way of think. The structure of the decree do not reflect their territorial order, neither their institutional, social and spiritual dynamics corresponding to their universe views. For the Arhuaco people, the decree does not has an indigenous soul but *bunachu9* (Pueblo Arhuaco, 2011).

A second element is the lack of reparation policies adjusted to the cultural reality of the Arhuaco people. In this sense, the territory in its physical and spiritual ambit is the first element for their cultural conservation. This is why it must be considered as victim and subject of reparation according to the Law of Origin. The Arhuaco People in relation of this reality manifest:

During the formulation process of the program to guarantee fundamental rights within the frame of the sentence 004 of 2009 (Constitutional court), the indigenous groups of the Sierra Nevada were able to consolidate a document where stated. 1) The government should guarantee the fundamental rights and the historical demands for territorial rights and other rights in relation with our culture diminish by many years of armed conflict. In this order, a reparation with an especial focus according to our vision and thoughts it can be realized with the certification and the return of the ancestral territory, through the ancestral black line (Linea Negra) entitled to peasants and landlords that limits the political autonomy in the territory. (Pueblo Arhuaco, 2011)

Based on the previous facts, under the worldview of the Arhuaco people, only can be understood the policies of justice, reparation and guarantee of non-repetition by the healing and balance of the ancestral territory. This position is because functionaries as well as the institutions of justice in the territory are in charge of the spiritual balance. In addition, any damage done to a human being, it is a damage done to the vital cycles of nature and to the destiny of each human being. In this sense, any reparation policy that will is not adjusted to a

Having the aim to repair the victims of the armed conflict, the intention of the decree to repair etnic groups under a differential focus is to respect the cultural difference. For the Arhuaco people, a full reparation will be done when the ancestral territory marked by the black line (línea negra) is return to the Arhuaco people. For us the territory is part of the collective live as a group and is in relation with our Mother Nature, language, philosophy and daily acts as expressions of the spirituality of the earth. We are product of the earth. In this sense, all the damage done to the natives plants, animal and persons affect the live. The territorial recovery means the new beginnig of all the indigenous victims, the satisfaction of the Mother Nature and to the entire Arhuaco indigenous groups. A reparation policy focus on money or services to the victim families, does not has the culural differentiation needed for the especial groups. Instead, the reparation of the territory permit to recovery the balance of holy places, envigorate the natural dynamics of the earth, repair all the alteration suffered and finally serve to accomplish our mission in life: serve to the humanity. (Pueblo Arhuaco, 2011)

Another challenge that faces the reparation decree is its implementation. For the Arhuaco people, the institution where the decisions are taken are related with the mission of keeping the balance in the political spaces, This is why the institutional spaces from the central state such as the ministries, does not provide the possibility to apply a fully reparation policy according to cultural singularities. This situation explains the reasons why the Arhuaco people are reluctant to be part of this institutional spaces, that will undermine their own institutional spaces driving them into forced procedures and decisions and thus their undermining their culture. (Pueblo Arhuaco, 2011).

It is conclude that the difficulties in the implementation of the decree for the Arhuaco people mainly are caused because of the lack of knowledge about their culture. This will be resumated in what Uprimy and Guzmn says "the challenges of the transitional justice in Colombia is "to put in dialogue the logic of the State and the ordinary justice with the logic and view from the victims: a transitional justice from below" (2010: 20).

FUTURE RESEARCH, DIRECTIONS, AND CONCLUSION

The first contribution of this work is methodological: the research is focused at the confluence of various disciplines (sociology of law, anthropology, international relations) and it mobilized materials of various natures, which make it possible to work starting from scales and different temporalities, through an ethnographic "multi-site" method.

The second contribution is empirical. In Latin America as in other contexts, the international and indigenous legal experts in the present time remain a badly known population and the authors hope that this work will be able to contribute to break certain stereotypes. (For instance, the imaginary of indigenous representatives like a "porter" of a different rationality; the imaginary of one homogeneous indigenous communities; this conception forget the social positions, resources and capitals).

These legal practices are based in a quasi-exclusive way on the conventional debates of international law, applied to specific populations: Indigenous peoples. In this sense, this social universe is sometimes represented like an exotic space of reflection and contact between two opposite worlds: the "indigenous" and the "diplomats". In this social space, the agents with the most legitimate capitals are the specialists in international law. Thus, the paper analyzes the transnational dimension of the legal mobilization. These social spaces represent the emergence and convergence of national and local legal practices, claims and progressive discourses.

This process represents an interaction between national and international law, different interest of transnational economic agents and the production of "indigenous autonomy discourse" and legal indigenous institutions (for example indigenous jurisdictions, indigenous circumscription and "indigenous peace zones") in the context of the *peace-building* and "good governance" discourse, based on the "field" of the transitional justice. This let to focus in the imbrications between "indigenous causes", production legal levels of universal law and transformations, in the context of post-colonial domination relations.

The second part of the paper have focused on the activities of the Colombian Indigenous leaders at the UN in Geneva, and in particular, on the uses they make of international law. The authors have briefly analyzed the various registers they used to further their cause and the articulation and the role played by competing agents (NGOs, UN experts, academics and Indigenous representatives) of the local, national and international networks (as an example of the boomerang pattern). Once again, it appeared important to outline. The fieldwork has shown that the Indigenous leaders were able to appropriate the discourse of international law but remained within a context of strong domination in the context of "symbolic violence" for the legal production. The professional practices and activities of multi-level advocacy networks for Indigenous Peoples in Bogotá, Cauca, Paris, Melbourne and Geneva were important to focus. This "ethnographic study multi-site" has shown the reproduction in the international level of national and local legal hierarchy. It was important to show how this professional practice broke the « illusion » of the transcultural legal co-production and represent the consolidation of international legal expertise about indigenous populations.

The third part emphasized briefly that NGOs, Victim's Associations, and Indigenous organizations could use simultaneously both national and international laws to defend Indigenous rights at the local level (in particular in cases of forced displacements due to violence and the claims in the context of transitional justice). The authors have shown that for a same case of abuse, the groups involved attempted to use a variety of law systems: international law, victim's law, human rights law, transitional justice mechanisms and indigenous law, as the authors wrote through the cases. In addition, they have made both a "formal" use of these laws (in the legitimate courts –ordinary jurisdiction- and international spaces) and an "alternative" one (setting up unofficial courts and tribunals including indigenous personalities, academics, international lawyers, etc. Furthermore, the articulation between transitional justice mechanisms and their Cosmo view). Those unofficial courts and views of justice, truth and reparation can be understood as a form of law and "peace-building" production "from below". However, these practices are strongly dominated in a context where the dominant economic agents attempt to set up a legal reform, which will allow for the dismantling of "multicultural justice" in the context of the importation and appropriation of transitional justice practices and discourses in the twenty first century.

As Paige Arthur remarks, some legal and political experts have not recognize that many of the countries in which transitional justice practitioners work are not only societies coming to terms with past human rights violations, they are also societies coming to terms with ethnic, religious or linguistics divisions that may have been at the root of the violations themselves (Arthur, 2010).

Colombia is a case in which political redress in the forms of institutional reforms, the protection of the rights of truth, justice, reparation and non-repetition of minority groups or preferential policies of memorialization might seek in addition to redress just for mass atrocity. Therefore, there will be two types of transitional justice through an 'identity lens': justice for past and human rights abuse, and justice for systematic institutional marginalization on the basis of one or various identities (Arthur, 2010).

Finally, in the last part of the paper there are some thoughts about the impacts and recommendations for future actions of the transitional justice in Colombia from the cases presented. The articulation between the Transitional Justice and the Special Indigenous Jurisdiction is very complex. This text focused on truth commissions and the own forms of memory and justice of the indigenous groups. These groups require special lines of action to guarantee the right to justice, truth, reparation and guarantees of non-repetition in accordance with their specificities and cultural reality.

It is important to note that according to the diversity of indigenous groups, setting up a "Truth Commission" is not part of its own Mayor Law procedures. It is understood that the need for truth commissions is an initiative of the central state for the inclusion of complex perspectives of

Figure 1. Judicial fields

Different uses of juridical fields in UN
Indigenous Colombian Delegation
Geneva
UN

OIA : Abadio Green (president)

Strategies:

1. Denunciation action of indigenous people's rights violations
2. Denunciation of Indigenous displacements forced due to violence
3. Denunciation of Drugs Policies and Colombian Plan
4. Denunciation of economic projetc implantation in Colombia

Wayúu people: Luz Mila (indigenous lawyer)

Strategies :

1. Alternatifve projects presentation
2. Denunciation of control policies of illegal plantations
3. Appropriation process of international law and uses of prior, free and informed consultation

(169th Convention)

CRIC: Aparicio Ríos (Human Rights program)

1. Denunciation of global economic model and the human rights violations for the transnationals economics agents
2. Presentation of indigenous and alternative economic development models
3. Presentation of autonomy and ethno-development project
4. Plans of life

the indigenous groups in the Transitional Justice process. It is important to provide an articulation of the meanings and concepts of justice, truth, reparation and guarantees of non-repetition from the cultural equivalent of each indigenous group, in order to avoid imposing an institutional definition or regulation. The respect for the oral traditions of each group is vital. An important issue is the analysis of the different concepts of indigenous justice (harmony, balance) and truth, peace and reparation (rebalancing the equilibrium) for each Indigenous group. The model of Truth Commission proposed must be intercultural. These models should have representatives and spiritual leaders of all indigenous groups. For these models also are needed critical voices of women, grandparents and indigenous children. The proposed model of Truth Commission must be Intercultural without violating the culture, language, worldview and Mayor Law application of the indigenous groups. It is important to analyze the position of each indigenous group in the decision of being part or not in the process of a Truth Commission, ensuring a free, prior and informed consent. In an eventual agreement, it must be considered the way in which the group will participate.

Once created the Truth Commission should become an effective space to research the problematic experienced by the indigenous groups. The establishment of the truth is essential to any process of repair. It is important to establish special mechanisms for the participation of the indigenous groups who do not have solid organizational structures and lack of social mobilization. This will be accomplished encouraging a direct participation from the social base and not by "mega representatives" (organizations representing a multiplicity of groups but have no proximity to the social bases in territory).

The processes in order to build mechanisms such as the Truth Commission must have the time and the resources to ensure the construction from the social bases. The various indigenous leaders consulted during the development of this research said that they have not been taken into account in the context of peace negotiations with the guerrillas. The concept of truth it seems necessary to build peace.

When is socialize the experience of truth commissions developed in others parts of the world, all those interviewed and consulted call for the current authorities of the Colombian State to apologize to the indigenous groups for all the acts committed against them. The truth commission must be accompanied by the creation of special programs for indigenous peoples on issues of healing and harmonization in the context of reintegration. It is fundamental to work in the area of legal training of judges and in the education for peace and transitional justice for indigenous groups.

REFERENCES

Arhuaco, P. (2007). *Atlas Arhuaco*. Comité de Educación del Pueblo Arhuaco.

Pueblo Arhuaco. (2011). *Posisición del Pueblo Arhuaco frente al Decreto Ley 4633 – Ley de Victimas Indígenas-*. Documento elaborado en el kadukwu de Me'chacha, Noviembre.

Pueblo Arhuaco. (2012). *Normas y criterios generales del Pueblo Arhuaco*. Documento aprobado en Asamblea General del Pueblo Arhuaco, Agosto.

Pueblo Arhuaco. (2012a). *Fundamento tradicional y cultural del Pueblo Arhuaco (Política General)*. Documento aprobado en Asamblea General del Pueblo Arhuaco, Agosto.

Pueblo Arhuaco. (2012b). *Documento Arhuaco frente a la consulta del Proyecto de Ley de Tierras y Desarrollo Rural*. Documento elaborado por el Equipo Coordinador de la Consulta Previa de Ley de Tierras y Desarrollo Rural.

Pueblo Arhuaco. (2013). *Consideraciones de los Directivos del Pueblo Arhuaco frente al documento expedido por autoridades del Pueblo Kankuamo*. Documento elaborado por las Directiva General del Pueblo *Arhuaco*, Agosto.

Arthur, P. (2009). How 'Transitions' Reshaped Human Rights: A Conceptual History of Transitional Justice. *Human Rights Quarterly*, *31*(2), 321–367. doi:10.1353/hrq.0.0069

Arthur, P. (Ed.). (2010). *Identities in Transition: Challenges for Transitional Justice in Divided Societies*. Cambridge University Press. doi:10.1017/CBO9780511976858

Arthur, P., González, E., Lam, Y., Rice, J., Rodríguez-Garavito, C., & Yashar, D. (2013). *Fortaleciendo los derechos indígenas a través de comisiones de la verdad*. Bogotá: ICTJ.

Bell, C. (2009). Transitional Justice, Interdisciplinarity, and the State of the 'Field' or 'Non-Field'. *International Journal of Transitional Justice*, *3*(1), 5–27. doi:10.1093/ijtj/ijn044

Benavides, F. (2013). *Justicia en epocas de transicion: Conceptos, modelos, debates y experiencias*. Colombia: Grupo Editorial Ibañez.

Bonilla, D. (Ed.), (2009). *Teoría del derecho y trasplantes jurídicos*. Siglo del Hombre Editores.

Colmenares, R. (1983). *Del Derecho Consuetudinario Guajiro al Estado Social de Derecho Multiétnico en Venezuela. Revista de la Facultad de Ciencias Jurídicas y Políticas, (70)*. Maracaibo, Venezuela: Universidad del Zulia.

Colmenares, R. (2006). Sistema de Justicia Penal Formal y el Derecho Consuetudinario Wayuu. *Frónesis*, 13(1), 57–69. Retrieved from http://www.scielo.org.ve/scielo.php?pid=S1315-62682006000100006&script=sci_arttext

Comisión Nacional de Reparación y Reconciliación (CNRR). (2010). *La masacre de Bahía Portete: mujeres wayuu en la mira*. Bogotá, Colombia: Alfaguara.

De Greiff, P. (2011). Algunas reflexiones acerca del desarrollo de la Justicia Transicional. *Anuario de Derechos Humanos*, Universidad de Chile, (7).

Congreso de la Republica de Colombia. (2011). Decreto Ley "*Por medio del cual se dictan medidas de asistencia, atención, reparación integral y de restitución de derechos territoriales a las víctimas pertenecientes a los Pueblos y Comunidades indígenas*" (4633 de 2011). Ministerio del interior, 9 de diciembre.

Dezalay, Y., & Garth, B. (2002). La Internacionalización de las luchas por el poder. La competencia entre abogados y economistas por transformar los Estados latinoamericanos. Clave de Sur. 1ª ed. ILSA, Bogotá D.C. Colombia.

Guerra Curvelo, W. (2002). *La ley en la sociedad wayúu. La disputa y la palabra*. Bogotá: Ministerio de Cultura.

International Center for Transitional Justice (ICTJ). (2010). Indigenous Voices and Truth Commissions. Retrieved from https://www.ictj.org/sites/default/files/IPTC-March-2010-Meeting-Summary-Materials.pdf

Keck, M., & Sikkink, K. (1998). *Activists beyond Borders. Advocacy Networks in International Politics*. Cornell University.

Merry, S. (2007). *The practice of human rights: tracking law between the global and the local*. New York: Cambridge University Press.

Mesa de Trabajo Mujer y Conflicto Armado. (2006). *Memoria de mujeres. Guía para documentar y hacer visible el impacto de la violencia contra mujeres, jóvenes y niñas, en contextos de conflicto armado*. Bogotá: Ediciones Antropos.

Orentlicher, D. (1991). Settling Accounts: The Duty to Prosecute Human Rights Violations of a Prior Regime. *The Yale Law Journal*, *100*(8), 2537–2615. doi:10.2307/796903

Orentlicher, D. (2005). Conjunto de principios actualizado para la protección y la promoción de los derechos humanos mediante la lucha contra la impunidad.

Orentlicher, D. (2007). Settling Accounts Revisited: Reconciling Global Norms with Local Agency. *International Journal of Transitional Justice*, *1*(1), 10–22. doi:10.1093/ijtj/ijm010

Perafán, C., Azcárate, L., & Zea, H. (2000). *Sistema jurídicos, tukano, chamí, guambiano, sikuani*. Bogotá: Arfos Ltda.

Pontón, E. (2014). Crítica a los mecanismos institucionales de reparación a víctimas indígenas – Caso de análisis: el Pueblo Wayuu. Repositorio institucional Universidad del Rosario. Bogotá.

Rodríguez-Garavito, C., & Lam, Y. (2013). Enfrentando las violaciones de los derechos de los pueblos indígenas al territorio, la tierra y los recursos naturales durante conflictos y transiciones. ICTJ. Fortaleciendo los derechos indígenas a través de comisiones de la verdad, Bogotá.

Sanchéz, E. (2007). *Derechos Propios-Ejercicio de la Jurisdicción Especial Indígena en Colombia*. Bogotá: Instituto de Estudios del Ministerio Público.

Santamaría, A. (2008). *Redes transnacionales y emergencia de la diplomacia indígena: Un estudio a partir del caso colombiano*. Bogotá: Universidad del Rosario.

Suescun, A. (1998). *Derecho y sociedad en la historia de Colombia*. Tomo I. El Derecho Chibcha (Siglo IX-Siglo XVI).

Teitel, R. (2000). *Transitional Justice*. Oxford University Press.

Teitel, R. (2003). Transitional Justice Genealogy. Harvard Human Rights Journal, 16, 69-94.

Uprimny, R., & Guzmán, D. (2010). *Justicia Transicional desde abajo y con perspectiva de Género*. UNIFEM.

ENDNOTES

1 Christine Bell argues in her article *Transitional Justice, Interdisciplinarity and the State of the 'Field' or 'Non-Field'* that "there is a hidden politics to how transitional justice has been constructed as an interdisciplinary field that obscures tensions between the range of practices and goals that it now incorporates" (Bell, 2009).

2 In 2000 the term 'transitional justice' came to describe "the conception of justice in periods of political transition", characterized by legal responses to the wrongdoings of repressive predecessor regimes (Teitel, 2000, 2003: 1). At the same time, in order to discuss how successor regimes should deal with the human rights abuses of the authoritarian predecessors, and to strengthen the protection of human rights 'transitional justice', as Bell writes, "became a label under which nongovernmental organizations (NGOs) worked and university courses, centers and institutes were established". The founding meeting of the main transitional justice NGO, the International Center for Transitional Justice (ICTJ) in 2000 and the creation of normative guidelines at UN are examples of this kind of label (Bell, 2009: 9).

3 This is a good example of "the boomerang pattern" as Keck and Sikkink mention. Some transnational advocacy networks link activists in developed countries with others in or from less developed countries, to intend to

'affect the behavior of states'. Thus, when the links between the state and domestic actors are in conflict, domestic NGOs or different agents and local experts may directly seek international allies to try "to bring pressure" on their states from outside. This kind of strategy is called the 'boomerang pattern', common in indigenous rights campaigns, "where the target of their activity is to change a state's behavior". (Keck and Sikkink, 1998).

4 To see more articles about the international indigenous participation at UN: Angela Santamaria *Redes transnacionales y emergencia de la diplomacia indígena. Un estudio a partir del caso colombiano,* 2008; Irène Bellier, *Usages et déclinaisons internationales del'"autochtonie" dans le contexte des Nations Unies* (2009), and *Les peuples autochtones aux Nations unies: un nouvel acteur dans la fabrique des normes internationales* (2012), Mónica Acosta, *Los líderes indígenas arhuacos como "empresarios políticos": un análisis desde su participación en los mecanismos de los pueblos indígenas de la ONU,* 2012.

5 Social leader from the Embera indigenous group. Nowadays is a Colombian Senator elected (2014) through the especial electoral indigenous circumscription,

6 Social leader of the Arhuaco Indigenous group. Nowadays is part of the Andine Parliament elected with 199.239 votes in 2014.

7 Social leader from the Kuna indigenous group. Ph.D. in Education from the Universidad Bolivariana de Medellin.

8 The actual president of the National Indigenous Colombian Organization (ONIC) is Luis Fernando Arias, from the Kankuamo Indigenous group.

9 Non indigenous person.

Chapter 21
Criminal Interests within Political Insurgencies:
The Case for Development-Centred Counterinsurgency

Oscar Palma
Universidad del Rosario, Colombia

ABSTRACT

Insurgencies are progressive and systematic insurrections with political aims. They are usually aimed at the creation of a new state, the liberation of a nation from foreign intervention, the transformation of the political system, or the imposition of a certain way of life. Whereas this political character sets them apart from common criminals, whose main objective is personal profit; in practice, most insurgencies are a combination of criminal and political interests. Solutions that address political grievances or criminal motivations separately, leaving one of them aside, are highly likely to fail, perpetuating violence. Development-centred counterinsurgency seems to be an ideal framework to confront this type of insurgencies. The case of Colombia is examined to observe achievements, failures and challenges.

INTRODUCTION

Although the conceptualization of political violence and criminality creates differentiated dimensions to describe the nature of non-state violent actors, it is not always easy to observe this distinction in the real world. Depicting armed actors as monolithic and unitary agents might not always be precise, and could even lead into bad policy making. Insurgencies and terrorists have political interests by definition, but in many cases it is possible to observe fighters who are more motivated by profit. Instead of waging war because they believe in an altruist goal, they do it as way of living.

This reality imposes a challenge for policy-makers. If only the political elements of conflict are addressed (the grievances of the insurgency), then interests in profit will remain, perpetuating violence. Remnants of the organization could prevail, or new armed groups could be formed. By contrast, if policies are only formulated to erode

DOI: 10.4018/978-1-4666-9675-4.ch021

profiting interest, unattended social and political demands will likely perpetuate violence.

This chapter argues that, as a consequence of the existence of political and economic interests within a single insurgent organization, states need to recur to a strand of counterinsurgency practice which could be denominated 'development-centred counterinsurgency'. This model seeks to fight insurgents not only militarily, but by recurring to practices that resemble nation-building. It is not here argued that there aren't other possible solutions to conflicts when insurgencies exist. Negotiations or appeasement are examples of possible strategic paths. But it is not the interest of this document to discuss the best possible strategy. Instead, it focuses on best practices when confrontation of the insurgency is necessary.

For this analysis, there will be a differentiated exploration of case studies. After discussing literature regarding economic interests in conflict, the Taliban, the Kurdistan Worker's Party, and the Revolutionary Armed Forces of Colombia will be analysed to describe how it is possible to observe criminal interests within the organization. Following an explanation of the idea of development-centred counterinsurgency, the case of Colombia is explored to observe achievements, failures and challenges of this type of counterinsurgency policies, hoping to offer more light for the study of other cases.

BACKGROUND: ECONOMIC INTERESTS IN CONFLICTS

The interest of individuals in making profit out of wars is not a new feature in warfare. Centuries before the so-called *new wars*, supposedly waged for economic incentives and not for political motivations, combatants were already interested in looting.[1] From Julius Caesar to Bismarck, including the conquistadores, the feudal barons and the condottieri, interests in profit had always been common (Lewison, 1936).

The study of economic interests in conflict has almost become a sub-discipline in Development and Security Studies. It is a common theme explored in the post-Cold War era, especially to understand dilemmas throughout the developing world. Several authors such as David Keen (1998, 2006), David Malone and Jake Sherman (2005), Paul Collier and Anke Hoeffler (1998, 1999, 2000) and Mats Berdal (2009) have explained how in specific cases economic interests precede political motivations in the causation and endurance of conflict.[2] The control of regions where specific commodities are produced generates competition between diverse groups and forces that recur to violence to guarantee this domination. In many cases, in the absence of state institutions, a criminal economy emerges. As explained by Keen, "conflicts can create war economies, often in regions controlled by rebels or warlords and linked to international trading networks; members of armed gangs can benefit from looting; and regimes can use violence to deflect opposition, reward supporters or maintain their access to resources" (Keen; 1998, 11).

When this is the case, it is common to see a transformation within the groups themselves: an interest in continue waging war for the sake of profits, instead of winning it to achieve a political goal. "Defeating the enemy or bringing the fighting to an end appears to have become less important for key parties involved than securing the benefits from the continuation of conflict" (Arson, 2005, 4).

This discussion created a certain dichotomy between explanations of conflict based on economic interests in the one hand, and on political agendas in the other; a debate commonly known as greed vs. grievance. Through a series of World Bank sponsored studies, Collier and Hoeffler argued at some point that conflicts were exclusively caused by combatant's greed; but a more appropriate conclusion is that rebellions are "motivated by a blend of an altruistic desire to rectify the grievances of a group, and a selfish desire to loot the resources of others" (Keen, 1998).

The idea of internal conflict as exclusively caused by economic agendas, then, gave way to an explanation in which causation of war remains to be political, but interest in profit is an aggravating factor; transforming, deepening, fuelling violence and making conflict longer; a key obstacle to conflict-solving.

Increasingly, civil wars that appear to have begun with political aims have mutated into conflicts in which short-term economic benefits are paramount. While ideology and identity remain important in understanding conflict, they may not tell the whole story. Portraying civil wars as simply revolutionary struggles between opposing sides obscures the emerging political economy form which the combatants can benefit. (Keen, 1998, 11)

This is why, as it was argued by Mats Berdal, a political economy perspective linking political and economic agendas, and explaining the interdependence of economic and political variables, is more appropriate to understand this type of situations (Berdal, 2009, 79-81). Economic dilemmas have political implications just as political issues have economic repercussions. Karen Ballentine and Jake Sherman agree with this perspective:

conceptualizing explanations of armed conflict in terms of greed and grievance has imposed an unnecessary limiting dichotomy on what is, in reality, a highly diverse, complex set of incentive and opportunity structures that vary across time and location. (Ballentine and Sherman, 2003, 8)

With this reality as background, it is difficult to describe organizations as pursuing monolithic ends. Can an insurgency interested in profits still be considered political? Or should they be understood as a criminalized entity? Ballentine and Sherman proposed that it is necessary to go beyond the level of the organization as a unitary group, to examine the behaviour of combatants and insurgents, discovering diversified interests and objectives. The famous analogy of 'opening the box' in International Relations to discover what's inside the state, and how different actors within it are the key to unravel state's behaviour, is also valuable here. For a true understanding of insurgencies, it is necessary to 'open the box' to discover the motivations of individuals, groups and sectors within the organization. This is a correct approach to think about insurgencies in scenarios where specific commodities fuel conflict. Building appropriate responses, especially in terms of policy-making, must go beyond simplistic visions formed through monolithic concepts such as narcoterrorism, terrorism or criminality.

The global criminal economy offers armed groups plenty of sources to profit, especially through transnational smuggling networks. Products like diamonds, drugs, gold, and coltan, more than oil and timber among others, have proved to be ideal, because they are both easily lootable and highly profitable.[3]

Svante Cornell, Director at Central Asia-Caucasus Institute at Johns Hopkins University, argued that narcotics and diamonds have a stronger influence on the duration of conflict than oil, gas, timber or minerals. Narcotics, particularly, tend to favour non-state actors disproportionately because of its illegality, allowing them to strengthen their operational capabilities and even to increase their legitimacy with producing communities (Cornell, 2005). Narco-trafficking is in fact the largest source of profit for both criminal groups and terrorism, accounting for 2% of the global economy according to the International Monetary Fund, and 7% of international trade following United Nations statistics (Shelley and Picarelly, 2005, 312).

Narcotics offer a good example on how political and economic variables interact. The existence of war economies generates political effects that are favourable to insurgencies. Vanda Felbab-Brown, a researcher at Brookings Institution, demonstrated that legitimacy is not only constructed through ideological affinity. In the case of narcotics, the insurgency provides the structure and stability in regions where it is *de facto* authority, allowing communities to make a way of living (Felbab-Brown, 2010, 17). By reciprocity, the insurgency wins freedom of action, popular support and legitimacy (Felbab-Brown, 2010, 17). The counterinsurgent is consequentially unpopular in areas of coca or opium cultivation, and it is generally observed as the enemy, because a disruption of the war economy, implies a risk to the survival of local communities.

The Triadic Character of Insurgencies

It has been argued that insurgencies display a triadic character that can't be defined exclusively in political or criminal terms, especially those which operate in areas where commodities like narcotics sustain a criminal economy (Palma, 2015). They demonstrate three dimensions existing simultaneously: political, criminal and military. Whereas these three describe the functions of the insurgency, the former two speak about the motivations of insurgents. This means that within the organization, as observed by Ballentine and Sherman, it is possible to find individuals motivated by profit, by a political objective, and even those looking for both.

The political dimension includes all of those who are fighting to achieve a goal that can be defined as political. There could of course be endless discussions about what is and what isn't political, but that is obviously not the objective in this chapter. Colin Gray explains that politics "refers to the process of struggle over the right or authority to govern the 'body politic' and hence decide on the distribution of civic burdens and rewards" (Gray, 1999, p.55). It is sufficient to say that those who intend to transform the ways in which society is organized and ruled, and the way in which power is exercised, purse a political objective. But beyond political motivations, there are also those who perform 'political' tasks. Insurgencies do not only wage war, they also spread their discourse and ideas, and look to increase their support, in some cases through political parties. These functions include the development of popular assemblies and smaller local meetings; indoctrination of individuals; dissemination of ideas by word of mouth; and the spread of propaganda through pamphlets or radio stations. Today, all of these tasks extend to cyberspace and include online social networks.

The military dimension is composed by proper combatants, insurgents who are waging war. They may be motivated by a specific political objective, or by profit, but still, as combatants, they are part of this dimension. This means that the three dimensions overlap. Tasks in the military dimensions resemble those of conventional military institutions: recruiting and finding adequate personnel, developing training and specialization, executing operations, building logistical chains, securing communication channels, establishing internal control and discipline, and obtaining intelligence.

The criminal dimension is formed by all insurgents whose motivation is to profit from war, and those who perform activities related to the production or trade of the commodities that fuel their interests. In the case of narcotics, for example, these activities include providing raw materials; cultivating coca or poppy; processing them into narcotics; collecting taxes from peasant and dealers; selling and transporting to shipment points; money laundering and providing security to the infrastructure.

The triadic character framework of analysis describes the realities of the Taliban, the Kurdistan Worker's Party, and the Revolutionary Armed Forces of Colombia. Understanding this character is vital to determine appropriate policy responses.

The Taliban

It is commonly believed that the Taliban-led insurgency remains focused on its strategic goals: controlling the population, expanding insurgent influence, driving out coalition forces, defeating the Afghan National Security Forces, and undermining the central Afghan Government (US Department of State, 2011, 53). In general terms this is still true, but when the 'box is opened' it is possible to find interests in profit by certain Taliban commanders, and sectors within the insurgency.

Political and military structures are clearly identifiable within the organization. The highest political authority is the *shura*, a collegiate body that discusses strategic and political issues (Rashid, 2002, 189-191). The national-level *shura* is replicated through the regional and tribal levels, by local *shura* councils. By 2014, the military wing was led by Mullah Mohammed Omar. His closest advisor was a Chief of the General Staff, who was joined by the Chiefs of Staff of the Army and the Air Force (Rashid, 2002, 196). The insurgency itself was composed by two types of combatants: those who resemble a *lashkar,* militants who fight by their own will without any payment, and those who are paid professional soldiers recruited among former communist rebels (Rashid, 2002, 198). In that sense, several combatants might be more interested on receiving their payments, than on winning their war.

But observing the Taliban as a unified movement is not necessarily appropriate. The insurgency has evolved into a more structurally diversified organization on both sides of the Afghan-Pakistani border, and less of a cohesive hierarchical monolithic body. There seems to be at least three main factions: Mullah Omar's faction, strong in the central region with a very militaristic approach; the Seraajudin Haqqani faction, also present in central Afghanistan; and the Lashkaar-i-Dadullah Shaheed faction with limited contact with the population, but stronger in the South. It is said to be close to Pakistan's Military Intelligence (Tariq, 2009, 51).

"Because of this diversity, it is often described as a loosely structured organization where regional commanders maintain relatively high degrees of independence to conduct operations and raise funds" (Peters, 2009, 8). According to Gretchen Peters, a journalist and researcher who has done extensive field research in Afghanistan, "operational autonomy of local commanders increased considerably in the post-2001 phase" (Peters, 2009, 8). This autonomy is vital to discover profiting interests within the organization. Since local commanders are the key to the insurgency's structure, Taliban's actions will basically depend on their interests and priorities, and lower-level commanders were actually the ones in charge of taxing and extorting money from local populations, keeping funds for local operations (US Department of Defense, 2011, 53).

This decentralization of the Taliban became evident as most fighters and sub-commanders operating in their districts reportedly felt disconnected from senior insurgent leaders. They observed them as living safely outside major conflict areas, while making profit out of war (US Department of Defense, 2011, 53). This is especially the case because in terms of money flows, the Taliban remained a strict hierarchy, with the top tiers concentrating most of the wealth (Peters, 2009a, 8). According to a report produced by the US Department of Defense in 2011, "the dissonance between Pakistan-based senior leadership and the rank-and-file insurgents located in Afghanistan should not be overstated, but it does suggest that seams within the insurgency may be widening" (US Department of Defense, 2011, 53).

The United States Peace Institute (USIP) explains that "it is no longer possible to treat the insurgency and the drug trade as separate matters, to be handled by military and law enforcement, respectively." (Peters, 2009b, 1). Taliban commanders on the village level have expanded their activities related to drugs from collecting extortion and charging protection fees to running heroin refineries and engaging in kidnapping and other smuggling schemes (Peters, 2009b, 1):

In areas where the Taliban are dominant, the village-level Taliban subcommander will hand out written receipts for the amount of opium collected, and farmers interviewed for this study *said the Taliban leadership was strict in assigning each commander's control zone. Researchers for this study heard multiple cases in which farmers complained to the Taliban leadership of being overcharged, and the Quetta Shura responded by punishing the subcommanders. Likewise, Taliban commanders keep track of how much farmers and other members of the local community are earning by maintaining informants in each community, paying the equivalent of $10 a tip for information. In areas where there was no clear dominant force, there are reports of fighting between Taliban commanders, criminal gangs, and corrupt officials, who all appear to prey on the farmers. (Peters, 2009b, 18)*

USIP declares "that insurgent actors in many Afghan villages today behave more like mafiosi than mujahideen. More than 80 percent of those surveyed believe Taliban commanders in the South now fight for profit rather than religion or ideology. And according to recent NATO military intelligence, as few as 5 percent of insurgent commanders now fight for ideological reasons" (Peters, 2009b, 5).

Like many insurgencies, the Taliban profits from taxation, extortion, smuggling, drug trafficking, and foreign donations, but the bulk of it, proceeds from drug trafficking. The second-generation Taliban, the one that has evolved from its removal from power in 2001, "has a more pragmatic approach than their ideologically more purist first-generation forbearers: they exploit the opium business, they avidly use suicide operations, they embrace the media for their own propaganda, and they use new technologies, even digital films and music" (Rid and Hecker; 2009).

The Taliban has several methods of profiting from the drug trade. The first one is the *ushr,* an imposed tax rate of 10% on poppy cultivation. It is collected at the village level by the Taliban subcommander (Peters, 2009a, 8). Besides *ushr*, the Taliban collects a percentage of every drug shipment, in some cases as high as 20% (Peters, 2009a, 10). There is also money received from protection to thousands of poppy merchants. The latter seems to be the most profitable of them all (Peters, 2009a, 20). The Taliban also collected taxes at drug refineries located near the Pakistan and Iran borders. Eventually, some Taliban commanders began running refineries themselves: "Militants 'oversaw heroin production' at as many as fifty heroin labs—and the number of labs in operation expanded during their time in power. Some employed as many as sixty men" (Peters, 2009a, 21).

In sum, as Gretchen Peters argued, it is impossible to explain the resurgence of the Taliban after 2010 without observing the economic miracle that financed their comeback (Peters, 2009a, 7). Taliban insurgents and drug-dealers managed to place an agricultural product of a country with lagging trade networks and infrastructure into the global economy; they succeeded in creating both farming and exporting networks.

The Kurdistan Peoples Party

The case of the PKK is not different. The organization also demonstrates a triadic character composed by political, criminal and military dimensions. Its original goal was to establish a Kurdish state in South-eastern Turkey, where about half of the world's 30 million Kurds live. In recent years, that goal evolved away from the reclamation of total independence, into increasing autonomy for the region (Curtis and Karakan, 2002, 18). Like in the case of the Taliban, its involvement with drug trafficking has also changed the organization's nature.

Regarding its political structure, the PKK has three directing institutions: The President and the Council of the Presidency, the Central Committee, and the Central Discipline Committee (Roth and Sever, 906). The Central Committee governs PKK activities, while the Central Disciplinary Board monitors discipline of its members. Members of these bodies are elected by the Party Congress which is the assembly of all members. The structure is replicated at the provincial, regional and local levels to form Provincial Committees, Local Committees, and Cells. The PKK also counts on an international political wing known as the ERNK (National Liberation Front of Kurdistan). It is in charge of all the diplomatic and propaganda actions, especially in Europe. This organization works as an umbrella for student groups and cultural institutions.

In terms of its military dimension, the PKK counts with a military branch known as the ARGK (Kurdistan's People Liberation Army), with bases in Armenia, Azerbaijan, Iran, Iraq, Syria and Turkey. It was believed to have between 4000 and 5000 combatants, with probably 15000 at its peak (Mannes, 2004, 183). It also had an intelligence and counterintelligence agency, and specialized terrorist units, such as the Metropolitan Teams for Terror (Mannes, 2004).

As it was described by a Europol report, the PKK has been involved in drug trafficking, human smuggling, illegal immigration, identity theft, money laundering and fraud (Kenes, 2011). A study prepared by the Research Division of the Library of Congress of the United States defines de PKK as a "terrorist organization with various illegal trafficking and money-laundering activities that depend heavily on links in Western Europe. Because it is known to have dealt extensively with criminal organizations in trafficking both arms and narcotics, the PKK has been an important nexus of criminal activities with terrorism" (Kurtis & Karakan, 2002, 18).

Frank Urbancic, deputy counterterrorism coordinator at the US State Department described the PKK as "the mafia all over Europe (...) it has an octopus-like structure carrying out criminal activities, including drug and people smuggling to raise funds, as well as fronts that provide cover for the organization's criminal and terror activities" (Onay, 2008).

Besides drugs, an important volume of the organization's funds comes from a sophisticated people-smuggling network transporting refugees from northern Iraq to Italy. The three most frequently routes are Istanbul-Milan, Istanbul-Bosnia-Milan, and Turkey-Tunisia-Malta-Italy (Curtis & Karakan, 2002, 20). Evidence also demonstrates that the PKK supplied arms to other Kurdish terrorist groups and to the Tamil Tigers (Curtis and Karakan, 2002, 20).

With narcotics, the PKK operates as a multilevel business organization involved in all phases of the production/distribution chain. The first phase, laboratory production from the morphine base, is usually done in Pakistan; the final phase, retail sales, is done in European streets with people on the PKK payroll (Curtis & Karakan, 2002, 21; Cornell, 2005, 625). It asserted a dominating role in the trade of heroin along the Balkan route from Afghanistan through Iran and Turkey to Western Europe, with Istanbul as a transhipment point (Curtis & Karakan, 2002, 21). Kurdish networks in Western Europe played a crucial role in marketing and distribution (Cornell, 2005, 625). Interpol documented drug trade by several Kurdish clans based in Germany, Italy, the Netherlands, and Spain with ties to the PKK (Curtis & Karakan, 2002, 21). Like it seems to be the case with the Taliban, the PKK also operates heroin laboratories in Turkey and northern Iraq (Curtis & Karakan, 2002, 21). 833 suspected PKK members were arrested from 1984 to 2010 on drug-dealing related charges (Sunday's Saman, 2011).

Tensions between the criminal and the political character of the organization can be evidenced with PKK's leader Abdullah Ocalan's declaration:

I am aware that my brother (Osman) is collecting money from people who conduct drug trafficking. In addition, there are some structures called customs units of the organization and located along the borders. They collect the money as well... On the borders a certain amount of money is collected from traffickers as a tax. Apart from that, I did not accept the proposal of drug trafficking in Iran/Maku region, although I knew it would provide a high level of income. Despite this fact, I learned that some people in the organization, in particular my brother, Osman Ocalan, were trafficking drugs to Europe through Iran, Zagros, and Romania. I warned them not to get involved in this. However, at certain points, it is obvious that I could not control the organization very well. (Roth and Sever, 908)

Revolutionary Armed Forces of Colombia

Just like in the case of the Taliban and the PKK, FARC also displays behaviours that demonstrate the existence of three dimensions. The organization dates from the 1950s as a self-defence group of liberal armed peasants defending against the Conservative government, in an era of partisan violence. With the emergence of communism in Colombia, the group is formally created by 1964 as an armed branch of the Colombian Communist Party. Until the 1980s its political agenda was clear: social equality, land distribution, peasant rights, political representation, and opposition to the oligarchy.

It could be said that its political dimension was composed by all insurgents, but the military dimension only by combatants in the jungles and mountains, excluding communists in the cities. But this structural arrangement changed with the end of the Cold War. A rupture with the Communist Party, forced FARC to assume both the political and military tasks. In a first attempt, the creation of a Political Party known as *Union Patriotica* opened a door for the insurgency to participate in national politics. The extermination of this Party by extremist right-wing forces, motivated the creation of a clandestine organization known as the *Partido Comunista Colombiano Clandestino*. The latter, together with the *Movimiento Bolivariano*, and possibly with the newer peasant-based *Marcha Patriotica*, expresses FARC's political dimension.

The criminal dimension only appeared when narcotics became a notorious enterprise in Colombia. Through the drug cartels, especially Medellin, the extensive plantation of coca was introduced in Colombian soil, with a variant of the leaves cultivated in Peru. FARC was initially sceptic about peasants seeding coca leaves, but their conviction and the insurgency's scepticism to cultivation created a gap between them. Thinking about consequences for its legitimacy, the insurgency finally accepted the production of cocaine in territories of their dominion, conditioned to a 10% tax charged to drug-dealers, and to the cultivation of other daily life products.

FARC's participation in narco-trafficking would progressively increase through the years, changing combatants' interests within war. FARC eliminated intermediaries between peasant producers and buyers, becoming more dominant through the production/trade chain. From simply charging taxes and providing security to drug producers, they became the most important sellers in the country. It is not clear how deeply involved they are with transnational trafficking. But it is known that they have agreements with international cartels, including the Mexicans, for selling. FARC sells directly to some of the most sophisticated Colombian traders (micro-cartels).

It is a widespread believe that FARC has lost its political horizon, becoming a criminal enterprise; a hypercartel (Guzman & Muñoz, 2004). During Alvaro Uribe's government a particular discourse which depicts insurgents as a bunch of bandits and terrorists, interested only in drug-dealing, became widely popular. But this vision might be quite extreme. Explaining FARC today purely as a criminal organization might ignore several social grievances, which could trigger future violence if unaddressed. Several senior commanders still demonstrate concern for the political issues and goals. In fact, Alfonso Cano, former FARC Commander who was killed in a military operation, made all efforts to emphasise the political character of the organization prioritising political actions and institutions. He promoted the *Movimiento Bolivariano por la Nueva Colombia* as a wide and opened movement to reach social and political sectors seeking their support. He proposed a plan to adapt to the strong state offensive conducted during the Uribe administration. Besides several strategic and tactical military dispositions, this comprehensive programme known as *Plan Renacer Revolucionario de las Masas,* focused deeply on regaining support from the masses through political action.

This does not mean that the organization is free from tensions between its political and criminal dimensions. Cano had to send a strong message to several of his commanders who were peacefully living a life of luxury in safe havens, instead of fighting in Colombia. It became publicly known that FARC was not happy with Grannobles's behaviour, a member of the Secretariat who had apparently been living as a drug-dealer in Venezuela. A similar case is presented by Oliver Solarte, former finance commander of the 48th front, "a proper drug-dealer who controlled the entire business in the region and who behaved like a criminal more than like an insurgent."[4] Similarly, Gener Garcia Molina (a.k.a. John 40), who controlled finances in the province of Guainía, was removed from the 43rd Front Command because of his excessive behaviour (Vox Populi, 2012, December 4).

However, the fact that there is a new peace process in which FARC is discussing specific social grievances, speaks about the existence of a political agenda. An understanding of the organization as having three dimensions, then, bears a stronger explanatory power than simply qualifying it as a criminal organization.

A useful metaphor in this explanation could be a Marlboro cigarette. The insurgency is the entire cigarette. It is composed of two parts, the yellow filter, smaller and representing the top hierarchy. Commanders are more aligned to a political vision, and to the interest in achieving their original objectives. A longer white tobacco tube, represents the middle ranks and the bulk of combatants who would be more motivated by profit. But this division might not be strict, some commanders might be interested in profits just as lower-rank militants could be fighting for a political objective. In that sense, a more realistic image is that of a spotted Marlboro cigarette; white spots on the filter, representing those commanders interested in wealth, and yellow spots along the white tube, as an analogy of combatants motivated by an ideal.

THINKING ABOUT COUNTERINSURGENCY

As it can be observed, these organizations are combinations of political and criminal interests. An understanding of the organization as a monolithic entity would fail to explain the nature of the struggle and would consequentially lead into bad policy-making. Solutions need to address social, political and profit-based motivations simultaneously. States would make considerable mistakes if they, for example, address only political grievances. In that case they would leave an opened window, an opportunity, for those with an economic motivation to continue exploiting violence to their favour. This means, groups within the organization will fail to lay down their weapons, or that new groups will emerge. By contrast, if only the elements that generate profiting interests are addressed, unattended political grievances could continue to generate violence on the long term.

When thinking about solutions to the problem, it is unavoidable to land in the field of counterinsurgency and nation-building, including sustainable development. They might look like contrasting enterprises: making war against an organization, and trying to construct a sustainable community. Truth is they are both sides of the same coin. Counterinsurgency theory has evolved to a point in which it is difficult to strictly divide it from nation-building.

It is not ignored that the state has several possibilities to solve conflicts beyond making war. The negotiation table is always a possibility; mediation, concessions and appeasement, are always options. In most cases, however states must face the challenge of fighting an armed organization, and this is why it is necessary to discuss appropriate ways to address insurgency scenarios. It is the case of the three organizations discussed in this chapter.

Without going deeply into theory, it is not incorrect to say that counterinsurgency practice has progressively evolved to incorporate elements of sustainable development and nation building. Evidently, experiences before 20th Century would be incompatible with today's efforts to pacify communities in conflict, and to build nations. During the Napoleonic era, insurrections were suppressed by force, excess and brutality. In Calabria entire towns were garrisoned, while in Spain summary executions were applied to people who were absent from home on the assumption they were active guerrilla members. Public meetings were forbidden, holidays suspended and clerics deported. It was decreed that for every Frenchman killed, four insurgents would be hanged, and if there weren't any, civilians would take their place (Beckett, 2001, p.27). The infamous *Colonnes infernales* (infernal columns) terrorized civilians through assassinations, deportations, fires, confiscations, abusing of woman and drowning of priests (Beckett, 2001). During the Franco-Prussian war, retaliatory measures by the Prussians against French communities included the burning of houses, and the imposition of forced contributions for civilians (Howard, 2001). Bismarck himself urged that villages be burned to terrorize the French into rapid submission (Beckett, 2001).

British response to colonial insurgencies was not an exception. In the Boer Wars, there were orders to burn down or blow up all the houses next to railways, bridges or telegraphic lines that were attacked. Collective fines were decreed, and civilians were forced to ride trains as human shields. Martial Law was declared increasing tensions between the Army and local politicians. 30,000 farmhouses were destroyed by 1902 (Beckett, 2001, p.39). By 1900 an internment system was extended through all the Boer Republics, and the population was entirely removed from their places of origin. 28000 Boer civilians were garrisoned in 40 concentration camps, and 16000 to 20000 died. Similar mechanisms of extermination were applied by the Germans in South and East Africa (1904-1907). There, between 50 to 80 per cent of African tribes were eliminated (Merom, 2003).

It was with the American global expansion after 1898 that the evolution of counterinsurgency towards a 'civic action' approach popularized. Its purpose was to win support from the community in order to break the bond between insurgents and the population. In that sense 'attraction' programmes were created, combining political and military elements. Specific health, education, public services and recreation missions were established to carry their benefits to vulnerable population. Through propaganda, the idea was to convince the population that the state was better than the insurgents; in other words, to win the hearts and minds of the population by demonstrating that the state would bring more benefits than the rebels. But as several experiences would later demonstrate, this wasn't enough.

The era of Maoism and national liberation movements served as the platform to the construction of a proper body of counterinsurgency theory, mainly by former Officers who had considerable field experience. French and British officers like David Galula (1964), Robert Thompson (1966) and Frank Kitson (1971) came to be known as classic theorists. They explained the struggle against insurgents not as a military effort, but as a state political action which required participation of all state institutions. It was understood as a competition between two parties to gain support of the masses. This is why legitimacy became the most important factor in this competition, and the reason why state's actions shouldn't disrupt people's lives. By contrast, they should be focused in guaranteeing a better life for communities. Counterinsurgency became more about selling an idea to the population than killing every single rebel. This became a wide and accepted perspective during the Cold War, but in a context of criminalized economies and profiting interests, as it is proved by the Colombian case, more was necessary.

The classical theorists created the base for the formulation of a development-centred vision of counterinsurgency, although they never went as far as to relate it with the practice of nation-building. It was with the experiences of the United States and the United Kingdom in Afghanistan and Iraq that the idea of a 'comprehensive approach' emerged through the global counterinsurgency thought, bringing together security, economic and information elements as pillars of a political strategy. The idea that a struggle against insurgencies was not an affair of the military, but a matter of state policy was revisited by theoreticians and practitioners such as General George Casey, Carter Malkasian, Daniel Marston, General David Petraeus, and Coronel John Nagl, among many others, to conclude that the effort of all state institutions in security and development was necessary for a successful counterinsurgency strategy. This vision deeply penetrated American and British doctrine, and it was influential in Colombia as well. In American doctrine, development activities (economic pillar). are defined as "immediate humanitarian relief and the provision of essential services, as well as longer-term programs to develop the infrastructure and capacity for legitimate agricultural, industrial, educational, medical, commercial and governmental activities" (United States Government Interagency Counterinsurgency Initiative, 2009, 17).

With the appointment of General George Casey as head of operations in Iraq, a counterinsurgency model known as 'clear-hold-build' began to be implemented, deepening the development component of the equation (Malkasian and Marston, 2009). In general terms the model seeks to clear areas of insurgency, to maintain a stable presence of security institutions in those areas, and to build state institutions and the capabilities for the communities for sustainable development.

It is the 'build' component which makes counterinsurgency similar, if not identical, to nation-building. Once the insurgency is expelled and the presence of security institutions is guaranteed, the campaign turns into development. The objective is to build capabilities for communities to achieve social and economic sustainability within the law, with a permanent presence of all state institutions. This is a step beyond civic action campaigns aimed at winning the hearts and minds of the population. Whereas medical, educational or other types of civic campaigns might be temporary, the aim of local development is sustainability through time, reducing dependence on particular state campaigns and empowering local communities. It is this particular component of a counterinsurgency campaign that makes the elimination of criminal economies a vital part of an overall strategy to defeat insurgents.

In the case of narcotics, Vanda Felbab-Brown very well explained how counterinsurgency actions and antinarcotics are constantly at odds. As it has been explained, communities who live in areas of coca or poppy plantations find sustenance on the criminal economy. Their lives are possible because drug-dealing exists. When the state is trying to win people's support as it attacks the insurgency, it may also erode the economy through which they find a way of living, generating rejection and resentment towards its actions (Felbab-Brown; 2010). This is why an overall comprehensive strategy is necessary. It is not appropriate to simply remove the insurgency from the area and to disrupt the criminal economy, without providing sustainable options for communities to integrate to the nation. This is why counterinsurgency will never be effective in these cases if it doesn't include a 'build' component. It is not enough to sell state propaganda or to carry temporary missions to convince people that insurgents are 'the bad ones'; achieving local development, with the participation of all state institutions, is an absolute 'must' when criminal economies exist.

This type of policy action is also relevant considering the micro-dynamics of conflict, or what Stathis Kalyvas has called violence in civil war, as opposed to the civil war itself. On the micro level, violence doesn't only erupt because of ideological discussions between political actors. In many cases violence emerges as a consequence of local dynamics of tension between groups, communities, families and allegiances towards specific actors (2006). Breaking allegiances with illicit agents, and building legitimacy for state institutions, who could provide a sense of order within the law, is precisely the objective of this approach. Pretending that the state will be powerful and disruptive enough to finalize tensions at the personal level is an illusion. But systemic violence at the local level might be resolved through the presence of state institutions and their legitimate action within the law. As Kalyvas has stated: "contrary to widespread perception, allegiances may be endogenous to the war, [and] military control of a locale may result in popular collaboration" (Kalyvas, 2006, 5).

Now, this does not necessarily mean that the state is the one and only institution with a mandate to build sustainable communities as a top-down exercise. In one hand, the state itself is also composed by many sectors, institutions, groups, and individuals with their own particular interest in conflict. There might even be spoilers within the state, or among political sectors, willing to perpetuate conflict as much as insurgents. In a counterinsurgency campaign the state might end up fuelling the cycles of violence instead of breaking them. In the other hand, society itself, social organizations and institutions, could have a stronger and more effective role in nation and community building than the state itself. In the interest of limiting the discussion in this paper, its focus is on state action, without intending to ignore other approaches.

Development-Centred Counterinsurgency in Colombia

The historical inexistence of state institutions in isolated regions in Colombia motivated the growth of illegal armed groups, and their transformation into de facto authorities. FARC, particularly, became strong through the 1980s and 1990s, becoming a dominant territorial actor in Southeastern Colombia. During the administration of Ernesto Samper (1994-1998) FARC managed to launch considerably strong attacks against the Military Forces in this region, demonstrating a solid military capability (Ospina, 2006). Through peace negotiations conducted with President Andres Pastrana (1998-2002), FARC grew stronger. The organization used a demilitarized zone the size of Switzerland to increase its military capabilities and its dominion over the coca business. But also, during this period the Military Forces were increasing their capabilities with resources from Plan Colombia (Pardo, 2004; Valencia, 2002).

The state was ready for a strong offensive against the rebels. With the first administration of Alvaro Uribe (2002-2006) the Democratic Security Policy was implemented to increase territorial control, and to attack FARC frontally in its core areas. The military build-up was combined with a group of Military Officers which revolutionized the way war was conducted in Colombia, with the implementation of Joint Commands, for example; and with the understanding of the struggle as an affair of the state requiring participation of all state institutions, and not an exclusive problem of the Military Forces (Spencer, 2011). Results can be understood as positive if the weakness of FARC by the end of this period is observed, but it is necessary to recognize that the campaign was not exempted from abuses, excesses and human rights violations. Large areas of the territory were cleared of insurgency, and to a considerable extent, many of those areas were 'hold' by the state, with the presence of the National Police force. The challenge was to achieve the 'build' side of the clear-hold-build model.

It was necessary to disrupt the war economy, mainly based on cocaine production, to replace it with sustainable legal economies which offered real opportunities for peasants to make a living. But the dilemma is not as simple. The problem itself is not cocaine production. The problem is the lack of economic and social infrastructure in marginalized regions, through which communities could become integrated with society. If cocaine disappeared, with the absence of such infrastructure, criminal economies would persist with other commodities and sources. By 2012, it was already becoming evident that illegal mining, gold, coltan and even timber, were potential sources for illicit economies to flourish, promoted by armed groups including criminal bands (BACRIMs) (El Tiempo, 2012).

This analysis is aggravated by the micro-dynamics of conflict, or what Stathis Kalyvas has called violence in civil war as opposed to the civil war itself. On the micro level, violence doesn't only erupt because of ideological discussions between political actors. In many cases violence emerges as a consequence of local dynamics of tension between groups, families and loyalties towards specific actors.

The strategy thus needed to guarantee that insurgents would not return and that state institutions would provide services and infrastructure to communities. This was the logic behind the *Politica de Consolidacion de la Seguridad Democratica* (PCSD), which was implemented during Alvaro Uribe's second administration (2006-2010). It has the same logic of 'stability operations' implemented by the United States in Afghanistan.

This Policy categorized three types of regions: zones of control, where insurgency was still strong and action of the Military Forces was required ('clear' stage); zones of stabilization or transition, where the military forces already had control but security needed to be enhanced ('hold' stage); and consolidation, where security had been achieved and institutions needed be developed to increase population welfare ('build' stage) (Ministerio de Defensa Nacional, 2007) (see Figure 1[5]).

For the purpose of 'building', the stage which incorporated development into counterinsurgency, the Presidency created the *Centro de Coordinación de Acción Integral* (CCAI). It was in charge of coordinating more than 20 national agencies and ministries for action in marginalized regions. Before the CCAI, state entities acted by themselves, with no coordination or without following a strategic central guideline. With the agency, once an area was stabilized and ready for consolidation,

Figure 1.

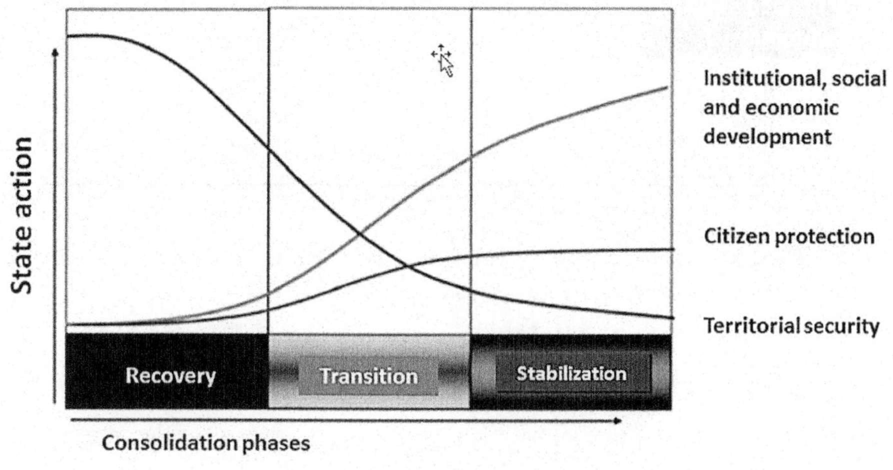

Figure 2.

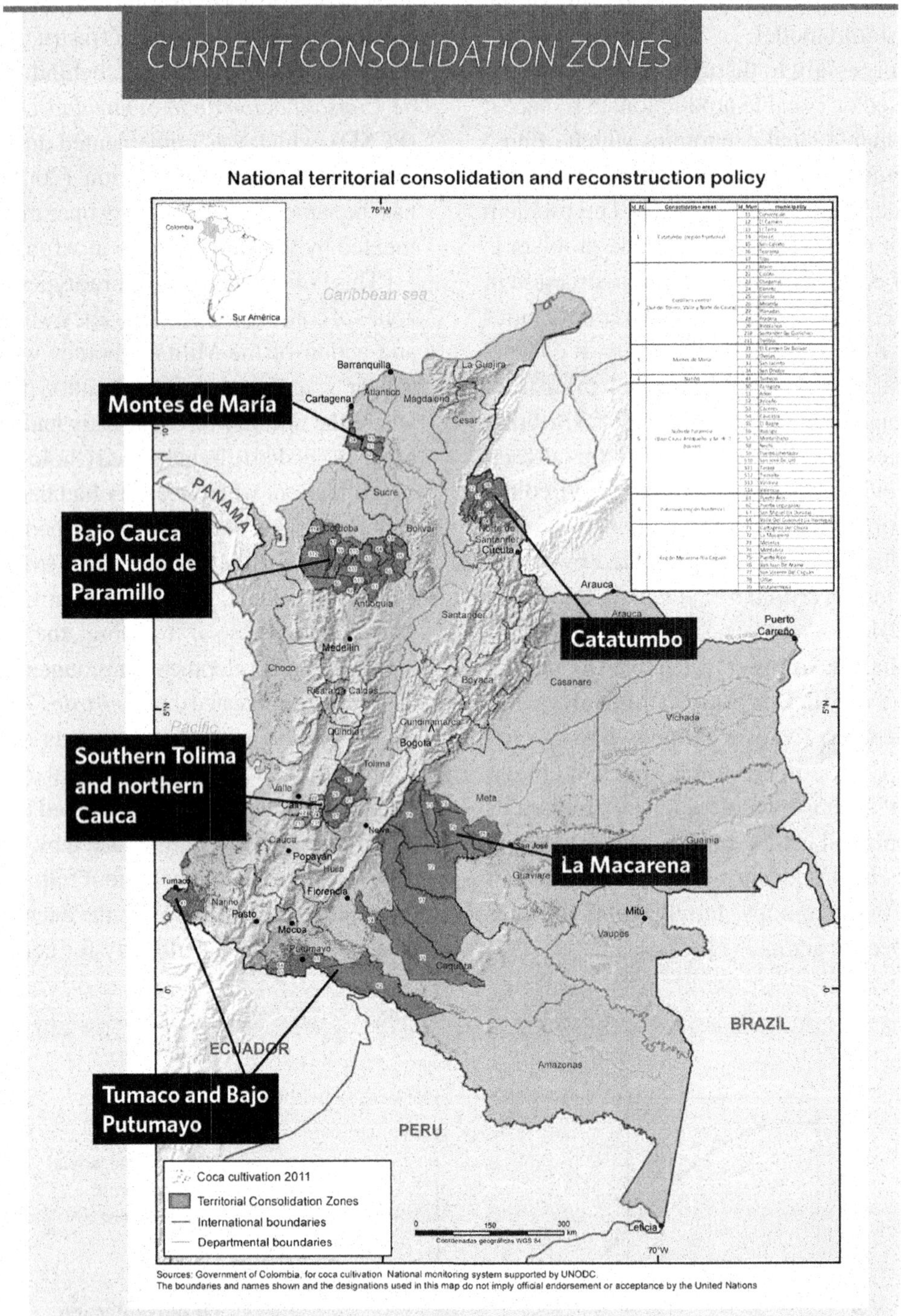

Map Source: United Nations Office on Drugs and Crime. Green areas indicate 2011 coca cultivation.

Figure 3.

Id_zc	Consolidation areas	Id_mun	Municipality
1	Catatumbo (region fronteriza)	11	Convención
		12	El Carmen
		13	El Tarra
		14	Hacarí
		15	San Calixto
		16	Teorama
		17	Tibú
2	Cordillera Central	21	Ataco
	(sur del Tolima, Valle y Norte del Cauca)	22	Caloto
		23	Chaparral
		24	Corinto
		25	Florida
		26	Miranda
		27	Planadas
		28	Pradera
		29	Río Blanco
		210	Santander de Quilichao
		211	Toribio
3	Montes de María	31	El Carmen de Bolivar
		32	Ovejas
		33	San Jacinto
		34	San Onofre
4	Nariño	41	Tumaco
5	Nudo de Paramillo (Bajo Cauca antioqueño y sur de Bolivar)	50	Zaragoza
		51	Anorí
		52	Briceño
		53	Cáceres
		54	Caucasia
		55	El bagre
		56	Ituango
		57	Montelibano
		58	Nechí
		59	Puerto Liberador
		510	San José de Uri
		511	Tarazá
		512	Tierra Alta
		513	Valdivia
		514	Valencia
6	Putumayo (region fronteriza)	61	Puerto Asís
		62	Puerto Leguízamo
		63	San Miguel (la Dorada)
		64	Valle del Guamuéz (La Hormiga)
7	Región Macarena- Río Caguan	71	Cartagena del Chairá
		72	La Macarena
		73	Mesetas
		74	Montañita
		75	Puerto Rico
		76	San Juan de Arama
		77	San Vicente del Caguan
		78	Uribe
		79	Vistahermosa

a task force would design an inter-institutional action plan. In the field, the task forced was transformed into a *Centro de Fusion* (Joint or Fusion Centre) through which actions and quick impact projects were implemented, guaranteeing coordination of all institutions within a strategy. There were initially 9 zones to be intervened, but at the end of the Uribe administration there were 15 planned regions for intervention, including former guerrilla havens such as La Macarena in the Southeast, Sierra Nevada de Santa Marta in the North and Montes de Maria in the Northwest (see Figures 2 and 3[6]).

There was a relative level of success in La Macarena and Montes de Maria, which served as pilot project areas. Just in La Macarena, the National Police was present in all municipalities within the zone, "guerrilla attacks and acts of sabotage dropped sharply, as did homicides and other measures of violent crime. According to Colombia's police and the United Nations Office on Drugs and Crime (UNODC), 77 percent of coca grown in the PCIM region was eradicated between 2007 and 2010, and in some (though certainly not all) cases, authorities offered families whose crops were eradicated access to food security and other short-term assistance" (Isacson, 2012). 538 quick impact projects were completed in La Macarena, ranging from small road improvements to the construction of schools and clean water infrastructure. New police stations opened in six towns (Isacson, 2012)

A proper bottom-up decision process was implemented by the CCAI allowing meetings between community leaders, government officials, and the military, allowing the population to decide which projects they saw as a priority for development. By 2010, US$254 million had gone into the non-military side of the Consolidation effort in La Macarena (Isacson, 2012).

Unfortunately, the strategy never fully materialized, and its level of priority for the state seems to have fallen down. Whereas there were advances in La Macarena and Montes de Maria, the rest of the consolidation areas never took off properly. There are several explanations.

CCAI was a national 'cabinet' level agency placed within the orbit of the Presidency of the Republic, and not responding to a specific Ministry. It was more of a coordination centre than a proper executive agency. The lack of a budget of its own made it difficult to advance. Ministries still determined their actions, supported with their own budgets. In many cases, executive institutions were not fully convinced of the need to focus on consolidation projects, so the institutional response to development in selected areas was rather slow:

the National Police's deployment is slow once territorial recovery has been secured," [(...)] there had been a "lack of response on the part of the Agrarian Bank" to provide credit to farmers in La Macarena, and "INCODER [the Agriculture Ministry's land-distribution agency] has failed to respond by titling productive un-owned land." A government source told the Colombian investigative journalism site La Silla Vacía (The Empty Chair) that "[d]uring the Uribe government the Transportation Ministry never wanted to get seriously involved.

The lag in effective participation of civilian ministries, such as the Ministry of Agriculture, and other actors undermines the PCIM [La Macarena Integrated Consolidation Plan] model of integrated state action," noted a January 2010 cable. "The current ad hoc inter-institutional process will result in poorly coordinated interventions that lack a long-term, structural impact.

It took "nearly two years of lobbying to secure" the presence of a special prosecutor and two investigators from Colombia's Prosecutor General's Office. (Isacson, 2012, 11)

Besides the lack of institutional will, the build component of a counterinsurgency campaign is always costly. It turned out to be far more expensive than authorities expected, discouraging the strategy as a political alternative. This is not only the case in Colombia, but also in Afghanistan. US authorities have suffered the consequences of expensive 'stabilization operations', weakening the desire of officials to continue following the course of nation-building:

frustration with both the Colombian and Afghan models may be justified, as they have been more costly than expected and — as we shall see — military-to-civilian transitions have been difficult to implement. Troublingly, though, it is not clear whether reforms are imminent, or what will be replacing them. (Isacson, 2012, 2)

Whereas the United States might at some point forget about the mess in Afghanistan, and decide to stop financing efforts in this country, Colombian authorities have no choice. They must provide a solution to the problem of insurgencies and criminal economies. If the plans for 'consolidation', as they have been formulated, are abandoned, they need to be replaced with others. Truth is, on the long term, security will be absent in Colombia if local development in sensitive areas is not achieved. *Building through development is not an option in the struggle against armed groups, it is a must.*

In the Colombian case there was also the dilemma of leadership and a change in priorities. The Administration of Juan Manuel Santos has chosen the path of negotiations with FARC as the way to end the fifty year-long war. This has demanded that all state efforts be focused on the peace process, leaving the 'consolidation' strategy, as a second-level priority. The head of the strategy was Sergio Jaramillo, former deputy Minister of Defense under Santos, but as soon as negotiations began, he was destined to Havana as the High Peace Commissioner. The agency became an administrative unit within the *Departamento para la Prosperidad Social*. Territorially, and as a way to address the historical grievances of the peasants, efforts have been focused on land redistribution and restitution, and the Military Forces have intensified counterinsurgency military actions in specific regions through a plan known as *Espada de Honor*. This offensive carries no civilian components of 'hold' and 'build', remaining far from a development-centred counterinsurgency model.

This does not mean that the peace process is a mistake. Its results could be rewarding in the demobilization of the Western hemisphere's oldest insurgent group, and the construction of bases to end the armed conflict. But even if the process comes to a positive end, the local nation-building component will be necessary in marginalized areas that have been riddled by crime and conflict for decades. As it has been said repetitively through this chapter, leaving criminal interests unattended will foster more violence in the future. This is what would happen if the build component of the equation is ignored.

But even if a successful negotiation erases the country's current guerrilla groups from the map, Colombia will still face yawning gaps of governance and justice in vast areas of this map. These gaps will breed further violence and make land restitution dangerous for many beneficiaries, if Colombia lacks a plan to fill them. The Consolidation program — if it could achieve a true civilian transition — appeared to be such a plan. That is why its apparent decline is so disturbing. (Isacson, 2012, 2)

If negotiations with FARC fail, then it is obvious that the state will need to reinforce its counterinsurgency strategy. Fighting guerrilla members and destroying coca fields, without providing a sustainable economic alternative for communities, is very much reinforcing an unending circle of violence, leading nowhere.

FUTURE RESEARCH DIRECTIONS

There are at least three directions in which research could go forward from this point. Firstly, more comparative cases with non-state armed organizations could offer lights about the idea of a triadic character within organizations, and how criminal interests can be observed structurally within the insurgency: the configuration of specific units in certain areas where such interests are more easily observable, or a more generalized spread of such interests. Secondly, it is important to conduct more field research in specific areas where this type of strategies are applied. It is necessary to evaluate the strengths and weaknesses of this type of strategy, and the performance of particular state institutions in the field. Finally, and specifically for the case of Colombia, it could be studied, how this type of strategies can be applied in a context in which insurgencies have signed a peace agreement with the government. Criminality, especially related do drug-dealing, are likely to continue, and could even intensify as reluctant combatants continue to profit from illicit markets. State building in isolated regions will still be necessary and so the approach could provide interesting perspectives on the solution.

CONCLUSION

Insurgencies are not monolithic organizations. Trying to understand armed actors through unitary concepts such as criminality, terrorism, or banditry, tend to be misleading. The cases of the Taliban, the Kurdistan Worker's Party, and the Revolutionary Armed Forces of Colombia, demonstrate that to have a better explanation of the nature and the character of these organizations, it is necessary to 'open the box' and to dig deeper within, to discover diverse interests, motivations and functions that combatants and insurgents have. Through this approach, it is possible to observe that there are political and criminal motivations within a single organization. Whereas some rebels are convinced of the necessity to wage war in order to achieve an altruist political goal, others make war only to obtain profits.

This implies that to address conflicts where insurgencies operate it is necessary to respond to both types of motivations. If a solution is thought only in political terms, a fraction of the organization will persist pursuing profiting ends, either as a continuation of the same organization, or as a new entity. By contrast, if the problem is depicted as one of criminality, political grievances will run unattended, probably motivating future violence. In the end, successful policy requires confronting the insurgency responding both to political and criminal interests simultaneously. This takes us to the concept of development-centred counterinsurgency.

Although there is no specific definition of the concept, counterinsurgency has evolved during the last century to become a practice that combines military force and civilian action, leading into policies that could well be classified as nation-building. This type of campaign is ideal since it seeks to clear areas of insurgency, and to build state institutions in order to incorporate into society those marginalized communities which have depended on criminal economies. Insurgencies make profit from criminal economies, especially when commodities like narcotics are the base. Consequently, to erode the profiting interests of insurgents, and to avoid others from joining the organization as a way of living, it is necessary to disrupt those economies, replacing them with licit economic and social structures.

This is not an easy task. Both the United States in Afghanistan and Colombia have implemented development-centred counterinsurgency policies with low success. They have both recurred to the clear-hold-build models, in which the build component is aimed at creating sustainable legal economies. Whereas the United States referred to them as stability operations, Colombia implemented a policy known as Consolidation.

The experience of Colombia in specific pilot regions like La Macarena and Montes de Maria offers practical examples for the solutions of other cases of insurgency, from the point of view of development-centred counterinsurgency. In these regions, the state managed to clear the area of insurgents, holding it through the presence of military and police forces, avoiding the return of the rebels, and investing in quick impact projects to build economic structures, eroding criminal economies which had lasted for decades.

Unfortunately, the lack of will of certain state institutions, the elevated costs of development-centred counterinsurgency, the institutional weakness of the coordinating national agency, and the change of priorities of the office of the President, implied a relative decline of the Consolidation Policy. This is a mistake. The 'build' side of the equation is necessary with or without an agreement with FARC; if criminal economies are not disrupted, armed actors will continue to exist. If the government wants to forget about consolidation as it has been formulated, then it needs to come up with a viable alternative.

REFERENCES

Arnson, C. (2005). *Rethinking the Economics of War, the Intersection of Need, Creed and Greed*. Washington: The Woodrow Wilson Centre Press.

Ballentine, K., & Sherman, J. (2003). The Political Economy of Armed Conflict, Beyond Greed and Grievance. London: Boulder.

Becket, I. (2001). *Modern Insurgencies and Counterinsurgencies: Guerrillas and Opponents since 1750*. London: Routledge. doi:10.4324/9780203402450

Berdal, M. (2009). *Building Peace After War*. London: Routedge.

Berdal, M., & Malone, D. (2000). *Greed and Grievance: Economic Agendas in Civil Wars*. Boulder, Colorado: Lynne Rienner.

Bülent, K. (2011, September 30). European PKK. *Today's Zaman*. Retrieved from http://www.todayszaman.com/mobile_detailc.action?newsId=261416

Collier, P. (2000a). Doing Well out of a War: An Economic Perspective. In M. Berdal & D. Malone (Eds.), *Greed and Grievance: Economic Agendas in Civil Wars* (pp. 91–112). Boulder, Colorado: Lynne Rienner.

Collier, P. (2000b). Rebellion as a Quasi-Criminal Activity. *The Journal of Conflict Resolution*, *44*(6), 839–853. doi:10.1177/0022002700044006008

Collier, P., & Hoeffler, A. (1998). *On Economic Causes of Civil War*. Washington: World Bank.

Collier, P., & Hoeffler, A. (1999). *Justice-Seeking and Loot-Seeking in Civil War*. Washington: World Bank.

Collier, P., & Hoeffler, A. (2000). *Greed and Grievance in Civil War*. Washington: World Bank.

Cornell, S. (2005). The Interaction of Narcotics and Conflict. *Journal of Peace Research*, *42*(6), 751–760. doi:10.1177/0022343305057895

Curtis, G., & Karakan, T. (2002). *The Nexus Among Terrorists, Narcotics, Traffickers, weapons proliferators, and Traffickers, Weapons Proliferators and Organized Crime Networks in Western Europe*. Washington: Library of the Congress.

El Tiempo. (2012, September 11). Mineria Ilegal Desplaza a la coca en ocho regiones. *El Tiempo*. Retrieved from http://www.eltiempo.com/justicia/ARTICULO-WEB-NEW_NOTA_INTERIOR-12214227.html

Felbab-Brown, V. (2010). *Shooting Up, Counterinsurgency and the War on Drugs*. Washington: Brookings Institution Press.

Galula, D. (1964). *Counterinsurgency Warfare*. Westport, CT: Praeger.

Gray, C. (1999). *Modern Strategy*. Oxford: Oxford University Press.

Howard, M. (2001). *The Franco-Prussian War*. London: Routledge.

Isacson, A. (2012). *Consolidating Consolidation*. Washington: Washington Office on Latin America.

Kaldor, M. (2005). *New and Old Wars*. Cambridge: Polity.

Kalyvas, S. (2006). *The Logic of Violence in Civil War*. Cambridge: Cambridge University Press. doi:10.1017/CBO9780511818462

Keen, D. (1998). *The Economic Functions of Civil Wars*. Oxford: Oxford University Press.

Keen, D. (2006). *Endless War? Hidden Functions of the War on Terror*. Ann Arbor: Pluto Press.

Keen, D.; Berdal, M. (1997). Violence and Economic Agendas in Civil Wars: Some Policy Implications. *Millennium Journal of International Studies 26(3)*.795-818

Kitson, F. (1971). *Low Intensity Operations: Subversion, Insurgency, Peacekeeping*. London: Faber and Faber.

Lewison, R. (1936). *The Profits of War through the Ages*. London: George Routledge and Sons Ltd.

Malkasian, C., & Marston, D. (2008). Counterinsurgency in Modern Warfare. Oxford: Osprey.

Mannes, A. (2004). *Profiles in terror: the Guide to Middle East Terrorist Organizations*. Lanham: Rowan and Littlefield.

Merom, G. (2003). *How Democracies lose Small Wars*. Cambridge: Cambridge University Press. doi:10.1017/CBO9780511808227

Ministerio de Defensa Nacional. (2007). *Politica de Consolidacion de la Seguridad Democratica*. Bogota: Ministerio de Defensa Nacional.

Munkler, H. (2006). *The New Wars*. Cambridge: Polity.

Navias, M., & Moreman, T. (1994). Limited War and Developing Countries. In L. Freedman (Ed.), *War* (pp. 310–314). Oxford: Oxford University Press.

O'Neill, B. (1980). *Insurgency in the Modern World*. Boulder: Westview Press.

Onay, A. (2008, February 21) PKK Criminal Networks and Fronts in Europe. *Policy Watch No. 1344*. Washington: The Washington Institute.

Ospina, C. (2006). Insights from Colombia's Long War: Counterinsurgency Lessons Learned. *Journal of Counterterrorism and Homeland Security International*, *12*(3), 26–33.

Palma, O. (2015). Transnational Networks of Insurgency and Crime: Explaining the spread of commercial insurgencies beyond national borders. *Small Wars & Insurgencies*, *26*(3), 476–496. doi: 10.1080/09592318.2014.982885

Pardo, R. (2004). *Historia de las Guerras*. Bogota: Ediciones B.

Peters, G. (2009a). The Taliban and the Opium Trade. In A. Giustozzi (Ed.), *Decoding the Taliban: Insights from the Afghan Field* (pp. 7–22). New York: Columbia University Press.

Peters, G. (2009b). *How opium profits the Taliban*. Washington: United States Institute of Peace.

Rashid, A. (2002). *Los Taliban*. Barcelona: Ediciones Peninsula.

Rid, T., & Hecker, M. (2009). *War 2.0 Irregular Warfare in the Information Age*. London: Praeger.

Ross, M. (2004) Oil, Drugs and Diamonds: The Varying Role of Natural Resources in Civil War. In K. Ballentine, & J. Sherman (Eds.), The Political Economy of Armed Conflict, Beyond Greed and Grievance (pp. 47-72). London: Boulder.

Roth, M., & Sever, M. (2007). The Kurdish Worker's Party (PKK) as a Criminal Syndicate: Funding Terrorism through Organized Crime, A Case Study. *Studies in Conflict and Terrorism*, *30*(10), 901–920. doi:10.1080/10576100701558620

Shelley, L., & Picarelly, J. (2005). Methods not Motives: Implications of the Convergence of International Organized Crime and Terrorism. *Police Practice and Research*, *3*(4), 305–318. doi:10.1080/1561426022000032079

Spencer, D. (2011). *Colombia Camino a la Recuperación: Seguridad y Gobernabilidad 1982-2010*. Washington: Center for Hemispheric Defense Studies.

Sunday's Zaman. (2011, May 10) Turkish police report reveals PKKs role in drug trafficking. *Today's Zaman*. Retrieved from http://www.todayszaman.com/news-243511-police-report-reveals-pkks-role-in-drug-smuggling-from-1984-to-2010.html

Tariq Elias, M. O. (2009). The resurgence of the Taliban in Kabul: Logan and Wardak. In A. Giustozzi (Ed.), *Decoding the Taliban: Insights from the Afghan Field* (pp. 43–56). New York: Columbia University Press.

Thompson, R. (1966). *Defeating Communist Insurgencies: Experiences from Malaya and Vietnam*. Michigan: Chatto and Windus.

US Department of Defense (2011, April) *Report on Progress Towards Security and Stability in Afghanistan*. Washington: Department of Defense.

US Government Interagency Counterinsurgency Initiative. (2009). *Counterinsurgency Guide*. Washington: Bureau of Political-Military Affairs.

Valencia, L. (2002). *Adios a la Politica, Bienvenida la Guerra*. Bogota: Intermedio.

ADDITIONAL READING

For more information on the Colombian conflict and the emergence of guerrillas read:

Baron, L. (2006). *Historias no Oficiales de Guerra y de Paz*. Bogota: CINEP.

Guillermoprieto, A. (2000). *Las Guerras en Colombia*. Bogota: Alguilar.

Valencia, L. (2002). *Adios a la Politica, Bienvenida la Guerra*. Bogota: Intermedio.

Vargas, A. (2008). *El Papel de las Fuerzas Armadas en la Politica Antidrogas Colombiana*. Bogota: Universidad Nacional de Colombia.

Vargas, R. (1994). *Drogas, Poder y Región en Colombia*. Bogota: Cinep.

Vargas, R. (2005). *Narcotrafico, Guerra y Politica Antidrogas*. Bogota: Grupo TH.

For up to date information on the Colombian conflict and the state of armed actors refer to reports published by Ariel Avila, Fundación Ideas para la Paz and the International Crisis Group.

Beckett, I. (2001). *Modern Insurgencies and Counterinsurgencies*. London: Routledge.

Beckett, I., & Pimlott, J. (1985). *Armed Forces and Modern Counterinsurgency*. London: Croom Helm.

Benbow, T., & Thornton, R. (2008). *Dimensions of Counterinsurgency: Applying Experience to Practice*. Oxon: Routledge.

Berger, M., & Borer, D. (2008). *The Long War, Counterinsurgency, Insurgency and Collapsing States*. London: Routledge.

Cassidy, R. (2006). *Counterinsurgency and the Global War on Terror: Military Culture and Irregular War*. Westport: Praeger.

Guzman, I., & Muñoz, J. (2004). *The Hyper Cartel, The Real Story Behind the Finances of Colombian Terrorist Groups*. Bogota: Circa-DKF.

Matta, L. (1999). Colombia y las FARC-EP. Txalaparta: Nafarroa.

Medina, C. (2011). *FARC-EP Flujos y reflujos, la guerra en las regiones*. Bogota: Universidad Nacional de Colombia.

Merom, G. (2003). *How Democracies Lose Small Wars*. Cambridge: Cambridge University Press.

Metz, S., & Millen, R. (2004). *Insurgency and Counterinsurgency in the 21st Century: Reconceptualizing Threat and Response*. Washington: US Army War College Strategic Studies Institute.

Pizarro, E. (2004). Una Democracia Asediada. Bogota: Norma.

Pizarro, E. (2011). Las FARC 1949-2011 De guerrilla campesina a máquina de guerra. Bogota: Norma.

Rangel, A. (1998). Colombia: Guerra en el fin de Siglo. Bogota: Universidad de los Andes.

Record, J. (2007). *Beating Goliath: Why Insurgencies Win*. Washington: Potomac Books.

Santos, J. (2009). *Jaque al Terror: Los Años Horribles de las FARC*. Bogota: Planeta.

Villamarin, L. (2007). *El Cartel de las FARC*. Bogota: Arango Asociados.

KEY TERMS AND DEFINITIONS

Commercial or Criminal Insurgency: Describes an insurgency movement whose political motivation has been perverted by criminal interests. It hasn't necessarily become a criminal organization itself, but it has become impossible to determine if their objectives are purely political or criminal.

Counterinsurgency: A comprehensive and progressive political strategy designed by a state in order to defeat an insurgency, and using all the dimensions of power including military force.

Criminality: Like terrorists, criminals use violence as a means to attaining a specific end. However, while the violent act might be similar –kidnapping, shooting, arson, for example –the purpose or motivation is not. Whether the criminal employs violence as a means to obtain money, to acquire material goods, or to kill or injure a specific victim for pay, he is acting primarily for selfish personal motivation (usually material gain). (Hoffman, 1998)

Fuerzas Armadas Revolucionarias de Colombia (FARC): (Revolutionary Armed Forces of Colombia) Marxist-Leninist insurgency fighting the Colombian state since the 1950s. Many believe their political ideals have been lost, and their existence is explained today by their interests in profiting from drug dealing and other criminal activities.

Guerrilla: It is a mode of war referring to the exploitation of the environment in order to wear the enemy down; more than fighting it frontally, fighting it for a long period in order to wear it down instead of defeating it directly; and conducting actions through a sequence of attacks and retreats, using basic instruments instead of advanced technologies (Navias & Moreman, 1994)

Hybrid Organization: It is an organization which combines political and criminal interests, a commercial insurgency is a type of hybrid organization.

Insurgency: A struggle between a non-ruling group and the ruling authorities in which the former consciously employs political resources (organizational skills, propaganda, and/or demonstrations) and instruments of violence to establish legitimacy for some aspect of the political system it considers illegitimate. Legitimacy and illegitimacy refer to whether or not existing aspects of politics are considered moral or immoral (or, to simplify, right or wrong) by the population or selected elements therein." (O'Neill, 1980, p.1)

PKK: The Kurdistan Workers Party, is an originally Marxist-Leninist organization fighting the Turkish state in order to obtain the liberation of Kurds. In recent years and after the arrest of its most prominent leader Abdullah Ocalan, it has abandoned the Marxist-Leninist doctrine, to engage on 'Democratic Confederalism'. It has also been signalled of being corrupted by criminal interests, disrupting its political nature.

Taliban: Islamist insurgency operating in Pakistan and Afghanistan seeking the creation of an Islamic state in territories of their dominion. Although history points at its creation in Pakistan, they reached power in Afghanistan implementing their own regime based on the sharia. They hosted Al Qaeda within their territory, and as a consequence, the international coalition removed them from power after the 911 attacks in the United States. Since then, they have been waging an insurgent war against the international coalition and the Afghan government, largely funded by the opium and heroin markets.

Terrorism: Although it is a contested concept. One of the more accepted academic definitions is provided by Bruce Hoffman: "the deliberate creation and exploitation of fear through violence or the threat of violence in the pursuit of political change. All terrorist acts involve violence or the threat of violence. Terrorism is specifically designed to have far-reaching psychological effects beyond the immediate victim(s) or object of the terrorist attack." (Hoffman, 1998)

Triadic Character: It is a description of the character of commercial insurgencies, and possibly of other hybrid organizations. This type of organizations have military, political and criminal dimensions, based on different types of motivations and functions that militants have within organizations.

ENDNOTES

1 Main authors on New Wars include Mary Kaldor (2006) and Herfried Munkler (2005)

2 See also Berdal and Keen (1997), Collier (2000a, 2000b), Berdal and Malone (2000)

3 Ross argues that lootable sources like diamonds and drugs are more likely to lead to war than unlootable sources like oil and timber. Ross (2004).

4 Interview with former Deputy Minister of Defence and current High Peace Commissioner, Sergio Jaramillo, Bogota, July 2010.

5 Taken from Isacson, 2012, 10.

6 Taken from Isacson, 2012, 10. Original source as cited in the article: United Nations Office on Drugs and Crime.

Chapter 22
Might the Keys to Peace Open the Doors to Extractivism? Reflections on Colombia's Post-Conflict Extractive Economy

Richard Clayton Doughman
Universidad del Rosario, Colombia

ABSTRACT

The present paper explores what the ongoing peace talks between the Colombian government and the Fuerzas Armadas Revolucionarias de Colombia – Ejército Popular (FARC-EP) may mean to Colombia's growing extractive economy. Militarization during the decades-long conflict and the spike in rural, state and paramilitary violence under former President Alvaro Uribe Vélez's (2000-2008) have left an unequal land structure favorable to resource extraction by foreign multinational corporations. Concessions for mining and oil exploration now cover a large percentage of Colombian territory, and the policy environment has become ever more welcoming to foreign capital. While armed conflict has opened new territories for resource exploitation, the instability it has created could deter long-term foreign investment. This paper hypothesizes that current President Juan Manuel Santos's pursuit of peace with the FARC-EP aims to enhance conditions for intensified resource extraction in Colombia in consonance with the regional trend toward a recolonization of Latin America's natural commons.

INTRODUCTION

In September 2012, the Government of Colombia under President Juan Manuel Santos announced the signing of a General Accord to End the Armed Conflict in Colombia, formally entering into peace negotiations with the *Fuerzas Armadas Revolucionarios de Colombia – Ejército del Pueblo* (FARC-EP). Though talks to agree upon an agenda for the peace process began in secret earlier in 2012, the public announcement of peace talks marked a surprising shift in recent policy toward the guerrilla group. Santos's bid to end the country's civil war comes after a period marked by the bloodiest fighting in the history of the decades-long conflict. Santos himself, both as President

DOI: 10.4018/978-1-4666-9675-4.ch022

and earlier as Minister of Defense under former President Alvaro Uribe Velez (2002-2010), has backed an aggressive military offensive against the guerrilla group that drastically reduced the guerrilla's ranks while killing a number of its top military officers in a series of highly publicized and controversial, precision strikes.[1]

The military's campaign to reassert control over the nation's territory and the glut of paramilitary violence that has accompanied it have left behind a wake of gross human rights violations: massacres, torture, forced migration, mass graves, rape and the intimidation of local communities. Since 1985 over 5.7 million Colombians have suffered forced displacement within the country leaving behind over 6.5 million hectares in abandoned lands. Over the past 15 years, conflict has displaced an average of 296,988 Colombians each year, consistently placing the county among the world leaders in this category (Consultoría para los Derechos Humanos y el Desplazamiento, 2013).

Parallel to the country's militarization, former President Uribe advanced a series of neoliberal reform policies aimed at opening Colombia to foreign investment, particularly investment in the exploitation of the country's wealth of natural resources. As military and paramilitary forces gained control of new territories, foreign capital poured into the country's growing oil, mining and biofuels sectors, often in the very territories refugees had fled. Between 2002 and 2010 over $57 billion in foreign direct investment (FDI) entered Colombia, with over $30 billion in the mining and oil sectors alone[2]. The annual average of FDI during Uribe's presidency was over twice that of the previous five-year period. (Banco de la República, 2014). Eager to shake its label as a failing state, Colombia looked to replicate the same export boom enjoyed by many of its Latin American neighbors who have ridden sustained, high commodity prices to rapid rates of economic growth, though often at the cost of heavy, primary sector dependence, social conflict and environmental destruction.

President Santos's economic policies have largely been a continuation of his predecessor's. His 2010 National Development Plan names the agribusiness, transportation infrastructure and mining/energy sectors as among the "locomotives" that will drive economic growth and turn Colombia into a competitive player in the world economy. While peace talks are ongoing, no cease-fire has been declared; violence still grips the nation's countryside, and guerrilla groups often target economic infrastructure despite substantial efforts by the armed forces to protect it. Security risks associated with operating in Colombia weigh down efforts to lure foreign investment, thereby limiting capital accumulation based on raw material extraction and export.

This paper seeks to explore the potential impacts of the Colombian government's peace negotiations with the FARC on the country's extractive economy. It recognizes the fundamental role that state and paramilitary violence have played in the expansion of the extractive economy over the past decade, acting as a guarantee for territorial control and allowing capital to penetrate areas of the country where previous conditions limited accumulation. At the same time, it suggests that the current peace talks reflect the Santos administration's recognition that continued violence is no longer functional to medium and long-term capital accumulation in Colombia, and that the administration's pursuit of peace aims to establish better conditions for capital accumulation through intensified resource extraction.

The paper consists of six sections, including this introduction. The background section serves as a brief, conceptual prelude defining key terms and placing Colombia in the context of an international division of labor within the capitalist world-system, under which Latin America is a periphery relegated to the subordinate role of a provider of raw materials for the central economies. The third section describes the historical relationship between state and paramilitary violence and increasing FDI in Colombia during Uribe's presidency. It also recounts the major policy reforms that sought to hasten the influx of foreign capital into Colombia. The fourth section outlines the dual nature of the Santos presidency, examining the prominent role of extractive activities in his National Development Plan and the militarization of the nation's economic infrastructure as well as his gestures of peace, including the 2011 Victim's Land Restitution Law. The fifth section analyzes those elements of the peace negotiations that have come to light thus far in terms of their implications for Colombia's extractive economy. The conclusion offers some final thoughts on the potential contradictions between a post-conflict economy based on resource extraction and hopes of lasting peace.

BACKGROUND

Violence plays a fundamental role in the expansion of the capitalist relations and therefore in capitalist accumulation. Karl Marx vividly describes the violence perpetrated by the state and legitimized by law that enabled the separation of the peasantry from the land in the original accumulation of capital (Marx, 1990). Rosa Luxemburg later observes that parallel to the clean-functioning economic laws that guide capital's appropriation of the surplus value created by workers in Europe, capitalist expansion in the colonies employs the blunter instruments of, "force, fraud, oppression [and] looting" (Luxemburg, 1951, 452). David Harvey (2003) too, identifies both the more subtle form of capitalist accumulation based on the expanded reproduction of capitalist relations through salaried labor and its more violent counterpart, the "accumulation based on predation, fraud and violence" which he titles "accumulation by dispossession." He aptly notes that the two forms of accumulation have operated side-by-side throughout the history of capitalism, with one looming larger than the other at given times and in certain places. For Harvey, a defining characteristic of the neoliberal expression of capitalism has been the rise of accumulation by dispossession as the preeminent form of capitalist accumulation in the years following the crisis of over-accumulation of the early 1970s (Harvey, 2003).

Accumulation by dispossession gained novel forms with the neoliberal economic policies pushed upon Latin America through the right-wing, military dictatorships in the Southern Cone beginning in the mid-1970s, violently truncating processes of national development based on industrialization and import substitution. The ensuing debt-crises and rapid inflation suffered by the majority of Latin American nations in the 1980s would serve as a lever to introduce further reforms the following decade in the way of structural adjustment programs proffered by the International Monetary Fund (IMF) and the World Bank. Following the guidelines of the Washington Consensus, the restructuring of the national debt for many countries was made contingent upon initiatives that reduced public spending in social services, privatized national companies, public utilities and pension programs at wholesale prices, liberalized trade, expanded exports and deregulated capital flows, all the while undermining guarantees for labor in an effort to restore the profit rate for private capital in the region.

One of the major effects of neoliberal policies has been the return to commodity export dependence in the Latin American economies (see Table 1). The limits placed on productive public investment by the structural adjustment programs, the rise of new industrial centers in Asia and the flooding of Latin American markets with cheap imported goods under free trade agreements, have undermined national industry while placing a premium on exports as a means to bring in foreign currency. The result has been a boom in Latin America's extractive economy in which economic growth is predicated on the extraction of the region's natural commons and their sale on the world market. Raw materials flow from the region toward the industrial centers of the

Table 1. Primary product exports as a percent of total exports in Latin America (selected countries)

	1998	2003	2008	2013
Argentina	65.1%	73.2%	68.8%	66.9%
Bolivia	70.3%	83.2%	94.2%	96.0%
Brazil	45.3%	48.2%	55.2%	63.6%
Chile	82.7%	80.9%	84.0%	86.1%
Colombia	67.7%	64.0%	67.6%	82.4%
Ecuador	89.5%	88.6%	91.3%	93.3%
Mexico	14.8%	18.5%	26.4%	23.8%
Paraguay	86.4%	87.3%	90.7%	91.9%
Peru	75.9%	78.5%	83.9%	85.4%
Venezuela	81.5%	83.7%	95.6%*	--
All of Latin America and Caribbean	41.5%	43.7%	55.5%	53.0%

*Includes Re-exportation
Source: CEPALSTAT, 2014

world's central economies, and increasingly serve as the material base for speculation on financial markets. Raw material exports have accounted for roughly 90% of the economic growth experienced by countries such as Venezuela, Ecuador, Chile, Peru and Bolivia in recent years and between 60% and 70% of growth in Colombia, Uruguay, Argentina and Brasil (Machado, 2013). The seas of transgenic soybean crops spreading across the Southern Cone and the clusters of open-pit mines bored into the Andes bear witness to this trend.

Acosta (2012, 85) defines extractivism as "those activities which remove large volumes of natural resources almost exclusively for export with little or no processing." Although mining and oil extraction are perhaps the most obvious of these activities, export agriculture, biofuels production, timber exports, commercial fishing, tourism, biopiracy and carbon markets may all fit the definition under the right conditions. Within this understanding, extractivism in Latin American dates back to European colonization and the extraction of precious metals by dint of coerced slave and indigenous labor to finance Europe's growing mercantile economy. As such, extractivism is inscribed within an international division of labor that is constitutive of the capitalist world-system. Speaking broadly, central economies, specialized in high value added processes serve as the dynamic centers of capital accumulation while the peripheral economies, marked by subordination to and dependence on the central economies, specialize in the supply of raw materials. That today foreign capital and multinational corporations dominate nearly all extractive activities in the region only reinforces its neocolonial nature.

The recent peak in world commodity prices has led to a rapid territorial expansion of extractive activities. Cloaking large-scale projects in a discourse of development, economic growth and progress, governments of all political colors have sought to reap the benefits of the commodities boom; the stauncher neoliberal regimes in Colombia, Mexico, Peru, Chile and Paraguay have funneled profits toward a national elite, while progressive governments in Venezuela, Ecuador, Argentina, Brasil and Bolivia, have followed a "neo-extractivist" model in which greater state control over resources allows broader redistribution of the benefits (Acosta, 2012). Regardless of the model, the mode of capital accumulation remains unchanged. Foreign capital and multinational corporations profit as extractive activities colonize ever-broader swaths of territory in the region, forcing local populations off their lands, subjecting them to ecological destruction and environmental contamination, and aggravating poverty and social inequality as already vulnerable populations lose access to and control over the natural commons[3] on which their livelihoods depend. The impacts of extractivism have grown as projects expand to unprecedented scales, and corporations employ new technologies (i.e. open pit mining and hydraulic fracturing) to exploit previously unprofitable resources while using loose regulatory controls to externalize the environmental and social costs. Extractivism, taken as a whole, constitutes a recolonization of Latin America's natural commons (Seoane et al., 2010).

The extractivist offensive has sparked social and environmental conflict, often pitting social movements and local populations against governments and companies on the other. The forcible appropriation of territory by private companies for extractive activities, the radical transformations in terms of land use and the environmental degradation that these activities imply provoke fierce resistance in affected territories (Svampa, 2010) (Delgado, 2012). In the mining sector alone the Latin American Mining Conflict Observatory (OCMAL) reports 202 conflicts affecting over 300 communities across Latin America. Resistance to extractive activities has given rise to a throng of local and national social, environmental and indigenous movements, often linked through international networks, employing direct action, legislative campaigns and tactical litigation to protect their territories.

The resistance with which resource extraction inevitably meets has prompted the United States, acting in its own strategic interests as well as those of its transnational corporations, to seek a greater measure of territorial control in the region. Latin America has historically served as a strategic resource reserve vital to the United States' economic interests. U.S. designed security policies for the region from the U.S. Policy Regarding Hemisphere Defense of 1949 to the National Security Doctrine of the late 1960s have always noted the importance of protecting and maintaining the northward flow of raw materials (Delgado & Romano, 2011). The proliferation of U.S. controlled or staffed military bases and forward operating sites in the region over the past decade fit into a strategy designed to assert territorial control and discipline local populations. Writing of the Merida Initiative and Plan Colombia, Ceceña et al. (2007, 14-15) explain,

These plans are thought of from a military perspective and begin with reconnaissance of the territories, and from there, strategies of total control are designed. Borders are redefined according to security objectives; normative structures respond not to the criteria of the population's welfare or caring for the nation's patrimony as in other times, but rather to the criteria of control and discipline.

The militarization of Mexico and Colombia in the past decade under the auspices of the War on Drugs are the most striking examples, but even under more progressive governments, organizations and movements who resist extractive projects are often subject to judicial persecution and criminalization (Korol, 2011)(Palau, M., 2009)[4]. The application of militarized security regimes to resource-rich territories has its logical end; what Delgado and Romano (2010, 97) refer to as the "securitization of the natural environment" guarantees "access to as well as the extraction and transportation of strategic resources, in spite of any spikes in social and environmental problems."

For its abundant natural resources and strategic geography with ports on both the Atlantic and Pacific Oceans, Colombia has merited special attention from the United States. Colombia is listed by the Convention on Biological Diversity as a "megadiverse" country, in which nearly 10% of the world's biodiversity is found (Convention on Biological Diversity, 2014). Its inferred gold resource reserves have grown to a total 90 million troy ounces as of 2013 (Rettberg and Ortiz, 2014). Its estimated oil reserves are 2.4 billion barrels

(U.S. Energy Information Administration, 2014) and its the sixth leading exporter of coal in the world (Unidad de Planeación Minero Energética, 2005). A recent World Bank report, referring to the country's eastern plains region, listed Colombia as a country with large quantities of unforested lands suitable for cultivation (Deininger et al., 2011), while the country's investment promotion portal, Proexport, advertises up to 7.4 million hectares of land suitable for biofuels development (Proexport Colombia, 2014). Access to these and other recourses has made territorial control in Colombia a priority for the U.S. Between 2000 and 2012, the United States sent $9.85 billion to Colombia in the form of grants and loans. Of this, $2.44 billion came directly in the form of official military aid and another $4.29 billion was channeled through the U.S. State Department and U.S. Agency for International Development (USAID) under the Andean Counterdrug Initiative, which also financed Colombian police and military operations (U.S. Overseas Loans and Grants, 2014). The country's militarization under Plan Colombia as well as the impacts of violence on resource extraction will be dealt with in the following section.

ARMED CONFLICT AND EXTRACTIVISM ESCALATE UNDER PRESIDENT ALVARO URIBE VELEZ

Following the failed peace process under President Andrés Pastrana (1998-2002), Alvaro Uribe was elected in 2002 promising aggressive action against the guerrilla. In the context of the global war on terror, Uribe framed the combat not in terms of an internal conflict with historical roots and a possible political solution, but rather in terms of a just-cause against narco-terrorist organizations operating within Colombia's borders, whose elimination could only come through arms. Within days of being sworn into office, he declared a state of exception in the entire country that would last for 180 days, during which time, he issued a series of decrees bolstering the surveillance and repressive capacities of the state while giving the armed forces looser rein to act against the civil population.

Funds flowing in from the U.S. through Plan Colombia, earmarked for counter-narcotics operations were effectively redirected towards modernizing Colombia's police and armed forces to combat terrorism, with the FARC and the *Ejército de Liberación Nacional* (ELN) as the principle targets. Concomitantly, tributary reforms raised funding for security, and Colombia's military spending surged throughout the first decade of the millennium, passing from just over $3 billion in 2000 (3.7% of the GDP) to nearly $10.5 billion (4.6% of the GDP) in 2008 (Delgado & Romano, 2011). In same period, the military's ranks swelled, adding more than 82,000 troops in 25 brigades ("Pie de fuerza", 2009).

The militarization of the Colombian state was realized through the Policy of Defense and Democratic Security, which following the Doctrine of Integral Action, effectively subordinated the political and social actions of the state to military objectives (Betancur & Osario 2013). Reasserting state control over the totality of Colombian territory became a top priority. Seven areas of the country, many of them in strategic or resource-rich territories, were initially declared Regions of Rehabilitation and Consolidation. Currently, the Administrative Unit for Territorial Consolidation defines these regions as "territories of great environmental or strategic value, with high potential for social and economic development, located in zones that have been affected by armed conflict and illegal crops and weak institutional presence" (Unidad Administrativa para la Consolidación Territorial, 2014).

This number was eventually expanded to include 11 different regions (see Figure 1) in which the Colombian military was granted expanded powers including powers to intercept communications, raid homes, and capture and detain

Figure 1. Consolidation regions in Colombia
Source: www.consolidacion.gov.co

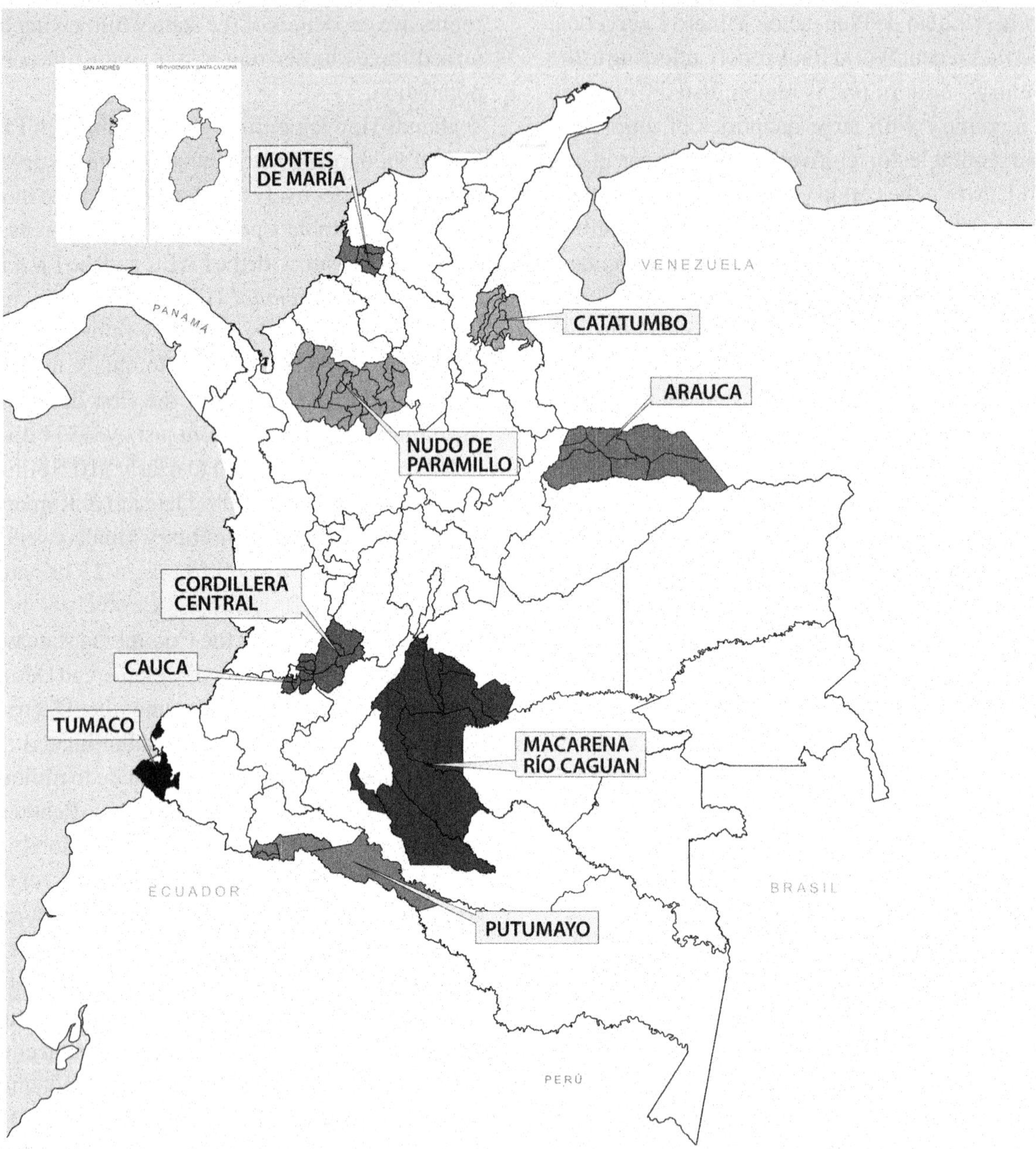

individuals suspected of having ties to armed groups, all without court order. The freedom of action enjoyed by the military in these regions permitted a series of abuses by the armed forces including mass and arbitrary detentions and the persecution of labor leaders and human rights activists, often in coordination with paramilitaries.

In Colombia's militarized climate, paramilitary groups flourished. Ostensibly, operating independently of the state—though often coordinating with high-ranking officers in the Colombian armed forces and linked to prominent politicians[5]—paramilitary groups employed a strategy of expansion based on terror. Active in urban and rural areas, paramilitary groups used forced displacement, torture and massacres to intimidate local residents and low-level officials, many times taking over municipal governments in order to establish territorial control and discipline the local population (Yeste & Fernandez, 2005). Paramilitary groups effectively stretch the range of action of the State, while masking the state's responsibility in illegal acts, allowing those with power, both formal and informal, to pursue economic and military goals with near perfect impunity (Delgado & Romano, 2011).

The violence sweeping the Colombian countryside took an enormous human toll. The Colombian Commission of Jurists states that between July 2001 and June 2009 over 20,558 Colombians were killed in non-combat situations by homicide and forced disappearance resulting from socio-political violence; in cases where the presumed author of these crimes is known, 16.98% are attributed to directly state forces, 61.34% to paramilitary forces aided by state complicity or negligence and 21.68% to guerrilla groups (Comisión Colombiana de Juristas, 2011). State forces committed over 3,500 extra-judicial executions between 2002 and 2010 (Coordinación Colombia – Europa – Estados Unidos, 2012). Between 2000 and 2010 over 2.9 million Colombians were forcibly displaced from their lands and homes (Observatorio Nacional de Desplazamiento Forzado, 2010), with paramilitary groups again playing the dominant role[6] (González, 2013).

The forced displacement of the rural population aggravated Colombia's already unequal land structure and strengthened the local landed elite's hold on the countryside. Calculating rural property concentration while accounting for landowners with more than one property, Ibañez and Muñoz (2011) observe that Colombia's land Gini coefficient[7] rose from .877 to .891 in the ten-year span, placing it among the most unequal countries in the world[8]. Houghton (2008, 25-26) writes of the role of the nation's land-holding elite in paramilitarism, as that of functionally linking Colombian territory to international finance capital by guaranteeing access to material resources. The "landed estate" acts as an "agent of control over strategic resources" that allows transnational corporations to translate state-issued concessions into the material base for future cycles of capital appreciation through speculation.

The Colombian government hastened this process through a series of measures designed to create investor confidence and attract foreign capital as territorial control expanded. Reforms to the Mining Code in 2001, reduced the state to the role of promoting and regulating mining activities, and at the same time, it trimmed the paperwork necessary to gain concessions. It also declared mining to be an activity of "Public Utility and Social Interest," thereby granting it priority in conflicts over land use and preemptively disarming local resistance. Institutional reforms gutted previously existing regulatory structures to create the National Mining Agency and the National Hydrocarbons Agency, entities designed to streamline the licensing process for potential investors. Finally, by conceding rights to the first party to apply through formal channels, the new mining code benefits private companies while ignoring claims by artisan miners and ethnic groups who have historically mined their territories. Consequently, the number of mining titles issued by the state has soared; national mining authorities approved 93% of the applications received, issuing 6,000 concessions between 2002 and 2010, often ignoring the limits of indigenous and afro-Colombian territories as well as forest reserves and other protected ecosystems (Frasser and Restrepo, 2012).

Labor reforms in 2002 dealt a blow to worker's collective bargaining power, undercutting basic labor rights, while creating an ever more flexible labor market. Later policies favored labor outsourcing though Associated Labor Cooperatives—frequent in a range of extractive sectors from sugarcane harvesting to cut flowers and mining—giving companies greater flexibility in labor contracting while eliminating their responsibilities to pay social security. Tributary reforms created generous exemptions for export-oriented companies, eliminating tariffs on imported capital goods and taxes on reinvested profits. The number of free trade zones grew from 11 in 2002 to 89 in 2010 (www.primerocolombia.com); meanwhile Uribe signed a rush of trade agreements[9] hoping to open up export markets.

Other attempts by the Uribe administration to promote extractive exports were struck down by the country's Constitutional Court, including tax breaks for the oil palm biofuels sector, the Forestry Law in 2006 and the Rural Development Statute a year later. Nonetheless, the success of Uribe's crusade to create investor confidence and legal certainty for private investment can be measured by foreign capital's response.

According to Colombia's national bank, FDI in Colombia grew from \$2.1 billion in 2002 to over \$6.7 billion in 2010, reaching a peak of nearly \$10.6 billion in 2008. FDI in the oil and mining sectors grew by 613% and 385% respectively in the same period, while FDI in the financial services sector increased more than four-fold. Oil exports rose by over 500% to over \$16 billion in 2010. Coal exports climbed by over 600% to over \$6 billion and gold exports jumped 22-fold (Banco de la Republica, 2014).

Yet the export boom and violence are inextricably linked. The Program for Land Restitution has designated over 1.75 million hectares of land to be returned to victims of forced displacement. Of these lands, over 80,000 hectares have already been ceded to mining companies for mineral exploration or exploitation, while claims for another 130,000 hectares are pending approval (see Figures 2 and 3) (Garay et al., 2013). Part of a biofuels complex controlled by a national elite and particularly favored by the Uribe administration, oil palm plantations grew in planted area from 134,000 to 303,000 hectares between 1996 and 2008, often usurping lands with a violent past. With a potential for profits and government subsidies, oil palm plantations offered a tempting opportunity to invest funds earned by armed groups in drug trafficking.

Finally, number of multinational corporations involved in extractive activities have been tied to paramilitary groups in recent years; OXY, Chiquita Brand Bananas, and BP are among the best known though certainly not the only cases (Becerra Ostos, 2009) ("Banana Para-Republic", 2007) (Rosetti, 2006). Though companies allege that armed groups extort payments, payments to paramilitary organizations are especially suspicious when threats and violence coincide directly with a corporation's interests in a specific territory, for example: the assassination or intimidation of union leaders or the forced displacement of local populations from mineral-rich lands. Armed groups, including drug traffickers, guerrillas, paramilitaries and BACRIM, have also found their way directly into the value chain of mining activities, particularly in the alluvial gold mining operations in the country's Pacific region, either financing equipment, operating dredges or laundering money through Colombia's deregulated gold market (Rettberg and Ortiz, 2014). According to Colombia's Comptroller General, 80% of human rights violations occur in municipalities where oil and mineral extraction are present. In the same vein, 78% of crimes against union leaders and 87% of the cases of forced displacement occur in these same municipalities (Garay et al., 2013).

The preceding section has outlined the ways in which state and paramilitary violence as means to assert territorial control were prerequisite to the establishment and expansion of a development model based on intensive resource extraction in Colombia under the Uribe administration. The following section details the continued growth by the extractivist sector under President Santos, even as the government engages in peace talks with the FARC-EP.

Figure 2. Granted mining concessions and focus areas for land restitution in specific Colombian municipalities
Source: (Garay et al., 2013).

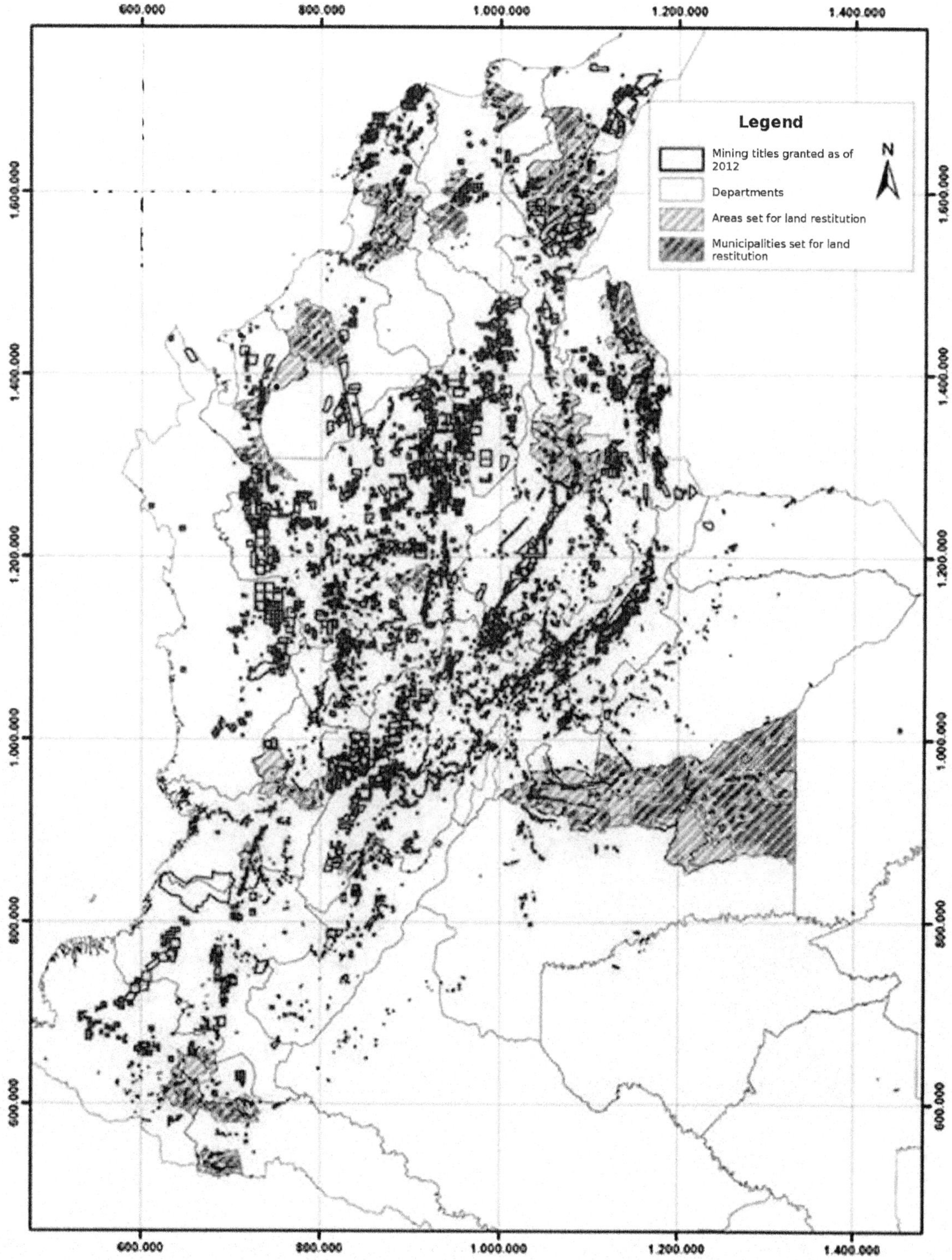

Figure 3. Granted and requested mining concessions and focus areas for land restitution in specific Colombian municipalities
Source: (Garay et al. 2013).

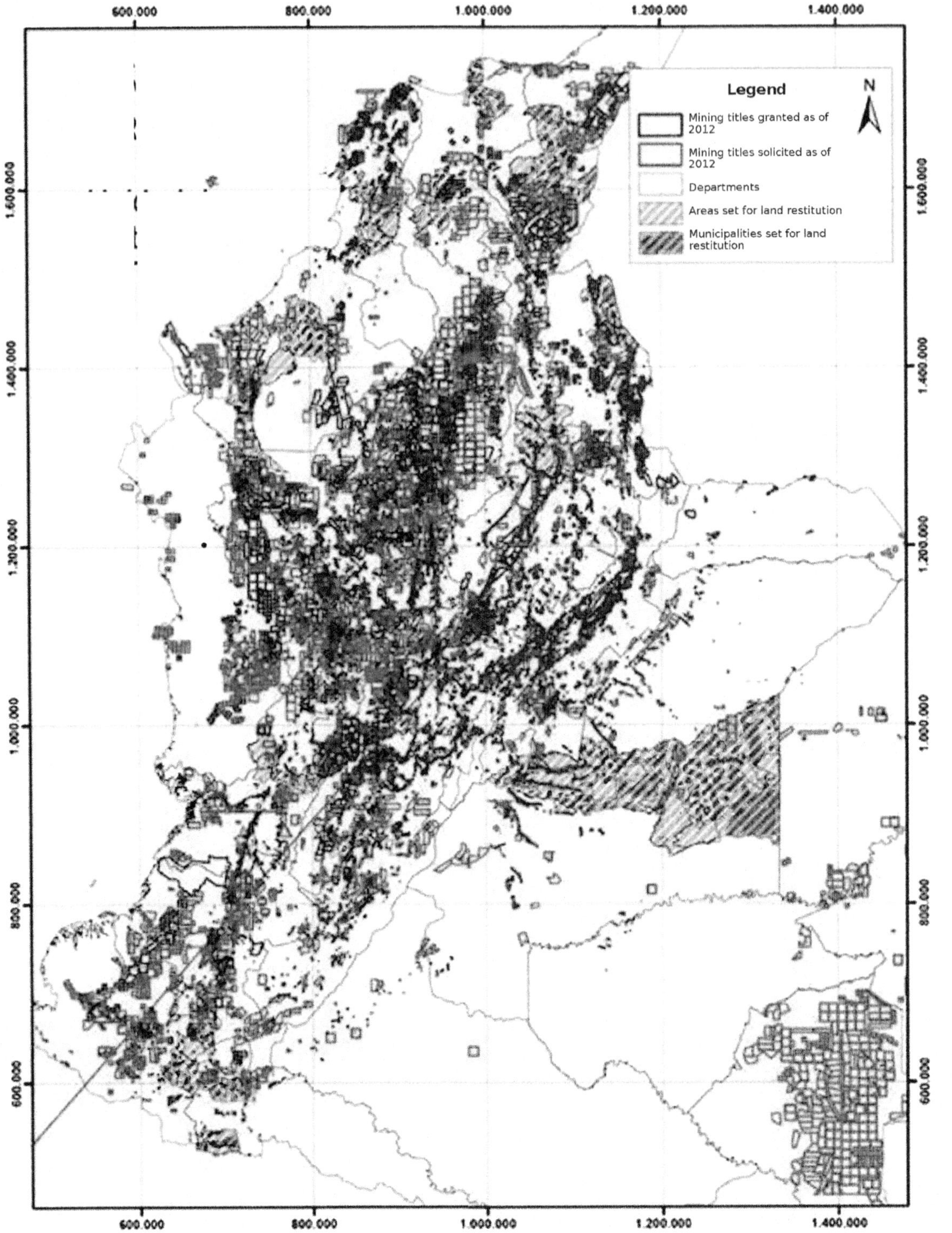

TRANSITIONS AND CONTINUITY UNDER SANTOS

As has been shown thus far, violence was both forerunner and companion to economic expansion based on extractivism in Colombia; under President Uribe, accumulation by dispossession took on a particularly murderous form. Here, it will be argued that by the time President Juan Manuel Santos was sworn into office the model of plunder based on mass state and paramilitary violence had largely run its course, and that changing conditions began to show the previous model's limits. Violence in the countryside had opened up new territories and new opportunities to capital accumulation in the country, but continued violence and instability threatened to hamper their being realized in the medium and long term. Additionally, Colombia's heavy baggage of human rights violations made it less attractive than some of its neighbors, when trying to lure foreign investment. The guerrilla threat had also changed, as nearly a decade of intense fighting had decimated its ranks. This section analyzes the continuities and the points of inflection in the transition between Uribe's presidency and that of Juan Manuel Santos beginning in 2010; in doing so, it seeks to understand, at least partially, what at the time was a surprising decision by Santos to enter into peace dialogues with the FARC-EP, considering that as Minister of Defense he had been a zealous advocate of a military solution to the conflict.

When the Constitutional Court struck down Uribe's bid to change the Constitution to allow for a third consecutive term, Santos became the leading candidate to take his place. During the campaign Santos gave every indication of staying the course plotted by Uribe. Yet, not a full year into office, while garnering support for a bill that sought to compensate the nation's millions of victims, he began speaking of "armed conflict" in Colombia, a departure from the previous discourse that identified the guerrilla as a "narco-terrorist threat" that needed to be exterminated. The subtle shift in terminology tacitly recognized the guerrillas as counterparts in a political struggle; it also marked the first cracks in what would grow into a heated rift between Santos and Uribe. When recently asked in an electoral debate if he had betrayed the former president by pursuing peace with the FARC-EP, Santos responded that he had "betrayed corruption, betrayed paramilitary cronyism, and betrayed illegal wiretaps[10]"("Yo traicioné", 2014) The statement is telling in that, aside from displaying the bitterness that has come between Santos and Uribe, it sheds light on Santos's labors to improve the country's image. Below, it will be argued that this retouching of Colombia's image forms part of a calculated effort to improve investor confidence, and thereby deepen the economic process of accumulation through extraction started under Uribe[11]; in part it explains Santos's motivations for entering into peace talks with the FARC-EP. To develop this point, three critical aspects of the Uribe-Santos transition will be analyzed: President Santos's 2010 National Development Plan, the changed nature of Colombia's conflict, and finally the Law for Victims and Land Restitution, which created a legal framework for recognizing victims of the armed conflict and compensating them.

The National Development Plan

President Santos presented his National Development Plan in November of 2010, and it was approved by Congress in April the following year titled, "Prospertity for All," the plan promised "more jobs, less poverty and more security," (Departamento Nacional de Planeación, 2010). Laden with talk of competitiveness, transparency, and improving the business environment, the plan seeks to carry on Colombia's export-based growth, while making Colombia more legible and more accessible to foreign capital. At its core Santos's National Development Plan defines economic growth as the driving force of prosperity, and thus proposes hitching the Colombian economy to "five locomotives" for dynamic growth: the mining and energy sector, the housing sector, transport infrastructure, the agro-industrial sector, and scientific and technological innovation. Seizing on the metaphor for 19th century progress, the plan describes the locomotives in different phases of heating their engines (innovation), getting up to speed (agro-industry) or already chugging along (housing, mining and energy, transport infrastructure) (Departamento Nacional de Planeación, 2010). The analysis below will focus on the plan's designs for the agro-industrial, the mining and energy, and the transport infrastructure sectors as part of the country's extractive economy.

Tellingly, the president's plan to speed up the agro-industrial locomotive is defined not in terms of improving food security—much less food sovereignty—by rather on the current climate of the high global demand and rising prices of agricultural commodities. Elements of the plan point toward the converting the Orinoco region in eastern Colombia into an agro-export power. Deininger and Byerlee (2011) in a World Bank report list Colombia among other nations with a relatively large amount of unforested, available land apt for agricultural production. The vast, open plains of the eastern Orinoco region, long neglected by the Colombian government, and racked by violence over the past decade, have recently become a target for land-grabbing by international investors. The allure is based on the region's potential to become an agro-export zone based on flex crop[12] production. The region is being compared to the Brasilian *Cerrado,* scene of the Brasilian miracle, where vast tracts of "underutilized" land with infertile soil were planted to soybeans and other industrial monocultures through intensive soil improvement with petrochemical fertilizers. Agro-food giant, Cargill, along with the Brasilian Company, Monica Seeds and others have bought up tracts as large as 30,000 hectares often using as many as 30 front companies to skirt regulations that limit property size in the region to under 1000 hectares (Oxfam, 2013). The Family Agricultural Unit (UAF) is a legal figure that sets maximum property sizes depending on the region in an effort to promote family agriculture and slow land concentration. The Uribe administration tried to do away with the UAF with a Rural Development Law, which was later struck down by the courts; Santos's plan states the need to, "establish mechanisms to facilitate private investment in agroindustrial projects by creating agribusiness development zones and by making the restrictions associated with the UAF more flexible" (Departamento Nacional de Planeación, 2010, 16). In this line, a number of recent congressional bills introduced by the president have taken aim at the figure.

Santos plan for agroindustry also contains an institutional push to promote the use of certified seeds. Directly tied to the free trade agreement signed with the U.S., the policy brings Colombia up to date in its adherence to the protocol of UPOV 91[13] protecting the intellectual property rights of large seed firms. It has already created conflict with rural producers, including the forcible confiscation and destruction of non-certified seeds, and it was a central point in the agrarian strikes of 2013 and 2014.

The plan's stated goals of incorporating new technological packages, widening export markets, formalizing rural property and increasing the use of hybrid and transgenic seeds would indicate the expansion of a model of capital-intensive and export-oriented, industrial agriculture dominated by multinational corporations. Projects in the region fueling the transport infrastructure locomotive (discussed below) such as the navigability projects on the Meta River system suggest that Santos views the Orinoco Region as Colombia's chance to capitalize on the agro-export boom that has propelled economic growth in Brasil, Argentina and Paraguay, though the social and environmental costs of this model have been amply shown[14].

The mining and energy locomotive hasn't slowed under Santos despite a brief moratorium on new licenses due to backlogs. The National Development plan seeks to facilitate activities in the mining and oil sectors, emphasizing legal certainty, infrastructure, institutional efficiency, paperwork reduction and the formalization of the mining sector, in which both armed groups and artisan miners exploit resources illegally. The plan hinges on the government's ability to increase the legibility of the sector, and thereby offer greater security for foreign investment, while continuing to expand production.

With regards to mining, the development plan follows the guidelines set down in a 2006 strategic planning document titled, "Colombia, a mining country," which lays out a comprehensive strategy to expand the sector in the medium-term. Reducing the administrative hoops companies must jump through has been determined a priority, as diagnoses have suggested that the complexities of Colombia's mining bureaucracy have hindered competitiveness with neighboring countries (Unidad de Planeación Minero Energética, 2006). The Ministry of Mining and Energy is also faced with the enormous task of trying to regulate the avalanche of concessions doled out by the previous administration. By its own calculation, the government exercises fiscal control over only 55% of the mining titles ceded for exploration and exploitation (Departamento Nacional de Planeación, 2010). Parallel to this, the Santos administration has also tried to formalize the sector by attacking illegal mining. The problem has been that under current law, the term illegal applies both to artisan miners, operating without a permit as well as mining operations controlled by guerillas, paramilitaries or drug lords. The campaign to formalize mining has blatantly sought to legitimate large-scale, often open-pit mining operations run by foreign companies proclaiming them to be environmentally and socially responsible; small, medium and artisan miners have been stigmatized as illegal, without distinguishing them from armed groups. One result has been an increase in conflict in the sector as informal minors joined the agrarian strike of 2013-2014.

The sheer number of mining concessions, many of which overlap with protected areas and indigenous and Afro-Colombian territories, has created conflict as projects that were in prospection or exploration move toward production. A rash of plebiscites in local communities has challenged the national government's authority to determine land use, and thereby force large-scale extractive projects on unwilling territories.[15] Undeterred, the national government has asserted its authority on the grounds that, although communities have certain autonomy to determine land use in their territories, the national state is the sole owner of mineral rights, and mining's status as an activity of "public utility" makes exploitation a priority. Similarly, conflict has flared around hydroelectric projects such as the Quimbo dam being built in the Department of Huila, where the displaced community has opposed both the national government and Endesa, the Spanish company in charge of construction. The project is part of a broader expansion of Colombia's electric infrastructure necessary to accommodate energy-intensive mining operations.

The National Development Plan sets concrete goals for the mining sector: increase annual coal output from 73 million to 124 million metric tons, increase gold production from 48 to 72 metric tons per year. It also proposes cutting the time required to obtain a mining concession from 514 days to only 90 days, inviting doubt as to the state's ability to seriously evaluate the social and environmental impacts of proposed projects.

Oil extraction and gas extraction, concentrated in the nation's east and along the Caribbean, are also slated for expansion. The plan aims to increase production from 990,600 barrels a day of oil and gas to over 1.4 million barrels, while greatly increasing the number of exploratory wells drilled and the carrying capacity of the nation's gas and oil pipelines. In 2014, the Ministry of

Mines and Energy has made moves to expand the use of hydraulic fracturing in gas extraction, including in sensitive paramos. The security implications of the hydrocarbon sector's growth will be discussed below.

The transport infrastructure locomotive is designed to be both an engine of growth and employment in and of itself while also laying rail for the other locomotives. Though many of Colombia's rural areas languish for a lack of paved secondary and tertiary roads, the transport infrastructure proposed by Santos aims to speed and ease the flow of goods and commodities along the major corridors of the country's transportation grid, particularly the flows from the resource-rich heartlands toward the nation's ports. The major transport corridors tagged for development coincide with the major axes identified in the Initiative for South American Regional Infrastructure Integration (IIRSA); financed in large part by the World Bank, the Interamerican Development Bank and the Bank of Brasil, IIRSA is a network of transportation megaprojects on a continental scale that would channel capital and resource flows, linking continental heartlands to ports to speed and cheapen resource extraction[16] The National Planning department, defines these integration and development axes as:

multinational strips of territory that include certain quantities of natural resources, human settlements, productive areas and logistical services. This strip is joined to transport, energy and communications infrastructures that facilitate the flow of goods and services, persons and information both within a territory as well as to and from other territories. (Departamento de Planeación Nacional, 2012)

The country's limited infrastructure is named as a limiting factor on its competitiveness, which is why the Santos administration has contracted the construction over 2000 km of divided highways, calling them "the Highways of Prosperity." The same plan calls for major improvements to seaports, airports, border crossings and rail systems. The plan also calls for improving the navigation of the Magdalena River to allow for a nearly threefold increase in cargo capacity along the nation's principle river system. With all of these projects, the government has made a special point of securing private capital's participation, creating new sites for capital accumulation in Colombia. For example, over half the 2012 budget for the Ministry of Transport was dedicated to works on the nation's privatized highway network, while under 12% was put toward tertiary roads (Ministerio de Hacienda, 2014). Nonetheless, given their scale, the projects inevitably collide with the interests of local communities who are often displaced and whose territories are dramatically transformed.

The Changed Security Environment

Although the ambitious development plan marks a line of continuity with the Uribe administration, the security environment in which it has unfolded has changed significantly. The decade-long state and paramilitary offensive has decimated the guerrillas' ranks. Between 2002 and 2010, the number of FARC-EP militants dropped from 20,766 to 8,978. Similarly, the ELN's ranks fell from 4,130 to 1,294 militants in the same period. By the beginning of 2014 the FARC-EP and ELN's numbers stood at a mere 6,672 and 1,485 militants respectively, which shows that even while peace talks with the FARC-EP have been ongoing, the government offensive against the guerillas hasn't relented. ("El ocaso", 2014). Both guerrilla organizations have suffered irreversible decline; the majority of their losses have resulted from members killed in combat by state forces, but there has also been a concerted effort to weaken the organizations by promoting demobilization and limiting their financing though the destruction of illegal crops (Decisive Point, 2014). The thinning of the ranks was accompanied by a number strategic assassinations of high-ranking members of the FARC-EP, such as that of High Commander Alfonso Cano in 2011. The increased intelligence capacity of the state and the threat of strategic strikes, forced members of the guerrilla's commanding body to flee the country. From there, a steady depletion of the group's middle ranks followed. From 2008 onward, the guerrilla was no longer able to openly confront state forces; it changed tactics, exposed itself less, dissolved its ranks to mobilize a more clandestine network of operatives and attacked "softer" targets in the civilian population and economic infrastructure (Decisive Point, 2014).

The continued strikes against economic infrastructure are more than just a nuisance. For example, the oil industry suffered 30 attacks on infrastructure in the first four months of 2014 alone ("Eln ataca", 2014). The 770 km-long pipeline that connects the Caño-Limón oilfield in Arauca to Coveñas on the Caribbean coast has suffered 20 attacks alone. One explosion has had the pipeline shut down for over a month, lowering exports by approximately 2.5 million barrels, raising the transport costs by around $27 a barrel and costing the industry roughly $8 million each day (Sandoval Duarte, 2014). The construction of the Bicentennial Pipeline, connecting the same oil field with the coast, but with five times the capacity, has suffered numerous delays due to attacks despite two army battalions dedicated to its protection ("El país pierde", 2012). Guerrillas regularly attack high-tension electrical towers, and the train that transports coal from the Cerrejón mine in Guajira to Puerto Bolivar on the coast was attacked multiple times in the space of a month in 2013 (Riohacha, 2013). Armed groups often kidnap technicians working on projects or extort payments from oil and mining operators hoping to move through territories or to avoid attacks, these extortion payments only raise the costs of companies operating in Colombia.

Violence and the additional operational costs it implies can often discourage foreign investment, particularly in the already high risk field of oil and mineral prospection. While celebrating the success of gold exploration in Colombia, the Metals Economics Group 2012 report, "Tendancies in World Exploration," makes a more general observation of the "value of easy access to prospecting, both in geographical and political terms," and admonishes that "junior mining companies that trade on the stock exchange are often hesitant to explore in countries that haven't protected their interests historically" (Metals Economic Group, 2012, 5). High gold prices may warrant exploration in riskier areas, but when prices fall, capital withdraws from these countries first. The point underscores the competitive nature of attracting foreign investment for peripheral countries; for mining companies that have to convince investors of a sure thing, doubts about long-term stability in a country can be a turn-off that causes capital to look elsewhere. The U.S. State Department notes in its 2013 Investment Climate Statement that lingering violence in Colombia "remains a serious problem" (www.state.gov).

To protect private and state investment in infrastructure the government has created specialized and newly equipped Energy and Transport Battalions (ETB) within the armed forces, whose sole mission is to protect mining, energy and transport infrastructure. As Minister of Defense, Juan Carlos Pinzón has stated, "Today there are many more points to take care of, many more investments to tend to which is great news for the country, but it implies doubling the capacity of State Forces" (www.mindefensa.gov.co). All told, more than 80,000 troops—over 30% of the total armed forces—make up the 21 battalions distributed between the protection of mining operations, oil operations and roadways ("El sector", 2013). The ETBs effectively privatize a portion of the armed forces, placing public at the disposal of private interests. In some cases, as in the Pacific Rubiales oilfield, troops are quartered within the corporate premises and rely on the company for certain provisions. Oriented more toward protecting foreign investment than providing for public safety, ETB troops have been responsible for aggressions toward local populations (Comisión Intereclesial de Justicia y Paz, 2008). Labeling them as guerrilla militants, Colombian military personnel have detained, threatened and killed local leaders opposed to extractive activities (Gisbert and Pinto, 2014) (Colombia Solidarity Campaign, 2013). In any case, the expanded presence of the ETBs make clear that, peace talks notwithstanding, militarization remains a prerrequisite to capital accumulation in Colombia.

The Law for Victims and Land Restitution

Colombia's armed conflict has forced over 5.7 million Colombians to flee their homes, collectively abandoning over 6.5 million hectares (Consultoría para los Derechos Humanos y el Desplazamiento, 2013). In 2011, the Colombian Congress passed the Law for Victims and Land Restitution, which allowed for international humanitarian law to be applied to victims of the armed conflict. The law sets out an ambitious program for tending to and compensating victims of the armed conflict and returning their lands. It establishes conditions for integral reparations, including guarantees for protection against being re-victimized. The law established a fund for victims and a specialized bureaucratic structure, the Integral Victims Reparation Unit. Though widely seen as positive step in terms of recognizing the victims, the program has received a number of criticisms as well, especially for not recognizing victims of events prior to established cut-off dates of 1985 for victims in general, and of 1991 for victims of forced displacement specifically.

However, the law may have perverse effects, intended or not. How effective authorities will be in identifying the responsible parties of forced displacement is not yet known. Victims who hope to be awarded reparations must first renounce any suits filed against the state or civil suits against the those responsible for their forced displacement, which could limit deeper criminal investigations against those responsible. Those third parties who can show that they exercised good faith in buying or occupying a victim's lands can't be held accountable and would be entitled to compensation if the lands they had purchased were returned to victims. The frequent use of front men and other intermediaries to purchase despoiled properties means that many of the real authors and direct beneficiaries of forced displacement could enjoy impunity and even compensation from the state; the front men themselves enjoy immunity under the law. Some sources suggest that the law contemplates returning only 2 million hectares while a census taken by the nation's comptroller estimates that the area of lands abandoned by victims ranges upward of 7.6 million hectares (Controlaría General de la República, 2013b). Titles to despoiled lands not identified as such by the law's provisions would gain legitimacy; this situation is particularly worrisome for indigenous and Afro-Colombian groups, who don't possess legal titles to their abandoned lands (Amnesty International, 2012). Also, the emphasis on giving legal title to lands returned to victims is functional to creating a more transparent land market; though it may grant greater legal security to the victim on the surface, it also grants greater legal security to prospective buyers should a recipient of reparation decide to sell, for security or other reasons. The risk here is the effective legalization of previous land plundering, and the creation of a legal firewall that protects eventual buyers, in good faith and otherwise, from future claims. In this vein, the relatively short period—10 years—in which the government sets out to resolve these cases hint of a quick fix to clarify Colombia's murky land market.

Progress on land restitution has been plodding; though the Victim's Unit boasted of tending to over 157,000 victims in its first year, to date, over 6.4 million victims have officially registered, and the number of victims continues to rise. In terms of land restitution, as of October, 2013 the Special Administrative Unit for Returning Despoiled Lands (UAEGRTD) estimated a total of 286,409 potential cases; it had received a total of 43,590 petitions for restitution of which only 425 had received a final determination. These 425 sentences returned a total of 12,133 hectares to approximately 1216 persons (Controlaría General de la República, 2013a).

Other limiting factors spring from beyond the contents of the law itself. Between 2012 and 2013, over 500 persons reported receiving threats for applying for land restitution; many of these threats come directly from guerilla or paramilitary movements while others speak of newly formed "Anti-Restitution Armies." According to the Land Restitution Unit, since 2011 there have been 434 violent acts against those who petition for land restitution (Massé & Comargo, 2013, 3-4). Also, though the law guarantees protection and basic material conditions for the well-being for recipients of restitution, it's difficult to determine what guarantees they might enjoy in practice, which will have a direct impact on their ability to permanently re-settle on their lands. The general state of poverty that affects rural Colombia, including a lack of social services and infrastructure, hinders resettlement. In many cases, despoiled lands have undergone dramatic transformations—deforested and planted to oil palm, for example—which again reduces the chances that restituted lands regain their previous economic and social function. Finally, those who have since purchased or occupied despoiled lands have very real economic and political interests at stake, and violence remains an option at the disposal of not only of armed groups but also corporations and the rural elite. Taken together, serious obstacles must be overcome if the Victims and Land Restitution Law is to favor the victims of forced displacement and afford them the opportunity to enjoy the use of their lands for any duration. At the same time, the law leaves open the possibility of whitewashing Colombia's blood-stained land market by granting impunity to land usurpers while legalizing their plunder.

* * *

The intention of the preceding section has been to point out continuities and discontinuities between the presidencies of Uribe and Santos. Economic policy, as shown by the National Development Plan, has built on previous growth in the extractive sector. While continuing an aggressive military strategy toward the guerrilla, Santos has opened the possibility of peace negotiations; he has taken steps to formally recognize victims of the armed conflict, and has distanced himself from Uribe and associations with paramilitary groups. If a rise in foreign direct investment, is any indicator, the Santos administration has succeeded to this point in promoting a capital-friendly environment while repairing damage to Colombia's image in the international community and providing greater political and legal certainty for foreign capital. FDI rose each year from $6.7 billion in 2010 to over $16.7 billion in 2013. Again, investments in extractive activities accounted for over half of this total, with the oil and mining sectors alone bringing in over $7.8 billion. In this period, oil production rose from 805,000 to over 1 million barrels a day; coal production jumped from 74.3 to 89.4 metric tons (U.S. Energy Information Administration, 2014). Gold production climbed each year from 1.7 million troy ounces in 2010 to over 2.2 million troy ounces in 2013 (Unidad de Planeación Minero Energética, 2014). The numbers would suggest that Santos's gestures of peace and strides toward legible institutions have sped the pace of capital accumulation in Colombia. In the following section, analysis will center on the possible implications of the peace process on Colombia's extractive sector.

PEACE AND EXTRACTIVISM

Given the limited nature of the information that has issued forth from Havana, analysis is necessarily speculative, but there are some elements in the jointly-announced agreement that offer hints as to the nature of discussion between the FARC-EP and the Colombian government as well as a glimpse at possible post-conflict scenarios. Analysis here will focus on the First Joint Report released from the negotiating table, as it is the most directly relevant to the future of Colombia's extractive economy. The contents of the report, under the heading, "Toward a New Colombian Countryside: Integral Rural Reform," result from the completion of the first point of the five-point agenda[17]. The following is an attempt to read between the lines of the report in order to project its possible implications for extractivism in Colombia. Rural reform is central to the conflict's resolution as the origins of the armed conflict can be traced in large part to Colombia's historically unequal land structure.

The agreement emphasizes the importance of the welfare of the rural population including *campesino*, indigenous and Afro-Colombian communities; it also promises to "reactivate the *campesino*, family and community economies" (FARC-EP & Gobierno Nacional de Colombia, 2013). The document recognizes the concept of *buen vivir*, or living well, a concept that has become a guiding principle of social movements in the region. *Buen vivir* subordinates economic development objectives to the precepts of living well, including respect for human dignity and diversity as well as for the subjective rights of nature. However, the agreement also leaves ample room for more established notions of economic development based on growth, suggesting that stimulus given to small agriculture would not in any way harm "other forms of agricultural production" necessary to rural development in the context of globalization. The agreement would seem to hint at a future in which large-scale and family-scale agriculture live side-by-side. While in theory, stern regulations ought to be capable of checking the roughshod expansion of agribusiness, in practice this has proven difficult, especially within a liberalized land market. The steady creep of industrial monocultures across the continent has pushed hundreds of thousands of families off their land as rising prices drive agro-export growth. Though the agreement calls for the strengthening of *Campesino* Reserves—redoubts for family agriculture sheltered from the forces of the transnational agri-foods complex—questions remain as to their dimensions: will they be large enough to harbor Colombia's significant rural population? Will they be strong enough to hold market the at bay? What will become families and their lands in areas not designated as reserves? The stress placed on export-driven growth over the past two administrations and experiences across the region indicate that export agriculture could very well colonize those lands not explicity protected, leading to vast expanses of Colombian territory being planted to flex crop monocultures to satisfy the demands of global markets and finance capital, with all the social and ecological consequences that these crops imply for the rural population.

The agreement calls for a redistribution of rural lands aimed at democratizing access to land and, at least partially, reverting Colombia's concentrated land structure. A land fund would be created from current fiscal and uncultivated lands as well as those lands that were illegally obtained in the past. Along with redistribution would come the formalization of rural property under a land-titling program that would include an update to Colombia's land registry. This last measure would certainly draw the ire of the rural elite, exposing cases of despoiled lands as well as raising tax liabilities. While there's no doubt that a renewed land registry is necessary, the question is whether the formalization of private property and titling programs can guarantee that Colombia's rural population remains rooted in the countryside. Will formal property rights be enough to secure land tenure for *campesino* populations, or conversely, will formalization speed the commodification of rural land and promote further concentration by offering greater legal certainty for foreign land grabbing? Independent of property rights, the strongest safeguards against rural exodus would seem the agreement's pledges to increase public investment in rural roads, health care, education, credit and seed capital for family agriculture.

Nevertheless, even significant rural investment will have a limited effect in guaranteeing livelihoods if Colombia's *campesinos* are forced to compete with dumping from subsidized U.S. agriculture as permitted in current free trade agreement. The plight of Mexico's corn farmers should serve as a sobering example of the dangers of trade liberalization. Unless the free trade agreement with the U.S. can be renegotiated, Colombian *campesinos* will face falling farm-gate prices for their products, a situation that could jeopardize another key point in the peace negotiations, the production of illegal crops. Low farm-gate prices for corn in Mexico have stimulated a shift to more lucrative poppy and marijuana crops. Such a possibility would certainly exist in Colombia, and would create incentives for further violence in spite of peace with the FARC.

The generous protections for intellectual property rights offered by the free trade agreement with the U.S. present another obstacle to the agreement on rural reform, as the latter pledges to protect and promote the use of native seeds. As part of the UPOV convention of 1991, the government has passed a number of resolutions criminalizing the use and exchange of non-certified seeds, an ancestral practice at the very root of all agriculture, not only *campesino* and indigenous agriculture. The forced commodification of seeds has already created conflict with rural producers. The question will then be, how much flexibility will the government have to make good on its pledge to protect native seeds, when trade agreements would appear to bind its hands on the issue.

Though the agreement with the FARC-EP promotes local participation in creating land-use plans, it recognizes the national government's power to determine land use. Used effectively, this power could convert the vast stretches of fertile lands currently grazed by cattle on the ranches of the rural elite to dense, food-producing, small-scale agriculture. However, under Santos, nationally determined priorities have trumped the local will, as mining, oil exploration and hydroelectric projects have been imposed upon bristling populations, creating new sites of social conflict. A discussion of mining is conspicuously absent in the first agreement, and the government has refused put it on the negotiating table. Conflicts over land use are already heated as rural communities continue to be displaced or transformed by large-scale mining operations. Peace with the FARC-EP offers little guarantee that these conflicts won't continue to spill over into violence. A post-conflict scenario could see the blossoming of vibrant social movements like those that have grown across the region in opposition to neoliberal extractivism. The agrarian strike and the strength of Colombia's indigenous movement show that such movements have already taken root here; what guarantees can be offered that these movements won't be the future victims of violence and state repression, as has been the case under far more progressive governments in Argentina, Bolivia and Ecuador?

These are only some of the questions that loom in a potential post-conflict Colombia, but they point to some of the unresolved tensions and contradictions apparent in the first joint report from the negotiating table. In the end, whether or not the Havana peace negotiations can be a springboard to lasting peace, will hinge upon their ability to change a development model that feeds on violence, against both humanity and nature.

FUTURE RESEARCH DIRECTIONS

The commitment of the dominant political class to a development agenda based on extractivism and the ongoing nature of the peace talks with both the FARC and the ELN leave open a number of channels for future research on the relationship between violence and extractivism in Colombia. At the country level more research is needed to empirically link the stores of existing data on military, paramilitary and guerrilla violence and human rights violations to the expansion of the extractive economy on territorially specific, case-by-case basis. Such research would go a long way in identifying responsible parties as well as beneficiaries in cases of forced displacement and land grabbing. It will also provide important clues for monitoring the effectiveness of the Victim's Land Restitution Law and other post-conflict policy measures aimed at compensating victims of the armed conflict. As talks to end hostilities with the FARC and ELN unfold, future research must analyze how and to what degree the development agenda can be the subject of peace negotiations in the context of armed conflict, and questions will inevitably be raised as to the legitimacy of attempts by such agreements to orient or re-orient the national economic model.

More broadly, David Harvey's concept of accumulation by dispossession offers a useful tool for understanding neoliberal capitalism's demand for territorial expansion and how it necessarily leads to political and social conflicts over land and resource use. Future research must go further in examining the role of the neoliberal development model based on extractivism in proliferating territorial conflict and instability in the Global South. Identifying instances where the extractivist model is an underlying cause in armed conflict will illuminate its role in conditioning and shaping peace processes as they emerge.

CONCLUSION

As has been shown, the current model of economic development in Latin America and the driving force behind its recent economic growth, has been the ever more intense extraction of the region's natural commons and their sale on the world market to satisfy the voracious demand for raw materials of the world's central economies. Extractivism is predicated on territorial control, which has led to increasing militarization in the region in an effort to guarantee access to strategic resources. The spike in violence that has ravaged Colombia since the collapse of the previous peace process in Caguán, forms part of the five-decade long conflict, but it also reflects a renewed state offensive—accompanied by paramilitary forces—to assert control over the national territory and thereby create new spaces for capital accumulation in Colombia. Nor was the guerrilla immune to this logic as it sought to benefit from coca production. As new territories were bent to an extractivist logic, investment soared and primary exports rose. Under President Uribe, accumulation by dispossession took on its bloodiest form, but far from disappearing under President Santos, it has merely scrubbed itself a little cleaner. If anything, foreign capital's continued exploitation of Colombian resources demanded greater legibility and stability. If paramilitary violence has declined, militarization has gained greater focus, with over 30% of Colombian troops dedicated to protecting mining, energy and transport infrastructure. Stronger institutions have translated into greater might when imposing new projects on unwilling territories. As Colombia tries desperately to catch up with its neighbors in cashing in on the extractivist boom, continued armed conflict only clutters the road.

In this context, and without reducing the entire peace process to simple question of economic expediency, this paper has sought to ask: To what degree are the current government's peace negotiations with the FARC-EP motivated by a need to guarantee better conditions for capital accumulation through resource extraction in Colombia? From that question springs another: how realistic can lasting peace be, unless current notions of development are decolonized, and stripped of the modern and eurocentric vision that somehow infinite accumulation and infinite progress can be achieved merely by opening new holes in the earth and digging ever deeper? Without attempting a comprehensive answer, I would suggest only that the violence inherent in the current development model doesn't begin with the deployment of troops or the taking up of arms, but rather in the instrumentalization of nature, her transformation into natural resources by pure, economic rationality. Unless this vision can be changed, the Colombia's *campesinos,* Afro and indigenenous peoples will merely be seen as obstacles to progress, and despite any formal peace, Colombia will continue to be haunted by endless conflict.

REFERENCES

Acosta, A. (2012). Extractivismo y neoextractivismo: dos caras de la misma maldición. In M. Lang & D. Mokrani (Eds.), *Más alla del desarrollo* (pp. 83–121). Quito: Abya Yala Ediciones.

Amnesty International. (2012). Colombia: La ley de víctimas y de restitución de tierras. Retrieved from https://www.amnesty.org/download/Documents/20000/amr230182012es.pdf

Banana Para-Republica. (2007). *Semana*. Retrieved from http://www.semana.com/nacion/articulo/banana-para-republic/84015-3

Banco de la República. (2014). *Flujos de Inversión Directa* [Data file]. Retrieved from http://www.banrep.gov.co/es/inversion-directa

Becerra Ostos, S. J. (2009). Paramilitarismo y neoliberalismo en Barrancabermeja: El caso de la privatización de Ecopetrol 1980-2000. *Ciencia Política*, (7), 125–149.

Betancur, J. C., & Osario Pérez, F. E. (2013). Participación de grupos étnicos y nuevas agendas del desarrollo en Colombia. In C. Barreira, J. V. Tavares dos Santos, J. Zuluaga Nieto, R. González Arana, & F. González Ortiz (Eds.), *Conflictos sociales, luchas sociales y políticas de seguridad ciudadana*. (pp. 77-112). Retrieved from http://biblioteca.clacso.edu.ar/clacso/gt/20131007104153/ConflictosSociales.pdf

Ceceña, A. E., Aguilar, P., & Motto, C. (2007). *Territorialidad de la Dominación*. Observatorio Latinoamericano de Geopolítica. Retrieved from http://www.geopolitica.ws/media/uploads/IIRSA.pdf

CEPALSTAT. (2014). *Exportaciones de productos primarios según su participación en el total* [Data file]. Retrieved from http://interwp.cepal.org/sisgen/ConsultaIntegrada.asp?idIndicador=1910&idioma=e

Colombia Solidarity Campaign. (2013). *La Colosa: Una muerte anunciada*. Retrieved from http://www.colombiasolidarity.org.uk/campaign-media/51-press/610-colombia-solidarity-campaign-lanza-informe-qla-colosa-una-muerte-anunciadaq

Comisión Colombiana de Juristas. (2011). *Colombia: situación de las violaciones al derecho a la vida julio de 2001 a junio de 2009*. Retrieved from http://www.coljuristas.org/documentos/cifras/cif_2011-06-06.pdf

Consultoría para los Derechos Humanos y el Desplazamiento. (2013). La crisis humanitaria en Colombia persiste. El Pacífico en disputa: Informe de desplazamiento forzado en 2012 [Document CODHES no. 26]. Retrieved from http://www.abcolombia.org.uk/downloads/Informe_Desplazamiento_2012_La_Crisis_Humanitaria_.pdf

Controlaría General de la República. (2013a). *II Informe de seguimiento al proceso restitución de tierras*. Retrieved from http://www.contraloria.gov.co/documents/155638087/161616579/Restituci%C3%B3n+de+Tierras+II+2013.pdf/93c00df9-4e7a-43a4-9e11-75dc5f426246?version=1.0

Controlaría General de la República. (2013b). *Encuesta nacional de víctimas*. Retrieved from http://www.contraloriagen.gov.co/documents/155638087/161621822/Libro_ENV_CGR-2013_(16-01-2015).pdf

Convention on Biodiversity. (2014). *Colombia - Overview*. Retrieved from www.cbd.int

Coordinación Colombia-Europa-Estados Unidos. (2012). *Ejecuciones extrajudiciales en Colombia.* Retrieved from http://www.justf.org/files/presentations/1209_CCEEUU.pdf

Decisive Point. (2014). *Contraterrorismo: La victoria silencioso del Estado*. Retrieved from Decisive Point website http://www.decisive-point.org/images/documentos/Contraterrorismo_La%20victoria_silencionsa_del_Estado_2014.pdf

Deininger, K., Byerlee, D., Lindsay, J., Norton, A., Selod, H., & Stickler, M. (2011). *Rising Global Interest in Farmland: Can it yield sustainable benefits?* Retrieved from the World Bank website http://siteresources.worldbank.org/DEC/Resources/Rising-Global-Interest-in-Farmland.pdf

Delgado Ramos, G. C. (2012). Extractivismo minero, conflicto y resistencia social. *Realidad Económica*, (265), 60–84.

Delgado Ramos, G. C., Romano, S. M. (2011). Plan Colombia e Iniciativa Mérida: negocio y seguridad interna. *El Cotidiano,* (170), 89–100.

Departamento Nacional de Planeación. (2010). *Plan Nacional de Desarrollo 2010-2014: Prosperidad para todos.* Retrieved from https://colaboracion.dnp.gov.co/CDT/PND/PND2010-2014%20Tomo%20I%20CD.pdf

Doughman, R. (2011). *La chipa y la soja*. Asunción: BASE-IS.

¿El ocaso de las Farc y Eln? (2014). *El Espectador.* Retrieved from www.elespectador.com

El país pierde US$ 1 millón al día por ataques a oleoductos. (2012). *El Tiempo*. Retrieved from www.eletiempo.com

El sector minero-energético está en la mira de guerrilla. (2013, February 2). *El Universal*. Retrieved from www.eluniversal.com.co

Eln ataca nuevo tramo de oleoducto Caño Limón-Coveñas. (2014, May 2). *El Espectador.* Retrieved from www.elespectador.com

Frasser Lozano, C. C., & Restrepo Plaza, L. M. (2012). Sector minero en Colombia: ¿El auge para quién? *El Observador Regional, 23.*

Fuerzas Armadas y Revolucionarias de Colombia Ejercito del Pueblo, & Gobierno Nacional de la República de Colombia. (2013). *Primer informe conjunto de la mesa de conversaciones entre el Gobierno de la República y las Fuerzas Armadas Aevolucionarias de Colombia-Ejercito del Pueblo, FARC-EP*. Retrieved from https://www.mesadeconversaciones.com.co/sites/default/files/Informe%20%20Conjunto%201-%20Mesa%20de%20Conversaciones%20-Gobierno%20y%20Farc%20-%20Version%20Espa_ol.pdf

Garay Salamanca, J. L., Cabrera Leal, M., Espitia Zamora, J. E., Morales, J. F., Negrete Montes, R. E., & Pardo Becerra, L. Á. ... Vargas Valencia, F. (2013). Minería en Colombia: Fundamentos para superar el modelo extractivista. Bogotá: Controlaría General de la Republica.

Gisbert, T., & Pinto, M. J. (2014, May). Colombia: Militarización al servicio del Extractivismo. *Noticias de los Especuladores de La Guerra, (41)*. Retrieved from http://www.wri-irg.org/node/23117

González Posso, C. (2013). La verdad en el abandono forzado y el despojo de tierras.

Harvey, D. (2003). *The New Imperialism*. New York: Oxford University Press.

Houghton, J. (2008). Desterritorialización y pueblos indígenas. In J.Houghton (Ed.), *La tierra contra la muerte: Conflictos territoriales de los pueblos indígenas en Colombia*. Retrieved from http://observatorioetnicocecoin.org.co/cecoin/files/Tierra_contra_la_muerte.pdf

Ibañez, A. M., & Muñoz, J. C. (2011). La persistencia de la concentración de la tierra en Colombia: ¿Qué pasó entre 2000 y 2010? *Notas de Política, (9)*.

Korol, C. (2011). La dimensión represiva y militar del modelo de desarrollo. In M. Palau (Ed.), *La dimensión represiva y militar del modelo de desarrollo*. Asunción, Paraguay: BASE-IS.

Luxemburg, R. (1951). *The Accumulation of Capital*. London: Routledge and Kegan Paul.

Machado Aráoz, H. (2013). En las encrucijadas del extractivismo: gobiernos progresistas vs. movimientos del Buen Vivir y el (eco)socialismo del siglo XXI. *Revista Herramienta, (53)*. Retrieved from http://www.herramienta.com.ar/autores/machado-araoz-horacio

Marx, K. (1990). *Capital* (Vol. I). St. Ives, England: Penguin.

Massé, F., & Camargo Castro, J. (2013). Actores armados ilegales y procesos de restitución y reclamación de tierras: VI informe del área de DDR 2013. Retrieved from http://www.verdadabierta.com/documentos/negocios-ilegales/tierras/1139-informe-actores-armados-ilegales-y-procesos-de-restitucion-y-recuperacion-de-tierras-centro-internacional-de-toledo-para-la-paz

Metals Economic Group. (2012). Tendencias de la exploración mundial 2012. Retrieved from http://www.convencionminera.com/perumin31/images/perumin/recursos/OLD/Exploraci%d0%b2n%20MEG%20Tendencias%20de%20la%20exploraci%d0%b2n%20mundial.pdf

Ministerio de Hacienda. (2014). *Proyecto Presupuesto General de la Nación*. Retrieved from www.minhacienda.gov.co/HomeMinhacienda(presupuestogeneraldelanacion/ProyectoPGN/2014

Observatorio Nacional de Desplazamiento Forzado. (2010). *Dinámica del desplazamiento forzado*. Retrieved from Agencia Presidencial para la Acción Social y la Cooperación Internacional: www.dps.gov.co/documentos/Retornos/Informe%20Desplazamiento%20Forzado%a%20Junio%202010.pdf

Oxfam. (2013). *Divide y comprarás: una nueva forma de concentrar tierras baldías en Colombia*. Retrieved from http://oxf.am/Uzh#sthash.x6szVnXf.dpuf

Palau, M. (2009). Gobierno de Lugo: ¿Escenario de construcción de alternativas? In L. Rojas Villagra (Ed.), *Gobierno Lugo: herencia, gestión y desafíos*. Asunción: BASE-IS.

Palau, T., Cabello, D., Maeyens, A., Rulli, J., & Segovia, D. (2009). Los Refugiados del Modelo Agro Exportador (2nd ed.). Asunción: BASE-IS.

Pie de fuerza militar llegó a su techo. (2009, January 30). *El Tiempo. Bogotá*. Retrieved from http://www.eltiempo.com/archivo/documento/CMS-4785562

Proexport Colombia. (2014). *Inversión en el sector de Biocombustibles en Colombia*. Retrieved from www.inviertaencolombia.com.co

Rettberg, A., & Ortiz-Riomalo, J. F. (2014). Conflicto dorado: Canales y mecanismo de la relación entre minería de oro, conflicto armado y criminalidad en Colombia. Retrieved from http://papers.ssrn.com/sol3/Delivery.cfm/SSRN_ID2418883_code1341307.pdf?abstractid=2418883&mirid=1&type=2

Riohacha. (2012, October 13). Atentados contra infraestructura minero - energética en La Guajira. *El Tiempo*. Retrieved from www.eltiempo.com

Rosetti, N. (2006). Multinacionales y paramilitares en Colombia: una conversación con Juan Carlos Galvis y Marta Hinestroza. *El Viejo Topo, 220*. Retrieved from www.elviejotopo.com

Sandoval Duarte, H. (2014, April 27). Oleoducto de la discordia. *El Espectador.* Retrieved from www.elespectador.com

Seoane, J., Taddei, E., & Algranati, C. (2010). *Recolonización de Bienes Comunes de la Naturaleza y Alternativas desde los Pueblos*. Buenos Aires: Diálogo de los Pueblos and Grupo GEAL.

Svampa, M. (2010). Hacia una gramática de las luchas en America Latina: movilización plebeya, demandas de autonomía y giro eco-territorial. *Revista Internacional de FIlosofía Política*, 1–28. Retrieved from http://dialnet.unirioja.es/servlet/articulo?codigo=3315848&orden=359476&info=link

Svampa, M. (2012). Extractivismo neodesarrollista y movimientos sociales. ¿Un giro-ecoterritorial hacia nuevas alternativas? In M. Lang & D. Mokrani (Eds.), *Más alla del desarrollo* (pp. 185–218). Quito: Abya Yala Ediciones.

Teubal, M. (2009). Expansión de la Soja Transgénica en la Argentina. In M. Pérez (Ed.), Promesas y peligros de la liberalización del comercio agrícola: Lecciones desde América Latina (pp. 70–90). Retrieved from ase.tufts.edu/gdae/Pubs/rp/wg/.../PromesaPeligroBookJune09.pdf

Unidad Administrativa para la Consolidación Territorial. (2014). *Regiones en Consolidación*. Retrieved from http://www.consolidacion.gov.co/?q=content/regiones-en-consolidaci%C3%B3n

Unidad de Planeación Minero Energética. (2005). *La cadena del carbón*. Bogotá: Unidad de Planeación Minero Energético.

Unidad de Planeación Minero Energética. (2006). Colombia País Minero: Plan Nacional para el Desarrollo Minero, 2019. Bogotá.

Unidad de Planeación Minero Energética. (2014). *Histórico de producción de Oro* [Dataset]. Retrieved from http://www.upme.gov.co/generador-consultas/Consulta_Series.aspx?idModulo=4&tipoSerie=116&grupo=355&Fechainicial=01/01/1931&Fechafinal=31/12/2015

U.S. Energy Information Administration. (2014). *Country Analysis Brief Overview*. Washington, D.C. Retrieved from www.eia.gov

U.S. Overseas Loans and Grants. (2014). *U.S. Economic Assistance to Colombia FY2001-FY2012*. Retrieved from http://gbk.eads.usaidallnet.gov/

Yeste, M. P., & Fernández, L. P. (2005). *El conflicto en Colombi*a. Retrieved from http://e-archivo.uc3m.es/bitstream/handle/10016/17382/06_conflictos_colombia_2006.pdf?sequence=1

Yo traicioné la corrupción, el amiguismo con el paramilitarismo y las chuzadas: Santos. (2014, May 23). *El Espectador*. Retrieved from www.elespectador.com

KEY TERMS AND DEFINITIONS

Accumulation by Dispossession: Developed by David Harvey and derived from Marx's description of the primitive accumulation of capital, the term refers to the fraudulent or forceful appropriation of natural or social commons by capital and their subsequent conversion into commodities.

Commodity Export Dependence: A condition within an international division of labor in which peripheral national economies rely heavily on the export of raw materials with little or no valued added, placing them on unequal terms of exchange with central nations that export high value-added goods.

Extractivism: A term of growing use in Latin America academia and social movements to describe economic activities that remove of large amounts of a nation's natural commons for sale on the world market with little or no processing. Extractivism has increasingly formed the base of Latin American economies under neoliberalism.

Militarization: Refers not only to the strategic placement of troops and military installations in a given territory, but also a re-conception of that territory in purely military terms, that is a territory to be secured against an enemy threat.

Natural Commons: A purposeful re-definition by many social movements of the purely instrumental category "natural resources" used in development literature. The term refers to elements in the natural environment, held in common and sheltered from the market, because their value to the well-being of the community exceeds any monetary value that could be ascribed to them.

Neo-Extractivism: The term refers specifically to policies followed by certain left-leaning Latin American governments that have come to power outwardly rejecting neoliberal policies such as privatization and monetary orthodoxy, but have relied heavily on extractivist activities as a means of financing social reforms. Ecuador under Correa, Venezuela under Chávez, Argentina under the Kirchners, and Bolivia under Morales are some obvious examples.

Recolonization: Making reference to the region's colonial past, the term describes the advances of foreign capital in appropriating Latin America's natural and social commons under neoliberal policies.

ENDNOTES

1 Raul Reyes, a member of the FARC secretariat, was killed while encamped across the Putumayo River in Ecuadorian territory. While celebrated by the government, the airstrike and following ground attack triggered a diplomatic conflict between Colombia, Ecuador and Venezuela.

2 All figures are in U.S. Dollars unless otherwise noted.

3 The term "natural commons" is a purposeful re-definition by many social movements of the purely instrumental category of natural resources. It stems from the more general concept of the commons, "an idea that incorporates a number of different visions and asserts the need to shield from the market those resources whose value exceeds any price by virtue of their natural, social and cultural heritage. Their inalienable character derives from their being held in common, shared and therefore linked to the very definition of community" (Svampa, 2012, 192).

4 The wave of anti-terrorism laws passed by a number of Latin American countries in recent years has been an effective tool in incarcerating and bringing judicial processes against leaders of social movements, whose forms of protest often include blocking roads.

5 Retired Colombian General Rito Alejo Del Río was found guilty in 2012 of "joining with and protecting" paramilitaries from the United Self-Defense Forces of Colombia. Former President of the Senate and cousin of President Alvaro Uribe is currently serving time for his links to paramilitary groups. Jorge Noguera, director of the the nation's

top intelligence agency, the Administrative Department of Security (DAS) from 2002 to 2006 was sentenced to 25 years in prison for his relations with paramilitaries and providing information that led directly to homicide. These instances represent only the most noteworthy cases of the broader phenomena of *parapolïtica,* under which paramilitary organizations infested all levels and branches of government.

6 The 2005 Law for Justice and Peace provided incentives for members of paramilitary forces to demobilize. Many, who otherwise might have faced long sentences if brought to justice, accepted alternative sentences of five to eight years. While the law as well as prior negotiations the AUC have led to significant demobilization by paramilitary forces, in many cases, the victims right to truth has been ignored. For example, in 2008, 14 paramilitary leaders were extradited to the U.S. on drug trafficking charges, and thereby avoided testifying as to their crimes and their connections with government officials. Additionally, though nominatively disbanded the AUC fragmented into a number of criminal bands (BACRIM) which have continued operating in Colombian territory, under new names: los Águilas Negtras, los Rastrojos, los Urabeños.

7 The land Gini coefficient measures the degree of concentration in landed property on a scale of 0 to 1, where 0 represents perfectly equal distribution, and 1 represents maximal inequality.

8 The authors add that large landowners' use of front men to buy property partially masks land concentration and that these numbers are likely to under-represent the degree of actual concentration.

9 The list includes; Honduras, El Salvador and Guatemala, Norway, Switzerland, Iceland, Lichtenstein, MERCOSUR, Chile, the U.S. and Canada.

10 This last betrayal is a reference to the illegal wiretapping activities carried out by the DAS under former President Uribe.

11 In this context, its worth noting that the U.S. - Colombia Free Trade Agreement, signed in 2006, could only be ratified by the U.S. Congress once U.S. Democrats overcame concerns about Colombia's chronic human rights violations under Uribe.

12 The term flex crop denotes crops which offer flexibility in terms of potential markets as the can alternatively serve as food, feed or fuel. Corn and soy are primary examples, but sugarcane and oil palm also fit the bill.

13 "The UPOV system of plant variety protection came into being with the adoption of the International Convention for the Protection of New Varieties of Plants by a Diplomatic Conference in Paris on December 2, 1961. This was the point at which there was recognition of the intellectual property rights of plant breeders in their varieties on an international basis." (www.upov.int)

14 See (Doughman 2011), (Palau, T. et al., 2009), (Teubal, 2009)

15 In July 2013, 99% of the voters rejected mining activity in a plebiscite in the municipality of Piedras, Tolima, where the South African Company, AngloGold Ashanti is planning to place its waste dump and extract gold from pulverized rock using cyanide leaching. The population of Tauramena, Casanare spoke out in similar proportions against oil exploration in the municipality in December of 2013.

16 See (Ceceña, Aguilar & Motto, 2007).

17 It should be remembered that, as stipulated by the General Agreement that governs the negotiations, no point is agreed upon until all points are agreed upon.

Chapter 23 Caguan's and Havana's Peace Talks: Strategic Retreat or Stalemate Driven?

Felipe Zarama
Universidad del Rosario, Colombia

ABSTRACT

Different to previous attempts, negotiations currently under way in Havana between the Government and FARC, since 2012, were preceded by a decline in both parties' contentious tactics. This chapter seeks to analyze the relation between the conflict cycle and the start of a peace process, through the Colombian experience, and Dean Pruitt and Sun Lee Kim's perceived stalemate concept. It is argued that Havana dialogues are likely to be successful on the grounds that it seems that both parties share a mutual perception of stalemate. Finally, it is suggested that the context in which dialogues arose may also have an impact in an eventual DDR process.

INTRODUCTION

Since its inception in 1964, four main processes have been put in place seeking a peaceful settlement between the Colombian government and the Revolutionary Armed Forces of Colombia (FARC). The first round of dialogue was launched by Belisario Betancur's administration (1982-1986) in 1984, in La Uribe (Meta Department). Even though a bilateral cease-fire was in place for almost four years, La Uribe's peace dialogues ended without an agreement. The second endeavor to peacefully end the conflict was the Caracas-Tlaxcala dialogues, carried out in both Venezuelan and Mexican cities, during César Gaviria's administration, in the early 1990s. After another failure and a subsequent escalation, President Andrés Pastrana was elected in 1998 with a clear mandate to seek negotiations with the guerrilla groups, mainly FARC. This attempt at negotiation, also known as Caguan's peace talks, started in 1999 after President Pastrana gave the order to the Military Forces to abandon an area of approximately 42,000 km^2 for the purpose of hosting the peace dialogues in that zone.

After three years of negotiations, few real advances, and the declining support of the population, President Pastrana suspended the dialogues

DOI: 10.4018/978-1-4666-9675-4.ch023

ending the Demilitarized Zone (DZ) in February 2002. This marked the beginning of a new escalation of violence period in the Colombian conflict, mainly driven by the state's initiative and opposed by FARC's declining military power (Echandía, 2012c)[1].

In subsequent years, the Armed Forces have been able to recover the strategic advantage in the war against the insurgent groups. In particular, regarding FARC's situation, the security forces have not only been able to regain the initiative, as is shown by Echandía (2008), but they have inflicted major losses in the rebels' command structure. Furthermore, one of the rebel group's strengths in the last decades, such as the conception and implementation of its Strategic Plan aimed to seize power, has now been minimized to the point of becoming a liability for them.

In spite of the fact that FARC has practically given up its pretension to seize power, the group has adapted to this new situation with the purpose of keeping its strategic rearguard, which allows it to survive as an armed actor. The result from this adaptation process, natural in guerrilla groups, has allowed FARC to maintain a considerable firepower. Higher mobility and smaller units, the increased usage of landmines, and a strategic retreat towards the borders have produced a decline in the efficiency of security forces' strategies against the rebels.

Presumably, bearing that context in mind, President Santos announced, on August 2012, that "exploratory talks" were taking place between the Government and FARC with the purpose of establishing a new attempt at a peace dialogue. The parties agreed a set of ruling principles during this new approach: no demilitarization zone, a six points' concise agenda, and no cease-fire. Even though one can find these elements in previous negotiation processes, it is to be highlighted that the rebel group yielded to negotiate without a demilitarization zone, which explicitly evidenced their declining power as they gave up a concession previously made by former administrations. FARC also renounced its historical position regarding the agenda, which previously consisted in a broad encompassing set of issues, including Colombia's economic model and the profound causes of the conflict. A small agenda is therefore not a minor compromise. Notwithstanding the fact that President Santos initially stated that Havana rounds would also differ in terms of the time to reach an agreement which would be measured in months and not years, the process will probably surpass three years. This has been interpreted as a miscalculation on the part of the Head of State, rather than as a failure of Havana's peace dialogues.

The Havana scenario is, thence, substantially different from previous efforts to reach an agreement with the guerrilla. Something in the conflict dynamics probably has changed in recent years. This could explain the start and governing principles of this new attempt at reaching a peaceful solution to the conflict. Thus, in what way does the cycle of the conflict (escalation, stalemate, de-escalation) relate to the beginning of the negotiations between the Colombian Government and FARC in Caguan's (1999-2002) and Havana's (2012-the present) currently under way peace talks?

Therefore, it is suggested in this article that there is a perceived stalemate of the conflict by the Government and FARC, which would explain why the parties have decided to get involved in a new attempt to reach a peaceful settlement. The purpose of this chapter also seeks to suggest a view that may explain why the parties have reached a compromise in the aforementioned ruling principles, from which several scholars have inferred that Havana's peace talks are likely to be successful.

In order to fulfill this purpose, the chapter will examine both Caguan's and Havana's peace talks, the last two attempts at reaching a peaceful solution. The chapter is divided in two main parts that correspond to both processes and the conflict cycle that preceded their inception. From a methodological point of view, it is intended to analyze the conflict cycle in terms of the use of contentious tactics, access to or depletion of resources, social support and the willingness to fight. The main chapter's argument is that perception of stalemate by conflict parties may have leaned them towards a peace process, following Dean Pruitt and Sun Lee Kim's concept. Nevertheless, in Pruitt and Kim's perspective, the perception of stalemate is not necessarily found on the two parties' discourse, but rather on conflict cycle and parties' behavior.

BACKGROUND

This chapter does not attempt to examine the deep causes of the conflict, or how violence and the political order are related. Prominent pundits such as Francisco Gutiérrez Sanín, Daniel Pécaut, and Gónzalo Sánchez, among others, have taken care of these issues. Nor is it interested in explaining the whole conflict system (Richani, 2001). It rather wishes to suggest a plausible explanation to the question of why the Colombian Government and the FARC *guerrilla* have decided to negotiate again.

During President Uribe's administration, the Government stated repeatedly that the military victory against FARC was close, although several scholars have pointed out that this was misleading. Among them, Camilo Echandía (2009) insisted that the guerrilla adapted itself to a negative power correlation. Irene Cabrera (2012), in her study about the presence of the guerrilla in the border zones, finds that the armed group was able to keep the military initiative in those areas. In the border zones, FARC's actions have exceeded the ones launched by the Armed Forces. However, in the overall balance since the 2000s, the Army has regained the initiative that was obtained by the rebels in the 1990s.

Ariel Ávila (2012), former researcher at Corporación Nuevo Arco Iris, ascertained that in spite of the fact that the Military Forces have considerably harmed FARC's commanding structure, the rebels have not necessarily been defeated. This is mostly due to the fact that, according to him, the military impact of some of the commanders' neutralization and their role in military terms for the insurgent group has often been overrated. Another view advanced in the collective book *Una vieja guerra en un nuevo contexto (An Old War in a New Context)*, is that FARC was militarily defeated in the northern part of the country, and yet, it effectively expanded in the southern region (Vásquez, 2011).

Previously, Corporación Observatorio por la Paz (2009) researchers have come up with a shocking idea: FARC won the war in 1999, but they did not translate a military edge into a political victory; the same happened to the government in 2008. Eduardo Pizarro Leongómez (2011) has even suggested that the current state of the long Colombian armed conflict involves two losers: a fifty years old insurgency that has not been able to seize power, and, by the same token, a government that has not been capable of defeating it. Therefore, no party can consider itself as the winner. According to this scholar, the Colombian conflict reached a "mutual hurling stalemate" referring to Zartman's concept.

Perceived Stalemate: A Beacon of Light from the Conflict Resolution Theory

In the book *Social Conflict*, Dean Pruitt and Sun Her Kim study how conflicts escalate and deescalate. The authors define the escalation process as a moment in which "one of the participants in conflict is using heavier tactics than before –is putting greater pressure on the other participant" (Pruitt & Kim, 2004, p. 88). Pruitt and Kim (2004) also understand that an actor-driven escalation is to be considered as an escalation of the conflict as a whole, due to the fact that the use of heavier tactics by a party leads the other to reciprocate.

According to these authors there are three models through which a conflict of diverging interests may turn into the employment of heavier tactics: the contender-defender model, the conflict spiral model, and the structural change model. Nevertheless, the purpose of this article is not to determine how the escalation process of the Colombian armed conflict first began, but to identify the stage (escalation, stalemate or de-escalation) at which it currently is, and how this relates to the undergoing negotiation process.

In spite of the escalation and regardless of how complex a conflict may become, these scholars affirm that conflicts always end. They identify five ways in which a conflict ends: first when "one party succeeds in overwhelming the other and the other yields"; secondly, because "one party is able to take advantage of the other"; thirdly, both parties avoid conflict turning into other activities; fourthly, "a powerful third party (or parties) enters the scene and imposes a settlement; and finally, the parties negotiate a settlement of the conflict" (Pruitt & Kim, 2004, p. 172).

According to Pruitt & Kim (2004, p. 172) "negotiation and a mediation ordinarily grow out of *perceived stalemate* [italics by Pruitt & Kim], a situation in which one (or better, both) of the parties perceives that it cannot make further progress in the conflict at an acceptable cost or risk". Following the authors, there are four main reasons why a party may consider that the conflict has reached a stalemate stage: failure of contentious tactics, exhaustion of necessary resources, loss of social support, and unacceptable costs or risks.

Pruitt and Kim find that "contentious tactics that were used with some success in the past may begin to fail because they have lost their bite" (Pruitt & Kim, 2004, p. 173). A reason for this to happen is that a conflict is a process, with changing dynamics, where parties mutate and adapt. Through time, a party may adapt to the contentious tactics of the other, rendering party tactics less effective.

The resource exhaustion as a driver for stalemate is related to the depletion of all kinds of resources: energy –understood as "the physical and/or psychological stamina necessary to maintain a struggle" (Pruitt & Kim, 2004, p. 174)–, money, and time. Another cause for stalemate is the loss of political capital and social support. Conflict is a political and military battle, both realms being fundamental to wage a war. Without military power one cannot carry out or even start the struggle, but it works as well for the political support of the population. Finally, a party may conclude that the conflict has reached the stalemate because "the costs or risks associated with continued struggle will be so great that further escalation must be avoided" (Pruitt & Kim, 2004, p. 174).

With regard to the parties' acknowledgement of stalemate, there are a few considerations to be raised, as the authors of this theory have pointed out. The first consideration is that parties may take a while in recognizing that the conflict is reaching a stalemate. Two facts may help them to recognize this: the occurrence of a shocking event, or a change in leadership (2004). In the stage previous to acknowledging the stalemate, parties will usually continue to employ heavy contentious tactics trying to defeat the adversary.

The original aspect of this chapter is then to suggest an explanation to the occurrence and shape of the current peace talks and to test Pruitt & Kim's theory in the Colombian conflict scenario. It will be also vindicated that previous attempts at reaching a peaceful settlement failed primarily due to the absence of stalemate. Instead, on those previous experiences, escalation prevailed.

CAGUAN PEACE TALKS: A STRATEGIC RETREAT?

In this section, the main argument is that an escalation stage led by FARC expansion preceded peace dialogues held between the Government and that rebel group in 1999 at San Vicente del Caguan, Meta Department. Contrary to Pruitt and Kim's perspective, contentious tactics were not declining in efficacy in 1998. Rather, increasing access by both parties, to resources –financial and human– during the time that dialogues lasted, was a premonition of its failure and a subsequent escalation. It is therefore argued that this escalation was a structural factor that prevented the dialogues from being successful.

In spite of the fact that the first generation guerillas' inception was in 1964, the Colombian armed conflict escalated within the decade of the 1980s as the country entered into the drug production and trafficking world network (Echandía, 2008). The drug business brought two sources of violence. The first one was the violence related to the fight against drug cartels, which declared a war against the Colombian state mainly through terrorist attacks in order to avoid extradition to the United States. The other one is related to drug trafficking that allowed insurgent and paramilitary groups to grow and to actually oppose a structural threat to the state (Raisbeck, 2014). Moreover, as Raisbeck pointed out, a study by Echeverry *et al* (2001) shows that it is in the 1980s that the armed conflict really reached a peak in terms of intensity. Echeverry and his colleagues compare Colombia's death rate per thousand inhabitants' with neighboring countries and find that it was not until the 1980s that the former increased dramatically surpassing those from neighboring countries. Really, the armed conflict has only escalated during the last three decades.

In this decade, FARC's Seventh Conference took place. Undoubtedly, the results of this rebel convention is a turning point in insurgency history in Colombia, as it propelled FARC as the most powerful armed group in the forthcoming decades. It was then, when the rebels developed a plan to take over Bogota, Colombia's capital. This consisted in strategically unraveling their Fronts[2] to siege the capital through the Eastern stream of the Andes Mountains. The group also realized that in order to seize power it needed at least 15,000 men (Silva, 1999). In 1993 at the Eighth Conference, the group ratified its strategic goal and created the Blocks[3], which are a set of Fronts that operate in a broad region under the command of one of the Secretariat Members (Echandía, 2013).

Two years after FARC's strategic turning point, the first attempt to reach a peaceful settlement with that group were the peace talks launched by President Belisario Betancur (1982-1986). Negotiations started in 1984 at La Uribe, a town in Meta Department where FARC had, at that time, their headquarters, also known as Casa Verde. An agreement was signed in order to advance in a large agenda and to put a bilateral cease-fire in place (González Posso, 2004). The rebel group was broadly in touch with the media, a situation that allowed them to spread their views and ideals nationally as well as worldwide. This process was definitely a showcase for FARC.

The dialogues were conducted along other guerrilla groups. An insurgents' coordination platform was conceived, the Simon Bolivar Guerrilla Coordinator –CGSB– (*la Coordinadora Guerrillera Simón Bolívar*). This platform gathered the following rebel groups: FARC, ELN, 19th April Movement (M-19), Popular Revolutionary Army (EPL), Quintin-Lame Revolutionary Movement (QL) and the Workers Self-Defense Force (ADO)[4].

Peace dialogues at La Uribe failed because of several factors that prevented a positive outcome. The first one was Betancur's weakness, due to the lack of political support from all ranks regarding the approach to the guerrillas in order to seek the conflict´s peaceful settlement. Not only had the military forces disagreed with it, but even the members of the President's own party also dissented in that regard, as well as the main economic groups (González Posso, 2013). It can therefore be stated that a broad consensus regarding the peace talks was nonexistent.

The Betancur administration lost even more power and legitimacy, after the Justice Palace seizure in November 1985 by an M-19 commando.

With the purpose of conducting a political trial to the President, M-19 fighters took over the Supreme Court Headquarters, whose constitutional committee was at the time discussing the Colombian nationals' extradition constitutionality. The Military Forces responded with heavy fire, which turned the place into a tragedy. This event reduced President Betancur's political capital, and isolated him even more in his endeavors to seek a peaceful settlement (González Posso, 2013).

Another failure of this process was that the cease fire was not really respected by both sides. Along with the peace talks, vigilante paramilitary groups progressively killed, presumably with the complicity of some state agents, the members of the recently created FARC's political arm, the Patriotic Union (UP). The rebels' political party inception was part of La Uribe' dialogues, as "the Betancur Administration considered that the creation of this party and the 'democratic opening' was a successful path to lean FARC's intentions towards civil life" (González Posso, 2004, p. 49).

The UP experience was terrible. More than 2,000 members (among them three presidential candidates) were systematically killed from 1986 to 1993 (Nasi, 2006). In spite of the fact that political-based "genocide" is an ambiguous category for the international humanitarian law, what undoubtedly did happen was that this group's military branch overshadowed the political one (González Posso, 2004, and Pécaut quoted by Echandía).

Even more, Betancur's proposal came at a bad time for FARC. The guerrilla had recently conceived their Strategic Plan to seize power. Actually, as Mauricio Silva argues, Jacobo Arenas had to convince the rebels to be part of the process (Jiménez, Silva, & Patiño, 2009). The rebel group was by that time thinking about taking over Bogota, through progressively abandoning guerilla warfare towards movements and then positions warfare. Nevertheless, Arenas knew the political costs of opting-out of that process.

In spite of this, the Betancur administration signed a renewal of the cease fire agreement in March 1986, a few months before its mandate ended. In 1986, running for the Liberal Party, Virgilio Barco was elected President (1986-1990). As González Posso (2004, p. 49) characterizes it, "the Barco administration received the dialogues as an awkward inheritance that could not project towards more lasting and firm agreements." The cease fire continued until June 1987, after an ambush in Puerto Rico, Caqueta Department, where 26 military effectives and one civilian were killed.

On the second part of his mandate, the Barco administration launched a reincorporation to civil life program, aiming to demobilize the guerrilla groups (Nasi, 2006). Part of this strategy was due to the fact that the state was in an open battle with drug cartels, thus undermining the capacity of the Colombian security forces to tackle both insurgent and cartel threats. This administration pursued another attempt to reach an agreement with the guerrilla. Probably because of what happened with UP, FARC returned the gesture with heavy contentious tactics. From this point on, the Colombian armed conflict began to de-escalate with second-generation guerrilla groups (*c.f.* endnote # vi), as well as it started to escalate with first-generation rebel groups. The demobilization process, which formally ended in the next presidential period, was thus successful with the M-19, ADO, most of the EPL, and QL. Nevertheless, FARC and ELN opted out of this process.

Under President César Gaviria's term, two points are to be raised. The first one is the air raids on Casa Verde, FARC's Headquarters in December 1990. In spite of the fact that the security forces were able to seize the 26-year-old bunker, Casa Verde operation did not produce a single casualty in FARC's military staff. It cannot, therefore, be considered an entirely successful operation for the Colombian armed forces.

The second fact, in Gaviria's administration, relevant to this chapter, is the approaching dialogues carried out in Caracas and Tlaxcala between the Colombian government and a renewed CGSB –the umbrella organization conceived in La Uribe as a platform that brought together several guerilla groups with the purpose of presenting a common position in front of the government. The CGSB participated in the Caracas-Tlaxcala Talks, joining together FARC, ELN, and EPL rebel groups, all of which comprised the totality of the insurgency. The rest of the groups by that time had already reached an agreement for their demobilization. Some of them were even part of the Constitutional Assembly of 1991.

In June 1991, the first round of the negotiations, where the parties reached an agreement on a ten-issue agenda, was launched in Caracas, Venezuela. These dialogues were conceived as a result of the failure of La Uribe's, and were likewise influenced by the success of demobilization agreements with other groups. Due to Casa Verde's bombardment, both parties decided to meet on international soil (González Posso, 2004).

As Camilo González Posso (2004) pointed out, four rounds of dialogues took place in Caracas between June and November 1991. The parties never agreed on the mechanisms for monitoring an eventual cease fire agreement. In March 1992, and after four rounds in the Venezuelan capital, the parties met in Tlaxcala. Nonetheless, from that point on, and until September, the process went into several crises. The most striking one was the kidnapping and subsequent assassination of former minister Argelino Durán Quintero by the EPL and the disappearance and assassination of Daniel García, a FARC's diplomatic envoy. Both facts "led to mutual recriminations, whose outcome was a joint statement, which officially put an end to the conversations" (González Posso, 2004, p. 50).

After the end of the second attempt to reach a peace settlement, an escalation started again led by both sides. As stated before, the UP's fatal pursuit by paramilitary groups and death squads lasted at least until 1993. According to González Posso (2004, p. 50), the extermination of FARC's political party members was also a consequence of two issues: "on the one side, the intransigence of reactionary right-wing oriented forces, but on the other side, it was also the result of the combination of all kinds of struggle strategy –civil and armed, and what has been known as *la combinación de todas las formas de lucha*– fostered by some left-wing segment of the society". This approach to insurgency means that the insurgent groups wage war against the state in all realms (military, political, economic, legal, and others). Nevertheless, as it was stated before, FARC's military branch outweighed the political one.

Another explanation of the political branch offset results from Jacobo Arenas' death in 1990, according to Otty Patiño, a former M-19 militant (Jiménez, Silva, & Patiño, 2009). Jacobo Arenas was the political master of FARC's engine. He was a former member of the Colombian Communist Party (PCC) who joined the rebel group and became its main strategic mind. The authors of the book *Guerras inútiles* find that Arenas' extinction was a determining factor for FARC's political arm offset (Corporación Observatorio por la Paz, 2009). Nevertheless and according to them, through the following years the rebel group's Strategic Plan conceived at the Seventh Conference, of which Arenas was the mastermind, compensated the absence of its architect.

After Caracas-Tlaxcala Peace Talks, FARC began to implement the aforementioned strategy, which sought to take over Bogota. In order to do so, the rebel group esteemed necessary to deploy 15,000 troops over the Eastern Andes (Silva, 1999). This military goal also explains why the guerrilla moved on illicit drug plantation zones and began to implement a strategy of economic actions –kidnapping and all kinds of extortion, aiming to obtain more financial resources that would allow them to afford the struggle (Silva, 1999).

Due to the implementation of their Strategic Plan, FARC was in fact able to produce a military shift in their favor. Between 1987 and 2003 as can be seen on Figure 1, the number of armed contacts initiated by the insurgent group exceeded the ones that were carried out by the Military Forces' initiative. Except for short periods of time in 1993 and 1995, the attacks perpetrated by the rebels' militants exceeded the operations launched by the Colombian State (see Figure 1). It is certain that the correlation between the action launched by the former and the latter was even greater in 1991 than the same index in the period from 1996 and 2002. Notwithstanding the fact that the power balance only truly shifted in FARC's favor during those six years, Mauricio Silva (1999) described how the armed group was able to carry out qualitative important firepower: simultaneous attacks to military bases and towns seizures, whose pinnacle was the seizure of Mitu, Vaupes Department, in November 1998, just before the beginning of Caguan's peace dialogues.

According to this author, the last types of actions differ substantially from the others. From that point, FARC was able to deploy large quantities of fighters, whole Fronts in order to produce a huge impact on the enemy. Silva also considers that FARC was successful both by employing a high number of manpower as well as by the National Army´s lack of discipline (Silva, 1999, p. 229).

In 1994 Ernesto Samper (1994-1998), Liberal Party's candidate, was elected. At the beginning if his administration, the Government made some moves in order to seek a peaceful settlement. La Uribe, in Meta Department, was again selected to host the peace dialogues. Nonetheless, as it can be appreciated on Figure 1, in 1995 FARC increased their military actions. In particular, those actions took place in Huila, Cundinamarca, Putumayo, Cauca, and Guaviare Departments, which "responded to the purpose of diluting Army's offensive on Meta Department, the proposed zone by the Government as the stage to start the dialogues" (Echandía, 2013, p. 42).

Samper's attempts at starting peace dialogues with the guerrilla failed due to three reasons. The first one was that the military plan implemented by FARC was being successful. As Echandía (2013, p. 42) stated, "During the Samper administration,

Figure 1. Power balance between the Colombian state and FARC guerrilla: 1990-2011
Source: Author's elaboration. Data from Human Rights Observatory of the Human Rights and International Humanitarian Law Presidential Program and Echandía (2012).

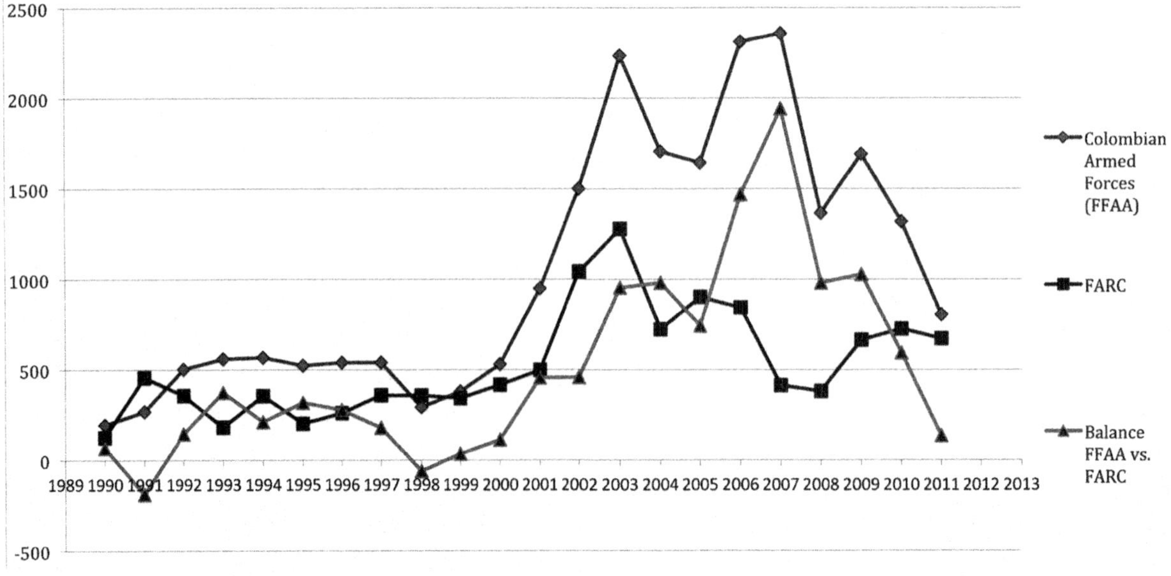

FARC was able to advance in the Strategic Plan conceived at the Seventh Conference and renewed at the Eighth Conference, which sought to control territories and to put together a regular army to reach the strategic equilibrium with the state". Additionally, the rebel group rejected the offerings made by President Samper's administration on the grounds that the government did not have the authority to negotiate (Echandía, 2013). The president wasted all of his political capital to remain in office, after the scandals about drug traffickers financing his campaign broke out. Samper made it through the impeachment process in Congress, but he turned into a weak president. Even on international grounds, the United States withdrew President Samper's visa.

Due to the evidence of drug resources financing the campaign, the United States took away Colombia's certification, which meant that the financial aid could only be used against drug traffickers. This meant on the ground, that "helicopters, coming from the United Sates as part of their financial support, could not be used for counter-insurgent tasks. They were stocked in their bases while National Army isolated units were seized and annihilated by FARC fighters" (Corporación Observatorio por la Paz, 2009, p. 172).

This situation was translated into a military advantage for the rebel group in detriment of the government. Not only was the rebel group able to concentrate an important amount of manpower to attack Army's and National Police's positions all across the country, but also during the 1990s they increased their capacity to simultaneously attack several places. These types of actions were evidenced in the simultaneous assault of Bogota´s nearby towns of La Calera and Pasca by 53 and 54 FARC Fronts (Corporación Observatorio por la Paz, 2009).

In 1997, FARC achieved a great political victory, a consequence of the military advantage. The Samper administration agreed to demilitarize Cartagena del Chairá, Caqueta Department, with the purpose of releasing 60 soldiers and 10 marines kidnapped at Las Delicias Base' seizure (Corporación Observatorio por la Paz, 2009, p. 169).

On this presidential period, it was possible for the rebel group to alter the balance of power. It escalated the conflict with the purpose of transforming its traditional guerilla warfare into a war of movements (Echandía, 2008). In Kim & Pruitt terms, the guerrilla was putting greater pressure on the government.

Samper's mandate ended with no peace talks in place and with a strengthened FARC. In that context, the 1998 presidential campaign focused on the possibility of dialogues. Both candidates had proposals on how to approach FARC and ELN, the two remaining guerrilla groups other than a small splinter faction of EPL that did not demobilize in the 1990s. While, Horacio Serpa, the Liberal party and governing party´s candidate, chose to reach ELN guerrilla first (Corporación Observatorio por la Paz, 2009), the opposition candidate, Andrés Pastrana chose approaching FARC first. As was mentioned previously, Pastrana's campaign advisor and subsequent lead negotiator, Victor G. Ricardo's appearance on the newspapers after a meeting with *Manuel Marulanda Vélez*[5], FARC's Chief Commander, turned the edge (Semana, 1998). This gesture, that took place on the time between the first and second run-off, gave the Conservative Party candidate an advantage, causing Andrés Pastrana to become the next Colombian president.

An initiative, named "The Mandate for Peace", calling for the government to seek a peaceful settlement with the guerillas, came out in the parliamentary and forthcoming presidential elections. As the authors of *Guerras inútiles* pointed out: "the electoral debate for succeeding President Ernesto Samper happened in the middle of an offensive by the FARC fulfilling their Strategic Plan, and with a fearful public opinion, fed up with war, and desirous for peace" (Corporación Observatorio por la Paz, 2009, p. 174).

Thus, a strategic calculation was made by Pastrana and his advisors. They realized that the Government was in a weak position, and a negotiation was needed in order to strengthen the state. Victor G. Ricardo, former Presidential High Commissioner for Peace and the main negotiator and mastermind behind the Caguan's peace talks, describes the strategic decision as following:

The real reason why in candidate Pastrana's campaign we started thinking about a peace proposal had to do with the circumstances that the nation was facing at the time, and the possibilities of the state, which was really hurt by several attacks carried out by the guerrilla. (...) To sum up, state's capacities were very limited. (Ricardo, 2014)

As can be read from the former High Commissioner for Peace's (*Alto Comisionado para la Paz*) opinion, the balance of power between the government and FARC shifted in favor of the latter. The state decided to negotiate to buy some time. Researchers from the Corporación Observatorio por la Paz described this strategic decision as following:

President Pastrana's strategy regarding FARC had several elements: 1. A harsh antidrug policy focused on fighting coca crops. 2. A negotiation process with FARC without major concessions other than the territories already described. 3. Reengineering the Military Forces. He was able to persuade US government that the FARC had turned into a drug "cartel" and, therefore, military support should be focused on fighting that type of economy in the South of the country, where the main plantations were located; as a consequence of this perception Plan Colombia was created. (Corporación Observatorio por la Paz, 2009, p. 175)

According to Pruitt & Kim, a negotiation process may arise when there is a perceived stalemate by the parties. Nonetheless, peace dialogues may also be carried out when one of the parties has a military edge. In this case, the weak party might seek a negotiation process as a strategic retreat, in order to gather forces and strengthen itself. Also in Pruitt & Kim's terms, escalation occurs when a party is putting pressure on the other through increased use of contentious tactics, in which the overwhelmed party may seek a negotiation in order to achieve a cease fire. Normally, rebel groups decided strategically to advance in peace dialogues when state's reprisal is compromising their survival. What is interesting regarding the Caguan's Peace Talks (1999-2001) is that, from Ricardo's standpoint, the party that needed space and time to strengthen was the Colombian Government.

According to González Posso (2013), both parties employed the peace talks held between 1999 and 2001 at the Demilitarized Zone (DZ) to advance in their military strategies. The rebels conceived the DZ as a means to their military strategy. Caguan's DZ actually corresponded, more or less, to FARC's strategic heartland. It is therefore not surprising that the rebel group employed this demilitarized territory with the purpose of seizing Bogota, as their Strategic Plan predicted.

As for the government, it needed time to recompose and strengthen the military forces. Along with the DZ, both parties agreed to carry out the negotiations in the middle of the confrontation. No cease fire, except on the DZ, was in place. As stated by the former High Commissioner for Peace, this was a complex issue to explain to public opinion. "The people did not understand why the FARC not only continued to attack the security forces, but also remained kidnapping and extorting" (Ricardo, 2014).

FARC's military intentions at the peace talks carried out by the Pastrana administration, as Echandía described them, were the following. First, the rebel group wanted to wage a political war of attraction regarding the DZ, which made the Government the recipient of several critics. Secondly, the rebel sought to expand its territorial control from the DZ –which was part of its strategic heartland– and to advance in their strategic plan. Lastly, FARC wanted to break the siege that paramilitary forces held on San Martín, Granada, San Juan de Arama, and Fuente de Oro, in Meta Department (Echandía, 2012c)

On the other hand, the Armed Forces were able to neutralize FARC's military purpose of employing the DZ tactically. As for the Military Forces and the Police, "from 1999 on, the security forces began to retake the initiative thanks to increasing mobility and higher air reaction capacity" (Echandía, 2008, p. 7).

Caguan Peace Talks' methodology consisted in a series of negotiations regarding several issues. The parties decided that on the *Common Agenda for the Change towards a New Colombia*, they should reach an agreement on all the issues that an endorsement mechanism (a referendum or a Constituent Assembly) should subsequently tackle. In spite of the fact that Ricardo states that when he quit his position –as the main Government negotiator– the Colombian Government and the guerrilla were close to a compromise on a cease fire agreement, several scholars (Nasi, 2006) argue that the negotiations "were just dialogues between the Government and the guerrilla delegates that had only reached a certainly broad agreement on issues to be discussed, but nothing was concrete" (Corporación Observatorio por la Paz, 2009, p. 177).

In regards to kidnapping, the guerrilla killed three and abducted four members of the National Congress during the period that the peace process was in place. The Liberal representatives Consuelo González de Perdomo, Orlando Beltrán Cuéllar, Liberal Senator Luis Eladio Pérez, and Conservative Representative Oscar Tulio Lizcano were abducted in order to pressure the Government for a prisoners' swap agreement (Semana, 2001). Other politicians and high profile persons were kidnapped as well, including Ramiro Carranza from the Administrative Department for Security (DAS), and former minister Fernando Araújo.

FARC's kidnapping strategy was threefold. First was the economic motive which targeted wealthy sectors in order to accrue financial resources to finance its struggle. Secondly, the abduction of Military and Police members had the purpose of affecting the enemy, and to present themselves as a regular army in a strategic equilibrium with the state. Most of 500 public forces held in FARC's power were taken at the town seizures between 1996 and 1998. The rebel group has argued since then that Military and Police staff under their custody have been retained and have not been kidnapped, due to the fact that the motive is to foster a prisoner swap and not an economic one (González Posso, 2013). Finally, FARC kidnapped politicians and high profile targets in order to pressure the Government, and specifically to force a prisoners-for-kidnapped exchange.

In September 2001, due to several factors, the peace dialogues entered a critical state from which they never recovered. On September 21st the former Minister of Culture, Consuelo Araújo Noguera also known as "La Cacica", was abducted by a FARC commando near Valledupar, Cesar Department. The Military Forces exerted pressure in order to liberate her, but five days later the rebel group commando chose to execute the former minister. This issue led to a significant crisis.

Hernando Gómez Buendía, one of the main analysts of the Colombian armed conflict, describes how the process became agonic from September 2001 to January 2002. In November 2011, the Liberal candidate Horacio Serpa visited the DZ with the purpose of supporting the peace dialogues. However, he was interpreted as an electoral move. The sum of Araújo's murder, Serpa's visit to the zone, and the changing international context, triggered by the terrorist attacks of 9-11, President Pastrana was forced into a position where he could no longer maintain the DZ in the same terms (Gómez Buendía, 2001). This led the president to authorize the Military Forces to exert control over the zone. Taking advantage of the vagueness of Caguan's ruling principles, "this actually meant a decrease in the warranties that led the FARC to freeze the process" (Gómez Buendía, 2001).

On January 2002, President Pastrana ordered FARC to evacuate the DZ in 48 hours. But thanks to an international mediation led by the United Nations Representative in Colombia and ten members of the diplomatic corps, the dialogues were extended for a month. Nevertheless, on February 20th, 2002 members of FARC's Teofilo Forero Mobile Column hijacked an Avianca airplane covering the Neiva (Huila Department) – Bogotá route and then kidnapped Senator Jorge Gechem Turbay. The president, "frustrated and exhausted by the rebel group's apathy to yield in favor of a peace settlement, announced the end of the dialogues that night" (Corporación Observatorio por la Paz, 2009, p. 191). At midnight, the military operations were launched aiming to regain control of the five towns comprising the DZ.

From that point on, an offensive against FARC began. From February through August, the last months of Pastrana's presidential period, FARC demonstrated the power they had acquired. Power accumulated by the guerrilla prior to Caguan's peace talks, was increased even more during the three years that those dialogues lasted. Dialogues failed because the conflict did not reach a stalemate, rather it escalated. No decline in the contentious tactics employed by the parties. No deprivation of resources as both parties increased their financing during time that dialogues lasted. Yet, a decline social support for FARC was evidenced, since a large segment of the population perceived that Caguan's failure was in part FARC's unwillingness to yield in favor of a peaceful solution. Instead, the Government received a mandate to militarily address the conflict.

THE STATE REGAINS THE STRATEGIC EDGE

In this section, the main argument is that conflict between FARC and the Colombian Government escalated after Caguan's failure. Both parties strengthened during the time that dialogues lasted. Nevertheless, the Military Forces were able to significantly hit FARC rebel territorial presence and commanding structure. State's action was also able to produce an impact on insurgent's financing. Caguan's failure and increased use of terrorism had also diminished FARC's social support.

After Caguan's failure, another escalation period began. This time it was led by the Military Forces' offensive. A military reengineering was put in place while the dialogues were under way. More resources for the Colombian state became available from U.S. cooperation, and from an increase in tax collection for waging the war against rebels. Also, in Pruitt and Kim's terms, social support for FARC was declining after Caguan's failure, while President Uribe won the elections with a mandate to address the conflict militarily. This shift from the point of view of public opinion was the result of FARC's unwillingness to lean in favor of a peace agreement. In this section it is, therefore, argued that rebels' miscalculation of state power led them to believe that seizing the capital was an achievable goal.

In spite of FARC's power, military reengineering carried out by President Pastrana's administration was a major success. The Armed Forces were modernized, strengthened, and their size rose in manpower. As Echandía (2008, p. 7) pointed out, "[b]etween 1999 and 2001, combats initiated by the Military Forces registered a continuous growth that was significantly accelerated from 2002 on". This shift in security forces' behavior was possible thanks to the aforementioned transformation.

Notwithstanding, FARC "tended to overestimate its military capability and tried to escalate the violent conflict believing that they were able to maintain a regular confrontation with the state's regular forces", as is argued by Fernán González (2011). Politically, the rebel intensified its kidnapping policy in order to pressure the Government. In particular, the rebel group increased politicians' abductions, such as the actions in Antioquia Department where Governor Guillermo Gaviria and his Peace Commissioner and former Minister Gilberto Echeverri were kidnapped and subsequently executed. The presidential candidate Ingrid Betancourt and Clara Rojas, her vice-presidential formula, Luis Eladio Pérez, and former Meta Department Governor Alan Jara, were also abducted during that period. But, undoubtedly, the most impressive action carried out by FARC was the kidnapping of twelve Valle del Cauca's Departmental Assembly Deputies by a commando of FARC's Western Bloc. Simulating a bomb threat and presenting themselves as Army soldiers, they took twelve deputies and kidnapped them. In the aftermath, the rebel group made official the request for demilitarizing the towns of Florida and Pradera, in Valle del Cauca Department, for the purpose of negotiating a kidnapped and prisoners' swap (Corporación Observatorio por la Paz, 2009).

During Uribe Vélez's administrations (2002-2006 and 2006-2010), the rebel group insisted on demilitarizing Florida and Pradera. According to Corporación Observatorio por la Paz researchers (2009), FARC's strategic goal in its demand of these Valle del Cauca towns' military withdrawal was the demilitarization action itself. FARC cloaked this interest with the claim for a "Humanitarian Agreement", which initially was intended to cover a larger set of issues than a kidnapped and prisoners' swap. Nevertheless, Uribe's administration did not yield to rebels' demands, appearing as insensitive to the relatives of those who were abducted (Corporación Observatorio por la Paz, 2009).

During this two-term administration, a military offensive, which was in turn possible thanks to Pastrana's Military Forces' reengineering, was put in place aiming at mainly tackling FARC's Eastern and Southern Blocs. A public policy was designed and named the Defense and Democratic Security Policy, which became Uribe's hallmark. Its main purpose was to regain the military initiative and regain control of territory. The public policy's name, as Rubén Sánchez and Federmán Rodríguez (2005) affirmed, responded to the Government's wish to avoid being compared to the National Defense paradigm that was used in the past to legitimatize military dictatorships in the Western hemisphere.

The Democratic Security Policy was, therefore, the legal and institutional framework. Along with Plan Colombia, the United States' military aid sponsored program conceived under Pastrana's mandate (Rojas, 2013), this public policy instituted a tax on the wealthiest patrimony in order to finance the cost of the war against insurgent groups (International Crisis Group, 2006). This meant that the Military Forces and the National Police were even more strengthened in this process. As per the National Police, the goal of presence in all 1,098 municipalities' urban-areas was achieved in 2004 (International Crisis Group, 2006). In 2002, just when the dialogues at Caguan ended, 158 municipalities had no police authority in their jurisdiction (Ávila, 2008).

In strategic terms some changes were also made. The Government put in place "an aggressive stimuli program to combatants' desertion, from which the Military Forces were able to gather valuable information from guerilla fighters that turned themselves in" (Corporación Observatorio por la Paz, 2009, p. 189). As it is stated by this research center, the demobilization program was not only an important instrument in undermining FARC's manpower capacity, but was also a very important source of intelligence. Along with that program, a whole strategy was put in place with the purpose of gathering intelligence. Additionally, a Cooperation Network was also put in place, which consisted in a reward-based program aiming to receive any kind of information from civilians that could be helpful for the security forces. Finally, the Military Forces created "battalions composed of peasant-soldiers borne from the confrontation areas" (Corporación Observatorio por la Paz, 2009, p. 189), which allowed the state to offset the guerrilla's edge, based on rebel fighters' knowledge of the terrain in which the battles took place, in those zones.

The military strategy, designed to achieve the goal that the Democratic Security Policy established, was the Patriot Plan. Juanita Léon defines the latter in the following terms:

Regarding FARC's objective to strangle the nation's political and economic core, the new goal of the Military Forces was to recover the State's authority all across the territory, starting from the country's productive center and expanding it [the offensive] towards the South, where the guerrilla's heartland is located. (León, 2005, p. 251)

The rebel group was able to locate 1,000 fighters in Cundinamarca Department, where the capital is situated. This compound was divided into eight Fronts, one Company and three Mobile Columns by the end of the year 2000 (León, 2005, p. 250). FARC practically sieged Bogota, a situation that misled them to think that they were close to winning the war. The Patriot Plan was then implemented to overcome the strategic equilibrium that the rebel group was able to reach at the end of the 1990s.

Operation Liberty One was implemented by the Armed Forces to expel the rebels from Cundinamarca. The Military Forces, through their reengineering process, created two platforms in order to adapt themselves to the guerrilla warfare. The first one were the Mobile Brigades whose aim was to patrol and close the municipalities' entries from which guerrilla fighters gather food and water supplies (León, 2005). The Army also created a new elite body named Rapid Deployment Forces (FUDRA), composed of high professionalized and specialized men accompanied by airborne support to quickly engage in combat with the enemy. If Mobile Brigades were in charge of the patrolling tasks, "the main combat effort was made by FUDRA soldiers" (León, 2005, p. 254).

After a year of military pressure, the security forces were able to take down FARC's commander in Cundinamarca Department. The Army eliminated Luis Alexis Castellanos (A.K.A *Manguera*), Javier Gutiérrez, and Carlos A. Osorio Velásquez (A.K.A. *Marco Aurelio Buendía*), who had been the masterminds of the Cundinamarca takeover plan. Actually, *Buendía* led in 1994 FARC's action against La Calera town, located in the surrounding area of Colombia's capital. He was also one of the brains behind the indiscriminate kidnapping strategy named the "miraculous catch". No matter who could get abducted because of this strategy, it was mainly implemented in the Bogota-Los Llanos highway, one of the country's main food supplying corridors for the capital. Since Operation Liberty One, FARC started to lose power and, therefore, began failing in maintaining territorial control.

As Echandía (2012a, p. 59) shows, the military forces' offensive against the rebel group triggered "a reduction in both FARC's armed actions and territorial presence". Apart from the Cundinamarca operation, the security forces launched with its Caribbean Joint Task Force (FTCC) important operations aiming to neutralize FARC's Caribbean Bloc. The military efforts led to taking down *Martin Caballero*, FARC's Caribbean Bloc leader and Secretariat's member in 2007 (Echandía, 2012d, p. 57). The FTCC was able to recover and expel the rebel group from the Montes de Maria region, located in the south of the Bolivar Department and a strategic position on the grounds of its connection with the Magdalena River.

According to Echandía (2012d) military forces' actions in the eastern part of the country's, Los Llanos region and in particular in the Arauca Department, were able to produce a significant reduction in FARC's military capacity. In all theaters of operation, the military forces were able to inflict damage on the rebel group.

Undoubtedly, paramilitaries played a role in counterinsurgency through terror and displacement, aiming to diminish the guerrilla's social base. Although, they were not part of a deliberate central strategy of the state, paramilitary groups also served the purposes and ends of the Government. They remained autonomous financially from the state through a large variety of actions, mainly drug trafficking. The relation of paramilitaries groups with drug traffickers is also a complex one. Undeniably, the latter were involved in the former's inception (Medina Gallego, 1990), but once big cartels were extinct, paramilitaries took over the business and became by that strategic choice an enemy to the state's antidrug policy (Duncan, 2008). Some have argued that since the military offensive was aimed mainly at FARC and, in particular, at its Eastern Bloc, paramilitaries' actions were focused on ELN and geographically circumscribed to the North-Eastern bounds of Colombia (Corporación Observatorio por la Paz, 2009).

During the time that Caguan's peace talks lasted, paramilitary groups grew considerably. The role of paramilitary groups in counterinsurgency tasks has been a central concern in literature but not the only one. Edwin Cruz (2007, p. 118) tracks four approaches that have been used to analyze paramilitaries' groups in Colombia: "First, as a tool for counterinsurgency or a state-directed 'dirty-war'; second, as a violent services provider for local and regional actors; thirdly, paramilitary groups have also been considered as independent actors from the state; and finally, as rent-seeking groups and co-opted by drug traffickers". According to this author, paramilitaries are essentially complex actors, since in all paramilitary groups one could find all four trends, in addition to the fact that their configuration varied depending on the region where they operated. The different regional factions were only gathered into a single national umbrella in 1997. At that time, one of these regional groups – Cordoba and Uraba's United Peasants Self-defense (ACCU) – took over the leadership with the purpose of presenting an amalgam as another conflict party. In other words, the purpose was to appear as a legitimate political actor.

Paramilitary groups' territorial expansion followed a different pattern from FARC's. The latter were born on the periphery, at the agricultural frontier. In early stages on these lands, the insurgents built their strategic heartland and began their expansion towards other peripheral and semi-peripheral zones, such as Uraba. This semi-peripheral zone located on the north eastern part of Colombia, hosted in the 70s a significant union movement that sprouted from unfair working conditions at the banana plantations. In that context, the Popular Liberation Army (EPL) another left-wing insurgent group that made its stronghold by establishing close relations with the union movement and then forcing patrons to improve working conditions (León, 2005).

Carlos Castaño, ACCU commander, succeeded in expelling guerrilla groups from Uraba region from 1995 until approximately 1998. In 1997, Castaño took over the United Self-Defense Forces (AUC), the national federation of paramilitary groups. In spite of his past in the Medellin drug cartel, Castaño represented the counterinsurgent arm versus other commanders that were more interested in criminal activities, mainly drug trafficking. As noted by Gustavo Duncan (2008), from 1997 to 2001 was Castaño's golden age. The paramilitary project as a counterinsurgent force was successful in expelling guerrilla groups from Uraba, the south of Bolivar Department and the Madgdalena Medio region where they succeeded in expelling ELN from Barrancabermeja (González, Bolívar, & Vázquez, 2002). This oil-industry key city located at the Magdalenian river basin was a stronghold for ELN (Duncan, 2008).

In these regions, paramilitary groups were to create hegemony through the imposition of a monopoly of violence through massacres and population displacement, and progressively in open combats with the insurgents as their military capacity grew (Duncan, 2008). These groups targeted any suspected insurgents' supporter, but once they succeeded militarily, a political and criminal project began. Duncan (2008) has defined this kind of behavior as a mafia project, since it intended to control any criminal activity, even from small gangs, or small robbery and paradoxically drug abuse. This form of territorial control ironically paved the way to gain support from the indigenous population that could enjoy peace from this armed law and order.

In spite of the fact that paramilitary tactics were incredibly effective aiming at rebels' social bases, once AUC intended to fight FARC forces in its strategic heartland it encountered a formidable army, as Gustavo Duncan (2008) pointed out. From 2001 until the beginning of dialogues with President Uribe's administration paramilitary counterinsurgent project stagnated. As several authors asserted, this situation was also a consequence of the paramilitary's criminal arm outweigh of the counterinsurgent one. The latter was represented by Castaño and Salvatore Mancuso –a former breeder that became one of the main AUC commanders. Castaño, at the dawn of his golden age, lost so much power in the organization that he only played a secondary role in the approaches with the President Uribe's administration. Even more, one commander actually demanded Castaño's exclusion as a condition to sit at the negotiations table (Duncan, 2008). The former leader would disappear and be considered dead on other paramilitary commanders' order.

Fernando Cubides (2006, p. 56), a scholar that has studied the paramilitary phenomena, has criticized the timing that the Government chose to seek the AUC's demobilization: "What all analysts, without any exception, considered to be the natural order in terms of the negotiation, its logic sequence, was inverted: since the paramilitaries existed in function of the guerrilla, disabling the former, contributing to its disappearance, implied reaching, previously, some sort negotiated solution with the latter". Even though it is not the purpose of this chapter, it might be stated that in terms of Pruitt and Kim's perceived stalemate concept, paramilitaries' insurgent project stagnated when they tried to fight in an open combat with FARC at its historic rearguard. Additionally, the criminal branch overbore the insurgent one and may have led the Government to meet at Santafé de Ralito, Cordoba Department, in spite of the fact that the insurgent issue was not solved. Once the agreement was concluded 30,000 paramilitary fighters' were demobilized and most, but not all, of the groups that were gathered under the AUC umbrella (Duncan, 2008) as well. A group called Casanare Peasants Self-Defense Forces (ACC), and Block Cacique Pipintá in Caldas Department or the Colombian Popular Revolutionary Antiterrorist Army (ERPAC), among others, opted-out and were never part of the negotiations (Echandía, 2012b).

In spite of the fact that AUC demobilization brought a significant reduction of violence in Colombia, some of the former paramilitaries and the ones that opted out of the Ralito's process have returned to illegal pursuits, mainly criminal activity associated with drug trafficking and illegal mining (Echandía, 2012b). These groups were called by the Government as emerging criminal bands (BACRIM). Even though some claim they are still carrying out counter-insurgent tasks, its role is not significant and some of these emerging bands have even established ties with insurgent groups for illegal financing.

FARC's social support suffered from paramilitaries' actions. Nevertheless, in the dispute for territorial control with the paramilitary groups, FARC also employed terror tactics, such as massacres and displacement (Echandía, 2012b). This behavior produced an impact on guerrilla's social support, which reduced significantly over 2000s. In addition, FARC progressively used more terrorist tactics as the guerrilla was considerably weakened on the military realm. Although, this was a FARC's miscalculation, as embracing terrorism to harm the Government made it easier for the latter to call the former a terrorist threat, especially after 9-11. As the International Crisis Group (2006) noted, this also meant that the rebels lost ground on the international arena, taking into consideration that FARC was included in US and European terrorist organizations lists.

As for the government´s military offensive, in President Uribe's first term, it was able to force the rebels to withdraw from the major cities and return to their strategic heartland. Located in the Colombian jungles and mountains of the south of the country, these zones historically under FARC control, served the rebel group as a safe haven to hide from the security forces, and to gather financial and human resources. These territories in Cauca, Putumayo, Nariño, Caquetá, and Meta Departments were, and still are, characterized by the presence of coca plantations, from which the rebels have not only been able to extract resources, but also to recruit new fighters. Mostly, in President Uribe's second term and President Santos' first, Military Forces were also able to strike FARC's commanding structure. Echandía (2012d, p. 60) sums up the military offensive carried out by the Government against FARC in the following terms:

The military offensive impact against FARC is expressed in their 50% manpower loss, including nine members of the Central Command Structure (Estado Mayor Central), among them five members of the Secretariat, and a considerable amount of middle-ranking officials have left the ranks either by death, capture, or demobilization.

With respect to the elimination of high-ranking officials' that Echandía referred to, along with the aforementioned killings of FARC's commanders in Cundinamarca, the security forces were able to directly harm the rebel's command structure since 2003. Among them *El Negro Acacio*, FARC's 16 Front commander and one of the masterminds behind the drug trafficking activities aiming to finance the group, was neutralized by the security forces (Echandía, 2012d). As this scholar pointed out - *Simón Trinidad's* capture, alias *Karina*'s demobilization, and *Iván Ríos*' assassination by his security staff leader–all of these losses produced a significant vacuum in the rebel group's leadership.

Nonetheless, it was not until *Operación Fénix* (Phoenix Operation) that *Raúl Reyes* became the first Secretariat member that the security forces were able to neutralize (Echandía, 2012d). This operation carried out in March 2008, on a FARC's Ecuadorian-based base camp, consisted in a precise airstrike where the second in the chain of command and first negotiator during the Caguan Peace Talks was hit. *Reyes*' elimination was the beginning of the end of the group's traditional Central Command Structure.

Later in March 2008, *Manuel Marulanda Vélez* also known as *Tirofijo,* FARC's historical High Commander, was announced to be dead from natural causes by nowadays group's leader, Timoleón Jiménez A.K.A. *Timochenko. Marulanda* was one of the rebel group's founders. He became a rebel symbol and the incarnation of FARC's military branch, in opposition to Jacobo Arenas that represented the political one, as has been stated before (Jiménez, Silva, & Patiño, 2009).

Due to security forces' reengineering –which increased the mobility, enhanced the technology, improved the intelligence power, strengthened airborne capabilities, and built up a framework to cooperate and to carry out joint operations between all the Forces (Army, Navy, Air Force, and National Police)– the Colombian state was able to hit all FARC Fronts' rearguards (Corporación Observatorio por la Paz, 2009, p. 199).

Another key issue was important in striking FARC's power: the defeat of their kidnapping policy. The military pressure and intelligence improvements were decisive in beating rebel group's abduction strategy as a tool for pressuring the Government. The first one, was *Operación Jaque* (Check Operation) that was able to infiltrate the group's communications and liberate former presidential candidate Ingrid Betancourt, three United States civilian contractors, and several members of the security forces that had been abducted during the rebel towns' seizures (Corporación Observatorio por la Paz, 2009).

According to Daniel Pécaut, a French scholar that has been studying Colombia and its armed conflict for years, *Operación Jaque* "made evident the vulnerability of a formerly hermitic organization" (Pécaut, 2008 quoted by Echandia, 2002). Just before the end of Uribe Vélez's mandate,

Operation Camaleon was able to liberate four soldiers and policemen that were held by the guerrilla for more than ten years (Echandía, 2012d, p. 59).

Nonetheless, as several authors recognize, the major stepback in FARC's kidnapping strategy was the assassination of eleven of the twelve Valle del Cauca deputies that were abducted in 2002 (Corporación Observatorio por la Paz, 2009) (Echandía, 2012d). As the researchers of the Corporación Observatorio para la Paz affirmed, on July 2007 the rebel group informed that the cross-fire between a non-identified armed group and the FARC's squad that was holding the deputies in custody was responsible for these deaths (Corporación Observatorio por la Paz, 2009, pp. 196-197). The Government vehemently denied that military operations were taking place at the time and place where the combats with the rebel' squad had been presumably held. Later, the intelligence gathered from wiretapped emails between FARC's commanders, confirmed that two units of the rebel group had accidentally clashed, which was misread, by the squad that was holding the kidnapped deputies, as a military operation aiming to free them. The abducted deputies received close distance shots, from which it was also inferred that the hostages were executed. As stated before, many scholars coincide that this episode was a huge political defeat for the rebel group. But particularly, this incident meant that the Colombian civilian population turned against FARC. It also made impossible the rebels' political end of pressuring the Government for a humanitarian prisoners' swap, and finally resulted in a huge social mobilization against the rebels' kidnapping policy in February 2008 (Corporación Observatorio por la Paz, 2009, p. 197).

Apart from major losses that the rebel group suffered in its main command structure, and the defeat of their kidnapping policy, FARC was also neutralized by the security forces in their efforts to recover the position they had formerly held in Cundinamarca and the south of Bolivar Department (Echandía, 2012d).

At the beginning of the first term of Juan Manuel Santos' administration (2010-2014), FARC received one of the most important hits in their history. Through a joint operation with highly precise armament, "the military forces took *Jorge Briceño* down, the highest FARC military strategist, member of the Secretariat, and one of the most powerful commanders of the organization" (Echandía, 2012d, p. 59). Also known as *Mono Jojoy*, the Oriental Bloc commander was in charge of the most powerful structure of the organization. This military unit carried out the Mitú seizure, in which the rebels were able to gather close to 1,000 fighters around Vaupés Department's capital. Massive and indiscriminate kidnapping operations, also known as "miraculous catch", in the Bogota-Villavicencio highway also are part of important Oriental Bloc actions. Undoubtedly, *Mono Jojoy*'s death was a major loss for the rebel group.

In spite of the fact that *Jojoy*'s neutralization was an important victory for the security forces, the most significant raid against the FARC was Odiseo Operation, which led the military forces to take *Alfonso Cano* down. The importance of this episode lies in the fact that it "was the first time that the FARC lost their commander in chief in combat" (Echandía, 2012d, p. 59).

All of the successful attacks against FARC leaders were framed within a high-value target strategy implemented by the Military Forces. In Echandía's (2008) terms, the strategic impact of neutralizing *Reyes, Jojoy,* and *Cano* was to break FARC's invulnerability. In particular, this operation ended with the perception that their leaders were always safe. Furthermore, Democratic Security Policy's success is due to affecting FARC's strategic heartland, which no more constituted a safe haven for the rebels' commanding structure. The rebel group also proved to be incapable of diluting the pressure that was exerted by the Military Forces in order to siege and neutralize rebel leaders (Echandía, 2012d).

STAGNATION AND PERCEIVED STALEMATE OF THE COLOMBIAN ARMED CONFLICT

In this section, the main argument is that conflict between FARC and the Colombian Government stagnated at end of the 2000s. After the offensive carried out by the Military Forces –which effectively harmed rebel's manpower, commanding structure and finances– the effectiveness of state contentious tactics began to fall due to FARC's adaptation process. The rebel group reorganized in smaller units, with higher mobility, and increasing the use of landmines and snipers to stop the Military's mobility. In Pruitt and Kim's terms, contentious tactics began to fail, along with other key variables, and this may have led to a stalemate. In 2012 the parties formally decided to enter into a new attempt at peacefully ending the conflict. It may therefore be argued that a perception of a stalemate, or otherwise refusing to continue the fight at such an unacceptable costs or risks, would explain why the Government and FARC finally reached the decision to establish the peace talks in Havana.

It is an undeniable fact that FARC have been considerably weakened, "which is expressed in the loss of 50% of their members, a forced retreat towards a zone in which they are not safe anymore, and an ostensible drop in their armed power and capacity of maneuver" (Echandía, 2008, p. 13). In spite of FARC's strategic inferiority, the rebel group was able to adapt itself to this situation. In 2009, when Cano was still alive, the rebel group issued a new strategic plan: *Plan Renacer* (Reborn Plan). The rebels have since increased the usage of landmines, snipers, and a growing employment of the militias that can carry out attacks and immediately disguise themselves within the civil population (Echandía, 2012c). The group's strategic goal has come to guarantee the survival of their strategic heartland, in the understanding that it is impossible for them to recover the military initiative that they once had (Echandía, 2012c).

The rebel group has also introduced some changes in its daily operation, in order to recover from the important losses suffered in the last decade. In recent times, FARC's Secretariat and Central Command Structure have been releasing and softening the control and communications over middle-rank officials, gaining autonomy, and allowing the units to maintain the operations (Echandía, 2009). As is also described by Echandía (2009, p. 66), in the adaptation process the group has also introduced new kinds of armed structures: "the creation of Mobile Blocs and the possibility of putting together joint area commands or 'interfronts', [which are] structures established from mobile fronts and columns in order to carry out [armed] actions and that have the ability to react to offensives launched by the Military Forces".

As Echandía (2009) stated, this military and operational adaptation has allowed FARC to maintain a considerable firepower. Regarding its armed structures, the Eastern Bloc was the most combated, but remains active. As per the Western Bloc, it is the only FARC structure that has increased its territorial control in the Pacific (Echandía, 2009), where the coca plantations have increased in recent years.

It is certain that the Colombian state has been able to reduce FARC power significantly, but in no way has it been able to terminate it. The rebel group has maintained a considerable power of action. Since 2008 the group has also been able to preserve its membership, in spite of the Government's efforts to demobilize, capture, and neutralize rebel fighters. As can be read from Figure 2, the rebel group has been able to maintain at least 8,000 men in arms, which allows it to survive and to keep a considerable firepower.

The rebel group has returned to the guerrilla warfare model. Carrying out sabotage and ambushes' operations, and avoiding frontal combat with the Armed Forces has become the new guideline in rebels' repertoire. According to the Human Rights Observatory, since 2008, FARC has been able to maintain more than 500 armed

Figure 2. FARC manpower evolution
Source: Human Rights Observatory, Human Rights and International Humanitarian Law Presidential Program, retrieved from Echandía (2012) and Semana (2012).

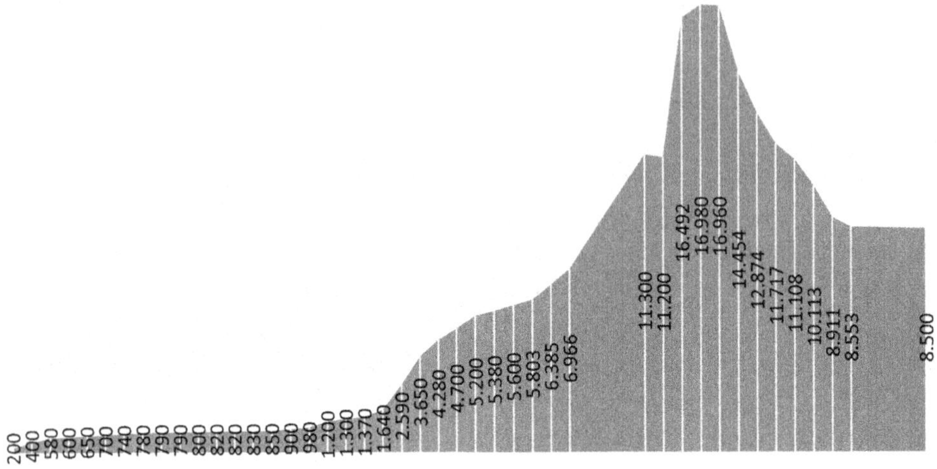

actions per year. Nevertheless, as demonstrated by Echandía, the rebel group has been capable of maintaining its firepower but it has not recovered the capabilities to launch other actions, as they were able to perform long ago (Echandía, 2012d).

The main achievement of the military offensive carried out by the Colombian state was breaking FARC's territorial control, mainly in the municipalities' urban areas. Using data and methodology (Restrepo, Spagat, & Vargas, 2005) from the Bogota-based Conflict Analysis Resource Center (CERAC) and the Electoral Observation Mission (MOE), Figure 3, Figure 4, Figure 5, and Figure 6 show the evolution of guerrilla presence cross-referenced with rebels' armed actions (i.e. unilateral actions and combats, following CERAC's methodology). The areas highlighted in dark grey correspond to territories in which the guerrilla was present and that where armed actions took place. On the other hand, the areas in which the guerrilla was present but no armed actions were conducted by the insurgents groups, are highlighted in light grey. In spite of the fact that data includes all insurgent groups (FARC, ELN and EPL), territorial control by all guerrilla groups has been broken by the state action, with paramilitaries' coalescing in some cases. This may be inferred since, towns with territorial presence but no armed actions (light grey area) can be considered as areas in which guerrilla groups insulated those area from the state's action. Guerrilla presence and no combats or unilateral actions (or armed actions) is, therefore, an indicator of territorial control by insurgent groups. Areas highlighted in dark grey may show that there is dispute for those towns' control, since no group can claim those as insulated areas from the others' armed actions.

For the purposes of this chapter, two points are to be raised. In spite of the fact that guerrilla's presence –expressed in terms of the number of territories in which the guerrilla is present and it conducted armed actions– grew significantly from 1998 to 2002 (the time that Caguan's dialogues lasted), the number of territories in which the guerrilla is present and that did not host armed actions dropped. This could be interpreted as evidence that, even though, FARC strengthened in the DZ, the Colombian state also became stronger. Secondly, it is also evident that Armed Forces' offensive has been successful in undermining rebels' territorial presence and control.

Figure 3. Number of Municipalities with guerrilla presence and armed actions: 1998
Source: Data from Conflict Analysis Resource Center (CERAC) and the Electoral Observation Mission (MOE).[6]

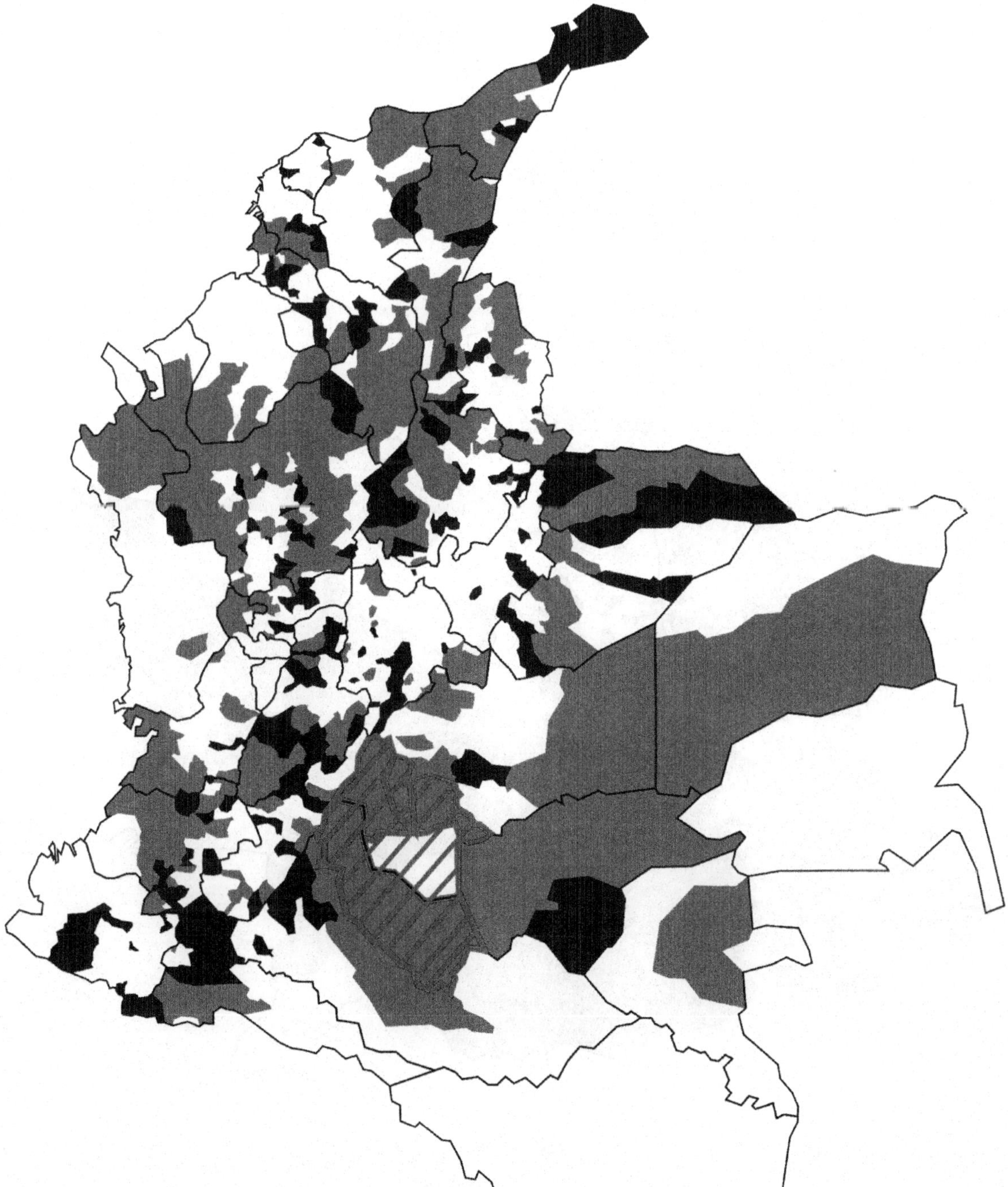

Figure 4. Number of Municipalities with guerrilla presence and armed actions: 2002
Source: Data from Conflict Analysis Resource Center (CERAC) and the Electoral Observation Mission (MOE).

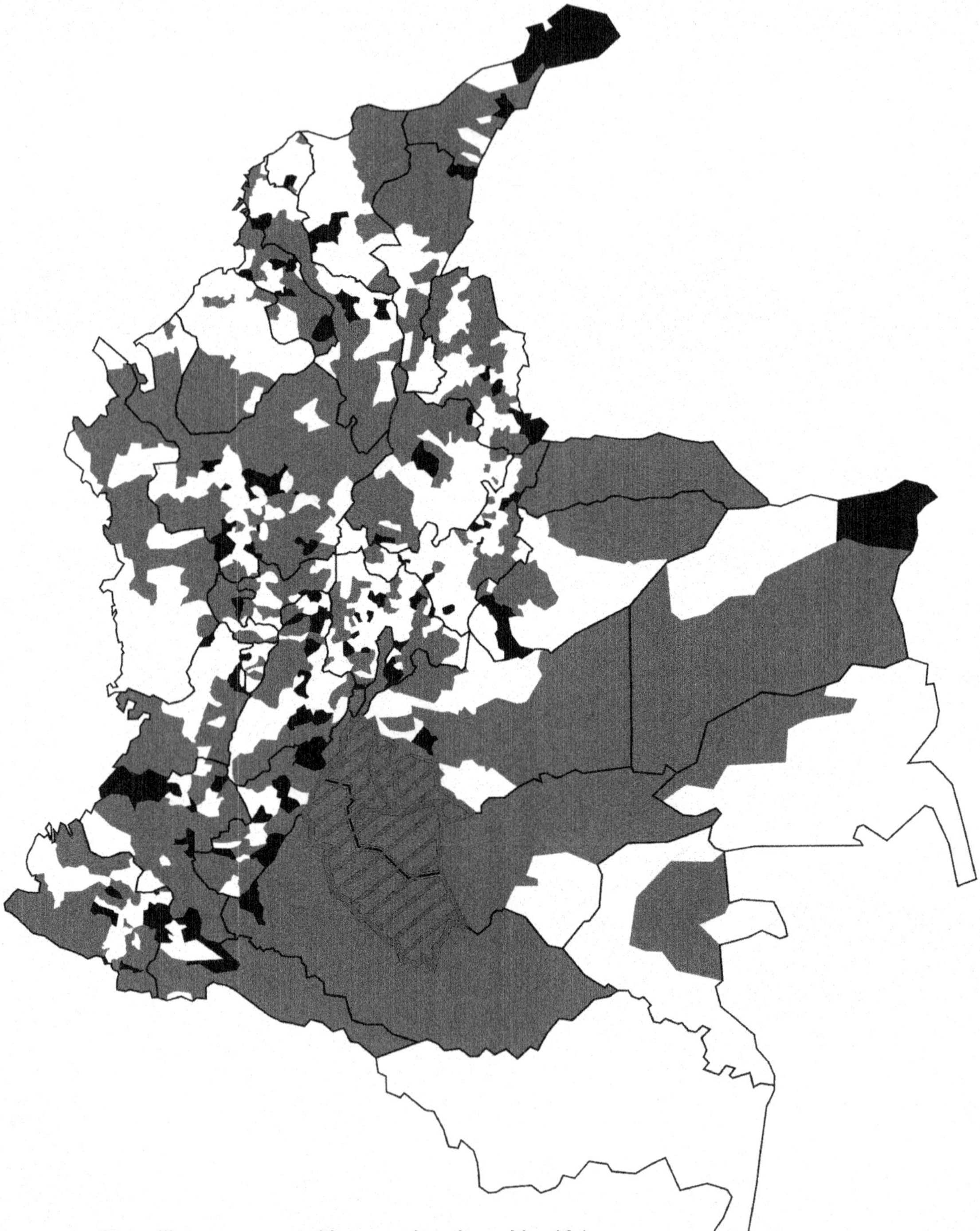

Figure 5. Number of Municipalities with guerrilla presence and armed actions: 2007
Source: Data from Conflict Analysis Resource Center (CERAC) and the Electoral Observation Mission (MOE).

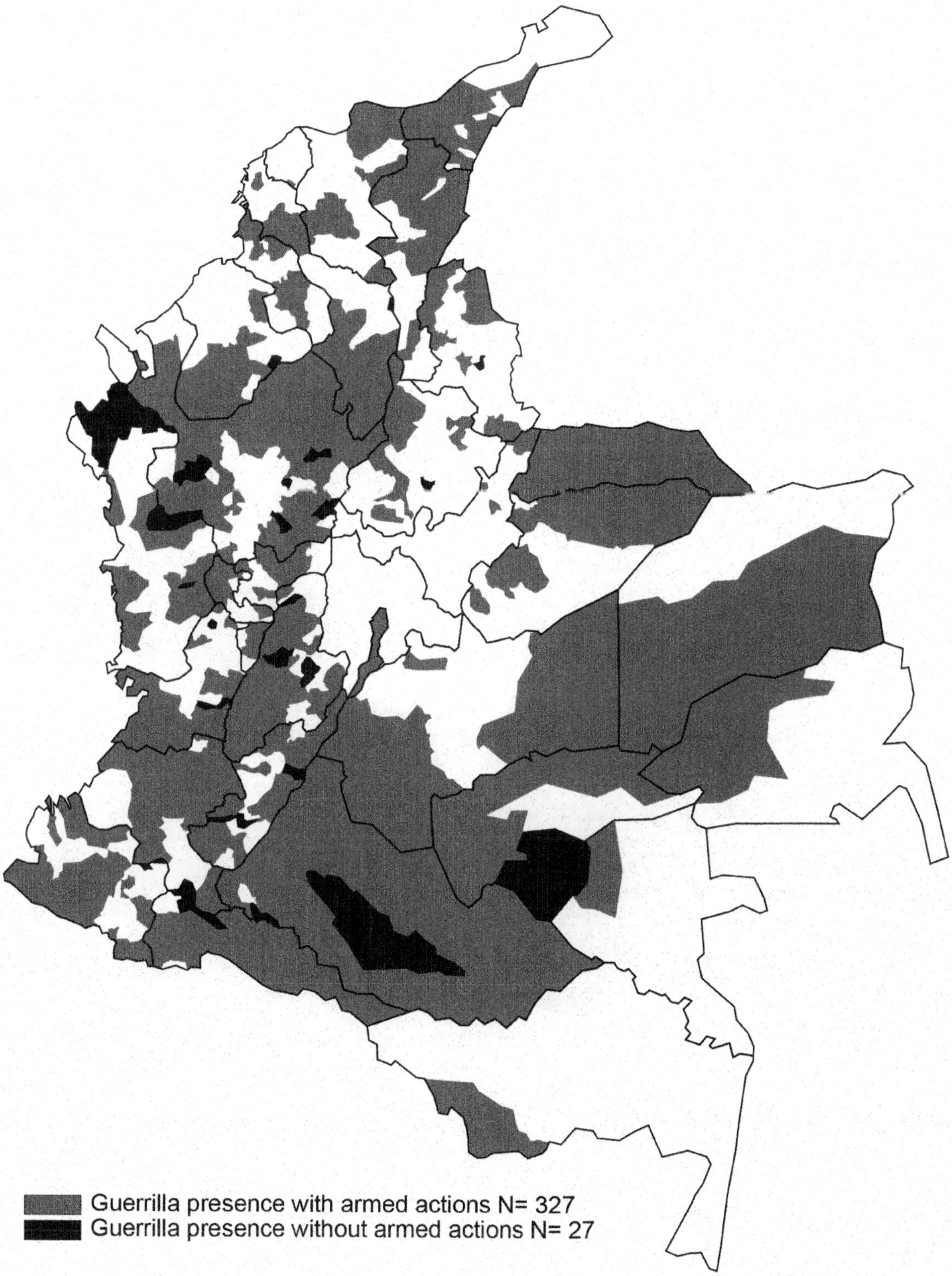

Figure 6. Number of Municipalities with guerrilla presence and armed actions: 2011
Source: Data from Conflict Analysis Resource Center (CERAC) and the Electoral Observation Mission (MOE).

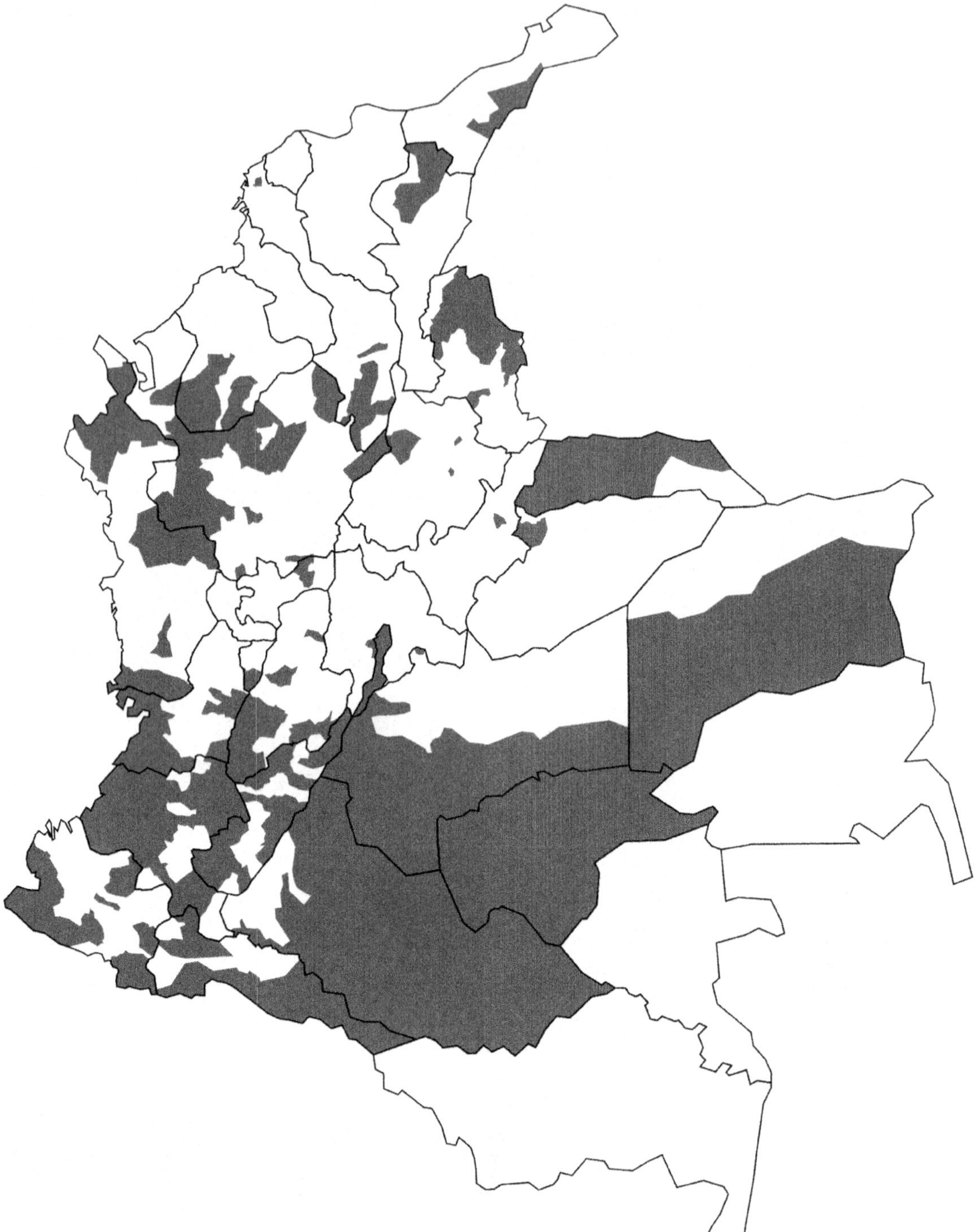

With regards to the former, it dropped from 401 towns in 1998, to 327 municipalities in 2007 and finally it reached 169 in 2011. Regarding the other variable, rebel-controlled towns were reduced from 105 municipalities in 2002, to 27 in 2007, and none in 2011. This also confirms that rebels have not been able to recover the power they once had, but neither are they terminated. In addition, it is not true that insurgents, and mainly FARC, have strengthened during Havana's peace talks, unlike what happened in Caguan's dialogues. For instance, The National Police is still present in the urban areas of all municipalities.

Regarding the rebel group's funding, state action, via Plan Colombia, has been effective in reducing the amount of coca crops' hectares from 145,000 ha in 2001 to 48,000 ha in 2013. Alexandra Guáqueta (2003) demonstrates that there is a correlation between increase of coca and poppy crops and the growth evidenced in armed groups' fighters. In spite of the 67% reduction in plantations, FARC has managed to maintain a substantial armed contingent.

According to Jeremy McDermott (2013), researcher at InSight Crime –a research center on conflict and crime– the Colombian Government estimates that FARC controls about 60% of all coca plantations in Colombia. As per McDermott's calculations, the guerrilla, in order to maintain 8,000 fighters and 30,000 militia members, needs at least USD $200 million dollars per year. The most realistic calculation is hence that the rebel group receives at least that amount from drug trafficking and other activities. Alfredo Rangel's calculation states that FARC's drug income dropped by 40% after *Negro Acacio*'s death (Rangel quoted by International Crisis Group, 2009, p. 12). The International Crisis Group (2009, p. 12) estimates that the rebel group's income for drug trafficking activities, accounted for one billion dollars, has dropped to 600 or 500 million dollars in 2007. As McDermott claims, certainly the rebel group has lost important financial resources due to the security forces' efforts, but it has also been able to maintain the necessary cash flow to finance its activities.

The rebel group in the last decade has intensified its involvement in illegal mining, as this practice has grown in Colombia, mainly driven by international gold price increasing in recent years. According to a research carried out by *Semana* magazine, one kilogram of gold is worth 18 times of the cost of the same amount of cocaine in the Colombian market (Racines, 2014). The rebels, along with other armed groups and gangs, have been collecting illegal taxes from mining sites. Most of them, if not all, are informal mines that have no mining titles, and usually are located in areas of rebel influence. According to *Semana*'s data, from 300 towns that host non-authorized extraction, 75 municipalities coincide with coca crops plantations, and FARC is actually present in 72 of them.

In regards to the other party's financing, the Colombian State has not only been capable of maintaining the financial resources necessary to maintain the war effort. As one may notice on Figure 7, the Security and Defense budget has regularly increased since 2001. This is an important factor, considering Pruitt & Kim's theory about the perceived stalemate driven by the deprivation of resources. It can therefore be established that no deprivation of resources could produce a stalemate in the Colombian conflict.

It seems that since FARC units have had different involvement in illegal financing activities, risks to criminalization, or to abandon a demobilization process at any stage, may foreseeably depend on a given Front or Block's participation on drug trafficking or illegal mining. Undoubtedly, there is evidence of a few rebels entering the criminalization path (Delgado, 2014) (Semana, 2014) (Semana, 2014). Another source for violence recycling might be the ties that the rebels have established with criminal organizations in Colombia and abroad. Domestically, FARC's units have been coalescing

Figure 7. Colombian state Defense budget
Source: Data from the National Defense Ministry

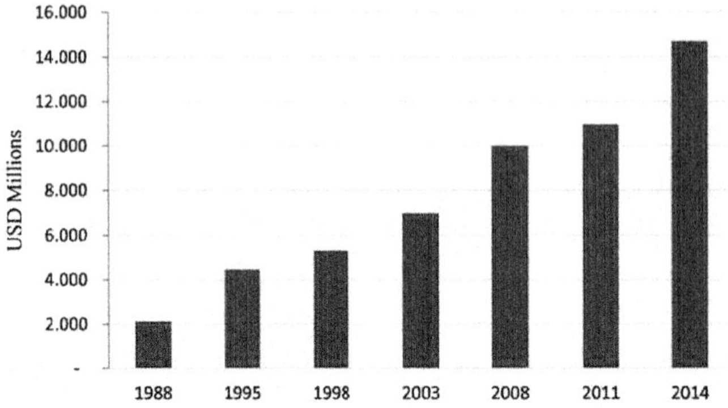

in the last years with former-paramilitary gangs, the also known as criminal emergent bands. One example of such shady alliance has occurred in the South, where FARC has been working with the North of Valle Cartel's private army for drug trafficking purposes (El Espectador, 2010). In another region as McDermott states, criminal emergent bands have been providing ammunition to the rebels in exchange for drugs (McDermott, 2013). Internationally, it is suspected that the rebel group has developed close ties with some Mexican cartels, and not only for drug trafficking but also for training purposes (Semana, 2015).

In the same line of thought, FARC's financing strategy through drugs' production has led to a criminalization trend in some Fronts. According to Jeremy McDermott, the guerrilla's main Fronts that are dedicated to drug production and smuggling are Front 10th, Front 16th, Front 29th, Front 30th Front 33rd, Front 48th and Front 57th (McDermott, 2013). This researcher has warned of the possibilities of criminalization after a demobilization agreement that will probably be reached. Certainly, the aforementioned Fronts are more likely to enter this path, which can be aggravated with the middle-ranking official burden of war in recent times.

It may also be important to consider another variable that can lead to a conflict stalemate, according to Pruitt & Kim. Such would be the case of the loss of social support. As per Corporación Observatorio para la Paz, FARC's indiscriminate kidnapping policy (Figure 8), and the use of improvised rockets to attack Military bases and Police

Figure 8. FARC's attributed kidnappings
Source: Data from the National Defense Ministry

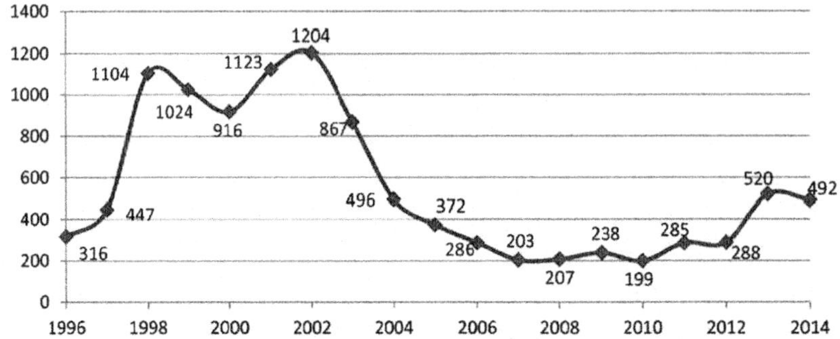

stations with gas cylinders –known for their lack of accuracy– have produced important civilian casualties. Teófilo Vásquez (2011) has pointed out, FARC's strategic retreat towards rural areas is effective for surviving state's offensive, but it has an inherent cost in terms of closeness to the population. Vásquez also adds that in terms of social support, after the end of the Cold War it became difficult for the insurgents to congregate large segments of the population, in particular urban-based citizens. Even radical left-wing individuals in the cities were increasingly more reluctant to support insurgent activities, according to this scholar. In addition, the effects of using terrorism as a strategy also harmed rebel's social support, as it was aforementioned. Nevertheless, the rebel group has not been totally devoid from social support, as several rural segments still back it (Vásquez, 2011).

In relation to the Colombian state's social support, two facts are relevant. First, it has had significant difficulties in gaining legitimacy in traditional FARC-controlled territories, in which an alternative governance system has been working for several years (León, 2013). Furthermore, human rights violations, such as summary executions that were presented as combat results, have had a clear impact in the legitimacy of the government's security forces.

Regarding depletion of time as a driver for stalemate, it would appear that both parties have issues concerning this matter. At one end, FARC has important time-related issues. Even though the rebels have been able to survive from the Colombian state offensive and lasted for more than 50 years, the guerrilla is having trouble with its membership and commanding chain of command. Firstly, the demobilization program and airborne superiority have considerably decimated rebel fighters. In addition to that, high profile strategy has not only taken FARC's commanding structure, but also guerrilla commanders have since fled the country towards the borders in order to avoid an almost certain death. Remote control of the war, which has been aggravated because several FARC commanders are in Havana for the peace dialogues, is still producing a huge impact. As is shown by Pizarro Leongómez (2011), "[n]owadays, the extreme dispersion of FARC's Fronts–in the context of Military Forces' strengthening and territorial control– is not only generating a serious disruption in the chain of command and internal discipline, but it is also producing huge difficulties in guns and ammunition supply".

Even though FARC has managed to survive, it appears that time is shrinking it. The guerrilla's survival can usually be considered as a victory, since it is not defeated. Guerrilla warfare is about a lengthy process asymmetric fight, which includes attack-and-hide actions that seek to overstretch state's capabilities. This way guerrilla groups maximize resources, as they strive to harm the enemy with few resources. Nevertheless, as can be inferred from Pizarro Leongómez's argument, dispersion may also affect insurgents, since it makes units' supply and political work harder. Relying on militia members may allow FARC to survive as an armed actor, but it seems difficult to reach a strategic equilibrium with the state. Another process that may have overborne time as an insurgent's advantage is criminalization. This path may affect fighters' disciple.[7]

In regards with the Government, apparently President Santos considered that the alternative for peace dialogues was better than the military approach because it would probably take too long to reach a successful outcome using force. When the President Santos (2012) addressed the country after the Framework Agreement for Ending the Conflict was concluded with FARC, he stated that "[a]ny responsible statesman knows that he cannot let got a possibility like this [Havana's peace dialogues] to end the conflict". The Head of State later on that same speech added: "we did not combat for combating; we engage in combat to reach peace" (Santos, 2012).

It seems therefore that conflict between the Government and FARC has reached a stalemate.

Contentious tactics have lost their taste, in Pruitt and Kim's terms. Nevertheless, cash flow seems to not be a problem for either one of the parties. Social support for FARC declined in national public opinion, in spite of the fact that they still have keen supporters mainly in areas where they maintain an influence. The conflict may have stagnated, but has by no means de-escalated.

Have Both Parties Perceived the Stalemate?

One can find several facts that may be read in terms of recognition of stalemate by both parties, in spite of the fact that in Pruitt and Kim's theoretical perspective there is no reference to the perception stage other than the change of leadership or a shocking event as triggering factors for realizing the stalemate. As per the Government, in the previous administration, President Uribe refrained to recognize that Colombia was in an armed conflict. According to the former President, the state was fighting a highly organized criminal structure, since, in his view, FARC was only a drug trafficking and terrorist organization. President Santos served in that administration as its Defense Minister for almost three years, coalescing with that framework. Nevertheless, Santos' administration introduced two laws that were aimed at building a transitional justice framework. This framework, which comprised the Victims and Restitution Law and the Legal Framework for the Peace, was put through in order to address the situation of thousands of paramilitary fighters who were on a legal loophole. It was also understood that both laws would lay the foundations for an eventual negotiation with remaining guerrilla groups. The Victims and Restitution Law actually recognized that Colombia was in conflict. Such recognition may be read as a move towards a peace process by the Government, as states are often reluctant to negotiate with terrorists. More so, FARC has always refused to acknowledge itself as a terrorist organization. This could be therefore interpreted as a tacit recognition or perception of stalemate. Furthermore, according to Ávila (2012) the Victims and Restitution Law and the Legal Framework for the Peace were part of a Government strategy to lean FARC in favor of a negotiated solution named "democratic asphyxiation". Repairing victims and increased access to rights should increase pressure on FARC.

As per FARC's recognition of stalemate one may refer to a document published on the rebel's official website about the dialogues entitled "Why we decided to negotiate with Santos" (FARC-EP Peace Delegation, s.f.). The rebel group explained the decision as following:

State's offensive over the last 14 years, along with Colombia and Patriot Plans, has been able to cause us harm, some of it considerable, but it is far from putting us in inferiority conditions or in defeat. (...) We have never been so far from surrendering or turning ourselves in. So, if we accepted to sit at the negotiations table with the Government, we did it with our own concept: to find a solution, of a civilized and peaceful nature, to the serious political, economic, and social problems that the Colombian people are suffering." (FARC-EP Peace Delegation, s.f.)

As can be read from FARC's document, the rebel group recognizes it has been struck, but it also advocates that by no means it has been defeated. It can be therefore inferred that the group has perceived that the conflict has reached a stalemate. In the same document, FARC's Peace Delegation *(s.f.)* adds "[b]esides, one has to recognize that Santos, unlike Uribe, accepted that Colombia was immersed in an armed conflict and not a terrorist threat. Likewise, this conflict has old causes that have to be solved. Having recognized that, was already important to us and for the Colombian people".

SOLUTIONS AND RECOMMENDATIONS

As has been shown, it may be inferred that the struggle between the Government and FARC rebels reached a stalemate. It seems not too far-fetched to think that the mutual perception of the conflict stage could have been at the core of the strategic calculations made by the parties involved in order to pursue a peaceful settlement. A conflict in such scenario increases the likelihood of a peace process inception, and raises as well its chances of reaching a successful outcome. Nevertheless, as Pruitt and Kim have acknowledged, a party well aware of the stalemate may still try to militarily win the war. It is therefore important that peace dialogues do not continue indefinitely as this might turn into a strategic advantage for the rebels. Stalemate is neither a warranty for the process' success, nor does it ensure that major crises cannot occur. Actually, Havana's peace talks have seen several crises but they have neither meant the end of the process, or have seriously affected it, as happened in the Caguan experience. Stalemate-driven peace dialogues may be more resilient, but not immune to crises.

In regards to conflict resolution, an important question may be raised as well. Are conflicts doomed to reach a stalemate –which would have to be perceived by the parties– in order to end the confrontation? Does a mediator have to wait in order for this to happen? It might be stated that at least, third parties should foster stalemate rather than escalation. One shortcoming of Pruitt and Kim's perspective is that it does not necessarily predict when a conflict stagnates, neither when the parties' perception might occur. Another important limitation of this perspective is that it does not explain, or foretell about, how violence would reproduce in a post-conflict scenario. Pruitt and Kim's concept scope does not embody this issue, in spite that rebel fighters' criminalization might also be also considered as a dynamic that may lead a conflict to a stalemate, or even to be a triggering factor for the parties to perceive that stagnated situation.

FUTURE RESEARCH DIRECTIONS

In both academic and public scenarios it is common to encounter concerns about an eventual demobilization of FARC fighters and the possibilities of violence reproduction in a post-conflict scenario. This more recent debate has had a previous argument about the criminalization of armed groups in Colombia. Increasing funding coming from drug trafficking and illegal mining has led many to think that the core of the conflict has changed, turning rebels into greed seekers.

In academia, the aforementioned debate that has been prevalent in Colombia, is embedded in the economic agendas in civil wars' debate that arose since the mid-1990s, concerning conflicts in the post-Cold War period and the increasing role of resources in contemporary civil wars. Several scholars agree that Mery Kaldor's article on what she called "new wars" introduced this debate. According to Cynthia Arson's (2005) –who advances a great literature review on the subject–, Kaldor conferred novelty to contemporary wars on the grounds that, nowadays, conflicts occur in the context of, and profit from, globalization. Also that there is an increasing blurriness between war and organized crime, a growing dependence on both local and transnational networks, and the fact that the new conflict scenarios are fostering a war economy of plundering, black market transactions, and external assistance. According to several scholars, one underlying feature of contemporary wars is that, since foreign financing declined due to the end of the bipolar confrontation, there is an increasingly important role of resources in explaining conflicts' inception and duration (Ballentine & Sherman, 2003) (Arnson, 2005).

Undoubtedly, one of the most influential works, even today, is the research carried out by Paul Collier and his colleagues at the World Bank's Development Research Group. As many have pointed out, Collier's thinking experienced an evolution since his first work with Anke Hoeffler. Initially they pointed out that that armed groups' agendas were a blend of a desire to rectify grievances and greedy interests to loot resources. In subsequent works Collier and his colleagues went further by suggesting that an actual causal link between economic factors –such as the existence of primary lootable commodities, rapid economic decline prior to violence eruption, or diaspora transfers– and conflict existed. Criticism did not wait. As Arson (2005) pointed out, most of Collier's critique was grounded on the usefulness of statistical correlations for determining the risks of conflict eruption, rather than presenting causal relations. Critics led greed thesis' authors to present in forthcoming years a more nuanced perspective on economic factors, this time as drivers of more feasible or durable wars (Arnson, 2005).

Following Arnson (2005), one the first trends in the armed groups' economic agendas debate were the findings that resources not only played an important role in financing but they could redefine the struggle itself, as was argued by David Keen. Berdal further advanced this argument in company of David Malone. Berdal and Malone stated that the appearance of war economies has had an impact on the parties, changing the very core of fight from defeating the enemy, to economically driven interests in a continuous fighting at profitable level (Berdal & Malone, 2000). This means that fighters often may encounter incentives to continue the struggle.

Cynthia Arnson and William Zartman coordinated *Rethinking the Economics of War*. In Zartman's contribution, the author proposes a continuum with the purpose of overcoming the issue of combining grievances explanations with greed thesis. Zartman's formula need, creed, and greed allows one to address conflicts produced by "political repression and economic deprivation ("need"), generalized belief and identity feelings ("creed")—and particularly, selective deprivation and discrimination based on those beliefs and identities—and personal or factional ambitions of private gain ("greed")" (Arnson, 2005, p. 11). In the same line of thought, Arnson (2005) proposes a circular correlation between war and resources: the latter creates opportunities for war and the former generates economic opportunities.

According to Berdal (2005), Ballentine and Sherman's book contribution to the ongoing debate of greed versus grievances is that they sought to assess through a qualitative approach to particular cases the relative importance of economic factors in the onset and duration of conflicts (Ballentine & Sherman, 2003). Following Berdal (2005), Michael Pugh and Neil Cooper's contribution lies in the inclusion of the regional context as an important factor when dealing with both ongoing and terminated conflicts.

An important part of the literature on Disarmament, Demobilization and Reintegration (DDR) has grown in the last years, particularly focused on mechanisms that can foster full reintegration of former combatants. As Jairo Munive (2013) has pointed out in an *International Peacekeeping* article, in the 2000s an important set of literature grew on the subject of DDR templates, especially driven by the United Nations and its Integrated Disarmament, Demobilization and Reintegration Standards. Berdal and David Ucko (2013) in an introductory article of a special issue of the same journal, made the same distinction between DDR mechanisms or templates, and context and politics as approaches to dealing with protracted periods or armed conflict where reintegration process take place.

Regarding the Colombian conflict analysis contribution to the greed versus grievances debate one has to refer to Nazih Richani's (2001) work using a systems of war approach. Alexandra Guáqueta's (2003) study on political and economic dimensions of the Colombian armed conflict and

Marc Chernick's (2005) contribution to Arnson and Zartman's book. Guáqueta and Chernick coincide that the Colombian conflict cannot be labeled as one exclusively based on the greed thesis, in spite of the fact that resources (particularly drugs, gold, and oil) have played a significant role in civil war escalation and duration, although its longevity cannot "be reduced to the boom-and-bust cycles of legal and illegal commodity exports" (Chernick, 2005, p. 204). Authors of the collective book *Una vieja guerra en un nuevo contexto (An old war in a new context)* in their study of conflict dynamics in a macro southern region suggest that Colombia is an old war in a new context. The purpose is to dialogue with the economic agendas in civil wars debate, otherwise known as "new wars" (Vásquez, 2011). As it stressed in González's book conclusion chapter (2011), the Colombian conflict can be defined as "an old war in a new context". Nevertheless, not all the conflict regions follow the same pattern. Historic rearguards such as Caguan surroundings, may not be truly analyzed trough the "new wars" paradigm. Nevertheless, southern Pacific region might be close to the pattern claimed by scholars of the economic agendas in civil wars, as it has enter the conflict dynamic more recently and coupled with the expansion of illicit crops and drug production.

In academic literature on the Colombian armed conflict, the issue of the role of resources in the duration of the conflict has therefore been tackled. But not much has been advanced on the *context* as a factor that can positively or negatively affect the outcomes of a demobilization process. Bearing that in mind, the Colombian case seems to be an excellent scenario to test the context variable as a determinant factor for DDR process' success or failure. Markets of violence literature offers an explanation to the question of why violence kept going in post-conflict scenarios in spite of the fact that conflicts were formally over. Georg Elwert (s.f.) defines this concept as "economic areas dominated by civil wars, warlords or robbery, in which [a] self-perpetuating system emerges and links non-violent commodity markets with the violent acquisition of goods". Markets of violence often arise in or from civil wars, as one of its main characteristics is the existence of oligopolies of violence, which means the erosion of the monopoly of violence (Guerrero, 2003). Another important feature and the main difference with economies of war is the role of coaction, threat, and terror as regulatory mechanisms of market (Guerrero, 2003).

In January 2015, FARC rebels declared an indefinite unilateral cease fire aiming to pressure the Government to agree to a bilateral ceasefire. Santos' administration, after recognizing that the group proved to refrain from attacking since the aforementioned proclamation, agreed on a de-escalation compromise deciding to stop air raids against FARC campsites. In spite of the fact that in recent years, rebels' commanders have had to relinquish control over middle-ranking officials, who have taken the burden of war, the ceasefire pledge was actually maintained. This episode leads one to grant FARC's structure a more compact nature than it was initially accorded by scholars and analysts.

What can be inferred from this episode for the eventually forthcoming DDR process? It seems less likely that FARC will return to the use of violence from a splinter faction, as might be foreseen from the observed behavior of rebels during the unilateral undetermined ceasefire. This differs from the previous experience of the demobilization of paramilitary groups, in which a splinter faction did arise opting-out in the negotiation of the peace process itself. Nevertheless, even if the possibility that an opting-out group from FARC is less expected, it does not mean that violence will not reappear in a different way. It rather seems more likely that violence will not necessarily end, but will continue through the persistence of markets of violence.

Markets of violence literature deals with the expansion of the violence-specialized labor market after a demobilization process. In such market, labor force is characterized by the specialization in the use of violence (Elwert, s.f.). A goal of markets of violence is decreasing the price of violence. Therefore, a price reduction might occur if one takes into account that markets of violence often arise in the middle of wars or from them. On the other side of the coin, one has to take into account not only the offer but also the demand for violence. If the price for violence is cheaper, it becomes more likely that demands for violent services arise. Political violence, in particular with electoral aims, might be reproduced through this process. Thus, such a hypothetical scenario cannot be totally disregarded.

CONCLUSION

As it has been argued during this chapter, both parties' contentious tactics are declining in efficacy. This decline is not deep enough to produce a descent into a de-escalation stage. Both contentious tactics still produce harm in the other actor, but they are not capable of producing the other's rendition or a strategic edge that could mean the end of the conflict as Pruitt & Kim have affirmed. It is interesting to point out, that the stalemate can be considered a stagnation process of the conflict. This means that the conflict neither escalates nor de-escalates. The fact that both parties' cash flow has not been affected also contributes to the stalemate stage, as it does not let the conflict to decrease in the use of contentious tactics.

It might not be too far-fetched to think that in Santos' strategic calculations, the costs associated to militarily winning the war could have been too high, causing him to choose the peace talks instead. As it has been stated before, FARC has been able to maintain a considerable firepower because of the opportunities that the borders offered to illegal financing and to shelter from the state's military offensive. Moreover, as it was evident during the previous administration, it is too costly for Colombia to involve neighboring countries in the fight against the rebels, and to perform unilateral actions (such as the bombardment on Reyes' camp in Ecuador) – at least not without assuming costs for the Colombian economy and its foreign policy.

The perception of the stagnation of the conflict by the Colombian Government and the FARC could have been triggered –following Pruitt & Kim's provisions– by the shifts in the parties' leadership. As it has been shown during this article, the military offensive against FARC's central command structure was able to produce the replacement of the commanders that negotiated during Caguan's Peace Talks. According to Ricardo, at a meeting in Caguan, *Cano* once told him that if it had been for him, he would never have negotiated in 1998, because he was almost certain that FARC were very close to seizing power. Nevertheless, when *Cano* issued Reborn Plan a few years after *Marualnda*'s death, this war plan was aimed at surviving as an armed actor and then seeking a negotiation with the Government (Ávila, 2012). Rebel commanders from urban origin are more prone to a political solution, than historical fighters that were at Marquetalia, FARC's inception. *Cano* may have been more willing than *Marulanda* to lean in favor of a peace dialogues. Similarly, Santos' arrival to the presidency could be considered as producing the same effect in the Government camp as well. It is to be highlighted that even though *Cano* was eliminated, his successor *Timochenko* decided to continue with a peace solution (Estado Mayor Conjunto de las FARC-EP, 2013)

Finally, as the Havana Talks formally began on August 2012, it can therefore be inferred that both parties have realized that in order to pursue the armed struggle they have to bear unacceptable costs or risks. It is relevant to raise the point that FARC accepted to conduct the negotiations in less favorable terms than in the past. In particular, they accepted to carry out the peace dialogues without a demilitarized territory, different to what they claimed during Uribe Vélez's administration. During that presidential term, the rebel group demanded that the Government clear Florida and Pradera towns in Valle del Cauca Department. At the other end, it is not an irrelevant fact that the current president was the former Defense Minister that led the most important raids against the rebel group. It seems hard to believe that someone that collected important hits against the rebels, both as President and as Defense Minister, would dismiss the opportunity to overwhelm the insurgents militarily.

Finally, as Pruitt & Kim acknowledge, the perceived stalemate is not a guarantee for the success of the peace talks. Both parties may still try to escalate the war to gain a strategic edge. Nevertheless, Havana Peace Talks is likely to produce a successful outcome, given the current stage of the conflict. Dialogues currently under way are likely to be successful based on how the parties *decided* to embrace a new attempt at peacefully end the conflict: the mutual perception of stalemate. Thus, the perceived stalemate increases the likelihood of effectiveness in a given negotiation process. The importance of Pruitt & Kim's theory resides in that last point.

A stalemate condition in a conflict may be considered as part of the context that can influence a forthcoming DDR process. Such scenario not only increases the likelihood of a negotiation, but may lean fighters' intentions to a more lasting peace as it reduces the incentives for keeping the armed struggle. Nevertheless, stalemate is not a straightforward condition for success. Following Zartman's continuum, a rebel group may transit from a grievances-driven group to a rent-seeking one. It seems important that the path to criminalization may redefine fighters' incentives to continue the struggle, as findings of the economic agendas in civil wars debate have shown. It seems plausible, that the Colombian Government also decided to advance in peace dialogues to avoid further FARC's criminalization. The rebel group commander in chief recognized that in recent times some commanders may have been influenced by drug trafficking rents (Delgado, 2014).

Nevertheless, two episodes that presented powerful incentives for spoilers were overcome. General Ruben Darío Alzate, the Army's Titan Joint Task Forces Commander, and two companions were kidnapped in Choco on November 16th, 2014 by FARC's 34th Front. Through the mediation of Cuba's and Norway's delegates, the rebel group released the General, his companions, and two soldiers that had been abducted in Arauca Department two weeks before as a result of combats held in that area. Another episode that spoilers could have eventually exploited was FARC's declaration of unilateral indefinite ceasefire on January 2015. A splinter faction could sabotage the rebel group's pledge, but this is not what happened. The armed group respected the ceasefire forcing President Santos to give the order to advance in a de-escalation agreement with the rebel group.

Thus, a path towards criminalization in FARC officials has been evidenced although not all the organization has entered this trend. Havana's peace talks are likely to be successful, in spite of the fact that, when the author was finishing this chapter, core issues about transitional justice were still being discussed – such as victims' rights and DDR agreement. Even more, these issues have taken more time in negotiation than previous agreements on rural reforms, political participation for former the rebels, and the drugs problem. Few considerations are to be raised. First, terminating the conflict with FARC will not necessarily mean the end of violence, as markets of violence literature states. Nevertheless, this does not mean that peace talks are doomed to failure as it was suggested by Raisbeck (2014), who claimed that dialogues will not be successful if drug trafficking was not resolved. Havana's peace talks' success should be assessed in terms of the extinction of FARC as a political armed group, and not necessarily by the continuation of markets of violence. Additionally, these dialogues may turn into a very interesting point for comparing DDR process and fighters' return to war, which can shed light on the question of why violence persists in post-conflict states.

ACKNOWLEDGMENT

The author held the position of Young-Researcher at the Politics and Internationals Affairs Studies Center (CEPI) of Universidad del Rosario (Bogotá) between March 2014 and March 2015, period in which he carried out the present research.

The author thanks Professor Freddy Cante for his comments on this chapter and the opportunity to participate in this collective book. He is really grateful with Professor Andrés Molano and Mauricio Palma, his friends and colleagues, for their commitment in the improvement of this chapter and their mentorship. He is also truly thankful with Prof. Rebeca Donoso, for the evenings she spent with the author improving the chapter style, and basically teaching to him. Finally, the author also thanks his colleague Camilo Vargas, who helped him elaborating the maps that are included in this chapter. He is also thankful with Human Rights Observatory, Human Rights and International Humanitarian Law Presidential Program and the National Ministry of Defense for providing data that was used as evidence in this chapter.

REFERENCES

Arnson, C. (2005). The Political Economy of War: Situating the Debate. In C. Arnson, & I. Zartman, Rethinking the Economics of War (pp. 1-22). Washington; Baltimore: Woodrow Wilson Center Press: The John Hopkins University Press.

Ávila, A. (2008). FARC: Dinámica reciente de la guerra. *Arcanos*, 14, 4-21.

Ávila, A. (2012, January). Las FARC: la guerra que el país no quiere ver. A*rcanos,* 17, 36-59.

Ballentine, K., & Sherman, J. (2003). Introduction. In K. Ballentine & J. Sherman (Eds.), *The Political Economy of Armed Conflict* (pp. 1–15). Boulder: Lynne Rienner.

Beltrán, A. (2009). FARC-EP: una reflexión sobre su organización política y militar. In C. Medina (Ed.), *FARC-EP: temas y problemas nacionales 1958-2008* (pp. 71–102). Bogota: Universidad Nacional de Colombia.

Berdal, M. (2005). Beyond greed and grievance – and not too soon. *Review of International Studies, 31*(04), 687–698. doi:10.1017/S0260210505006698

Berdal, M., & Malone, D. (2000). Introduction. In M. Berdal, & D. Malone (Eds.), Greed & Grievance (pp. 1-15). Boulder: Lynne Rienner.

Berdal, M., & Ucko, D. (2013). Introduction to the DDR Forum: Rethinking the Reintegration of Former Combatants. *International Peacekeeping, 20*(3), 316–320. doi:10.1080/13533312.2013.843971

Cabrera, I. (2012). Conflictos armados en zonas de frontera: análisis a partir del caso colombiano. In C. Echandía (Ed.), *Prolongación sin solución? Perspectivas sobre la paz y la guerra en Colombia* (pp. 75–122). Bogotá: Universidad Externado.

Chernick, M. (2005). Economic Resources and Internal armed Conflicts: Lessons from the Colombian Case. In C. Arnson, & W. Zartman (Eds.), Rethinking the Economics of War. The Intersection of Need, Creed, and Greed (pp. 178-205). Washington; Baltimore: Woodrow Wilson Center Press: The Johns Hopkins Univeristy Press.

Corporación Observatorio por la Paz. (2009). *Guerra inútiles. Una historia de las FARC*. Bogotá: Intermedio.

Cruz, E. (2007). Los estudios sobre paramilitarismo en Colombia. *Análisis Político (Bogotá)*, 60, 117–134.

Cubides, F. (2006). Proceso inconcluso, verdades a medias: Para un balance de las negociaciones del gobierno Uribe con los paramilitares. *Análisis Político (Bogotá)*, 57, 55–64.

Delgado, J. (2014, December 4). Desescalar las hostilidades: Apremiante aspiración estratégica de las Farc. *Observatorio de Política y Estrategia en América Latina (OPEAL)*. Retrieved from http://opeal.net/index.php?option=com_k2&view=item&id=2159:desescalar-las-hostilidades-apremiante-aspiracion-estrategica-de-las-farc&Itemid=144

Duncan, G. (2008). *Los señores de la guerra*. Bogota: Planeta.

Echandía, C. (2008). El fin de la invulnerabilidad de las FARC. *Nueva Sociedad, 217*.

Echandía, C. (2009). Subestimación del riesgo estratégico en el conflicto colombiano. *Zero*, 33, 62-67.

Echandía, C. (2012a). La experiencia del Caguán. Punto de partida del debilitamiento de las Farc. *Zero,* 28, 54-61.

Echandía, C. (2012b). Organizaciones armadas y violencia global en Colombia. In E. Bechara (Ed.), ¿Prolongación sin solución? (pp. 123-157). Bogotá: Universidad Externado de Colombia.

Echandía, C. (2012c). Colombie: Évolution du conflit armé à partir de l'analyse de la territorialité et des stratégies des FARC (1990-2011). *Problemes d'Amerique Latine, 83*(1), 101–116. doi:10.3917/pal.083.0101

Echandía, C. (2012d). Cambios en la conducta de las FARC en medio de la ofensiva militar en su contra. In E. Bechara (Ed.), *Prolongación sin solución? Perspectivas sobre la guerra y la paz en Colombia*. Bogotá: Universidad Externado de Colombia.

Echandía, C. (2013). De la Uribe a La Habana. *Revista Zero*, 36-43.

Echeverry, J., Salazar, N., & Navas, V. (2001, February 12). ¿Nos Parecemos al Resto del Mundo? El Conflicto Colombiano en el Contexto Internacional. *ARCHIVOS DE MACROECONOMÍA,* 143, 1-54.

El Espectador. (2010, March 9). *Cabecilla de Farc habla de alianza con Los Rastrojos*. Obtenido de El Espectador: http://www.elespectador.com/noticias/judicial/audio-cabecilla-de-farc-habla-de-alianza-los-rastrojos

Elwert, G. (n. d.). *Intervention in Markets of Violence*. Freie Univeritāt Berlin. Retrieved from http://www.oei.fu-berlin.de/en/projekte/cscca/downloads/ge_pub_marketsofviolence.pdf

Estado Mayor Conjunto de las FARC-EP. (2013, May 27). *De Marquetalia A La Habana: 49 años luchando por la paz*. Delegación de Paz FARC-EP. Retrieved from http://www.pazfarc-ep.org/index.php/noticias-comunicados-documentos-farc-ep/estado-mayor-central-emc/4-de-marquetalia-la-habana-49-anos-luchando-por-la-paz

Gómez Buendía, H. (2001, October 29). *La crisis*. Semana. Retrieved from http://www.semana.com/opinion/articulo/la-crisis/49075-3

González, F. (2011). A manera de síntesis conclusiva. In T. Vásquez, A. Vargas, & J. A. Restrepo (Eds.), *Una vieja guerra en un nuevo contexto* (pp. 429–446). Bogota: Editorial Pontificia Universidad Javeriana.

González, F., Bolívar, I., & Vázquez, T. (2002). *Violencia política en Colombia*. Bogota: CINEP.

González Posso, C. (2004). Negociaciones con las FARC 1982-2002. *Accord,* 14, 48-53.

González Posso, C. (2013). *En La Habana: El laberinto con salida*. Instituto de estudios para el desarrollo y la paz (Indepaz). Retrieved from http://www.indepaz.org.co/wp-content/uploads/2013/02/LABERINTO-CON-SALIDA-1.pdf

Guáqueta, A. (2003). The Colombian Conflict: Political and economic Dimensions. In K. Ballentine & J. Sherman (Eds.), *The Political Economy of Armed Conflict* (pp. 73–101). Boulder: Lynne Rienner.

Guerrero, J. (2003). Mercados de violencia, mercados ilegales y guerras civiles en América Latina en los años noventa: Tesis para un estudio etnográfico de las economías de guerra. *Palimpsesto*, *III*, 32–45.

International Crisis Group. (2006, October 20). Tougher Challenges Ahead for Colombia's Uribe. *Latin America Briefing*, 11, 1-20. Retrieved from http://www.crisisgroup.org/en/regions/latin-america-caribbean/andes/colombia/b011-tougher-challenges-ahead-for-colombias-uribe.aspx

International Crisis Group. (2009, March 26th). *Ending Colombia's FARC conflict: dealing the right card.* Retrieved from http://www.crisisgroup.org/~/media/Files/latin-america/colombia/30_ending_colombias_farc_conflict___dealing_the_right_card.pdf

Jiménez, Á., Silva, M., & Patiño, O. (2009, August 22). "Cano es el Pastrana de las Farc" Entrevista a Álvaro Jiménez, Mauricio Silva, Otty Patiño (J. León, Interviewer). Retrieved from http://lasillavacia.com/historia/3863

León, J. (2005). *País de Plomo. Crónicas de la guerra*. Bogota: Aguilar.

León, J. (2013, April 24). *¿Se consolida el poder militar en el Programa de Consolidación?* Retrieved from http://lasillavacia.com/node/43873

McDermott, J. (2013, May 20). *Actividades Criminales de las FARC y las Ganancias de la Guerrilla.* InSight Crime. Retrieved from http://es.insightcrime.org/investigaciones/actividades-criminales-farc-y-ganancias-de-la-guerrilla

Medina Gallego, C. (1990). *Autodefensas, Paramilitares y Narcotraficantes en Colombia*. Bogotá: Editorial Documentos Periodísticos.

Munive, J. (2013). Context Matters: The Conventional DDR Template is Challenged in South Sudan. *International Peacekeeping*, *20*(5), 559–599. doi:10.1080/13533312.2013.853962

Nasi, C. (2006). Spoilers in Colombia: Actors and Strategies. In E. Newman & O. Richmond (Eds.), *Challenges to peacebuilding: Managing spoilers during conflict resolution* (pp. 219–241). Tokyo, New York: United Nations University Press.

Newman, E., & Richmon, O. (2006). Introduction. Obstacles to peace processes: Understanding spoiling. In E. Newman, & O. Richmon (Eds.), Challenges to peacebuilding: managing spoilers during conflict resolution (pp. 1-19). New York: United Nations University.

Peace Delegation, F. A. R. C.-E. P. (n. d.). *Why we decided to negotiate with Santos.* Retrieved from http://www.pazfarc-ep.org/index.php/cronologia

Pizarro Leongómez, E. (2011). *Las Farc (1949-2011): De guerrilla campesina máquina de guerra*. Bogotá: Edtorial Norma.

Pizarro Loengómez, E. (2011). *Las Farc (1949-2011). De guerilla campesina a maquinaria de guerra*. Bogota: Editorial Norma.

Pruitt, D. G., & Kim, S. H. (2004). *Social Conflict. Esclation, Stalemate, and Settlement.* Boston: McGraw-Hill.

Racines, K. (2014). Minería ilegal en Colombia. *Semana Sostenible*, 22-23.

Raisbeck, D. (2014, June 3). *Con Santos o con Zuluaga, la guerra contra las drogas garantiza el fracaso de las negociaciones de paz.* Retrieved from http://es.panampost.com/daniel-raisbeck/2014/06/03/con-santos-o-con-zuluaga-la-guerra-contra-las-drogas-garantiza-el-fracaso-de-las-negociaciones-de-paz/

Restrepo, J., Spagat, M., & Vargas, J. (2005). The Severity of the Colombian Conflict: Cross-Country Datasets versus New Micro Data. *Journal of Peace Research*, 43(1), 99–115.

Ricardo, V. G. (2014, August 27). The Caguan's Peace Talks (F. Zarama, Interviewer).

Richani, N. (2001). The Political Economy of Colombia's Protracted Civil War. *The Journal of Conflict Studies*, *XXI*(2).

Rojas, D. (2013). Much more than a war on drugs: Elementos para un balance del Plan Colombia. *Análisis Político (Bogotá)*, (77): 113–132.

Rueda, M. I. (1991, January 4). *El atentado a Iragori*. Semana. Retrieved from http://www.semana.com/nacion/articulo/el-atentado-iragori/16110-3

Sánchez, R., & Rodríguez, F. (2005). Una aproximación al estudio de la seguridad. *Ensayos sobre Defensa y Seguridad*, 79-115.

Santos, J. (2012, September 4). *Alocución del Presidente de la República, Juan Manuel Santos sobre el 'Acuerdo General para la Terminación del Conflicto*. Retrieved from http://wsp.presidencia.gov.co/Prensa/2012/Septiembre/Paginas/20120904_01.aspx

Semana. (1998, July 27). *El voto de Tirofijo*. Retrieved from http://www.semana.com/nacion/articulo/el-voto-de-tirofijo/36608-3

Semana. (2001, November 11). *Contra la pared*. Retrieved from http://www.semana.com/nacion/articulo/contra-pared/47939-3

Semana. (2012, September 18). *Cifras de la guerra en Colombia*. Retrieved from http://www.semana.com/especiales/cifras-guerra-colombia/index.html

Semana. (2014, December 22). *¿Quién es 'Megatrónico', el otro capo de las FARC?* Retrieved from http://www.semana.com/nacion/articulo/alias-megatronico-el-capo-invisible-de-las-farc/413135-3

Semana. (2014, October 23). *'Marquitos Figueroa' cayó por sus ocho mujeres*. Retrieved from http://www.semana.com/nacion/articulo/marquitos-figueroa-fue-capturado-por-sus-mujeres/406788-3

Semana. (2015, May 18). *Lo que une a los narcos mexicanos con las FARC*. Retrieved from http://www.semana.com/nacion/articulo/farc-narcos-mexicanos-unidos-por-narcotrafico-armas/428241-3

Silva, M. (1999). Desarrollos y cuestiones militares en las FARC. In C. O. Paz (Ed.), Las verdaderas intenciones de las FARC (pp. 228-239). Bogotá: Intermedio editores.

Vásquez, T. (2011). Capítulo 3: La dinámica macroregional del conflicto armado. In T. Vásquez, A. Vargas, & J. A. Restrepo (Eds.), *Una vieja guerra en un nuevo contexto* (pp. 299–339). Bogota: Editorial Pontificia Universidad Javeriana.

KEY TERMS AND DEFINITIONS

Escalation: Conflict cycle in which a conflict party is putting greater pressure on the other through the increase use of contentious tactics, which invites the other party to reciprocate.

Greedy or Rent-Seekers Armed Groups: Warlords, gangs, or rebels that control resources' exploitation, or receive revenues through the imposition of illegal taxing on workers or firms. The income from these activities may alter their incentives, fostering the continuation rather than the end of the struggle.

Markets of Violence: Economic areas dominated by civil wars in the context of oligopolies of violence, in which a violent regulated self-perpetuating system emerges that links non-violent commodity markets with the violent acquisition of goods; violence itself can become a tradable good.

Spoilers: Leaders and parties that try to sabotage a negotiation process through violent or non-violent means, as they perceive that a given peace settlement threatens their power, worldview or interests.

Stalemate: A stagnation stage of a conflict, in which a conflict nor escalates nor de-escalates. Mutual perception by the parties may lead them to start a negotiation process in order to avoid unbearable costs or risks.

ENDNOTES

1 Some of the references used by the author have not been officially translated into English yet. Therefore, for the purposes of this chapter, the author has chosen to translate the quotes himself to make it easier for the reader to follow the line of argument or evidence provided.

2 After the Seventh Conference, FARC's military structure is composed as follows: *the basic unit is the Squad, composed of 12 men. Two squads plus their commanders make a Guerrilla. The union of two Guerrillas, plus their respective commander and his replacement, make a Company. More than two Companies, plus their management, compose a Column. The bigger military structure in a region receives the name of Front and it would be composed of two or more Columns and its management.* (Beltrán, 2009, p. 77)

3 A Block is a military structure gathering five or more Fronts; it was not conceived until the Eighth Conference.

4 Scholars usually divide in two groups the guerrilla movements in Colombia: the first and second generation movements. The former gathers the ones issued in the 1960s – such as the FARC, the ELN, and the EPL – that were inspired in the Cuban Revolution. As for the latter, these are groups inspired by the Sandinist Nicaraguan Revolution and can be defined as democratic openness groups.

5 The author has chosen to put the alias names of all the FARC combatants in italics to show that they are not their real names. This has been done in order not to confuse the readers whenever there is an apostrophe that is being used as a possessive.

6 Conflict Analysis Resource Center (CERAC) conducts a follow-up of armed groups' actions in Colombia to produce the Colombian Armed Conflict Data Base, which can be accessed at cerarc.org.co. The Data Base is not census-based, and therefore it is subject to updates by CERAC. CERAC's methodology may be consulted in Restrepo, Spagat, & Vargas (2005). The maps were elaborated by Camilo Vargas, Coordinator of the Democracy Political-Electoral Observatory of the Electoral Observation Mission (MOE). Some of data may also be consulted on www.datoselectorales.org.

7 The ideas expressed in this paragraph came from a dialogue that the author held with Professor Andrés Molano. Time shrinking for guerrilla groups is an issue that requires more analysis and testing. It may be the subject of future work by Professor Molano and the author.

Compilation of References

Aalen, L., & Tronvoll, K. (2009). The End of Democracy? Curtailing Political and Civil Rights in Ethiopia. *Review of African Political Economy, 36*(120), 193–207. doi:10.1080/03056240903065067

ABC news. (2014). *Iraqi Army, Militants Clash West of Baghdad*. Retrieved from http://abcnews.go.com/International/wireStory/iraq-humanitarian-crisis-highest-level-24967762

Abdalla, M., Dias Barros, D., & Berthet Ribeiro, M. (Eds.), (2014). *Spaces in Movement: New Perspectives on Migration in African Settings*. Köln: Köppe.

Abdulazeez, N. (2013). *Ethnic conflict in the Middle East, Causes, Reconciliation and Negotiation*. Kent: Parker.

Abelshauser, W. (2004). Deutsche Wirtschaftsgeschichte nach 1945, München: becksche Reihe.

Abregú, M. (2008). Human Rights for All: From the Struggle against Authoritarianism to the Construction of an All-Inclusive Democracy - A View from the Southern Cone and Andean Region. *Sur International Journal of Human Rights, 5*(8), 7–41.

Acosta, A. (2012). Extractivismo y neoextractivismo: dos caras de la misma maldición. In M. Lang & D. Mokrani (Eds.), *Más alla del desarrollo* (pp. 83–121). Quito: Abya Yala Ediciones.

Afpel, R., & Simon, B. (Eds.). (1996). *Minefields in their hearts. The mental health of children in war and communal violence*. New Haven: Yale University Press.

African Union Commission of Inquiry on South Sudan (CISS). (2014 June 26-27). Interim Report, African Union, Assembly of the Union, Twenty-Third Ordinary Session, Assembly/AU/19(XXIII).

African Union Panel of the Wise. (2013, February). Peace, Justice, and Reconciliation in Africa: Opportunities and Challenges in the Fight Against Impunity. The African Union Series. International Peace Institute.

African Union Peace and Security Council (AUPSC). (2013, December 30). Communiqué. 411th Meeting of the Peace and Security Council at the Level of Heads of State and Government on the Situation in South Sudan. PSC/AHG/COMM.1 (CDXI).

Aftrol Staff Writer. (2008). Rwanda's Commonwealth accession questioned. *Afrol News*. Retrieved from http://www.afrol.com/articles/33812

Agamben, G. (2000) Sovereign Police. In V. Binetti, & C. Casarino, (trans.), Means Without End: notes on politics. Minneapolis: University of Minnesota Press.

Agamben, G. (2004). (A. Hidalgo, Ed.), *Infancia e historia*. Buenos Aires.

Agamben, G. (2005). *State of Exception* (K. Attel, Trans.). Chicago: University of Chicago Press. doi:10.1215/9780822386735-013

Agencia Catalana de Cooperació al Desenvolupament. (2008). *Indonesia (Aceh). Aguswandi. (2008). The Political Process in Aceh: A New Beginning? Conciliation Resources Accord, 20*. London: Conciliation Resources.

Agencia Colombiana para la Reintegración. (2014). *Estrategia de Reintegración*. Bogotá, Colombia: Presentación Power Point.

Agencia Colombiana para la Reintegración. (2014). Evolución del Proceso de Reintegración. Bogotá: ACR. Retrieved from: www.reintegracion.gov.co

Agencia Colombiana para la Reintegración. (2014). *Memorias III Congreso de Responsabilidad Social. Justicia Transicional y Escenarios de Reconciliación,* Universidad Externado De Colombia, Colombia.

Agencia Colombiana para la Reintegración. (2014). Por la paz soy capaz. Informe de gestión ACR, enero–diciembre 2013. Bogotá, Colombia.

Agencia Colombiana para la Reintegración. (2015). *First Global Disarmament, Demovilization and Reintegration (DDR).* Colombia: Summit. Agencia Colombiana para la Reintegración.

Agreement on a Cessation of Hostilities between the Government of the Republic of South Sudan and the South Sudan Democratic Movement/Defense Army Cobra Faction. (2014, January 23). Retrieved from http://www.gurtong.net/LinkClick.aspx?fileticket=mvVHdl-Wsd4=&tabid=124.

Agreement on Permanent Ceasefire and Security Arrangements Implementation Modalities between the Government of the Sudan (GoS) and the Sudan People's Liberation Movement/Sudan People's Liberation Army (SPLM/SPLA) during the Pre-Interim and Interim Periods, signed in Naivasha, Kenya on 31 December 2004.

Agreement to Resolve the Crisis in South Sudan. (2014, May 9). Retrieved from http://www.southsudan.igad.int/attachments/article/249/Agreement%20to%20Resolve%20the%20crisis%20in%20S.%20Sudan,%209%20May'14.pdf.

Aguila, G. (2010). State violence and repression in Rosario during the Argentine dictatorship, 1976-83. In M. Esparza, H.R. Huttenbach, & D. Feierstein (Eds.), *State Violence and Genocide in Latin America* (pp. 137-151). Oxfordshire, UK: Routledge.

Al Arabiya. (2014, July 5). Iranian pilot killed fighting in Iraq, state media report. Retrieved from https://english.alarabiya.net/en/News/middle-east/2014/07/05/Iranian-pilot-killed-fighting-in-Iraq-state-media-reports.html

Al Jazeera. (2010). *Iraq's most powerful coalitions.* Retrieved from http://www.aljazeera.com/focus/iraqelection2010/2010/03/20103493048404203.html

Al Sharq Al Awsat. (2011). *The national alliances discuss "Sunni Insurgency" and "Al Sader" calls Tikrit to retreat federalism.*http://www.aawsat.com/details.asp?section=4&issueno=12023&article=647358&feature=

Alfredson, T., & Cungu', A. (2008). *Negotiation Theory and Practice: A review of literature.* Retrieved from http://www.fao.org/docs/up/easypol/550/4-5_negotiation_background_paper_179en.pdf

Aljazeera. (2008, October 11). Exiled Aceh Leader Returns. Retrieved from http://www.aljazeera.com/news/asia-pacific/2008/10/2008101144652814370.html

Al-Khafaji, I. (2004). *In Search of Legitimacy: The Post-Rentier Iraqi State.* Retrieved from http://conconflicts.ssrc.org/archives/iraq/khafaji/

Al-Khatib, M. K. (n. d.). *Mi'at 'Am min al-'Adhab [One Hundred Years of Suffering].* Beirut: Manshurat.

Al-Marashi, I. (2003). An Insight into the Mindset of Iraq's Security Apparatus. *Intelligence and National Security, 18*(3), 1–23. doi:10.1080/02684520412331306900

AlSayyad, N. (2004). Urban Informality as a ,New' Way of Life. In A. Roy & N. AlSayyad (Eds.), *Urban Informality. Transnational Perspectives from the Middle East, Latin America and South Asia* (pp. 7–30). Lanham, MD: Lexington Books.

Alta Consejería para la Reintegración. (2010). Desarme, Desmovilización y Reintegración en Colombia. Lecciones aprendidas y resultados del proceso 2002-2010. Bogotá, Colombia.

Amnesty International. (2002). *Kingdom of Cambodia: Urgent need for Judicial Reform.* Retrieved from http://www.unhcr.org/refworld/pdfid/3deb63334.pdf

Amnesty International. (2011). *Days of rage: Protests and Repression in Iraq.* Retrieved from http://www.amnesty.ca/sites/default/files/mde140132011en.pdf

Amnesty International. (2012). Colombia: La ley de víctimas y de restitución de tierras. Retrieved from https://www.amnesty.org/download/Documents/20000/amr230182012es.pdf

Anceschi, L., Gervasio, G., & Teti, A. (2014). *Informal Power in the Greater Middle East. Hidden Geographies.* London: Routledge.

Anderson, L., & Stansfield, G. (Eds.), (2005). *The Future of Iraq. Dictatorship, Democracy, or Division?* Macmillan.

Angelova, I. (2014). *Rebel-Held Suburbs of Damascus: Resilience Mechanisms in the Face of Chemical Attacks. Policy Alternatives*. Arab Reform Initiative.

Aptel, C., & Ladisch, V. (2011). *Through a new lens: a child-sensitive approach to transitional justice*. New York: International Center for Transitional Justice.

Arabic, B. B. C. (2012). Iraq asks states whom participated in Baghdad meeting to drop his debts. Retrieved from http://www.bbc.co.uk/arabic/middleeast/2012/03/120327_iraq_arabs_summit.shtml

Arcanos 2011. (n. d.). Retrieved from http://www.arcoiris.com.co/2012/05/arcanos-17/

Archard, D. (1993). *Children. Rights and childhood*. New York: Routledge.

Arendt, H. (1996). *Essai sur la Violence* (trans. plus foreword by M.-I. B. de Launay). *La Nature du Totalitarisme*. Paris: Bibliothèque philosophique Payot.

Arendt, H. (1958a). *The Human Condition*. Chicago: University of Chicago Press.

Arendt, H. (1958b). *The Origins of Totalitarianism*. Cleveland: The World Publishing Company.

Arendt, H. (1965/1977). *Eichman in Jerusalem: a report on the banality of evil*. London: Penguin.

Arendt, H. (1999). *Eichmann en Jerusalén: un estudio sobre la banalidad del mal*. Barcelona: Lumen.

Arendt, H. (2006). *Eichmann in Jerusalem: A Report on the Banality of Evil*. London: Penguin Classics.

Arhuaco, P. (2007). *Atlas Arhuaco*. Comité de Educación del Pueblo Arhuaco.

Arnson, C. (2005). The Political Economy of War: Situating the Debate. In C. Arnson, & I. Zartman, Rethinking the Economics of War (pp. 1-22). Washington; Baltimore: Woodrow Wilson Center Press: The John Hopkins University Press.

Arnson, C. (2005). *Rethinking the Economics of War, the Intersection of Need, Creed and Greed*. Washington: The Woodrow Wilson Centre Press.

Arthur, P. (2009). How 'Transitions' Reshaped Human Rights: A Conceptual History of Transitional Justice. *Human Rights Quarterly*, *31*(2), 321–367. doi:10.1353/hrq.0.0069

Arthur, P. (Ed.). (2010). *Identities in Transition: Challenges for Transitional Justice in Divided Societies*. Cambridge University Press. doi:10.1017/CBO9780511976858

Arthur, P., González, E., Lam, Y., Rice, J., Rodríguez-Garavito, C., & Yashar, D. (2013). *Fortaleciendo los derechos indígenas a través de comisiones de la verdad*. Bogotá: ICTJ.

Ashdow, P. (2014). Western Intervention over Isis won't prevent the Break-up of Iraq. Retrieved from http://www.theguardian.com/commentisfree/2014/aug/14/western-intervention-isis-iraq-muslim

Aspinall, E. (2008 April). Peace without Justice? The Aceh Peace Process in Indonesia. Centre for Humanitarian Dialogue, Helsinki.

Aspinall, E. (2009). Combatants to contractors: The political economy of peace in Aceh. *Indonesia*.

Assmann, J. (1988). Kollektives Gedächtnis und kulturelle Identität. In J. Assmann, & T. Hölscher (Ed.), Kultur und Gedächtnis. Frankfurt: Suhrkamp.

Assmann, J. (2013). Das kulturelle Gedächtnis. Schrift, Erinnerung und politische Identität in frühen Hochkulturen (7th ed.). München: C.H. Beck.

Aswat Al Iraq. (2012). *First independent human rights organization, historical accomplishment-UNAMI*. Retrieved from http://en.aswataliraq.info/(S(ucrz3s55x5512p3hnjk0pj55))/Default1.aspx?page=article_page&id=147956

Audi, A. (2004-05). Iraq's New Investment laws and the Standard of Civilisation: A case study on the limits of international law. *The Georgetown Law Journal*, *93*, 335–364.

Aumann, R. (2005, December 8). Nobel Prize Organization. Retrieved from http://www.nobelprize.org/nobel_prizes/economic-sciences/laureates/2005/aumann-lecture.html

Ávila, A. (2008). FARC: Dinámica reciente de la guerra. *Arcanos*, 14, 4-21.

Ávila, A. (2012, January). Las FARC: la guerra que el país no quiere ver. *Arcanos, 17*, 36-59.

Bader-Blau, S. (2007). Iraqi Unions vs. Big *Oil. Middle East Report (New York, N.Y.), 37*, 16–21.

Bahrain, K. P. M. G. (2004). *Development Fund for Iraq: Report of Factual Findings in connection with Disbursements For the period from 1 January 2004 to 28 June 2004*. Baghdad: International Advisory and Monitoring Board of the Development Fund for Iraq and the Project and Contracting Office.

Ballentine, K., & Sherman, J. (2003). The Political Economy of Armed Conflict, Beyond Greed and Grievance. London: Boulder.

Ballentine, K., & Sherman, J. (2003). Introduction. In K. Ballentine & J. Sherman (Eds.), *The Political Economy of Armed Conflict* (pp. 1–15). Boulder: Lynne Rienner.

Banana Para-Republica. (2007). *Semana*. Retrieved from http://www.semana.com/nacion/articulo/banana-para-republic/84015-3

Banco de la República. (2014). *Flujos de Inversión Directa* [Data file]. Retrieved from http://www.banrep.gov.co/es/inversion-directa

Barber, B. (Ed.). (2009). *Adolescents and war. How youth deal with political violence*. New York: Oxford University Press. doi:10.1093/acprof:oso/9780195343359.001.0001

Barron, P. (2009). The limits of DDR: Reintegration lessons from Aceh. *Small Arms Survey Yearbook*, 249–283.

Barsalou, J. & Baxter, V. (2007, January). *The Urge To Remember, The Role of Memorials in Social Reconstruction and Traditional Justice*. United States Institute of Peace, Stabilization and Reconstruction Series No. 5.

Bastiat, F. (2004). *Essays on Political Economy*. New York: G. P. Putnams and Sons.

Batatu, H. (1978). *The Old Social Classes and the Revolutionary Movements of Iraq. A Study of Iraq's Old Landed and Commercial Classes and of its Communists, Ba'athists, and Free Officers*. Princeton: Princeton University Press.

Batatu, H. (1978). *The Old Social Classes and the Revolutionary Movements of Iraq*. Princeton, NJ: Princeton University Press.

Bayart, J.-F., Ellis, S., & Hibou, B. (1999). *The Criminalization of the State in Africa*. Oxford: James Currey.

BBC News Latin America. (2015, January 15). Q&A: Colombia Peace Talks. Retrieved from http://www.bbc.com/news/world-latin-america-19875363

BBC. (2011). *Iraq crisis: Where will ISIS attack next?* Retrieved from http://www.bbc.com/news/world-middle-east-27846706

BBC. (2011). *Iraq war in figures*. Retrieved from http://www.bbc.co.uk/news/world-middle-east-11107739

BBC. (2014). Iraq Kurdistan independence referendum planned. Retrieved from http://www.bbc.com/news/world-middle-east-28103124

BBC. (2014). Iraq Profile. Retrieved from http://www.bbc.com/news/world-middle-east-14546763

Becerra Ostos, S. J. (2009). Paramilitarismo y neoliberalismo en Barrancabermeja: El caso de la privatización de Ecopetrol 1980-2000. *Ciencia Política*, (7), 125–149.

Beck, C. (2007). Re-paving the road to peace: Analysis of the implementation of DD&R in Aceh Province, Indonesia. Bonn: Bonn International Center for Conversion. Retrieved from https://www.bicc.de/uploads/tx_bicctools/brief35.pdf

Becket, I. (2001). *Modern Insurgencies and Counterinsurgencies: Guerrillas and Opponents since 1750*. London: Routledge. doi:10.4324/9780203402450

Bell, C. (2009). The "New" law of Transitional Justice. In K. Ambos, J. Large, & M. Wierda (Eds.), Building a future on Peace and Justice (pp. 105-126). Springer.

Bell, C. (2009). Transitional Justice, Interdisciplinarity, and the State of the 'Field' or 'Non-Field'. *International Journal of Transitional Justice, 3*(1), 5–27. doi:10.1093/ijtj/ijn044

Bellin, E. (2004). The Robustness of Authoritarianism in the Middle East: Exceptionalism in Comparative Perspective. *Comparative Politics, 36*(2), 139–157. doi:10.2307/4150140

Bello, M. N. (Ed.), (2004). Desplazamiento forzado, Dinámicas de guerra, exclusión y desarraigo. Bogotá: Universidad Nacional de Colombia, sede Bogotá.

Beltrán, A. (2009). FARC-EP: una reflexión sobre su organización política y militar. In C. Medina (Ed.), *FARC-EP: temas y problemas nacionales 1958-2008* (pp. 71–102). Bogota: Universidad Nacional de Colombia.

Benary, E. (2011, September 22). We are the Palestinians and they are the Arabs. Retrieved from http://cjhsla.org/2011/09/22/we-are-the-palestinians-and-they-are-the-arabs/

Benavides, F. (2013). *Justicia en epocas de transicion: Conceptos, modelos, debates y experiencias*. Colombia: Grupo Editorial Ibañez.

Bengio, O. (2003). Pitfalls of Instant Democracy. In M. Eisenstadt & E. Mathewson (Eds.), *U.S. Policy in Post-Saddam Iraq: Lessons from the British Experience* (pp. 15–26). Washington, DC: Washington Institute for Near East Policy.

Benjamin, W. (1978). Critique of violence. In P Demetz (Ed.), *Reflections*. New York: Shoken Books.

Benjamin, W. (1978). Critique of Violence. In P. Demetz (Ed.), *Reflections: Essays, Aphorisms*. Autobiographical Writings, New York: Schoken Books.

Benjamin, W. (2009). *On the Concept of History*. New York: Classic Books America.

Benjamin, W. (2012). *Critique de la Violence* (Original work published 1921). Paris: Petite Bibliothèque Payot.

Bensssousan, G. (2010). *Auschwitz por herencia? Sobre un buen uso de la memoria*. Barcelona: Anthropos.

Berdal, M., & Malone, D. (2000). Introduction. In M. Berdal, & D. Malone (Eds.), Greed & Grievance (pp. 1-15). Boulder: Lynne Rienner.

Berdal, M. (2005). Beyond greed and grievance – and not too soon. *Review of International Studies, 31*(04), 687–698. doi:10.1017/S0260210505006698

Berdal, M. (2009). *Building Peace After War*. London: Routedge.

Berdal, M., & Malone, D. (2000). *Greed and Grievance: Economic Agendas in Civil Wars*. Boulder, Colorado: Lynne Rienner.

Berdal, M., & Ucko, D. (2013). Introduction to the DDR Forum: Rethinking the Reintegration of Former Combatants. *International Peacekeeping, 20*(3), 316–320. doi:10.1080/13533312.2013.843971

Berger, P. L., & Luckmann, T. (1966). *The Social Construction of Reality. A Treatise in the Sociology of Knowledge*. New York: Anchor Books.

Bernal, V. (2013). Civil Society and Cyberspace: Reflections on Dehai, Asmarino, and Awate. *Africa Today, 60*(2), 21–36. doi:10.2979/africatoday.60.2.21

Betancur, J. C., & Osario Pérez, F. E. (2013). Participación de grupos étnicos y nuevas agendas del desarrollo en Colombia. In C. Barreira, J. V. Tavares dos Santos, J. Zuluaga Nieto, R. González Arana, & F. González Ortiz (Eds.), *Conflictos sociales, luchas sociales y políticas de seguridad ciudadana*. (pp. 77-112). Retrieved from http://biblioteca.clacso.edu.ar/clacso/gt/20131007104153/ConflictosSociales.pdf

Bierce, A. (2004). *The Devil's Dictionary*. Washington: Bloomsbury.

Blair, E. (2012). *Un itinerario de investigación sobre la violencia. Contribución a una sociología de la ciencia*. Medellín: Editorial Universidad de Antioquia.

Bloomfield, D., Barnes, T., & Huyse, L. (Eds.), (2003). *Reconciliation after Violent Conflict. A Handbook*. Stockholm: International Institute for Democracy and Electoral Assistance.

Blumer, H. (1969). *Symbolic Interactionism: Perspective and Method*. New Jersey: Prentice Hall.

Bocco, R., & Meier, D. (2005). Penser la Notion de Frontière au Moyen-Orient. *A Contrario*, 2/3, 3-10.

Bocco, R. (1995). *'Asabiyât* Tribales et États au Moyen-Orient. Confrontations et Connivences. *Monde Arabe Maghreb-Machrek, 147*, 3–12.

Boetié, E. d. (2003). *El discurso de la servidumbre voluntaria, o el contra uno*. Bogotá: Universidad Nacional de Colombia.

Bonilla, D. (Ed.), (2009). *Teoría del derecho y trasplantes jurídicos*. Siglo del Hombre Editores.

Borbet, A. (2010). *Die Zahl der Opfer des DDR-Regimes*. Erfurt: Landeszentrale für politische Bildung Thüringen.

Borer, T. A., Darby, J., McEvoy-Levy, S., & RIREC Project on Post-Accord Peace Building. (2006). *Peacebuilding after peace accords: The challenges of violence, truth, and youth*. Notre Dame, Ind: University of Notre Dame Press.

Boulding, K. (1981). *A Preface to Grants Economics: the Economy of Love and Fear*. New York: Praeger.

Boulding, K. (1989). *Three Faces of Power: A General Theory*. London: Sage Publications.

Bourdieu, P. (1987). The Force of Law: Toward a Sociology of the Juridical Field. Hastings Law Journal, 38.

Bourdieu, P., & Wacquant, L. (2005). Una invitación a la sociología reflexiva. Buenos Aires, Argentina: Siglo XXI Editores.

Bourdieu, P. (1979). *La Distinction. Critique Sociale du Jugement*. Paris: Les Éditions de Minuit.

Bourrat, F. (dir.) (2012). La Place et le Rôle des Armées dans le Monde Arabe Contemporain. In Les Champs de Mars, 23. Paris: La Documentation Française (Institut de Recherche Stratégique de l'École militaire).

Bozarslan, H. (2008). *Une Histoire de la Violence au Moyen-Orient, de la Fin de l'Empire Ottoman à Al-Qaida*. Paris: La Découverte.

Bozzini, D. (2011). Low-tech Surveillance and the Despotic State in Eritrea. *Surveillance & Society*, *9*, 93–113.

Bracher, K. D. (1955). Die Auflösung der Weimarer Republik. Eine Studie zum Problem des Machtverfalls in der Demokratie. Villingen: Ring-Verlag.

Brähler, E., Decker, O., & Kiess, J. (2014). *Die stabilisierte Mitte. Rechtsextreme Einstellungen in Deutschland 2014*. Amadeo Antonio Stiftung.

Brahm, E. (2003). *Hurting Stalemate Stage*. Retrieved from http://www.beyondintractability.org/essay/stalemate/

Braukämper, A. (2012). *Das umstrittene Gedächtnis. Die Erinnerung an Nationalsozialismus, Faschismus und Krieg in Europa seit 1945 (The disputed memory. Remembering National Socialism, Fascism and War in Europe after 1945)*. Paderborn: Schoenings.

Braun, H. (2008). *Mataron a Gaitán. Vida pública y Violencia urbana en Colombia*. Madrid: Editora Aguilar.

Brett, R., & Malagón, L. (2013). Overcoming the original sin of the "original condition:" How reparations may contribute to emancipatory peacebuilding. *Human Rights Review (Piscataway, N.J.)*, *14*(3), 257–271. doi:10.1007/s12142-013-0271-5

Bucaille, L. (Dir.). (2013). Femmes combattantes (dossier). *Critique Internationale*, *60*, 7–88.

Bülent, K. (2011, September 30). European PKK. *Today's Zaman*. Retrieved from http://www.todayszaman.com/mobile_detailc.action?newsId=261416

Cabrera, I. (2012). Conflictos armados en zonas de frontera: análisis a partir del caso colombiano. In C. Echandía (Ed.), *Prolongación sin solución? Perspectivas sobre la paz y la guerra en Colombia* (pp. 75–122). Bogotá: Universidad Externado.

Caillé, A., Senellart, M., & Lazerri, C. (Eds.), (2007). Histoire Raisonnée de la Philosophie Morale et Politiquees. Paris: Flammarion.

Cairns, E. (1996). *Children and political violence*. Cambridge: Blackwell Publishers.

Cairns, E., McLernon, F., Moore, W., & Hakvoort, I. (2006). The impact of the peace process in Northern Ireland on children's and adolescents' ideas about war and peace. In S. McEvoy-Levy (Ed.), *Troublemakers or Peacemakers? Youth and post-accord peace building* (pp. 117–138). Notre Dame, IN: University of Notre Dame Press.

Camau, M. (2006). Globalisation Démocratique et Exception Autoritaire Arabe. *Critique Internationale*, *30*(1), 59–81. doi:10.3917/crii.030.0059

Campbell, J. (1976). *Successful Negotiation: Trieste*. Princeton: Princeton University Press.

Caracol Radio. (2005) Oral Interview with Orlando Fals Borda Orlando due to the book Violence in Colombia. *El Heraldo*. Ediciones 21, 22 y 23 de Febrero de 2000. Retrieved from www.caracol.com.co/oir.aspx?Id=168502

Cárdenas, J & ACR (2015). Evolución del proceso de reintegración. Fortaleza institucional basada en la experiencia y lecciones aprendidas. Bogotá: ACR.

Carillo, M. (2012, August 29). Time is right, but past failures haunt Colombia's peace talks. *CNN*. Retrieved from http://edition.cnn.com/2012/08/28/world/americas/colombia-farc-peace-talks/

Castillejo, A. (2009). *Los archivos del dolor. Ensayos sobre la violencia y el recuerdo en la Sudáfrica contemporánea*. Bogotá: Universidad de los Andes CESU.

Castillejo, A. (2009). Los archivos el dolor. Ensayos sobre la violencia y el recuerdo en la Sudáfrica contemporánea. Bogotá: Universidad de los Andes.

Castillejo, A.C. (2007). La Globalización del Testimonio:Silencio endémico y los usos de la palabra. *Revista Antípoda*, 4.

Castillo, M. (2012, August 29). Time is right, but past failures haunt Colombia Peace Talks. *CNN Latin America*. Retrieved from http://edition.cnn.com/2012/08/28/world/americas/colombia-farc-peace-talks/

Caylus, H. (2012). Le Choix d'une Démilitarisation Brutale: le Cas de l'Armée Irakienne. In F. Bourrat (Ed.), La Place et le Rôle des Armées dans le Monde Arabe Contemporain (pp. 97-117). In Les Champs de Mars, 23. Paris: La Documentation Française (Institut de Recherche Stratégique de l'École militaire).

Ceceña, A. E., Aguilar, P., & Motto, C. (2007). *Territorialidad de la Dominación*. Observatorio Latinoamericano de Geopolítica. Retrieved from http://www.geopolitica.ws/media/uploads/IIRSA.pdf

Centre de Gestions des Conflits. (2001). *Les juridictions Gacaca et le processus de réconciliation nationale*. Kigali.

Centro de Memoria Histórica. (2013). *Basta ya! Colombia: memorias de guerra y dignidad (General Report)*. Bogotá, Colombia: Grupo de Memoria Histórica.

Centro Nacional de Memoria Histórica. (2012). ¡Basta Ya!. Colombia: Memorias de guerra y dignidad. Informe general Grupo Memoria Histórica. DPS.

Centro Nacional de Memoria Histórica. (2013). Basta Ya. Colombia: memorias de guerra y dignidad. Bogotá: Imprenta Nacional.

CEPALSTAT. (2014). *Exportaciones de productos primarios según su participación en el total* [Data file]. Retrieved from http://interwp.cepal.org/sisgen/ConsultaIntegrada.asp?idIndicador=1910&idioma=e

Çetinsaya, G. (2005). *Ottoman Administration of Iraq, 1890 – 1908*. London, New York: Routledge.

Chabal, P. (2009). *Africa: the politics of suffering and smiling*. London: Zed Books.

Chabal, P., & Daloz, J.-P. (1999). *Afrika Works. Disorder as political instrument*. Oxford: James Currey.

Chamblis, W., & Michalowsky, R. (2010). *State Crime in the Global Age*. Collumpton.

Chernick, M. (2005). Economic Resources and Internal armed Conflicts: Lessons from the Colombian Case. In C. Arnson, & W. Zartman (Eds.), Rethinking the Economics of War. The Intersection of Need, Creed, and Greed (pp. 178-205). Washington; Baltimore: Woodrow Wilson Center Press: The Johns Hopkins Univeristy Press.

Chouet, A. (1995). L'Espace Tribal Alaouite à l'Épreuve du Pouvoir. La Désintégration par le Politique. *Monde Arabe Maghreb-Machrek*, *147*, 93–119.

Christine, B. (2003). Human rights and minority protection. In J. Darby & R. MacGinty (Eds.), *Contemporary Peacemaking Conflict, violence and Peace Processes*. New York: Palgrave Macmillan.

Ciorciari, J. D., & Heindel, A. (in press). Experiments in International Criminal Justice: Lessons from the Khmer Rouge Tribunal. *Michigan Journal of International Law*.

Civico, A. (2012, Spring) This has been a cruel war: paramilitary violence and democracy in Colombia. Paper presented in the panel What is Political about Violence in Post- Conflict Latin America? American Ethnological Society.

Clamp, K. L., & Doak, J. (2012). More than words: Restorative Justice Concepts in Transitional Justice Settings. *International Criminal Law Review*, *12*(3), 339–360. doi:10.1163/157181212X648824

Clark, P. (2009). The Rules (and Politics) of Engagement: The Gacaca Courts and Post-Genocide Justice, Healing and Reconciliation in Rwanda. In P. Clark, & Z. Kaufman (Eds.), After Genocide (pp. 297-319).

Coalition Provisional Authority (2003a). Order Number 12, Trade Liberalisation Policy, CPA/ORD/7 June 2003/12: 1, emphasis in the original.

Coalition Provisional Authority (2003b). Order Number 81, Patent, Industrial Design, Undisclosed Information, Integrated Circuits and Plant Variety, CPA/ORD/26 April 04/81: 1, emphasis in the original.

Cohen, S. (2004). *States of Denial*. Oxford University Press.

Coleman, R., Sim, J., Tombs, S., & Whyte, D. (2009). Introduction. In R. Coleman, J. Sim, S. Tombs, & D. Whyte (Eds.), *State, Power, Crime*. London: Sage. doi:10.4135/9781446269527.n1

Collier, P. (2000a). Doing Well out of a War: An Economic Perspective. In M. Berdal & D. Malone (Eds.), *Greed and Grievance: Economic Agendas in Civil Wars* (pp. 91–112). Boulder, Colorado: Lynne Rienner.

Collier, P. (2000b). Rebellion as a Quasi-Criminal Activity. *The Journal of Conflict Resolution*, *44*(6), 839–853. doi:10.1177/0022002700044006008

Collier, P., & Hoeffler, A. (1998). *On Economic Causes of Civil War*. Washington: World Bank.

Collier, P., & Hoeffler, A. (1999). *Justice-Seeking and Loot-Seeking in Civil War*. Washington: World Bank.

Collier, P., & Hoeffler, A. (2000). *Greed and Grievance in Civil War*. Washington: World Bank.

Colliers, R. (2003) Imports Inundate Iraq under new U.S. Policy, San Francisco Chronicle, 10th July.

Colmenares, R. (2006). Sistema de Justicia Penal Formal y el Derecho Consuetudinario Wayuu. *Frónesis*, 13(1), 57–69. Retrieved from http://www.scielo.org.ve/scielo.php?pid=S1315-62682006000100006&script=sci_arttext

Colmenares, R. (1983). *Del Derecho Consuetudinario Guajiro al Estado Social de Derecho Multiétnico en Venezuela. Revista de la Facultad de Ciencias Jurídicas y Políticas, (70)*. Maracaibo, Venezuela: Universidad del Zulia.

Colombia Solidarity Campaign. (2013). *La Colosa: Una muerte anunciada*. Retrieved from http://www.colombiasolidarity.org.uk/campaign-media/51-press/610-colombia-solidarity-campaign-lanza-informe-qla-colosa-una-muerte-anunciadaq

Comisión Colombiana de Juristas. (2011). *Colombia: situación de las violaciones al derecho a la vida julio de 2001 a junio de 2009*. Retrieved from http://www.coljuristas.org/documentos/cifras/cif_2011-06-06.pdf

Comisión Nacional de Rearación y Reconciliación, CNRR, (2010), May.

Comisión Nacional de Reparación y Reconciliación (CNRR). (2010). *La masacre de Bahía Portete: mujeres wayuu en la mira*. Bogotá, Colombia: Alfaguara.

COMISIÓN NACIONAL DE REPARACIÓN Y RECONCILIACIÓN, CNRR. . (2011). Mujeres y Guerra. Victimas y resistentes en el Caribe Colombiano. Informe del Grupo de Memoria Histórica coordinado por María Emma Wills. Taurus, Fundación Semana.

Comisión Nacional de Reparación y Reconciliación. (2009). Recordar y narrar el conflicto. Herramientas para reconstruir memoria histórica. Bogotá: Fotoletras S.A.

Conflictrecovery.org. (2007). Support to Aceh Reintegration and Peace Agency. Retrieved from http://www.conflictrecovery.org/bin/Annexe_I-a.pdf

Congreso de la Republica de Colombia. (2011). Decreto Ley "*Por medio del cual se dictan medidas de asistencia, atención, reparación integral y de restitución de derechos territoriales a las víctimas pertenecientes a los Pueblos y Comunidades indígenas*" (4633 de 2011). Ministerio del interior, 9 de diciembre.

Constitución Política de Colombia, 1991

Consultoría para los Derechos Humanos y el Desplazamiento. (2013). La crisis humanitaria en Colombia persiste. El Pacífico en disputa: Informe de desplazamiento forzado en 2012 [Document CODHES no. 26]. Retrieved from http://www.abcolombia.org.uk/downloads/Informe_Desplazamiento_2012_La_Crisis_Humanitaria_.pdf

Controlaría General de la República. (2013a). *II Informe de seguimiento al proceso restitución de tierras*. Retrieved from http://www.contraloria.gov.co/documents/155638087/161616579/Restituci%C3%B3n+de+Tierras+II+2013.pdf/93c00df9-4e7a-43a4-9e11-75dc5f426246?version=1.0

Controlaría General de la República. (2013b). *Encuesta nacional de víctimas.* Retrieved from http://www.contraloriagen.gov.co/documents/155638087/161621822/Libro_ENV_CGR-2013_(16-01-2015).pdf

Convention on Biodiversity. (2014). *Colombia - Overview.* Retrieved from www.cbd.int

Conze, E., Frei, N., Hayes, P., & Zimmermann, M. (Eds.), (2010). *Das Amt und die Vergangenheit. Deutsche Diplomaten im Dritten Reich und in der Bundesrepublik.* München: Karl Blessing Verlag.

Cook, S. A. (2007). *Ruling but not Governing: the Military and Political Development in Egypt, Algeria and Turkey.* Baltimore: John Hopkins University Press.

Coordinación Colombia-Europa-Estados Unidos. (2012). *Ejecuciones extrajudiciales en Colombia.* Retrieved from http://www.justf.org/files/presentations/1209_CCEEUU.pdf

Copnall, J. (2014). *A Poisonous Thorn in Our Hearts: Sudan and South Sudan's Bitter and Incomplete Divorce.* London: Hurst Publishers.

Cornell, S. (2005). The Interaction of Narcotics and Conflict. *Journal of Peace Research, 42*(6), 751–760. doi:10.1177/0022343305057895

Corporación Observatorio por la Paz. (2009). *Guerra inútiles. Una historia de las FARC.* Bogotá: Intermedio.

Correa De Andreis, A. (2001). *La mirada que mira la mirada. Un caso de alianza en la Ciénaga Grande de Santa Marta.* Barranquilla: Universidad del Norte.

Correa, C., Guillerot, J., & Magarrell, L. (2009). Reparations and victim participation: a look at the Truth Commission Experience. In C. Ferstman (Ed.), *M. Goetz., & A. Stephens. Reparations for victims of genocide, war crimes and crimes against humanity. Systems in place and Systems in the Making* (pp. 383–414). The Netherlands: Martinus Nijhoff Publishers. doi:10.1163/ej.9789004174498.i-576.103

Coughlan, J., Ghouse, S., & Smith, R. (2012). The Legacy of the Khmer Rouge Tribunal: Maintaining the Status Quo of Cambodia's Judicial and Legal System. *Amsterdam Law Forum, (4)*, 17-35.

Cour Suprême. (2001). *Manuel explicatif sur la loi organique portant création des juridictions Gacaca.*

CPA Order 89. (2003). Amendments to the Labor Code Law No. 71, 1987.

Crawford-Browne, S., Basha, S., & Alexander, K. (2005). Obstacles to Transitional Justice in Sudan. In B. Raftopoulos & K. Alexander (Eds.), *Peace in the Balance: The Crisis in Sudan* (pp. 139–157). Cape Town, South Africa: Institute for Justice and Reconciliation.

Crenzel, E. (2008). Present Pasts: Memory (ies) of State Terrorism in the Southern Cone of Latin America. In F. Lessa (Ed.), *The Memory of State Terrorism in the Southern Cone.*

Crowther, S. (2013). *The Election and the ECCC.* Cambodia Tribunal Monitor.

Cruz, E. (2007). Los estudios sobre paramilitarismo en Colombia. *Análisis Político (Bogotá)*, 60, 117–134.

Cubides, F. (2006). Proceso inconcluso, verdades a medias: Para un balance de las negociaciones del gobierno Uribe con los paramilitares. *Análisis Político (Bogotá)*, 57, 55–64.

Curtis, G., & Karakan, T. (2002). *The Nexus Among Terrorists, Narcotics, Traffickers, weapons proliferators, and Traffickers, Weapons Proliferators and Organized Crime Networks in Western Europe.* Washington: Library of the Congress.

Czempiel, E.-O. (1994). *Die Reform der UNO. Möglichkeiten und Missverständnisse.* München: Beck.

Dabasha, H. (2011). *Shi'ism. A Religion of Protest. Harvard.* Harvard University Press.

Dai, Y. (2008). Transformation of the Islamic Da'wa Party in Iraq: From the Revolutionary Period to the Diaspora Era. *Asian and African Area Studies, 7*(2), 238–267.

Dallaire, R. & Beardsley, B. (2003). Shake hands with the devil: the failure of humanity in Rwanda.

Dallaire, R. (2010). *They fight like soldiers they die like children. The global quest to eradicate the use of child soldiers.* New York: Walker & Company.

Das Veena. (2008). Trauma y Testimonio. In A. Ortega Francisco (Ed.), Veena Das: Sujetos del dolor, agentes de dignidad. Bogotá: Universidad Javeriana, Instituto pensar, Universidad Nacional de Colombia, Colección CES.

Davis, E. (2005). History Matters: Past as Prologue in Building Democracy in Iraq. *Orbis*, *49*(2), 229–244. doi:10.1016/j.orbis.2005.01.004

Davis, E. (2005). *Memories of state, politics, history and collective identity in modern Iraq*. Berkeley, CA: University of California Press.

Dawisha, A. (2012). Post Occupation Iraq. The Brittleness of political Institutions. *The Woodrow Wilson International Center for Scholars: Occasional Paper Series,* Spring, 1-15.

Dawisha, A. (2009). *Iraq. A Political History from Independence to Occupation*. Princeton: Princeton University Press.

De Greiff, P. (2011). Algunas reflexiones acerca del desarrollo de la Justicia Transicional. *Anuario de Derechos Humanos*, Universidad de Chile, (7).

De Greiff, P. (2012). Theorizing Transitional Justice. In M. Williams, R. Nagy, & J. Elster (Eds.), Transitional Justice (pp.31-77). New York: New York University Press.

De Greiff, P. (2006). Justice and Reparations. In P. De Greiff (Ed.), *The Handbook of Reparations* (pp. 451–477). New York: Oxford University Press. doi:10.1093/0199291926.003.0013

de la República de Colombia, C. (2005). Ley 975 de 2005 por la cual se dictan disposiciones para la reincorporación de miembros de grupos armados organizados al margen de la ley que contribuyan de manera efectiva a la consecusión de la paz nacional y se dictan otras disposiciones para acuerdos humanitarios. Colombia.

de Souza Santos, B. (1995). *Towards a New Common Sense: law, science and politics in the paradigmatic transition*. London: Routledge.

de Vigny, A.-V. (1949). B. Grillet (Ed.), *Servitude et Grandeur Militaires*. Paris: Librairie Larousse (collection Classiques Larousse).

De Waals, F. (2007). *Chimpanzee Politics: Power and Sex among Apes*. Baltimore: Johns Hopkins University Press.

Decisive Point. (2014). *Contraterrorismo: La victoria silencioso del Estado*. Retrieved from Decisive Point website http://www.decisive-point.org/images/documentos/Contraterrorismo_La%20victoria_silencionsa_del_Estado_2014.pdf

Deininger, K., Byerlee, D., Lindsay, J., Norton, A., Selod, H., & Stickler, M. (2011). *Rising Global Interest in Farmland: Can it yield sustainable benefits?* Retrieved from the World Bank website http://siteresources.worldbank.org/DEC/Resources/Rising-Global-Interest-in-Farmland.pdf

Del Pino, P., & Jelin, E. (2003). *Luchas locales, comunidades e identidades*. Madrid: Siglo XXI Editores.

Delgado Ramos, G. C. (2012). Extractivismo minero, conflicto y resistencia social. *Realidad Económica*, (265), 60–84.

Delgado Ramos, G. C., Romano, S. M. (2011). Plan Colombia e Iniciativa Mérida: negocio y seguridad interna. *El Cotidiano,* (170), 89–100.

Delgado, J. (2014, December 4). Desescalar las hostilidades: Apremiante aspiración estratégica de las Farc. *Observatorio de Política y Estrategia en América Latina (OPEAL)*. Retrieved from http://opeal.net/index.php?option=com_k2&view=item&id=22159:desescalar-las-hostilidades-apremiante-aspiracion-estrategica-de-las-farc&Itemid=144

Deng, D. K. (2014, July). *Memory, Healing and Transformation in South Sudan*. Transitional Justice Working Paper. South Sudan Law Society.

Departamento Nacional de Planeación. (2010). *Plan Nacional de Desarrollo 2010-2014: Prosperidad para todos*. Retrieved from https://colaboracion.dnp.gov.co/CDT/PND/PND2010-2014%20Tomo%20I%20CD.pdf

Der Spiegel. (1970) Kniefall angemessen oder übertrieben? *Der Spiegel*, 1970(51).

Derrida, J. (1995). *Archive Fever: A Freudian Impression*. Chicago: Chicago University Press.

Dershowitz, A. (2002, January 22). Want to torture? Get a warrant. *San Francisco Chronicle*.

Des Forges, A. (1999). *Leave None to Tell the Story: Genocide in Rwanda*. New York: Human Rights Watch.

Deutsche Welle. (2014). Kurdistan, public referendum towards independency. Retrieved from http://www.dw.de/كردستان-استفتاء-شعبي-باتجاه-الاستقلال/a-17757172

Dezalay, Y., & Garth, B. (2002). La Internacionalización de las luchas por el poder. La competencia entre abogados y economistas por transformar los Estados latinoamericanos. Clave de Sur. 1ª ed. ILSA, Bogotá D.C. Colombia.

Di Certo, B. (2012, June 4). Top officials eyed in KRT probe: report. *Phnom Penh Post*, 1, 6.

Diaz, C. (2009) Colombia's bid for justice and peace. In K. Ambos, J. Large, M. Wierda (Eds.), Building a future on Peace and Justice (pp. 469-501). Springer. Berlin

Digneffe, F., & Fierens, J. (2003). *Justice et gacaca. L'expérience rwandaise et le genocide*. Namur: Presses Universitaires de Namur.

Dodge, T. (2003). *Inventing Iraq. The Failure of Nation-Building and a History Denied.* New York: Columbia University Press.

Dodge, T. (2003). *Inventing Iraq: The Failure of Nation-Building and a History Denied.* New York: Columbia University Press.

Dodge, T. (2005). *IRAQ'S FUTURE The aftermath of regime change*. London: Routledge.

Dodge, T. (2013). State and society in Iraq ten years after regime change: The rise of a new authoritarianism. *International Affairs*, *89*(2), 241–257. doi:10.1111/1468-2346.12016

Doerry, M. (2006). "Nirgendwo und überall zu Haus": Gespräche mit Überlebenden des Holocaust. München. In Ders. Erziehung zur Mündigkeit (7th ed.). Frankfurt/Main. Retrieved from http://signale.cornell.edu/text/meaning-working-through-past

Doki, C. (2013, May 2). Scant hope for South Sudan's latest amnesty offer to rebels. *The Niles*. Retrieved from http://www.hrw.org/sites/default/files/reports/southsudan0814_ForUpload.pdf.

Doughman, R. (2011). *La chipa y la soja*. Asunción: BASE-IS.

Druliolle, V. (2011). Remembering and its Places in Post-dictatorship Argentina. In F. Lessa (Ed.), *The Memory of State Terrorism in the Southern Cone.*

Drummond-Mundal, L., & Cave, D. (2006). Children as the seeds of peace: Exploring children's potential contribution to conflict transformation and peacebuilding. Draft submitted to *The Journal of Peacebuilding and Development.* (Unpublished manuscript).

Duncan, G. (2008). *Los señores de la guerra*. Bogota: Planeta.

Echandía Castilla, C. (2000). El conflicto armado colombiano en los años noventa: cambios en las estrategias y efectos económicos. *Revista Colombia Internacional*, 49 – 50, 117 – 134

Echandía, C. (2008). El fin de la invulnerabilidad de las FARC. *Nueva Sociedad, 217.*

Echandía, C. (2009). Subestimación del riesgo estratégico en el conflicto colombiano. *Zero*, 33, 62-67.

Echandía, C. (2012a). La experiencia del Caguán. Punto de partida del debilitamiento de las Farc. *Zero,* 28, 54-61.

Echandía, C. (2012b). Organizaciones armadas y violencia global en Colombia. In E. Bechara (Ed.), ¿Prolongación sin solución? (pp. 123-157). Bogotá: Universidad Externado de Colombia.

Echandía, C. (2013). De la Uribe a La Habana. *Revista Zero*, 36-43.

Echandía, C. (2012c). Colombie: Évolution du conflit armé à partir de l'analyse de la territorialité et des stratégies des FARC (1990-2011). *Problemes d'Amerique Latine*, *83*(1), 101–116. doi:10.3917/pal.083.0101

Echandía, C. (2012d). Cambios en la conducta de las FARC en medio de la ofensiva militar en su contra. In E. Bechara (Ed.), *Prolongación sin solución? Perspectivas sobre la guerra y la paz en Colombia.* Bogotá: Universidad Externado de Colombia.

Echeverry, J., Salazar, N., & Navas, V. (2001, February 12). ¿Nos Parecemos al Resto del Mundo? El Conflicto Colombiano en el Contexto Internacional. *ARCHIVOS DE MACROECONOMÍA,* 143, 1-54.

Eckert, J. (2012). Rumours of Rights. In J. Eckert, B. Donahoe, Ch. Strümpell, & Z. Ö. Biner (Eds.), *Law against the State. Ethnographic Forays into Law's Transformations* (pp. 147–170). Cambridge: Cambridge University Press. doi:10.1017/CBO9781139043786.007

Edmonds, M., Mills, G., & McNamee, T. (2009). Disarmament, Demobilization, and Reintegration and Local Ownership in the Great Lakes: The Experience of Rwanda, Burundi, and the Democratic Republic of Congo. *African Security*, *2*(1), 29–58. doi:10.1080/19362200902766383

Eisenstadt, S. N. (1973). *Traditional Patrimonialism and Modern Neopatrimonialism*. Thousand Oaks, London: SAGE Publications.

El Colombiano. (2012, November 8). ONU condenó masacre de 10 campesinos en Santa Rosa de Osos. Retrieved from http://www.elcolombiano.com/BancoConocimiento/S/santa_rosa_de_osos_masacre_de_campesinos_fue_condenada_por_la_onu/santa_rosa_de_osos_masacre_de_campesinos_fue_condenada_por_la_onu.asp

El Espectador. (2010, March 9). *Cabecilla de Farc habla de alianza con Los Rastrojos*. Obtenido de El Espectador: http://www.elespectador.com/noticias/judicial/audio-cabecilla-de-farc-habla-de-alianza-los-rastrojos

¿El ocaso de las Farc y Eln? (2014). *El Espectador*. Retrieved from www.elespectador.com

El país pierde US$ 1 millón al día por ataques a oleoductos. (2012). *El Tiempo*. Retrieved from www.eletiempo.com

El sector minero-energético está en la mira de guerrilla. (2013, February 2). *El Universal*. Retrieved from www.eluniversal.com.co

El Tiempo. (2012, September 11). Mineria Ilegal Desplaza a la coca en ocho regiones. *El Tiempo*. Retrieved from http://www.eltiempo.com/justicia/ARTICULO-WEB-NEW_NOTA_INTERIOR-12214227.html

El Tiempo. (2015, June). ONU condenó masacre de 10 campesinos en Santa Rosa de Osos Retrieved from http://www.eltiempo.com/contenido/politica/justicia/ARCHIVO/ARCHIVO-15997016-0.pdf

Elhag, N. (2008). A Tale of Two Wars: The Militarization of Dinka and Nuer Identities in South Sudan. In J. Abbink & A. van Dokkum (Eds.), *Dilemmas of Development: Conflicts of Interest and their Resolutions in Modernizing Africa* (pp. 164–186). Leiden: African Studies Centre.

Elias, N. (1969/1982). *The Civilizing Process: Sociogenetic and Psychogenetic Investigations*. Oxford: Blackwell.

Eln ataca nuevo tramo de oleoducto Caño Limón- Coveñas. (2014, May 2). *El Espectador*. Retrieved from www.elespectador.com

Elster, J. (2012). Justice, Truth, Peace. In M. Williams, R. Nagy, & J. Elster (Eds.), Transitional Justice (pp.78-97). New York: New York University Press.

Elwert, G. (n. d.). *Intervention in Markets of Violence*. Freie Univerität Berlin. Retrieved from http://www.oei.fu-berlin.de/en/projekte/cscca/downloads/ge_pub_marketsofviolence.pdf

Eribon, D. (1982). Entrevista a Pierre Bourdieu. Retrieved from http://pierre-bourdieu.blogspot.com/2008/01/entrevista-pierre-bourdieu-qu-significa.html

Esposito, D. & Crocker, B. (2004, January). *To Guarantee the Peace: An Action Strategy for a Post-Conflict Sudan*. Centre for Strategic and International Studies.

Essed, Ph., Frerks, G., & Schrijvers, J. (2004). Introduction. Refugees, Agency and Social Transformation. In P. Essed, G. Frerks, & J. Schrijvers (Eds.), Refugees and the Transformation of Societies. Agency, Policies, Ethics and Politics. New York, Oxford: Berghahn.

Estado Mayor Conjunto de las FARC-EP. (2013, May 27). *De Marquetalia A La Habana: 49 años luchando por la paz*. Delegación de Paz FARC-EP. Retrieved from http://www.pazfarc-ep.org/index.php/noticias-comunicados-documentos-farc-ep/estado-mayor-central-emc/4-de-marquetalia-la-habana-49-anos-luchando-por-la-paz

EU Council Secretariat. (2006). EU Monitoring Mission in Aceh. Retrieved from http://www.eeas.europa.eu/csdp/missions-and-operations/aceh-amm/pdf/15122006_factsheet_aceh-amm_en.pdf

European Security Review. (2005). Aceh Monitoring Mission: a New Challenge for ESDP. Retrieved from eeas.europa.eu/us/docs/infopack_06_en.pdf

Extraordinary Chambers in the Courts of Cambodia (2014, August 7). *Case 002/01 Judgment* (Doc 002/19-09-2007/ECCC/TC).

Extraordinary Chambers in the Courts of Cambodia. (2009, August 18). *Considerations of the Pre-Trial Chamber Regarding the Disagreement Between the Co-Prosecutors Pursuant to Internal Rule 71* (Doc. 001/18-11-2008-ECCC/PTC).

Extraordinary Chambers in the Courts of Cambodia. (2010). *Judgment in Case 001* (Doc. 001/18-07/ECCC/TC).

Extraordinary Chambers in the Courts of Cambodia. (2010, September 9). *Second Decision on Nuon Chea's and Ieng Sary's Appeal Against OCIJ Order on Request to Summon Witnesses, Opinion of Judges Downing and Marchi-Uhel* (Doc. 002/19-09-2007-EEEC-OPIJ (PTC 50)).

Extraordinary Chambers in the Courts of Cambodia. (2012). *Appeal Judgment in Case 0001* (Doc. 001/18-07-2007-ECCC/SC).

Extraordinary Chambers in the Courts of Cambodia. (2013, December 24). *Case 0002/02 Trial Chamber Workplan* (Doc. E301/5).

Fals Borda, O., Guzmá, G., & Umaña, E. (1962). *La violencia en Colombia*. Bogotá: Universidad Nacional.

FAO. (2014, November 21). FAO. Retrieved from http://www.fao.org/news/story/en/item/45210/icode/

Farago, F. (1998). *Les Grands Courants de la Pensée Politique*. Paris: Armand Colin.

Farouk-Souglett, M., & Suglett, P. (2001). *Iraq since 1958. From Revolution to Dictatorship*. New York: I. B. Tauris.

Farson, R. (1974). *Birthrights*. New York: Macmillan Publishing Co., Inc.

Felbab-Brown, V. (2010). *Shooting Up, Counterinsurgency and the War on Drugs*. Washington: Brookings Institution Press.

Feldman, N. (2004). *What We Owe Iraq: War and the Ethics of Nation Building*. Princeton: Princeton University Press.

Fernández, C., García-Durán, M., & Sarmiento, F. (2004). Peace mobilisation in Colombia: 1978 – 2002. Retrieved from http://www.c-r.org/accord-article/peace-mobilisation-colombia-1978-2002

Feyerabend, P. (1999). *The Conquest of Abundance: A Tale of Abstraction versus the Richnes of Being*. Chicago: Chicago University Press.

Fidler, D. (2001). The Return of the Standard of Civilisation. *Chicago Journal of International Law*, *2*(1), 147.

Filkins, D. (2014, April 28). Letter from Iraq. What We Left Behind. *The New*.

Firchow, P., Ginty, R., & M., (2013). Reparations and Peacebuilding: Issues and Controversies. *Human Rights Review (Piscataway, N.J.)*, *14*(3), 231–239. doi:10.1007/s12142-013-0275-1

Fischer, T., & Lorenz, M. N. (Eds.). (2009). *Lexikon der Vergangenheitsbewältigung in Deutschland. Debatten- und Diskursgeschichte des Nationalsozialismus nach 1945* (2nd ed.). Bielefeld: Transkript.

Fogoto, M. (2012, August 5). Is Erbil's Growth Spurt Hype or for Real? *Alpha Magazine*, 10-14.

Foucault, M. (1966). *Les Mots et les Choses (Une Archéologie des Sciences Humaines)*. Paris: Gallimard.

Francis, P. (18 de June de 2015). Papal Encyclicals on line. Obtenido de papalencyclicas: http://www.papalencyclicals.net/

Frankfurter Allgemeine Zeitung (FAZ). (2014a). In Sippenhaft. *FAZ*, 137.

Frankfurter Allgemeine Zeitung (FAZ). (2014b). Lasst euch euren freien Willen nicht nehmen. *FAZ*, 149.

Frankfurter Allgemeine Zeitung (FAZ). (2014c). Klarheit im Urteil. *FAZ*, 149.

Frankfurter Allgemeine Zeitung (FAZ). (2014d). Extremistisches Material? *FAZ*, 150.

Frankfurter Allgemeine Zeitung (FAZ). (2014e). Wie meine Familie von den Nazis enteignet wurde. *FAZ*, 150.

Frankfurter Allgemeine Zeitung (FAZ). (2014f). Der berühmteste Deserteur der Wehrmacht. FAZ, 151.

Frankfurter Allgemeine Zeitung (FAZ). (2014g). Geknechtet und überfordert. *FAZ*, 155.

Frankfurter Allgemeine Zeitung (FAZ). (2014h). Steinmeiers Widerstandskämpferin. FAZ, 157.

Frankfurter Allgemeine Zeitung am Sonntag (FAZamSO). (2014a). Was wurde aus Hans Kammler? *FAZamSo*, 24.

Frankfurter Allgemeine Zeitung am Sonntag (FAZamSo). (2014b). Bunker als Wohnhaus. FAZamSo, 27.

Frank, T. (2000). *One Market Under God: Extreme Capitalism, Market Populism, and the End of Economic Democracy*. New York: Doubleday.

Frasser Lozano, C. C., & Restrepo Plaza, L. M. (2012). Sector minero en Colombia: ¿El auge para quién? *El Observador Regional, 23.*

Freedson, J. (2011). *Bridging the accountability gap: new approaches to addressing violations against children in armed conflict*. Cambridge: Conflict Dynamics International.

Freeman, M. (2007). Why it remains important to take children's rights seriously. *International Journal of Children's Rights, 15*(1), 5–23. doi:10.1163/092755607X181711

Freemann, R. B., & Medoff, J. (1984). *What Do Unions Do?* New York: Basic Books.

Friedman, G., & Himmelstein, J. (2013). *Konflikte fordern uns heraus. Mediation als Brücke zur Verständigung*. Frankfurt am Main: Wolfgang Metzner Verlag.

Friedman, Y. (2010). *The Nusayri-Alawis: An Introduction to the Religion, History, and Identity of the Leading Minority in Syria*. Leiden: Brill.

Froedin, L. (2008). The Challenges of Reintegration in Aceh. Retrieved from http://www.c-r.org/es/node/1125

Fuerzas Armadas y Revolucionarias de Colombia Ejercito del Pueblo, & Gobierno Nacional de la República de Colombia. (2013). *Primer informe conjunto de la mesa de conversaciones entre el Gobierno de la República y las Fuerzas Armadas Aevolucionarias de Colombia-Ejercito del Pueblo, FARC-EP*. Retrieved from https://www.mesadeconversaciones.com.co/sites/default/files/Informe%20%20Conjunto%201-%20Mesa%20de%20Conversaciones%20-Gobierno%20y%20Farc%20-%20Version%20Espa_ol.pdf

Galeano, E. (1995). *Ser como ellos y otros artículos*. Bogotá: Tercer Mundo Editores.

Galtung, J. (1967). Theories of peace: a synthetic approach to peace thinking. TRANSCEND International. Retrieved from http://www.transcend.org/files/Galtung_Book_unpub_Theories_of_Peace_-_A_Synthetic_Approach_to_Peace_Thinking_1967.pdf

Galtung, J. (1998). Konflikttransformation mit friedlichen Mitteln. *Die Methode der Transzendenz*. Retrieved from http://www.transcend.at/methode.html

Galtung, J. (1969). Violence, peace and peace research. *Journal of Peace Research*, *6*(3), 167–191, Retrieved fromhttp://www.jstor.org/discover/10.2307/422690?uid=3737864&uid=2129&uid=2&uid=70&uid=4&sid=21105242745363. doi:10.1177/002234336900600301

Galtung, J. (1976). Three realistic approaches to peace: Peacekeeping, peacemaking and peacebuilding. *Impact of Science on Society*, *26*, 103–115.

Galtung, J. (1996). *Peace by Peaceful Means: Peace and Conflict, Development and Civilization*. London: SAGE Publications Ltd.

Galtung, J. (2000). Leaving the Twentieth Century, Entering the twenty-first: Some Basic conflict Formations. In *J. Galtung and C. Jacobsen, searching for Peace the Road to TRANSCEND*. London: Pluto Press.

Galtung, J. (2006). Theoretical challenges of peace building with and for youth. In S. McEvoy-Levy (Ed.), *Troublemakers or Peacemakers? Youth and post-accord peace building* (pp. 259–279). Notre Dame, IN: University of Notre Dame Press.

Galtung, J. (2007). *Konflikte und Konfliktlösungen. Die Transcend-Methode und ihre Anwendung*. Berlin: Kai Homilius Verlag.

Galula, D. (1964). *Counterinsurgency Warfare*. Westport, CT: Praeger.

Gampel, Y. (2002). El dolor de lo social. Psicoanálisis APdeBA. Vol. XXIV - N° 1/2.

Garay Salamanca, J. L., Cabrera Leal, M., Espitia Zamora, J. E., Morales, J. F., Negrete Montes, R. E., & Pardo Becerra, L. Á. … Vargas Valencia, F. (2013). Minería en Colombia: Fundamentos para superar el modelo extractivista. Bogotá: Controlaría General de la Republica.

Garbarino, J., & Kostelny, K. (1996). What do we need to know to understand children in war and community violence? In R. Afpel, & B. Simon (Eds.), Minefields in their hearts. The mental health of children in war and communal violence. New Haven: Yale University Press.

García Acuña, Y. (2008). *Familias en Colombia. Transiciones hacia el siglo XXI*. Barranquilla: Ediciones Universidad Simón Bolívar.

García Márquez, G. (2007). Cien años de soledad, Edición conmemorativa. Bogotá: Real Academia Española, Asociación de Academias de la Lengua española

García, Y. (2012). *Rutas por la memoria. Voces de Nueva Venecia y El Salado*. Barranquilla: Universidad Simón Bolívar -Colciencias.

Gebreluel, G., & Tronvoll, K. (2013, October 15). Is the Horn of Africa facing another collapsing state? Eritrea's refugee crisis threatens to undermine the stability of the secretive country. *Al Jazeera*. Retrieved from http://www.aljazeera.com/indepth/opinion/2013/10/horn-africa-facing-another-collapsing-state-20131061177564655.html

Geertz, C. (1977). The Integrative Revolution: Primordial Sentiments and Civil Politics in the New States. In C. Geertz (Ed.), *The Interpretation of Cultures* (pp. 255–310). New York: Basic Books.

Geisser, V., & Krefa, A. (2011). L'Uniforme ne Fait plus le Régime, les Militaires Arabes face aux 'Révolutions'. *La Revue Internationale et Stratégique*, *83*(3), 93–102. doi:10.3917/ris.083.0093

Gellner, E. (1981). *Muslim Society*. Cambridge: Cambridge University Press.

Georgescu-Roegen, N. (1971). *The Entropy Law and the Economic Process*. Boston: Harvard University Press. doi:10.4159/harvard.9780674281653

Georgescu-Roegen, N. (1976). *Energy and Economic Myths: Institutional and Economic Essays*. Toronto: Pergamon Press Inc.

Gessner, V. (1998). Globalisation and Legal Certainty. In V. Gessner & A. Budak (Eds.), *Emerging Legal Certainty: empirical studies on the globalisation of law, Aldershot*. Dartmouth.

Ghai, Y. (2003). Territorial options. In J. Darby & R. MacGinty (Eds.), *Contemporary Peacemaking Conflict, violence and Peace Processes*. New York: Palgrave Macmillan.

Ghassûb, M., & Sinclair-Webb, E. (2000). *Imagined Masculinities: Male Identity and Culture in the Modern Middle East*. Londres: Saqi Books.

Giordano, R. (1987). *Die zweite Schuld oder Von der Last Deutscher zu sein*. Hamburg: Rasch und Röhring Verlag.

Giraldo, J. (1996). Colombia: The Genocidal Democracy. Common Courage Press.

Gisbert, T., & Pinto, M. J. (2014, May). Colombia: Militarización al servicio del Extractivismo. *Noticias de los Especuladores de La Guerra, (41)*. Retrieved from http://www.wri-irg.org/node/23117

Glick-Schiller, N., & Fouron, G. (2001). *Georges Woke Up Laughing: Long-Distance Nationalism and the Search for Home*. Durham, NC: Duke University Press. doi:10.1215/9780822383239

Goldsmith, E. (1985). Is development the Solution or the Problem. *The Ecologist*, 210–219.

Gómez Buendía, H. (2001, October 29). *La crisis*. Semana. Retrieved from http://www.semana.com/opinion/articulo/la-crisis/49075-3

Gomez Santamaria, S.M. (2010) Constructions of the Violent State: The Case of Extrajudicial Executions of Civilians by State Military Forces in Antioquia, Colombia. Oñati Socio-Legal Series, 1(1).

Gomez Suarez, A. (2007). Perpetrator Blocs, genocidal mentalities and geographies: the destruction of Union Patriotica in Colombia and its lessons for genocide studies. *Journal of Genocide Research, 9(4)*. London: Routledge. doi:10.1080/14623520701644440

Gomez, C. (2014, October 6) Victims of Colombia conflict fight to be recognized as such. Quartz. Retrieved from http://qz.com/274647/victims-of-colombias-conflict-fight-to-be-recognized-as-such/

Gómez, S. G. (2013). Contextualización teórica e histórica de la reintegración social y económica de desmovilizados en Colombia. *Poliantea, 6*(11).

González Posso, C. (2004). Negociaciones con las FARC 1982-2002. *Accord,* 14, 48-53.

González Posso, C. (2013). *En La Habana: El laberinto con salida*. Instituto de estudios para el desarrollo y la paz (Indepaz). Retrieved from http://www.indepaz.org.co/wp-content/uploads/2013/02/LABERINTO-CON-SALIDA-1.pdf

González Posso, C. (2013). La verdad en el abandono forzado y el despojo de tierras.

González, F. (2011). A manera de síntesis conclusiva. In T. Vásquez, A. Vargas, & J. A. Restrepo (Eds.), *Una vieja guerra en un nuevo contexto* (pp. 429–446). Bogota: Editorial Pontificia Universidad Javeriana.

González, F., Bolívar, I., & Vázquez, T. (2002). *Violencia política en Colombia*. Bogota: CINEP.

Gonzalez-Quijano, Y. (2012). *Arabités Numériques. Le Printemps du Web Arabe*. Arles: Actes Sud/Sindbad.

Government of Southern Sudan Presidential Decree No. 44/2006. (2006 June). Retrieved from http://www.unmis.unmissions.org/Portals/UNMIS/CPA%20Monitor/Annexes/Annex%204427%20-%20GoSS%20Commissioners.pdf.

Government of Southern Sudan Presidential Decree No. 46/2006. (2006, June 27). Retrieved from http://www.unmis.unmissions.org/Portals/UNMIS/CPA%20Monitor/Annexes/Annex%2044%20-%20GoSS%20Commissioners.pdf.

Government of Southern Sudan Presidential Decree No. 48/2006. (2006, June 27). Retrieved from http://www.unmis.unmissions.org/Portals/UNMIS/CPA%20Monitor/Annexes/Annex%2044%20-%20GoSS%20Commissioners.pdf.

Graw, K., & Schielke, S. (Eds.). (2012). *The Global Horizon. Expectations of Migration in Africa and the Middle East*. Leuven: Leuven University Press.

Gray, C. (1999). *Modern Strategy*. Oxford: Oxford University Press.

Greenpeace. (2007, February 9). Greenpeace Org. Abolish Nuclear Weapons: The Vital Statistics. Retrieved from http://www.greenpeace.org/international/en/campaigns/peace/abolish-nuclear-weapons/the-vital-statistics/

Gres Toso S. (2007). Historiografía, memoria y política. Observaciones para un debate. *Cyber Humanitatis,* 41.

Gresle, F. (dir.) (2005). *Sociologie du Milieu Militaire. Les Conséquences de la Professionnalisation sur les Armées et l'Identité Militaire*. Paris: L'Harmattan.

Guáqueta, A. (2003). The Colombian Conflict: Political and economic Dimensions. In K. Ballentine & J. Sherman (Eds.), *The Political Economy of Armed Conflict* (pp. 73–101). Boulder: Lynne Rienner.

Gubrium, J. F., & Goldstein, J. A. (2001). *Handbook of interview research*. London: Sage. doi:10.4135/9781412973588

Guerra Curvelo, W. (2002). *La ley en la sociedad wayúu. La disputa y la palabra*. Bogotá: Ministerio de Cultura.

Guerrero, J. (2003). Mercados de violencia, mercados ilegales y guerras civiles en América Latina en los años noventa: Tesis para un estudio etnográfico de las economías de guerra. *Palimpsesto, III*, 32–45.

Gugliemucci, A. (2007). *La Objetivación de las Memorias Públicas sobre la última dictadura militar. Revista Antípoda. Número 4*. Uniandes Bogotá.

Haddad, F. (2011). *Sectarianism in Iraq. Antagonistic Views of Unity*. London: Hurst & Co.

Haj, S. (1997). *The Making of Iraq. 1900 – 1963. Capital, Power, and Ideology*. Albany, NY: State University of New York Press.

Halbwachs, M. (2004). La memoria colectiva, Zaragoza: Prensa Universitarias de Zaragoza. Retrieved from http://es.scribd.com/doc/36199740/Halbwachs-Maurice-La-Memoria-Colectiva

Hamber, B., & Kelly, G. (2005). A place for reconciliation? Conflict and locality in Northern Ireland. *Democratic Dialogue*, Report 18.

Hamburger Institut für Sozialforschung (Ed.). (2001). *Verbrechen der Wehrmacht. Dimensionen des Vernichtungskrieges 1941 – 1944. Begleitbroschüre zur Ausstellung*. Hamburg: Hamburger Edition.

Hannoyer, J. (Coord.) (1999). Guerres Civiles. Économies de la Violence, Dimensions de la Civilité. Paris: Karthala / Beirut: CERMOC.

Hardin, G. (1993). *Living Within Limits: Ecology, Economics, and Population Taboos*. New York: Oxford University Press.

Harmon-Gross, E. (2009). *Seeking Resettlement and Navigating Transnational Politics. The Intersection of Policies, Human Rights and Individuals in Shimelba Refugee Camp* [MA Thesis]. University of Tennessee. Retrieved from http://trace.tennessee.edu/utk_gradthes/84

Hart, K. (1973). Informal Income Opportunities and Urban Employment in Ghana. *The Journal of Modern African Studies, 11*(1), 61–89. doi:10.1017/S0022278X00008089

Hart, K. (2010). Africa's urban revolution and the informal economy. In V. Padayachee (Ed.), *The Political Economy of Africa* (pp. 371–388). London, New York: Routledge.

Harvey, D. (2003). *The New Imperialism*. New York: Oxford University Press.

Harwood, M. (2005, April). Pinkertons at the CPA. *Washington Monthly*. Retrieved from http://www.washingtonmonthly.com/features/2005/0504.harwood.html

Hassan, B. J. (2009, June 22). Rwanda: Letter from Hassan B. Jallow to Kenneth Roth. Retrieved from http://reliefweb.int/report/rwanda/rwanda-letter-hassan-b-jallow-kenneth-roth-22-jun-2009

Hassan, H. (2012, July 16). A Bamascus loyalist defects as violence affects the tribes. *The National*. Retrieved from http://www.thenational.ae/thenationalconversation/comment/a-damascus-loyalist-defects-as-violence-affects-the-tribes

Hayek, F. (1991). *The Fatal Conceit: The Errors of Socialism*. Chicago: University of Chicago Press.

Hazan, P. (2009). Reconciliation. In V. Chetail (Ed.), *Post-Conflict Peacebuilding: A Lexicon* (pp. 256–266). Oxford: Oxford University Press.

Helsing, J. (2006). Young people's activism and the transition to peace. Bosnia, Northern Ireland and Israel. In S. McEvoy-Levy (Ed.), *Troublemakers or Peacemakers? Youth and post-accord peace building* (pp. 195–216). Notre Dame, IN: University of Notre Dame Press.

Hepner, T. R. (2009). Seeking Asylum in a Transnational Social Field. New Refugees and Struggles for Autonomy and Rights. In D. O'Kane & T. R. Hepner (Eds.), *Biopolitics, Militarism and Development. Eritrea in the Twenty-First Century* (pp. 115–133). New York: Berghahn.

Hersh, S. M. (2003, December 15). Moving Targets. Will the counter-insurgency plan in Iraq repeat the mistakes of Vietnam? *The New Yorker.*

Hessisch-Niedersächsische Allgemeine (HNA). (2014). Ruinen des Grauens.

Hessisch-Niedersächsische Allgemeine (HNA). (2014b). Jeder zweite hat genug von DDR-Geschichte.

Heydebrand, W. (2001). From Globalisation of Law to Law Under Globalisation. In D. Nelken, & J. Feest (Eds.), Adapting Legal Cultures (p. 119). Oxford: Hart.

Heym, S. (1984). Schwarzenberg, München: btb Verlag.

Hiltermann, J. (2010). *Kurds no closer to taking Kirkuk after Iraqi elections*. Foreign Policy. International crisis group. Retrieved from http://www.crisisgroup.org/en/regions/middle-east-north-africa/iraq-iran-gulf/iraq/kurds-no-closer-to-taking-kirkuk-after-iraqi-elections.aspx

Hiltermann, J. (2012). *A Kurdish Wedge between Iraq and Turkey*. International Crisis Group. Retrieved from http://www.crisisgroup.org/en/regions/middle-east-north-africa/iraq-iran-gulf/iraq/op-eds/hiltermann-a-kurdish-wedge-between-iraq-turkey.aspx

Hiltermann, J. (2012). *Ruling Baghdad*. The National Interest. Retrieved from http://nationalinterest.org/commentary/ruling-baghdad-3604

Hintjens, H. (2009). Reconstructing political identities in Rwanda. In P Clark, & Z.D. Kaufman (Eds.), After Genocide (pp. 82-85).

Hirsch, F. (1977). *Social Limits to Growth*. London: Routledge & Kegan Paul Ltd.

Hirschman, A. (1982). *Shifting Involvements: private interest and public action*. Princeton: Princeton University Press.

Hirschman, A. (2013). *The Essential Hirschman*. Princeton: Princeton University Press.

Hirt, N., & Mohammad, A. S. (2013). 'Dreams Don't Come True in Eritrea'. Anomie and Family Disintegration due to the Structural Militarization of Society. *The Journal of Modern African Studies*, *51*(1), 139–168. doi:10.1017/S0022278X12000572

Hoadley, S. (1996). *The 1995 NPT Conference: An Application of Zartman's multilateral negotiation theory* (The Australian National University, Research School of Pacific Studies, Peace Research Centre: Working Paper 164) Canberra: National Library of Australia.

Holguin, J. (2010). Communitarian Reintegration in DDR Programs: An Analysis of the Communitarian Component of the Reintegration Program in Colombia, 2002-2008 [Doctoral dissertation]. University of Notre Dame.

Holtmann, E., & Wiesenthal, H. (2009): *Transition. Transformation. Posttransformation.* Jena: SFB 580 Mitteilungen, 31.

Honwana, A. (2012). *The Time of Youth. Work, Social Change, and Politics in Africa*. Sterling, VA: Kumarian Press.

Horn, H. v. (2005). *Die Vereinten Nationen nach 60 Jahren: Ein Sanierungsfall? Mit Kriegseinsätzen zur neuen Welt-UN-Ordnung*. Retrieved from http://www.ag-friedensforschung.de/themen/UN-Reform/horn.html

Horst, C. (2006). *Transnational Nomads. How Somalis Cope with Refugee Life in the Dadaab Camps of Kenya*. New York, Oxford: Berghahn.

Houghton, J. (2008). Desterritorialización y pueblos indígenas. In J.Houghton (Ed.), *La tierra contra la muerte: Conflictos territoriales de los pueblos indígenas en Colombia*. Retrieved from http://observatorioetnicocecoin.org.co/cecoin/files/Tierra_contra_la_muerte.pdf

Howard, M. (2001). *The Franco-Prussian War*. London: Routledge.

Human Right Watch. (2006). *Iraq: Saddam Hussein Put to Death*. Retrieved from http://www.hrw.org/news/2006/12/29/iraq-saddam-hussein-put-death

Human Rights Watch. (2010). *Iraq's 2010 National Election, A human rights Platform for Candidates*. Retrieved from http://www.hrw.org/news/2010/02/25/iraq-s-2010-national-elections

Human Rights Watch. (2014, August). *South Sudan's New War: Abuses by Government and Opposition Forces*. Report. Retrieved from http://www.hrw.org/sites/default/files/reports/southsudan0814_ForUpload.pdf.>

Human Rights Watch. (2015). Rol de los altos mandos en Falsos positivos: evidencias de responsabilidad de generales y coroneles del Ejército Colombiano por ejecuciones de civiles. Human Rights Watch. Retrieved from http://www.eltiempo.com/contenido/politica/justicia/ARCHIVO/ARCHIVO-15997016-0.pdf

Huyssen, A. (2000). En busca del tiempo futuro. *Revista Puentes, 1*(2). Argentina.

Ibañez, A. M., & Muñoz, J. C. (2011). La persistencia de la concentración de la tierra en Colombia: ¿Qué pasó entre 2000 y 2010? *Notas de Política, (9).*

IEPRI. (2006). Nuestra guerra sin nombre. Transformaciones del conflicto en Colombia. Bogotá: Norma.

IFC. (2006). Founding declaration of the Congress of Freedom in Iraq (in French). Retrieved from http://solidariteirak.org/spip.php?article301

IMAB. (2005). Statement by the International Advisory and Monitoring Board on the Development Fund for Iraq, 23rd May.

IMAB. (2005). Statement by the International Advisory and Monitoring Board on the Development Fund for Iraq, 4th November.

Impunity Watch. (2012, November 12). Paramilitary Drug Gang Slaughters 10 Farmworkers. Retrieved from http://impunitywatch.com/paramilitary-drug-gang-slaughters-10-farmworkers/

Informe de la Comisión de Organismos de Derechos Humanos sobre la Masacre en la Ciénaga Grande de Santa Marta. (2000, December 22). Retrieved from http://www.derechos.org/nizkor/colombia/doc/cienaga.html

Instituto Colombiano de Bienestar Familiar. (2013). *Reparación con sentido. Guía pedagógica*. Bogotá: Author.

International Center for Transitional Justice (ICTJ). (2010). Indigenous Voices and Truth Commissions. Retrieved from https://www.ictj.org/sites/default/files/IPTC-March-2010-Meeting-Summary-Materials.pdf

International Center for Transitional Justice. (2012). Feature Series: Colombia's Justice and Peace Process. Retrieved from https://www.ictj.org/news/feature-series-colombia%E2%80%99s-justice-and-peace-process

International Center for Transitional Justices. Middle East and North Africa, Iraq (2012). *Background: A Repressive Recent History*. Retrieved from http://ictj.org/our-work/regions-and-countries/iraq

International Crisis Group. (2006, October 20). Tougher Challenges Ahead for Colombia's Uribe. *Latin America Briefing*, 11, 1-20. Retrieved from http://www.crisisgroup.org/en/regions/latin-america-caribbean/andes/colombia/b011-tougher-challenges-ahead-for-colombias-uribe.aspx

International Crisis Group. (2007, July 26). *A Strategy for Comprehensive Peace in Sudan*. Africa Report N°130.

International Crisis Group. (2009, March 26th). *Ending Colombia's FARC conflict: dealing the right card*. Retrieved from http://www.crisisgroup.org/~/media/Files/latin-america/colombia/30_ending_colombias_farc_conflict___dealing_the_right_card.pdf

International Crisis Group. (2013). *International Crisis Group: Eritrea. Scenarios for Future Transition*. Africa Report No. 200.

International Crisis Group. (2014, April 10). *South Sudan: A Civil War by Any Other Name*. Africa Report N°217.

International Crisis Group. (2015 July 27). *South Sudan: keeping Faith with the IGAD Peace Process*. Africa Report N°228.

International Crisis Group. (2104) *The Iraq's Jihadi Jack-in-the-Box*. Retrieved from http://www.crisisgroup.org/en/regions/middle-east-north-africa/iraq-iran-gulf/iraq/b038-iraq-s-jihadi-jack-in-the-box.aspx

International Crisis Group. Middle East Report N°12. (2012). *Iraq's Secular Opposition: The Rise and Decline of Al-Iraqiya*. Brussels/Baghdad. Retrieved from http://www.crisisgroup.org/en/regions/middle-east-north-africa/iraq-iran-gulf/iraq/127-iraqs-secular-opposition-the-rise-and-decline-of-al-iraqiya.aspx

International Organization for Migration. (2012). *Internal Displacement of Christian Families in Northern Iraq Subsides, Emigration rises*: IOM Report. Retrieved from http://www.iom.int/cms/en/sites/iom/home/news-and-views/press-briefing-notes/pbn-2012/pbn-listing/internal-displacement-of-christian-famil.html

International Republican Institute. (2014). *Survey of Cambodian Public Opinion*. Retrieved from http://www.iri.org/sites/default/files/Cambodian%20Poll%209%20Final%20PUBLIC.pdf

Iraq Body Count. (2012). *Documented civilian deaths from violence*. Retrieved from http://www.iraqbodycount.org/database/

Iraq Media, N. E. T. (2012). *Ministry of Planning announces unemployment rate reduced to 11%*. Retrieved from http://imn.iq/news/view.16192/

Iraq Revenue Watch. (2003). *Iraq Keeping Secrets: America and Iraq's public finances. Iraq Revenue Watch, report no. 3*. New York: Open Society Institute.

Iraqi Council of representative (2012). *Constitution*. Retrieved from http://parliament.iq/english/index.php?newlang=english

Isacson, A. (2012). *Consolidating Consolidation*. Washington: Washington Office on Latin America.

ITUC. (2011). International Trade Union Confederation, *2011 Annual Survey of violations of trade union rights - Iraq*. Retrieved from http://www.refworld.org/docid/4ea66205c.html

ITUC. (2012). International Trade Union Confederation, *2012 Annual Survey of Violations of Trade Union Rights – Iraq*. Retrieved from http://www.refworld.org/docid/4fd88946c.html

Iturralde, M. (2010). Democracies without Citizenship: Crime and Punishment in Latin America. *New Criminal Law Review: An International and Interdisciplinary Journal, 13(2)*. University of California Press. doi:10.1525/nclr.2010.13.2.309

Jabar, F. A. (2003). *The Shi'ite Movement in Iraq*. London: Saqi Books.

Jackson, M. (2006). *The Politics of Storytelling. Violence, Transgression and Intersubjectivity*. Copenhagen: Museum Tusculanum Press.

Jakob, T. E. (2014). The Islamic State in Iraq. The Key Lies in Baghdad (in German). Retrieved from http://www.fokus-nahost.de/?p=161360

Jelin, E. (2001). Los trabajos de la memoria. Madrid: Siglo XXI Editores.

Jelin, E. (2002). *Trabajos de la memoria*. Madrid: Siglo XXI Editores.

Jelin, E. (2007). Familiares, víctimas y ciudadan@s: Las luchas por la legitimidad de a palabra. *Cadernos Pagu, 29*, 37–60.

Jimenez Becerra, A., & Guerra García, F. (2009). Las luchas por la memoria. Bogotá: Instituto por la Pedagogía, la Paz y el Conflicto Urbano, IPAZUD, Universidad Distrital francisco José de Caldas.

Jiménez, Á., Silva, M., & Patiño, O. (2009, August 22). "Cano es el Pastrana de las Farc" Entrevista a Álvaro Jiménez, Mauricio Silva, Otty Patiño (J. León, Interviewer). Retrieved from http://lasillavacia.com/historia/3863

Johnson, D. H. (2011). Twentieth Century Civil Wars. In J. Ryle, J. Willis, & S. Baldo (Eds.), The Sudan Handbook (pp. 207-222). London: Rift Valley Institute.

Jones, N. (2014, October 7). Mail Online. Retrieved from http://www.dailymail.co.uk/home/moslive/article-2091670/Hitler-Stalin-The-murderous-regimes-world.html

Juba Declaration on Unity and Integration between the Sudan People's Liberation Army (SPLA) and the South Sudan Defence Forces (SSDF). (2006, January 8). Retrieved from http://www.peacemaker.un.org/sudan-juba-declaration2006.

Kadhem, F. J. (2012). *The Sacred and the Secular: The 'ulama of Najaf in Iraqi politics between 1950 and 1980* [Unpublished doctoral dissertation]. University of Exeter.

Kaës, R. (1996). *El sujeto y la herencia. Transmisión de la vida psíquica entre generaciones*. Buenos Aires: Amorrortu Editores.

Kagame, G. (2008). UN Security Council extends ICTR mandate. *New Times*, 1–2.

Kaldor, M. (2005). *New and Old Wars*. Cambridge: Polity.

Kalecki, M. (1971). *Selected Essays on the Dynamic of Capitalist Economy 1933-1970*. Boston: Cambridge University Press.

Kalyvas, S. (2006). *The Logic of Violence in Civil War*. Cambridge: Cambridge University Press. doi:10.1017/CBO9780511818462

Kamm, H. (2002). *Cambodia. Reports from a Stricken Land*. New York, NY: Arcade Publisher.

Kammler, J. (1985). Ich habe die Metzelei satt und laufe über ... Kasseler Soldaten zwischen Verweigerung und Widerstand (1939 – 1945); Kasseler Quellen und Studien, Schriftenreihe des Magistrats der Stadt Kassel 6, Fuldabrück: Hesse GmbH.

Kampfner, J (2003, May26). Blair Was Told it Would be Illegal to Occupy Iraq. New Statesman.

Kant, I. (1795). *Perpetual Peace: A Philosophical Sketch*. Retrieved from https://www.mtholyoke.edu/acad/intrel/kant/kant1.htm

Kant, I. (1963). *To perpetual peace: a philosophical sketch*. New York: Hackett Publishing.

Karger, A. (2012). Verzeihen – Reconciliation – Versöhnung. Versuch einer Differenzierung verschiedener Konzepte. In A. Karger (Ed.), *Vergessen, vergelten, vergeben, versöhnen? Weiterleben mit dem Trauma, Psychoanalytische Blätter 30*. Göttingen: Vandenhoeck & Ruprecht Verlag.

Katz, P. (2011). A new "normal" Political complicity: exclusionary violence and the delegation of Argentine Jewish associations during the Argentine dirty war. International Journal of Transitional Justice, 5(3).

Kaufman, A. (2015, June 19). Wake-up Call: Ami does his best Bibi impression [Video]. *972 Mag*. Retrieved from http://972mag.com/amik

Kaufman, S. (2006). *Lo legado y lo propio. Lazos familiares y transmisión de memorias. En Jelin, E. & Kaufman, S. (Comps). Subjetividad y figuras de la memoria*. Buenos Aires: Siglo XXI Editora Iberoamericana, Siglo XXI de España Editores.

Keane, J. (1996). *Reflections on Violence*. London: Verso.

Keck, M., & Sikkink, K. (1998). *Activists beyond Borders. Advocacy Networks in International Politics*. Cornell University.

Keen, D.; Berdal, M. (1997). Violence and Economic Agendas in Civil Wars: Some Policy Implications. *Millennium Journal of International Studies 26(3)*.795-818

Keen, D. (1998). *The Economic Functions of Civil Wars*. Oxford: Oxford University Press.

Keen, D. (2006). *Endless War? Hidden Functions of the War on Terror*. Ann Arbor: Pluto Press.

Kelly, C. (2004). The War on Jurisdiction: Troubling questions about Executive Order 13303. *Arizona Law Review*, *46*(483).

Kemper, Y. (2005). *Youth in war to peace transitions. Approaches of International Organizations*. Berlin: Berghof Research Center for Constructive Conflict Management.

Kerr, R. & Lincoln, J. (2007). *The Special Court for Sierra Leone: Outreach, Legacy, and Impact, Draft Interim Report*. War Crimes Research Group Department of War Studies, King's College London.

Keynes, J. M. (2003). *The General Theory of Employment, Interest and Money*. London: Macmillan.

Kibreab, G. (2004). Pulling the Wool over the Eyes of the Strangers. Refugee Deceit and Trickery in Institutionalized Settings. *Journal of Refugee Studies*, *17*(1), 1–26. doi:10.1093/jrs/17.1.1

Kibreab, G. (2009). Forced Labour in Eritrea. *The Journal of Modern African Studies*, *47*(1), 41–72. doi:10.1017/S0022278X08003650

Kiernan, B. (2005). *The Pol Pot Regime: Race, Power and Genocide in Cambodia under the Khmer Rouge 1975-1979*. New Haven: Yale University Press.

Kirk, J. (2010). Gender, forced migration and education. Identities and experiences of refugee women teachers. *Gender and Education*, *22*(2), 161–176. doi:10.1080/09540251003606925

Kitson, F. (1971). *Low Intensity Operations: Subversion, Insurgency, Peacekeeping*. London: Faber and Faber.

Knight, F. (1982). *Freedom and Reform: Essays in Economics and Social Philosophy*. Indianapolis: Liberty Fund.

Knörr, J. (2005). Introduction. In J. Knörr (Ed.), Childhood and Migration (pp. 9-21). Bielefeld: transcript.

Korol, C. (2011). La dimensión represiva y militar del modelo de desarrollo. In M. Palau (Ed.), *La dimensión represiva y militar del modelo de desarrollo*. Asunción, Paraguay: BASE-IS.

Kostelny, K. (2006). A culture-based, integrative approach. Helping war-affected children. In N. Boothby, A. Strang, & M. Wessells (Eds.), *A world turned upside down. Social ecological approaches to children in war zones* (pp. 19–38). United States of America: Kumarian Press, Inc.

Köttig, M. (2009). Die Bedeutung der intergenerationalen Weitergabe in Familien- und Lebensgeschichten rechtsextrem orientierter junger Frauen. In H. Radebold, W. Bohlleber, & J. Zinnecker (Eds.), *Transgenerationale Weitergabe kriegsbelasteter Kindheiten. Interdisziplinäre Studien zur Nachhaltigkeit historischer Erfahrungen über vier Generationen 2* (pp. 201–214). Weinheim, München: Beltz Juventa.

Kramer, A. E., & Robertson, C. (2008, September 10). Iraq Cancels Six No-Bid Oil Contracts. *New York Times*.

Kramer, R., & Michalowski, R. (2005). War, Aggression and State Crime. *The British Journal of Criminology*, *45*(4), 446–469. doi:10.1093/bjc/azi032

La Rosa, A.-M., & Philippe, X. (2009). Transitional Justice. In V. Chetail (Ed.), *Post-Conflict Peacebuilding: A Lexicon* (pp. 1–28). Oxford: Oxford University Press.

LabourNet UK. (2004). The 'Yellow' Unions in Saddam's Iraq. Workers Democratic Trade Union Movement (WDTUM) in Iraq. Retrieved from http://www.labournet.net/world/0408/ukiraq03.html

Lacapra, D. (2006). Historia en transito. Experiencia, identidad, teoría crítica. permanente Buenos Aires: Fondo de Cultura Económica de la Argentina.

Ladisch, V., & Ramirez-Barat, C. (2014). Between Protection and Participation: Involving Children and Youth in Transitional Justice Processes. In C. Ramirez-Barat (Ed.), *Transitional Justice, culture and society. Beyond outreach* (pp. 173–210). New York: Social Science Research Council.

Lafargue, P. (1989). *The Right to Be Lazy*. Chicago: Charles H. Kerr Publishing Company.

Lambourne, W. (2009). Transitional Justice and Peacebuilding after mass violence. *The International Journal of Transitional Justice*, *3*(1), 28–48. doi:10.1093/ijtj/ijn037

Laplante, L. (2010). Evaluating Truth Commissions and Reparations through the Eyes of Victims. *L'observateur des Nations Unies*, *28*(1), 167–176.

Laplante, L. (2012). Negotiating reparations rights: The participatory and symbolic quotients. *Buffalo Human Rights Law Review*, *19*, 217–250.

Laplante, L. J. (2011). Reviewed Work: Reconciliation(s): Transitional Justice in Postconflict Societies by Joanna R. Quinn. *Law & Society Review*, *45*(1), 230–232. doi:10.1111/j.1540-5893.2011.00433_5.x

Laplante, L., & Theidon, K. (2006). *Transitional Justice in times of conflict: Colombia's Ley de Justicia y Paz. Michigan Journal of International Law*, 49.

Latouche, S. (2010). *Farewell to Growth*. Cambridge: Polity Press.

Law 1448 de 2011. Ley de Víctimas y Restitución de Tierras. Decree 250 de 2004. Decree 2244 del 20 de junio de 2011. Decree 790, 20 Abril de 2012. Sentence T-025 de 2004.

Law 387 de julio of 1997. Por la cual se dictan medidas para la prevención de desplazamiento forzado; la atención, protección y estabilización socioeconómica de los desplazados internos por la violencia en Colombia.

Law 975 de 2005. (2005). Ley de Justicia y Paz

Lawson, A., & Halford, S. (2004). Fuelling Suspicion: the Coalition and Iraq's oil billions. London: Christian Aid.

Le Gac, D. (1991). *La Syrie du Général Assad*. Bruxelles: Éditions Complexe.

Lechner, N., & Güell, P. (2006). Construcción social de las memorias en la transición chilena. In Jelin, E. & Kaufman, S. (Comps). Subjetividad y figuras de la memoria. Ciudad Autónoma de Buenos Aires: Siglo XXI Editora Iberoamericana.

Lederach, J. (1997). *Building Peace: Sustainable Reconciliation in Divided Societies*. Washington, DC: United States Institute of Peace.

Lederach, J. (2005). *Moral Imagination: the art and soul of building peace*. New York: Oxford University Press. doi:10.1093/0195174542.001.0001

Lemke, T. (2005). A Zone of Indistinction – A Critique of Giorgio Agamben's Concept of Biopolitics, Outlines. *Critical Social Studies*, *7*(1), 9.

León, J. (2013, April 24). *¿Se consolida el poder militar en el Programa de Consolidación?* Retrieved from http://lasillavacia.com/node/43873

León, J. (2005). *País de Plomo. Crónicas de la guerra*. Bogota: Aguilar.

Lesa, F. (2011). *Beyond Transitional Justice: Exploring continuities in Human Rights Abuses in Argentina between 1976 and 2010. Journal of Human Rights Practice, 3(1), 25-48*. Oxford University Press.

Leverrier, I. (2014). *Joumana Maarouf's Letters from Syria*. Retrieved from http://syrie.blog.lemonde.fr/2014/04/08/les-lettres-de-syrie-de-joumana-maarouf-en-librairie/

Lewison, R. (1936). *The Profits of War through the Ages*. London: George Routledge and Sons Ltd.

Lichterbeck, P. (2009). *Der Aufbruch von Kigali* (p. 5). Der Tagesspiegel.

Liempt, I. v. (2007). *Navigating Borders. Inside Perspectives on the Process of Human Smuggling into the Netherlands*. Amsterdam: Amsterdam University Press. doi:10.5117/9789053569306

Lijphart, A. (1977). *Democracy in Plural Societies. A Comarative Exploration*. London: Yale University Press.

Lindell, I. (2010). Introduction. The changing politics of informality – collective organizing, alliances and scales of engagement. In I. Lindell (Ed.), *Africa's informal workers. Collective agency, alliances and transnational organizing in urban Africa* (pp. 1–32). London, New York: Zed Books.

Lindemann, T. (2008). Faucons et Colombes. Le Choix Stratégique des Forces Armées entre Intérêt Corporatiste et Identités Militaires. *Revue Internationale de Politique Comparée*, *1/15*(1), 55–76. doi:10.3917/ripc.151.0055

Linz, J. J. (2000). *Totalitarian and Authoritarian Regimes*. Boulder, London: Lynne Rienner Publishers.

Lipset, S. M., & Rokkan, S. (1967). *Party Systems and Voter Alignments. Cross-National Perspectives*. New York: Free Press.

Llewellyn, J., & Philpott, D. (2014). *Restorative Justice, Reconciliation and Peacebuilding*. New York: Oxford University Press. doi:10.1093/acprof:oso/9780199364862.001.0001

Longman, T. (2008). Justice at the grassroots? Gacaca trials in Rwanda. In N. Roht-Arriaza & J. Mariezcurrena (Eds.), *Transitional justice in the twenty-first century. Beyond truth versus justice* (pp. 206–228). Cambridge.

Lüdeke, F. (2012). *'Der weibliche Flüchtling' zwischen Bild und Aushandlung: Eine Feldforschung in Shimelba/Äthiopien* [MA Thesis]. Bayreuth University, Germany

Luizard, P.-J. (2002). *La question irakienne*. Paris: Fayard.

Lund, A. (2012). *Syrian Jihadism. UIbrief, 13*. Stockholm: Swedish Institute of International Affairs.

Luxemburg, R. (1951). *The Accumulation of Capital*. London: Routledge and Kegan Paul.

Lyderson, K. (2010). Iraqi Electricity Union Offices Raided Under Minister's Draconian Decree. Retrieved from https://www.globalpolicy.org/political-issues-in-iraq/oil-in-iraq/49337-iraqi-electricity-union-offices-raided-under-ministers-draconian-decree.html

Maalouf, A. (2004). *Identidades asesinas* (F. Villaverde, Trans.). Madrid: Alianza Editorial.

Machado Aráoz, H. (2013). En las encrucijadas del extractivismo: gobiernos progresistas vs. movimientos del Buen Vivir y el (eco)socialismo del siglo XXI. *Revista Herramienta, (53)*. Retrieved from http://www.herramienta.com.ar/autores/machado-araoz-horacio

Maddison, A. (2001, April 1). The World Economy: A Millennial Perspective. *The Unbroken window.com*. Retrieved from http://theunbrokenwindow.com/Development/MADDISON%20The%20World%20Economy--A%20Millennial.pdf

Maddison, A. (2014 November 1). World Economy. Retrieved from http://www.theworldeconomy.org/

Maher, D., & Thomson, A. (2011). The terror that underpins the ´peace:´ the political economy of Colombia's paramilitary demobilization process. In E. Herring, & D. Stokes (Eds.), Critical studies on terrorism, 4(1), 95-113.

Malamud-Goti, J. (1995). Punishing Human Rights Abuses in fledgling democracies: The case of Argentina. In N. Roht-Arriaza (Ed.), Impunity and Human Rights in International Law and Practice (pp. 160-170). Oxford University Press.

Maldonado, C. E., & Gómez-Cruz, N.(2015).Biological Hypercomputation: A New Research Problem in Complexity Theory.Complexity, 20(4), 8-18.

Maldonado, C. E. (2002). *Filosofía de la sociedad civil*. Bogotá: Siglo del Hombre Editores.

Maldonado, C. E., & Gómez-Cruz, N. (2012). The Complexification of Engineering. *Complexity*, *17*(4), 8–15. doi:10.1002/cplx.20395

Maldonado, C. E., & Gómez-Cruz, N. A. (2014). Synchronicity Among Biological and Computational Levels of an Organism: Quantum Biology and Complexity. *Procedia Computer Science*, *36*, 177–184. doi:10.1016/j.procs.2014.09.076

Malkasian, C., & Marston, D. (2008). Counterinsurgency in Modern Warfare. Oxford: Osprey.

Malkki, L. (1995). *Purity and exile. Violence, memory, and national cosmology among Hutu refugees in Tanzania*. Chicago: University of Chicago Press.

Mannes, A. (2004). *Profiles in terror: the Guide to Middle East Terrorist Organizations*. Lanham: Rowan and Littlefield.

Manrique Gil, M. (2014, March). South Sudan: The Roots and Prospects of a Multifaceted Crisis. European Parliament, Directorate-General for External Policies DG EXPO/B/PolDep/Note/2014_55.

Mapping Militant Organizations Project. (2012). *Iraq*. Retrieved from http://www.stanford.edu/group/mappingmilitants/cgi-bin/maps/view/iraq

Marcus, H. (1994). *A History of Ethiopia*. Berkeley: University of California Press.

Margulis, L., & Sagan, D. (2003). *Acquiring Genomes: A Theory of the Origin of Species*. New York: Basic Books.

Marle, V. (2007) Constitution as Archive. In S. Veitch (Ed.), Law and the Politics of Reconciliation. Hampshire, England: Ashgate.

Marr, P. (1970). Iraq's Leadership Dilemma: A Study in Leadership Trends. *The Middle East Journal*, *24*(3), 283–301.

Marr, P. (2004). *The Modern History of Iraq*. Boulder: Westview Press.

Marteen, D., & Zambrano, M. (2010). Citizenship Deferred: The politics of Victimhood, Land Restitution and Gender Justice in the Colombian (Post?) Conflict. International Journal of Transitional Justice, 4(2), 189-206.

Marx, K. (1973). *Manifiesto of the Communist Party*. New York: Inter Publisher.

Marx, K. (1990). *Capital* (Vol. I). St. Ives, England: Penguin.

Marx, K. (1993). *The Capital: A Critique of Political Economy* (Vol. 3). New York: Penguin Classics.

Massé, F., & Camargo Castro, J. (2013). Actores armados ilegales y procesos de restitución y reclamación de tierras: VI informe del área de DDR 2013. Retrieved from http://www.verdadabierta.com/documentos/negocios-ilegales/tierras/1139-informe-actores-armados-ilegales-y-procesos-de-restitucion-y-recuperacion-de-tierras-centro-internacional-de-toledo-para-la-paz

Mattei, U. (2003). A Theory of Imperial Law: A study on U.S. hegemony and the Latin resistance. *Global Jurist Frontiers*, *3*(2), 4. doi:10.2202/1535-1653.1088

Mayumi, K. (2012). *The Origin of Ecological Economics: The Bioeconomics of Georgescu-Roegen*. New York: Routledge.

Mazurana, D., & Carlson, K. (2010). *Children and reparation: past lessons and new directions*. Innocenti Working Paper, UNICEF, Florence.

Mazurana, D., & Carlson, K. (2009). Reparations as a Means for Recognizing and Addressing Crimes and Grave Rights Violations against Girls and Boys during Situations of Armed Conflict and under Authoritarian and Dictatorial Regimes. In R. Rubio-Marín (Ed.), *The Gender of Reparations: Unsettling Sexual Hierarchies While Redressing Human Rights Violations* (pp. 162–214). Cambridge: Cambridge University Press. doi:10.1017/CBO9780511596711.007

Mbembe, A. (2001). *On the Postcolony*. Berkeley: University of California Press.

McDermott, J. (2013, May 20). *Actividades Criminales de las FARC y las Ganancias de la Guerrilla*. InSight Crime. Retrieved from http://es.insightcrime.org/investigaciones/actividades-criminales-farc-y-ganancias-de-la-guerrilla

McEvoy-Levy, S. (2006). Conclusion. Youth and post-accord peace building. In S. McEvoy-Levy (Ed.), *Troublemakers or Peacemakers? Youth and post-accord peace building* (pp. 281–305). Notre Dame, IN: University of Notre Dame Press.

McEvoy-Levy, S. (2006). Introduction: youth and the post-accord environment. In S. McEvoy-Levy (Ed.), *Troublemakers or Peacemakers? Youth and post-accord peace building* (pp. 1–26). Notre Dame, IN: University of Notre Dame Press.

McGarry, J., & O'Leary, B. (2008). Iraq's constitution of 2005: Liberal Consociation as political prescription. In S. Choudhry (Ed.), *Constitutional design for divided societies: integration of accommodation?* Oxford: Oxford University press.

Meconnen, D. R., & Estefanos, M. (2011). *From Sawa to the Sinai Desert. The Eritrean Tragedy of Human Trafficking*. Discussion Paper. Retrieved from http://ssrn.com/abstract=2055303

Medina Gallego, C. (1990). *Autodefensas, Paramilitares y Narcotraficantes en Colombia*. Bogotá: Editorial Documentos Periodísticos.

Meek, S., & Malan, M. (2004). Identifying lessons from DDR experiences in Africa: workshop report. *Institute for Security Studies* (Monograph 106).

Meertens, D. (2004). Género, Desplazamiento, Derechos. In M. N. Bello (Ed.), *Desplazamiento forzado. Dinámicas de guerra, exclusión y desarraigo*. Bogotá: Universidad Nacional de Colombia.

Meiksins-Wood, E. (1998). The Agrarian Origins of Capitalism. *Monthly Review (New York, N.Y.)*, *50*(3), 14. doi:10.14452/MR-050-03-1998-07_2

Meiksins-Wood, E. (2003). *Empire of Capital* (pp. 97–99). London: Verso.

Meir, G. (1969, June 15). Interview. *Sunday Times*, 4.

Melish, T. (2010). Maximum Feasible Participation of the Poor: New Governance, New Accountability, and a 21st Century War on the Sources of Poverty. *Yale Human Rights and Development Law Journal*, *13*(1), 1–134.

Memorandum of Understanding between the Government of the Republic of Indonesia and the Free Aceh Movement. (2005). Retrieved from http://news.bbc.co.uk/2/shared/bsp/hi/pdfs/15_08_05_aceh.pdf

Merleau-Ponty, M. (1979). *Le Visible et l'Invisible, followed by Notes de Travail*. Paris: Gallimard. (Original work published 1964)

Merom, G. (2003). *How Democracies lose Small Wars*. Cambridge: Cambridge University Press. doi:10.1017/CBO9780511808227

Merry, S. (2007). *The practice of human rights: tracking law between the global and the local*. New York: Cambridge University Press.

Mesa de Trabajo Mujer y Conflicto Armado. (2006). *Memoria de mujeres. Guía para documentar y hacer visible el impacto de la violencia contra mujeres, jóvenes y niñas, en contextos de conflicto armado*. Bogotá: Ediciones Antropos.

Mesa Mujer y Conflicto armado. Informe sobre la violencia sociopolitical contra mujeres, jóvenes y niñas en Colombia (2005, November). Retrieved from http://www.coljuristas.org/documentos/libros_e_informes/v_informe_mesa_mujer_y_conflicto.pdf

Metals Economic Group. (2012). Tendencias de la exploración mundial 2012. Retrieved from http://www.convencionminera.com/perumin31/images/perumin/recursos/OLD/Exploraci%d0%b2n%20MEG%20Tendencias%20de%20la%20exploraci%d0%b2n%20mundial.pdf

Miano, M. (2013). Toward a Child-Oriented Approach to Reparations: Reflecting on the Rights and Needs of Child Victims of Armed Conflict. *PRAXIS The Fletcher Journal of Human Security*, *28*, 28–45.

Michaud, G. (pseudonym for Seurat, M.). (1983). L'État de Barbarie: Syrie 1979-1982. *Esprit (Paris, France)*, (November): 16–30.

Michaud, Y. (2012). *La Violence* (7th ed.). Paris: PUF.

Mignorance, F. (2006). The flow of palm oil Colombia / Belgium/ Europe. A study from human Rights perspective. Human Rights Everywhere. Retrieved from http://www.cbc.collectifs.net/doc/informe_en_v3-1.pdf

Ministerio de Defensa Nacional. (2007). *Politica de Consolidacion de la Seguridad Democratica*. Bogota: Ministerio de Defensa Nacional.

Ministerio de Defensa Nacional. Republica de Colombia (2006). Programa de Atención Humanitaria para el desmovilizado. Retrieved from https://www.mindefensa.gov.co

Ministerio de Hacienda. (2014). *Proyecto Presupuesto General de la Nación*. Retrieved from www.minhacienda.gov.co/HomeMinhacienda(presupuestogeneraldelanacion/ProyectoPGN/2014

Mishan, E. (1993). *The Cost of Economic Growth* (Revised Edition). London: Praeger Publishers.

Monbiot, G. (2013, March 11). My search for a smartphone that is not soaked in blood. *The Guardian*. Retrieved from http://www.theguardian.com/commentisfree/2013/mar/11/search-smartphone-soaked-blood

Morel, A., Wratanabe, M., & Wrobe, R. (2009). Delivering assistance to conflict-affected communities: the BRA-KDP program in Aceh. *World Bank*. Retrieved from http://documentos.bancomundial.org/curated/es/2009/12/12022794/delivering-assistance-conflict-affected-communities-bra-kdp-program-aceh

Morris, L. (2014). A letter from Sistani turned the tide against Iraq's leader. *Washington Post*. Retrieved from http://www.washingtonpost.com/world/middle_east/a-letter-from-sistani-turned-the-tide-against-iraqs-leader/2014/08/13/3b3426cf-60ee-4856-ad26-d01a9c6cc9c3_story.html

Morrow, J. (2005). *Iraq's Constitutional Process II. A Lost Opportunity. Special Report 155*. Washington, DC: United States Institute of Peace.

Muesi, F. (2008, September6). Rwanda's input to solve part of UNAMID's problems – Karake. *New Times*, •••, 3.

Muhsin, A. (2003). Address of the UK Representative of the Workers' Democratic Trade Unions of Iraq before the TUC in Sheffield on 23.09.2003 [Speech]. Retrieved from http://www.labournet.net/ukunion/0310/shefftuc1.html

Multi-Stakeholder Review. (2009). *Multi-Stakeholder Review of Post-Conflicting in Aceh – Identifying the Foundations for Sustainable Peace and Development in Aceh* (Vol. 2). Washington, DC: World Bank.

Munive, J. (2013). Disarmament, Demobilisation and Reintegration in South Sudan: The Limits of Conventional Peace and Security Templates. Danish Institute for International Studies, 2013:07.

Munive, J. (2013). Context Matters: The Conventional DDR Template is Challenged in South Sudan. *International Peacekeeping*, *20*(5), 559–599. doi:10.1080/13533312.2013.853962

Munkler, H. (2006). *The New Wars*. Cambridge: Polity.

Murray, J. (1986). Understanding Competing theories of negotiation. Negotiation Journal, 1986(April). Retrieved from http://repository.law.ttu.edu/bitstream/handle/10601/1634/Negotiations.pdf?sequence=1

Mustill, L. J. (1988). The New Lex Mercatoria: The first twenty five years. *Arbitration International*, *4*(2), 86–119. doi:10.1093/arbitration/4.2.86

Mutara, E. (2009, March 7). 156 genocide survivors and witnesses killed. The New Times.

Nader, L. (2005). The Americanisation of International Law. In F. von Benda-Beckman, K. von Benda-Beckman, & A. Griffiths (Eds.), Mobile People, Mobile Law: expanding legal relations in a contracting world (pp. 200-201). Aldershot: Ashgate.

Nader, L. (2007). Promise or Plunder? A Past and Future Look at Law and Development.Global Jurist, 7(1).

Nakash, Y. (1996). *The Shi'is of Iraq*. Princeton: Princeton University Press.

Nasi, C. (2006). Spoilers in Colombia: Actors and Strategies. In E. Newman & O. Richmond (Eds.), *Challenges to peacebuilding: Managing spoilers during conflict resolution* (pp. 219–241). Tokyo, New York: United Nations University Press.

Nasr, V. (2006). *The Shia Revival. How Conflicts within Islam will shape the Future*. New York: W. W. Norton & Company.

National Platform for Peace and Reconciliation (NPPR). (2014, April). Retrieved from http://www.reconciliation-southsudan.org/index.php?option=com_content&view=featured&Itemid=101.

Natsios, A. S. (2012). *Sudan, South Sudan & Darfur: What Everyone Needs to Know*. New York: Oxford University Press.

Navias, M., & Moreman, T. (1994). Limited War and Developing Countries. In L. Freedman (Ed.), *War* (pp. 310–314). Oxford: Oxford University Press.

Neebe, R. (1981). Großindustrie, Staat und NSDAP 1930-1933. Göttingen: Vandenhoeck + Ruprecht GmbH.

Netz-gegen-Nazis.de. (n. d.). Data from the Website. Retrieved from http://www.netz-gegen-nazis.de/artikel/rechtsextremismus-zahlen-755

Newman, E., & Richmon, O. (2006). Introduction. Obstacles to peace processes: Understanding spoiling. In E. Newman, & O. Richmon (Eds.), Challenges to peacebuilding: managing spoilers during conflict resolution (pp. 1-19). New York: United Nations University.

Ngoga, M. (2008). The institutionalisation of impunity: A judicial perspective on the Rwandan Genocide. In P. Clark & Z. D. Kaufman (Eds.), *After genocide: Transitional justice, post-conflict reconstruction and reconciliation in Rwanda and beyond, London* (pp. 326–327). Hurst.

Nietzsche, F. (2003). *Beyond Good and Evil*. New York: Penguin Classics.

No Author. (2011). Syrian Tribes Start Creating Unrest. Sheikhs are Using Force to Oppress the Youth. *Al-Sharq al-Awsat*. Retrieved from http://www.aawsat.com/details.asp?section=4&article=647031&issueno=12021

Nosworthy, D. (Ed.). (2009). *Seen, but not Heard: Placing Children and Youth on the Security Governance Agenda*. Zurich: LIT Verlag.

Nouwen, S. (2006). Hybrid courts: The Hybrid Category of a New Type of International Crimes Courts. *Utrecht Law Review*, *2*(2), 190–214. doi:10.18352/ulr.32

Nussio, E., & Howe, K. (2010). What if the FARC Demobilizes? *International Journal Stability of Security and Development*, *1*(1), 58–67. doi:10.5334/sta.aj

Nye, J. (2007). *Understanding international conflicts an Introduction to Theory and History* (6th ed.). New York, London: PEARSON/ LONGMAN.

O'leary, B. (2009). How to Get Out of Iraq with Integrity. Pennsylvania: University of Pennsylvania Press.

O'Neill, B. (1980). *Insurgency in the Modern World*. Boulder: Westview Press.

Oberti, A. (2006). La memoria y sus sombras. In E. Jelin & S. Kaufman (Eds.), *Comps). Subjetividad y figuras de la memoria*. Buenos Aires: Siglo XXI Editora Iberoamericana, Siglo XXI de España Editores.

Observatorio Nacional de Desplazamiento Forzado. (2010). *Dinámica del desplazamiento forzado*. Retrieved from Agencia Presidencial para la Acción Social y la Cooperación Internacional: www.dps.gov.co/documentos/Retornos/Informe%20Desplazamiento%20Forzado%a%20Junio%202010.pdf

Oette, L. (2011). Law Reform in Times of Peace Processes and Transitional Justice: The Sudanese Dimension. In L. Oette (Ed.), *Criminal Law Reform and Transitional Justice, Human Rights Perspectives for Sudan* (pp. 11–31). Surrey, UK: Ashgate.

Office of the United Nations High Commissioner for Human Rights. (2008). *Rule of Law Tools for Post-conflict States: Maximizing the Legacy of Hybrid Courts*. Doc. E.08.XIV.12.

Onay, A. (2008, February 21) PKK Criminal Networks and Fronts in Europe. *Policy Watch No. 1344*. Washington: The Washington Institute.

Online, R. P. (2010). BdV hat nur noch rund 550.000 Mitglieder. Retrieved from http://www.rp-online.de/politik/deutschland/bdv-hat-nur-noch-rund-550000-mitglieder-aid-1.478970

Open Society Justice Initiative. (2010). *Salvaging Judicial Independence: the Need for a Principled Completion Plan for the Extraordinary Chambers in the Courts of Cambodia*. Retrieved from http://www.opensocietyfoundations.org/reports/salvaging-judicial-independence-need-principled-completion-plan-extraordinary-chambers-courts

Open Society Justice Initiative. (2012). *The Future of Cases 003/004 at the Extraordinary Chambers in the Courts of Cambodia*. Retrieved from http://www.opensocietyfoundations.org/sites/default/files/eccc-report-cases3and4-100112_0.pdf

OpenStax. (2014 November 28). World Energy Use. Retrieved from http://cnx.org/contents/031da8d3-b525-429c-80cf-6c8ed997733a@8.9:51/College_Physics

Orentlicher, D. (2005). Conjunto de principios actualizado para la protección y la promoción de los derechos humanos mediante la lucha contra la impunidad.

Orentlicher, D. (1991). Settling Accounts: The Duty to Prosecute Human Rights Violations of a Prior Regime. *The Yale Law Journal*, *100*(8), 2537–2615. doi:10.2307/796903

Orentlicher, D. (2007). Settling Accounts Revisited: Reconciling Global Norms with Local Agency. *International Journal of Transitional Justice*, *1*(1), 10–22. doi:10.1093/ijtj/ijm010

Ospina, C. (2006). Insights from Colombia's Long War: Counterinsurgency Lessons Learned. *Journal of Counterterrorism and Homeland Security International*, *12*(3), 26–33.

OXFAM International. (2014, January 20). Working for the Few: Political Capture and Economic Inequality. Retrieved from http://www.oxfam.org/sites/www.oxfam.org/files/file_attachments/bp-working-for-few-political-capture-economic-inequality-200114-en_3.pdf

Oxfam. (2013). *Divide y comprarás: una nueva forma de concentrar tierras baldías en Colombia*. Retrieved from http://oxf.am/Uzh#sthash.x6szVnXf.dpuf

Palau, T., Cabello, D., Maeyens, A., Rulli, J., & Segovia, D. (2009). Los Refugiados del Modelo Agro Exportador (2nd ed.). Asunción: BASE-IS.

Palau, M. (2009). Gobierno de Lugo: ¿Escenario de construcción de alternativas? In L. Rojas Villagra (Ed.), *Gobierno Lugo: herencia, gestión y desafíos*. Asunción: BASE-IS.

Palma, O. (2015). Transnational Networks of Insurgency and Crime: Explaining the spread of commercial insurgencies beyond national borders. *Small Wars & Insurgencies*, *26*(3), 476–496. doi:10.1080/09592318.2014.982885

Panezi, M. (2007). Source of Law in Transition: re-visiting general principles of international law. *Ancilla Iuris*, 66-79.

Pardo, R. (2004). *Historia de las Guerras*. Bogota: Ediciones B.

Parker, N., & Salman, R. (2013). Notes from the Underground: The Rise of Nouri al-Maliki and the New Islamists. *World Policy Journal*, *30*(1), 63–76. doi:10.1177/0740277513482618

Passerini, L. (2006). *Memoria y utopía. La primacía de la intersubjetividad* (1st ed.). España: Publicacions de la Universitat de València.

Peacaut, D. (1978). Orden y Violencia en Colombia 1930-1954. Bogotá. CEREC. Siglo XXI.

Peace and Reconciliation Commission Act of 2012. (2012 May 4). Retrieved from http://www.peacecommission.org/wp-content/uploads/2014/03/Peace-and-Reconciliation-Commission-Act-2012.pdf.

Peace Delegation, F. A. R. C.-E. P. (n. d.). *Why we decided to negotiate with Santos*. Retrieved from http://www.pazfarc-ep.org/index.php/cronologia

Pecaut, D. (1997). *Pasado, presente y futuro de la violencia. Análisis Político. No 30*. Enero-Abril.

People's World. (2006). Gripping narrative of an Iraqi trade unionist. Retrieved from http://www.peoplesworld.org/gripping-narrative-of-an-iraqi-trade-unionist/

Perafán, C., Azcárate, L., & Zea, H. (2000). *Sistema jurídicos, tukano, chamí, guambiano, sikuani*. Bogotá: Arfos Ltda.

Peters, G. (2009a). The Taliban and the Opium Trade. In A. Giustozzi (Ed.), *Decoding the Taliban: Insights from the Afghan Field* (pp. 7–22). New York: Columbia University Press.

Peters, G. (2009b). *How opium profits the Taliban*. Washington: United States Institute of Peace.

Pfetsch, F. R. (2006). *Verhandeln in Konflikten. Grundlage – Theorie – Praxis*. Wiesbaden: VS Verlag für Sozialwissenschaften.

Pham, P., Vinck, P., & Hen, S. (2011). *After the first trial: a Population based Survey on Knowledge and Perceptions of Justice and the ECCC*. Berkley University Human Rights Centre.

Picture 1 - http://www.move-magazin.eu/wp-content/uploads/2011/07/Kniefall-von-Warschau-Copyright-Deutscher-Bundestag.jpg, 20.09.2014

Pie de fuerza militar llegó a su techo. (2009, January 30). *El Tiempo. Bogotá*. Retrieved from http://www.eltiempo.com/archivo/documento/CMS-4785562

Piot, Ch. (2010). Border Practices. In A.-M. Makhulu, B. Buggenhagen, & S. Jackson (Eds.), Hard Work, Hard Times. Global Volatility and African Subjectivities (pp. 150-164). Berkeley, & Los Angeles: University of California Press.

Pizarro Leongómez, E. (2011). *Las Farc (1949-2011): De guerrilla campesina máquina de guerra*. Bogotá: Edtorial Norma.

Pizarro Loengómez, E. (2011). *Las Farc (1949-2011). De guerilla campesina a maquinaria de guerra*. Bogota: Editorial Norma.

Polanyi, K. (2001). *The Great Transformaton: The Poltical and Economic Origins of our Time*. Boston: Beacon Press.

Pollak, M. (1992). Memoria e identidad social. In memoria, olvido, silencio. La producción social de identidades frente a situaciones límites. Introducción Ludmila da Silva Catela (2006). La Plata: Buenos Aires: Ediciones Al Margen.

Pontón, E. (2014). Crítica a los mecanismos institucionales de reparación a víctimas indígenas – Caso de análisis: el Pueblo Wayuu. Repositorio institucional Universidad del Rosario. Bogotá.

Popper, K. (1945). The Open Society and its Enemies. London: Routledge.

Posso, C. M. (2004). Alternatives to War: Colombia's Peace Process. Conciliation Resources. Retrieved from http://www.c-r.org/accord-article/negotiations-farc-1982-2002

Presidential Decree No. 03/2013. (2013, April 15). RSS/RO/J/03/2013. Retrieved from http://www.sudantribune.com/IMG/pdf/presidential_decree_reducing_powers_of_the_vp.pdf.

Presidential Decree No. 04/2013. (2013, April 15). RSS/RO/J/04/2013. Retrieved from http://www.sudantribune.com/IMG/pdf/presidential_decree_reducing_powers_of_the_vp.pdf.

Presidential Decree No. 49/2013. (2013, July 23). RSS/RD/J/49/2013. Retrieved from http://www.gurtong.net/LinkClick.aspx?fileticket=ZOejD0c-c1w%3d&tabid=124.

Presidential Decree No. 50/2013. (2013, July 23). RSS/RD/J/50/2013. Retrieved from http://www.gurtong.net/LinkClick.aspx?fileticket=7cD-9Y4z904%3d&tabid=124.

Proexport Colombia. (2014). *Inversión en el sector de Biocombustibles en Colombia*. Retrieved from www.inviertaencolombia.com.co

Proposed Compromise Agreement on the Resolution of the Conflict in the Republic of South Sudan. Retrieved from http://southsudan.igad.int.

Pruitt, D. G., & Kim, S. H. (2004). *Social Conflict. Esclation, Stalemate, and Settlement*. Boston: McGraw-Hill.

Prunier G. (2008). *The Rwanda crisis: History of a genocide* (6th ed., p. 312). London: Colombia University Press.

Prunier, G. (2009). *From genocide to continental war. The 'Congolese' conflict and the crisis of contemporary Africa*. London: Hurst & Co.

Pueblo Arhuaco. (2011). *Posisición del Pueblo Arhuaco frente al Decreto Ley 4633 – Ley de Victimas Indígenas-*. Documento elaborado en el kadukwu de Me'chacha, Noviembre.

Pueblo Arhuaco. (2012). *Normas y criterios generales del Pueblo Arhuaco*. Documento aprobado en Asamblea General del Pueblo Arhuaco, Agosto.

Pueblo Arhuaco. (2012a). *Fundamento tradicional y cultural del Pueblo Arhuaco (Política General)*. Documento aprobado en Asamblea General del Pueblo Arhuaco, Agosto.

Pueblo Arhuaco. (2012b). *Documento Arhuaco frente a la consulta del Proyecto de Ley de Tierras y Desarrollo Rural*. Documento elaborado por el Equipo Coordinador de la Consulta Previa de Ley de Tierras y Desarrollo Rural.

Pueblo Arhuaco. (2013). *Consideraciones de los Directivos del Pueblo Arhuaco frente al documento expedido por autoridades del Pueblo Kankuamo*. Documento elaborado por las Directiva General del Pueblo *Arhuaco*, Agosto.

Pugel, J. (2009). Measuring Reintegration in Liberia: Assessing the Gap between Outputs and Outcome. In R. Muggah (Ed.), *Security and Post-Conflict Reconstruction: Dealing with Fighters in the Aftermath of War* (p. 90). Abingdon, Great Britain: Routledge.

Quartz. (2014). Victims of Colombia's Conflict Fight to be Recognized as such. Retrieved from http://qz.com/274647/victims-of-colombias-conflict-fight-to-be-recognized-as-such/

Quehl, H. (2005). *Kämpferinnen und Kämpfer im eritreischen Unabhängigkeitskrieg 1961-1991. Faktoren der Diversität und der Koherenz. Eine historische Untersuchung zur Alltagsgeschichte des Krieges*. Felsberg: Edition Eins.

Quehl, H. (2014). Interviews - All interviews were conducted by the author in May 2014.

Quehl, H. (2003). Oral History on War. Tagadelti in and after Eritrea's War of Independence. In E.-M. Bruchhaus (Ed.), *Hot Spot Horn of Africa. Between Integration and Disintegration* (pp. 136–147). Münster: LIT.

Quehl, H. (2013). Zum Umbau von Kriegsgesellschaften. Eritrea, Kurdistan und Nicaragua zwischen Pragmatismus, Isolation und Assimilation. In B. Greiner, T. Müller, & K. Voß (Eds.), *Erbe des Kalten Krieges. Studien zum Kalten Krieg* (Vol. 6, pp. 480–498). Hamburg: Hamburger Edition.

Racines, K. (2014). Minería ilegal en Colombia. *Semana Sostenible*, 22-23.

Radtke, K. (2006). Die Finanzierung von Bürgerkriegen aus der Diaspora. Eritreer in Frankfurt und Tamilen in Toronto. In K. Inhetveen (Ed.), *Flucht als Politik. Berichte von fünf Kontinenten* (pp. 163–182). Köln: Köppe.

Rae, J. (2010). *The sociological theory of capital, being a complete reprint of the new principles of political economy, 1834*. New York: Nabu Press.

Raghavan, L. (2014). *Mahatma Gandhi and Buddha's Path to Enlightenment*. Washington: Theosophy Trust Books.

Raisbeck, D. (2014, June 3). *Con Santos o con Zuluaga, la guerra contra las drogas garantiza el fracaso de las negociaciones de paz*. Retrieved from http://es.panampost.com/daniel-raisbeck/2014/06/03/con-santos-o-con-zuluaga-la-guerra-contra-las-drogas-garantiza-el-fracaso-de-las-negociaciones-de-paz/

Ramírez-Barat, C. (2012). *Engaging children and youth in transitional justice processes: guidance for outreach programs*. New York: International Center for transitional Justice.

Raphael, S. (2010). Paramilitarism and state terrorism in Colombia. In R. Jackson, E. Murphy, & S. Poynting (Eds.), *Contemporary state terrorism: theory and practice*. London: Routledge.

Rashid, A. (2002). *Los Taliban*. Barcelona: Ediciones Peninsula.

Rayburn, J. (2014). *Iraq after America: Strongmen, Sectarians, Resistance*. Washington, DC: Hoover Institution Press.

Reátegui. (2009). En: International Center for Transitional Justice Colombia (2009). *Recordar en conflicto: iniciativas no oficiales de memoria en Colombia*. Bogotá: Unión Europea.

Re-Dedication of and Implementation Modalities (2014). The Cessation of Hostilities Agreement signed on 23rd January 2014 between the Government of the Republic of South Sudan and the Sudan People's Liberation Movement/Army (In Opposition), signed on 25 August 2014 in Addis Ababa.

Regan, P. (2000). *Third party interventions and the duration of interstate conflicts*. Retrieved from http://web.worldbank.org/archive/website01241/WEB/IMAGES/THIRDPAR.PDF

Reilly, B. (2003). Democratic validation. In J. Darby & R. MacGinty (Eds.), *Contemporary Peacemaking Conflict, violence and Peace Processes*. New York: Palgrave Macmillan.

Restrepo, J., Spagat, M., & Vargas, J. (2005). The Severity of the Colombian Conflict: Cross-Country Datasets versus New Micro Data. *Journal of Peace Research*, 43(1), 99–115.

Rettberg, A., & Ortiz-Riomalo, J. F. (2014). Conflicto dorado: Canales y mecanismo de la relación entre minería de oro, conflicto armado y criminalidad en Colombia. Retrieved from http://papers.ssrn.com/sol3/Delivery.cfm/SSRN_ID2418883_code1341307.pdf?abstractid=2418883&mirid=1&type=2

Revault d'Allonnes, M. (1995). *Ce que l'Homme Fait à l'Homme. Essai sur le Mal Politique*. Paris: Flammarion.

Reyes Mate, M. (2011). *Auschwitz, justicia y deber de memoria*. Fronterad. Retrieved from http://fronterad.com/?q=auschwitz-justicia-y-deber-de-la-memoria&page=0,0

Reynolds, M. O. (1988). A Critique of What Do Unions Do? *The Review of Austrian Economics*, *2*(1), 259–271. doi:10.1007/BF01539312

Riaño, P. (2006). *Jóvenes, memoria y violencia en Medellín. Una antropología del recuerdo y el olvido*. Medellín: Editorial Universidad de Antioquia, ICAHN.

Riaño, P. (2007). Memorias Metodológicas. Revista de Estudios Sociales.

Ricardo, V. G. (2014, August 27). The Caguan's Peace Talks (F. Zarama, Interviewer).

Ricardo, D. (2004). *Principles of Political Economy and Taxation*. London: Dover Publications.

Richani, N. (2001). The Political Economy of Colombia's Protracted Civil War. *The Journal of Conflict Studies*, *XXI*(2).

Ricoeur, P. (2008). La memoria, la historia, el olvido. Buenos Aires: Fondo de Cultura Económica.

Ricoeur, P. (2000). *La memoria, la historia, el olvido*. Buenos Aires: Fondo de Cultura Económica.

Rid, T., & Hecker, M. (2009). *War 2.0 Irregular Warfare in the Information Age*. London: Praeger.

Rifkin, J. (1981). *Entropy: A New World View*. New York: Bantham.

Rifkin, J. (2009). *El siglo de la biotecnología: el comercio genético y el nacimiento de un mundo feliz*. Barcelona: Paidós.

Riohacha. (2012, October 13). Atentados contra infraestructura minero - energética en La Guajira. *El Tiempo*. Retrieved from www.eltiempo.com

Robben, A. (2005). *Political Violence and Trauma in Argentina*. University of Pennsylvania Press. doi:10.9783/9780812203318

Robinson, J. (1972). The second crises of economic theory. *The American Economic Review*, 62(1/2), 1-10.

Rodríguez-Garavito, C., & Lam, Y. (2013). Enfrentando las violaciones de los derechos de los pueblos indígenas al territorio, la tierra y los recursos naturales durante conflictos y transiciones. ICTJ. Fortaleciendo los derechos indígenas a través de comisiones de la verdad, Bogotá.

Rojas, D. (2013). Much more than a war on drugs: Elementos para un balance del Plan Colombia. *Análisis Político (Bogotá)*, (77): 113–132.

Rolston, B. (2007). Demobilization and reintegration of ex-combatants: The Irish case in international perspective. *Social & Legal Studies*, *16*(2), 259–280. doi:10.1177/0964663907076534

Rosetti, N. (2006). Multinacionales y paramilitares en Colombia: una conversación con Juan Carlos Galvis y Marta Hinestroza. *El Viejo Topo, 220*. Retrieved from www.elviejotopo.com

Ross, M. (2004) Oil, Drugs and Diamonds: The Varying Role of Natural Resources in Civil War. In K. Ballentine, & J. Sherman (Eds.), The Political Economy of Armed Conflict, Beyond Greed and Grievance (pp. 47-72). London: Boulder.

Roth, M., & Sever, M. (2007). The Kurdish Worker's Party (PKK) as a Criminal Syndicate: Funding Terrorism through Organized Crime, A Case Study. *Studies in Conflict and Terrorism*, *30*(10), 901–920. doi:10.1080/10576100701558620

Rubio-Marín, R., & De Greiff, P. (2007). Women and reparations. *The International Journal of Transitional Justice*, *1*(3), 318–337. doi:10.1093/ijtj/ijm035

Rückerl, A. (1979). *Die Strafverfolgung von NS-Verbrechen 1945 – 1978. Eine Dokumentation*. Karlsruhe: C.F. Müller Juristischer Verlag.

Rudaw. (2014). Barzani's meeting with the minister of foreign affairs of Iran. Retrieved from http://rudaw.net/sorani/kurdistan/270820142

Rueda, M. I. (1991, January 4). *El atentado a Iragori.* Semana. Retrieved from http://www.semana.com/nacion/articulo/el-atentado-iragori/16110-3

Russell, K., & Sambanis, N. (2014). Maliki Isn't the Problem. The Roots of Sectarianism in Iraq. In: *Foreign Affairs*. Retrieved from http://www.foreignaffairs.com/articles/141599/kevin-russell-and-nicholas-sambanis/maliki-isnt-the-problem

Russell, B. (1935). *Praise of Idleness and other essays.* London: George Allen & Unwin.

Sábato, E. (1951). Hombres y engranajes. Buenos Aires: Emicé editores.

Sánchez, R., & Rodríguez, F. (2005). Una aproximación al estudio de la seguridad. *Ensayos sobre Defensa y Seguridad*, 79-115.

Sanchéz, E. (2007). *Derechos Propios-Ejercicio de la Jurisdicción Especial Indígena en Colombia.* Bogotá: Instituto de Estudios del Ministerio Público.

Sánchez, G. (2003). *Guerras, Memoria e Historia*. Medellín: La Carreta Histórica.

Sánchez, G., & Meertens, D. (1983). *Bandoleros, gamonales y campesinos. El caso de la Violencia en Colombia.* Bogotá: El Áncora Editores.

Sandoval Duarte, H. (2014, April 27). Oleoducto de la discordia. *El Espectador.* Retrieved from www.elespectador.com

Santamaría, A. (2008). *Redes transnacionales y emergencia de la diplomacia indígena: Un estudio a partir del caso colombiano*. Bogotá: Universidad del Rosario.

Santiago, C (2006). From Insular Cases to Camp X-Ray: Agamben's state of exception and United States territorial law. *Studies in Law, Politics and Society*, 39, 15-55.

Santos, J. (2012, September 4). *Alocución del Presidente de la República, Juan Manuel Santos sobre el 'Acuerdo General para la Terminación del Conflicto.* Retrieved from http://wsp.presidencia.gov.co/Prensa/2012/Septiembre/Paginas/20120904_01.aspx

Saramago, J. (1992). *El evangelio según Jesucristo.* Barcelona: Seix Barral.

Sartre, J.-P. (1968). *Search for a method.* New York: Random House.

Sassoon, J. (2012). *Saddam Hussein's Ba'ath Party. Inside an Authoritarian Regime*. New York, Cambridge: Cambridge University Press.

Saul, J. R. (1993). *Voltaire Bastard's: The Dictatorship of Reason in the West.* New York: Vintage.

Scharpf, F. W. (1988). The Joint-Decision Trap: Lessons from German Federalism and European Integration. *Public Administration*, *66*(3), 239–278. doi:10.1111/j.1467-9299.1988.tb00694.x

Scheffer, D. (2008). The Extraordinary Chambers in the Courts of Cambodia. In C. Bassiouni (Ed.), International Criminal Law (Vol. III, pp. 219-256). Martinus Nijhoff, Netherlands.

Schelling, T. (2005, December 10). Nobel Prize. Retrieved from http://www.nobelprize.org/nobel_prizes/economic-sciences/laureates/2005/schelling-lecture.pdf

Schelling, T. (1985). *Choice and Consequence: perspectives of an errant economist.* Boston: Harvard University Press.

Schielke, S. (2012). Engaging the world on the Alexandria waterfront. In K. Graw & S. Schielke (Eds.), *The Global Horizon. Expectations of Migration in Africa and the Middle East* (pp. 175–193). Leuven: Leuven University Press.

Schlumberger, O. (2008). Structural Reform, Economic Order, and Development: Patrimonial Capitalism. *Review of International Political Economy*, *15*(4), 622–649. doi:10.1080/09692290802260670

Schmemann, S. (2014, June 20). In Refugee Statistics, a Stark Tale of Global Strife. *The New York Times*. Retrieved from http://www.nytimes.com/2014/06/22/opinion/sunday/in-refugee-statistics-a-stark-tale-of-global-strife.html?_r=0

Schmitt, C. (2003). *The Nomos of the Earth: in the international law of the jus publicum Europaeum* (Original work published 1950). New York: Telos.

Schneider, C. (2006). *Der Warschauer Kniefall. Ritual, Ereignis und Erzählung (Historische Kulturwissenschaften 9).* Konstanz: UVK.

Schrey, D. & Meisenberg, S. (2013). The Contribution of the Khmer Rouge Tribunal to Reconciliation, Remembrance and Memoralisation in Cambodia. *KAS International Reports,* 2013(4), 75-94.

Schumpeter, J. (2008). *Capitalism, Socialism and Democracy*. New York: Harper Perennial Modern Classics.

Schuster, L. (2005). The Continuing Mobility of Migrants in Italy. Shifting between Places and Statuses. *Journal of Ethnic and Migration Studies*, *31*(4), 757–774. doi:10.1080/13691830500109993

Scott, J. (1990). *Domination and the Arts of Resistance: Hidden Transcripts*. New Haven: Yale University Press.

Scott, J. W. (2015). Experiência. *Revista de Estudios de Gênero. La Ventana*, *2*(13), 42–74.

Sebasoni, S. (2001, December 18-31). Gacaca: Une justice que le peuple rwandais comprend. *Grands Lacs Hebdo* (pp. 25f).

Seibert-Fohr, A. (2012). Transitional Justice in Post-Conflict Situations. In R. Wolfrum (Ed.), *The Max Planck Encyclopedia of Public International Law* (Vol. IX, pp. 1042–1049). Oxford: Oxford University Press.

Semana. (1998, July 27). *El voto de Tirofijo.* Retrieved from http://www.semana.com/nacion/articulo/el-voto-de-tirofijo/36608-3

Semana. (2001, November 11). *Contra la pared.* Retrieved from http://www.semana.com/nacion/articulo/contra-pared/47939-3

Semana. (2012, March 28). Asesinatos de Manuel Ruiz y su hijo, otro golpe a la restitución de tierras. Retrieved from http://www.semana.com/nacion/articulo/asesinatos-manuel-ruiz-su-hijo-otro-golpe-restitucion-tierras/255592-3

Semana. (2012, September 18). *Cifras de la guerra en Colombia.* Retrieved from http://www.semana.com/especiales/cifras-guerra-colombia/index.html

Semana. (2014, December 22). *¿Quién es 'Megatrónico', el otro capo de las FARC?* Retrieved from http://www.semana.com/nacion/articulo/alias-megatronico-el-capo-invisible-de-las-farc/413135-3

Semana. (2014, October 23). *'Marquitos Figueroa' cayó por sus ocho mujeres.* Retrieved from http://www.semana.com/nacion/articulo/marquitos-figueroa-fue-capturado-por-sus-mujeres/406788-3

Semana. (2015, May 18). *Lo que une a los narcos mexicanos con las FARC.* Retrieved from http://www.semana.com/nacion/articulo/farc-narcos-mexicanos-unidos-por-narcotrafico-armas/428241-3

Sen, A. (2009). *The Idea of Justice.* Boston: Harvard University Press.

Sendker, L. (1990). *Eritreische Flüchtlinge im Sudan. Zwischen Assimilation und Segregation* (Vol. 70). Hamburg: Institut für Afrika-Kunde.

Seoane, J., Taddei, E., & Algranati, C. (2010). *Recolonización de Bienes Comunes de la Naturaleza y Alternativas desde los Pueblos.* Buenos Aires: Diálogo de los Pueblos and Grupo GEAL.

Seri, G. (2010). Vicious Legacies? State violence in Argentina. In M. Esparza, H. R. Huttenbach, & D. Feierstein (Eds.), *State Violence and Genocide in Latin America* (pp. 182–195). Oxfordshire, UK: Routledge.

Servilien, M. S. (2007). Le Rwanda. Reconstruire une nation (pp. 9-29, 160-178).

Shakespeare, W. (2004). *The Merchant of Venice.* New York: Washington Square Press.

Shelley, L., & Picarelly, J. (2005). Methods not Motives: Implications of the Convergence of International Organized Crime and Terrorism. *Police Practice and Research*, *3*(4), 305–318. doi:10.1080/1561426022000032079

Silva, M. (1999). Desarrollos y cuestiones militares en las FARC. In C. O. Paz (Ed.), Las verdaderas intenciones de las FARC (pp. 228-239). Bogotá: Intermedio editores.

Simmel, G. (1995). *Le Conflit* (Original work published 1908). Strasbourg: Circé.

Simmel, G. (1999). *Sociologie. Études sur les Formes de Socialisation* (Original work published 1908). Paris: PUF.

Singer, P. W. (2006). *Children at war.* Berkeley: University of California Press.

Sisk, D. T. (2003). Power–sharing after civil wars: matching Problem to Solutions. In J. Darby & R. MacGinty (Eds.), *Contemporary Peacemaking Conflict, violence and Peace Processes*. New York: Palgrave Macmillan.

Sitzungsbericht über die 26. Stadtverordnetenversammlungs in: Kammler, J., Krause-Villmar, D. (1984). Volksgemeinschaft und Volksfeinde. Kassel 1933 -1945. Eine Dokumentation. Kassel in der Zeit des Nationalsozialismus I, Fuldabrück: Hesse GmbH.

Skaar, E. (2001). *Judicial Independence and Human Rights Policies in Argentina and Chile*. Bergen, Norway: Chr Michelsen Institute.

Skalník, P. (1989). Outwitting the State. An Introduction. In P. Skalník (Ed.), *Outwitting the State* (pp. 1–22). New Brunswick: Transaction Publ.

Sluglett, P. (2007). *Britain in Iraq*. New York: Columbia University Press.

Small Arms Survey 2006: Unfinished Business. (2006). Small Arms Survey. Geneva: Graduate Institute of International and Development Studies. Retrieved from http://www.smallarmssurvey.org/

Smith, A. (2003). *Wealth of Nations*. New York: Oxford University Press.

Sorel, G. (1972). *Réflexions sur la Violence* (Original work published 1908). Paris: Marcel Rivière.

Sosa, C. (2011). Queering Acts of Mourning in the Aftermath of Argentina's Dictatorship: The Mothers of Plaza de Mayo. In F. Lessa (Ed.), *The Memory of State Terrorism in the Southern Cone*.

South Sudan Peace and Reconciliation Commission. (2013, January). Strategic Plan 2013-2015. Retrieved from http://www.cmi.fi/images/stories/publications/reports/2013/SSPRC_SP%202013-2015_FINAL.pdf.

Southern Sudan Human Rights Commission Act of 2009. (2009). Retrieved from http://www.icnl.org/research/library/files/South%20Sudan/SSHumanRights%20CommissionAct2009.pdf.

Spencer, D. (2011). *Colombia Camino a la Recuperación: Seguridad y Gobernabilidad 1982-2010*. Washington: Center for Hemispheric Defense Studies.

Stankovic, T., & Torjesen, S. (2010). *Fresh Insights on Disarmament, Demobilization and Reintegration: A Survey for Practitioners. Norwegian Institute of International Affairs*. Oslo: NUPI.

Steele, A. D. (2008). *Special report reconciliation strategies in Iraq*. United States Institute of Peace. Retrieved from http://www.usip.org/publications/reconciliation-strategies-iraq

Stewart, R. (2014). *Incorporating Cultural and Religious Practices into Transitional Justice: Lessons Related to Islam in Tunisia and Aceh, Indonesia*. McGill University. Retrieved from http://www.mei.edu/content/map/incorporating-cultural-and-religious-practices-transitional-justice-lessons-related-islam-tunisia

Stokes, D. (2006). Iron Fists in Iron Gloves: The Political Economy of US Terrocracy Promotion in Colombia. *British Journal of Politics and International Relations*, *8*(3), 368–387. doi:10.1111/j.1467-856X.2006.00219.x

Strauss, L. (1997). De la Tyrannie, followed by Correspondance avec Alexandre Kojève (1932-1965). Paris: Éditions Gallimard (NRF, Bibliothèque de philosophie).

Streit, M. E., Mummert, U., & Kiwit, D. (2000). *Cognition, Rationality and Institutions. Berlin et al.* Springer. doi:10.1007/978-3-642-59783-1

Strutynski, P. (2005). *UN-Reform – ein Schritt zurück*. Retrieved from http://www.ag-friedensforschung.de/themen/UNO/reform5.html

Suchkova, M. (2011). *The importance of a participatory reparations process and its relationships to the principles of reparation (Reparations Unit, Briefing Paper No.5)*. Colchester: University of Essex.

Sudan Tribune. (2013, December 25). *Kiir denounces Killing of Civilians on Tribal Basis, says "Criminals" to be punished*. Retrieved from <http://www.sudantribune.com/IMG/pdf/president_salva_kiir_christmas_message.pdf.>

Sudan Tribune. (2013, November 15). Audio Recording. Retrieved from <http://www.sudantribune.com/spip.php?article48818.>

Suescun, A. (1998). *Derecho y sociedad en la historia de Colombia*. Tomo I. El Derecho Chibcha (Siglo IX-Siglo XVI).

Sujatmiko, I. G. (2012). Conflict Transformation and Social Reconciliation: The Case of Aceh, Indonesia. *Asian Social Science*, *8*(2). doi:10.5539/ass.v8n2p104

Sullivan, M. (2013). *Maliki's Authoritarian Regime. Middle East Security Report No. 10.* Washington, DC: Institute for the Study of War.

Sunday's Zaman. (2011, May 10) Turkish police report reveals PKKs role in drug trafficking. *Today's Zaman.* Retrieved from http://www.todayszaman.com/news-243511-police-report-reveals-pkks-role-in-drug-smuggling-from-1984-to-2010.html

Svampa, M. (2010). Hacia una gramática de las luchas en America Latina: movilización plebeya, demandas de autonomía y giro eco-territorial. *Revista Internacional de FIlosofía Política*, 1–28. Retrieved from http://dialnet.unirioja.es/servlet/articulo?codigo=3315848&orden=359476&info=link

Svampa, M. (2012). Extractivismo neodesarrollista y movimientos sociales. ¿Un giro-ecoterritorial hacia nuevas alternativas? In M. Lang & D. Mokrani (Eds.), *Más alla del desarrollo* (pp. 185–218). Quito: Abya Yala Ediciones.

Swedish International Development Cooperation Agency. (2006). *Manual for Conflict Analysis.* Retrieved from http://www2.sida.se/sida/jsp/sida.jsp?d=118&a=3351&language=en_US&searchWords=manual%20for%20conflict%20analysis%2020th%20October%202012

Tapiéro, N. (1956). *Les Idées Réformistes d'al-Kawâkibî, 1265-1320–1849-1902. Contribution à l'Étude de l'Islam Moderne.* Paris: Les Éditions arabes.

Tariq Elias, M. O. (2009). The resurgence of the Taliban in Kabul: Logan and Wardak. In A. Giustozzi (Ed.), *Decoding the Taliban: Insights from the Afghan Field* (pp. 43–56). New York: Columbia University Press.

Taussig, M. T. (1987). *Shamanism, Colonialism, and the Wild Man: A Study in Terror and Healing.* Chicago: University of Chicago Press. doi:10.7208/chicago/9780226790114.001.0001

Taylor, (1999) A Juridical Frankenstein, or death in the hands of the state. In A. Sarat (Ed.), *The Killing State: Capital Punishment, Law, Politics and Culture* (pp. 60-80). New York: Oxford University Press.

Teitel, R. (2003). Transitional Justice Genealogy. Harvard Human Rights Journal, 16, 69-94.

Teitel, R.G. (2000). *Transitional Justice.* Oxford University Press

Teitel, R. (2000). *Transitional Justice.* Oxford University Press.

Temkin, A. Y. (2012). Equations for the Quantum Mind Evolution in the Struggle for Life. NeuroQuantology, June(2), 305-310. doi:10.14704/nq.2012.10.2.535

Tesfagiorgis, M. (2013). From Troubled Homes to Human Organ Harvesters. The Odysee of African Refugees in North Africa. In D. R. Mekonnen, & M. Tesfagiorgis (Eds.), The Horn of Africa at the Brink of the 21st Century. Coping with Fragmentation, Isolation and Marginalization in a Globalizing Environment (pp. 61-98). Felsberg: Edition Eins.

Tesfaye, L. (2011). *Stationen mobiler Fluchtgeschichten: Migration als Verhandlungsfeld zwischen Kontrollregimen, Handlungsräumen und der Verwirklichung persönlicher Lebensvorstellungen am Beispiel eritreischer Flüchtlinge in Äthiopien* [MA Thesis]. Munich University.

Teubal, M. (2009). Expansión de la Soja Transgénica en la Argentina. In M. Pérez (Ed.), Promesas y peligros de la liberalización del comercio agrícola: Lecciones desde América Latina (pp. 70–90). Retrieved from ase.tufts.edu/gdae/Pubs/rp/wg/.../PromesaPeligroBookJune09.pdf

Teubner, G. (2002). Breaking Frames: Economic globalisation and the emergence of lex mercatoria. *European Journal of Social Theory*, *5*(2), 199–217. doi:10.1177/13684310222225414

The Agreement on Security Arrangements (Chapter VI), signed in Naivasha, Kenya on 25 September 2003.

The Agreement on Wealth Sharing (Chapter III), signed in Naivasha, Kenya on 7 January 2004.

The Comprehensive Peace Agreement of 2005. (2005). Retrieved from http://www.unmis.unmissions.org/Portals/UNMIS/Documents/General/cpa-en.pdf consisting of, *inter alia,*

The Court Report. Issue 71. (2014, April).

The Court Report. Issue 83. (2015, March).

The Court Report. Issue 84. (2015, April).

The guardian (2014). Obama hails 'promising step forward' as Iraq names new prime minister http://www.theguardian.com/world/live/2014/aug/11/iraq-crisis-us-air-strikes-help-kurds-retake-territory-live-updates

The Local Government Act of 2009. (2009).Retrieved from http://mlgi.org.za/resources/local-government-database/by-country/sudan/sub-national-legislation/The%20Local%20Government%20Act%202009.pdf/view

The Machakos Protocol (Chapter I), signed in Machakos, Kenya on 20 July 2002.

The Protocol on Power Sharing (Chapter II), signed in Naivasha, Kenya on 26 May 2004.

The Sudd Institute. (2013, June 7). *Peace and Reconciliation in South Sudan: A Conversation for Justice and Stability.* Retrieved from http://www.suddinstitute.org/assets/Publications/National-Reconciliation-formatted-Sudd-Institute.pdf.

The Washington Times. (2002, March 19) FARC leaders indicted in US. Retrieved from http://www.washingtontimes.com/news/2002/mar/19/20020319-041134-7938r/

Thiele, H.-G. (Ed.). (1997). Die Wehrmachtsausstellung. Dokumentation einer Kontroverse. Dokumentation der Fachtagung in Bremen am 26. Februar 1997 und der Bundestagsdebatten am 13. März und 24. April 1997, Bremen: Bundeszentrale für politische Bildung.

Thomas, D., & Wall, J. (Eds.). (2011). *Children and armed conflict. Cross-disciplinary investigations*. Great Britain: Palgrave Macmillan.

Thompson, R. (1966). *Defeating Communist Insurgencies: Experiences from Malaya and Vietnam*. Michigan: Chatto and Windus.

Tibi, B. (2005). *Islam between Culture and Politics* (2nd ed.). Basingstoke (Hampshire) / New York: Palgrave Macmillan. doi:10.1057/9780230204157

Tickamyer, A., & Bohon, S. (2000). The Informal Economy. In E. F. Borgatta, & Rh. Montgomery (Eds), *Encyclopedia of Sociology* (2nd ed., Vol. 2, pp. 1337-1344). New York: Macmillan.

Tilly, C. (1985). War Making and State Making as Organized Crime. In *P. B. Evans, D. Rueschemeyer, & T. Skocpol (dir.), Bringing the State back* (pp. 169–187). Cambridge: Cambridge University Press. doi:10.1017/CBO9780511628283.008

Todorov, J. (2000). *Los abusos de la memoria*. Buenos Aires: Paidós.

Tomuschat, C., De Coti, O. L., & Tojo, A. B. (1999, February 25). *Guatemala, Memory of Silence*. Report of the Commission for Historical Clarification. Conclusions and Recommendations. Retrieved from www.aaas.org/sites/default/files/migrate/uploads/mos_en.pdf.

Torres, L., Niland, L., & Allen, P. (2013, September 26). IPCC Climate Change Figures: then and now-interactive. *The Guardian*. Retrieved from http://www.theguardian.com/environment/interactive/2013/sep/26/ipcc-climate-change-figures-then-and-now-interactive

Traverso, E. (2007). *El pasado, instrucciones de uso. Historia, memoria, política*. Madrid: Marcial Pons. Ediciones Jurídicas y Sociales.

Treiber, M. (2013b, September 11-13). Flucht aus Eritrea und die Zersetzung des Sozialen. *Rundbrief KDV im Krieg*. Connection e.V. Internationale Arbeit für Kriegsdienstverweigerer und Deserteure,

Treiber, M. (2013c). Leaving Eritrea, Entering the World – Migrants in the Making. In M. Tesfagiorgis, & D. R. Mekonnen (Eds), *The Horn of Africa at the Brink of the 21st Century. Coping with Fragmentation, Isolation and Marginalization in a Globalizing Environment* (pp. 127-138). Felsberg: Edition Eins.

Treiber, M. (2005). *Der Traum vom guten Leben. Die eritreische warsay-Generation im Asmara der zweiten Nachkriegszeit*. Münster: LIT.

Treiber, M. (2007). Dreaming of a good life. Young urban refugees from the Horn of Africa between refusal of politics and political asylum seeking. In H. P. Hahn & G. Klute (Eds.), *Cultures of Migration. African perspectives* (pp. 239–260). Berlin: LIT.

Treiber, M. (2009). Trapped in Adolescence. The Post-War Urban Generation. In D. O'Kane & T. R. Hepner (Eds.), *Biopolitics, Militarism, and the Developmental State: Eritrea in the 21st Century* (pp. 92–114). New York: Berghahn.

Treiber, M. (2010). The Choice between Clean and Dirty. Discourses of Aesthetics, Morality and Progress in Post-revolutionary Asmara, Eritrea. In E. Dürr & R. Jaffe (Eds.), *Urban Pollution. Cultural Meanings, Social Practices* (pp. 123–143). Oxford: Berghahn.

Treiber, M. (2013a). Lessons for Life. Two migratory portraits from Eritrea. In A. Triulzi & R. McKenzie (Eds.), *Long Journeys. African Migrants on the Road* (pp. 187–212). Leiden: Brill. doi:10.1163/9789004250390_011

Treiber, M. (2013d). Grasping Kiflu's Fear – Informality and Existentialism in Migration from North-East Africa. *Modern Africa. Politics. Historia y Sociedad (Rio Piedras, San Juan, P.R.), 1*(2), 111 139.

Treiber, M. (2014). Becoming by Moving. Khartoum and Addis Ababa as migratory stages between Eritrea and 'something. In M. Abdalla, D. Dias Barros Denise, & M. Berthet Ribeiro (Eds.), *Spaces in Movement: New Perspectives on Migration in African Settings* (pp. 189–205). Köln: Köppe.

Treiber, M., & Tesfaye, L. (2008). Step by Step. Migration from Eritrea. In E.-M. Bruchhaus & M. Sommer (Eds.), *Hot Spot Horn of Africa revisited. Approaches to make sense of conflict* (pp. 280–295). Berlin: LIT.

Tripp, C. (2007). *A History of Iraq*. New York, Cambridge: Cambridge University Press. doi:10.1017/CBO9780511804304

Triulzi, A., & McKenzie, R. L. (Eds.). (2013). *Long Journeys. African Migrants on the Road*. Leiden: Brill. doi:10.1163/9789004250390

Trobisch-Lütge, S. (2010). *Das späte Gift. Folgen politischer Traumatisierung in der DDR und ihre Behandlung*, 2. Gießen: Psychosozial-Verlag.

Tudor, O. (2004). TUC report of an ICFTU fact-finding visit. Retrieved from http://www.tuc.org.uk/international-issues/iraq-appeal/iraq-unions-and-law

U.S. Department of Defense. (2006). *Measuring Stability and Security in Iraq. Report to Congress*. Retrieved from http://www.defense.gov/home/features/Iraq_Reports/

U.S. Department of Defense. (2008). *Measuring Stability and Security in Iraq. Report to Congress*. Retrieved from http://www.defense.gov/home/features/Iraq_Reports/

U.S. Department of State. (1999). *Saddam Hussein's Iraq*. Retrieved from http://www2.gwu.edu/~nsarchiv/NSAEBB/NSAEBB167/13.pdf

U.S. Department of State. (2002). *Future of Iraq Project*. Retrieved from http://www2.gwu.edu/~nsarchiv/NSAEBB/NSAEBB198/

U.S. Energy Information Administration. (2014). *Country Analysis Brief Overview*. Washington, D.C. Retrieved from www.eia.gov

U.S. Overseas Loans and Grants. (2014). *U.S. Economic Assistance to Colombia FY2001-FY2012*. Retrieved from http://gbk.eads.usaidallnet.gov/

Ueberschär, G. R. (Ed.), (2008). Der Nationalsozialismus vor Gericht. Die alliierten Prozesse gegen Kriegsverbrecher und Soldaten 1943-1952 (3rd ed.). Frankfurt/Main: Fischer Taschenbuch Verlag. Retrieved from http://www.wortbedeutung.info/Versöhnung/

UN General Assembly. (1998, July 17). Rome Statute of the International Criminal Court. Retrieved from http://legal.un.org/icc/statute/99_corr/cstatute.htm.

UN High Commissioner for Refugees. (2007). *Refugee Protection and Mixed Migration. A 10-Point Plan of Action*. Retrieved from http://www.unhcr.org/4742a30b4.html

UN High Commissioner for Refugees. (2011a). *Eligibility Guidelines for Assessing the International Protection Need of Asylum Seekers from Eritrea*. Retrieved from www.refworld.org

UN High Commissioner for Refugees. (2011b). *UNHCR Resettlement Handbook*. Retrieved from http://www.refworld.org/docid/4ecb973c2.html

UN Security Council Resolution 1593 (2005, March 31). UN Doc. S/RES/1593. Retrieved from http://www.un.org/en/ga/search/view_doc.asp?symbol=S/RES/1593(2005).

UN Security Council Resolution 1996 (2011, July 8). UN Doc. S/RES/1996 (2011). Retrieved from http://www.un.org/en/ga/search/view_doc.asp?symbol=S/RES/1996(2011).

UN Security Council Resolution 2132 (2013, December 24). UN Doc. S/RES/2132. Retrieved from http://www.un.org/en/ga/search/view_doc.asp?symbol=S/RES/2132(2013).

UN-General Assembly. (2000). *Resolution 55/2: United Nations Millennium Declaration* Retrieved November 18, 2014, from http://www.un.org/millennium/declaration/ares552e.pdf

UN-General Assembly. (2005). *Resolution adopted by the General Assembly: 60/1. 2005 World Summit Outcome* – (A/60/L.1) Retrieved from http://www.un.org/womenwatch/ods/A-RES-60-1-E.pdf

UNHCR. (2014). *UNHCR country operations profile - Iraq*. Retrieved from http://www.unhcr.org/pages/49e486426.html

UN-High-Level Panel on Threats. Challenges and Change (2004). *A more secure World: Our shared responsibility* (A/59/565). Retrieved from http://www.un.org/en/peacebuilding/pdf/historical/hlp_more_secure_world.pdf

UNICEF. (2004). *Adolescent programming experiences during conflict and post-conflict. Case studies*. New York: Author.

UNICEF. (2014). *Under Siege. The devastating impact on children of three years of conflict in Syria*. New York: Author.

Unidad Administrativa para la Consolidación Territorial. (2014). *Regiones en Consolidación*. Retrieved from http://www.consolidacion.gov.co/?q=content/regiones-en-consolidaci%C3%B3n

Unidad de Planeación Minero Energética. (2005). *La cadena del carbón*. Bogotá: Unidad de Planeación Minero Energético.

Unidad de Planeación Minero Energética. (2006). Colombia País Minero: Plan Nacional para el Desarrollo Minero, 2019. Bogotá.

Unidad de Planeación Minero Energética. (2014). *Histórico de producción de Oro* [Dataset]. Retrieved from http://www.upme.gov.co/generadorconsultas/Consulta_Series.aspx?idModulo=4&tipoSerie=116&grupo=355&Fechainicial=01/01/1931&Fechafinal=31/12/2015

Unidad para la Atención y Reparación Integral a las Víctimas. (2015). *Registro Único de Víctimas*. Retrieved from http://www.unidadvictimas.gov.co/index.php/en/

United Nations Assistant Mission for Iraq. (2012). *Iraqi Constitution*. Retrieved from http://www.uniraq.org/documents/iraqi_constitution.pdf

United Nations Development Programme. (2007). *Special Audit: Audit of Human Resources Management at the ECCC* (Report No. RCM0172). Retrieved on 05 October 2014, from http://www.unakrt-online.org/Docs/Other/2007-06-04%20UNDP%20Special%20Audit%20of%20ECCC%20HR.pdf

United Nations Mission In South Sudan. (2014, February 21). *Interim Report on Human Rights: Crisis in South Sudan, Report Coverage 15 December 2013–31 January 2014*. Human Rights Division. Retrieved from http://unmiss.unmissions.org/Default.aspx?tabid=5805&language=en-US.

United Nations Mission In South Sudan. (2014, May 8). *Conflict in South Sudan: A Human Rights Report*. Human Rights Division. Retrieved from http://unmiss.unmissions.org/Default.aspx?tabid=5805&language=en-US.

United Nations Mission In South Sudan. (2015, June 29). *Flash Human Rights Report on the Escalation of Fighting in Greater Upper Nile. April/May 2015*. Retrieved from http://unmiss.unmissions.org/Default.aspx?tabid=5805&language=en-US.

United Nations. (1945). *Charter of the United Nations: We the people of the United Nations...United for a better World*, Retrieved from http://www.unrol.org/files/UNcharter.pdf

United Nations. (1981). *Secretary-General's Report to the General Assembly, (A/36/215)*. New York: Author.

United Nations. (1989). *Convention on the Rights of the Child, (Adopted by General Assembly Resolution 44/25)*. New York: Author.

United Nations. (1996). Impact of armed conflict on children (Report from the expert of the Secretary-General Graça Machel, (General Assembly resolution A/51/306). New York: Author.

United Nations. (2004). *Report of Secretary-General on Khmer Rouge Trials* (Doc. A/59/432). Retrieved from http://www.unakrt-online.org/documents/report-secretary-general-khmer-rouge-trials-1

United Nations. (2004). *The Rule of Law and Transitional Justice in Conflict and Post-Conflict Societies.* Report of the Secretary General to the Security Council (S/2004/616 (2004)).

United Nations. (2004). *The rule of law and transitional justice in conflict and post-conflict societies: Report of the Secretary-General to the Security Council, (S/2004/616)*. New York: Author.

United Nations. (2004, October 6). Press Release of the Secretary-General. Department of Public Information (SG/SM/9519, SC/8210). Retrieved from http://www.un.org/News/Press/docs/2004/sgsm9519.doc.htm

United Nations. (2005). *Guidelines on justice in matters involving child victims and witnesses of crime, (Ecosoc Resolution 2005/20)*. New York: Author.

United Nations. (2008). *United Nations Peacekeeping Operations. Principles and Guidelines*. New York: Author.

United Nations. (2011). *The Rule of Law and Transitional Justice in Conflict and Post-Conflict Societies.* Report of the Secretary General to the Security Council (S/2011/634 (2011).

United Nations. (2014). *Working Group on Children and Armed Conflict. Conclusions on children and armed conflict in the Syrian Arab Republic, (S/AC.51/2014/4)*. New York: Author.

United Nations. (2014, July 25). Report of the Secretary-General on South Sudan (S/2014/537).

United Nations. (2014, May 12). Secretary-General's Briefing to the Security Council on South Sudan. Statement. Retrieved from <http://www.un.org/sg/statements/index.asp?nid=7666.

United Nations. (2015, July 1). Press Release. Department of Public Information (SC/11958). Retrieved 30 June 2015 from http://www.un.org/press/en/2015/sc11958.doc.htm.

UNOCHA. (2014). *Iraq*. Retrieved from http://www.unocha.org/iraq

UNPO. (2014). *Urgent Action For Iraq's Vulnerable Components Needed.* Retrieved from http://www.unpo.org/article/17220

UNSDN. (2013). Indonesian National Program for Community Empowerment. Retrieved from http://unsdn.org/indonesian-national-program-for-community-empowerment/

UN-Secretary General - Annan. K., (2005). *In larger Freedom: Towards development, security and human rights for all* (A/59/2005) Retrieved from http://www.un.org/en/ga/search/view_doc.asp?symbol=A/59/2005

UN-Secretary General - Boutros-Ghali. (1992). *Report of the Secretary-General. An Agenda for Peace. Preventive diplomacy, peacemaking and peace keeping* (A/47/277-S/24111). Retrieved from http://www.unrol.org/files/a_47_277.pdf

UN-Secretary General - Boutros-Ghali. (1994). *Report of the Secretary-General. Agenda für Entwicklung* (A/48/935). Retrieved from https://www.globalpolicy.org/component/content/article/226-initiatives/32314-an-agenda-for-development-report-of-the-secretary-general.html

UN-Security Council. (2000). *Report of the Panel on United Nations Peace Operations. The Brahimi Report* A/55/305-S/2000/809. Retrieved from http://www.unrol.org/files/brahimi%20report%20peacekeeping.pdf

Uppsala Conflict Data Program. (2015, February 25). UCDP Conflict Encyclopedia. Retrieved from www.ucdp.uu.se/database

Uppsala University World Bank. (2006). *GAM Reintegration Needs Assessment: Enhancing Peace through Community-Level Development Programming*. Jakarta: The World Bank.

Uppsala University, Department of Peace and Conflict Research. (2012). Definitions. Available fromhttp://www.pcr.uu.se/research/ucdp/definitions/#Ceasefire_agreements

Uprimny, R., & Saffon, M. (2007). *Uses and abuses of Transitional Justice discourse in Colombia*. PRIO Policy Brief 6, Oslo International Peace Research Institute.

Uprimny, R., Sanchez, C., & Guzman, D. (2010). Informe sobre Colombia. En Las victimas y la Justicia Transicional. Fundación para el debido proceso legal. Washington D.C.

Uprimny, R., & Guzmán, D. (2010). *Justicia Transicional desde abajo y con perspectiva de Género*. UNIFEM.

Uprimny, R., & Guzmán-Rodríguez, D. (2010). En búsqueda de un concepto transformador y participativo para las reparaciones en contextos transicionales. *International Law: Revista Colombiana de Derecho Internacional, 17*, 231–286.

Uribe, C. (2011). *Amnistias y responsabilidad de la corte penal internacional. Lecciones del proceso de Paz con la AUC. In G. Gallego, & M. González (Eds.), Conflicto armado interno derechos humanos e impunidad.*

Uribe, M. V. (1990). *Matar, rematar y contramatar: las masacres de la violencia en el Tolima, 1948-1964*. Bogotá: CINEP, Controversia.

US Department of Defense (2011, April) *Report on Progress Towards Security and Stability in Afghanistan*. Washington: Department of Defense.

US Government Interagency Counterinsurgency Initiative. (2009). *Counterinsurgency Guide*. Washington: Bureau of Political-Military Affairs.

USIP. (2006). *Weak Viability The Iraqi Federal State and the Constitutional Amendment Process*. Retrieved from http://www.usip.org/files/resources/Morrow_SR168.pdf

Valencia, L. (2002). *Adios a la Politica, Bienvenida la Guerra*. Bogota: Intermedio.

Valter, S. (2012). Rivalités et Complémentarités au Sein des Forces Armées: le Facteur Confessionnel en Syrie. *Les Champs de Mars*, 23, 79-96.

Valter, S. (2014). La Justice Chariatique en Syrie 'Libérée'. *Confluences Méditerranée, 90*(3), 155–173. doi:10.3917/come.090.0155

Van Dam, N. (1996). *The Struggle for Power in Syria. Politics and Society under Asad and the Ba'th Party*. Londres: I.B. Tauris.

Van Zyl, P. (2005). Promoting Transitional Justice in Post-Conflict Societies. In A. Bryden, & H. Hanggi (Eds.), *Security Governance in Post-Conflict Peacebuilding* (pp. 209–231). Geneva: Geneva Centre for the Democratic Control of Armed Forces.

Varennes, D. F. (2003). Peace Accords and Ethnic Conflicts: a comparative Analysis of content and approaches. In J. Darby & R. MacGinty (Eds.), *Contemporary Peacemaking Conflict, violence and Peace Processes*. New York: Palgrave Macmillan.

Vásquez, T. (2011). Capítulo 3: La dinámica macroregional del conflicto armado. In T. Vásquez, A. Vargas, & J. A. Restrepo (Eds.), *Una vieja guerra en un nuevo contexto* (pp. 299–339). Bogota: Editorial Pontificia Universidad Javeriana.

Veblen, T. (1953). *The Theory of the Leisure Class: an Economic Study of Institutions*. New York: The MacMillan Company.

Veblen, T. (1964). *An Inquiry into the Nature of Peace*. New York: Kelley.

Veblen, T. (2009). *The Theory of the Leisure Class*. New York: Oxford University Press.

VerdadAbierta.com. (2015, January). Los retos de la Ley de Justicia y Paz en su noveno año. Retrieved from http://www.verdadabierta.com/justicia-y-paz/legislacion/5563-los-retos-de-la-ley-de-justicia-y-paz-en-su-noveno-ano

Verdeja, E. (2010). Political Violence, justice and reconciliation in Latin America. In M. Esparza, H. R. Huttenbach, & D. Feierstein (Eds.), *State Violence and Genocide in Latin America* (pp. 169–181). Oxfordshire, UK: Routledge.

Verón, E. (2002). *Construir el acontecimiento. Los medios de comunicación masiva y el accidente en la central nuclear de Three Mile Island.* Barcelona: Gedisa.

Viñar, M. (2006). *Violencia social y realidad en psicoanálisis. En Puget Janine y Käes René, (Compils).* Buenos Aires: Editorial Lumen SRL.

Visser, R. (2008). Iraqi Shiite Factionalism and Iran's Role in the Basra Fighting. Terrorism Focus, 5(14).

Visser, R. (2010). *Once More, Washington Puts the Cart before the Horse in Iraq.* Retrieved from https://gulfanalysis.wordpress.com/2010/12/15/once-more-washington-puts-the-cart-before-the-horse-in-iraq/

Völter, B. (2009). Generationenforschung und transgenerationale Weitergabe aus biografietheoretischer Perspektive. In H. Radebold, W. Bohlleber, & J. Zinnecker (Eds.), *Transgenerationale Weitergabe kriegsbelasteter Kindheiten. Interdisziplinäre Studien zur Nachhaltigkeit historischer Erfahrungen über vier Generationen Weinheim* (pp. 95–106). München: Beltz Juventa.

Waibel, H. (2011). *Diener vieler Herren. Ehemalige NS-Funktionäre in der SBZ/DDR.* Frankfurt: Peter Lang Verlag.

Waldorf, L. (2006). Mass Justice for Mass Atrocity: Rethinking Local Justice as Transitional Justice. *Temple Law Review, 79*(1), 1–87.

Walker, M. (2003). The Making of Modern Iraq. *The Wilson Quarterly, 27*, 29–40.

Wallach, J. (1995). *The Desert Queen. The Extraordinary Life of Gertrude Bell.* New York: Anchor Books.

Wallensteen, P. (2007). Understanding Conflict Resolution (2nd ed.). London: SAGE publication.

Walzer, M. (2006). *Just and Unjust Wars: A Moral Argument with Historical Illustrations.* New York: Basic Books.

Wang, Y. (Ed.), (2012, November 9). Colombian paramilitary gang kills 10 peasant. Xinhuanet.com. Retrieved from http://news.xinhuanet.com/english/world/2012-11/09/c_131961167.htm

Ward, C. J. (2011). *The Coalition Provisional Authority's Experience with Governance in Iraq: Lessons Identified.* United States Institute for Peace Special Report No.139. Washington D.C., United States Institute of Peace.

Warner, L. A. (2013). Armed Group Amnesty and Military Integration in South Sudan. *The Rusi Journal, 158*(6), 40–47.

Webb, S. (2003). U.S. military attacks Iraqi trade unions. Retrieved from http://www.peoplesworld.org/u-s-military-attacks-iraqi-trade-unions/

Wessells, M. (2007). *Child soldiers: From violence to prevention.* Boston: Harvard University Press.

Wessells, M., & Jonah, D. (2006). Recruitment and reintegration of former youth soldiers in Sierra Leone. Challenges of reconciliation and post-accord peace building. In S. McEvoy-Levy (Ed.), *Troublemakers or Peacemakers? Youth and post-accord peace building* (pp. 27–47). Notre Dame, IN: University of Notre Dame Press.

Westin, Ch., & Hassanen, S. (Eds.), (2014). *People on the Move. Experiences of forced migration, with examples from various parts of the world.* Trenton, NJ: Red Sea Press.

WFP. (2014 October 1). Hunger Statistics. Retrieved from http://www.wfp.org/hunger/stats

White, S. (2002). Being, becoming and relationship: Conceptual challenges of a child rights approach in development. *Journal of International Development, 14*(8), 1095–1104. doi:10.1002/jid.950

Whyte, D. (2009). Crimes of the Powerful: a reader (Readings in Criminology and Criminal Justice). Open University Press.

Whyte, D. (2007). The Crimes of Neo-liberal Rule in Occupied Iraq. *The British Journal of Criminology, 47*(2), 177–195. doi:10.1093/bjc/azl065

Whyte, D. (2008). Hire an American! Tyranny and Corruption in Occupied Iraq. *Social Justice (San Francisco, Calif.), 35*(3).

Whyte, S. R. (2009). Epilogue. In L. Haram & C. Bawa Yamba (Eds.), *Dealing with Uncertainty in Contemporary African Lives* (pp. 213–216). Uppsala: Nordic Africa Institute.

Wibabara, C. (2014). *Gacaca Courts versus the International Criminal Tribunal for Rwanda and the National Courts* (pp. 107–159). Baden-Baden.

Williams, M. H. (2013). *The Multicultural Dilemma. Migration, ethnic politics, and state intermediation*. New York: Routledge.

Wilson, A. T. (1931). *A Clash of Loyalties. Mesopotamia 1914-1917. A Personal and Historical Record*. London: Humphrey & Milford.

Wilson, A. T. (1932). *A Clash of Loyalties. Mesopotamia 1917-1920. A Personal and Historical Record*. London: Humphrey & Milford.

Wolffsohn, M., & Brechenmacher, T. (2005). *Denkmalsturz? Brandts Kniefall*. München: Olzog.

Wolgast, E. (1997). Vergangenheitsbewältigung in der unmittelbaren Nachkriegszeit. In R. Carola (Ed.), Forschungsmagazin der Universität Heidelberg. Retrieved from http://www.uni-heidelberg.de/uni/presse/RuCa3_97/wolgast.htm

Woodhead, M., & Montgomery, H. (Eds.), (2003) Understanding childhood: an interdisciplinary approach. United Kingdom: John & Sons Ltd.

World Bank Indicators. (2015, February 2) Retrieved from http://data.worldbank.org/indicator/NY.GDP.MKTP.KD.ZG

World Bank. (2004, July 26). State Owned Enterprises Reform In Iraq (Working Paper No. 2). *The World Bank*.

World Bank. (2014, November 20). Poverty Overview. Retrieved from http://www.worldbank.org/en/topic/poverty/overview#1

World Health Organization. (2014). VISION 2020. Retrieved from http://www.theeye.co.rw/vision_2020.php

Yeste, M. P., & Fernández, L. P. (2005). *El conflicto en Colombi*a. Retrieved from http://e-archivo.uc3m.es/bitstream/handle/10016/17382/06_conflictos_colombia_2006.pdf?sequence=1

Yo traicioné la corrupción, el amiguismo con el paramilitarismo y las chuzadas: Santos. (2014, May 23). *El Espectador*. Retrieved from www.elespectador.com

Young, J. (2006). *The South Sudan Defense Forces in the Wake of the Juba Declaration. Small Arms Survey*. Graduate Institute of International Studies.

Zambrano Carlos Vladimir (2006). *Memoria colectiva y Comunidad Política, Propedéutica Etnográfica-Constructivista,* Bogotá: Universidad Nacional, sede Bogotá, Instituto Unidad de Investigaciones Jurídico-Sociales Gerardo Molina, UNIJUS

Zartman, I. W. (1997). Introduction: Toward the Resolution of International Conflicts. In I. W. Zartman, & J.L. Rasmussen. (Ed.), Peacemaking in international Conflict. Methods and Techniques. Washington, D.C.: United States Institute of Peace Press.

Zartman, I. W. (1999). *Negotiations as a Mechanism for Resolution in the Arab-Israeli conflict* (Davis Occasional Papers 72). Jerusalem: The Leonard Davis Institute for International Relations.

Zartman, I. W. (2004, September 2). *Mutually Exciting Opportunities and Durable Settlements*. Paper presented at the annual meeting of the American Political Science Association, Hilton Chicago and the Palmer House, Chicago, IL. Retrieved from http://www.allacademic.com/meta/p60174_index.html

Zartman, I. W. (1975). Negotiation: Theory and Reality. *Journal of International Affairs*, *29*(1), 69–77.

Zartman, I. W. (2001). The timing of peace initiatives: Hurting stalemates and ripe moments. *The Global Review of Ethnopolitics*, *1*(1), 8–18. doi:10.1080/14718800108405087

Zewde, B. (2001). *A History of Modern Ethiopia 1855-1991*. Oxford: James Currey.

Zoellick, R. B. (2005). *The Hard Work Of Peace. Prepared For Delivery University Of Khartoum, Sudan On 9 November 2005*. Sudan. Retrieved from .http://2001-2009.State.Gov/S/D/Former/Zoellick/Rem/56654.Htm

About the Contributors

Fredy Cante is a researcher and Full Professor, Centro de Estudios Políticos Internacionales, Facultad de Ciencia Política y de Gobierno de la Universidad del Rosario. Academic Qualification: Economist, Universidad Nacional de Colombia. 1993. PhD in Economic Science, Universidad Nacional de Colombia. Doctoral Thesis: Individual Freedom and Feasible Opportunities. 2009. Visiting Scholar: Columbia University, New York, during autumn of 2001. Department: Institute for Social and Economic Research and Policy (ISERP). Output: Individual Rights and Strategic Interaction (working paper). Tutor: Jon Elster, Department of Political Science. Short courses about nonviolent political action: Fletcher Summer Institute for the advanced study in nonviolent conflict, Organized by The International Center on Nonviolent Conflict and Tufts University, Boston, July 2006. Teaching nonviolent political action, organized by The International Center on Nonviolent Conflict, Istanbul, August 2010. Experience and research: nonviolent political action, civil war, and collective action.

Hartmut Quehl has studied History, Political Sciences and Islamic Studies in Marburg, Freiburg, Damascus and Hanover. Since 2008 he is director of the Felsberg Institute for Education and Academic Research (FIBW). His research interest lays on peace and conflict research, post-conflict reconstruction, social and everyday life history of wartimes, oral history and qualitative empiricism. His current research is on the transformation of victorious liberation fronts into governments during the cold war and the post-cold war era, and on the changing faces of violent conflict after the cold war, both under comparative aspects.

* * *

Nazar Jamil Abdulazeez, holds MA degree in International Relations from KENT university/the UK. Nazar has been working as a civil society activist since early 2000 in Iraq. He was rewarded by (Prince of the UK) for his work during Iraqi Crisis after 2003 and by the Prime Minister – Kurdistan Regional Governorate/ Iraq in 2008. Since 2014, Nazar has been working as Coordinator for NGOs humanitarian Response in Kurdistan Region of Iraq. Additionally, Nazar is the founding father of the Kurdish institute for Victimology and fighting genocide in Iraq and member of Felesber institute for education and academic research in Germany since 2008.

Monica Acosta is a doctoral student and a lawyer and internationalist of Rosario University, Bogota, Colombia. She is interested in issues of gender and transitional justice, transnational collective action, indigenous women participation and their leadership in international organizations. Her doctoral research is focused on indigenous women in transitional justice in Colombia. She is a member of the Intercultural School of Indigenous Peoples, where she teaches about international political participation and transitional justice based on the rights of Indigenous Peoples.

Javier Alonso Cárdenas is a Professor and currently working on a Ph.D. in Political Science at Universidad de los Andes (Bogotá, Colombia). His research interests are peace building, Disarmament, Demobilization and Reintegration (DDR) programs. He also has worked on history of ideas, conceptual history, and the relationship between history of occidental thought and literature. He has been professor of Political Theory and Research methods on Political Science and International Relations at Universidad del Rosario (Bogotá, Colombia).

Richard Clayton Doughman holds a Masters in Latin American Studies from the Universidad Nacional de Cuyo, Mendoza, Argentina. Human Sciences Professor at the Universidad del Rosario, Bogota, Colombia.

Sinthya Rubio Escolar is pursuing a PhD in Advanced Studies in Human Rights from the Universidad Carlos III de Madrid. She holds a MA in Advanced Studies in Human Rights from the same institution; and a BA in International Relations from the Universidad del Norte, Colombia. Her current research work focuses on reparations for children and youth. She is currently working at Unidad para la Atención y Reparación Integral a las Víctimas, a government entity based in Colombia, where she is in charge of reparations for children and youth.

Hauke Feickert is an Independent Lecturer at the Centre for Near- and Middle Eastern Studies at the University of Marburg, Germany. He writes regularly on developments in Iraq in the German Middle East magazine "Zenith" and has published in German academic media, like "Die Blaetter" or the "Hessian Foundation for Peace and Conflict Studies". His academic work focuses on U.S. foreign- and security policy. His research interests also include Iraqi history in the 20th century, the evolvement of Iraqi party politics, state building, and democracy development in authoritarian countries. He holds a PhD in political science from the University of Bonn with a work comparing U.S. policy towards Iraq and the British policy in Mesopotamia after the First World War.

Mauricio Alejandro Fernández studied political science and is researcher of the Center of International and Political Studies (CEPI) of the Faculty of Political Sciences and Government of the University of Rosario, in Bogota, Colombia. His research agenda focuses on the geographical studies, urban and regional development and disparities, cultural studies and social movements. He has been involved in pedagogical initiatives in teaching at indigenous territories and promoting Participatory and Intercultural Action Research.

Yomaira García-Acuña is a Psychologist, who did master studies in social development in the National Autonomous University of Mexico, UNAM. She is a specialist in family therapy from the Family Institute in Mexico and she is the author of the books Families in Colombia: Transitions to the XXIst

Century (Familias en Colombia: Transiciones hacia el Siglo XX) and Routes through Memories (Rutas por la Memoria)., She is currently doing her PhDin Social Sciences at the Universidad Nacional General Sarmiento-Instituto de Desarrollo Económico y Social (UNGS-IDES), Argentina. Senior Professor and researcher of the Universidad Simón Bolívar, Colombia.

María Angélica Garzón is a Social and Human Sciences PhD candidate, Universidad Nacional de Colombia. Researcher interested in topics related with the return of population and reconstruction of collective memory, Bogotá, Colombia. She currently teaches at the Universidad Pedagógica y Tecnológica de Colombia UPTC in the area of social sciences.

Gerd Hankel, PhD, M.A., is a legal scholar and guest fellow at the Hamburg Institute for Social Research. He studied at the Universities of Granada (Spain), Mainz, and Bremen and holds degrees in Romance languages and literature and in law. From 2000 to the end of 2001 he was on the team of researchers from various disciplines that created the Institute's exhibition *Crimes of the German Wehrmacht: Dimensions of a War of Annihilation 1941-1944*. Gerd Hankel's current research focuses on dealing with the legal aspects of the genocide and the reconciliation process in Rwanda, on International Humanitarian Law and its implementation especially in the Great Lakes Region in Africa.

Daniel Heilmann's research focuses on public international law and comparative constitutional law. He has worked for various international organizations and he advises governments in South-East Asia, Subsaharan Africa and in the Middle East concerning legal matters and parliamentary affairs.

Thomas Erich Jakob first studied Political Science, Economics, and Islamic Science. Dr. Jakob then graduated at the Friedrich Alexander University (FAU) in 2012 and became research assistant at the Center for Iraq Studies (CIS) in Erlangen, Germany. In spring 2015 he changed to the Philipps University Marburg for PhD research.

Carlos Eduardo Maldonado has a Ph.D. in philosophy (KULeuven, Belgium); Visiting Positions: Visiting Scholar (University of Pittsburgh, U.S.A., Visiting Research Professor (The Catholic University of America; Washington, D.C.); Visiting Scholar (University of Cambridge, UK).Honorary Doctorate (University of Timisoara, Rumania). Full Professor, School of Political Science and Government, Universidad del Rosario (Bogotá, Colombia).

Oscar Palma is an Assistant Professor of International Relations, Universidad del Rosario. PhD London School of Economics, MA University of Leicester. Lecturer Escuela Superior de Guerra, Colombia.

Nadia Stefania Pérez is a Political Science and Government student at Universidad del Rosario. Her research interests include peace-building, democracy, social development, education and democracy.

Paula A. Timcke Rey Sociologist (Dipl. Soz. Ludwig-Maximilians-Universität München), is the Latin American Representative of the Felsberg Institute for Education and Academic Research (FI) in Bogotá, Colombia. Her work focuses on violence, armed conflict and internal displacement in Colombia, as well as collective memory, qualitative social research and CAQDAS. Timcke has taught at the Rosario University and has researched at the National Center for Historical Memory (CNMH), both in

Bogotá, Colombia. Currently she works on fostering academic relations between German and Colombian research and education institutions and is a member of the ICRoV (International Consortium of Research on Violence).

Gustavo Rojas- Paez lectures legal theory at Universidad Libre, Colombia. He has an MA in Legal Sociology from the IISL-Oñati. He is a PhD candidate in Jurisprudence at Freiburg University, Germany. He is part of the research group Law State and Society coordinated by Dr Nhorys Torregroza at Universidad Libre, school of Law, Colombia. He is an editor of Oñati Sociolegal Series, Vol. 4, No. 1, 2014.

Angela Santamaria (PhD) is faculty and Intercultural School of Indigenous Peoples member, Bogotá, Colombia. Her research agenda focuses on the development of practice oriented theory about collective action, and women indigenous activism. Her preferred approach is research oriented "participative action" and engaged ethnographic and collaborative research. Her current research projects focus on: the conceptualization of indigenous women leadership in Amazonia and Sierra Nevada de Santa Marta (Colombia); the role of cultural diversity and gender in collective leadership. She has been involved in a number of initiatives to teach in indigenous territories and promote Participatory and Intercultural Action Research.

Kathrin Maria Scherr is the Head of the Sub-Saharan Africa Operations at the Max Planck Foundation for International Peace and the Rule of Law (MPFPR) in Heidelberg, Germany. She is responsible for designing and implementing legal projects in the Sub-Saharan Africa region, which support on-going constitutional processes and assist in the stabilisation of legal systems through the provision of capacity-building programmes for legal actors. Kathrin holds a Ph.D. in Comparative Public Law from the European University Institute (EUI), Florence, Italy, an M.A. in International Relations and International Economics from the Johns Hopkins University, School of Advanced International Studies (SAIS), Washington DC and a law degree and advanced degree in EU law from the University of Graz, Austria. She previously worked at the Legal Vice Presidency Unit and the Financial and Private Sector Development Unit, Europe and Central Asia (ECA), of the World Bank, at the European Court of Justice, and the Committee on Legal Affairs and Human Rights of the Parliamentary Assembly of the Council of Europe.

Magnus Treiber holds a PhD in Anthropology from Munich University. His doctoral thesis describes the life-worlds of young urbanites in Eritrea's capital Asmara. Magnus Treiber taught at Munich, Bayreuth and Addis Ababa universities in Germany and Ethiopia. Political culture in the Horn of Africa, migration studies, anthropological theory and methodology are his main fields of interest.

Sergio Triana has broad experience on peace building, security and Disarmament, Demobilization and Reintegration (DDR) in Asia, Africa, Latin America and the Caribbean. Currently he is studying in the University of Cambridge a Phd in Criminology and his research focus is the analysis of the Contexts that generate high risk of recidivism in ex-combatants of illegal armed groups in Colombia. His professional experiences combined with his academic background – focused on European public policy at SciencesPo (Paris) in a Master of Public Affairs and US public administration at Columbia University in a Master of Public Administration– serve to marry theory with practice with respect to peacebuilding, crime prevention and reintegration programs articulated with institutional capacity of the State, economic development and social policy. He has been part of the following publications, i. "Global DDR Summit South-South Cooperation analysis, 2013" (ACR – IOM & USAID, 2014), ii. "3rd Forum of Social Responsibility: Transitional Justice and Reconciliation" (ACR and Nogal Foundation, 2014), iii. "The Modernization of the State in Latin America and the Caribbean and the role of the Development Banks –Spanish-" (IDB &WB, 2011), iv. "Strategy for Institutions for Growth and Social Welfare" (IDB, 2011), v. "Counter drug trafficking policy: Policy shift by thinking in the country producers" (Asuntosdelsur.org, 2009), vi. "Strategy for the protection of vulnerable populations" (Columbia University, 2009), and vii. "Operational Youth Development Action Plan -Colombia, Ecuador & Perú-" (IDB, 2007). Mr. Triana has focused his experience in recent years on peace building and DDR in the African and Asian region by being the head of the technical missions (South-South cooperation) of the Republic of Colombia in the Republics of Indonesia, Timor L'Este and Congo. As the International Affairs and knowledge advisor to the General Director of the Colombian Agency for Reintegration (ACR) – Presidency of the Republic of Colombia-, he was the manager of the Global DDR Summit in Santa Marta, 2013, and the Knowledge Management System on DDR and Peace Building (ACR, IOM, & USAID).

Stéphane Valter is a senior lecturer (authorized to supervise researches) in Arabic language and civilization at Le Havre University (France) – Institute of Oriental Languages and Civilizations (ILCO). He obtained the 'agrégation' (an academic qualification for state teachers) for Arabic in 1989. He was administrative and scientific secretary at the French Institute for Arabic Studies in Damascus (IFEAD) from 1992 to 1997. He got a doctorate in political science (Arab world program) at the Institut d'études politiques (IEP) of Paris in 1998. He is a member of (the peer reviewed journal) Maghreb Machrek's editorial board, and a member of Syria Studies' editorial board (an on-line refereed journal, The Centre for Syrian Studies, University of St-Andrews, Scotland). Last book: Jean-François Daguzan and S. Valter (under the direction of), Armées et sociétés: le printemps arabe entre révolution et réaction, Paris, Fondation pour la recherche stratégique, ESKA, September 2014, 316 pages.

David Whyte is Professor of Socio-legal Studies at the University of Liverpool. His most recent books are How Corrupt is Britain? (ed., Pluto, 2015) and The Corporate Criminal (co-authored with Steve Tombs, Routledge, 2015). He is on the Executive Committee of the Institute of Employment Rights and a member of the Advisory Board of Corporate Watch.

Mirjam Wolfstein has studied Political Sciences and History at the Uni Kassel. 2008 she was a researcher for a representative in the German Parliament. Since 2009 she is a researcher of the Felsberg Institute for Education and Academic Research (FIBW). The main research interest lays on peace and conflict research, negotiation theories and migration especially unaccompanied minors. Her Focus areas are in the Near and Middle Eastern areas.

Felipe Zarama is the Operative Coordinator of the Policy and Strategy in Latin America Observatory at the Hernán Echavarría Olózaga Institute of Political Science. He formerly held the position of Young-Researcher at the Politics and Internationals Affairs Studies Center (CEPI) of Universidad del Rosario (Bogotá) between March 2014 and March 2015, period in which he carried out the present research.

Index

N

P

R

S

T

U

W

Y

Z

CPSIA information can be obtained at www.ICGtesting.com
Printed in the USA
BVOW09*0005301215

431197BV00007B/73/P

9 781466 6967